arihant
SUCCESS AND NOTHING LESS
ARIHANT PRAKASHAN (SERIES), MEERUT

AF819980

Skills in Mathematics

JEE Main & Advanced

Vector & 3D Geometry

Amit M Agarwal

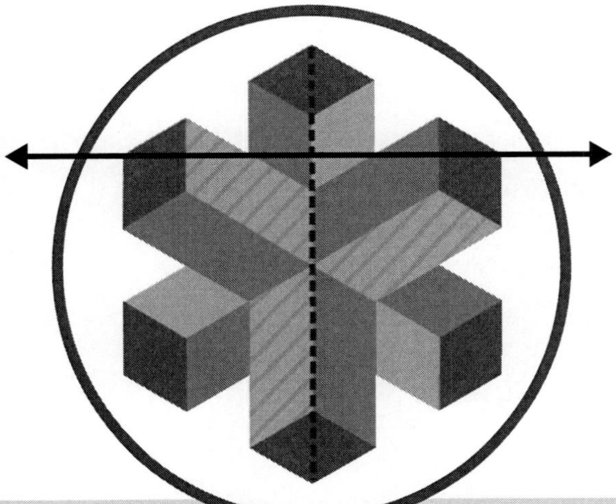

Arihant Prakashan (Series), Meerut

卐 **Administrative & Production Offices**

Regd. Office

'Ramchhaya' 4577/15, Agarwal Road, Darya Ganj, New Delhi -110002
Tele: 011- 47630600, 43518550

卐 **Head Office**

Kalindi, TP Nagar, Meerut (UP) - 250002 Tel: 0121-7156203, 7156204

卐 **Sales & Support Offices**

Agra, Ahmedabad, Bengaluru, Bareilly, Chennai, Delhi, Guwahati, Hyderabad, Jaipur, Jhansi, Kolkata, Lucknow, Nagpur & Pune.

卐 **PO No :** TXT-XX-XXXXXXX-X-XX

Published by Arihant Publications (India) Ltd.

For further information about the books published by Arihant, log on to www.arihantbooks.com or e-mail at info@arihantbooks.com

Follow us on

Preface

It is a matter of great pride and honour for me to have received such an overwhelming response to the previous editions of this book from the readers. In a way, this has inspired me to revise this book thoroughly as per the changed pattern of JEE Main & Advanced. I have tried to make the contents more relevant as per the needs of students, many topics have been re-written, a lot of new problems of new types have been added. All possible efforts are made to remove all the printing errors that had crept in previous editions. The book is now in such a shape that the students would feel at ease while going through the problems, which will in turn clear their concepts too.

A Summary of changes that have been made in Revised & Enhanced Edition

- Theory has been completely updated so as to accommodate all the changes made in JEE Syllabus & Pattern in recent years.
- The most important point about this new edition is, now the whole text matter of each chapter has been divided into small milestones with practice exercise in each milestones. This will help reader in step by step Pearning
- Theory of each milestone is more precise with **JEE focus Points** and **JEE Spike**.
- **JEE Scanners** are incorporated in theory for more synced learning with JEE Main and Advanced PYQs.
- Just after completion of theory, Solved Examples of all JEE types have been given, providing the students a complete understanding of all the formats of JEE questions & the level of difficulty of questions generally asked in JEE.
- Along with exercises given with each Milestone, following three exercises have been given at the end of each chapter.
- Practice Milestone 1- JEE Main Pattern Exercises.
- Practice Milestone 2- JEE Advanced Pattern Exercises.
- Practice Milestone 3- Challenging Problems Exercises.
- Previous Years questions asked in JEE Main and Advanced have been incorporated in all the exercises.

However I have made the best efforts and put my all teaching experience in revising this book. Still I am looking forward to get the valuable suggestions and criticism from my own fraternity i.e. the fraternity of JEE teachers. I strongly beleive that

"YOU CAN DO ANYTHING IF YOU SET YOUR MIND TO IT, I TEACH GEOMETRY TO JEE ASPIRANTS BUT BELIEVE THE MOST IMPORTANT FORMULA IS COURAGE + DREAMS = SUCCESS"

I would also like to motivate the students to send their suggestions or the changes that they want to be incorporated in this book. All the suggestions given by you all will be kept in prime focus at the time of next revision of the book.

Amit M Agarwal

Enhanced Features

JEE Focus Points

- The coordinates of point P may also be expressed as (lr, mr, nr).
- $l|\mathbf{r}|$, $m|\mathbf{r}|$, $n|\mathbf{r}|$ are projections of $\mathbf{r}$ on X, Y and Z-axes respectively.
- The numbers lr, mr and nr, proportional to the direction cosines, are called the direction ratios of $\mathbf{r}$ and are denoted by a, b and c respectively.
- If $\mathbf{r} = a\hat{\mathbf{i}} + b\hat{\mathbf{j}} + c\hat{\mathbf{k}}$, then a, b and c are direction ratios of the given vector. Also, if $a^2 + b^2 + c^2 = 1$, then a, b and c will be direction cosines of given vector.
- If vector is equally inclined to axes OX, OY and OZ. Then, $\cos\alpha = \cos\beta = \cos\gamma$ i.e. $\alpha = \beta = \gamma$

Concept Inside Video

A collection of Key Points/Results prime from JEE Preparation point of View. These are further elaborated with support videos.

JEE SPIKE

If vectors $x_1\mathbf{a} + y_1\mathbf{b} + z_1\mathbf{c}$, $x_2\mathbf{a} + y_2\mathbf{b} + z_2\mathbf{c}$ and $x_3\mathbf{a} + y_3\mathbf{b} + z_3\mathbf{c}$ are coplanar(where $\mathbf{a}$, $\mathbf{b}$ and $\mathbf{c}$ are non-coplanar).

Then, $\begin{vmatrix} x_1 & y_1 & z_1 \\ x_2 & y_2 & z_2 \\ x_3 & y_3 & z_3 \end{vmatrix} = 0$

Seypregated Most Valuable Pointes for JEE preparation

JEE SCANNER

Example Similar to PYQ Asked in JEE Main 2023

Let the position vector of the points A, B and C be $\hat{i} - \hat{j} + \hat{k}$, $\alpha\hat{i} + 2\hat{j} - \hat{k}$ and $8\hat{i} + (\alpha - 6)\hat{j} + 3\hat{k}$. Let the set $S = \{x \in R$: the points A, B and C be coplanar$\}$. Then, the value of $\Sigma_{\alpha \in S}(\alpha + 2)^2$ is ....

Sol. Given that $A(1, -1, 1)$, $B(\alpha, 2, -1)$ and $C(8, \alpha - 6, 3)$

Now, $\begin{vmatrix} 1 & -1 & 1 \\ \alpha & 2 & -1 \\ 8 & \alpha - 6 & 3 \end{vmatrix} = 0$

Skill Builder

For Sol.

Let the position vector of the points A, B and C be $\hat{i} + \hat{j} + \hat{k}$, $a\hat{i} - 3\hat{j} + \hat{k}$ and $6\hat{i} + (a - 6)\hat{j} + 3\hat{k}$. Let the set $S = \{x \in R$: the

- **For more practice** See Q.12 of Milestone Practice 3.

Unmatched Concept elevation tool helpful in syncing recant JEE Main & Advanced PYQs with theory and provide additional practice through Skill builders.

Contents

Syllabus

JEE Main

Three Dimensional Geometry

Coordinates of a point in space, distance between two points, section formula, direction ratios and direction cosines, angle between two intersecting lines. Skew lines, the shortest distance between them and its equation. Equations of a line

Vector Algebra

Vectors and scalars, addition of vectors, components of a vector in two dimensions and three dimensional space, scalar and vector products, scalar.

JEE Advanced

Three Dimensions

Distance between two points, direction cosines and direction ratios, equation of a straight line in space, skew lines, shortest distance between two lines, equation of a plane, distance of a point from a plane, angle between two lines, angle between two planes, angle between a line and the plane, coplanar lines.

Vectors

Addition of vectors, scalar multiplication, dot and cross products, scalar and vector triple products, and their geometrical interpretations.

1

“

Mathematics is not about numbers, equations, computations or algorithms, it is about understanding.

-William Paul Thurston

Vector Algebra

Learning Milestones

Milestone 1 Basics of Vector Algebra and Direction Cosines

- Scalar and Vector Quantities
- Representation of Vectors
- Types of Vectors
- Position Vector of a Point in Space
- Direction Cosines
- Rectangular Resolution of a Vector in 2D and 3D Systems

Milestone 2 Algebra of Vectors

- Addition of Vectors
- Subtraction of Vectors
- Vector Joining Two Points
- Multiplication of a Vector by a Scalar
- Section Formula
- Vector Along the Bisector of the Angle between Two Vectors
- Magnitude of Resultant of Two Vectors

Milestone 3 Collinearity and Coplanarity

- Linear Combination of Vectors
- Collinearity and Coplanarity of Vectors
- Theorem of Coplanar Vectors
- Theorem of Non-coplanar Vectors
- Linear Independence and Dependence of Vectors

Practice Milestones

Practice Milestone 1- JEE Main Pattern

Practice Milestone 2 - JEE Advanced Pattern

Practice Milestone 3 - Challenging Problems

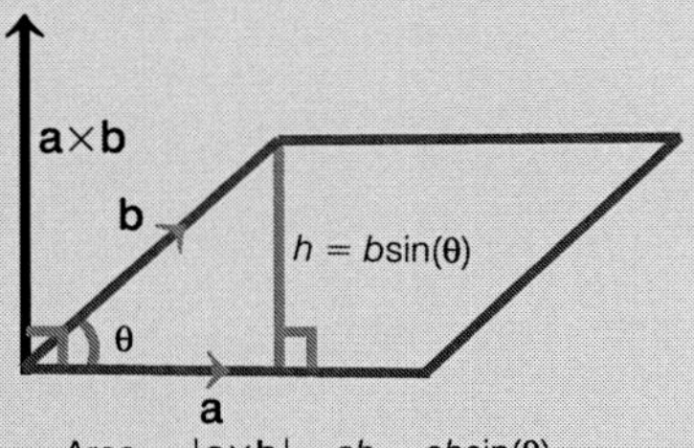

Area $= |\mathbf{a}\times\mathbf{b}| = ah = ab\sin(\theta)$

Milestone 1 Basics of Vector Algebra and Direction Cosines

• Scalar and Vector Quantities • Representation of Vectors • Types of Vectors • Position Vector of a Point in Space • Direction Cosines • Rectangular Resolution of a Vector in 2D and 3D Systems

Vectors represent one of the most important mathematical systems, which is used to handle certain types of problems in Geometry, Mechanics and other branches of Applied Mathematics, Physics and Engineering.

1.1 Scalar and Vector Quantities

Physical quantities are divided into two categories-Scalar quantities and Vector quantities. Those quantities which have only magnitude are called scalar quantities or briefly scalars. Examples of scalar quantities are mass, volume, density, work, temperature etc.

Second kind of quantities are those which have both magnitude and direction, such quantities are called vectors. Displacement, velocity, acceleration, momentum, weight, force etc., are examples of vector quantities.

Example 1. Classify the following measures as scalars and vectors :

(i) 20 m North-West

(ii) 10 Newton

(iii) 30 km/h

(iv) 50m/s towards North

(v) 10^{-19} coulomb

Sol. (i) Directed distance -Vector

(ii) Force-Vector

(iii) Speed-Scalar

(iv) Velocity-Vector

(v) Electric charge-Scalar

1.2 Representation of Vectors

Geometrically, a vector is represented by a directed line segment. For example, $\mathbf{a} = \mathbf{AB}$. Here, A is called the **initial point** and B is called the **terminal point** or **tip**.

A directed line segment with initial point A and terminal point B is denoted by **AB** or $\overrightarrow{AB}$. Vectors are also denoted by small letters with an arrow above it e.g. $\vec{a}, \vec{b}, \vec{c}$ etc. or by small bold letters e.g. **a, b, c** etc.

Here, in the figure $\mathbf{a} = \mathbf{AB}$ and magnitude or modulus of $\mathbf{a}$ is expressed as $|\mathbf{a}| = |\mathbf{AB}| = AB$ (Distance between initial and terminal points).

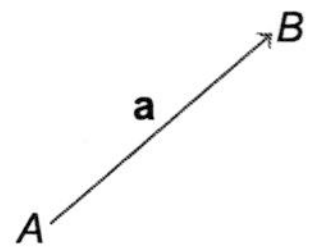

1. The magnitude of a vector is always a non-negative real number.
2. Every vector **AB** has the following three characteristics

   Length The length of **AB** will be denoted by $|\mathbf{AB}|$ or AB.

   Support The line of unlimited length of which AB is a segment is called the support of the vector **AB**.

   Sense The sense of **AB** is from A to B and that of **BA** is from B to A. Thus, the sense of a directed line segment is from its initial point to the terminal point.

Example 2. Represent graphically,

(i) A displacement of 60 km, 40° East of North

(ii) A displacement of 50 km South-East

Sol. (i) The vector **OP** represent the required vector.

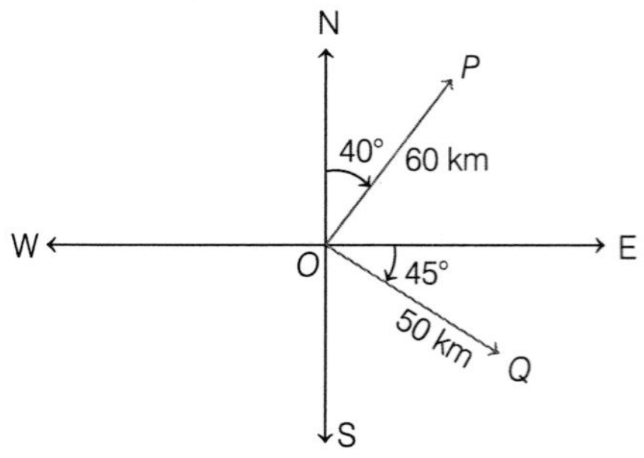

(ii) The vector **OQ** represent the required vector.

1.3 Types of Vectors

1. **Zero or null vector** A vector whose magnitude is zero is called zero or null vector and it is represented by **0**.
2. **Unit vector** A vector whose modulus is unity, is called a unit vector. The unit vector in the direction of a vector **a** is denoted by $\hat{\mathbf{a}}$, read as **a** cap.

   Thus, $|\hat{\mathbf{a}}| = 1$.

$$\hat{\mathbf{a}} = \frac{\mathbf{a}}{|\mathbf{a}|} = \frac{\text{Vector}}{\text{Magnitude of } \mathbf{a}}$$

3. **Like and unlike vectors** Vectors are said to be like when they have the same sense of direction and unlike when they have opposite directions.

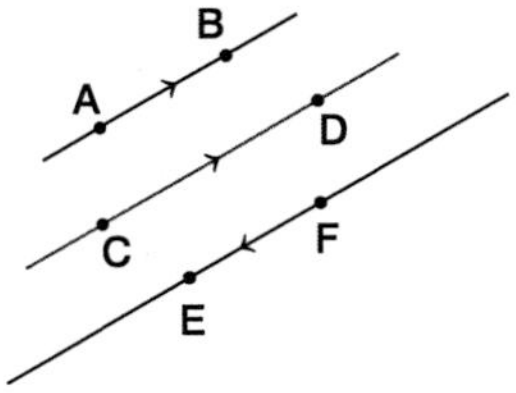

   Here, **AB** and **CD** are like vectors. **FE** and **AB**, **FE** and **CD** are unlike vectors.
4. **Collinear or parallel vectors** Vectors having the same or parallel supports are called collinear vectors.

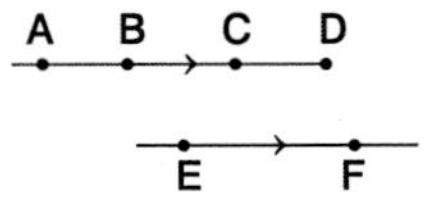

   Here, **AB**, **CD** and **EF** are collinear vectors. **AB** and **DC** are also collinear.
5. **Coinitial vectors** Vectors having the same initial point are called coinitial vectors.

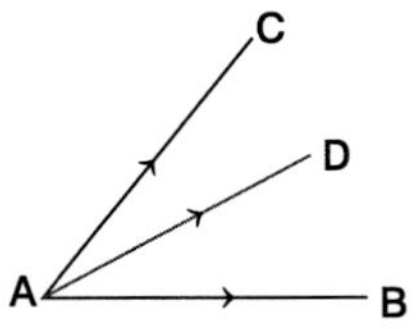

   In figure, **AB**, **AD** and **AC** are coinitial vectors with the same initial point *A*.
6. **Coplanar vectors** A system of vectors is said to be coplanar, if they lie in the same plane or their supports are parallel to the same plane.

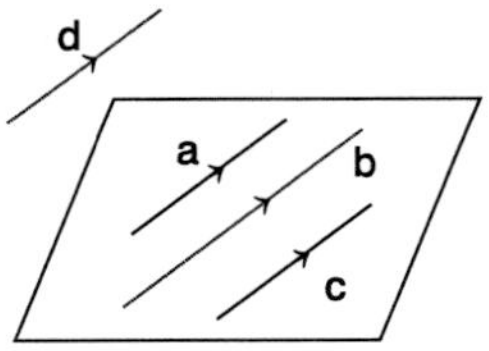

   In figure, **a, b, c** and **d** are coplanar. Whereas **a, b** and **c** lie on the same plane, **d** is parallel to the plane of **a**, **b** and **c**.
7. **Coterminous vectors** Vectors having the same terminal points are called coterminous vectors.

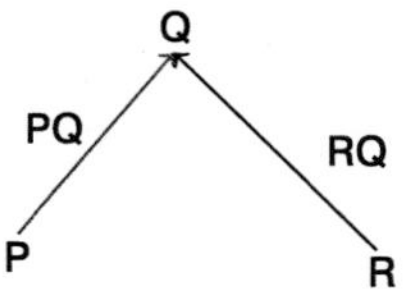

   Here, **PQ** and **RQ** are coterminous vector.
8. **Negative of a vector** The vector which has the same magnitude as the given vector **a** but opposite direction, is called the negative of **a** and is denoted by −**a**. Thus, if **PQ** = **a**, then **QP** = − **a**.

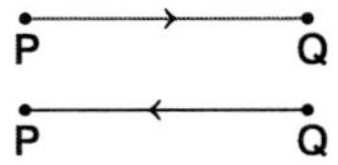

9. **Reciprocal of a vector** A vector having the same direction as that of a given vector **a** but magnitude equal to the reciprocal of the given vector is known as the reciprocal of *a* and is denoted by $\mathbf{a}^{-1}$. Thus, if $|\mathbf{a}| = a$, then $|\mathbf{a}^{-1}| = 1/a$.
10. **Localised vector** A vector which is drawn parallel to a given vector through a specified point in space is called a localised vector. For example, a force acting on a rigid body is a localised vector as its effect depends on the line of action of the force.
11. **Free vectors** If the value of a vector depends only on its length and direction and is independent of its position in the space, it is called a free vector.
12. **Equality of vectors** Two vectors **a** and **b** are said to be equal, if

    (i) $|\mathbf{a}| = |\mathbf{b}|$

    (ii) they have the same or parallel support.

    (iii) they have the same sense.

    Two unit vectors may not be equal unless they have the same direction.

Example 3. In the following figure, which of the vectors are:

(i) collinear (ii) equal

(iii) coinitial (iv) collinear but not equal

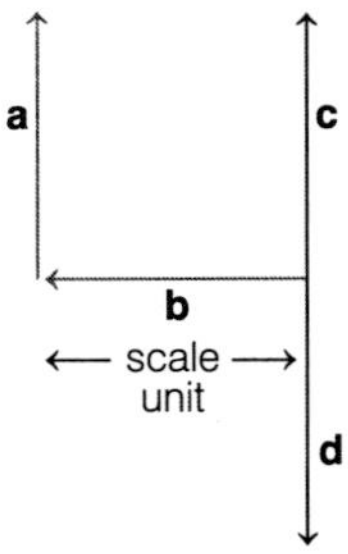

Sol. (i) **a**, **c** and **d** are collinear vectors.

(ii) **a** and **c** are equal vectors.

(iii) **b**, **c** and **d** are coinitial vectors.

(iv) **a** and **d** are collinear but they are not equal, as their directions are not same.

1.4 Position Vector of a Point in Space

Let O be the fixed point in space and $X'OX$, $Y'OY$ and $Z'OZ$ be three lines perpendicular to each other at O. Then, these three lines called X-axis, Y-axis and Z-axis which constitute the rectangular coordinate system.

The planes XOY, YOZ and ZOX, called the XY-plane, the YZ-plane and the ZX-plane, respectively.

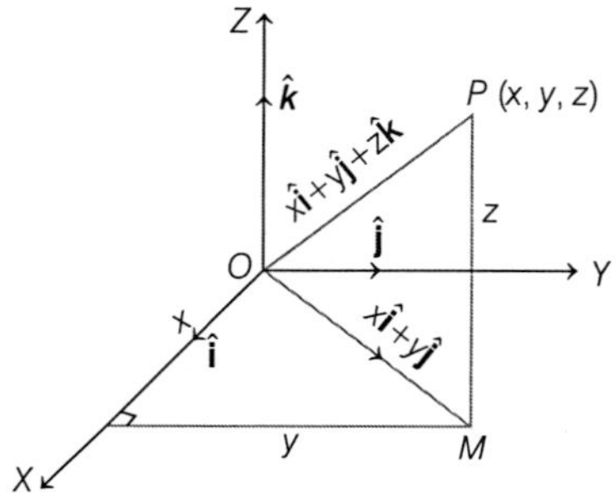

Now, let P be any point in space. Then, position of P is given by triad (x, y, z) where x, y, z are perpendicular distance from YZ-plane, ZX-plane, and XY-plane respectively.

The vector **OP** is called the position vector of point P with respect to the origin O and written as

$$\mathbf{OP} = x\hat{\mathbf{i}} + y\hat{\mathbf{j}} + z\hat{\mathbf{k}}$$

where $\hat{\mathbf{i}}$, $\hat{\mathbf{j}}$ and $\hat{\mathbf{k}}$ are unit vectors parallel to X-axis, Y-axis and Z-axis. We usually denote position vector by $\mathbf{r}$.

JEE Focus Points

- If A and B are any two points in space having coordinates (x_1, y_1, z_1) and (x_2, y_2, z_2) respectively, then distance between the points A and B
$= \sqrt{(x_2 - x_1)^2 + (y_2 - y_1)^2 + (z_2 - z_1)^2}$.
- Using distance formula, the magnitude of OP (or r) is given by
$$|\mathrm{OP}| = \sqrt{(x-0)^2 + (y-0)^2 + (z-0)^2}$$
$$= \sqrt{x^2 + y^2 + z^2}$$
- Two vectors are equal if they have same components i.e. if $\mathbf{a} = a_1\hat{\mathbf{i}} + a_2\hat{\mathbf{j}} + a_3\hat{\mathbf{k}}$ and $\mathbf{b} = b_1\hat{\mathbf{i}} + b_2\hat{\mathbf{j}} + b_3\hat{\mathbf{k}}$ are equal, then $a_1 = b_1$, $a_2 = b_2$ and $a_3 = b_3$.

Example 4. Find a unit vector parallel to the vector $-3\hat{\mathbf{i}} + 4\hat{\mathbf{j}}$.

Sol. Let $\mathbf{a} = -3\hat{\mathbf{i}} + 4\hat{\mathbf{j}}$

Then, $|\mathbf{a}| = \sqrt{(-3)^2 + (4)^2} = 5$

$\therefore$ Unit vector parallel to $\mathbf{a} = \hat{\mathbf{a}} = \dfrac{1}{|\mathbf{a}|}\cdot\mathbf{a}$

$$= \frac{-3\hat{\mathbf{i}} + 4\hat{\mathbf{j}}}{5} = \frac{-3}{5}\hat{\mathbf{i}} + \frac{4}{5}\hat{\mathbf{j}}$$

Example 5. If one side of a square be represented by the vectors $3\hat{\mathbf{i}} + 4\hat{\mathbf{j}} + 5\hat{\mathbf{k}}$, then find the area of the square.

Sol. Let $\mathbf{a} = 3\hat{\mathbf{i}} + 4\hat{\mathbf{j}} + 5\hat{\mathbf{k}}$, then

$$|\mathbf{a}| = \sqrt{3^2 + 4^2 + 5^2} = \sqrt{9 + 16 + 25} = 5\sqrt{2} \text{ units}$$

Thus, the length of a side of square $= 5\sqrt{2}$ units

Hence, area of square $= (5\sqrt{2})^2 = 25 \times 2 = 50$ sq units

Example 6. A vector **x** has components $(3p - 1)$ and 1 with respect to rectangular cartesian system. This system is rotated through a certain angle about the origin in the counter clockwise sense. If with respect to new system, **x** has components $(2p + 1)$ and 1, then find the value of p.

Sol. We have, $\mathbf{x} = (3p - 1)\hat{\mathbf{i}} + \hat{\mathbf{j}}$

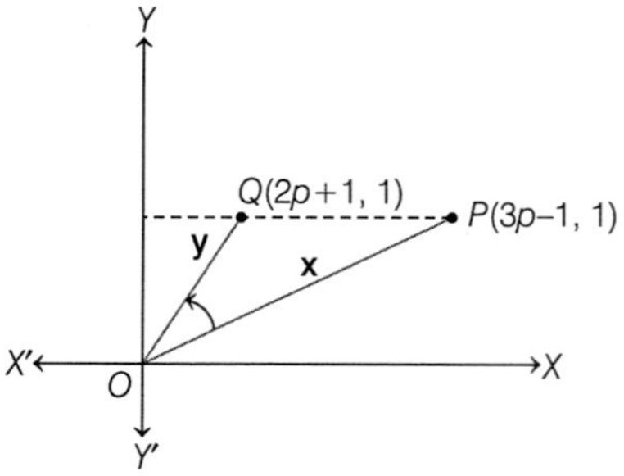

After rotation, let $\mathbf{y} = (2p + 1)\hat{\mathbf{i}} + \hat{\mathbf{j}}$ and magnitude of **x** and **y** will be same.

$$\therefore \quad |\mathbf{x}| = |\mathbf{y}|$$

$$\Rightarrow \quad \sqrt{(3p-1)^2 + (1)^2} = \sqrt{(2p+1)^2 + (1)^2}$$

$$\Rightarrow \quad (3p-1)^2 + 1 = (2p+1)^2 + 1$$

$$\Rightarrow \quad 9p^2 + 1 - 6p = 4p^2 + 1 + 4p$$

$$\Rightarrow \quad 5p^2 = 10p$$

$$\Rightarrow \quad 5p(p-2) = 0$$

$$\Rightarrow \quad p = 0, 2$$

1.5 Direction Cosines

Let **r** be the position vector of a point $P(x, y, z)$. Then, direction cosines of **r** are the cosines of angles α, β and γ that the vector **r** makes with the positive direction of X, Y and Z-axes respectively. We usually denote direction cosines by l, m and n respectively.

Thus, we have the following

$$\cos\alpha = l = \frac{x}{\sqrt{x^2+y^2+z^2}} = \frac{x}{|\mathbf{r}|} = \frac{x}{r}$$

$$\cos\beta = m = \frac{y}{\sqrt{x^2+y^2+z^2}} = \frac{y}{|\mathbf{r}|} = \frac{y}{r}$$

and $$\cos\gamma = n = \frac{z}{\sqrt{x^2+y^2+z^2}} = \frac{z}{|\mathbf{r}|} = \frac{z}{r}$$

Clearly, $\boldsymbol{l^2 + m^2 + n^2 = 1}$.

Here, $\alpha = \angle POX, \beta = \angle POY, \gamma = \angle POZ$ and $\hat{\mathbf{i}}, \hat{\mathbf{j}}$ and $\hat{\mathbf{k}}$ are the unit vectors along OX, OY and OZ respectively.

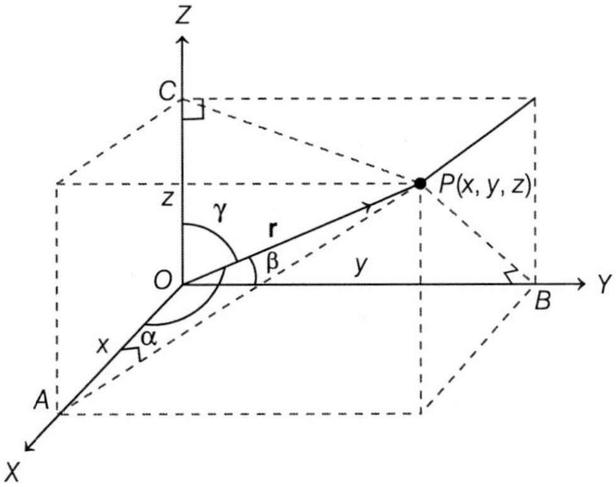

JEE Focus Points

Concept Inside Video

- The coordinates of point P may also be expressed as (lr, mr, nr).
- $l|\mathbf{r}|, m|\mathbf{r}|, n|\mathbf{r}|$ are projections of **r** on X, Y and Z-axes respectively.
- The numbers lr, mr and nr, proportional to the direction cosines, are called the direction ratios of **r** and are denoted by a, b and c respectively.
- If $\mathbf{r} = a\hat{\mathbf{i}} + b\hat{\mathbf{j}} + c\hat{\mathbf{k}}$, then a, b and c are direction ratios of the given vector. Also, if $a^2 + b^2 + c^2 = 1$, then a, b and c will be direction cosines of given vector.
- If vector is equally inclined to axes OX, OY and OZ. Then, $\cos\alpha = \cos\beta = \cos\gamma$ i.e. $\alpha = \beta = \gamma$

Example 7. Show that the vector $\hat{\mathbf{i}} + \hat{\mathbf{j}} + \hat{\mathbf{k}}$ is equally inclined to the axes OX, OY and OZ.

Sol. Let $\mathbf{a} = \hat{\mathbf{i}} + \hat{\mathbf{j}} + \hat{\mathbf{k}}$

If **a** makes angles α, β, γ with X, Y and Z-axes respectively.

Then, $$\cos\alpha = \frac{1}{\sqrt{1^2+1^2+1^2}} = \frac{1}{\sqrt{3}},$$

and $$\cos\beta = \frac{1}{\sqrt{3}} \text{ and } \cos\gamma = \frac{1}{\sqrt{3}}$$

Hence, **a** is equally inclined to all the axes.

Example 8. A line makes angle 60° with Y-axis and Z-axis, then find the angle which it makes with X-axis.

Sol. $\because l = \cos\alpha,\ m = \cos\beta = \cos 60° = \frac{1}{2}$

and $n = \cos\gamma = \cos 60° = \frac{1}{2}$

Now, $$l^2 + m^2 + n^2 = 1$$

$$\Rightarrow \quad l^2 + \left(\frac{1}{2}\right)^2 + \left(\frac{1}{2}\right)^2 = 1$$

$$\Rightarrow \quad (l)^2 = \frac{1}{2}$$

$\therefore\ l = \frac{1}{\sqrt{2}} = \cos\alpha = \cos 45°$

So, the angle which it makes with X-axis is 45°.

1.6 Rectangular Resolution of a Vector in 2D and 3D Systems

In Two Dimensional System

Any vector **r** in two dimensional system can be expressed as $\mathbf{r} = x\hat{\mathbf{i}} + y\hat{\mathbf{j}}$. The vectors $x\hat{\mathbf{i}}$ and $y\hat{\mathbf{j}}$ are called the perpendicular component vectors of **r**.

The scalars x and y are called the components or resolved parts of **r** in the directions of X-axis and Y-axis, respectively and the ordered pair (x, y) is known as coordinates of point whose position vector is **r**.

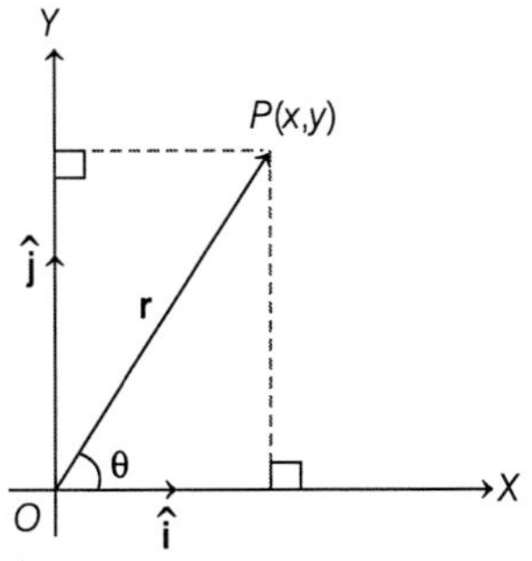

Also, the magnitude of $\mathbf{r} = \sqrt{x^2+y^2}$ and if θ is the inclination of **r** with the X-axis, then

$$\theta = \tan^{-1}\left(\frac{y}{x}\right).$$

Unit vector along $\mathbf{r} = \frac{\mathbf{r}}{|\mathbf{r}|} = \frac{x}{\sqrt{x^2+y^2}}\hat{\mathbf{i}} + \frac{y}{\sqrt{x^2+y^2}}\hat{\mathbf{j}}$

$$= \cos\theta\hat{\mathbf{i}} + \sin\theta\hat{\mathbf{j}}$$

Thus, in two dimensional system, unit vector along a direction ($\mathbf{r}$) making an angle θ with the positive direction of X-axis in anti-clockwise direction is $\cos\theta\hat{\mathbf{i}} + \sin\theta\hat{\mathbf{j}}$.

Similarly, unit vector along a direction ($\mathbf{r}$) making an angle θ with the positive direction of X-axis in clockwise direction is $\cos\theta\hat{\mathbf{i}} - \sin\theta\hat{\mathbf{j}}$.

Example 9. Let **AB** be a vector in two dimensional plane with the magnitude 4 units and making an angle of 30° with X-axis and lying in the first quadrant. Find the components of **AB** along the two axes of coordinates. Hence, represent **AB** in terms of unit vectors $\hat{\mathbf{i}}$ and $\hat{\mathbf{j}}$.

Sol. Let us consider A as origin. From the diagram, it can be seen that the component of **AB** along X-axis

$$= AB\cos 30° = 4\cos 30° = 4 \times \frac{\sqrt{3}}{2} = 2\sqrt{3}$$

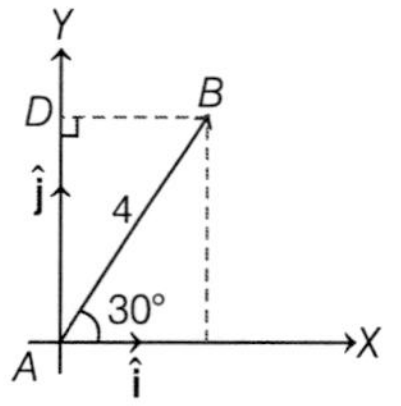

and the component of **AB** along Y-axis

$$= AB\sin 30° = 4 \times \frac{1}{2} = 2$$

Hence, $\mathbf{AB} = 2\sqrt{3}\,\hat{\mathbf{i}} + 2\hat{\mathbf{j}}$

In three Dimensional System

Any vector $\mathbf{r}$ in three dimensional system can be expressed as $\mathbf{r} = x\hat{\mathbf{i}} + y\hat{\mathbf{j}} + z\hat{\mathbf{k}}$.

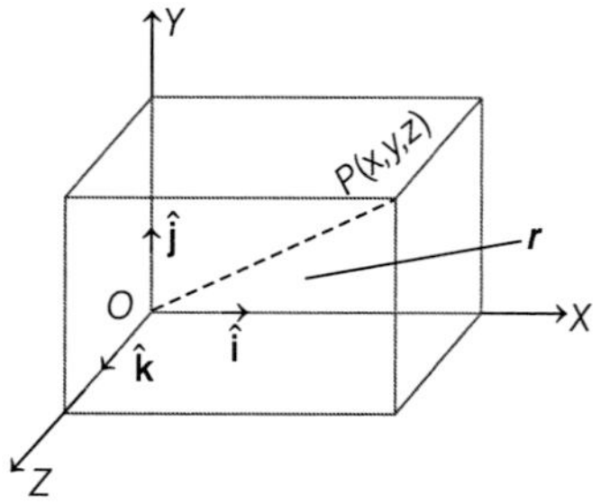

The vectors $x\hat{\mathbf{i}}, y\hat{\mathbf{j}}$ and $z\hat{\mathbf{k}}$ are called the right angled components of $\mathbf{r}$.

The scalars x, y and z are called the components or resolved parts of $\mathbf{r}$ in the directions of X-axis, Y-axis and Z-axis, respectively and ordered triplet (x, y, z) is known as coordinates of P whose position vector is $\mathbf{r}$. Also, the magnitude or modulus of $\mathbf{r}$

$$= |\mathbf{r}| = \sqrt{x^2+y^2+z^2}.$$

Unit vector along $\mathbf{r} = \frac{\mathbf{r}}{|\mathbf{r}|}$

$$= \frac{x}{|\mathbf{r}|}\hat{\mathbf{i}} + \frac{y}{|\mathbf{r}|}\hat{\mathbf{j}} + \frac{z}{|\mathbf{r}|}\hat{\mathbf{k}}$$

$$= l\hat{\mathbf{i}} + m\hat{\mathbf{j}} + n\hat{\mathbf{k}}$$

where, l, m, n are the direction cosines of $\mathbf{r}$.

Thus, $\hat{\mathbf{r}} = l\hat{\mathbf{i}} + m\hat{\mathbf{j}} + n\hat{\mathbf{k}}$ and $\mathbf{r} = |\mathbf{r}|(l\hat{\mathbf{i}} + m\hat{\mathbf{j}} + n\hat{\mathbf{k}})$

Example 10. Let **PQ** be the vector in three dimensional plane with initial point $P \equiv (3, 12, 6)$ and terminal point $Q \equiv (-4, -3, 2)$ as shown below. Express **PQ** in both component form and vector form. Also, find unit vectors along **PQ**.

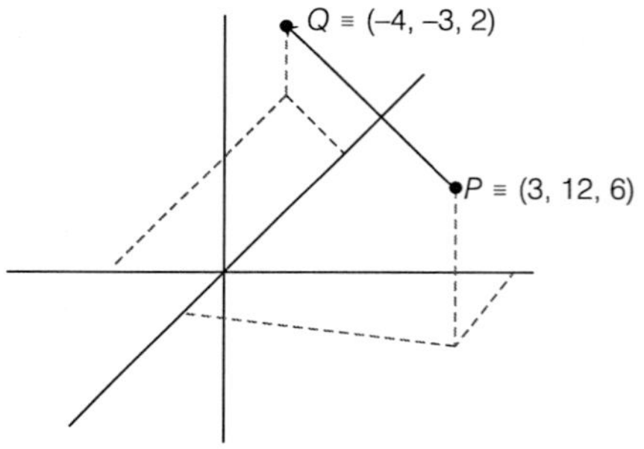

Sol. In scalar component form,

$$PQ = (x_2 - x_1, y_2 - y_1, z_2 - z_1)$$
$$= (-4-3, -3-12, 2-6)$$
$$= (-7, -15, -4)$$

In vector form,

$$\mathbf{PQ} = -7\hat{\mathbf{i}} - 15\hat{\mathbf{j}} - 4\hat{\mathbf{k}}$$

Now, unit vector along **PQ** is

$$\mathbf{PQ} = \frac{-7\hat{\mathbf{i}} - 15\hat{\mathbf{j}} - 4\hat{\mathbf{k}}}{\sqrt{(-7)^2 + (-15)^2 + (4)^2}}$$

$$= \frac{-(7\hat{\mathbf{i}} + 15\hat{\mathbf{j}} + 4\hat{\mathbf{k}})}{\sqrt{290}}$$

Milestone Practice 1.1

1. Find the perimeter of a triangle with sides $3\hat{i}+4\hat{j}+5\hat{k}$, $4\hat{i}-3\hat{j}-5\hat{k}$ and $7\hat{i}+\hat{j}$.

2. If vector $x\hat{i}+2\hat{j}$ be obtained by rotating the vector $2\hat{i}+(x-4)\hat{j}$ by a certain angle about the origin in counter clockwise sense. Find the value of x.

3. A vector of modulus 3 is equally inclined to X and Z-axes at an angle $\frac{\pi}{4}$. The length of projection of the vector on the Y-axis, is

(a) 1 (b) 0
(c) 2 (d) None of these

4. If a unit vector **a** makes angles $\frac{\pi}{3}$ with $\hat{i}$, $\frac{\pi}{4}$ with $\hat{j}$ and an acute angle θ with $\hat{k}$, then find the angle θ and hence the components of **a**.

5. Write the direction ratios of the vector $\mathbf{r}=\hat{i}-\hat{j}+2\hat{k}$ and hence calculate its direction cosines.

6. A vector **a** has length 28 and direction ratios are proportional to 6, −3, 2. The components of **a** on the coordinates axes, if the line makes an acute angle with X-axis is equal to

(a) 24, 8, 12 (b) − 12, 8, 12
(c) 24, − 12, − 8 (d) 24, −12, 8

7. If a line makes an angle of $\frac{\pi}{4}$ with the positive directions of each of X-axis and Y-axis. The angle that the line makes with the positive direction of the Z-axis, is

(a) $\frac{\pi}{4}$ (b) $\frac{\pi}{3}$
(c) $\frac{\pi}{2}$ (d) 2π

8. A line makes the same angle θ with each of the X and Z-axes. If the angle β, which it makes with Y-axis such that $\sin^2\beta = 3\sin^2\theta$. Find the value of $\cos^2\theta$.

Answer Key

1. $15\sqrt{2}$
2. 2
3. (b)
4. $\frac{1}{2}, \frac{1}{\sqrt{2}}, \frac{1}{2}$
5. $\frac{1}{\sqrt{6}}, \frac{-1}{\sqrt{6}}, \frac{2}{\sqrt{6}}$
6. (d)
7. (c)
8. $\frac{3}{5}$

For Detailed Solution

Milestone 2 Algebra of Vectors

• Addition of Vectors • Subtraction of Vectors • Vector Joining Two Points • Multiplication of a Vector by a Scalar • Section Formula • Vector Along the Bisector of the Angle between Two Vectors • Magnitude of Resultant of Two Vectors

1.7 Addition of Vectors (Resultant of Vectors)

Vector addition is the operation of adding two or more vectors together into a vector sum.

It may be added geometrically, the vector that gets connected to the head of the first to the tail of the second is the vector sum of **a** and **b**.

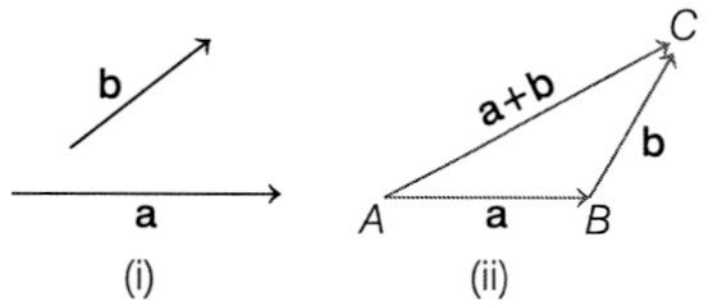

1. Triangle Law of Addition

If two vectors are represented by two consecutive sides of a triangle, then their sum is represented by the third side of the triangle, but in opposite direction. This is known as the triangle law of addition of vectors.

Thus, if $\mathbf{AB} = \mathbf{a}$, $\mathbf{BC} = \mathbf{b}$ and $\mathbf{AC} = \mathbf{c}$, then

$$\mathbf{AB} + \mathbf{BC} = \mathbf{AC} \text{ i.e. } \mathbf{a} + \mathbf{b} = \mathbf{c}$$

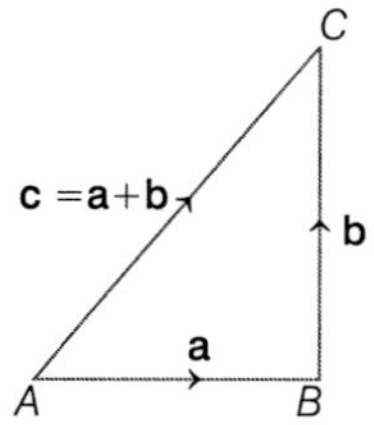

In ΔABC, we have

$$\mathbf{AB} + \mathbf{BC} = \mathbf{AC}$$

$$\Rightarrow \quad \mathbf{AB} + \mathbf{BC} = -\mathbf{CA}$$

$$\Rightarrow \quad \mathbf{AB} + \mathbf{BC} + \mathbf{CA} = \mathbf{0} \;\Rightarrow\; \mathbf{AA} = \mathbf{0}$$

This means that when the sides of a triangle are taken in order, it leads to zero resultant as the initial and terminal points get coincided.

So, if two vectors are represented in magnitude and direction by the two sides of a triangle taken in the same order, then their sum is represented by the third side of the triangle in reverse order.

2. Parallelogram Law of Addition

If two vectors are represented by two adjacent sides of a parallelogram, then their sum is represented by the diagonal of the parallelogram whose initial point is the same as the initial point of the given vectors. This is known as parallelogram law of vector addition.

Thus, if $\mathbf{OA} = \mathbf{a}, \mathbf{OB} = \mathbf{b}$ and $\mathbf{OC} = \mathbf{c}$

Then, $\mathbf{OA} + \mathbf{OB} = \mathbf{OC}$

i.e. $\mathbf{a} + \mathbf{b} = \mathbf{c}$,

where OC is a diagonal of the parallelogram $OACB$.

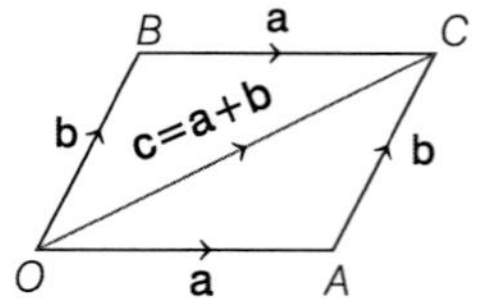

JEE Focus Points

- The magnitude of $\mathbf{a} + \mathbf{b}$ is not equal to the sum of the magnitudes of **a** and **b**.
- From the figure, we have

$\mathbf{OA} + \mathbf{AC} = \mathbf{OC}$ [by triangle law of vector addition]

or $\mathbf{OA} + \mathbf{OB} = \mathbf{OC}$ [$\because \mathbf{AC} = \mathbf{OB}$]

which is the parallelogram law. Thus, we may say that the two laws of vector addition are equivalent to each other.

3. Polygon Law of Addition

If the number of vectors are represented by the sides of a polygon taken in order, the resultant is represented by the closing side of the polygon taken in the reverse order.

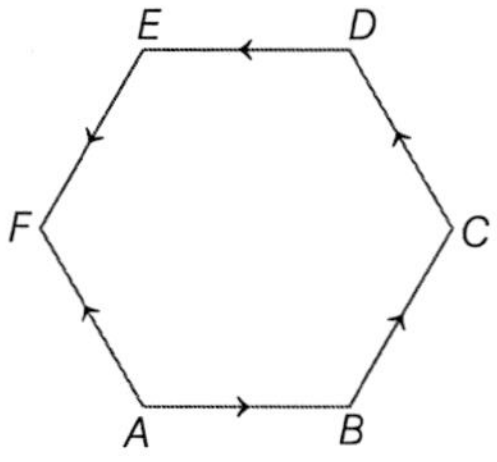

In the figure,

$$\mathbf{AB} + \mathbf{BC} + \mathbf{CD} + \mathbf{DE} + \mathbf{EF} = \mathbf{AF}$$

4. Addition in Component Form

If the vectors are defined in terms of $\hat{\mathbf{i}}, \hat{\mathbf{j}}$ and $\hat{\mathbf{k}}$, i.e. if $\mathbf{a} = a_1\hat{\mathbf{i}} + a_2\hat{\mathbf{j}} + a_3\hat{\mathbf{k}}$ and $\mathbf{b} = b_1\hat{\mathbf{i}} + b_2\hat{\mathbf{j}} + b_3\hat{\mathbf{k}}$, then their sum is defined as

$$\mathbf{a} + \mathbf{b} = (a_1 + b_1)\hat{\mathbf{i}} + (a_2 + b_2)\hat{\mathbf{j}} + (a_3 + b_3)\hat{\mathbf{k}}$$

Properties of Vector Addition

Vector addition has the following properties

(i) **Closure** The sum of two vectors is always a vector.

(ii) **Commutativity** For any two vectors **a** and **b**,

$\Rightarrow \quad \mathbf{a} + \mathbf{b} = \mathbf{b} + \mathbf{a}$

(iii) **Associativity** For any three vectors **a**, **b** and **c**,

$\Rightarrow \quad \mathbf{a} + (\mathbf{b} + \mathbf{c}) = (\mathbf{a} + \mathbf{b}) + \mathbf{c}$

(iv) **Identity** Zero vector is the identity for addition. For any vector **a**.

$\Rightarrow \quad \mathbf{0} + \mathbf{a} = \mathbf{a} = \mathbf{a} + \mathbf{0}$

(v) **Additive inverse** For every vector **a** its negative vector $-\mathbf{a}$ exists such that $\mathbf{a} + (-\mathbf{a}) = (-\mathbf{a}) + \mathbf{a} = \mathbf{0}$ i.e. $(-\mathbf{a})$ is the additive inverse of the vector **a**.

Example 11. If S is the mid-point of side QR of a ΔPQR, then prove that $\mathbf{PQ} + \mathbf{PR} = 2\,\mathbf{PS}$.

Sol. Clearly, by triangle law of addition, we have

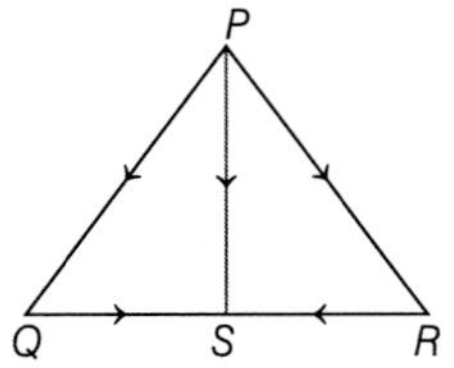

$$\mathbf{PQ} + \mathbf{QS} = \mathbf{PS} \quad \text{...(i)}$$

and $$\mathbf{PR} + \mathbf{RS} = \mathbf{PS} \quad \text{... (ii)}$$

On adding Eqs. (i) and (ii), we get

$$(\mathbf{PQ} + \mathbf{QS}) + (\mathbf{PR} + \mathbf{RS}) = 2\mathbf{PS}$$

$$\Rightarrow (\mathbf{PQ} + \mathbf{PR}) + (\mathbf{QS} + \mathbf{RS}) = 2\mathbf{PS} \Rightarrow \mathbf{PQ} + \mathbf{PR} + 0 = 2\mathbf{PS}$$

[$\because S$ is the mid-point of **QR** and directions of **QS** and **RS** are opposite $\therefore$ $\mathbf{QS} = -\mathbf{RS}$]

Hence, $\mathbf{PQ} + \mathbf{PR} = 2\mathbf{PS}$ **Hence proved.**

Example 12. If $ABCDEF$ is a regular hexagon, then prove that $\mathbf{AD} + \mathbf{EB} + \mathbf{FC} = 4\mathbf{AB}$.

Sol. We have,

$$\mathbf{AD} + \mathbf{EB} + \mathbf{FC} = (\mathbf{AB} + \mathbf{BC} + \mathbf{CD}) + (\mathbf{ED} + \mathbf{DC} + \mathbf{CB}) + \mathbf{FC}$$
$$= \mathbf{AB} + (\mathbf{BC} + \mathbf{CB}) + (\mathbf{CD} + \mathbf{DC}) + \mathbf{ED} + \mathbf{FC}$$

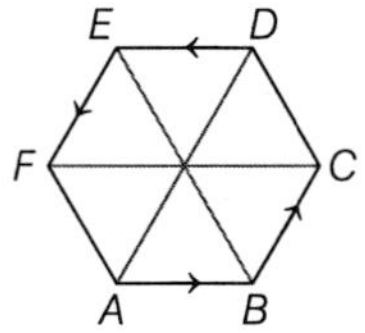

$$= \mathbf{AB} + \mathbf{0} + \mathbf{0} + \mathbf{AB} + 2\mathbf{AB} = 4\mathbf{AB}$$

[$\because$ $\mathbf{ED} = \mathbf{AB}, \mathbf{FC} = 2\mathbf{AB}$]

Hence proved.

Example 13. Find the unit vector parallel to the resultant vector of $2\hat{\mathbf{i}} + 4\hat{\mathbf{j}} - 5\hat{\mathbf{k}}$ and $\hat{\mathbf{i}} + 2\hat{\mathbf{j}} + 3\hat{\mathbf{k}}$.

> **Decoding the Question**
> The unit vector parallel to resultant vector of **a** and **b** is $\dfrac{(\mathbf{a} + \mathbf{b})}{|\mathbf{a} + \mathbf{b}|}$.

Sol. Resultant vector, $\mathbf{r} = (2\hat{\mathbf{i}} + 4\hat{\mathbf{j}} - 5\hat{\mathbf{k}}) + (\hat{\mathbf{i}} + 2\hat{\mathbf{j}} + 3\hat{\mathbf{k}})$

$$= 3\hat{\mathbf{i}} + 6\hat{\mathbf{j}} - 2\hat{\mathbf{k}}$$

Unit vector parallel to $\mathbf{r} = \dfrac{1}{|\mathbf{r}|}\mathbf{r}$

$$= \frac{1}{\sqrt{3^2 + 6^2 + (-2)^2}}(3\hat{\mathbf{i}} + 6\hat{\mathbf{j}} - 2\hat{\mathbf{k}}) = \frac{1}{7}(3\hat{\mathbf{i}} + 6\hat{\mathbf{j}} - 2\hat{\mathbf{k}})$$

1.8 Subtraction of Vectors

If **a** and **b** are two vectors, then their subtraction $\mathbf{a} - \mathbf{b}$ is defined as $\mathbf{a} - \mathbf{b} = \mathbf{a} + (-\mathbf{b})$, where $-\mathbf{b}$ is the negative of **b** having magnitude equal to that of **b** and direction opposite to **b**.

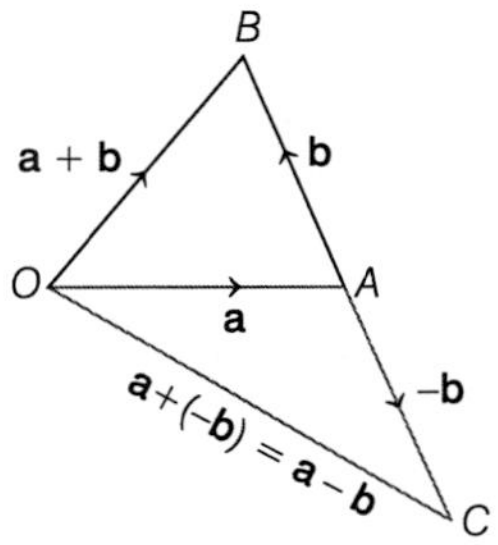

If $\mathbf{a} = a_1\hat{\mathbf{i}} + a_2\hat{\mathbf{j}} + a_3\hat{\mathbf{k}}$

and $\mathbf{b} = b_1\hat{\mathbf{i}} + b_2\hat{\mathbf{j}} + b_3\hat{\mathbf{k}}$

Then, $\mathbf{a} - \mathbf{b} = (a_1 - b_1)\hat{\mathbf{i}} + (a_2 - b_2)\hat{\mathbf{j}} + (a_3 - b_3)\hat{\mathbf{k}}$

Properties of Vector Subtraction

(i) $\mathbf{a} - \mathbf{b} \neq \mathbf{b} - \mathbf{a}$

(ii) $(\mathbf{a} - \mathbf{b}) - \mathbf{c} \neq \mathbf{a} - (\mathbf{b} - \mathbf{c})$

(iii) Since, any one side of a triangle is less than the sum and greater than the difference of the other two sides, so for any two vectors **a** and **b**, we have

(a) $|\mathbf{a} + \mathbf{b}| \leq |\mathbf{a}| + |\mathbf{b}|$ (b) $|\mathbf{a} + \mathbf{b}| \geq |\mathbf{a}| - |\mathbf{b}|$

(c) $|\mathbf{a} - \mathbf{b}| \leq |\mathbf{a}| + |\mathbf{b}|$ (d) $|\mathbf{a} - \mathbf{b}| \geq |\mathbf{a}| - |\mathbf{b}|$

1.9 Vector Joining Two Points

In the adjoining figure, P and Q are any two points such that $\mathbf{OP} = x_1\hat{\mathbf{i}} + y_1\hat{\mathbf{j}} + z_1\hat{\mathbf{k}}$ and $\mathbf{OQ} = x_2\hat{\mathbf{i}} + y_2\hat{\mathbf{j}} + z_2\hat{\mathbf{k}}$

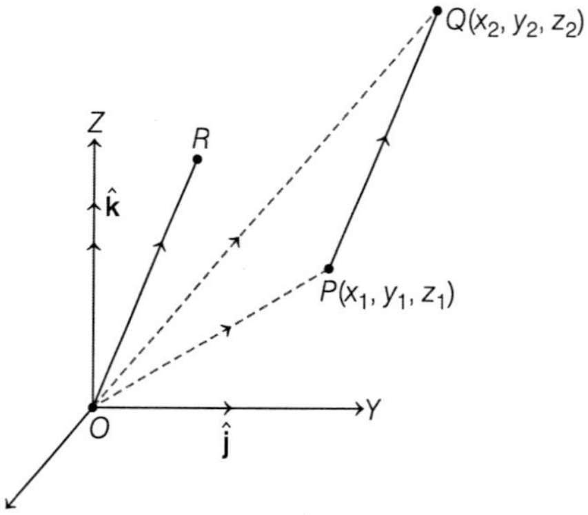

Now, **PQ** is shifted at origin without rotation such that $|\mathbf{PQ}| = |\mathbf{OR}|$

$$\therefore \quad \mathbf{PQ} = \mathbf{OR} = (x_2 - x_1)\hat{\mathbf{i}} + (y_2 - y_1)\hat{\mathbf{j}} + (z_2 - z_1)\hat{\mathbf{k}}$$
$$= (x_2\hat{\mathbf{i}} + y_2\hat{\mathbf{j}} + z_2\hat{\mathbf{k}}) - (x_1\hat{\mathbf{i}} + y_1\hat{\mathbf{j}} + z_1\hat{\mathbf{k}})$$
$$= \mathbf{OQ} - \mathbf{OP}$$

$\Rightarrow \mathbf{OQ} = \mathbf{OP} + \mathbf{PQ}$ [triangle law of addition]

$\Rightarrow \mathbf{OQ} = \mathbf{OP} + \mathbf{OR}$ [$\because \mathbf{PQ} = \mathbf{OR}$]

Example 14. If the position vectors of **A** and **B** respectively $\hat{\mathbf{i}} + 3\hat{\mathbf{j}} - 7\hat{\mathbf{k}}$ and $5\hat{\mathbf{i}} - 2\hat{\mathbf{j}} + 4\hat{\mathbf{k}}$, then find **AB**.

Sol. Let O be the origin, then we have

$\mathbf{OA} = \hat{\mathbf{i}} + 3\hat{\mathbf{j}} - 7\hat{\mathbf{k}}$

and $\mathbf{OB} = 5\hat{\mathbf{i}} - 2\hat{\mathbf{j}} + 4\hat{\mathbf{k}}$

Now, $\mathbf{AB} = \mathbf{OB} - \mathbf{OA} = (5\hat{\mathbf{i}} - 2\hat{\mathbf{j}} + 4\hat{\mathbf{k}}) - (\hat{\mathbf{i}} + 3\hat{\mathbf{j}} - 7\hat{\mathbf{k}})$

$= 4\hat{\mathbf{i}} - 5\hat{\mathbf{j}} + 11\hat{\mathbf{k}}$

Example 15. Vectors drawn from the origin O to the points A, B and C are respectively **a**, **b** and **4a – 3b**. Find **AC** and **BC**.

Sol. We have, $\mathbf{OA} = \mathbf{a}$, $\mathbf{OB} = \mathbf{b}$ and $\mathbf{OC} = 4\mathbf{a} - 3\mathbf{b}$

Clearly, $\mathbf{AC} = \mathbf{OC} - \mathbf{OA} = (4\mathbf{a} - 3\mathbf{b}) - (\mathbf{a})$

$= 3\mathbf{a} - 3\mathbf{b}$

and $\mathbf{BC} = \mathbf{OC} - \mathbf{OB} = (4\mathbf{a} - 3\mathbf{b}) - (\mathbf{b})$

$= 4\mathbf{a} - 4\mathbf{b}$

Example 16. Let α, β and γ be distinct real numbers. Show that the points with position vectors $\alpha\hat{\mathbf{i}} + \beta\hat{\mathbf{j}} + \gamma\hat{\mathbf{k}}, \beta\hat{\mathbf{i}} + \gamma\hat{\mathbf{j}} + \alpha\hat{\mathbf{k}}$ and $\gamma\hat{\mathbf{i}} + \alpha\hat{\mathbf{j}} + \beta\hat{\mathbf{k}}$ form an equilateral triangle.

Decoding the Question

Consider ΔABC is an equilateral triangle if $|AB| = |BC| = |AC|$.

Sol. Let the given points be A, B and C with position vectors $\alpha\hat{\mathbf{i}} + \beta\hat{\mathbf{j}} + \gamma\hat{\mathbf{k}}, \beta\hat{\mathbf{i}} + \gamma\hat{\mathbf{j}} + \alpha\hat{\mathbf{k}}$ and $\gamma\hat{\mathbf{i}} + \alpha\hat{\mathbf{j}} + \beta\hat{\mathbf{k}}$.

As, α, β and γ are distinct real numbers, therefore ABC form a triangle.

Clearly, $\mathbf{AB} = \mathbf{OB} - \mathbf{OA}$

$= (\beta\hat{\mathbf{i}} + \gamma\hat{\mathbf{j}} + \alpha\hat{\mathbf{k}}) - (\alpha\hat{\mathbf{i}} + \beta\hat{\mathbf{j}} + \gamma\hat{\mathbf{k}})$

$= (\beta - \alpha)\hat{\mathbf{i}} + (\gamma - \beta)\hat{\mathbf{j}} + (\alpha - \gamma)\hat{\mathbf{k}}$

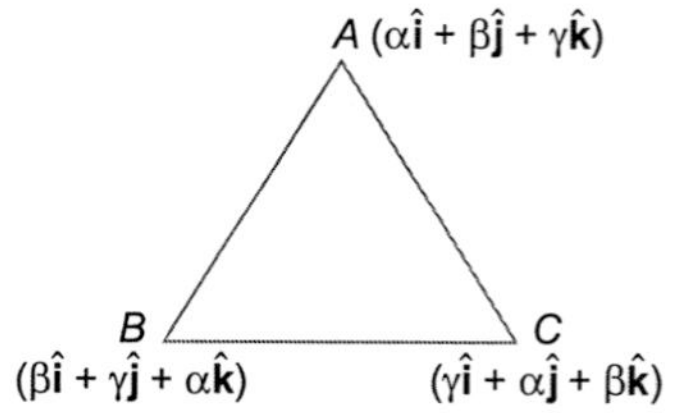

Now, $|\mathbf{AB}| = \sqrt{(\beta - \alpha)^2 + (\gamma - \beta)^2 + (\alpha - \gamma)^2}$

Similarly, $\mathbf{BC} = \mathbf{CA} = \sqrt{(\beta - \alpha)^2 + (\gamma - \beta)^2 + (\alpha - \gamma)^2}$

$\therefore \Delta ABC$ is an equilateral triangle. **Hence proved.**

Example 17. The two adjacent sides of a parallelogram are $2\hat{\mathbf{i}} + 4\hat{\mathbf{j}} - 5\hat{\mathbf{k}}$ and $\hat{\mathbf{i}} + 2\hat{\mathbf{j}} + 3\hat{\mathbf{k}}$. Find the unit vectors along the diagonals of the parallelogram.

Sol. Let $OACB$ be the given parallelogram and let the adjacent sides OA and OB be represented by $a = 2\hat{\mathbf{i}} + 4\hat{\mathbf{j}} - 5\hat{\mathbf{k}}$ and $b = \hat{\mathbf{i}} + 2\hat{\mathbf{j}} + 3\hat{\mathbf{k}}$ respectively.

Now, the vectors along the two diagonals are

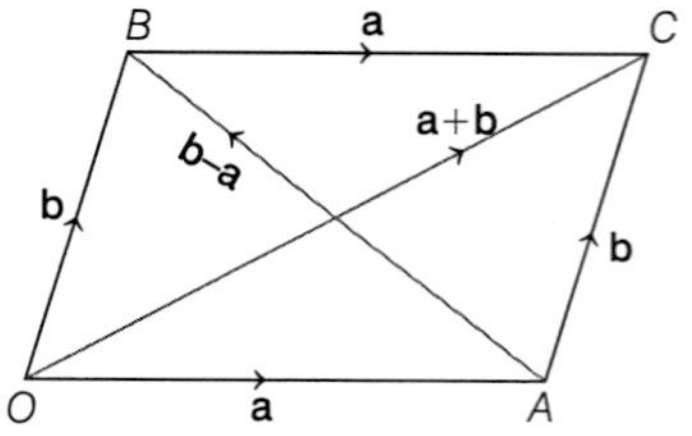

$$\mathbf{d}_1 = \mathbf{a} + \mathbf{b} = 3\hat{\mathbf{i}} + 6\hat{\mathbf{j}} - 2\hat{\mathbf{k}}$$

and $$\mathbf{d}_2 = \mathbf{b} - \mathbf{a} = -\hat{\mathbf{i}} - 2\hat{\mathbf{j}} + 8\hat{\mathbf{k}}$$

The required unit vectors are

$$\hat{\mathbf{n}}_1 = \frac{\mathbf{d}_1}{|\mathbf{d}_1|} = \frac{3\hat{\mathbf{i}} + 6\hat{\mathbf{j}} - 2\hat{\mathbf{k}}}{\sqrt{3^2 + 6^2 + (-2)^2}} = \frac{3}{7}\hat{\mathbf{i}} + \frac{6}{7}\hat{\mathbf{j}} - \frac{2}{7}\hat{\mathbf{k}}$$

and $$\hat{\mathbf{n}}_2 = \frac{d_2}{|d_2|} = \frac{-\hat{\mathbf{i}} - 2\hat{\mathbf{j}} + 8\hat{\mathbf{k}}}{\sqrt{(-1)^2 + (-2)^2 + 8^2}} = \frac{-1}{\sqrt{69}}\hat{\mathbf{i}} - \frac{2}{\sqrt{69}}\hat{\mathbf{j}} + \frac{8}{\sqrt{69}}\hat{\mathbf{k}}$$

Example 18. If the vectors $\mathbf{AB} = 4\hat{\mathbf{i}} + 3\hat{\mathbf{j}} + 2\hat{\mathbf{k}}$ and $\mathbf{AC} = 6\hat{\mathbf{i}} + \hat{\mathbf{j}} - 2\hat{\mathbf{k}}$ are the sides of a ΔABC, then find the length of the median through A.

Sol. In ΔABC, $\mathbf{AB} + \mathbf{BC} + \mathbf{CA} = 0$

$$\Rightarrow \quad \mathbf{AB} + \mathbf{BC} = \mathbf{AC} \qquad [\because \mathbf{CA} = -\mathbf{AC}]$$

$$\Rightarrow \quad \mathbf{BC} = \mathbf{AC} - \mathbf{AB}$$

$$\Rightarrow \quad \mathbf{BM} = \frac{\mathbf{AC} - \mathbf{AB}}{2} \qquad \text{...(i)}$$

[$\because M$ is the mid-point of BC]

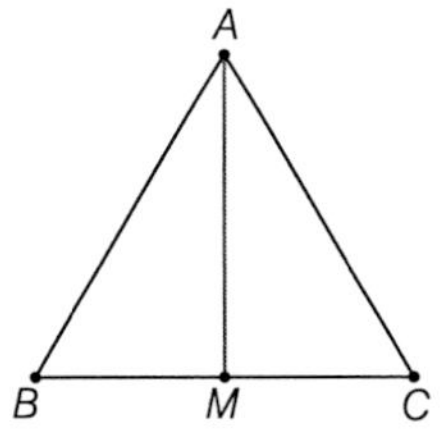

In ΔABM, $\mathbf{AB} + \mathbf{BM} + \mathbf{MA} = 0$

$$\Rightarrow \quad \mathbf{AB} + \mathbf{BM} = \mathbf{AM}$$

$$\Rightarrow \quad \mathbf{AB} + \frac{\mathbf{AC} - \mathbf{AB}}{2} = \mathbf{AM}$$

$$\Rightarrow \quad \frac{2\mathbf{AB} + \mathbf{AC} - \mathbf{AB}}{2} = \mathbf{AM} \Rightarrow \frac{\mathbf{AB} + \mathbf{AC}}{2} = \mathbf{AM}$$

$$\Rightarrow \quad \mathbf{AM} = \frac{(4\hat{\mathbf{i}} + 3\hat{\mathbf{j}} + 2\hat{\mathbf{k}}) + (6\hat{\mathbf{i}} + \hat{\mathbf{j}} - 2\hat{\mathbf{k}})}{2}$$

$$\Rightarrow \quad \mathbf{AM} = 5\hat{\mathbf{i}} + 2\hat{\mathbf{j}}$$

$$\Rightarrow \quad |\mathbf{AM}| = \sqrt{25 + 4} = \sqrt{29}$$

Time Saving Technique

Use $AM = \frac{AB + AC}{2}$, If AM is the median of ΔABC.

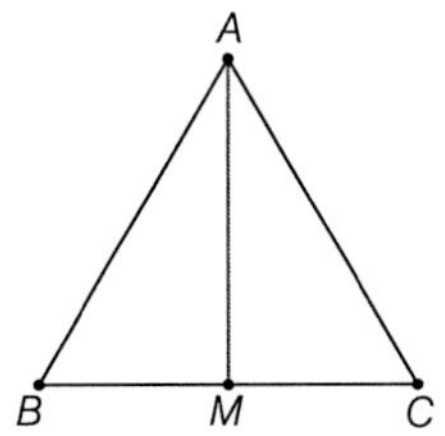

$$\Rightarrow AM = \frac{(4\hat{i} + 3\hat{j} + 2\hat{k}) + (6\hat{i} + \hat{j} - 2\hat{k})}{2} = 5\hat{i} + 2\hat{j}$$

Hence, $|AM| = \sqrt{29}$

1.10 Multiplication of a Vector by a Scalar

If $\mathbf{a}$ is a vector and m is a scalar (i.e. a real number), then $m\,\mathbf{a}$ is a vector whose magnitude is m times that of $\mathbf{a}$ and whose direction is the same as that of $\mathbf{a}$, if m is positive and opposite to that of $\mathbf{a}$, if m is negative.

$\therefore$ Magnitude of $ma = |m\mathbf{a}| = ma$

$\Rightarrow m$ (magnitude of $\mathbf{a}$) $= m\,|\mathbf{a}|$

Again, if $\mathbf{a} = a_1\hat{\mathbf{i}} + a_2\hat{\mathbf{j}} + a_3\hat{\mathbf{k}}$,

then $\quad m\,\mathbf{a} = (ma_1)\,\hat{\mathbf{i}} + (ma_2)\hat{\mathbf{j}} + (ma_3)\,\hat{\mathbf{k}}$

Properties of Multiplication of Vectors by a Scalar

The following are properties of multiplication of vectors by scalars, for vectors **a**, **b** and scalars m, n

(i) $m(-\mathbf{a}) = (-m)\,\mathbf{a} = -(m\mathbf{a})$

(ii) $(-m)(-\mathbf{a}) = m\,\mathbf{a}$

(iii) $m(n\mathbf{a}) = (mn)\,\mathbf{a} = n(m\mathbf{a})$

(iv) $(m + n)\,\mathbf{a} = m\mathbf{a} + n\mathbf{a}$

(v) $m(\mathbf{a} + \mathbf{b}) = m\,\mathbf{a} + m\,\mathbf{b}$

Example 19. For a non-zero vector **a**, find the set of real numbers, satisfying $|(5 - x)\mathbf{a}| < |2\mathbf{a}|$.

Sol. We have, $\quad |(5 - x)\,\mathbf{a}| < |2\mathbf{a}|$

$$|5 - x|\,|\mathbf{a}| < 2\,|\mathbf{a}|$$

$$\Rightarrow \quad |5 - x| < 2$$

$$\Rightarrow \quad -2 < 5 - x < 2$$

$$\Rightarrow \quad 3 < x < 7$$

1.11 Section Formula

Let A and B be two points with position vectors **a** and **b** respectively. Let P be a point on AB dividing it in the ratio $m : n$.

Internal Division

If P divides AB internally in the ratio $m : n$. Then, the position vector of P is given by $\mathbf{OP} = \frac{m\mathbf{b} + n\mathbf{a}}{m + n}$.

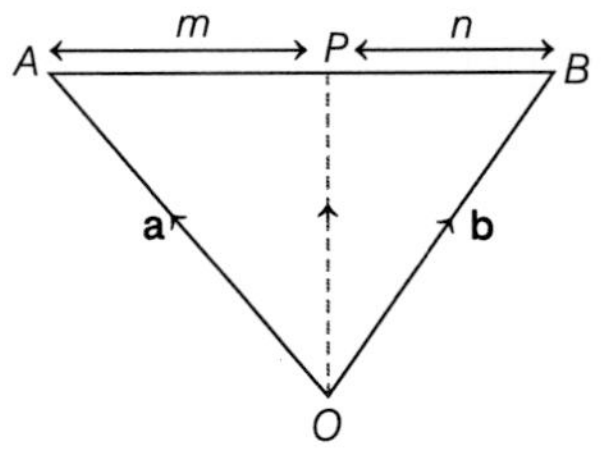

Proof

Let O be the origin. Then, $\mathbf{OA} = \mathbf{a}$ and $\mathbf{OB} = \mathbf{b}$. Let r be the position vector of P which divides AB internally in the ratio $m : n$. Then,

$$\frac{AP}{PB} = \frac{m}{n}$$

or $$n\mathbf{AP} = m\mathbf{PB}$$

or $$n\,(\text{PV of } P - \text{PV of } A) = m\,(\text{PV of } B - \text{PV of } P)$$

or $$n(\mathbf{r} - \mathbf{a}) = m(\mathbf{b} - \mathbf{r})$$

or $$n\mathbf{r} - n\mathbf{a} = m\mathbf{b} - m\mathbf{r}$$

or $$\mathbf{r}(n + m) = m\mathbf{b} + n\mathbf{a}$$

or $$\mathbf{r} = \frac{m\mathbf{b} + n\mathbf{a}}{m + n}$$

or $$\mathbf{OP} = \frac{m\mathbf{b} + n\mathbf{a}}{m + n}$$

External Division

If P divides AB externally in the ratio $m : n$. Then, the position vector of P is given by $\mathbf{OP} = \dfrac{m\mathbf{b} - n\mathbf{a}}{m - n}$.

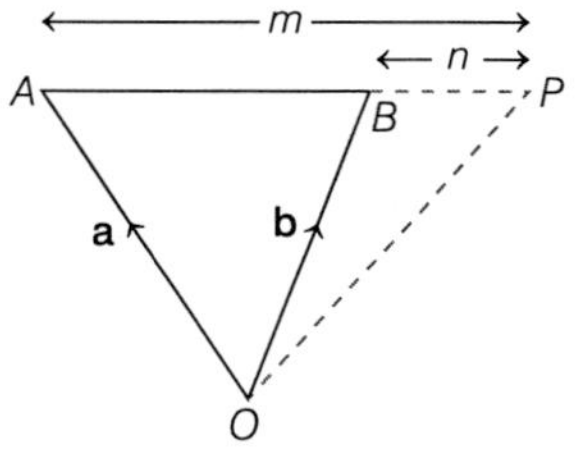

Proof

Let O be the origin. Then, $\mathbf{OA} = \mathbf{a}$, $\mathbf{OB} = \mathbf{b}$. Let $\mathbf{r}$ be the position vector of point P dividing AB externally in the ratio $m : n$.

Then, $$\frac{AP}{BP} = \frac{m}{n}$$

or $$nAP = mBP$$

or $$n\mathbf{AP} = m\mathbf{BP}$$

or $$n\,(\text{PV of } P - \text{PV of } A) = m\,(\text{PV of } P - \text{PV of } B)$$

or $$n(\mathbf{r} - \mathbf{a}) = m(\mathbf{r} - \mathbf{b})$$

or $$n\mathbf{r} - n\mathbf{a} = m\mathbf{r} - m\mathbf{b}$$

or $$r(m - n) = m\mathbf{b} - n\mathbf{a}$$

or $$\mathbf{r} = \frac{m\mathbf{b} - n\mathbf{a}}{m - n}$$

or $$\mathbf{OP} = \frac{m\mathbf{b} - n\mathbf{a}}{m - n}$$

JEE SPIKE

In ΔABC, having vertices $A(\mathbf{a})$, $B(\mathbf{b})$ and $C(\mathbf{c})$

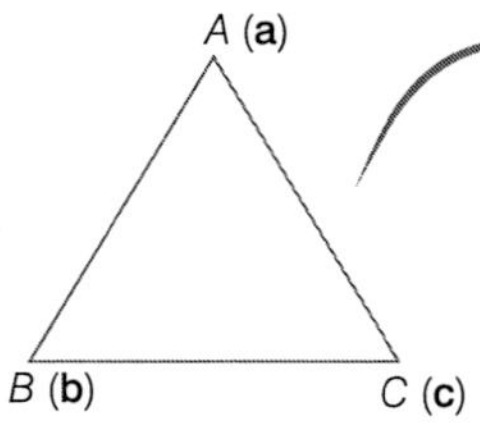

Concept Inside Video

(i) Position vector of mid-point of AB is $\dfrac{\mathbf{a} + \mathbf{b}}{2}$.

(ii) Position vector of centroid is $\dfrac{\mathbf{a} + \mathbf{b} + \mathbf{c}}{3}$.

(iii) Position vector of incentre is $\dfrac{BC\cdot \mathbf{a} + AC\cdot \mathbf{b} + AB\cdot \mathbf{c}}{AB + BC + AC}$.

(iv) Position vector of orthocentre is $\dfrac{\tan A\cdot \mathbf{a} + \tan B\cdot \mathbf{b} + \tan C\cdot \mathbf{c}}{\tan A + \tan B + \tan C}$.

(v) Position vector of circumcentre is $\dfrac{\sin 2A\cdot \mathbf{a} + \sin 2B\cdot \mathbf{b} + \sin 2C\cdot \mathbf{c}}{\sin 2A + \sin 2B + \sin 2C}$.

Example 20. Find the position vectors of the points which divide the join of points $A\,(2\mathbf{a} - 3\mathbf{b})$ and $B\,(3\mathbf{a} - 2\mathbf{b})$ internally and externally in the ratio $2 : 3$.

Sol. Let P be a point which divide AB internally in the ratio $2 : 3$. Then, by section formula, position vector of P is given by

$$\mathbf{OP} = \frac{2(3\mathbf{a} - 2\mathbf{b}) + 3(2\mathbf{a} - 3\mathbf{b})}{2 + 3}$$

$$= \frac{6\mathbf{a} - 4\mathbf{b} + 6\mathbf{a} - 9\mathbf{b}}{5} = \frac{12}{5}\mathbf{a} - \frac{13}{5}\mathbf{b}$$

Similarly, the position vector of the point (P') which divides AB externally in the ratio $2 : 3$ is given by

$$\mathbf{OP'} = \frac{2(3\mathbf{a} - 2\mathbf{b}) - 3(2\mathbf{a} - 3\mathbf{b})}{2 - 3}$$

$$= \frac{6\mathbf{a} - 4\mathbf{b} - 6\mathbf{a} + 9\mathbf{b}}{-1} = \frac{5\mathbf{b}}{-1} = -5\mathbf{b}$$

Example 21. If D, E and F are the mid-points of the sides BC, CA and AB respectively of the ΔABC and O be any point, then prove that

$$\mathbf{OA} + \mathbf{OB} + \mathbf{OC} = \mathbf{OD} + \mathbf{OE} + \mathbf{OF}$$

Sol. Since, D is the mid-point of BC, therefore by section formula, we have

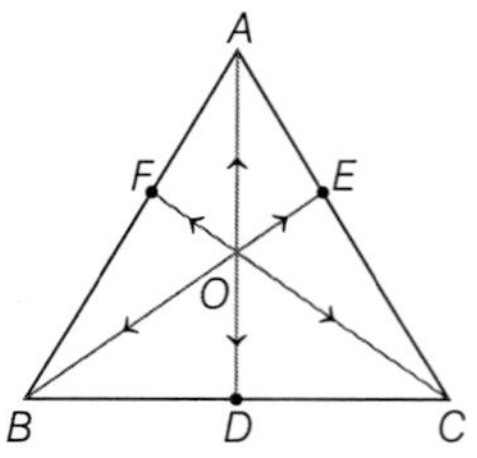

$$\mathbf{OD} = \frac{\mathbf{OB} + \mathbf{OC}}{2}$$

$\Rightarrow \quad \mathbf{OB} + \mathbf{OC} = 2\mathbf{OD}$ ...(i)

Similarly, $\quad \mathbf{OC} + \mathbf{OA} = 2\mathbf{OE}$ ...(ii)

and $\quad \mathbf{OB} + \mathbf{OA} = 2\mathbf{OF}$ ...(iii)

On adding Eqs. (i), (ii) and (iii), we get

$$2(\mathbf{OA} + \mathbf{OB} + \mathbf{OC}) = 2(\mathbf{OD} + \mathbf{OE} + \mathbf{OF})$$

$$\Rightarrow \quad \mathbf{OA} + \mathbf{OB} + \mathbf{OC} = \mathbf{OD} + \mathbf{OE} + \mathbf{OF}$$

Hence proved.

Example 22. If $\mathbf{OA} = 2\hat{i} + 2\hat{j} + \hat{k}$, $\mathbf{OB} = 2\hat{i} + 4\hat{j} + 4\hat{k}$ and the length of the internal bisector of $\angle AOB$ of ΔAOB is k, then find the value of $18k^2$.

Sol. We have, $\mathbf{OA} = 2\hat{\mathbf{i}} + 2\hat{\mathbf{j}} + \hat{\mathbf{k}}$

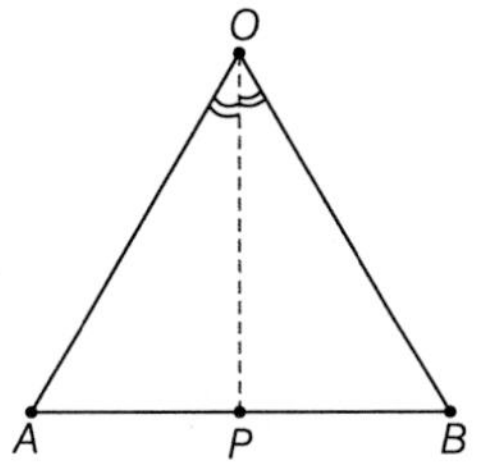

$\therefore \quad |\mathbf{OA}| = \sqrt{4+4+1} \Rightarrow |\mathbf{OA}| = 3$

$|\mathbf{OB}| = 2\hat{\mathbf{i}} + 4\hat{\mathbf{j}} + 4\hat{\mathbf{k}}$

$\therefore \quad |\mathbf{OB}| = \sqrt{4+16+16} = \sqrt{36} = 6$

Let the angle bisector of $\angle AOB$ intersect the side AB at P. Then, P divide the line segment AB internally in 3 : 6 i.e. 1 : 2.

$$\therefore \quad |\mathbf{OP}| = \frac{1(\mathbf{OB}) + 2(\mathbf{OA})}{1+2}$$

$$= \frac{(2\hat{\mathbf{i}} + 4\hat{\mathbf{j}} + 4\hat{\mathbf{k}}) + 2(2\hat{\mathbf{i}} + 2\hat{\mathbf{j}} + \hat{\mathbf{k}})}{3}$$

$$= \frac{6\hat{\mathbf{i}} + 8\hat{\mathbf{j}} + 6\hat{\mathbf{k}}}{3} = 2\hat{\mathbf{i}} + \frac{8\hat{\mathbf{j}}}{3} + 2\hat{\mathbf{k}}$$

$$\therefore \quad |\mathbf{OP}| = \sqrt{4 + \frac{64}{9} + 4}$$

$$= \sqrt{\frac{36+64+36}{9}} = \sqrt{\frac{136}{9}} = k$$

$$\Rightarrow \quad 18k^2 = 18 \times \frac{136}{9} = 272$$

Example 23. The position vectors of the vertices A, B and C of a triangle are $\hat{i} - \hat{j} - 3\hat{k}$, $2\hat{i} + \hat{j} - 2\hat{k}$ and $-5\hat{i} + 2\hat{j} - 6\hat{k}$, respectively. Find the length of the bisector AD of the $\angle BAC$, where D is on the segment BC.

> **Decoding the Question**
>
> In ΔABC, AD is internal bisector of $\angle BAC$, then $\frac{AB}{AC} = \frac{BD}{DC}$.

Sol. $|\mathbf{AB}| = |(2\hat{\mathbf{i}} + \hat{\mathbf{j}} - 2\hat{\mathbf{k}}) - (\hat{\mathbf{i}} - \hat{\mathbf{j}} - 3\hat{\mathbf{k}})|$

$$= |\hat{\mathbf{i}} + 2\hat{\mathbf{j}} + \hat{\mathbf{k}}| = \sqrt{1^2 + 2^2 + 1^2} = \sqrt{6}$$

$$|\mathbf{AC}| = |(-5\hat{\mathbf{i}} + 2\hat{\mathbf{j}} - 6\hat{\mathbf{k}}) - (\hat{\mathbf{i}} - \hat{\mathbf{j}} - 3\hat{\mathbf{k}})| = |-6\hat{\mathbf{i}} + 3\hat{\mathbf{j}} - 3\hat{\mathbf{k}}|$$

$$= \sqrt{(-6)^2 + 3^2 + (-3)^2} = \sqrt{54} = 3\sqrt{6}$$

$$|\mathbf{BD}| : |\mathbf{DC}| = |\mathbf{AB}| : |\mathbf{AC}| = \frac{\sqrt{6}}{3\sqrt{6}} = \frac{1}{3}$$

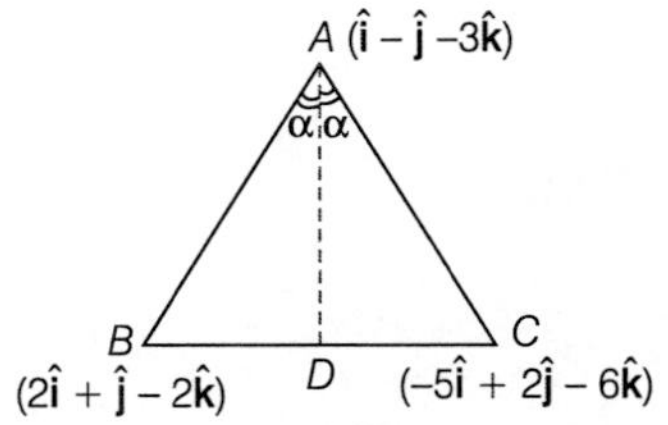

$$\therefore \text{ Position vector of } D = \frac{1(-5\hat{\mathbf{i}} + 2\hat{\mathbf{j}} - 6\hat{\mathbf{k}}) + 3(2\hat{\mathbf{i}} + \hat{\mathbf{j}} - 2\hat{\mathbf{k}})}{1+3}$$

$$= \frac{1}{4}(\hat{\mathbf{i}} + 5\hat{\mathbf{j}} - 12\hat{\mathbf{k}})$$

$\therefore \quad \mathbf{AD}$ = Position vector of D – Position vector of A

$$\mathbf{AD} = \frac{1}{4}(\hat{\mathbf{i}} + 5\hat{\mathbf{j}} - 12\hat{\mathbf{k}}) - (\hat{\mathbf{i}} - \hat{\mathbf{j}} - 3\hat{\mathbf{k}}) = \frac{1}{4}(-3\hat{\mathbf{i}} + 9\hat{\mathbf{j}})$$

$$= \frac{3}{4}(-\hat{\mathbf{i}} + 3\hat{\mathbf{j}})$$

$$|\mathbf{AD}| = \frac{3}{4}\sqrt{(-1)^2 + 3^2} = \frac{3}{4}\sqrt{10}$$

Example 24. The median AD of the ΔABC is bisected at E and BE meets AC at F. Then, find the ratio of $AF : AC$.

Sol. Let position vector of A w.r.t. B is $\mathbf{a}$ and that of C w.r.t. B is $\mathbf{c}$.

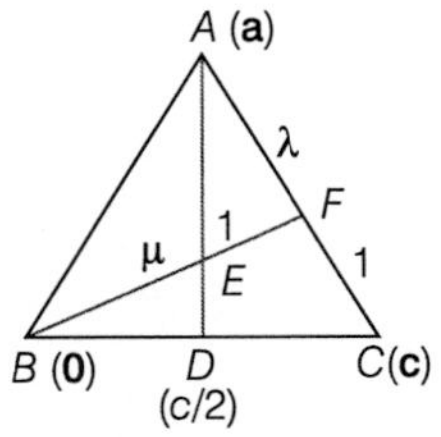

$$\text{Position vector of } D \text{ w.r.t. } B = \frac{0 + \mathbf{c}}{2} = \frac{\mathbf{c}}{2}$$

$$\text{Position vector of } E = \frac{\mathbf{a} + \frac{\mathbf{c}}{2}}{2} = \frac{\mathbf{a}}{2} + \frac{\mathbf{c}}{4} \quad \text{...(i)}$$

Let $AF : FC = \lambda : 1$ and $BE : EF = \mu : 1$

$$\text{Position vector of } F = \frac{\lambda\mathbf{c} + \mathbf{a}}{1 + \lambda}$$

Now, position vector of

$$E = \frac{\mu\left(\frac{\lambda\mathbf{c} + \mathbf{a}}{1+\lambda}\right) + 1 \cdot 0}{\mu + 1}$$

$$= \frac{\mu}{(1+\lambda)(1+\mu)} \cdot \mathbf{a} + \frac{\lambda\mu}{(1+\lambda)(1+\mu)} \cdot \mathbf{c} \quad \text{...(ii)}$$

From Eqs. (i) and (ii), we get

$$\frac{\mathbf{a}}{2}+\frac{\mathbf{c}}{4}=\frac{\mu}{(1+\lambda)(1+\mu)}\mathbf{a}+\frac{\lambda\mu}{(1+\lambda)(1+\mu)}\mathbf{c}$$

On comparing both sides, we get

$$\frac{1}{2}=\frac{\mu}{(1+\lambda)(1+\mu)} \text{ and } \frac{1}{4}=\frac{\lambda\mu}{(1+\lambda)(1+\mu)} \Rightarrow \lambda=\frac{1}{2}$$

$$\therefore \quad \frac{AF}{AC}=\frac{AF}{AF+FC}=\frac{\lambda}{1+\lambda}=\frac{\frac{1}{2}}{\frac{3}{2}}=\frac{1}{3}$$

JEE SCANNER

Example Similar to PYQ Asked in JEE Main 2023

In ΔABC, if the points H and O are the circumcentre and the orthocentre respectively, then the value of **HA + HB + HC** *is equal to*

(a) **HO** (b) **HG** (c) **HC** (d) **HB**

Sol. (a) $\mathbf{HA}+\mathbf{HB}+\mathbf{HC}=\mathbf{a}+\mathbf{b}+\mathbf{c}$

and $\quad \mathbf{HG}=\dfrac{\mathbf{a}+\mathbf{b}+\mathbf{c}}{3} \Rightarrow \mathbf{a}+\mathbf{b}+\mathbf{c}=3\mathbf{HG}=\mathbf{HO}$

Hence, G is the centroid of triangle.

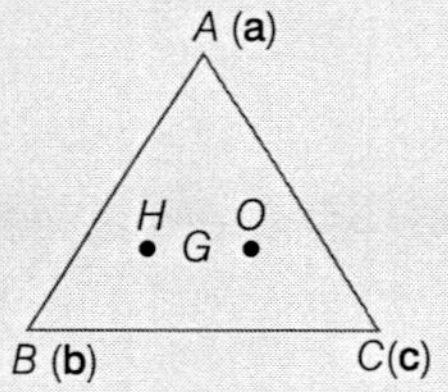

Skill Builder

In ΔPQR, if the points D and E are the circumcentre and the orthocentre respectively, then the value of **DP + DQ + DR** is equal to

For Sol.

(a) **DG** (b) **DE** (c) **DP** (d) **DR**

■ **For more practice** See Q.15 of Milestone Practice 2.

1.12 Vector Along the Bisector of the Angle between Two Vectors

Let $\hat{\mathbf{a}}$ and $\hat{\mathbf{b}}$ be the unit vectors along the vector $\mathbf{AB}(\mathbf{a})$ and $\mathbf{AC}(\mathbf{b})$, respectively.

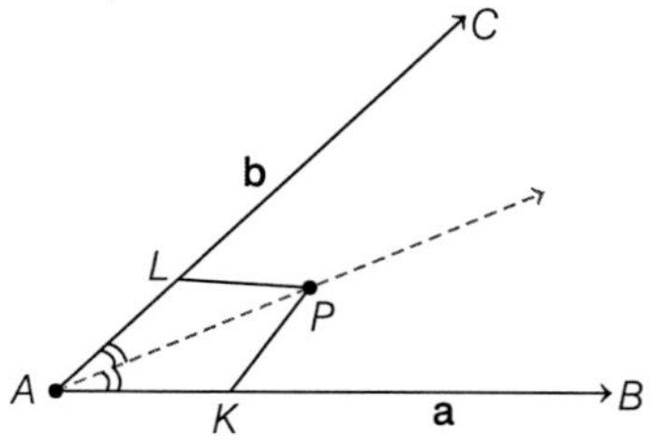

$\therefore\ |\mathbf{AK}|=|\mathbf{AL}|$ and $AKPL$ is a rhombus.

The bisector of $\angle BAC$ is $\hat{\mathbf{a}}+\hat{\mathbf{b}}$

So, a vector along the bisector of angle between $\mathbf{a}$ and $\mathbf{b}$ is $\lambda\left(\dfrac{\mathbf{a}}{|\mathbf{a}|}+\dfrac{\mathbf{b}}{|\mathbf{b}|}\right)$.

Similarly, a vector along the external bisector is $\lambda\left(\dfrac{\mathbf{a}}{|\mathbf{a}|}-\dfrac{\mathbf{b}}{|\mathbf{b}|}\right)$.

Example 25. Find the vector **c**, directed along the internal bisector of the angle between the vectors $\mathbf{a}=7\hat{\mathbf{i}}-4\hat{\mathbf{j}}-4\hat{\mathbf{k}}$ and $\mathbf{b}=-2\hat{\mathbf{i}}-\hat{\mathbf{j}}+2\hat{\mathbf{k}}$ with $|\mathbf{c}|=5\sqrt{6}$.

Sol. Let $\mathbf{a}=7\hat{\mathbf{i}}-4\hat{\mathbf{j}}-4\hat{\mathbf{k}}$ and $\mathbf{b}=-2\hat{\mathbf{i}}-\hat{\mathbf{j}}+2\hat{\mathbf{k}}$

$$\text{Now, required vector } \mathbf{c}=\lambda\left(\frac{\mathbf{a}}{|\mathbf{a}|}+\frac{\mathbf{b}}{|\mathbf{b}|}\right)$$

$$=\lambda\left(\frac{7\hat{\mathbf{i}}-4\hat{\mathbf{j}}-4\hat{\mathbf{k}}}{9}+\frac{-2\hat{\mathbf{i}}-\hat{\mathbf{j}}+2\hat{\mathbf{k}}}{3}\right)$$

$$\mathbf{c}=\frac{\lambda}{9}(\hat{\mathbf{i}}-7\hat{\mathbf{j}}+2\hat{\mathbf{k}})$$

$$|\mathbf{c}|^2=\frac{\lambda^2}{81}\times 54=150 \quad \text{[given]}$$

$$\Rightarrow \quad \lambda=\pm 15$$

$$\Rightarrow \quad \mathbf{c}=\pm\frac{5}{3}(\hat{\mathbf{i}}-7\hat{\mathbf{j}}+2\hat{\mathbf{k}})$$

1.13 Magnitude of Resultant of Two Vectors

Let **R** be the resultant of two vectors **P** and **Q**. Then,

$\mathbf{R}=\mathbf{P}+\mathbf{Q}$

$$|\mathbf{R}|=R=\sqrt{P^2+Q^2+2PQ\cos\theta}$$

where, $|\mathbf{P}|=P, |\mathbf{Q}|=Q,\ \tan\alpha=\dfrac{Q\sin\theta}{P+Q\cos\theta}$

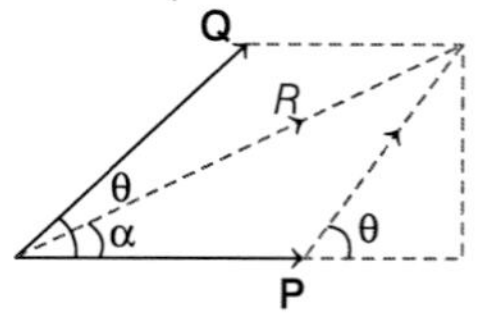

Deduction When $|\mathbf{P}|=|\mathbf{Q}|$, i.e. $P=Q$

$$\tan\alpha=\frac{P\sin\theta}{P+P\cos\theta}=\frac{\sin\theta}{1+\cos\theta}=\tan\frac{\theta}{2}$$

$$\therefore \quad \alpha=\frac{\theta}{2}$$

Hence, the angular bisector of two unit vectors **a** and **b** is along the vector sum $\mathbf{a}+\mathbf{b}$.

JEE Focus Points

- The internal bisector of the angle between any two vectors is along the vector sum of the corresponding unit vectors.
- The external bisector of the angle between two vectors is along the vector difference of the corresponding unit vectors.

Concept Inside Video

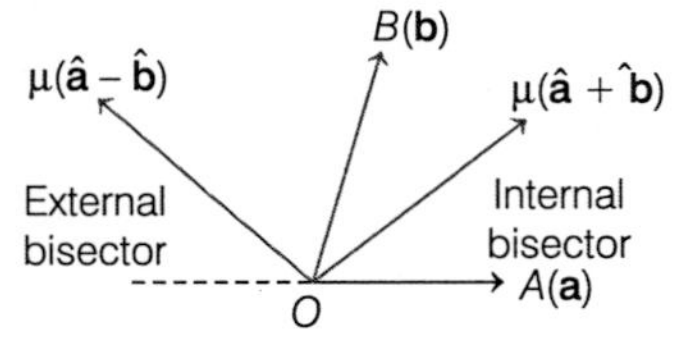

Example 26. The sum of two forces is 18 N and resultant whose direction is at right angles to the smaller force is 12 N. Find the magnitude of the two forces.

Sol. We have, $|\mathbf{P}|+|\mathbf{Q}|=18\text{N}; |\mathbf{R}|=|\mathbf{P}+\mathbf{Q}|=12\text{ N}$

$$\alpha = 90^\circ$$

$$P + Q\cos\theta = 0$$

$$\Rightarrow \quad Q\cos\theta = -P$$

Now. $R^2 = P^2 + Q^2 + 2PQ\cos\theta$

$$\Rightarrow \quad R^2 = P^2 + Q^2 + 2P(-P) = Q^2 - P^2$$

$$= (Q+P)(Q-P)$$

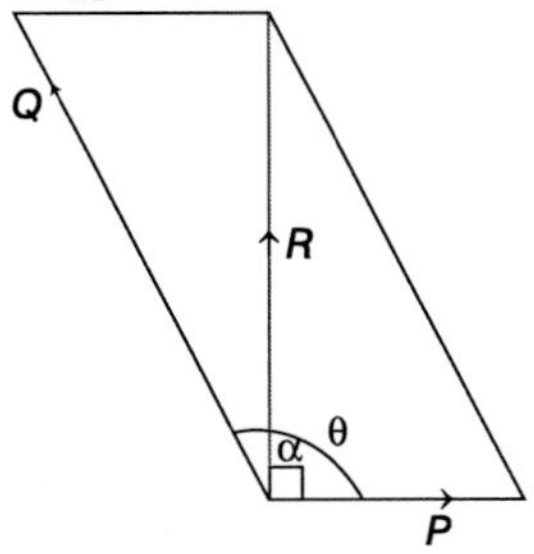

$$\Rightarrow \quad 12^2 = (P+Q)(Q-P) = 18(Q-P)$$

$$\Rightarrow \quad Q - P = 8 \text{ and } Q + P = 18$$

$$\Rightarrow \quad Q = 13, P = 5$$

$\therefore$ Magnitude of two forces are 5 N and 13 N.

Example 27. Find the length of longer diagonal of the parallelogram constructed on $5\mathbf{a}+2\mathbf{b}$ and $\mathbf{a}-3\mathbf{b}$, when it is given that $|\mathbf{a}|=2\sqrt{2}, |\mathbf{b}|=3$ and angle between **a** and **b** is $\dfrac{\pi}{4}$.

Sol. Length of the two diagonals will be

$$d_1 = |(5\mathbf{a}+2\mathbf{b})+(\mathbf{a}-3\mathbf{b})|$$

and $\quad d_2 = |(5\mathbf{a}+2\mathbf{b})-(\mathbf{a}-3\mathbf{b})|$

$$\Rightarrow \quad d_1 = |6\mathbf{a}-\mathbf{b}|, d_2 = |4\mathbf{a}+5\mathbf{b}|$$

Thus,

$$d_1 = \sqrt{|6\mathbf{a}|^2 + |-\mathbf{b}|^2 + 2|6\mathbf{a}||-\mathbf{b}|\cos(\pi - \pi/4)}$$

$$= \sqrt{36(2\sqrt{2})^2 + 9 + 12\cdot 2\sqrt{2}\cdot 3\cdot\left(-\frac{1}{\sqrt{2}}\right)} = 15$$

$$d_2 = \sqrt{|4\mathbf{a}|^2 + |5\mathbf{b}|^2 + 2|4\mathbf{a}||5\mathbf{b}|\cos\frac{\pi}{4}}$$

$$= \sqrt{16\times 8 + 25\times 9 + 40\times 2\sqrt{2}\times 3\times\frac{1}{\sqrt{2}}} = \sqrt{593}$$

$\therefore$ Length of the longer diagonal $= \sqrt{593}$

Example 28. ΔABC is an isosceles triangle right angled at A. Forces of magnitude $2\sqrt{2}$, 5 and 6 act along **BC**, **CA** and **AB** respectively. The magnitude of their resultant force is

(a) 4 (b) 5

(c) $11+2\sqrt{2}$ (d) 30

Sol. (b) $R\cos\theta = 6\cos 0^\circ + 2\sqrt{2}\cos(180^\circ - B) + 5\cos 270^\circ$

$$R\cos\theta = 6 - 2\sqrt{2}\cos B \qquad \text{...(i)}$$

$$R\sin\theta = 6\sin 0^\circ + 2\sqrt{2}\sin(180^\circ - B) + 5\sin 270^\circ$$

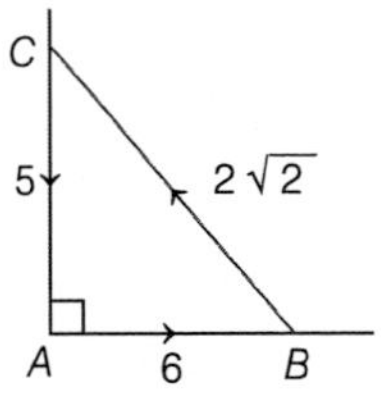

$$R\sin\theta = 2\sqrt{2}\sin B - 5 \qquad \text{...(ii)}$$

From Eqs. (i) and (ii), we get

$$R^2 = 36 + 8\cos^2 B - 24\sqrt{2}\cos B + 8\sin^2 B + 25 - 20\sqrt{2}\sin B$$

$$= 61 + 8(\cos^2 B + \sin^2 B) - 24\sqrt{2}\cos B - 20\sqrt{2}\sin B$$

$\because ABC$ is a right angled isosceles triangle.

i.e. $\quad \angle B = \angle C = 45^\circ$

$$\therefore \quad R^2 = 61 + 8(1) - 24\sqrt{2}\frac{1}{\sqrt{2}} - 20\sqrt{2}\cdot\frac{1}{\sqrt{2}} = 25$$

$$\therefore \quad R = 5$$

Milestone Practice 1.2

1. Find a unit vector in the direction of the resultant of the vectors $\hat{i}+2\hat{j}+3\hat{k}$, $-\hat{i}+2\hat{j}+\hat{k}$ and $3\hat{i}+\hat{j}$.

2. Find the direction cosines of the resultant of the vectors $(\hat{i}+\hat{j}+\hat{k})$, $(-\hat{i}+\hat{j}+\hat{k})$, $(\hat{i}-\hat{j}+\hat{k})$ and $(\hat{i}+\hat{j}-\hat{k})$.

3. In a regular hexagon *ABCDEF*, show that **AE** is equal to **AC** + **AF** − **AB** .

4. In any ΔABC, a point *P* is on the side *BC*. If **PQ** is the resultant of the vectors **AP**, **PB** and **PC**, then prove that *ABQC* is a parallelogram and *Q* is a fixed point.

5. In a regular hexagon *ABCDEF*, the value of **AB** + **AC** + **AD** + **AE** + **AF** is equal to

   (a) **AD** (b) 2**AD** (c) 3**AD** (d) 4**AD**

6. The position vectors of *A*, *B*, *C*, *D* are **a**, **b**, 2**a** + 3**b** and **a** − 2**b**, respectively. Show that **DB** = 3**b** − **a** and **AC** = **a** + 3**b**.

7. If $P(-1, 2)$ and $Q(3, -7)$ are two points, express the vector **PQ** in terms of unit vectors $\hat{i}$ and $\hat{j}$. Also, find distance between point *P* and *Q*. What is the unit vector in the direction of **PQ**?

8. Show that the points *A*, *B* and *C* with position vectors $\mathbf{a}=3\hat{j}-4\hat{j}-4\hat{k}$, $\mathbf{b}=2\hat{i}-\hat{j}+\hat{k}$ and $\mathbf{c}=\hat{i}-3\hat{j}-5\hat{k}$ respectively, form the vertices of a right angled triangle.

9. If $\mathbf{a}=\hat{i}+2\hat{j}+2\hat{k}$ and $\mathbf{b}=3\hat{i}+6\hat{j}+2\hat{k}$, then find a vector in the direction of **a** and having magnitude as $|\mathbf{b}|$.

10. Find the position vector of a point *P* which divides the line joining two points *A* and *B* whose position vectors are $\hat{i}+2\hat{j}-\hat{k}$ and $-\hat{i}+\hat{j}+\hat{k}$ respectively, in the ratio 2 : 1.

    (i) internally (ii) externally

11. If the position vector of one end of the line segment *AB* be $2\hat{i}+3\hat{j}-\hat{k}$ and the position vector of its middle point be $3(\hat{i}+\hat{j}+\hat{k})$, then the position vector of the other end, is

    (a) $2\hat{i}+3\hat{j}+7\hat{k}$ (b) $4\hat{i}+\hat{j}+7\hat{k}$
    (c) $4\hat{i}+3\hat{j}+\hat{k}$ (d) $4\hat{i}+3\hat{j}+7\hat{k}$

12. Let *ABCD* be a parallelogram whose diagonals intersect at *P* and let *O* be the origin. Then, show that **OA** + **OB** + **OC** + **OD** = 4**OP**.

13. Let **a**, **b** and **c** the position vectors of *A*, *B* and *C*, respectively of ΔABC. If $|\mathbf{a}-\mathbf{b}|=4$, $|\mathbf{b}-\mathbf{c}|=2$ and $|\mathbf{c}-\mathbf{a}|=3$, then the distance between the centroid and the incentre of triangle is

    (a) $\frac{4}{9}$ (b) $\frac{1}{3}$ (c) $\frac{3}{8}$ (d) $\frac{2}{5}$

14. In a ΔABC, *D* and *E* are points on *BC* and *AC* respectively. Such that $BD = 2DC$ and $AE = 3EC$. Let *P* be the point of intersections of *AD* and *BE*. Find $\frac{BP}{PE}$ using vector methods.

15. If the points *H* and *O* are respectively the circumcentre and the orthocentre of ΔPQR, then find the value of $\frac{\mathbf{HP}+\mathbf{HQ}+\mathbf{HR}}{2}$.

16. Find unit vector bisecting the angle between vectors, positive *X*-axis and positive *Z*-axis.

17. Find the unit vector **c** if $-\hat{i}+\hat{j}-\hat{k}$ bisects the angle between vectors **c** and $3\hat{i}+4\hat{j}$.

18. $A(1, -1, -3)$, $B(2, 1, -2)$ and $C(-5, 2, -6)$ are the position vectors of the vertices of a ΔABC, then the length of the bisector of its internal angle at *A* is equal to

    (a) $\frac{2\sqrt{10}}{5}$ (b) $\frac{5\sqrt{10}}{2}$ (c) $\frac{3\sqrt{10}}{4}$ (d) $\frac{2\sqrt{10}}{9}$

19. Two forces F_1 and F_2 of magnitude 6*F* and 8*F* respectively are at an angle θ with each other. If the force F_2 is halved, then their resultant also get halved. Then, find the angle θ.

Answer Key

1. $\frac{3\hat{i}+5\hat{j}+4\hat{k}}{5\sqrt{2}}$ 2. $\frac{1}{\sqrt{3}}, \frac{1}{\sqrt{3}}, \frac{1}{\sqrt{3}}$ 5. (c) 7. $4\hat{i}-9\hat{j}, \sqrt{97}, \frac{4\hat{i}-9\hat{j}}{\sqrt{97}}$ 9. $\frac{7}{3}(\hat{i}+2\hat{j}+2\hat{k})$

10. (i) $\frac{-\hat{i}+4\hat{j}+\hat{k}}{3}$ (ii) $-3\hat{i}+3\hat{k}$ 11. (d) 13. (b) 14. $\frac{8}{3}$

15. $\frac{\mathbf{HO}}{2}$ 16. $\pm\frac{1}{\sqrt{2}}(\hat{i}+\hat{k})$ 17. $\frac{-1}{15}(11\hat{i}+10\hat{j}+2\hat{k})$ 18. (c)

19. Cannot determined

For Detailed Solution

Milestone 3 Collinearity and Coplanarity

• Linear Combination of Vectors • Collinearity and Coplanarity of Vectors • Theorem of Coplanar Vectors • Theorem of Non-coplanar Vectors • Linear Independence and Dependence of Vectors

1.14 Linear Combination of Vectors

A vector **r** is said to be a linear combination of vectors **a, b** and **c**... etc., if there exist scalars x, y and z etc. such that $\mathbf{r} = x\mathbf{a} + y\mathbf{b} + z\mathbf{c} + \ldots$

e.g. Vectors $\mathbf{r}_1 = 2\mathbf{a} + \mathbf{b} + 3\mathbf{c}$ and $\mathbf{r}_2 = \mathbf{a} + 3\mathbf{b} + \sqrt{2}\mathbf{c}$ are linear combinations of the vectors **a**, **b** and **c**.

1.15 Collinearity and Coplanarity of Vectors

Relation between Two Collinear Vectors (or Parallel Vectors)

Let **a** and **b** be two collinear vectors and let $\hat{\mathbf{x}}$ be the unit vector in the direction of **a**. Then, the unit vector in the direction of **b** is $\hat{\mathbf{x}}$ or $-\hat{\mathbf{x}}$ as **a** and **b** are like or unlike parallel vectors. Now, $\mathbf{a} = |\mathbf{a}|\,\hat{\mathbf{x}}$ and $\mathbf{b} = \pm|\mathbf{b}|\,\hat{\mathbf{x}}$.

$$\therefore \quad \mathbf{a} = \left(\frac{|\mathbf{a}|}{|\mathbf{b}|}\right)|\mathbf{b}|\,\hat{\mathbf{x}} \Rightarrow \mathbf{a} = \pm\left(\frac{|\mathbf{a}|}{|\mathbf{b}|}\right)\mathbf{b}$$

$$\Rightarrow \quad \mathbf{a} = \lambda\mathbf{b}, \text{ where } \lambda = \pm\frac{|\mathbf{a}|}{|\mathbf{b}|}$$

Thus, if **a** and **b** are collinear vectors, then $\mathbf{a} = \lambda\mathbf{b}$ or $\mathbf{b} = \lambda\mathbf{a}$ for some scalar λ i.e. there exist two non-zero scalar quantities x and y so that $x\mathbf{a} + y\mathbf{b} = \mathbf{O}$

An Important Theorem

Theorem Vectors **a** and **b** are two non-zero, non-collinear vectors and x, y are two scalars such that $x\mathbf{a} + y\mathbf{b} = 0$.

Then, $\quad x = 0, y = 0$

Proof It is given that

$$x\mathbf{a} + y\mathbf{b} = 0 \qquad \ldots\text{(i)}$$

Suppose that $x \neq 0$, then dividing both sides of Eq. (i) by the scalar x, we get

$$\mathbf{a} = -\frac{y}{x}\mathbf{b} \qquad \ldots\text{(ii)}$$

Now, $\frac{y}{x}$ is a scalar, because x and y are scalars.

Hence, Eq. (ii) expresses **a** as product of **b** by a scalar, so that **a** and **b** are collinear.

Thus, we arrive at a contradiction because **a** and **b** are given to be non-collinear.

Thus, our supposition that $x \neq 0$, is wrong.

Hence, $x = 0$. Similarly, $y = 0$

JEE Focus Points

Concept Inside Video

- $x\mathbf{a} + y\mathbf{b} = 0 \Rightarrow \begin{cases} \mathbf{a} = 0, \mathbf{b} = 0 \\ \text{or} \\ x = 0, y = 0 \\ \text{or} \\ \mathbf{a} \parallel \mathbf{b} \end{cases}$
- If **a** and **b** are two non-collinear (or non-parallel) vectors, then $x_1\mathbf{a} + y_1\mathbf{b} = x_2\mathbf{a} + y_2\mathbf{b}$
  $\Rightarrow \quad x_1 = x_2$ and $y_1 = y_2$
  Proof $x_1\mathbf{a} + y_1\mathbf{b} = x_2\mathbf{a} + y_2\mathbf{b}$
  $\Rightarrow \quad (x_1 - x_2)\mathbf{a} + (y_1 - y_2)\mathbf{b} = 0$
  $\Rightarrow \quad x_1 - x_2 = 0$ and $y_1 - y_2 = 0$
  [$\because$ **a** and **b** are non-collinear]
  $\Rightarrow \quad x_1 = x_2$ and $y_1 = y_2$
  If $\mathbf{a} = a_1\hat{\mathbf{i}} + a_2\hat{\mathbf{j}} + a_3\hat{\mathbf{k}}$ and $\mathbf{b} = b_1\hat{\mathbf{i}} + b_2\hat{\mathbf{j}} + b_3\hat{\mathbf{k}}$, then $\mathbf{a} \parallel \mathbf{b}$
  $\Rightarrow \quad \frac{a_1}{b_1} = \frac{a_2}{b_2} = \frac{a_3}{b_3}$

Test of Collinearity of Three Points

(i) Three points A, B and C are collinear, if $\mathbf{AB} = \lambda\mathbf{BC}$

(ii) Three points with position vectors **a, b** and **c** are collinear iff there exist scalars x, y and z not all zero such that

$$x\mathbf{a} + y\mathbf{b} + z\mathbf{c} = 0,$$

where $x + y + z = 0$

Proof Let us suppose that points A, B and C are collinear and their position vectors are **a, b** and **c** respectively. Let C divide the join of **a** and **b** in the ratio $y : x$.

Then, $\mathbf{c} = \dfrac{x\mathbf{a} + y\mathbf{b}}{x + y}$

or $x\mathbf{a} + y\mathbf{b} - (x + y)\mathbf{c} = 0$

or $x\mathbf{a} + y\mathbf{b} + z\mathbf{c} = 0$,

where $z = -(x + y)$

Also, $x + y + z = x + y - (x + y) = 0$

Conversely, let $x\mathbf{a} + y\mathbf{b} + z\mathbf{c} = 0$,

where $x + y + z = 0$.

Therefore,

$$x\mathbf{a} + y\mathbf{b} = -z\mathbf{c} = (x + y)\mathbf{c} \qquad [\because x + y = -z]$$

or $\mathbf{c} = \dfrac{x\mathbf{a} + y\mathbf{b}}{x + y}$

This relation shows that **c** divides the join of **a** and **b** in the ratio $y : x$.

Hence, the three points A, B and C are collinear.

(iii) If $\mathbf{a} = a_1\hat{\mathbf{i}} + a_2\hat{\mathbf{j}}$, $\mathbf{b} = b_1\hat{\mathbf{i}} + b_2\hat{\mathbf{j}}$ and $\mathbf{c} = c_1\hat{\mathbf{i}} + c_2\hat{\mathbf{j}}$, then the points with position vector **a**, **b** and **c** will be collinear iff $\begin{vmatrix} a_1 & a_2 & 1 \\ b_1 & b_2 & 1 \\ c_1 & c_2 & 1 \end{vmatrix} = 0$.

Proof The points with position vector **a**, **b** and **c** will be collinear iff there exist scalars x, y and z not all zero such that,

$$x(a_1\hat{\mathbf{i}} + a_2\hat{\mathbf{j}}) + y(b_1\hat{\mathbf{i}} + b_2\hat{\mathbf{j}}) + z(c_1\hat{\mathbf{i}} + c_2\hat{\mathbf{j}}) = 0$$

and $x + y + z = 0$

$$\Rightarrow \quad xa_1 + yb_1 + zc_1 = 0$$
$$xa_2 + yb_2 + zc_2 = 0$$
$$x + y + z = 0$$

Thus, the points will be collinear iff the above system of equations have non-trivial solution

Hence, the points will be collinear

$$\text{iff} \begin{vmatrix} a_1 & b_1 & c_1 \\ a_2 & b_2 & c_2 \\ 1 & 1 & 1 \end{vmatrix} = 0 \text{ or } \begin{vmatrix} a_1 & a_2 & 1 \\ b_1 & b_2 & 1 \\ c_1 & c_2 & 1 \end{vmatrix} = 0.$$

Example 29. Show that the points $A(1, 2, 3)$, $B(3, 4, 7)$ and $C(-3, -2, -5)$ are collinear. Find the ratio in which point C divides AB.

> **Decoding the Question**
> First use, if three points A, B, C are collinear, then $\mathbf{AB} = \lambda\mathbf{BC}$.
> After this, apply internal section formula.

Sol. Clearly, $\mathbf{AB} = (3 - 1)\hat{\mathbf{i}} + (4 - 2)\hat{\mathbf{j}} + (7 - 3)\hat{\mathbf{k}}$

$$= 2\hat{\mathbf{i}} + 2\hat{\mathbf{j}} + 4\hat{\mathbf{k}}$$

and $\mathbf{BC} = (-3 - 3)\hat{\mathbf{i}} + (-2 - 4)\hat{\mathbf{j}} + (-5 - 7)\hat{\mathbf{k}}$

$$= -6\hat{\mathbf{i}} - 6\hat{\mathbf{j}} - 12\hat{\mathbf{k}}$$
$$= -3(2\hat{\mathbf{i}} + 2\hat{\mathbf{j}} + 4\hat{\mathbf{k}}) = -3\mathbf{AB}$$

$\because \quad \mathbf{BC} = -3\mathbf{AB}$

$\therefore$ A, B and C are collinear.

Now, let C divide AB in the ratio $k : 1$, then

$$\mathbf{OC} = \frac{k\mathbf{OB} + 1 \cdot \mathbf{OA}}{k + 1}$$

$$\Rightarrow \quad -3\hat{\mathbf{i}} - 2\hat{\mathbf{j}} - 5\hat{\mathbf{k}} = \frac{k(3\hat{\mathbf{i}} + 4\hat{\mathbf{j}} + 7\hat{\mathbf{k}}) + (\hat{\mathbf{i}} + 2\hat{\mathbf{j}} + 3\hat{\mathbf{k}})}{k + 1}$$

$$\Rightarrow \quad -3\hat{\mathbf{i}} - 2\hat{\mathbf{j}} - 5\hat{\mathbf{k}} = \left(\frac{3k + 1}{k + 1}\right)\hat{\mathbf{i}} + \left(\frac{4k + 2}{k + 1}\right)\hat{\mathbf{j}} + \left(\frac{7k + 3}{k + 1}\right)\hat{\mathbf{k}}$$

$$\Rightarrow \quad \frac{3k + 1}{k + 1} = -3; \ \frac{4k + 2}{k + 1} = -2 \text{ and } \frac{7k + 3}{k + 1} = -5$$

From all relations, we get

$$k = \frac{-2}{3}$$

Hence, C divides AB externally in the ratio $2 : 3$.

Example 30. If the position vectors of A, B, C and D are $2\hat{\mathbf{i}} + \hat{\mathbf{j}}$, $\hat{\mathbf{i}} - 3\hat{\mathbf{j}}$, $3\hat{\mathbf{i}} + 2\hat{\mathbf{j}}$ and $\hat{\mathbf{i}} + \lambda\hat{\mathbf{j}}$ respectively and $\mathbf{AB} \parallel \mathbf{CD}$, then find the value of λ.

Sol. $\mathbf{AB} = (\hat{\mathbf{i}} - 3\hat{\mathbf{j}}) - (2\hat{\mathbf{i}} + \hat{\mathbf{j}}) = -\hat{\mathbf{i}} - 4\hat{\mathbf{j}}$;

$\mathbf{CD} = (\hat{\mathbf{i}} + \lambda\hat{\mathbf{j}}) - (3\hat{\mathbf{i}} + 2\hat{\mathbf{j}}) = -2\hat{\mathbf{i}} + (\lambda - 2)\hat{\mathbf{j}}$;

$\mathbf{AB} \parallel \mathbf{CD} \Rightarrow \mathbf{AB} = x\,\mathbf{CD}$, where x is a non-zero scalar.

$$-\hat{\mathbf{i}} - 4\hat{\mathbf{j}} = x\{-2\hat{\mathbf{i}} + (\lambda - 2)\hat{\mathbf{j}}\}$$

$$\Rightarrow \quad -1 = -2x, \ -4 = (\lambda - 2)x$$

$$\Rightarrow \quad x = \frac{1}{2} \text{ and } \lambda = -6$$

Example 31. The points with position vectors $60\hat{\mathbf{i}} + 3\hat{\mathbf{j}}$, $40\hat{\mathbf{i}} - 8\hat{\mathbf{j}}$ and $a\hat{\mathbf{i}} - 52\hat{\mathbf{j}}$ are collinear, then find the value of a.

Sol. The three points are collinear if

$$\begin{vmatrix} 60 & 3 & 1 \\ 40 & -8 & 1 \\ a & -52 & 1 \end{vmatrix} = 0$$

$$\Rightarrow \quad 60(-8 + 52) - 3(40 - a) + (-2080 + 8a) = 0$$
$$\Rightarrow \quad 2640 - 120 + 3a - 2080 + 8a = 0$$
$$\Rightarrow \quad 11a = -440$$
$$\Rightarrow \quad a = -40$$

JEE SCANNER

Example Similar to PYQ Asked in JEE Main 2019

If **a** *and* **b** *are non-collinear vectors, then the value of x for which vectors* $\alpha = (x-2)\mathbf{a} + \mathbf{b}$ *and* $\beta = (3+2x)\mathbf{a} - 2\mathbf{b}$ *are collinear is equal to*

(a) $\frac{3}{5}$ (b) $\frac{1}{8}$ (c) $\frac{1}{4}$ (d) $\frac{2}{7}$

Sol. (c) Since, the vectors α and β are collinear.

$\therefore$ There exist scalar λ such that

$$\alpha = \lambda\beta$$

$$\Rightarrow \quad (x-2)\mathbf{a} + \mathbf{b} = \lambda\{(3+2x)\mathbf{a} - 2\mathbf{b}\}$$

$$\Rightarrow \quad (x-2-\lambda(3+2x))\mathbf{a} + (1+2\lambda)\mathbf{b} = \mathbf{0}$$

$$\Rightarrow \quad x-2-\lambda(3+2x) = 0 \text{ and } 1+2\lambda = 0$$

$$\Rightarrow \quad x-2-\lambda(3+2x) = 0 \text{ and } \lambda = -\frac{1}{2}$$

$$\Rightarrow \quad x-2+\frac{1}{2}(3+2x) = 0$$

$$\Rightarrow \quad 4x-1 = 0 \Rightarrow x = \frac{1}{4}$$

Skill Builder

For Sol.

If **a** and **b** are non-collinear vectors, then the value of μ for which $\alpha = (\mu - 3)\mathbf{a} + 2\mathbf{b}$ and $\beta = (2\mu + 3)\mathbf{a} - 4\mathbf{b}$ are collinear is equal to

(a) $\frac{3}{4}$ (b) $\frac{-3}{4}$ (c) $\frac{2}{5}$ (d) $\frac{-1}{4}$

■ **For more practice** See Q.6 of Milestone Practice 3.

Example 32. Let **a**, **b** and **c** be three non-zero vectors such that no two of these are collinear. If the vector $\mathbf{a}+2\mathbf{b}$ is collinear with **c** and $\mathbf{b}+3\mathbf{c}$ is collinear with **a**, then find the value of $\mathbf{a}+2\mathbf{b}+6\mathbf{c}$.

Sol. As $\mathbf{a}+2\mathbf{b}$ and **c** are collinear $\mathbf{a}+2\mathbf{b} = \lambda\mathbf{c}$ ...(i)

Again, $\mathbf{b}+3\mathbf{c}$ is collinear with **a**.

$$\therefore \quad \mathbf{b}+3\mathbf{c} = \mu\mathbf{a} \quad \text{...(ii)}$$

where λ and μ are any non-zero scalar.

Now, $\mathbf{a}+2\mathbf{b}+6\mathbf{c} = (\mathbf{a}+2\mathbf{b}) + 6\mathbf{c} = \lambda\mathbf{c} + 6\mathbf{c}$

$$= (\lambda+6)\mathbf{c} \quad \text{...(iii)}$$

Also, $\mathbf{a}+2\mathbf{b}+6\mathbf{c} = \mathbf{a} + 2(\mathbf{b}+3\mathbf{c})$

$$= \mathbf{a} + 2\mu\mathbf{a} = (2\mu+1)\mathbf{a} \quad \text{...(iv)}$$

From Eqs. (iii) and (iv), we get

$$(\lambda+6)\mathbf{c} = (2\mu+1)\mathbf{a}$$

But **a** and **c** are non-zero and non-collinear vectors,

$$\therefore \quad \lambda+6 = 0 = 2\mu+1$$

Hence, $\mathbf{a}+2\mathbf{b}+6\mathbf{c} = 0$

Example 33. If vectors $\mathbf{a} = x\hat{\mathbf{i}} - \hat{\mathbf{j}} + z\hat{\mathbf{k}}$ and $\mathbf{b} = \hat{\mathbf{i}} + y\hat{\mathbf{j}} - \hat{\mathbf{k}}$ are collinear such that $\mathbf{a} = \lambda\mathbf{b}$, then find the possible unit vector parallel to the vector $x\hat{\mathbf{i}} + y\hat{\mathbf{j}} + z\hat{\mathbf{k}}$.

Sol. Given, **a** and **b** are collinear.

$$\therefore \quad \frac{x}{1} = \frac{-1}{y} = \frac{z}{-1} = \lambda$$

$$\Rightarrow \quad x = \lambda, y = \frac{-1}{\lambda} \text{ and } z = -\lambda$$

Now, unit vector parallel to vector $x\hat{\mathbf{i}} + y\hat{\mathbf{j}} + z\hat{\mathbf{k}}$ will be

$$\frac{\pm\{x\hat{\mathbf{i}} + y\hat{\mathbf{j}} + z\hat{\mathbf{k}}\}}{\sqrt{x^2+y^2+z^2}} = \frac{\pm\left\{\lambda\hat{\mathbf{i}} - \frac{1}{\lambda}\hat{\mathbf{j}} - \lambda\hat{\mathbf{k}}\right\}}{\sqrt{\lambda^2 + \left(-\frac{1}{\lambda}\right)^2 + (-\lambda)^2}}$$

$$= \frac{\pm\{\lambda^2\hat{\mathbf{i}} - \hat{\mathbf{j}} - \lambda^2\hat{\mathbf{k}}\}}{\sqrt{2\lambda^4+1}}$$

1.17 Theorem of Coplanar Vectors

Let **a** and **b** be two non-zero, non-collinear vectors. Then, any vector **r** coplanar with **a** and **b** can be uniquely expressed as a linear combination $x\mathbf{a} + y\mathbf{b}$; x and y being scalars.

Proof We take any point O in the plane of **a** and **b**.

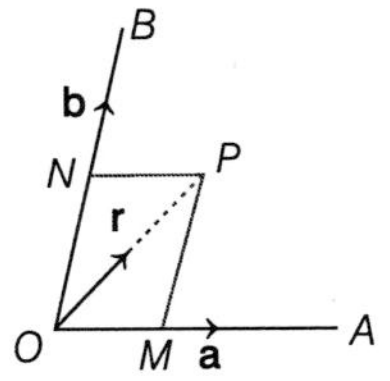

Let $\quad \mathbf{OA} = \mathbf{a}, \mathbf{OB} = \mathbf{b}$ and $\mathbf{OP} = \mathbf{r}$

Clearly, OA, OB and OP are coplanar.

Through P, we draw lines PM and PN, parallel to OB and OA respeetively meeting OA and OB at M and N respectively.

We have, $\mathbf{OP} = \mathbf{OM} + \mathbf{MP}$

$$= \mathbf{OM} + \mathbf{ON} \; [\because MP = ON \text{ and } MP \,||\, ON] \quad \text{...(i)}$$

Now, **OM** and **OA** are collinear vectors

$\mathbf{OM} = x\,\mathbf{OA} = x\mathbf{a}$, where x is scalar.

Similarly, $\mathbf{ON} = y\,\mathbf{OB} = y\mathbf{b}$, where y is a scalar.

Hence, from Eq. (i),

$$\mathbf{OP} = x\mathbf{a} + y\mathbf{b} \text{ or } \mathbf{r} = x\mathbf{a} + y\mathbf{b}$$

Uniqueness If possible, let $\mathbf{r} = x\mathbf{a} + y\mathbf{b}$ and $\mathbf{r} = x'\mathbf{a} + y'\mathbf{b}$ be two different ways of representing r.

Then, we have $\quad x\mathbf{a} + y\mathbf{b} = x'\mathbf{a} + y'\mathbf{b}$

$$\Rightarrow \quad (x-x')\mathbf{a} + (y-y')\mathbf{b} = 0$$

But **a** and **b** are non-collinear vectors

$$\therefore \quad x - x' = 0 \text{ and } y - y' = 0$$

$$\Rightarrow \quad x' = x \text{ and } y' = y$$

Thus, the uniqueness in established.

Test of Coplanarity of Three Vectors

(i) Three vectors **a, b, c** are coplanar iff any one of them is a linear combination of the remaining two i.e. iff $\mathbf{a} = x\mathbf{b} + y\mathbf{c}$, where x and y are scalars.

(ii) If three vectors $\mathbf{a} = a_1\hat{\mathbf{i}} + a_2\hat{\mathbf{j}} + a_3\hat{\mathbf{k}}$, $\mathbf{b} = b_1\hat{\mathbf{i}} + b_2\hat{\mathbf{j}} + b_3\hat{\mathbf{k}}$ and $\mathbf{c} = c_1\hat{\mathbf{i}} + c_2\hat{\mathbf{j}} + c_3\hat{\mathbf{k}}$ are coplanar,

then $\begin{vmatrix} a_1 & a_2 & a_3 \\ b_1 & b_2 & b_3 \\ c_1 & c_2 & c_3 \end{vmatrix} = 0.$

If vectors **a**,**b** and **c** are coplanar, then there exist scalars x and y such that $\mathbf{c} = x\mathbf{a} + y\mathbf{b}$.

Hence, $c_1\hat{\mathbf{i}} + c_2\hat{\mathbf{j}} + c_3\hat{\mathbf{k}} = x(a_1\hat{\mathbf{i}} + a_2\hat{\mathbf{j}} + a_3\hat{\mathbf{k}}) + y(b_1\hat{\mathbf{i}} + b_2\hat{\mathbf{j}} + b_3\hat{\mathbf{k}})$

Now, $\hat{\mathbf{i}}, \hat{\mathbf{j}}$ and $\hat{\mathbf{k}}$ are non-coplanar and hence independent.

Then, $c_1 = xa_1 + yb_1, c_2 = xa_2 + yb_2$

and $c_3 = xa_3 + yb_3$

The above system of equations in terms of x and y is consistent. Thus,

$$\begin{vmatrix} a_1 & b_1 & c_1 \\ a_2 & b_2 & c_2 \\ a_3 & b_3 & c_3 \end{vmatrix} = 0 \text{ or } \begin{vmatrix} a_1 & a_2 & a_3 \\ b_1 & b_2 & b_3 \\ c_1 & c_2 & c_3 \end{vmatrix} = 0.$$

JEE SPIKE

If vectors $x_1\mathbf{a} + y_1\mathbf{b} + z_1\mathbf{c}$, $x_2\mathbf{a} + y_2\mathbf{b} + z_2\mathbf{c}$ and $x_3\mathbf{a} + y_3\mathbf{b} + z_3\mathbf{c}$ are coplanar(where **a, b** and **c** are non-coplanar).

Then, $\begin{vmatrix} x_1 & y_1 & z_1 \\ x_2 & y_2 & z_2 \\ x_3 & y_3 & z_3 \end{vmatrix} = 0$

Example 34. Check whether the given three vectors are coplanar or non-coplanar.

$$-2\hat{\mathbf{i}} - 2\hat{\mathbf{j}} + 4\hat{\mathbf{k}}, -2\hat{\mathbf{i}} + 4\hat{\mathbf{j}} - 2\hat{\mathbf{k}}, 4\hat{\mathbf{i}} - 2\hat{\mathbf{j}} - 2\hat{\mathbf{k}}$$

Sol. Now, consider

$$\begin{vmatrix} -2 & -2 & 4 \\ -2 & 4 & -2 \\ 4 & -2 & -2 \end{vmatrix} = -2(-8-4) + 2(4+8) + 4(4-16)$$
$$= 24 + 24 - 48 = 0$$

$\therefore$ The vectors are coplanar.

Test of Coplanarity of Four Points

(i) To prove that four points $A(\mathbf{a}), B(\mathbf{b}), C(\mathbf{c})$ and $D(\mathbf{d})$ are coplanar, it is just sufficient to prove that vectors **AB**, **AC** and **AD** are coplanar.

(ii) Four points with position vectors **a, b**, **c** and **d** are coplanar if there exist scalars x, y, z and u (sum of any two is not zero) such that $x\mathbf{a} + y\mathbf{b} + z\mathbf{c} + u\mathbf{d} = 0$, where $x + y + z + u = 0$.

(iii) Four points with position vectors $\mathbf{a} = a_1\hat{\mathbf{i}} + a_2\hat{\mathbf{j}} + a_3\hat{\mathbf{k}}, \mathbf{b} = b_1\hat{\mathbf{i}} + b_2\hat{\mathbf{j}} + b_3\hat{\mathbf{k}}$, $\mathbf{c} = c_1\hat{\mathbf{i}} + c_2\hat{\mathbf{j}} + c_3\hat{\mathbf{k}}$ and $\mathbf{d} = d_1\hat{\mathbf{i}} + d_2\hat{\mathbf{j}} + d_3\hat{\mathbf{k}}$

will be coplanar, iff $\begin{vmatrix} d_1 - a_1 & d_2 - a_2 & d_3 - a_3 \\ b_1 - a_1 & b_2 - a_2 & b_3 - a_3 \\ c_1 - a_1 & c_2 - a_2 & c_3 - a_3 \end{vmatrix} = 0$

Example 35. The sum of all values of λ, for which the points whose position vectors are $2\hat{\mathbf{i}} - 3\hat{\mathbf{j}} + 5\hat{\mathbf{k}}$, $4\hat{\mathbf{i}} - 2\hat{\mathbf{j}} + 3\hat{\mathbf{k}}$, $(\lambda + 1)\hat{\mathbf{i}} + 2\hat{\mathbf{k}}$ and $8\hat{\mathbf{i}} + (\lambda - 8)\hat{\mathbf{j}} + 6\hat{\mathbf{k}}$ are coplanar is equal to

(a) 17 (b) $-\frac{17}{2}$ (c) -17 (d) $\frac{17}{2}$

Sol. (d) Let the vectors be $\mathbf{A} = 2\hat{\mathbf{i}} - 3\hat{\mathbf{j}} + 5\hat{\mathbf{k}}$, $\mathbf{B} = 4\hat{\mathbf{i}} - 2\hat{\mathbf{j}} + 3\hat{\mathbf{k}}$, $\mathbf{C} = (\lambda + 1)\hat{\mathbf{i}} + 2\hat{\mathbf{k}}$, $\mathbf{D} = 8\hat{\mathbf{i}} + (\lambda - 8)\hat{\mathbf{j}} + 6\hat{\mathbf{k}}$

The given four points are coplanar, then

$$\begin{vmatrix} 8-2 & \lambda - 8 + 3 & 6-5 \\ 4-2 & -2+3 & 3-5 \\ \lambda + 1 - 2 & 0+3 & 2-5 \end{vmatrix} = 0$$

$$\Rightarrow \begin{vmatrix} 6 & \lambda - 5 & 1 \\ 2 & 1 & -2 \\ \lambda - 1 & 3 & -3 \end{vmatrix} = 0$$

$$\Rightarrow 6(-3+6) - (\lambda - 5)(-6 + 2\lambda - 2) + 1(6 - \lambda + 1) = 0$$
$$\Rightarrow 6 \times 3 + (5 - \lambda)(2\lambda - 8) - \lambda + 7 = 0$$
$$\Rightarrow 18 + 10\lambda - 40 - 2\lambda^2 + 8\lambda - \lambda + 7 = 0$$
$$\Rightarrow -2\lambda^2 + 17\lambda - 15 = 0$$
$$\Rightarrow 2\lambda^2 - 17\lambda + 15 = 0$$

Therefore, sum of roots $= -\frac{b}{a} = \frac{17}{2}$

1.18 Theorem on Non-coplanar Vectors

Theorem 1

If **a, b, c**, are three non-zero, non-coplanar vectors and x, y, z are three scalars such that

$$x\mathbf{a} + y\mathbf{b} + z\mathbf{c} = 0.$$

Then, $x = y = z = 0.$

Proof It is given that $x\mathbf{a} + y\mathbf{b} + z\mathbf{c} = 0$ ...(i)

Suppose that $x \neq 0$

Then, Eq. (i) can be written as

$$x\mathbf{a} = -y\mathbf{b} - z\mathbf{c} \Rightarrow \mathbf{a} = -\frac{y}{x}\mathbf{b} - \frac{z}{x}\mathbf{c} \quad \text{...(ii)}$$

Now, $\frac{y}{x}$ and $\frac{z}{x}$ are scalars because x, y and z are scalars.

Thus, Eq. (ii) expresses **a** as a linear combination of **b** and **c**.

Hence, **a** is coplanar with **b** and **c** which is contrary to our hypothesis because **a**,**b** and **c** are given to be non-coplanar.

Thus, our supposition that $x \neq 0$ is wrong.

Hence, $x = 0$

Similarly, we can prove that $y = 0$ and $z = 0$

Theorem 2

If **a**,**b** and **c** are non-coplanar vectors, then any vector **r** can be uniquely expressed as a linear combination $x\mathbf{a} + y\mathbf{b} + z\mathbf{c}$; x, y and z being scalars.

or

Any vector in space can be expressed as a linear combination of three non-coplanar vectors.

Proof Take any point O.

Let **a, b, c** be any three non-coplanar vectors and **r** be any vector in space.

Let **OA** = **a**, **OB** = **b**, **OC** = **c**, **OP** = **r**

Here, the three lines OA, OB, OC are not coplanar. Hence, they determine three different planes BOC, COA and AOB when taken in pairs.

Through P, draw planes parallel to these planes BOC, COA and AOB meeting OA, OB and OC in L, E and N respectively. Thus, we obtain a parallelopiped with OP as diagonal and three coterminous edges OL, OE and ON along OA, OB and OC, respectively.

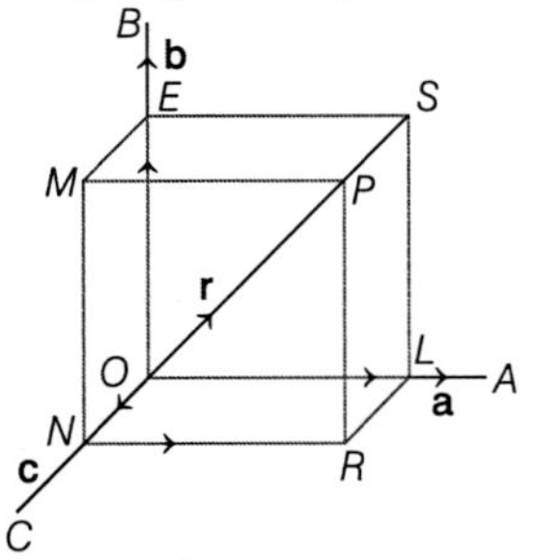

$\therefore$ **OL** is collinear with **OA**.

$\therefore$ **OL** = x **OA** = x **a**, where x is a scalar.

Similarly, **OE** = y **b** and **ON** = z**c**,

where y and z are scalars.

Now, **OP** = **OR** + **RP** = (**ON** + **NR**) + **RP**

= **ON** + **OL** + **OE** [$\because$ **NR** = **OL** and **RP** = **OE**]

= **OL** + **OE** + **ON** = $x\mathbf{a} + y\mathbf{b} + z\mathbf{c}$

Thus, $\mathbf{r} = x\mathbf{a} + y\mathbf{b} + z\mathbf{c}$

Hence, **r** can be expressed as a linear combination of **a**, **b** and **c**.

Uniqueness If possible let

$$\mathbf{r} = x\mathbf{a} + y\mathbf{b} + z\mathbf{c} \text{ and } \mathbf{r} = x'\mathbf{a} + y'\mathbf{b} + z'\mathbf{c}$$

be two different ways of representing **r**, then we have

$$x\mathbf{a} + y\mathbf{b} + z\mathbf{c} = x'\mathbf{a} + y'\mathbf{b} + z'\mathbf{c}$$

$$\Rightarrow \quad (x - x')\mathbf{a} + (y - y')\mathbf{b} + (z - z')\mathbf{c} = 0$$

Now **a**, **b** and **c** are non-coplanar vectors

$$\therefore \quad x - x' = 0, y - y' = 0 \text{ and } z - z' = 0$$

$$\Rightarrow \quad x = x', y = y' \text{ and } z = z'$$

Hence, the uniqueness is established.

JEE SCANNER

Example Similar to PYQ Asked in JEE Main 2023

Let the position vector of the points A, B and C be $\hat{i} - \hat{j} + \hat{k}$, $\alpha\hat{i} + 2\hat{j} - \hat{k}$ *and* $8\hat{i} + (\alpha - 6)\hat{j} + 3\hat{k}$. *Let the set* $S = \{x \in R$ *: the points A, B and C be coplanar}. Then, the value of* $\Sigma_{\alpha \in S} (\alpha + 2)^2$ *is ....*

Sol. Given that $A(1, -1, 1)$, $B(\alpha, 2, -1)$ and $C(8, \alpha - 6, 3)$

$$\text{Now, } \begin{vmatrix} 1 & -1 & 1 \\ \alpha & 2 & -1 \\ 8 & \alpha - 6 & 3 \end{vmatrix} = 0$$

Expand the determinant along the first row

$$1(6 + \alpha - 6) + (3\alpha + 8) + (\alpha^2 - 6\alpha - 16) = 0$$

On simplifying, we get

$$\alpha^2 - 2\alpha - 8 = 0 \Rightarrow \alpha^2 - 4\alpha + 2\alpha - 8 = 0$$

$$\Rightarrow \alpha(\alpha - 4) + 2(\alpha - 4) = 0 \Rightarrow \alpha = -2 \text{ and } 4$$

We have two values of α.

$$\Rightarrow \quad \Sigma_{\alpha \in S} (\alpha + 2)^2 = (4 + 2)^2 + (-2 + 2)^2 = 36 + 0 = 36$$

Hence, $\Sigma_{\alpha \in S} (\alpha + 2)^2 = 36$

Skill Builder

Let the position vector of the points A, B and C be $\hat{i} + \hat{j} + \hat{k}$, $a\hat{i} - 3\hat{j} + \hat{k}$ and $6\hat{i} + (a - 6)\hat{j} + 3\hat{k}$. Let the set $S = \{x \in R$: the point A, B and C be coplanar}. Then, the value of $\Sigma_{a \in S}(a + 2)^2$ is ....

For Sol.

■ **For more practice** See Q.12 of Milestone Practice 3.

Example 36. If the vectors $4\hat{i} + 11\hat{j} + m\hat{k}$, $7\hat{i} + 2\hat{j} + 6\hat{k}$ and $\hat{i} + 5\hat{j} + 4\hat{k}$ are coplanar, then find the value of m.

Sol. Since, the three vectors are coplanar, one will be a linear combination of the other two.

$$\therefore \quad 4\hat{i} + 11\hat{j} + m\hat{k} = x(7\hat{i} + 2\hat{j} + 6\hat{k}) + y(\hat{i} + 5\hat{j} + 4\hat{k})$$

where x and y are non-zero scalars.

$$\Rightarrow \quad 4 = 7x + y \quad \ldots(i)$$
$$11 = 2x + 5y \quad \ldots(ii)$$
$$m = 6x + 4y \quad \ldots(iii)$$

From Eqs. (i) and (ii), we get $x = \frac{3}{11}$ and $y = \frac{23}{11}$

From Eq. (iii), we get $m = 6 \times \frac{3}{11} + 4 \times \frac{23}{11} = 10$

Alternate Solution

Since, vectors $4\hat{i} + 11\hat{j} + m\hat{k}$, $7\hat{i} + 2\hat{j} + 6\hat{k}$ and $\hat{i} + 5\hat{j} + 4\hat{k}$ are coplanar.

$$\therefore \begin{vmatrix} 4 & 11 & m \\ 7 & 2 & 6 \\ 1 & 5 & 4 \end{vmatrix} = 0$$

$$\Rightarrow 4(8 - 30) - 11(28 - 6) + m(35 - 2) = 0$$
$$\Rightarrow -88 - 11 \times 22 + 33m = 0$$
$$\Rightarrow -8 - 22 + 3m = 0$$
$$\Rightarrow 3m = 30 \Rightarrow m = 10$$

Example 37. Let the vectors $\mathbf{r}_1 = \hat{i} + \hat{j} + \alpha\hat{k}$, $\mathbf{r}_2 = \hat{i} + \beta\hat{j} + \hat{k}$ and $\mathbf{r}_3 = \gamma\hat{i} + \hat{j} + \hat{k}$ be coplanar. If the vectors $\mathbf{s}_1 = (\alpha + \beta)\hat{i} + \gamma\hat{j} + \gamma\hat{k}$, $\mathbf{s}_2 = \alpha\hat{i} + (\beta + \gamma)\hat{j} + \alpha\hat{k}$ and $\mathbf{s}_3 = \beta\hat{i} + \beta\hat{j} + (\gamma + \alpha)\hat{k}$ are also coplanar, then find the value of $\left(\frac{\alpha + \beta + \gamma}{2}\right)$.

Sol. Given, $\mathbf{r}_1 = \hat{\mathbf{i}} + \hat{\mathbf{j}} + \alpha\hat{\mathbf{k}}$, $\mathbf{r}_2 = \hat{\mathbf{i}} + \beta\hat{\mathbf{j}} + \hat{\mathbf{k}}$ and $\mathbf{r}_3 = \gamma\hat{\mathbf{i}} + \hat{\mathbf{j}} + \hat{\mathbf{k}}$ are coplanar.

Now, using the condition of coplanar, we get

$$\begin{vmatrix} 1 & 1 & \alpha \\ 1 & \beta & 1 \\ \gamma & 1 & 1 \end{vmatrix} = 0$$

Expanding the determinant along R_1

$$\Rightarrow \quad (\beta - 1) - (1 - \gamma) + \alpha(1 - \beta\gamma) = 0$$
$$\Rightarrow \quad \alpha + \beta + \gamma = 2 + \alpha\beta\gamma \quad \ldots(i)$$

Also, given that $\mathbf{s}_1 = (\alpha + \beta)\hat{\mathbf{i}} + \gamma\hat{\mathbf{j}} + \gamma\hat{\mathbf{k}}$,

$$\mathbf{s}_2 = \alpha\hat{\mathbf{i}} + (\beta + \gamma)\hat{\mathbf{j}} + \alpha\hat{\mathbf{k}}$$

and $\mathbf{s}_3 = \beta\hat{\mathbf{i}} + \beta\hat{\mathbf{j}} + (\gamma + \alpha)\hat{\mathbf{k}}$ are coplanar.

Again, using the coplanar condition, we get

$$\Rightarrow \begin{vmatrix} \alpha + \beta & \gamma & \gamma \\ \alpha & \beta + \gamma & \alpha \\ \beta & \beta & \gamma + \alpha \end{vmatrix} = 0$$

On applying row transformations, $R_3 \to R_3 - (R_1 + R_2)$

$$\Rightarrow \begin{vmatrix} \alpha + \beta & \gamma & \gamma \\ \alpha & \beta + \gamma & \alpha \\ -2\alpha & -2\gamma & 0 \end{vmatrix} = 0$$

Expand the determinant along R_1,

$$\Rightarrow (\alpha + \beta)(0 + 2\alpha\gamma) - \gamma(0 + 2\alpha^2) + \gamma(-2\alpha\gamma + 2\alpha(\beta + \gamma)) = 0$$
$$\Rightarrow \quad 2\alpha^2\gamma + 2\alpha\beta\gamma - 2\alpha^2\gamma - 2\alpha\gamma^2 + 2\alpha\beta\gamma + 2\alpha\gamma^2 = 0$$
$$\Rightarrow \quad \alpha\beta\gamma = 0$$
$$\therefore \quad \alpha + \beta + \gamma = 2 \quad \text{[from Eq. (i)]}$$

Hence, $\frac{\alpha + \beta + \gamma}{2} = 1$

Example 38. Show that the points $P(\mathbf{a} + 2\mathbf{b} + \mathbf{c})$, $Q(\mathbf{a} - \mathbf{b} - \mathbf{c})$, $R(3\mathbf{a} + \mathbf{b} + 2\mathbf{c})$ and $S(5\mathbf{a} + 3\mathbf{b} + 5\mathbf{c})$ are coplanar given that **a**, **b** and **c** are non-coplanar.

Sol. To show that P, Q, R, S are coplanar, we will show that **PQ**, **PR**, **PS** are coplanar.

$$\mathbf{PQ} = -3\mathbf{b} - 2\mathbf{c}$$
$$\mathbf{PR} = 2\mathbf{a} - \mathbf{b} + \mathbf{c}$$
$$\mathbf{PS} = 4\mathbf{a} + \mathbf{b} + 4\mathbf{c}$$

Let $\mathbf{PQ} = x\mathbf{PR} + y\mathbf{PS}$

$$\Rightarrow \quad -3\mathbf{b} - 2\mathbf{c} = x(2\mathbf{a} - \mathbf{b} + \mathbf{c}) + y(4\mathbf{a} + \mathbf{b} + 4\mathbf{c})$$
$$\Rightarrow \quad -3\mathbf{b} - 2\mathbf{c} = (2x + 4y)\mathbf{a} + (-x + y)\mathbf{b} + (x + 4y)\mathbf{c}$$

As the vectors **a, b, c** are non-coplanar, we can equate their coefficients.

$$\Rightarrow \quad 0 = 2x + 4y$$
$$\Rightarrow \quad -3 = -x + y$$
$$\Rightarrow \quad -2 = x + 4y$$

$x = 2, y = -1$ is the unique solution for the above system of equations.

$$\Rightarrow \quad \mathbf{PQ} = 2\mathbf{PR} - \mathbf{PS}$$

PQ, **PR**, **PS** are coplanar because **PQ** is a linear combination of **PR** and **PS**.

$\Rightarrow$ The points **P, Q, R, S** are also coplanar.

Time Saving Technique

For the vectors **PQ**, **PR** and **PS** to be coplanar, we must have

$$\begin{vmatrix} 0 & -3 & -2 \\ 2 & -1 & 1 \\ 4 & 1 & 4 \end{vmatrix} = 0 \text{ which is true.}$$

$\therefore$ The **PQ, PR, PS** are coplanar.

Hence, the points P, Q, R, S are also coplanar.

Example 39. Check whether the points $\mathbf{a} = 2\hat{i} - \hat{j} + \hat{k}$, $\mathbf{b} = \hat{i} + 3\hat{j} - \hat{k}$, $\mathbf{c} = -2\hat{i} + \hat{j} - 3\hat{k}$ and $\mathbf{d} = 3\hat{i} + 2\hat{j} + 5\hat{k}$ form a tetrahedron or not.

Sol. Let given points be $A(\mathbf{a}), B(\mathbf{b}), C(\mathbf{c})$ and $D(\mathbf{d})$.

$$\therefore \quad \mathbf{AB} = (\hat{\mathbf{i}} + 3\hat{\mathbf{j}} - \hat{\mathbf{k}}) - (2\hat{\mathbf{i}} - \hat{\mathbf{j}} + \hat{\mathbf{k}}) = -\hat{\mathbf{i}} + 4\hat{\mathbf{j}} - 2\hat{\mathbf{k}}$$
$$\mathbf{AC} = (-2\hat{\mathbf{i}} + \hat{\mathbf{j}} - 3\hat{\mathbf{k}}) - (2\hat{\mathbf{i}} - \hat{\mathbf{j}} + \hat{\mathbf{k}}) = -4\hat{\mathbf{i}} + 2\hat{\mathbf{j}} - 4\hat{\mathbf{k}}$$
$$\text{and } \mathbf{AD} = (3\hat{\mathbf{i}} + 2\hat{\mathbf{j}} + 5\hat{\mathbf{k}}) - (2\hat{\mathbf{i}} - \hat{\mathbf{j}} + \hat{\mathbf{k}})$$
$$= \hat{\mathbf{i}} + 3\hat{\mathbf{j}} + 4\hat{\mathbf{k}}$$

Now, determinant of coefficients of **AB, AC** and **AD** is

$$\begin{vmatrix} -1 & 4 & -2 \\ -4 & 2 & -4 \\ 1 & 3 & 4 \end{vmatrix} = -1(8+12) - 4(-16+4) - 2(-12-2)$$

$$= -1(20) - 4(-12) - 2(-14)$$
$$= -20 + 48 + 28$$
$$= 56 \neq 0$$

Hence, the given points are non-coplanar. So, these points form a tetrahedron in 3-D space.

1.19 Linear Independence and Dependence of Vectors

1. Linearly Independent Vectors

A set of non-zero vectors $\mathbf{a}_1, \mathbf{a}_2 ...., \mathbf{a}_n$ is said to be linearly independent, if

$$x_1\mathbf{a}_1 + x_2\mathbf{a}_2 + ... + x_n\mathbf{a}_n = 0$$
$$\Rightarrow \quad x_1 = x_2 = ... = x_n = 0.$$

2. Linearly Dependence Vectors

A set of vector $\mathbf{a}_1, \mathbf{a}_2 ...., \mathbf{a}_n$ is said to be linearly dependent, if there exist scalars $x_1, x_2, ..., x_n$ not all zero such that $x_1\mathbf{a}_1 + x_2\mathbf{a}_2 + ... + x_n\mathbf{a}_n = 0$

Properties of Linearly Independent and Dependent Vectors

(i) A super set of a linearly dependent set of vectors is linearly dependent.

(ii) A subset of a linearly independent set of vectors is linearly independent.

(iii) Two non-zero, non-collinear vectors are linearly independent.

(iv) Any two collinear vectors are linearly dependent.

(v) Any three non-coplanar vectors are linearly independent.

(vi) Any three coplanar vectors are linearly dependent.

(vii) Three vectors $\mathbf{a} = a_1\hat{\mathbf{i}} + a_2\hat{\mathbf{j}} + a_3\hat{\mathbf{k}}$, $\mathbf{b} = b_1\hat{\mathbf{i}} + b_2\hat{\mathbf{j}} + b_3\hat{\mathbf{k}}$ and $\mathbf{c} = c_1\hat{\mathbf{i}} + c_2\hat{\mathbf{j}} + c_3\hat{\mathbf{k}}$ will be linearly dependent vectors iff $\begin{vmatrix} a_1 & a_2 & a_3 \\ b_1 & b_2 & b_3 \\ c_1 & c_2 & c_3 \end{vmatrix} = 0.$

(viii) More than three vectors in 3-dimensional space are always linearly dependent.

Example 40. If $\mathbf{a} = \hat{i} + \hat{j} + \hat{k}$, $\mathbf{b} = 4\hat{i} + 3\hat{j} + 4\hat{k}$ and $\mathbf{c} = \hat{i} + \alpha\hat{j} + \beta\hat{k}$ are linearly dependent vectors and $|\mathbf{c}| = \sqrt{3}$, then find the value of α and β.

Sol. The given vectors are linearly dependent, hence there exist scalars x, y and z not all zero, such that

$$x\mathbf{a} + y\mathbf{b} + z\mathbf{c} = 0$$

i.e. $x(\hat{\mathbf{i}} + \hat{\mathbf{j}} + \hat{\mathbf{k}}) + y(4\hat{\mathbf{i}} + 3\hat{\mathbf{j}} + 4\hat{\mathbf{k}}) + z(\hat{\mathbf{i}} + \alpha\hat{\mathbf{j}} + \beta\hat{\mathbf{k}}) = 0$

i.e. $(x + 4y + z)\hat{\mathbf{i}} + (x + 3y + \alpha z)\hat{\mathbf{j}} + (x + 4y + \beta z)\hat{\mathbf{k}} = 0$

$\Rightarrow \quad x + 4y + z = 0,\ x + 3y + \alpha z = 0,\ x + 4y + \beta z = 0$

For non-trivial solution $\begin{vmatrix} 1 & 4 & 1 \\ 1 & 3 & \alpha \\ 1 & 4 & \beta \end{vmatrix} = 0$

$\Rightarrow \quad \beta = 1$

$\because \quad |\mathbf{c}|^2 = 3$

$\Rightarrow \quad 1 + \alpha^2 + \beta^2 = 3$

$\Rightarrow \quad \alpha^2 = 2 - \beta^2 = 2 - 1 = 1$

$\therefore \quad \alpha = \pm 1$

Time Saving Technique

$|\mathbf{c}| = \sqrt{1 + \alpha^2 + \beta^2} = \sqrt{3} \Rightarrow \alpha^2 + \beta^2 = 2$

$\because$ **a**, **b** and **c** are linearly dependent, hence $\begin{vmatrix} 1 & 1 & 1 \\ 4 & 3 & 4 \\ 1 & \alpha & \beta \end{vmatrix} = 0$

$\Rightarrow \quad \beta = 1$

$\therefore \quad \alpha^2 = 1$

$\Rightarrow \quad \alpha = \pm 1$

Milestone Practice 1.3

1. If the position vectors of the points A, B and C be $\mathbf{a}$, $\mathbf{b}$ and $3\mathbf{a}-2\mathbf{b}$ respectively, then prove that the points A, B and C are collinear. Also, find the ratio in which point C divides AB.

2. The position vectors of four points P, Q, R and S are $2\mathbf{a}+4\mathbf{c}$, $5\mathbf{a}+3\sqrt{3}\mathbf{b}+4\mathbf{c}$, $-2\sqrt{3}\mathbf{b}+\mathbf{c}$ and $2\mathbf{a}+\mathbf{c}$ respectively, prove that PQ is parallel to RS. Then, find $PQ:RS$.

3. Three points A, B and C have position vectors i.e. $\hat{\mathbf{i}}+x\hat{\mathbf{j}}+3\hat{\mathbf{k}}$, $2\hat{\mathbf{i}}+3\hat{\mathbf{j}}-4\hat{\mathbf{k}}$ and $y\hat{\mathbf{i}}-7\hat{\mathbf{j}}+10\hat{\mathbf{k}}$, respectively. If they are collinear, then (x, y) is equal to
   (a) $(1, 0)$ (b) $(-2, 0)$ (c) $(-1, 0)$ (d) $(0, -2)$

4. Find the condition that the three points whose position vectors, $\mathbf{a}=a\hat{\mathbf{i}}+b\hat{\mathbf{j}}+c\hat{\mathbf{k}}$, $\mathbf{b}=\hat{\mathbf{i}}+c\hat{\mathbf{j}}$ and $\mathbf{c}=-\hat{\mathbf{i}}-\hat{\mathbf{j}}$ are collinear.

5. Let $\mathbf{a}=\hat{\mathbf{i}}-2\hat{\mathbf{j}}+3\hat{\mathbf{k}}$, $\mathbf{b}=3\hat{\mathbf{i}}+3\hat{\mathbf{j}}-\hat{\mathbf{k}}$ and $\mathbf{c}=\lambda\hat{\mathbf{i}}+\hat{\mathbf{j}}+(2\lambda-1)\hat{\mathbf{k}}$. If $\mathbf{c}$ is parallel to the plane of the vector $\mathbf{a}$ and $\mathbf{b}$, then find the value of λ.

6. Vectors $\mathbf{a}$ and $\mathbf{b}$ are non-collinear. Find for what values of x vectors $\mathbf{c}=(x-2)\mathbf{a}+\mathbf{b}$ and $\mathbf{d}=(2x+1)\mathbf{a}-\mathbf{b}$ are collinear?

7. Let $\mathbf{a}$, $\mathbf{b}$, $\mathbf{c}$ be three vectors of which every pair is non-collinear. If the vectors $\mathbf{a}+\mathbf{b}$ and $\mathbf{b}+\mathbf{c}$ are collinear with $\mathbf{c}$ and $\mathbf{a}$ respectively, then the value of $\mathbf{a}+\mathbf{b}+\mathbf{c}$ is
   (a) $\mathbf{0}$ (b) 0 (c) $\mathbf{a}$ (d) $2\mathbf{b}$

8. If $\mathbf{a}$ and $\mathbf{b}$ are non-collinear vectors $\mathbf{A}=(p+4q)\mathbf{a}+(2p+q+1)\mathbf{b}$ and $\mathbf{B}=(-2p+q+2)\mathbf{a}+(2p-3q-1)\mathbf{b}$ and if $3\mathbf{A}=2\mathbf{B}$, then find the value of p^2+q^2.

9. If the vectors $2\hat{\mathbf{i}}-\hat{\mathbf{j}}+\hat{\mathbf{k}}$, $\hat{\mathbf{i}}+2\hat{\mathbf{j}}-3\hat{\mathbf{k}}$ and $3\hat{\mathbf{i}}+a\hat{\mathbf{j}}+5\hat{\mathbf{k}}$ are coplanar, then find the value of a.

10. Show that the vectors $\mathbf{a}-2\mathbf{b}+3\mathbf{c}$, $-2\mathbf{a}+3\mathbf{b}-4\mathbf{c}$ and $-\mathbf{b}+2\mathbf{c}$ are coplanar vector, where $\mathbf{a}$, $\mathbf{b}$, $\mathbf{c}$ are non-coplanar vectors.

11. Given three non-zero, non-coplanar vectors $\mathbf{a}$, $\mathbf{b}$ and $\mathbf{c}$. $\mathbf{r}_1=p\mathbf{a}+q\mathbf{b}+\mathbf{c}$ and $\mathbf{r}_2=\mathbf{a}+p\mathbf{b}+q\mathbf{c}$. If the vectors $\mathbf{r}_1+2\mathbf{r}_2$ and $2\mathbf{r}_1+\mathbf{r}_2$ are collinear, then find the value of p^2+q^2.

12. Let S be the set of all (λ, μ) for which the vector $\lambda\hat{\mathbf{i}}-3\hat{\mathbf{j}}+\hat{\mathbf{k}}$, $3\hat{\mathbf{i}}-\mu\hat{\mathbf{j}}+2\hat{\mathbf{k}}$ and $4\hat{\mathbf{i}}-5\hat{\mathbf{j}}+\hat{\mathbf{k}}$, where $\mu-\lambda=3$ and coplanar, then the value of $\Sigma_{(\lambda,\mu)\in S}(\lambda+\mu)$, is
    (a) 20 (b) 28 (c) 29 (d) 30

13. If $\mathbf{a}$, $\mathbf{b}$ and $\mathbf{c}$ are non-coplanar vectors, then prove that the four points $2\mathbf{a}+3\mathbf{b}-\mathbf{c}$, $\mathbf{a}-2\mathbf{b}+3\mathbf{c}$, $3\mathbf{a}+4\mathbf{b}-2\mathbf{c}$ and $\mathbf{a}-6\mathbf{b}+6\mathbf{c}$ are coplanar.

14. Prove that the points $6\hat{\mathbf{i}}-7\hat{\mathbf{j}}$, $16\hat{\mathbf{i}}-19\hat{\mathbf{j}}-4\hat{\mathbf{k}}$, $3\hat{\mathbf{j}}-6\hat{\mathbf{k}}$ and $2\hat{\mathbf{i}}+5\hat{\mathbf{j}}+10\hat{\mathbf{k}}$ form a tetrahedron in 3-D space.

15. Point to $A(\mathbf{a})$, $B(\mathbf{b})$, $C(\mathbf{c})$ and $D(\mathbf{d})$ are related as $x\mathbf{a}+y\mathbf{b}+z\mathbf{c}+w\mathbf{d}=\mathbf{0}$ and $x+y+z+w=\mathbf{0}$, where x, y, z and w are scalars (sum of any two of x, y, z and w is not zero). If A, B, C and D are concyclic, then find the value of $\dfrac{|xy||\mathbf{a}-\mathbf{b}|^2}{|wz||\mathbf{c}-\mathbf{d}|^2}$.

16. If A, B, C, P and Q are five coplanar points, where $\mathbf{PA}+\mathbf{PB}+\mathbf{PC}+\mathbf{AQ}+\mathbf{BQ}+\mathbf{CQ}$ is $\lambda\mathbf{PQ}$, then the value of λ^2 is
    (a) 3 (b) 9
    (c) 27 (d) None of these

17. If vector $(\mathbf{a}, \mathbf{b}, \mathbf{c})$ are non-zero, non-coplanar vectors, determine whether the vectors $\mathbf{r}_1=2\mathbf{a}-3\mathbf{b}+\mathbf{c}$, $\mathbf{r}_2=3\mathbf{a}-5\mathbf{b}+2\mathbf{c}$ and $\mathbf{r}_3=4\mathbf{a}-5\mathbf{b}+\mathbf{c}$ are linearly independent or dependent.

Answer Key

1. 2 : 3	2. 3 : 2	3. (b)	4. $a-2b=1$	5. $\frac{-1}{11}$
6. $\frac{1}{3}$	7. (a)	8. 5	9. -4	11. 2
12. (b)	15. 1	16. (b)	17. Linearly dependent	

For Detailed Solution

JEE Pattern EXAMPLES

Single Option Correct Type Questions

Example 1 *A unit vector* **a** *makes an angle* $\frac{\pi}{4}$ *with Z-axis. If* $\mathbf{a}+\hat{\mathbf{i}}+\hat{\mathbf{j}}$ *is a unit vector, then* **a** *is equal to*

(a) $\frac{\hat{\mathbf{i}}}{2}+\frac{\hat{\mathbf{j}}}{2}+\frac{\hat{\mathbf{k}}}{\sqrt{2}}$ (b) $\frac{\hat{\mathbf{i}}}{2}+\frac{\hat{\mathbf{j}}}{2}-\frac{\hat{\mathbf{k}}}{\sqrt{2}}$

(c) $-\frac{\hat{\mathbf{i}}}{2}-\frac{\hat{\mathbf{j}}}{2}+\frac{\hat{\mathbf{k}}}{\sqrt{2}}$ (d) None of these

Sol. (c) Let $\mathbf{a}=l\hat{\mathbf{i}}+m\hat{\mathbf{j}}+n\hat{\mathbf{k}}$, where $l^2+m^2+n^2=1$.

a makes an angle $\frac{\pi}{4}$ with Z-axis.

$$\therefore \quad n=\frac{1}{\sqrt{2}},\ l^2+m^2=\frac{1}{2} \quad \text{...(i)}$$

$$\therefore \quad \mathbf{a}=l\hat{\mathbf{i}}+m\hat{\mathbf{j}}+\frac{\hat{\mathbf{k}}}{\sqrt{2}}$$

$$\mathbf{a}+\hat{\mathbf{i}}+\hat{\mathbf{j}}=(l+1)\hat{\mathbf{i}}+(m+1)\hat{\mathbf{j}}+\frac{\hat{\mathbf{k}}}{\sqrt{2}}$$

Its magnitude is 1, hence $(l+1)^2+(m+1)^2=\frac{1}{2}$ ...(ii)

From Eqs. (i) and (ii), we get

$$2lm=\frac{1}{2} \Rightarrow l=m=-\frac{1}{2}$$

Hence, $\mathbf{a}=-\frac{\hat{\mathbf{i}}}{2}-\frac{\hat{\mathbf{j}}}{2}+\frac{\hat{\mathbf{k}}}{\sqrt{2}}$

Example 2 *A vector* **a** *has the components* $2p$ *and* 1 *w.r.t. a rectangular cartesian system. This system is rotated through a certain angle about the origin in the counter clockwise sense. If with respect to a new system,* **a** *has components* $(p+1)$ *and* 1, *then*

(a) $p=0$ (b) $p=1$ or $p=-\frac{1}{3}$

(c) $p=-1$ or $p=\frac{1}{3}$ (d) $p=1$ or $p=-1$

Sol. (b) We have, $\mathbf{a}=2p\hat{\mathbf{i}}+\hat{\mathbf{j}}$

On rotation, let **b** be the vector with components $(p+1)$ and 1 so that

$$\mathbf{b}=(p+1)\hat{\mathbf{i}}+\hat{\mathbf{j}}$$

Now, $|\mathbf{a}|=|\mathbf{b}| \Rightarrow a^2=b^2$

$$\Rightarrow \quad 4p^2+1=(p+1)^2+1$$

$$\Rightarrow \quad 4p^2=(p+1)^2$$

$$\Rightarrow \quad 2p=\pm(p+1)$$

$$\Rightarrow \quad 3p=-1 \text{ or } p=1$$

$$\therefore \quad p=-\frac{1}{3} \text{ or } p=1$$

JEE SCANNER

Example 3 Similar to PYQ Asked in JEE Main 2019

Two forces A and B of magnitude 2F and 3F respectively are at an angle θ with each other. If the force B is doubled, then their resultant also get doubled. Then, the angle θ is

(a) $\frac{2\pi}{3}$ (b) $\frac{\pi}{4}$

(c) $\frac{\pi}{2}$ (d) None of these

Sol. (a) $R^2=A^2+B^2+2AB\cos\theta$

$$=4F^2+9F^2+12F^2\cos\theta$$

$$=13F^2+12F^2\cos\theta \quad \text{...(i)}$$

when force B is doubled,

Now, $4R^2=4F^2+36F^2+24F^2\cos\theta$

Put the value of R^2 from Eq. (i), we get

$$4(13F^2+12F^2\cos\theta)=4F^2+36F^2+24F^2\cos\theta$$

$$\Rightarrow \quad 24F^2\cos\theta=-12F^2$$

$$\Rightarrow \quad \cos\theta=-\frac{1}{2} \Rightarrow \theta=\frac{2\pi}{3}$$

Skill Builder

Two force f_1 and f_2 of magnitude $4F$ and $6F$ respectively are at an angle θ with each other. If the force f_1 is one-fourth and f_2 is halved, then their resultant also get half, then the angle θ is

(a) $\frac{\pi}{3}$ (b) $\frac{\pi}{4}$

(c) $\frac{\pi}{2}$ (d) $\frac{2\pi}{3}$

For Sol.

Example 4 *A line segment has length 63 and direction ratios are 3, – 2 and 6. The components of line vector are*

(a) –27, 18, 54 (b) 27, – 18, 54
(c) 27, – 18, – 54 (d) –27, – 18, – 54

Sol. (b) Let the components of line segment on axes are x, y and z.

So, $x^2 + y^2 + z^2 = 63^2$

Now, $\frac{x}{3} = \frac{y}{-2} = \frac{z}{6} = k$ (let)

$\because \quad (3k)^2 + (-2k)^2 + (6k)^2 = 63^2 \Rightarrow k = \pm\frac{63}{7} = \pm 9$

$\therefore$ Components are (27, – 18, 54) or (–27, 18, – 54).

Example 5 *If the vectors* $6\hat{\mathbf{i}} - 2\hat{\mathbf{j}} + 3\hat{\mathbf{k}}, 2\hat{\mathbf{i}} + 3\hat{\mathbf{j}} - 6\hat{\mathbf{k}}$ *and* $3\hat{\mathbf{i}} + 6\hat{\mathbf{j}} - 2\hat{\mathbf{k}}$ *form a triangle, then it is*

(a) right angled (b) obtuse angled
(c) equilateral (d) isosceles

Sol. (b) **AB** = Position vectors of B – Position vector of A

$= (2\hat{\mathbf{i}} + 3\hat{\mathbf{j}} - 6\hat{\mathbf{k}}) - (6\hat{\mathbf{i}} - 2\hat{\mathbf{j}} + 3\hat{\mathbf{k}}) = -4\hat{\mathbf{i}} + 5\hat{\mathbf{j}} - 9\hat{\mathbf{k}}$

$\Rightarrow |\mathbf{AB}| = \sqrt{16 + 25 + 81} = \sqrt{122}$

$\mathbf{BC} = \hat{\mathbf{i}} + 3\hat{\mathbf{j}} + 4\hat{\mathbf{k}}$

$\Rightarrow |\mathbf{BC}| = \sqrt{1 + 9 + 16} = \sqrt{26}$ and $\mathbf{AC} = -3\hat{\mathbf{i}} + 8\hat{\mathbf{j}} - 5\hat{\mathbf{k}}$

$\Rightarrow |\mathbf{AC}| = \sqrt{98}$

Therefore, $AB^2 = 122$, $BC^2 = 26$ and $AC^2 = 98$

$\Rightarrow \quad AB^2 + BC^2 = 26 + 122 = 148$

Since, $AC^2 < AB^2 + BC^2$, therefore ΔABC is an obtuse angled triangle.

Example 6 *The vector* $\hat{\mathbf{i}} + x\hat{\mathbf{j}} + 3\hat{\mathbf{k}}$ *is rotated through an angle* θ *and is doubled in magnitude. It now becomes* $4\hat{\mathbf{i}} + (4x - 2)\hat{\mathbf{j}} + 2\hat{\mathbf{k}}$. *Then, the values of x is*

(a) 1 (b) – 2 (c) 2 (d) $\frac{2}{3}$

Sol. (c) Let $\alpha = \hat{\mathbf{i}} + x\hat{\mathbf{j}} + 3\hat{\mathbf{k}}$

$\beta = 4\hat{\mathbf{i}} + (4x - 2)\hat{\mathbf{j}} + 2\hat{\mathbf{k}}$

Given, $2|\alpha| = |\beta|$

$\Rightarrow \quad 2\sqrt{10 + x^2} = \sqrt{20 + 4(2x - 1)^2}$

$\Rightarrow \quad 10 + x^2 = 5 + (4x^2 - 4x + 1)$

$\Rightarrow \quad 3x^2 - 4x - 4 = 0 \Rightarrow x = 2, -\frac{2}{3}$

Example 7 *If* **A** *and* **B** *are two vectors and k be any scalar quantity greater than zero, if*

$$\alpha|\mathbf{A} + \mathbf{B}|^2 \le (1 + k)|\mathbf{A}|^2 + \left(1 + \frac{1}{k}\right)|\mathbf{B}|^2,$$

then the value of α^2 *is*

(a) 4 (b) 1 (c) 0 (d) 9

Decoding the Question
Use AM $\geq$ GM for a and b as $\frac{a+b}{2} \geq \sqrt{ab}$.

Sol. (b) We know,

$$(1 + k)|\mathbf{A}|^2 + \left(1 + \frac{1}{k}\right)|\mathbf{B}|^2$$

$$= |\mathbf{A}|^2 + k|\mathbf{A}|^2 + |\mathbf{B}|^2 + \frac{1}{k}|\mathbf{B}|^2 \quad \text{...(i)}$$

Also, $k|\mathbf{A}|^2 + \frac{1}{k}|\mathbf{B}|^2 \geq 2\left(k|\mathbf{A}|^2 \cdot \frac{1}{k}|\mathbf{B}|^2\right)^{\frac{1}{2}} = 2|\mathbf{A}| \cdot |\mathbf{B}|$ ...(ii)

So, $(1 + k)|\mathbf{A}|^2 + \left(1 + \frac{1}{k}\right)|\mathbf{B}|^2 \geq |\mathbf{A}|^2 + |\mathbf{B}|^2 + 2|\mathbf{A}| \cdot |\mathbf{B}|$

$= (|\mathbf{A}| + |\mathbf{B}|)^2$ [using Eqs. (i) and (ii)]

and also, $|\mathbf{A}| + |\mathbf{B}| \geq |\mathbf{A} + \mathbf{B}|$

Now, $(1 + k)|\mathbf{A}|^2 + \left(1 + \frac{1}{k}\right)|\mathbf{B}|^2 \geq |\mathbf{A} + \mathbf{B}|^2$

Hence, $\alpha^2 = 1$

Example 8 *The position vectors of the points A, B and C are* $(2\hat{\mathbf{i}} + \hat{\mathbf{j}} - \hat{\mathbf{k}}), (3\hat{\mathbf{i}} - 2\hat{\mathbf{j}} + \hat{\mathbf{k}})$ *and* $(\hat{\mathbf{i}} + 4\hat{\mathbf{j}} - 3\hat{\mathbf{k}})$ *respectively. These points.*

(a) form an isosceles triangle
(b) form a right angled triangle
(c) are collinear
(d) form a scalene triangle

Sol. (c) $\mathbf{AB} = (3 - 2)\hat{\mathbf{i}} + (-2 - 1)\hat{\mathbf{j}} + (1 + 1)\hat{\mathbf{k}}$

$= \hat{\mathbf{i}} - 3\hat{\mathbf{j}} + 2\hat{\mathbf{k}}$

$\mathbf{BC} = (1 - 3)\hat{\mathbf{i}} + (4 + 2)\hat{\mathbf{j}} + (-3 - 1)\hat{\mathbf{k}}$

$= -2\hat{\mathbf{i}} + 6\hat{\mathbf{j}} - 4\hat{\mathbf{k}}$

$\mathbf{CA} = (2 - 1)\hat{\mathbf{i}} + (1 - 4)\hat{\mathbf{j}} + (-1 + 3)\hat{\mathbf{k}}$

$= \hat{\mathbf{i}} - 3\hat{\mathbf{j}} + 2\hat{\mathbf{k}}$

$|\mathbf{AB}| = \sqrt{1 + 9 + 4} = \sqrt{14}$

$|\mathbf{BC}| = \sqrt{4 + 36 + 16} = \sqrt{56}$

$= 2\sqrt{14}$

$|\mathbf{CA}| = \sqrt{1 + 9 + 4} = \sqrt{14}$

So, $|\mathbf{AB}| + |\mathbf{AC}| = |\mathbf{BC}|$ and angle between AB and BC is 180°.

So, points A, B and C cannot form an isosceles triangle.

Hence, A, B and C are collinear.

Example 9 *In a* ΔABC, *if* $2\mathbf{AC} = 3\mathbf{CB}$, *then* $2\mathbf{OA} + 3\mathbf{OB}$ *is equal to*

(a) 5**OC** (b) –**OC**
(c) **OC** (d) None of these

Sol. (a) $2\mathbf{OA} + 3\mathbf{OB} = 2(\mathbf{OC} + \mathbf{CA}) + 3(\mathbf{OC} + \mathbf{CB})$

$= 5\mathbf{OC} + 2\mathbf{CA} + 3\mathbf{CB}$

$= 5\mathbf{OC}$ $[\because 2\mathbf{CA} = -3\mathbf{CB}]$

Example 10 *If* **a**, **b**, **c** *and* **d** *be the position vectors of the points A, B, C and D respectively, referred to same origin O such that no three of these points are collinear and* $\mathbf{a}+\mathbf{c}=\mathbf{b}+\mathbf{d}$, *then quadrilateral ABCD is a*

(a) square (b) rhombus
(c) rectangle (d) parallelogram

Sol. (d) Given, $\mathbf{a}+\mathbf{c}=\mathbf{b}+\mathbf{d} \Rightarrow \frac{1}{2}(\mathbf{a}+\mathbf{c})=\frac{1}{2}(\mathbf{b}+\mathbf{d})$

Here, mid-points of **AC** and **BD** coincide, where **AC** and **BD** are diagonals. In addition, we know that, diagonals of a parallelogram bisect each other.

Hence, quadrilateral is parallelogram.

Example 11 *P is a point on the side BC of the* ΔABC *and Q is a point such that* **PQ** *is the resultant of* **AP**, **PB** *and* **PC**. *Then, ABQC is a*

(a) square (b) rectangle
(c) parallelogram (d) trapezium

Sol. (c) $\mathbf{AP}+\mathbf{PB}+\mathbf{PC}=\mathbf{PQ}$ or $\mathbf{AP}+\mathbf{PB}=\mathbf{PQ}+\mathbf{CP}$

$\Rightarrow \quad \mathbf{AB}=\mathbf{CQ}$

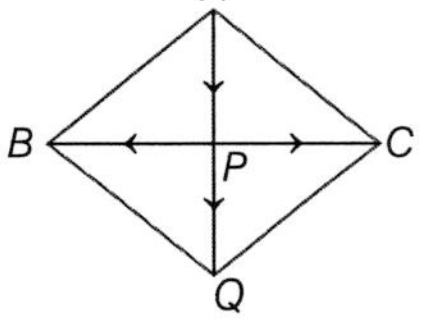

Hence, it is a parallelogram.

Example 12 *If ABCD is a parallelogram and the position vectors of A, B and C are* $\hat{\mathbf{i}}+3\hat{\mathbf{j}}+5\hat{\mathbf{k}}$, $\hat{\mathbf{i}}+\hat{\mathbf{j}}+\hat{\mathbf{k}}$ *and* $7\hat{\mathbf{i}}+7\hat{\mathbf{j}}+7\hat{\mathbf{k}}$, *then the position vector of D will be*

(a) $7\hat{\mathbf{i}}+5\hat{\mathbf{j}}+3\hat{\mathbf{k}}$ (b) $7\hat{\mathbf{i}}+9\hat{\mathbf{j}}+11\hat{\mathbf{k}}$
(c) $9\hat{\mathbf{i}}+11\hat{\mathbf{j}}+13\hat{\mathbf{k}}$ (d) $8\hat{\mathbf{i}}+8\hat{\mathbf{j}}+8\hat{\mathbf{k}}$

Sol. (b) Let position vector of D be $x\hat{\mathbf{i}}+y\hat{\mathbf{j}}+z\hat{\mathbf{k}}$, then $\mathbf{AB}=\mathbf{DC}$.

$\Rightarrow \quad -2\hat{\mathbf{j}}-4\hat{\mathbf{k}}=(7-x)\hat{\mathbf{i}}+(7-y)\hat{\mathbf{j}}+(7-z)\hat{\mathbf{k}}$

$\Rightarrow \quad x=7, y=9 \text{ and } z=11$

Hence, position vector of D will be $7\hat{\mathbf{i}}+9\hat{\mathbf{j}}+11\hat{\mathbf{k}}$.

Example 13 *P is the point of intersection of the diagonals of the parallelogram ABCD. If O is any point, then* $\mathbf{OA}+\mathbf{OB}+\mathbf{OC}+\mathbf{OD}$ *is equal to*

(a) **OP** (b) 2**OP** (c) 3**OP** (d) 4**OP**

Sol. (d) We know that P will be the mid-point of AC and BD.

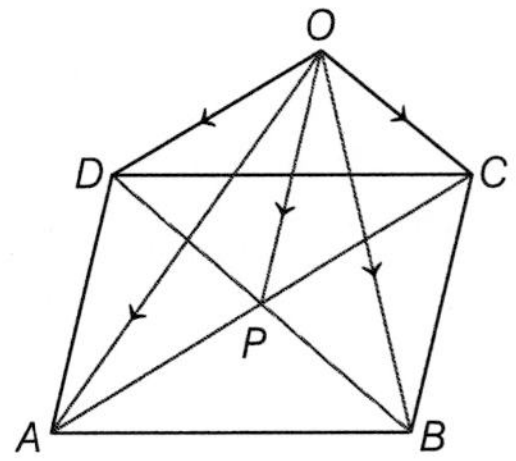

$\therefore \quad \mathbf{OA}+\mathbf{OC}=2\mathbf{OP}$ ...(i)

and $\quad \mathbf{OB}+\mathbf{OD}=2\mathbf{OP}$ ...(ii)

On adding Eqs. (i) and (ii), we get

$$\mathbf{OA}+\mathbf{OB}+\mathbf{OC}+\mathbf{OD}=4\mathbf{OP}$$

Example 14 *If C is the middle point of AB and P is any point outside AB, then*

(a) $\mathbf{PA}+\mathbf{PB}=\mathbf{PC}$
(b) $\mathbf{PA}+\mathbf{PB}=2\mathbf{PC}$
(c) $\mathbf{PA}+\mathbf{PB}+\mathbf{PC}=0$
(d) $\mathbf{PA}+\mathbf{PB}+2\mathbf{PC}=0$

Sol. (b) $\mathbf{PA}+\mathbf{PB}=(\mathbf{PA}+\mathbf{AC})+(\mathbf{PB}+\mathbf{BC})-(\mathbf{AC}+\mathbf{BC})$

$=\mathbf{PC}+\mathbf{PC}-(\mathbf{AC}-\mathbf{CB})=2\mathbf{PC}-0 \quad [\because \mathbf{AC}=\mathbf{CB}]$

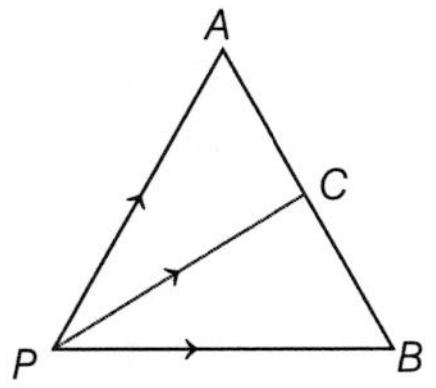

$\therefore \quad \mathbf{PA}+\mathbf{PB}=2\mathbf{PC}$

Example 15 *If O be the circumcentre and O′ be the orthocentre of the* ΔABC, *then* $\mathbf{O'A}+\mathbf{O'B}+\mathbf{O'C}$ *is equal to*

(a) $\mathbf{OO'}$ (b) $2\mathbf{O'O}$ (c) $2\mathbf{OO'}$ (d) 0

Sol. (b)

$\mathbf{O'A}=\mathbf{O'O}+\mathbf{OA}$

$\mathbf{O'B}=\mathbf{O'O}+\mathbf{OB}$

$\mathbf{O'C}=\mathbf{O'O}+\mathbf{OC}$

$\Rightarrow \mathbf{O'A}+\mathbf{O'B}+\mathbf{O'C}=3\mathbf{O'O}+\mathbf{OA}+\mathbf{OB}+\mathbf{OC}$

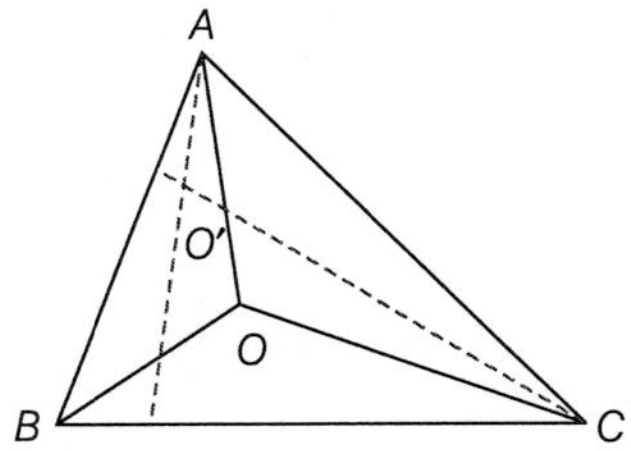

Since, $\quad \mathbf{OA}+\mathbf{OB}+\mathbf{OC}=\mathbf{OO'}=-\mathbf{O'O}$

$\therefore \quad \mathbf{O'A}+\mathbf{O'B}+\mathbf{O'C}=2\mathbf{O'O}$

Example 16 *Five points given by A, B, C, D and E are in a plane. Three forces* **AC**, **AD** *and* **AE** *at A and three forces* **CB**, **DB** *and* **EB** *act at B. Then, their resultant is*

(a) 2**AC** (b) 3**AB**
(c) 3**DB** (d) 2**BC**

Sol. (b) Points A, B, C, D and E are in a plane.

Resultant $=(\mathbf{AC}+\mathbf{AD}+\mathbf{AE})+(\mathbf{CB}+\mathbf{BD}+\mathbf{EB})$

$=(\mathbf{AC}+\mathbf{CB})+(\mathbf{AD}+\mathbf{DB})+(\mathbf{AE}+\mathbf{EB})$

$=\mathbf{AB}+\mathbf{AB}+\mathbf{AB}$

$=3\mathbf{AB}$

Example 17 *If the vectors represented by the sides AB and BC of the regular hexagon ABCDEF be* **a** *and* **b**, *then the vector represented by* **AE** *will be*

(a) $2\mathbf{b}-\mathbf{a}$ (b) $\mathbf{b}-\mathbf{a}$ (c) $2\mathbf{a}-\mathbf{b}$ (d) $\mathbf{a}+\mathbf{b}$

Sol. (a) As in figure, $\mathbf{AB}=\mathbf{a}$, $\mathbf{BC}=\mathbf{b}$,

So, $\mathbf{AD}=2\mathbf{b}$ and $\mathbf{ED}=\mathbf{a}$

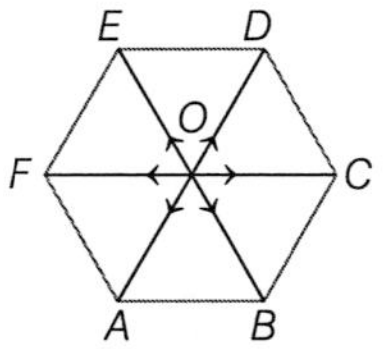

Now, $\mathbf{AE}+\mathbf{ED}=\mathbf{AD} \Rightarrow \mathbf{AE}=\mathbf{AD}-\mathbf{ED}=2\mathbf{b}-\mathbf{a}$

Example 18 *If* **a** *and* **b** *are the position vectors of A and B respectively, then the position vector of a point C on AB produced such that* $\mathbf{AC}=3\mathbf{AB}$ *is*

(a) $3\mathbf{a}-\mathbf{b}$ (b) $3\mathbf{b}-\mathbf{a}$
(c) $3\mathbf{a}-2\mathbf{b}$ (d) $3\mathbf{b}-2\mathbf{a}$

Sol. (d) Since, given that $\mathbf{AC}=3\mathbf{AB}$. It means that point C divides AB externally.

Thus, $\mathbf{AC}:\mathbf{BC}=3:2$

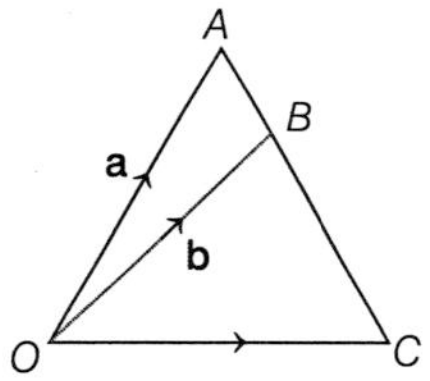

Hence, $\mathbf{OC}=\dfrac{3\cdot\mathbf{b}-2\cdot\mathbf{a}}{3-2}=3\mathbf{b}-2\mathbf{a}$

Example 19 *Let A and B be points with position vectors* **a** *and* **b** *with respect to the origin O. If the point C on OA is such that* $2\mathbf{AC}=\mathbf{CO}$, *CD is parallel to OB and* $|\mathbf{CD}|=3|\mathbf{OB}|$, *then* **AD** *is equal to*

(a) $3\mathbf{b}-\dfrac{\mathbf{a}}{2}$ (b) $3\mathbf{b}+\dfrac{\mathbf{a}}{2}$

(c) $3\mathbf{b}-\dfrac{\mathbf{a}}{3}$ (d) $3\mathbf{b}+\dfrac{\mathbf{a}}{3}$

Sol. (c) Since, $\mathbf{OA}=\mathbf{a}$, $\mathbf{OB}=\mathbf{b}$ and $2\mathbf{AC}=\mathbf{CO}$

By section formula, $\mathbf{OC}=\dfrac{2}{3}\mathbf{a}$

Therefore, $|\mathbf{CD}|=3|\mathbf{OB}|$

$\Rightarrow \mathbf{CD}=3\mathbf{b}$

$\Rightarrow \mathbf{OD}=\mathbf{OC}+\mathbf{CD}=\dfrac{2}{3}\mathbf{a}+3\mathbf{b}$ $[\because \mathbf{CD}=\mathbf{OD}-\mathbf{OC}]$

Hence, $\mathbf{AD}=\mathbf{OD}-\mathbf{OA}=\dfrac{2}{3}\mathbf{a}+3\mathbf{b}-\mathbf{a}$

$=3\mathbf{b}-\dfrac{1}{3}\mathbf{a}$

JEE SCANNER

Example 20 Similar to PYQ Asked in JEE Main 2024

Let O be the origin and the position vectors of P and Q be $2\hat{i}+\hat{j}+2\hat{k}$ *and* $4\hat{i}+4\hat{j}+2\hat{k}$ *respectively. If the internal bisector of* $\angle POQ$ *meets the line PQ at R, then the length of OR is*

(a) $\dfrac{2}{3}\sqrt{34}$ (b) $\dfrac{3}{2}\sqrt{34}$ (c) $\dfrac{3}{2}\sqrt{31}$ (d) $\dfrac{2}{3}\sqrt{31}$

Sol. (a) We have, $\mathbf{OP}=2\hat{i}+\hat{j}+2\hat{k}$ and $\mathbf{OQ}=4\hat{i}+4\hat{j}+2\hat{k}$

$|\mathbf{OP}|=\sqrt{4+1+4}=\sqrt{9}=3$

$|\mathbf{OQ}|=\sqrt{16+16+4}=\sqrt{36}=6$

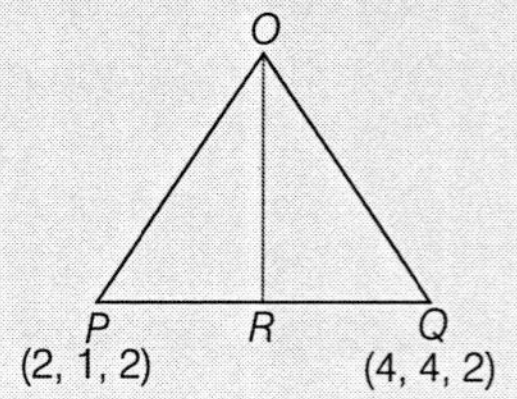

$\Rightarrow \dfrac{OP}{OQ}=\dfrac{3}{6}=\dfrac{1}{2} \Rightarrow \dfrac{PR}{QR}=\dfrac{1}{2}$

$\therefore \mathbf{OR}=\dfrac{1(4\hat{i}+4\hat{j}+2\hat{k})+2(2\hat{i}+\hat{j}+2\hat{k})}{1+2}=\dfrac{8\hat{i}+6\hat{j}+6\hat{k}}{3}$

Hence, $|\mathbf{OR}|=\dfrac{\sqrt{64+36+36}}{3}=\dfrac{\sqrt{136}}{3}=\dfrac{2\sqrt{34}}{3}$

Skill Builder

For Sol.

Let O be the origin and the position vectors of A and B be $3\hat{i}+4\hat{j}$ and $10\hat{i}+10\hat{j}+5\hat{k}$, respectively. If the internal bisector of $\angle AOB$ meets the line AB at C and the length of OC is l, then $16l^2$ is equal to

(a) 3480 (b) 435 (c) 1740 (d) 870

Example 21 *If D, E and F are respectively, the mid-points of AB, AC and BC in* ΔABC, *then* $\mathbf{BE}+\mathbf{AF}$ *is equal to*

(a) $\mathbf{DC}$ (b) $\dfrac{1}{2}\mathbf{BF}$ (c) $2\mathbf{BF}$ (d) $\dfrac{3}{2}\mathbf{BF}$

Sol. (a) $\mathbf{BE}+\mathbf{AF}=\mathbf{OE}-\mathbf{OB}+\mathbf{OF}-\mathbf{OA}$

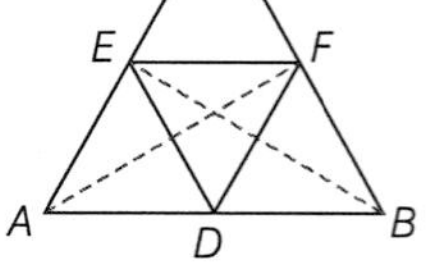

$=\dfrac{\mathbf{OA}+\mathbf{OC}}{2}-\mathbf{OB}+\dfrac{\mathbf{OB}+\mathbf{OC}}{2}-\mathbf{OA}$

$=\mathbf{OC}-\dfrac{\mathbf{OA}+\mathbf{OB}}{2}=\mathbf{OC}-\mathbf{OD}=\mathbf{DC}$

Example 22 *In a quadrilateral PQRS,* $\mathbf{PQ} = a$, $\mathbf{QR} = b$, $\mathbf{SP} = a - b$. *If M is the mid-point of* $\mathbf{QR}$ *and X is a point of* $\mathbf{SM}$ *such that,* $\mathbf{SX} = \frac{4}{5}\mathbf{SM}$, *then*

(a) $\mathbf{PX} = \frac{1}{5}\mathbf{PR}$ (b) $\mathbf{PX} = \frac{3}{5}\mathbf{PR}$

(c) $\mathbf{PX} = \frac{2}{5}\mathbf{PR}$ (d) None of these

Sol. (b) If we take point P as the origin, the position vectors of Q and S are $\mathbf{a}$ and $\mathbf{b} - \mathbf{a}$ respectively.

In ΔPQR, we have

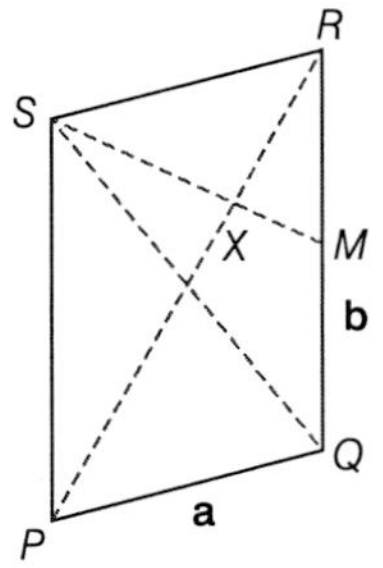

$$\mathbf{PR} = \mathbf{PQ} + \mathbf{QR} \Rightarrow \mathbf{PR} = \mathbf{a} + \mathbf{b}$$

$\therefore$ Position vector of $R = \mathbf{a} + \mathbf{b}$

$$\Rightarrow \quad \text{PV of } M = \frac{\mathbf{a} + (\mathbf{a} + \mathbf{b})}{2} = \left(\mathbf{a} + \frac{1}{2}\mathbf{b}\right)$$

Now, $$SX = \frac{4}{5}SM$$

$$\Rightarrow \quad XM = SM - SX = SM - \frac{4}{5}SM = \frac{1}{5}SM$$

$$\therefore \quad SX : XM = 4 : 1$$

$$\Rightarrow \quad \text{PV of } X = \frac{4\left(\mathbf{a} + \frac{1}{2}\mathbf{b}\right) + 1(\mathbf{b} - \mathbf{a})}{4 + 1} = \frac{3\mathbf{a} + 3\mathbf{b}}{5}$$

$$\Rightarrow \quad \mathbf{PX} = \frac{3}{5}(\mathbf{a} + \mathbf{b})$$

$$\Rightarrow \quad \mathbf{PX} = \frac{3}{5}\mathbf{PR}$$

Example 23 *Orthocentre of an equilateral triangle ABC is the origin O. If* $\mathbf{OA} = \mathbf{a}$, $\mathbf{OB} = \mathbf{b}$, $\mathbf{OC} = \mathbf{c}$, *then* $\mathbf{AB} + 2\mathbf{BC} + 3\mathbf{CA}$ *is equal to*

(a) $3\mathbf{c}$ (b) $3\mathbf{a}$ (c) $\mathbf{0}$ (d) $3\mathbf{b}$

Sol. (b) For an equilateral triangle, centroid is the same as orthocentre

$$\therefore \quad \frac{\mathbf{OA} + \mathbf{OB} + \mathbf{OC}}{3} = \mathbf{0}$$

$$\therefore \quad \mathbf{OA} + \mathbf{OB} + \mathbf{OC} = \mathbf{0}$$

Now, $\mathbf{AB} + 2\mathbf{BC} + 3\mathbf{CA}$

$$= \mathbf{OB} - \mathbf{OA} + 2\mathbf{OC} - 2\mathbf{OB} + 3\mathbf{OA} - 3\mathbf{OC}$$
$$= -\mathbf{OB} + 2\mathbf{OA} - \mathbf{OC}$$
$$= -(\mathbf{OB} + \mathbf{OA} + \mathbf{OC}) + 3\mathbf{OA}$$
$$= 3\mathbf{OA} = 3\mathbf{a}$$

JEE SCANNER

Example 24 Similar to PYQ Asked in JEE Main 2024

Let the position vectors of the vertices P, Q and R of a triangle be $3\hat{i} + 2\hat{j} + \hat{k}$, $\hat{i} + 2\hat{j} - \hat{k}$ *and* $\hat{i} + \hat{k}$ *respectively. Let* l_1, l_2 *and* l_3 *be the lengths of perpendicular drawn from the orthocenter of the triangle on the sides PQ, QR and RP respectively, then* $l_1^2 + l_2^2 + l_3^2$ *equals*

(a) $\frac{1}{2}$ (b) 1 (c) 4 (d) 2

Sol. (d) Given, position vectors of the vertices P, Q and R are $3\hat{\mathbf{i}} + 2\hat{\mathbf{j}} + \hat{\mathbf{k}}$, $\hat{\mathbf{i}} + 2\hat{\mathbf{j}} - \hat{\mathbf{k}}$ and $\hat{\mathbf{i}} + \hat{\mathbf{k}}$ respectively.

So, coordinates of $P \equiv (3, 2, 1)$, $Q \equiv (1, 2, -1)$ and $R \equiv (1, 0, 1)$

l_1 : Length of perpendicular drawn from orthocentre of ΔPQR on PQ.

l_2 : Length of perpendicular drawn from orthocentre of ΔPQR on QR.

l_3 : Length of perpendicular drawn from orthocentre of ΔPQR on RP.

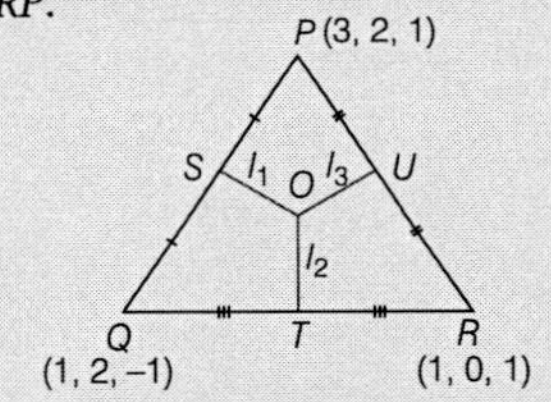

Now, $PQ = \sqrt{(3-1)^2 + (2-2)^2 + (1+1)^2} = \sqrt{4 + 0 + 4} = 2\sqrt{2}$

$QR = \sqrt{(1-1)^2 + (2-0)^2 + (-1-1)^2} = \sqrt{0 + 4 + 4} = 2\sqrt{2}$

$RP = \sqrt{(1-3)^2 + (0-2)^2 + (1-1)^2} = \sqrt{4 + 4 + 0} = 2\sqrt{2}$

This represents ΔPQR is an equilateral triangle. As we know that in an equilateral triangle, orthocentre and centroid will be same (coincide).

So, centroid $\equiv \left(\frac{5}{3}, \frac{4}{3}, \frac{1}{3}\right)$

Let S be the mid-point of $PQ = (2, 2, 0)$

$$\therefore l_1 = \sqrt{\left(\frac{5}{3} - 2\right)^2 + \left(\frac{4}{3} - 2\right)^2 + \left(\frac{1}{3} - 0\right)^2}$$

$$= \sqrt{\left(\frac{-1}{3}\right)^2 + \left(\frac{-2}{3}\right)^2 + \left(\frac{1}{3}\right)^2} = \sqrt{\frac{1}{9} + \frac{4}{9} + \frac{1}{9}} = \sqrt{\frac{2}{3}} = l_2 = l_3$$

Hence, $l_1^2 + l_2^2 + l_3^2 = \frac{2}{3} + \frac{2}{3} + \frac{2}{3} = \frac{6}{3} = 2$

Skill Builder

Let the position vectors of the vertices A, B and C of a triangle be $3\hat{i} + 3\hat{j} + \hat{k}$, $2\hat{i} + 3\hat{j} + 2\hat{k}$, $2\hat{i} + 2\hat{j} + \hat{k}$ respectively. Let l_1, l_2 and l_3 be the lengths of perpendicular drawn from the orthocenter of the triangle on the sides AB, BC and CA respectively. Then, $2(l_1^2 + l_2^2 + l_3^2)$ equals

For Sol.

(a) $\frac{1}{2}$ (b) 2 (c) 1 (d) 4

Example 25 *ABCDEF is a regular hexagon in the XY-plane with vertices in the anticlockwise direction. If* $\mathbf{AB} = 2\hat{\mathbf{i}}$, *then* $\mathbf{CD}$ *is*

(a) $\hat{\mathbf{i}} + \sqrt{3}\hat{\mathbf{j}}$ (b) $\hat{\mathbf{i}} + 2\hat{\mathbf{j}}$

(c) $-\hat{\mathbf{i}} + \sqrt{3}\hat{\mathbf{j}}$ (d) None of these

Sol. (c)

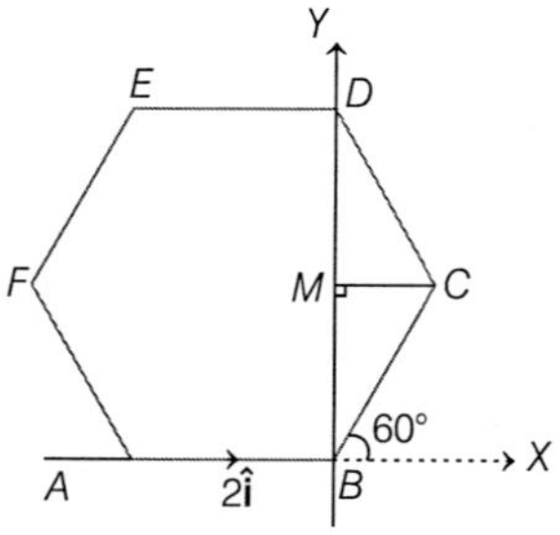

$\mathbf{AB}$ is along the X-axis and BD is along the Y-axis.

$\mathbf{AB} = 2\hat{\mathbf{i}} \Rightarrow AB = BC = CD = \ldots\ldots\ldots = 2$

From the figure, $BM = BC\sin 60° = 2\sin 60° = \sqrt{3}$

$\therefore \quad \mathbf{BD} = 2\sqrt{3}\hat{\mathbf{j}}$

$\mathbf{BC} = BC\cos 60°\hat{\mathbf{i}} + BC\sin 60°\hat{\mathbf{j}} = \hat{\mathbf{i}} + \sqrt{3}\hat{\mathbf{j}}$

$\mathbf{CD} = \mathbf{BD} - \mathbf{BC} = 2\sqrt{3}\hat{\mathbf{j}} - (\hat{\mathbf{i}} + \sqrt{3}\mathbf{j})$

$= -\hat{\mathbf{i}} + \sqrt{3}\hat{\mathbf{j}}$

Example 26 *The vertices of triangle are A*(1, 1, 2), *B*(4, 3, 1) *and C*(2, 3, 5). *A vector representing the internal bisector of the* $\angle A$ *is*

(a) $\hat{\mathbf{i}} + \hat{\mathbf{j}} + 2\hat{\mathbf{k}}$ (b) $2\hat{\mathbf{i}} - 2\hat{\mathbf{j}} + \hat{\mathbf{k}}$

(c) $2\hat{\mathbf{i}} + 2\hat{\mathbf{j}} + \hat{\mathbf{k}}$ (d) None of these

Sol. (c) From the figure, we have

$\mathbf{b} = \mathbf{AC} = \hat{\mathbf{i}} + 2\hat{\mathbf{j}} + 3\hat{\mathbf{k}}$

and $\mathbf{c} = \mathbf{AB} = 3\hat{\mathbf{i}} + 2\hat{\mathbf{j}} - \hat{\mathbf{k}}$

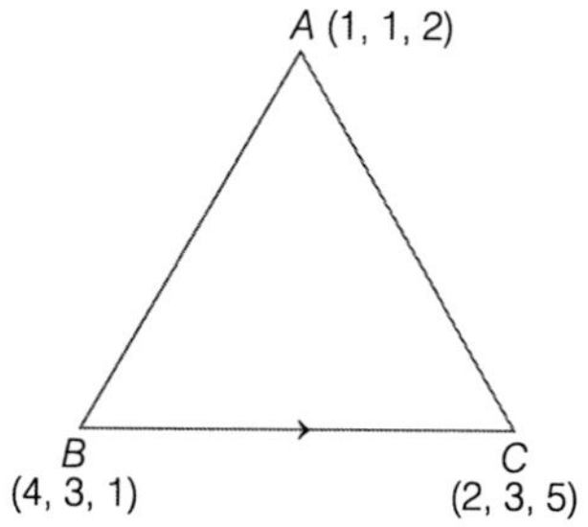

$\therefore$ Unit vector along the bisector of $\angle A$ is given by

$$= \frac{\mathbf{b} + \mathbf{c}}{2} = \frac{(\hat{\mathbf{i}} + 2\hat{\mathbf{j}} + 3\hat{\mathbf{k}}) + (3\hat{\mathbf{i}} + 2\hat{\mathbf{j}} - \hat{\mathbf{k}})}{2}$$

$$= \frac{4\hat{\mathbf{i}} + 4\hat{\mathbf{j}} + 2\hat{\mathbf{k}}}{2} = 2\hat{\mathbf{i}} + 2\hat{\mathbf{j}} + \hat{\mathbf{k}}$$

$\therefore$ A vector along the internal bisector of $\angle A = 2\hat{\mathbf{i}} + 2\hat{\mathbf{j}} + \hat{\mathbf{k}}$

Example 27 *Let* $\mathbf{a}$, $\mathbf{b}$ *and* $\mathbf{c}$ *be three non-zero vectors which are pair-wise non-collinear. If* $\mathbf{a} + 3\mathbf{b}$ *is collinear with* $\mathbf{c}$ *and* $\mathbf{b} + 2\mathbf{c}$ *is collinear with* $\mathbf{a}$, *then* $\mathbf{a} + 3\mathbf{b} + 6\mathbf{c}$ *is*

(a) $\mathbf{b}$ (b) $\mathbf{a} + \mathbf{c}$ (c) 0 (d) $\mathbf{c}$

Sol. (c) Given, $\mathbf{a} + 3\mathbf{b}$ is collinear with $\mathbf{c}$,

$\therefore \quad \mathbf{a} + 3\mathbf{b} = k_1\mathbf{c}$ ...(i)

Also, $\mathbf{b} + 2\mathbf{c}$ is collinear with $\mathbf{a}$,

$\therefore \quad \mathbf{b} + 2\mathbf{c} = k_2\mathbf{a}$ ...(ii)

From Eq. (i), we get

$\mathbf{a} + 3\mathbf{b} + 6\mathbf{c} = (k_1 + 6)\mathbf{c}$ ...(iii)

From Eq. (ii), we get

$3\mathbf{b} + 6\mathbf{c} = 3k_2\mathbf{a} \Rightarrow \mathbf{a} + 3\mathbf{b} + 6\mathbf{c} = (1 + 3k_2)\mathbf{a}$ ...(iv)

From Eqs. (iii) and (iv), we get

$(k_1 + 6)\mathbf{c} = (1 + 3k_2)\mathbf{a}$

Since, $\mathbf{a}$ and $\mathbf{c}$ are non-collinear,

$\therefore \quad k_1 + 6 = 0 = 1 + 3k_2$

From Eq. (iv), we get

$\mathbf{a} + 3\mathbf{b} + 6\mathbf{c} = 0$

JEE SCANNER

Example 28 Similar to PYQ Asked in JEE Main 2024

Let $\mathbf{a}$, $\mathbf{b}$ *and* $\mathbf{c}$ *be three non-zero vectors such that* $\mathbf{b}$ *and* $\mathbf{c}$ *are non-collinear. If* $\mathbf{a} + 6\mathbf{b}$ *is collinear with* $\mathbf{c}$, $\mathbf{b} + 10\mathbf{c}$ *is collinear with* $\mathbf{a}$ *and* $\mathbf{a} + \alpha\mathbf{b} + \beta\mathbf{c} = 0$, *then* $\alpha + \beta$ *is equal to*

(a) -60 (b) 60 (c) 66 (d) -50

Sol. (c) We have, $\mathbf{a} + 6\mathbf{b} = \lambda\mathbf{c}$ ...(i)

and $\mathbf{b} + 10\mathbf{c} = \mu\mathbf{a}$, ...(ii)

where λ and μ are scalars.

From Eq. (i), we have

$\mathbf{a} = \lambda\mathbf{c} - 6\mathbf{b}$

$\therefore \quad \mathbf{b} + 10\mathbf{c} = \mu(\lambda\mathbf{c} - 6\mathbf{b})$ [from Eq. (ii)]

$\Rightarrow \quad \frac{\mathbf{b}}{\mu} + \frac{10}{\mu}\mathbf{c} = \lambda\mathbf{c} - 6\mathbf{b}$

$\therefore \quad \frac{10}{\mu} = \lambda$ and $\frac{1}{\mu} = -6$

$\Rightarrow \quad \mu = -\frac{1}{6} \Rightarrow \lambda = -60$

$\therefore \ \mathbf{a} + 6\mathbf{b} + 60\mathbf{c} = 0 \Rightarrow \alpha = 6$ and $\beta = 60$

$\therefore \alpha + \beta = 6 + 60 = 66$

Skill builder

Let $\mathbf{a}$, $\mathbf{b}$ and $\mathbf{c}$ be three non-zero vectors such that $\mathbf{b}$ and $\mathbf{c}$ are non-collinear. If $\mathbf{a} + 3\mathbf{b}$ is collinear with $\mathbf{c}$, $\mathbf{b} + 9\mathbf{c}$ is collinear with $\mathbf{a}$ and $\mathbf{a} + \alpha\mathbf{b} + \beta\mathbf{c} = 0$, then $\alpha + \beta$ is equal to

(a) 27 (b) 30

(c) 24 (d) -24

For Sol.

Example 29 *In a trapezium, the vector* $\mathbf{BC} = \lambda \mathbf{AD}$. *We will then find that* $\mathbf{p} = \mathbf{AC} + \mathbf{BD}$ *is collinear with* $\mathbf{AD}$. *If* $\mathbf{p} = \mu\, \mathbf{AD}$, *then*

(a) $\mu = \lambda + 1$ (b) $\lambda = \mu + 1$
(c) $\lambda + \mu = 1$ (d) $\mu = 2 + \lambda$

Sol. (a) We have, $\mathbf{p} = \mathbf{AC} + \mathbf{BD} = \mathbf{AC} + \mathbf{BC} + \mathbf{CD}$

$$= \mathbf{AC} + \lambda\mathbf{AD} + \mathbf{CD}$$
$$= \lambda\mathbf{AD} + (\mathbf{AC} + \mathbf{CD}) = \lambda\, \mathbf{AD} + \mathbf{AD}$$
$$= (\lambda + 1)\mathbf{AD}$$

Therefore, $\mathbf{p} = \mu\, \mathbf{AD} \Rightarrow \mu = \lambda + 1$

Example 30 *Let a, b and c be distinct non-negative numbers and the vectors* $a\hat{\mathbf{i}} + a\hat{\mathbf{j}} + c\hat{\mathbf{k}}$, $\hat{\mathbf{i}} + \hat{\mathbf{k}}$, $c\hat{\mathbf{i}} + c\hat{\mathbf{j}} + b\hat{\mathbf{k}}$ *lie in a plane, then the quadratic equation* $ax^2 + 2cx + b = 0$ *has*

(a) real and equal roots
(b) real and unequal roots
(c) unreal roots
(d) both roots real and positive

Sol. (a) $a\hat{\mathbf{i}} + a\hat{\mathbf{j}} + c\hat{\mathbf{k}}$, $\hat{\mathbf{i}} + \hat{\mathbf{k}}$ and $c\hat{\mathbf{i}} + c\hat{\mathbf{j}} + b\hat{\mathbf{k}}$ are coplanar

$$\therefore \begin{vmatrix} a & a & c \\ 1 & 0 & 1 \\ c & c & b \end{vmatrix} = 0 \Rightarrow c^2 - ab = 0 \qquad \text{...(i)}$$

For equation $ax^2 + 2cx + b = 0$

$$D = 4c^2 - 4ab = 0 \qquad \text{[using Eq. (i)]}$$

So, roots are real and equal.

Example 31 *The number of distinct real values of* λ *for which the vectors* $\lambda^3\hat{\mathbf{i}} + \hat{\mathbf{k}}$, $\hat{\mathbf{i}} - \lambda^3\hat{\mathbf{j}}$ *and* $\hat{\mathbf{i}} + (2\lambda - \sin\lambda)\hat{\mathbf{j}} - \lambda\hat{\mathbf{k}}$ *are coplanar is*

(a) 0 (b) 1 (c) 2 (d) 3

Sol. (a) Put $\Delta = 0 \Rightarrow \lambda^7 + \lambda^3 + 2\lambda - \sin\lambda = 0$

Let $f(\lambda) = \lambda^7 + \lambda^3 + 2\lambda - \sin\lambda$

$\Rightarrow f'(\lambda) = (7\lambda^6 + 3\lambda^2 + 2 - \cos\lambda) > 0, \forall \in R$

$\therefore$ $f(\lambda) = 0$ has only one real solution which is $\lambda = 0$.

Example 32 *The points* $A(2 - x, 2, 2)$, $B(2, 2 - y, 2)$, $C(2, 2, 2 - z)$ *and* $D(1, 1, 1)$ *are coplanar, then locus of* $P(x, y, z)$ *is*

(a) $\frac{1}{x} + \frac{1}{y} + \frac{1}{z} = 1$ (b) $x + y + z = 1$

(c) $\frac{1}{1-x} + \frac{1}{1-y} + \frac{1}{1-z} = 1$ (d) None of these

Sol. (a) Here, $\mathbf{AB} = x\hat{\mathbf{i}} - y\hat{\mathbf{j}}$; $\mathbf{AC} = x\hat{\mathbf{i}} - z\hat{\mathbf{k}}$; $\mathbf{AD} = (x - 1)\hat{\mathbf{i}} - \hat{\mathbf{j}} - \hat{\mathbf{k}}$

As, these vectors are coplanar.

$$\Rightarrow \begin{vmatrix} x & -y & 0 \\ x & 0 & -z \\ x-1 & -1 & -1 \end{vmatrix} = 0 \Rightarrow \frac{1}{x} + \frac{1}{y} + \frac{1}{z} = 1$$

JEE SCANNER

Example 33 Similar to PYQ Asked in JEE Main 2023 & 21

If the four points $2\hat{\mathbf{i}} + 3\hat{\mathbf{j}} - \hat{\mathbf{k}}$, $\hat{\mathbf{i}} + 2\hat{\mathbf{j}} + 3\hat{\mathbf{k}}$, $3\hat{\mathbf{i}} + 4\hat{\mathbf{j}} - 2\hat{\mathbf{k}}$ *and* $\hat{\mathbf{i}} - \lambda\hat{\mathbf{j}} + 6\hat{\mathbf{k}}$ *are coplanar, then the value of* λ *is*

(a) −4 (b) 3 (c) −2 (d) 4

Sol. (c) The given four points are coplanar.

$$\begin{vmatrix} 1-2 & -\lambda-3 & 6+1 \\ 1-2 & 2-3 & 3+1 \\ 3-2 & 4-3 & -2+1 \end{vmatrix} = 0$$

$$\Rightarrow \begin{vmatrix} -1 & -\lambda-3 & 7 \\ -1 & -1 & 4 \\ 1 & 1 & -1 \end{vmatrix} = 0$$

$$\Rightarrow -1(1-4) + (\lambda+3)(1-4) + 7(-1+1) = 0$$

$$\Rightarrow 3 - 3\lambda - 9 = 0 \Rightarrow -3\lambda = 6$$

Hence, $\lambda = -2$

Skill Builder

If the four points $3\hat{\mathbf{i}} + 4\hat{\mathbf{j}} - \hat{\mathbf{k}}$, $\hat{\mathbf{i}} + 3\hat{\mathbf{j}} + 9\hat{\mathbf{k}}$, $2\hat{\mathbf{i}} + 3\hat{\mathbf{j}} - 5\hat{\mathbf{k}}$ and $\hat{\mathbf{i}} - \alpha\hat{\mathbf{j}} + 3\hat{\mathbf{k}}$ are coplanar, then the value of α is

(a) $\frac{-8}{3}$ (b) $\frac{-4}{3}$

(c) $\frac{8}{3}$ (d) $\frac{2}{9}$

For Sol.

Example 34 $\mathbf{p} = 2\mathbf{a} - 3\mathbf{b}$, $\mathbf{q} = \mathbf{a} - 2\mathbf{b} + \mathbf{c}$ *and* $\mathbf{r} = -3\mathbf{a} + \mathbf{b} + 2\mathbf{c}$, *where* $\mathbf{a}$, $\mathbf{b}$, $\mathbf{c}$ *being non-zero non-coplanar vectors, then the vector* $-2\mathbf{a} + 3\mathbf{b} - \mathbf{c}$ *is equal to*

(a) $\mathbf{p} - 4\mathbf{q}$ (b) $\frac{-7\mathbf{q} + \mathbf{r}}{5}$

(c) $2\mathbf{p} - 3\mathbf{q} + \mathbf{r}$ (d) $4\mathbf{p} - 2\mathbf{r}$

Sol. (b) Let $-2\mathbf{a} + 3\mathbf{b} - \mathbf{c} = x\mathbf{p} + y\mathbf{q} + z\mathbf{r}$,

where x, y and z are scalars.

$$\Rightarrow -2\mathbf{a} + 3\mathbf{b} - \mathbf{c} = (2x + y - 3z)\mathbf{a} + (-3x - 2y + z)\mathbf{b} + (y + 2z)\mathbf{c}$$

$\therefore$ $2x + y - 3z = -2$, $-3x - 2y + z = 3$ and $y + 2z = -1$

On solving these, we get

$$x = 0, y = -\frac{7}{5}, z = \frac{1}{5}$$

$$\therefore -2\mathbf{a} + 3\mathbf{b} - c = \frac{(-7\mathbf{q} + \mathbf{r})}{5}$$

Time Saving Technique

Check alternates one-by-one

i.e. (a) $\mathbf{p} - 4\mathbf{q} = -2\mathbf{a} + 5\mathbf{b} - 4\mathbf{c}$ (b) $\frac{-7\mathbf{q} + \mathbf{r}}{5} = -2\mathbf{a} + 3\mathbf{b} - \mathbf{c}$

(c) $2\mathbf{p} - 3\mathbf{q} + \mathbf{r} = -2\mathbf{a} + \mathbf{b} - \mathbf{c}$ (d) $4\mathbf{p} - 2\mathbf{r} = 14\mathbf{a} - 14\mathbf{b} - 4\mathbf{c}$

Example 35 *If the vectors* $\mathbf{a}_1$ *and* $\mathbf{a}_2$ *are linearly independent satisfying*

$$(\sqrt{3}\tan x+1)\,\mathbf{a}_1+(\sqrt{3}\sec x-2)\,\mathbf{a}_2=0,$$

then the value of x is

(a) $\frac{5\pi}{6}$ (b) $\frac{7\pi}{6}$ (c) $\frac{11\pi}{6}$ (d) $\frac{13\pi}{6}$

Sol. (c) Given, $(\sqrt{3}\tan x+1)\,\mathbf{a}_1+(\sqrt{3}\sec x-2)\,\mathbf{a}_2=0$

Since, $\mathbf{a}_1$ and $\mathbf{a}_2$ are linearly independent,

$\therefore\ \sqrt{3}\tan x+1=0$ and $\sqrt{3}\sec x-2=0$

$$\Rightarrow \quad \tan x=-\frac{1}{\sqrt{3}} \text{ and } \sec x=\frac{2}{\sqrt{3}}$$

$$\Rightarrow \quad \tan x=-\tan\frac{\pi}{6} \text{ and } \cos x=\frac{\sqrt{3}}{2}$$

$$\Rightarrow \quad \tan x=\tan\left(\pi-\frac{\pi}{6}\right) \text{ or } \tan\left(2\pi-\frac{\pi}{6}\right)$$

$$=\tan\frac{5\pi}{6} \text{ or } \tan\frac{11\pi}{6}$$

$$\text{and } \cos x=\cos\frac{\pi}{6} \text{ or } \cos\left(2\pi-\frac{\pi}{6}\right)=\cos\frac{\pi}{6} \text{ or } \cos\frac{11\pi}{6}$$

$$\Rightarrow \quad x=\frac{11\pi}{6}$$

More than One Correct Option Type Questions

Example 36 $\mathbf{a}, \mathbf{b}$ *and* $\mathbf{c}$ *are three coplanar unit vectors such that* $\mathbf{a}+\mathbf{b}+\mathbf{c}=0$. *If three vectors* $\mathbf{p}, \mathbf{q}$ *and* $\mathbf{r}$ *are parallel to* $\mathbf{a}, \mathbf{b}$ *and* $\mathbf{c}$ *respectively, and have integral but different magnitudes, then among the following options,* $|\mathbf{p}+\mathbf{q}+\mathbf{r}|$ *can take a value equal to*

(a) 1 (b) 0 (c) $\sqrt{3}$ (d) 2

Sol. (c,d) Let $\mathbf{a}, \mathbf{b}$ and $\mathbf{c}$ lie in the XY-plane.

Let $\mathbf{a}=\hat{\mathbf{i}}$, $\mathbf{b}=-\frac{1}{2}\hat{\mathbf{i}}+\frac{\sqrt{3}}{2}\hat{\mathbf{j}}$ and $\mathbf{c}=-\frac{1}{2}\hat{\mathbf{i}}-\frac{\sqrt{3}}{2}\hat{\mathbf{j}}$

Therefore, $|\mathbf{p}+\mathbf{q}+\mathbf{r}|=|\lambda\mathbf{a}+\mu\mathbf{b}+\nu\mathbf{c}|$

$$=\left|\lambda\hat{\mathbf{i}}+\mu\left(-\frac{1}{2}\hat{\mathbf{i}}+\frac{\sqrt{3}}{2}\hat{\mathbf{j}}\right)+\nu\left(-\frac{1}{2}\hat{\mathbf{i}}-\frac{\sqrt{3}}{2}\hat{\mathbf{j}}\right)\right|$$

$$=\left|\left(\lambda-\frac{\mu}{2}-\frac{\nu}{2}\right)\hat{\mathbf{i}}+\frac{\sqrt{3}}{2}(\mu-\nu)\,\hat{\mathbf{j}}\right|$$

$$=\sqrt{\left(\lambda-\frac{\mu}{2}-\frac{\nu}{2}\right)^2+\frac{3}{4}(\mu-\nu)^2}$$

$$=\sqrt{\lambda^2+\mu^2+\nu^2-\lambda\mu-\lambda\nu-\mu\nu}$$

$$=\frac{1}{\sqrt{2}}\sqrt{(\lambda-\mu)^2+(\mu-\nu)^2+(\nu-\lambda)^2}$$

$$=\frac{1}{\sqrt{2}}\sqrt{1+1+4}=\sqrt{3}$$

$\Rightarrow\ |\mathbf{p}+\mathbf{q}+\mathbf{r}|$ can take a value equal to $\sqrt{3}$ and 2.

Example 37 *A, B, C and D are four points such that* $\mathbf{AB}=m(2\hat{\mathbf{i}}-6\hat{\mathbf{j}}+2\hat{\mathbf{k}})$, $\mathbf{BC}=(\hat{\mathbf{i}}-2\hat{\mathbf{j}})$ *and* $\mathbf{CD}=n(-6\hat{\mathbf{i}}+15\hat{\mathbf{j}}-3\hat{\mathbf{k}})$. *If CD intersects AB at some point E, then*

(a) $m\geq\frac{1}{2}$ (b) $n\geq\frac{1}{3}$ (c) $m=n$ (d) $m<n$

Sol. (a, b) Let $\mathbf{EB}=p\,\mathbf{AB}$ and $\mathbf{CE}=q\,\mathbf{CD}$

Then, $0<p$ and $q\leq 1$

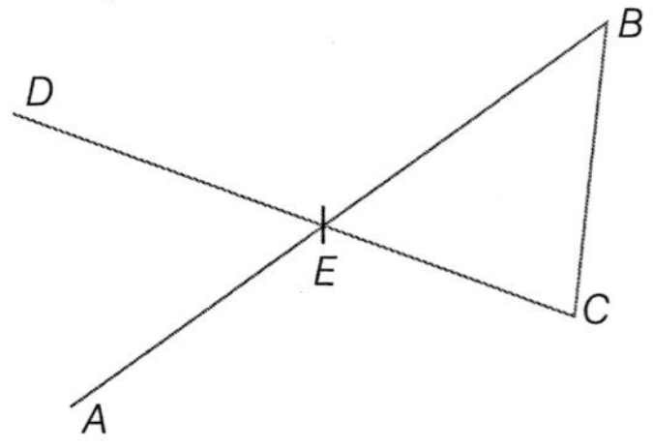

Since, $\mathbf{EB}+\mathbf{BC}+\mathbf{CE}=\mathbf{0}$

$$pm(2\hat{\mathbf{i}}-6\hat{\mathbf{j}}+2\hat{\mathbf{k}})+(\hat{\mathbf{i}}-2\hat{\mathbf{j}})+qn(-6\hat{\mathbf{i}}+15\hat{\mathbf{j}}-3\hat{\mathbf{k}})=\mathbf{0}$$

$$\Rightarrow (2pm+1-6qn)\hat{\mathbf{i}}+(-6pm-2+15qn)\hat{\mathbf{j}}+(2pm-3qn)\hat{\mathbf{k}}=\mathbf{0}$$

$$\Rightarrow \quad 2pm-6qn+1=\mathbf{0},$$

$$-6pm-2+15qn=\mathbf{0},\ 2pm-3qn=\mathbf{0}$$

Solving these, we get

$$p=\frac{1}{(2m)} \quad\text{and}\quad q=\frac{1}{(3n)}$$

$$\therefore \quad 0<\frac{1}{(2m)}\leq 1 \quad\text{and}\quad 0<\frac{1}{(3n)}\leq 1$$

$$\Rightarrow \quad m\geq\frac{1}{2} \quad\text{and}\quad n\geq\frac{1}{3}$$

Example 38 *The vectors* $x\hat{\mathbf{i}}+(x+1)\hat{\mathbf{j}}+(x+2)\hat{\mathbf{k}}$, $(x+3)\hat{\mathbf{i}}+(x+4)\hat{\mathbf{j}}+(x+5)\hat{\mathbf{k}}$ *and* $(x+6)\hat{\mathbf{i}}+(x+7)\hat{\mathbf{j}}+(x+8)\hat{\mathbf{k}}$ *are coplanar if x is equal to*

(a) 1 (b) −3 (c) 4 (d) 0

Decoding the Question

Apply here test of coplanarity of three vectors i.e. if $\mathbf{a}=a_1\hat{\mathbf{i}}+a_2\hat{\mathbf{j}}+a_3\hat{\mathbf{k}}$, $\mathbf{b}=b_1\hat{\mathbf{i}}+b_2\hat{\mathbf{j}}+b_3\hat{\mathbf{k}}$ and $\mathbf{c}=c_1\hat{\mathbf{i}}+c_2\hat{\mathbf{j}}+c_3\hat{\mathbf{k}}$ are coplanar, then $\begin{vmatrix} a_1 & a_2 & a_3 \\ b_1 & b_2 & b_3 \\ c_1 & c_2 & c_3 \end{vmatrix}=0$.

Sol. (a, b, c, d) As, given vectors are coplanar, then

$$\begin{vmatrix} x & x+1 & x+2 \\ x+3 & x+4 & x+5 \\ x+6 & x+7 & x+8 \end{vmatrix}=0$$

Applying $C_2\to C_2-C_1$ and $C_3\to C_3-C_1$, we have

$$\begin{vmatrix} x & 1 & 2 \\ x+3 & 1 & 2 \\ x+6 & 1 & 2 \end{vmatrix}=0$$

Hence, $x\in R$.

Example 39 *Given three vectors* $\mathbf{a}, \mathbf{b}$, *and* $\mathbf{c}$ *are non-zero and non-coplanar vectors. Then, which of the following are coplanar?*

(a) $\mathbf{a}+\mathbf{b}, \mathbf{b}+\mathbf{c}, \mathbf{c}+\mathbf{a}$ (b) $\mathbf{a}-\mathbf{b}, \mathbf{b}+\mathbf{c}, \mathbf{c}+\mathbf{a}$

(c) $\mathbf{a}+\mathbf{b}, \mathbf{b}-\mathbf{c}, \mathbf{c}+\mathbf{a}$ (d) $\mathbf{a}+\mathbf{b}, \mathbf{b}+\mathbf{c}, \mathbf{c}-\mathbf{a}$

Sol. (b, c, d) $\mathbf{c}+\mathbf{a}=(\mathbf{b}+\mathbf{c})+(\mathbf{a}-\mathbf{b})$

$\mathbf{a}+\mathbf{b}=(\mathbf{b}-\mathbf{c})+(\mathbf{c}+\mathbf{a})$

$\mathbf{b}+\mathbf{c}=(\mathbf{a}+\mathbf{b})+(\mathbf{c}-\mathbf{a})$

So, vectors in options (b), (c) and (d) are coplanar.

Example 40 *In a four-dimensional space where unit vectors along the axes are* $\hat{\mathbf{i}}, \hat{\mathbf{j}}, \hat{\mathbf{k}}$ *and* $\hat{\mathbf{i}}$, *and* $\mathbf{a}_1, \mathbf{a}_2, \mathbf{a}_3, \mathbf{a}_4$ *are four non-zero vectors such that no vector can be expressed as a linear combination of others and* $(\lambda-1)(\mathbf{a}_1-\mathbf{a}_2)+\mu(\mathbf{a}_2+\mathbf{a}_3)+\gamma(\mathbf{a}_3+\mathbf{a}_4-2\mathbf{a}_2)+\mathbf{a}_3+\delta\mathbf{a}_4=0$, *then*

(a) $\lambda=1$ (b) $\mu=-\frac{2}{3}$

(c) $\gamma=\frac{2}{3}$ (d) $\delta=\frac{1}{3}$

Sol. (a, b, d)

$(\lambda-1)(\mathbf{a}_1-\mathbf{a}_2)+\mu(\mathbf{a}_2+\mathbf{a}_3)+\gamma(\mathbf{a}_3+\mathbf{a}_4-2\mathbf{a}_2)+\mathbf{a}_3+\delta\mathbf{a}_4=\mathbf{0}$

i.e. $(\lambda-1)\mathbf{a}_1+(1-\lambda+\mu-2\gamma)\mathbf{a}_2+(\mu+\gamma+1)\mathbf{a}_3+(\gamma+\delta)\mathbf{a}_4=\mathbf{0}$

Since, $\mathbf{a}_1, \mathbf{a}_2, \mathbf{a}_3$ and $\mathbf{a}_4$ are linearly independent, we have

$\lambda-1=0, 1-\lambda+\mu-2\gamma=0,$

$\mu+\gamma+1=0$ and $\gamma+\delta=0$

i.e. $\lambda=1, \mu=2\gamma,$

and $\mu+\gamma+1=0 \Rightarrow 3\gamma+1=0$

and $\gamma+\delta=0 \Rightarrow \delta=-\gamma$

Hence, $\lambda=1, \mu=-\frac{2}{3}, \gamma=-\frac{1}{3}, \delta=\frac{1}{3}$

Passage Based Questions

Passage I
(Ex. Nos. 41 to 42)

ABCD is a parallelogram. L is a point on BC which divides BC in the ratio 1:2. AL intersects BD at P. M is a point on DC which divides DC in the ratio 1:2 and AM intersects BD at Q.

Example 41 *Points P divides AL in the ratio*

(a) 1: 2 (b) 1: 3

(c) 3 : 1 (d) 2 : 1

Example 42 *Point Q divides DB in the ratio*

(a) 1: 2 (b) 1: 3

(c) 3 : 1 (d) 2 : 1

Sol. (Ex. Nos. 41-42)

41. (c)

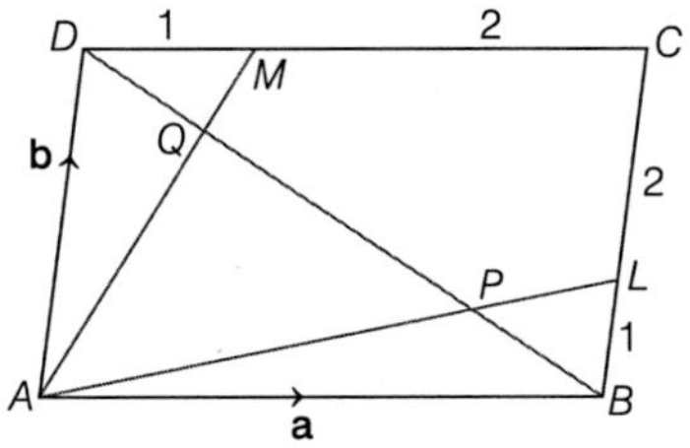

$\mathbf{BL}=\frac{1}{3}\mathbf{b}$ $[\because \mathbf{BC}=\mathbf{AD}=\mathbf{b}]$

$\therefore$ $\mathbf{AL}=\mathbf{a}+\frac{1}{3}\mathbf{b}$

Let $\mathbf{AP}=\lambda\mathbf{AL}$ and P divides DB in the ratio $\mu:1-\mu$.

Then, $\mathbf{AP}=\lambda\mathbf{a}+\frac{\lambda}{3}\mathbf{b}$ ...(i)

Also, $\mathbf{AP}=\mu\mathbf{a}+(1-\mu)\mathbf{b}$ ...(ii)

From Eqs. (i) and (ii),

$\lambda\mathbf{a}+\frac{\lambda}{3}\mathbf{b}=\mu\mathbf{a}+(1-\mu)\mathbf{b}$

$\therefore$ $\lambda=\mu$

and $\frac{\lambda}{3}=1-\mu$

$\therefore$ $\lambda=\frac{3}{4}$

$\therefore$ $\mathbf{AP}=\frac{3}{4}\mathbf{AL} \Rightarrow \mathbf{AP}:\mathbf{PL}=3:1$

42. (b) Hence, P divides AL in the ratio 3 : 1 and P divides DB in the ratio 3 : 1. Similarly, Q divides DB in the ratio 1 : 3.

Thus, $DQ=\frac{1}{4}DB$ and $PB=\frac{1}{4}DB$

Passage II
(Ex. Nos. 43 to 44)

Let A, B, C, D, E represent vertices of a regular pentagon ABCDE. Given the position vector of these vertices be $\mathbf{a}, \mathbf{a}+\mathbf{b}, \mathbf{b}, \lambda\mathbf{a}$ *and* $\lambda\mathbf{b}$ *respectively.*

Example 43 *The ratio* $\frac{AD}{BC}$ *is equal to*

(a) $1-\cos\frac{3\pi}{5}:\cos\frac{3\pi}{5}$ (b) $1+2\cos\frac{2\pi}{5}:\cos\frac{\pi}{5}$

(c) $1+2\cos\frac{\pi}{5}:2\cos\frac{\pi}{5}$ (d) None of these

Example 44 *AD divides EC in the ratio*

(a) $\cos\frac{2\pi}{5}:1$ (b) $\cos\frac{3\pi}{5}:1$

(c) $1:2\cos\frac{\pi}{5}$ (d) 1: 2

Sol. (Ex. Nos. 43-44)

Decoding the Question

Use sine rule formula, $\frac{a}{\sin A} = \frac{b}{\sin B} = \frac{c}{\sin C}$.

Given *ABCDE* is a regular pentagon.

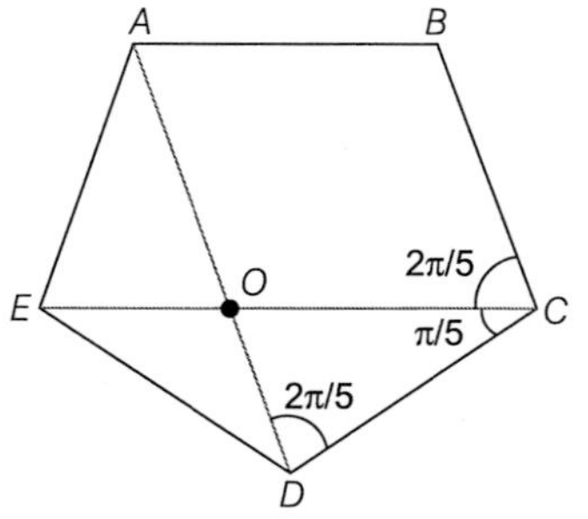

Let position vector of points *A* and *C* be **a** and **b**, respectively.

AD is parallel to *BC* and *AB* is parallel to *EC*.

Therefore,

AOCB is a parallelogram and position vector of *B* is $\mathbf{a} + \mathbf{b}$.

The position vectors of *E* and *D* are $\lambda\mathbf{b}$ and $\lambda\mathbf{a}$ respectively.

Also, $OA = BC = AB = OC = 1$ (let)

Therefore, *AOCB* is rhombus.

$$\angle ABC = \angle AOC = \frac{3\pi}{5}$$

and $$\angle OAB = \angle BCO = \pi - \frac{3\pi}{5} = \frac{2\pi}{5}$$

Further, $$OA = AE = 1 \text{ and } OC = CD = 1$$

Thus, ΔEAO and ΔOCD are isosceles.

In ΔOCD, using sine rule we get.

$$\frac{OC}{\sin\frac{2\pi}{5}} = \frac{OD}{\sin\frac{\pi}{5}} \Rightarrow OD = \frac{1}{2\cos\frac{\pi}{5}} = OE$$

$$\Rightarrow \quad AD = OA + OD = 1 + \frac{1}{2\cos\frac{\pi}{5}}$$

43. (c) $\frac{AD}{BC} = 1 + \frac{1}{2\cos\frac{\pi}{5}} = \frac{1 + 2\cos\frac{\pi}{5}}{2\cos\frac{\pi}{5}}$

44. (c) $\frac{OE}{OC} = \frac{1}{2\cos\frac{\pi}{5}}$

Passage III
(Ex. Nos. 45 to 46)

In a parallelogram OABC vectors **a**, **b**, **c** *respectively, the position vectors of vertices A, B, C with reference to O as origin. A point E is taken on the side BC which divides it in the ratio of* 2 : 1. *Also, the line segment AE intersects the line bisecting the angle* $\angle AOC$ *internally at point P. If CP when extended meets AB at point F, then*

Example 45 *The position vector of point P is*

(a) $\frac{|\mathbf{a}||\mathbf{c}|}{3|\mathbf{c}| + 2|\mathbf{a}|}\left(\frac{\mathbf{a}}{|\mathbf{a}|} + \frac{\mathbf{c}}{|\mathbf{c}|}\right)$ (b) $\frac{3|\mathbf{a}||\mathbf{c}|}{3|\mathbf{c}| + 2|\mathbf{a}|}\left(\frac{\mathbf{a}}{|\mathbf{a}|} + \frac{\mathbf{c}}{|\mathbf{c}|}\right)$

(c) $\frac{2|\mathbf{a}||\mathbf{c}|}{3|\mathbf{c}| + 2|\mathbf{a}|}\left(\frac{\mathbf{a}}{|\mathbf{a}|} + \frac{\mathbf{c}}{|\mathbf{c}|}\right)$ (d) None of these

Example 46 *The ratio in which F divides AB is*

(a) $\frac{2|\mathbf{a}|}{||\mathbf{a}| - 3|\mathbf{c}||}$ (b) $\frac{|\mathbf{a}|}{||\mathbf{a}| - 3|\mathbf{c}||}$

(c) $\frac{3|\mathbf{a}|}{||\mathbf{a}| - 3|\mathbf{c}||}$ (d) $\frac{3|\mathbf{c}|}{3||\mathbf{c}| - |\mathbf{a}||}$

Sol. (Ex. Nos. 45-46)

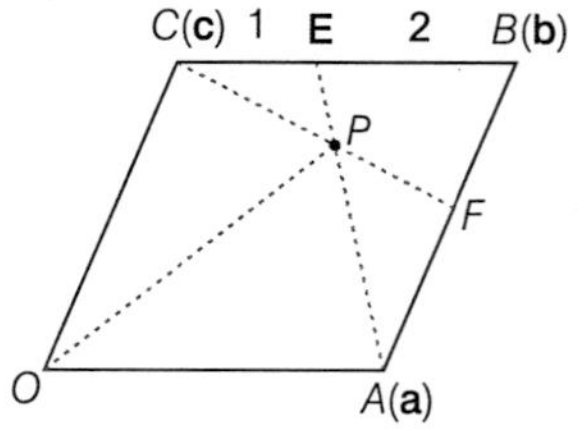

Let the position vector of *A* and *C* be **a** and **c** respectively. Therefore,

Position vector of

$$\boldsymbol{B} = \mathbf{b} = \mathbf{a} + \mathbf{c} \quad \text{...(i)}$$

Also, position vector of

$$E = \frac{\mathbf{b} + 2\mathbf{c}}{3} = \frac{\mathbf{a} + 3\mathbf{c}}{3} \quad \text{...(ii)}$$

Now, point *P* lies on angle bisector of $\angle AOC$. Thus,

Position vector of point

$$P = \lambda\left(\frac{\mathbf{a}}{|\mathbf{a}|} + \frac{\mathbf{b}}{|\mathbf{b}|}\right) \quad \text{...(iii)}$$

Also, let *P* divides *EA* in ratio $\mu : 1$.

Therefore, Position vector of *P*

$$= \frac{\mu\mathbf{a} + \frac{\mathbf{a} + 3\mathbf{c}}{3}}{\mu + 1} = \frac{(3\mu + 1)\mathbf{a} + 3\mathbf{c}}{3(\mu + 1)} \quad \text{...(iv)}$$

Comparing Eqs. (iii) and (iv), we get

$$\lambda\left(\frac{\mathbf{a}}{|\mathbf{a}|} + \frac{\mathbf{c}}{|\mathbf{c}|}\right) = \frac{(3\mu + 1)\mathbf{a} + 3\mathbf{c}}{3(\mu + 1)}$$

$$\Rightarrow \quad \frac{\lambda}{|\mathbf{a}|} = \frac{3\mu + 1}{3(\mu + 1)} \text{ and } \frac{\lambda}{|\mathbf{c}|} = \frac{1}{\mu + 1}$$

$$\Rightarrow \quad \frac{3|\mathbf{c}| - |\mathbf{a}|}{3|\mathbf{a}|} = \mu$$

$$\Rightarrow \quad \frac{\lambda}{|\mathbf{c}|} = \frac{1}{\frac{3|\mathbf{c}| - |\mathbf{a}|}{3|\mathbf{a}|} + 1} \Rightarrow \lambda = \frac{3|\mathbf{a}||\mathbf{c}|}{3|\mathbf{c}| + 2|\mathbf{a}|}$$

45. (b) So, position vector of *P* is $\frac{3|\mathbf{a}||\mathbf{c}|}{3|\mathbf{c}| + 2|\mathbf{a}|}\left(\frac{\mathbf{a}}{|\mathbf{a}|} + \frac{\mathbf{c}}{|\mathbf{c}|}\right)$.

46. (d) Let F divides AB in ratio $t:1$, then position vector of F is $\frac{t\mathbf{b}+\mathbf{a}}{t+1}$

Now, points C, P, F are collinear,

Then, $\quad \mathbf{CF} = m\mathbf{CP}$

$$\Rightarrow \frac{t(\mathbf{a}+\mathbf{c})}{t+1} - \mathbf{c} = m\left\{\frac{3|\mathbf{a}||\mathbf{c}|}{3|\mathbf{c}|+2|\mathbf{a}|}\left(\frac{\mathbf{a}}{|\mathbf{a}|}+\frac{\mathbf{c}}{|\mathbf{c}|}\right) - \mathbf{c}\right\}$$

Comparing coefficients, we get

$$\frac{t}{t+1} = m\frac{3|\mathbf{c}|}{3|\mathbf{c}|+2|\mathbf{a}|}$$

and $$\frac{-1}{t+1} = m\frac{|\mathbf{a}|-3|\mathbf{c}|}{3|\mathbf{c}|+2|\mathbf{a}|}$$

$$t = \frac{3|\mathbf{c}|}{3|\mathbf{c}|-|\mathbf{a}|}$$

Stem Based Questions

Stem I

(Ex. Nos. 47 to 48)

Consider three non-zero and non-coplanar vectors $\mathbf{a}$, $\mathbf{b}$ *and* $\mathbf{c}$ *such that* $\mathbf{x}_1 = m\mathbf{a}+n\mathbf{b}+\mathbf{c}$ *and* $\mathbf{x}_2 = \mathbf{a}+m\mathbf{b}+n\mathbf{c}$. *If vectors* $\mathbf{x}_1+2\mathbf{x}_2$ *and* $2\mathbf{x}_1+\mathbf{x}_2$ *are collinear, then*

Example 47 *Value of m is equal to ....*

Example 48 *Value of n is equal to ....*

Sol. Given, $\mathbf{x}_1 = m\mathbf{a}+n\mathbf{b}+\mathbf{c}$ and $\mathbf{x}_2 = \mathbf{a}+m\mathbf{b}+n\mathbf{c}$

$\therefore \mathbf{x}_1+2\mathbf{x}_2 = (m\mathbf{a}+n\mathbf{b}+\mathbf{c})+2(\mathbf{a}+m\mathbf{b}+n\mathbf{c})$

$= (m+2)\mathbf{a}+(2m+n)\mathbf{b}+(1+2n)\mathbf{c}$ ...(i)

and $2\mathbf{x}_1+\mathbf{x}_2 = 2(m\mathbf{a}+n\mathbf{b}+\mathbf{c})+\mathbf{a}+m\mathbf{b}+n\mathbf{c}$

$= (2m+1)\mathbf{a}+(m+2n)\mathbf{b}+(n+2)\mathbf{c}$ ...(ii)

Since, $\mathbf{x}_1+2\mathbf{x}_2$ and $2\mathbf{x}_1+\mathbf{x}_2$ are collinear.

$\therefore \quad \mathbf{x}_1+2\mathbf{x}_2 = \lambda(2\mathbf{x}_1+\mathbf{x}_2)$

$\Rightarrow (m+2)\mathbf{a}+(2m+n)\mathbf{b}+(1+2n)\mathbf{c}$

$= \lambda\{(2m+1)\mathbf{a}+(m+2n)\mathbf{b}+(n+2)\mathbf{c}\}$

$$\Rightarrow \frac{m+2}{2m+1} = \frac{2m+n}{m+2n} = \frac{1+2n}{n+2} = \lambda$$

$$= \frac{m+2+2m+n+1+2n}{2m+1+m+2n+n+2}$$

$$= \frac{3m+3n+3}{3m+3n+3} = 1$$

$$\Rightarrow \frac{m+2}{2m+1} = \frac{2m+n}{m+2n} = \frac{1+2n}{n+2} = 1$$

$$\Rightarrow \frac{m+2}{2m+1} = 1, \frac{1+2n}{n+2} = 1$$

$\Rightarrow \quad m+2 = 2m+1, 1+2n = n+2$

$\Rightarrow \quad m = 1, n = 1$

Thus, **47.** (1) **48.** (1)

Stem II

(Ex. Nos. 49 to 50)

If x_1 *and* x_2 *are two values of x for which the unit vector* $x\hat{\mathbf{i}}+y\hat{\mathbf{j}}+\frac{1}{2}\hat{\mathbf{k}}$ *is linearly dependent with* $\hat{\mathbf{i}}+2\hat{\mathbf{j}}$ *and* $\hat{\mathbf{j}}-2\hat{\mathbf{k}}$, *then*

Example 49 *Value of* x_1+x_2 *is ....*

Example 50 *Value of* $80|x_1x_2|$ *is ....*

> **Decoding the Question**
> We know that any two collinear vectors are linearly dependent. So, if **a** is linearly dependent with **b** and **c**, then $\mathbf{a} = \lambda_1\mathbf{b}+\lambda_2\mathbf{c}$. Use this for solving the example.

Sol. Since, $x\hat{\mathbf{i}}+y\hat{\mathbf{j}}+\frac{1}{2}\hat{\mathbf{k}}$ is linearly dependent with $\hat{\mathbf{i}}+2\hat{\mathbf{j}}$ and $\hat{\mathbf{j}}-2\hat{\mathbf{k}}$.

Therefore, $x\hat{\mathbf{i}}+y\hat{\mathbf{j}}+\frac{1}{2}\hat{\mathbf{k}} = \lambda_1(\hat{\mathbf{i}}+2\hat{\mathbf{j}})+\lambda_2(\hat{\mathbf{j}}-2\hat{\mathbf{k}})$

$$\Rightarrow \quad x\hat{\mathbf{i}}+y\hat{\mathbf{j}}+\frac{1}{2}\hat{\mathbf{k}} = \lambda_1\hat{\mathbf{i}}+(2\lambda_1+\lambda_2)\hat{\mathbf{j}}+(-2\lambda_2)\hat{\mathbf{k}}$$

$$\Rightarrow \quad x = \lambda_1, y = 2\lambda_1+\lambda_2$$

and $$\frac{1}{2} = -2\lambda_2 \Rightarrow \lambda_2 - -\frac{1}{4} \Rightarrow y = 2x-\frac{1}{4} \quad \text{...(i)}$$

Now, $x\hat{\mathbf{i}}+y\hat{\mathbf{j}}+\frac{1}{2}\hat{\mathbf{k}}$ is unit vector.

$$\therefore \quad x^2+y^2+\frac{1}{4} = 1$$

$$\Rightarrow \quad x^2+\left(2x-\frac{1}{4}\right)^2 = \frac{3}{4} \quad \text{[using (i)]}$$

$$\Rightarrow \quad x^2+4x^2+\frac{1}{16}-x = \frac{3}{4} \Rightarrow 5x^2-x-\frac{11}{16} = 0$$

$$\therefore \quad x_1+x_2 = \frac{1}{5} = 0.2 \text{ and } x_1x_2 = \frac{-11}{80}$$

$$\therefore \quad 80|x_1x_2| = 11$$

Thus, **49.** (0.2) **50.** (11)

Single Integer Answer Type Questions

Example 51 *P and Q have position vectors* **a** *and* **b** *relative to the origin O and X, Y divide* **PQ** *internally and externally respectively in the ratio 2 : 1. Vector* **XY** *is* $\lambda\mathbf{a}+\mu\mathbf{b}$, *then the value of* $|\lambda+\mu|$ *is*

Sol. (0) Since, X and Y divide **PQ** internally and externally in the ratio 2 : 1, then $X = \frac{2\mathbf{b}+\mathbf{a}}{3}$ and $Y = 2\mathbf{b}-\mathbf{a}$

$\therefore$ **XY** = Position vector of Y-Position vector of X

$$= 2\mathbf{b}-\mathbf{a}-\frac{2\mathbf{b}+\mathbf{a}}{3} = \frac{4\mathbf{b}}{3}-\frac{4\mathbf{a}}{3}$$

On comparing it with $\lambda \mathbf{a} + \mu \mathbf{b}$, we get

$$\lambda = -\frac{4}{3} \text{ and } \mu = \frac{4}{3}$$

$$\therefore \quad |\lambda + \mu| = \left|\frac{-4}{3} + \frac{4}{3}\right| = 0$$

Example 52 *If $A(1, -1, -3)$, $B(2, 1, -2)$ and $C(-5, 2, -6)$ are the position vectors of the vertices of ΔABC. The length of the bisector of its internal angle at A is $\frac{\lambda\sqrt{10}}{4}$, then value of λ is*

Sol. (3) We have, $\mathbf{AB} = \hat{\mathbf{i}} + 2\hat{\mathbf{j}} + \hat{\mathbf{k}}$, $\mathbf{AC} = -6\hat{\mathbf{i}} + 3\hat{\mathbf{j}} - 3\hat{\mathbf{k}}$

$$\Rightarrow \quad |\mathbf{AB}| = \sqrt{6} \text{ and } |\mathbf{AC}| = 3\sqrt{6}$$

Clearly, point D divides BC in the ratio $AB : AC$, i.e. $1 : 3$

$$\therefore \text{ Position vector of } D = \frac{(-5\hat{\mathbf{i}} + 2\hat{\mathbf{j}} - 6\hat{\mathbf{k}}) + 3(2\hat{\mathbf{i}} + \hat{\mathbf{j}} - 2\hat{\mathbf{k}})}{1+3}$$

$$= \frac{1}{4}(\hat{\mathbf{i}} + 5\hat{\mathbf{j}} - 12\hat{\mathbf{k}})$$

$$\therefore \quad \mathbf{AD} = \frac{1}{4}(\hat{\mathbf{i}} + 5\hat{\mathbf{j}} - 12\hat{\mathbf{k}}) - (\hat{\mathbf{i}} - \hat{\mathbf{j}} - 3\hat{\mathbf{k}}) = \frac{3}{4}(-\hat{\mathbf{i}} + 3\hat{\mathbf{j}})$$

$$\Rightarrow \quad |\mathbf{AD}| = AD = \frac{3}{4}\sqrt{10}$$

$$\therefore \quad \lambda = 3$$

Example 53 *Let ABC be a triangle whose centroid is G, orthocentre is H and circumcentre is the origin 'O'. If D is any point in the plane of the triangle such that no three of O, A, C and D are collinear satisfying the relation $\mathbf{AD} + \mathbf{BD} + \mathbf{CH} + 3\mathbf{HG} = \lambda\mathbf{HD}$, then what is the value of the scalar 'Δ'.*

Sol. (2) LHS $= \mathbf{d} - \mathbf{a} + \mathbf{d} - \mathbf{b} + \mathbf{h} - \mathbf{c} + 3(\mathbf{g} - \mathbf{h})$

$$= 2\mathbf{d} - (\mathbf{a} + \mathbf{b} + \mathbf{c}) + 3\frac{(\mathbf{a} + \mathbf{b} + \mathbf{c})}{3} - 2\mathbf{h}$$

$$= 2\mathbf{d} - 2\mathbf{h} = 2(\mathbf{d} - \mathbf{h}) = 2\mathbf{HD}$$

$$\Rightarrow \quad \lambda = 2$$

Example 54 *Let $\mathbf{a}$, $\mathbf{b}$ and $\mathbf{c}$ be unit vectors such that $\mathbf{a} + \mathbf{b} - \mathbf{c} = 0$. If the area of triangle formed by vectors $\mathbf{a}$ and $\mathbf{b}$ is A, then what is the value of $16A^2$?*

Sol. (3) Given, $\mathbf{a} + \mathbf{b} = \mathbf{c}$

Now, vector $\mathbf{c}$ is along the diagonal of the parallelogram which has adjacent side vectors $\mathbf{a}$ and $\mathbf{b}$. Since, $\mathbf{c}$ is also a unit vector, triangle formed by vectors $\mathbf{a}$ and $\mathbf{b}$ is an equilateral triangle.

Then, Area of triangle $= \frac{\sqrt{3}}{4}$

$$\Rightarrow \quad A^2 = \frac{3}{16}$$

$$\Rightarrow \quad 16A^2 = 3$$

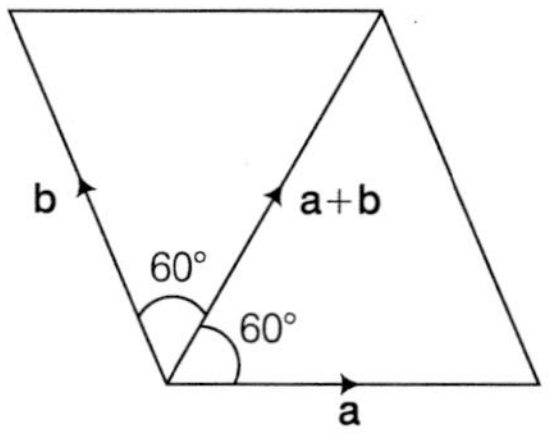

Example 55 *Find the least positive integral value of x for which the angle between vectors $\mathbf{a} = x\hat{\mathbf{i}} - 3\hat{\mathbf{j}} - \hat{\mathbf{k}}$ and $\mathbf{b} = 2x\hat{\mathbf{i}} + x\hat{\mathbf{j}} - \hat{\mathbf{k}}$ is acute.*

Sol. (2) Let $\mathbf{a} = x\hat{\mathbf{i}} - 3\hat{\mathbf{j}} - \hat{\mathbf{k}}$ and $\mathbf{b} = 2x\hat{\mathbf{i}} + x\hat{\mathbf{j}} - \hat{\mathbf{k}}$ be the adjacent sides of the parallelogram.

Now, angle between $\mathbf{a}$ and $\mathbf{b}$ is acute, i.e. $|\mathbf{a} + \mathbf{b}| > |\mathbf{a} - \mathbf{b}|$

$$\Rightarrow |3x\hat{\mathbf{i}} + (x-3)\hat{\mathbf{j}} - 2\hat{\mathbf{k}}|^2 > |-x\hat{\mathbf{i}} - (x+3)\hat{\mathbf{j}}|^2$$

or $\quad 9x^2 + (x-3)^2 + 4 > x^2 + (x+3)^2$

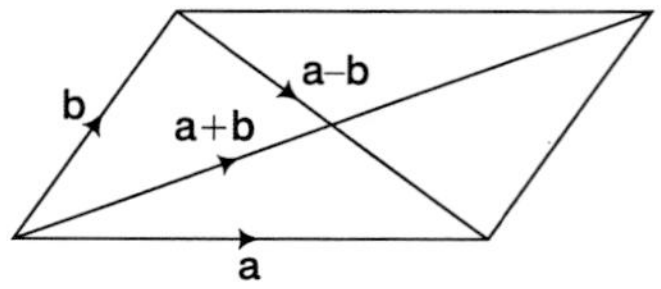

or $\quad 8x^2 - 12x + 4 > 0$ or $2x^2 - 3x + 1 > 0$

or $\quad (2x-1)(x-1) > 0 \Rightarrow x < \frac{1}{2}$ or $x > 1$

Hence, the least positive integral value is 2.

Example 56 *If the points $a(\cos\alpha\,\hat{\mathbf{i}} + \sin\alpha\,\hat{\mathbf{j}})$, $b(\cos\beta\,\hat{\mathbf{i}} + \sin\beta\,\hat{\mathbf{j}})$ and $c(\cos\gamma\,\hat{\mathbf{i}} + \sin\gamma\,\hat{\mathbf{j}})$ are collinear, then the value of $|z|$ is ....*
(where $z = bc\sin(\beta - \gamma) + ca\sin(\gamma - \alpha) + ab\sin(\alpha - \beta) + 3\hat{\mathbf{i}}$)

Decoding the Question

If $\mathbf{a} = a_1\hat{\mathbf{i}} + a_2\hat{\mathbf{j}}$, $\mathbf{b} = b_1\hat{\mathbf{i}} + b_2\hat{\mathbf{j}}$ and $\mathbf{c} = c_1\hat{\mathbf{i}} + c_2\hat{\mathbf{j}}$ are collinear,

then $\begin{vmatrix} a_1 & a_2 & 1 \\ b_1 & b_2 & 1 \\ c_1 & c_2 & 1 \end{vmatrix} = 0$

Sol. (3) $\begin{vmatrix} a\cos\alpha & a\sin\alpha & 1 \\ b\cos\beta & b\sin\beta & 1 \\ c\cos\gamma & c\sin\gamma & 1 \end{vmatrix} = 0$

$$\Rightarrow bc\sin(\gamma - \beta) + ac\sin(\alpha - \gamma) + ab\sin(\beta - \alpha) = 0$$

$$\Rightarrow \quad |z| = 3$$

Numerical Value Type Questions

Example 57 *A particle in equilibrium is subjected to four forces*

$\mathbf{F}_1 = -10\hat{\mathbf{k}}$, $\mathbf{F}_2 = u\left(\frac{4}{13}\hat{\mathbf{i}} - \frac{12}{13}\hat{\mathbf{j}} + \frac{3}{13}\hat{\mathbf{k}}\right)$

$\mathbf{F}_3 = v\left(-\frac{4}{13}\hat{\mathbf{i}} - \frac{12}{13}\hat{\mathbf{j}} + \frac{3}{13}\hat{\mathbf{k}}\right)$ *and* $\mathbf{F}_4 = w(\cos\theta\,\hat{\mathbf{i}} + \sin\theta\,\hat{\mathbf{j}})$

If the values of u, v and w in terms of θ are $\frac{65}{3} + k_1\cot\theta$, $\frac{65}{3} + k_2\cot\theta$ *and* $k_3\operatorname{cosec}\theta$ *respectively, then value of* $(k_1 + k_2 + k_3)$ *is ....*

Sol. (40) Since, the particle is in equilibrium.

$$\mathbf{F}_1 + \mathbf{F}_2 + \mathbf{F}_3 + \mathbf{F}_4 = 0$$

$$-10\hat{\mathbf{k}} + u\left(\frac{4}{13}\hat{\mathbf{i}} - \frac{12}{13}\hat{\mathbf{j}} + \frac{3}{13}\hat{\mathbf{k}}\right) + v\left(-\frac{4}{13}\hat{\mathbf{i}} - \frac{12}{13}\hat{\mathbf{j}} + \frac{3}{13}\hat{\mathbf{k}}\right) + w(\cos\theta\hat{\mathbf{i}} + \sin\theta\hat{\mathbf{j}}) = 0$$

$$\Rightarrow \left(\frac{4u}{13} - \frac{4v}{13} + w\cos\theta\right)\hat{\mathbf{i}} + \left(\frac{-12}{13}u - \frac{12}{13}v + w\sin\theta\right)\hat{\mathbf{j}} + \left(\frac{3}{13}u + \frac{3}{13}v - 10\right)\hat{\mathbf{k}} = 0$$

$$\Rightarrow \frac{4u}{13} - \frac{4v}{13} + w\cos\theta = 0 \quad \text{...(i)}$$

$$-\frac{12}{13}u - \frac{12}{13}v + w\sin\theta = 0 \quad \text{...(ii)}$$

$$\frac{3}{13}u + \frac{3}{13}v - 10 = 0 \quad \text{...(iii)}$$

From Eq. (iii), we get $u + v = \frac{130}{3}$

From Eq. (ii), we get

$$-\frac{12}{13}(u + v) + w\sin\theta = 0$$

$$\Rightarrow -\frac{12}{13}\left(\frac{130}{3}\right) + w\sin\theta = 0$$

$$\Rightarrow w = \frac{40}{\sin\theta} = 40\operatorname{cosec}\theta$$

On substituting the value of w in Eq. (i), we get

$$u - v = -130\cot\theta$$

and $u + v = \frac{130}{3}$

On solving, we get

$$u = \frac{65}{3} - 65\cot\theta$$

$$v = \frac{65}{3} + 65\cot\theta \quad \text{and} \quad w = 40\operatorname{cosec}\theta$$

$$\therefore k_1 + k_2 + k_3 = -65 + 65 + 40 = 40$$

Example 58 *Find the non-negative integer value of λ such that x, y, z ≠ (0, 0, 0) and* $(\hat{\mathbf{i}} + \hat{\mathbf{j}} + 3\hat{\mathbf{k}})\,x + (3\hat{\mathbf{i}} - 3\hat{\mathbf{j}} + \hat{\mathbf{k}})\,y + (-4\hat{\mathbf{i}} + 5\hat{\mathbf{j}})z = \lambda(x\hat{\mathbf{i}} + y\hat{\mathbf{j}} + z\hat{\mathbf{k}})$, *where* $\hat{\mathbf{i}}, \hat{\mathbf{j}}$ *and* $\hat{\mathbf{k}}$ *are unit vectors along the coordinate axes.*

Sol. (0) Here,

$$(\hat{\mathbf{i}} + \hat{\mathbf{j}} + 3\hat{\mathbf{k}})x + (3\hat{\mathbf{i}} - 3\hat{\mathbf{j}} + \hat{\mathbf{k}})y + (-4\hat{\mathbf{i}} + 5\hat{\mathbf{j}})z = \lambda(x\hat{\mathbf{i}} + y\hat{\mathbf{j}} + z\hat{\mathbf{k}})$$

On comparing the coefficients of $\hat{\mathbf{i}}, \hat{\mathbf{j}}$ and $\hat{\mathbf{k}}$, we get

$$x + 3y - 4z = \lambda x$$

$$\Rightarrow (1-\lambda)x + 3y - 4z = 0 \quad \text{...(i)}$$

$$x - 3y + 5z = \lambda y$$

$$\Rightarrow x - (3+\lambda)y + 5z = 0 \quad \text{...(ii)}$$

$$3x + y = \lambda z$$

$$\Rightarrow 3x + y - \lambda z = 0 \quad \text{...(iii)}$$

The Eqs. (i), (ii) and (iii) will have a non-trivial solution, if

$$\begin{vmatrix} 1-\lambda & 3 & -4 \\ 1 & -(3+\lambda) & 5 \\ 3 & 1 & -\lambda \end{vmatrix} = 0$$

$$[\because (x, y, z) \neq (0, 0, 0) \quad \therefore \Delta = 0]$$

$$\Rightarrow (1-\lambda)\{\lambda(3+\lambda) - 5\} - 3\{-\lambda - 15\} - 4\{1 + 3(\lambda + 3)\} = 0$$

$$\Rightarrow (1-\lambda)\{\lambda^2 + 3\lambda - 5\} - 3\{-\lambda - 15\} - 4\{3\lambda + 10\} = 0$$

$$\Rightarrow \lambda^3 + 2\lambda^2 + \lambda = 0$$

$$\Rightarrow \lambda(\lambda^2 + 2\lambda + 1) = 0$$

$$\Rightarrow \lambda(\lambda + 1)^2 = 0$$

$$\therefore \lambda = 0 \text{ or } \lambda = -1$$

Example 59 *If G is the centroid of the ΔABC and if G′ is the centroid of another ΔA′B′C′ such that* $AA' + BB' + CC' = pGG'$, *then value of* $3p^2$ *is equal to ....*

Sol. (27) Here,

G is centroid of ΔABC and G' is centroid of $\Delta A'B'C'$, shown as in figure.

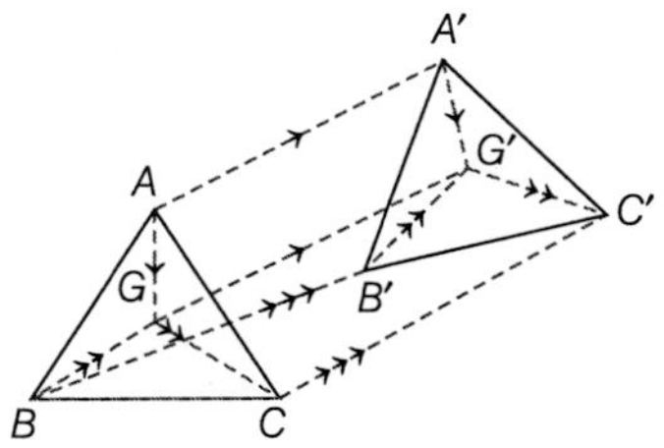

Clearly, $\mathbf{AA'} = \mathbf{AG} + \mathbf{GG'} + \mathbf{G'A'}$ (polygon law)

$\mathbf{BB'} = \mathbf{BG} + \mathbf{GG'} + \mathbf{G'B'}$

$\mathbf{CC'} = \mathbf{CG} + \mathbf{GG'} + \mathbf{G'C'}$

On adding these

$$\mathbf{AA'} + \mathbf{BB'} + \mathbf{CC'} = 3\mathbf{GG'} + (\mathbf{AG} + \mathbf{BG} + \mathbf{CG}) + (\mathbf{G'A'} + \mathbf{G'B'} + \mathbf{G'C'})$$

$$= 3\mathbf{GG'} + (\mathbf{AG} + 2\mathbf{DG}) + (\mathbf{G'A'} + 2\mathbf{G'D'})$$

[using **AD** and **A′D′** as the medians of ΔABC and $\Delta A'B'C'$, respectively]

$$= 3\mathbf{GG'} + (\mathbf{AG} + \mathbf{GA}) + \mathbf{G'A'} + \mathbf{A'G'}$$

$$= 3\mathbf{GG'} + O + O$$

$$\therefore \mathbf{AA'} + \mathbf{BB'} + \mathbf{CC'} = 3\mathbf{GG'}$$

Time Saving Technique

We know by triangle law

$$\mathbf{AA'} = \mathbf{OA'} - \mathbf{OA}$$

$$\mathbf{BB'} = \mathbf{OB'} - \mathbf{OB}$$

$$\mathbf{CC'} = \mathbf{OC'} - \mathbf{OC}$$

$$\Rightarrow \mathbf{AA'} + \mathbf{BB'} + \mathbf{CC'} = (\mathbf{OA'} + \mathbf{OB'} + \mathbf{OC'}) - (\mathbf{OA} + \mathbf{OB} + \mathbf{OC})$$

$$= 3\mathbf{OG'} - 3\mathbf{OG}$$

$$= 3\mathbf{GG'}$$

$\therefore$ Value of $3p^2$ is $3(3)^2 = 27$

Example 60 *If D, E and F be three points on the sides BC, CA and AB, respectively of a ΔABC. such that the points D, E and F are collinear and* $\frac{\mathbf{BD}}{\mathbf{CD}} \cdot \frac{\mathbf{CE}}{\mathbf{AE}} \cdot \frac{\mathbf{AF}}{\mathbf{BF}} = 20\lambda$*, then the value of λ is .... (Menelau's theorem)*

Sol. (0.05) Here, D, E and F be the points on the sides **BC**, **CA** and **AB** respectively of ΔABC. Such that points D, E and F are collinear, as shown in the adjoining figure.

Let B as the origin, $\mathbf{BA} = \mathbf{a}$ and $\mathbf{BC} = \mathbf{c}$

Then, $\mathbf{BF} = k\mathbf{a}$ and $\mathbf{BD} = l\mathbf{c}$

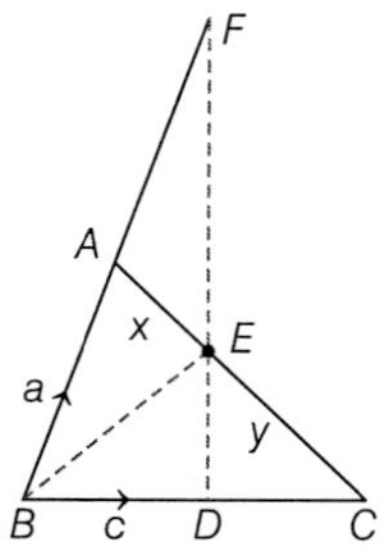

where, k and l are scalars.

$$\therefore \quad \frac{BD}{BC} = l \text{ and } \frac{BF}{BA} = k \quad \text{...(i)}$$

i.e. $BC : BD = 1 : l$

$$\Rightarrow \frac{BC}{BD} - 1 = \frac{1}{l} - 1 \Rightarrow \frac{DC}{BD} = \frac{1-l}{l}$$

$$\Rightarrow \frac{BD}{DC} = \frac{l}{1-l} \quad \text{...(i)}$$

and $$\frac{BA}{BF} = \frac{1}{k}$$

$$\Rightarrow 1 - \frac{BA}{BF} = 1 - \frac{1}{k}$$

$$\Rightarrow \frac{AF}{BF} = \frac{k-1}{k} \quad \text{...(ii)}$$

Now, let E divide the line AC in the ratio of $x : y$.

$$\text{So that } \mathbf{BE} = \frac{x\mathbf{c} + y\mathbf{a}}{x+y} = \frac{x \cdot \frac{\mathbf{BD}}{l} + y \cdot \frac{\mathbf{BF}}{k}}{x+y} \quad \text{...(iii)}$$

$$\Rightarrow \mathbf{BE} - \frac{x}{l(x+y)}\mathbf{BD} - \frac{y}{k(x+y)}\mathbf{BF} = 0$$

Since, D, E and F are collinear.

Sum of coefficients must be zero.

$$\text{Hence, } 1 - \frac{x}{l(x+y)} - \frac{y}{k(x+y)} = 0$$

$$\Rightarrow (x+y) - \frac{x}{l} - \frac{y}{k} = 0$$

$$\Rightarrow x + y = \frac{x}{l} + \frac{y}{k}$$

$$\Rightarrow x\left(1 - \frac{1}{l}\right) = y\left(\frac{1}{k} - 1\right)$$

$$\Rightarrow x\left(\frac{l-1}{l}\right) = y\left(\frac{1-k}{k}\right)$$

$$\Rightarrow \frac{l}{l-1} \cdot \frac{y}{x} \cdot \frac{k-1}{k} = 1$$

$$\Rightarrow \frac{BD}{DC} \cdot \frac{CE}{AE} \cdot \frac{AF}{BF} = 1 \quad \text{[using Eqs. (i), (ii) and (iii)]}$$

$$\therefore \lambda = \frac{1}{20} = 0.05$$

Example 61 *ABCD a parallelogram, A_1 and B_1 are mid-points of sides BC and CD, respectively. If* $\mathbf{AA}_1 + \mathbf{AB}_1 = t\mathbf{AC}$*, then $2\,|t|$ is equal to ....*

Sol. (3) Let A be the origin and position vector of B and D are respectively **a** and **b**, then

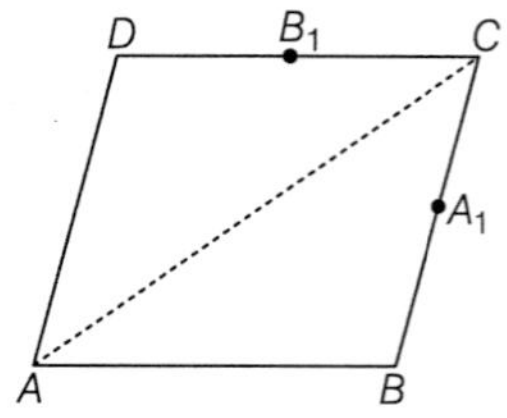

$$\mathbf{AB} = \mathbf{a}, \ \mathbf{AD} = \mathbf{b}$$

$$\therefore \quad \mathbf{AC} = \mathbf{a} + \mathbf{b}$$

$$\mathbf{AA}_1 = \frac{(\mathbf{a}+\mathbf{b}) + \mathbf{a}}{2} = \mathbf{a} + \frac{\mathbf{b}}{2}$$

$$\text{and} \quad \mathbf{AB}_1 = \frac{\mathbf{b} + (\mathbf{a}+\mathbf{b})}{2} = \frac{\mathbf{a}}{2} + \mathbf{b}$$

Since, $\quad \mathbf{AA}_1 + \mathbf{AB}_1 = t\mathbf{AC}$

$\Rightarrow \left(\mathbf{a} + \frac{\mathbf{b}}{2}\right) + \left(\frac{\mathbf{a}}{2} + \mathbf{b}\right) = t(\mathbf{a} + \mathbf{b})$

$\Rightarrow \frac{3}{2}(\mathbf{a} + \mathbf{b}) = t(\mathbf{a} + \mathbf{b}) \Rightarrow t = \frac{3}{2} = 2|t| = 3$

Example 62 *If the vectors* $x\hat{\mathbf{i}} + \hat{\mathbf{j}} + \hat{\mathbf{k}}, \hat{\mathbf{i}} + y\hat{\mathbf{j}} + \hat{\mathbf{k}}$ *and* $\hat{\mathbf{i}} + \hat{\mathbf{j}} + z\hat{\mathbf{k}}$ *are coplanar, where* $x \neq 1, y \neq 1$ *and* $z \neq 1$ *such that* $\frac{1}{1-x} + \frac{1}{1-y} + \frac{1}{1-z} = a$, *then value of* $10a^2$ *is ....*

Sol. (10) The vectors are coplanar, if we can find two scalars λ and μ such that

$$(x\hat{\mathbf{i}} + \hat{\mathbf{j}} + \hat{\mathbf{k}}) = \lambda(\hat{\mathbf{i}} + y\hat{\mathbf{j}} + \hat{\mathbf{k}}) + \mu(\hat{\mathbf{i}} + \hat{\mathbf{j}} + z\hat{\mathbf{k}})$$

$\Rightarrow \quad x = \lambda + \mu, 1 = \lambda y + \mu, 1 = \lambda + \mu z$

$\Rightarrow \quad x = \lambda + \mu, y = \frac{1-\mu}{\lambda}, z = \frac{1-\lambda}{\mu}$

$\Rightarrow \quad 1 - x = 1 - \lambda - \mu, 1 - y = \frac{\lambda - 1 + \mu}{\lambda},$

$1 - z = \frac{\mu - 1 + \lambda}{\mu}$

$\therefore \quad \frac{1}{1-x} + \frac{1}{1-y} + \frac{1}{1-z} = \frac{1}{1-\lambda-\mu} + \frac{\lambda}{\lambda+\mu-1} + \frac{\mu}{\lambda+\mu-1}$

$= \frac{-1+\lambda+\mu}{\lambda+\mu-1} = 1$

$\therefore \quad \frac{1}{1-x} + \frac{1}{1-y} + \frac{1}{1-z} = 1$

$\therefore \quad 10a^2 = 10(1)^2 = 10$

Alternate Solution

Thus, above problem could also be solved as

$$\begin{vmatrix} x & 1 & 1 \\ 1 & y & 1 \\ 1 & 1 & z \end{vmatrix} = 0 \Rightarrow \begin{vmatrix} x-1 & 0 & 1-z \\ 0 & y-1 & 1-z \\ 1 & 1 & z \end{vmatrix} = 0$$

[using $R_1 \to R_1 - R_3$ and $R_2 \to R_2 - R_3$]

$$\Rightarrow (x-1)(y-1)(z-1)\begin{vmatrix} 1 & 0 & -1 \\ 0 & 1 & -1 \\ \frac{-1}{1-x} & \frac{-1}{1-y} & \frac{-z}{1-z} \end{vmatrix} = 0$$

$\left[\text{using } R_1 \to \frac{1}{x-1}R_1, R_2 \to \frac{1}{y-1}R_2, R_3 \to \frac{1}{z-1}R_3\right]$

$\Rightarrow \quad -\frac{1}{(1-x)}(1) + \frac{1}{(1-y)}(-1) - \frac{z}{(1-z)}(1) = 0$ [expanding along R_3]

$\Rightarrow \quad \frac{-1}{(1-x)} - \frac{1}{(1-y)} + \frac{(1-z)-1}{(1-z)} = 0$

$\Rightarrow \quad \frac{1}{1-x} + \frac{1}{1-y} + \frac{1}{1-z} = 1$

we get, $a = 1$

Then, $10a^2 = 10 \times 1 = 10$

Example 63 *If* $\mathbf{r}_1, \mathbf{r}_2$ *and* $\mathbf{r}_3$ *are the position vectors of three collinear points and scalars l and m exists such that* $\mathbf{r}_3 = l\,\mathbf{r}_1 + m\mathbf{r}_2$, *then value of* $10(l + m)$ *is equal to ....*

Sol. (10) Let A, B and C be the three points whose position vectors referred to O are $\mathbf{r}_1$, $\mathbf{r}_2$ and $\mathbf{r}_3$, respectively.

$$\mathbf{AB} = \mathbf{OB} - \mathbf{OA} = \mathbf{r}_2 - \mathbf{r}_1$$

$$\mathbf{BC} = \mathbf{OC} - \mathbf{OB} = \mathbf{r}_3 - \mathbf{r}_2$$

Now, if A, B and C are collinear points, then **AB** and **AC** are in the same line and $\mathbf{BC} = \lambda(\mathbf{AC})$

$\Rightarrow \quad (\mathbf{r}_3 - \mathbf{r}_2) = \lambda(\mathbf{r}_2 - \mathbf{r}_1)$

$\Rightarrow \quad \mathbf{r}_3 = -\lambda\mathbf{r}_1 + (\lambda + 1)\mathbf{r}_2$

$\Rightarrow \quad \mathbf{r}_3 = -l\,\mathbf{r}_1 + m\mathbf{r}_2$

where, $l = -\lambda$ and $m = \lambda + 1$

$\Rightarrow \quad 10(l + m) = 10[-\lambda + (\lambda + 1)] = 10$

Example 64 *If (2, 3, 9), (5, 2, 1), (1, λ, 8) and (λ, 2, 3) are coplanar, then the sum of all possible value of λ are* $\frac{p}{q}$, *where p and q are coprime, then* $(p + q)$ *is equal to ....*

Sol. (65) Let $A(2, 3, 9)$, $B(5, 2, 1)$, $C(1, \lambda, 8)$ and $D(\lambda, 2, 3)$ be coplanar.

$$\therefore \quad \begin{vmatrix} 5-2 & 2-3 & 1-9 \\ 1-2 & \lambda-3 & 8-9 \\ \lambda-2 & 2-3 & 3-9 \end{vmatrix} = 0$$

$$\Rightarrow \quad \begin{vmatrix} 3 & -1 & -8 \\ -1 & \lambda-3 & -1 \\ \lambda-2 & -1 & -6 \end{vmatrix} = 0$$

$\Rightarrow 3(-6\lambda + 18 - 1) + 1(6 + \lambda - 2) - 8(1 - \lambda^2 + 5\lambda - 6) = 0$

$\Rightarrow \quad -18\lambda + 51 + 4 + \lambda + 40 + 8\lambda^2 - 40\lambda = 0$

$\Rightarrow \quad 8\lambda^2 - 57\lambda + 95 = 0$

Sum of all possible value of $\lambda = \frac{57}{8}$

$\therefore \quad p = 57, q = 8 \Rightarrow p + q = 57 + 8 = 65$

Example 65 *Let S be the set of all* (λ, μ) *for which the vectors* $\lambda\hat{\mathbf{i}} + \hat{\mathbf{j}} + \hat{\mathbf{k}}, \hat{\mathbf{i}} + 3\hat{\mathbf{j}} + \hat{\mathbf{k}}$ *and* $2\hat{\mathbf{i}} + 2\hat{\mathbf{j}} + \mu\hat{\mathbf{k}}$, *where* $\lambda - \mu = -1$ *are coplanar, then* $\Sigma_{(\lambda, \mu) \in S}\, 80(\lambda^2 + \mu^2)$ *is equal to ....*

Sol. (480) The given equations are coplanar

$$\Rightarrow \quad \begin{vmatrix} \lambda & 1 & 1 \\ 1 & 3 & 1 \\ 2 & 2 & \mu \end{vmatrix} = 0$$

$\Rightarrow \lambda(3\mu - 2) - 1(\mu - 2) + 1(2 - 6) = 0$

$\Rightarrow \quad 3\lambda\mu - 2\lambda - \mu + 2 - 4 = 0$

$\Rightarrow \quad 3\lambda\mu - 2\lambda - \mu - 2 = 0$

$\Rightarrow \quad 3\lambda\mu - 2\lambda - \mu = 2 \quad$ ...(i)

and $\quad \lambda - \mu = -1$

So, from Eq. (i), we get

$$3(\mu-1)\mu-2(\mu-1)-\mu=2$$

$\Rightarrow \quad (3\mu-3)\mu-2\mu+2-\mu=2$

$\Rightarrow \quad 3\mu^2-3\mu-3\mu=0$

$\Rightarrow \quad 3\mu^2-6\mu=0 \Rightarrow 3\mu(\mu-2)=0$

$\therefore \quad \mu=0, 2$

So, $\lambda=-1, 1$

$\therefore \ \Sigma_{\lambda,\mu\in S}\, 80(\lambda^2+\mu^2)=80[(1+1)+(0+4)]$

$=80[2+4]$

$=80\times 6=480$

Matching Type Questions

Example 66 *In the Cartesian plane, a man starts at origin and walks a distance of 3 units of the North-East direction and reaches a point P. From P, he walks a distance of 4 units in the North-West direction to reach a point Q. Construct the parallelogram OPQR with PO and PQ as adjacent sides. Let M be the mid-point of PQ.*

Column I	Column II
A. The position vector of P is	(p) $\frac{3}{\sqrt{2}}(\hat{i}+\hat{j})$
B. The position vector of R is	(q) $\frac{1}{\sqrt{2}}(\hat{i}+5\hat{j})$
C. The position vector of M is	(r) $2\sqrt{2}(-\hat{i}+\hat{j})$
D. If the line OM meets the diagonal PR in the point T, then **OT** equals	(s) $\frac{\sqrt{2}}{3}(\hat{i}+5\hat{j})$

Sol. A → p, B → r, C → q, D → s

(A) Let $\hat{i}$ and $\hat{j}$ be the unit vectors along **OX** and **OY** respectively.

Now, $OP=3$ and $\angle XOP=45^\circ$ implies that

$$\mathbf{OP}=(3\cos 45^\circ)\hat{i}+(3\sin 45^\circ)\hat{j}=\frac{3}{\sqrt{2}}(\hat{i}+\hat{j})$$

(B) Again, $\angle XOR=135^\circ$ and $OR=4$ implies that

$$\mathbf{OR}=\frac{4}{\sqrt{2}}(-\hat{i}+\hat{j})=2\sqrt{2}(-\hat{i}+\hat{j})$$

(C) The position vector of Q is given by

$$\mathbf{OP}+\mathbf{PQ}=\mathbf{OP}+\mathbf{OR}=\frac{1}{\sqrt{2}}(-\hat{i}+7\hat{j})$$

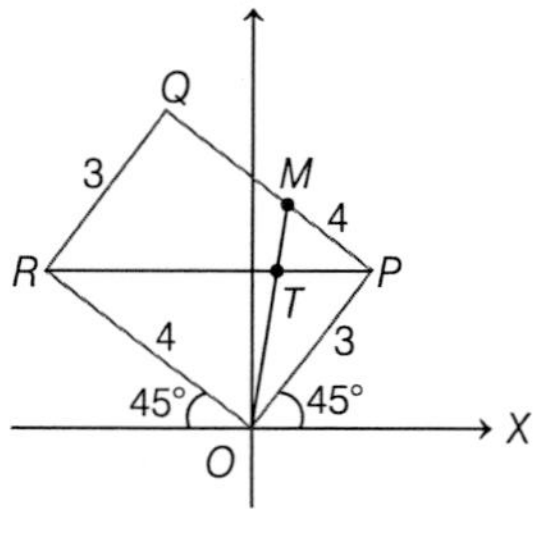

$$\therefore \quad \mathbf{OM}=\frac{\left(\frac{3}{\sqrt{2}}\right)(\hat{i}+\hat{j})+\left(\frac{1}{\sqrt{2}}\right)(-\hat{i}+7\hat{j})}{2}$$

$$=\frac{2\hat{i}+10\hat{j}}{2\sqrt{2}}=\frac{\hat{i}+5\hat{j}}{\sqrt{2}}$$

(D) Now, $PT:RT=1:2$

Therefore, $\mathbf{OT}=\dfrac{1(\mathbf{OR})+2(\mathbf{OP})}{3}$

$$=\frac{\left(\frac{4}{\sqrt{2}}\right)(-\hat{i}+\hat{j})+2\left[\left(\frac{3}{\sqrt{2}}\right)(\hat{i}+\hat{j})\right]}{3}=\frac{\sqrt{2}}{3}(\hat{i}+5\hat{j})$$

Example 67 *Let O, G and O′ be the circumcentre, centroid and orthocentre of a ΔABC respectively. AL and BM are perpendiculars from A and B on sides BC and CA respectively. Let AD be the median and OD is perpendicular to side BC and S be any point in the plane of ΔABC.*

Column I	Column II
A. **OA + OB + OC** is equal to	(p) **2AO**
B. **O′A + O′B + O′C** is equal to	(q) **OO′**
C. **AO′ + O′B + O′C** is equal to	(r) **3SG**
D. **SA + SB + SC** is equal to	(s) **2O′O**

Sol. A → q, B → s, C → p, D → r

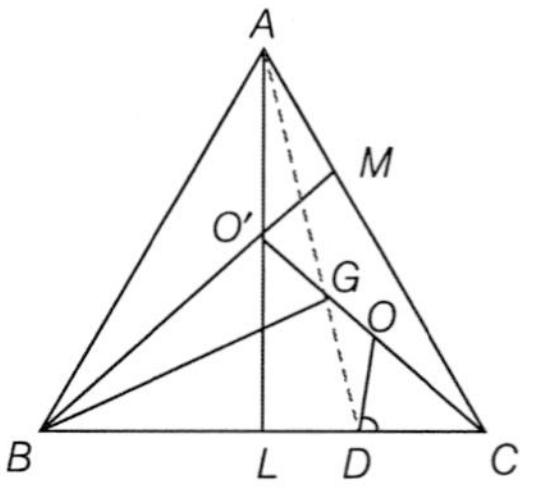

(A) $\dfrac{\mathbf{OA}+\mathbf{OB}+\mathbf{OC}}{3}=\mathbf{OG}=\dfrac{1}{3}\mathbf{OO'}$

$\therefore \ \mathbf{OA}+\mathbf{OB}+\mathbf{OC}=\mathbf{OO'}\to q$

(B) $\dfrac{\mathbf{O'A}+\mathbf{O'B}+\mathbf{O'C}}{3}=\mathbf{O'G}=\dfrac{2}{3}\mathbf{O'O}$

$\therefore \ \mathbf{O'A}+\mathbf{O'B}+\mathbf{O'C}=2\mathbf{O'O}\to s$

(C) $\mathbf{O'B}+\mathbf{O'C}=2\mathbf{O'D}$

$=2(\mathbf{O'A}+\mathbf{AO}+\mathbf{OD})$

$=2\mathbf{O'A}+2\mathbf{AO}+\mathbf{AO'}$

$=-2\mathbf{AO'}+2\mathbf{AO}+\mathbf{AO'}$

$=-\mathbf{AO'}+2\mathbf{AO}$

$\therefore \ \mathbf{O'B}+\mathbf{O'C}+\mathbf{AO'}=2\mathbf{AO}$

(D) $\dfrac{\mathbf{SA}+\mathbf{SB}+\mathbf{SC}}{3}=\mathbf{SG}$

$\therefore \ \mathbf{SA}+\mathbf{SB}+\mathbf{SC}=3\mathbf{SG}$

EXERCISE 1

JEE Main Pattern

Single Option Correct Type Questions

1. The vectors $\mathbf{AB} = 3\hat{\mathbf{i}} + 4\hat{\mathbf{k}}$ and $\mathbf{AC} = 5\hat{\mathbf{i}} - 2\hat{\mathbf{j}} + 4\hat{\mathbf{k}}$ are the sides of a ΔABC. The length of the median through A is

(a) $\sqrt{18}$ (b) $\sqrt{72}$
(c) $\sqrt{33}$ (d) $\sqrt{288}$

2. If $OP = 8$ and $\mathbf{OP}$ makes angles 45° and 60° with OX-axis and OY-axis respectively, then $\mathbf{OP}$ is equal to

(a) $8(\sqrt{2}\hat{\mathbf{i}} + \hat{\mathbf{j}} \pm \hat{\mathbf{k}})$ (b) $4(\sqrt{2}\hat{\mathbf{i}} + \hat{\mathbf{j}} \pm \hat{\mathbf{k}})$
(c) $\frac{1}{4}(\sqrt{2}\hat{\mathbf{i}} + \hat{\mathbf{j}} \pm \hat{\mathbf{k}})$ (d) $\frac{1}{8}(\sqrt{2}\hat{\mathbf{i}} + \hat{\mathbf{j}} \pm \hat{\mathbf{k}})$

3. Let $\mathbf{a}, \mathbf{b}$ and $\mathbf{c}$ be three units vectors such that $3\mathbf{a} + 4\mathbf{b} + 5\mathbf{c} = \mathbf{0}$. Then, which of the following statements is true?

(a) $\mathbf{a}$ is parallel to $\mathbf{b}$
(b) $\mathbf{a}$ is perpendicular to $\mathbf{b}$
(c) $\mathbf{a}$ is neither parallel nor perpendicular to $\mathbf{b}$
(d) None of the above

4. A line passes through the points whose position vectors are $\hat{\mathbf{i}} + \hat{\mathbf{j}} - 2\hat{\mathbf{k}}$ and $\hat{\mathbf{i}} - 3\hat{\mathbf{j}} + \hat{\mathbf{k}}$. The position vector of a point on it at unit distance from the first point is

(a) $\frac{1}{5}(5\hat{\mathbf{i}} + \hat{\mathbf{j}} - 7\hat{\mathbf{k}})$ (b) $\frac{1}{5}(4\hat{\mathbf{i}} + 9\hat{\mathbf{j}} - 15\hat{\mathbf{k}})$
(c) $(\hat{\mathbf{i}} - 4\hat{\mathbf{j}} + 3\hat{\mathbf{k}})$ (d) $\frac{1}{5}(\hat{\mathbf{i}} - 4\hat{\mathbf{j}} + 3\hat{\mathbf{k}})$

5. If D, E and F are the middle points of the sides BC, CA and AB of the ΔABC, then $\mathbf{AD} + \mathbf{BE} + \mathbf{CF}$ is

(a) a zero vector (b) a unit vector
(c) Both (a) and (b) (d) None of these

6. If P and Q are the middle points of the sides BC and CD of the parallelogram $ABCD$, then $\mathbf{AP} + \mathbf{AQ}$ is equal to

(a) $\mathbf{AC}$ (b) $\frac{1}{2}\mathbf{AC}$
(b) $\frac{2}{3}\mathbf{AC}$ (d) $\frac{3}{2}\mathbf{AC}$

7. The figure formed by the four points $\hat{\mathbf{i}} + \hat{\mathbf{j}} - \hat{\mathbf{k}}$, $2\hat{\mathbf{i}} + 3\hat{\mathbf{j}}$, $3\hat{\mathbf{i}} + 5\hat{\mathbf{j}} - 2\hat{\mathbf{k}}$ and $\hat{\mathbf{k}} - \hat{\mathbf{j}}$ is

(a) rectangle (b) parallelogram
(c) trapezium (d) None of these

8. A and B are two points. The position vector of A is $6\mathbf{b} - 2\mathbf{a}$. A point P divides the line AB in the ratio 1 : 2. If $\mathbf{a} - \mathbf{b}$ is the position vector of P, then the position vector of B is given by

(a) $7\mathbf{a} - 15\mathbf{b}$ (b) $7\mathbf{a} + 15\mathbf{b}$
(c) $15\mathbf{a} - 7\mathbf{b}$ (d) $15\mathbf{a} + 7\mathbf{b}$

9. If $ABCD$ is parallelogram, $\mathbf{AB} = 2\hat{\mathbf{i}} + 4\hat{\mathbf{j}} - 5\hat{\mathbf{k}}$ and $\mathbf{AD} = \hat{\mathbf{i}} + 2\hat{\mathbf{j}} + 3\hat{\mathbf{k}}$, then the unit vector in the direction of $\mathbf{BD}$ is

(a) $\frac{1}{\sqrt{69}}(\hat{\mathbf{i}} + 2\hat{\mathbf{j}} - 8\hat{\mathbf{k}})$ (b) $\frac{1}{69}(\hat{\mathbf{i}} + 2\hat{\mathbf{j}} - 8\hat{\mathbf{k}})$
(c) $\frac{1}{\sqrt{69}}(-\hat{\mathbf{i}} - 2\hat{\mathbf{j}} + 8\hat{\mathbf{k}})$ (d) $\frac{1}{69}(-\hat{\mathbf{i}} - 2\hat{\mathbf{j}} + 8\hat{\mathbf{k}})$

10. If A, B and C are the vertices of a triangle whose position vectors are $\mathbf{a}$, $\mathbf{b}$ and $\mathbf{c}$ and G is the centroid of the ΔABC, then $\mathbf{GA} + \mathbf{GB} + \mathbf{GC}$ is

(a) $\mathbf{0}$ (b) $\mathbf{A} + \mathbf{B} + \mathbf{C}$
(c) $\frac{\mathbf{a} + \mathbf{b} + \mathbf{c}}{3}$ (d) $\frac{\mathbf{a} + \mathbf{b} - \mathbf{c}}{3}$

11. If $ABCDEF$ is regular hexagon, then $\mathbf{AD} + \mathbf{EB} + \mathbf{FC}$ is equal to

(a) $\mathbf{0}$ (b) $2\mathbf{AB}$
(c) $3\mathbf{AB}$ (d) $4\ \mathbf{AB}$

12. $ABCDE$ is a pentagon. Forces $\mathbf{AB}$, $\mathbf{AE}$, $\mathbf{DC}$ and $\mathbf{ED}$ act at a point. Which force should be added to this system to make the resultant $2\mathbf{AC}$?

(a) $\mathbf{AC}$ (b) $\mathbf{AD}$
(c) $\mathbf{BC}$ (d) $\mathbf{BD}$

13. If $ABCDEF$ is a regular hexagon and $\mathbf{AB} + \mathbf{AC} + \mathbf{AD} + \mathbf{AE} + \mathbf{AF} = \lambda\mathbf{AD}$, then λ is equal to

(a) 2 (b) 3 (c) 4 (d) 6

14. Let us define the length of a vector $a\hat{\mathbf{i}} + b\hat{\mathbf{j}} + c\hat{\mathbf{k}}$ as $|a| + |b| + |c|$. This definition coincides with the usual definition of length of a vector $a\hat{\mathbf{i}} + b\hat{\mathbf{j}} + c\hat{\mathbf{k}}$ if and only if

(a) $a = b = c = 0$
(b) any two of a, b and c are zero
(c) any one of a, b and c is zero
(d) $a + b + c = 0$

15. If $\hat{\mathbf{i}} - 3\hat{\mathbf{j}} + 5\hat{\mathbf{k}}$ bisects the angle between $\hat{\mathbf{a}}$ and $-\hat{\mathbf{i}} + 2\hat{\mathbf{j}} + 2\hat{\mathbf{k}}$, where $\hat{\mathbf{a}}$ is a unit vector, then

(a) $\hat{\mathbf{a}} = \frac{1}{105}(41\hat{\mathbf{i}} + 88\hat{\mathbf{j}} - 40\hat{\mathbf{k}})$

(b) $\hat{\mathbf{a}} = \frac{1}{105}(41\hat{\mathbf{i}} + 88\hat{\mathbf{j}} + 40\hat{\mathbf{k}})$

(c) $\hat{\mathbf{a}} = \frac{1}{105}(-41\hat{\mathbf{i}} + 88\hat{\mathbf{j}} - 40\hat{\mathbf{k}})$

(d) $\hat{\mathbf{a}} = \frac{1}{105}(41\hat{\mathbf{i}} - 88\hat{\mathbf{j}} - 40\hat{\mathbf{k}})$

16. Given three vectors $\mathbf{a} = 6\hat{\mathbf{i}} - 3\hat{\mathbf{j}}$, $\mathbf{b} = 2\hat{\mathbf{i}} - 6\hat{\mathbf{j}}$ and $\mathbf{c} = -2\hat{\mathbf{i}} + 21\hat{\mathbf{j}}$ such that $\alpha = \mathbf{a} + \mathbf{b} + \mathbf{c}$. Then, the resolution of the vector α into components with respect to $\mathbf{a}$ and $\mathbf{b}$ is given by

(a) $3\mathbf{a} - 2\mathbf{b}$ (b) $3\mathbf{b} - 2\mathbf{a}$

(c) $2\mathbf{a} - 3\mathbf{b}$ (d) $\mathbf{a} - 2\mathbf{b}$

17. 'I' is the incentre of ΔABC whose corresponding sides are a, b, c respectively. $a\,\mathbf{IA} + b\,\mathbf{IB} + c\,\mathbf{IC}$ is always equal to

(a) $\mathbf{0}$ (b) $(a + b + c)\mathbf{BC}$

(c) $(\mathbf{a} + \mathbf{b} + \mathbf{c})\mathbf{AC}$ (d) $(a + b + c)\mathbf{AB}$

18. If $4\hat{\mathbf{i}} + 7\hat{\mathbf{j}} + 8\hat{\mathbf{k}}$, $2\hat{\mathbf{i}} + 3\hat{\mathbf{j}} + 4\hat{\mathbf{k}}$ and $2\hat{\mathbf{i}} + 5\hat{\mathbf{j}} + 7\hat{\mathbf{k}}$ are the position vectors of the vertices A, B and C respectively of ΔABC. The position vector of the point where the bisector of $\angle A$ meets BC is

(a) $\frac{1}{3}(6\hat{\mathbf{i}} + 13\hat{\mathbf{j}} + 18\hat{\mathbf{k}})$ (b) $\frac{2}{3}(6\hat{\mathbf{i}} + 12\hat{\mathbf{j}} - 8\hat{\mathbf{k}})$

(c) $\frac{1}{3}(-6\hat{\mathbf{i}} - 8\hat{\mathbf{j}} - 9\hat{\mathbf{k}})$ (d) $\frac{2}{3}(-6\hat{\mathbf{i}} - 12\hat{\mathbf{j}} + 8\hat{\mathbf{k}})$

19. A, B, C and D have position vectors $\mathbf{a}, \mathbf{b}, \mathbf{c}$ and $\mathbf{d}$, respectively, such that $\mathbf{a} - \mathbf{b} = 2(\mathbf{d} - \mathbf{c})$. Then,

(a) AB and CD bisect each other

(b) BD and AC bisect each other

(c) AB and CD trisect each other

(d) BD and AC trisect each other

20. If $\hat{\mathbf{i}} - 3\hat{\mathbf{j}} + 5\hat{\mathbf{k}}$ bisects the angle between $\hat{\mathbf{a}}$ and $-\hat{\mathbf{i}} + 2\hat{\mathbf{j}} + 2\hat{\mathbf{k}}$, where $\hat{\mathbf{a}}$ is a unit vector, then $\hat{\mathbf{a}} = \frac{\lambda\hat{\mathbf{i}} + \mu\hat{\mathbf{j}} + \gamma\hat{\mathbf{k}}}{105}$, then the value of $\lambda^2 - 2\mu + \gamma$ is

(a) 1857 (b) 1897

(c) 1817 (d) 1465

21. Given a cube $ABCD$, $A_1B_1C_1D_1$ with lower base $ABCD$, upper base $A_1B_1C_1D_1$ and the lateral edges AA_1, BB_1, CC_1 and DD_1; M and M_1 are the centres of the faces $ABCD$ and $A_1B_1C_1D_1$, respectively. O is a point on the line MM_1 such that $\mathbf{OA} + \mathbf{OB} + \mathbf{OC} + \mathbf{OD} = \mathbf{OM}_1$. If $\mathbf{OM} = \lambda\mathbf{OM}_1$, then λ is equal to

(a) $\frac{1}{16}$ (b) $\frac{1}{8}$

(c) $\frac{1}{4}$ (d) $\frac{1}{2}$

22. If the vector $\mathbf{b}$ is collinear with the vector $\mathbf{a} = (2\sqrt{2}, -1, 4)$ and $|\mathbf{b}| = 10$, then

(a) $\mathbf{a} \pm \mathbf{b} = \mathbf{0}$ (b) $\mathbf{a} \pm 2\mathbf{b} = \mathbf{0}$

(c) $2\mathbf{a} \pm \mathbf{b} = \mathbf{0}$ (d) None of these

23. If $\mathbf{a}$ and $\mathbf{b}$ are two non-collinear vectors and $x\mathbf{a} + y\mathbf{b} = \mathbf{0}$

(a) $x = 0$, but y is not necessarily zero

(b) $y = 0$, but x is not necessarily zero

(c) $x = 0$, $y = 0$

(d) None of the above

24. A transversal cuts the sides OL, OM and diagonal ON of a parallelogram at A, B and C respectively, then the value of $\left(\frac{OL}{OA} + \frac{OM}{OB}\right)$ is

(a) $\frac{OC}{ON}$ (b) $\frac{ON}{OC}$

(c) $\frac{CN}{OC}$ (d) $\frac{OC}{CN}$

25. Let $\mathbf{a}, \mathbf{b}, \mathbf{c}$ are three non-coplanar vectors such that $\mathbf{r}_1 = \mathbf{a} - \mathbf{b} + \mathbf{c}$, $\mathbf{r}_2 = \mathbf{b} + \mathbf{c} - \mathbf{a}$, $\mathbf{r}_3 = \mathbf{c} + \mathbf{a} + \mathbf{b}$ and $\mathbf{r} = 2\mathbf{a} - 3\mathbf{b} + 4\mathbf{c}$, if $\mathbf{r} = x_1\mathbf{r}_1 + x_2\mathbf{r}_2 + x_3\mathbf{r}_3$, then

(a) $x_1 + x_2 = 4$ (b) $x_2 + x_3 = \frac{1}{2}$

(c) $x_1 + x_3 = \frac{3}{2}$ (d) $x_1x_2x_3 = -\frac{5}{4}$

26. If three points A, B and C are collinear, whose position vectors are $\hat{\mathbf{i}} - 2\hat{\mathbf{j}} - 8\hat{\mathbf{k}}$, $5\hat{\mathbf{i}} - 2\hat{\mathbf{k}}$ and $11\hat{\mathbf{i}} + 3\hat{\mathbf{j}} + 7\hat{\mathbf{k}}$ respectively, then the ratio in which B divides AC is

(a) 1 : 2 (b) 2 : 3

(c) 2 : 1 (d) 1 : 1

27. If $\mathbf{a}$ and $\mathbf{b}$ are two non-zero and non-collinear vectors, then $\mathbf{a} + \mathbf{b}$ and $\mathbf{a} - \mathbf{b}$ are

(a) linearly dependent vectors

(b) linearly independent vectors

(c) linearly dependent and independent vectors

(d) None of the above

28. If $\mathbf{x}$ and $\mathbf{y}$ are two non-collinear vectors and ABC is a triangle with side lengths a, b and c satisfying $(20a - 15b)\mathbf{x} + (15b - 12c)\mathbf{y} + (12c - 20a)(\mathbf{x} \times \mathbf{y}) = \mathbf{0}$, then ΔABC is

(a) an acute angled triangle

(b) an obtuse angled triangle

(c) a right angled triangle

(d) a scalene triangle

29. If $\mathbf{x}$ and $\mathbf{y}$ are two non-collinear vectors and a, b and c represent the sides of a ΔABC satisfying $(a - b)\mathbf{x} + (b - c)\mathbf{y} + (c - a)(\mathbf{x} \times \mathbf{y}) = 0$, then ΔABC is (where $\mathbf{x} \times \mathbf{y}$ is perpendicular to the plane of $\mathbf{x}$ and $\mathbf{y}$)

(a) an equilateral triangle

(b) an obtuse angled triangle

(c) a right angled triangle

(d) a scalene triangle

30. Vectors $\mathbf{a} = \hat{\mathbf{i}} + 2\hat{\mathbf{j}} + 3\hat{\mathbf{k}}$, $\mathbf{b} = 2\hat{\mathbf{i}} - \hat{\mathbf{j}} + \hat{\mathbf{k}}$ and $\mathbf{c} = 3\hat{\mathbf{i}} + \hat{\mathbf{j}} + 4\hat{\mathbf{k}}$ are so placed that the end point of one vector is the starting point of the next vector. Then the vectors are
(a) not coplanar
(b) coplanar but cannot form a triangle
(c) coplanar and form a triangle
(d) coplanar and can form a right angled triangle

31. *A, B, C, D* and *E* are five coplanar points, then **DA** + **DB** + **DC** + **AE** + **BE** + **CE** is equal to
(a) **DE** (b) 3**DE** (c) 2**DE** (d) 4**ED**

32. Four non-zero vectors will always be
(a) linearly dependent (b) linearly independent
(c) either (a) or (b) (d) None of these

33. The number of integral values of p for which $(p+1)\hat{\mathbf{i}} - 3\hat{\mathbf{j}} + p\hat{\mathbf{k}}$, $p\hat{\mathbf{i}} + (p+1)\hat{\mathbf{j}} - 3\hat{\mathbf{k}}$ and $-3\hat{\mathbf{i}} + p\hat{\mathbf{j}} + (p+1)\hat{\mathbf{k}}$ are linearly dependent vectors is
(a) 0 (b) 1 (c) 2 (d) 3

34. If the vectors **a** and **b** are linearly independent satisfying $(\sqrt{3}\tan\theta + 1)\,\mathbf{a} + (\sqrt{3}\sec\theta - 2)\,\mathbf{b} = 0$, then the most general value of θ are
(a) $n\pi - \frac{\pi}{6}, n \in Z$ (b) $2n\pi \pm \frac{11\pi}{6}, n \in Z$
(c) $n\pi \pm \frac{\pi}{6}, n \in Z$ (d) $2n\pi + \frac{11\pi}{6}, n \in Z$

35. $\mathbf{a} = \hat{\mathbf{i}} + \hat{\mathbf{j}} + \hat{\mathbf{k}}$, $\mathbf{b} = 4\hat{\mathbf{i}} + 3\hat{\mathbf{j}} + 4\hat{\mathbf{k}}$ and $\mathbf{c} = \hat{\mathbf{i}} + x_1\hat{\mathbf{j}} + x_2\hat{\mathbf{k}}$ are linearly dependent vectors and $|\mathbf{c}| = 2$, then the value of $729x_1^4 + 343x_1^2x_2^2 + 81x_2^2 + 15$ is
(a) 3668 (b) 3697 (c) 6394 (d) 3698

Numerical Value Type Questions

36. In a ΔABC, $\angle A = 30°$. H is the orthocentre and D is the mid-point of BC. Segment HD is produced to T such that $HD = DT$. Then, the length of $BC = \lambda AT$, then λ is equal to ....

37. If the vectors $2\hat{\mathbf{i}} + 3\hat{\mathbf{j}} + \hat{\mathbf{k}}$, $-2\hat{\mathbf{i}} + 4\hat{\mathbf{j}} - 2\hat{\mathbf{k}}$ and $\lambda\hat{\mathbf{i}} + \mu\hat{\mathbf{j}} + 4\hat{\mathbf{k}}$ are coplanar and $2\mu - \lambda = 22$, then $\lambda + \mu$ is ....

38. If vectors $\mathbf{AB} = -3\hat{\mathbf{i}} + 4\hat{\mathbf{k}}$ and $\mathbf{AC} = 5\hat{\mathbf{i}} - 2\hat{\mathbf{j}} + 4\hat{\mathbf{k}}$ are the sides of ΔABC, the median through A is AD, then the value of $|AD|$ is ....

39. Let S be the set of all values of λ such that $x, y, z = (0, 0, 0)$ and $(\hat{\mathbf{i}} + \hat{\mathbf{j}} + 3\hat{\mathbf{k}})x + (3\hat{\mathbf{i}} - 3\hat{\mathbf{j}} + \hat{\mathbf{k}})y + (-4\hat{\mathbf{i}} + 5\hat{\mathbf{j}})z = \lambda(x\hat{\mathbf{i}} + y\hat{\mathbf{j}} + z\hat{\mathbf{k}})$, where $\hat{\mathbf{i}}$, $\hat{\mathbf{j}}$ and $\hat{\mathbf{k}}$ are unit vector along the coordinate axes, then $\sum_{\lambda \in S} (\lambda + 5)^2$ is equal to ....

40. $ABCD$ is a parallelogram and A_1 and B_1 are the mid-points of side BC and CD respectively, if $\mathbf{AA}_1 + \mathbf{AB}_1 = \lambda\mathbf{AC}$, then value of λ is ....

41. The point with position vector $60\hat{\mathbf{i}} + 3\hat{\mathbf{j}}$, $40\hat{\mathbf{i}} - 8\hat{\mathbf{j}}$, $a\hat{\mathbf{i}} - 52\hat{\mathbf{j}}$ are collinear, then value of a^2 is ....

42. The median AD of the ΔABC is bisected at E and BE meets AC at F. Then, ratio of $FC : AF$ is ....

43. Let S be the set of all (α, β) for which $\mathbf{a} = 3\hat{\mathbf{i}} - 7\hat{\mathbf{j}} - 4\hat{\mathbf{k}}$, $\mathbf{b} = \alpha\hat{\mathbf{i}} - \beta\hat{\mathbf{j}} + \hat{\mathbf{k}}$ and $\mathbf{c} = \hat{\mathbf{i}} + \hat{\mathbf{j}} + 2\hat{\mathbf{k}}$ are linearly dependent vectors and $|\mathbf{b}| = \sqrt{14}$, then $\Sigma_{(\alpha, \beta) \in S} (\alpha^3 + \beta^3)$ is ....

44. The position vectors of the points P, Q, R and S are $3\hat{\mathbf{i}} - 2\hat{\mathbf{j}} - \hat{\mathbf{k}}$, $2\hat{\mathbf{i}} + 3\hat{\mathbf{j}} - 4\hat{\mathbf{k}}$, $-\hat{\mathbf{i}} + \hat{\mathbf{j}} + 2\hat{\mathbf{k}}$ and $4\hat{\mathbf{i}} + 5\hat{\mathbf{j}} + \alpha\hat{\mathbf{k}}$ It is known that these points are coplanar, then the value of -17α must be ....

45. If unit vector $a\hat{\mathbf{i}} + b\hat{\mathbf{j}} + \frac{1}{2}\hat{\mathbf{k}}$ is linearly dependent with $\hat{\mathbf{i}} + 2\hat{\mathbf{j}}$ and $\hat{\mathbf{j}} - 2\hat{\mathbf{k}}$, then value of $16|5a^2 - a|$ is equal to ....

Previous Year Questions

46. The position vectors of the vertices A, B and C of a triangle are $2\hat{\mathbf{i}} - 3\hat{\mathbf{j}} + 3\hat{\mathbf{k}}$, $2\hat{\mathbf{i}} + 2\hat{\mathbf{j}} + 3\hat{\mathbf{k}}$ and $-\hat{\mathbf{i}} + \hat{\mathbf{j}} + 3\hat{\mathbf{k}}$, respectively. Let l denotes the length of the angle bisector AD of $\angle BAC$, where D is on the line segment BC, then $2l^2$ equals **[Single Correct Type, 2024 Main]**
(a) 49 (b) 42
(c) 45 (d) 50

47. Let the position vectors of the vertices A, B and C of a triangle be $2\hat{\mathbf{i}} + 2\hat{\mathbf{j}} + \hat{\mathbf{k}}$, $\hat{\mathbf{i}} + 2\hat{\mathbf{j}} + 2\hat{\mathbf{k}}$ and $2\hat{\mathbf{i}} + \hat{\mathbf{j}} + 2\hat{\mathbf{k}}$, respectively. Let l_1, l_2 and l_3 be the lengths of perpendiculars drawn from the orthocenter of the triangle on the sides AB, BC and CA respectively, then $l_1^2 + l_2^2 + l_3^2$ equals **[Single Correct Type, 2024 Main]**
(a) $\frac{1}{5}$ (b) $\frac{1}{4}$
(c) $\frac{1}{3}$ (d) $\frac{1}{2}$

48. Let **a**, **b** and **c** be three non-zero vectors such that **b** and **c** are non-collinear. If $\mathbf{a} + 5\mathbf{b}$ is collinear with $\mathbf{c}$, $\mathbf{b} + 6\mathbf{c}$ is collinear with **a** and $\mathbf{a} + \alpha\mathbf{b} + \beta\mathbf{c} = \mathbf{0}$, then $\alpha + \beta$ is equal to **[Single Correct Type, 2024 Main]**
(a) −25 (b) 35
(c) 30 (d) −30

49. Let O be the origin and the position vectors of A and B be $2\hat{\mathbf{i}}+2\hat{\mathbf{j}}+\hat{\mathbf{k}}$ and $2\hat{\mathbf{i}}+4\hat{\mathbf{j}}+4\hat{\mathbf{k}}$, respectively. If the internal bisector of $\angle AOB$ meets the line AB at C, then the length of OC is **[Single Correct Type, 2024 Main]**

(a) $\frac{3}{2}\sqrt{34}$ (b) $\frac{2}{3}\sqrt{34}$
(c) $\frac{3}{2}\sqrt{31}$ (d) $\frac{2}{3}\sqrt{31}$

50. Let $ABCD$ be a quadrilateral. If E and F are the mid-points of the diagonals AC and BD respectively and $(\mathbf{AB}-\mathbf{BC})+(\mathbf{AD}-\mathbf{DC})=k\mathbf{FE}$, then k is equal to **[Single Correct Type, 2023 Main]**

(a) 4 (b) -2
(c) 2 (d) -4

51. Let S be the set of all (λ,μ) for which the vectors $\lambda\hat{\mathbf{i}}-\hat{\mathbf{j}}+\hat{\mathbf{k}}$, $\hat{\mathbf{i}}+2\hat{\mathbf{j}}+\mu\hat{\mathbf{k}}$ and $3\hat{\mathbf{i}}-4\hat{\mathbf{j}}+5\hat{\mathbf{k}}$, where $\lambda-\mu=5$ are coplanar, then $\sum_{(\lambda,\,\mu)\in S}80(\lambda^2+\mu^2)$ is equal to **[Single Correct Type, 2023 Main]**

(a) 2210 (b) 2130
(c) 2290 (d) 2370

52. Let a, b and c be three distinct real numbers, none equal to one. If the vectors $a\hat{\mathbf{i}}+\hat{\mathbf{j}}+\hat{\mathbf{k}}$, $\hat{\mathbf{i}}+b\hat{\mathbf{j}}+\hat{\mathbf{k}}$ and $\hat{\mathbf{i}}+\hat{\mathbf{j}}+c\hat{\mathbf{k}}$ are coplanar, then $\frac{1}{1-a}+\frac{1}{1-b}+\frac{1}{1-c}$ is equal to **[Single Correct Type, 2023 Main]**

(a) 2 (b) -1 (c) -2 (d) 1

53. For any vector $\mathbf{a}=a_1\hat{\mathbf{i}}+a_2\hat{\mathbf{j}}+a_3\hat{\mathbf{k}}$, with $10|a_i|<1$, $i=1,2,3$, consider the following statements

(A) $\max\{|a_1|,|a_2|,|a_3|\}\le|\mathbf{a}|$

(B) $|\mathbf{a}|\le 3\max\{|a_1|,|a_2|,|a_3|\}$ **[Single Correct Type, 2023 Main]**

(a) Neither (A) nor (B) is true
(b) Both (A) and (B) are true
(c) Only (B) is true
(d) Only (A) is true

54. Let **a, b** and **c** be three non-zero vectors such that **b** and **c** are non-collinear. If $\mathbf{a}+5\mathbf{b}$ is collinear with $\mathbf{c}$, $\mathbf{b}+6\mathbf{c}$ is collinear with **a** and $\mathbf{a}+\alpha\mathbf{b}+\beta\mathbf{c}=\mathbf{0}$, then $\alpha+\beta$ is equal to **[Single Correct Type, 2024 Main]**

(a) -25 (b) 35 (c) 30 (d) -30

55. An arc PQ of a circle subtends a right angle at its centre O. The mid-point of the arc PQ is R. If $\mathbf{OP}=\mathbf{u}$, $\mathbf{OR}=\mathbf{v}$ and $\mathbf{OQ}=\alpha\mathbf{u}+\beta\mathbf{v}$, then α,β^2 are the roots of the equation **[Single Correct Type, 2023 Main]**

(a) $3x^2-2x-1=0$ (b) $3x^2+2x-1=0$
(c) $x^2-x-2=0$ (d) $x^2+x-2=0$

56. Let the vectors $\mathbf{u}_1=\hat{\mathbf{i}}+\hat{\mathbf{j}}+a\hat{\mathbf{k}}$, $\mathbf{u}_2=\hat{\mathbf{i}}+b\hat{\mathbf{j}}+\hat{\mathbf{k}}$, and $\mathbf{u}_3=c\hat{\mathbf{i}}+\hat{\mathbf{j}}+\hat{\mathbf{k}}$ be coplanar. If the vectors $\mathbf{v}_1=(a+b)\hat{\mathbf{i}}+c\hat{\mathbf{j}}+c\hat{\mathbf{k}}$, $\mathbf{v}_2=a\hat{\mathbf{i}}+(b+c)\hat{\mathbf{j}}+a\hat{\mathbf{k}}$ and $\mathbf{v}_3=b\hat{\mathbf{i}}+b\hat{\mathbf{j}}+(c+a)\hat{\mathbf{k}}$ are also coplanar, then $6(a+b+c)$ is equal to **[Single Correct Type, 2023 Main]**

(a) 0 (b) 4
(c) 12 (d) 6

57. If the points with position vectors $\alpha\hat{\mathbf{i}}+10\hat{\mathbf{j}}+13\hat{\mathbf{k}}$, $6\hat{\mathbf{i}}+11\hat{\mathbf{j}}+11\hat{\mathbf{k}}$, $\frac{9}{2}\hat{\mathbf{i}}+\beta\hat{\mathbf{j}}-8\hat{\mathbf{k}}$ are collinear, the $(19\alpha-6\beta)^2$ is equal to **[Single Correct Type, 2023 Main]**

(a) 36 (b) 25
(c) 49 (d) 16

58. The sum of all values of α, for which the points whose position vectors are $\hat{\mathbf{i}}-2\hat{\mathbf{j}}+3\hat{\mathbf{k}}$, $2\hat{\mathbf{i}}-3\hat{\mathbf{j}}+4\hat{\mathbf{k}}$, $(\alpha+1)\hat{\mathbf{i}}+2\hat{\mathbf{k}}$ and $9\hat{\mathbf{i}}+(\alpha-8)\hat{\mathbf{j}}+6\hat{\mathbf{k}}$ are coplanar, is equal to **[Single Correct Type, 2023 Main]**

(a) -2 (b) 2
(c) 6 (d) 4

59. If the vectors $\mathbf{a}=\lambda\hat{\mathbf{i}}+\mu\hat{\mathbf{j}}+4\hat{\mathbf{k}}$, $\mathbf{b}=-2\hat{\mathbf{i}}+4\hat{\mathbf{j}}-2\hat{\mathbf{k}}$ and $\mathbf{c}=2\hat{\mathbf{i}}+3\hat{\mathbf{j}}+\hat{\mathbf{k}}$ are coplanar and the projection of **a** on the vector **b** is $\sqrt{54}$ units, then the sum of all possible values of $\lambda+\mu$ is equal to **[Single Correct Type, 2023 Main]**

(a) 0 (b) 6
(c) 24 (d) 18

60. Let **a, b, c** be three non-zero non-coplanar vectors. Let the position vectors of four points A, B, C and D be $\mathbf{a}-\mathbf{b}+\mathbf{c}$, $\lambda\mathbf{a}-3\mathbf{b}+4\mathbf{c}$, $-\mathbf{a}-2\mathbf{b}-3\mathbf{c}$ and $2\mathbf{a}-4\mathbf{b}+6\mathbf{c}$ respectively. If **AB**, **AC** and **AD** are coplanar, then λ is **[Numerical Value Type, 2023 Main]**

61. If the four points, whose position vectors are $3\hat{\mathbf{i}}-4\hat{\mathbf{j}}+2\hat{\mathbf{k}}$, $\hat{\mathbf{i}}+2\hat{\mathbf{j}}-\hat{\mathbf{k}}$, $-2\hat{\mathbf{i}}-\hat{\mathbf{j}}+3\hat{\mathbf{k}}$ and $5\hat{\mathbf{i}}-2\alpha\hat{\mathbf{j}}+4\hat{\mathbf{k}}$ are coplanar, then α is equal to **[Single Correct Type, 2023 Main]**

(a) $\frac{73}{17}$ (b) $-\frac{107}{7}$
(c) $-\frac{73}{17}$ (d) $\frac{107}{7}$

62. If (2, 3, 9), (5, 2, 1), (1, λ, 8) and (λ, 2, 3) are coplanar, then the product of all possible values of λ is **[Single Correct Type, 2022 Main]**

(a) $\frac{21}{2}$ (b) $\frac{59}{8}$
(c) $\frac{57}{8}$ (d) $\frac{95}{8}$

63. Let the vectors $\mathbf{a} = (1+t)\hat{\mathbf{i}} + (1-t)\hat{\mathbf{j}} + \hat{\mathbf{k}}$, $\mathbf{b} = (1-t)\hat{\mathbf{i}} + (1+t)\hat{\mathbf{j}} + 2\hat{\mathbf{k}}$ and $\mathbf{c} = t\hat{\mathbf{i}} - t\hat{\mathbf{j}} + \hat{\mathbf{k}}, t \in R$ be such that for $\alpha, \beta, \gamma \in R$, $\alpha\mathbf{a} + \beta\mathbf{b} + \gamma\mathbf{c} = \mathbf{0}$ $\Rightarrow \alpha = \beta = \gamma = 0$. Then, the set of all values of t is

[Single Correct Type, 2022 Main]

(a) a non-empty finite set
(b) equal to N
(c) equal to $R - \{0\}$
(d) equal to R

64. Let A, B, C be the points whose position vectors respectively are $\mathbf{a} = \hat{\mathbf{i}} + 4\hat{\mathbf{j}} + 3\hat{\mathbf{k}}$, $\mathbf{b} = 2\hat{\mathbf{i}} + \alpha\hat{\mathbf{j}} + 4\hat{\mathbf{k}}$, $\mathbf{c} = 3\hat{\mathbf{i}} - 2\hat{\mathbf{j}} + 5\hat{\mathbf{k}}$. If α is the smallest positive integer for which **a, b, c** are non-collinear, then the length of the median, ΔABC, through A is

[Single Correct Type, 2022 Main]

(a) $\frac{\sqrt{82}}{2}$ (b) $\frac{\sqrt{62}}{2}$
(c) $\frac{\sqrt{69}}{2}$ (d) $\frac{\sqrt{66}}{2}$

65. Let the vectors $(2+a+b)\hat{\mathbf{i}} + (a+2b+c)\hat{\mathbf{j}} - (b+c)\hat{\mathbf{k}}$, $(1+b)\hat{\mathbf{i}} + 2b\hat{\mathbf{j}} - b\hat{\mathbf{k}}$ and $(2+b)\hat{\mathbf{i}} + 2b\hat{\mathbf{j}} + (1-b)\hat{\mathbf{k}}, \forall a, b, c \in R$ be coplanar. Then, which of the following is true?

[Single Correct Type, 2021 Main]

(a) $2b = a + c$ (b) $3c = a + b$
(c) $a = b + 2c$ (d) $2a = b + c$

66. If vectors $\mathbf{a}_1 = x\hat{\mathbf{i}} - \hat{\mathbf{j}} + \hat{\mathbf{k}}$ and $\mathbf{a}_2 = \hat{\mathbf{i}} + y\hat{\mathbf{j}} + z\hat{\mathbf{k}}$ are collinear, then a possible unit vector parallel to the vector $x\hat{\mathbf{i}} + y\hat{\mathbf{j}} - z\hat{\mathbf{k}}$ is **[Single Correct Type, 2021 Main]**

(a) $\frac{1}{\sqrt{2}}(-\hat{\mathbf{j}} + \hat{\mathbf{k}})$ (b) $\frac{1}{\sqrt{3}}(\hat{\mathbf{i}} + \hat{\mathbf{j}} - k\hat{\mathbf{k}})$
(c) $\frac{1}{\sqrt{2}}(\hat{\mathbf{i}} - \hat{\mathbf{j}})$ (d) $\frac{1}{\sqrt{3}}(\hat{\mathbf{i}} - \hat{\mathbf{j}} + \hat{\mathbf{k}})$

67. If (1, 5, 35), (7, 5, 5), (1, λ, 7) and (2λ, 1, 2) are coplanar, then the sum of all possible values of λ is

[Single Correct Type, 2021 Main]

(a) $\frac{44}{5}$ (b) $-\frac{44}{5}$
(c) $\frac{39}{5}$ (d) $-\frac{39}{5}$

68. Let $\alpha \in R$ and the three vectors $\mathbf{a} = \alpha\hat{\mathbf{i}} + \hat{\mathbf{j}} + 3\hat{\mathbf{k}}$, $\mathbf{b} = 2\hat{\mathbf{i}} + \hat{\mathbf{j}} - \alpha\hat{\mathbf{k}}$ and $\mathbf{c} = \alpha\hat{\mathbf{i}} - 2\hat{\mathbf{j}} + 2\hat{\mathbf{k}}$. Then, the set $S = \{\alpha : \mathbf{a}, \mathbf{b}$ and $\mathbf{c}$ are coplanar$\}$

[Single Correct Type, 2019 Main]

(a) is singleton
(b) contains exactly two positive numbers
(c) is empty
(d) contains exactly two numbers only one of which positive

69. If a unit vector **a** makes angles $\frac{\pi}{3}$ with $\hat{\mathbf{i}}$, $\frac{\pi}{4}$ with $\hat{\mathbf{j}}$ and $\theta \in (0, \pi)$ with $\hat{\mathbf{k}}$, then a value of θ is

[Single Correct Type, 2019 Main]

(a) $\frac{5\pi}{6}$ (b) $\frac{\pi}{4}$
(c) $\frac{5\pi}{12}$ (d) $\frac{2\pi}{3}$

70. The sum of the distinct real values of μ for which the vectors $\mu\hat{\mathbf{i}} + \hat{\mathbf{j}} + \hat{\mathbf{k}}$, $\hat{\mathbf{i}} + \mu\hat{\mathbf{j}} + \hat{\mathbf{k}}$, $\hat{\mathbf{i}} + \hat{\mathbf{j}} + \mu\hat{\mathbf{k}}$ are coplanar, is

[Single Correct Type, 2019 Main]

(a) 0 (b) -1 (c) 1 (d) 2

71. Let $\alpha = (\lambda - 2)\mathbf{a} + \mathbf{b}$ and $\beta = (4\lambda - 2)\mathbf{a} + 3\mathbf{b}$, be two given vectors where vectors **a** and **b** are non-collinear. The value of λ for which vectors α and β are collinear, is

[Single Correct Type, 2019 Main]

(a) -4 (b) -3 (c) 4 (d) 3

EXERCISE 2
JEE Advanced Pattern

Single Option Correct Type Questions

1. If $\mathbf{b}$ is a vector whose initial point divides the join of $5\hat{\mathbf{i}}$ and $5\hat{\mathbf{j}}$ in the ratio $k:1$ and whose terminal point in the origin and $|\mathbf{b}| \leq \sqrt{37}$, then k lies in the interval

(a) $[-6, -1/6]$ (b) $(-\infty, -6] \cup [-1/6, \infty)$
(c) $[0, 6]$ (d) None of these

2. If $\mathbf{a}$ and $\mathbf{b}$ are two unit vectors and θ is the angle between them, then the unit vector along the angular bisector of $\mathbf{a}$ and $\mathbf{b}$ will be given by

(a) $\dfrac{\mathbf{a}-\mathbf{b}}{2\cos(\theta/2)}$ (b) $\dfrac{\mathbf{a}+\mathbf{b}}{2\cos(\theta/2)}$
(c) $\dfrac{\mathbf{a}-\mathbf{b}}{\cos(\theta/2)}$ (d) None of these

3. The position vectors of the points P and Q with respect to the origin O are $\mathbf{a} = \hat{\mathbf{i}} + 3\hat{\mathbf{j}} - 2\hat{\mathbf{k}}$ and $\mathbf{b} = 3\hat{\mathbf{i}} - \hat{\mathbf{j}} - 2\hat{\mathbf{k}}$, respectively. If M is a point on PQ, such that OM is the bisector of $\angle POQ$, then $\mathbf{OM}$ is

(a) $2(\hat{\mathbf{i}} - \hat{\mathbf{j}} + \hat{\mathbf{k}})$ (b) $2\hat{\mathbf{i}} + \hat{\mathbf{j}} - 2\hat{\mathbf{k}}$
(c) $2(-\hat{\mathbf{i}} + \hat{\mathbf{j}} - \hat{\mathbf{k}})$ (b) $2(\hat{\mathbf{i}} + \hat{\mathbf{j}} + \hat{\mathbf{k}})$

4. $ABCD$ is a quadrilateral. E is the point of intersection of the line joining the mid-points of the opposite sides. If O is any point and $\mathbf{OA} + \mathbf{OB} + \mathbf{OC} + \mathbf{OD} = x\mathbf{OE}$, then x is equal to

(a) 3 (b) 9
(c) 7 (d) 4

5. In the ΔOAB, M is the mid-point of AB, C is a point on OM, such that $2\mathbf{OC} = \mathbf{CM}$. X is a point on the side OB such that $\mathbf{OX} = 2\mathbf{XB}$. The line XC is produced to meet OA in Y. Then, $\dfrac{OY}{YA}$ is equal to

(a) $\dfrac{1}{3}$ (b) $\dfrac{2}{7}$ (c) $\dfrac{3}{2}$ (d) $\dfrac{2}{5}$

6. Points X and Y are taken on the sides QR and RS, respectively of a parallelogram $PQRS$, so that $\mathbf{QX} = 4\mathbf{XR}$ and $\mathbf{RY} = 4\mathbf{YS}$. The line XY cuts the line PR at Z. Then, $\mathbf{PZ}$ is

(a) $\dfrac{21}{25}\mathbf{PR}$ (b) $\dfrac{16}{25}\mathbf{PR}$
(c) $\dfrac{17}{25}\mathbf{PR}$ (d) None of these

7. $OABCDE$ is a regular hexagon of side 2 units in the XY-plane. O being the origin and OA taken along the X-axis. A point P is taken on a line parallel to Z-axis through the centre of the hexagon at a distance of 3 units from O. Then, the vector $\mathbf{AP}$ is

(a) $-\hat{\mathbf{i}} + 3\hat{\mathbf{j}} + \sqrt{5}\hat{\mathbf{k}}$
(b) $\hat{\mathbf{i}} - \sqrt{3}\hat{\mathbf{j}} + 5\hat{\mathbf{k}}$
(c) $-\hat{\mathbf{i}} + \sqrt{3}\hat{\mathbf{j}} + \sqrt{5}\hat{\mathbf{k}}$
(d) $\hat{\mathbf{i}} + \sqrt{3}\hat{\mathbf{j}} + \sqrt{5}\hat{\mathbf{k}}$

8. Find the value of λ so that the points P, Q, R and S on the sides OA, OB, OC and AB, respectively, of a regular tetrahedron $OABC$ are coplanar. It is given that $\dfrac{OP}{OA} = \dfrac{1}{3}, \dfrac{OQ}{OB} = \dfrac{1}{2}, \dfrac{OR}{OC} = \dfrac{1}{3}$ and $\dfrac{OS}{AB} = \lambda$.

(a) $\lambda = \dfrac{1}{2}$ (b) $\lambda = -1$
(c) $\lambda = 0$ (d) for no value of λ

9. On the XY-plane, where O is the origin, given points, $A(1, 0)$, $B(0, 1)$ and $C(1, 1)$. Let P, Q and R be moving point on the line OA, OB, OC respectively such that $\mathbf{OP} = 45t(\mathbf{OA})$, $\mathbf{OQ} = 60t(\mathbf{OB})$, $\mathbf{OR} = (1-t)(\mathbf{OC})$ with $t > 0$. If the three points P, Q and R are collinear, then the value of t is equal to

(a) $\dfrac{1}{106}$ (b) $\dfrac{7}{187}$
(c) $\dfrac{1}{100}$ (d) None of these

10. If $\mathbf{a}, \mathbf{b}$ and $\mathbf{c}$ are three non-coplanar vectors such that $\mathbf{a} + \mathbf{b} + \mathbf{c} = \alpha\mathbf{d}$ and $\mathbf{b} + \mathbf{c} + \mathbf{d} = \beta\mathbf{a}$, then $\mathbf{a} + \mathbf{b} + \mathbf{c} + \mathbf{d}$ is equal to

(a) $\mathbf{0}$ (b) $\alpha\mathbf{a}$
(c) $\beta\mathbf{b}$ (d) $(\alpha + \beta)\mathbf{c}$

More than One Correct Option Type Questions

11. If the resultant of three forces $\mathbf{F}_1 = p\hat{\mathbf{i}} + 3\hat{\mathbf{j}} - \hat{\mathbf{k}}$, $\mathbf{F}_2 = 6\hat{\mathbf{i}} - \hat{\mathbf{k}}$ and $\mathbf{F}_3 = -5\hat{\mathbf{i}} + \hat{\mathbf{j}} + 2\hat{\mathbf{k}}$ acting on a particle has a magnitude equal to 5 units, then the value of p is

(a) -6 (b) -4
(c) 2 (d) 4

12. Let ABC be a triangle, the position vectors of whose vertices are $7\hat{\mathbf{j}}+10\hat{\mathbf{k}}$, $-\hat{\mathbf{i}}+6\hat{\mathbf{j}}+6\hat{\mathbf{k}}$ and $-4\hat{\mathbf{i}}+9\hat{\mathbf{j}}+6\hat{\mathbf{k}}$. Then, ΔABC is

(a) isosceles (b) equilateral
(c) right angled (d) None of these

13. The sides of a parallelogram are $2\hat{\mathbf{i}}+4\hat{\mathbf{j}}-5\hat{\mathbf{k}}$ and $\hat{\mathbf{i}}+2\hat{\mathbf{j}}+3\hat{\mathbf{k}}$. The unit vector parallel to one of the diagonals is

(a) $\frac{1}{7}(3\hat{\mathbf{i}}+6\hat{\mathbf{j}}-2\hat{\mathbf{k}})$

(b) $\frac{1}{7}(3\hat{\mathbf{i}}-6\hat{\mathbf{j}}-2\hat{\mathbf{k}})$

(c) $\frac{1}{\sqrt{69}}(\hat{\mathbf{i}}+2\hat{\mathbf{j}}+8\hat{\mathbf{k}})$

(d) $\frac{1}{\sqrt{69}}(-\hat{\mathbf{i}}-2\hat{\mathbf{j}}+8\hat{\mathbf{k}})$

14. If $A(-4,0,3)$ and $B(14,2,-5)$, then which one of the following points lie on the bisector of the angle between **OA** and **OB** (O is the origin of reference)?

(a) (2, 2, 4) (b) (2, 11, 5)
(c) (−3, −3, −6) (d) (1, 1, 2)

15. If D, E and F are the mid-points of the sides BC, CA and AB, respectively of a ΔABC and O is any point. Then, which of the following option is correct?

(a) $\mathbf{AD}+\mathbf{BE}+\mathbf{CF}=\mathbf{0}$

(b) $\mathbf{OE}+\mathbf{OF}+\mathbf{DO}=\mathbf{OA}$

(c) $\mathbf{AD}+\frac{2}{3}\mathbf{BE}+\frac{1}{3}\mathbf{CF}=\frac{1}{2}\mathbf{AC}$

(d) $\mathbf{AD}+\frac{1}{3}\mathbf{BE}+\frac{1}{3}\mathbf{CF}=\frac{1}{2}\mathbf{AC}$

16. If $\mathbf{DA}=\mathbf{a}$, $\mathbf{AB}=\mathbf{b}$ and $\mathbf{CB}=\lambda\mathbf{a}$, where $\lambda>0$ and X, Y are mid-points of DB and AC respectively, such that $|\mathbf{a}|=17$ and $|\mathbf{XY}|=4$, then λ is equal to

(a) $\frac{8}{17}$ (b) $\frac{9}{17}$
(c) $\frac{25}{17}$ (d) $\frac{4}{17}$

17. Let $\mathbf{a}=(1,1,-1)$, $\mathbf{b}=(5,-3,-3)$ and $\mathbf{c}=(3,-1,2)$. If $\mathbf{r}$ is collinear with $\mathbf{c}$ and has length $\frac{|\mathbf{a}+\mathbf{b}|}{2}$, then $\mathbf{r}$ equal to

(a) $-3\mathbf{c}$ (b) $-\mathbf{c}$
(c) $\mathbf{c}$ (d) $\frac{2}{3}\mathbf{c}$

18. If $A(\mathbf{a})$, $B(\mathbf{b})$ and $C(\mathbf{c})$ are three collinear points such that $(\cos^2\alpha)\mathbf{a}+(\sin^2\beta)\mathbf{b}-(2\sec^2\gamma)\mathbf{c}=\mathbf{0}$, then

(a) A is mid-point of AC
(b) C is mid-point of AB
(c) A divides CB externally in the ratio 1 : 2
(d) B divides AC internally in the ratio 1 : 2

19. If non-zero vectors **a** and **b** are equally inclined to coplanar vector **c**, then **c** can be

(a) $\frac{|\mathbf{a}|}{|\mathbf{a}|+2|\mathbf{b}|}\mathbf{a}+\frac{|\mathbf{b}|}{|\mathbf{a}|+|\mathbf{b}|}\mathbf{b}$

(b) $\frac{|\mathbf{b}|}{|\mathbf{a}|+|\mathbf{b}|}\mathbf{a}+\frac{|\mathbf{a}|}{|\mathbf{a}|+|\mathbf{b}|}\mathbf{b}$

(c) $\frac{|\mathbf{a}|}{|\mathbf{a}|+2|\mathbf{b}|}\mathbf{a}+\frac{|\mathbf{b}|}{|\mathbf{a}|+2|\mathbf{b}|}\mathbf{b}$

(d) $\frac{|\mathbf{b}|}{2|\mathbf{a}|+|\mathbf{b}|}\mathbf{a}+\frac{|\mathbf{a}|}{2|\mathbf{a}|+|\mathbf{b}|}\mathbf{b}$

20. If **a**, **b** and **c** are non-coplanar vectors and λ is a real number, then the vectors $\mathbf{a}+2\mathbf{b}+3\mathbf{c}$, $\lambda\mathbf{b}+\mu\mathbf{c}$ and $(2\lambda-1)\mathbf{c}$ are coplanar when

(a) $\mu\in R$ (b) $\lambda=\frac{1}{2}$
(c) $\lambda=0$ (d) no value of λ

Passage Based Questions

Passage I

(Q. Nos. 21 and 22)

- Let $OABCD$ be a pentagon in which the sides OA and CB are parallel and the sides OD and AB are parallel. Also, $OA:CB=2:1$ and $OD:AB=1:3$.

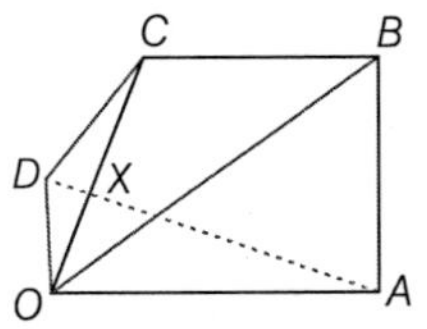

21. The ratio $\frac{OX}{XC}$ is

(a) 3/4 (b) 1/3
(c) 2/5 (d) 1/2

22. The ratio $\frac{AX}{XD}$ is

(a) 5/2 (b) 6
(c) 7/3 (d) 4

Passage II

(Q. Nos. 23 and 24)

- Consider the regular hexagon $ABCDEF$ with centre at O (origin).

23. $\mathbf{AD}+\mathbf{EB}+\mathbf{FC}$ is equal to

(a) 2**AB** (b) 3**AB**
(c) 4**AB** (d) None of these

24. Five forces **AB**, **AC**, **AD**, **AE**, **AF** act at the vertex A of a regular hexagon $ABCDEF$. Then, their resultant is

(a) 3**AO** (b) 2**AO**
(c) 4**AO** (d) 6**AO**

Passage III
(Q. Nos. 25 to 26)

- Three points A, B and C have position vectors $-2\mathbf{a}+3\mathbf{b}+5\mathbf{c}$, $\mathbf{a}+2\mathbf{b}+3\mathbf{c}$ and $7\mathbf{a}-\mathbf{c}$ with reference to an origin O. Answer the following questions.

25. Which of the following is true?
(a) $2\mathbf{OA}-3\mathbf{OB}+\mathbf{OC}=\mathbf{0}$
(b) $2\mathbf{OA}+7\mathbf{OB}+9\mathbf{OC}=\mathbf{0}$
(c) $\mathbf{OA}+\mathbf{OB}+\mathbf{OC}=\mathbf{0}$
(d) None of the above

26. B divided AC in ratio
(a) 2 :1
(b) 2 : 3
(c) 2 : −3
(d) 1 : 2

Passage IV
(Q. Nos. 27 and 28)

- If two vectors **OA** and **OB** are there, then their resultant $\mathbf{OA}+\mathbf{OB}$ can be found by completing the parallelogram $OACB$ and $\mathbf{OC}=\mathbf{OA}+\mathbf{OB}$. Also, if $|\mathbf{OA}|=|\mathbf{OB}|$, then the resultant will bisect the angle between them.

27. A vector **C** directed along internal bisector of angle between vectors $\mathbf{A}=7\hat{\mathbf{i}}-4\hat{\mathbf{j}}-4\hat{\mathbf{k}}$ and $\mathbf{B}=-2\hat{\mathbf{i}}-\hat{\mathbf{j}}+2\hat{\mathbf{k}}$ with $|\mathbf{C}|=5\sqrt{6}$ is
(a) $\frac{5}{3}(\hat{\mathbf{i}}-\hat{\mathbf{j}}+\hat{\mathbf{k}})$
(b) $\frac{5}{3}(\hat{\mathbf{i}}-7\hat{\mathbf{j}}+2\hat{\mathbf{k}})$
(c) $\frac{5}{3}(5\hat{\mathbf{i}}+5\hat{\mathbf{j}}+2\hat{\mathbf{k}})$
(d) $\frac{5}{3}(-5\hat{\mathbf{i}}+5\hat{\mathbf{j}}+2\hat{\mathbf{k}})$

28. If internal and external bisectors of $\angle A$ of ΔABC meet the base BC at D and E respectively, then (D and E lie on same side of B)
(a) $BC=\frac{BD+BE}{4}$
(b) $BC^2=BD\times DE$
(c) $\frac{2}{BC}=\frac{1}{BD}+\frac{1}{BE}$
(d) None of these

Stem Based Questions

Stem I
(Q. Nos. 29 and 30)

- The vector $\mathbf{a}=x\hat{\mathbf{i}}+4\hat{\mathbf{j}}+y\hat{\mathbf{k}}$ lies in the plane of vectors $\mathbf{b}=\hat{\mathbf{i}}+\hat{\mathbf{j}}$ and $\mathbf{c}=\hat{\mathbf{j}}+\hat{\mathbf{k}}$ and bisects the angle between **b** and **c**, then

29. Value of x is ....

30. Value of y is ....

Stem II
(Q. Nos. 31 and 32)

- In a four-dimensional space where unit vectors along the axes are $\hat{\mathbf{i}}, \hat{\mathbf{j}}, \hat{\mathbf{k}}$ and $\hat{\mathbf{l}}$, and $\mathbf{a}_1, \mathbf{a}_2, \mathbf{a}_3, \mathbf{a}_4$ are four non-zero vectors such that no vector can be expressed as a linear combination of other and $(x_1-1)(\mathbf{a}_1-\mathbf{a}_2)+x_2(\mathbf{a}_2+\mathbf{a}_3)$ $+x_3(\mathbf{a}_3+\mathbf{a}_4-2\mathbf{a}_2)+\mathbf{a}_3+x_4\mathbf{a}_4=\mathbf{0}$, then

31. Value of $6(x_1+x_2)$ is equal to ......

32. Value of $18|x_3x_4|$ is equal to ......

Stem III
(Q. Nos. 33 and 34)

- Suppose that **p**, **q** and **r** are three non-coplanar vectors in R^3. Let the components of a vector **s** along **p**, **q** and **r** be 4, 3 and 5, respectively. If the components of this vector **s** along $(-\mathbf{p}+\mathbf{q}+\mathbf{r})$, $(\mathbf{p}-\mathbf{q}+\mathbf{r})$ and $(-\mathbf{p}-\mathbf{q}+\mathbf{r})$ and x, y and z, respectively. Then,

33. The value of $2|z|$ is ....

34. The value of $2(x+y)$ is ....

Single Integer Type Questions

35. If the resultant of three forces $\mathbf{F}_1=p\hat{\mathbf{i}}+3\hat{\mathbf{j}}-\hat{\mathbf{k}}$, $\mathbf{F}_2=-5\hat{\mathbf{i}}+\hat{\mathbf{j}}+2\hat{\mathbf{k}}$ and $\mathbf{F}_3=6\hat{\mathbf{i}}-\hat{\mathbf{k}}$ acting on a particle has a magnitude equal to 5 units. Then, the magnitude of difference in the values of p is ....

36. Vectors along the adjacent sides of parallelogram are $\mathbf{a}=\hat{\mathbf{i}}+2\hat{\mathbf{j}}+\hat{\mathbf{k}}$ and $\mathbf{b}=2\hat{\mathbf{i}}+4\hat{\mathbf{j}}+\hat{\mathbf{k}}$. Find the length of the longer diagonal of the parallelogram.

37. If $\mathbf{a}+\mathbf{b}$ is along the angle bisector of **a** and **b**, where $|\mathbf{a}|=\lambda|\mathbf{b}|$, then the number of digits in value of λ is ......

38. Let **p** be the position vector of orthocentre and **g** is the position vector of the centroid of ΔABC, where circumcentre is the origin. If $\mathbf{p}=k\mathbf{g}$, then the value of k is ......

39. In a ΔABC, a line is drawn passing through centroid dividing AB internally in ratio 2 : 1 and AC in $\lambda:1$ (internally). The value of λ is ......

40. A vector **a** has component $2p$ and 1 with respect to a rectangular cartesian system. The system is rotated through a certain angle about the origin in the counter clockwise sense. If with respect to the new system, **a** has components $(p+1)$ and 1, where p take the values p_1 and p_2. Then, the value of $3|p_1+p_2|$ is ......

41. If vectors $\mathbf{a}=\hat{\mathbf{i}}+2\hat{\mathbf{j}}-\hat{\mathbf{k}}$, $\mathbf{b}=2\hat{\mathbf{i}}-\hat{\mathbf{j}}+\hat{\mathbf{k}}$ and $\mathbf{c}=\lambda\hat{\mathbf{i}}+\hat{\mathbf{j}}+2\hat{\mathbf{k}}$ are coplanar, then find the value of $(\lambda-4)$.

Numerical Value Type Questions

42. If the magnitude of $\mathbf{r}_1 - \mathbf{r}_2$ is m, when $|\mathbf{r}_1| = 5$ and points North-East while $|\mathbf{r}_2| = 5$ but points North-West, then the value of m^2 is ....

43. Let $OACB$ be a parallelogram with O at the origin and OC a diagonal. Let D be the mid-point of OA. If BD and CO intersects in the same ratio $k_1 : k_2$, then value of $(k_1 + k_2)^2$ is ....

44. ΔABC is a triangle with the point P on side BC such that $3\mathbf{BP} = 2\mathbf{PC}$, the point Q is on the line $\mathbf{CA}$ such that $4\mathbf{CQ} = \mathbf{QA}$. If the ratio in which the line joining the common point R of $\mathbf{AP}$ and $\mathbf{BQ}$ and the point S divides $\mathbf{AB}$ is $\lambda_1 : \lambda_2$, then $(\lambda_1 - \lambda_2)$ is equal to ....

45. In a ΔABC internal angle bisectors AI, BI and CI are produced to meet opposite sides in A', B' and C', respectively. If the maximum value of $\dfrac{AI \cdot BI \cdot CI}{AA' \cdot BB' \cdot CC'}$ is $\dfrac{k_1}{k_2}$, then the value of $(k_1 k_2)$ is ....

46. Let $OABCD$ be a pentagon in which the sides OA and CB are parallel and the sides OD and AB are parallel. Also, $OA : CB = 2 : 1$ and $OD : AB = 1 : 3$. If the diagonals OC and AD meet at X. If $OX : OC = m : n$, then the value of $\left(\dfrac{m}{n}\right)$ is ....

47. In the XY-plane, O is the origin, given point are $A(1, 0)$, $B(0, 1)$ and $C(1, 1)$. Let P, Q and R are moving points on the line OA, OB, OC respectively, such that $\mathbf{OP} = 50x(\mathbf{OA})$, $\mathbf{OQ} = 75x(\mathbf{OB})$ and $\mathbf{OR} = (1 - x)(\mathbf{OC})$ with $x > 0$. If the points P, Q and R are collinear, then value of $465x$ is ....

48. If unit vector $a\hat{\mathbf{i}} + b\hat{\mathbf{j}} + \frac{1}{2}\hat{\mathbf{k}}$ is linearly dependent with $\hat{\mathbf{i}} + 2\hat{\mathbf{j}}$ and $\hat{\mathbf{j}} - 2\hat{\mathbf{k}}$, then value of $5a^2 - a$ is equal to ....

Matching Type Questions

49. $\mathbf{a}$ and $\mathbf{b}$ form the consecutive sides of a regular hexagon $ABCDEF$.

Column I	Column II
a. If $\mathbf{CD} = x\mathbf{a} + y\mathbf{b}$, then	p. $x = -2$
b. If $\mathbf{CE} = x\mathbf{a} + y\mathbf{b}$, then	q. $x = -1$
c. If $\mathbf{AE} = x\mathbf{a} + y\mathbf{b}$, then	r. $y = 1$
d. If $\mathbf{AD} = -x\mathbf{b}$, then	s. $y = 2$

50. $ABCDEF$ is a regular hexagon in the XY-plane with vertices in the anti-clockwise direction and $\mathbf{AB} = 2\hat{\mathbf{i}}$

Column I	Column II
a. **AC**	p. $-\hat{\mathbf{i}} + \sqrt{3}\hat{\mathbf{j}}$
b. **AD**	q. $-3\hat{\mathbf{i}} + \sqrt{3}\hat{\mathbf{j}}$
c. **CD**	r. $2\hat{\mathbf{i}} + 2\sqrt{3}\hat{\mathbf{j}}$
d. **CE**	s. $3\hat{\mathbf{i}} + \sqrt{3}\hat{\mathbf{j}}$

Previous Year Questions

51. Three lines $L_1 : \mathbf{r} = \lambda\hat{\mathbf{i}}, \lambda \in R$, $L_2 : \mathbf{r} = \hat{\mathbf{k}} + \mu\hat{\mathbf{j}}, \mu \in R$ and $L_3 : \mathbf{r} = \hat{\mathbf{i}} + \hat{\mathbf{j}} + v\hat{\mathbf{k}}, v \in R$ and given for which point(s) Q on L_2 can we find a point P on L_1 and a point R on L_3 so that P, Q and R are collinear?

[More than One Option Correct, 2019 Adv.]

(a) $\hat{\mathbf{k}} + \frac{1}{2}\hat{\mathbf{j}}$

(b) $\hat{\mathbf{k}} + \hat{\mathbf{j}}$

(c) $\hat{\mathbf{k}}$

(d) $\hat{\mathbf{k}} - \frac{1}{2}\hat{\mathbf{j}}$

EXERCISE 3

Challenging Problems

Subjective Type Questions

1. If G is the centroid of the ΔABC and if G' is the centroid of another $\Delta A'B'C'$, then prove that
$\mathbf{AA'} + \mathbf{BB'} + \mathbf{CC'} = 3\mathbf{GG'}$.

2. If O is the circumcentre and O' is the orthocenter of ΔABC prove that

   (i) $\mathbf{SA} + \mathbf{SB} + \mathbf{SC} = 3\mathbf{SG}$, where S is any point in the plane of ΔABC.

   (ii) $\mathbf{OA} + \mathbf{OB} + \mathbf{OC} = \mathbf{OO'}$

   (iii) $\mathbf{O'A} + \mathbf{O'B} + \mathbf{O'C} = 2\mathbf{O'O}$

   (iv) $\mathbf{AO'} + \mathbf{O'B} + \mathbf{O'C} = \mathbf{AP}$

   where, **AP** is diameter of the circumcircle.

3. If $\mathbf{c} = 3\mathbf{a} + 4\mathbf{b}$ and $2\mathbf{c} = \mathbf{a} - 3\mathbf{b}$, show that

   (i) $\mathbf{c}$ and $\mathbf{a}$ have the same direction and $|\mathbf{c}| > |\mathbf{a}|$.

   (ii) $\mathbf{c}$ and $\mathbf{b}$ have opposite direction and $|\mathbf{c}| > |\mathbf{b}|$.

4. Let $\mathbf{A}(t) = f_1(i)\hat{\mathbf{i}} + f_2(t)\hat{\mathbf{j}}$ and $\mathbf{B}(t) = g_1(t)\hat{\mathbf{i}} + g_2(t)\hat{\mathbf{j}}$ $t \in [0, 1]$, where f_1, f_2, g_1 and g_2 are continuous functions. If $\mathbf{A}(t)$ and $\mathbf{B}(t)$ are non-zero vectors for all t and $\mathbf{A}(0) = 2\hat{\mathbf{i}} + 3\hat{\mathbf{j}}$, $\mathbf{A}(1) = 6\hat{\mathbf{i}} + 2\hat{\mathbf{j}}$, $\mathbf{B}(0) = 3\hat{\mathbf{i}} + 2\hat{\mathbf{j}}$ and $\mathbf{B}(1) = 2\hat{\mathbf{i}} + 6\hat{\mathbf{j}}$. Then, show that $\mathbf{A}(t)$ and $\mathbf{B}(t)$ are parallel for some t.

5. Prove that if $\cos\alpha \neq 1$, $\cos\beta \neq 1$ and $\cos\gamma \neq 1$, then the vectors $\mathbf{a} = \hat{\mathbf{i}}\cos\alpha + \hat{\mathbf{j}} + \hat{\mathbf{k}}$, $\mathbf{b} = \hat{\mathbf{i}} + \hat{\mathbf{j}}\cos\beta + \hat{\mathbf{k}}$, $\mathbf{c} = \hat{\mathbf{i}} + \hat{\mathbf{j}} + \hat{\mathbf{k}}\cos\gamma$ can never be coplanar.

6. If $\mathbf{r}_1, \mathbf{r}_2$ and $\mathbf{r}_3$ are the position vectors of three collinear points and scalars l and m exists such that $\mathbf{r}_3 = l\,\mathbf{r}_1 + m\mathbf{r}_2$, then show that $l + m = 1$.

7. Let $OACB$ be a parallelogram with O at the origin and OC a diagonal. Let D be the mid-point of OA. Using vector methods prove that BD and CO intersects in the same ratio. Determine this ratio.

8. ΔABC is a triangle with the point P on side BC such that $3\mathbf{BP} = 2\mathbf{PC}$, the point Q is on the line **CA** such that $4\mathbf{CQ} = \mathbf{QA}$. Find the ratio in which the line joining the common point R of **AP** and **BQ** and the point S divides **AB**.

9. Let $\mathbf{r}_1, \mathbf{r}_2, \mathbf{r}_3, \ldots, \mathbf{r}_n$ be the position vectors of points $P_1, P_2, P_3, \ldots, P_n$ relative to an origin O. Show that if the vectors equation $a_1\mathbf{r}_1 + a_2\mathbf{r}_2 + \ldots + a_n\mathbf{r}_n = \mathbf{0}$ holds, then a similar equation will also hold good with respect to any other origin O', if $a_1 + a_2 + a_3 + \ldots + a_n = 0$.

10. If $\mathbf{u}$, $\mathbf{v}$ and $\mathbf{w}$ is a linearly independent system of vectors, examine the system $\mathbf{p}, \mathbf{q}$ and $\mathbf{r}$, where
$\mathbf{p} = (\cos a)\mathbf{u} + (\cos b)\mathbf{v} + (\cos c)\mathbf{w}$
$\mathbf{q} = (\sin a)\mathbf{u} + (\sin b)\mathbf{v} + (\sin c)\mathbf{w}$
$\mathbf{r} = \sin(x + a)\mathbf{u} + \sin(x + b)\mathbf{v} + \sin(x + c)\mathbf{w}$ for linearly dependent.

Answer Keys

Exercise 1

1. (c)	2. (b)	3. (d)	4. (a)	5. (a)	6. (d)	7. (c)	8. (a)	9. (c)	10. (a)
11. (d)	12. (c)	13. (b)	14. (b)	15. (d)	16. (c)	17. (a)	18. (a)	19. (d)	20. (c)
21. (c)	22. (c)	23. (c)	24. (b)	25. (b)	26. (b)	27. (b)	28. (c)	29. (a)	30. (b)
31. (b)	32. (a)	33. (b)	34. (d)	35. (d)	36. (0.5)	37. (24)	38. (4.23)	39. (57)	40. (1.5)
41. (1600)	42. (2 : 1)	43. (35)	44. (146)	45. (11)	46. (c)	47. (d)	48. (b)	49. (b)	50. (d)
51. (c)	52. (d)	53. (b)	54. (b)	55. (c)	56. (c)	57. (a)	58. (b)	59. (c)	60. (26/17)
61. (a)	62. (d)	63. (c)	64. (a)	65. (a)	66. (d)	67. (a)	68. (c)	69. (d)	70. (b)
71. (a)									

Exercise 2

1. (b)	2. (b)	3. (b)	4. (d)	5. (b)	6. (a)	7. (c)	8. (b)	9. (b)	10. (a)
11. (b,c)	12. (a,c)	13. (a,d)	14. (a,c,d)	15. (a,b,c)	16. (b,c)	17. (b,c)	18. (b,c)	19. (b,d)	20. (a,b,c)
21. (c)	22. (b)	23. (c)	24. (d)	25. (a)	26. (d)	27. (b)	28. (c)	29. (2)	30. (2)
31. (2)	32. (2)	33. (7)	34. (17)	35. (6)	36. (7)	37. (1)	38. (3)	39. (2)	40. (2)
41. (9)	42. (50)	43. (9)	44. (5)	45. (216)	46. (0.29)	47. (15)	48. (0.69)		

49. a → q, r ; b → p, r; c → q,s; d → p

50. a → s; b → r; c → p; d → q

51. (a,d)

Solutions

Exercise 1 - JEE Main Pattern

1. PV of $\mathbf{AD} = \dfrac{(3+5)\hat{\mathbf{i}} + (0-2)\hat{\mathbf{j}} + (4+4)\hat{\mathbf{k}}}{2} = 4\hat{\mathbf{i}} - \hat{\mathbf{j}} + 4\hat{\mathbf{k}}$

$|\mathbf{AD}| = \sqrt{16+16+1} = \sqrt{33}$

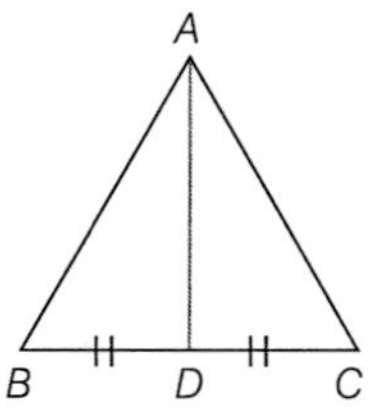

2. **Decoding the Question**

First, find the value of γ by applying $\cos^2\alpha + \cos^2\beta + \cos^2\gamma = 1$, where α, β and γ are angles which vectors makes with three axes. After this apply $\mathbf{OP} = |\mathbf{OP}|(\cos\alpha\hat{\mathbf{i}} + \cos\beta\hat{\mathbf{j}} + \cos\gamma\hat{\mathbf{k}})$.

Let $\alpha = 45°$, $\beta = 60°$ and $OP = |\mathbf{OP}| = 8$.

Let γ be the angle which vector **OP** makes with Z-axis.

$\because \quad \cos^2\alpha + \cos^2\beta + \cos^2\gamma = 1$

$\therefore \cos^2 45° + \cos^2 60° + \cos^2\gamma = 1$

$\Rightarrow \quad \left(\dfrac{1}{\sqrt{2}}\right)^2 + \left(\dfrac{1}{2}\right)^2 + \cos^2\gamma = 1$

$\Rightarrow \quad \cos^2\gamma = \dfrac{1}{4} \Rightarrow \cos\gamma = \pm\dfrac{1}{2}$

$\Rightarrow \quad \gamma = 60°$ or $120°$

Now, $\mathbf{OP} = |\mathbf{OP}|(\cos 45°\hat{\mathbf{i}} + \cos 60°\hat{\mathbf{j}} + \cos 60°\hat{\mathbf{k}})$

or $\quad \mathbf{OP} = |\mathbf{OP}|(\cos 45°\hat{\mathbf{i}} + \cos 60°\hat{\mathbf{j}} + \cos 120°\hat{\mathbf{k}})$

$\Rightarrow \quad \mathbf{OP} = 8\left(\dfrac{1}{\sqrt{2}}\hat{\mathbf{i}} + \dfrac{1}{2}\hat{\mathbf{j}} + \dfrac{1}{2}\hat{\mathbf{k}}\right)$

or $\quad \mathbf{OP} = 8\left(\dfrac{1}{\sqrt{2}}\hat{\mathbf{i}} + \dfrac{1}{2}\hat{\mathbf{j}} - \dfrac{1}{2}\hat{\mathbf{k}}\right)$

$\Rightarrow \quad \mathbf{OP} = 4(\sqrt{2}\hat{\mathbf{i}} + \hat{\mathbf{j}} \pm \hat{\mathbf{k}})$

3. $3\mathbf{a} + 4\mathbf{b} + 5\mathbf{c} = \mathbf{0}$

Hence, **a**, **b** and **c** are coplanar.

No other conclusion can be derived from it.

4.

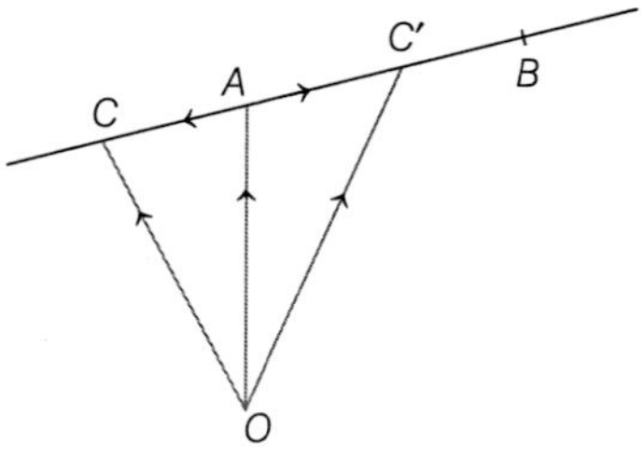

We have, $A(\hat{\mathbf{i}} + \hat{\mathbf{j}} - 2\hat{\mathbf{k}})$ and $B(\hat{\mathbf{i}} - 3\hat{\mathbf{j}} + \hat{\mathbf{k}})$

On line AB points C and C' are at distance 1 unit from A.

OC = **OA** + **AC**, where **AC** is unit vector in direction of **AB**

$\therefore \quad \mathbf{OC} = \mathbf{OA} + \dfrac{\mathbf{AB}}{|\mathbf{AB}|}$

$\Rightarrow \quad \mathbf{OC} = (\hat{\mathbf{i}} + \hat{\mathbf{j}} - 2\hat{\mathbf{k}}) + \dfrac{(-4\hat{\mathbf{j}} + 3\hat{\mathbf{k}})}{5}$

$\Rightarrow \quad \mathbf{OC} = \dfrac{1}{5}(5\hat{\mathbf{i}} + \hat{\mathbf{j}} - 7\hat{\mathbf{k}})$

Similarly, $\quad \mathbf{OC'} = \mathbf{OA} - \dfrac{\mathbf{AB}}{|\mathbf{AB}|}$

$\mathbf{OC'} = \dfrac{1}{5}(5\hat{\mathbf{i}} + 9\hat{\mathbf{j}} - 13\hat{\mathbf{k}})$

5. $\quad \mathbf{AD} = \mathbf{OD} - \mathbf{OA}$

$= \dfrac{\mathbf{b}+\mathbf{c}}{2} - \mathbf{a} = \dfrac{\mathbf{b}+\mathbf{c}-2\mathbf{a}}{2}$

[where, O is the origin for reference]

Similarly, $\quad \mathbf{BE} = \mathbf{OE} - \mathbf{OB} = \dfrac{\mathbf{c}+\mathbf{a}}{2} - \mathbf{b} = \dfrac{\mathbf{c}+\mathbf{a}-2\mathbf{b}}{2}$

and $\quad \mathbf{CF} = \dfrac{\mathbf{a}+\mathbf{b}-2\mathbf{c}}{2}$

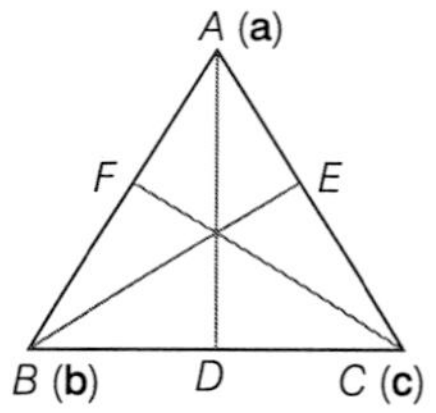

Now, $\mathbf{AD} + \mathbf{BE} + \mathbf{CF} = \dfrac{\mathbf{b}+\mathbf{c}-2\mathbf{a}}{2} + \dfrac{\mathbf{c}+\mathbf{a}-2\mathbf{b}}{2} + \dfrac{\mathbf{a}+\mathbf{b}-2\mathbf{c}}{2} = \mathbf{0}$

6. $\mathbf{AP} = \mathbf{AB} + \mathbf{BP} = \mathbf{AB} + \dfrac{1}{2}\mathbf{BC} = \mathbf{AB} + \dfrac{1}{2}\mathbf{AD}$ ...(i)

$\mathbf{AQ} = \mathbf{AD} + \mathbf{DQ} = \mathbf{AD} + \dfrac{1}{2}\mathbf{DC} = \mathbf{AD} + \dfrac{1}{2}\mathbf{AB}$ ... (ii)

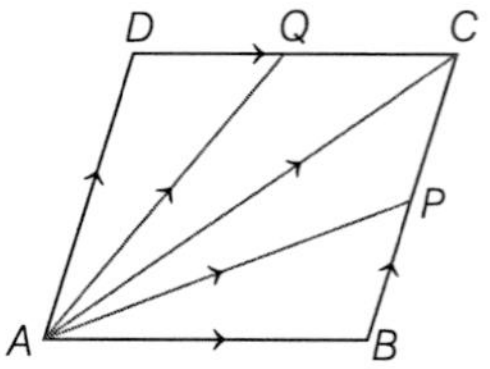

By Eqs. (i) and (ii), we get

$\mathbf{AP} + \mathbf{AQ} = \dfrac{3}{2}(\mathbf{AB} + \mathbf{AD}) = \dfrac{3}{2}(\mathbf{AB} + \mathbf{BC}) = \dfrac{3}{2}\mathbf{AC}$

7. Let $A \equiv (1, 1, -1)$, $B \equiv (2, 3, 0)$, $C \equiv (3, 5, -2)$ and $D \equiv (0, -1, 1)$.
So, $\mathbf{AB} = (1, 2, 1)$, $\mathbf{BC} = (1, 2, -2)$, $\mathbf{CD} = (-3, -6, 3)$
and $\mathbf{DA} = (1, 2, -2)$.
Clearly, $\mathbf{BC} \parallel \mathbf{DA}$ but AB is not parallel to CD.
So, it is a trapezium.

8. $\mathbf{OP} = \dfrac{1\,(\mathbf{OB}) + 2\,(6\,\mathbf{b} - 2\mathbf{a})}{1 + 2}$

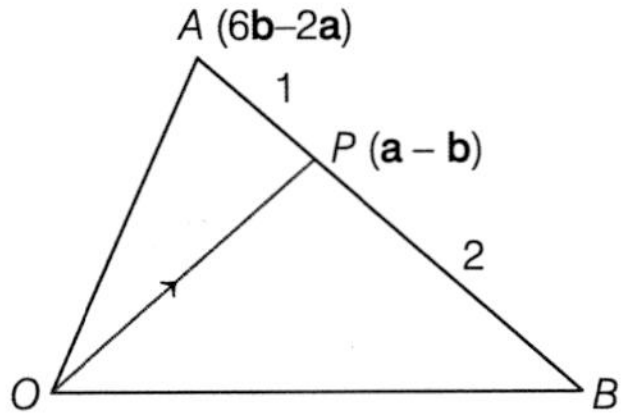

$\Rightarrow\ 3(\mathbf{a} - \mathbf{b}) = \mathbf{OB} + 12\,\mathbf{b} - 4\mathbf{a} \ \Rightarrow\ \mathbf{OB} = 7\mathbf{a} - 15\,\mathbf{b}$

9. Since, $\mathbf{AB} + \mathbf{BD} = \mathbf{AD}$

$$\mathbf{BD} = \mathbf{AD} - \mathbf{AB} = (\hat{\mathbf{i}} + 2\hat{\mathbf{j}} + 3\hat{\mathbf{k}}) - (2\hat{\mathbf{i}} + 4\hat{\mathbf{j}} - 5\hat{\mathbf{k}}) = -\hat{\mathbf{i}} - 2\hat{\mathbf{j}} + 8\hat{\mathbf{k}}$$

Hence, unit vector in the direction of **BD** is

$$\frac{-\hat{\mathbf{i}} - 2\hat{\mathbf{j}} + 8\hat{\mathbf{k}}}{|-\hat{\mathbf{i}} - 2\hat{\mathbf{j}} + 8\hat{\mathbf{k}}|} = \frac{-\hat{\mathbf{i}} - 2\hat{\mathbf{j}} + 8\hat{\mathbf{k}}}{\sqrt{69}}$$

10. Position vectors of vertices A, B and C of the ΔABC = $\mathbf{a}, \mathbf{b}$ and $\mathbf{c}$. We know that position vector of centroid of the triangle, $\mathbf{G} = \dfrac{\mathbf{a} + \mathbf{b} + \mathbf{c}}{3}$.

Therefore, $\mathbf{GA} + \mathbf{GB} + \mathbf{GC}$

$$= \left(\mathbf{a} - \frac{\mathbf{a} + \mathbf{b} + \mathbf{c}}{3}\right) + \left(\mathbf{b} - \frac{\mathbf{a} + \mathbf{b} + \mathbf{c}}{3}\right) + \left(\mathbf{c} - \frac{\mathbf{a} + \mathbf{b} + \mathbf{c}}{3}\right)$$

$$= \frac{1}{3}(2\mathbf{a} - \mathbf{b} - \mathbf{c} + 2\mathbf{b} - \mathbf{a} - \mathbf{c} + 2\mathbf{c} - \mathbf{a} - \mathbf{b}) = \mathbf{0}$$

11. A regular hexagon $ABCDEF$.

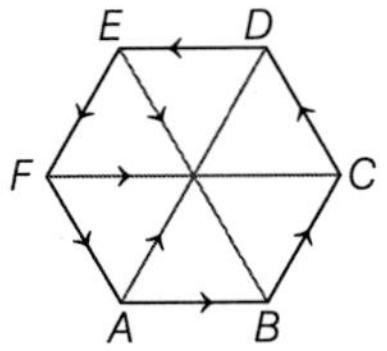

We know from the hexagon that **AD** is parallel to **BC** or $\mathbf{AD} = 2\mathbf{BC}$, **FA** is parallel to **EB** or $\mathbf{EB} = 2\mathbf{FA}$ and **FC** is parallel to **AB** or $\mathbf{FC} = 2\mathbf{AB}$.

Thus, $\mathbf{AD} + \mathbf{EB} + \mathbf{FC} = 2\mathbf{BC} + 2\mathbf{FA} + 2\mathbf{AB}$
$= 2(\mathbf{FA} + \mathbf{AB} + \mathbf{BC}) = 2(\mathbf{FC})$
$= 2(2\mathbf{AB}) = 4\mathbf{AB}$

12. $\mathbf{AE} + \mathbf{ED} + \mathbf{DC} + \mathbf{AB} = \mathbf{AD} + \mathbf{DC} + \mathbf{AB} = \mathbf{AC} + \mathbf{AB}$

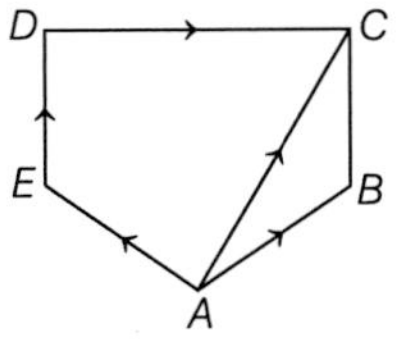

Obviously, if **BC** is added to this system, then it will be
$\mathbf{AC} + \mathbf{AB} + \mathbf{BC} = \mathbf{AC} + \mathbf{AC} = 2\mathbf{AC}$.

13. By triangle law, $\mathbf{AB} = \mathbf{AD} - \mathbf{BD}, \mathbf{AC} = \mathbf{AD} - \mathbf{CD}$

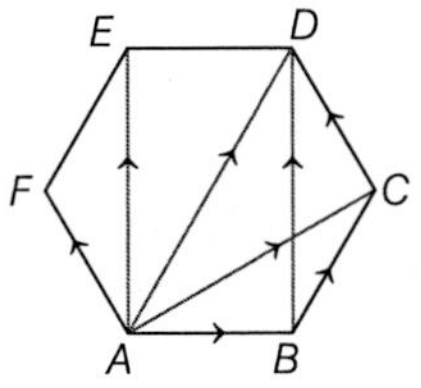

Therefore,

$$\mathbf{AB} + \mathbf{AC} + \mathbf{AD} + \mathbf{AE} + \mathbf{AF}$$
$$= 3\mathbf{AD} + (\mathbf{AE} - \mathbf{BD}) + (\mathbf{AF} - \mathbf{CD}) = 3\mathbf{AD}$$

Hence, $\lambda = 3$ $\quad [\because \mathbf{AE} = \mathbf{BD}, \mathbf{AF} = \mathbf{CD}]$

14. $|a| + |b| + |c| = \sqrt{a^2 + b^2 + c^2}$
$\Leftrightarrow\ 2|ab| + 2|bc| + 2|ca| = 0$
$\Leftrightarrow\ ab = bc = ca = 0 \Leftrightarrow$ any two of a, b and c are zero

15.

> **Decoding the Question**
> If **p** bisects the angles between unit vector $\hat{\mathbf{a}}$ and **b**, then we can find $\hat{\mathbf{a}}$ by use formula $\lambda \mathbf{p} = \hat{\mathbf{a}} + \dfrac{\mathbf{b}}{|\mathbf{b}|}$.

We must have $\lambda(\hat{\mathbf{i}} - 3\hat{\mathbf{j}} + 5\hat{\mathbf{k}}) = \hat{\mathbf{a}} + \dfrac{2\hat{\mathbf{k}} + 2\hat{\mathbf{j}} - \hat{\mathbf{i}}}{3}$

Therefore, $\quad 3\hat{\mathbf{a}} = 3\lambda(\hat{\mathbf{i}} - 3\hat{\mathbf{j}} + 5\hat{\mathbf{k}}) - (2\hat{\mathbf{k}} + 2\hat{\mathbf{j}} - \hat{\mathbf{i}})$
$= \hat{\mathbf{i}}(3\lambda + 1) - \hat{\mathbf{j}}(2 + 9\lambda) + \hat{\mathbf{k}}(15\lambda - 2)$

or $\quad 3|\hat{\mathbf{a}}| = \sqrt{(3\lambda + 1)^2 + (2 + 9\lambda)^2 + (15\lambda - 2)^2}$

or $\quad 9 = (3\lambda + 1)^2 + (2 + 9\lambda)^2 + (15\lambda - 2)^2$

or $\quad 315\lambda^2 - 18\lambda = 0 \Rightarrow \lambda = 0, \dfrac{2}{35}$

If $\lambda = 0$, $\hat{\mathbf{a}} = \dfrac{1}{3}(\hat{\mathbf{i}} - 2\hat{\mathbf{j}} - 2\hat{\mathbf{k}})$ (not acceptable)

For $\lambda = \dfrac{2}{35}$, $\hat{\mathbf{a}} = \dfrac{41}{105}\hat{\mathbf{i}} - \dfrac{88}{105}\hat{\mathbf{j}} - \dfrac{40}{105}\hat{\mathbf{k}}$

16. $\alpha = \mathbf{a} + \mathbf{b} + \mathbf{c} = 6\hat{\mathbf{i}} + 12\hat{\mathbf{j}}$
Let $\alpha = x\mathbf{a} + y\mathbf{b} \Rightarrow 6x + 2y = 6$ and $-3x - 6y = 12$
$\therefore \quad x = 2, y = -3$
$\therefore \quad \alpha = 2\mathbf{a} - 3\mathbf{b}$

17. Let the incentre be at the origin and be $A(\mathbf{p}), B(\mathbf{q})$ and $C(\mathbf{r})$.
Then, $\quad \mathbf{IA} = \mathbf{p}, \mathbf{IB} = \mathbf{q}$ and $\mathbf{IC} = \mathbf{r}$
Incentre I is $\dfrac{ap + bq + cr}{a + b + c}$, where $p = BC$, $q = AC$ and $r = AB$
Incentre is at the origin. Therefore,

$$\frac{a\mathbf{p} + b\mathbf{q} + c\mathbf{r}}{a + b + c} = \mathbf{0},$$

or $\quad a\mathbf{p} + b\mathbf{q} + c\mathbf{r} = \mathbf{0} \Rightarrow a\mathbf{IA} + b\mathbf{IB} + c\mathbf{IC} = \mathbf{0}$

18. Let the bisector of $\angle A$ meets BC at D, then AD divides BC in the ratio $AB : AC$.
$\therefore$ Position vectors of D

$$= \frac{|\mathbf{AB}|(2\hat{\mathbf{i}} + 5\hat{\mathbf{j}} + 7\hat{\mathbf{k}}) + |\mathbf{AC}|(2\hat{\mathbf{i}} + 3\hat{\mathbf{j}} + 4\hat{\mathbf{k}})}{|\mathbf{AB}| + |\mathbf{AC}|}$$

Here, $|\mathbf{AB}| = |-2\hat{\mathbf{i}} - 4\hat{\mathbf{j}} - 4\hat{\mathbf{k}}| = 6$

and $|\mathbf{AC}| = |-2\hat{\mathbf{i}} - 2\hat{\mathbf{j}} - \hat{\mathbf{k}}| = 3$

$\therefore$ Position vector of $D = \dfrac{6(2\hat{\mathbf{i}} + 5\hat{\mathbf{j}} + 7\hat{\mathbf{k}}) + 3(2\hat{\mathbf{i}} + 3\hat{\mathbf{j}} + 4\hat{\mathbf{k}})}{6+3}$

$= \dfrac{18\hat{\mathbf{i}} + 39\hat{\mathbf{j}} + 54\hat{\mathbf{k}}}{9}$

$= \dfrac{1}{3}(6\hat{\mathbf{i}} + 13\hat{\mathbf{j}} + 18\hat{\mathbf{k}})$

19. $\mathbf{a} - \mathbf{b} = 2(\mathbf{d} - \mathbf{c})$

$\therefore \quad \dfrac{\mathbf{a} + 2\mathbf{c}}{2+1} = \dfrac{\mathbf{b} + 2\mathbf{d}}{2+1}$

Hence, AC and BD trisect each other as LHS is the position vector of a point trisecting A an C, and RHS that of B and D.

20. $\alpha(\hat{\mathbf{i}} - 3\hat{\mathbf{j}} + 5\hat{\mathbf{k}}) = \hat{\mathbf{a}} + \dfrac{2\hat{\mathbf{k}} + 2\hat{\mathbf{j}} - \hat{\mathbf{i}}}{3}$

$\Rightarrow 3\hat{\mathbf{a}} = \alpha(3\hat{\mathbf{i}} - 9\hat{\mathbf{j}} + 15\hat{\mathbf{k}}) - 2\hat{\mathbf{k}} - 2\hat{\mathbf{j}} + \hat{\mathbf{i}}$

$\Rightarrow 3\hat{\mathbf{a}} = (3\alpha + 1)\hat{\mathbf{i}} - (9\alpha + 2)\hat{\mathbf{j}} + (15\alpha - 2)\hat{\mathbf{k}}$

$\therefore 3|\hat{\mathbf{a}}| = (3\alpha + 1)\hat{\mathbf{i}} - (9\alpha + 2)\hat{\mathbf{j}} + (15\alpha - 2)\hat{\mathbf{k}}$

$\Rightarrow \quad 3 = \sqrt{(3\alpha + 1)^2 + (9\alpha + 2)^2 + (15\alpha - 2)^2}$

$\Rightarrow \quad 9 = 315\alpha^2 - 18\alpha + 9$

$\therefore \quad \alpha = 0, \dfrac{2}{35}$

For $\alpha = 0$, $\hat{\mathbf{a}} = \dfrac{\hat{\mathbf{i}} - 2\hat{\mathbf{j}} - 2\hat{\mathbf{k}}}{3}$ (not acceptable)

For $\alpha = \dfrac{2}{35}$, $\hat{\mathbf{a}} = \dfrac{2}{35}(\hat{\mathbf{i}} - 3\hat{\mathbf{j}} + 5\hat{\mathbf{k}}) - \dfrac{(2\hat{\mathbf{k}} + 2\hat{\mathbf{j}} - \hat{\mathbf{i}})}{3}$

$= \dfrac{1}{105}(41\hat{\mathbf{i}} - 88\hat{\mathbf{j}} - 40\hat{\mathbf{k}})$

On comparing, we get

$\lambda = 41, \mu = -88, \gamma = -40$

$\lambda^2 - 2\mu + \gamma = (41)^2 + 2(88) - 40$

$= 1681 + 176 - 40$

$= 1817$

21. $\mathbf{OM}_1 = \mathbf{OA} + \mathbf{OB} + \mathbf{OC} + \mathbf{OD}$

$= \mathbf{OM} + \mathbf{MA} + \mathbf{OM} + \mathbf{MB} + \mathbf{OM} + \mathbf{MC} + \mathbf{OM} + \mathbf{MD}$

$= 4\mathbf{OM} + (\mathbf{MA} + \mathbf{MC}) + (\mathbf{MB} + \mathbf{MD})$

$= 4\mathbf{OM}$ $\quad [\because \mathbf{MA} = -\mathbf{MC}, \mathbf{MB} = -\mathbf{MD}]$

$\Rightarrow \mathbf{OM} = \left(\dfrac{1}{4}\right)\mathbf{OM}_1$

$\therefore \quad \lambda = \dfrac{1}{4}$

22. It is given that $\mathbf{b}$ is collinear with the vector $\mathbf{a}$.

$\therefore \quad \mathbf{b} = \lambda\mathbf{a}$ ...(i)

$= 2\sqrt{2}\lambda\hat{\mathbf{i}} - \lambda\hat{\mathbf{j}} + 4\lambda\hat{\mathbf{k}}$

Also, $|\mathbf{b}| = 10$

$\Rightarrow \quad \sqrt{(2\sqrt{2}\lambda)^2 + (-\lambda)^2 + (4\lambda)^2} = 10$

$\Rightarrow \quad 25\lambda^2 = 100$

$\Rightarrow \quad \lambda = \pm 2$ ... (ii)

From Eqs. (i) and (ii), we have

$\mathbf{b} = \pm 2\mathbf{a} \Rightarrow 2\mathbf{a} \pm \mathbf{b} = \mathbf{0}$

23. If $\mathbf{a}$ and $\mathbf{b}$ are two non-zero, non-collinear vectors and x and y are two scalars such that $x\mathbf{a} + y\mathbf{b} = \mathbf{0}$, then $x = 0$ and $y = 0$ because one will be a scalar multiple of the other and hence collinear which is a contradiction.

24. We have,

$\mathbf{ON} = \mathbf{OL} + \mathbf{LN} = \mathbf{OL} + \mathbf{OM}$

Let $\mathbf{OL} = x\mathbf{OA}$, $\mathbf{OM} = y\mathbf{OB}$ and $\mathbf{ON} = z\mathbf{OC}$

So, $|\mathbf{OL}| = x|\mathbf{OA}|$, $|\mathbf{OM}| = y|\mathbf{OB}|$ and $|\mathbf{ON}| = z|\mathbf{OC}|$

$\therefore \quad x = \dfrac{OL}{OA}, y = \dfrac{OM}{OB}$ and $z = \dfrac{ON}{OC}$

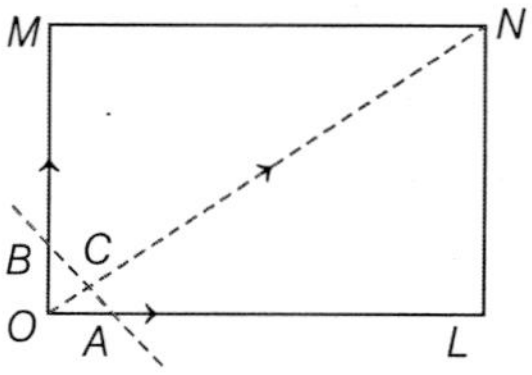

$z\,\mathbf{OC} = x\,\mathbf{OA} + y\,\mathbf{OB}$

$\Rightarrow \quad x\mathbf{OA} + y\mathbf{OB} - z\mathbf{OC} = \mathbf{0}$

$\therefore$ Points A, B and C are collinear, the sum of the coefficients of their PV must be zero.

$\Rightarrow \quad x + y - z = 0$

i.e. $\dfrac{OL}{OA} + \dfrac{OM}{OB} = \dfrac{ON}{OC}$

25. Given, $\mathbf{r}_1 = \mathbf{a} - \mathbf{b} + \mathbf{c}$, $\mathbf{r}_2 = \mathbf{b} + \mathbf{c} - \mathbf{a}$, $\mathbf{r}_3 = \mathbf{c} + \mathbf{a} + \mathbf{b}$

and $\mathbf{r} = 2\mathbf{a} - 3\mathbf{b} + 4\mathbf{c}$

Now, $\mathbf{r} = x_1\mathbf{r}_1 + x_2\mathbf{r}_2 + x_3\mathbf{r}_3$

$\Rightarrow \quad 2\mathbf{a} - 3\mathbf{b} + 4\mathbf{c} = x_1(\mathbf{a} - \mathbf{b} + \mathbf{c}) + x_2(\mathbf{b} + \mathbf{c} - \mathbf{a}) + x_3(\mathbf{c} + \mathbf{a} + \mathbf{b})$

$\Rightarrow \quad 2\mathbf{a} - 3\mathbf{b} + 4\mathbf{c} = (x_1 - x_2 + x_3)\mathbf{a} + (-x_1 + x_2 + x_3)\mathbf{b} + (x_1 + x_2 + x_3)\mathbf{c}$

On equating coefficients of $\mathbf{a}$, $\mathbf{b}$ and $\mathbf{c}$, we get

$x_1 - x_2 + x_3 = 2$ ...(i)

$-x_1 + x_2 + x_3 = -3$ ...(ii)

and $x_1 + x_2 + x_3 = 4$ ...(iii)

On solving Eqs. (i), (ii) and (iii), we get

$x_1 = \dfrac{7}{2}$, $x_2 = 1$ and $x_3 = -\dfrac{1}{2}$

$\therefore x_2 + x_3 = 1 - \dfrac{1}{2} \Rightarrow x_2 + x_3 = \dfrac{1}{2}$

26. Let the B divide AC in ratio $\lambda : 1$, then

$5\hat{\mathbf{i}} - 2\hat{\mathbf{k}} = \dfrac{\lambda(11\hat{\mathbf{i}} + 3\hat{\mathbf{j}} + 7\hat{\mathbf{k}}) + \hat{\mathbf{i}} - 2\hat{\mathbf{j}} - 8\hat{\mathbf{k}}}{\lambda + 1}$

$\Rightarrow \quad 3\lambda - 2 = 0$

$\Rightarrow \quad \lambda = \dfrac{2}{3}$, i.e. ratio $= 2 : 3$

27. Since, **a** and **b** are non-collinear, so **a** + **b** and **a** − **b** will also be non-collinear.
Hence, **a** + **b** and **a** − **b** are linearly independent vectors.

28. Since, **x**, **y** and **x** × **y** are linearly independent, we have
$$20a - 15b = 15b - 12c = 12c - 20a = 0$$
$$\Rightarrow \quad \frac{a}{3} = \frac{b}{4} = \frac{c}{5}$$
$$\Rightarrow \quad c^2 = a^2 + b^2$$
Hence, ΔABC is right angled.

29. As **x**, **y** and **x** × **y** are non-collinear vectors, vectors are linearly independent.
Hence,
$$a - b = 0 = b - c = c - a$$
$$\text{or } a = b = c$$
Therefore, the triangle is equilateral.

30. Given, $\mathbf{a} = \hat{\mathbf{i}} + 2\hat{\mathbf{j}} + 3\hat{\mathbf{k}}$, $\mathbf{b} = 2\hat{\mathbf{i}} - \hat{\mathbf{j}} + \hat{\mathbf{k}}$ and $\mathbf{c} = 3\hat{\mathbf{i}} + \hat{\mathbf{j}} + 4\hat{\mathbf{k}}$.
Now, $\mathbf{a} + \mathbf{b} = 3\hat{\mathbf{i}} + \hat{\mathbf{j}} + 4\hat{\mathbf{k}} = \mathbf{c}$
$$\therefore \quad \mathbf{a} + \mathbf{b} = \mathbf{c}$$
This show that vectors are coplanar but cannot form a triangle.

31. A, B, C, D and E are five coplanar points.
$$\mathbf{DA} + \mathbf{DB} + \mathbf{DC} + \mathbf{AE} + \mathbf{BE} + \mathbf{CE}$$
$$= (\mathbf{DA} + \mathbf{AE}) + (\mathbf{DB} + \mathbf{BE}) + (\mathbf{DC} + \mathbf{CE})$$
$$= \mathbf{DE} + \mathbf{DE} + \mathbf{DE} = 3\mathbf{DE}$$

32. Four or more than four non-zero vectors are always linearly dependent.

33. The vectors are linearly dependent
$$\Rightarrow \quad \begin{vmatrix} p+1 & -3 & p \\ p & p+1 & -3 \\ -3 & p & p+1 \end{vmatrix} = 0$$
$$\Rightarrow \quad (2p-2)\begin{vmatrix} 1 & -3 & p \\ 1 & p+1 & -3 \\ 1 & p & p+1 \end{vmatrix} = 0$$
$$\Rightarrow \quad 2(p-1)\begin{vmatrix} 1 & -3 & p \\ 0 & p+4 & -3-p \\ 0 & p+3 & 1 \end{vmatrix} = 0$$
$$\Rightarrow \quad 2(p-1)(p+4+(p+3)^2) = 0$$
$$\Rightarrow \quad (p-1)(p^2+7p+13) = 0$$
Roots of $p^2 + 7p + 13 = 0$ are (imaginary)
$$\therefore \quad p = 1$$
Only integral value of p is 1.

34. **Decoding the Question**
Apply the condition of linearly independent i.e. **a** and **b** are said to be linearly independent
if $\quad \mathbf{a}x_1 + \mathbf{b}x_2 = 0 \Rightarrow x_1 = x_2 = 0.$

$\sqrt{3}\tan\theta + 1 = 0$ and $\sqrt{3}\sec\theta - 2 = 0$
$$\Rightarrow \quad \theta = \frac{11\pi}{6} \Rightarrow \theta = 2n\pi + \frac{11\pi}{6}, n \in Z$$

35. Clearly **a**, **b** and **c** must be coplanar
$$\Rightarrow \quad \mathbf{c} = \lambda\mathbf{a} + \mu\mathbf{b}$$
$$\Rightarrow \hat{\mathbf{i}} + x_1\hat{\mathbf{j}} + x_2\hat{\mathbf{k}} = \lambda(\hat{\mathbf{i}} + \hat{\mathbf{j}} + \hat{\mathbf{k}}) + \mu(4\hat{\mathbf{i}} + 3\hat{\mathbf{j}} + 4\hat{\mathbf{k}})$$
$\therefore \quad 1 = \lambda + 4\mu$, $x_1 = \lambda + 3\mu$ and $x_2 = \lambda + 4\mu$
$\therefore x_2 = 1$
Given, $|\mathbf{c}| = 2 \Rightarrow \sqrt{1 + x_1^2 + x_2^2} = 2$
$$\Rightarrow 2 + x_1^2 = 4$$
$$\therefore \quad x_1^2 = 2$$
Then, $729x_1^4 + 343x_1^2x_2^2 + 81x_2^2 + 15$
$$= 729(2)^2 + 343(2)(1)^2 + 81(1)^2 + 15$$
$$= 2916 + 686 + 81 + 15 = 3698$$

36. Let the origin of reference be the circumcentre of the triangle.
Let **OA** = **a**, **OB** = **b**, **OC** = **c** and **OT** = **t**
Then, $|\mathbf{a}| = |\mathbf{b}| = |\mathbf{c}| = R$
Again, **OA** + **OB** + **OC** = **OA** + 2**OD** = **OA** + **AH** = **OH**
∴The position vector of H is **a** + **b** + **c**.

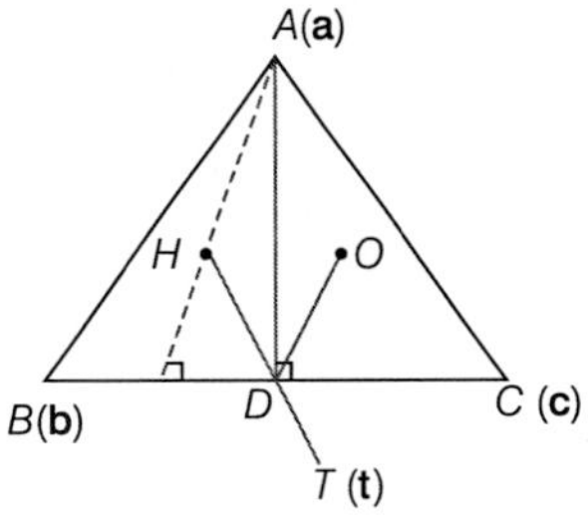

Since, D is the mid-point of HT, we have
$$\frac{\mathbf{a} + \mathbf{b} + \mathbf{c} + \mathbf{t}}{2} = \frac{\mathbf{b} + \mathbf{c}}{2} \Rightarrow \mathbf{t} = -\mathbf{a}$$
$\therefore$ **AT** = −2**a** or $AT = |-2\mathbf{a}| = 2|\mathbf{a}| = 2R$
But $BC = 2R\sin A = R$
$$\therefore \quad AT = 2BC \Rightarrow BC = \frac{1}{2}AT$$
Hence, $\lambda = \frac{1}{2} = 0.5$

37. Given vectors $2\hat{\mathbf{i}} + 3\hat{\mathbf{j}} + \hat{\mathbf{k}}$, $-2\hat{\mathbf{i}} + 4\hat{\mathbf{j}} - 2\hat{\mathbf{k}}$ and $\lambda\hat{\mathbf{i}} + \mu\hat{\mathbf{j}} + 4\hat{\mathbf{k}}$ are coplanar
$$\therefore \quad \begin{vmatrix} 2 & 3 & 1 \\ -2 & 4 & -2 \\ \lambda & \mu & 4 \end{vmatrix} = 0$$
$$\Rightarrow \quad 2(16 + 2\mu) + 2(12 - \mu) + \lambda(-6 - 4) = 0$$
$$\Rightarrow \quad 32 + 4\mu + 24 - 2\mu - 10\lambda = 0$$
$$\Rightarrow \quad 2\mu - 10\lambda + 56 = 0$$
$$\Rightarrow \quad \mu - 5\lambda + 28 = 0 \quad \text{...(i)}$$
Also, given $\quad 2\mu - \lambda - 22 = 0 \quad$ ...(ii)
On solving Eqs. (i) and (ii), we get
$$\lambda + \mu = 24$$

38. **AB** + **AC** = 2**AD**
$$\therefore \quad \mathbf{AD} = \frac{1}{2}(\mathbf{AB} + \mathbf{AC})$$

$$\Rightarrow \quad \mathbf{AD} = \frac{1}{2}[-3\hat{\mathbf{i}} + 4\hat{\mathbf{k}} + 5\hat{\mathbf{i}} - 2\hat{\mathbf{j}} + 4\hat{\mathbf{k}}]$$

$$= \frac{1}{2}[2\hat{\mathbf{i}} - 2\hat{\mathbf{j}} + 8\hat{\mathbf{k}}]$$

$$= \hat{\mathbf{i}} - \hat{\mathbf{j}} + 4\hat{\mathbf{k}}$$

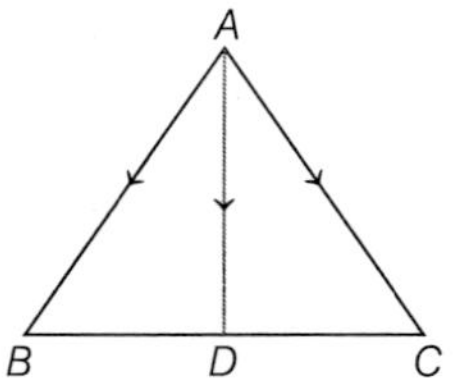

Length of $|AD| = \sqrt{(1)^2 + (-1)^2 + (4)^2}$

$= \sqrt{1 + 1 + 16} = \sqrt{18} = 3\sqrt{2}$

$= 3 \times 1.41 = 4.23$

39. Given, $(\hat{\mathbf{i}} + \hat{\mathbf{j}} + 3\hat{\mathbf{k}})x + (3\hat{\mathbf{i}} - 3\hat{\mathbf{j}} + \hat{\mathbf{k}})y + (-4\hat{\mathbf{i}} + 5\hat{\mathbf{j}})z$

$$= \lambda(x\hat{\mathbf{i}} + y\hat{\mathbf{j}} + z\hat{\mathbf{k}})$$

Comparing coefficient of $\hat{\mathbf{i}}$,

$$x + 3y - 4z = \lambda x \Rightarrow (1 - \lambda)x + 3y - 4z = 0 \quad \text{...(i)}$$

Similarly, for $\hat{\mathbf{j}}$ and $\hat{\mathbf{k}}$, we get

$$x - (3 + \lambda)y + 5z = 0 \quad \text{...(ii)}$$

and $$3x + y - \lambda z = 0 \quad \text{...(iii)}$$

All the above three equation are satisfied for x, y and z not for all zero, if

$$\begin{vmatrix} 1-\lambda & 3 & -4 \\ 1 & -(3+\lambda) & 5 \\ 3 & 1 & -\lambda \end{vmatrix} = 0$$

$$\Rightarrow \quad \lambda^3 + 2\lambda^2 + \lambda = 0$$

$$\Rightarrow \quad \lambda(\lambda + 1)^2 = 0$$

$\therefore \quad \lambda = 0, -1, -1$

$$\sum_{\lambda \in S} (\lambda + 5)^2 = (0 + 5)^2 + (-1 + 5)^2 + (-1 + 5)^2$$

$$= 25 + 16 + 16 = 57$$

40. Let the position vector of A, B and D be $\mathbf{0}$, $\mathbf{b}$ and $\mathbf{d}$, respectively.

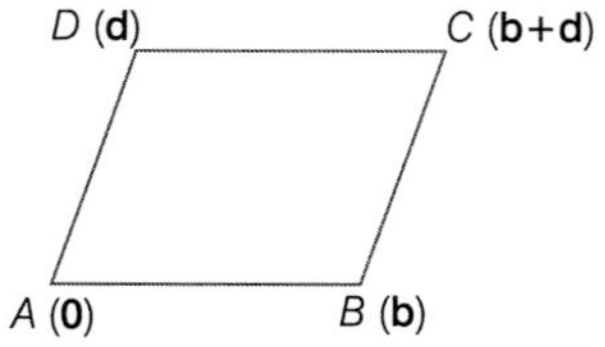

The position vector of $C = \mathbf{b} + \mathbf{d}$

Position vector of $A_1 = \mathbf{b} + \frac{\mathbf{d}}{2}$

and position vector of $B_1 = \mathbf{d} + \frac{\mathbf{b}}{2}$

$$= \mathbf{AA}_1 + \mathbf{AB}_1 = \frac{3}{2}(\mathbf{b} + \mathbf{d}) = \frac{3}{2}\mathbf{AC}$$

$\therefore \lambda = \frac{3}{2} = 1.5$

41. Given vector $60\hat{\mathbf{i}} + 3\hat{\mathbf{j}}$, $40\hat{\mathbf{i}} - 8\hat{\mathbf{j}}$ and $a\hat{\mathbf{i}} - 52\hat{\mathbf{j}}$ are collinear.

$$\therefore \ (40\hat{\mathbf{i}} - 8\hat{\mathbf{j}}) - (60\hat{\mathbf{i}} + 3\hat{\mathbf{j}}) = \lambda[(a\hat{\mathbf{i}} - 52\hat{\mathbf{j}}) - (40\hat{\mathbf{i}} - 8\hat{\mathbf{j}})]$$

$$-20\hat{\mathbf{i}} - 11\hat{\mathbf{j}} = \lambda(a - 40)\hat{\mathbf{i}} - \lambda(44\hat{\mathbf{j}})$$

$\therefore \lambda(a - 40) = -20$ and $-11 = -44\lambda$

$$\lambda = \frac{1}{4}$$

$$\therefore \quad \frac{1}{4}(a - 40) = -20$$

$$\Rightarrow \quad a - 40 = -80$$

$$\Rightarrow \quad a = -40$$

$$\Rightarrow \quad a^2 = (-40)^2 = 1600$$

42. Taking A be the origin.

Let position vector of B and C be $\mathbf{b}$ and $\mathbf{c}$, respectively.

position vector of D is $\frac{\mathbf{b} + \mathbf{c}}{2}$

and position vector of $E = \frac{\mathbf{b} + \mathbf{c}}{4}$

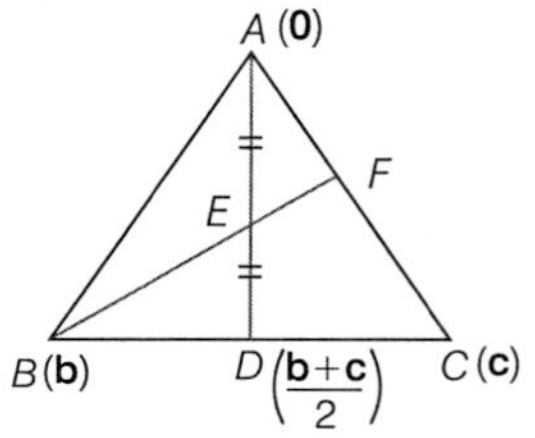

Let $AF : FC = \lambda : 1$

Then, position vector of $F = \frac{\lambda \mathbf{c}}{\lambda + 1}$ ...(i)

Let $BF : EF = \mu : 1$

position vector of F is $\frac{\mu\left(\frac{\mathbf{b} + \mathbf{c}}{4}\right) - \mathbf{b}}{\mu - 1}$ ...(ii)

Comparing position vector of F in Eqs. (i) and (ii), we have

$$\frac{\lambda \mathbf{c}}{\lambda + 1} = \frac{\frac{\mu(\mathbf{b} + \mathbf{c})}{4} - \mathbf{b}}{\mu - 1}$$

Since, vector $\mathbf{b}$ and $\mathbf{c}$ are independent, we have

$$\frac{\lambda}{\lambda + 1} = \frac{\mu}{4(\mu - 1)} \text{ and } \frac{\mu - 4}{4(\mu - 1)} = 0$$

$$\Rightarrow \quad \lambda = \frac{1}{2} \text{ and } \mu = 4$$

$$\therefore \quad AF : FC = \frac{1}{2} \text{ or } FC : AF = 2 : 1$$

43. Given vector $\mathbf{a} = 3\hat{\mathbf{i}} - 7\hat{\mathbf{j}} - 4\hat{\mathbf{k}}$, $\mathbf{b} = \alpha\hat{\mathbf{i}} - \beta\hat{\mathbf{j}} + \hat{\mathbf{k}}$ and $\mathbf{c} = \hat{\mathbf{i}} + \hat{\mathbf{j}} + 2\hat{\mathbf{k}}$ are linearly dependent, hence there exists scalars x, y and z are not all zero such that $x\mathbf{a} + y\mathbf{b} + z\mathbf{c} = 0$.

$$x(3\hat{\mathbf{i}} - 7\hat{\mathbf{j}} - 4\hat{\mathbf{k}}) + y(\alpha\hat{\mathbf{i}} - \beta\hat{\mathbf{j}} + \hat{\mathbf{k}}) + z(\hat{\mathbf{i}} + \hat{\mathbf{j}} + 2\hat{\mathbf{k}}) = 0$$

$$\Rightarrow (3x + \alpha y + z)\hat{\mathbf{i}} + (-7x - \beta y + z)\hat{\mathbf{j}} + (-4x + y + 2z)\hat{\mathbf{k}} = 0$$

$$\Rightarrow 3x + \alpha y + z = 0, 7x + \beta y - z = 0, 4x - y - 2z = 0$$

For non-trivial solution,
$$\begin{vmatrix} 3 & \alpha & 1 \\ 7 & \beta & -1 \\ 4 & -1 & -2 \end{vmatrix} = 0$$

$\Rightarrow \quad 3(-2\beta - 1) - \alpha(-14 + 4) + 1(-7 - 4\beta) = 0$

$\Rightarrow \quad -6\beta - 3 + 10\alpha - 7 - 4\beta = 0$

$\Rightarrow \quad 10\alpha - 10\beta = 10$

$\Rightarrow \quad \alpha - \beta = 1 \qquad$ ...(i)

Also, given $|\mathbf{b}| = \sqrt{14}$

$\therefore \quad \alpha^2 + \beta^2 + 1 = 14 \Rightarrow \alpha^2 + \beta^2 = 13 \qquad$ ...(ii)

On solving Eqs. (i) and (ii), we get

$$\alpha = 3 \text{ and } \beta = 2$$

$\therefore (\alpha^3 + \beta^3) = 3^3 + 2^3 = 27 + 8 = 35$

44. $\because \quad \mathbf{PQ} = (2\hat{\mathbf{i}} + 3\hat{\mathbf{j}} - 4\hat{\mathbf{k}}) - (3\hat{\mathbf{i}} - 2\hat{\mathbf{j}} - \hat{\mathbf{k}}) = -\hat{\mathbf{i}} + 5\hat{\mathbf{j}} - 3\hat{\mathbf{k}}$

$\mathbf{PR} = (-\hat{\mathbf{i}} + \hat{\mathbf{j}} + 2\hat{\mathbf{k}}) - (3\hat{\mathbf{i}} - 2\hat{\mathbf{j}} - \hat{\mathbf{k}}) = -4\hat{\mathbf{i}} + 3\hat{\mathbf{j}} + 3\hat{\mathbf{k}}$

and $\mathbf{PS} = (4\hat{\mathbf{i}} + 5\hat{\mathbf{j}} + \alpha\hat{\mathbf{k}}) - (3\hat{\mathbf{i}} - 2\hat{\mathbf{j}} - \hat{\mathbf{k}}) = \hat{\mathbf{i}} + 7\hat{\mathbf{j}} + (\alpha + 1)\hat{\mathbf{k}}$

Vector **PQ**, **PR** and **PS** will be coplanar.

$$\Rightarrow \begin{vmatrix} -1 & 5 & -3 \\ -4 & 3 & 3 \\ 1 & 7 & \alpha + 1 \end{vmatrix} = 0 \Rightarrow 17\alpha + 146 = 0 \Rightarrow -17\alpha = 146$$

45. Given, $a\hat{\mathbf{i}} + b\hat{\mathbf{j}} + \frac{1}{2}\hat{\mathbf{k}}$ is linearly dependent with $\hat{\mathbf{i}} + 2\hat{\mathbf{j}}$ and $\hat{\mathbf{j}} - 2\hat{\mathbf{k}}$.

$\therefore \quad a\hat{\mathbf{i}} + b\hat{\mathbf{j}} + \frac{1}{2}\hat{\mathbf{k}} = x(\hat{\mathbf{i}} + 2\hat{\mathbf{j}}) + y(\hat{\mathbf{j}} - 2\hat{\mathbf{k}})$

$\Rightarrow \quad a\hat{\mathbf{i}} + b\hat{\mathbf{j}} + \frac{1}{2}\hat{\mathbf{k}} = x\hat{\mathbf{i}} + (2x + y)\hat{\mathbf{j}} - 2y\hat{\mathbf{k}}$

On equating coefficients of $\hat{\mathbf{i}}$, $\hat{\mathbf{j}}$ and $\hat{\mathbf{k}}$, we get

$a = x \qquad$ ...(i)

$b = 2x + y \qquad$ ...(ii)

and $\quad \frac{1}{2} = -2y \Rightarrow y = -\frac{1}{4} \qquad$ ...(iii)

Also, given $\left|a\hat{\mathbf{i}} + b\hat{\mathbf{j}} + \frac{1}{2}\hat{\mathbf{k}}\right| = 1 \Rightarrow \sqrt{a^2 + b^2 + \frac{1}{4}} = 1$

$\Rightarrow \quad a^2 + b^2 = 1 - \frac{1}{4} \Rightarrow a^2 + b^2 = \frac{3}{4}$

$\Rightarrow \quad a^2 + \left(2a - \frac{1}{4}\right)^2 = \frac{3}{4} \qquad$ [using Eqs. (i), (ii) and (ii)]

$\Rightarrow \quad a^2 + 4a^2 + \frac{1}{16} - a = \frac{3}{4} \Rightarrow 5a^2 - a = \frac{3}{4} - \frac{1}{16}$

$\Rightarrow \quad 5a^2 - a = \frac{11}{16} \Rightarrow 16(5a^2 - a) = 11$

46. Given position vectors of the vertices A, B, C of ΔABC are $2\hat{\mathbf{i}} - 3\hat{\mathbf{j}} + 3\hat{\mathbf{k}}$, $2\hat{\mathbf{i}} + 2\hat{\mathbf{j}} + 3\hat{\mathbf{k}}$ and $-\hat{\mathbf{i}} + \hat{\mathbf{j}} + 3\hat{\mathbf{k}}$ respectively.

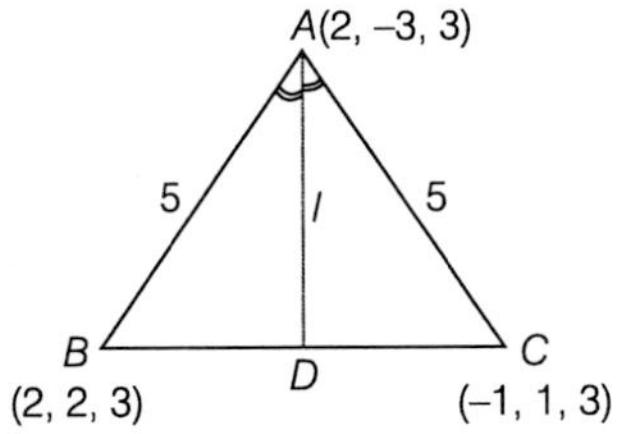

So, coordinates of $A \equiv (2, -3, 3)$, $B \equiv (2, 2, 3)$ and $C \equiv (-1, 1, 3)$

Now, $AB = 5$ and $AC = 5$

As we know that

$$\frac{BD}{DC} = \frac{AB}{AC} \Rightarrow \frac{BD}{DC} = \frac{5}{5} = \frac{1}{1} \Rightarrow BD = DC$$

i.e. D is mid-point of BC.

Now, $\quad D \equiv \left(\frac{2-1}{2}, \frac{2+1}{2}, \frac{3+3}{2}\right) \equiv \left(\frac{1}{2}, \frac{3}{2}, 3\right)$

Hence, $\quad l = AD$

$$= \sqrt{\left(2 - \frac{1}{2}\right)^2 + \left(-3 - \frac{3}{2}\right)^2 + (3-3)^2}$$

$$= \sqrt{\frac{9}{4} + \frac{81}{4}} = \sqrt{\frac{90}{4}} = \sqrt{\frac{45}{2}}$$

$\therefore \quad 2l^2 = 2 \times \frac{45}{2} = 45$

47. **Decoding the Question**

First check whether the triangle is an equilateral or not. If triangle is an equilateral, then we know that here orthocenter and centroid will be same.

Given, position vectors of the vertices A, B, C are $2\hat{\mathbf{i}} + 2\hat{\mathbf{j}} + \hat{\mathbf{k}}$, $\hat{\mathbf{i}} + 2\hat{\mathbf{j}} + 2\hat{\mathbf{k}}$ and $2\hat{\mathbf{i}} + \hat{\mathbf{j}} + 2\hat{\mathbf{k}}$, respectively.

So, coordinates of $A \equiv (2, 2, 1)$, $B \equiv (1, 2, 2)$ and $C \equiv (2, 1, 2)$

l_1: Length of perpendicular drawn from orthocentre of ΔABC on AB.

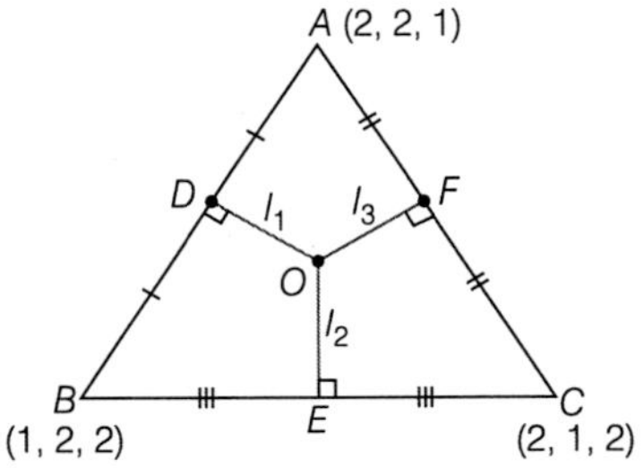

l_2: Length of perpendicular drawn from orthocentre of ΔABC on BC.

l_3: Length of perpendicular drawn from orthocentre of ΔABC on CA.

Now, $AB = \sqrt{(2-1)^2 + (2-2)^2 + (1-2)^2} = \sqrt{1 + 0 + 1} = \sqrt{2}$

$BC = \sqrt{(1-2)^2 + (2-1)^2 + (2-2)^2} = \sqrt{1 + 1 + 0} = \sqrt{2}$

$CA = \sqrt{(2-2)^2 + (1-2)^2 + (2-1)^2} = \sqrt{0 + 1 + 1} = \sqrt{2}$

This represents ΔABC is an equilateral triangle.

As we known that, in an equilateral triangle, orthocentre and centroid will be same [coincide].

So, centroid $\equiv \left(\frac{5}{3}, \frac{5}{3}, \frac{5}{3}\right)$

Let D be the mid-point of $AB = \left(\frac{3}{2}, 2, \frac{3}{2}\right)$

$\therefore \; l_1 = \sqrt{\frac{1}{36} + \frac{1}{9} + \frac{1}{36}} = \frac{1}{\sqrt{6}} = l_2 = l_3$

Hence, $l_1^2 + l_2^2 + l_3^2 = \frac{1}{6} + \frac{1}{6} + \frac{1}{6} = 3\left(\frac{1}{6}\right) = \frac{1}{2}$

48. We have, $\mathbf{a} + 5\mathbf{b} = \lambda\mathbf{c}$ ...(i)

and $\mathbf{b} + 6\mathbf{c} = \mu\mathbf{a}$ ...(ii)

From Eq. (i), we have,

$$\mathbf{a} = \lambda\mathbf{c} - 5\mathbf{b}$$

$\therefore \quad \mathbf{b} + 6\mathbf{c} = \mu(\lambda\mathbf{c} - 5\mathbf{b})$ [from Eq. (ii)]

$$\Rightarrow \frac{\mathbf{b}}{\mu} + \frac{6}{\mu}\mathbf{c} = \lambda\mathbf{c} - 5\mathbf{b}$$

$$\therefore \frac{6}{\mu} = \lambda \text{ and } \frac{1}{\mu} = -5$$

$$\Rightarrow \mu = -\frac{1}{5}$$

$$\Rightarrow \lambda = -30$$

$\therefore \quad \mathbf{a} + 5\mathbf{b} + 30\mathbf{c} = \mathbf{0}$ [from Eq. (i)]

$$\Rightarrow \alpha = 5 \text{ and } \beta = 30$$

$$\therefore \alpha + \beta = 5 + 30 = 35$$

49. We have, $\mathbf{OA} = 2\hat{\mathbf{i}} + 2\hat{\mathbf{j}} + \hat{\mathbf{k}}$

$$\mathbf{OB} = 2\hat{\mathbf{i}} + 4\hat{\mathbf{j}} + 4\hat{\mathbf{k}}$$

$$|\mathbf{OA}| = \sqrt{4 + 4 + 1} = \sqrt{9} = 3$$

$$|\mathbf{OB}| = \sqrt{4 + 16 + 16} = 6$$

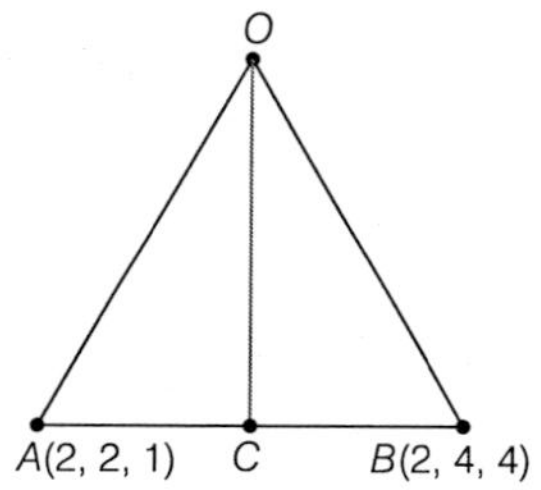

$$\Rightarrow \frac{OA}{OB} = \frac{3}{6} = \frac{1}{2}$$

$$\Rightarrow \frac{AC}{BC} = \frac{1}{2}$$

$$\therefore \mathbf{OC} = \frac{1 \times (2\hat{\mathbf{i}} + 4\hat{\mathbf{j}} + 4\hat{\mathbf{k}}) + 2(2\hat{\mathbf{i}} + 2\hat{\mathbf{j}} + \hat{\mathbf{k}})}{1 + 2}$$

$$= \frac{6\hat{\mathbf{i}} + 8\hat{\mathbf{j}} + 6\hat{\mathbf{k}}}{3}$$

$$\therefore |\mathbf{OC}| = \frac{\sqrt{36 + 64 + 36}}{3}$$

$$= \frac{\sqrt{136}}{3} = \frac{2\sqrt{34}}{3}$$

50. Let the position vectors of vertices A, B, C and D of quadrilateral $ABCD$ be **a**, **b**, **c** and **d**, respectively.

E is the mid-point of AC.

$\therefore$ Position vector of $E = \frac{1}{2}(\mathbf{a} + \mathbf{c})$

F is the mid-point of BD.

$\therefore$ Position vector of $F = \frac{1}{2}(\mathbf{b} + \mathbf{d})$

$\therefore$ **EF** = (position vector of F) – (position vector of E)

$$= \frac{1}{2}(\mathbf{b} + \mathbf{d}) - \frac{1}{2}(\mathbf{a} + \mathbf{c}) = \frac{1}{2}(\mathbf{b} + \mathbf{d} - \mathbf{a} - \mathbf{c})$$

Now, $\mathbf{AB} + \mathbf{AD} + \mathbf{CB} + \mathbf{CD} = (\mathbf{b} - \mathbf{a}) + (\mathbf{d} - \mathbf{a}) + (\mathbf{b} - \mathbf{c}) + (\mathbf{d} - \mathbf{c})$

$$= 2(\mathbf{b} + \mathbf{d} - \mathbf{a} - \mathbf{c}) = 2 \times 2\mathbf{EF}$$

$$\Rightarrow \mathbf{AB} + \mathbf{AD} + \mathbf{CD} + \mathbf{CB} = 4\mathbf{EF}$$

$$\Rightarrow \mathbf{AB} + (-\mathbf{BC}) + \mathbf{AD} + (-\mathbf{DC}) = 4\mathbf{EF} = -4\mathbf{FE}$$

$$\Rightarrow (\mathbf{AB} - \mathbf{BC}) + (\mathbf{AD} - \mathbf{DC}) = -4\mathbf{FE} = k\mathbf{FE}$$

$$\Rightarrow k = -4$$

51. The given equation are coplanar.

$$\Rightarrow \begin{vmatrix} \lambda & -1 & 1 \\ 1 & 2 & \mu \\ 3 & -4 & 5 \end{vmatrix} = 0$$

$$\Rightarrow \lambda[10 + 4\mu] + 1[5 - 3\mu] + 1[-10] = 0$$

$\Rightarrow \quad 4\lambda\mu + 10\lambda - 3\mu = 5$ ...(i)

And $\lambda - \mu = 5 \Rightarrow \lambda = 5 + \mu$

Putting the value of λ in Eq. (i), we get

$$4(5 + \mu)\mu + 10(5 + \mu) - 3\mu = 5$$

$$\Rightarrow 4\mu^2 + 27\mu + 45 = 0$$

$$\Rightarrow 4\mu^2 + 15\mu + 12\mu + 45 = 0$$

$$\therefore \mu = -3, \frac{-15}{4}$$

$$\Rightarrow \lambda = 2, \frac{5}{4}$$

$$\therefore \sum_{(\lambda, \mu) \in S} 80(\lambda^2 + \mu^2) = 80\left[(9 + 4) + \frac{225}{16} + \frac{25}{16}\right]$$

$$= 80\left[13 + \frac{125}{8}\right]$$

$$= 10 \times 229$$

$$= 2290$$

52. Since, vectors are coplanar.

That means the determinant is equal to zero.

$$\Rightarrow \begin{vmatrix} a & 1 & 1 \\ 1 & b & 1 \\ 1 & 1 & c \end{vmatrix} = 0$$

$$\Rightarrow \begin{vmatrix} a-1 & 1-b & 0 \\ 0 & b-1 & 1-c \\ 1 & 1 & c \end{vmatrix} = 0$$

$[R_1 \to R_1 - R_2 \text{ and } R_2 \to R_2 - R_3]$

Expand the determinant along C_1,

$$\Rightarrow (a-1)[c(b-1) - (1-c)] + 1[(1-b)(1-c)] = 0$$

$$\Rightarrow c(a-1)(b-1) - (a-1)(1-c) + (1-b)(1-c) = 0$$

$$\Rightarrow c(1-a)(1-b) + (1-a)(1-c) + (1-b)(1-c)$$
$$+ (1-a)(1-b)(1-c) = (1-a)(1-b)(1-c)$$

$$\Rightarrow (1-a)(1-b) + (1-a)(1-c) + (1-b)(1-c)$$
$$= (1-a)(1-b)(1-c)$$

$$\Rightarrow \frac{1}{1-a} + \frac{1}{1-b} + \frac{1}{1-c} = 1$$

53. We have, $10|a_i| < 1, i = 1,2,3$

Let $|a_1| \ge |a_2| \ge |a_3|$

$$|\mathbf{a}| = \sqrt{a_1^2 + a_2^2 + a_3^2} \ge \sqrt{a_1^2}$$

$\therefore \quad |\mathbf{a}| \geq |a_1|$ or $\max\{|a_1|, |a_2|, |a_3|\}$

Hence, (A) is true.

$$|\mathbf{a}| = \sqrt{a_1^2 + a_2^2 + a_3^2} \leq \sqrt{a_1^2 + a_1^2 + a_1^2} = \sqrt{3}|a_1|$$

$\therefore \ |\mathbf{a}| = \sqrt{3}|a_1| < 3|a_1|$

$\therefore \ |\mathbf{a}| < 3\max\{|a_1|, |a_2|, |a_3|\}$

Hence, (B) is also true.

54. We have,

$$\mathbf{a} + 5\mathbf{b} = \lambda\mathbf{c} \qquad \text{...(i)}$$

and $$\mathbf{b} + 6\mathbf{c} = \mu\mathbf{a} \qquad \text{...(ii)}$$

From Eq. (i), we have,

$$\mathbf{a} = \lambda\mathbf{c} - 5\mathbf{b}$$

$\therefore \quad \mathbf{b} + 6\mathbf{c} = \mu(\lambda\mathbf{c} - 5\mathbf{b})$ [from Eq. (ii)]

$\Rightarrow \quad \dfrac{\mathbf{b}}{\mu} + \dfrac{6}{\mu}\mathbf{c} = \lambda\mathbf{c} - 5\mathbf{b}$

$\therefore \quad \dfrac{6}{\mu} = \lambda$ and $\dfrac{1}{\mu} = -5$

$\Rightarrow \quad \mu = -\dfrac{1}{5}$

$\Rightarrow \quad \lambda = -30$

$\therefore \quad \mathbf{a} + 5\mathbf{b} + 30\mathbf{c} = 0$

$\Rightarrow \quad \alpha = 5$ and $\beta = 30$

$\therefore \quad \alpha + \beta = 5 + 30 = 35$

55. An arc PQ of a circle subtends a right angle at its centre O. The mid-point of an arc PQ is R.

So, $\mathbf{PR} = \mathbf{RQ}$ also given that

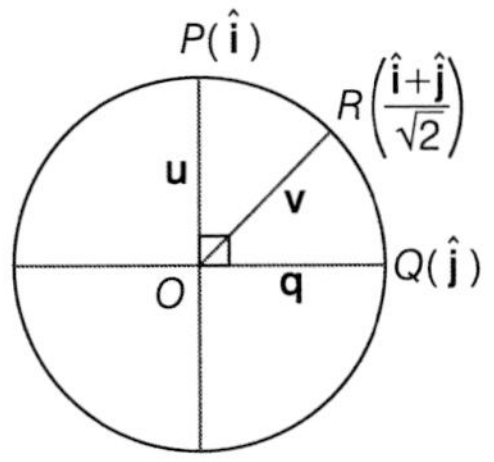

Let $\mathbf{OP} = \mathbf{u}$

$\mathbf{OQ} = \alpha\mathbf{u} + \beta\mathbf{v} = \mathbf{q}$

$\mathbf{OR} = \mathbf{v}$

Clearly, $\mathbf{q} = \hat{\mathbf{j}}, \ \mathbf{u} = \hat{\mathbf{i}}, \ \mathbf{v} = \dfrac{\hat{\mathbf{i}} + \hat{\mathbf{j}}}{\sqrt{2}}$ [say]

Now, given $\mathbf{q} = \alpha\mathbf{u} + \beta\mathbf{v}$

$\Rightarrow \quad \hat{\mathbf{j}} = \alpha(\hat{\mathbf{i}}) + \beta\left(\dfrac{\hat{\mathbf{i}} + \hat{\mathbf{j}}}{\sqrt{2}}\right)$

$\Rightarrow \quad \hat{\mathbf{j}} = \hat{\mathbf{i}}\left(\alpha + \dfrac{\beta}{\sqrt{2}}\right) + \dfrac{\beta}{\sqrt{2}}\hat{\mathbf{j}}$

On comparing both sides, we get

$$\alpha + \beta/\sqrt{2} = 0$$

and $$\frac{\beta}{\sqrt{2}} = 1$$

$\Rightarrow \quad \alpha = -\beta/\sqrt{2}, \ \beta = \sqrt{2}$

$\Rightarrow \quad \alpha = -1, \ \beta^2 = 2$

Now, α and β^2 are roots of the quadratic equation is $x^2 - x - 2 = 0$.

56. Given, $\mathbf{u}_1 = \hat{\mathbf{i}} + \hat{\mathbf{j}} + a\hat{\mathbf{k}}$, $\mathbf{u}_2 = \hat{\mathbf{i}} + b\hat{\mathbf{j}} + \hat{\mathbf{k}}$ and $\mathbf{u}_3 = c\hat{\mathbf{i}} + \hat{\mathbf{j}} + \hat{\mathbf{k}}$ are coplanar.

Also, given that $\mathbf{v}_1 = (a+b)\hat{\mathbf{i}} + c\hat{\mathbf{j}} + c\hat{\mathbf{k}}$, $\mathbf{v}_2 = a\hat{\mathbf{i}} + (b+c)\hat{\mathbf{j}} + a\hat{\mathbf{k}}$ and $\mathbf{v}_3 = b\hat{\mathbf{i}} + b\hat{\mathbf{j}} + (c+a)\hat{\mathbf{k}}$ are coplanar.

Now, using the condition of coplanar, we get

$$\Rightarrow \quad \begin{vmatrix} 1 & 1 & a \\ 1 & b & 1 \\ c & 1 & 1 \end{vmatrix} = 0$$

$\Rightarrow \ (b-1) - (1-c) + a(1-bc) = 0$

$\Rightarrow \quad a + b + c = 2 + abc \qquad \text{...(i)}$

Again, using the coplanar condition, we get

$$\Rightarrow \quad \begin{vmatrix} a+b & c & c \\ a & b+c & a \\ b & b & c+a \end{vmatrix} = 0$$

$$\Rightarrow \quad \begin{vmatrix} a+b & c & c \\ a & b+c & a \\ -2a & -2c & 0 \end{vmatrix} = 0 \quad [R_3 \to R_3 - (R_1 + R_2)]$$

$\Rightarrow (a+b)(0 + 2ac) - c(0 + 2a^2) + c(-2ac + 2a(b+c)) = 0$

$\Rightarrow \quad 2a^2c + 2abc - 2a^2c - 2ac^2 + 2abc + 2ac^2 = 0$

$\Rightarrow \quad abc = 0$

$\therefore \quad a + b + c = 2$ [from Eq. (i)]

$\therefore \quad 6(a + b + c) = 12$

57. Let $\mathbf{a} = \alpha\hat{\mathbf{i}} + 10\hat{\mathbf{j}} + 13\hat{\mathbf{k}}$, $\mathbf{b} = 6\hat{\mathbf{i}} + 11\hat{\mathbf{j}} + 11\hat{\mathbf{k}}$

and $\mathbf{c} = \dfrac{9}{2}\hat{\mathbf{i}} + \beta\hat{\mathbf{j}} - 8\hat{\mathbf{k}}$

If $P(\mathbf{a})$, $Q(\mathbf{b})$, $R(\mathbf{c})$ are collinear, then $\mathbf{PQ} \parallel \mathbf{QR} \parallel \mathbf{PR}$

Now, $\mathbf{PQ} = (6 - \alpha)\hat{\mathbf{i}} + \hat{\mathbf{j}} - 2\hat{\mathbf{k}}$

$$\mathbf{QR} = -\frac{3}{2}\hat{\mathbf{i}} + (\beta - 11)\hat{\mathbf{j}} - 19\hat{\mathbf{k}}$$

$$\mathbf{PQ} \parallel \mathbf{QR} = \frac{6 - \alpha}{-\frac{3}{2}} = \frac{1}{\beta - 11} = \frac{2}{19}$$

$\Rightarrow \quad 19\alpha = 117 \Rightarrow 6\beta = 123$

$\therefore (19\alpha - 6\beta)^2 = (117 - 123)^2 = 36$

58. Let the vectors be $\mathbf{A} = \hat{\mathbf{i}} - 2\hat{\mathbf{j}} + 3\hat{\mathbf{k}}$, $\mathbf{B} = 2\hat{\mathbf{i}} - 3\hat{\mathbf{j}} + 4\hat{\mathbf{k}}$, $\mathbf{C} = (\alpha + 1)\hat{\mathbf{i}} + 2\hat{\mathbf{k}}$ and $\mathbf{D} = 9\hat{\mathbf{i}} + (\alpha - 8)\hat{\mathbf{j}} + 6\hat{\mathbf{k}}$.

We know that if the vectors are coplanar, then

$$[\mathbf{AB} \ \ \mathbf{AC} \ \ \mathbf{AD}] = 0$$

$\Rightarrow \mathbf{AB} = (2\hat{\mathbf{i}} - 3\hat{\mathbf{j}} + 4\hat{\mathbf{k}}) - (\hat{\mathbf{i}} - 2\hat{\mathbf{j}} + 3\hat{\mathbf{k}}) = \hat{\mathbf{i}} - \hat{\mathbf{j}} + \hat{\mathbf{k}}$

$\Rightarrow \mathbf{AC} = ((\alpha + 1)\hat{\mathbf{i}} + 2\hat{\mathbf{k}}) - (\hat{\mathbf{i}} - 2\hat{\mathbf{j}} + 3\hat{\mathbf{k}}) = \alpha\hat{\mathbf{i}} + 2\hat{\mathbf{j}} - \hat{\mathbf{k}}$

$\Rightarrow \mathbf{AD} = (9\hat{\mathbf{i}} + (\alpha - 8)\hat{\mathbf{j}} + 6\hat{\mathbf{k}}) - (\hat{\mathbf{i}} - 2\hat{\mathbf{j}} + 3\hat{\mathbf{k}})$

$= 8\hat{\mathbf{i}} + (\alpha - 6)\hat{\mathbf{j}} + 3\hat{\mathbf{k}}$

Now, $\begin{vmatrix} 1 & -1 & 1 \\ \alpha & 2 & -1 \\ 8 & \alpha-6 & 3 \end{vmatrix} = 0$

$\Rightarrow 1(6+\alpha-6)+(3\alpha+8)+(\alpha^2-6\alpha-16)=0$

On simplifying, we get

$$\alpha^2-2\alpha-8=0$$

Therefore, sum of the roots is $-(-2)=2$.

59. $\begin{vmatrix} \lambda & \mu & 4 \\ -2 & 4 & -2 \\ 2 & 3 & 1 \end{vmatrix} = 0$

$\Rightarrow \lambda(10)-\mu(2)+4(-14)=0$

$\Rightarrow \quad 10\lambda-2\mu=56 \quad$ ...(i)

$\Rightarrow \quad 5\lambda-\mu=28$

$$\frac{\mathbf{a}\cdot\mathbf{b}}{|\mathbf{b}|}=\sqrt{54}$$

$\Rightarrow \quad \dfrac{-2\lambda+4\mu-8}{\sqrt{24}}=\sqrt{54}$

$\Rightarrow \quad -2\lambda+4\mu-8=\sqrt{54\times 24} \quad$ ...(ii)

On solving Eqs. (i) and (ii), we get

$$\lambda+\mu=24$$

60. $\mathbf{AB}=(\lambda-1)\mathbf{a}-2\mathbf{b}+3\mathbf{c}$

$\mathbf{AC}=-2\mathbf{a}-\mathbf{b}-4\mathbf{c}$

$\mathbf{AD}=\mathbf{a}-3\mathbf{b}+5\mathbf{c}$

$\therefore \quad \begin{vmatrix} \lambda-1 & -2 & 3 \\ -2 & -1 & -4 \\ 1 & -3 & 5 \end{vmatrix} = 0$

$\Rightarrow (\lambda-1)(-5-12)+2(-10+4)+3(6+1)=0$

$\Rightarrow \quad -17\lambda+17-12+21=0$

$\Rightarrow \quad \lambda=\dfrac{26}{17}$

61. Let $P(3,-4,2)$, $R(-2,-1,3)$, $Q(1,2,-1)$, $S(5,-2\alpha,4)$

P, Q, R, S are coplanar points, then

$$\begin{vmatrix} 1-3 & 2+4 & -1-2 \\ -2-3 & -1+4 & 3-2 \\ 5-3 & -2\alpha+4 & 4-2 \end{vmatrix}=0$$

$\Rightarrow \quad \alpha=\dfrac{73}{17}$

62. $A(2,3,9)$; $B(5,2,1)$; $C(1,\lambda,8)$; $D(\lambda,2,3)$

$\therefore \quad [\mathbf{AB}\ \ \mathbf{AC}\ \ \mathbf{AD}]=0$

$\Rightarrow \quad \begin{vmatrix} 3 & -1 & -8 \\ -1 & \lambda-3 & -1 \\ \lambda-2 & -1 & -6 \end{vmatrix}=0$

$\Rightarrow 3[-6(\lambda-3)-1]-8[1-(\lambda-3)(\lambda-2)]+[6+(\lambda-2)]=0$

$\Rightarrow \quad 3(-6\lambda+17)-8(-\lambda^2+5\lambda-5)+(\lambda+4)=8$

$\Rightarrow \quad 8\lambda^2-57\lambda+95=0$

$\therefore \ \lambda_1\lambda_2=\dfrac{95}{8}$

63. According to given condition in question; **a**, **b** and **c** are linearly independent vectors .

So, scalar triple product of **a**, **b** and **c** are non-zero, i.e. $[\mathbf{a}\,\mathbf{b}\,\mathbf{c}]\neq 0$.

$\Rightarrow \quad \begin{vmatrix} 1+t & 1-t & 1 \\ 1-t & 1+t & 2 \\ t & -t & 1 \end{vmatrix}\neq 0$

$\Rightarrow \quad \begin{vmatrix} 1+t & 2 & 1 \\ 1-t & 2 & 2 \\ t & 0 & 1 \end{vmatrix}\neq 0 \quad$ [applying $C_2\to C_1+C_2$]

$\Rightarrow \quad 2\begin{vmatrix} 1+t & 1 & 1 \\ 1-t & 1 & 2 \\ t & 0 & 1 \end{vmatrix}\neq 0 \quad$ [taking 2 as common from C_2]

$\Rightarrow \quad 2[(1+t)-(1-t-2t)-t]\neq 0$

$\Rightarrow \quad 2(3t)\neq 0$

$\Rightarrow \quad t\neq 0$

Hence, $t\in R-\{0\}$

64. $\mathbf{OA}=\mathbf{a}=\hat{\mathbf{i}}+4\hat{\mathbf{j}}+3\hat{\mathbf{k}}$,

$\mathbf{OB}=\mathbf{b}=2\hat{\mathbf{i}}+\alpha\hat{\mathbf{j}}+4\hat{\mathbf{k}}$,

$\mathbf{OC}=\mathbf{c}=3\hat{\mathbf{i}}-2\hat{\mathbf{j}}+5\hat{\mathbf{k}}$

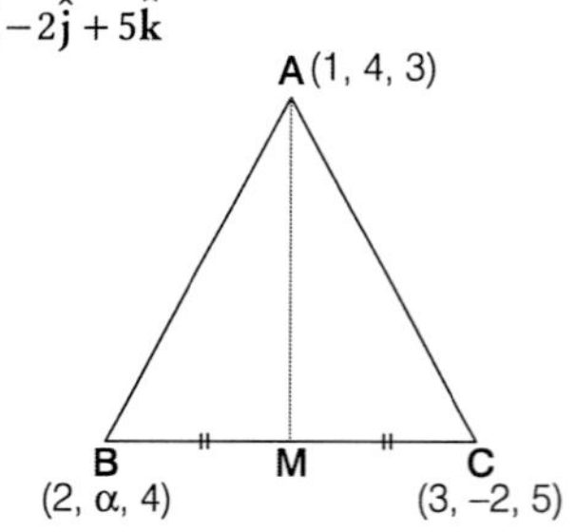

$$\mathbf{AB}=\mathbf{b}-\mathbf{a}=\hat{\mathbf{i}}+(\alpha-4)\hat{\mathbf{j}}+\hat{\mathbf{k}}$$

$$\mathbf{AC}=\mathbf{c}-\mathbf{a}=2\hat{\mathbf{i}}-6\hat{\mathbf{j}}+2\hat{\mathbf{k}}$$

$\mathbf{AB}\,||\,\mathbf{AC}$, if $\dfrac{1}{2}=\dfrac{\alpha-4}{-6}=\dfrac{1}{2}$

$\Rightarrow \quad \alpha-4=-3$

$\Rightarrow \quad \alpha=1$

a, **b** and **c** are non-collinear for $\alpha=2$ (smallest positive integer)

Mid-point of $BC=M\left(\dfrac{2+3}{2},\dfrac{2-2}{2},\dfrac{4+5}{2}\right)$

$$=M\left(\frac{5}{2},0,\frac{9}{2}\right)$$

$$AM=\sqrt{\left(\frac{5}{2}-1\right)^2+(0-4)^2+\left(\frac{9}{2}-3\right)^2}$$

$$=\sqrt{\frac{9}{4}+16+\frac{9}{4}}$$

$$=\sqrt{\frac{82}{4}}$$

$$=\frac{\sqrt{82}}{2}$$

65. If the vectors are coplanar,

$$\begin{vmatrix} a+b+2 & a+2b+c & -b-c \\ 1+b & 2b & -b \\ 2+b & 2b & 1-b \end{vmatrix} = 0$$

$$\therefore \quad \begin{vmatrix} a+1 & a+c & -c \\ b+1 & 2b & -b \\ 1 & 0 & 1 \end{vmatrix} = 0$$

$$[R_3 \to R_3 - R_2, R_1 \to R_1 - R_2]$$

$\Rightarrow (a+1)2b - (a+c)(2b+1) - c(-2b) = 0$

$\Rightarrow 2ab + 2b - 2ab - a - 2bc - c + 2bc = 0$

$\Rightarrow \quad 2b - a - c = 0$

Hence, $2b = a + c$

66. Given, $\mathbf{a}_1 = x\hat{\mathbf{i}} - \hat{\mathbf{j}} + \hat{\mathbf{k}}$ and $\mathbf{a}_2 = \hat{\mathbf{i}} + y\hat{\mathbf{j}} + z\hat{\mathbf{k}}$ are collinear, then

$\frac{x}{1} = \frac{-1}{y} = \frac{1}{z} = \lambda$ (say)

This gives $x = \lambda, y = -\frac{1}{\lambda}, z = \frac{1}{\lambda}$

Then, unit vector parallel to vector $x\hat{\mathbf{i}} + y\hat{\mathbf{j}} + z\hat{\mathbf{k}}$ will be

$$= \frac{\pm\left((\lambda)\hat{\mathbf{i}} - \left(\frac{1}{\lambda}\right)\hat{\mathbf{j}} + \left(\frac{1}{\lambda}\right)\hat{\mathbf{k}}\right)}{\sqrt{(\lambda)^2 + \left(\frac{-1}{\lambda}\right)^2 + \left(\frac{1}{\lambda}\right)^2}}$$

$$= \pm\frac{(\lambda^2\hat{\mathbf{i}} - \hat{\mathbf{j}} + \hat{\mathbf{k}})\lambda}{\lambda\sqrt{\lambda^4 + 2}}$$

$$= \pm\frac{(\lambda^2\hat{\mathbf{i}} - \hat{\mathbf{j}} + \hat{\mathbf{k}})}{\sqrt{\lambda^4 + 2}}$$

Take $\lambda = 1$,

$$= \frac{\pm(\hat{\mathbf{i}} - \hat{\mathbf{j}} + \hat{\mathbf{k}})}{\sqrt{3}}$$

67. Let $A(1, 5, 35)$, $B(7, 5, 5)$, $C(1, \lambda, 7)$, $D(2\lambda, 1, 2)$ are coplanar.

$$[\mathbf{AB} \quad \mathbf{AC} \quad \mathbf{AD}] = 0$$

$$\Rightarrow \quad \begin{vmatrix} 6 & 0 & -30 \\ 0 & \lambda-5 & -28 \\ 2\lambda-1 & -4 & -33 \end{vmatrix} = 0$$

$$\Rightarrow \quad \begin{vmatrix} 1 & 0 & -5 \\ 0 & \lambda-5 & -28 \\ 2\lambda-1 & -4 & -33 \end{vmatrix} = 0$$

$\Rightarrow (-33\lambda + 165 - 112) + 5(\lambda - 5)(2\lambda - 1) = 0$

$\Rightarrow \quad 53 - 33\lambda + 5(2\lambda^2 - 11\lambda + 5) = 0$

$\Rightarrow \quad 10\lambda^2 - 88\lambda + 78 = 0$

$\Rightarrow \quad 5\lambda^2 - 44\lambda + 39 = 0$

$\therefore \quad \lambda_1 + \lambda_2 = \frac{44}{5}$

Hence, the sum of all possible values of λ is $\frac{44}{5}$.

68. For these vectors to be coplanar,

$$[\mathbf{a} \quad \mathbf{b} \quad \mathbf{c}] = 0$$

$$\Rightarrow \quad \begin{vmatrix} \alpha & 1 & 3 \\ 2 & 1 & -\alpha \\ \alpha & -2 & 2 \end{vmatrix} = 0 \Rightarrow \begin{vmatrix} 0 & 3 & 1 \\ 2 & 1 & -\alpha \\ \alpha & -2 & 2 \end{vmatrix} = 0$$

$$[\because R_1 \to R_1 - R_3]$$

$\Rightarrow \quad -3(4 + \alpha^2) + 1(-4 - \alpha) = 0$

$\Rightarrow \quad 3\alpha^2 + \alpha + 16 = 0$

$\Rightarrow \quad \alpha = \frac{-1 \pm \sqrt{-191}}{6}$

Not possible for real number α.

Hence, S is empty.

69. Given unit vector $\mathbf{a}$ makes an angle $\frac{\pi}{3}$ with $\hat{\mathbf{i}}$, $\frac{\pi}{4}$ with $\hat{\mathbf{j}}$ and $\theta \in (0, \pi)$ with $\hat{\mathbf{k}}$.

Now, we know that $\cos^2\alpha + \cos^2\beta + \cos^2\gamma = 1$, where α, β, γ are angles made by the vectors with $\hat{\mathbf{i}}$, $\hat{\mathbf{j}}$ and $\hat{\mathbf{k}}$, respectively.

$\therefore \quad \cos^2\left(\frac{\pi}{3}\right) + \cos^2\left(\frac{\pi}{4}\right) + \cos^2\theta = 1$

$\Rightarrow \quad \frac{1}{4} + \frac{1}{2} + \cos^2\theta = 1$

$\Rightarrow \quad \cos^2\theta = \frac{1}{4} \Rightarrow \cos\theta = \pm\frac{1}{2}$

$\Rightarrow \quad \cos\theta = \cos\left(\frac{\pi}{3}\right)$ or $\cos\left(\frac{2\pi}{3}\right)$

$\Rightarrow \quad \theta = \frac{\pi}{3}$ or $\frac{2\pi}{3}$

So, θ is $\frac{2\pi}{3}$, according to options.

70. If the three vectors are coplanar, then

$$\begin{vmatrix} \mu & 1 & 1 \\ 1 & \mu & 1 \\ 1 & 1 & \mu \end{vmatrix} = 0$$

$\Rightarrow \quad \mu(\mu^2 - 1) - 1(\mu - 1) + 1(1 - \mu) = 0$

$\Rightarrow \quad \mu^3 - \mu - \mu + 1 + 1 - \mu = 0$

$\Rightarrow \quad \mu^3 - 3\mu + 2 = 0$

$\Rightarrow \quad (\mu - 1)(\mu^2 + \mu - 2) = 0$

$\Rightarrow \quad (\mu - 1)(\mu - 1)(\mu + 2) = 0$

$\Rightarrow \quad \mu = 1, 1, -2$

So, distinct real value of μ are 1 and -2.

Hence, sum of the distinct real values of μ is -1.

71. Two vectors $\mathbf{c}$ and $\mathbf{b}$ are said to be collinear if we can write $\mathbf{c} = \lambda\mathbf{b}$ for some non-zero scalar λ.

Let the vectors $\alpha = (\lambda - 2)\mathbf{a} + \mathbf{b}$ and $\beta = (4\lambda - 2)\mathbf{a} + 3\mathbf{b}$ are collinear, where $\mathbf{a}$ and $\mathbf{b}$ are non-collinear.

$\therefore$ We can write $\alpha = k\beta$, for some $k \in R - \{0\}$

$\Rightarrow \quad (\lambda - 2)\mathbf{a} + \mathbf{b} = k[(4\lambda - 2)\mathbf{a} + 3\mathbf{b}]$

$\Rightarrow \quad [(\lambda - 2) - k(4\lambda - 2)]\mathbf{a} + (1 - 3k)\mathbf{b} = 0$

Now, as $\mathbf{a}$ and $\mathbf{b}$ are non-collinear, therefore they are linearly independent and hence

$$(\lambda - 2) - k(4\lambda - 2) = 0 \text{ and } 1 - 3k = 0$$

$\Rightarrow \ \lambda - 2 = k(4\lambda - 2)$ and $3k = 1$

$\Rightarrow \ \lambda - 2 = \frac{1}{3}(4\lambda - 2) \qquad \left[\because 3k = 1 \Rightarrow k = \frac{1}{3}\right]$

$\Rightarrow 3\lambda - 6 = 4\lambda - 2 \Rightarrow \lambda = -4$

Exercise 2 - JEE Advanced Pattern

1. The point that divides $5\hat{\mathbf{i}}$ and $5\hat{\mathbf{j}}$ in the ratio of $k : 1$ is $\frac{(5\hat{\mathbf{j}})k + (5\hat{\mathbf{i}})1}{k+1}$

$$\therefore \quad \mathbf{b} = \frac{5\hat{\mathbf{i}} + 5k\hat{\mathbf{j}}}{k+1}$$

Also, $\quad |\mathbf{b}| \le \sqrt{37}$

$$\Rightarrow \quad \frac{1}{k+1}\sqrt{25 + 25k^2} \le \sqrt{37} \text{ or } 5\sqrt{1+k^2} \le \sqrt{37}(k+1)$$

On squaring both sides, we get

$$25(1 + k^2) \le 37(k^2 + 2k + 1)$$

or $6k^2 + 37k + 6 \ge 0$ or $(6k+1)(k+6) \ge 0$

$$k \in (-\infty, -6] \cup \left[-\frac{1}{6}, \infty\right)$$

2. Vector in the direction of angular bisector of $\mathbf{a}$ and $\mathbf{b}$ is $\frac{\mathbf{a} + \mathbf{b}}{2}$.

Unit vector in this direction is $\frac{\mathbf{a} + \mathbf{b}}{|\mathbf{a} + \mathbf{b}|}$.

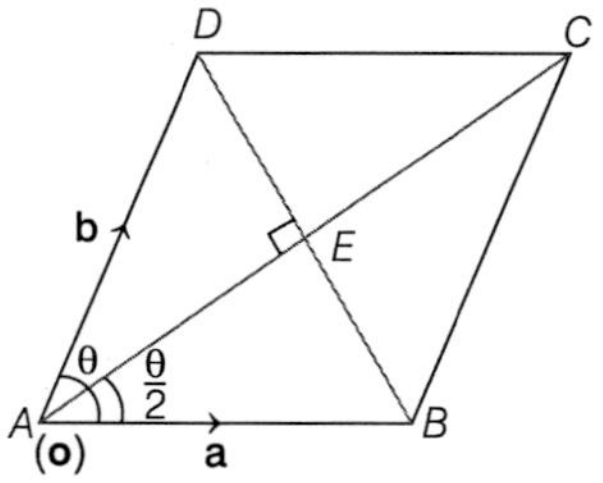

From the figure, position vector of E is $\frac{\mathbf{a} + \mathbf{b}}{2}$.

Now, in ΔAEB, $AE = AB\cos\frac{\theta}{2} \Rightarrow \left|\frac{\mathbf{a} + \mathbf{b}}{2}\right| = \cos\frac{\theta}{2}$

Hence, unit vector along the bisector is $\frac{\mathbf{a} + \mathbf{b}}{2\cos(\theta/2)}$.

3. **Decoding the Question**

First check the type of triangle. If it is an isosceles triangle then we know that angle bisector, also bisects the opposite side of the angle.

Since, $|\mathbf{OP}| = |\mathbf{OQ}| = \sqrt{14}$ i.e. $|\mathbf{a}| = |\mathbf{b}| = \sqrt{14}$

ΔOPQ is an isosceles.

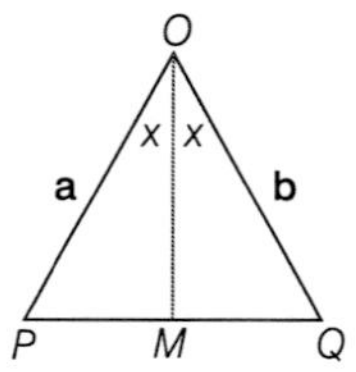

Hence, the internal bisector OM is perpendicular to PQ and M is the mid-point of P and Q. Therefore,

$$\mathbf{OM} = \frac{1}{2}(\mathbf{OP} + \mathbf{OQ}) = \frac{1}{2}(\mathbf{a} + \mathbf{b})$$

$$= \frac{1}{2}[(\hat{\mathbf{i}} + 3\hat{\mathbf{j}} - 2\hat{\mathbf{k}}) + (3\hat{\mathbf{i}} - \hat{\mathbf{j}} - 2\hat{\mathbf{k}})]$$

$$= 2\hat{\mathbf{i}} + \hat{\mathbf{j}} - 2\hat{\mathbf{k}}$$

4.

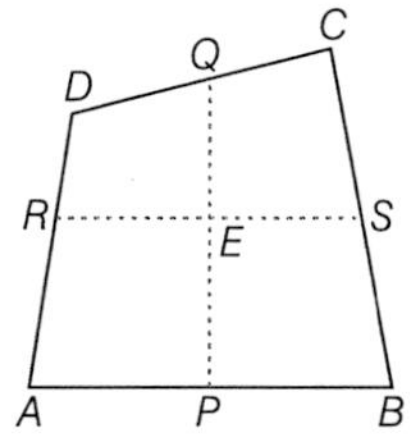

Let $\quad \mathbf{OA} = \mathbf{a}, \mathbf{OB} = \mathbf{b}, \mathbf{OC} = \mathbf{c}$ and $\mathbf{OD} = \mathbf{d}$

Therefore, $\mathbf{OA} + \mathbf{OB} + \mathbf{OC} + \mathbf{OD} = \mathbf{a} + \mathbf{b} + \mathbf{c} + \mathbf{d}$

P, the mid-point of **AB**, is $\frac{\mathbf{a} + \mathbf{b}}{2}$.

Q, the mid-point of **CD**, is $\frac{\mathbf{c} + \mathbf{d}}{2}$.

Therefore, the mid-point of **PQ** is $\frac{\mathbf{a} + \mathbf{b} + \mathbf{c} + \mathbf{d}}{4}$.

Similarly, the mid-point of **RS** is $\frac{\mathbf{a} + \mathbf{b} + \mathbf{c} + \mathbf{d}}{4}$

i.e. $\quad \mathbf{OE} = \frac{\mathbf{a} + \mathbf{b} + \mathbf{c} + \mathbf{d}}{4} \Rightarrow x = 4$

5.

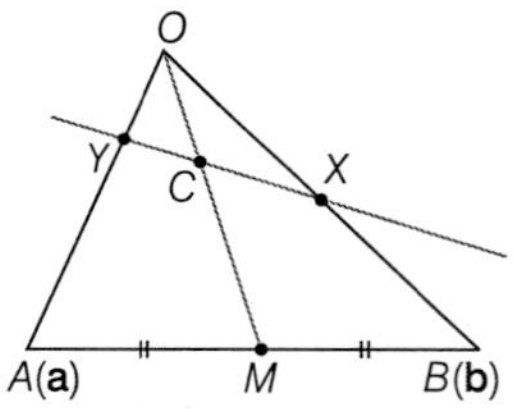

$$\mathbf{OA} = \mathbf{a}, \ \mathbf{OB} = \mathbf{b}$$

$$\therefore \quad \mathbf{OM} = \frac{\mathbf{a} + \mathbf{b}}{2}$$

$$\therefore \quad \mathbf{OC} = \frac{\mathbf{a} + \mathbf{b}}{6}$$

$$\mathbf{OX} = \frac{2}{3}\mathbf{b}$$

Let $\quad \frac{OY}{YA} = \lambda$

$$\therefore \quad \mathbf{OY} = \frac{\lambda}{\lambda + 1}\mathbf{a}$$

Now, points Y, C and X are collinear.

$$\therefore \quad \mathbf{YC} = m\mathbf{CX}$$

$$\therefore \quad \frac{\mathbf{a} + \mathbf{b}}{6} - \frac{\lambda}{\lambda + 1}\mathbf{a} = m\frac{2\mathbf{b}}{3} - m\frac{\mathbf{a} + \mathbf{b}}{6}$$

Comparing coefficients of $\mathbf{a}$ and $\mathbf{b}$,

$$\therefore \quad \frac{1}{6} - \frac{\lambda}{\lambda + 1} = -\frac{m}{6} \text{ and } \frac{1}{6} = \frac{2m}{3} - \frac{m}{6}$$

$$\therefore \quad m = \frac{1}{3} \text{ and } \lambda = \frac{2}{7}$$

6. PV of X is $\dfrac{4(\mathbf{a}+\mathbf{b})+\mathbf{a}}{5}=\dfrac{5\mathbf{a}+4\mathbf{b}}{5}$

PV of Y is $\dfrac{4\mathbf{b}+\mathbf{a}+\mathbf{b}}{5}=\dfrac{\mathbf{a}+5\mathbf{b}}{5}$

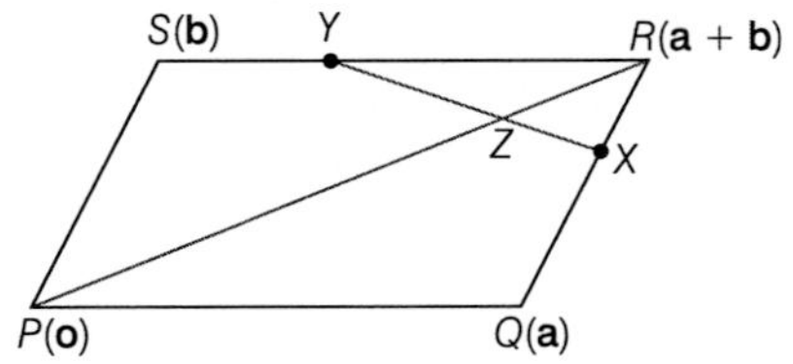

Now, $\quad \mathbf{PZ}=m\mathbf{PR}$

$\mathbf{PZ}=m(\mathbf{a}+\mathbf{b})$

Let Z divided YX in the ratio $\lambda:1$.

$$\text{PV of } Z=\frac{\lambda\mathbf{OX}+\mathbf{OY}}{\lambda+1}$$

$$\therefore \quad \mathbf{PZ}=\frac{\lambda\left(\dfrac{5\mathbf{a}+4\mathbf{b}}{5}\right)+\dfrac{\mathbf{a}+5\mathbf{b}}{5}}{\lambda+1}$$

$$=m(\mathbf{a}+\mathbf{b})$$

Comparing coefficients of **a** and **b**,

$$m=\frac{5\lambda+1}{5(\lambda+1)} \text{ and } m=\frac{4\lambda+5}{5(\lambda+1)}$$

$$\therefore \quad \lambda=4$$

$$\therefore \quad \mathbf{PZ}=\frac{4\left(\dfrac{5\mathbf{a}+4\mathbf{b}}{5}\right)+\dfrac{\mathbf{a}+5\mathbf{b}}{5}}{4+1}$$

$$=\frac{21(\mathbf{a}+\mathbf{b})}{25}=\frac{21}{25}\mathbf{PR}$$

7.

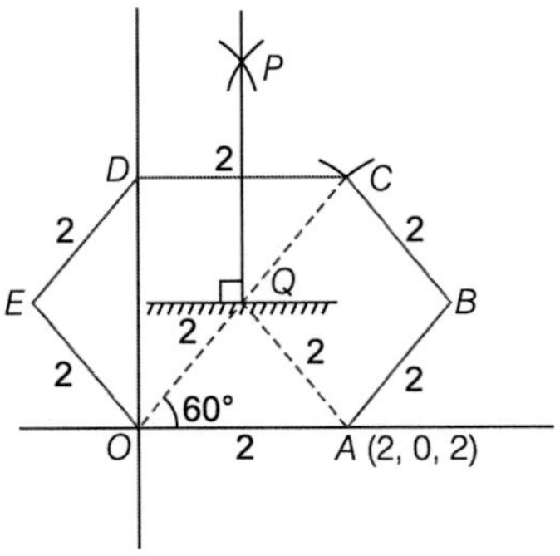

Here, coordinate of Q are $(2\cos 60°, 2\sin 60°)$

$\Rightarrow \quad Q(1, \sqrt{3}, 0)$

$\therefore \quad P(1, \sqrt{3}, z)$

$$OP=3$$

$\Rightarrow \quad \sqrt{1+3+z^2}=3 \text{ or } z^2=5$

$$z=\sqrt{5}$$

$\therefore \quad P(1, \sqrt{3}, \sqrt{5}) \Rightarrow \mathbf{OP}=\hat{\mathbf{i}}+\sqrt{3}\,\hat{\mathbf{j}}+\sqrt{5}\hat{\mathbf{k}}$

Now, $\mathbf{AP}=\mathbf{OP}-\mathbf{OA}=\hat{\mathbf{i}}+\sqrt{3}\,\hat{\mathbf{j}}+\sqrt{5}\hat{\mathbf{k}}-2\hat{\mathbf{i}}$

$$=-\hat{\mathbf{i}}+\sqrt{3}\,\hat{\mathbf{j}}+\sqrt{5}\hat{\mathbf{k}}$$

8. Let $\mathbf{OA}=\mathbf{a}, \mathbf{OB}=\mathbf{b}$ and $\mathbf{OC}=\mathbf{c}$,

then $\mathbf{AB}=\mathbf{b}-\mathbf{a}$ and $\mathbf{OP}=\dfrac{1}{3}\mathbf{a}$.

$$\mathbf{OQ}=\frac{1}{2}\mathbf{b},\ \mathbf{OR}=\frac{1}{3}\mathbf{c}.$$

Since, P, Q, R and S are coplanar, then

$$\mathbf{PS}=\alpha\mathbf{PQ}+\beta\mathbf{PR}$$

(**PS** can be written as a linear combination of **PQ** and **PR**)

$$=\alpha(\mathbf{OQ}-\mathbf{OP})+\beta(\mathbf{OR}-\mathbf{OP})$$

i.e. $\mathbf{OS}-\mathbf{OP}=-(\alpha+\beta)\dfrac{\mathbf{a}}{3}+\dfrac{\alpha}{2}\mathbf{b}+\dfrac{\beta}{3}\mathbf{c}$

$\Rightarrow \quad \mathbf{OS}=(1-\alpha-\beta)\dfrac{\mathbf{a}}{3}+\dfrac{\alpha}{2}\mathbf{b}+\dfrac{\beta}{3}\mathbf{c}$ ... (i)

Given $\quad \mathbf{OS}=\lambda\mathbf{AB}=\lambda(\mathbf{b}-\mathbf{a})$ ...(ii)

From Eq. (i) and Eq. (ii), $\beta=0, \dfrac{1-\alpha}{3}=-\lambda$ and $\dfrac{\alpha}{2}=\lambda$

$\Rightarrow \quad 2\lambda=1+3\lambda$ or $\lambda=-1$

9. Again, it is given that the point P, Q and R are collinear.

$\Rightarrow \quad \mathbf{PQ}=\lambda\mathbf{QR}$

$\Rightarrow \quad 15t(4\hat{\mathbf{j}}-3\hat{\mathbf{i}})=\lambda[(1-t)(\hat{\mathbf{i}}+\hat{\mathbf{j}})-60t\hat{\mathbf{j}}]$

$\Rightarrow \quad =\lambda[(1-t)\hat{\mathbf{i}}+(1-61t)\hat{\mathbf{j}}]$

$\Rightarrow \quad \dfrac{45t}{t-1}=\dfrac{60t}{1-61t}$

$\Rightarrow \quad \dfrac{3t}{t-1}=\dfrac{4t}{1-61t}$

$\Rightarrow \quad 3(1-61t)=4(t-1)$

$\Rightarrow \quad 3-183t=4t-4 \Rightarrow 187t=7$

$\therefore \quad t=\dfrac{7}{187}$

10. We have, $\quad \mathbf{a}+\mathbf{b}+\mathbf{c}=\alpha\mathbf{d}$

and $\quad \mathbf{b}+\mathbf{c}+\mathbf{d}=\beta\mathbf{a}$

$\therefore \quad \mathbf{a}+\mathbf{b}+\mathbf{c}+\mathbf{d}=(\alpha+1)\mathbf{d}$

and $\quad \mathbf{a}+\mathbf{b}+\mathbf{c}+\mathbf{d}=(\beta+1)\mathbf{a}$

$\Rightarrow \quad (\alpha+1)\mathbf{d}=(\beta+1)\mathbf{a}$

If $\alpha\neq-1$, then $(\alpha+1)\mathbf{d}=(\beta+1)\mathbf{a}$

$\Rightarrow \quad \mathbf{d}=\dfrac{\beta+1}{\alpha+1}\mathbf{a}$

$\Rightarrow \quad \mathbf{a}+\mathbf{b}+\mathbf{c}=\alpha\mathbf{d}$

$\Rightarrow \quad \mathbf{a}+\mathbf{b}+\mathbf{c}=\alpha\left(\dfrac{\beta+1}{\alpha+1}\right)\mathbf{a}$

$\Rightarrow \quad \left[1-\dfrac{\alpha(\beta+1)}{\alpha+1}\right]\mathbf{a}+\mathbf{b}+\mathbf{c}=\mathbf{0}$

a, b and **c** are coplanar which is contradiction to the given condition.

$\therefore \quad \alpha=-1$

and so $\mathbf{a}+\mathbf{b}+\mathbf{c}+\mathbf{d}=\mathbf{0}$

11. Let **R** be the resultant.

Then, $\mathbf{R}=\mathbf{F}_1+\mathbf{F}_2+\mathbf{F}_3=(p+1)\hat{\mathbf{i}}+4\hat{\mathbf{j}}$

Given, $|\mathbf{R}|=5$.

Therefore, $(p+1)^2+16=25$

or $\quad p+1=\pm3$ or $p=2,-4$

12. We have, $\mathbf{AB} = -\hat{\mathbf{i}} - \hat{\mathbf{j}} - 4\hat{\mathbf{k}},\ \mathbf{BC} = -3\hat{\mathbf{i}} + 3\hat{\mathbf{j}}$

and $\mathbf{CA} = 4\hat{\mathbf{i}} - 2\hat{\mathbf{j}} + 4\hat{\mathbf{k}}$.

Therefore, $|\mathbf{AB}| = |\mathbf{BC}| = 3\sqrt{2}$ and $|\mathbf{CA}| = 6$

Clearly, $|\mathbf{AB}|^2 + |\mathbf{BC}|^2 = |\mathbf{AC}|^2$

Hence, the triangle is right angled isosceles triangle.

13. Let $\mathbf{a} = 2\hat{\mathbf{i}} + 4\hat{\mathbf{j}} - 5\hat{\mathbf{k}}$

and $\mathbf{b} = \hat{\mathbf{i}} + 2\hat{\mathbf{j}} + 3\hat{\mathbf{k}}$.

Then, the diagonals of the parallelogram are

$$\mathbf{p} = \mathbf{a} + \mathbf{b} \text{ and } \mathbf{q} = \mathbf{b} - \mathbf{a},$$

i.e. $\mathbf{p} = 3\hat{\mathbf{i}} + 6\hat{\mathbf{j}} - 2\hat{\mathbf{k}}$ and $\mathbf{q} = -\hat{\mathbf{i}} - 2\hat{\mathbf{j}} + 8\hat{\mathbf{k}}$

So, unit vectors along the diagonals are

$$\frac{1}{7}(3\hat{\mathbf{i}} + 6\hat{\mathbf{j}} - 2\hat{\mathbf{k}}) \text{ and } \frac{1}{\sqrt{69}}(-\hat{\mathbf{i}} - 2\hat{\mathbf{j}} + 8\hat{\mathbf{k}})$$

14. $\mathbf{OA} = -4\hat{\mathbf{i}} + 3\hat{\mathbf{k}};\ \mathbf{OB} = 14\hat{\mathbf{i}} + 2\hat{\mathbf{j}} - 5\hat{\mathbf{k}}$

$$\mathbf{a} = \frac{-4\hat{\mathbf{i}} + 3\hat{\mathbf{k}}}{5};\ \mathbf{b} = \frac{14\hat{\mathbf{i}} + 2\hat{\mathbf{j}} - 5\hat{\mathbf{k}}}{15}$$

$$\mathbf{r} = \frac{\lambda}{15}[-12\hat{\mathbf{i}} + 9\hat{\mathbf{k}} + 14\hat{\mathbf{i}} + 2\hat{\mathbf{j}} - 5\hat{\mathbf{k}}]$$

$$= \frac{\lambda}{15}[2\hat{\mathbf{i}} + 2\hat{\mathbf{j}} + 4\hat{\mathbf{k}}] = \frac{2\lambda}{15}[\hat{\mathbf{i}} + \hat{\mathbf{j}} + 2\hat{\mathbf{k}}]$$

15. Consider the point O as origin, we have

$$\mathbf{f} = \frac{\mathbf{a}+\mathbf{b}}{2},\ \mathbf{e} = \frac{\mathbf{a}+\mathbf{c}}{2} \text{ and } \mathbf{d} = \frac{\mathbf{b}+\mathbf{c}}{2}$$

Here, $\mathbf{d} + \mathbf{e} + \mathbf{f} = \mathbf{a} + \mathbf{b} + \mathbf{c}$ ...(i)

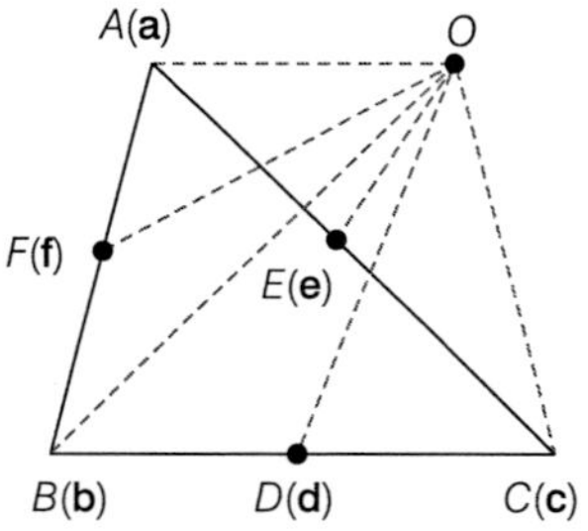

(a) $\mathbf{AD} + \mathbf{BE} + \mathbf{CF} = (\mathbf{d} - \mathbf{a}) + (\mathbf{e} - \mathbf{b}) + (\mathbf{f} - \mathbf{c})$

$= (\mathbf{d} + \mathbf{e} + \mathbf{f}) - (\mathbf{a} + \mathbf{b} + \mathbf{c}) = \mathbf{0}$ [using Eq. (i)]

$\Rightarrow \mathbf{AD} + \mathbf{BE} + \mathbf{CF} = \mathbf{0}$

(b) Here, $\mathbf{OE} + \mathbf{OF} + \mathbf{DO} = \mathbf{e} + \mathbf{f} - \mathbf{d}$

$$= \frac{\mathbf{c}+\mathbf{a}}{2} + \frac{\mathbf{a}+\mathbf{b}}{2} - \frac{\mathbf{b}+\mathbf{c}}{2} = \mathbf{a} = \mathbf{OA}$$

$\therefore \mathbf{OE} + \mathbf{OF} + \mathbf{OD} = \mathbf{OA}$

(c) Here, $\mathbf{AD} + \frac{2}{3}\mathbf{BE} + \frac{1}{3}\mathbf{CF} = (\mathbf{d} - \mathbf{a}) + \frac{2}{3}(\mathbf{e} - \mathbf{b}) + \frac{1}{3}(\mathbf{f} - \mathbf{c})$

$$= \frac{\mathbf{b}+\mathbf{c}}{2} - \mathbf{a} + \frac{2}{3}\left(\frac{\mathbf{c}+\mathbf{a}}{2} - \mathbf{b}\right) + \frac{1}{3}\left(\frac{\mathbf{a}+\mathbf{b}}{2} - \mathbf{c}\right)$$

$$= \mathbf{a}\left(-1 + \frac{1}{3} + \frac{1}{6}\right) + \mathbf{b}\left(\frac{1}{2} - \frac{2}{3} + \frac{1}{6}\right) + \mathbf{c}\left(\frac{1}{2} + \frac{1}{3} - \frac{1}{3}\right)$$

$$= -\frac{1}{2}\mathbf{a} + \frac{1}{2}\mathbf{c} = \frac{1}{2}(\mathbf{c} - \mathbf{a}) = \frac{1}{2}\mathbf{AC}$$

$\therefore \mathbf{AD} + \frac{2}{3}\mathbf{BE} + \frac{1}{3}\mathbf{CF} = \frac{1}{2}\mathbf{AC}$

16. We have, $\mathbf{DA} = \mathbf{a}$, $\mathbf{AB} = \mathbf{b}$ and $\mathbf{CB} = \lambda\mathbf{a}$

Given, X and Y are the mid-points of DB and AC.

Then, $\mathbf{OX} = \frac{\mathbf{OB} + \mathbf{OD}}{2},\ \mathbf{OY} = \frac{\mathbf{OA} + \mathbf{OC}}{2}$

$$\Rightarrow \mathbf{XY} = \mathbf{OY} - \mathbf{OX} = \frac{\mathbf{OA} + \mathbf{OC} - \mathbf{OB} - \mathbf{OD}}{2}$$

$$= \frac{\mathbf{DA} + \mathbf{BC}}{2} = \frac{\mathbf{a} - \lambda\mathbf{a}}{2}$$

$$\Rightarrow \mathbf{XY} = \frac{(1-\lambda)\mathbf{a}}{2}$$

$\therefore |\mathbf{XY}| = \pm\left(\frac{1-\lambda}{2}\right)a = 4$ [given]

$\Rightarrow \frac{(1-\lambda)}{2}17 = 4$ [taking +ve sign]

$$\Rightarrow 1 - \lambda = \frac{8}{17}$$

$$\therefore \lambda = \frac{9}{17}$$

and $-\left(\frac{1-\lambda}{2}\right)a = 4$ [taking –ve sign]

$$\Rightarrow (\lambda - 1)17 = 8$$

$$\Rightarrow \lambda = \frac{25}{17}$$

17. We have, $\mathbf{r} = \lambda\mathbf{c}$

$$\therefore |\mathbf{r}| = |\lambda||\mathbf{c}|$$

$$\frac{|\mathbf{a} + \mathbf{b}|}{2} = |\lambda||\mathbf{c}|$$

$$\therefore |6\hat{\mathbf{i}} - 2\hat{\mathbf{j}} - 4\hat{\mathbf{k}}| = 2|\lambda||3\hat{\mathbf{i}} - \hat{\mathbf{j}} + 2\hat{\mathbf{k}}|$$

$$\sqrt{56} = 2|\lambda|\sqrt{14}$$

$$\therefore \lambda = \pm 1$$

$$\therefore \mathbf{r} = \pm\mathbf{c}$$

18. We have, $\cos^2\alpha + \sin^2\beta - 2\sec^2\gamma = 0$

$$\Rightarrow \cos^2\alpha + \sin^2\beta = 2\sec^2\gamma$$

$$\Rightarrow \cos^2\alpha + \sin^2\beta = 2$$

and $\sec^2\gamma = 1$

$$\Rightarrow \cos^2\alpha = 1, \sin^2\beta = 1$$

and $\sec^2\gamma = 1$

$$\therefore \mathbf{a} + \mathbf{b} - 2\mathbf{c} = \mathbf{0} \Rightarrow \mathbf{a} = \frac{2\mathbf{c} - \mathbf{b}}{2-1} \text{ or } \mathbf{c} = \frac{\mathbf{a}+\mathbf{b}}{2}$$

19. Since, $\mathbf{a}$ and $\mathbf{b}$ are equally inclined to $\mathbf{c}$, therefore $\mathbf{c}$ must be of the form $t\left(\frac{\mathbf{a}}{|\mathbf{a}|} + \frac{\mathbf{b}}{|\mathbf{b}|}\right)$

Now, $\frac{|\mathbf{b}|}{|\mathbf{a}| + |\mathbf{b}|}\mathbf{a} + \frac{|\mathbf{a}|}{|\mathbf{a}| + |\mathbf{b}|}\mathbf{b} = \frac{|\mathbf{a}||\mathbf{b}|}{|\mathbf{a}| + |\mathbf{b}|}\left(\frac{\mathbf{a}}{|\mathbf{a}|} + \frac{\mathbf{b}}{|\mathbf{b}|}\right)$

Also, $\frac{|\mathbf{b}|}{2|\mathbf{a}| + |\mathbf{b}|}\mathbf{a} + \frac{|\mathbf{a}|}{2|\mathbf{a}| + |\mathbf{b}|}\mathbf{b} = \frac{|\mathbf{a}||\mathbf{b}|}{2|\mathbf{a}| + |\mathbf{b}|}\left(\frac{\mathbf{a}}{|\mathbf{a}|} + \frac{\mathbf{b}}{|\mathbf{b}|}\right)$

Other two vectors cannot be written in the from $t\left(\frac{\mathbf{a}}{|\mathbf{a}|} + \frac{\mathbf{b}}{|\mathbf{b}|}\right)$.

20. For coplanar vectors, $\begin{vmatrix} 1 & 2 & 3 \\ 0 & \lambda & \mu \\ 0 & 0 & 2\lambda - 1 \end{vmatrix} = 0$

or $(2\lambda - 1)\lambda = 0$

or $\lambda = 0, \frac{1}{2}$

and $\mu \in R$

Solutions (Q.Nos. 21-22)

Let the position vectors of A, B, C and D be $\mathbf{a}, \mathbf{b}, \mathbf{c}$ and $\mathbf{d}$, respectively. Then,

$OA : CB = 2 : 1$

$\Rightarrow \quad \mathbf{OA} = 2\mathbf{CB}$

$\Rightarrow \quad \mathbf{a} = 2(\mathbf{b} - \mathbf{c})$ ... (i)

and $OD : AB = 1 : 3$

$3\mathbf{OD} = \mathbf{AB}$

$\Rightarrow \quad 3\mathbf{d} = (\mathbf{b} - \mathbf{a}) = \mathbf{b} - 2(\mathbf{b} - \mathbf{c})$ [using Eq. (i)]

$= -\mathbf{b} + 2\mathbf{c}$ ... (ii)

Let $OX : XC = \lambda : 1$ and $AX : XD = \mu : 1$

Now, X divides OC in the ratio $\lambda : 1$.

Therefore, PV of $X = \frac{\lambda \mathbf{c}}{\lambda + 1}$ ...(iii)

X also divided AD in the ratio $\mu : 1$.

Therefore, PV of $X = \frac{\mu \mathbf{d} + \mathbf{a}}{\mu + 1}$ ...(iv)

From Eqs. (iii) and (iv), we get

$$\frac{\lambda \mathbf{c}}{\lambda + 1} = \frac{\mu \mathbf{d} + \mathbf{a}}{\mu + 1}$$

or $\left(\frac{\lambda}{\lambda + 1}\right)\mathbf{c} = \left(\frac{\mu}{\mu + 1}\right)\mathbf{d} + \left(\frac{1}{\mu + 1}\right)\mathbf{a}$

or $\left(\frac{\lambda}{\lambda + 1}\right)\mathbf{c} = \left(\frac{\mu}{\mu + 1}\right)\left(\frac{-\mathbf{b} + 2\mathbf{c}}{3}\right) + \left(\frac{1}{\mu + 1}\right)2(\mathbf{b} - \mathbf{c})$

[using Eqs. (i) and (ii)]

or $\left(\frac{\lambda}{\lambda + 1}\right)\mathbf{c} = \left(\frac{6 - \mu}{3(\mu + 1)}\right)\mathbf{b} + \left(\frac{2\mu}{3(\mu + 1)} - \frac{2}{\mu + 1}\right)\mathbf{c}$

or $\left(\frac{\lambda}{\lambda + 1}\right)\mathbf{c} = \left(\frac{6 - \mu}{3(\mu + 1)}\right)\mathbf{b} + \left(\frac{2\mu - 6}{3(\mu + 1)}\right)\mathbf{c}$

or $\left(\frac{6 - \mu}{3(\mu + 1)}\right)\mathbf{b} + \left(\frac{2\mu - 6}{3(\mu + 1)} - \frac{\lambda}{\lambda + 1}\right)\mathbf{c} = \mathbf{0}$

or $\frac{6 - \mu}{3(\mu + 1)} = 0$

and $\frac{2\mu - 6}{3(\mu + 1)} - \frac{\lambda}{\lambda + 1} = 0$

[as **b** and **c** are non-collinear]

or $\mu = 6, \lambda = \frac{2}{5}$

Hence, $OX : XC = 2 : 5$ and $AX / XD = \frac{\mu}{1} = \frac{6}{1}$

21. (c) **22.** (b)

Solutions (Q.Nos. 23-24)

Consider the regular hexagon $ABCDEF$ with centre at O (origin).

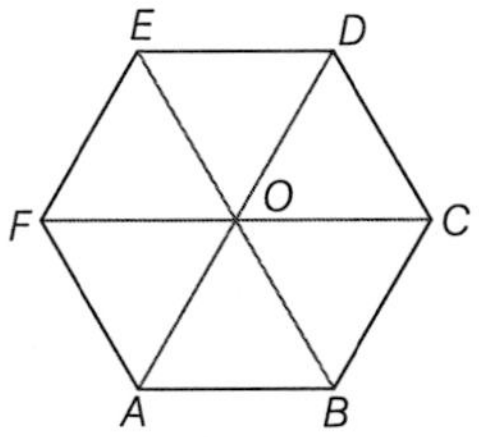

$\mathbf{AD} + \mathbf{EB} + \mathbf{FC} = 2\mathbf{AO} + 2\mathbf{OB} + 2\mathbf{OC}$

$= 2(\mathbf{AO} + \mathbf{OB}) + 2\mathbf{OC}$

$= 2\mathbf{AB} + 2\mathbf{AB}$ [$\because \mathbf{OC} = \mathbf{AB}$]

$= 4\mathbf{AB}$

$\mathbf{R} = \mathbf{AB} + \mathbf{AC} + \mathbf{AD} + \mathbf{AE} + \mathbf{AF}$

$= \mathbf{ED} + \mathbf{AC} + \mathbf{AD} + \mathbf{AE} + \mathbf{CD}$

[$\because$ **AB** = **ED** and **AF** = **CD**]

$= (\mathbf{AC} + \mathbf{CD}) + (\mathbf{AE} + \mathbf{ED}) + \mathbf{AD}$

$= \mathbf{AD} + \mathbf{AD} + \mathbf{AD}$

$= 3\mathbf{AD}$

$= 6\mathbf{AO}$

23. (c) **24.** (d)

Solutions (Q.Nos. 25-26)

25. $2\mathbf{OA} - 3\mathbf{OB} + \mathbf{OC} = 2(-2\mathbf{a} + 3\mathbf{b} + 5\mathbf{c}) - 3(\mathbf{a} + 2\mathbf{b} + 3\mathbf{c}) + (7\mathbf{a} - \mathbf{c})$

$= \mathbf{0}$

26. (d) $\because \; 2\mathbf{OA} - 3\mathbf{OB} + \mathbf{OC} = \mathbf{0}$

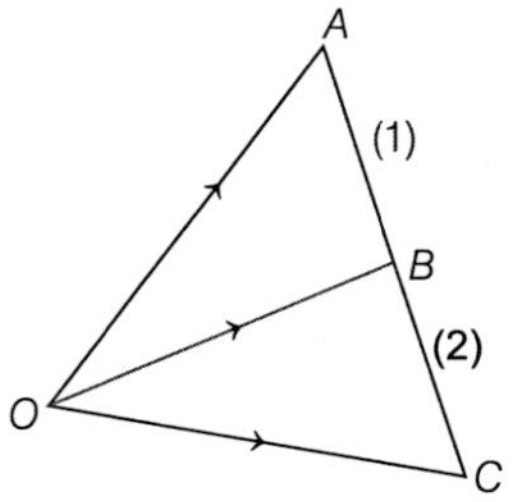

$\Rightarrow \quad \mathbf{OB} = \frac{2\mathbf{OA} + \mathbf{OC}}{3}$

$\Rightarrow$ B Divides AC in 1 : 2.

25. (a) **26.** (d)

Solutions (Q.Nos. 27-28)

27. Here, $\mathbf{C} = t(\hat{\mathbf{A}} + \hat{\mathbf{B}}) = t\left(\frac{7\hat{\mathbf{i}} - 4\hat{\mathbf{j}} - 4\hat{\mathbf{k}}}{9} + \frac{(-2\hat{\mathbf{i}} - \hat{\mathbf{j}} + 2\hat{\mathbf{k}})}{3}\right)$

$\Rightarrow \quad \mathbf{C} = t\left(\frac{\hat{\mathbf{i}} - 7\hat{\mathbf{j}} + 2\hat{\mathbf{k}}}{9}\right)$

Also, $|\mathbf{C}| = 5\sqrt{6}$

$\Rightarrow \frac{t}{9}.\sqrt{1 + 49 + 4} = 5\sqrt{6} \Rightarrow \frac{t}{9}\cdot 3\sqrt{6} = 5\sqrt{6}$

$\therefore \quad t = 15 \Rightarrow \mathbf{C} = \frac{15}{9}(\hat{\mathbf{i}} - 7\hat{\mathbf{j}} + 2\hat{\mathbf{k}})$

or $\mathbf{C} = \frac{5}{3}(\hat{\mathbf{i}} - 7\hat{\mathbf{j}} + 2\hat{\mathbf{k}})$

28. Here, $\dfrac{AB}{AC}=\dfrac{BD}{DC}$ and $\dfrac{AB}{AC}=\dfrac{BE}{CE}$

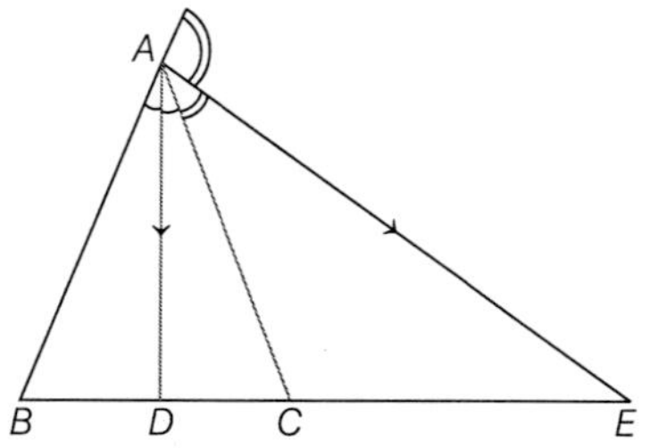

$$\Rightarrow \quad \frac{BD}{DC}=\frac{BE}{CE} \Rightarrow \frac{BD}{BC-BD}=\frac{BE}{BE-BC}$$

$$\Rightarrow \quad BD\cdot BE - BD\cdot BC = BC\cdot BE - BD\cdot BE$$

$$\Rightarrow \quad 2BD\cdot BE=(BD+BE)\cdot BC \text{ or } \frac{2}{BC}=\frac{1}{BD}+\frac{1}{BE}$$

27. (b) **28.** (c)

Solutions (Q.Nos. 29-30)

Given, **a** bisects the angle between **b** and **c**.

$$\therefore \quad \mathbf{a}=\lambda\left(\frac{\mathbf{b}}{|\mathbf{b}|}+\frac{\mathbf{c}}{|\mathbf{c}|}\right)$$

$$\Rightarrow x\hat{\mathbf{i}}+4\hat{\mathbf{j}}+y\hat{\mathbf{k}}=\lambda\left(\frac{\hat{\mathbf{i}}+\hat{\mathbf{j}}}{\sqrt{2}}+\frac{\hat{\mathbf{j}}+\hat{\mathbf{k}}}{\sqrt{2}}\right)$$

$$\Rightarrow x\hat{\mathbf{i}}+4\hat{\mathbf{j}}+y\hat{\mathbf{k}}=\lambda\left(\frac{\hat{\mathbf{i}}+2\hat{\mathbf{j}}+\hat{\mathbf{k}}}{\sqrt{2}}\right)$$

On equating the coefficient of $\hat{\mathbf{i}},\hat{\mathbf{j}}$ and $\hat{\mathbf{k}}$, we get

$$x=\frac{\lambda}{\sqrt{2}}, 4=\frac{2\lambda}{\sqrt{2}} \text{ and } y=\frac{\lambda}{\sqrt{2}}$$

$$\Rightarrow \quad x=\frac{\lambda}{\sqrt{2}}, \lambda=2\sqrt{2} \text{ and } y=\frac{\lambda}{\sqrt{2}}$$

$$\therefore \quad x=\frac{2\sqrt{2}}{\sqrt{2}} \text{ and } y=\frac{2\sqrt{2}}{\sqrt{2}} \Rightarrow x=2 \text{ and } y=2$$

29. (2) **30.** (2)

Solutions (Q.Nos. 31-32)

We have,

$$(x_1-1)(\mathbf{a}_1-\mathbf{a}_2)+x_2(\mathbf{a}_2+\mathbf{a}_3)+x_3(\mathbf{a}_3+\mathbf{a}_4-2\mathbf{a}_2)+\mathbf{a}_3+x_4\mathbf{a}_4=\mathbf{0}$$

$$\Rightarrow (x_1-1)\mathbf{a}_1+(1-x_1+x_2-2x_3)\mathbf{a}_2 + (x_2+x_3+1)\mathbf{a}_3+(x_3+x_4)\mathbf{a}_4=\mathbf{0}$$

Since, $\mathbf{a}_1,\mathbf{a}_2,\mathbf{a}_3$ and $\mathbf{a}_4$ are linearly independent, therefore

$$x_1-1=0 \Rightarrow x_1=1 \quad \text{...(i)}$$

$$1-x_1+x_2-2x_3=0 \Rightarrow x_2-2x_3=0 \quad \text{...(ii)}$$

$$x_2+x_3+1=0 \quad \text{...(iii)}$$

and $$x_3+x_4=0 \quad \text{...(iv)}$$

On solving Eqs. (i), (ii), (iii) and (iv), we get

$$x_1=1,\ x_2=\frac{-2}{3},\ x_3=-\frac{1}{3} \text{ and } x_4=\frac{1}{3}$$

31. (2) $6(x_1+x_2)=6\left(1-\dfrac{2}{3}\right)=6\times\dfrac{1}{3}=2$

32. (2) $18\,|x_3x_4|=18\left|\dfrac{-1}{9}\right|=2$

Solutions (Q.Nos. 33-34)

According to the question,

$$\mathbf{s}=4\mathbf{p}+3\mathbf{q}+5\mathbf{r}$$

and $\mathbf{s}=x(-\mathbf{p}+\mathbf{q}+\mathbf{r})+y(\mathbf{p}-\mathbf{q}+\mathbf{r})+z(-\mathbf{p}-\mathbf{q}+\mathbf{r})$

$$\therefore \quad -x+y-z=4 \quad \text{...(i)}$$

$$x-y-z=3 \quad \text{...(ii)}$$

$$x+y+z=5 \quad \text{...(iii)}$$

On adding Eqs. (i) and (ii), we get

$$z=-\frac{7}{2}$$

On adding Eqs. (ii) and (iii), we get

$$x=4$$

On adding Eqs. (i) and (iii), we get

$$y=\frac{9}{2}$$

Hence, $2|z|=7$ and $2(x+y)=17$

33. (7) **34.** (17)

35. Let **R** be the resultant. Then,

$$\mathbf{R}=\mathbf{F}_1+\mathbf{F}_2+\mathbf{F}_3=(p+1)\hat{\mathbf{i}}+4\hat{\mathbf{j}}$$

Given, $|\mathbf{R}|=5$, Therefore, $R^2=25$

$$\because \quad (p+1)^2+16=25 \text{ or } p+1=\pm 3 \text{ or } p=2,-4$$

$\therefore$ Difference $=2-(-4)=6$

36. Vectors along the sides are $\mathbf{a}=\hat{\mathbf{i}}+2\hat{\mathbf{j}}+\hat{\mathbf{k}}$ and $\mathbf{b}=2\hat{\mathbf{i}}+4\hat{\mathbf{j}}+\hat{\mathbf{k}}$

Clearly, the vector along the longer diagonal is

$$\mathbf{a}+\mathbf{b}=3\hat{\mathbf{i}}+6\hat{\mathbf{j}}+2\hat{\mathbf{k}}$$

Hence, length of the longer diagonal is

$$|\mathbf{a}+\mathbf{b}|=|3\hat{\mathbf{i}}+6\hat{\mathbf{j}}+2\hat{\mathbf{k}}|=7$$

37. Since, angle bisector of **a** and **b**.

$$\Rightarrow \quad h(\hat{\mathbf{a}}+\hat{\mathbf{b}})=h\left(\frac{\mathbf{a}}{|\mathbf{a}|}+\frac{\mathbf{b}}{|\mathbf{b}|}\right) \quad \text{... (i)}$$

Given, **a** + **b** is along angle bisector.

$$\Rightarrow \quad \mu\left(\frac{\mathbf{a}}{|\mathbf{a}|}+\frac{\mathbf{b}}{|\mathbf{b}|}\right)=\mathbf{a}+\mathbf{b}$$

only, when $|\mathbf{a}|=|\mathbf{b}|=\mu$

$$\therefore \quad |\mathbf{a}|=|\mathbf{b}| \Rightarrow \lambda=1$$

38.

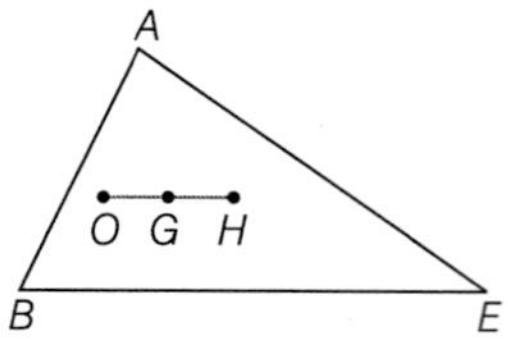

Here, O is circumcentre = **O**, G is centroid = **g**

H is orthocentre = **p**

Since, $$\frac{\mathbf{OG}}{\mathbf{GH}}=\frac{1}{2}$$

$$\Rightarrow \quad \frac{\mathbf{g}}{\mathbf{p}-\mathbf{g}}=\frac{1}{2}$$

$$\Rightarrow \quad 2\mathbf{g}=\mathbf{p}-\mathbf{g} \text{ or } \mathbf{p}=3\mathbf{g}$$

$$\therefore \quad k=3$$

39. $\mathbf{XG} = k\mathbf{GY}$

$$\frac{\mathbf{b}+\mathbf{c}}{3} - \frac{2\mathbf{b}}{3} = k\left(\frac{\lambda \mathbf{c}}{1+\lambda} - \frac{\mathbf{b}+\mathbf{c}}{3}\right), k = 1$$

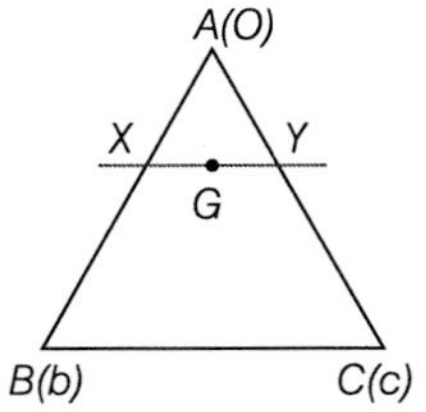

$$\frac{2\mathbf{c}}{3} = \frac{\lambda}{1+\lambda}\mathbf{c} \Rightarrow \frac{\lambda}{1+\lambda} = \frac{2}{3} \Rightarrow \lambda = 2$$

40. We have, $\mathbf{a} = 2p\hat{\mathbf{i}} + \hat{\mathbf{j}}$

Let $\mathbf{b}$ be the vector obtained from $\mathbf{a}$ by rotating the axes. Then, the components of $\mathbf{b}$ are $p+1$ and 1.

Therefore, $\mathbf{b} = (p+1)\hat{\alpha} + \hat{\beta}$,

where $\hat{\alpha}$ and $\hat{\beta}$ are unit vectors along the new axes.

But $|\mathbf{b}| = |\mathbf{a}|$

$\Rightarrow$ $4p^2 + 1 = (p+1)^2 + 1$

$\Rightarrow$ $3p^2 - 2p - 1 = 0 \Rightarrow p = 1, -\frac{1}{3}$

$\Rightarrow$ $p_1 = 1$ and $p_2 = -\frac{1}{3}$

$\therefore$ $3|p_1 + p_2| = 3\left|1 - \frac{1}{3}\right| = 2$

41. Vector $\mathbf{a} = \hat{\mathbf{i}} + 2\hat{\mathbf{j}} - \hat{\mathbf{k}}, \mathbf{b} = 2\hat{\mathbf{i}} - \hat{\mathbf{j}} + \hat{\mathbf{k}}, \mathbf{c} = \lambda\hat{\mathbf{i}} + \hat{\mathbf{j}} + 2\hat{\mathbf{k}}$ are coplanar.

$$\Rightarrow \begin{vmatrix} 1 & 2 & -1 \\ 2 & -1 & 1 \\ \lambda & 1 & 2 \end{vmatrix} = 0 \text{ or } \lambda - 3 + 2(-5) = 0 \text{ or } \lambda = 13$$

$\therefore$ $\lambda - 4 = 13 - 4 = 9$

42. Here, $\mathbf{r}_1 = \mathbf{OA}$ pointing North-East and $\mathbf{r}_2 = \mathbf{OB}$ pointing North-West. Where, $|\mathbf{OA}| = |\mathbf{OB}| = 5$.

As shown in figure,

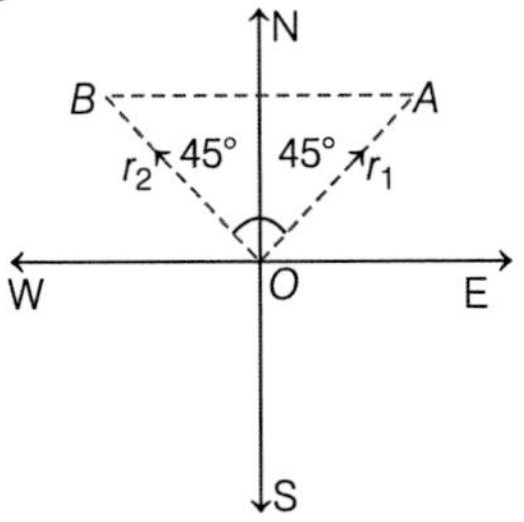

$\therefore$ $\angle BOA = 90°$

$\Rightarrow$ $\mathbf{r}_1 - \mathbf{r}_2 = \mathbf{BA}$ [using triangle law]

Clearly, $\angle BOA$ is right angled at O.

$\therefore$ $BA^2 = OA^2 + OB^2 = 5^2 + 5^2 = 50$

$\Rightarrow$ $|BA| = 5\sqrt{2}$ or $|\mathbf{r}_1 - \mathbf{r}_2| = 5\sqrt{2}$

$\therefore$ $m^2 = 50$

43. Let $OACB$ be a parallelogram shown as

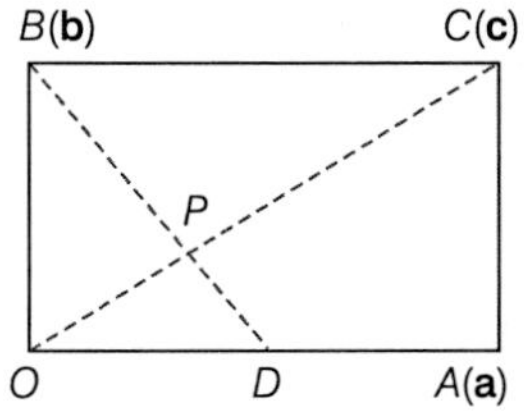

Here, $\mathbf{OD} = \frac{1}{2}\mathbf{BC}$

$\Rightarrow$ $\mathbf{OP} + \mathbf{PD} = \frac{1}{2}(\mathbf{BP} + \mathbf{PC})$ [using Δ law]

$\Rightarrow$ $2\mathbf{OP} + 2\mathbf{PD} = \mathbf{BP} + \mathbf{PC}$

$-2\mathbf{PO} + 2\mathbf{PD} = -\mathbf{PB} + \mathbf{PC}$

$\Rightarrow$ $\mathbf{PB} + 2\mathbf{PD} = \mathbf{PC} + 2\mathbf{PO}$

$\Rightarrow$ $\frac{\mathbf{PB} + 2\mathbf{PD}}{1+2} = \frac{\mathbf{PC} + 2\mathbf{PO}}{1+2}$

The common point P of BD and CO divides each in the ratio $2:1$.

$\therefore (k_1 + k_2)^2 = (2+1)^2 = 9$

44. Let S be the point of intersection of $\mathbf{AB}$ and $\mathbf{CR}$. Let A be the origin and the position vectors of the points B, C, P, Q, R and S be $\mathbf{b}, \mathbf{c}, \mathbf{p}, \mathbf{q}, \mathbf{r}$ and $\mathbf{s}$ respectively.

$\therefore$ $\mathbf{p} = \frac{3\mathbf{b} + 2\mathbf{c}}{5}$ ...(i)

and $\mathbf{q} = \frac{4\mathbf{c}}{5}$ ...(ii)

$\Rightarrow$ $\frac{5\mathbf{p} - 3\mathbf{b}}{2} = \frac{5\mathbf{q}}{4} \Rightarrow 10\mathbf{p} - 6\mathbf{b} = 5\mathbf{q}$

i.e. $10\mathbf{p} = 5\mathbf{q} + 6\mathbf{b} \Rightarrow \frac{10\mathbf{p}}{11} = \frac{5\mathbf{q} + 6\mathbf{b}}{11} = \mathbf{r}$

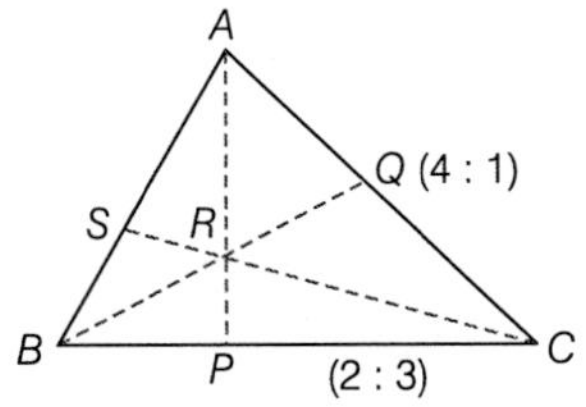

$\Rightarrow$ $\frac{11\mathbf{r}}{10} = \mathbf{p} = \frac{3\mathbf{b} + 2\mathbf{c}}{5}$ [using Eq. (i)]

$11\mathbf{r} = 6\mathbf{b} + 4\mathbf{c}$

$11\mathbf{r} - 4\mathbf{c} = 6\mathbf{b}$

$\frac{11\mathbf{r} - 4\mathbf{c}}{7} = \frac{6}{7}\mathbf{b} = \mathbf{s}$, thus S divides AB in the ratio $6:1$.

$\therefore (\lambda_1 - \lambda_2) = 5$

45. Since, angle bisectors divides opposite side in the ratio of sides containing the angle.

$\Rightarrow$ $BA' = \frac{ac}{b+c}$ and $CA' = \frac{ab}{a+c}$

Now, BI is also angle bisector of $\angle B$ for $\Delta ABA'$.

$\Rightarrow$ $\frac{AI}{AI'} = \frac{b+c}{a}$

$$\Rightarrow \quad \frac{AI}{AA'} = \frac{b+c}{a+b+c}$$

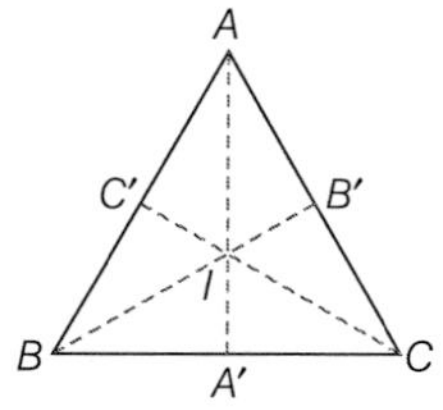

Similarly, $\dfrac{BI}{BB'} = \dfrac{a+c}{a+b+c}$ and $\dfrac{CI}{CC'} = \dfrac{a+b}{a+b+c}$

$$\Rightarrow \quad \frac{AI \cdot BI \cdot CI}{AA' \cdot BB' \cdot CC'} = \frac{(b+c)(a+c)(a+b)}{(a+b+c)(a+b+c)(a+b+c)} \quad \text{...(i)}$$

As we know **AM** $\geq$ **GM**, we get

$$\frac{\frac{b+c}{a+b+c} + \frac{c+a}{a+b+c} + \frac{a+b}{a+b+c}}{3} \geq \left[\frac{(a+b)(b+c)(c+a)}{(a+b+c)^3}\right]^{\frac{1}{3}}$$

$$\Rightarrow \quad \frac{2(a+b+c)}{3(a+b+c)} \geq \left[\frac{(a+b)(b+c)(c+a)}{(a+b+c)^3}\right]^{1/3}$$

$$\Rightarrow \quad \frac{(a+b)(b+c)(c+a)}{(a+b+c)^3} \leq \frac{8}{27} \quad \text{...(ii)}$$

From Eqs. (i) and (ii), we get

$$\frac{AI \cdot BI \cdot CI}{AA' \cdot BB' \cdot CC'} \leq \frac{8}{27}$$

$\therefore k_1 \cdot k_2 = 216$

46. Let O be the origin of reference.

Let the position vectors of A, B, C and D be **a**, **b**, **c** and **d**, respectively.

Then, $\quad OA : CB = 2 : 1$

$$\Rightarrow \quad \frac{OA}{CB} = \frac{2}{1} \Rightarrow OA = 2CB$$

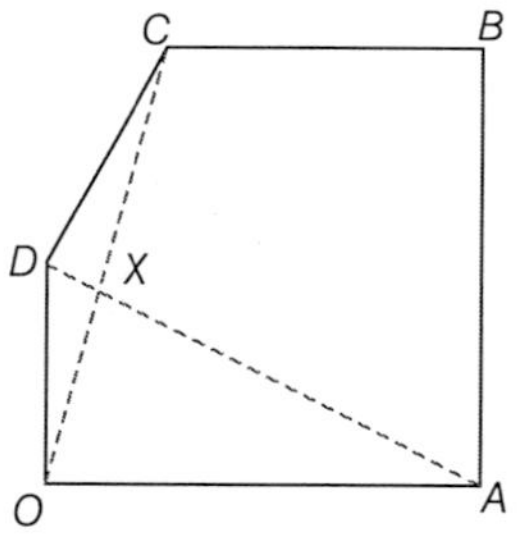

$\Rightarrow \quad \mathbf{OA} = 2\mathbf{CB}$

$\Rightarrow \quad \mathbf{a} = 2(\mathbf{b} - \mathbf{c}) \quad \text{...(i)}$

and $\quad OD : AB = 1 : 3$

$$\Rightarrow \quad \frac{OD}{AB} = \frac{1}{3} \Rightarrow 3OD = AB$$

$\Rightarrow \quad 3\mathbf{OD} = \mathbf{AB}$

$\Rightarrow \quad 3\mathbf{d} = (\mathbf{b} - \mathbf{a}) = \mathbf{b} - 2(\mathbf{b} - \mathbf{c}) \quad$ [using Eq. (i)]

$\Rightarrow \quad 3\mathbf{d} = -\mathbf{b} + 2\mathbf{c} \quad \text{...(ii)}$

Let $OX : XC = \lambda : 1$ and $AX : XD = \mu : 1$

Now, X divides OC in the ratio $\lambda : 1$. Therefore,

$$\text{PV of } X = \frac{\lambda \mathbf{c}}{\lambda + 1} \quad \text{...(iii)}$$

X also divides AD in the ratio $\mu : 1$

$$\text{PV of } X = \frac{\mu \mathbf{d} + \mathbf{a}}{\mu + 1}$$

From Eqs. (iii) and (iv), we get

$$\frac{\lambda \mathbf{c}}{\lambda + 1} = \frac{\mu \mathbf{d} + \mathbf{a}}{\mu + 1}$$

$$\Rightarrow \quad \left(\frac{\lambda}{\lambda+1}\right)\mathbf{c} = \left(\frac{\mu}{\mu+1}\right)\mathbf{d} + \left(\frac{1}{\mu+1}\right)\mathbf{a}$$

$$\Rightarrow \quad \left(\frac{\lambda}{\lambda+1}\right)\mathbf{c} = \left(\frac{\mu}{\mu+1}\right)\left(\frac{-\mathbf{b}+2\mathbf{c}}{3}\right) + \left(\frac{1}{\mu+1}\right)2(\mathbf{b}-\mathbf{c})$$

[using Eqs. (i) and (ii)]

$$\Rightarrow \quad \left(\frac{\lambda}{\lambda+1}\right)\mathbf{c} = \left(\frac{2}{\mu+1} - \frac{\mu}{3(\mu+1)}\right)\mathbf{b} + \left(\frac{2\mu}{3(\mu+1)} - \frac{2}{\mu+1}\right)\mathbf{c}$$

$$\Rightarrow \quad \left(\frac{\lambda}{\lambda+1}\right)\mathbf{c} = \left(\frac{6-\mu}{3(\mu+1)}\right)\mathbf{b} + \left(\frac{2\mu-6}{3(\mu+1)}\right)\mathbf{c}$$

$$\Rightarrow \quad \left(\frac{6-\mu}{3(\mu+1)}\right)\mathbf{b} + \left(\frac{2\mu-6}{3(\mu+1)} - \frac{\lambda}{\lambda+1}\right)\mathbf{c} = \mathbf{0}$$

$$\Rightarrow \quad \frac{6-\mu}{3(\mu+1)} = 0 \text{ and } \frac{2\mu-6}{3(\mu+1)} - \frac{\lambda}{\lambda+1} = 0$$

[since, **b** and **c** are non-collinear]

$$\Rightarrow \quad \mu = 6 \text{ and } \lambda = \frac{2}{5}$$

Hence, $\quad OX : XC = 2 : 5$

$$\therefore \frac{m}{n} = 0.29$$

47. We have, $\mathbf{OA} = \hat{\mathbf{i}} + 0\hat{\mathbf{j}} = \hat{\mathbf{i}}$, $\mathbf{OB} = 0\hat{\mathbf{i}} + \hat{\mathbf{j}} = \hat{\mathbf{j}}$ and $\mathbf{OC} = \hat{\mathbf{i}} + \hat{\mathbf{j}}$

$\therefore \quad \mathbf{OP} = 50x(\mathbf{OA}) = 50x\hat{\mathbf{i}}$

$\mathbf{OQ} = 75x(\mathbf{OB}) = 75x\hat{\mathbf{j}}$

$\mathbf{OR} = (1-x)(\mathbf{OC}) = (1-x)(\hat{\mathbf{i}} + \hat{\mathbf{j}})$

Given, that P, Q and R are collinear.

$\therefore \quad \mathbf{PQ} = t\,\mathbf{QR}$

$\Rightarrow 75x\hat{\mathbf{j}} - 50x\hat{\mathbf{i}} = t\,[(1-x)(\hat{\mathbf{i}} + \hat{\mathbf{j}}) - 75x\hat{\mathbf{j}}]$

$\Rightarrow 75x\hat{\mathbf{j}} - 50x\hat{\mathbf{i}} = t\,[(1-x)\hat{\mathbf{i}} + (1-76x)\hat{\mathbf{j}}]$

On equating coefficient of $\hat{\mathbf{i}}$ and $\hat{\mathbf{j}}$ both sides, we get

$$-50x = t(1-x) \quad \text{...(i)}$$

and $$75x = t(1-76x) \quad \text{...(ii)}$$

From Eqs. (i) and (ii), we get

$$-\frac{2}{3} = \frac{1-x}{1-76x} \Rightarrow -2 + 152x = 3 - 3x$$

$$\Rightarrow \quad 155x = 5 \Rightarrow 465x = 15$$

48. Since, $a\hat{\mathbf{i}} + b\hat{\mathbf{j}} + \frac{1}{2}\hat{\mathbf{k}}$ is linearly dependent with $\hat{\mathbf{i}} + 2\hat{\mathbf{j}}$ and $\hat{\mathbf{j}} - 2\hat{\mathbf{k}}$

$$\therefore a\hat{\mathbf{i}} + b\hat{\mathbf{j}} + \frac{1}{2}\hat{\mathbf{k}} = x(\hat{\mathbf{i}} + 2\hat{\mathbf{j}}) + y(\hat{\mathbf{j}} - 2\hat{\mathbf{k}})$$

$$\Rightarrow a\hat{\mathbf{i}} + b\hat{\mathbf{j}} + \frac{1}{2}\hat{\mathbf{k}} = x\hat{\mathbf{i}} + (2x+y)\hat{\mathbf{j}} - 2y\hat{\mathbf{k}}$$

On equating both sides, we get

$$a = x, b = 2x + y, \frac{1}{2} = -2y \quad \text{...(i)}$$

Also, $\left|a\hat{\mathbf{i}}+b\hat{\mathbf{j}}+\frac{1}{2}\hat{\mathbf{k}}\right|=1 \Rightarrow a^2+b^2=\frac{3}{4}$

$\Rightarrow \quad a^2+\left(2a-\frac{1}{4}\right)^2=\frac{3}{4}$ [using Eq. (i)]

$\Rightarrow \quad 5a^2-a=\frac{11}{16}=0.69$

49.

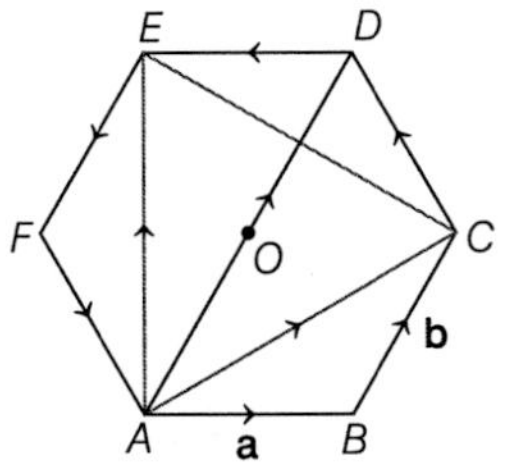

$\mathbf{AB}=\mathbf{a},\ \mathbf{BC}=\mathbf{b}$

$\therefore \quad \mathbf{AC}=\mathbf{AB}+\mathbf{BC}=\mathbf{a}+\mathbf{b}$ ... (i)

$\mathbf{AD}=2\mathbf{BC}=2\mathbf{b}$ ... (ii)

[because AD is parallel to BC and twice in length]

$\mathbf{CD}=\mathbf{AD}-\mathbf{AC}=2\mathbf{b}-(\mathbf{a}+\mathbf{b})=\mathbf{b}-\mathbf{a}$

$\mathbf{FA}=-\mathbf{CD}=\mathbf{a}-\mathbf{b}$ ... (iii)

$\mathbf{DE}=-\mathbf{AB}=-\mathbf{a}$ ... (iv)

$\mathbf{EF}=-\mathbf{BC}=-\mathbf{b}$ ... (v)

$\mathbf{AE}=\mathbf{AD}+\mathbf{DE}=2\mathbf{b}-\mathbf{a}$ ... (vi)

$\mathbf{CE}=\mathbf{CD}+\mathbf{DE}=\mathbf{b}-\mathbf{a}-\mathbf{a}=\mathbf{b}-2\mathbf{a}$ ... (vii)

50. We have, $\mathbf{AB}=2\hat{\mathbf{i}}$

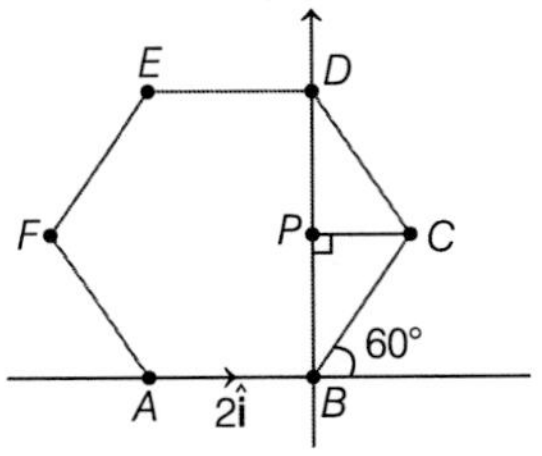

$\therefore \quad BP=BC\sin 60°=2\times\frac{\sqrt{3}}{2}=\sqrt{3}$

$\therefore \quad \mathbf{BD}=2\sqrt{3}\hat{\mathbf{j}}$

Now, $\mathbf{BC}=BC\cos 60°\hat{\mathbf{i}}+BC\sin 60°\hat{\mathbf{j}}=\hat{\mathbf{i}}+\sqrt{3}\hat{\mathbf{j}}$

$\therefore \quad \mathbf{AC}=\mathbf{AB}+\mathbf{BC}=2\hat{\mathbf{i}}+(\hat{\mathbf{i}}+\sqrt{3}\hat{\mathbf{j}})=3\hat{\mathbf{i}}+\sqrt{3}\hat{\mathbf{j}}$

$\therefore \quad \mathbf{AD}=\mathbf{AB}+\mathbf{BD}=2\hat{\mathbf{i}}+2\sqrt{3}\hat{\mathbf{j}}$

Also, $\mathbf{CD}=\mathbf{BD}-\mathbf{BC}=2\sqrt{3}\hat{\mathbf{j}}-(\hat{\mathbf{i}}+\sqrt{3}\hat{\mathbf{j}})$

$\Rightarrow \quad \mathbf{CD}=-\hat{\mathbf{i}}+\sqrt{3}\hat{\mathbf{j}}$

and $\mathbf{CE}=\mathbf{CD}+\mathbf{DE}$
$=(-\hat{\mathbf{i}}+\sqrt{3}\hat{\mathbf{j}})+(-2\hat{\mathbf{i}})=-3\hat{\mathbf{i}}+\sqrt{3}\hat{\mathbf{j}}$

51. Let $P(a, 0, 0)$, $Q(0, b, 1)$ and $R(1, 1, c)$ be points on the line L_1, L_2 and L_3 respectively. P, Q, R are collinear if

$$\frac{-a}{1}=\frac{b}{1-b}=\frac{1}{c-1}$$

As long as $b \neq 0, 1$, we can have a unique a and c. Thus, Q can't be collinear at $(0, 1, 1)$ and $(0, 0, 1)$.

Exercise 3 - Challenging Problems

1. Here, G is centroid of ΔABC and G' is centroid of $\Delta A'B'C'$, shown as in figure.

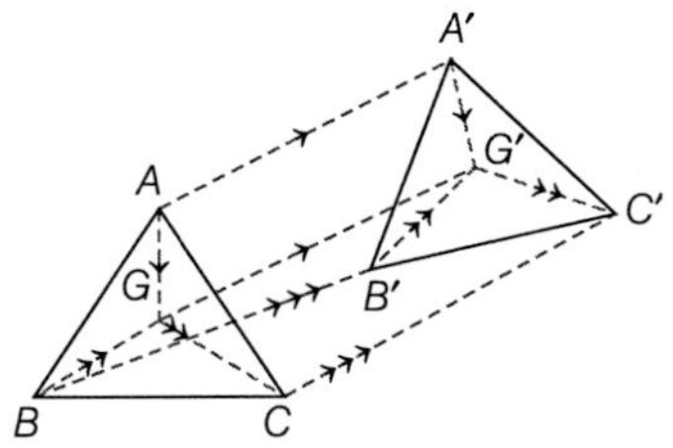

Clearly, $\mathbf{AA}'=\mathbf{AG}+\mathbf{GG}'+\mathbf{G}'\mathbf{A}'$ (polygon law)

$\mathbf{BB}'=\mathbf{BG}+\mathbf{GG}'+\mathbf{G}'\mathbf{B}'$

$\mathbf{CC}'=\mathbf{CG}+\mathbf{GG}'+\mathbf{G}'\mathbf{C}'$

On adding these

$\mathbf{AA}'+\mathbf{BB}'+\mathbf{CC}'=3\mathbf{GG}'+(\mathbf{AG}+\mathbf{BG}+\mathbf{CG})$
$+(\mathbf{G}'\mathbf{A}'+\mathbf{G}'\mathbf{B}'+\mathbf{G}'\mathbf{C}')$

$=3\mathbf{GG}'+(\mathbf{AG}+2\mathbf{DG})+(\mathbf{G}'\mathbf{A}'+2\mathbf{G}'\mathbf{D}')$

[using $\mathbf{AD}$ and $\mathbf{A}'\mathbf{D}'$ as the medians of ΔABC and $\Delta A'B'C'$, respectively]

$=3\mathbf{GG}'+(\mathbf{AG}+\mathbf{GA})+\mathbf{G}'\mathbf{A}'+\mathbf{A}'\mathbf{G}'$

$=3\mathbf{GG}'+\mathbf{0}+\mathbf{0}$

$\therefore \ \mathbf{AA}'+\mathbf{BB}'+\mathbf{CC}'=3\mathbf{GG}'$

Time Saving Technique

We know by triangle law,

$\mathbf{AA}'=\mathbf{OA}'-\mathbf{OA}$

$\mathbf{BB}'=\mathbf{OB}'-\mathbf{OB}$

$\mathbf{CC}'=\mathbf{OC}'-\mathbf{OC}$

$\Rightarrow \quad \mathbf{AA}'+\mathbf{BB}'+\mathbf{CC}'=(\mathbf{OA}'+\mathbf{OB}'+\mathbf{OC}')-(\mathbf{OA}+\mathbf{OB}+\mathbf{OC})$

$=3\mathbf{OG}'-3\mathbf{OG}=3\mathbf{GG}'$

2. Let G be the centroid of ΔABC, first we shall show that circumcentre O, orthocenter O' and centroid G are collinear and $O'G=2OG$.

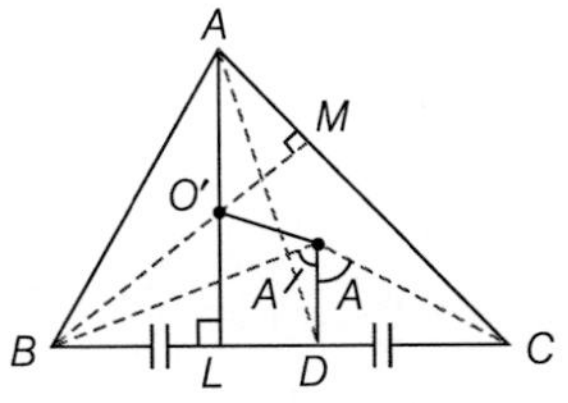

Let AL and BM be perpendiculars on the sides BC and CA, respectively.

Let AD be the median and OD be the perpendicular from O on side BC. If R is the circumradius of circumcircle of ΔABC, then $OB=OC=R$.

In ΔOBD, we have

$OD=R\cos A$ ...(i)

In ΔABM,

$AM=AB\cos A=c\cos A$ ...(ii)

Form $\Delta AO'M$, $AO' = AM\sec(90° - C)$

$$= c\cos A \text{ cosec } C$$

$$= \frac{c}{\sin C}\cdot \cos A = 2R\cos A \quad \left[\because \frac{a}{\sin A} = \frac{b}{\sin B} = \frac{c}{\sin C} = 2R\right]$$

$$AO' = 2(OD) \quad \ldots\text{(iii)}$$

Now, $\Delta AGO'$ and ΔOGD are similar.

$$\therefore \quad \frac{OG}{O'G} = \frac{GD}{GA} = \frac{OD}{AO'} = \frac{1}{2} \quad \text{[using Eq. (iii)]}$$

$$\Rightarrow \quad 2OG = O'G$$

(i) We have, $\mathbf{SA} + \mathbf{SB} + \mathbf{SC} = \mathbf{SA} + (\mathbf{SB} + \mathbf{SC})$

$$= \mathbf{SA} + 2\mathbf{SD} \quad [\because D \text{ is the mid-point of } \mathbf{BC}]$$

$$= (1+2)\mathbf{SG} = 3\mathbf{SG}$$

(ii) On replacing S by O in Eq. (i), we get

$$\mathbf{OA} + \mathbf{OB} + \mathbf{OC} = 3\mathbf{OG}$$

$$= 2\mathbf{OG} + \mathbf{OG} = \mathbf{GO'} + \mathbf{OG}$$

$$= \mathbf{OG} + \mathbf{GO'} = \mathbf{OO'}$$

(iii) $\mathbf{O'A} + \mathbf{O'B} + \mathbf{O'C} = 3\mathbf{O'G}$ [from Eq. (i)]

$$= 2\mathbf{O'G} + \mathbf{O'G}$$

$$= 2\mathbf{O'G} + 2\mathbf{GO} \quad [\because 2\mathbf{OG} = \mathbf{O'G}]$$

$$= 2\mathbf{O'O}$$

(iv) $\mathbf{AO} + \mathbf{O'B} + \mathbf{O'C} = 2\mathbf{AO'} + (\mathbf{O'A} + \mathbf{O'B} + \mathbf{O'C})$

$$= 2\mathbf{AO'} + 2\mathbf{O'O} \quad \text{[from Eq. (iii)]}$$

$$= 2(\mathbf{AO'} + \mathbf{O'O}) = 2\mathbf{AO} = \mathbf{AP}$$

$[\because \mathbf{AO}$ is the circumradius of $\Delta ABC]$

3. We have, $\mathbf{c} = 3\mathbf{a} + 4\mathbf{b}$ and $2\mathbf{c} = \mathbf{a} - 3\mathbf{b}$

$$\Rightarrow \quad 2(3\mathbf{a} + 4\mathbf{b}) = \mathbf{a} - 3\mathbf{b}$$

$$\Rightarrow \quad 5\mathbf{a} = -11\mathbf{b}$$

$$\Rightarrow \quad \mathbf{a} = -\frac{11}{5}\mathbf{b} \text{ and } \mathbf{b} = -\frac{5}{11}\mathbf{a}$$

(i) $\mathbf{c} = 3\mathbf{a} + 4\mathbf{b} = 3\mathbf{a} + 4\left(-\frac{5}{11}\mathbf{a}\right)$ $\left[\text{using } \mathbf{b} = -\frac{5}{11}\mathbf{a}\right]$

$$= 3\mathbf{a} - \frac{20}{11}\mathbf{a} = \frac{13}{11}\mathbf{a}$$

which shows that **c** and **a** have the same direction.

And $\mathbf{c} = \frac{13}{11}\mathbf{a}$

$$\Rightarrow |\mathbf{c}| = \frac{13}{11}|\mathbf{a}| \Rightarrow |\mathbf{c}| > |\mathbf{a}|$$

(ii) We have, $\mathbf{c} = 3\mathbf{a} + 4\mathbf{b}$ and $\mathbf{a} = -\frac{11}{5}\mathbf{b}$

$$\mathbf{c} = 3\left(-\frac{11}{5}\mathbf{b}\right) + 4\mathbf{b} = -\frac{33}{5}\mathbf{b} + 4\mathbf{b}$$

$$\mathbf{c} = -\frac{13}{5}\mathbf{b}$$

This shows **c** and **b** have opposite directions.

Also, $|\mathbf{c}| = \left|-\frac{13}{5}\mathbf{b}\right| = \frac{13}{5}|\mathbf{b}| \Rightarrow |\mathbf{c}| > |\mathbf{b}|$

4. If $\mathbf{A}(t)$ and $\mathbf{B}(t)$ are non-zero vectors for all t and $\mathbf{A}(0) = 2\hat{\mathbf{i}} + 3\hat{\mathbf{j}}$, $\mathbf{A}(1) = 6\hat{\mathbf{i}} + 2\hat{\mathbf{j}}$, $\mathbf{B}(0) = 3\hat{\mathbf{i}} + 2\hat{\mathbf{j}}$, and $\mathbf{B}(1) = 2\hat{\mathbf{i}} + 6\hat{\mathbf{j}}$.

In order to prove that $\mathbf{A}(t)$ and $\mathbf{B}(t)$ are parallel vectors for some values of t. It is sufficient to show that $\mathbf{A}(t) = \lambda\mathbf{B}(t)$ for some λ.

$$\Leftrightarrow \quad \{f_1(t)\hat{\mathbf{i}} + f_2(t)\hat{\mathbf{j}}\} = \lambda\{g_1(t)\hat{\mathbf{i}} + g_2(t)\hat{\mathbf{j}}\}$$

$$\Leftrightarrow \quad f_1(t) = \lambda g_1(t) \text{ and } f_2(t) = \lambda g_2(t)$$

$$\Leftrightarrow \quad \frac{f_1(t)}{f_2(t)} = \frac{g_1(t)}{g_2(t)}$$

$$\Leftrightarrow \quad f_1(t)g_2(t) - f_2(t)g_1(t) = 0 \quad \text{for some } t \in [0, 1]$$

Let $f(t) = f_1(t)g_2(t) - f_2(t)g_1(t)$, $t \in [0, 1]$

Since, f_1, f_2, g_1 and g_2 are continuous functions.

$\therefore F(t)$ is also a continuous function.

Also, $f(0) = f_1(0)g_2(0) - g_1(0)f_2(0)$

$$= 2\times 2 - 3\times 3 = 4 - 9 = -5 < 0$$

and $f(1) = f_1(1)g_2(1) - g_1(1)f_2(1)$

$$= 6\times 6 - 2\times 2 = 32 > 0$$

Thus, $F(t)$ is a continuous function on $[0, 1]$ such that $F(0)\cdot F(1) < 0$.

$\therefore$ By intermediate value theorem, there exists some $t \in (0, 1)$ such that

$$f(t) = 0$$

$$\Rightarrow \quad f_1(t)g_2(t) - f_2(t)g_1(t) = 0$$

$$\Rightarrow \quad \mathbf{A}(t) = \lambda\mathbf{B}(t) \text{ for some } \lambda.$$

Hence, $\mathbf{A}(t)$ and $\mathbf{B}(t)$ are parallel vectors.

5. Suppose that, a, b and c are coplanar.

$$\Rightarrow \quad \begin{vmatrix} \cos\alpha & 1 & 1 \\ 1 & \cos\beta & 1 \\ 1 & 1 & \cos\gamma \end{vmatrix} = 0$$

On applying $R_2 \to R_2 - R_1$ and $R_3 \to R_3 - R_1$

$$\Rightarrow \quad \begin{vmatrix} \cos\alpha & 1 & 1 \\ 1-\cos\alpha & \cos\beta - 1 & 0 \\ 1-\cos\alpha & 0 & \cos\gamma - 1 \end{vmatrix} = 0$$

$$\Rightarrow \cos\alpha(\cos\beta - 1)(\cos\gamma - 1) - (1-\cos\alpha)(\cos\gamma - 1) - (1-\cos\alpha)(\cos\beta - 1) = 0$$

On dividing throughout by $(1-\cos\alpha)(1-\cos\beta)(1-\cos\gamma)$, we get

$$\frac{\cos\alpha}{1-\cos\alpha} + \frac{1}{1-\cos\beta} + \frac{1}{1-\cos\gamma} = 0$$

$$\Rightarrow \quad \frac{-(1-\cos\alpha)+1}{1-\cos\alpha} + \frac{1}{1-\cos\beta} + \frac{1}{1-\cos\gamma} = 0$$

$$\Rightarrow \quad -1 + \frac{1}{(1-\cos\alpha)} + \frac{1}{(1-\cos\beta)} + \frac{1}{(1-\cos\gamma)} = 0$$

$$\frac{1}{1-\cos\alpha} + \frac{1}{1-\cos\beta} + \frac{1}{1-\cos\gamma} = 1$$

$$\Rightarrow \text{cosec}^2\frac{\alpha}{2} + \text{cosec}^2\frac{\beta}{2} + \text{cosec}^2\frac{\gamma}{2} = 2, \text{ which is not possible.}$$

As, $\text{cosec}^2\frac{\alpha}{2} \geq 1$, $\text{cosec}^2\frac{\beta}{2} \geq 1$

and $\text{cosec}^2\frac{\gamma}{2} \geq 1$

$\because$ They never be coplanar.

6. Let A, B and C be the three points whose position vectors referred to O are $\mathbf{r}_1$, $\mathbf{r}_2$ and $\mathbf{r}_3$, respectively.

$$\mathbf{AB} = \mathbf{OB} - \mathbf{OA} = \mathbf{r}_2 - \mathbf{r}_1$$
$$\mathbf{BC} = \mathbf{OC} - \mathbf{OB} = \mathbf{r}_3 - \mathbf{r}_2$$

Now, if A, B and C are collinear points, then **AB** and **BC** are in the same line and $\mathbf{BC} = \lambda\,(\mathbf{AB})$

$\Rightarrow \quad (\mathbf{r}_3 - \mathbf{r}_2) = \lambda(\mathbf{r}_2 - \mathbf{r}_1)$

$\Rightarrow \quad \mathbf{r}_3 = -\lambda\mathbf{r}_1 + (\lambda + 1)\,\mathbf{r}_2$

$\because \quad \mathbf{r}_3 = l\mathbf{r}_1 + m\mathbf{r}_2$

where, $\quad l = -\lambda$ and $m = \lambda + 1$

$\Rightarrow \quad l + m = -\lambda + (\lambda + 1) = 1$

7. Let $OACB$ be a parallelogram shown as

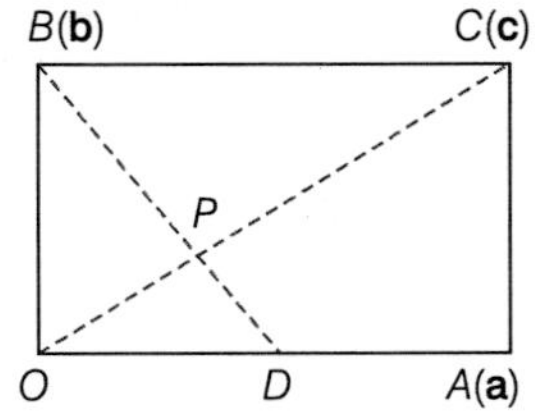

Here, $\quad \mathbf{OD} = \dfrac{1}{2}\mathbf{BC}$

$\Rightarrow \quad \mathbf{OP} + \mathbf{PD} = \dfrac{1}{2}(\mathbf{BP} + \mathbf{PC}) \quad$ [using Δ law]

$\Rightarrow \quad 2\mathbf{OP} + 2\mathbf{PD} = \mathbf{BP} + \mathbf{PC}$

$\quad -2\mathbf{PO} + 2\mathbf{PD} = -\mathbf{PB} + \mathbf{PC}$

$\Rightarrow \quad \mathbf{PB} + 2\mathbf{PD} = \mathbf{PC} + 2\mathbf{PO}$

$\Rightarrow \quad \dfrac{\mathbf{PB} + 2\mathbf{PD}}{1+2} = \dfrac{\mathbf{PC} + 2\mathbf{PO}}{1+2}$

The common point P of BD and CO divides each in the ratio 2 : 1.

8. Let S be the point of intersection of **AB** and **CR**. Let A be the origin and the position vectors of the points B, C, P, Q, R and S be $\mathbf{b}, \mathbf{c}, \mathbf{p}, \mathbf{q}, \mathbf{r}$ and $\mathbf{s}$ respectively.

$\therefore \quad \mathbf{p} = \dfrac{3\mathbf{b} + 2\mathbf{c}}{5} \quad$ ...(i)

and $\quad \mathbf{q} = \dfrac{4\mathbf{c}}{5} \quad$ ...(ii)

$\Rightarrow \quad \dfrac{5\mathbf{p} - 3\mathbf{b}}{2} = \dfrac{5\mathbf{q}}{4}$

$\Rightarrow \quad 10\mathbf{p} - 6\mathbf{b} = 5\mathbf{q}$

i.e. $\quad 10\mathbf{p} = 5\mathbf{q} + 6\mathbf{b}$

$\Rightarrow \quad \dfrac{10\mathbf{p}}{11} = \dfrac{5\mathbf{q} + 6\mathbf{b}}{11} = \mathbf{r}$

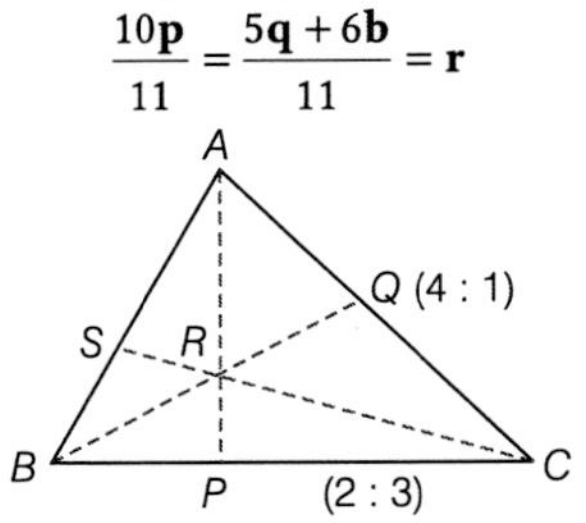

$\Rightarrow \quad \dfrac{11\mathbf{r}}{10} = \mathbf{p} = \dfrac{3\mathbf{b} + 2\mathbf{c}}{5} \quad$ [using Eq. (i)]

$\Rightarrow \quad 11\mathbf{r} = 6\mathbf{b} + 4\mathbf{c}$

$\Rightarrow \quad 11\mathbf{r} - 4\mathbf{c} = 6\mathbf{b}$

$\dfrac{11\mathbf{r} - 4\mathbf{c}}{7} = \dfrac{6}{7}\mathbf{b} = \mathbf{s}$, thus S divides AB in the ratio 6 : 1.

9. Let the position vector of O' with reference to O as the origin be α.

Then, $\quad \mathbf{OO'} = \alpha$

Now, $\mathbf{O'}P_i$ = Position vector of P_i

$\quad$ − Position vector of $O' = \mathbf{r}_i - \alpha \quad$ ...(i)

$i = 1, 2, \ldots\ldots, n$

Let the position vectors of $P_1, P_2, P_3, \ldots\ldots, P_n$ with respect to O' as the origin be $\mathbf{R}_1, \mathbf{R}_2, \ldots, \mathbf{R}_n$ respectively.

Then, $\quad \mathbf{R}_i = \mathbf{O'}P_i = \mathbf{r}_i - \alpha,\ i = 1, 2, \ldots\ldots, n \quad$ [using Eq. (i)]

Now, $a_1\mathbf{R}_1 + a_2\mathbf{R}_2 + \ldots\ldots + a_n\mathbf{R}_n = \mathbf{0}$

$\Rightarrow \quad \sum_{i=1}^{n} a_i\mathbf{R}_i = \mathbf{0} \Rightarrow \sum_{i=1}^{n} a_i(\mathbf{r}_i - \alpha) = \mathbf{0}$

$\Rightarrow \quad \sum_{i=1}^{n} a_i\mathbf{r}_i - \sum_{i=1}^{n} a_i\,\alpha = \mathbf{0}$

$\Rightarrow \quad \mathbf{0} - \alpha\left(\sum_{i=1}^{n} a_i\right) = \mathbf{0} \quad \left[\because \sum_{i=1}^{n} a_i\mathbf{r}_i = \mathbf{0} \text{ (given)}\right]$

$\Rightarrow \quad \sum_{i=1}^{n} a_i = 0$

Thus, $\sum_{i=1}^{n} a_i\mathbf{R}_i = \mathbf{0}$ will hold good, if $\sum_{i=1}^{n} a_i = 0$.

10. Let l, m and n be scalars such that

$$l\mathbf{p} + m\mathbf{q} + n\mathbf{r} = \mathbf{0}$$

$\Rightarrow l\{(\cos a)\mathbf{u} + (\cos b)\mathbf{v} + (\cos c)\mathbf{w}\} + m\{(\sin a)\mathbf{u} + (\sin b)\mathbf{v} + (\sin c)\mathbf{w}\} + n\{\sin(x + a)\mathbf{u} + \sin(x + b)\mathbf{v} + \sin(x + c)\mathbf{w}\} = \mathbf{0}$

$\Rightarrow \{l\cos a + m\sin a + n\sin(x + a)\}\mathbf{u} + \{l\cos b + m\sin b + n\sin(x + b)\}\mathbf{v} + \{l\cos c + m\sin c + n\sin(x + c)\}\mathbf{w} = \mathbf{0}$

$\Rightarrow \quad l\cos a + m\sin a + n\sin(x + a) = 0 \quad$ ...(i)

$\quad l\cos b + m\sin b + n\sin(x + b) = 0 \quad$ ...(ii)

$\quad l\cos c + m\sin c + n\sin(x + c) = 0 \quad$ ...(iii)

This is a homogeneous system of linear equations in l, m and n.

The determinant of the coefficient matrix is

$$\Delta = \begin{vmatrix} \cos a & \sin a & \sin(x+a) \\ \cos b & \sin b & \sin(x+b) \\ \cos c & \sin c & \sin(x+c) \end{vmatrix} = \begin{vmatrix} \cos a & \sin a & 0 \\ \cos b & \sin b & 0 \\ \cos c & \sin c & 0 \end{vmatrix} = 0$$

[using $C_3 \to C_3 - \sin x\, C_1 - \cos x\, C_2$]

$\Rightarrow$ So, the above system of equations has non-trivial solutions also. This means that l, m and n may attain non-zero values also.

Hence, the given system of vectors is a linearly dependent system of vectors.

2

> *What is Mathematics? It is only a systematic effort of solving puzzles pored by nature.*
>
> **–Shakuntla Devi**

Product of Vectors

Learning Milestones

Milestone 1 Scalar or Dot Product

- Scalar or Dot Product of Two Vectors
- Angle Between Two Vectors
- Scalar Product in Terms of Components
- Components of a Vector Along and Perpendicular to Another Vector
- Application of Dot Product in Mechanics

Milestone 2 Vector or Cross Product

- Vector or Cross Product of Two Vectors
- Area of Parallelogram and Triangle
- Moment of a Force and Couple Moment of a Force
- Moment of a Couple
- Rotation About an Axis

Milestone 3 Scalar Triple Product

- Definition
- Volume of Tetrahedron

Milestone 4 Vector Triple Product

- Definition
- Reciprocal System of Vectors
- Solving of Vector Equations

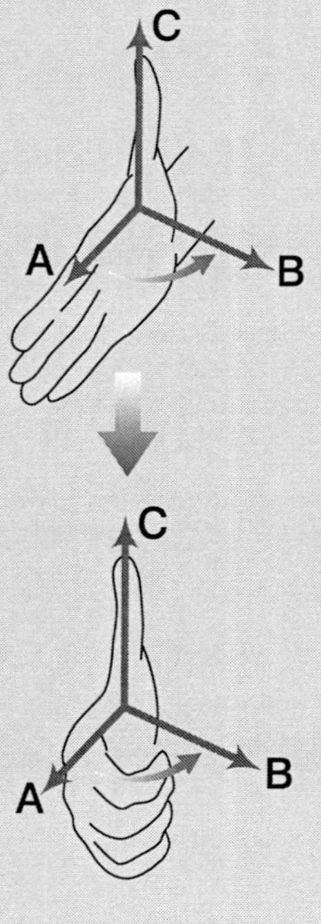

Practice Milestones

Practice Milestone 1- JEE Main Pattern
Practice Milestone 2 - JEE Advanced Pattern
Practice Milestone 3 - Challenging Problems

Milestone 1 Scalar or Dot Product

• Scalar or Dot Product of Two Vectors • Angle Between Two Vectors • Scalar Product in Terms of Components • Components of a Vector Along and Perpendicular to Another Vector • Application of Dot Product in Mechanics

Product of two vectors is processed by two methods.

(i) Scalar product (ii) Vector product

In this milestone, we study the scalar product.

2.1 Scalar or Dot Product of Two Vectors

When the product of two vectors results in a scalar quantity, then it is called **scalar product**. It is also known as **dot product** because we denote it by putting a **dot** (·) between two vectors.

2.2 Angle between Two Vectors

If **a** and **b** are two non-zero vectors and θ be the angle between them, then their scalar product (or dot product) is denoted by $\mathbf{a}\cdot\mathbf{b}$ and is defined as the scalar $|\mathbf{a}||\mathbf{b}|\cos\theta$, where $|\mathbf{a}|$ and $|\mathbf{b}|$ are modulii of **a** and **b** respectively and $0 \le \theta \le \pi$.

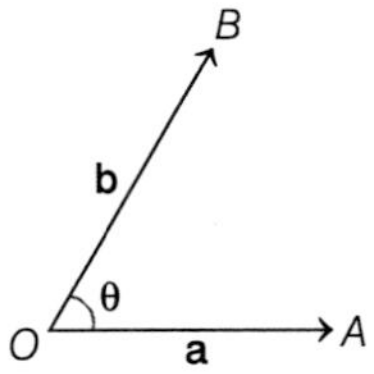

We know that $\mathbf{a}\cdot\mathbf{b} = |\mathbf{a}||\mathbf{b}|\cos\theta$

$$\therefore \quad \cos\theta = \frac{\mathbf{a}\cdot\mathbf{b}}{|\mathbf{a}||\mathbf{b}|} \Rightarrow \theta = \cos^{-1}\left(\frac{\mathbf{a}\cdot\mathbf{b}}{|\mathbf{a}||\mathbf{b}|}\right)$$

JEE Focus Points

Concept Inside Video

- $\mathbf{a}\cdot\mathbf{b} \in R$
- $\mathbf{a}\cdot\mathbf{b} \le |\mathbf{a}||\mathbf{b}|$
- If **a** is perpendicular to **b**, then $\mathbf{a}\cdot\mathbf{b} = 0$
- $\mathbf{a}\cdot\mathbf{b} = 0 \Rightarrow \mathbf{a} = 0$ or $\mathbf{b} = 0$ or $\mathbf{a} \perp \mathbf{b}$
- $\mathbf{a}\cdot\mathbf{b} > 0$ if the angle between **a** and **b** is acute.
- $\mathbf{a}\cdot\mathbf{b} < 0$ if the angle between **a** and **b** is obtuse.
- If the two vectors have same direction, then $\theta = 0$;
  $\therefore \quad \cos\theta = 1$ and $\mathbf{a}\cdot\mathbf{b} = |\mathbf{a}||\mathbf{b}|$
- If the two vectors have opposite direction, then $\theta = \pi$;
  $\therefore \quad \cos\theta = -1$ and $\mathbf{a}\cdot\mathbf{b} = -|\mathbf{a}||\mathbf{b}|$
- If **a** and **b** are unit vectors, then $|\mathbf{a}| = 1, |\mathbf{b}| = 1$;
  $\therefore \quad \mathbf{a}\cdot\mathbf{b} = \cos\theta$
- If $\mathbf{a} = a_1\hat{\mathbf{i}} + a_2\hat{\mathbf{j}} + a_3\hat{\mathbf{k}}$ and $\mathbf{b} = b_1\hat{\mathbf{i}} + b_2\hat{\mathbf{j}} + b_3\hat{\mathbf{k}}$, then $\mathbf{a}\cdot\mathbf{b} = a_1b_1 + a_2b_2 + a_3b_3$.

Example 1. Find the angle θ between the vectors $\mathbf{a} = 2\hat{\mathbf{i}} + 2\hat{\mathbf{j}} - \hat{\mathbf{k}}$ and $\mathbf{b} = 6\hat{\mathbf{i}} - 3\hat{\mathbf{j}} + 2\hat{\mathbf{k}}$.

Sol. Angle between **a** and **b** is given by

$$\cos\theta = \frac{\mathbf{a}\cdot\mathbf{b}}{|\mathbf{a}||\mathbf{b}|}$$

$$= \frac{(2\hat{\mathbf{i}} + 2\hat{\mathbf{j}} - \hat{\mathbf{k}})\cdot(6\hat{\mathbf{i}} - 3\hat{\mathbf{j}} + 2\hat{\mathbf{k}})}{\sqrt{2^2 + 2^2 + (-1)^2}\cdot\sqrt{6^2 + (-3)^2 + 2^2}}$$

$$= \frac{12 - 6 - 2}{3\cdot 7}$$

$$= \frac{4}{21}$$

Hence, $\theta = \cos^{-1}\left(\frac{4}{21}\right)$

Example 2. If the vectors $\mathbf{a} = (c\log_2 x)\hat{\mathbf{i}} - 6\hat{\mathbf{j}} + 3\hat{\mathbf{k}}$ and $\mathbf{b} = (\log_2 x)\hat{\mathbf{i}} + 2\hat{\mathbf{j}} + (2c\log_2 x)\hat{\mathbf{k}}$ make an obtuse angle for any $x \in (0, \infty)$. Then, determine the interval to which c belongs.

Sol. Given, $\mathbf{a} = (c\log_2 x)\hat{\mathbf{i}} - 6\hat{\mathbf{j}} + 3\hat{\mathbf{k}}$

and $\mathbf{b} = (\log_2 x)\hat{\mathbf{i}} + 2\hat{\mathbf{j}} + (2c\log_2 x)\hat{\mathbf{k}}$

$$\mathbf{a}\cdot\mathbf{b} = (c\log_2 x)(\log_2 x) - (6)(2) + 3(2c\log_2 x)$$

$$= c(\log_2 x)^2 - 12 + 6c\log_2(x)$$

Now, **a** and **b** make an obtuse angle.

$\therefore \quad \mathbf{a}\cdot\mathbf{b} < 0$

$\Rightarrow c(\log_2 x)^2 - 12 + 6c\log_2 x < 0, \forall x > 0$

Put $\log_2 x = y$

$\therefore \; cy^2 - 12 + 6cy < 0$

$\Rightarrow cy^2 + 6cy - 12 < 0, \forall y \in R$

$\Rightarrow \quad c < 0$ and $36c^2 + 48c < 0$

$[\because ax^2 + bx + c < 0, \forall x \in R$ iff $a < 0$ and $D < 0]$

$\Rightarrow \quad c < 0$ and $12c(3c + 4) > 0$

$\Rightarrow \quad c \in \left(-\frac{4}{3}, 0\right)$

Properties of Scalar Product

(i) **Commutativity** The scalar product of two vector is commutative i.e. $\mathbf{a} \cdot \mathbf{b} = \mathbf{b} \cdot \mathbf{a}$.

(ii) **Distributivity of scalar product over vector addition** The scalar product of vectors is distributive over vector addition i.e.

(a) $\mathbf{a} \cdot (\mathbf{b} + \mathbf{c}) = \mathbf{a} \cdot \mathbf{b} + \mathbf{a} \cdot \mathbf{c}$ (left distributivity)

(b) $(\mathbf{b} + \mathbf{c}) \cdot \mathbf{a} = \mathbf{b} \cdot \mathbf{a} + \mathbf{c} \cdot \mathbf{a}$ (right distributivity)

(iii) Let $\mathbf{a}$ and $\mathbf{b}$ be two non-zero vectors, if $\mathbf{a} \cdot \mathbf{b} = 0 \Leftrightarrow \mathbf{a} \perp \mathbf{b}$.

As $\hat{\mathbf{i}}, \hat{\mathbf{j}}$ and $\hat{\mathbf{k}}$ are mutually perpendicular unit vectors along the coordinate axes, therefore

$\hat{\mathbf{i}} \cdot \hat{\mathbf{j}} = \hat{\mathbf{j}} \cdot \hat{\mathbf{i}} = 0, \hat{\mathbf{j}} \cdot \hat{\mathbf{k}} = \hat{\mathbf{k}} \cdot \hat{\mathbf{j}} = 0; \hat{\mathbf{k}} \cdot \hat{\mathbf{i}} = \hat{\mathbf{i}} \cdot \hat{\mathbf{k}} = 0$

(iv) For any vector $\mathbf{a}, \mathbf{a} \cdot \mathbf{a} = |\mathbf{a}|^2 = \mathbf{a}^2$.

As $\hat{\mathbf{i}}, \hat{\mathbf{j}}$ and $\hat{\mathbf{k}}$ are unit vectors along the coordinate axes, therefore $\hat{\mathbf{i}} \cdot \hat{\mathbf{i}} = |\hat{\mathbf{i}}|^2 = 1, \hat{\mathbf{j}} \cdot \hat{\mathbf{j}} = |\hat{\mathbf{j}}|^2 = 1$ and $\hat{\mathbf{k}} \cdot \hat{\mathbf{k}} = |\hat{\mathbf{k}}|^2 = 1$.

(v) If m is a scalar and $\mathbf{a}$ and $\mathbf{b}$ be any two vectors, then $(m\mathbf{a}) \cdot \mathbf{b} = m(\mathbf{a} \cdot \mathbf{b}) = \mathbf{a} \cdot (m\mathbf{b})$.

(vi) If m and n are scalars and $\mathbf{a}$ and $\mathbf{b}$ be two vectors, then $(m\mathbf{a}) \cdot n\mathbf{b} = mn(\mathbf{a} \cdot \mathbf{b}) = (mn\mathbf{a}) \cdot \mathbf{b} = \mathbf{a} \cdot (mn\mathbf{b})$

(vii) For any vectors $\mathbf{a}$ and $\mathbf{b}$, we have

(a) $\mathbf{a} \cdot (-\mathbf{b}) = -(\mathbf{a} \cdot \mathbf{b}) = (-\mathbf{a}) \cdot \mathbf{b}$

(b) $(-\mathbf{a}) \cdot (-\mathbf{b}) = \mathbf{a} \cdot \mathbf{b}$

(viii) For any two vectors $\mathbf{a}$ and $\mathbf{b}$, we have

(a) $|\mathbf{a} + \mathbf{b}|^2 = |\mathbf{a}|^2 + |\mathbf{b}|^2 + 2\mathbf{a} \cdot \mathbf{b}$

(b) $|\mathbf{a} - \mathbf{b}| = |\mathbf{a}|^2 + |\mathbf{b}|^2 - 2\mathbf{a} \cdot \mathbf{b}$

(c) $(\mathbf{a} + \mathbf{b}) \cdot (\mathbf{a} - \mathbf{b}) = |\mathbf{a}|^2 - |\mathbf{b}|^2$

(d) $|\mathbf{a} + \mathbf{b}| = |\mathbf{a}| + |\mathbf{b}| \Rightarrow \mathbf{a} \parallel \mathbf{b}$

(e) $|\mathbf{a} + \mathbf{b}|^2 = |\mathbf{a}|^2 + |\mathbf{b}|^2 \Rightarrow \mathbf{a} \perp \mathbf{b}$

(f) $|\mathbf{a} + \mathbf{b}| = |\mathbf{a} - \mathbf{b}| \Rightarrow \mathbf{a} \perp \mathbf{b}$

JEE Focus Points

Concept Inside Video

- Let $\mathbf{r} = x\hat{\mathbf{i}} + y\hat{\mathbf{j}} + z\hat{\mathbf{k}}$ where x, y and z are the cartesian components of the vector $\mathbf{r}$ along the three coordinate axes taking dot product with $\hat{\mathbf{i}}, \hat{\mathbf{j}}$ and $\hat{\mathbf{k}}$ respectively, we have

$$\mathbf{r} \cdot \hat{\mathbf{i}} = x, \ \mathbf{r} \cdot \hat{\mathbf{j}} = y,$$
$$\mathbf{r} \cdot \hat{\mathbf{k}} = z$$
$$\therefore \quad \mathbf{r} = (\mathbf{r} \cdot \hat{\mathbf{i}})\hat{\mathbf{i}} + (\mathbf{r} \cdot \hat{\mathbf{j}})\hat{\mathbf{j}} + (\mathbf{r} \cdot \hat{\mathbf{k}})\hat{\mathbf{k}}$$

- $|\mathbf{a} \cdot \mathbf{b}|^2 \le |\mathbf{a}|^2 |\mathbf{b}|^2$

Maximum value of $\mathbf{a} \cdot \mathbf{b} = |\mathbf{a}||\mathbf{b}|$

and minimum value of $\mathbf{a} \cdot \mathbf{b} = -|\mathbf{a}||\mathbf{b}|$

Example 3. If $|\mathbf{a}| = 3, |\mathbf{b}| = 4$, then find the value of λ for which $\mathbf{a} + \lambda\mathbf{b}$ is perpendicular to $\mathbf{a} - \lambda\mathbf{b}$.

Sol. $\because \quad (\mathbf{a} + \lambda\mathbf{b}) \cdot (\mathbf{a} - \lambda\mathbf{b}) = 0$

$\Rightarrow \quad |\mathbf{a}^2| - \lambda(\mathbf{a} \cdot \mathbf{b}) + \lambda(\mathbf{b} \cdot \mathbf{a}) - \lambda^2 |\mathbf{b}|^2 = 0$

$\Rightarrow \quad |\mathbf{a}|^2 - \lambda^2 |\mathbf{b}|^2 = 0$

$\Rightarrow \quad \lambda = \pm \dfrac{|\mathbf{a}|}{|\mathbf{b}|} = \pm \dfrac{3}{4}$

Projection of a Vector on Other Vector

In Figure, projection of $\mathbf{a}$ on $\mathbf{b} = PQ$,

where $PQ = AB \cos\theta$

Projection of $\mathbf{a}$ on $\mathbf{b}$ may be positive or negative, it is positive or negative according as the angle between $\mathbf{a}$ and $\mathbf{b}$ is acute or obtuse.

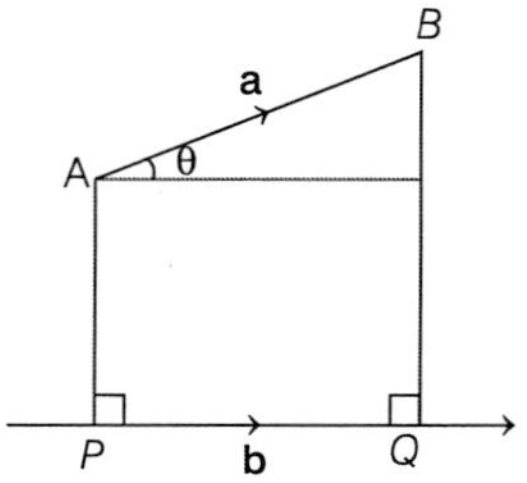

Geometrical Interpretation of Scalar Product

Let $\mathbf{a}$ and $\mathbf{b}$ be two vectors represented by **OA** and **OB** respectively. Let θ be the angle between **OA** and **OB**. Draw $BL \perp OA$ and $AM \perp OB$.

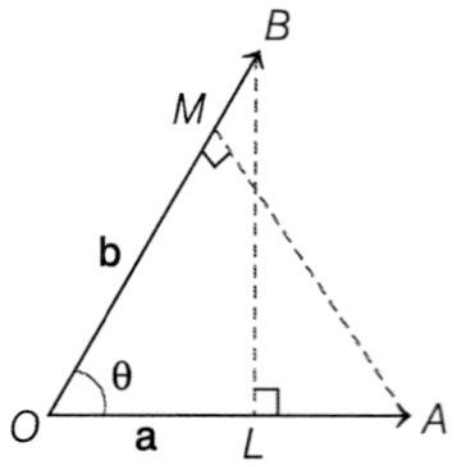

From ΔOBL and ΔOAM, we have

$$OL = OB \cos\theta \text{ and } OM = OA \cos\theta.$$

Here, OL and OM are known as projection of $\mathbf{b}$ on $\mathbf{a}$ and $\mathbf{a}$ on $\mathbf{b}$ respectively.

Now, $\mathbf{a} \cdot \mathbf{b} = |\mathbf{a}||\mathbf{b}|\cos\theta$

$= |\mathbf{a}|(OB\cos\theta) = |\mathbf{a}|(OL)$

= (Magnitude of $\mathbf{a}$) (Projection of $\mathbf{b}$ on $\mathbf{a}$) ...(i)

Again, $\mathbf{a} \cdot \mathbf{b} = |\mathbf{a}||\mathbf{b}|\cos\theta$

$= |\mathbf{b}|(|\mathbf{a}|\cos\theta) = |\mathbf{b}|(OA\cos\theta) = |\mathbf{b}|(OM)$

$\mathbf{a} \cdot \mathbf{b}$ = (Magnitude of $\mathbf{b}$) (Projection of $\mathbf{a}$ on $\mathbf{b}$) ...(ii)

Thus, geometrically interpreted, **the scalar product of two vectors is the product of modulus of either vector and the projection of the other in its direction.**

JEE Focus Points

- Projection of **a** on **b** $= \dfrac{\mathbf{a}\cdot\mathbf{b}}{|\mathbf{b}|}$

  $= \mathbf{a}\cdot\dfrac{\mathbf{b}}{|\mathbf{b}|} = \mathbf{a}\cdot\hat{\mathbf{b}}$

Concept Inside Video

- Projection of **b** on **a** $= \dfrac{\mathbf{a}\cdot\mathbf{b}}{|\mathbf{a}|}$

  $= \mathbf{b}\cdot\dfrac{\mathbf{a}}{|\mathbf{a}|} = \mathbf{b}\cdot\hat{\mathbf{a}}$

- If the vectors $-\mathbf{a}$ and **b** are shown as below, then the angle between their direction is $\pi - \theta$, where $\angle AOB = \theta$

  $-\mathbf{a}\cdot\mathbf{b} = |\mathbf{a}||\mathbf{b}|\cos(\pi-\theta) = -|\mathbf{a}||\mathbf{b}|\cos\theta$

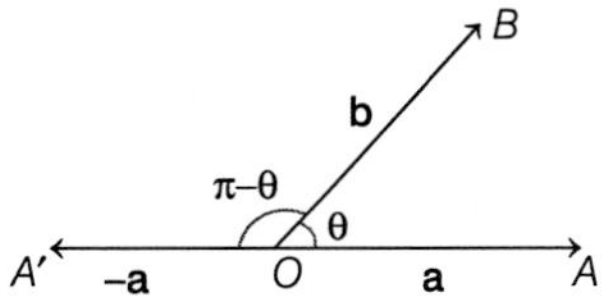

Example 4. Find the projection of $\mathbf{a} = 2\hat{\mathbf{i}} + 3\hat{\mathbf{j}} - 2\hat{\mathbf{k}}$ on $\mathbf{b} = \hat{\mathbf{i}} + 2\hat{\mathbf{j}} + 3\hat{\mathbf{k}}$.

Sol. Projection of **a** on $\mathbf{b} = \mathbf{a}\cdot\dfrac{\mathbf{b}}{|\mathbf{b}|}$

$$= \frac{(2\hat{\mathbf{i}} + 3\hat{\mathbf{j}} - 2\hat{\mathbf{k}})\cdot(\hat{\mathbf{i}} + 2\hat{\mathbf{j}} + 3\hat{\mathbf{k}})}{|\hat{\mathbf{i}} + 2\hat{\mathbf{j}} + 3\hat{\mathbf{k}}|}$$

$$= \frac{2+6-6}{\sqrt{14}}$$

$$= \frac{2}{\sqrt{14}}$$

Example 5. If $\mathbf{a} = \hat{\mathbf{i}} + 3\hat{\mathbf{j}} + 7\hat{\mathbf{k}}$ and $\mathbf{b} = 7\hat{\mathbf{i}} - \hat{\mathbf{j}} + 8\hat{\mathbf{k}}$, then find the projection of **b** on **a**.

Sol. Given, $\mathbf{a} = \hat{\mathbf{i}} + 3\hat{\mathbf{j}} + 7\hat{\mathbf{k}}$

and $\mathbf{b} = 7\hat{\mathbf{i}} - \hat{\mathbf{j}} + 8\hat{\mathbf{k}}$

Now, projection of **b** on $\mathbf{a} = \dfrac{\mathbf{a}\cdot\mathbf{b}}{|\mathbf{a}|}$

$$= \frac{(\hat{\mathbf{i}} + 3\hat{\mathbf{j}} + 7\hat{\mathbf{k}})\cdot(7\hat{\mathbf{i}} - \hat{\mathbf{j}} + 8\hat{\mathbf{k}})}{\sqrt{1+9+49}}$$

$$= \frac{7-3+56}{\sqrt{59}}$$

$$= \frac{60}{\sqrt{59}}$$

2.3 Scalar Product in Terms of Components

If $\mathbf{a} = a_1\hat{\mathbf{i}} + a_2\hat{\mathbf{j}} + a_3\hat{\mathbf{k}}$ and $\mathbf{b} = b_1\hat{\mathbf{i}} + b_2\hat{\mathbf{j}} + b_3\hat{\mathbf{k}}$, then $\mathbf{a}\cdot\mathbf{b} = a_1b_1 + a_2b_2 + a_3b_3$.

Thus, **scalar product of two vectors is equal to the sum of the products of their corresponding components.**

In particular, $\mathbf{a}\cdot\mathbf{a} = |\mathbf{a}|^2 = a_1^2 + a_2^2 + a_3^2$.

Angle between two vectors in term of component

$$\cos\theta = \frac{a_1b_1 + a_2b_2 + a_3b_3}{\sqrt{a_1^2 + a_2^2 + a_3^2}\sqrt{b_1^2 + b_2^2 + b_3^2}}$$

$$\Rightarrow \quad \theta = \cos^{-1}\left\{\frac{a_1b_1 + a_2b_2 + a_3b_3}{\sqrt{a_1^2 + a_2^2 + a_3^2}\sqrt{b_1^2 + b_2^2 + b_3^2}}\right\}$$

Condition of two vectors being parallel

Let $\mathbf{a} = a_1\hat{\mathbf{i}} + a_2\hat{\mathbf{j}} + a_3\hat{\mathbf{k}}$ and $\mathbf{b} = b_1\hat{\mathbf{i}} + b_2\hat{\mathbf{j}} + b_3\hat{\mathbf{k}}$.

If **a** and **b** be parallel, then

$$\mathbf{a} = \lambda\mathbf{b} \text{ or } \frac{a_1}{b_1} = \frac{a_2}{b_2} = \frac{a_3}{b_3}$$

Condition of two vectors being perpendicular

Let $\mathbf{a} = a_1\hat{\mathbf{i}} + a_2\hat{\mathbf{j}} + a_3\hat{\mathbf{k}}$ and $\mathbf{b} = b_1\hat{\mathbf{i}} + b_2\hat{\mathbf{j}} + b_3\hat{\mathbf{k}}$.

If **a** and **b** be perpendicular to each other, then

$$a_1b_1 + a_2b_2 + a_3b_3 = 0$$

Example 6. If $\mathbf{a} = 5\hat{\mathbf{i}} - \hat{\mathbf{j}} + 7\hat{\mathbf{k}}$ and $\mathbf{b} = \hat{\mathbf{i}} - \hat{\mathbf{j}} + \lambda\hat{\mathbf{k}}$, then find λ such that $\mathbf{a}+\mathbf{b}$ and $\mathbf{a}-\mathbf{b}$ are orthogonal.

Sol. Clearly, $\mathbf{a}+\mathbf{b} = (5\hat{\mathbf{i}} - \hat{\mathbf{j}} + 7\hat{\mathbf{k}}) + (\hat{\mathbf{i}} - \hat{\mathbf{j}} + \lambda\hat{\mathbf{k}})$

$= 6\hat{\mathbf{i}} - 2\hat{\mathbf{j}} + (7+\lambda)\hat{\mathbf{k}}$

and $\mathbf{a}-\mathbf{b} = (5\hat{\mathbf{i}} - \hat{\mathbf{j}} + 7\hat{\mathbf{k}}) - (\hat{\mathbf{i}} - \hat{\mathbf{j}} + \lambda\hat{\mathbf{k}}) = 4\hat{\mathbf{i}} + (7-\lambda)\hat{\mathbf{k}}$

Since, $\mathbf{a}+\mathbf{b}$ and $\mathbf{a}-\mathbf{b}$ are orthogonal.

$\therefore \quad (\mathbf{a}+\mathbf{b})\cdot(\mathbf{a}-\mathbf{b}) = 0$

$\Rightarrow \quad [6\hat{\mathbf{i}} - 2\hat{\mathbf{j}} + (7+\lambda)\hat{\mathbf{k}}]\cdot(4\hat{\mathbf{i}} + (7-\lambda)\hat{\mathbf{k}}) = 0$

$\Rightarrow \quad 6\times 4 - 2\times 0 + (7+\lambda)(7-\lambda) = 0$

$\Rightarrow \quad 24 + 49 - \lambda^2 = 0$

$\Rightarrow \quad \lambda^2 = 73$

$\Rightarrow \quad \lambda = \pm\sqrt{73}$

Example 7. Let $\mathbf{a} = \hat{\mathbf{i}} + \hat{\mathbf{j}} + \sqrt{2}\,\hat{\mathbf{k}}$, $\mathbf{b} = b_1\hat{\mathbf{i}} + b_2\hat{\mathbf{j}} + \sqrt{2}\hat{\mathbf{k}}$ and $\mathbf{c} = 5\hat{\mathbf{i}} + \hat{\mathbf{j}} + \sqrt{2}\,\hat{\mathbf{k}}$ be three vectors such that the projection of **b** on **a** is $|\mathbf{a}|$ and $\mathbf{a}+\mathbf{b}$ is perpendicular to **c**, then find $|\mathbf{b}|$.

Sol. Given, projection of $\mathbf{b}$ on $\mathbf{a} = \dfrac{\mathbf{b}\cdot\mathbf{a}}{|\mathbf{a}|} = |\mathbf{a}| \Rightarrow \mathbf{b}\cdot\mathbf{a} = |\mathbf{a}|^2$

$$\Rightarrow (b_1\hat{\mathbf{i}} + b_2\hat{\mathbf{j}} + \sqrt{2}\hat{\mathbf{k}})\cdot(\hat{\mathbf{i}} + \hat{\mathbf{j}} + \sqrt{2}\hat{\mathbf{k}}) = 1^2 + 1^2 + (\sqrt{2})^2$$

$$\Rightarrow b_1 + b_2 + 2 = 4$$

$$\Rightarrow b_1 + b_2 = 2 \quad \text{...(i)}$$

Also, given $\mathbf{a} + \mathbf{b}$ is perpendicular to $\mathbf{c}$.

$$\therefore (\mathbf{a} + \mathbf{b})\cdot\mathbf{c} = 0$$

$$\Rightarrow [(\hat{\mathbf{i}} + \hat{\mathbf{j}} + \sqrt{2}\hat{\mathbf{k}}) + (b_1\hat{\mathbf{i}} + b_2\hat{\mathbf{j}} + \sqrt{2}\hat{\mathbf{k}})]\cdot(5\hat{\mathbf{i}} + \hat{\mathbf{j}} + \sqrt{2}\hat{\mathbf{k}}) = 0$$

$$\Rightarrow [(1 + b_1)\hat{\mathbf{i}} + (1 + b_2)\hat{\mathbf{j}} + 2\sqrt{2}\hat{\mathbf{k}}]\cdot(5\hat{\mathbf{i}} + \hat{\mathbf{j}} + \sqrt{2}\hat{\mathbf{k}}) = 0$$

$$\Rightarrow 5 + 5b_1 + 1 + b_2 + 4 = 0$$

$$\Rightarrow 5b_1 + b_2 = -10 \quad \text{...(ii)}$$

On solving Eqs. (i) and (ii), we get

$$b_1 = -3 \text{ and } b_2 = 5$$

$$\therefore \quad \mathbf{b} = -3\hat{\mathbf{i}} + 5\hat{\mathbf{j}} + \sqrt{2}\hat{\mathbf{k}}$$

Hence, $|\mathbf{b}| = \sqrt{9 + 25 + 2} = \sqrt{36} = 6$

Example 8. If $\mathbf{a}+\mathbf{b}+\mathbf{c} = 0$, $|\mathbf{a}| = 3$, $|\mathbf{b}| = 5$ and $|\mathbf{c}| = 7$, then find the angle between $\mathbf{a}$ and $\mathbf{b}$.

Sol. Given, $\mathbf{a} + \mathbf{b} + \mathbf{c} = 0$

$$\Rightarrow \mathbf{a} + \mathbf{b} = -\mathbf{c}$$

Taking magnitude both sides, we get

$$|\mathbf{a} + \mathbf{b}| = |-\mathbf{c}|$$

$$\Rightarrow |\mathbf{a} + \mathbf{b}|^2 = |-\mathbf{c}|^2$$

$$\Rightarrow |\mathbf{a}|^2 + |\mathbf{b}|^2 + 2|\mathbf{a}||\mathbf{b}|\cos\theta = |\mathbf{c}|^2$$

$$\Rightarrow 3^2 + 5^2 + 2(3)(5)\cos\theta = 7^2$$

$$\Rightarrow 9 + 25 + 30\cos\theta = 49$$

$$\Rightarrow 30\cos\theta = 49 - 34 = 15$$

$$\Rightarrow \cos\theta = \frac{15}{30} = \frac{1}{2} \Rightarrow \theta = \frac{\pi}{3}$$

Example 9. If $\mathbf{a}$, $\mathbf{b}$ and $\mathbf{c}$ are unit vectors such that $\mathbf{a}+\mathbf{b}+\mathbf{c} = 0$, then find the value of $\mathbf{a}\cdot\mathbf{b}+\mathbf{b}\cdot\mathbf{c}+\mathbf{c}\cdot\mathbf{a}$.

Sol. Given, $\mathbf{a} + \mathbf{b} + \mathbf{c} = 0$

On squaring both sides, we get

$$(\mathbf{a} + \mathbf{b} + \mathbf{c})^2 = 0^2$$

$$\Rightarrow (\mathbf{a} + \mathbf{b} + \mathbf{c})\cdot(\mathbf{a} + \mathbf{b} + \mathbf{c}) = 0$$

$$\Rightarrow |\mathbf{a}|^2 + |\mathbf{b}|^2 + |\mathbf{c}|^2 + 2\mathbf{a}\cdot\mathbf{b} + 2\mathbf{b}\cdot\mathbf{c} + 2\mathbf{c}\cdot\mathbf{a} = 0$$

$$\Rightarrow 1 + 1 + 1 + 2(\mathbf{a}\cdot\mathbf{b} + \mathbf{b}\cdot\mathbf{c} + \mathbf{c}\cdot\mathbf{a}) = 0$$

$$\Rightarrow \mathbf{a}\cdot\mathbf{b} + \mathbf{b}\cdot\mathbf{c} + \mathbf{c}\cdot\mathbf{a} = -\frac{3}{2}$$

Example 10. Let $\mathbf{a}$, $\mathbf{b}$ and $\mathbf{c}$ be vectors of length 10, 12 and 15, respectively. If $\mathbf{a}$ is perpendicular to $(\mathbf{b}+\mathbf{c})$, $\mathbf{b}$ to $(\mathbf{c}+\mathbf{a})$ and $\mathbf{c}$ to $(\mathbf{a}+\mathbf{b})$, then find the length of $(\mathbf{a}+\mathbf{b}+\mathbf{c})$.

Sol. We have, $|\mathbf{a}| = 10$, $|\mathbf{b}| = 12$ and $|\mathbf{c}| = 15$

Since, $\mathbf{a} \perp (\mathbf{b} + \mathbf{c})$

$$\Rightarrow \mathbf{a}\cdot(\mathbf{b} + \mathbf{c}) = 0$$

$$\Rightarrow \mathbf{a}\cdot\mathbf{b} + \mathbf{a}\cdot\mathbf{c} = 0 \quad \text{...(i)}$$

$\mathbf{b} \perp (\mathbf{a} + \mathbf{c})$

$$\Rightarrow \mathbf{b}\cdot(\mathbf{a} + \mathbf{c}) = 0$$

$$\Rightarrow \mathbf{b}\cdot\mathbf{a} + \mathbf{b}\cdot\mathbf{c} = 0 \quad \text{...(ii)}$$

and also, $\mathbf{c} \perp (\mathbf{a} + \mathbf{b})$

$$\Rightarrow \mathbf{c}\cdot(\mathbf{a} + \mathbf{b}) = 0$$

$$\Rightarrow \mathbf{c}\cdot\mathbf{a} + \mathbf{c}\cdot\mathbf{b} = 0 \quad \text{...(iii)}$$

On adding Eqs. (i), (ii) and (iii), we get

$$2(\mathbf{a}\cdot\mathbf{b} + \mathbf{b}\cdot\mathbf{c} + \mathbf{c}\cdot\mathbf{a}) = 0 \quad \text{...(iv)}$$

Now, $|\mathbf{a} + \mathbf{b} + \mathbf{c}|^2 = |\mathbf{a}|^2 + |\mathbf{b}|^2 + |\mathbf{c}|^2 + 2(\mathbf{a}\cdot\mathbf{b} + \mathbf{b}\cdot\mathbf{c} + \mathbf{c}\cdot\mathbf{a})$

$$\Rightarrow |\mathbf{a} + \mathbf{b} + \mathbf{c}|^2 = 100 + 144 + 225 + 0 \quad \text{[using Eq. (iv)]}$$

$$\Rightarrow |\mathbf{a} + \mathbf{b} + \mathbf{c}| = \sqrt{469} \text{ units}$$

Time Saving Technique

We can apply this property $|\mathbf{a}+\mathbf{b}+\mathbf{c}| = \sqrt{|\mathbf{a}|^2+|\mathbf{b}|^2+|\mathbf{c}|^2}$ iff $\mathbf{a}\cdot\mathbf{b}+\mathbf{b}\cdot\mathbf{c}+\mathbf{c}\cdot\mathbf{a} = 0$ to get the answer directly

$$= \sqrt{100+144+225} = \sqrt{469}$$

Example 11. Let $a, b, c \in R$ be such that $a^2 + b^2 + c^2 = 1$, if $a\cos\theta = b\cos\left(\theta + \dfrac{2\pi}{3}\right) = c\cos\left(\theta + \dfrac{4\pi}{3}\right)$, where $\theta = \dfrac{\pi}{2}$, then find the angle between the vector $a\hat{\mathbf{i}} + b\hat{\mathbf{j}} + c\hat{\mathbf{k}}$ or $b\hat{\mathbf{i}} + c\hat{\mathbf{j}} + a\hat{\mathbf{k}}$.

Sol. Given, $a\cos\theta = b\cos\left(\theta + \dfrac{2\pi}{3}\right) = c\cos\left(\theta + \dfrac{4\pi}{3}\right) = \lambda$

$$a = \frac{\lambda}{\cos\theta}, b = \frac{\lambda}{\cos\left(\theta + \frac{2\pi}{3}\right)}, c = \frac{\lambda}{\cos\left(\theta + \frac{4\pi}{3}\right)}$$

$$\Rightarrow \frac{1}{a} + \frac{1}{b} + \frac{1}{c} = \frac{1}{\lambda}\left[\cos\theta + \cos\left(\theta + \frac{2\pi}{3}\right) + \cos\left(\theta + \frac{4\pi}{3}\right)\right]$$

$$= \frac{1}{\lambda}\left[\cos\theta + 2\cos\left(\frac{\theta + \frac{2\pi}{3} + \theta + \frac{4\pi}{3}}{2}\right)\cos\left(\frac{\theta + \frac{2\pi}{3} - \theta - \frac{4\pi}{3}}{2}\right)\right]$$

$$= \frac{1}{\lambda}\left[\cos\theta + 2\cos\left(\frac{2\theta + \frac{6\pi}{3}}{2}\right)\cos\left(-\frac{2\pi}{3}\right)\right]$$

$$= \frac{1}{\lambda}\left[\cos\theta - 2\times\frac{1}{2}\cos(\pi + \theta)\right] = \frac{1}{\lambda}(\cos\theta + \cos\theta) = 0$$

$$\therefore \quad \frac{1}{a} + \frac{1}{b} + \frac{1}{c} = 0 \Rightarrow ab + bc + ca = 0$$

Now, angle between vector

$a\hat{\mathbf{i}} + b\hat{\mathbf{j}} + c\hat{\mathbf{k}}$ and $b\hat{\mathbf{i}} + c\hat{\mathbf{j}} + a\hat{\mathbf{k}} = ab + bc + ca = 0$

$\therefore$ Angle between vector is $\dfrac{\pi}{2}$ or $90°$.

JEE SCANNER

Example Similar to PYQ Asked in JEE Main 2021

The scalar product of the vector $\mathbf{a}=\hat{i}+\hat{j}+\hat{k}$ *with a unit vector along the sum of the vector* $\mathbf{b}=2\hat{i}+4\hat{j}-5\hat{k}$ *and* $\mathbf{c}=\lambda\hat{i}+2\hat{j}+3\hat{k}$ *is equal to 1, then the value of* λ *is ......*

Sol. Given, $\mathbf{a}=\hat{i}+\hat{j}+\hat{k}$, $\mathbf{b}=2\hat{i}+4\hat{j}-5\hat{k}$, $\mathbf{c}=\lambda\hat{i}+2\hat{j}+3\hat{k}$

$$\mathbf{b}+\mathbf{c}=(2+\lambda)\hat{i}+6\hat{j}-2\hat{k}$$

Unit vector along the sum of the vector **b** and **c**

$$=\frac{(2+\lambda)\hat{i}+6\hat{j}-2\hat{k}}{\sqrt{(2+\lambda)^2+(6)^2+(-2)^2}}$$

Now, $(\hat{i}+\hat{j}+\hat{k})\cdot\dfrac{[(2+\lambda)\hat{i}+6\hat{j}-2\hat{k}]}{\sqrt{(2+\lambda)^2+36+4}}=1$

$\Rightarrow \quad (2+\lambda)+6-2=\sqrt{(2+\lambda)^2+40}$

$\Rightarrow \quad (\lambda+6)^2=(2+\lambda)^2+40$

$\Rightarrow \quad \lambda^2+12\lambda+36=4+4\lambda+\lambda^2+40$

$\Rightarrow \quad 8\lambda=8 \Rightarrow \lambda=1$

Skill Builder

The scalar product of vector $\mathbf{a}=2\hat{i}+5\hat{j}-7\hat{k}$ with a unit vector along the sum of the vector $\mathbf{b}=7\hat{i}+5\hat{j}+3\hat{k}$ and $\mathbf{c}=\mu\hat{i}+4\hat{j}-5\hat{k}$ is equal to 2, then the value of $[|\mu|]$ is .... (where $[\cdot]$ is the greatest integer function and $|\cdot|$ is modulus function)

For Sol.

■ **For more practice** See Q.7 of Milestone Practice 1.

Example 12. Let **a**, **b**, **c** be unit vectors, where $|\mathbf{a}-\mathbf{b}|^2+|\mathbf{b}-\mathbf{c}|^2+|\mathbf{c}+\mathbf{a}|^2=3$, then find the value of $|\mathbf{a}+2\mathbf{b}+3\mathbf{c}|$.

Sol. We have, $\quad |a-b|^2+|b-c|^2+|c+a|^2=3 \quad$ ...(i)

$\Rightarrow 2[|\mathbf{a}|^2+|\mathbf{b}|^2+|\mathbf{c}|^2]-2\mathbf{a}\cdot\mathbf{b}-2\mathbf{b}\cdot\mathbf{c}+2\mathbf{c}\cdot\mathbf{a}=3$

$\Rightarrow 3+|\mathbf{a}|^2+|\mathbf{b}|^2+|\mathbf{c}|^2-2\mathbf{a}\cdot\mathbf{b}-2\mathbf{b}\cdot\mathbf{c}+2\mathbf{c}\cdot\mathbf{a}=3$

$\Rightarrow \quad |\mathbf{a}|^2+|\mathbf{b}|^2+|\mathbf{c}|^2-2\mathbf{a}\cdot\mathbf{b}-2\mathbf{b}\cdot\mathbf{c}+2\mathbf{c}\cdot\mathbf{a}=0$

$\Rightarrow \quad |\mathbf{a}+\mathbf{c}-\mathbf{b}|^2=0$

$\Rightarrow \quad \mathbf{b}=\mathbf{a}+\mathbf{c}$ ...(ii)

From Eq. (i), $\quad |\mathbf{c}|^2|+|\mathbf{a}|^2+|\mathbf{a}+\mathbf{c}|^2=3 \quad$ [using Eq. (ii)]

$\Rightarrow \quad |\mathbf{a}+\mathbf{c}|^2=1$

$\Rightarrow \quad \mathbf{a}\cdot\mathbf{c}=-\dfrac{1}{2}$

So, $|\mathbf{a}+2\mathbf{b}+3\mathbf{c}|^2=|3\mathbf{a}+5\mathbf{c}|^2 \quad$ [from Eq. (i)]

$\Rightarrow \quad |3\mathbf{a}+5\mathbf{c}|^2=9|\mathbf{a}|^2+25|\mathbf{c}|^2+30\mathbf{a}\cdot\mathbf{c}$

$=9+25-15=19$

Example 13. Dot product of a vector with vectors, $3\hat{i}-5\hat{k}$, $2\hat{i}+7\hat{j}$ and $\hat{i}+\hat{j}+\hat{k}$ are respectively −1, 6 and 5, find the vector.

Sol. Let $\mathbf{a}=3\hat{i}-5\hat{k}$, $\mathbf{b}=2\hat{i}+7\hat{j}$, $\mathbf{c}=\hat{i}+\hat{j}+\hat{k}$

Let $\mathbf{d}=x\hat{i}+y\hat{j}+z\hat{k}$ be vector such that its dot product with **a**, **b** and **c** are −1, 6 and 5 respectively, then $\mathbf{d}\cdot\mathbf{a}=-1$

$\Rightarrow \quad (x\hat{i}+y\hat{j}+z\hat{k})\cdot(3\hat{i}-5\hat{k})=-1$

$\Rightarrow \quad 3x-5z=-1$ ...(i)

Similarly, $\quad \mathbf{d}\cdot\mathbf{b}=6$

$\Rightarrow \quad (x\hat{i}+y\hat{j}+z\hat{k})\cdot(2\hat{i}+7\hat{j})=6$

$\Rightarrow \quad 2x+7y=6$ ...(ii)

and $\quad \mathbf{d}\cdot\mathbf{c}=5$

$\Rightarrow \quad (x\hat{i}+y\hat{j}+z\hat{k})\cdot(\hat{i}+\hat{j}+\hat{k})=5$

$\Rightarrow \quad x+y+z=5$ ...(iii)

On solving Eqs. (i), (ii) and (iii), we get

$x=3, y=0$ and $z=2$

$\therefore$ Required vector $\mathbf{d}=3\hat{i}+2\hat{k}$

Example 14. If $a+2b+3c=4$, then find the least value of $a^2+b^2+c^2$.

Sol. Let $\mathbf{u}=a\hat{i}+b\hat{j}+c\hat{k}$, $\mathbf{v}=\hat{i}+2\hat{j}+3\hat{k}$

$$\mathbf{u}\cdot\mathbf{v}=(a\hat{i}+b\hat{j}+c\hat{k})\cdot(\hat{i}+2\hat{j}+3\hat{k})=a+2b+3c$$

Now, $\quad \cos\theta=\dfrac{\mathbf{u}\cdot\mathbf{v}}{|\mathbf{u}||\mathbf{v}|}$

$\Rightarrow \quad \cos\theta=\dfrac{a+2b+3c}{\sqrt{a^2+b^2+c^2}\sqrt{1^2+2^2+3^2}}$

$\Rightarrow \quad \cos^2\theta=\dfrac{(a+2b+3c)^2}{14(a^2+b^2+c^2)}\le 1 \quad [\because \cos^2\theta\le 1]$

$\Rightarrow \quad a^2+b^2+c^2\ge\dfrac{(a+2b+3c)^2}{14}=\dfrac{16}{14}=\dfrac{8}{7}$

Hence, the least value of $a^2+b^2+c^2$ is $\dfrac{8}{7}$.

Example 15. Find the unit vector which makes an angle of 45° with the vector $2\hat{i}+2\hat{j}-\hat{k}$ and an angle of 60° with the vector $\hat{j}-\hat{k}$.

Sol. Let the unit vector be $\mathbf{c}=c_1\hat{i}+c_2\hat{j}+c_3\hat{k}$ so that it makes an angle of 45° with $2\hat{i}+2\hat{j}-\hat{k}$.

Given, $\cos 45°=\dfrac{(c_1\hat{i}+c_2\hat{j}+c_3\hat{k})\cdot(2\hat{i}+2\hat{j}-\hat{k})}{\sqrt{c_1^2+c_2^2+c_3^2}\sqrt{4+4+1}}$

$\Rightarrow \quad \dfrac{1}{\sqrt{2}}=\dfrac{2c_1+2c_2-c_3}{3} \quad [\because c_1^2+c_2^2+c_3^2=1]$

$\Rightarrow \quad 2c_1+2c_2-c_3=\dfrac{3}{\sqrt{2}}$ ...(i)

Also, it makes an angle of 60° with $\hat{\mathbf{j}} - \hat{\mathbf{k}}$.

$$\Rightarrow \quad \frac{c_2 - c_3}{\sqrt{2}} = \cos 60° \quad [\because |\hat{\mathbf{j}} - \hat{\mathbf{k}}| = \sqrt{2} \text{ and } |\mathbf{c}| = 1]$$

$$\Rightarrow \quad c_2 - c_3 = \frac{\sqrt{2}}{2} \quad \text{...(ii)}$$

$$\Rightarrow \quad c_1^2 + c_2^2 + c_3^2 = 1 \quad \text{...(iii)}$$

$$[\text{using } |\mathbf{c}| = |c_1\hat{\mathbf{i}} + c_2\hat{\mathbf{j}} + c_3\hat{\mathbf{k}}| = 1]$$

From Eq. (ii), $c_2 = \frac{1}{\sqrt{2}} + c_3$

and from Eq. (i), $c_1 = \frac{-c_3}{2} + \frac{1}{2\sqrt{2}}$

On substituting in Eq. (iii), we get

$$\frac{c_3^2}{4} + \frac{1}{2} + \frac{2c_3}{\sqrt{2}} + \frac{1}{8} - \frac{c_3}{2\sqrt{2}} + c_3^2 + c_3^2 = 1$$

$$\Rightarrow \quad \frac{9}{4}c_3^2 + \frac{3c_3}{2\sqrt{2}} + \frac{5}{8} = 1$$

$$\Rightarrow \quad c_3 = -\frac{1}{\sqrt{2}}, \frac{1}{3\sqrt{2}}$$

Hence, the required vectors are

$$\left(\frac{1}{\sqrt{2}}, 0, -\frac{1}{\sqrt{2}}\right) \text{ and } \left(\frac{1}{3\sqrt{2}}, \frac{4}{3\sqrt{2}}, \frac{1}{3\sqrt{2}}\right).$$

Example 16. A vector $\mathbf{a} = (x, y, z)$ of length $2\sqrt{3}$ which makes equal angles with the vectors $\mathbf{b} = (y, -2z, 3x)$ and $\mathbf{c} = (2z, 3x, y)$ and is perpendicular to $\mathbf{d} = (1, -1, 2)$ and makes an obtuse angle with Y-axis. Find the vector.

Sol. Since, $\mathbf{a}$ is perpendicular to $\mathbf{d}$, so $\mathbf{a} \cdot \mathbf{d} = 0$

$$\Rightarrow \quad x - y + 2z = 0 \quad \text{...(i)}$$

$\because \quad |\mathbf{b}| = |\mathbf{c}|$

$\Rightarrow \mathbf{a} \cdot \mathbf{b} = \mathbf{a} \cdot \mathbf{c}$ as $\mathbf{a}$ makes equal angles with $\mathbf{b}$ and $\mathbf{c}$.

$$\therefore \quad xy - 2yz + 3xz = 2xz + 3xy - yz$$

$$\Rightarrow \quad xz - 2xy - yz = 0 \quad \text{...(ii)}$$

Also, we have $x^2 + y^2 + z^2 = 12$ ...(iii)

and $y < 0$

From Eq. (i), $y = x + 2z$

Substitute the value of y in Eq. (ii), we get

$$xz - 2x(x + 2z) - (x + 2z)z = 0$$

$$\Rightarrow \quad xz - 2x^2 - 4xz - xz - 2z^2 = 0$$

$$\Rightarrow \quad -2x^2 - 4xz - 2z^2 = 0$$

$$\Rightarrow \quad x^2 + 2xz + z^2 = 0$$

$$\Rightarrow \quad (x + z)^2 = 0$$

$$\Rightarrow \quad x = -z$$

$$\therefore \quad y = -z + 2z = z$$

Now, substitute the value of x and y in Eq. (iii), we get

$$(-z)^2 + (z)^2 + z^2 = 12$$

$$\Rightarrow \quad z^2 = 4$$

$$\Rightarrow \quad z = \pm 2$$

but $y < 0$ and $y = z$

So, $z = -2 = y$ and $x = 2$.

Example 17. Let a unit vector $\mathbf{u} = x\hat{\mathbf{i}} + y\hat{\mathbf{j}} + z\hat{\mathbf{k}}$ make angles $\frac{\pi}{2}, \frac{\pi}{3}$ and $\frac{2\pi}{3}$ with the vectors $\frac{1}{\sqrt{2}}\hat{\mathbf{i}} + \frac{1}{\sqrt{2}}\hat{\mathbf{k}}$, $\frac{1}{\sqrt{2}}\hat{\mathbf{j}} + \frac{1}{\sqrt{2}}\hat{\mathbf{k}}$ and $\frac{1}{\sqrt{2}}\hat{\mathbf{i}} + \frac{1}{\sqrt{2}}\hat{\mathbf{j}}$, respectively. If $\mathbf{v} = \frac{1}{\sqrt{2}}\hat{\mathbf{i}} + \frac{1}{\sqrt{2}}\hat{\mathbf{j}} + \frac{1}{\sqrt{2}}\hat{\mathbf{k}}$, then find the value of $|\mathbf{u} - \mathbf{v}|^2$.

Sol. $\because$ Unit vector $\mathbf{u} = x\hat{\mathbf{i}} + y\hat{\mathbf{j}} + z\hat{\mathbf{k}}$ makes $\frac{\pi}{2}, \frac{\pi}{3}$ and $\frac{2\pi}{3}$ with the vectors $\frac{1}{\sqrt{2}}\hat{\mathbf{i}} + \frac{1}{\sqrt{2}}\hat{\mathbf{k}}, \frac{1}{\sqrt{2}}\hat{\mathbf{j}} + \frac{1}{\sqrt{2}}\hat{\mathbf{k}}$ and $\frac{1}{\sqrt{2}}\hat{\mathbf{i}} + \frac{1}{\sqrt{2}}\hat{\mathbf{j}}$, respectively.

Taking dot products of unit vector $\mathbf{u}$ with given vector respectively, we have

$$\frac{x}{\sqrt{2}} + \frac{z}{\sqrt{2}} = |\mathbf{u}| \sqrt{\frac{1}{2} + \frac{1}{2}} \cos\frac{\pi}{2} = 0$$

$$\Rightarrow \quad x + z = 0 \quad \text{...(i)}$$

and $$\frac{y}{\sqrt{2}} + \frac{z}{\sqrt{2}} = |\mathbf{u}| \sqrt{\frac{1}{2} + \frac{1}{2}} \cos\frac{\pi}{3}$$

$$\Rightarrow \quad \frac{y + z}{\sqrt{2}} = \frac{1}{2}$$

$$\Rightarrow \quad y + z = \frac{1}{\sqrt{2}} \quad \text{...(ii)}$$

and $$\frac{x}{\sqrt{2}} + \frac{y}{\sqrt{2}} = |\mathbf{u}| \sqrt{\frac{1}{2} + \frac{1}{2}} \cos\frac{2\pi}{3}$$

$$\Rightarrow \quad \frac{x + y}{\sqrt{2}} = 1 \times 1 \times \frac{-1}{2}$$

$$\Rightarrow \quad x + y = \frac{-1}{\sqrt{2}} \quad \text{...(iii)}$$

On solving Eqs. (i), (ii) and (iii), we get

$$y = 0, x = \frac{-1}{\sqrt{2}} \text{ and } z = \frac{1}{\sqrt{2}}$$

$$\mathbf{u} = \frac{-1}{\sqrt{2}}\hat{\mathbf{i}} + \frac{1}{\sqrt{2}}\hat{\mathbf{k}} \text{ and } \mathbf{v} = \frac{1}{\sqrt{2}}\hat{\mathbf{i}} + \frac{1}{\sqrt{2}}\hat{\mathbf{j}} + \frac{1}{\sqrt{2}}\hat{\mathbf{k}}$$

$$\therefore \quad \mathbf{u} - \mathbf{v} = -\sqrt{2}\hat{\mathbf{i}} - \frac{1}{\sqrt{2}}\hat{\mathbf{j}}$$

Hence, $|\mathbf{u} - \mathbf{v}|^2 = (-\sqrt{2})^2 + \left(\frac{-1}{\sqrt{2}}\right)^2 = 2 + \frac{1}{2} = \frac{5}{2}$

2.4 Components of a Vector Along and Perpendicular to Another Vector

Let **a** and **b** be two vectors represented by **OA** and **OB** and let θ be the angle between **a** and **b**. Draw $BM \perp OA$, as shown,

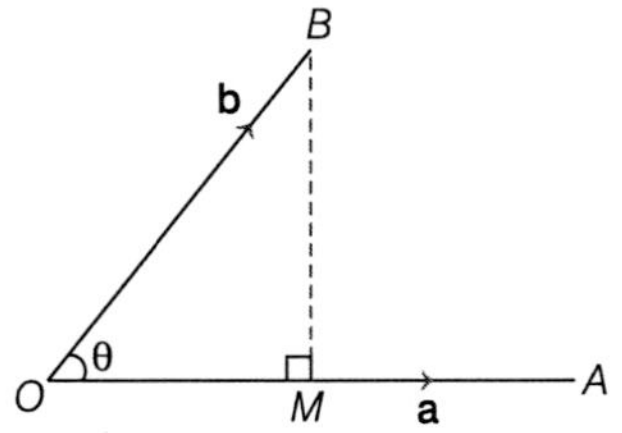

$\therefore \quad \mathbf{b} = \mathbf{OM} + \mathbf{MB}$

$\Rightarrow \quad \mathbf{OM} = (OM)\hat{\mathbf{a}} = (OB\cos\theta)\,\hat{\mathbf{a}} = (|\mathbf{b}|\cos\theta)\,\hat{\mathbf{a}}$

$$= \left(|\mathbf{b}|\frac{(\mathbf{a}\cdot\mathbf{b})}{|\mathbf{a}||\mathbf{b}|}\right)\hat{\mathbf{a}} = \left(\frac{\mathbf{a}\cdot\mathbf{b}}{|\mathbf{a}|}\right)\hat{\mathbf{a}} = \frac{(\mathbf{a}\cdot\mathbf{b})\,\mathbf{a}}{|\mathbf{a}||\mathbf{a}|} = \left(\frac{\mathbf{a}\cdot\mathbf{b}}{|\mathbf{a}|^2}\right)\mathbf{a}$$

$$\mathbf{b} = \mathbf{OM} + \mathbf{MB}$$

$$\mathbf{MB} = \mathbf{b} - \mathbf{OM} = \mathbf{b} - \left(\frac{\mathbf{a}\cdot\mathbf{b}}{|\mathbf{a}|^2}\right)\mathbf{a}$$

Thus, the components of **b** along and perpendicular to **a** are $\left(\frac{\mathbf{a}\cdot\mathbf{b}}{|\mathbf{a}|^2}\right)\mathbf{a}$ and $\mathbf{b} - \left(\frac{\mathbf{a}\cdot\mathbf{b}}{|\mathbf{a}|^2}\right)\mathbf{a}$, respectively.

Length of perpendicular from a point $P(\alpha, \beta, \gamma)$ to the line joining $A(x_1, y_1, z_1)$ and $B(x_2, y_2, z_2)$.

$$\Rightarrow \quad PL = \left|\mathbf{b} - \frac{\mathbf{b}\cdot\mathbf{a}}{|\mathbf{a}|^2}\mathbf{a}\right|$$

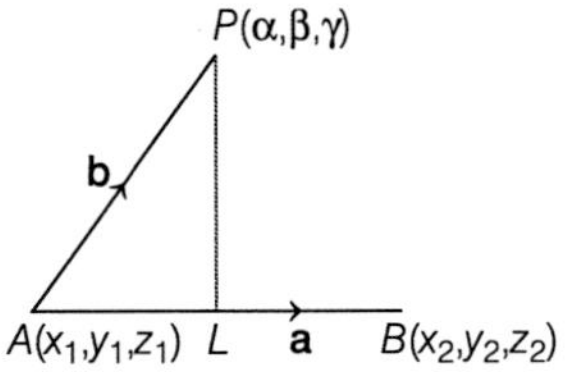

where, $\mathbf{b} = (\alpha - x_1)\,\hat{\mathbf{i}} + (\beta - y_1)\,\hat{\mathbf{j}} + (\gamma - z_1)\,\hat{\mathbf{k}}$

and $\quad \mathbf{a} = (x_2 - x_1)\,\hat{\mathbf{i}} + (y_2 - y_1)\,\hat{\mathbf{j}} + (z_2 - z_1)\,\hat{\mathbf{k}}$

Example 18. Find the vector component of a vector $2\hat{i} + 3\hat{j} + 6\hat{k}$ along and perpendicular to non-zero vector $2\hat{i} + \hat{j} + 2\hat{k}$.

Sol. Let $\mathbf{a} = 2\hat{\mathbf{i}} + 3\hat{\mathbf{j}} + 6\hat{\mathbf{k}}$ and $\mathbf{b} = 2\hat{\mathbf{i}} + \hat{\mathbf{j}} + 2\hat{\mathbf{k}}$

Now, vector component of **a** along $\mathbf{b} = \dfrac{(\mathbf{a}\cdot\mathbf{b})}{|\mathbf{b}|^2}\cdot\mathbf{b}$

$$= \frac{[(2\hat{\mathbf{i}} + 3\hat{\mathbf{j}} + 6\hat{\mathbf{k}})\cdot(2\hat{\mathbf{i}} + \hat{\mathbf{j}} + 2\hat{\mathbf{k}})]}{(4+1+4)}(2\hat{\mathbf{i}} + \hat{\mathbf{j}} + 2\hat{\mathbf{k}})$$

$$= \left(\frac{4+3+12}{9}\right)(2\hat{\mathbf{i}} + \hat{\mathbf{j}} + 2\hat{\mathbf{k}}) = \frac{19}{9}(2\hat{\mathbf{i}} + \hat{\mathbf{j}} + 2\hat{\mathbf{k}})$$

and vector component of **a** perpendicular to **b**

$$= \mathbf{a} - \frac{\mathbf{a}\cdot\mathbf{b}}{|\mathbf{b}|^2}\mathbf{b} = (2\hat{\mathbf{i}} + 3\hat{\mathbf{j}} + 6\hat{\mathbf{k}}) - \left(\frac{19}{9}(2\hat{\mathbf{i}} + \hat{\mathbf{j}} + 2\hat{\mathbf{k}})\right)$$

$$= \frac{1}{9}(-20\hat{\mathbf{i}} + 8\hat{\mathbf{j}} + 16\hat{\mathbf{k}})$$

JEE SCANNER

Example Similar to PYQ Asked in JEE Main 2021

If $\alpha = 3\hat{i} + 4\hat{j} + 5\hat{k}$ and $\beta = 2\hat{i} + \hat{j} - 4\hat{k}$, let β_1 be parallel to α and β_2 be perpendicular to α and $\beta = \beta_1 + \beta_2$, then the value of $5\beta_2\cdot(2\hat{i} + \hat{j} - \hat{k})$ is equal to

(a) 50 (b) 52

(c) 53 (d) 55

Sol. (a) It is given that β_1 is parallel to α

$$\therefore \quad \beta_1 = \lambda\alpha = \lambda(3\hat{\mathbf{i}} + 4\hat{\mathbf{j}} + 5\hat{\mathbf{k}})$$

It is also given that $\beta = \beta_1 + \beta_2$

$$\beta_2 = \beta - \beta_1 = \beta - \lambda\alpha$$

It is also given that β_2 is perpendicular to α

$$\therefore \quad \beta_2\cdot\alpha = 0 \Rightarrow (\beta - \lambda\alpha)\cdot\alpha = 0$$

$$\beta\cdot\alpha - \lambda(\alpha\cdot\alpha) = 0$$

$$\lambda = \frac{\beta\cdot\alpha}{|\alpha|^2} = \frac{(2\hat{\mathbf{i}} + \hat{\mathbf{j}} - 4\hat{\mathbf{k}})\cdot(3\hat{\mathbf{i}} + 4\hat{\mathbf{j}} + 5\hat{\mathbf{k}})}{(\sqrt{3^2 + 4^2 + 5^2})^2}$$

$$\lambda = \frac{6 + 4 - 20}{(\sqrt{50})^2} = \frac{-10}{50} = \frac{-1}{5}$$

$$\therefore \quad \beta_1 = \frac{-1}{5}(3\hat{\mathbf{i}} + 4\hat{\mathbf{j}} + 5\hat{\mathbf{k}})$$

$$\beta_2 = (2\hat{\mathbf{i}} + \hat{\mathbf{j}} - 4\hat{\mathbf{k}}) + \left(\frac{3}{5}\hat{\mathbf{i}} + \frac{4}{5}\hat{\mathbf{j}} + \frac{5}{5}\hat{\mathbf{k}}\right)$$

$$\beta_2 = \frac{1}{5}(13\hat{\mathbf{i}} + 9\hat{\mathbf{j}} - 15\hat{\mathbf{k}})$$

$$\therefore \; 5\beta_2\cdot(2\hat{\mathbf{i}} + \hat{\mathbf{j}} - \hat{\mathbf{k}}) = \frac{5}{5}(13\hat{\mathbf{i}} + 9\hat{\mathbf{j}} - 15\hat{\mathbf{k}})\cdot(2\hat{\mathbf{i}} + \hat{\mathbf{j}} - \hat{\mathbf{k}})$$

$$= 26 + 9 + 15 = 50$$

Skill Builder

If $\mathbf{a} = \hat{i} + 2\hat{j} + 2\hat{k}$ and $\mathbf{b} = 5\hat{i} - 3\hat{j} + 2\hat{k}$, let $\mathbf{b}_1$ be parallel to **a** and $\mathbf{b}_2$ be perpendicular to **a** and $\mathbf{b} = \mathbf{b}_2 - \mathbf{b}_1$, then the value of $3\mathbf{b}_2\cdot(\hat{i} + \hat{j} + \hat{k})$ is equal to

(a) 1 (b) 6

(c) 7 (d) 5

For Sol.

■ **For more practice** See Q.13 of Milestone Practice 1.

Example 19. Find the perpendicular distance of the point $P(1, 0, 1)$ to the line through the points $A(2, 3, 4)$ and $B(-1, 1, -2)$.

Sol. Let $\mathbf{b} = \mathbf{AP} = -\hat{\mathbf{i}} - 3\hat{\mathbf{j}} - 3\hat{\mathbf{k}}$ and $\mathbf{a} = \mathbf{AB} = -3\hat{\mathbf{i}} - 2\hat{\mathbf{j}} - 6\hat{\mathbf{k}}$

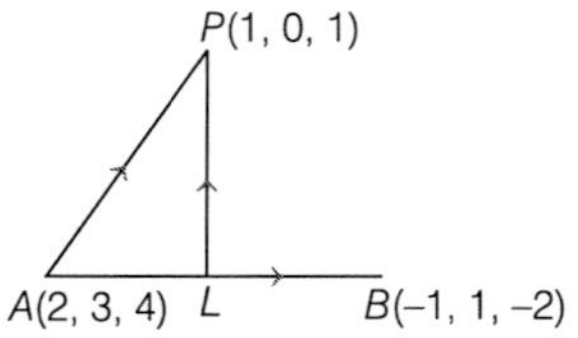

$\therefore$ Projection of $\mathbf{b}$ on $\mathbf{a}$ is $\dfrac{\mathbf{b}\cdot\mathbf{a}}{|\mathbf{a}|^2}\mathbf{a}$

Here, $\mathbf{b}\cdot\mathbf{a} = (-\hat{\mathbf{i}} - 3\hat{\mathbf{j}} - 3\hat{\mathbf{k}})\cdot(-3\hat{\mathbf{i}} - 2\hat{\mathbf{j}} - 6\hat{\mathbf{k}}) = 3 + 6 + 18 = 27$

and $|\mathbf{a}|^2 = (-3)^2 + (-2)^2 + (-6)^2 = 9 + 4 + 36 = 49$

$$\therefore \quad \frac{\mathbf{b}\cdot\mathbf{a}}{|\mathbf{a}|^2}\mathbf{a} = \frac{27}{49}(-3\hat{\mathbf{i}} - 2\hat{\mathbf{j}} - 6\hat{\mathbf{k}})$$

$$\therefore \quad \mathbf{LP} = \mathbf{b} - \frac{\mathbf{b}\cdot\mathbf{a}}{|\mathbf{a}|^2}\mathbf{a} = (-\hat{\mathbf{i}} - 3\hat{\mathbf{j}} - 3\hat{\mathbf{k}}) - \frac{27}{49}(-3\hat{\mathbf{i}} - 2\hat{\mathbf{j}} - 6\hat{\mathbf{k}})$$

$$= \frac{(-49\hat{\mathbf{i}} - 147\hat{\mathbf{j}} - 147\hat{\mathbf{k}}) + (81\hat{\mathbf{i}} + 54\hat{\mathbf{j}} + 162\hat{\mathbf{k}})}{49}$$

$$= \frac{32\hat{\mathbf{i}} - 93\hat{\mathbf{j}} + 15\hat{\mathbf{k}}}{49}$$

$\therefore$ Required perpendicular distance

$$|\mathbf{LP}| = \frac{1}{49}\sqrt{(32)^2 + (-93)^2 + (15)^2}$$

$$= \frac{1}{49}\sqrt{1024 + 8649 + 225} = \frac{\sqrt{9898}}{49}$$

2.5 Application of Dot Product in Mechanics (Work done)

A force acting on a particle is said to do work, if the particle is displaced in a direction which is not perpendicular to force.

Let a particle be placed at O and a force $\mathbf{f}$ represented by $\mathbf{OB}$ be acting on the particle at O. Due to the application of force $\mathbf{f}$, the particle is displaced in the direction of $\mathbf{OA}$. Let $\mathbf{OA}$ be the displacement.

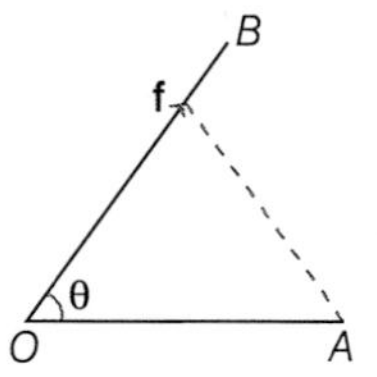

Then, the component of $\mathbf{OA}$ in the the direction of force $\mathbf{f}$ is, $|\mathbf{OA}|\cos\theta$

Work done $= |\mathbf{f}|\,|\mathbf{OA}|\cos\theta = \mathbf{f}\cdot\mathbf{OA} = \mathbf{f}\cdot\mathbf{d}$, where $\mathbf{d} = \mathbf{OA}$

$\therefore$ Work done $=$ (Force) $\cdot$ (Displacement)

JEE SPIKE

The work done by the resultant of a number of forces $\mathbf{f}_1, \mathbf{f}_2, \mathbf{f}_3, \ldots \mathbf{f}_n$, when its point of application experiences a number of consecutive displacements $\mathbf{d}_1, \mathbf{d}_2, \mathbf{d}_3, \ldots \mathbf{d}_n$ is equal to the product of sum of the forces and single displacement from the beginning to the end.

Concept Inside Video

Case I The sum of work done by the forces separately

i.e. work done $= \mathbf{f}_1\,\mathbf{d} + \mathbf{f}_2\,\mathbf{d} + \ldots + \mathbf{f}_n\,\mathbf{d}$

$= \mathbf{R}\cdot\mathbf{d}$ (where $\mathbf{R} = \mathbf{f}_1 + \mathbf{f}_2 + \ldots + \mathbf{f}_n$

Case II The work done by the force in single displacement from the beginning to the end.

i.e. work done $= \mathbf{f}(\mathbf{d}_1 + \mathbf{d}_2 + \ldots + \mathbf{d}_n)$

Example 20. Two forces $\mathbf{f}_1 = 3\hat{\mathbf{i}} - 2\hat{\mathbf{j}} + \hat{\mathbf{k}}$ and $\mathbf{f}_2 = \hat{\mathbf{i}} + 3\hat{\mathbf{j}} - 5\hat{\mathbf{k}}$ acting on a particle at A move it to B. Find the work done if the position vector of A and B are $-2\hat{\mathbf{i}} + 5\hat{\mathbf{k}}$ and $3\hat{\mathbf{i}} - 7\hat{\mathbf{j}} + 2\hat{\mathbf{k}}$.

Sol. Let $\mathbf{R}$ be the resultant of two forces $\mathbf{f}_1$ and $\mathbf{f}_2$ and $\mathbf{d}$ be the displacement.

Then, $\mathbf{R} = (3\hat{\mathbf{i}} - 2\hat{\mathbf{j}} + \hat{\mathbf{k}}) + (\hat{\mathbf{i}} + 3\hat{\mathbf{j}} - 5\hat{\mathbf{k}})$

$= 4\hat{\mathbf{i}} + \hat{\mathbf{j}} - 4\hat{\mathbf{k}}$

and $\mathbf{d} = (3\hat{\mathbf{i}} - 7\hat{\mathbf{j}} + 2\hat{\mathbf{k}}) - (-2\hat{\mathbf{i}} + 5\hat{\mathbf{k}})$

$= 5\hat{\mathbf{i}} - 7\hat{\mathbf{j}} - 3\hat{\mathbf{k}}$

$\therefore$ The total work done $=$ The work done by resultant

$= \mathbf{R}\cdot\mathbf{d} = (4\hat{\mathbf{i}} + \hat{\mathbf{j}} - 4\hat{\mathbf{k}})\cdot(5\hat{\mathbf{i}} - 7\hat{\mathbf{j}} - 3\hat{\mathbf{k}})$

$= 20 - 7 + 12$

$= 25$ units

Example 21. Forces of magnitudes 5 and 3 units acting in the directions $6\hat{\mathbf{i}} + 2\hat{\mathbf{j}} + 3\hat{\mathbf{k}}$ and $3\hat{\mathbf{i}} - 2\hat{\mathbf{j}} + 6\hat{\mathbf{k}}$, respectively act on a particle which is displaced from the point $(2, 2, -1)$ to $(4, 3, 1)$. Find the work done by the forces.

Sol. Let $\mathbf{R}$ be the resultant of two forces and $\mathbf{d}$ be the displacement.

$$\text{Then,} \quad \mathbf{R} = 5\frac{(6\hat{\mathbf{i}} + 2\hat{\mathbf{j}} + 3\hat{\mathbf{k}})}{\sqrt{36 + 4 + 9}} + 3\frac{(3\hat{\mathbf{i}} - 2\hat{\mathbf{j}} + 6\hat{\mathbf{k}})}{\sqrt{9 + 4 + 36}}$$

$$= \frac{1}{7}(39\hat{\mathbf{i}} + 4\hat{\mathbf{j}} + 33\hat{\mathbf{k}})$$

and $\mathbf{d} = (4\hat{\mathbf{i}} + 3\hat{\mathbf{j}} + \hat{\mathbf{k}}) - (2\hat{\mathbf{i}} + 2\hat{\mathbf{j}} - \hat{\mathbf{k}})$

$= 2\hat{\mathbf{i}} + \hat{\mathbf{j}} + 2\hat{\mathbf{k}}$

$\therefore$ Total work done $= \mathbf{R}\cdot\mathbf{d}$

$$= \frac{1}{7}(78 + 4 + 66)$$

$$= \frac{148}{7} \text{ units}$$

Milestone Practice 2.1

1. If $\mathbf{r}\cdot\hat{\mathbf{i}}=\mathbf{r}\cdot\hat{\mathbf{j}}=\mathbf{r}\cdot\hat{\mathbf{k}}$ and $|\mathbf{r}|=3$, then find vector $\mathbf{r}$.

2. If $\mathbf{a}\cdot\hat{\mathbf{i}}=\mathbf{a}\cdot(\hat{\mathbf{i}}+\hat{\mathbf{j}})=\mathbf{a}\cdot(\hat{\mathbf{i}}+\hat{\mathbf{j}}+\hat{\mathbf{k}})$, then find the unit vector $\mathbf{a}$.

3. If $\mathbf{a}+\mathbf{b}=2\hat{\mathbf{i}}$ and $2\mathbf{a}-\mathbf{b}=\hat{\mathbf{i}}-\hat{\mathbf{j}}$, then the cosine of the angle between $\mathbf{a}$ and $\mathbf{b}$ is equal to
   (a) $\cos^{-1}\left(\frac{5}{4}\right)$ (b) $\cos^{-1}\left(\frac{1}{4}\right)$
   (c) $\cos^{-1}\left(\frac{4}{5}\right)$ (d) $\cos^{-1}\left(\frac{1}{5}\right)$

4. Find the angle between the vectors $\mathbf{a}+\mathbf{b}$ and $\mathbf{a}-\mathbf{b}$, if $\mathbf{a}=2\hat{\mathbf{i}}-\hat{\mathbf{j}}+3\hat{\mathbf{k}}$ and $\mathbf{b}=3\hat{\mathbf{i}}+\hat{\mathbf{j}}-2\hat{\mathbf{k}}$.

5. If $|\mathbf{a}|+|\mathbf{b}|=|\mathbf{c}|$ and $\mathbf{a}+\mathbf{b}=\mathbf{c}$, then the angle between $\mathbf{a}$ and $\mathbf{b}$ is equal to
   (a) $0°$ (b) $45°$ (c) $60°$ (d) $90°$

6. If *P, Q, R* and *S* are four distinct points in space such that $\mathbf{PQ}$ is not perpendicular to $\mathbf{RS}$ and satisfies $\mathbf{PQ}\cdot\mathbf{RS}=\lambda(|\mathbf{PS}|^2+|\mathbf{QR}|^2-|\mathbf{PR}|^2-|\mathbf{QS}|^2)$, then find the value of λ.

7. In isosceles ΔPQR, $|\mathbf{PQ}|=|\mathbf{QR}|=8$, a point S divides PQ internally in the ratio $1:3$, then the angle between $\mathbf{RS}$ and $\mathbf{RP}$ is equal to (where $|\mathbf{RP}|=12$)
   (a) $\frac{3\sqrt{7}}{8}$ (b) $\frac{\sqrt{7}}{8}$ (c) $\frac{\sqrt{7}}{3}$ (d) $\frac{8\sqrt{7}}{3}$

8. Vector $\mathbf{a}$, $\mathbf{b}$ and $\mathbf{c}$ are of the same length and when taken pair-wise they form equal angles. If $\mathbf{a}=\hat{\mathbf{i}}+\hat{\mathbf{j}}$ and $\mathbf{b}=\hat{\mathbf{j}}+\hat{\mathbf{k}}$, then find vector $\mathbf{c}$.

9. Let $\mathbf{a}=4\hat{\mathbf{i}}+3\hat{\mathbf{j}}$ and $\mathbf{b}$ be two vectors perpendicular to each other in *XY*-plane, then find the vectors in the same plane having projection 1 and 2 along $\mathbf{a}$ and $\mathbf{b}$.

10. Let S be the set of all $a\in R$ for which the angle between the vectors $\mathbf{u}=a(\log_e b)\,\hat{\mathbf{i}}-8\hat{\mathbf{j}}+2\hat{\mathbf{k}}$ and $\mathbf{v}=(\log_e b)\,\hat{\mathbf{i}}+3\hat{\mathbf{j}}+3a(\log_e b)\hat{\mathbf{k}}$, $(b>1)$ is acute. Then, find the value of S.

11. An arc AB of a circle subtends a right angle at its centre O. The mid-point of the arc AB is C. If $\mathbf{OA}=\mathbf{a}$, $\mathbf{OC}=\mathbf{b}$ and $\mathbf{OB}=\alpha\mathbf{a}+\beta\mathbf{b}$ and α,β^2 are the roots of the equation. Then, find the equation.

12. If the projection of vector $x\hat{\mathbf{i}}-\hat{\mathbf{j}}+\hat{\mathbf{k}}$ on vector $2\hat{\mathbf{i}}-\hat{\mathbf{j}}+5\hat{\mathbf{k}}$ is $\frac{1}{\sqrt{30}}$, then the value of x is equal to
   (a) $\frac{2}{5}$ (b) $-\frac{2}{5}$
   (c) $\frac{5}{2}$ (d) $-\frac{5}{2}$

13. Let $\mathbf{a}=5\hat{\mathbf{i}}+2\hat{\mathbf{j}}+3\hat{\mathbf{k}}$ and $\mathbf{b}=2\hat{\mathbf{i}}-\hat{\mathbf{j}}+4\hat{\mathbf{k}}$. Let $\mathbf{b}_1$ be parallel to $\mathbf{a}$ and $\mathbf{b}_2$ be perpendicular to $\mathbf{a}$. If $\mathbf{b}=\mathbf{b}_1+\mathbf{b}_2$, then find the value of $19\mathbf{b}_2\cdot(\hat{\mathbf{i}}+\hat{\mathbf{j}}+\hat{\mathbf{k}})$.

14. The vector components of a vector $2\hat{\mathbf{i}}+3\hat{\mathbf{j}}+6\hat{\mathbf{k}}$ along and perpendicular to the non-zero vector $2\hat{\mathbf{i}}+\hat{\mathbf{j}}+2\hat{\mathbf{k}}$ is equal to
   (a) $(-5\hat{\mathbf{i}}+2\hat{\mathbf{j}}+4\hat{\mathbf{k}})$ (b) $\frac{1}{9}(-5\hat{\mathbf{i}}+2\hat{\mathbf{j}}+4\hat{\mathbf{k}})$
   (c) $\frac{4}{9}(-5\hat{\mathbf{i}}+2\hat{\mathbf{j}}+4\hat{\mathbf{k}})$ (d) $\frac{1}{4}(-5\hat{\mathbf{i}}+2\hat{\mathbf{j}}+4\hat{\mathbf{k}})$

15. The projection of the vector $6\hat{\mathbf{i}}+\hat{\mathbf{j}}-3\hat{\mathbf{k}}$ on the line joining the points $(3,-4,2)$ and $(6,3,-5)$ is equal to
   (a) $\frac{46}{107}$ (b) $\frac{46}{\sqrt{107}}$
   (c) $\frac{\sqrt{46}}{107}$ (d) $\sqrt{\frac{46}{107}}$

16. If $\mathbf{OA}=\hat{\mathbf{i}}+2\hat{\mathbf{j}}+2\hat{\mathbf{k}}$ turns through a right angle passing through the positive *X*-axis on the way, then show that the vector in its new position is $\frac{4\hat{\mathbf{i}}-\hat{\mathbf{j}}-\hat{\mathbf{k}}}{\sqrt{2}}$.

17. A particle is acted upon by constant forces $4\hat{\mathbf{i}}+\hat{\mathbf{j}}-3\hat{\mathbf{k}}$ and $3\hat{\mathbf{i}}+\hat{\mathbf{j}}-\hat{\mathbf{k}}$ which displace it from a point $\hat{\mathbf{i}}+2\hat{\mathbf{j}}+3\hat{\mathbf{k}}$ to the point $5\hat{\mathbf{i}}+4\hat{\mathbf{j}}+\hat{\mathbf{k}}$. Find the work done by the forces in standard units.

Answer Key

1. $\pm\sqrt{3}(\hat{\mathbf{i}}+\hat{\mathbf{j}}+\hat{\mathbf{k}})$
2. $\hat{\mathbf{i}}$
3. (c)
4. $\frac{\pi}{2}$
5. (a)
6. $\frac{1}{2}$
7. (a)
8. $\hat{\mathbf{i}}+\hat{\mathbf{k}}$ and $\frac{-1}{3}\hat{\mathbf{i}}+\frac{4}{3}\hat{\mathbf{j}}-\frac{1}{3}\hat{\mathbf{k}}$
9. $-\frac{2}{5}\hat{\mathbf{i}}+\frac{11}{5}\hat{\mathbf{j}}$
10. ϕ
11. $x^2-x-2=0$
12. (d)
13. -5
14. (c)
15. (b)
17. 40 units

For Detailed Solution

Milestone 2 Vector or Cross Product

• Vector or Cross Product of Two Vectors • Properties of Vector Product • Geometrical Interpretation of Vector Product • Area of Parallelogram and Triangle • Moment of a Force and Couple Moment of a Force • Moment of a Couple • Rotation About an Axis

2.6 Vector or Cross Product of Two Vectors

When the product of two vectors results in a vector quantity, then this product is called **vector product**. It is also known as **cross product** because we denote it by putting a **cross** ($\times$) between two vectors.

Angle Between Two Vectors

Let **a** and **b** be two non-zero and non- parallel vectors. Then, the vector product $\mathbf{a} \times \mathbf{b}$ is defined as a vector whose magnitude is

$$|\mathbf{a}||\mathbf{b}|\sin\theta$$

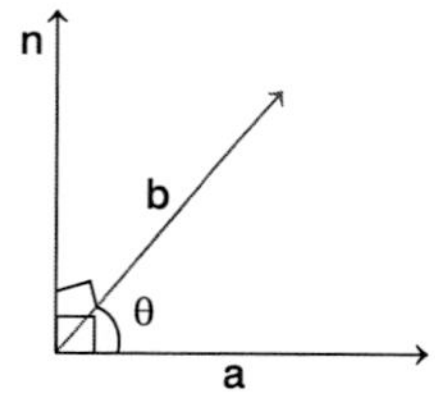

where, θ is the angle between **a** and **b** whose direction is perpendicular to the plane of **a** and **b** in such a way that **a**, **b** and this direction constitute a right handed system.

In other words, $\mathbf{a} \times \mathbf{b} = |\mathbf{a}||\mathbf{b}|\sin\theta\, \hat{\mathbf{n}}$,
where θ is the angle between **a** and **b** ($0 \le \theta \le \pi$), $\hat{\mathbf{n}}$ is a unit vector perpendicular to the plane of **a** and **b** such that **a**, **b** and $\hat{\mathbf{n}}$ form a right handed system.

Concept Inside Video

JEE Focus Points

- Vector product is also known as **outer product**.
- θ is restricted to be in the interval $[0, \pi]$.
- If θ be the angle between vector **a** and **b**, then $\sin\theta = \dfrac{|\mathbf{a} \times \mathbf{b}|}{|\mathbf{a}||\mathbf{b}|}$.
- If **a** and **b** are collinear i.e. $\theta = 0°$ or π, then direction of $\hat{\mathbf{n}}$ is not well defined. So, in this case also we defined $\mathbf{a} \times \mathbf{b} = \mathbf{0}$.
- The vector product of any vector with itself is **0**. Thus, $\mathbf{a} \times \mathbf{a} = 0, \mathbf{b} \times \mathbf{b} = 0$ etc.
- If $\mathbf{a} \times \mathbf{b} = 0$, then either $\mathbf{a} = 0$ or $\mathbf{b} = 0$ or **a** is parallel to **b** ($\mathbf{a} = \lambda \mathbf{b}$).
- If $|\mathbf{a} \times \mathbf{b}| = |\mathbf{a}||\mathbf{b}|$, then **a** is perpendicular to **b**.
- If **a** and **b** are unit vector, then $|\mathbf{a} \times \mathbf{b}| = \sin\theta$.
- $|\mathbf{a} \times \mathbf{b}|^2 \le |\mathbf{a}|^2 |\mathbf{b}|^2$ **(cauchy-schwarz inequality).**

Example 22. If $|\mathbf{a}| = 2, |\mathbf{b}| = 5$ and $|\mathbf{a} \times \mathbf{b}| = 8$, then find the value of $(\mathbf{a} \cdot \mathbf{b})^2$.

Sol. We have, $|\mathbf{a}| = 2, |\mathbf{b}| = 5$ and $|\mathbf{a} \times \mathbf{b}| = 8$.

Let θ be the angle between **a** and **b**.

Then,
$$\sin\theta = \frac{|\mathbf{a} \times \mathbf{b}|}{|\mathbf{a}||\mathbf{b}|} = \frac{8}{2 \times 5} = \frac{4}{5}$$

Now,
$$\cos\theta = \pm\sqrt{1 - \sin^2\theta} = \pm\sqrt{1 - \frac{16}{25}} = \pm\frac{3}{5}$$

$$\mathbf{a} \cdot \mathbf{b} = |\mathbf{a}||\mathbf{b}|\cos\theta = \pm\left(2 \times 5 \times \frac{3}{5}\right) = \pm 6$$

$$\Rightarrow \quad (\mathbf{a} \cdot \mathbf{b})^2 = (6)^2 = 36$$

Example 23. Let **a**, **b** and **c** be three vectors such that $\mathbf{a} \ne 0, |\mathbf{a}| = |\mathbf{c}| = 1, |\mathbf{b}| = 4$ and $|\mathbf{b} \times \mathbf{c}| = \sqrt{15}$, if $\mathbf{b} - 2\mathbf{c} = \lambda\mathbf{a}$, then find the value of $\dfrac{\lambda}{2}$.

Sol. Let the angle beween **b** and **c** be α, then

$$|\mathbf{b} \times \mathbf{c}| = \sqrt{15}$$

$$\Rightarrow \quad |\mathbf{b}||\mathbf{c}|\sin\alpha = \sqrt{15}$$

$$\Rightarrow \quad \sin\alpha = \frac{\sqrt{15}}{4}$$

$$\Rightarrow \quad \cos\alpha = \frac{1}{4}$$

Now,
$$\mathbf{b} - 2\mathbf{c} = \lambda\mathbf{a}$$

$$\Rightarrow \quad |\mathbf{b} - 2\mathbf{c}|^2 = \lambda^2 |\mathbf{a}|^2$$

$$\Rightarrow \quad |\mathbf{b}|^2 + 4|\mathbf{c}|^2 - 4\cdot\mathbf{b}\cdot\mathbf{c} = \lambda^2|\mathbf{a}|^2$$

$$\Rightarrow \quad 16 + 4 - 4\{|\mathbf{b}||\mathbf{c}|\cos\alpha\} = \lambda^2$$

$$\Rightarrow \quad 16 + 4 - 4\times 4\times 1\times\frac{1}{4} = \lambda^2$$

$$\Rightarrow \quad \lambda^2 = 16 \text{ or } \lambda = \pm 4$$

Hence, $\dfrac{\lambda}{2} = \pm 2$

2.7 Properties of Vector Product

(i) Vector product is not commutative i.e. if **a** and **b** are any two vectors, then $\mathbf{a}\times\mathbf{b} \neq \mathbf{b}\times\mathbf{a}$, however $\mathbf{a}\times\mathbf{b} = -(\mathbf{b}\times\mathbf{a})$.

(ii) Vector product is not associative.
i.e. $\quad \mathbf{a}\times(\mathbf{b}\times\mathbf{c}) \neq (\mathbf{a}\times\mathbf{b})\times\mathbf{c}$

(iii) If **a** and **b** are two vectors and m is a scalar, then

$$m\mathbf{a}\times\mathbf{b} = m(\mathbf{a}\times\mathbf{b}) = \mathbf{a}\times m\mathbf{b}$$

(iv) If **a** and **b** are two vectors and m and n are scalars, then

$$m\mathbf{a}\times n\mathbf{b} = mn(\mathbf{a}\times\mathbf{b}) = m(n\mathbf{a}\times\mathbf{b}) = n(m\mathbf{a}\times\mathbf{b})$$

(v) Distributivity of vector product over vector addition. Let **a**, **b** and **c** be any three vectors. Then,

(a) $\mathbf{a}\times(\mathbf{b}+\mathbf{c}) = \mathbf{a}\times\mathbf{b} + \mathbf{a}\times\mathbf{c}$ (left distributivity)

(b) $(\mathbf{b}+\mathbf{c})\times\mathbf{a} = \mathbf{b}\times\mathbf{a} + \mathbf{c}\times\mathbf{a}$ (right distributivity)

(vi) For any three vectors **a**, **b** and **c**, we have

$$\mathbf{a}\times(\mathbf{b}-\mathbf{c}) = \mathbf{a}\times\mathbf{b} - \mathbf{a}\times\mathbf{c}$$

(vii) The vector product of any vector (zero or non-zero) with zero vector is a zero vector

i.e. $\quad \mathbf{a}\times\mathbf{0} = \mathbf{0}\times\mathbf{a} = \mathbf{0}$

(viii) The vector product of two non-zero vectors is zero vector iff they are parallel (collinear).

i.e. $\mathbf{a}\times\mathbf{b} = \mathbf{0} \Leftrightarrow \mathbf{a}\,||\,\mathbf{b}$, **a** and **b** are non-zero vectors.

It follows from the above property that $\mathbf{a}\times\mathbf{a} = \mathbf{0}$ for every non-zero vector **a** which in turn implies that $\hat{\mathbf{i}}\times\hat{\mathbf{i}} = \hat{\mathbf{j}}\times\hat{\mathbf{j}} = \hat{\mathbf{k}}\times\hat{\mathbf{k}} = \mathbf{0}$.

(ix) Vector product of orthonormal triad of unit vectors $\hat{\mathbf{i}}$, $\hat{\mathbf{j}}$ and $\hat{\mathbf{k}}$ using the definition of the vector product obtain

$$\hat{\mathbf{i}}\times\hat{\mathbf{j}} = \hat{\mathbf{k}},\ \hat{\mathbf{j}}\times\hat{\mathbf{k}} = \hat{\mathbf{i}},\ \hat{\mathbf{k}}\times\hat{\mathbf{i}} = \hat{\mathbf{j}},$$

$$\hat{\mathbf{j}}\times\hat{\mathbf{i}} = -\hat{\mathbf{k}},\ \hat{\mathbf{k}}\times\hat{\mathbf{j}} = -\hat{\mathbf{i}},\ \hat{\mathbf{i}}\times\hat{\mathbf{k}} = -\hat{\mathbf{j}}$$

(x) $\mathbf{a}\cdot(\mathbf{a}\times\mathbf{b}) = \mathbf{b}\cdot(\mathbf{a}\times\mathbf{b}) = 0$

(xi) If $\mathbf{a} = a_1\hat{\mathbf{i}} + a_2\hat{\mathbf{j}} + a_3\hat{\mathbf{k}}$ and $\mathbf{b} = b_1\hat{\mathbf{i}} + b_2\hat{\mathbf{j}} + b_3\hat{\mathbf{k}}$

$$\mathbf{a}\times\mathbf{b} = \begin{vmatrix} \hat{\mathbf{i}} & \hat{\mathbf{j}} & \hat{\mathbf{k}} \\ a_1 & a_2 & a_3 \\ b_1 & b_2 & b_3 \end{vmatrix}$$

$$= (a_2b_3 - a_3b_2)\hat{\mathbf{i}} + (a_3b_1 - a_1b_3)\hat{\mathbf{j}} + (a_1b_2 - a_2b_1)\hat{\mathbf{k}}$$

(xii) The unit vector perpendicular to the plane of **a** and **b** is $\dfrac{\mathbf{a}\times\mathbf{b}}{|\mathbf{a}\times\mathbf{b}|}$ and a vector of magnitude λ perpendicular to the plane **a** and **b** is $\pm\lambda\dfrac{(\mathbf{a}\times\mathbf{b})}{(\mathbf{a}\times\mathbf{b})}$.

(xiii) **Lagrange's identity** If **a** and **b** are any two vectors, then

$$|\mathbf{a}\times\mathbf{b}|^2 = |\mathbf{a}|^2|\mathbf{b}|^2 - (\mathbf{a}\cdot\mathbf{b})^2$$

or $\quad |\mathbf{a}\times\mathbf{b}|^2 + (\mathbf{a}\cdot\mathbf{b})^2 = |\mathbf{a}|^2|\mathbf{b}|^2$

Example 24. If $\mathbf{a} = 2\hat{\mathbf{i}} + 3\hat{\mathbf{j}} - 5\hat{\mathbf{k}}$ and $\mathbf{b} = m\hat{\mathbf{i}} + n\hat{\mathbf{j}} + 12\hat{\mathbf{k}}$ and $\mathbf{a}\times\mathbf{b} = \mathbf{0}$. Then, find the values of m and n.

Sol. Clearly, $\mathbf{a}\times\mathbf{b} = \begin{vmatrix} \hat{\mathbf{i}} & \hat{\mathbf{j}} & \hat{\mathbf{k}} \\ 2 & 3 & -5 \\ m & n & 12 \end{vmatrix}$

$$= (36 + 5n)\hat{\mathbf{i}} - (24 + 5m)\hat{\mathbf{j}} + (2n - 3m)\hat{\mathbf{k}}$$

Since, $\quad \mathbf{a}\times\mathbf{b} = \mathbf{0}$

$\therefore (36 + 5n)\hat{\mathbf{i}} - (24 + 5m)\hat{\mathbf{j}} + (2n - 3m)\hat{\mathbf{k}} = 0\hat{\mathbf{i}} + 0\hat{\mathbf{j}} + 0\hat{\mathbf{k}}$

On comparing the coefficients of $\hat{\mathbf{i}}$, $\hat{\mathbf{j}}$ and $\hat{\mathbf{k}}$, we get

$$36 + 5n = 0 \quad \text{...(i)}$$

$$-(24 + 5m) = 0 \quad \text{...(ii)}$$

and $\quad 2n - 3m = 0 \quad$ ...(iii)

On solving Eqs. (i), (ii) and (iii), we get

$$n = -\frac{36}{5}$$

and $\quad m = -\dfrac{24}{5}$

Time Saving Technique

$$\mathbf{a}\times\mathbf{b} = 0 \Rightarrow \mathbf{a} = \lambda\mathbf{b}$$

$$\therefore \quad \frac{2}{m} = \frac{3}{n} = \frac{-5}{12}$$

$$m = \frac{-24}{5} \text{ and } n = \frac{-36}{5}$$

JEE SCANNER

Example Similar to PYQ Asked in JEE Main 2024

If $\mathbf{a}=-4\hat{\mathbf{i}}+\hat{\mathbf{j}}+3\hat{\mathbf{k}}$, $\mathbf{b}=\hat{\mathbf{i}}+2\hat{\mathbf{j}}-5\hat{\mathbf{k}}$ *and* $\mathbf{c}=(((\mathbf{a}\times\mathbf{b})\times\hat{\mathbf{j}})\times\hat{\mathbf{j}})\times\hat{\mathbf{j}}$. *Then, the value of* $\mathbf{c}\cdot(\hat{\mathbf{i}}-\hat{\mathbf{j}}-\hat{\mathbf{k}})$ *is*

(a) −5 (b) −11 (c) 11 (d) 5

Sol. Given, $\mathbf{a}=-4\hat{\mathbf{i}}+\hat{\mathbf{j}}+3\hat{\mathbf{k}}$ and $\mathbf{b}=\hat{\mathbf{i}}+2\hat{\mathbf{j}}-5\hat{\mathbf{k}}$

$$\mathbf{a}\times\mathbf{b}=\begin{vmatrix}\hat{\mathbf{i}} & \hat{\mathbf{j}} & \hat{\mathbf{k}}\\ -4 & 1 & 3\\ 1 & 2 & -5\end{vmatrix}$$

$$=(-5-6)\hat{\mathbf{i}}-(20-3)\hat{\mathbf{j}}+(-8-1)\hat{\mathbf{k}}=-11\hat{\mathbf{i}}-17\hat{\mathbf{j}}-9\hat{\mathbf{k}}$$

$$\Rightarrow \quad (\mathbf{a}\times\mathbf{b})\times\hat{\mathbf{j}}=\begin{vmatrix}\hat{\mathbf{i}} & \hat{\mathbf{j}} & \hat{\mathbf{k}}\\ -11 & -17 & -9\\ 0 & 1 & 0\end{vmatrix}=9\hat{\mathbf{i}}-11\hat{\mathbf{k}}$$

$$\Rightarrow \quad ((\mathbf{a}\times\mathbf{b})\times\hat{\mathbf{j}})\times\hat{\mathbf{j}}=\begin{vmatrix}\hat{\mathbf{i}} & \hat{\mathbf{j}} & \hat{\mathbf{k}}\\ 0 & 9 & -11\\ 0 & 1 & 0\end{vmatrix}=11\hat{\mathbf{i}}$$

$$\Rightarrow (((\mathbf{a}\times\mathbf{b})\times\hat{\mathbf{j}})\times\hat{\mathbf{j}})\times\hat{\mathbf{j}}=11(\hat{\mathbf{i}}\times\hat{\mathbf{j}})=11\hat{\mathbf{k}}$$

$$\therefore \quad \mathbf{c}=11\hat{\mathbf{k}}$$

Hence, $\mathbf{c}\cdot(\hat{\mathbf{i}}-\hat{\mathbf{j}}-\hat{\mathbf{k}})=-11$

Skill Builder

If $\mathbf{a}=2\hat{\mathbf{i}}-\hat{\mathbf{j}}+\hat{\mathbf{k}}$, $\mathbf{b}=3\hat{\mathbf{i}}+2\hat{\mathbf{j}}-\hat{\mathbf{k}}$ and $\mathbf{c}=(((\mathbf{a}\times\mathbf{b})\times\hat{\mathbf{k}})\times\hat{\mathbf{k}})\times\hat{\mathbf{k}}$. Then, the value of $\mathbf{c}\cdot(\hat{\mathbf{i}}+\hat{\mathbf{j}}+\hat{\mathbf{k}})$ is

For Sol.

(a) 7 (b) −6
(c) 5 (d) −7

■ **For more practice** See Q.12 of Milestone Practice 2.

Example 25. If **a** is any vector, then find the value of $(\mathbf{a}\times\hat{\mathbf{i}})^2+(\mathbf{a}\times\hat{\mathbf{j}})^2+(\mathbf{a}\times\hat{\mathbf{k}})^2$.

Sol. Let $\mathbf{a}=a_1\hat{\mathbf{i}}+a_2\hat{\mathbf{j}}+a_3\hat{\mathbf{k}}$

$$\therefore \quad \mathbf{a}\times\hat{\mathbf{i}}=(a_1\hat{\mathbf{i}}+a_2\hat{\mathbf{j}}+a_3\hat{\mathbf{k}})\times\hat{\mathbf{i}}=-a_2\hat{\mathbf{k}}+a_3\hat{\mathbf{j}}$$

$$(\mathbf{a}\times\hat{\mathbf{i}})^2=(\mathbf{a}\times\hat{\mathbf{i}})\cdot(\mathbf{a}\times\hat{\mathbf{i}})$$
$$=(-a_2\hat{\mathbf{k}}+a_3\hat{\mathbf{j}})\cdot(-a_2\hat{\mathbf{k}}+a_3\hat{\mathbf{j}})$$
$$=a_2^2+a_3^2$$

Similarly, $(\mathbf{a}\times\hat{\mathbf{j}})^2=a_3^2+a_1^2$

and $\quad (\mathbf{a}\times\hat{\mathbf{k}})^2=a_1^2+a_2^2$

$$\therefore (\mathbf{a}\times\hat{\mathbf{i}})^2+(\mathbf{a}\times\hat{\mathbf{j}})^2+(\mathbf{a}\times\hat{\mathbf{k}})^2=2(a_1^2+a_2^2+a_3^2)$$
$$=2|\mathbf{a}|^2$$

Example 26. If $x_1^2+x_2^2+x_3^2=1$, $x_1,x_2,x_3\in R$, then find the maximum value of

$$(6x_1-5x_2)^2+(7x_2-6x_3)^2+(5x_3-7x_1)^2.$$

Sol. Let $\mathbf{a}=x_1\hat{\mathbf{i}}+x_2\hat{\mathbf{j}}+x_3\hat{\mathbf{k}}$ and $\mathbf{b}=5\hat{\mathbf{i}}+6\hat{\mathbf{j}}+7\hat{\mathbf{k}}$

$$\therefore \quad \mathbf{a}\times\mathbf{b}=\begin{vmatrix}\hat{\mathbf{i}} & \hat{\mathbf{j}} & \hat{\mathbf{k}}\\ x_1 & x_2 & x_3\\ 5 & 6 & 7\end{vmatrix}$$

$$=\hat{\mathbf{i}}(7x_2-6x_3)-\hat{\mathbf{j}}(7x_1-5x_3)+\hat{\mathbf{k}}(6x_1-5x_2)$$
$$=\hat{\mathbf{i}}(7x_2-6x_3)+\hat{\mathbf{j}}(5x_3-7x_1)+\hat{\mathbf{k}}(6x_1-5x_2)$$

Since, $|\mathbf{a}\times\mathbf{b}|^2\le|\mathbf{a}|^2|\mathbf{b}|^2$ [Cauchy Schwarz inequality]

$$\therefore (7x_2-6x_3)^2+(5x_3-7x_1)^2+(6x_1-5x_2)^2$$
$$\le(x_1^2+x_2^2+x_3^2)(25+36+49)$$

$$\Rightarrow (7x_2-6x_3)^2+(5x_3-7x_1)^2+(6x_1-5x_2)^2\le 110$$

Hence, the maximum value is 110.

Example 27. Let $\mathbf{a}=3\hat{\mathbf{i}}+2\hat{\mathbf{j}}+\hat{\mathbf{k}}$, $\mathbf{b}=2\hat{\mathbf{i}}-\hat{\mathbf{j}}+3\hat{\mathbf{k}}$ and **c** be a vector such that $(\mathbf{a}+\mathbf{b})\times\mathbf{c}=2(\mathbf{a}\times\mathbf{b})+24\hat{\mathbf{j}}-6\hat{\mathbf{k}}$ and $(\mathbf{a}-\mathbf{b}+\hat{\mathbf{i}})\cdot\mathbf{c}=-3$, then find $|\mathbf{c}|^2$.

Sol. Given, $\mathbf{a}=3\hat{\mathbf{i}}+2\hat{\mathbf{j}}+\hat{\mathbf{k}}$ and $\mathbf{b}=2\hat{\mathbf{i}}-\hat{\mathbf{j}}+3\hat{\mathbf{k}}$

$$\therefore \quad \mathbf{a}\times\mathbf{b}=\begin{vmatrix}\hat{\mathbf{i}} & \hat{\mathbf{j}} & \hat{\mathbf{k}}\\ 3 & 2 & 1\\ 2 & -1 & 3\end{vmatrix}=7\hat{\mathbf{i}}-7\hat{\mathbf{j}}-7\hat{\mathbf{k}}$$

Let $\mathbf{c}=x\hat{\mathbf{i}}+y\hat{\mathbf{j}}+z\hat{\mathbf{k}}$

$$\because \quad (\mathbf{a}+\mathbf{b})\times\mathbf{c}=2(\mathbf{a}\times\mathbf{b})+24\hat{\mathbf{j}}-6\hat{\mathbf{k}}$$

$$\Rightarrow (5\hat{\mathbf{i}}+\hat{\mathbf{j}}+4\hat{\mathbf{k}})\times\mathbf{c}=2(7\hat{\mathbf{i}}-7\hat{\mathbf{j}}-7\hat{\mathbf{k}})+24\hat{\mathbf{j}}-6\hat{\mathbf{k}}$$

$$\Rightarrow (5\hat{\mathbf{i}}+\hat{\mathbf{j}}+4\hat{\mathbf{k}})\times(x\hat{\mathbf{i}}+y\hat{\mathbf{j}}+z\hat{\mathbf{k}})=14\hat{\mathbf{i}}+10\hat{\mathbf{j}}-20\hat{\mathbf{k}}$$

$$\Rightarrow \quad \begin{vmatrix}\hat{\mathbf{i}} & \hat{\mathbf{j}} & \hat{\mathbf{k}}\\ 5 & 1 & 4\\ x & y & z\end{vmatrix}=14\hat{\mathbf{i}}+10\hat{\mathbf{j}}-20\hat{\mathbf{k}}$$

$$\Rightarrow (z-4y)\hat{\mathbf{i}}+(4x-5z)\hat{\mathbf{j}}+(5y-x)\hat{\mathbf{k}}=14\hat{\mathbf{i}}+10\hat{\mathbf{j}}-20\hat{\mathbf{k}}$$

On comparing the coefficient of $\hat{\mathbf{i}}$, $\hat{\mathbf{j}}$ and $\hat{\mathbf{k}}$, we get

$$z-4y=14 \quad \text{...(i)}$$
$$4x-5z=10 \quad \text{...(ii)}$$
$$5y-x=-20 \quad \text{...(iii)}$$

On solving Eqs. (i), (ii) and (iii), we get

$$x=5, y=-3 \text{ and } z=2$$

Hence, $|\mathbf{c}|^2=x^2+y^2+z^2$
$$=25+9+4$$
$$=38$$

Example 28. Let **a** and **b** be unit vectors such that $|\mathbf{a}+\mathbf{b}|=\sqrt{3}$. Then, find the value of $(2\mathbf{a}+5\mathbf{b})\cdot(3\mathbf{a}+\mathbf{b}+\mathbf{a}\times\mathbf{b})$.

Sol. $(2\mathbf{a}+5\mathbf{b})\cdot(3\mathbf{a}+\mathbf{b}+\mathbf{a}\times\mathbf{b})$

$$=6\mathbf{a}\cdot\mathbf{a}+17\mathbf{a}\cdot\mathbf{b}+5\mathbf{b}\cdot\mathbf{b}=11+17\mathbf{a}\cdot\mathbf{b}$$

$[\because \mathbf{a}\cdot(\mathbf{a}\times\mathbf{b})=\mathbf{b}\cdot(\mathbf{a}\times\mathbf{b})=0$, as $\mathbf{a}$ and $\mathbf{b}$ are perpendicular to $\mathbf{a}\times\mathbf{b}]$

From given, $|\mathbf{a}+\mathbf{b}|=\sqrt{3}$

On squaring both sides, we get

$$\Rightarrow \quad |\mathbf{a}+\mathbf{b}|^2=3$$

$$\Rightarrow \quad |\mathbf{a}|^2+|\mathbf{b}|^2+2\mathbf{a}\cdot\mathbf{b}=3 \Rightarrow \mathbf{a}\cdot\mathbf{b}=\frac{1}{2}$$

Hence, $(2\mathbf{a}+5\mathbf{b})\cdot(3\mathbf{a}+\mathbf{b}+\mathbf{a}\times\mathbf{b})=11+\frac{17}{2}=\frac{39}{2}$

Example 29. Find the unit vector perpendicular to the vectors $6\hat{i}+2\hat{j}+3\hat{k}$ and $3\hat{i}-6\hat{j}-2\hat{k}$.

Sol. Let $\mathbf{a}=6\hat{\mathbf{i}}+2\hat{\mathbf{j}}+3\hat{\mathbf{k}}$ and $\mathbf{b}=3\hat{\mathbf{i}}-6\hat{\mathbf{j}}-2\hat{\mathbf{k}}$

$$\mathbf{a}\times\mathbf{b}=\begin{vmatrix}\hat{\mathbf{i}} & \hat{\mathbf{j}} & \hat{\mathbf{k}}\\ 6 & 2 & 3\\ 3 & -6 & -2\end{vmatrix}$$

$$=14\hat{\mathbf{i}}+21\hat{\mathbf{j}}-42\hat{\mathbf{k}}=7(2\hat{\mathbf{i}}+3\hat{\mathbf{j}}-6\hat{\mathbf{k}})$$

$$|\mathbf{a}\times\mathbf{b}|=7|2\hat{\mathbf{i}}+3\hat{\mathbf{j}}-6\hat{\mathbf{k}}|=7\times7$$

$$\therefore \quad \frac{\mathbf{a}\times\mathbf{b}}{|\mathbf{a}\times\mathbf{b}|}=\frac{1}{7}(2\hat{\mathbf{i}}+3\hat{\mathbf{j}}-6\hat{\mathbf{k}})$$

which is a unit vector perpendicular to $\mathbf{a}$ and $\mathbf{b}$.

Example 30. Let $\mathbf{a}$, $\mathbf{b}$ and $\mathbf{c}$ be three vectors such that $|\mathbf{a}|=\sqrt{28}, 2|\mathbf{b}|=|\mathbf{c}|=2$ and $2(\mathbf{a}\times\mathbf{b})=3(\mathbf{c}\times\mathbf{a})$. If the angle between $\mathbf{b}$ and $\mathbf{c}$ is $\frac{2\pi}{3}$, then find the value of $\left(\frac{\mathbf{a}\times\mathbf{c}}{\mathbf{a}\cdot\mathbf{b}}\right)^2$.

Sol. $\because \quad 2(\mathbf{a}\times\mathbf{b})=3(\mathbf{c}\times\mathbf{a})$

$$\Rightarrow 2(\mathbf{a}\times\mathbf{b})+3(\mathbf{a}\times\mathbf{c})=0$$

$$\Rightarrow \quad \mathbf{a}\times(2\mathbf{b}+3\mathbf{c})=0$$

$$\therefore \quad \mathbf{a}=\lambda(2\mathbf{b}+3\mathbf{c})$$

$$\Rightarrow \quad |\mathbf{a}|^2=\lambda^2|2\mathbf{b}+3\mathbf{c}|^2$$

$$\Rightarrow \quad |\mathbf{a}|^2=\lambda^2(4|\mathbf{b}|^2+9|\mathbf{c}|^2+12\mathbf{b}\cdot\mathbf{c})$$

$$\Rightarrow \quad 28=\lambda^2(4(1)+9\times4+12\times1\times2\times\left(-\frac{1}{2}\right)$$

$$\Rightarrow \quad 28=\lambda^2(4+36-12)$$

$$\Rightarrow \quad 28=28\lambda^2$$

$$\Rightarrow \quad \lambda=\pm1$$

$$\therefore \quad \mathbf{a}=\pm(2\mathbf{b}+3\mathbf{c})$$

Now, $\quad \dfrac{|\mathbf{a}\times\mathbf{c}|}{|\mathbf{a}\cdot\mathbf{b}|}=\dfrac{2|\mathbf{b}\times\mathbf{c}|}{2\mathbf{b}\cdot\mathbf{b}+3\mathbf{c}\cdot\mathbf{b}}$

$$\left[\begin{array}{l}\because \mathbf{a}\times\mathbf{c}=\pm(2\mathbf{b}\times\mathbf{c}+3\mathbf{c}\times\mathbf{c})=2(\mathbf{b}\times\mathbf{c})\\ \mathbf{a}\cdot\mathbf{b}=2\mathbf{b}\cdot\mathbf{b}+3\mathbf{c}\cdot\mathbf{b}\end{array}\right]$$

$$\therefore \quad |\mathbf{b}\times\mathbf{c}|^2=|\mathbf{b}|^2|\mathbf{c}|^2-(\mathbf{b}\cdot\mathbf{c})^2$$

$$=1(4)-\left[1(2)\left(-\frac{1}{2}\right)\right]^2$$

$$=4-1=3$$

$$\frac{|\mathbf{a}\times\mathbf{c}|}{|\mathbf{a}\cdot\mathbf{b}|}=\frac{2\times\sqrt{3}}{2(1)(1)+3(2)(1)\left(-\frac{1}{2}\right)}$$

$$=\frac{2\sqrt{3}}{2-3}$$

$$=-2\sqrt{3}$$

So, $\left(\dfrac{\mathbf{a}\times\mathbf{c}}{\mathbf{a}\cdot\mathbf{b}}\right)^2=(2\sqrt{3})^2=12$

JEE SCANNER

Example Similar to PYQ Asked in JEE Main 2023

If $\mathbf{a}=2\hat{i}+\hat{k}$, $\mathbf{b}=\hat{i}+\hat{j}+\hat{k}$ and $\mathbf{c}=4\hat{i}-3\hat{j}+7\hat{k}$ be three vectors, if $\mathbf{r}$ is a vector such that $\mathbf{r}\times\mathbf{b}=\mathbf{c}\times\mathbf{b}$ and $\mathbf{r}\cdot\mathbf{a}=0$, then $7|\mathbf{r}|^2$ is equal to ....

Sol. Given, $\quad \mathbf{r}\times\mathbf{b}=\mathbf{c}\times\mathbf{b}$

$$\mathbf{r}\times\mathbf{b}-\mathbf{c}\times\mathbf{b}=0$$

$$(\mathbf{r}-\mathbf{c})\times\mathbf{b}=0$$

$\Rightarrow \mathbf{r}-\mathbf{c}$ is parallel to $\mathbf{b}$.

$\Rightarrow \mathbf{r}-\mathbf{c}=\lambda\mathbf{b}$, for some scalar λ.

$$\Rightarrow \quad \mathbf{r}=\mathbf{c}+\lambda\mathbf{b} \quad \text{...(i)}$$

Also given, $\quad \mathbf{r}\cdot\mathbf{a}=0$

$$\therefore \quad (\mathbf{c}+\lambda\mathbf{b})\cdot\mathbf{a}=0$$

$$\Rightarrow \quad \mathbf{c}\cdot\mathbf{a}+\lambda(\mathbf{b}\cdot\mathbf{a})=0$$

$$\lambda=-\left(\frac{\mathbf{c}\cdot\mathbf{a}}{\mathbf{b}\cdot\mathbf{a}}\right)=-\left[\frac{(4\hat{\mathbf{i}}-3\hat{\mathbf{j}}+7\hat{\mathbf{k}})\cdot(2\hat{\mathbf{i}}+\hat{\mathbf{k}})}{(\hat{\mathbf{i}}+\hat{\mathbf{j}}+\hat{\mathbf{k}})\cdot(2\hat{\mathbf{i}}+\hat{\mathbf{k}})}\right]$$

$$\lambda=-\left(\frac{8+7}{2+0+1}\right)=\frac{-15}{3}=-5$$

On putting λ in Eq. (i), we get

$$\mathbf{r}=\mathbf{c}-5\mathbf{b}=(4\hat{\mathbf{i}}-3\hat{\mathbf{j}}+7\hat{\mathbf{k}})-5(\hat{\mathbf{i}}+\hat{\mathbf{j}}+\hat{\mathbf{k}})$$

$$=-\hat{\mathbf{i}}-8\hat{\mathbf{j}}+2\hat{\mathbf{k}}$$

$$|\mathbf{r}|^2=1+64+4=69$$

$$7|\mathbf{r}|^2=7\times69=483$$

Skill Builder

If $\mathbf{a}=3\hat{i}-\hat{k}$, $\mathbf{b}=\hat{i}+2\hat{j}+3\hat{k}$ and $\mathbf{c}=3\hat{i}-4\hat{j}+7\hat{k}$ be three vectors, if $\mathbf{r}$ is a vector such that $\mathbf{r}\times\mathbf{b}=\mathbf{c}\times\mathbf{b}$ and $\mathbf{r}\cdot\mathbf{a}=0$, then $8|\mathbf{r}|^2$ is equal to ....

For Sol.

■ **For more practice** See Q.8 of Milestone Practice 2.

Example 31. If $\mathbf{a}=\hat{\mathbf{i}}+\hat{\mathbf{j}}+\hat{\mathbf{k}}$, $\mathbf{c}=\hat{\mathbf{j}}-\hat{\mathbf{k}}$ are given vector, then find vector $\mathbf{b}$ satisfying equation $\mathbf{a}\times\mathbf{b}=\mathbf{c}$ and $\mathbf{a}\cdot\mathbf{b}=3$.

Sol. Let $\mathbf{b}=x\hat{\mathbf{i}}+y\hat{\mathbf{j}}+z\hat{\mathbf{k}}$, then

$$\mathbf{a}\times\mathbf{b}=\mathbf{c}$$

$$\Rightarrow \begin{vmatrix}\hat{\mathbf{i}} & \hat{\mathbf{j}} & \hat{\mathbf{k}}\\ 1 & 1 & 1\\ x & y & z\end{vmatrix}=\hat{\mathbf{j}}-\hat{\mathbf{k}}$$

$$\Rightarrow (z-y)\hat{\mathbf{i}}+(x-z)\hat{\mathbf{j}}+(y-x)\hat{\mathbf{k}}=\hat{\mathbf{j}}-\hat{\mathbf{k}}$$

$$\Rightarrow z-y=0, x-z=1, y-x=-1$$

$$\Rightarrow y=z, z=x-1\, y=x-1$$

Also, given that $\mathbf{a}\cdot\mathbf{b}=3$

$$\Rightarrow (\hat{\mathbf{i}}+\hat{\mathbf{j}}+\hat{\mathbf{k}})\cdot(x\hat{\mathbf{i}}+y\hat{\mathbf{j}}+z\hat{\mathbf{k}})=3$$

$$\Rightarrow x+y+z=3$$

$$\Rightarrow x+x-1+x-1=3$$

$$\Rightarrow 3x=5$$

$$\Rightarrow x=\frac{5}{3}$$

Now, $y=x-1$

$$\Rightarrow y=\frac{5}{3}-1=\frac{2}{3},$$

$$z=\frac{2}{3}$$

Here, $\mathbf{b}=\frac{5}{3}\hat{\mathbf{i}}+\frac{2}{3}\hat{\mathbf{j}}+\frac{2}{3}\hat{\mathbf{k}}$

Example 32. If $\mathbf{a}$ and $\mathbf{b}$ are vectors such that $|\mathbf{a}+\mathbf{b}|=\sqrt{29}$ and $\mathbf{a}\times(2\hat{\mathbf{i}}+3\hat{\mathbf{j}}+4\hat{\mathbf{k}})=(2\hat{\mathbf{i}}+3\hat{\mathbf{j}}+4\hat{\mathbf{k}})\times\mathbf{b}$, then a possible value of $(\mathbf{a}+\mathbf{b})\cdot(-7\hat{\mathbf{i}}+2\hat{\mathbf{j}}+3\hat{\mathbf{k}})$ is

(a) 0 (b) 3
(c) ± 4 (d) 8

Sol. (c) Here, $\mathbf{a}\times(2\hat{\mathbf{i}}+3\hat{\mathbf{j}}+4\hat{\mathbf{k}})=(2\hat{\mathbf{i}}+3\hat{\mathbf{j}}+4\hat{\mathbf{k}})\times\mathbf{b}$

$$\Rightarrow \mathbf{a}\times(2\hat{\mathbf{i}}+3\hat{\mathbf{j}}+4\hat{\mathbf{k}})-(2\hat{\mathbf{i}}+3\hat{\mathbf{j}}+4\hat{\mathbf{k}})\times\mathbf{b}=0$$

$$\Rightarrow (\mathbf{a}+\mathbf{b})\times(2\hat{\mathbf{i}}+3\hat{\mathbf{j}}+4\hat{\mathbf{k}})=0$$

$$\Rightarrow \mathbf{a}+\mathbf{b}=\lambda(2\hat{\mathbf{i}}+3\hat{\mathbf{j}}+4\hat{\mathbf{k}}) \quad \text{...(i)}$$

Since, $|\mathbf{a}+\mathbf{b}|=\sqrt{29}$

$$\Rightarrow \pm\lambda\sqrt{4+9+16}=\sqrt{29}$$

$$\Rightarrow \lambda=\pm 1$$

$$\therefore \mathbf{a}+\mathbf{b}=\pm(2\hat{\mathbf{i}}+3\hat{\mathbf{j}}+4\hat{\mathbf{k}})$$

Now, $(\mathbf{a}+\mathbf{b})\cdot(-7\hat{\mathbf{i}}+2\hat{\mathbf{j}}+3\hat{\mathbf{k}})=\pm(-14+6+12)$

$$=\pm 4$$

JEE SCANNER

Example Similar to PYQ Asked in JEE Main 2023

Let A, B and C be points with position vector $2\hat{\mathbf{i}}-\hat{\mathbf{j}}+\hat{\mathbf{k}}$, $\hat{\mathbf{i}}+2\hat{\mathbf{j}}+3\hat{\mathbf{k}}$ and $3\hat{\mathbf{i}}+\hat{\mathbf{j}}+2\hat{\mathbf{k}}$ respectively, then the shortest distance between point B and plane OAC is

(a) $3\sqrt{\frac{2}{7}}$ units (b) $2\sqrt{\frac{7}{5}}$ units
(c) $2\sqrt{\frac{3}{7}}$ units (d) $2\sqrt{\frac{5}{7}}$ units

Sol. Shortest distance between B and plane OAC is perpendicular distance of point B on the plane OAC at point M.

Now, BM = Projection vector $\mathbf{AB}$ on vector perpendicular to the plane.

Now, vector perpendicular to the plane is $\mathbf{OA}\times\mathbf{OC}=\mathbf{a}\times\mathbf{c}$.

$$\mathbf{BM}=\frac{\mathbf{OB}\cdot(\mathbf{a}\times\mathbf{c})}{|\mathbf{a}\times\mathbf{c}|}=\frac{\mathbf{b}\cdot(\mathbf{a}\times\mathbf{c})}{|\mathbf{a}\times\mathbf{c}|}$$

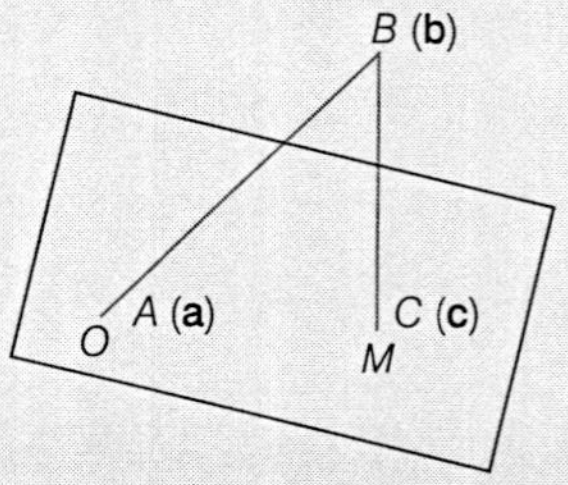

Now, $\mathbf{a}\times\mathbf{c}=\begin{vmatrix}\hat{\mathbf{i}} & \hat{\mathbf{j}} & \hat{\mathbf{k}}\\ 2 & -1 & 1\\ 3 & 1 & 2\end{vmatrix}=-3\hat{\mathbf{i}}-\hat{\mathbf{j}}+5\hat{\mathbf{k}}$

$$\therefore \mathbf{b}\cdot(\mathbf{a}\times\mathbf{c})=(\hat{\mathbf{i}}+2\hat{\mathbf{j}}+3\hat{\mathbf{k}})\cdot(-3\hat{\mathbf{i}}-\hat{\mathbf{j}}+5\hat{\mathbf{k}})$$

$$=-3-2+15=10$$

and $|\mathbf{a}\times\mathbf{c}|=|-3\hat{\mathbf{i}}-\hat{\mathbf{j}}+5\hat{\mathbf{k}}|=\sqrt{9+1+25}$

$$=\sqrt{35}$$

Hence, $BM=\frac{10}{\sqrt{35}}=2\sqrt{\frac{5}{7}}$ units

Skill Builder

Let P, Q and R be points with position vector $3\hat{\mathbf{i}}-\hat{\mathbf{j}}+3\hat{\mathbf{k}}$, $\hat{\mathbf{i}}+\hat{\mathbf{j}}+\hat{\mathbf{k}}$ and $2\hat{\mathbf{i}}+\hat{\mathbf{j}}-3\hat{\mathbf{k}}$ respectively, then the shortest distance between point Q and plane OPR is

(a) $\frac{4}{5}\sqrt{5}$ units (b) $\frac{2}{5}\sqrt{5}$ units
(c) $\frac{4}{5}\sqrt{13}$ units (d) $\frac{2}{5}\sqrt{3}$ units

For Sol.

■ **For more practice** See Q.19 of Milestone Practice 2.

Example 33. Let $\mathbf{a}=2\hat{\mathbf{i}}+\hat{\mathbf{j}}-2\hat{\mathbf{k}}$ and $\mathbf{b}=\hat{\mathbf{i}}+\hat{\mathbf{j}}$. If $\mathbf{c}$ is a vector such that $\mathbf{a}\cdot\mathbf{c}=|\mathbf{c}|, |\mathbf{c}-\mathbf{a}|=2\sqrt{2}$ and the angle between $(\mathbf{a}\times\mathbf{b})$ and $\mathbf{c}$ is $\frac{\pi}{6}$, then final the value of $|(\mathbf{a}\times\mathbf{b})\times\mathbf{c}|$.

Sol. Given, $\mathbf{a}=2\hat{\mathbf{i}}+\hat{\mathbf{j}}-2\hat{\mathbf{k}}$ and $\mathbf{b}=\hat{\mathbf{i}}+\hat{\mathbf{j}}$

$$|\mathbf{a}|^2=4+1+4=9$$

$$|\mathbf{c}-\mathbf{a}|=2\sqrt{2} \Rightarrow |\mathbf{c}-\mathbf{a}|^2=(2\sqrt{2})^2$$

$$\Rightarrow |\mathbf{c}|^2+|\mathbf{a}|^2-2\mathbf{c}\cdot\mathbf{a}=8$$

$$\Rightarrow |\mathbf{c}|^2+9-2|\mathbf{c}|=8 \quad [\because \mathbf{c}\cdot\mathbf{a}=|\mathbf{c}|]$$

$$\Rightarrow |\mathbf{c}|^2-2|\mathbf{c}|+1=0$$

$$\Rightarrow (|\mathbf{c}|-1)^2=0 \Rightarrow |\mathbf{c}|=1$$

Now, $$\mathbf{a}\times\mathbf{b}=\begin{vmatrix}\hat{\mathbf{i}} & \hat{\mathbf{j}} & \hat{\mathbf{k}}\\ 2 & 1 & -2\\ 1 & 1 & 0\end{vmatrix}=2\hat{\mathbf{i}}-2\hat{\mathbf{j}}+\hat{\mathbf{k}}$$

$$\Rightarrow |\mathbf{a}\times\mathbf{b}|=\sqrt{4+4+1}=3$$

$$\Rightarrow |(\mathbf{a}\times\mathbf{b})\times\mathbf{c}|=|\mathbf{a}\times\mathbf{b}||\mathbf{c}|\sin\frac{\pi}{6}=3\times1\times\frac{1}{2}=\frac{3}{2}$$

Example 34. Let $\mathbf{a}=3\hat{\mathbf{i}}+5\hat{\mathbf{j}}+4\hat{\mathbf{k}}$, $\mathbf{b}=2\hat{\mathbf{i}}-\hat{\mathbf{j}}-3\hat{\mathbf{k}}$ and $\mathbf{c}=-\hat{\mathbf{i}}+3\hat{\mathbf{j}}+2\hat{\mathbf{k}}$. If $\mathbf{d}$ is a vector perpendicular to both $\mathbf{b}$ and $\mathbf{c}$ and $\mathbf{a}\cdot\mathbf{d}=36$, then find the value of $|\mathbf{a}\times\mathbf{d}|^2$.

Decoding the Question

If $\mathbf{d}$ is perpendicular to both $\mathbf{b}$ and $\mathbf{c}$, then $\mathbf{d}=\lambda(\mathbf{b}\times\mathbf{c})$, where λ is arbitrary constant and also use Lagrange's identity formula

$$|\mathbf{a}\times\mathbf{b}|^2=|\mathbf{a}|^2|\mathbf{b}|^2-(\mathbf{a}\cdot\mathbf{b})^2$$

Sol. Given that $\mathbf{a}=3\hat{\mathbf{i}}+5\hat{\mathbf{j}}+4\hat{\mathbf{k}}, \mathbf{b}=2\hat{\mathbf{i}}-\hat{\mathbf{j}}-3\hat{\mathbf{k}}$

and $\mathbf{c}=-\hat{\mathbf{i}}+3\hat{\mathbf{j}}+2\hat{\mathbf{k}}$

Let us find $\mathbf{b}\times\mathbf{c}$

$$\Rightarrow \mathbf{b}\times\mathbf{c}=\begin{vmatrix}\hat{\mathbf{i}} & \hat{\mathbf{j}} & \hat{\mathbf{k}}\\ 2 & -1 & -3\\ -1 & 3 & 2\end{vmatrix}=(-2+9)\hat{\mathbf{i}}-(4-3)\hat{\mathbf{j}}+(6-1)\hat{\mathbf{k}}$$

$$\Rightarrow \mathbf{b}\times\mathbf{c}=7\hat{\mathbf{i}}-\hat{\mathbf{j}}+5\hat{\mathbf{k}}$$

Since, $\mathbf{d}$ is perpendicular to both $\mathbf{b}$ and $\mathbf{c}$

$$\therefore \quad \mathbf{d}=\lambda(7\hat{\mathbf{i}}-\hat{\mathbf{j}}+5\hat{\mathbf{k}})$$

Also, $\mathbf{a}\cdot\mathbf{d}=36$

$$\Rightarrow \lambda(3\hat{\mathbf{i}}+5\hat{\mathbf{j}}+4\hat{\mathbf{k}})\cdot(7\hat{\mathbf{i}}-\hat{\mathbf{j}}+5\hat{\mathbf{k}})=36$$

$$\Rightarrow 36\lambda=36$$

$$\therefore \lambda=1$$

Now, let us apply **Lagrange's identity** which is as follows.

$$\therefore |\mathbf{a}\times\mathbf{d}|^2=|\mathbf{a}|^2|\mathbf{d}|^2-(\mathbf{a}\cdot\mathbf{d})^2$$

$$=|3\hat{\mathbf{i}}+5\hat{\mathbf{j}}+4\hat{\mathbf{k}}|^2|7\hat{\mathbf{i}}-\hat{\mathbf{j}}+5\hat{\mathbf{k}}|^2-(36)^2$$

$$=3750-1296=2454$$

2.8 Geometrical Interpretation of Vector Product

If $\mathbf{a}$ and $\mathbf{b}$ are two non-zero, non-parallel vectors represented by **OA**, **OB** respectively and let θ be the angle between them. Complete the parallelogram $OACB$. Draw $BL \perp OA$.

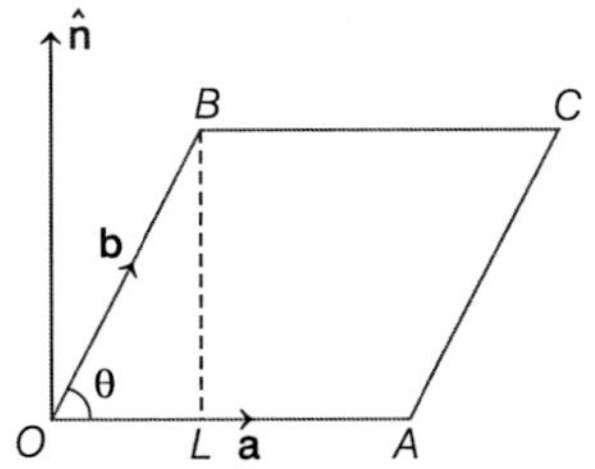

In ΔOBL, $\quad \sin\theta=\frac{BL}{OB}$

$$\Rightarrow BL=OB\sin\theta=|\mathbf{b}|\sin\theta$$

Now, $$\mathbf{a}\times\mathbf{b}=|\mathbf{a}||\mathbf{b}|\sin\theta\,\mathbf{n}=(OA)(BL)\,\mathbf{n}$$

$$=(\text{Base}\times\text{Height})\,\mathbf{n}$$

$$=(\text{Area of parallelogram } OACB)\,\mathbf{n}$$

$$=\text{Vector area of the parallelogram } OACB$$

Thus, $\mathbf{a}\times\mathbf{b}$ is a vector whose magnitude is equal to the area of the parallelogram having $\mathbf{a}$ and $\mathbf{b}$ as its adjacent sides and whose direction $\mathbf{n}$ is perpendicular to the plane of $\mathbf{a}$ and $\mathbf{b}$ such that $\mathbf{a}$, $\mathbf{b}$ and $\mathbf{n}$ form a right handed system.

Infact, $\mathbf{a}\times\mathbf{b}$ is the vector area of that face of the parallelogram which is towards the observe in given figure.

2.9 Area of Parallelogram and Triangle

(i) The area of a parallelogram with adjacent sides $\mathbf{a}$ and $\mathbf{b}$ is $|\mathbf{a}\times\mathbf{b}|$.

(ii) The area of a parallelogram with diagonals $\mathbf{d}_1$ and $\mathbf{d}_2$ is $\frac{1}{2}|\mathbf{d}_1\times\mathbf{d}_2|$.

(iii) The area of a plane quadrilateral $ABCD$ is $\frac{1}{2}|\mathbf{AC}\times\mathbf{BD}|$, where AC and BD are its diagonals.

(iv) The area of a triangle with adjacent sides $\mathbf{a}$ and $\mathbf{b}$ is $\frac{1}{2}|\mathbf{a}\times\mathbf{b}|$.

(v) The area of a ΔABC is $\frac{1}{2}|\mathbf{AB}\times\mathbf{AC}|$

or $\frac{1}{2}|\mathbf{BC}\times\mathbf{BA}|$ or $\frac{1}{2}|\mathbf{CB}\times\mathbf{CA}|$

(vi) If **a**, **b** and **c** are position vectors of a ΔABC, then its area $= \frac{1}{2}|(\mathbf{a}\times\mathbf{b})+(\mathbf{b}\times\mathbf{c})+(\mathbf{c}\times\mathbf{a})|$

(vii) Three points with position vector **a**, **b** and **c** are collinear, if $[(\mathbf{a}\times\mathbf{b})+(\mathbf{b}\times\mathbf{c})+(\mathbf{c}\times\mathbf{a})]=0$.

Example 35. Find the area of the triangle with vertices $A(1, 2, 3), B(2, -1, 4)$ and $C(4, 5, -1)$.

Sol. The adjacent sides **AB** and **AC** of ΔABC given as

$$\mathbf{AB} = (2-1)\hat{\mathbf{i}}+(-1-2)\hat{\mathbf{j}}+(4-3)\hat{\mathbf{k}} = \hat{\mathbf{i}}-3\hat{\mathbf{j}}+\hat{\mathbf{k}}$$

and $\mathbf{AC} = (4-1)\hat{\mathbf{i}}+(5-2)\hat{\mathbf{j}}+(-1-3)\hat{\mathbf{k}} = 3\hat{\mathbf{i}}+3\hat{\mathbf{j}}-4\hat{\mathbf{k}}$

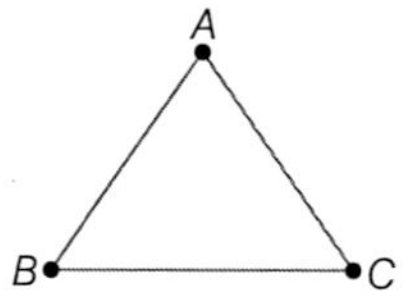

Now, $\mathbf{AB}\times\mathbf{AC} = \begin{vmatrix} \hat{\mathbf{i}} & \hat{\mathbf{j}} & \hat{\mathbf{k}} \\ 1 & -3 & 1 \\ 3 & 3 & -4 \end{vmatrix}$

$$= \hat{\mathbf{i}}(12-3)-\hat{\mathbf{j}}(-4-3)+\hat{\mathbf{k}}(3+9)$$

$$= 9\hat{\mathbf{i}}+7\hat{\mathbf{j}}+12\hat{\mathbf{k}}$$

$\therefore \quad |\mathbf{AB}\times\mathbf{AC}| = \sqrt{81+49+144} = \sqrt{274}$

$\therefore$ Area of $\Delta ABC = \frac{1}{2}|\mathbf{AB}\times\mathbf{AC}|$

$$= \frac{1}{2}\sqrt{274} \text{ sq units}$$

Example 36. Show that the perpendicular distance of the point **c** from the joining of **a** and **b** is

$$\frac{|\mathbf{b}\times\mathbf{c}+\mathbf{c}\times\mathbf{a}+\mathbf{a}\times\mathbf{b}|}{|\mathbf{b}-\mathbf{a}|}$$

Sol. Let ABC be a triangle and let **a**, **b** and **c** be the position of its vertices A, B and C respectively. Let CM be the perpendicular from C on AB.

Then, area of $\Delta ABC = \frac{1}{2}(AB)\cdot(CM) = \frac{1}{2}|\mathbf{AB}||\mathbf{CM}|$

Also, area of $\Delta ABC = \frac{1}{2}|\mathbf{a}\times\mathbf{b}+\mathbf{b}\times\mathbf{c}+\mathbf{c}\times\mathbf{a}|$

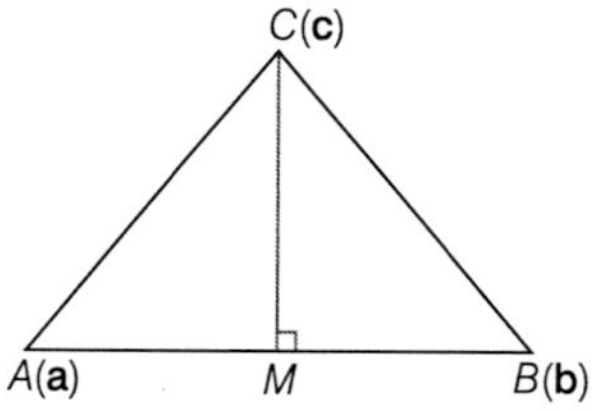

$\therefore \quad \frac{1}{2}|\mathbf{AB}||\mathbf{CM}| = \frac{1}{2}|\mathbf{a}\times\mathbf{b}+\mathbf{b}\times\mathbf{c}+\mathbf{c}\times\mathbf{a}|$

$\Rightarrow \quad \mathbf{CM} = \dfrac{|\mathbf{b}\times\mathbf{c}+\mathbf{c}\times\mathbf{a}+\mathbf{a}\times\mathbf{b}|}{|\mathbf{b}-\mathbf{a}|}$

Example 37. Let $\mathbf{a} = \hat{\mathbf{i}}+\mu\hat{\mathbf{j}}+3\hat{\mathbf{k}}$ and $\mathbf{b} = 3\hat{\mathbf{i}}-\mu\hat{\mathbf{j}}+\hat{\mathbf{k}}$. If the area of the parallelogram whose adjacent sides are represented by the vectors **a** and **b** is 24 sq units, then find the value of $\mathbf{a}\cdot\mathbf{b}$.

Sol. Given, $\mathbf{a} = \hat{\mathbf{i}}+\mu\hat{\mathbf{j}}+3\hat{\mathbf{k}}, \ \mathbf{b} = 3\hat{\mathbf{i}}-\mu\hat{\mathbf{j}}+\hat{\mathbf{k}}$

$\therefore$ Area of parallelogram $= |\mathbf{a}\times\mathbf{b}|$

$\Rightarrow \quad 24 = |(\hat{\mathbf{i}}+\mu\hat{\mathbf{j}}+3\hat{\mathbf{k}})\times(3\hat{\mathbf{i}}-\mu\hat{\mathbf{j}}+\hat{\mathbf{k}})|$

$\Rightarrow \quad 24 = |(4\mu)\hat{\mathbf{i}}+8\hat{\mathbf{j}}-(4\mu)\hat{\mathbf{k}}|$

$\Rightarrow \quad 576 = 16\mu^2+64+16\mu^2$

$\Rightarrow \quad 576 = 32\mu^2+64$

$\Rightarrow \quad 18 = \mu^2+2$

$\therefore \quad \mu^2 = 16$

$\therefore \quad \mathbf{a} = \hat{\mathbf{i}}+\mu\hat{\mathbf{j}}+3\hat{\mathbf{k}}$ and $\mathbf{b} = 3\hat{\mathbf{i}}-\mu\hat{\mathbf{j}}+\hat{\mathbf{k}}$

Hence, $\quad \mathbf{a}\cdot\mathbf{b} = 3-\mu^2+3 = 6-\mu^2 = 6-16 = -10$

JEE SCANNER

Example Similar to PYQ Asked in JEE Main 2023

If $A(1,5,2), B(-3,-1,\lambda), C(1,3,-2)$ and $D(4,5,0)$, $|\lambda|\le 10$ are the vertices of quadrilateral ABCD and its area is $\frac{\sqrt{309}}{2}$ sq units, then the value of $(1-4\lambda)$ is ......

Sol. $A(1, 5, 2), B(-3, -1, \lambda), C(1, 3, -2), D(4, 5\ 0)$

$$\text{Area} = \frac{1}{2}|\mathbf{BD}\times\mathbf{AC}| = \frac{\sqrt{309}}{2}$$

$$\mathbf{AC}\times\mathbf{BD} = \begin{vmatrix} \hat{\mathbf{i}} & \hat{\mathbf{j}} & \hat{\mathbf{k}} \\ 0 & -2 & -4 \\ 7 & 6 & -\lambda \end{vmatrix} = (2\lambda+24)\hat{\mathbf{i}}-(28)\hat{\mathbf{j}}+(14)\hat{\mathbf{k}}$$

$\mathbf{AC}\times\mathbf{BD} = (2\lambda+24)\hat{\mathbf{i}}-28\hat{\mathbf{j}}+14\hat{\mathbf{k}}$

Now, $|\mathbf{AC}\times\mathbf{BD}| = \sqrt{(2\lambda+24)^2+(-28)^2+(14)^2} = \sqrt{309}$

$\Rightarrow \lambda^2+24\lambda+389 = 309$

$\Rightarrow \lambda^2+24\lambda+80 = 0 \Rightarrow \lambda = -4, -20$

$\because \quad |\lambda|\le 10 \Rightarrow \lambda = -4$

Hence, $1-4\lambda = 1-4(-4) = 17$

Skill Builder

If $P(2,3,1), Q(-3,-1,\lambda), R(2,4,-1)$ and $S(2,5,0)$, are the vertices of quadrilateral $PQRS$ and its area is $\frac{5\sqrt{5}}{2}$ sq units, then the value of $(1+\lambda)$ is ....

For Sol.

■ **For more practice** See Q.16 of Milestone Practice 2.

Example 38. Let $OA = \mathbf{a}$, $OB = 12\mathbf{a} + 4\mathbf{b}$ and $OC = \mathbf{b}$, where O is the origin. If S is the paralellogram with adjacent sides OA and OC then, find $\left(\dfrac{\text{Area of the quadrilateral } OABC}{\text{Area of } S}\right)$.

Sol. $OA = \mathbf{a}, OB = 12\mathbf{a} + 4\mathbf{b}$ and $\mathbf{OC} = \mathbf{b}$ [given]

$\because$ S is parallelogram with adjacent sides OA and OC.

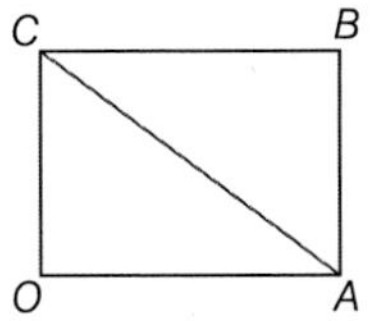

So, area of quadrilateral $OABC = \frac{1}{2}|\mathbf{d}_1 \times \mathbf{d}_2|$

$$= \frac{1}{2}|\mathbf{OB} \times \mathbf{AC}|$$
$$= \frac{1}{2}|(12\mathbf{a} + 4\mathbf{b}) \times (\mathbf{b} - \mathbf{a})|$$
$$= \frac{1}{2}|12(\mathbf{a} \times \mathbf{b}) - 4(\mathbf{b} \times \mathbf{a})|$$
$$= \frac{1}{2}|16(\mathbf{a} \times \mathbf{b})|$$
$$= 8|\mathbf{a} \times \mathbf{b}|$$

$\therefore$ Area of $S = |\mathbf{a} \times \mathbf{b}|$

Hence, $\dfrac{\text{Area of quadrilateral } OABC}{\text{Area of } S} = 8$

Example 39.

(i) Find the area of the quadrilateral whose diagonals are given by

$$3\hat{\mathbf{i}} + \hat{\mathbf{j}} - 2\hat{\mathbf{k}}, \hat{\mathbf{i}} - 3\hat{\mathbf{j}} + 4\hat{\mathbf{k}}$$

(ii) $A_1, A_2, \ldots, A_n$ are the vertices of a regular plane polygon with n sides. O is the centre. Show that

$$\sum_{i=1}^{n-1} (\mathbf{OA}_i \times \mathbf{OA}_{i+1}) = (1-n)(\mathbf{OA}_2 \times \mathbf{OA}_1)$$

Sol. (i) Area of the quadrilateral $= \frac{1}{2}|d_1 \times d_2|$

$$= \frac{1}{2}\begin{vmatrix} \hat{\mathbf{i}} & \hat{\mathbf{j}} & \hat{\mathbf{k}} \\ 3 & 1 & -2 \\ 1 & -3 & 4 \end{vmatrix} = \frac{1}{2}|-2\hat{\mathbf{i}} - 14\hat{\mathbf{j}} - 10\hat{\mathbf{k}}|$$

$$= \frac{1}{2}\sqrt{4 + 196 + 100} = \frac{10\sqrt{3}}{2} = 5\sqrt{3}$$

(ii) $A_1, A_2, \ldots, A_n$ are the vertices of a regular plane polygon of n sides and centre O.

Let $|\mathbf{OA}_i| = k, \forall\, i = 1 < 2, 3, \ldots, n$

Let $\hat{\mathbf{e}}_i$ be the unit vector along $\mathbf{OA}_i$

$$\mathbf{OA}_i = k\hat{\mathbf{e}}_i$$
$$\mathbf{OA}_i \times \mathbf{OA}_{i+1} = k\hat{\mathbf{e}}_i \times k\hat{\mathbf{e}}_{i+1} = k^2\hat{\mathbf{x}}_i$$

where, $\hat{\mathbf{x}}_i$ is a unit vector in the direction perpendicular to the plane of the polygon and $\hat{\mathbf{x}}_i = \hat{\mathbf{x}}_{i+1}$ for $i = 1, 2, 3, \ldots, n-1$

$$\therefore \quad \text{LHS} = \sum_{i=1}^{n-1} (\mathbf{OA}_i \times \mathbf{OA}_{i+1})$$
$$= k^2 \sum_{r=1}^{n-1} \hat{\mathbf{x}}_i$$
$$= k^2 (n-1)\hat{\mathbf{x}}_i$$
$$= (n-1)(\mathbf{OA}_i \times \mathbf{OA}_2)$$
$$= (1-n)(\mathbf{OA}_2 \times \mathbf{OA}_1)$$

2.10 Moment of a Force and Couple Moment of a Force

(i) **About a point** Let a force $\mathbf{F}$ be applied at a point P of a rigid body then, the moment of $\mathbf{F}$ about a point O measures the tendency of $\mathbf{F}$ to turn the body about point O. If this tendency of rotation about O is in anti-clockwise direction, the moment is positive, otherwise it is negative.

Let $\mathbf{r}$ be the position vector of P relative to O. Then, the moment or torque of $\mathbf{F}$ about the point O is defined as the vector $\mathbf{M} = \mathbf{r} \times \mathbf{F}$.

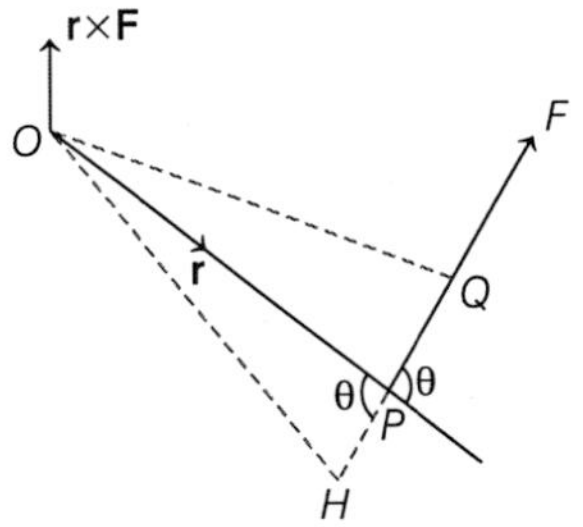

If several forces are acting through the same point P, then the vector sum of the moment of the separate forces about O is equal to the moment of their resultant force about O.

(ii) **About a line** The moment of a force $\mathbf{F}$ acting at a point P about a line L is a scalar given by $(\mathbf{r} \times \mathbf{F}) \cdot \hat{\mathbf{a}}$, where $\mathbf{a}$ is a unit vector in the direction of the line and $\mathbf{OP} = \mathbf{r}$, where O is any point on the line.

Thus, the moment of a force $\mathbf{F}$ about a line is the resolved part (component) along this line, of the moment of $\mathbf{F}$ about any point on the line.

JEE Focus Points

- Moment of a force F about a point $A = AB \times F$, where B is any point on F. [for part (i)]
- The moment of a force about a point is a vector while the moment about a straight line is a scalar quantity. [for part (ii)]

Concept Inside Video

Example 40. Find the moment about $(1, -1, -1)$ of the force $3\hat{i} + 4\hat{j} - 5\hat{k}$ acting at $(1, 0, -2)$.

Sol. Let $A \equiv (1, -1, -1)$, $B \equiv (1, 0, -2)$

and $\mathbf{F} = 3\hat{\mathbf{i}} + 4\hat{\mathbf{j}} - 5\hat{\mathbf{k}}$

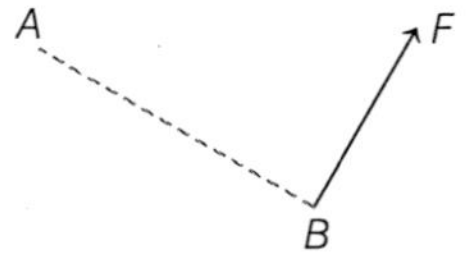

Then, moment of force **F** about A is given by $\mathbf{AB} \times \mathbf{F}$.

Here, $\mathbf{AB} = (\hat{\mathbf{i}} - 2\hat{\mathbf{k}}) - (\hat{\mathbf{i}} - \hat{\mathbf{j}} - \hat{\mathbf{k}}) = \hat{\mathbf{j}} - \hat{\mathbf{k}}$

$$\therefore \quad \mathbf{AB} \times \mathbf{F} = \begin{vmatrix} \hat{\mathbf{i}} & \hat{\mathbf{j}} & \hat{\mathbf{k}} \\ 0 & 1 & -1 \\ 3 & 4 & -5 \end{vmatrix}$$

$$= \hat{\mathbf{i}}(-5 + 4) - \hat{\mathbf{j}}(0 + 3) + \hat{\mathbf{k}}(0 - 3)$$

$$= -\hat{\mathbf{i}} - 3\hat{\mathbf{j}} - 3\hat{\mathbf{k}}$$

Example 41. Three forces $\hat{i} + 2\hat{j} - 3\hat{k}, 2\hat{i} + 3\hat{j} + 4\hat{k}$ and $\hat{i} - \hat{j} + \hat{k}$ acting on a particle at the point (0, 1, 2). Find the magnitude of the moment of the forces about the point $(1, -2, 0)$.

Sol. Total force $\mathbf{F} = (\hat{\mathbf{i}} + 2\hat{\mathbf{j}} - 3\hat{\mathbf{k}}) + (2\hat{\mathbf{i}} + 3\hat{\mathbf{j}} + 4\hat{\mathbf{k}}) + (\hat{\mathbf{i}} - \hat{\mathbf{j}} + \hat{\mathbf{k}})$

$$= 4\hat{\mathbf{i}} + 4\hat{\mathbf{j}} + 2\hat{\mathbf{k}}$$

Moment of the forces about

$$\mathbf{P} = \mathbf{r} \times \mathbf{F} = \mathbf{PA} \times \mathbf{F}$$

$$\mathbf{PA} = (0 - 1)\hat{\mathbf{i}} + (1 + 2)\hat{\mathbf{j}} + (2 - 0)\hat{\mathbf{k}}$$

$$= -\hat{\mathbf{i}} + 3\hat{\mathbf{j}} + 2\hat{\mathbf{k}}$$

$\therefore$ Moment about $P = (-\hat{\mathbf{i}} + 3\hat{\mathbf{j}} + 2\hat{\mathbf{k}}) \times (4\hat{\mathbf{i}} + 4\hat{\mathbf{j}} + 2\hat{\mathbf{k}})$

$$= \begin{vmatrix} \hat{\mathbf{i}} & \hat{\mathbf{j}} & \hat{\mathbf{k}} \\ -1 & 3 & 2 \\ 4 & 4 & 2 \end{vmatrix} = -2\hat{\mathbf{i}} + 10\hat{\mathbf{j}} - 16\hat{\mathbf{k}}$$

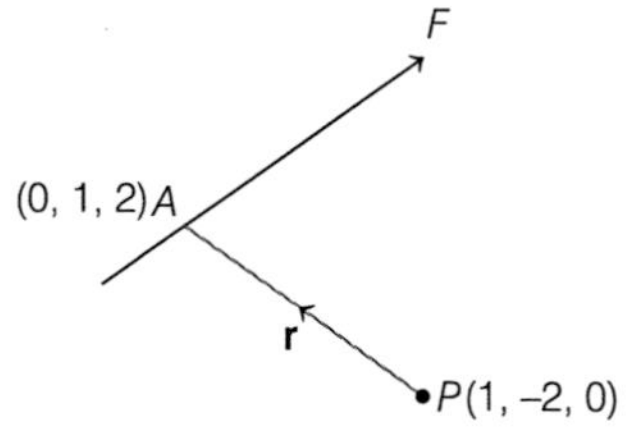

Magnitude of the moment $= |-2\hat{\mathbf{i}} + 10\hat{\mathbf{j}} - 16\hat{\mathbf{k}}|$

$$= 2\sqrt{1^2 + 5^2 + 8^2}$$

$$= 2\sqrt{90} = 6\sqrt{10}$$

Example 42. Find the moment about a line through the origin having the direction of $2\hat{i} - 2\hat{j} + \hat{k}$ due to 30 kg force acting at a point $(-4, 2, 5)$ in the direction of $12\hat{i} - 4\hat{j} - 3\hat{k}$.

Sol. Let **F** be the force. Then,

$$\mathbf{F} = \frac{30\,(12\hat{\mathbf{i}} - 4\hat{\mathbf{j}} - 3\hat{\mathbf{k}})}{\sqrt{144 + 16 + 9}} = \frac{30}{13}(12\hat{\mathbf{i}} - 4\hat{\mathbf{j}} - 3\hat{\mathbf{k}})$$

Suppose, the force **F** acts at point $P(-4, 2, 5)$ the moment of **F** acting at P about a line in the direction $2\hat{\mathbf{i}} - 2\hat{\mathbf{j}} + \hat{\mathbf{k}}$ is equal to the resolve part along the line of moment of **F** about a point on the line.

$$\therefore \quad \mathbf{r} = \mathbf{OP} = (-4\hat{\mathbf{i}} + 2\hat{\mathbf{j}} + 5\hat{\mathbf{k}}) - (0) = -4\hat{\mathbf{i}} + 2\hat{\mathbf{j}} + 5\hat{\mathbf{k}}$$

Let **M** be the moment **F** about O. Then,

$$\mathbf{M} = \mathbf{r} \times \mathbf{F} = \frac{30}{13}\begin{vmatrix} \hat{\mathbf{i}} & \hat{\mathbf{j}} & \hat{\mathbf{k}} \\ -4 & 2 & 5 \\ 12 & -4 & -3 \end{vmatrix}$$

$$= \frac{30}{13}(14\hat{\mathbf{i}} + 48\hat{\mathbf{j}} - 8\hat{\mathbf{k}})$$

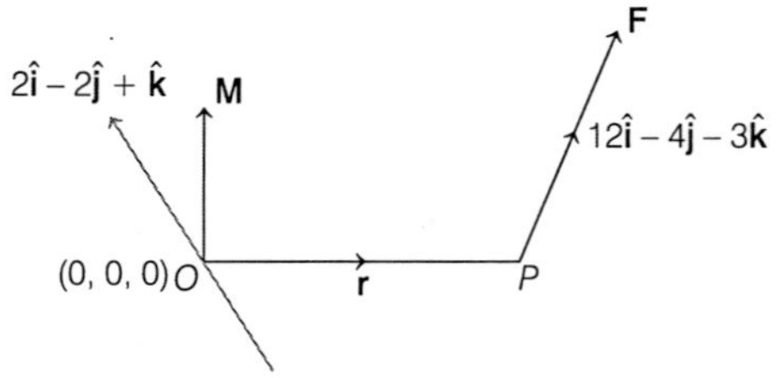

Let **a** be unit vector in the direction of $2\hat{\mathbf{i}} - 2\hat{\mathbf{j}} + \hat{\mathbf{k}}$. Then,

$$\mathbf{a} = \frac{2\hat{\mathbf{i}} - 2\hat{\mathbf{j}} + \hat{\mathbf{k}}}{\sqrt{4 + 4 + 1}} = \frac{1}{3}(2\hat{\mathbf{i}} - 2\hat{\mathbf{j}} + \hat{\mathbf{k}})$$

Thus, the moment of **F** about the given line

$$= \mathbf{M} \cdot \mathbf{a} = \frac{30}{13}(14\hat{\mathbf{i}} + 48\hat{\mathbf{j}} - 8\hat{\mathbf{k}}) \cdot \frac{1}{3}(2\hat{\mathbf{i}} - 2\hat{\mathbf{j}} + \hat{\mathbf{k}})$$

$$= -\frac{760}{13}$$

2.11 Moment of a Couple

A system consisting of a pair of equal unlike parallel forces is called a couple. The vector sum to two forces of a couple is always zero vector.

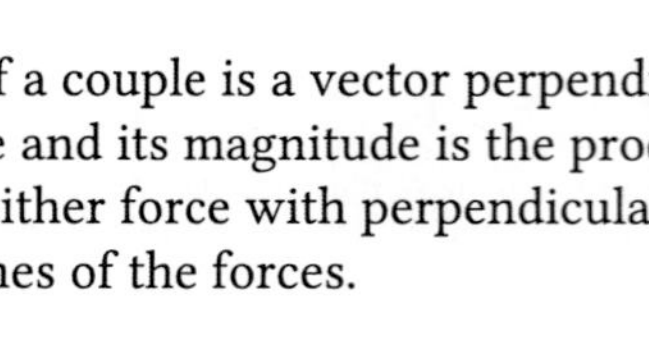

The moment of a couple is a vector perpendicular to the plane of couple and its magnitude is the product of the magnitude of either force with perpendicular distance between the lines of the forces.

$$\mathbf{M} = \mathbf{r} \times \mathbf{F},$$

where $\mathbf{r} = \mathbf{BA}$

$$|\mathbf{M}| = |\mathbf{BA} \times \mathbf{F}|$$
$$= |\mathbf{F}||\mathbf{BA}|\sin\theta,$$

where θ is the angle between **BA** and **F**

$$= |\mathbf{F}|(BN)$$
$$= |\mathbf{F}|\alpha$$

where, $\alpha = BN$ is the arm of the couple and '+' ve or '–' ve sign is to be taken accordingly as the forces indicate a counter anti-clockwise rotation or clockwise rotation.

Example 43. Find the moment of the couple formed by the forces $5\hat{\mathbf{i}} + \hat{\mathbf{k}}$ and $-5\hat{\mathbf{i}} - \hat{\mathbf{k}}$ acting at the points $(9, -1, 2)$ and $(3, -2, 1)$ respectively.

Sol. Moment of the couple,

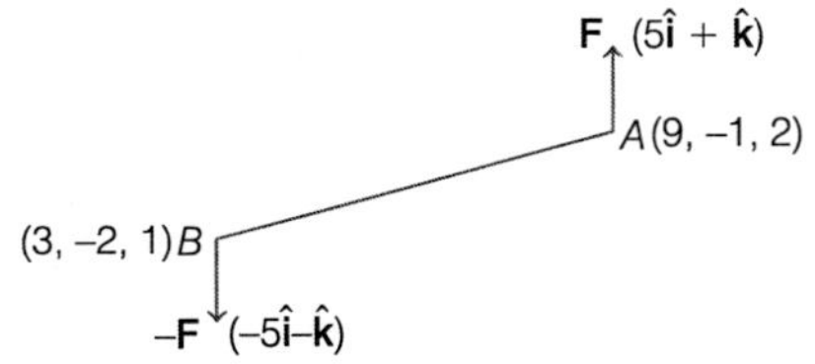

$$= \mathbf{BA} \times \mathbf{F} = \{(9-3)\hat{\mathbf{i}} + (-1+2)\hat{\mathbf{j}} + (2-1)\hat{\mathbf{k}}\} \times (5\hat{\mathbf{i}} + \hat{\mathbf{k}})$$

$$= (6\hat{\mathbf{i}} + \hat{\mathbf{j}} + \hat{\mathbf{k}}) \times (5\hat{\mathbf{i}} + \hat{\mathbf{k}})$$

$$= \begin{vmatrix} \hat{\mathbf{i}} & \hat{\mathbf{j}} & \hat{\mathbf{k}} \\ 6 & 1 & 1 \\ 5 & 0 & 1 \end{vmatrix}$$

$$= \hat{\mathbf{i}} - \hat{\mathbf{j}} - 5\hat{\mathbf{k}}$$

2.12 Rotation About an Axis

When a rigid body rotates about a fixed axis ON with an angular velocity ω, then velocity v of a particle P is given by

$$v = \omega \times \mathbf{r},$$

where, $\mathbf{r} = \mathbf{OP}$

and $\omega = |\omega|$ (unit vector along ON)

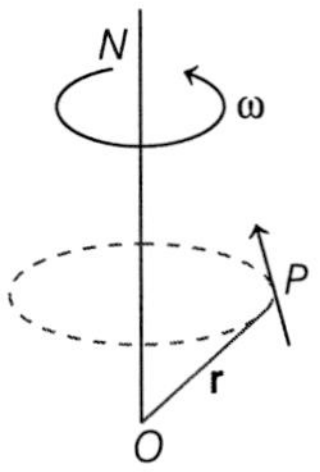

Example 44. A particle has an angular speed of 3 rad/s and the axis of rotation passes through the points (1, 1, 2) and $(1, 2, -2)$. Find the velocity of the particle at point $P(3, 6, 4)$.

> **Decoding the Question**
> First find unit vector along fixed axis, then apply $\mathbf{v} = \omega \times \mathbf{r}$ for velocity.

Sol. Clearly, $\mathbf{OA} = \hat{\mathbf{i}} + \hat{\mathbf{j}} + 2\hat{\mathbf{k}}$ and $\mathbf{OB} = \hat{\mathbf{i}} + 2\hat{\mathbf{j}} - 2\hat{\mathbf{k}}$

$\therefore$ $\mathbf{AB} = \hat{\mathbf{j}} - 4\hat{\mathbf{k}} \Rightarrow |\mathbf{AB}| = \sqrt{17}$

and $\mathbf{AP} = (3\hat{\mathbf{i}} + 6\hat{\mathbf{j}} + 4\hat{\mathbf{k}}) - (\hat{\mathbf{i}} + \hat{\mathbf{j}} + 2\hat{\mathbf{k}})$

$$= 2\hat{\mathbf{i}} + 5\hat{\mathbf{j}} + 2\hat{\mathbf{k}}$$

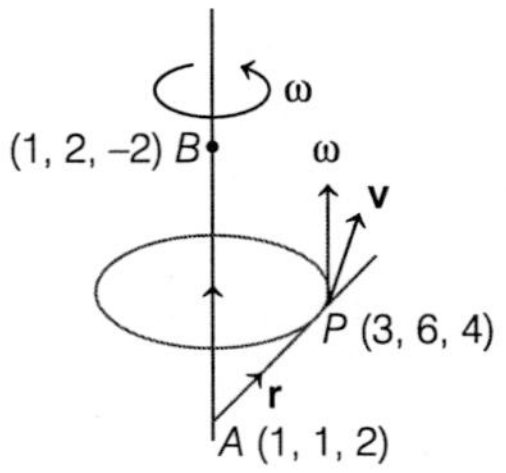

$\therefore$ $\omega = \dfrac{3}{\sqrt{17}}(\hat{\mathbf{j}} - 4\hat{\mathbf{k}})$ and $\mathbf{r} = 2\hat{\mathbf{i}} + 5\hat{\mathbf{j}} + 2\hat{\mathbf{k}}$

Now, $\mathbf{v} = \omega \times \mathbf{r} = \dfrac{3}{\sqrt{17}}(\hat{\mathbf{j}} - 4\hat{\mathbf{k}}) \times (2\hat{\mathbf{i}} + 5\hat{\mathbf{j}} + 2\hat{\mathbf{k}})$

$$= \frac{3}{\sqrt{17}}(22\hat{\mathbf{i}} - 8\hat{\mathbf{j}} - 2\hat{\mathbf{k}})$$

Example 45. A rigid body is spinning about a fixed point $(3, -2, -1)$ with an angular velocity of 4 rad/s, the axis of rotation being in the direction of $(1, 2, -2)$. Find the velocity of the particle at the point (4, 1, 1).

Sol. $\omega = 4\left(\dfrac{\hat{\mathbf{i}} + 2\hat{\mathbf{j}} - 2\hat{\mathbf{k}}}{\sqrt{1+4+4}}\right) = \dfrac{4}{3}(\hat{\mathbf{i}} + 2\hat{\mathbf{j}} - 2\hat{\mathbf{k}})$

$$\mathbf{r} = \mathbf{OP} - \mathbf{OA}$$
$$= (4\hat{\mathbf{i}} + \hat{\mathbf{j}} + \hat{\mathbf{k}}) - (3\hat{\mathbf{i}} - 2\hat{\mathbf{j}} - \hat{\mathbf{k}}) = \hat{\mathbf{i}} + 3\hat{\mathbf{i}} + 2\hat{\mathbf{k}}$$

$$\mathbf{v} = \omega \times \mathbf{r} = \frac{4}{3}(\hat{\mathbf{i}} + 2\hat{\mathbf{j}} - 2\hat{\mathbf{k}}) \times (\hat{\mathbf{i}} + 3\hat{\mathbf{j}} + 2\hat{\mathbf{k}})$$

$$= \frac{4}{3}(10\hat{\mathbf{i}} - 4\hat{\mathbf{j}} + \hat{\mathbf{k}})$$

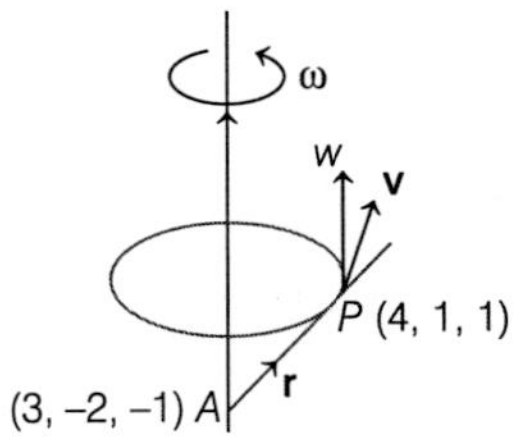

Milestone Practice 2.2

1. If $\mathbf{a}\times\mathbf{b}=\mathbf{c}\times\mathbf{d}$ and $\mathbf{a}\times\mathbf{c}=\mathbf{b}\times\mathbf{d}$, then show that $\mathbf{a}-\mathbf{d}$ is parallel to $\mathbf{b}-\mathbf{c}$.
2. If **a**, **b** and **c** are position vectors of the vertices of the ΔABC, then find $\dfrac{|(\mathbf{a}-\mathbf{c})\times(\mathbf{b}-\mathbf{a})|}{(\mathbf{c}-\mathbf{a})\cdot(\mathbf{b}-\mathbf{a})}$.
3. Let the vectors **a** and **b** be such that $|\mathbf{a}|=3$, $|\mathbf{b}|=\dfrac{\sqrt{2}}{3}$ and $\mathbf{a}\times\mathbf{b}$ is a unit vector, then the angle between **a** and **b** is equal to
   (a) $\dfrac{\pi}{3}$ (b) $\dfrac{\pi}{6}$ (c) $\dfrac{\pi}{2}$ (d) $\dfrac{\pi}{4}$
4. Let **OA** be vector parallel to line of intersection of planes P_1 and P_2 through origin. P_1 is parallel to the vectors $2\hat{j}+3\hat{k}$ and $4\hat{j}-3\hat{k}$ and P_2 is parallel to $\hat{j}-\hat{k}$ and $3\hat{i}+3\hat{j}$, then find the angle between vector **OA** and $2\hat{i}+\hat{j}-2\hat{k}$.
5. Let **a** and **b** be two unit vectors such that $\mathbf{a}\cdot\mathbf{b}=0$ for some $x, y\in R$, let $\mathbf{c}=x\mathbf{a}+y\mathbf{b}+(\mathbf{a}\times\mathbf{b})$. If $|\mathbf{c}|=2$ and the vector **c** is inclined at the same angle α to both **a** and **b**, then find the value of $8\cos^2\alpha$.
6. If **a** and **b** are non-parallel unit vectors and **c** is a vector in a plane perpendicular to **a** and **b** such that $|\mathbf{c}|=5$ and $|\mathbf{a}+\mathbf{b}|^2=|\mathbf{a}\times\mathbf{b}|$, then find the value of $\mathbf{a}\cdot\mathbf{b}$.
7. If $\mathbf{a}=2\hat{i}+3\hat{j}-\hat{k}$, $\mathbf{b}=-\hat{i}+2\hat{j}-4\hat{k}$, $\mathbf{c}=\hat{i}+\hat{j}+\hat{k}$, then find the value of $(\mathbf{a}\times\mathbf{b})\cdot(\mathbf{a}\times\mathbf{c})$.
8. Let $\mathbf{a}=-\hat{i}-\hat{k}$, $\mathbf{b}=-\hat{i}+\hat{j}$ and $\mathbf{c}=\hat{i}+2\hat{j}+3\hat{k}$ be three given vectors. If **r** is a vector such that $\mathbf{r}\times\mathbf{b}=\mathbf{c}\times\mathbf{b}$ and $\mathbf{r}\cdot\mathbf{a}=0$, then the value of $\mathbf{r}\cdot\mathbf{b}$ is equal to
   (a) 3 (b) 6 (c) 9 (d) 12
9. Two adjacent sides of a parallelogram $ABCD$ are given by $AB=2\hat{i}+10\hat{j}+11\hat{k}$ and $AD=-\hat{i}+2\hat{j}+2\hat{k}$. The side AD is rotated by an acute angle α in the plane of the parallelogram so that AD becomes AD'. If AD' make a right angle with the side AB, then find the value of $\cos\alpha$.
10. Let $\mathbf{a}=2\hat{i}+\hat{j}-2\hat{k}$, $\mathbf{b}=\hat{i}+\hat{j}$ and **c** be a vector such that $|\mathbf{c}-\mathbf{a}|=3$, $|(\mathbf{a}\times\mathbf{b})\times\mathbf{c}|=3$ and the angle between **c** and $\mathbf{a}\times\mathbf{b}$ is $30°$. Then, find the value of $\mathbf{a}\cdot\mathbf{c}$.
11. Find a vector of magnitude 15, which is perpendicular to both the vectors $4\hat{i}-\hat{j}+8\hat{k}$ and $-\hat{j}+\hat{k}$.
12. If **a** and **b** are vectors such that $|\mathbf{a}+\mathbf{b}|=\sqrt{29}$ and $\mathbf{a}\times(2\hat{i}+3\hat{j}+4\hat{k})=-(2\hat{i}+3\hat{j}+4\hat{k})\times\mathbf{b}$, then find the possible value of $(\mathbf{a}+\mathbf{b})\cdot(-7\hat{i}+2\hat{j}+3\hat{k})$.
13. In ΔABC, the side length BC, CA and AB are consecutive positive integers in increasing order. Let **a**, **b** and **c** be the position vectors of A, B and C, respectively. If $(\mathbf{c}-\mathbf{a})\cdot(\mathbf{b}-\mathbf{c})=0$, then the value of $|\mathbf{a}\times\mathbf{b}+\mathbf{b}\times\mathbf{c}+\mathbf{c}\times\mathbf{a}|$, is equal to
   (a) 3 (b) 6 (c) 9 (d) 12
14. A, B, C and D are four points in the space, then prove that
   $|\mathbf{AB}\times\mathbf{CD}+\mathbf{BC}\times\mathbf{AD}+\mathbf{CA}\times\mathbf{BD}|=4$ (area of ΔABC).
15. The area of the parallelogram having diagonals $3\hat{i}+\hat{j}-2\hat{k}$ and $\hat{i}-3\hat{j}+4\hat{k}$ is equal to
   (a) $5\sqrt{3}$ sq units (b) 5 sq units
   (c) $4\sqrt{3}$ sq units (d) $\sqrt{3}$ sq units
16. $P(1,4,3)$, $Q(-2,-1,\lambda)$, $R(1,3,-1)$ and $S(2,4,0)$ are the vertices of quadrilateral $PQRS$. If its area is $\dfrac{\sqrt{272}}{2}$ sq units, then find the value of $1-4\lambda$.
17. Find the moment of **F** about points $(2,-1,3)$, when force $\mathbf{F}=3\hat{i}+2\hat{j}-4\hat{k}$ is acting on point $(1,-1,2)$.
18. Let A, B and C be points with position vector $\hat{i}-2\hat{j}+\hat{k}$, $\hat{i}+\hat{j}-\hat{k}$ and $2\hat{i}+\hat{j}+\hat{k}$ respectively, then the shortest distance between point A and plane OBC is
   (a) $\sqrt{\dfrac{2}{7}}$ units (b) $\sqrt{\dfrac{7}{2}}$ units
   (c) $\sqrt{\dfrac{3}{7}}$ units (d) $\sqrt{\dfrac{7}{3}}$ units

Answer Key

2. $\tan\theta$	3. (d)	4. $\dfrac{\pi}{4}, \dfrac{3\pi}{4}$	5. 3	6. $-\dfrac{3}{5}$	7. -74
8. (c)	9. $\dfrac{\sqrt{17}}{9}$	10. 2	11. $\dfrac{15(-9\hat{i}-4\hat{j}+4\hat{k})}{\sqrt{113}}$	12. ±4	
13. (d)	15. (a)	16. 81	17. $-2\hat{i}-7\hat{j}-2\hat{k}$	18. (b)	

For Detailed Solution

Milestone 3 Scalar Triple Product

- Properties of Scalar Triple Product • Geometrical Interpretation of Scalar Triple Product
- Volume of Tetrahedron (A Pyramid having a Triangular Base)

The **scalar triple product** is defined for three vectors as the dot product of one of the vectors with the cross product of the other two. It is also called **mixed product** because here we multiply three vectors to get the product. It is always scalar.

If $\mathbf{a}, \mathbf{b}$ and $\mathbf{c}$ are any three vector, then their scalar triple product is defined as $(\mathbf{a} \times \mathbf{b}) \cdot \mathbf{c}$ or $\mathbf{a} \cdot (\mathbf{b} \times \mathbf{c})$.

We denoted it by $[\mathbf{a}, \mathbf{b}, \mathbf{c}]$.

2.13 Properties of Scalar Triple Product

(i) If $\mathbf{a}, \mathbf{b}$ and $\mathbf{c}$ are given by $\mathbf{a} = a_1\hat{\mathbf{i}} + a_2\hat{\mathbf{j}} + a_3\hat{\mathbf{k}}$, $\mathbf{b} = b_1\hat{\mathbf{i}} + b_2\hat{\mathbf{j}} + b_3\hat{\mathbf{k}}$ and $\mathbf{c} = c_1\hat{\mathbf{i}} + c_2\hat{\mathbf{j}} + c_3\hat{\mathbf{k}}$

Then, $$(\mathbf{a} \times \mathbf{b}) \cdot \mathbf{c} = \begin{vmatrix} a_1 & a_2 & a_3 \\ b_1 & b_2 & b_3 \\ c_1 & c_2 & c_3 \end{vmatrix}$$

(ii) $(\mathbf{a} \times \mathbf{b}) \cdot \mathbf{c} = \mathbf{a} \cdot (\mathbf{b} \times \mathbf{c})$ i.e. position of dot and cross can be interchanged without altering product. Hence, it is always represented by $[\mathbf{a}\ \mathbf{b}\ \mathbf{c}]$.

(iii) $[\mathbf{a}\ \mathbf{b}\ \mathbf{c}] = [\mathbf{b}\ \mathbf{c}\ \mathbf{a}] = [\mathbf{c}\ \mathbf{a}\ \mathbf{b}]$

(iv) $[\mathbf{a}\ \mathbf{b}\ \mathbf{c}] = -[\mathbf{b}\ \mathbf{a}\ \mathbf{c}]$

(v) $[k\mathbf{a}\ \mathbf{b}\ \mathbf{c}] = k[\mathbf{a}\ \mathbf{b}\ \mathbf{c}]$ and $[k_1\mathbf{a}\ \ k_2\mathbf{b}\ \ k_3\mathbf{c}] = k_1k_2k_3\,[\mathbf{a}\ \mathbf{b}\ \mathbf{c}]$

(vi) $[\mathbf{a} + \mathbf{b}\ \ \mathbf{c}\ \ \mathbf{d}] = [\mathbf{a}\ \mathbf{c}\ \mathbf{d}] + [\mathbf{b}\ \mathbf{c}\ \mathbf{d}]$

(vii) If $[\mathbf{a}\ \mathbf{b}\ \mathbf{c}] > 0$, then $\mathbf{a}, \mathbf{b}$ and $\mathbf{c}$ form a right handed system. On the other hand, if $[\mathbf{a}\ \mathbf{b}\ \mathbf{c}] < 0$, then $\mathbf{a}, \mathbf{b}$ and $\mathbf{c}$ form a left handed system.

(viii) The necessary and sufficient condition for three non-zero and non-collinear vectors $\mathbf{a}, \mathbf{b}$ and $\mathbf{c}$ to be coplanar is that $[\mathbf{a}\ \mathbf{b}\ \mathbf{c}] = 0$ i.e. $\mathbf{a}, \mathbf{b}$ and $\mathbf{c}$ are coplanar $\Leftrightarrow [\mathbf{a}\ \mathbf{b}\ \mathbf{c}] = 0$.

(ix) $[x_1\mathbf{a} + y_1\mathbf{b} + z_1\mathbf{c}, x_2\mathbf{a} + y_2\mathbf{b} + z_2\mathbf{c}, x_3\mathbf{a} + y_3\mathbf{b} + z_3\mathbf{c}]$

$$= \begin{vmatrix} x_1 & y_1 & z_1 \\ x_2 & y_2 & z_2 \\ x_3 & y_3 & z_3 \end{vmatrix} [\mathbf{a}\ \mathbf{b}\ \mathbf{c}]$$

JEE Focus Points

Concept Inside Video

- Four points A, B, C, D are coplanar, if $[\text{AB AC AD}] = 0$.
- Four points a, b, c and d are coplanar, if $[\mathbf{d}\ \mathbf{b}\ \mathbf{c}] + [\mathbf{d}\ \mathbf{c}\ \mathbf{a}] + [\mathbf{d}\ \mathbf{a}\ \mathbf{b}] = [\mathbf{a}\ \mathbf{b}\ \mathbf{c}]$ or $[\mathbf{a}\ \mathbf{b}\ \mathbf{c}] + [\mathbf{a}\ \mathbf{c}\ \mathbf{d}] + [\mathbf{a}\ \mathbf{d}\ \mathbf{b}] = [\mathbf{d}\ \mathbf{b}\ \mathbf{c}]$
- $[\mathbf{a}\ \mathbf{a}\ \mathbf{b}] = [\mathbf{b}\ \mathbf{b}\ \mathbf{a}] = [\mathbf{c}\ \mathbf{c}\ \mathbf{b}] = 0$
  i.e. if any two vectors are same, then vectors are coplanar.
- The value of the scalar product is zero if any two vectors are parallel.
- $[\mathbf{a}\ \mathbf{b}\ \mathbf{c}][\mathbf{a}\ \mathbf{b}\ \mathbf{c}] = \begin{bmatrix} \mathbf{a}\cdot\mathbf{a} & \mathbf{a}\cdot\mathbf{b} & \mathbf{a}\cdot\mathbf{c} \\ \mathbf{b}\cdot\mathbf{a} & \mathbf{b}\cdot\mathbf{b} & \mathbf{b}\cdot\mathbf{c} \\ \mathbf{c}\cdot\mathbf{a} & \mathbf{c}\cdot\mathbf{b} & \mathbf{c}\cdot\mathbf{c} \end{bmatrix} = [\mathbf{a}\times\mathbf{b}\ \ \mathbf{b}\times\mathbf{c}\ \ \mathbf{c}\times\mathbf{a}]$

Example 46. If $\mathbf{a} = 2\hat{\mathbf{i}} + 3\hat{\mathbf{j}} + 5\hat{\mathbf{k}}$, $\mathbf{b} = \hat{\mathbf{i}} - 2\hat{\mathbf{j}} + 2\hat{\mathbf{k}}$ and $\mathbf{c} = 2\hat{\mathbf{i}} - \hat{\mathbf{j}} + \hat{\mathbf{k}}$ are three vectors, then find the scalar triple product $[2\mathbf{a} - \mathbf{b}\ \ 2\mathbf{b} - \mathbf{c}\ \ 2\mathbf{c} - \mathbf{a}]$.

Sol. Given, $\mathbf{a} = 2\hat{\mathbf{i}} + 3\hat{\mathbf{j}} + 5\hat{\mathbf{k}}$, $\mathbf{b} = \hat{\mathbf{i}} - 2\hat{\mathbf{j}} + 2\hat{\mathbf{k}}$ and $\mathbf{c} = 2\hat{\mathbf{i}} - \hat{\mathbf{j}} + \hat{\mathbf{k}}$ are three vectors.

Now, $[2\mathbf{a} - \mathbf{b}\ \ 2\mathbf{b} - \mathbf{c}\ \ 2\mathbf{c} - \mathbf{a}]$

$$= (2\mathbf{a} - \mathbf{b}) \cdot \{(2\mathbf{b} - \mathbf{c}) \times (2\mathbf{c} - \mathbf{a})\}$$
$$= (2\mathbf{a} - \mathbf{b}) \cdot \{2\mathbf{b} \times (2\mathbf{c} - \mathbf{a}) - \mathbf{c} \times (2\mathbf{c} - \mathbf{a})\}$$
$$= (2\mathbf{a} - \mathbf{b}) \cdot \{4(\mathbf{b} \times \mathbf{c}) - 2(\mathbf{b} \times \mathbf{a}) - 2(\mathbf{c} \times \mathbf{c}) + \mathbf{c} \times \mathbf{a}\}$$
$$= (2\mathbf{a} - \mathbf{b}) \cdot \{4(\mathbf{b} \times \mathbf{c}) + 2(\mathbf{a} \times \mathbf{b}) - 0 + (\mathbf{c} \times \mathbf{a})\}$$
$$= 2\mathbf{a} \cdot \{4(\mathbf{b} \times \mathbf{c}) + 2(\mathbf{a} \times \mathbf{b}) + (\mathbf{c} \times \mathbf{a})\} - \mathbf{b} \cdot \{4(\mathbf{b} \times \mathbf{c}) + 2(\mathbf{a} \times \mathbf{b}) + (\mathbf{c} \times \mathbf{a})\}$$
$$= 8\mathbf{a} \cdot (\mathbf{b} \times \mathbf{c}) + 4\mathbf{a} \cdot (\mathbf{a} \times \mathbf{b}) + 2\mathbf{a} \cdot (\mathbf{c} \times \mathbf{a}) - 4\mathbf{b} \cdot (\mathbf{b} \times \mathbf{c}) - 2\mathbf{b} \cdot (\mathbf{a} \times \mathbf{b}) - \mathbf{b} \cdot (\mathbf{c} \times \mathbf{a})$$
$$= 8\,[\mathbf{a}\ \mathbf{b}\ \mathbf{c}] + 0 + 0 - 0 - 0 - [\mathbf{a}\ \mathbf{b}\ \mathbf{c}]$$
$$= 7[\mathbf{a}\ \mathbf{b}\ \mathbf{c}]$$

Now, $$[\mathbf{a}\ \mathbf{b}\ \mathbf{c}] = \begin{vmatrix} 2 & 3 & 5 \\ 1 & -2 & 2 \\ 2 & -1 & 1 \end{vmatrix}$$

$$= 2(-2 + 2) - 3(1 - 4) + 5(-1 + 4)$$
$$= 0 + 3 \times 3 + 5 \times 3 = 9 + 15 = 24$$

$\therefore \quad 7[\mathbf{a}\ \mathbf{b}\ \mathbf{c}] = 7 \times 24 = 168$

JEE SCANNER

Example Similar to PYQ Asked in JEE Main 2019

Let $\mathbf{b} = 2\hat{i} + \hat{j} - \hat{k}$, $\mathbf{c} = \hat{i} + 3\hat{k}$ *and* **a** *is a unit vector, then the maximum value of* $[\mathbf{a}\ \mathbf{b}\ \mathbf{c}]$ *is equal to*

(a) $\sqrt{59}$ (b) $\sqrt{57}$ (c) $\sqrt{58}$ (d) $\sqrt{50}$

Decoding the Question

$[\mathbf{a}\ \mathbf{b}\ \mathbf{c}]$ is maximum, when angle betwen **a** and $(\mathbf{b} \times \mathbf{c})$ is 0 and $|\mathbf{a} \cdot (\mathbf{b} \times \mathbf{c})| \le |\mathbf{a}||\mathbf{b} \times \mathbf{c}|$

Sol. We have, $\mathbf{b} = 2\hat{i} + \hat{j} - \hat{k}$ and $\mathbf{c} = \hat{i} + 3\hat{k}$

$$\mathbf{b} \times \mathbf{c} = \begin{vmatrix} \hat{i} & \hat{j} & \hat{k} \\ 2 & 1 & -1 \\ 1 & 0 & 3 \end{vmatrix} = 3\hat{i} - 7\hat{j} - \hat{k}$$

Now, $[\mathbf{a}\ \mathbf{b}\ \mathbf{c}] = \mathbf{a} \cdot (\mathbf{b} \times \mathbf{c}) = |\mathbf{a}||\mathbf{b} \times \mathbf{c}| \cos(\mathbf{a} \cdot (\mathbf{b} \times \mathbf{c}))$ is maximum at $(\mathbf{a} \cdot (\mathbf{b} \times \mathbf{c})) = 0$

$$\therefore \quad [\mathbf{a}\ \mathbf{b}\ \mathbf{c}]_{max} = 1 \times |3\hat{i} - 7\hat{j} - \hat{k}| \cos 0^\circ$$

$$= \sqrt{(3)^2 + (-7)^2 + (-1)^2} = \sqrt{9 + 49 + 1} = \sqrt{59}$$

Skill Builder

Let $\mathbf{b} = 3\hat{i} + \hat{j} - 2\hat{k}$, $\mathbf{c} = 3\hat{j} + \hat{k}$ and **a** is a unit vector, then the maximum value of $[\mathbf{a}\ \mathbf{b}\ \mathbf{c}]$ is equal to

(a) $\sqrt{137}$ (b) $\sqrt{139}$

(c) $\sqrt{58}$ (d) $\sqrt{133}$

For Sol.

- **For more practice** See Q.10 of Milestone Practice 3.

Example 47. Let **a**, **b** and **c** be three unit vectors and $\mathbf{a} \cdot \mathbf{b} = \mathbf{a} \cdot \mathbf{c} = 0$. If the angle between **b** and **c** is $\frac{\pi}{3}$, then find the value of $|[\mathbf{a}\ \mathbf{b}\ \mathbf{c}]|$.

Sol. Given, $\mathbf{a} \cdot \mathbf{b} = \mathbf{a} \cdot \mathbf{c}$

$\because$ **a** is perpendicular to **b** and **c**.

$$\therefore \quad \mathbf{a} = \lambda(\mathbf{b} \times \mathbf{c}) \Rightarrow |\mathbf{a}| = |\lambda(\mathbf{b} \times \mathbf{c})|$$

$$\Rightarrow \quad 1 = \left|\lambda |\mathbf{b}||\mathbf{c}| \sin\frac{\pi}{3}\right|$$

$$\Rightarrow \quad 1 = \left|\lambda \frac{\sqrt{3}}{2}\right|$$

$$\Rightarrow \quad |\lambda| = \frac{2}{\sqrt{3}}$$

Now, $|[\mathbf{a}\ \mathbf{b}\ \mathbf{c}]| = |\mathbf{a} \cdot (\mathbf{b} \times \mathbf{c})| = |\lambda(\mathbf{b} \times \mathbf{c}) \cdot (\mathbf{b} \times \mathbf{c})|$

$$= |\lambda(\mathbf{b} \times \mathbf{c})^2| = |\lambda||(\mathbf{b} \times \mathbf{c})|^2$$

$$= \frac{2}{\sqrt{3}}\left||\mathbf{b}||\mathbf{c}| \sin\frac{\pi}{3}\right|^2 = \frac{2}{\sqrt{3}}|\mathbf{b}|^2 |\mathbf{c}|^2 \sin^2\frac{\pi}{3}$$

$$= \frac{2}{\sqrt{3}}\left(\frac{\sqrt{3}}{2}\right)^2 = \frac{\sqrt{3}}{2}$$

Example 48. Let $\mathbf{a} = \hat{i} + 2\hat{j} + \hat{k}$, $\mathbf{b} = 3(\hat{i} - \hat{j} + \hat{k})$. Let **c** be the vector such that $\mathbf{a} \times \mathbf{c} = \mathbf{b}$ and $\mathbf{a} \cdot \mathbf{c} = 3$. Then, find $\mathbf{a} \cdot ((\mathbf{c} \times \mathbf{b}) - \mathbf{b} - \mathbf{c})$.

Sol. Given, $\mathbf{a} = \hat{i} + 2\hat{j} + \hat{k}$, $\mathbf{b} = 3(\hat{i} - \hat{j} + \hat{k})$ and $\mathbf{a} \times \mathbf{c} = \mathbf{b}$

$$\Rightarrow \quad (\mathbf{a} \times \mathbf{c}) \cdot \mathbf{b} = \mathbf{b} \cdot \mathbf{b} = |\mathbf{b}|^2 = 27$$

Now, $\mathbf{a} \cdot (\mathbf{c} \times \mathbf{b}) = [\mathbf{a}\ \mathbf{c}\ \mathbf{b}]$

$$= (\mathbf{a} \times \mathbf{c}) \cdot \mathbf{b} = 27$$

$$\Rightarrow \quad \mathbf{a} \cdot \mathbf{b} = 3 - 6 + 3 = 0$$

and $\mathbf{a} \cdot \mathbf{c} = 3$ [given]

Now, $\mathbf{a} \cdot ((\mathbf{c} \times \mathbf{b}) - \mathbf{b} - \mathbf{c}) = \mathbf{a} \cdot (\mathbf{c} \times \mathbf{b}) - \mathbf{a} \cdot \mathbf{b} - \mathbf{a} \cdot \mathbf{c}$

$$= 27 - 0 - 3$$

$$= 24$$

Example 49. Let $\mathbf{a} = x\hat{i} + 12\hat{j} - \hat{k}$, $\mathbf{b} = 2\hat{i} + 2x\hat{j} + \hat{k}$ and $\mathbf{c} = \hat{i} + \hat{k}$. If **b**, **c** and **a** in that order form a left handed system, then find the value of x.

Sol. Since, **b**, **c** and **a** form a left handed system, therefore $[\mathbf{b}\ \mathbf{c}\ \mathbf{a}] < 0$

$$\Rightarrow \quad \begin{vmatrix} 2 & 2x & 1 \\ 1 & 0 & 1 \\ x & 12 & -1 \end{vmatrix} < 0$$

$$\Rightarrow 2(0 - 12) - 2x(-1 - x) + 1(12 - 0) < 0$$

$$\Rightarrow \quad -24 + 2x + 2x^2 + 12 < 0$$

$$\Rightarrow \quad 2x^2 + 2x - 12 < 0$$

$$\Rightarrow \quad x^2 + x - 6 < 0$$

$$\Rightarrow \quad (x - 2)(x + 3) < 0$$

$$\Rightarrow \quad x \in (-3, 2)$$

Example 50. If **a** and **b** are non-zero and non-collinear vectors, then show that $\mathbf{a} \times \mathbf{b} = [\mathbf{a}\ \mathbf{b}\ \mathbf{i}]\hat{i} + [\mathbf{a}\ \mathbf{b}\ \mathbf{j}]\hat{j} + [\mathbf{a}\ \mathbf{b}\ \mathbf{k}]\hat{k}$

Sol. Let $\mathbf{a} \times \mathbf{b} = x\hat{i} + y\hat{j} + z\hat{k}$

$$\Rightarrow \quad (\mathbf{a} \times \mathbf{b}) \cdot \hat{i} = (x\hat{i} + y\hat{j} + z\hat{k}) \cdot \hat{i}$$

$$\Rightarrow \quad (\mathbf{a} \times \mathbf{b}) \cdot \hat{i} = x \quad \text{...(i)}$$

Similarly $(\mathbf{a} \times \mathbf{b}) \cdot \hat{j} = y$ ...(ii)

and $(\mathbf{a} \times \mathbf{b}) \cdot \hat{k} = z$ ...(iii)

On putting the values from Eqs. (i), (ii) and (iii), we get

$$\mathbf{a} \times \mathbf{b} = [\mathbf{a}\ \mathbf{b}\ \mathbf{i}]\hat{i} + [\mathbf{a}\ \mathbf{b}\ \mathbf{j}]\hat{j} + [\mathbf{a}\ \mathbf{b}\ \mathbf{k}]\hat{k}$$

Example 51. If **a**, **b** and **c** are any three vectors in space, then $(\mathbf{c} + \mathbf{b}) \times (\mathbf{c} + \mathbf{a}) \cdot (\mathbf{c} + \mathbf{b} + \mathbf{a}) = \lambda\,[\mathbf{a}\ \mathbf{b}\ \mathbf{c}]$. Find the value of λ.

Sol. Here, $[(\mathbf{c} + \mathbf{b}) \times (\mathbf{c} + \mathbf{a})] \cdot (\mathbf{c} + \mathbf{b} + \mathbf{a})$

$$= [(\mathbf{c} \times (\mathbf{c} + \mathbf{a}) + \mathbf{b} \times (\mathbf{c} + \mathbf{a})] \cdot (\mathbf{c} + \mathbf{b} + \mathbf{a})$$

$$= [(\mathbf{c} \times \mathbf{c}) + (\mathbf{c} \times \mathbf{a}) + (\mathbf{b} \times \mathbf{c}) + (\mathbf{b} \times \mathbf{a})] \cdot (\mathbf{c} + \mathbf{b} + \mathbf{a})$$

$$= [(\mathbf{c} \times \mathbf{a}) + (\mathbf{b} \times \mathbf{c}) + (\mathbf{b} \times \mathbf{a})] \cdot (\mathbf{c} + \mathbf{b} + \mathbf{a}) \quad [\because \mathbf{c} \times \mathbf{c} = 0]$$

$$= (\mathbf{c} \times \mathbf{a}) \cdot \mathbf{c} + (\mathbf{c} \times \mathbf{a}) \cdot \mathbf{b} + (\mathbf{c} \times \mathbf{a}) \cdot \mathbf{a} + (\mathbf{b} \times \mathbf{c}) \cdot \mathbf{c} + (\mathbf{b} \times \mathbf{c}) \cdot \mathbf{b}$$
$$+ (\mathbf{b} \times \mathbf{c}) \cdot \mathbf{a} + (\mathbf{b} \times \mathbf{a}) \cdot \mathbf{c} + (\mathbf{b} \times \mathbf{a}) \cdot \mathbf{b} + (\mathbf{b} \times \mathbf{a}) \cdot \mathbf{a}$$

$$= 0 + [\mathbf{c}\ \mathbf{a}\ \mathbf{b}] + 0 + 0 + 0 + [\mathbf{b}\ \mathbf{c}\ \mathbf{a}] + [\mathbf{b}\ \mathbf{a}\ \mathbf{c}] + 0 + 0$$

$= [\mathbf{a}\ \mathbf{b}\ \mathbf{c}] + [\mathbf{a}\ \mathbf{b}\ \mathbf{c}] - [\mathbf{a}\ \mathbf{b}\ \mathbf{c}]$

$= [\mathbf{a}\ \mathbf{b}\ \mathbf{c}] \quad [\because [\mathbf{c}\ \mathbf{a}\ \mathbf{b}] = [\mathbf{b}\ \mathbf{c}\ \mathbf{a}] = [\mathbf{a}\ \mathbf{b}\ \mathbf{c}], [\mathbf{b}\ \mathbf{a}\ \mathbf{c}] = -[\mathbf{a}\ \mathbf{b}\ \mathbf{c}]]$

Now, from question, we get

$\therefore \quad \lambda = 1$

Time Saving Technique

$$(\mathbf{c}+\mathbf{b}) \times (\mathbf{c}+\mathbf{a}) \cdot (\mathbf{c}+\mathbf{b}+\mathbf{c}) = \begin{vmatrix} 0 & 1 & 1 \\ 1 & 0 & 1 \\ 1 & 1 & 1 \end{vmatrix} [\mathbf{a}\ \mathbf{b}\ \mathbf{c}]$$

$$= (0(0-1) - 1(1-1) + (1-0))[\mathbf{a}\ \mathbf{b}\ \mathbf{c}]$$

$$= [\mathbf{a}\ \mathbf{b}\ \mathbf{c}]$$

$\therefore \quad \lambda = 1$

Example 52. For any three vectors **a**, **b** and **c**, $[\mathbf{a}+\mathbf{b}\ \ \mathbf{b}+\mathbf{c}\ \ \mathbf{c}+\mathbf{a}] = \lambda[\mathbf{a}\ \mathbf{b}\ \mathbf{c}]$. Then, find the value of λ.

Sol. We have, $[\mathbf{a}+\mathbf{b}\ \ \mathbf{b}+\mathbf{c}\ \ \mathbf{c}+\mathbf{a}]$

$= \{(\mathbf{a}+\mathbf{b}) \times (\mathbf{b}+\mathbf{c})\} \cdot (\mathbf{c}+\mathbf{a})$

$= \{\mathbf{a}\times\mathbf{b} + \mathbf{a}\times\mathbf{c} + \mathbf{b}\times\mathbf{b} + \mathbf{b}\times\mathbf{c}\} \cdot (\mathbf{c}+\mathbf{a})$

$= \{\mathbf{a}\times\mathbf{b} + \mathbf{a}\times\mathbf{c} + \mathbf{b}\times\mathbf{c}\} \cdot (\mathbf{c}+\mathbf{a}) \quad [\because \mathbf{b}\times\mathbf{b} = 0]$

$= (\mathbf{a}\times\mathbf{b})\cdot\mathbf{c} + (\mathbf{a}\times\mathbf{c})\cdot\mathbf{c} + (\mathbf{b}\times\mathbf{c})\cdot\mathbf{c}$

$\quad + (\mathbf{a}\times\mathbf{b})\cdot\mathbf{a} + (\mathbf{a}\times\mathbf{c})\cdot\mathbf{a} + (\mathbf{b}\times\mathbf{c})\cdot\mathbf{a}$

$= [\mathbf{a}\ \mathbf{b}\ \mathbf{c}] + 0 + 0 + 0 + 0 + [\mathbf{b}\ \mathbf{c}\ \mathbf{a}]$

$[\because [\mathbf{a}\ \mathbf{c}\ \mathbf{c}] = 0, [\mathbf{b}\ \mathbf{c}\ \mathbf{c}] = 0, [\mathbf{a}\ \mathbf{b}\ \mathbf{a}] = 0, [\mathbf{a}\ \mathbf{c}\ \mathbf{a}] = 0]$

$= [\mathbf{a}\ \mathbf{b}\ \mathbf{c}] + [\mathbf{a}\ \mathbf{b}\ \mathbf{c}] = 2[\mathbf{a}\ \mathbf{b}\ \mathbf{c}]$

$\therefore \quad \lambda = 2$

Example 53. If **a**, **b** and **c** are non-coplanar vectors and λ is a real number, then find the value of λ for which the vector $\mathbf{a}+2\mathbf{b}+3\mathbf{c}$, $\lambda\mathbf{b}+4\mathbf{c}$ and $(2\lambda-1)\mathbf{c}$ are non-coplanar.

Sol. Since, **a**, **b** and **c** are non-coplanar vectors.

$\therefore \quad [\mathbf{a}\ \mathbf{b}\ \mathbf{c}] \neq 0$

Now, $\mathbf{a}+2\mathbf{b}+3\mathbf{c}$, $\lambda\mathbf{b}+4\mathbf{c}$ and $(2\lambda-1)\mathbf{c}$ will be non-coplanar iff

$(\mathbf{a}+2\mathbf{b}+3\mathbf{c}) \cdot \{(\lambda\mathbf{b}+4\mathbf{c}) \times (2\lambda-1)\mathbf{c}\} \neq 0$

$\Rightarrow \quad (\mathbf{a}+2\mathbf{b}+3\mathbf{c}) \cdot \{\lambda(2\lambda-1)(\mathbf{b}\times\mathbf{c}) \neq 0$

$\Rightarrow \quad \lambda(2\lambda-1)[\mathbf{a}\ \mathbf{b}\ \mathbf{c}]\} \neq 0$

$\therefore \quad \lambda \neq 0, \frac{1}{2}$

Thus, given vectors will be non-coplanar for all values of λ except two values 0 and $\frac{1}{2}$.

Example 54. If x, y and z are distinct scalars such that $[x\mathbf{a}+y\mathbf{b}+z\mathbf{c},\ x\mathbf{b}+y\mathbf{c}+z\mathbf{a},\ x\mathbf{c}+y\mathbf{a}+z\mathbf{b}] = 0$, where **a**, **b** and **c** are non-coplanar vectors, then prove that $x+y+z=0$.

Sol. Given, **a**, **b** and **c** are non-coplanar.

$\therefore \quad [\mathbf{a}\ \mathbf{b}\ \mathbf{c}] \neq 0$

Now, consider $[x\mathbf{a}+y\mathbf{b}+z\mathbf{c},\ x\mathbf{b}+y\mathbf{c}+z\mathbf{a},\ x\mathbf{c}+y\mathbf{a}+z\mathbf{b}] = 0$

$$\Rightarrow \begin{vmatrix} x & y & z \\ z & x & y \\ y & z & x \end{vmatrix} [\mathbf{a}\ \mathbf{b}\ \mathbf{c}] = 0 \Rightarrow \begin{vmatrix} x & y & z \\ z & x & y \\ y & z & x \end{vmatrix} = 0 \quad [\because [\mathbf{a}\ \mathbf{b}\ \mathbf{c}] \neq 0]$$

$\Rightarrow \quad (x+y+z)(x^2+y^2+z^2-xy-yz-zx) = 0$

$\Rightarrow \quad \frac{1}{2}(x+y+z)\{(x-y)^2\} + (y-z)^2 + (z-x)^2\} = 0$

$\Rightarrow \quad x+y+z=0 \text{ or } x=y=z$

But x, y and z are distinct scalars.

$\therefore \quad x+y+z=0.$

2.14 Geometrical Interpretation of Scalar Triple Product

Let **a**, **b** and **c** be three vectors. Consider a parallelopiped having coterminous edges **OA**, **OB** and **OC** such that **OA** = **a**, **OB** = **b** and **OC** = **c**. Then, $\mathbf{a}\times\mathbf{b}$ is a vector perpendicular to the plane of **a** and **b**. Let ϕ be the angle between **c** and $\mathbf{a}\times\mathbf{b}$. If $\hat{\mathbf{n}}$ is a unit vector along $\mathbf{a}\times\mathbf{b}$, then ϕ is the angle between $\hat{\mathbf{n}}$ and **c**.

Now, $\quad [\mathbf{a}\ \mathbf{b}\ \mathbf{c}] = (\mathbf{a}\times\mathbf{b})\cdot\mathbf{c}$

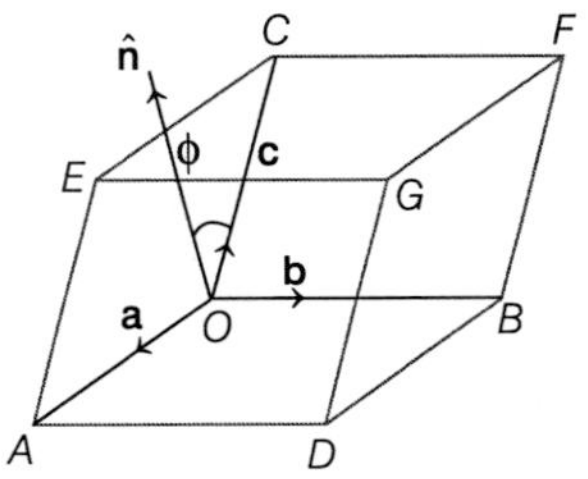

$= (\text{Area of parallelogram } OADB)\ \hat{\mathbf{n}}\cdot\mathbf{c}$

$= (\text{Area of parallelogram } OADB)\ (\hat{\mathbf{n}}\cdot\mathbf{c})$

$= (\text{Area of parallelogram } OADB)\ (|\mathbf{c}||\hat{\mathbf{n}}|\cos\phi)$

$= (\text{Area of parallelogram } OADB)\ (|\mathbf{c}|\cos\phi)$

$= (\text{Area of parallelogram } OADB)\ (OL)$

$= \text{Area of base} \times \text{height}$

$= \text{Volume of parallelopiped}$

Hence, **volume of parallelopiped** $= [\mathbf{a}\ \ \mathbf{b}\ \ \mathbf{c}]$

and height of parallelopiped $= \dfrac{\text{Volume of parallelopiped}}{\text{Area of base}}$

Example 55. Find the volume of the parallelopiped whose edges are represented by $\mathbf{a} = 2\hat{\mathbf{i}} - 3\hat{\mathbf{j}} + 4\hat{\mathbf{k}}$, $\mathbf{b} = \hat{\mathbf{i}} + 2\hat{\mathbf{j}} - \hat{\mathbf{k}}$ and $\mathbf{c} = 3\hat{\mathbf{i}} - \hat{\mathbf{j}} + 2\hat{\mathbf{k}}$.

Sol. Here, $[\mathbf{a}\ \mathbf{b}\ \mathbf{c}] = \begin{vmatrix} 2 & -3 & 4 \\ 1 & 2 & -1 \\ 3 & -1 & 2 \end{vmatrix} = 2(4-1) + 3(2+3) + 4(-1-6)$

$= 6 + 15 - 28 = -7$

$\therefore$ The volume of the parallelopiped $= |[\mathbf{a}\ \mathbf{b}\ \mathbf{c}]| = 7.$

Example 56. Find the altitude of a parallelopiped whose three coterminous edges are $\mathbf{a} = \hat{\mathbf{i}} + \hat{\mathbf{j}} + \hat{\mathbf{k}}$, $\mathbf{b} = 2\hat{\mathbf{i}} + 4\hat{\mathbf{j}} - \hat{\mathbf{k}}$ and $\mathbf{c} = \hat{\mathbf{i}} + \hat{\mathbf{j}} + 3\hat{\mathbf{k}}$ with **a** and **b** as the sides of the base of the parallelopiped.

Sol. Volume of parallelopiped $= |[\mathbf{a}\ \mathbf{b}\ \mathbf{c}]| = \begin{vmatrix} 1 & 1 & 1 \\ 2 & 4 & -1 \\ 1 & 1 & 3 \end{vmatrix}$

$$= 1(12+1) - 1(6+1) + 1(2-4) = 13 - 7 - 2 = 4 \text{ units}$$

$$\mathbf{a} \times \mathbf{b} = \begin{vmatrix} \hat{\mathbf{i}} & \hat{\mathbf{j}} & \hat{\mathbf{k}} \\ 1 & 1 & 1 \\ 2 & 4 & -1 \end{vmatrix}$$

$$= \hat{\mathbf{i}}(-1-4) - \hat{\mathbf{j}}(-1-2) + \hat{\mathbf{k}}(4-2) = -5\hat{\mathbf{i}} + 3\hat{\mathbf{j}} + 2\hat{\mathbf{k}}$$

$\therefore$ Area of base $= |\mathbf{a} \times \mathbf{b}| = \sqrt{25+9+4} = \sqrt{38}$

$\therefore$ Altitude of parallelopiped $= \dfrac{\text{Volume of parallelopiped}}{\text{Area of base}}$

$$= \frac{4}{\sqrt{38}} = \frac{2\sqrt{38}}{19} \text{ units}$$

Example 57. Let S be set of all λ for which the volume of a parallelopiped whose coterminus edges are given by $\mathbf{a} = \hat{\mathbf{i}} + \hat{\mathbf{j}} + \lambda\hat{\mathbf{k}}$, $\mathbf{b} = \hat{\mathbf{i}} + \hat{\mathbf{j}} + 3\hat{\mathbf{k}}$ and $\mathbf{c} = 2\hat{\mathbf{i}} + \hat{\mathbf{j}} + \hat{\mathbf{k}}$ be 1 cu unit, then find the value of $\sum_{\lambda \in S} \lambda^2$.

Sol. Volume of parallelopiped $= \mathbf{a} \cdot (\mathbf{b} \times \mathbf{c})$

$$\pm 1 = \begin{vmatrix} 1 & 1 & \lambda \\ 1 & 1 & 3 \\ 2 & 1 & 1 \end{vmatrix}$$

$\Rightarrow$ $\pm 1 = -\lambda + 3 \Rightarrow \lambda = 3 \pm 1 = 4, 2$

$\therefore$ $\sum_{\lambda \in S} \lambda^2 = 4^2 + 2^2 = 16 + 4 = 20$

Example 58. Let $\mathbf{PR} = 3\hat{\mathbf{i}} + \hat{\mathbf{j}} - 2\hat{\mathbf{k}}$ and $\mathbf{SQ} = \hat{\mathbf{i}} - 3\hat{\mathbf{j}} - 4\hat{\mathbf{k}}$ be diagonals of a parallelogram $PQRS$ and $\mathbf{PT} = \hat{\mathbf{i}} + 2\hat{\mathbf{j}} + 3\hat{\mathbf{k}}$ be another vector, then find the volume of parallelopiped determined by the vectors **PT**, **PQ** and **PS**.

Sol. Given, **PR** and **SQ** are diagonal of parallelogram $PQRS$.

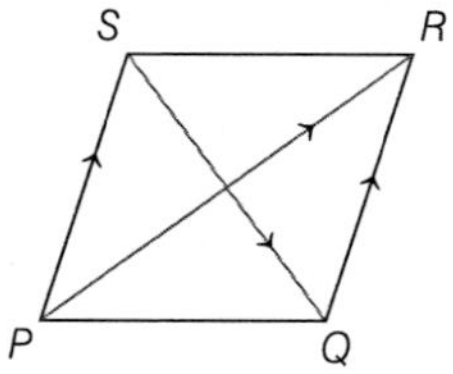

$\therefore$ $\mathbf{PR} = \mathbf{PQ} + \mathbf{QR}$ ...(i)

$\mathbf{SQ} = \mathbf{PQ} - \mathbf{PS}$ ...(ii)

or $\mathbf{PR} = \mathbf{PQ} + \mathbf{PS}$ $[\because \mathbf{QR} = \mathbf{PS}]$ ...(iii)

From Eqs. (ii) and (iii), we get

$$\mathbf{PQ} = \frac{\mathbf{PR} + \mathbf{SQ}}{2} \text{ and } \mathbf{PS} = \frac{\mathbf{PR} - \mathbf{SQ}}{2}$$

$\therefore$ $$\mathbf{PQ} = \frac{3\hat{\mathbf{i}} + \hat{\mathbf{j}} - 2\hat{\mathbf{k}} + \hat{\mathbf{i}} - 3\hat{\mathbf{j}} - 4\hat{\mathbf{k}}}{2} = \frac{4\hat{\mathbf{i}} - 2\hat{\mathbf{j}} - 6\hat{\mathbf{k}}}{2}$$

$$= 2\hat{\mathbf{i}} - \hat{\mathbf{j}} - 3\hat{\mathbf{k}}$$

$$\mathbf{PS} = \frac{3\hat{\mathbf{i}} + \hat{\mathbf{j}} - 2\hat{\mathbf{k}} - \hat{\mathbf{i}} + 3\hat{\mathbf{j}} + 4\hat{\mathbf{k}}}{2} = \frac{2\hat{\mathbf{i}} + 4\hat{\mathbf{j}} + 2\hat{\mathbf{k}}}{2}$$

$$= \hat{\mathbf{i}} + 2\hat{\mathbf{j}} + \hat{\mathbf{k}}$$

and $\mathbf{PT} = \hat{\mathbf{i}} + 2\hat{\mathbf{j}} + 3\hat{\mathbf{k}}$

$\therefore$ Volume of parallelopiped by the vector **PT**, **PQ** and **PS**

$$= \mathbf{PT} \cdot (\mathbf{PQ} \times \mathbf{PS})$$

$$= \begin{vmatrix} 1 & 2 & 3 \\ 2 & -1 & -3 \\ 1 & 2 & 1 \end{vmatrix}$$

$$= 1(-1+6) - 2(2+3) + 3(4+1)$$

$$= 5 - 10 + 15 = 10$$

2.15 Volume of Tetrahedron

(A pyramid having a triangular base)

If $OABC$ is a tetrahedron as shown in figure, where $\mathbf{OA} = \mathbf{a}$, $\mathbf{OB} = \mathbf{b}$, and $\mathbf{OC} = \mathbf{c}$.

Then, volume of tetrahedron $= \dfrac{1}{6}[\mathbf{a}\ \mathbf{b}\ \mathbf{c}]$

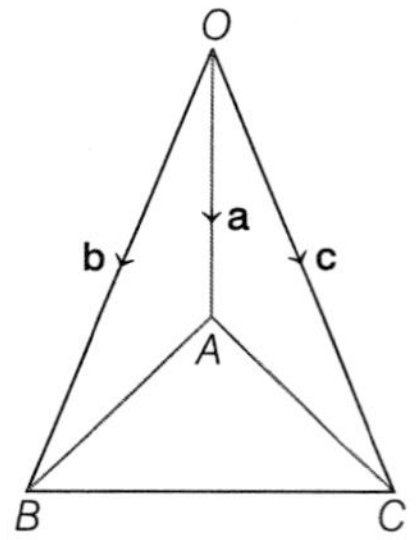

Volume of a tetrahedron in terms of the position vectors of its four vertices $A(\mathbf{a}), B(\mathbf{b}), C(\mathbf{c})$ and $D(\mathbf{d})$ is

$$\frac{1}{6}|(\mathbf{a} - \mathbf{d}) \cdot [(\mathbf{b} - \mathbf{d}) \times (\mathbf{c} - \mathbf{d})]|$$

JEE Focus Points

Concept Inside Video

- The six mid-points of the six edges of a tetrahedron lie in a sphere, if the pair of opposite edges are perpendicular to each other.
- Centre of the sphere is the centroid of the tetrahedron. $GA^2 + GB^2 + GC^2 + GO^2 = 12r^2$, G being the centroid.
- Any two edges of regular tetrahedron are perpendicular to each other.
- The angle between any two plane faces of a regular tetrahedron is $\cos^{-1}\dfrac{1}{3}$.
- Angle between the any edge and a face not containing the angle is $\cos^{-1}\sqrt{\dfrac{1}{3}}$ (for regular tetrahedron).
- The distance of any vertex from the opposite face of regular tetrahedron is $\sqrt{\dfrac{2}{3}}k$, k being the length of any edge.

Example 59. If $\mathbf{a}, \mathbf{b}$ and $\mathbf{c}$ are three non-coplanar uni-modular vectors, each inclined with other at an angle 30°, then find the volume of tetrahedron whose edges are $\mathbf{a}, \mathbf{b}$ and $\mathbf{c}$.

Sol. Since, the volume of tetrahedron with edges $\mathbf{a}$, $\mathbf{b}$ and $\mathbf{c}$ is $\frac{1}{6}[\mathbf{a}\ \mathbf{b}\ \mathbf{c}]$.

Where, $\mathbf{a}\cdot\mathbf{a} = \mathbf{b}\cdot\mathbf{b} = \mathbf{c}\cdot\mathbf{c} = 1$

and $\mathbf{a}\cdot\mathbf{c} = \mathbf{b}\cdot\mathbf{c} = \mathbf{a}\cdot\mathbf{c} = \frac{\sqrt{3}}{2}$ [given]

$$\therefore \quad V = \frac{1}{6}[\mathbf{a}\ \mathbf{b}\ \mathbf{c}]$$

$$\Rightarrow \quad V^2 = \frac{1}{36}[\mathbf{a}\ \mathbf{b}\ \mathbf{c}]^2$$

$$= \frac{1}{36}\begin{vmatrix} \mathbf{a}\cdot\mathbf{a} & \mathbf{a}\cdot\mathbf{b} & \mathbf{a}\cdot\mathbf{c} \\ \mathbf{b}\cdot\mathbf{a} & \mathbf{b}\cdot\mathbf{b} & \mathbf{b}\cdot\mathbf{c} \\ \mathbf{c}\cdot\mathbf{a} & \mathbf{c}\cdot\mathbf{b} & \mathbf{c}\cdot\mathbf{c} \end{vmatrix}$$

$$= \frac{1}{36}\begin{vmatrix} 1 & \frac{\sqrt{3}}{2} & \frac{\sqrt{3}}{2} \\ \frac{\sqrt{3}}{2} & 1 & \frac{\sqrt{3}}{2} \\ \frac{\sqrt{3}}{2} & \frac{\sqrt{3}}{2} & 1 \end{vmatrix} = \frac{1}{36}\left(\frac{3\sqrt{3}}{4} - \frac{5}{4}\right)$$

$$\therefore \quad V = \frac{1}{12}\sqrt{3\sqrt{3} - 5}$$

Example 60. Let $DABC$ be a tetrahedron such that $\mathbf{AD}$ is perpendicular to the base ABC and $\angle ABC = 30°$ and the volume is 18 cu units. If the value of $\mathbf{AB} + \mathbf{BC} + \mathbf{AD}$ is minimum, then find the length of $\mathbf{AC}$.

Sol. Volume of tetrahedron $= \frac{1}{6} \times \mathbf{AD}\cdot(\mathbf{AB}\times\mathbf{BC})$

$$= \frac{1}{6}\mathbf{AD}\cdot(|\mathbf{AB}||\mathbf{BC}|\sin 30°)$$

$$= \frac{1}{6}\mathbf{AD}\cdot\mathbf{AB}\cdot\mathbf{BC}\times\frac{1}{2}$$

$$= \frac{1}{12}\mathbf{AD}\cdot\mathbf{AB}\cdot\mathbf{BC}$$

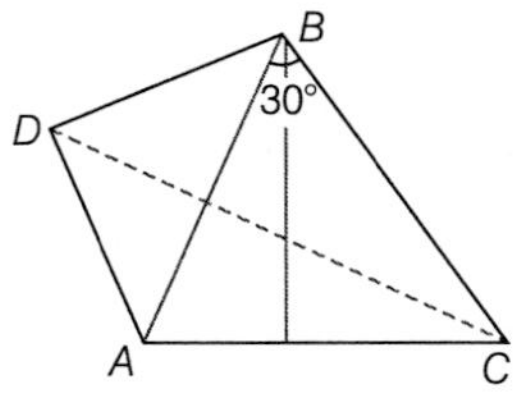

Volume of tetrahedron = 18

$$\therefore \quad 18 = \frac{1}{12}|\mathbf{AD}||\mathbf{AB}||\mathbf{BC}|$$

$$|\mathbf{AD}||\mathbf{AB}||\mathbf{BC}| = 216$$

Now, by AM ≥ GM

$$\frac{\mathbf{AB} + \mathbf{BC} + \mathbf{AD}}{3} \ge (|\mathbf{AB}||\mathbf{BC}||\mathbf{AD}|)^{1/3}$$

$$\mathbf{AB} + \mathbf{BC} + \mathbf{AD} \ge 18$$

So, the minimum value occurs when

$$\mathbf{AB} = \mathbf{BC} = \mathbf{AD} = 6$$

Hence, $\mathbf{AC} = \sqrt{\mathbf{AB}^2 + \mathbf{BC}^2 - 2\mathbf{AB}\ \mathbf{BC}\cos\theta}$

$$= \sqrt{6^2 + 6^2 - 2\times 6\times 6\times\cos 30°}$$

$$= \sqrt{36\left(1 + 1 - 2\times\frac{\sqrt{3}}{2}\right)} = 6\sqrt{2 - \sqrt{3}}$$

Milestone Practice 2.3

1. If $\mathbf{a}$ and $\mathbf{b}$ are two vectors such that $|\mathbf{a}\times\mathbf{b}| = 2$, then find the value of $[\mathbf{a}\ \ \mathbf{b}\ \ \mathbf{a}\times\mathbf{b}]$.

2. If $|\hat{\mathbf{a}} + \hat{\mathbf{b}} + \hat{\mathbf{a}}\times\hat{\mathbf{b}}| = |\hat{\mathbf{a}} - \hat{\mathbf{b}}|$, then the value of $|\hat{\mathbf{a}} - \hat{\mathbf{b}}|^2$ is equal to

   (a) sin 16° (b) sin 18°
   (c) 8 sin 18° (d) 8 sin 16°

3. If $\mathbf{a} = 3\sin\theta\,\hat{\mathbf{i}} - \cos\theta\,\hat{\mathbf{j}}$ and $\mathbf{b} = \frac{3\cos\theta}{3 + 2\cos 2\theta}\hat{\mathbf{i}} + \frac{\sin\theta}{3 + 2\cos 2\theta}\hat{\mathbf{j}}$ represent diagonals of a parallelogram such that area of the parallelogram is less than or equal to $\frac{3}{10}$, then find value of $[\mathbf{a}\ \ \mathbf{b}\ \ \mathbf{a}\times\mathbf{b}]$.

4. Examine whether the vectors $\mathbf{a} = 2\hat{\mathbf{i}} + 3\hat{\mathbf{j}} + 2\hat{\mathbf{k}}$, $\mathbf{b} = \hat{\mathbf{i}} - \hat{\mathbf{j}} + 2\hat{\mathbf{k}}$ and $\mathbf{c} = 3\hat{\mathbf{i}} + 2\hat{\mathbf{j}} + 4\hat{\mathbf{k}}$ form a left handed or a right handed system.

5. Let $\mathbf{a}$, $\mathbf{b}$ and $\mathbf{c}$ be three linearly independent vectors, find the value of $\frac{[\mathbf{a}+2\mathbf{b}-\mathbf{c}\ \ 2\mathbf{a}+\mathbf{b}+\mathbf{c}\ \ 4\mathbf{a}-\mathbf{b}+5\mathbf{c}]}{[\mathbf{a}\ \ \mathbf{b}\ \ \mathbf{c}]}$.

6. If $\mathbf{a}$, $\mathbf{b}$ and $\mathbf{c}$ are coplanar unit vectors, then find the value of $[2\mathbf{a} - \mathbf{b}\ \ 2\mathbf{b} - \mathbf{c}\ \ 2\mathbf{c} - \mathbf{a}]$.

7. If $\mathbf{a}$, $\mathbf{b}$ and $\mathbf{c}$ are non-coplanar vectors, then the value of $[\mathbf{a}+\mathbf{b}\ \ \mathbf{b}+\mathbf{c}\ \ \mathbf{c}+\mathbf{a}]$ is equal to

   (a) $[\mathbf{a}\ \ \mathbf{b}\ \ \mathbf{c}]$ (b) $2[\mathbf{a}\ \ \mathbf{b}\ \ \mathbf{c}]$
   (c) $3[\mathbf{a}\ \ \mathbf{b}\ \ \mathbf{c}]$ (d) None of these

8. If $[\mathbf{a}\ \mathbf{b}\ \mathbf{c}] = 2$, then find the value of $[(\mathbf{a} + 2\mathbf{b} - \mathbf{c})\ (\mathbf{a} - \mathbf{b})\ (\mathbf{a} - \mathbf{b} - \mathbf{c})]$.

9. If **a**, **b** and **c** are three non-coplanar vectors, then the value of $\frac{\mathbf{a}\cdot(\mathbf{b}\times\mathbf{c})}{\mathbf{b}\cdot(\mathbf{c}\times\mathbf{a})} + \frac{\mathbf{b}\cdot(\mathbf{c}\times\mathbf{a})}{\mathbf{c}\cdot(\mathbf{a}\times\mathbf{b})} + \frac{\mathbf{c}\cdot(\mathbf{a}\times\mathbf{b})}{\mathbf{a}\cdot(\mathbf{b}\times\mathbf{c})}$ is equal to

(a) 3 (b) 4 (c) 6 (d) 9

10. If the vectors $2\hat{i} - 3\hat{j}$, $\hat{i} + \hat{j} - \hat{k}$ and $3\hat{i} - \hat{k}$ form three concurrent edges of a parallelopiped , the the volume of the parallelopiped is equal to

(a) 4 cu units (b) 6 cu units
(c) 12 cu units (d) 14 cu units

11. If the volume of a parallelopiped whose adjacent edges are $\mathbf{a} = 2\hat{i} + 3\hat{j} + 4\hat{k}$, $\mathbf{b} = \hat{i} + \alpha\hat{j} + 2\hat{k}$, $\mathbf{c} = \hat{i} + 2\hat{j} + \alpha\hat{k}$ is 15, then find the value of α, where $\alpha > 0$.

12. Find the altitude of a parallelopiped whose three coterminous edges are vectors $\mathbf{A} = \hat{i} + \hat{j} + \hat{k}$, $\mathbf{B} = 2\hat{i} + 4\hat{j} - \hat{k}$ and $\mathbf{C} = \hat{i} + \hat{j} + 3\hat{k}$ with **A** and **B** as the sides of the base of the parallelopiped.

13. Let **a**, **b** and **c** be the unit vectors such that **a** and **b** are perpendicular and **c** is equally inclined to **a** and **b** at an angle θ. If $\mathbf{c} = x\mathbf{a} + y\mathbf{b} + z(\mathbf{a}\times\mathbf{b})$, then z is

(a) $1 + 2y^2$
(b) $x^2 + 3y$, $\sqrt{x^2 + y^2}$
(c) $\sqrt{1 - 2y^2}$, $\sqrt{1 - 2x^2}$
(d) $\sqrt{1 + 3y^2}$, $\sqrt{1 + x^4 + y^2}$

14. The position vector of the four angular points of a tetrahedron are $\mathbf{A}(\hat{j} + 2\hat{k})$, $\mathbf{B}(3\hat{i} + \hat{k})$, $\mathbf{C}(4\hat{i} + 3\hat{j} + 6\hat{k})$ and $\mathbf{D}(2\hat{i} + 3\hat{j} + 2\hat{k})$. Find the volume of the tetrahedron *ABCD*.

15. Let G_1, G_2 and G_3 be the centroids of the triangular faces *OBC*, *OCA* and *OAB* of a terahedron *OABC*. If V_1 denotes the volume of the tetrahedron *OABC* and V_2 that of the parallelopiped with $\mathbf{OG}_1, \mathbf{OG}_2$ and $\mathbf{OG}_3$ as three coterminous edges, if $\lambda V_1 = \mu V_2$, then the value of $\lambda + \mu$ is equal to

(a) 11
(b) 12
(c) 13
(d) 14

16. Consider the tetrahedron *ABCD* having vertices $A(1, -2, 0)$, $B(3, 1, 2)$, $C(-1, 1-1)$ and $D(1, 0, -1)$ find the distance of point *D* from plane *ABC*.

17. If $\mathbf{a} = \hat{i} + \hat{j} + \hat{k}$, $\mathbf{b} = \hat{i} - \hat{j} + \hat{k}$, $\mathbf{c} = \hat{i} + 2\hat{j} - \hat{k}$, then find the value of $\begin{vmatrix} \mathbf{a}\cdot\mathbf{a} & \mathbf{a}\cdot\mathbf{b} & \mathbf{a}\cdot\mathbf{c} \\ \mathbf{b}\cdot\mathbf{a} & \mathbf{b}\cdot\mathbf{b} & \mathbf{b}\cdot\mathbf{c} \\ \mathbf{c}\cdot\mathbf{a} & \mathbf{c}\cdot\mathbf{b} & \mathbf{c}\cdot\mathbf{c} \end{vmatrix}$.

18. **a**, **b** and **c** are three unit vectors and every two are inclined to each other at an angle $\cos^{-1}\left(\frac{3}{5}\right)$, if $\mathbf{a}\times\mathbf{b} = p\mathbf{a} + q\mathbf{b} + r\mathbf{c}$, where p, q and r are scalar, then the value of $55q^2$ is equal to

(a) 2 (b) 6 (c) 8 (d) 9

Answer Key

1. 4	2. (c)	3. $\frac{9}{25}$	4. coplanar	5. 0
6. 0	7. (b)	8. 6	9. (a)	10. (a)
11. $\frac{9}{2}$ or -1	12. $\frac{2\sqrt{38}}{19}$	13. (c)	14. 6 cu units	15. (c)
16. $\frac{16}{\sqrt{229}}$ units	17. 16	18. (d)		

For Detailed Solution

Milestone 4 Vector Triple Product

• Properties of Vector Triple Product • Reciprocal System of Vectors • Solving of Vector Equations

Let **a, b** and **c** be three vectors, then vector triple product of three vector **a**, **b** and **c** is defined as the cross product of vector **a** with the cross product of vector **b** and **c**

i.e. $\mathbf{a} \times (\mathbf{b} \times \mathbf{c})$.

Here, $\mathbf{a} \times (\mathbf{b} \times \mathbf{c})$ is coplanar with the vector **b** and **c** and are perpendicular to **a.**

Hence, we can write $\mathbf{a} \times (\mathbf{b} \times \mathbf{c})$ as linear combination of vector **b** and **c**.

i.e. $\mathbf{a} \times (\mathbf{b} \times \mathbf{c}) = l\,\mathbf{b} + m\mathbf{c}$ ...(i)

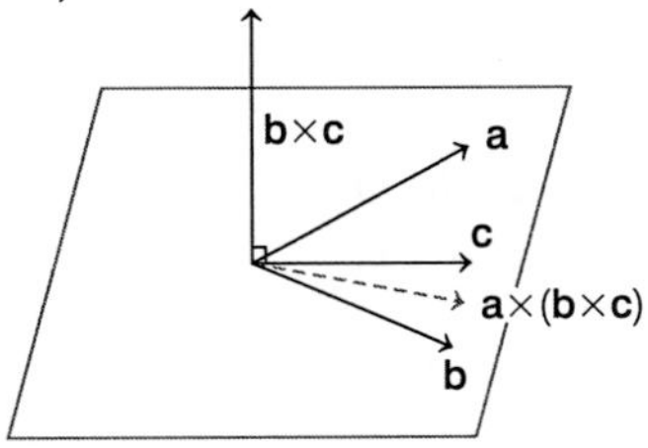

On taking scalar product of this equation with **a**, we get

$$0 = l(\mathbf{a} \cdot \mathbf{b}) + m(\mathbf{a} \cdot \mathbf{c})$$

$$\left[\begin{array}{l} \because \mathbf{a} \times (\mathbf{b} \times \mathbf{c}) \text{ is perpendicular to } \mathbf{a} \\ \therefore (\mathbf{a} \times (\mathbf{b} \times \mathbf{c}) \cdot \mathbf{a} = 0 \end{array}\right]$$

$$\Rightarrow \quad l(\mathbf{a} \cdot \mathbf{b}) = -m(\mathbf{a} \cdot \mathbf{c}) \Rightarrow \frac{l}{\mathbf{a} \cdot \mathbf{c}} = -\frac{m}{\mathbf{a} \cdot \mathbf{b}} = \lambda \text{ (say)}$$

$$\Rightarrow \quad l = \lambda(\mathbf{a} \cdot \mathbf{c}) \text{ and } m = -\lambda(\mathbf{a} \cdot \mathbf{b})$$

On substituting the value of l and m in Eq. (i), we get

$$\mathbf{a} \times (\mathbf{b} \times \mathbf{c}) = \lambda\,[(\mathbf{a} \cdot \mathbf{c})\mathbf{b} - (\mathbf{a} \cdot \mathbf{b})\,\mathbf{c}]$$

It is valid for every value of **a**, **b** and **c** because it is an identity.

If we choose the coordinate axes in such a way that

$$\mathbf{a} = a_1\hat{\mathbf{i}}, \mathbf{b} = b_1\hat{\mathbf{i}} + b_2\hat{\mathbf{j}} \text{ and } \mathbf{c} = c_1\hat{\mathbf{i}} + c_2\hat{\mathbf{j}} + c_3\hat{\mathbf{k}},$$

it is easy to show that $\lambda = 1$.

Hence, $\mathbf{a} \times (\mathbf{b} \times \mathbf{c}) = (\mathbf{a} \cdot \mathbf{c})\,\mathbf{b} - (\mathbf{a} \cdot \mathbf{b})\,\mathbf{c}$

Vector Triple Product Formula

$$\mathbf{a} \times (\mathbf{b} \times \mathbf{c}) = (\mathbf{a} \cdot \mathbf{c})\,\mathbf{b} - (\mathbf{a} \cdot \mathbf{b})\,\mathbf{c}$$

$$(\mathbf{a} \times \mathbf{b}) \times \mathbf{c} = (\mathbf{a} \cdot \mathbf{c})\,\mathbf{b} - (\mathbf{b} \cdot \mathbf{c})\,\mathbf{a}$$

In general, $\mathbf{c} \times (\mathbf{b} \times \mathbf{c}) \neq (\mathbf{a} \times \mathbf{b}) \times \mathbf{c}$

2.16 Properties of Vector Triple Product

(i) A vector triple product is a vector quantity.

(ii) If $\mathbf{r} = \mathbf{a} \times (\mathbf{b} \times \mathbf{c})$, then **r** is perpendicular to **a** and lie in the plane of **b** and **c**

(iii) Unit vector coplanar with **a** and **b** are perpendicular to **c** is $\pm \dfrac{(\mathbf{a} \times \mathbf{b}) \times \mathbf{c}}{|(\mathbf{a} \times \mathbf{b}) \times \mathbf{c}|}$

(iv) $[\mathbf{a} \times \mathbf{b} \;\; \mathbf{b} \times \mathbf{c} \;\; \mathbf{c} \times \mathbf{a}] = [\mathbf{a} \;\; \mathbf{b} \;\; \mathbf{c}]^2$

(v) $(\mathbf{a} \times \mathbf{b}) \cdot (\mathbf{c} \times \mathbf{d}) = (\mathbf{a} \cdot \mathbf{c})(\mathbf{b} \cdot \mathbf{d}) - (\mathbf{a} \cdot \mathbf{d})(\mathbf{b} \cdot \mathbf{c})$

$$= \begin{vmatrix} \mathbf{a} \cdot \mathbf{c} & \mathbf{a} \cdot \mathbf{d} \\ \mathbf{b} \cdot \mathbf{c} & \mathbf{b} \cdot \mathbf{d} \end{vmatrix}$$

This identity is known as **scalar product of four vector** also called Lagrange's identity.

(vi) $(\mathbf{a} \times \mathbf{b}) \times (\mathbf{c} \times \mathbf{d}) = [\mathbf{a}\,\mathbf{b}\,\mathbf{d}]\,\mathbf{c} - [\mathbf{a}\,\mathbf{b}\,\mathbf{c}]\,\mathbf{d}$

$$= [\mathbf{a}\,\mathbf{c}\,\mathbf{d}]\,\mathbf{b} - [\mathbf{b}\,\mathbf{c}\,\mathbf{d}]\,\mathbf{a}$$

This is identity is known as **vector product of four vectors**.

JEE SPIKE

- $\mathbf{a} \times (\mathbf{b} \times \mathbf{c}) = (\mathbf{a} \times \mathbf{b}) \times \mathbf{c}$, if some of all **a**, **b** and **c** are zero vectors or **a** and **c** are collinear.
- If $(\mathbf{a} \times \mathbf{b}) \cdot (\mathbf{c} \times \mathbf{d}) = 0$
  Then, plane containing **a**, **b** and **c**, **d** are perpendicular.
- If $(\mathbf{a} \times \mathbf{b}) \times (\mathbf{c} \times \mathbf{d}) = 0$
  Then, plane containing **a**, **b** and **c**, **d** are parallel.

Example 61. If $\mathbf{a} = \hat{\mathbf{i}} + \hat{\mathbf{j}} + \hat{\mathbf{k}}$, $\mathbf{b} = \hat{\mathbf{i}} + \hat{\mathbf{j}}$, $\mathbf{c} = \hat{\mathbf{i}}$ and $(\mathbf{a} \times \mathbf{b}) \times \mathbf{c} = \lambda\mathbf{a} + \mu\mathbf{b}$, then find $\lambda + \mu$.

Sol. $(\mathbf{a} \times \mathbf{b}) \times \mathbf{c} = \lambda\mathbf{a} + \mu\mathbf{b}$

$$\Rightarrow \quad (\mathbf{a} \cdot \mathbf{c})\,\mathbf{b} - (\mathbf{b} \cdot \mathbf{c})\,\mathbf{a} = \lambda\mathbf{a} + \mu\mathbf{b}$$

$$\Rightarrow \quad \lambda = -\,\mathbf{b} \cdot \mathbf{c},$$

$$\mu = \mathbf{a} \cdot \mathbf{c}$$

$\therefore \quad \lambda + \mu = \mathbf{a} \cdot \mathbf{c} - \mathbf{b} \cdot \mathbf{c}$

$= (\mathbf{a} - \mathbf{b}) \cdot \mathbf{c}$

$= \{(\hat{\mathbf{i}} + \hat{\mathbf{j}} + \hat{\mathbf{k}}) - (\mathbf{i} + \hat{\mathbf{j}})\} \cdot \hat{\mathbf{i}} = \hat{\mathbf{k}} \cdot \hat{\mathbf{i}} = 0$

$\therefore \quad \lambda + \mu = 0$

JEE SCANNER

Example Similar to PYQ Asked in JEE Main 2019

If **a**, **b** *and* **c** *are three non-parallel unit vectors such that* $\mathbf{a} \times (\mathbf{b} \times \mathbf{c}) = \frac{1}{2}\mathbf{b}$, *then the angles which* **a** *makes with* **b** *and* **c** *is*

(a) $\frac{\pi}{2}$ and $\frac{\pi}{6}$ (b) $\frac{\pi}{3}$ and $\frac{\pi}{2}$ (c) $\frac{\pi}{2}$ and $\frac{\pi}{3}$ (d) $\frac{\pi}{6}$ and $\frac{\pi}{2}$

Sol. We have, $\mathbf{a} \times (\mathbf{b} \times \mathbf{c}) = \frac{1}{2}\mathbf{b}$

$\Rightarrow \quad (\mathbf{a} \cdot \mathbf{c})\mathbf{b} - (\mathbf{a} \cdot \mathbf{b})\mathbf{c} = \frac{1}{2}\mathbf{b}$

$\Rightarrow \quad \mathbf{a} \cdot \mathbf{c} = \frac{1}{2}$ and $\mathbf{a} \cdot \mathbf{b} = 0$ [comparing **c** and **b**]

$\Rightarrow \quad \mathbf{a} \cdot \mathbf{c} = \frac{1}{2}$ and $\mathbf{a} \perp \mathbf{b}$

Suppose **a** makes angle θ with **c**.

Then, $\mathbf{a} \cdot \mathbf{c} = \frac{1}{2}$

$\Rightarrow \quad |\mathbf{a}||\mathbf{c}|\cos\theta = \frac{1}{2} \Rightarrow \cos\theta = \frac{1}{2}$ $[\because |\mathbf{a}||\mathbf{c}| \neq 0]$

$\Rightarrow \quad \theta = \frac{\pi}{3}$

Thus, **a** is perpendicular to **b** and makes an angle $\frac{\pi}{3}$ with **c**.

Time Saving Technique

In any question, if **a**, **b** and **c** are non-parallel unit vectors and $\mathbf{a} \cdot \mathbf{c} = \frac{1}{2}$ and $\mathbf{a} \cdot \mathbf{b} = 0$, then, we directly say that **a** is perpendicular to **b** and makes an angle $\frac{\pi}{3}$ with **c**.

Skill Builder

If **a**, **b** and **c** are three non-parallel unit vectors such that $\mathbf{a} \times (\mathbf{b} \times \mathbf{c}) = -\frac{\sqrt{3}}{2}\mathbf{c}$, then the angles which **a** makes with **b** and **c** is

(a) $\frac{\pi}{3}$ and $\frac{\pi}{2}$ (b) $\frac{\pi}{6}$ and $\frac{\pi}{2}$

(c) $\frac{\pi}{2}$ and $\frac{\pi}{6}$ (d) $\frac{\pi}{2}$ and $\frac{\pi}{3}$

For Sol.

■ **For more practice** See Q.6 of Milestone Practice 4.

Example 62. If $\mathbf{a} = -\hat{\mathbf{i}} + \hat{\mathbf{j}} + \hat{\mathbf{k}}$ and $\mathbf{b} = 2\hat{\mathbf{i}} + \hat{\mathbf{k}}$, then find the vector x satisfying the conditions.

(i) that it is coplanar with **a** and **b**.

(ii) it is perpendicular to **b**.

(iii) $\mathbf{a} \cdot \mathbf{x} = 7$

Sol. Since, **x** is in the plane of **a** and **b** and is perpendicular to **b**.

$\therefore \quad \mathbf{x} = \lambda \{\mathbf{b} \times (\mathbf{a} \times \mathbf{b})\}$

$\Rightarrow \quad \mathbf{x} = \lambda \{(\mathbf{b} \cdot \mathbf{b})\mathbf{a} - (\mathbf{b} \cdot \mathbf{a})\mathbf{b}\}$

$= \lambda \{5(-\hat{\mathbf{i}} + \hat{\mathbf{j}} + \hat{\mathbf{k}}) - (-1)(2\hat{\mathbf{i}} + \hat{\mathbf{k}})\}$

$= \lambda \{-5\hat{\mathbf{i}} + 5\hat{\mathbf{j}} + 5\hat{\mathbf{k}} + 2\hat{\mathbf{i}} + \hat{\mathbf{k}}\}$

$= \lambda \{-3\hat{\mathbf{i}} + 5\hat{\mathbf{j}} + 6\hat{\mathbf{k}}\}$

Now, $\mathbf{a} \cdot \mathbf{x} = 7$

$\therefore (-\hat{\mathbf{i}} + \hat{\mathbf{j}} + \hat{\mathbf{k}}) \cdot \{\lambda(-3\hat{\mathbf{i}} + 5\hat{\mathbf{j}} + 6\hat{\mathbf{k}})\} = 7 = \lambda(3 + 5 + 6) = 7$

$\lambda = \frac{7}{14} = \frac{1}{2}$

$\therefore \quad \mathbf{x} = -\frac{3}{2}\hat{\mathbf{i}} + \frac{5}{2}\hat{\mathbf{j}} + 3\hat{\mathbf{k}}$

Example 63. Let **a**, **b** and **c** be three non-zero vectors such that no two of them are collinear and $(\mathbf{a} \times \mathbf{b}) \times \mathbf{c} = \frac{1}{3}|\mathbf{b}||\mathbf{c}|\mathbf{a}$. If θ is the angle between vectors **b** and **c**, then find the value of $\sin\theta$.

Sol. Given, $(\mathbf{a} \times \mathbf{b}) \times \mathbf{c} = \frac{1}{3}|\mathbf{b}||\mathbf{c}|\mathbf{a}$

$\Rightarrow \quad -\mathbf{c} \times (\mathbf{a} \times \mathbf{b}) = \frac{1}{3}|\mathbf{b}||\mathbf{c}|\mathbf{a}$

$\Rightarrow \quad -(\mathbf{c} \cdot \mathbf{b}) \cdot \mathbf{a} + (\mathbf{c} \cdot \mathbf{a})\mathbf{b} = \frac{1}{3}|\mathbf{b}||\mathbf{c}|\mathbf{a}$

$\Rightarrow \left[\frac{1}{3}|\mathbf{b}||\mathbf{c}| + (\mathbf{c} \cdot \mathbf{b})\right]\mathbf{a} = (\mathbf{c} \cdot \mathbf{a})\mathbf{b}$

We know that if $\lambda\mathbf{a} + \mu\mathbf{b} = 0$ and **a**, **b** are not collinear, then $\lambda = 0$ and $\mu = 0$

$\therefore \quad \mathbf{c} \cdot \mathbf{b} + \frac{1}{3}|\mathbf{b}||\mathbf{c}| = 0$ and $\mathbf{c} \cdot \mathbf{a} = 0$

$\Rightarrow \quad |\mathbf{b}||\mathbf{c}|\cos\theta + \frac{1}{3}|\mathbf{b}||\mathbf{c}| = 0$

$\Rightarrow \quad |\mathbf{b}||\mathbf{c}|\left(\cos\theta + \frac{1}{3}\right) = 0$

$\Rightarrow \quad \cos\theta + \frac{1}{3} = 0$ $[\because |\mathbf{b}| \neq 0, |\mathbf{c}| \neq 0]$

$\Rightarrow \quad \cos\theta = -\frac{1}{3}$

$\Rightarrow \quad \sin\theta = \frac{\sqrt{8}}{3}$

$= \frac{2\sqrt{2}}{3}$

Example 64. If $\hat{i} \times [(\mathbf{a} - \hat{j}) \times \hat{i}] + \hat{j} \times [(\mathbf{a} - \hat{k}) \times \hat{j}] + \hat{k} \times [(\mathbf{a} - \hat{i}) \times \hat{k}] = 0,$

then find vector **a**.

Sol. $\hat{i} \times [(\mathbf{a} - \hat{j}) \times \hat{i}] = (\hat{i} \cdot \hat{i})(\mathbf{a} - \hat{j}) - (\hat{i} \cdot (\mathbf{a} - \hat{j}))\hat{i}$

$$= \mathbf{a} - \hat{j} - (\hat{i} \cdot \mathbf{a})\hat{i}$$

Similarly, $\hat{j} \times [(\mathbf{a} - \hat{k}) \times \hat{j})] = \mathbf{a} - \hat{k} - (\hat{j} \cdot \mathbf{a})\hat{j}$

and $\hat{k} \times [(\mathbf{a} - \hat{i}) \times \hat{k}] = \mathbf{a} - \hat{i} - (\hat{k} \cdot \mathbf{a})\hat{k}$

Now, $\hat{i} \times [(\mathbf{a} - \hat{j}) \times \hat{i}] + \hat{j} \times [(\mathbf{a} - \hat{k}) \times \hat{j}] + \hat{k} \times [(\mathbf{a} - \hat{i}) \times \hat{k}] = 0$

$\Rightarrow \quad \mathbf{a} - \hat{j} - (\hat{i} \cdot \mathbf{a})\hat{i} + \mathbf{a} - \hat{k} - (\hat{j} \cdot \mathbf{a})\hat{j} + \mathbf{a} - \hat{i} - (\hat{k} \cdot \mathbf{a})\hat{k} = 0$

$\Rightarrow \quad 3\mathbf{a} - (\hat{i} + \hat{j} + \hat{k}) - \mathbf{a} = 0$

$\Rightarrow \quad 2\mathbf{a} = \hat{i} + \hat{j} + \hat{k}$

$\Rightarrow \quad \mathbf{a} = \dfrac{\hat{i} + \hat{j} + \hat{k}}{2}$

Example 65. If **A**, **B** and **C** are vectors such that $|\mathbf{B}| = |\mathbf{C}|$, prove that

$$[\{(\mathbf{A} + \mathbf{B}) \times (\mathbf{A} + \mathbf{C})\} \times (\mathbf{B} \times \mathbf{C})] \cdot (\mathbf{B} + \mathbf{C}) = 0.$$

Sol. Let $\mathbf{R}_1 = \mathbf{A} + \mathbf{B}$, $\mathbf{R}_2 = \mathbf{A} + \mathbf{C}$ and $\mathbf{R}_3 = \mathbf{B} + \mathbf{C}$

$\therefore$ LHS $= [\{(\mathbf{A} + \mathbf{B}) \times (\mathbf{A} + \mathbf{C})\} \times (\mathbf{B} \times \mathbf{C})\}] \cdot (\mathbf{B} + \mathbf{C})$

$\Rightarrow \quad \{(\mathbf{R}_1 \times \mathbf{R}_2) \times (\mathbf{B} \times \mathbf{C})\} \cdot \mathbf{R}_3$

$\Rightarrow \quad [\{\mathbf{R}_1 \cdot (\mathbf{B} \times \mathbf{C})\} \mathbf{R}_2 - \{\mathbf{R}_2 \cdot (\mathbf{B} \times \mathbf{C}) \mathbf{R}_1\}] \cdot \mathbf{R}_3$

$\Rightarrow \quad [\mathbf{A} + \mathbf{B}\ \mathbf{B}\ \mathbf{C}][\mathbf{R}_2 \cdot \mathbf{R}_3] - [\mathbf{A} + \mathbf{C}\ \mathbf{B}\ \mathbf{C}](\mathbf{R}_1 \cdot \mathbf{R}_3)$

$\Rightarrow \quad \{[\mathbf{A}\ \mathbf{B}\ \mathbf{C}] + [\mathbf{B}\ \mathbf{B}\ \mathbf{C}]\}[(\mathbf{A} + \mathbf{C}) \cdot (\mathbf{B} + \mathbf{C})] - \{[\mathbf{A}\ \mathbf{B}\ \mathbf{C}] + [\mathbf{C}\ \mathbf{B}\ \mathbf{C}]\}[(\mathbf{A} + \mathbf{B}) \cdot (\mathbf{B} + \mathbf{C})]$

$\Rightarrow \quad [\mathbf{A}\ \mathbf{B}\ \mathbf{C}](\mathbf{A} \cdot \mathbf{B} + \mathbf{A} \cdot \mathbf{C} + \mathbf{C} \cdot \mathbf{B} + \mathbf{C} \cdot \mathbf{C}) - [\mathbf{A}\ \mathbf{B}\ \mathbf{C}](\mathbf{A} \cdot \mathbf{B} + \mathbf{A} \cdot \mathbf{C} + \mathbf{B} \cdot \mathbf{B} + \mathbf{B} \cdot \mathbf{C})$

$\Rightarrow \quad [\mathbf{A}\ \mathbf{B}\ \mathbf{C}](\mathbf{A} \cdot \mathbf{B} + \mathbf{A} \cdot \mathbf{C} + \mathbf{C} \cdot \mathbf{B} + |\mathbf{C}|^2 - \mathbf{A} \cdot \mathbf{B} - \mathbf{A} \cdot \mathbf{C} - |\mathbf{B}|^2 - \mathbf{B} \cdot \mathbf{C})$

$\Rightarrow \quad [\mathbf{A}\ \mathbf{B}\ \mathbf{C}](|\mathbf{C}|^2 - |\mathbf{B}|^2)$

$\Rightarrow \quad [\mathbf{A}\ \mathbf{B}\ \mathbf{C}](0) \qquad [\because |\mathbf{B}| = |\mathbf{C}|]$

$\Rightarrow \quad 0 = $ RHS

Example 66. If **b** and **c** are two vectors such that **a** is parallel to $\mathbf{b} \times \mathbf{c}$, $|\mathbf{a}| = 2$, $\mathbf{b} = 2\hat{i} + 3\hat{j} + \hat{k}$, $\mathbf{c} = \hat{i} + \hat{j} + 2\hat{k}$, then find the value of $(\mathbf{a} \times \mathbf{b}) \cdot (\mathbf{a} \times \mathbf{c})$.

Sol. Given, **a** parallel to $\mathbf{b} \times \mathbf{c}$

$\therefore \quad \mathbf{a} \times (\mathbf{b} \times \mathbf{c}) = 0$

$\Rightarrow \quad \mathbf{a} \cdot \mathbf{b} = 0 = \mathbf{a} \cdot \mathbf{c}$

$\because \quad \mathbf{b} \cdot \mathbf{c} = (2\hat{i} + 3\hat{j} + \hat{k}) \cdot (\hat{i} + \hat{j} + 2\hat{k})$

$$= 2 + 3 + 2 = 7$$

Now, $(\mathbf{a} \times \mathbf{b}) \cdot (\mathbf{a} \times \mathbf{c}) = |\mathbf{a}|^2 (\mathbf{b} \cdot \mathbf{c}) - (\mathbf{a} \cdot \mathbf{c})(\mathbf{b} \cdot \mathbf{a})$

$$= 4(7) - 0$$
$$= 28$$

Example 67. Let **a**, **b** and **c** be three non-zero vector such that $\mathbf{b} \cdot \mathbf{c} = 0$ and $\mathbf{a} \times (\mathbf{b} \times \mathbf{c}) = \dfrac{\mathbf{b} - \mathbf{c}}{2}$. If **d** be a vector such that $\mathbf{b} \cdot \mathbf{d} = \mathbf{a} \cdot \mathbf{b}$, then find the value of $(\mathbf{a} \times \mathbf{b}) \cdot (\mathbf{c} \times \mathbf{d})$.

Sol. Given, $\mathbf{a} \times (\mathbf{b} \times \mathbf{c}) = \dfrac{\mathbf{b} - \mathbf{c}}{2}$

$\therefore \quad (\mathbf{a} \cdot \mathbf{c})\,\mathbf{b} - (\mathbf{a} \cdot \mathbf{b})\,\mathbf{c} = \dfrac{1}{2}\mathbf{b} - \dfrac{1}{2}\mathbf{c}$

$\therefore \quad \mathbf{a} \cdot \mathbf{c} = \dfrac{1}{2}, \mathbf{a} \cdot \mathbf{b} = \dfrac{1}{2}$

Now, $\mathbf{a} \cdot \mathbf{b} = \mathbf{b} \cdot \mathbf{d} = \dfrac{1}{2}$

$$(\mathbf{a} \times \mathbf{b}) \cdot (\mathbf{c} \times \mathbf{d}) = (\mathbf{a} \cdot \mathbf{c})(\mathbf{b} \cdot \mathbf{d}) - (\mathbf{a} \cdot \mathbf{d})(\mathbf{b} \cdot \mathbf{c})$$
$$= \frac{1}{2} \times \frac{1}{2} - 0 = \frac{1}{4}$$

JEE SCANNER

Example Similar to PYQ Asked in JEE Main 2021

If **a**, **b** *and* **c** *are three vectors such that* $|\mathbf{a}| = 1$, $|\mathbf{b}| = 2$, $|\mathbf{c}| = 1$ *and* $\mathbf{a} \times (\mathbf{a} \times \mathbf{b}) + \mathbf{c} = 0$, *then the angle between* **a** *and* **b** *is equal to*

(a) $\dfrac{\pi}{6}$ (b) $\dfrac{\pi}{2}$ (c) $\dfrac{\pi}{4}$ (d) $\dfrac{\pi}{3}$

Sol. Let angle between **a** and **b** be θ.

$\therefore \quad \mathbf{a} \cdot \mathbf{b} = |\mathbf{a}||\mathbf{b}|\cos\theta$

Now, $\mathbf{a} \times (\mathbf{a} \times \mathbf{b}) + \mathbf{c} = 0 \Rightarrow (\mathbf{a} \cdot \mathbf{b})\mathbf{a} - (\mathbf{a} \cdot \mathbf{a})\mathbf{b} = -\mathbf{c}$

$\Rightarrow \quad 2\cos\theta\,\mathbf{a} - \mathbf{b} = -\mathbf{c} \Rightarrow |2\cos\theta\,\mathbf{a} - \mathbf{b}|^2 = |-\mathbf{c}|^2$

$\Rightarrow \quad 4\cos^2\theta\,|\mathbf{a}|^2 + |\mathbf{b}|^2 - 4\cos\theta\,|\mathbf{a}||\mathbf{b}|(\cos\theta) = |\mathbf{c}|^2$

$\Rightarrow \quad 4\cos^2\theta + (2)^2 - 4\cos\theta\,(1)(2)(\cos\theta) = (1)^2$

$\Rightarrow \quad 4\cos^2\theta + 4 - 8\cos^2\theta = 1$

$\Rightarrow \quad -4\cos^2\theta = -3$

$\Rightarrow \quad \cos^2\theta = \dfrac{3}{4}$

$\Rightarrow \quad \cos\theta = \dfrac{\sqrt{3}}{2}$

$\therefore \quad \theta = \dfrac{\pi}{6}$

Hence, the angle between **a** and **b** is $\dfrac{\pi}{6}$

Skill Builder

If **a**, **b** and c are three vectors such that $|\mathbf{a}| = 1$, $|\mathbf{b}| = 4$, $|\mathbf{c}| = 2$ and $\mathbf{a} \times (\mathbf{a} \times \mathbf{b}) + \mathbf{c} = 0$, then the angle between **a** and **b** is equal to

(a) $\dfrac{\pi}{3}$ (b) $\dfrac{\pi}{2}$

(c) $\dfrac{\pi}{6}$ (d) $\dfrac{\pi}{4}$

For Sol.

- **For more practice** See Q.6 of Milestone Practice 4.

2.17 Reciprocal System of Vectors

The two system of vectors are called reciprocal system of vectors if by taking dot product, we get unity.

i.e. $\mathbf{a}' \cdot \mathbf{a} = 1, \mathbf{b}' \cdot \mathbf{b} = 1$ and $\mathbf{c}' \cdot \mathbf{c} = 1$

If **a**, **b** and **c** be three non-coplanar vectors, then

$$\mathbf{a}' = \frac{\mathbf{b} \times \mathbf{c}}{[\mathbf{a}\ \mathbf{b}\ \mathbf{c}]},$$

$$\mathbf{b}' = \frac{\mathbf{c} \times \mathbf{a}}{[\mathbf{a}\ \mathbf{b}\ \mathbf{c}]}$$

and $$\mathbf{c}' = \frac{\mathbf{a} \times \mathbf{b}}{[\mathbf{a}\ \mathbf{b}\ \mathbf{c}]}$$

where, $\mathbf{a}', \mathbf{b}'$, and $\mathbf{c}'$ are said to be reciprocal system of vectors for the vector **a**, **b** and **c**.

JEE Focus Points

- If a, b, c and a′, b′, c′ are reciprocal system of vectors, then $\mathbf{a} \cdot \mathbf{a}' = \frac{\mathbf{a} \cdot (\mathbf{b} \times \mathbf{c})}{[\mathbf{a}\ \mathbf{b}\ \mathbf{c}]} = \frac{[\mathbf{a}\ \mathbf{b}\ \mathbf{c}]}{[\mathbf{a}\ \mathbf{b}\ \mathbf{c}]} = 1$

  Similarly, $\mathbf{b} \cdot \mathbf{b}' = \mathbf{c} \cdot \mathbf{c}' = 1$
- $\mathbf{a} \cdot \mathbf{b}' = \mathbf{a} \cdot \mathbf{c}' = \mathbf{b} \cdot \mathbf{a}' = \mathbf{b} \cdot \mathbf{a}' = \mathbf{c} \cdot \mathbf{a}' = \mathbf{c} \cdot \mathbf{b}' = 0$
- $[\mathbf{a}\ \mathbf{b}\ \mathbf{c}] \cdot [\mathbf{a}'\ \mathbf{b}'\ \mathbf{c}'] = 1$

  Concept Inside Video

  Proof We have,

  $$[\mathbf{a}'\ \mathbf{b}'\ \mathbf{c}'] = \left[\frac{\mathbf{b} \times \mathbf{c}}{[\mathbf{a}\ \mathbf{b}\ \mathbf{c}]}\ \frac{\mathbf{c} \times \mathbf{a}}{[\mathbf{a}\ \mathbf{b}\ \mathbf{c}]}\ \frac{\mathbf{a} \times \mathbf{b}}{[\mathbf{a}\ \mathbf{b}\ \mathbf{c}]}\right]$$

  $$= \frac{1}{[\mathbf{a}\ \mathbf{b}\ \mathbf{c}]^3}[\mathbf{b} \times \mathbf{c}\ \ \mathbf{c} \times \mathbf{a}\ \ \mathbf{a} \times \mathbf{b}] = \frac{1}{[\mathbf{a}\ \mathbf{b}\ \mathbf{c}]^3}[\mathbf{a}\ \mathbf{b}\ \mathbf{c}]^2 = \frac{1}{[\mathbf{a}\ \mathbf{b}\ \mathbf{c}]}$$

  $\therefore [\mathbf{a}'\ \mathbf{b}'\ \mathbf{c}'] \cdot [\mathbf{a}\ \mathbf{b}\ \mathbf{c}] = 1$
- The orthogonal triad of vectors $\hat{\mathbf{i}}, \hat{\mathbf{j}}$ and $\hat{\mathbf{k}}$ is self reciprocal.

  Let $\hat{\mathbf{i}}', \hat{\mathbf{j}}'$ and $\hat{\mathbf{k}}'$ be the system of vectors reciprocal to the system $\hat{\mathbf{i}}, \hat{\mathbf{j}}$ and $\hat{\mathbf{k}}$ then, we have

  $$\hat{\mathbf{i}}' = \frac{\hat{\mathbf{j}} \times \hat{\mathbf{k}}}{[\hat{\mathbf{i}}\ \hat{\mathbf{j}}\ \hat{\mathbf{k}}]} = \hat{\mathbf{i}}$$

  Similarly, $\hat{\mathbf{j}}' = \hat{\mathbf{j}}$ and $\hat{\mathbf{k}}' = \hat{\mathbf{k}}$
- a, b and c are non-coplanar iff a′, b′, c′ are non-coplanar.

  $\because \quad [\mathbf{a}\ \mathbf{b}\ \mathbf{c}][\mathbf{a}'\ \mathbf{b}'\ \mathbf{c}'] = 1$

  $\therefore \quad [\mathbf{a}'\ \mathbf{b}'\ \mathbf{c}'] = \frac{1}{[\mathbf{a}\ \mathbf{b}\ \mathbf{c}]}$

  So, $\quad [\mathbf{a}\ \mathbf{b}\ \mathbf{c}] \neq 0 \Leftrightarrow [\mathbf{a}'\ \mathbf{b}'\ \mathbf{c}'] \neq 0$

  Thus, a, b and c are non-coplanar iff [a′ b′ c′] are non-coplanar.

Example 68. Find the set of vectors reciprocal to the set of vectors $2\hat{\mathbf{i}} + 3\hat{\mathbf{j}} - \hat{\mathbf{k}}$, $\hat{\mathbf{i}} - \hat{\mathbf{j}} - 2\hat{\mathbf{k}}, -\hat{\mathbf{i}} + 2\hat{\mathbf{j}} + 2\hat{\mathbf{k}}$.

Sol. Let the given vector be **a**, **b**, **c**.

$$\text{Now, } [\mathbf{a}\ \mathbf{b}\ \mathbf{c}] = \begin{vmatrix} 2 & 3 & -1 \\ 1 & -1 & -2 \\ -1 & 2 & 2 \end{vmatrix}$$

$$= 2(-2+4) - 3(2-2) - 1(2-1) = 4 - 1 = 3$$

$$\mathbf{b} \times \mathbf{c} = \begin{vmatrix} \hat{\mathbf{i}} & \hat{\mathbf{j}} & \hat{\mathbf{k}} \\ 1 & -1 & -2 \\ -1 & 2 & 2 \end{vmatrix} = 2\hat{\mathbf{i}} + \hat{\mathbf{k}}$$

$$\mathbf{c} \times \mathbf{a} = \begin{vmatrix} \hat{\mathbf{i}} & \hat{\mathbf{j}} & \hat{\mathbf{k}} \\ -1 & 2 & 2 \\ 2 & 3 & -1 \end{vmatrix} = -8\hat{\mathbf{i}} + 3\hat{\mathbf{j}} - 7\hat{\mathbf{k}}$$

$$\mathbf{a} \times \mathbf{b} = \begin{vmatrix} \hat{\mathbf{i}} & \hat{\mathbf{j}} & \hat{\mathbf{k}} \\ 2 & 3 & -1 \\ 1 & -1 & -2 \end{vmatrix} = -7\hat{\mathbf{i}} + 3\hat{\mathbf{j}} - 5\hat{\mathbf{k}}$$

Hence, $$\mathbf{a}' = \frac{\mathbf{b} \times \mathbf{c}}{[\mathbf{a}\ \mathbf{b}\ \mathbf{c}]} = \frac{2\hat{\mathbf{i}} + \hat{\mathbf{k}}}{3}$$

$$\mathbf{b}' = \frac{\mathbf{c} \times \mathbf{a}}{[\mathbf{a}\ \mathbf{b}\ \mathbf{c}]} = \frac{-8\hat{\mathbf{i}} + 3\hat{\mathbf{j}} - 7\hat{\mathbf{k}}}{3}$$

and $$\mathbf{c}' = \frac{\mathbf{a} \times \mathbf{b}}{[\mathbf{a}\ \mathbf{b}\ \mathbf{c}]} = \frac{-7\hat{\mathbf{i}} + 3\hat{\mathbf{j}} - 5\hat{\mathbf{k}}}{3}$$

Example 69. If a, b and c are three non-coplanar vectors and p, q and r respectively are three reciprocal vectors, then prove that

$$(l\mathbf{a} + m\mathbf{b} + n\mathbf{c}) \cdot (l\mathbf{p} + m\mathbf{q} + n\mathbf{r}) = l^2 + m^2 + n^2.$$

Sol. Given, **p**, **q** and **r** are the reciprocal vectors of **a**, **b** and **c** respectively.

$$\therefore \quad \mathbf{p} = \frac{\mathbf{b} \times \mathbf{c}}{[\mathbf{a}\ \mathbf{b}\ \mathbf{c}]}$$

$$\mathbf{q} = \frac{\mathbf{c} \times \mathbf{a}}{[\mathbf{a}\ \mathbf{b}\ \mathbf{c}]}$$

and $$\mathbf{r} = \frac{\mathbf{a} \times \mathbf{b}}{[\mathbf{a}\ \mathbf{b}\ \mathbf{c}]}$$

$\Rightarrow \quad \mathbf{a} \cdot \mathbf{p} = 1, \mathbf{a} \cdot \mathbf{q} = 0, \mathbf{a} \cdot \mathbf{r} = 0$

$\mathbf{a} \cdot \mathbf{q} = 0, \mathbf{b} \cdot \mathbf{q} = 1, \mathbf{c} \cdot \mathbf{q} = 0$ ...(i)

and $\mathbf{a} \cdot \mathbf{r} = 0, \mathbf{b} \cdot \mathbf{r} = 0, \mathbf{c} \cdot \mathbf{r} = 1$

$\therefore (l\mathbf{a} + m\mathbf{b} + n\mathbf{c}) \cdot (l\mathbf{p} + m\mathbf{q} + n\mathbf{r}) = l^2 + m^2 + n^2$ [using Eq. (i)]

Example 70. If $\mathbf{a}' = \frac{\mathbf{b} \times \mathbf{c}}{[\mathbf{a}\ \mathbf{b}\ \mathbf{c}]}, \mathbf{b}' = \frac{\mathbf{c} \times \mathbf{a}}{[\mathbf{a}\ \mathbf{b}\ \mathbf{c}]}, \mathbf{c}' = \frac{\mathbf{a} \times \mathbf{b}}{[\mathbf{a}\ \mathbf{b}\ \mathbf{c}]}$, then show that $\mathbf{a} \times \mathbf{a}' + \mathbf{b} \times \mathbf{b}' + \mathbf{c} \times \mathbf{c}' = 0$, where a, b and c are non-coplanar.

Sol. Here, $\mathbf{a} \times \mathbf{a}' = \frac{\mathbf{a} \times (\mathbf{b} \times \mathbf{c})}{[\mathbf{a}\ \mathbf{b}\ \mathbf{c}]}$

$$\mathbf{a} \times \mathbf{a}' = \frac{(\mathbf{a} \cdot \mathbf{c})\mathbf{b} - (\mathbf{a} \cdot \mathbf{b})\mathbf{c}}{[\mathbf{a}\ \mathbf{b}\ \mathbf{c}]} \quad \text{...(i)}$$

Similarly, $\mathbf{b} \times \mathbf{b}' = \dfrac{(\mathbf{b} \cdot \mathbf{a})\,\mathbf{c} - (\mathbf{b} \cdot \mathbf{c})\,\mathbf{a}}{[\mathbf{a}\ \mathbf{b}\ \mathbf{c}]}$ ...(ii)

$$\mathbf{c} \times \mathbf{c}' = \frac{(\mathbf{c} \cdot \mathbf{b})\mathbf{a} - (\mathbf{c} \cdot \mathbf{a})\,\mathbf{b}}{[\mathbf{a}\ \mathbf{b}\ \mathbf{c}]} \quad \text{...(iii)}$$

$$\mathbf{a} \times \mathbf{a}' + \mathbf{b} \times \mathbf{b}' + \mathbf{c} \times \mathbf{c}'$$

$$= \frac{(\mathbf{a} \cdot \mathbf{c})\mathbf{b} - (\mathbf{a} \cdot \mathbf{b})\,\mathbf{c} + (\mathbf{b} \cdot \mathbf{a})\mathbf{c} - (\mathbf{b} \cdot \mathbf{c})\,\mathbf{a} + (\mathbf{c} \cdot \mathbf{b})\mathbf{a} - (\mathbf{c} \cdot \mathbf{a})\,\mathbf{b}}{[\mathbf{a}\ \mathbf{b}\ \mathbf{c}]}$$

$$= 0$$

Time Saving Technique

If $\mathbf{a}' = \dfrac{\mathbf{b} \times \mathbf{c}}{[\mathbf{a}\ \mathbf{b}\ \mathbf{c}]}, \mathbf{b}' = \dfrac{\mathbf{c} \times \mathbf{a}}{[\mathbf{a}\ \mathbf{b}\ \mathbf{c}]}, \mathbf{c}' = \dfrac{\mathbf{a} \times \mathbf{b}}{[\mathbf{a}\ \mathbf{b}\ \mathbf{c}]}$, then

$$\mathbf{a} \times \mathbf{a}' + \mathbf{b} \times \mathbf{b}' + \mathbf{c} \times \mathbf{c}' = 0$$

Example 71. If (e_1, e_2, e_3) and (e_1', e_2', e_3') are two sets of non-coplanar vectors such that $\hat{i} = 1, 2, 3$, we have

$$e_i \cdot e_j' = \begin{cases} 1, \text{ if } \hat{i} = \hat{j} \\ 0, \text{ if } \hat{i} \neq \hat{j} \end{cases}, \text{ then find the value of}$$

$[e_1, e_2, e_3], [e_1'\ e_2'\ e_3']$.

Sol. We have, $e_1 \cdot e_2' = 0, e_1 \cdot e_3' = 0$

$\Rightarrow \quad e_1 \perp e_2'$ and $e_1 \perp e_3'$

$\therefore \quad e_1 \,||\, (e_2' \times e_3')$

$\therefore \quad e_1 = \lambda\,(e_2' \times e_3')$ ...(i)

$$e_1 \cdot e_1' = \lambda (e_2' \times e_3') \cdot e_1'$$

$$1 = \lambda\ [e_1'\ e_2'\ e_3'] \quad [\because e_1 e_1' = 1, \text{ given}]$$

$$\lambda = \frac{1}{[e_1'\ e_2'\ e_3']}$$

From Eq. (i), $e_1 = \dfrac{e_2' \times e_3'}{[e_1'\ e_2'\ e_3']}$

Similarly, $e_2 = \dfrac{e_3' \times e_1'}{[e_1'\ e_2'\ e_3']}$ and $e_3 = \dfrac{e_1' \times e_2'}{[e_1'\ e_2'\ e_3']}$

$$\therefore \quad [e_1\ e_2\ e_3] = \frac{[e_2' \times e_3'\ e_3' \times e_1'\ e_1' \times e_2']}{[e_1'\ e_2'\ e_3']^3}$$

$\Rightarrow \quad [e_1, e_2, e_3][e_1'\ e_2'\ e_3']^3 = [e_2' \times e_3'\ e_3' \times e_1'\ e_1' \times e_2']$ ...(ii)

Now, $[e_2' \times e_3'\ e_3' \times e_1'\ e_1' \times e_2'] = [e_1'\ e_2'\ e_3']^2$ ...(iii)

$\therefore$ From Eqs. (ii) and (iii), we get

$$[e_1\ e_2\ e_3]\,[e_1'\ e_2'\ e_3']^3 = [e_1'\ e_2'\ e_3']^2$$

$$[e_1\ e_2\ e_3]\,[e_1'\ e_2'\ e_3'] = 1$$

2.18 Solving of Vector Equations

Solving a vector equation means determining an unknown vector (or a number of vectors satisfying the given conditions)

Generally, to solve vector equations we express the unknown as the linear combination of three non-coplanar vector as; $\mathbf{r} = x\mathbf{a} + y\mathbf{b} + z(\mathbf{a} \times \mathbf{b})$; as $\mathbf{a}$, $\mathbf{b}$ and $\mathbf{a} \times \mathbf{b}$ are non-coplanar and find x, y and z using given conditions.

Sometimes, we can directly solve the given condition, it would be more clear from some examples.

Example 72. Solve the vector equation $\mathbf{r} \times \mathbf{b} = \mathbf{a} \times \mathbf{b}$, $\mathbf{r} \cdot \mathbf{c} = 0$ provided that $\mathbf{c}$ is not perpendicular to $\mathbf{b}$.

Sol. Given, $\mathbf{r} \times \mathbf{b} = \mathbf{a} \times \mathbf{b}$

$\Rightarrow \quad (\mathbf{r} - \mathbf{a}) \times \mathbf{b} = 0$

Hence, $(\mathbf{r} - \mathbf{a})$ and $\mathbf{b}$ are parallel.

$\Rightarrow \quad \mathbf{r} - \mathbf{a} = t\mathbf{b}$ ...(i)

and we known $\mathbf{r} \cdot \mathbf{c} = 0$,

On taking dot product of Eq. (i) by $\mathbf{c}$, we get

$$\mathbf{r} \cdot \mathbf{a} - \mathbf{a} \cdot \mathbf{c} = t(\mathbf{b} \cdot \mathbf{c})$$

$\Rightarrow \quad 0 - \mathbf{a} \cdot \mathbf{c} = t(\mathbf{b} \cdot \mathbf{c})$

$\Rightarrow \quad t = -\left(\dfrac{\mathbf{a} \cdot \mathbf{c}}{\mathbf{b} \cdot \mathbf{c}}\right)$ ...(ii)

$\therefore$ From Eqs. (i) and (ii) solution of $\mathbf{r}$ is

$$\mathbf{r} = \mathbf{a} - \left(\frac{\mathbf{a} \cdot \mathbf{c}}{\mathbf{b} \cdot \mathbf{c}}\right)\mathbf{b}$$

Example 73. Solve for $\mathbf{x}$, such that $\mathbf{A} \cdot \mathbf{X} = \mathbf{C}$ and $\mathbf{A} \times \mathbf{X} = \mathbf{B}$ with $C \neq 0$.

Sol. We have, $\mathbf{A} \times \mathbf{X} = \mathbf{B}$

On taking vector product in both sides with $\mathbf{A}$, we get

$$\mathbf{A} \times \mathbf{B} = \mathbf{A} \times (\mathbf{A} \times \mathbf{X})$$

$$= (\mathbf{A} \cdot \mathbf{X})\,\mathbf{A} - (\mathbf{A} \cdot \mathbf{A})\,\mathbf{X}$$

$$= \mathbf{C}\mathbf{A} - |\,\mathbf{A}\,|^2\,\mathbf{X}$$

[using $\mathbf{A} \cdot \mathbf{X} = \mathbf{C}$ and $\mathbf{A} \cdot \mathbf{A} = |\,\mathbf{A}\,|^2$]

$\Rightarrow \quad |\,\mathbf{A}\,|^2\,\mathbf{X} = \mathbf{C}\mathbf{A} - \mathbf{A} \times \mathbf{B}$

or $\quad \mathbf{X} = \dfrac{\mathbf{C}\mathbf{A} + \mathbf{B} \times \mathbf{A}}{|\,\mathbf{A}\,|^2}$

Example 74. Solve the vector equation $\mathbf{r}\times\mathbf{a}+k\mathbf{r}=\mathbf{b}$, where $\mathbf{a}$ and $\mathbf{b}$ are two given vector and k is any scalar.

Sol. Since, $\mathbf{a}$, $\mathbf{b}$ and $\mathbf{a}\times\mathbf{b}$ are two non-coplanar vectors.

$$\mathbf{r} = x\mathbf{a} + y\mathbf{b} + z(\mathbf{a}\times\mathbf{b}) \quad \text{...(i)}$$

[where x, y and z scalars]

On putting $\mathbf{r}$ in $\mathbf{r}\times\mathbf{a} + k\mathbf{r} = \mathbf{b}$, we get

$$\{x\mathbf{a} + y\mathbf{b} + z(\mathbf{a}\times\mathbf{b})\}\times\mathbf{a} + k\{x\mathbf{a} + y\mathbf{b} + z(\mathbf{a}\times\mathbf{b})\} = \mathbf{b}$$

$$\Rightarrow y(\mathbf{b}\times\mathbf{a}) + z\{(\mathbf{a}\cdot\mathbf{a})\mathbf{b} - (\mathbf{a}\cdot\mathbf{b})\mathbf{a}\} + k\{x\mathbf{a} + y\mathbf{b} + z(\mathbf{a}\times\mathbf{b})\} = \mathbf{b}$$

$$\Rightarrow \{kx - z(\mathbf{a}\cdot\mathbf{b})\}\mathbf{a} + \{ky + z(\mathbf{a}\cdot\mathbf{a})\}\mathbf{b} + \{(-y + zk)\}(\mathbf{a}\times\mathbf{b}) = \mathbf{b}$$

$$\Rightarrow kx - z(\mathbf{a}\cdot\mathbf{b}) = 0,\ ky + z(\mathbf{a}\cdot\mathbf{a}) = 1$$

$$\Rightarrow -y + zk = 0$$

On solving these equations, we get

$$z = \frac{1}{k^2 + |\mathbf{a}|^2},\ x = \frac{\mathbf{a}\cdot\mathbf{b}}{k(|\mathbf{a}|^2 + k^2)}$$

and $$y = \frac{k}{k^2 + |\mathbf{a}|^2}$$

On putting theses value in Eq. (i), we get the solution,

$$\mathbf{r} = \frac{(\mathbf{a}\cdot\mathbf{b})\mathbf{a}}{k(k^2 + |\mathbf{a}|^2)} + \frac{k}{k^2 + |\mathbf{a}|^2}(\mathbf{b}) + \frac{1}{k^2 + |\mathbf{a}|^2}(\mathbf{a}\times\mathbf{b})$$

$$\mathbf{r} = \frac{1}{k^2 + |\mathbf{a}|^2}\left[\frac{(\mathbf{a}\cdot\mathbf{b})\mathbf{a}}{k} + (k)\mathbf{b} + (\mathbf{a}\times\mathbf{b})\right]$$ is required solution.

Example 75. Solve for vectors $\mathbf{A}$ and $\mathbf{B}$, where

$$\mathbf{A} + \mathbf{B} = \mathbf{a},\ \mathbf{A}\times\mathbf{B} = \mathbf{b},\ \mathbf{A}\cdot\mathbf{a} = 1$$

Sol. We have, $$\mathbf{A} + \mathbf{B} = \mathbf{a}$$

$$\Rightarrow \mathbf{A}\cdot\mathbf{a} + \mathbf{B}\cdot\mathbf{a} = \mathbf{a}\cdot\mathbf{a}$$

$$\Rightarrow 1 + \mathbf{B}\cdot\mathbf{a} = \mathbf{a}^2 \quad [\text{given } \mathbf{A}\cdot\mathbf{a} = 1]$$

$$\Rightarrow \mathbf{B}\cdot\mathbf{a} = \mathbf{a}^2 - 1 \quad \text{...(i)}$$

Also, $$\mathbf{A}\times\mathbf{B} = \mathbf{b}$$

$$\Rightarrow \mathbf{a}\times(\mathbf{A}\times\mathbf{B}) = \mathbf{a}\times\mathbf{b}$$

$$\Rightarrow (\mathbf{a}\cdot\mathbf{B})\mathbf{A} - (\mathbf{a}\cdot\mathbf{A})\mathbf{B} = \mathbf{a}\times\mathbf{b}$$

$$\Rightarrow (\mathbf{a}^2 - 1)\mathbf{A} - \mathbf{B} = \mathbf{a}\times\mathbf{b} \quad \text{...(ii)}$$

[using Eq. (i) and $\mathbf{a}\cdot\mathbf{A} = 1$]

and $$\mathbf{A} + \mathbf{B} = \mathbf{a}$$

From Eqs. (ii) and (iii), we get

$$\mathbf{A} = \frac{(\mathbf{a}\times\mathbf{b}) + \mathbf{a}}{\mathbf{a}^2}$$

and $$\mathbf{B} = \mathbf{a} - \left\{\frac{(\mathbf{a}\times\mathbf{b}) + \mathbf{a}}{\mathbf{a}^2}\right\}$$

$$= \frac{(\mathbf{b}\times\mathbf{a}) + \mathbf{a}(\mathbf{a}^2 - 1)}{\mathbf{a}^2}$$

Thus, $$\mathbf{A} = \frac{(\mathbf{a}\times\mathbf{b}) + \mathbf{a}}{\mathbf{a}^2}$$

and $$\mathbf{B} = \frac{(\mathbf{b}\times\mathbf{a}) + \mathbf{a}(\mathbf{a}^2 - 1)}{\mathbf{a}^2}$$

Milestone Practice 2.4

1. Find the value of $\alpha \times (\beta \times \gamma)$, where $\alpha = 2\hat{i} - 10\hat{j} + 2\hat{k}$, $\beta = 3\hat{i} + \hat{j} + 2\hat{k}$ and $\gamma = 2\hat{i} + \hat{j} + 3\hat{k}$.
2. Find the vector of length 3 units which is perpendicular to $\hat{i} + \hat{j} + \hat{k}$ and lies in the plane of $\hat{i} + \hat{j} + \hat{k}$ and $2\hat{i} - 3\hat{j}$.
3. Find the value of $(\mathbf{b} \times \mathbf{c}) \cdot (\mathbf{a} \times \mathbf{d}) + (\mathbf{c} \times \mathbf{a})(\mathbf{b} \times \mathbf{d}) + (\mathbf{a} \times \mathbf{b})(\mathbf{c} \times \mathbf{d})$.
4. If $\hat{i} \times (\mathbf{a} + \hat{i}) + \hat{j} \times (\mathbf{a} \times \hat{j}) + \hat{k} \times (\mathbf{a} \times \hat{k}) = \lambda \mathbf{a}$, then find the value of λ.
5. Prove that $[\mathbf{a} \times \mathbf{b} \;\; \mathbf{a} \times \mathbf{c} \;\; \mathbf{d}] = (\mathbf{a} \cdot \mathbf{d})[\mathbf{a}\;\mathbf{b}\;\mathbf{c}]$.
6. If **a**, **b** and **c** are non-coplanar unit vector such that $\mathbf{a} \times (\mathbf{b} \times \mathbf{c}) = \dfrac{\mathbf{b} + \mathbf{c}}{\sqrt{2}}$, **b** and **c** are non-parallel, then the angle between **a** and **b** is equal to
   (a) $\dfrac{\pi}{4}$ (b) $\dfrac{3\pi}{4}$
   (c) $\dfrac{\pi}{6}$ (d) $\dfrac{2\pi}{3}$
7. If **a**, **b** and **c** are three non-coplanar vectors and **r** is any arbitrary vector. Prove that $[\mathbf{b}\;\mathbf{c}\;\mathbf{r}]\mathbf{a} + [\mathbf{c}\;\mathbf{a}\;\mathbf{r}]\mathbf{b} + [\mathbf{a}\;\mathbf{b}\;\mathbf{r}]\mathbf{c} = [\mathbf{a}\;\mathbf{b}\;\mathbf{c}]\mathbf{r}$.
8. If $[\mathbf{a} \times \mathbf{b} \;\; \mathbf{b} \times \mathbf{c} \;\; \mathbf{c} \times \mathbf{a}]$ has the maximum value, then the value of $|(\mathbf{a} \times \mathbf{b}) \times \mathbf{c}|^2$ is equal to
   (a) -1 (b) 0
   (c) 1 (d) 2
9. Let $\mathbf{a} = a_1\hat{i} + a_2\hat{j} + a_3\hat{k}$, $\mathbf{b} = b_1\hat{i} + b_2\hat{j} + b_3\hat{k}$ and $\mathbf{c} = c_1\hat{i} + c_2\hat{j} + c_3\hat{k}$ be three non-zero vectors such that **c** is a unit vector perpendicular to both **a** and **b**. If the angle between **a** and **b** is $\dfrac{\pi}{6}$, then prove that
$$\begin{vmatrix} a_1 & a_2 & a_3 \\ b_1 & b_2 & b_3 \\ c_1 & c_2 & c_3 \end{vmatrix}^2 = \frac{1}{4}(a_1^2 + a_2^2 + a_3^2)(b_1^2 + b_2^2 + b_3^2).$$
10. Let **a** and **c** be unit vectors at an angle $\dfrac{\pi}{3}$ with each other. If $[\mathbf{a} \times (\mathbf{b} \times \mathbf{c})] \cdot (\mathbf{a} \times \mathbf{c}) = 5$, then the value of $[\mathbf{a}\;\mathbf{b}\;\mathbf{c}]$ is equal to
    (a) 10 (b) 11
    (c) 12 (d) None of these
11. If the vectors **b**, **c** and **d** are not coplanar, and $(\mathbf{a} \times \mathbf{b}) \times (\mathbf{c} \times \mathbf{d}) + (\mathbf{a} \times \mathbf{c}) \times (\mathbf{d} \times \mathbf{b}) + (\mathbf{a} \times \mathbf{d}) \times (\mathbf{b} \times \mathbf{c}) = \lambda\,[\mathbf{b}\;\mathbf{c}\;\mathbf{d}]\,\mathbf{a}$, then the value of λ is equal to
    (a) -2 (b) -1 (c) 0 (d) 1
12. Let **p**, **q** and **r** be three mutually perpendicular vectors of same magnitude. If a vector **x** satisfies the equation $\mathbf{p} \times [(\mathbf{x} - \mathbf{q}) \times \mathbf{p}] + \mathbf{q} \times [(\mathbf{x} - \mathbf{r}) \times \mathbf{q}] + \mathbf{r} \times [(\mathbf{x} - \mathbf{p}) \times \mathbf{r}] = 0$, then find the value of **x**.
13. A set of vectors reciprocal to the set of vectors $-\hat{i} + \hat{j} + \hat{k}$, $\hat{i} - \hat{j} + \hat{k}$, $\hat{i} + \hat{j} + \hat{k}$ is equal to
    (a) $\mathbf{a}' = \dfrac{\hat{i} + \hat{k}}{2}$, $\mathbf{b}' = \dfrac{-\hat{j} + \hat{k}}{2}$, $\mathbf{c}' = \dfrac{\hat{i} + \hat{j}}{2}$
    (b) $\mathbf{a}' = \dfrac{-\hat{i} + \hat{k}}{2}$, $\mathbf{b}' = \dfrac{\hat{j} + \hat{k}}{2}$, $\mathbf{c}' = \dfrac{\hat{i} + \hat{j}}{2}$
    (c) $\mathbf{a}' = \dfrac{-\hat{i} + \hat{k}}{2}$, $\mathbf{b}' = \dfrac{-\hat{j} + \hat{k}}{2}$, $\mathbf{c}' = \dfrac{\hat{i} + \hat{j}}{2}$
    (d) $\mathbf{a}' = \dfrac{-\hat{i} + \hat{k}}{2}$, $\mathbf{b}' = \dfrac{-\hat{j} + \hat{k}}{2}$, $\mathbf{c}' = \dfrac{\hat{i} - \hat{j}}{2}$
14. If **a**, **b**, **c** and **a**′, **b**′, **c**′ are reciprocal system of vectors, then prove that
$$\mathbf{a}' \times \mathbf{b}' + \mathbf{b}' \times \mathbf{c}' + \mathbf{c}' \times \mathbf{a}' = \frac{\mathbf{a} + \mathbf{b} + \mathbf{c}}{[\mathbf{a}\;\mathbf{b}\;\mathbf{c}]}.$$
15. Let **a**, **b** and **c** be non-coplanar vectors and let the equations **a**′, **b**′, **c**′ are reciprocal system of vector **a**, **b**, **c**, then prove that $\mathbf{a} \times \mathbf{a}' + \mathbf{b} \times \mathbf{b}' + \mathbf{c} \times \mathbf{c}'$ is null vector.
16. If **a**, **b** and **c** are three non-coplanar and non-zero vectors, then prove that $(\mathbf{a} \cdot \mathbf{a})\mathbf{b} \times \mathbf{c} + (\mathbf{a} \cdot \mathbf{b})\mathbf{c} \times \mathbf{a} + (\mathbf{a} \cdot \mathbf{c})\mathbf{a} \times \mathbf{b} = [\mathbf{b}\;\mathbf{c}\;\mathbf{a}]\mathbf{a}$.
17. If $\mathbf{a} = \mathbf{p} + \mathbf{q}$, $\mathbf{p} \times \mathbf{b} = 0$ and $\mathbf{q} \cdot \mathbf{b} = 0$, then prove that $\dfrac{\mathbf{b} \times (\mathbf{a} \times \mathbf{b})}{\mathbf{b} \cdot \mathbf{b}} = \mathbf{q}$.
18. Let $\mathbf{a} = \hat{i} - 3\hat{j} + 4\hat{k}$, $\mathbf{b} = 6\hat{i} + 4\hat{j} - 8\hat{k}$, and $\mathbf{c} = 5\hat{i} + 2\hat{j} + 5\hat{k}$ and a vector **r** satisfy the relation $\mathbf{r} \times \mathbf{b} = \mathbf{c} \times \mathbf{b}$, $\mathbf{r} \cdot \mathbf{a} = 0$, then show that $\dfrac{|\mathbf{b}|}{|\mathbf{r} - \mathbf{c}|} = 2$.
19. Solve $\mathbf{r} \times \mathbf{b} = \mathbf{a}$, where **a** and **b** are given vectors show that $\mathbf{a} \cdot \mathbf{b} = 0$.
20. Find **r**, if $\mathbf{r} \cdot \mathbf{a} = m$ and $\mathbf{r} \times \mathbf{b} = \mathbf{c} \times \mathbf{b}$, where $\mathbf{a} \cdot \mathbf{b} \neq 0$.

Answer Key

1. 0 2. $\dfrac{3}{\sqrt{114}}(7\hat{i} - 8\hat{j} + \hat{k})$ 3. 0 4. 2 6. (b) 8. (b) 10. (d)
11. (a) 12. $\dfrac{1}{2}(\mathbf{p} + \mathbf{q} + \mathbf{r})$ 13. (c) 20. $\dfrac{(\mathbf{a} \cdot \mathbf{b})\,\mathbf{c} - (m - \mathbf{a} \cdot \mathbf{c})\,\mathbf{b}}{\mathbf{a} \cdot \mathbf{b}}$

For Detailed Solution

JEE Pattern
EXAMPLES

Single Option Correct Type Questions

Example 1 *Angle between diagonals of a parallelogram whose sides are represented by* $\mathbf{a} = 2\hat{\mathbf{i}} + \hat{\mathbf{j}} + \hat{\mathbf{k}}$ *and* $\mathbf{b} = \hat{\mathbf{i}} - \hat{\mathbf{j}} - \hat{\mathbf{k}}$

(a) $\cos^{-1}\left(\frac{1}{3}\right)$ (b) $\cos^{-1}\left(\frac{1}{2}\right)$

(c) $\cos^{-1}\left(\frac{4}{9}\right)$ (d) $\cos^{-1}\left(\frac{5}{9}\right)$

Sol. (a) Let **c** and **d** be the diagonals of parallelogram.

Then, $\mathbf{c} = \mathbf{a} + \mathbf{b}$ and $\mathbf{d} = \mathbf{a} - \mathbf{b}$

$\Rightarrow \mathbf{c} = 3\hat{\mathbf{i}}$ and $\mathbf{d} = \hat{\mathbf{i}} + 2\hat{\mathbf{j}} + 2\hat{\mathbf{k}}$

Let θ be the angle between **c** and **d**.

Then, $$\cos\theta = \frac{\mathbf{c}\cdot\mathbf{d}}{|\mathbf{c}||\mathbf{d}|} = \frac{3\hat{\mathbf{i}}\cdot(\hat{\mathbf{i}} + 2\hat{\mathbf{j}} + 2\hat{\mathbf{k}})}{\sqrt{(3)^2}\sqrt{1^2+2^2+2^2}} = \frac{3}{3\times 3} = \frac{1}{3}$$

$\therefore \theta = \cos^{-1}\left(\frac{1}{3}\right)$

Example 2 *Let* $a, b > 0$ *and* $\alpha = \frac{\hat{\mathbf{i}}}{a} + \frac{4\hat{\mathbf{j}}}{b} + b\hat{\mathbf{k}}$ *and* $\beta = b\hat{\mathbf{i}} + a\hat{\mathbf{j}} + \frac{1}{b}\hat{\mathbf{k}}$*, then the maximum value of* $\frac{10}{5+\alpha\cdot\beta}$ *is*

(a) 1 (b) 2 (c) 4 (d) 8

Sol. (a) Given, $\alpha = \frac{\hat{\mathbf{i}}}{a} + \frac{4\hat{\mathbf{j}}}{b} + b\hat{\mathbf{k}}$ and $\beta = b\hat{\mathbf{i}} + a\hat{\mathbf{j}} + \frac{1}{b}\hat{\mathbf{k}}$

$$\alpha\cdot\beta = \left(\frac{\hat{\mathbf{i}}}{a} + \frac{4\hat{\mathbf{j}}}{b} + b\hat{\mathbf{k}}\right)\cdot\left(b\hat{\mathbf{i}} + a\hat{\mathbf{j}} + \frac{1}{b}\hat{\mathbf{k}}\right) = \frac{b}{a} + \frac{4a}{b} + 1$$

Now using AM $\geq$ GM on the two positive terms $\frac{b}{a}$ and $\frac{4a}{b}$, we have

$$\frac{\frac{b}{a} + \frac{4a}{b}}{2} \geq \sqrt{\frac{b}{a}\cdot\frac{4a}{b}}$$

$$\Rightarrow \frac{b}{a} + \frac{4a}{b} \geq 4 \Rightarrow \frac{b}{a} + \frac{4a}{b} + 1 \geq 5$$

Hence, the least value of $\alpha\cdot\beta$ is 5.

$\therefore$ Maximum value of $\frac{10}{5+\alpha\cdot\beta} = \frac{10}{5+5} = 1$

JEE SCANNER

Example 3 Similar to PYQ Asked in JEE Main 2024

Let $\mathbf{a} = 3\hat{\mathbf{i}} + 2\hat{\mathbf{j}} - \hat{\mathbf{k}}$, $\mathbf{b} = 2\hat{\mathbf{i}} + \hat{\mathbf{j}} + 2\hat{\mathbf{k}}$ *be two vectors. Let* $\mathbf{c} = x\hat{\mathbf{i}} + y\hat{\mathbf{j}} - \hat{\mathbf{k}}$ *be the vector such that* $(\mathbf{a}\times\mathbf{b})\cdot\mathbf{c} = 3$ *and* $\mathbf{a}\cdot\mathbf{c} = 9$*. Then,* $\mathbf{c}\cdot[(\mathbf{a}\times\mathbf{b}) - \mathbf{a} + 2\mathbf{c}]$ *is equal to*

(a) 9 (b) 6 (c) 12 (d) 3

Sol. (b) Given, $\mathbf{a} = 3\hat{\mathbf{i}} + 2\hat{\mathbf{j}} - \hat{\mathbf{k}}$, $\mathbf{b} = 2\hat{\mathbf{i}} + \hat{\mathbf{j}} + 2\hat{\mathbf{k}}$

and $\mathbf{c} = x\hat{\mathbf{i}} + y\hat{\mathbf{j}} - \hat{\mathbf{k}}$

Thus, $\mathbf{a}\times\mathbf{b} = 5\hat{\mathbf{i}} - 8\hat{\mathbf{j}} - \hat{\mathbf{k}}$ and $(\mathbf{a}\times\mathbf{b})\cdot\mathbf{c} = 3$ [given]

$\Rightarrow (5\hat{\mathbf{i}} - 8\hat{\mathbf{j}} - \hat{\mathbf{k}})\cdot(x\hat{\mathbf{i}} + y\hat{\mathbf{j}} - \hat{\mathbf{k}}) = 3$

$\Rightarrow 5x - 8y + 1 = 3$

$\Rightarrow 5x - 8y = 2$ ...(i)

Also, $\mathbf{a}\cdot\mathbf{c} = 9 \Rightarrow 3x + 2y + 1 = 9 \Rightarrow 3x + 2y = 8$ ...(ii)

From Eqs. (i) and (ii), we get $x = 2, y = 1$

$\therefore \mathbf{c} = 2\hat{\mathbf{i}} + \hat{\mathbf{j}} - \hat{\mathbf{k}}$

Consider, $\mathbf{c}\cdot[(\mathbf{a}\times\mathbf{b}) - \mathbf{a} + 2\mathbf{c}] = \mathbf{c}\cdot(\mathbf{a}\times\mathbf{b}) - \mathbf{c}\cdot\mathbf{a} + 2|\mathbf{c}|^2$

$= 3 - 9 + 12 = 6$

$[\because |\mathbf{c}| = \sqrt{(2)^2 + (1)^2 + (-1)^2} = \sqrt{6}]$

Skill Builder

Let $\mathbf{a} = 2\hat{\mathbf{i}} + 3\hat{\mathbf{j}} - 4\hat{\mathbf{k}}$, $\mathbf{b} = 3\hat{\mathbf{i}} - \hat{\mathbf{j}} + 5\hat{\mathbf{k}}$ and $\mathbf{c} = x\hat{\mathbf{i}} + y\hat{\mathbf{j}} - \hat{\mathbf{k}}$ be the vectors such that $(\mathbf{a}\times\mathbf{b})\cdot\mathbf{c} = 44$ and $\mathbf{a}\cdot\mathbf{c} = 17$. Then, $\mathbf{c}\cdot[(\mathbf{a}\times\mathbf{b}) - \mathbf{a} + 2\mathbf{c}]$ is equal to

(a) 115 (b) −27

(c) 27 (d) 81

For Sol.

Example 4 *Let the cosine of angle between the vectors* **p** *and* **q** *be* λ *such that* $2\mathbf{p} + \mathbf{q} = \hat{\mathbf{i}} + \hat{\mathbf{j}}$ *and* $\mathbf{p} + 2\mathbf{q} = \hat{\mathbf{i}} - \hat{\mathbf{j}}$*, then* λ *is equal to*

(a) $\frac{5}{9}$ (b) $-\frac{4}{5}$ (c) $\frac{3}{9}$ (d) $\frac{7}{9}$

Sol. (b) It is given that $2\mathbf{p} + \mathbf{q} = \hat{\mathbf{i}} + \hat{\mathbf{j}}$ and $\mathbf{p} + 2\mathbf{q} = \hat{\mathbf{i}} - \hat{\mathbf{j}}$

$\Rightarrow \mathbf{p} = \frac{1}{3}\hat{\mathbf{i}} + \hat{\mathbf{j}}$ and $\mathbf{q} = \frac{1}{3}\hat{\mathbf{i}} - \hat{\mathbf{j}}$

Let θ be the angle between $\mathbf{p}$ and $\mathbf{q}$. Then

$$\cos\theta = \frac{\mathbf{p}\cdot\mathbf{q}}{|\mathbf{p}||\mathbf{q}|} = \frac{\left(\frac{1}{3}\hat{\mathbf{i}}+\hat{\mathbf{j}}\right)\cdot\left(\frac{1}{3}\hat{\mathbf{i}}-\hat{\mathbf{j}}\right)}{\sqrt{\left(\frac{1}{3}\right)^2+(1)^2}\sqrt{\left(\frac{1}{3}\right)^2+(-1)^2}}$$

$$= \frac{\frac{1}{9}-1}{\sqrt{\frac{1}{9}+1}\sqrt{\frac{1}{9}+1}} = \frac{-\frac{8}{9}}{\frac{10}{9}} = -\frac{8}{10} = -\frac{4}{5}$$

Example 5 *Let* $\mathbf{u}$, $\mathbf{v}$ *and* $\mathbf{w}$ *be such that* $|\mathbf{u}|=1$, $|\mathbf{v}|=2$, $|\mathbf{w}|=3$. *If the projection* $\mathbf{v}$ *along* $\mathbf{u}$ *is equal to that of* $\mathbf{w}$ *along* $\mathbf{u}$. *Also,* $\mathbf{v}$ *and* $\mathbf{w}$ *are perpendicular to each other, then* $|\mathbf{u}-\mathbf{v}+\mathbf{w}|$ *equals.*

(a) $\sqrt{14}$ (b) $\sqrt{7}$ (c) 2 (d) 14

Sol. (a) We have, projection of $\mathbf{v}$ along $\mathbf{u}$ = projection of $\mathbf{w}$ along $\mathbf{u}$

$$\Rightarrow \frac{\mathbf{v}\cdot\mathbf{u}}{|\mathbf{u}|} = \frac{\mathbf{w}\cdot\mathbf{u}}{|\mathbf{u}|} \Rightarrow \mathbf{v}\cdot\mathbf{u} = \mathbf{w}\cdot\mathbf{u} \quad \text{... (i)}$$

Also, $\mathbf{v}$ and $\mathbf{w}$ are perpendicular to each other

$$\therefore \quad \mathbf{v}\cdot\mathbf{w} = 0 \quad \text{... (ii)}$$

Now, $|\mathbf{u}-\mathbf{v}+\mathbf{w}|^2 = |\mathbf{u}|^2+|\mathbf{v}|^2+|\mathbf{w}|^2-2(\mathbf{u}\cdot\mathbf{v}) - 2(\mathbf{v}\cdot\mathbf{w})+2(\mathbf{u}\cdot\mathbf{w})$

$$\Rightarrow |\mathbf{u}-\mathbf{v}+\mathbf{w}|^2 = 1+4+9 \Rightarrow |\mathbf{u}-\mathbf{v}+\mathbf{w}| = \sqrt{14}$$

Example 6 *If* $\mathbf{a}$, $\mathbf{b}$ *and* $\mathbf{c}$ *are unit vectors, then* $|\mathbf{a}-\mathbf{b}|^2+|\mathbf{b}-\mathbf{c}|^2+|\mathbf{c}-\mathbf{a}|^2$ *does not exceed*

(a) 4 (b) 9 (c) 8 (d) 6

Sol. (b) We have, $|\mathbf{a}-\mathbf{b}|^2+|\mathbf{b}-\mathbf{c}|^2+|\mathbf{c}-\mathbf{a}|^2$

$$= |\mathbf{a}| + |\mathbf{b}|^2 - 2(\mathbf{a}\cdot\mathbf{b}) + |\mathbf{b}|^2 + |\mathbf{c}|^2 - 2(\mathbf{b}\cdot\mathbf{c}) + |\mathbf{c}|^2 + |\mathbf{a}|^2 - 2(\mathbf{c}\cdot\mathbf{a})$$

$$= 2[|\mathbf{a}|^2+|\mathbf{b}|^2+|\mathbf{c}|^2-(\mathbf{a}\cdot\mathbf{b}+\mathbf{b}\cdot\mathbf{c}+\mathbf{c}\cdot\mathbf{a})]$$

$$= 2[3-(\mathbf{a}\cdot\mathbf{b}+\mathbf{b}\cdot\mathbf{c}+\mathbf{c}\cdot\mathbf{a})] = 6-2(\mathbf{a}\cdot\mathbf{b}+\mathbf{b}\cdot\mathbf{c}+\mathbf{c}\cdot\mathbf{a}) \quad \text{...(i)}$$

Now, $|\mathbf{a}+\mathbf{b}+\mathbf{c}|^2 \ge 0$

$$\Rightarrow |\mathbf{a}|^2+|\mathbf{b}|^2+|\mathbf{c}|^2+2(\mathbf{a}\cdot\mathbf{b}+\mathbf{b}\cdot\mathbf{c}+\mathbf{c}\cdot\mathbf{a}) \ge 0$$

$$\Rightarrow 3+2(\mathbf{a}\cdot\mathbf{b}+\mathbf{b}\cdot\mathbf{c}+\mathbf{c}\cdot\mathbf{a}) \ge 0$$

$$\Rightarrow \mathbf{a}\cdot\mathbf{b}+\mathbf{b}\cdot\mathbf{c}+\mathbf{c}\cdot\mathbf{a} \ge -\frac{3}{2}$$

$$\Rightarrow -2(\mathbf{a}\cdot\mathbf{b}+\mathbf{b}\cdot\mathbf{c}+\mathbf{c}\cdot\mathbf{a}) \le 3 \quad \text{...(ii)}$$

From Eqs. (i) and (ii), we get

$$|\mathbf{a}-\mathbf{b}|^2+|\mathbf{b}-\mathbf{c}|^2+|\mathbf{c}-\mathbf{a}|^2 \le 6+3$$

$$\Rightarrow |\mathbf{a}-\mathbf{b}|^2+|\mathbf{b}-\mathbf{c}|^2+|\mathbf{c}-\mathbf{a}|^2 \le 9$$

Example 7 *The vectors* $\mathbf{a} = 2\lambda^2\hat{\mathbf{i}}+4\lambda\hat{\mathbf{j}}+\hat{\mathbf{k}}$ *and* $\mathbf{b} = 7\hat{\mathbf{i}}-2\hat{\mathbf{j}}+\lambda\hat{\mathbf{k}}$ *make an obtuse angle whereas the angle between* $\mathbf{b}$ *and* $\hat{\mathbf{k}}$ *is acute and less than* $\pi/6$,

(a) $0<\lambda<\frac{1}{2}$ (b) $\lambda>\sqrt{159}$

(c) $-\frac{1}{2}<\lambda<0$ (d) null set

> **Decoding the Question**
> If **a** and **b** are non-zero vector and angle between **a** and **b** is obtuse, then $\mathbf{a}\cdot\mathbf{b}<0$.

Sol. (d) $(2\lambda^2\hat{\mathbf{i}}+4\lambda\hat{\mathbf{j}}+\hat{\mathbf{k}})\cdot(7\hat{\mathbf{i}}-2\hat{\mathbf{j}}+\lambda\hat{\mathbf{k}})<0 \Rightarrow 14\lambda^2-8\lambda+\lambda<0$

$$\Rightarrow 7\lambda(2\lambda-1)<0 \Rightarrow 0<\lambda<\frac{1}{2} \quad \text{...(i)}$$

Angle between $\mathbf{b}$ and $\hat{\mathbf{k}}$ is acute and less than $\frac{\pi}{6}$.

$$\mathbf{b}\cdot\hat{\mathbf{k}} = |\mathbf{b}|\cdot|\hat{\mathbf{k}}|\cos\theta \Rightarrow \lambda = \sqrt{53+\lambda^2}1\cdot\cos\theta$$

$$\Rightarrow \cos\theta = \frac{\lambda}{\sqrt{53+\lambda^2}}$$

$$\theta<\frac{\pi}{6} \Rightarrow \cos\theta>\cos\frac{\pi}{6}$$

$$\Rightarrow \cos\theta>\frac{\sqrt{3}}{2} \Rightarrow \frac{\lambda}{\sqrt{53+\lambda^2}}>\frac{\sqrt{3}}{2}$$

$$\Rightarrow 4\lambda^2-3(53+\lambda^2)>0 \Rightarrow \lambda^2>159$$

$$\Rightarrow \lambda>\sqrt{159} \text{ or } \lambda<-\sqrt{159} \quad \text{...(ii)}$$

From Eqs. (i) and (ii), $\lambda \in \phi$

$\therefore$ Domain of λ is null set.

Example 8 *In cartesian coordinates, the point A is* (x_1, y_1), *where* $x_1 = 1$ *on the curve* $y = x^2+x+10$. *Then, tangent at A cuts the X-axis at B. The value of the dot product* $\mathbf{OA}\cdot\mathbf{AB}$ *is*

(a) $-\frac{520}{3}$ (b) -148 (c) 140 (d) 12

Sol. (b) Given curve is $y = x^2+x+10$ ...(i)

When $x=1$, $y = 1^2+1+10 = 12$

$\therefore$ $A = (1, 12)$

$\therefore$ $\mathbf{OA} = \hat{\mathbf{i}}+12\hat{\mathbf{j}}$

From Eq. (i), $\frac{dy}{dx} = 2x+1$

Equation of tangent at A is $y-12 = \left(\frac{dy}{dx}\right)_{(1,12)}(x-1)$

$$\Rightarrow y-12 = (2\times1+1)(x-1) \Rightarrow y-12 = 3x-3$$

$$\therefore \quad y = 3(x+3)$$

This tangent cuts X-axis (i.e. $y=0$) at $(-3, 0)$

$\therefore$ $B = (-3, 0)$

$\mathbf{OB} = -3\hat{\mathbf{i}}+0\cdot\hat{\mathbf{j}} = -3\hat{\mathbf{i}}$,

$\therefore$ $\mathbf{OA}\cdot\mathbf{AB} = \mathbf{OA}\cdot(\mathbf{OB}-\mathbf{OA})$

$$= (\hat{\mathbf{i}}+12\hat{\mathbf{j}})\cdot(-3\hat{\mathbf{i}}-\hat{\mathbf{i}}-12\hat{\mathbf{j}}) = (\hat{\mathbf{i}}+12\hat{\mathbf{j}})\cdot(-4\hat{\mathbf{i}}-12\hat{\mathbf{j}})$$

$$= -4-144 = -148$$

Example 9 *In a tetrahedron OABC, the edges are of lengths,* $|OA| = |BC| = a$, $|OB| = |AC| = b$, $|OC| = |AB| = c$. *Let* G_1 *and* G_2 *be the centroids of the triangles ABC and AOC such that* $OG_1 \perp BG_2$, *then the value of* $\frac{a^2+c^2}{b^2}$ *is*

(a) 2 (b) 3 (c) 6 (d) 9

Sol. (b) $\mathbf{OG}_1 \cdot \mathbf{BG}_2 = 0$.

$$\Rightarrow \quad \frac{a+b+c}{3} \cdot \frac{a+c-3b}{3} = 0$$

$$\Rightarrow \quad a^2 + c^2 - 3b^2 + 2a \cdot c - 2b \cdot c - 2a \cdot b = 0$$

Now, $\quad |c-a|^2 = b^2, |c-b|^2 = a^2$ and $|a-b|^2 = c^2$

$$\therefore \quad 2a \cdot c = a^2 + c^2 - b^2,\ 2b \cdot c = b^2 + c^2 - a^2,$$
$$2a \cdot b = a^2 + b^2 - c^2$$

On putting in the above result, we get $2a^2 + 2c^2 - 6b^2 = 0$

$$\Rightarrow \quad \frac{a^2 + c^2}{b^2} = 3$$

Example 10 *If a, b, c and A, B, C $\in R - \{0\}$ such that $aA + bB + cC + \sqrt{(a^2+b^2+c^2)(A^2+B^2+C^2)} = 0$, then value of $\frac{aB}{bA} + \frac{bC}{cB} + \frac{cA}{aC}$ is*

(a) 3 (b) 4 (c) 5 (d) 6

Sol. (a) Let $\mathbf{r}_1 = a\hat{\mathbf{i}} + b\hat{\mathbf{j}} + c\hat{\mathbf{k}}$ and $\mathbf{r}_2 = A\hat{\mathbf{i}} + B\hat{\mathbf{j}} + C\hat{\mathbf{k}}$

$$\Rightarrow \quad \mathbf{r}_1 \cdot \mathbf{r}_2 = aA + bB + cC$$

$$\Rightarrow \quad |\mathbf{r}_1||\mathbf{r}_2| = \sqrt{(a^2+b^2+c^2)(A^2+B^2+C^2)}$$

$$\therefore \quad \mathbf{r}_1 \cdot \mathbf{r}_2 = -|\mathbf{r}_1||\mathbf{r}_2| \quad \text{[as given condition]}$$

$\Rightarrow$ $\mathbf{r}_1$ and $\mathbf{r}_2$ are anti-parallel.

$$\Rightarrow \quad \frac{a}{A} = \frac{b}{B} = \frac{c}{C} = k, \text{ where } k \text{ is any constant}$$

$$\Rightarrow \quad \frac{aB}{bA} + \frac{bC}{cB} + \frac{cA}{aC} = 3$$

Example 11 *If $(\mathbf{a} + 3\mathbf{b}) \cdot (7\mathbf{a} - 5\mathbf{b}) = 0$ and $(\mathbf{a} - 4\mathbf{b}) \cdot (7\mathbf{a} - 2\mathbf{b}) = 0$. Then, the angle between* **a** *and* **b** *is*

(a) 60° (b) 30°
(c) 90° (d) None of these

Sol. (a) We have, $\quad (\mathbf{a} + 3\mathbf{b}) \cdot (7\mathbf{a} - 5\mathbf{b}) = 0$

$$\Rightarrow \quad 7|\mathbf{a}|^2 + 16\mathbf{a} \cdot \mathbf{b} - 15|\mathbf{b}|^2 = 0 \quad \text{...(i)}$$

and $\quad (\mathbf{a} - 4\mathbf{b}) \cdot (7\mathbf{a} - 2\mathbf{b}) = 0$

$$\Rightarrow \quad 7|\mathbf{a}|^2 - 30\mathbf{a} \cdot \mathbf{b} + 8|\mathbf{b}|^2 = 0 \quad \text{...(ii)}$$

From Eqs. (i) and (ii), we get

$$\mathbf{a} \cdot \mathbf{b} = \frac{15|\mathbf{b}|^2 - 7|\mathbf{a}|^2}{16}$$

and $$\mathbf{a} \cdot \mathbf{b} = \frac{1}{30}(7|\mathbf{a}|^2 + 8|\mathbf{b}|^2)$$

$$\Rightarrow \quad \frac{15|\mathbf{b}|^2 - 7|\mathbf{a}|^2}{8} = \frac{1}{15}(7|\mathbf{a}|^2 + 8|\mathbf{b}|^2)$$

$$\Rightarrow \quad 15(15|\mathbf{b}|^2 - 7|\mathbf{a}|^2) = 8(7|\mathbf{a}|^2 + 8|\mathbf{b}|^2)$$

$$\Rightarrow \quad 225|\mathbf{b}|^2 - 105|\mathbf{a}|^2 = 56|\mathbf{a}|^2 + 64|\mathbf{b}|^2$$

$$\Rightarrow \quad 161|\mathbf{b}|^2 = 161|\mathbf{a}|^2 \Rightarrow |\mathbf{b}|^2 = |\mathbf{a}|^2$$

From Eq. (i), we get

$$16\mathbf{a} \cdot \mathbf{b} = 15|\mathbf{b}|^2 - 7|\mathbf{a}|^2 = 15|\mathbf{b}|^2 - 7|\mathbf{b}|^2$$

$$\Rightarrow \quad 16\mathbf{a} \cdot \mathbf{b} = 8|\mathbf{b}|^2$$

$$\Rightarrow \quad \mathbf{a} \cdot \mathbf{b} = \frac{1}{2}|\mathbf{b}|^2 \Rightarrow |\mathbf{a}||\mathbf{b}|\cos\theta = \frac{1}{2}|\mathbf{b}|^2 \Rightarrow \cos\theta = \frac{1}{2}$$

$[\because |\mathbf{b}|^2 = |\mathbf{a}|^2]$

$$\therefore \quad \theta = 60°$$

JEE SCANNER

Example 12 Similar to PYQ Asked in JEE Main 2024

Let $\mathbf{a} = a_1\hat{\mathbf{i}} + a_2\hat{\mathbf{j}} + a_3\hat{\mathbf{k}}$ and **b** *be a unit vector such that $|\mathbf{a}| = 5$ and $|\mathbf{a} \times \mathbf{c}| = 5$. If $\mathbf{c} = 3\mathbf{b} + 2(\mathbf{b} \times \mathbf{c})$, then the angle between* **a** *and* **c** *is equal to ....*

(a) $\cos^{-1}\left(\frac{\sqrt{2}}{3}\right)$ (b) $\cos^{-1}\left(\frac{2}{3}\right)$

(c) $\cos^{-1}\left(\frac{1}{3}\right)$ (d) $\cos^{-1}\left(\frac{2\sqrt{2}}{3}\right)$

Sol. Given, $|\mathbf{a}| = 5$, $|\mathbf{b}| = 1$ and $|\mathbf{a} \times \mathbf{c}| = 5$, and $\mathbf{c} = 3\mathbf{b} + 2(\mathbf{b} \times \mathbf{c})$

Dot product of c with b on both sides

$$\mathbf{b} \cdot \mathbf{c} = 3|\mathbf{b}|^2 + 2(\mathbf{b} \times \mathbf{c}) \cdot \mathbf{b} = 3 \cdot 1 = 3$$

and $\quad |c|^2 = 9|\mathbf{b}|^2 + 4|\mathbf{b} \times \mathbf{c}|^2$

$$\Rightarrow \quad |c|^2 = 9|\mathbf{b}|^2 + 4[|b|^2|c|^2 - (\mathbf{b} \cdot \mathbf{c})^2]$$

$$\Rightarrow \quad |c|^2 = 9 + 4[|c|^2 - 9] \Rightarrow |c|^2 = 9 + 4|c|^2 - 36$$

$$\Rightarrow \quad -3|c|^2 = -27 \Rightarrow |c|^2 = 9 \Rightarrow |c| = 3$$

Now, $\quad |\mathbf{a} \times \mathbf{c}| = 5 \Rightarrow |\mathbf{a}|^2|\mathbf{c}|^2 - (\mathbf{a} \cdot \mathbf{c})^2 = 25$

$$\Rightarrow \quad 25 \times 9 - (\mathbf{a} \cdot \mathbf{c})^2 = 25 \Rightarrow (\mathbf{a} \cdot \mathbf{c})^2 = 225 - 25 = 200$$

$$\Rightarrow \quad \mathbf{a} \cdot \mathbf{c} = \sqrt{200} = 10\sqrt{2}$$

$$\therefore \cos\theta = \frac{\mathbf{a} \cdot \mathbf{c}}{|\mathbf{a}||\mathbf{c}|} = \frac{10\sqrt{2}}{5 \times 3} = \frac{2\sqrt{2}}{3} \Rightarrow \theta = \cos^{-1}\left(\frac{2\sqrt{2}}{3}\right)$$

Skill Builder

Let $\mathbf{a} = a_1\hat{\mathbf{i}} + a_2\hat{\mathbf{j}} + a_3\hat{\mathbf{k}}$ and **b** be a unit vector such that $|\mathbf{a}| = 4$ and $|\mathbf{a} \times \mathbf{c}| = 6$. If $\mathbf{c} = 2\mathbf{b} + 5(\mathbf{b} \times \mathbf{c})$, then the angle between **a** and **c** is equal to ....

(a) $\cos^{-1}\left(\frac{\sqrt{7}}{4}\right)$ (b) $\cos^{-1}\left(\frac{2}{\sqrt{7}}\right)$

(c) $\cos^{-1}\left(\frac{\sqrt{2}}{7}\right)$ (d) $\cos^{-1}\left(\frac{\sqrt{7}}{2}\right)$

For Sol.

Example 13 *Let two non-collinear vectors* **a** *and* **b** *inclined at an angle $\frac{2\pi}{3}$ be such that $|\mathbf{a}| = 3$ and $|\mathbf{b}| = 2$. If a point P moves so that at any time t its position vector* **OP** *(where, O is the origin) is given as $\mathbf{OP} = \left(t + \frac{1}{t}\right)\mathbf{a} + \left(t - \frac{1}{t}\right)\mathbf{b}$, then least distance of P from the origin is*

(a) $\sqrt{2\sqrt{133} - 10}$ (b) $\sqrt{2\sqrt{133} + 10}$

(c) $\sqrt{5 + \sqrt{133}}$ (d) None of these

Sol. (b) We have, $|\mathbf{OP}|^2 = \left(t+\frac{1}{t}\right)^2 |\mathbf{a}|^2 + \left(t-\frac{1}{t}\right)^2 |\mathbf{b}|^2 + 2\left(t^2-\frac{1}{t^2}\right)|\mathbf{a}||\mathbf{b}|\cos\left(\frac{2\pi}{3}\right)$

$$\therefore \quad |\mathbf{OP}|^2 = 9\left(t+\frac{1}{t}\right)^2 + 4\left(t-\frac{1}{t}\right)^2 + 2\left(t^2-\frac{1}{t^2}\right)3\cdot 2\cdot\left(\frac{-1}{2}\right)$$

$$= 9\left(t^2+\frac{1}{t^2}+2\right) + 4\left(t^2+\frac{1}{t^2}-2\right) - 6\left(t^2-\frac{1}{t^2}\right)$$

$$= 7t^2 + \frac{19}{t^2} + 10$$

$$\Rightarrow \quad |\mathbf{OP}|^2 \ge 2\cdot\sqrt{7t^2\cdot\frac{19}{t^2}} + 10 \qquad [\because \text{AM} \ge \text{GM}]$$

$\therefore$ Minimum value of $|\mathbf{OP}| = \sqrt{10+2\sqrt{133}}$

Example 14 *If* $\mathbf{a}$, $\mathbf{b}$ *and* $\mathbf{c}$ *be non-zero vectors such that* $\mathbf{a}$ *is perpendicular to* $\mathbf{b}$ *and* $\mathbf{c}$ *and* $|\mathbf{a}|=1, |\mathbf{b}|=2, |\mathbf{c}|=1, \mathbf{b}\cdot\mathbf{c}=1$ *and there is a non-zero vector* $\mathbf{d}$ *coplanar with* $\mathbf{a}+\mathbf{b}$ *and* $2\mathbf{b}-\mathbf{c}$ *and* $\mathbf{d}\cdot\mathbf{a}=1$*, then minimum value of* $|\mathbf{d}|$ *is*

(a) $\frac{2}{\sqrt{13}}$ (b) $\frac{3}{\sqrt{13}}$ (c) $\frac{4}{\sqrt{5}}$ (d) $\frac{4}{\sqrt{13}}$

Sol. (d) $\mathbf{a}\cdot\mathbf{b} = \mathbf{a}\cdot\mathbf{c} = 0, |\mathbf{a}| = |\mathbf{c}| = 1, |\mathbf{b}| = 2$ and $\mathbf{b}\cdot\mathbf{c} = 1$

Let $\quad \mathbf{d} = x(\mathbf{a}+\mathbf{b}) + y(2\mathbf{b}-\mathbf{c})$

But $\quad \mathbf{d}\cdot\mathbf{a} = 1$

$\Rightarrow \quad x(1+0)+0 = 1 \Rightarrow x = 1$

$\Rightarrow \quad \mathbf{d} = \mathbf{a}+\mathbf{b}+y(2\mathbf{b}-\mathbf{c})$

$\Rightarrow \quad |\mathbf{d}|^2 = |\mathbf{a}|^2 + |\mathbf{b}|^2 + 2\mathbf{a}\cdot\mathbf{b} + y^2(2\mathbf{b}-\mathbf{c})^2 + 2y(\mathbf{a}+\mathbf{b})\cdot(2\mathbf{b}-\mathbf{c})$

$\Rightarrow \quad |\mathbf{d}|^2 = 1+4+y^2(16+1-4)+2y(8-1)$

$\qquad = 13y^2 - 14y + 5$

$$\therefore \quad |\mathbf{d}|_{\min} = \sqrt{\frac{4\times 13\times 5 - 14\times 14}{4\times 13}} = \frac{4}{\sqrt{13}}$$

Example 15 *A groove is in the form of a broken line ABC and the position vectors of the three points are respectively* $2\hat{\mathbf{i}}-3\hat{\mathbf{j}}+2\hat{\mathbf{k}}, 3\hat{\mathbf{i}}+2\hat{\mathbf{j}}-\hat{\mathbf{k}}$ *and* $\hat{\mathbf{i}}+\hat{\mathbf{j}}+\hat{\mathbf{k}}$*. A force of magnitude* $24\sqrt{3}$ *acts on a particle of unit mass kept at the point A and moves it along the groove to the point C. If the line of action of the force is parallel to the vector* $\hat{\mathbf{i}}+2\hat{\mathbf{j}}+\hat{\mathbf{k}}$ *all along, the number of units of work done by the force is*

(a) $144\sqrt{2}$ (b) $144\sqrt{3}$ (c) $72\sqrt{2}$ (d) $72\sqrt{3}$

Sol. (c) $\mathbf{F} = (24\sqrt{3})\dfrac{\hat{\mathbf{i}}+2\hat{\mathbf{j}}+\hat{\mathbf{k}}}{|\hat{\mathbf{i}}+2\hat{\mathbf{j}}+\hat{\mathbf{k}}|} = \dfrac{24\sqrt{3}}{\sqrt{6}}(\hat{\mathbf{i}}+2\hat{\mathbf{j}}+\hat{\mathbf{k}})$

$\qquad = 12\sqrt{2}(\hat{\mathbf{i}}+2\hat{\mathbf{j}}+\hat{\mathbf{k}})$

Displacement, $\mathbf{r}$ = Position Vector of C – Position Vector of A

$\qquad = (\hat{\mathbf{i}}+\hat{\mathbf{j}}+\hat{\mathbf{k}}) - (2\hat{\mathbf{i}}-3\hat{\mathbf{j}}+2\hat{\mathbf{k}})$

$\qquad = (-\hat{\mathbf{i}}+4\hat{\mathbf{j}}-\hat{\mathbf{k}})$

Work done by the force

$W = \mathbf{r}\cdot\mathbf{F} = (-\hat{\mathbf{i}}+4\hat{\mathbf{j}}-\hat{\mathbf{k}})\cdot 12\sqrt{2}(\hat{\mathbf{i}}+2\hat{\mathbf{j}}+\hat{\mathbf{k}})$

$\qquad = 12\sqrt{2}(-1+8-1) = 72\sqrt{2}$

JEE SCANNER

Example 16 Similar to PYQ Asked in JEE Main 2023

Let $\mathbf{a} = 2\lambda\hat{\mathbf{i}}+2\hat{\mathbf{j}}-2\hat{\mathbf{k}}$ *and* $\mathbf{b} = 6\hat{\mathbf{i}}-2\hat{\mathbf{j}}+4\hat{\mathbf{k}}$ *be two vectors and* λ *be an integer. Let c be a non-zero vector such that c is parallel to* $(\mathbf{a}+\mathbf{b}+\mathbf{c})$, $\mathbf{a}\cdot\mathbf{c} = -68$ *and* $\mathbf{b}\cdot\mathbf{c} = -80$*. Then, the value of* $\left[\dfrac{|\mathbf{c}\times\mathbf{b}|^2}{|\mathbf{a}|^2}\right]$ *is ....*

(where, $[\cdot]$ is the greatest integer function)

Sol. Since $\mathbf{c}$ is parallel to $(\mathbf{a}+\mathbf{b}+\mathbf{c})$.

$\therefore \quad (\mathbf{a}+\mathbf{b}+\mathbf{c})\times\mathbf{c} = 0 \Rightarrow (\mathbf{a}+\mathbf{b})\times\mathbf{c} = 0$

$\Rightarrow \quad \mathbf{c} = \mu(\mathbf{a}+\mathbf{b}) = \mu[(2\lambda\hat{\mathbf{i}}+2\hat{\mathbf{j}}-2\hat{\mathbf{k}})+(6\hat{\mathbf{i}}-2\hat{\mathbf{j}}+4\hat{\mathbf{k}})]$

$\qquad = 2\mu[(\lambda+3)\hat{\mathbf{i}}+\hat{\mathbf{k}}] \qquad$ ...(i)

Now, $\mathbf{a}\cdot\mathbf{c} = -68 \Rightarrow 2\lambda\cdot 2\mu(\lambda+3) - 2\cdot 2\mu = -68$

$\Rightarrow \qquad \mu\lambda(\lambda+3) - \mu = -17 \qquad$ ...(ii)

and $\quad \mathbf{b}\cdot\mathbf{c} = -80 \Rightarrow 6\cdot 2\mu(\lambda+3) + 4\cdot 2\mu = -80$

$\Rightarrow \qquad \lambda = \dfrac{-20-11\mu}{3\mu} \qquad$ ...(iii)

Put the value of λ is Eq. (ii), we get

$$\frac{\mu(-20-11\mu)}{3\mu}\left[\frac{-20-11\mu}{3\mu}+3\right] - \mu = -17$$

$\Rightarrow \qquad 13\mu^2 + 413\mu + 400 = 0$

$\Rightarrow \qquad \mu = -1, -\dfrac{400}{13} \Rightarrow \lambda = 3, -\dfrac{207}{60}$

$\because \lambda \in Z \quad \therefore \lambda = 3$ and $\mu = -1$

$\therefore \mathbf{c} = 2\mu[(\lambda+3)\hat{\mathbf{i}}+\hat{\mathbf{k}}] = -2(6\hat{\mathbf{i}}+\hat{\mathbf{k}}) = -12\hat{\mathbf{i}}-2\hat{\mathbf{k}}$

Now, $\mathbf{c}\times\mathbf{b} = \begin{vmatrix} \hat{\mathbf{i}} & \hat{\mathbf{j}} & \hat{\mathbf{k}} \\ -12 & 0 & -1 \\ 6 & -2 & 4 \end{vmatrix} = -4\hat{\mathbf{i}}+36\hat{\mathbf{j}}+24\hat{\mathbf{k}}$

and $\mathbf{a} = 6\hat{\mathbf{i}}+2\hat{\mathbf{j}}-2\hat{\mathbf{k}}$

$\therefore \qquad |\mathbf{a}| = \sqrt{36+4+4} = 2\sqrt{11}$

$\qquad |\mathbf{c}\times\mathbf{b}| = \sqrt{16+(36)^2+(24)^2} = 2\sqrt{118}$

Hence, $\left[\dfrac{|\mathbf{c}\times\mathbf{b}|^2}{|\mathbf{a}|^2}\right] = \left[\dfrac{(2\sqrt{118})^2}{(2\sqrt{11})^2}\right] = 10$

Skill Builder

Let $\mathbf{a} = \lambda\hat{\mathbf{i}}+\hat{\mathbf{j}}-\hat{\mathbf{k}}$ and $\mathbf{b} = 3\hat{\mathbf{i}}-\hat{\mathbf{j}}+2\hat{\mathbf{k}}$ be two vectors and λ be an integer. Let c be a non-zero vector such that c is parallel to $(\mathbf{a}+\mathbf{b}+\mathbf{c})$, $\mathbf{a}\cdot\mathbf{c} = -17$ and $\mathbf{b}\cdot\mathbf{c} = -20$. Then, the value of $\left[\dfrac{|\mathbf{c}\times\mathbf{b}|^2}{|\mathbf{a}|^2}\right]$ is ....

(where, $[\cdot]$ is the greatest integer function)

For Sol.

Example 17 *The coordinates of the mid-points of the sides of ΔPQR are $(3a, 0, 0)$, $(0, 3b, 0)$ and $(0, 0, 3c)$ respectively, then the area of ΔPQR is*

(a) $18\sqrt{b^2c^2 + c^2a^2 + a^2b^2}$ (b) $9\sqrt{b^2c^2 + c^2a^2 + a^2b^2}$

(c) $\frac{9}{2}\sqrt{b^2c^2 + c^2a^2 + a^2b^2}$ (d) $18\sqrt{ab + bc + ca}$

Sol. (a) Let L, M and N be the mid-points of the sides of ΔPQR.

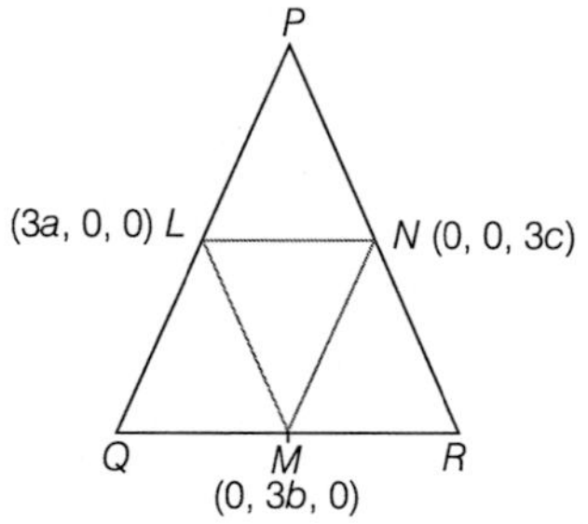

$$\text{Area of } \Delta LMN = \frac{1}{2}|\mathbf{MN} \times \mathbf{ML}|$$
$$= \frac{1}{2}|(-3b\hat{\mathbf{j}} + 3c\hat{\mathbf{k}}) \times (3a\hat{\mathbf{i}} - 3b\hat{\mathbf{j}})|$$
$$= \frac{1}{2}|9(bc\hat{\mathbf{i}} + ca\hat{\mathbf{j}} + ab\hat{\mathbf{k}})|$$
$$= \frac{9}{2}\sqrt{(bc)^2 + (ca)^2 + (ab)^2}$$

Now, area of $\Delta PQR = 4 \times$ (Area of ΔLMN)

$$= 4 \times \frac{9}{2}\sqrt{b^2c^2 + c^2a^2 + a^2b^2}$$
$$= 18\sqrt{b^2c^2 + c^2a^2 + a^2b^2}$$

Example 18 *Let ΔABC be a given triangle. If $|\mathbf{BA} - t\mathbf{BC}| \ge |\mathbf{AC}|$ for any $t \in R$, then ΔABC is*

(a) Equilateral (b) Right angled
(c) Isosceles (d) None of these

Sol. (b) $|\mathbf{BA}|^2 + t^2|\mathbf{BC}|^2 - 2\mathbf{BA}\cdot\mathbf{BC}\,t - |\mathbf{AC}|^2 \ge 0, \forall\, t \in R$

Discriminant of the quadratic equation ≤ 0

$$\Rightarrow 4(\mathbf{BA}\cdot\mathbf{BC})^2 - 4|\mathbf{BC}|^2|\mathbf{BA}|^2 + 4|\mathbf{BC}|^2|\mathbf{AC}|^2 \le 0 \quad \text{...(i)}$$

Using $(\mathbf{BA}\cdot\mathbf{BC})^2 - |\mathbf{BC}|^2|\mathbf{BA}|^2 = -|\mathbf{BA} \times \mathbf{BC}|^2$

$$= -|(\mathbf{BC} + \mathbf{CA}) \times \mathbf{BC}|^2$$
$$= -|\mathbf{CA} \times \mathbf{BC}|^2 \quad \text{...(ii)}$$

Using Eq. (ii) in Eq. (i).

$$|\mathbf{BC}|^2|\mathbf{AC}|^2 \le |\mathbf{AC} \times \mathbf{BC}|^2$$

But $|\mathbf{AC} \times \mathbf{BC}| = |\mathbf{AC}||\mathbf{BC}|\sin C$

$\Rightarrow \sin^2 C \ge 1$

$\Rightarrow \sin C = \pm 1$

$\Rightarrow \angle C = \frac{\pi}{2}$

Example 19 *If $a^2 + b^2 + c^2 = 1$ where $a, b, c \in R$, then the maximum value of $(4a - 3b)^2 + (5b - 4c)^2 + (3c - 5a)^2$ is*

(a) 25 (b) 50
(c) 144 (d) None of these

Sol. (b) Let $\mathbf{r}_1 = a\hat{\mathbf{i}} + b\hat{\mathbf{j}} + c\hat{\mathbf{k}}$, $\mathbf{r}_2 = 3\hat{\mathbf{i}} + 4\hat{\mathbf{j}} + 5\hat{\mathbf{k}}$

$$|\mathbf{r}_1 \times \mathbf{r}_2|^2 \le |\mathbf{r}_1|^2|\mathbf{r}_2|^2$$

Now, $$\mathbf{r}_1 \times \mathbf{r}_2 = \begin{vmatrix} \hat{\mathbf{i}} & \hat{\mathbf{j}} & \hat{\mathbf{k}} \\ a & b & c \\ 3 & 4 & 5 \end{vmatrix}$$

$$= \hat{\mathbf{i}}(5b - 4c) + \hat{\mathbf{j}}(3c - 5a) + \hat{\mathbf{k}}(4a - 3b)$$

So, from Eq. (i), we get

$$(5b - 4c)^2 + (3c - 5a)^2 + (4a - 3b)^2 \le 50$$

Example 20 *If $\mathbf{a}$, $\mathbf{b}$ and $\mathbf{c}$ are pth, qth, rth terms of HP and $\mathbf{u} = (q - r)\hat{\mathbf{i}} + (r - p)\hat{\mathbf{j}} + (p - q)\hat{\mathbf{k}}$, $\mathbf{v} = \frac{\hat{\mathbf{i}}}{a} + \frac{\hat{\mathbf{j}}}{b} + \frac{\hat{\mathbf{k}}}{c}$, then*

(a) $\mathbf{u}$ and $\mathbf{v}$ are parallel vectors.
(b) $\mathbf{u}$ and $\mathbf{v}$ are orthogonal vectors.
(c) $\mathbf{u}\cdot\mathbf{v} = 1$
(d) $\mathbf{u} \times \mathbf{v} = \hat{\mathbf{i}} + \hat{\mathbf{j}} + \hat{\mathbf{k}}$

Sol. (b) Let A be the first term and D be the common difference of the corresponding AP. Then,

$$\frac{1}{a} = A + (p - 1)D, \frac{1}{b} = A + (q - 1)D, \frac{1}{c} = A + (r - 1)D$$

$\Rightarrow$ $a^{-1}(q - r) + b^{-1}(r - p) + c^{-1}(p - q) = 0$

$\Rightarrow$ $\mathbf{v}\cdot\mathbf{u} = 0 \Rightarrow \mathbf{u} \perp \mathbf{v}$

Hence, $\mathbf{u}$ and $\mathbf{v}$ are orthogonal vectors.

Example 21 *If the vector product of a constant vector $\mathbf{OA}$ with variable vector $\mathbf{OB}$ in a fixed plane OAB be a constant vector, then the locus of B is*

(a) a straight line perpendicular to $\mathbf{OA}$.
(b) a circle with centre O radius equal to $|\mathbf{OA}|$.
(c) a straight line parallel to $\mathbf{OA}$.
(d) None of the above

Sol. (c) Let $A(\alpha, \beta)$ point be given and O be taken as the origin

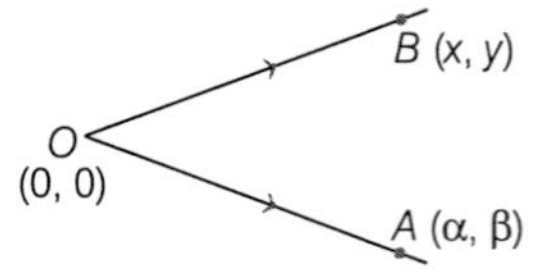

We have, $\mathbf{OA} = \alpha\hat{\mathbf{i}} + \beta\hat{\mathbf{j}}$ and $\mathbf{OB} = x\hat{\mathbf{i}} + y\hat{\mathbf{j}}$

Now, $|\mathbf{OA} \times \mathbf{OB}| = |(\alpha y - \beta x)\hat{\mathbf{k}}| = \text{constant}$

$\Rightarrow$ $\alpha y - \beta x = \text{constant}$

$\therefore$ Locus of $B(x, y)$ is a line parallel to OA because slope of

$$OA = \frac{\beta}{\alpha}$$

JEE SCANNER

Example 22 Similar to PYQ Asked in JEE Main 2024

Let $\mathbf{a} = \alpha\hat{i} + \hat{j} + \beta\hat{k}$ *and* $\mathbf{b} = \frac{2}{3}\hat{i} + \frac{2}{3}\hat{j} + \gamma\hat{k}$, *where* $\alpha, \beta, \gamma \in R$. *Let* $\mathbf{b}$ *be a unit vector and* $|\mathbf{a}| = 4$. *If* $(\mathbf{a}\cdot\mathbf{b}) = 2\sqrt{2}$, *then the value of* $\dfrac{135\gamma^2 |\mathbf{a}\times\mathbf{b}|^2}{(\alpha^2+\beta^2)\sqrt{2}\sin\theta}$ *is ....*

Sol. Given, $|\mathbf{a}| = 4, |\mathbf{b}| = 1$ and $\mathbf{a}\cdot\mathbf{b} = 2\sqrt{2}$

Since, $\mathbf{a}\cdot\mathbf{b} = 2\sqrt{2}$

$\Rightarrow |\mathbf{a}||\mathbf{b}|\cdot\cos\theta = 2\sqrt{2}$

$\Rightarrow 4\times 1\cdot\cos\theta = 2\sqrt{2}$

$\Rightarrow \cos\theta = \frac{2\sqrt{2}}{4} = \frac{1}{\sqrt{2}} \Rightarrow \theta = \frac{\pi}{4}$

Thus, the angle between $\mathbf{a}$ and $\mathbf{b}$ is $\frac{\pi}{4}$.

Also, $|\mathbf{a}|^2 = 4^2$

$\Rightarrow \alpha^2 + \beta^2 + 1 = 16 \Rightarrow \alpha^2 + \beta^2 = 15$

And $|\mathbf{b}|^2 = 1^2$

$\Rightarrow \frac{4}{9} + \frac{4}{9} + \gamma^2 = 1 \Rightarrow \gamma^2 = 1 - \frac{8}{9} = \frac{1}{9} \Rightarrow \gamma^2 = \frac{1}{9}$

Also, $|\mathbf{a}\times\mathbf{b}|^2 = |\mathbf{a}|^2|\mathbf{b}|^2 - (\mathbf{a}\cdot\mathbf{b})^2$

$= 16\times 1 - (2\sqrt{2})^2 = 8$

Consider, $\dfrac{\gamma^2|\mathbf{a}\times\mathbf{b}|^2}{(\alpha^2+\beta^2)\cdot\sin\theta} = \dfrac{\frac{1}{9}\times 8}{15\cdot\sin\frac{\pi}{4}} = \dfrac{\frac{8}{9}}{15\cdot\frac{1}{\sqrt{2}}} = \dfrac{8\sqrt{2}}{135}$

Hence, $\dfrac{135\gamma^2|\mathbf{a}\times\mathbf{b}|^2}{(\alpha^2+\beta^2)\sqrt{2}\sin\theta} = 8$

Skill Builder

Let $\mathbf{a} = x\hat{i} + \hat{j} + y\hat{k}$ and $\mathbf{b} = \frac{1}{2}\hat{i} + \frac{1}{2}\hat{j} + z\hat{k}$,, where $x, y, z \in R$. Let $\mathbf{b}$ be a unit vector and $|\mathbf{a}| = 6$. If $(\mathbf{a}\cdot\mathbf{b}) = 3\sqrt{3}$, then the value of $\dfrac{35z^2|\mathbf{a}\times\mathbf{b}|^2}{(x^2+y^2)\cdot\sin\theta}$ is ....

For Sol.

Example 23 *The vector* $\mathbf{r}$ *satisfying the conditions that*

I. *it is perpendicular to* $3\hat{i} + 2\hat{j} + 2\hat{k}$ *and* $18\hat{i} - 22\hat{j} - 5\hat{k}$

II. *it makes an obtuse angle with Y-axis.*

III. $|\mathbf{r}| = 14$

(a) $2(-2\hat{i} - 3\hat{j} + 6\hat{k})$ (b) $2(2\hat{i} - 3\hat{j} + 6\hat{k})$

(c) $4\hat{i} + 6\hat{j} - 12\hat{k}$ (d) None of these

Sol. (a) Let $\mathbf{a} = 3\hat{i} + 2\hat{j} + 2\hat{k}$ and $\mathbf{b} = 18\hat{i} - 22\hat{j} - 5\hat{k}$

Then, the required vector $\mathbf{r}$ is given by

$\mathbf{r} = \lambda(\mathbf{a}\times\mathbf{b})$

$\Rightarrow \mathbf{r} = \lambda(34\hat{i} + 51\hat{j} - 102\hat{k}) = 17\lambda(2\hat{i} + 3\hat{j} - 6\hat{k})$

Now, $|\mathbf{r}| = 14$

$\Rightarrow 119|\lambda| = 14$

$\Rightarrow |\lambda| = \frac{2}{17}$

Since, $\mathbf{r}$ makes an obtuse angle with Y-axis.

Therefore, $\lambda = -\frac{2}{17}$

Hence, $\mathbf{r} = -2(2\hat{i} + 3\hat{j} - 6\hat{k})$

or $\mathbf{r} = 2(-2\hat{i} - 3\hat{j} + 6\hat{k})$

Example 24 *For non-zero vectors* $\mathbf{a}, \mathbf{b}, \mathbf{c}$; $|(\mathbf{a}\times\mathbf{b})\cdot\mathbf{c}| = |\mathbf{a}||\mathbf{b}||\mathbf{c}|$ *holds if and only if*

(a) $\mathbf{a}\cdot\mathbf{b} = 0, \mathbf{b}\cdot\mathbf{c} = 0$ (b) $\mathbf{b}\cdot\mathbf{c} = 0, \mathbf{c}\cdot\mathbf{a} = 0$

(c) $\mathbf{c}\cdot\mathbf{a} = 0, \mathbf{a}\cdot\mathbf{b} = 0$ (d) $\mathbf{a}\cdot\mathbf{b} = \mathbf{b}\cdot\mathbf{c} = \mathbf{c}\cdot\mathbf{a} = 0$

Sol. (d) We have, $|(\mathbf{a}\times\mathbf{b})\cdot\mathbf{c}| = |\mathbf{a}||\mathbf{b}||\mathbf{c}|$

$\Rightarrow ||\mathbf{a}||\mathbf{b}||\mathbf{c}|\sin\theta\cos\alpha| = |\mathbf{a}||\mathbf{b}||\mathbf{c}|$

$\Rightarrow |\sin\theta||\cos\alpha| = 1$

$\Rightarrow \theta = \frac{\pi}{2}$ and $\alpha = 0$

$\Rightarrow \mathbf{a}\perp\mathbf{b}$ and $\mathbf{c}\,||\,\hat{\mathbf{n}}$

$\Rightarrow \mathbf{a}\perp\mathbf{b}$ and $\mathbf{c}\perp$ both $\mathbf{a}$ and $\mathbf{b}$

$\Rightarrow$ $\mathbf{a}, \mathbf{b}, \mathbf{c}$ are mutually perpendicular.

$\Rightarrow \mathbf{a}\cdot\mathbf{c} = \mathbf{b}\cdot\mathbf{c} = \mathbf{c}\cdot\mathbf{a} = 0$

Example 25 *If* $\mathbf{a}, \mathbf{b}$ *and* $\mathbf{c}$ *are three non-coplanar vectors, then* $3\mathbf{a} - 7\mathbf{b} - 4\mathbf{c}$, $3\mathbf{a} - 2\mathbf{b} + \mathbf{c}$ *and* $\mathbf{a} + \mathbf{b} + \lambda\mathbf{c}$ *will be coplanar, if* λ *is*

(a) -1 (b) 1 (c) 3 (d) 2

Sol. (d) Let $\alpha = 3\mathbf{a} - 7\mathbf{b} - 4\mathbf{c}$, $\beta = 3\mathbf{a} - 2\mathbf{b} + \mathbf{c}$ and $\gamma = \mathbf{a} + \mathbf{b} + \lambda\mathbf{c}$

For α, β and γ to be coplanar $[\alpha\ \beta\ \gamma] = 0$

$$\Rightarrow \begin{vmatrix} 3 & -7 & -4 \\ 3 & -2 & 1 \\ 1 & 1 & \lambda \end{vmatrix} [\mathbf{a}\ \mathbf{b}\ \mathbf{c}] = 0$$

$[3(-2\lambda - 1) + 7(3\lambda - 1) - 4(3 + 2)\,[\mathbf{a}\ \mathbf{b}\ \mathbf{c}]] = 0$

$\Rightarrow (15\lambda - 30)[\mathbf{a}\ \mathbf{b}\ \mathbf{c}] = 0$

Since, $\mathbf{a}, \mathbf{b}$ and $\mathbf{c}$ are non-coplanar.

$\therefore 15\lambda - 30 = 0 \Rightarrow \lambda = 2$

Example 26 *Let* $\mathbf{r} = (\mathbf{a}\times\mathbf{b})\sin x + (\mathbf{b}\times\mathbf{c})\cos y + (\mathbf{c}\times\mathbf{a})$, *where* $\mathbf{a}$, $\mathbf{b}$ *and* $\mathbf{c}$ *are non-zero non-coplanar vectors. If* $\mathbf{r}$ *is orthogonal to* $3\mathbf{a} + 5\mathbf{b} + 2\mathbf{c}$, *then the value of* $\sec^2 y + \mathrm{cosec}^2 x + \sec y\ \mathrm{cosec}\ x$ *is*

(a) 3 (b) 4 (c) 5 (d) 6

Sol. (a) $\mathbf{r}\cdot(3\mathbf{a}+5\mathbf{b}+2\mathbf{c})=0$

$\Rightarrow \mathbf{a}\cdot(\mathbf{b}\times\mathbf{c})[2\sin x+3\cos y+5]=0$

$\Rightarrow 2\sin x+3\cos y+5=0 \quad [\because \mathbf{a}\cdot(\mathbf{b}\times\mathbf{c})\neq 0]$

$\Rightarrow 2\sin x+3\cos y=-5$

$\Rightarrow \sin x=-1, \cos y=1$

$\Rightarrow \operatorname{cosec} x=-1, \sec y=-1$

Hence, $\sec^2 y+\operatorname{cosec}^2 x+\sec y \operatorname{cosec} x=3$

Example 27 *Let* $\mathbf{a}, \mathbf{b}$ *and* $\mathbf{c}$ *be three vectors such that* $[\mathbf{a}\ \mathbf{b}\ \mathbf{c}]=2$. *If* $\mathbf{r}=l(\mathbf{b}\times\mathbf{c})+m(\mathbf{c}\times\mathbf{a})+n(\mathbf{a}\times\mathbf{b})$ *is perpendicular to* $\mathbf{a}+\mathbf{b}+\mathbf{c}$, *then the value of* $(l+m+n)$ *is*

(a) 2 (b) 1 (c) 0 (d) None of these

Sol. (c) It is given that $\mathbf{r}$ perpendicular $(\mathbf{a}+\mathbf{b}+\mathbf{c})$

$\therefore \mathbf{r}\cdot(\mathbf{a}+\mathbf{b}+\mathbf{c})=0$

$\Rightarrow l[\mathbf{a}\ \mathbf{b}\ \mathbf{c}]+m[\mathbf{c}\ \mathbf{a}\ \mathbf{b}]+n[\mathbf{a}\ \mathbf{b}\ \mathbf{c}]=0$

$\Rightarrow 2(l+m+n)=0 \quad [\because [\mathbf{a}\ \mathbf{b}\ \mathbf{c}]=2]$

$\Rightarrow l+m+n=0$

Example 28 *If* $\mathbf{a}, \mathbf{b}$ *and* $\mathbf{c}$ *are non-coplanar vectors and* λ *is a real number, then* $[\lambda(\mathbf{a}+\mathbf{b})\ \ \lambda^2\mathbf{b}\ \ \lambda\mathbf{c}]=[\mathbf{a}\ \ \mathbf{b}+\mathbf{c}\ \ \mathbf{b}]$ *for*

(a) exactly two values of λ (b) exactly one value of λ

(c) no value of λ (d) exactly three values of λ

Decoding the Question

Let vector $\mathbf{a}=a_1\hat{\mathbf{i}}+a_2\hat{\mathbf{j}}+a_3\hat{\mathbf{k}}$, $\mathbf{b}=b_1\hat{\mathbf{i}}+b_2\hat{\mathbf{j}}+b_3\hat{\mathbf{k}}$ and $\mathbf{c}=c_1\hat{\mathbf{i}}+c_2\hat{\mathbf{j}}+c_3\hat{\mathbf{k}}$, then apply the properties of determinant.

Sol. (c) Given, $[\lambda(\mathbf{a}+\mathbf{b})\ \ \lambda^2\mathbf{b}\ \ \lambda\mathbf{c}]=[\mathbf{a}\ \ \mathbf{b}+\mathbf{c}\ \ \mathbf{b}]$

$$\Rightarrow \begin{vmatrix} \lambda(a_1+b_1) & \lambda(a_2+b_2) & \lambda(a_3+b_3) \\ \lambda^2 b_1 & \lambda^2 b_2 & \lambda^2 b_3 \\ \lambda c_1 & \lambda c_2 & \lambda c_3 \end{vmatrix} = \begin{vmatrix} a_1 & a_2 & a_3 \\ b_1+c_1 & b_2+c_2 & b_3+c_3 \\ b_1 & b_2 & b_3 \end{vmatrix}$$

$$\Rightarrow \lambda^4 \begin{vmatrix} a_1+b_1 & a_2+b_2 & a_3+b_3 \\ b_1 & b_2 & b_3 \\ c_1 & c_2 & c_3 \end{vmatrix} = \begin{vmatrix} a_1 & a_2 & a_3 \\ b_1+c_1 & b_2+c_2 & b_3+c_3 \\ b_1 & b_2 & b_3 \end{vmatrix}$$

[applying $R_1\to R_1-R_2$ in LHS and $R_2\to R_2-R_3$ in RHS]

$$\Rightarrow \lambda^4 \begin{vmatrix} a_1 & a_2 & a_3 \\ b_1 & b_2 & b_3 \\ c_1 & c_2 & c_3 \end{vmatrix} = -\begin{vmatrix} a_1 & a_2 & a_3 \\ b_1 & b_2 & b_3 \\ c_1 & c_2 & c_3 \end{vmatrix}$$

$\Rightarrow \lambda^4=-1$

Hence, no real value of λ exists.

Example 29 *If* $\mathbf{a}=\hat{\mathbf{i}}+\hat{\mathbf{j}}+\hat{\mathbf{k}}, \mathbf{b}=\hat{\mathbf{i}}-\hat{\mathbf{j}}+\hat{\mathbf{k}}, \mathbf{c}=\hat{\mathbf{i}}+2\hat{\mathbf{j}}-\hat{\mathbf{k}}$, *then the value of* $\begin{vmatrix} \mathbf{a}\cdot\mathbf{a} & \mathbf{a}\cdot\mathbf{b} & \mathbf{a}\cdot\mathbf{c} \\ \mathbf{b}\cdot\mathbf{a} & \mathbf{b}\cdot\mathbf{b} & \mathbf{b}\cdot\mathbf{c} \\ \mathbf{c}\cdot\mathbf{a} & \mathbf{c}\cdot\mathbf{b} & \mathbf{c}\cdot\mathbf{c} \end{vmatrix}$ *is*

(a) 2 (b) 4 (c) 16 (d) 64

Sol. (c) We have, $\mathbf{a}=\hat{\mathbf{i}}+\hat{\mathbf{j}}+\hat{\mathbf{k}}$, $\mathbf{b}=\hat{\mathbf{i}}-\hat{\mathbf{j}}+\hat{\mathbf{k}}$ and $\mathbf{c}=\hat{\mathbf{i}}+2\hat{\mathbf{j}}-\hat{\mathbf{k}}$

We know that $\begin{vmatrix} \mathbf{a}\cdot\mathbf{a} & \mathbf{a}\cdot\mathbf{b} & \mathbf{a}\cdot\mathbf{c} \\ \mathbf{b}\cdot\mathbf{a} & \mathbf{b}\cdot\mathbf{b} & \mathbf{b}\cdot\mathbf{c} \\ \mathbf{c}\cdot\mathbf{a} & \mathbf{c}\cdot\mathbf{b} & \mathbf{c}\cdot\mathbf{c} \end{vmatrix}=[\mathbf{a}\ \mathbf{b}\ \mathbf{c}]^2=\begin{vmatrix} 1 & 1 & 1 \\ 1 & -1 & 1 \\ 1 & 2 & -1 \end{vmatrix}^2$

$=[1(1-2)-1(-1-1)+1(2+1)]^2$

$=[-1+2+3]^2=[4]^2=16$

Example 30 *Let* $\mathbf{b}=-\hat{\mathbf{i}}+4\hat{\mathbf{j}}+6\hat{\mathbf{k}}$ *and* $\mathbf{c}=2\hat{\mathbf{i}}-7\hat{\mathbf{j}}-10\hat{\mathbf{k}}$. *If* $\mathbf{a}$ *be a unit vector and the scalar triple product* $[\mathbf{a}\ \mathbf{b}\ \mathbf{c}]$ *has the greatest value, then* $\mathbf{a}$ *is equal to*

(a) $\frac{1}{\sqrt{3}}(\hat{\mathbf{i}}+\hat{\mathbf{j}}+\hat{\mathbf{k}})$ (b) $\frac{1}{\sqrt{5}}(\sqrt{2}\hat{\mathbf{i}}-\hat{\mathbf{j}}-\sqrt{2}\hat{\mathbf{k}})$

(c) $\frac{1}{3}(2\hat{\mathbf{i}}+2\hat{\mathbf{j}}-\hat{\mathbf{k}})$ (d) $\frac{1}{\sqrt{59}}(3\hat{\mathbf{i}}-7\hat{\mathbf{j}}-\hat{\mathbf{k}})$

Sol. (c) $\mathbf{b}\times\mathbf{c}=2\hat{\mathbf{i}}+2\hat{\mathbf{j}}-\hat{\mathbf{k}}$

$[\mathbf{a}\ \mathbf{b}\ \mathbf{c}]=\mathbf{a}\cdot(2\hat{\mathbf{i}}+2\hat{\mathbf{j}}-\hat{\mathbf{k}})=1\cdot 3\cdot\cos\theta\leq 3$

The greatest value of $[\mathbf{a}\ \mathbf{b}\ \mathbf{c}]=3$, which is obtained when $\theta=0$.

So, $\mathbf{a}=\frac{\mathbf{b}\times\mathbf{c}}{|\mathbf{b}\times\mathbf{c}|}=\frac{2}{3}\hat{\mathbf{i}}+\frac{2}{3}\hat{\mathbf{j}}-\frac{1}{3}\hat{\mathbf{k}}$

Example 31 *The value of a so that the volume of parallelopiped formed by* $\hat{\mathbf{i}}+a\hat{\mathbf{j}}+\hat{\mathbf{k}}, \hat{\mathbf{j}}+a\hat{\mathbf{k}}$ *and* $a\hat{\mathbf{i}}+\hat{\mathbf{k}}$ *becomes minimum is*

(a) -3 b) 3 (c) $1/\sqrt{3}$ (d) $\sqrt{3}$

Decoding the Question

This example contains the application of differentiation. First calculate the volume of the parallelopiped and then apply second derivative test of differentiation while solving.

Sol. (c) Volume of the parallelopiped

$V=[\hat{\mathbf{i}}+a\hat{\mathbf{j}}+\hat{\mathbf{k}}\ \ \hat{\mathbf{j}}+a\hat{\mathbf{k}}\ \ a\hat{\mathbf{i}}+\hat{\mathbf{k}}]$

$=(\hat{\mathbf{i}}+a\hat{\mathbf{j}}+\hat{\mathbf{k}})\cdot\{(\hat{\mathbf{j}}+a\hat{\mathbf{k}})\times(a\hat{\mathbf{i}}+\hat{\mathbf{k}})\}$

$=(\hat{\mathbf{i}}+a\hat{\mathbf{j}}+\hat{\mathbf{k}})\cdot(\hat{\mathbf{i}}+a^2\hat{\mathbf{j}}-a\hat{\mathbf{k}})=1+a^3-a$

$\frac{dV}{da}=3a^2-1, \frac{d^2V}{da^2}=6a$

$\therefore \frac{dV}{da}=0$ (for minimum)

$\Rightarrow 3a^2-1=0 \Rightarrow a=\pm\frac{1}{\sqrt{3}}$

At $a=\frac{1}{\sqrt{3}}, \frac{d^2V}{da^2}=\frac{6}{\sqrt{3}}>0$

$\therefore V$ is minimum at $a=\frac{1}{\sqrt{3}}$

Example 32 *The position vectors of vertices of* ΔABC *are* $\mathbf{a}, \mathbf{b}, \mathbf{c}$ *and* $\mathbf{a}\cdot\mathbf{a}=\mathbf{b}\cdot\mathbf{b}=\mathbf{c}\cdot\mathbf{c}=3$. *If* $[\mathbf{a}\ \mathbf{b}\ \mathbf{c}]=0$, *then the position vectors of the orthocentre of* ΔABC *is*

(a) $\mathbf{a}+\mathbf{b}+\mathbf{c}$ (b) $\frac{1}{3}(\mathbf{a}+\mathbf{b}+\mathbf{c})$

(c) 0 (d) None of these

Sol. (a) Given, $[\mathbf{a}\ \mathbf{b}\ \mathbf{c}] = 0$

So, the points O, A, B and C are coplanar.

Also, $OA = OB = OC = \sqrt{3}$, hence origin O is the circumcentre.

Position vector of the centroid G is $\dfrac{\mathbf{a}+\mathbf{b}+\mathbf{c}}{3}$.

Now, orthocentre divides OG in the ratio of 3 : 2 externally.

So, position vectors of orthocentre is $\mathbf{a}+\mathbf{b}+\mathbf{c}$.

Example 33 *The vectors*

$$\mathbf{u} = (al + a_1 l_1)\hat{\mathbf{i}} + (am + a_1 m_1)\hat{\mathbf{j}} + (an + a_1 n_1)\hat{\mathbf{k}},$$

$$\mathbf{v} = (bl + b_1 l_1)\hat{\mathbf{i}} + (bm + b_1 m_1)\hat{\mathbf{j}} + (bn + b_1 n_1)\hat{\mathbf{k}}$$

and $$\mathbf{w} = (cl + c_1 l_1)\hat{\mathbf{i}} + (cm + c_1 m_1)\hat{\mathbf{j}} + (cn + c_1 n_1)\hat{\mathbf{k}}$$

(a) form an equilateral triangle
(b) are coplanar
(c) are collinear
(d) are mutually perpendicular

Sol. (b) We have, $[\mathbf{u}\ \mathbf{v}\ \mathbf{w}] = \begin{vmatrix} al + a_1 l_1 & am + a_1 m_1 & an + a_1 n_1 \\ bl + b_1 l_1 & bm + b_1 m_1 & bn + b_1 n_1 \\ cl + c_1 l_1 & cm + c_1 m_1 & cn + c_1 n_1 \end{vmatrix}$

$$\Rightarrow \quad [\mathbf{u}\ \mathbf{v}\ \mathbf{w}] = \begin{vmatrix} a & a_1 & 0 \\ b & b_1 & 0 \\ c & c_1 & 0 \end{vmatrix} \begin{vmatrix} l & m & n \\ l_1 & m_1 & n_1 \\ 0 & 0 & 0 \end{vmatrix} = 0$$

Hence, the given vectors are coplanar.

Example 34 *If* **a**, **b** *and* **c** *are three mutually perpendicular vectors, then the projection of the vectors* $l\dfrac{\mathbf{a}}{|\mathbf{a}|} + m\dfrac{\mathbf{b}}{|\mathbf{b}|} + n\dfrac{(\mathbf{a}\times\mathbf{b})}{|\mathbf{a}\times\mathbf{b}|}$ *along the angle bisector of the vectors* **a** *and* **b** *is*

(a) $\dfrac{l+m}{\sqrt{2}}$ (b) $\sqrt{l^2 + m^2 + n^2}$

(c) $\dfrac{\sqrt{l^2 + m^2}}{\sqrt{l^2 + m^2 + b^2}}$ (d) None of these

Sol. (a) A vector parallel to the bisector of the angle between the vectors **a** and **b** is

$$\frac{\mathbf{a}}{|\mathbf{a}|} + \frac{\mathbf{b}}{|\mathbf{b}|} = \hat{\mathbf{a}} + \hat{\mathbf{b}}$$

$\therefore$ Units vector along the bisector

$$= \frac{\hat{\mathbf{a}}+\hat{\mathbf{b}}}{|\hat{\mathbf{a}}+\hat{\mathbf{b}}|} = \frac{1}{\sqrt{2}}(\hat{\mathbf{a}}+\hat{\mathbf{b}})$$

$$(\hat{\mathbf{a}}+\hat{\mathbf{b}})^2 = |\mathbf{a}|^2 + |\hat{\mathbf{b}}|^2 + 2\hat{\mathbf{a}}\cdot\hat{\mathbf{b}} = 1 + 1 + 0 = 2$$

$\therefore$ Required projection

$$= \left[l\frac{\mathbf{a}}{|\mathbf{a}|} + m\frac{\mathbf{b}}{|\mathbf{b}|} + n\frac{\mathbf{a}\times\mathbf{b}}{|\mathbf{a}\times\mathbf{b}|}\right]\cdot\frac{1}{\sqrt{2}}(\hat{\mathbf{a}}+\hat{\mathbf{b}})$$

$$= \frac{1}{\sqrt{2}}(l+m)$$

$$\left[\because \frac{\mathbf{a}\cdot\hat{\mathbf{a}}}{|\mathbf{a}|} = \frac{\mathbf{b}\cdot\hat{\mathbf{b}}}{|\mathbf{b}|} = 1 \text{ and } \hat{\mathbf{a}}\cdot\hat{\mathbf{b}} = \hat{\mathbf{a}}\cdot(\mathbf{a}\times\mathbf{b}) = \hat{\mathbf{b}}\cdot(\hat{\mathbf{a}}\times\mathbf{b}) = 0\right]$$

JEE SCANNER

Example 35 Similar to PYQ Asked in JEE Adv. 2013

Consider the set of seven vectors $V = \{a\hat{\mathbf{i}} + b\hat{\mathbf{j}} + c\hat{\mathbf{k}},\ a, b, c \in \{0, 1\}\}$ *three non-coplanar vectors can be chosen from* V *in* P *ways, then* P *is ....*

Sol. Let (1, 1, 1), (0, 1, 1), (1, 0, 1) and (0, 0, 1) be vectors **a**, **b**, **c** and **d** and rest of the vectors are $-\mathbf{a}, -\mathbf{b}, -\mathbf{c}$ and $-\mathbf{d}$.

Now, we find the number of ways of selecting coplanar vectors.

Observe that out of any three coplanar vectors, two will be collinear (anti-parallel).

$\therefore$ Number of ways selecting the coplanar pair = 4

Number of ways selecting the third vector $= 3! = 6$

Total number of ways selecting three coplanar vectors
$$= 6 \times 4 = 24$$

Number of ways selecting three non-coplanar vectors
$$= {}^7C_3 - 24$$
$$= \frac{7!}{4!\,3!} - 24 = 35 - 24 = 11$$

Skill Builder

Consider the set of eight vectors $V = \{a\hat{\mathbf{i}} + b\hat{\mathbf{j}} + c\hat{\mathbf{k}},\ a, b, c \in \{-1, -1\}\}$ three non-coplanar vectors can be chosen from V in 2^P ways, then P is ....

For Sol.

Example 36 *If* V *is the volume of the parallelopiped having three coterminous edges as* **a**, **b** *and* **c**, *then the volume of parallelopiped having three coterminous edges as* $\alpha = (\mathbf{a}\cdot\mathbf{a})\mathbf{a} + (\mathbf{a}\cdot\mathbf{b})\mathbf{b} + (\mathbf{a}\cdot\mathbf{c})\mathbf{c}$, $\beta = (\mathbf{a}\cdot\mathbf{b})\mathbf{a} + (\mathbf{b}\cdot\mathbf{b})\mathbf{b} + (\mathbf{b}\cdot\mathbf{c})\mathbf{c}$ *and* $\gamma = (\mathbf{a}\cdot\mathbf{c})\mathbf{a} + (\mathbf{b}\cdot\mathbf{c})\mathbf{b} + (\mathbf{c}\cdot\mathbf{c})\mathbf{c}$ *is*

(a) V^3 (b) $3V$

(c) V^2 (d) $2V$

Sol. (a) We have, $|[\mathbf{a}\ \mathbf{b}\ \mathbf{c}]| = V$

Let V_1 be the volume of the parallelopiped formed by the vectors α, β and γ. Then,

$$V_1 = |[\alpha\ \beta\ \gamma]|$$

Now, $$[\alpha\ \beta\ \gamma] = \begin{vmatrix} \mathbf{a}\cdot\mathbf{a} & \mathbf{a}\cdot\mathbf{b} & \mathbf{a}\cdot\mathbf{c} \\ \mathbf{a}\cdot\mathbf{b} & \mathbf{b}\cdot\mathbf{b} & \mathbf{b}\cdot\mathbf{c} \\ \mathbf{a}\cdot\mathbf{c} & \mathbf{b}\cdot\mathbf{c} & \mathbf{c}\cdot\mathbf{c} \end{vmatrix} [\mathbf{a}\ \mathbf{b}\ \mathbf{c}]$$

$$\Rightarrow \quad [\alpha\ \beta\ \gamma] = [\mathbf{a}\ \mathbf{b}\ \mathbf{c}]^2\,[\mathbf{a}\ \mathbf{b}\ \mathbf{c}]$$

$$\Rightarrow \quad [\alpha\ \beta\ \gamma] = [\mathbf{a}\ \mathbf{b}\ \mathbf{c}]^3$$

$$\because \quad V_1 = |[\alpha\ \beta\ \gamma]|$$
$$= |[\mathbf{a}\ \mathbf{b}\ \mathbf{c}]^3| = V^3$$

Example 37 *Let* $\mathbf{r}, \mathbf{a}, \mathbf{b}$ *and* $\mathbf{c}$ *be four non-zero vectors such that* $\mathbf{r}\cdot\mathbf{a}=0$,

$|\mathbf{r}\times\mathbf{b}|=|\mathbf{r}||\mathbf{b}|, |\mathbf{r}\times\mathbf{c}|=|\mathbf{r}||\mathbf{c}|$, *then* $[\mathbf{a}\ \mathbf{b}\ \mathbf{c}]$ *is*

(a) $|\mathbf{a}||\mathbf{b}||\mathbf{c}|$ (b) $-|\mathbf{a}||\mathbf{b}|\mathbf{c}|$

(c) 0 (d) None of these

Sol. (c) Given, $\mathbf{r}\cdot\mathbf{a}=0$

$$|\mathbf{r}\times\mathbf{b}|=|\mathbf{r}||\mathbf{b}|$$

and $$|\mathbf{r}\times\mathbf{c}|=|\mathbf{r}||\mathbf{c}|$$

This shows $\mathbf{r}$ is perpendicular to both $\mathbf{b}$ and $\mathbf{c}$.

$\Rightarrow$ $\mathbf{r}$ is perpendicular to $\mathbf{a}$, $\mathbf{b}$ and $\mathbf{c}$

$\therefore$ $[\mathbf{a}\ \mathbf{b}\ \mathbf{c}]=0$

Example 38 *Let* $\mathbf{a}, \mathbf{b}$ *and* $\mathbf{c}$ *be three non-coplanar vectors and* $\mathbf{d}$ *be a non-zero vector which is perpendicular to* $\mathbf{a}+\mathbf{b}+\mathbf{c}$. *Now, if* $\mathbf{d}=(\sin x)(\mathbf{a}\times\mathbf{b})+(\cos y)(\mathbf{b}\times\mathbf{c})+2(\mathbf{c}\times\mathbf{a})$, *then the minimum value of* (x^2+y^2) *is*

(a) π^2 (b) $\frac{\pi^2}{2}$ (c) $\frac{\pi^2}{4}$ (d) $\frac{5\pi^2}{4}$

Sol. (d) Given, $\mathbf{d}\cdot(\mathbf{a}+\mathbf{b}+\mathbf{c})=0$

and $\mathbf{d}=\sin x(\mathbf{a}\times\mathbf{b})+\cos y(\mathbf{b}\times\mathbf{c})+2(\mathbf{c}\times\mathbf{a})$ ...(i)

$\because$ $\mathbf{a}\cdot\mathbf{d}=\cos y[\mathbf{a}\ \mathbf{b}\ \mathbf{c}]$ ... (ii)

$\mathbf{b}\cdot\mathbf{d}=2[\mathbf{b}\ \mathbf{c}\ \mathbf{a}]$ ... (iii)

$\mathbf{c}\cdot\mathbf{d}=\sin x[\mathbf{a}\ \mathbf{b}\ \mathbf{c}]$ ... (iv)

On adding Eqs. (ii), (iii) and (iv), we get

$$\mathbf{a}\cdot\mathbf{d}+\mathbf{b}\cdot\mathbf{d}+\mathbf{c}\cdot\mathbf{d}=(\cos y+2+\sin x)[\mathbf{a}\ \mathbf{b}\ \mathbf{c}]$$

$\because$ $\sin x+\cos y+2=0$

$\Rightarrow$ $\sin x+\cos y=-2$

$\Rightarrow$ $\sin x=-1$ and $\cos y=-1$

$[\because -1<\sin x\le 1 \text{ and } -1\le\cos y\le 1]$

Since, we have to find the minimum value of

$$x^2+y^2;\ x=-\frac{\pi}{2}, y=\pi$$

$\therefore$ $$x^2+y^2=\frac{\pi^2}{4}+\pi^2=\frac{5\pi^2}{4}$$

Example 39 *Let* $\mathbf{a}, \mathbf{b}$ *and* $\mathbf{c}$ *be three vectors of magnitude* 1, 1 *and* 2 *respectively. If* $\mathbf{a}\times(\mathbf{a}\times\mathbf{c})+\mathbf{b}=0$, *then the acute angle between* $\mathbf{a}$ *and* $\mathbf{c}$ *is*

(a) $\frac{\pi}{3}$ (b) $\frac{\pi}{4}$

(c) $\frac{\pi}{6}$ (d) None of these

Sol. (c) Given, $|\mathbf{a}|=1, |\mathbf{b}|=1$, and $|\mathbf{c}|=2$

Also, $\mathbf{a}\times(\mathbf{a}\times\mathbf{c})+\mathbf{b}=0$

$\Rightarrow$ $(\mathbf{a}\cdot\mathbf{c})\mathbf{a}-(\mathbf{a}\cdot\mathbf{a})\mathbf{c}+\mathbf{b}=0$

$\Rightarrow$ $(\mathbf{a}\cdot\mathbf{c})\mathbf{a}-\mathbf{c}+\mathbf{b}=0$ $[\because \mathbf{a}\cdot\mathbf{a}=|\mathbf{a}|^2=1]$

$\Rightarrow$ $(\mathbf{a}\cdot\mathbf{c})\mathbf{a}-\mathbf{c}=-\mathbf{b}$

$\Rightarrow$ $|(\mathbf{a}\cdot\mathbf{c})\mathbf{a}-\mathbf{c}|=|-\mathbf{b}|$

$\Rightarrow$ $|(\mathbf{a}\cdot\mathbf{c})\mathbf{a}-\mathbf{c}|^2=|\mathbf{b}|^2$

$\Rightarrow$ $|(\mathbf{a}\cdot\mathbf{c})\mathbf{a}|^2+|\mathbf{c}|^2-2\{(\mathbf{a}\cdot\mathbf{c})\mathbf{a}\cdot\mathbf{c}\}=|\mathbf{b}|^2$

$\Rightarrow$ $(\mathbf{a}\cdot\mathbf{c})^2|\mathbf{a}|^2+|\mathbf{c}|^2-2(\mathbf{a}\cdot\mathbf{c})(\mathbf{a}\cdot\mathbf{c})=|\mathbf{b}|^2$

$\Rightarrow$ $(\mathbf{a}\cdot\mathbf{c})^2\{|\mathbf{a}|^2-2\}+|\mathbf{c}|^2=|\mathbf{b}|^2$

$\Rightarrow$ $-(\mathbf{a}\cdot\mathbf{c})^2+4=1$

$\Rightarrow$ $\mathbf{a}\cdot\mathbf{c}=\pm\sqrt{3}$

$\Rightarrow$ $|\mathbf{a}||\mathbf{c}|\cos\theta=\sqrt{3}$

where, θ is an acute angle between $\mathbf{a}$ and $\mathbf{c}$.

$\Rightarrow$ $$\cos\theta=\frac{\sqrt{3}}{2}$$

$\therefore$ $$\theta=\frac{\pi}{6}$$

JEE SCANNER

Example 40 Similar to PYQ Asked in JEE Adv. 2018

Let $\mathbf{a}$ *and* $\mathbf{b}$ *be two unit vectors such that* $\mathbf{a}\cdot\mathbf{b}=0$ *for some* $x, y\in R$. *Let* $\mathbf{c}=x\mathbf{a}+y\mathbf{b}+(\mathbf{a}\times\mathbf{b})$, *if* $|\mathbf{c}|=3$ *and the vector* $\mathbf{c}$ *is inclined at the some angle* α *to both* $\mathbf{a}$ *and* $\mathbf{b}$, *then the value of* $9\cos^2\alpha$ *is ....*

Sol. Given, $|\mathbf{a}|=|\mathbf{b}|=1$, $\mathbf{a}\cdot\mathbf{b}=0$ and $\mathbf{c}=x\mathbf{a}+y\mathbf{b}+(\mathbf{a}\times\mathbf{b})$

Now, $\mathbf{c}\cdot\mathbf{a}=(x\mathbf{a}+y\mathbf{b}+(\mathbf{a}\times\mathbf{b}))\cdot\mathbf{a}$

$=x|\mathbf{a}|^2+y\mathbf{b}\cdot\mathbf{a}+(\mathbf{a}\times\mathbf{b})\cdot\mathbf{a}$

$=x\cdot 1+y\cdot 0+0=x$

and $\mathbf{c}\cdot\mathbf{b}=(x\mathbf{a}+y\mathbf{b}+(\mathbf{a}\times\mathbf{b}))\cdot\mathbf{b}$

$=x\mathbf{a}\cdot\mathbf{b}+y|\mathbf{b}|^2+(\mathbf{a}\times\mathbf{b})\cdot\mathbf{b}$

$=x\cdot 0+y\cdot 1+0$

$=y$

Since, $\mathbf{a}\cdot\mathbf{b}=0 \Rightarrow |\mathbf{a}||\mathbf{b}|\cos\theta=0$

$\Rightarrow$ $\cos\theta=0\Rightarrow\theta=\frac{\pi}{2}$

$\therefore$ $\mathbf{a}\times\mathbf{b}=|\mathbf{a}||\mathbf{b}|\sin\frac{\pi}{2}$ $\left[\because \theta=\frac{\pi}{2}\right]$

$=1$

$\Rightarrow|\mathbf{a}\times\mathbf{b}|=1$

Since, $\mathbf{c}\cdot\mathbf{a}=x\Rightarrow|\mathbf{c}||\mathbf{a}|\cos\alpha=x$

$\Rightarrow 3\cos\alpha=x$ ...(i)

Similarly, $\mathbf{c}\cdot\mathbf{d}=y\Rightarrow 3\cos\alpha=y$ ...(ii)

Now, $\mathbf{c}=x\mathbf{a}+y\mathbf{b}+(\mathbf{a}\times\mathbf{b})$

$|\mathbf{c}|^2=|x\mathbf{a}|^2+|y\mathbf{b}|^2+|\mathbf{a}\times\mathbf{b}|^2$

$(3)^2=x^2+y^2+1$

$9=9\cos^2\alpha+9\cos^2\alpha+1\Rightarrow 8=18\cos^2\alpha$

$\therefore 18\cos^2\alpha=3\Rightarrow 9\cos^2\alpha=4$

Skill Builder

Let $\mathbf{a}$ and $\mathbf{b}$ be two unit vectors such that $\mathbf{a}\cdot\mathbf{b}=0$ for some $x, y\in R$.
Let $\mathbf{c}=x\mathbf{a}+y\mathbf{b}+(\mathbf{a}\times\mathbf{b})$, if $|\mathbf{c}|=2$ and the vector $\mathbf{c}$ is inclined at the some angle α to both $\mathbf{a}$ and $\mathbf{b}$, then the value of $8\cos^2\alpha$ is ....

For Sol.

Example 41 *Let* $\mathbf{a} = 2\hat{\mathbf{i}} + \hat{\mathbf{j}} - 2\hat{\mathbf{k}}$ *and* $\mathbf{b} = \hat{\mathbf{i}} + \hat{\mathbf{j}}$. *If* $\mathbf{c}$ *is a vector such that* $\mathbf{a} \cdot \mathbf{c} = |\mathbf{c}|, |\mathbf{c} - \mathbf{a}| = 2\sqrt{2}$ *and the angle between* $\mathbf{a} \times \mathbf{b}$ *and* $\mathbf{c}$ *is 30°, then* $|(\mathbf{a} \times \mathbf{b}) \times \mathbf{c}|$ *is equal to*

(a) $\frac{2}{3}$ (b) $\frac{3}{2}$ (c) 2 (d) 3

Sol. (b) $|\mathbf{c} - \mathbf{a}| = 2\sqrt{2}$

$\Rightarrow \quad |\mathbf{c}|^2 + |\mathbf{a}|^2 - 2\mathbf{a} \cdot \mathbf{c} = 8$

$\Rightarrow \quad |\mathbf{c}|^2 + (\sqrt{9})^2 - 2|\mathbf{c}| = 8$

$\Rightarrow \quad |\mathbf{c}|^2 - 2|\mathbf{c}| + 1 = 0$

$\Rightarrow \quad (|\mathbf{c}| - 1)^2 = 0 \Rightarrow |\mathbf{c}| = 1$

Now, $\quad \mathbf{a} \times \mathbf{b} = 2\hat{\mathbf{i}} + 2\hat{\mathbf{j}} + \hat{\mathbf{k}}$

$\therefore \quad |\mathbf{a} \times \mathbf{b}| = \sqrt{4 + 4 + 1} = 3$

$\therefore \quad |(\mathbf{a} \times \mathbf{b}) \times \mathbf{c}| = |\mathbf{a} \times \mathbf{b}||\mathbf{c}| \sin 30°$

$= 3 \times 1 \times \frac{1}{2} = \frac{3}{2}$

Example 42 *Let* $\hat{\mathbf{a}}$ *and* $\hat{\mathbf{b}}$ *be two unit vectors such that* $\hat{\mathbf{a}} \cdot \hat{\mathbf{b}} = \frac{1}{3}$ *and* $\hat{\mathbf{a}} \times \hat{\mathbf{b}} = \hat{\mathbf{c}}$. *Also,* $\mathbf{F} = \alpha\hat{\mathbf{a}} + \beta\hat{\mathbf{b}} + \gamma\hat{\mathbf{c}}$, *where* α, β *and* γ *are scalars. If* $\alpha = k_1(\hat{\mathbf{F}} \cdot \hat{\mathbf{a}}) - k_2(\hat{\mathbf{F}} \cdot \hat{\mathbf{b}})$, *then the value of* $2(k_1 + k_2)$ *is*

(a) $2\sqrt{3}$ (b) $\sqrt{3}$

(c) 3 (d) 1

Sol. (c) $\quad \bar{\mathbf{F}} = \alpha\hat{\mathbf{a}} + \beta\hat{\mathbf{b}} + \gamma\hat{\mathbf{c}}$

$\therefore \quad \mathbf{F} \cdot (\hat{\mathbf{b}} \times \hat{\mathbf{c}}) = \alpha\, [\hat{\mathbf{a}}\ \hat{\mathbf{b}}\ \hat{\mathbf{c}}]$

$\therefore \quad \alpha = \frac{\hat{\mathbf{F}} \cdot (\hat{\mathbf{b}} \times \hat{\mathbf{c}})}{[\hat{\mathbf{a}}\hat{\mathbf{b}}\hat{\mathbf{c}}]}$

Now, $\quad \hat{\mathbf{b}} \times \hat{\mathbf{c}} = \hat{\mathbf{b}} \times (\hat{\mathbf{a}} \times \hat{\mathbf{b}}) = (\hat{\mathbf{b}} \cdot \hat{\mathbf{b}})\hat{\mathbf{a}} - (\hat{\mathbf{b}} \cdot \hat{\mathbf{a}})\hat{\mathbf{b}}$

$= \hat{\mathbf{a}} - \frac{1}{3}\hat{\mathbf{b}}$

$[\hat{\mathbf{a}}\ \hat{\mathbf{b}}\ \hat{\mathbf{c}}] = (\hat{\mathbf{a}} \times \hat{\mathbf{b}})^2 = |\hat{\mathbf{a}}|^2 |\hat{\mathbf{b}}|^2 - (\hat{\mathbf{a}} \cdot \hat{\mathbf{b}})^2 = 1 - \frac{1}{9} = \frac{8}{9}$

$\therefore \quad \alpha = \frac{9}{8}\left\{\hat{\mathbf{F}} \cdot \hat{\mathbf{a}} - \frac{1}{3}\hat{\mathbf{F}} \cdot \hat{\mathbf{b}}\right\}$

$\therefore \quad k_1 = \frac{9}{8}, k_2 = \frac{3}{8}$

$\Rightarrow \quad k_1 + k_2 = \frac{12}{8} = \frac{3}{2}$

$\therefore \quad 2(k_1 + k_2) = 3$

Example 43 *Let* $\mathbf{a} = \hat{\mathbf{i}} - \hat{\mathbf{j}}, \mathbf{b} = \hat{\mathbf{j}} - \hat{\mathbf{k}}$ *and* $\mathbf{c} = \hat{\mathbf{k}} - \hat{\mathbf{i}}$. *If* $\mathbf{d}$ *is a unit vector such that* $\mathbf{a} \cdot \mathbf{d} = 0 = [\mathbf{b}\ \mathbf{c}\ \mathbf{d}]$, *then* $\mathbf{d}$ *is equal to*

(a) $\pm\frac{(\hat{\mathbf{i}} + \hat{\mathbf{j}} - 2\hat{\mathbf{k}})}{\sqrt{6}}$ (b) $\pm\frac{(\hat{\mathbf{i}} + \hat{\mathbf{j}} - \hat{\mathbf{k}})}{\sqrt{3}}$

(c) $\pm\frac{(\hat{\mathbf{i}} + \hat{\mathbf{j}} + \hat{\mathbf{k}})}{\sqrt{3}}$ (d) $\pm\hat{\mathbf{k}}$

Sol. (a) We have, $\mathbf{a} \cdot \mathbf{d} = 0$ and $[\mathbf{b}\ \mathbf{c}\ \mathbf{d}] = 0$

$\Rightarrow \mathbf{a} \perp \mathbf{d}$ and $\mathbf{b}, \mathbf{c}, \mathbf{d}$ are coplanar.

$\Rightarrow \mathbf{d} \perp \mathbf{a}$ and $\mathbf{d}$ lies in the plane of $\mathbf{b}$ and $\mathbf{c}$, we know that the vector $\mathbf{r} = \mathbf{a} \times (\mathbf{b} \times \mathbf{c})$ is perpendicular to $\mathbf{a}$ and lies in the plane of $\mathbf{b}$ and $\mathbf{c}$.

$\therefore \quad \hat{\mathbf{d}} = \pm\frac{\mathbf{r}}{|\mathbf{r}|}$

Now, $\quad \mathbf{r} = \mathbf{a} \times (\mathbf{b} \times \mathbf{c})$

$\Rightarrow \quad \mathbf{r} = (\mathbf{a} \cdot \mathbf{c})\,\mathbf{b} - (\mathbf{a} \cdot \mathbf{b})\mathbf{c}$

$\Rightarrow \quad \mathbf{r} = -(\hat{\mathbf{j}} - \hat{\mathbf{k}}) + (\hat{\mathbf{k}} - \hat{\mathbf{i}}) = -\hat{\mathbf{i}} - \hat{\mathbf{j}} + 2\hat{\mathbf{k}}$

$\therefore \quad \hat{\mathbf{d}} = \pm\frac{\mathbf{r}}{|\mathbf{r}|} = \pm\frac{(-\hat{\mathbf{i}} - \hat{\mathbf{j}} + 2\hat{\mathbf{k}})}{\sqrt{1 + 1 + 4}}$

$= \pm\frac{\hat{\mathbf{i}} + \hat{\mathbf{j}} - 2\hat{\mathbf{k}}}{\sqrt{6}}$

Example 44 *The value for* $[\mathbf{a} \times (\mathbf{b} + \mathbf{c}), \mathbf{b} \times (\mathbf{c} - 2\mathbf{a}), \mathbf{c} \times (\mathbf{a} + 3\mathbf{b})]$ *is equal to*

(a) $[\mathbf{a}\ \mathbf{b}\ \mathbf{c}]^2$ (b) $7[\mathbf{a}\ \mathbf{b}\ \mathbf{c}]^2$

(c) $-5[\mathbf{a} \times \mathbf{b}\ \mathbf{b} \times \mathbf{c}\ \mathbf{c} \times \mathbf{a}]$ (d) None of these

Sol. (b) Let $\mathbf{a} \times \mathbf{b} = \mathbf{l}$, $\mathbf{b} \times \mathbf{c} = \mathbf{m}$ and $\mathbf{c} \times \mathbf{a} = \mathbf{n}$,

$\therefore \quad [\mathbf{a} \times (\mathbf{b} + \mathbf{c}), \mathbf{b} \times (\mathbf{c} - 2\mathbf{a}), \mathbf{c} \times (\mathbf{a} + 3\mathbf{b})]$

$= [\mathbf{l} - \mathbf{n}\quad \mathbf{m} + 2\mathbf{l}\quad \mathbf{n} - 3\mathbf{m}]$

$= \begin{vmatrix} 1 & 0 & -1 \\ 2 & 1 & 0 \\ 0 & -3 & 1 \end{vmatrix} [\mathbf{l}\ \mathbf{m}\ \mathbf{n}]$

$= 7[\mathbf{l}\ \mathbf{m}\ \mathbf{n}] = 7[\mathbf{a} \times \mathbf{b}\quad \mathbf{b} \times \mathbf{c}\quad \mathbf{c} \times \mathbf{a}] = 7[\mathbf{a}\ \ \mathbf{b}\ \ \mathbf{c}]^2$

Example 45 *If* $\mathbf{a}, \mathbf{b}, \mathbf{c}$ *and* $\mathbf{p}, \mathbf{q}, \mathbf{r}$ *are reciprocal system of vectors, then* $\mathbf{a} \times \mathbf{p} + \mathbf{b} \times \mathbf{q} + c \times \mathbf{r}$ *is equal to*

(a) $[\mathbf{a}\ \mathbf{b}\ \mathbf{c}]$ (b) $[\mathbf{p} + \mathbf{q} + \mathbf{r}]$

(c) 0 (d) $\mathbf{a} + \mathbf{b} + \mathbf{c}$

Sol. (c) $\mathbf{p} = \frac{\mathbf{b} \times \mathbf{c}}{[\mathbf{a}\ \mathbf{b}\ \mathbf{c}]}, \mathbf{q} = \frac{\mathbf{c} \times \mathbf{a}}{[\mathbf{a}\ \mathbf{b}\ \mathbf{c}]}, \mathbf{r} = \frac{\mathbf{a} \times \mathbf{b}}{[\mathbf{a}\ \mathbf{b}\ \mathbf{c}]}$

$\mathbf{a} \times \mathbf{p} = \mathbf{a} \times \frac{(\mathbf{b} \times \mathbf{c})}{[\mathbf{a}\ \mathbf{b}\ \mathbf{c}]}$

$= \frac{(\mathbf{a} \cdot \mathbf{c})\mathbf{b} - (\mathbf{a} \cdot \mathbf{b})\mathbf{c}}{[\mathbf{a}\ \mathbf{b}\ \mathbf{c}]}$

Similarly, $\quad \mathbf{b} \times \mathbf{q} = \frac{(\mathbf{a} \cdot \mathbf{b})\mathbf{c} - (\mathbf{b} \cdot \mathbf{c})\mathbf{a}}{[\mathbf{a}\ \mathbf{b}\ \mathbf{c}]}$

and $\quad \mathbf{c} \times \mathbf{r} = \frac{(\mathbf{b} \cdot \mathbf{c})\mathbf{a} - (\mathbf{a} \cdot \mathbf{c})\mathbf{b}}{[\mathbf{a}\ \mathbf{b}\ \mathbf{c}]}$

$\therefore \quad \mathbf{a} \times \mathbf{p} + \mathbf{b} \times \mathbf{q} + \mathbf{c} \times \mathbf{r}$

$= \frac{1}{[\mathbf{a}\ \mathbf{b}\ \mathbf{c}]}\{(\mathbf{a} \cdot \mathbf{c})\mathbf{b} - (\mathbf{a} \cdot \mathbf{b})\mathbf{c} + (\mathbf{a} \cdot \mathbf{b})\mathbf{c} - (\mathbf{b} \cdot \mathbf{c})\mathbf{a} + (\mathbf{b} \cdot \mathbf{c})\mathbf{a} - (\mathbf{a} \cdot \mathbf{c})\mathbf{b}\}$

$= \frac{1}{[\mathbf{a}\ \mathbf{b}\ \mathbf{c}]} \times \mathbf{0} = \mathbf{0}$

More than One Correct Option Type Questions

Example 46 *If* $\mathbf{a}$ *and* $\mathbf{b}$ *are non-zero vectors such that* $|\mathbf{a}+\mathbf{b}|=|\mathbf{a}-2\mathbf{b}|$, *then*

(a) $2\,\mathbf{a}\cdot\mathbf{b}=|\mathbf{b}|^2$

(b) $\mathbf{a}\cdot\mathbf{b}=|\mathbf{b}|^2$

(c) least value of $\mathbf{a}\cdot\mathbf{b}+\dfrac{1}{|\mathbf{b}|^2+2}$ is $\sqrt{2}$.

(d) least value of $\mathbf{a}\cdot\mathbf{b}+\dfrac{1}{|\mathbf{b}|^2+2}$ is $\sqrt{2}-1$.

Sol. (a, d) $|\mathbf{a}+\mathbf{b}|=|\mathbf{a}-2\mathbf{b}|$

$\Rightarrow \quad \mathbf{a}\cdot\mathbf{b}=\dfrac{|\mathbf{b}|^2}{2}$ [squaring both sides and solving]

Also, $\mathbf{a}\cdot\mathbf{b}+\dfrac{1}{|\mathbf{b}|^2+2}=\dfrac{|\mathbf{b}|^2+2}{2}+\dfrac{1}{|\mathbf{b}|^2+2}-1$

$\geq\sqrt{2}-1$ [using AM $\geq$ GM]

Example 47 *If* $\mathbf{z}_1=a\hat{\mathbf{i}}+b\hat{\mathbf{j}}$ *and* $\mathbf{z}_2=c\hat{\mathbf{i}}+d\hat{\mathbf{j}}$ *are two vectors in* $\hat{\mathbf{i}}$ *and* $\hat{\mathbf{j}}$ *system, where* $|\mathbf{z}_1|=|\mathbf{z}_2|=r$ *and* $\mathbf{z}_1\cdot\mathbf{z}_2=0$, *then* $\mathbf{w}_1=a\hat{\mathbf{i}}+c\hat{\mathbf{j}}$ *and* $\mathbf{w}_2=b\hat{\mathbf{i}}+d\hat{\mathbf{j}}$ *satisfy*

(a) $|\mathbf{w}_1|=r$

(b) $|\mathbf{w}_2|=r$

(c) $\mathbf{w}_1\cdot\mathbf{w}_2=0$

(d) $\mathbf{w}_1\times\mathbf{w}_2=0$

Sol. (a, b, c) $|z_1|=|z_2|=r$ and $\mathbf{z}_1\cdot\mathbf{z}_2=0$

$\Rightarrow \quad \sqrt{a^2+b^2}=\sqrt{c^2+d^2}=r$ ...(i)

and $\quad ac+bd=0$

as, $\quad ac=-bd$

$\Rightarrow \quad \dfrac{b}{a}=\dfrac{-c}{d}=\lambda$ ...(ii)

From Eqs. (i) and (ii), we get

$$a^2(1+\lambda^2)=d^2(1+\lambda^2)$$

$\Rightarrow \quad a^2=d^2$ and $b^2=c^2$

Now, $\quad |\mathbf{w}_1|=\sqrt{a^2+c^2}=\sqrt{d^2+b^2}=|\mathbf{w}_2|=r$

and $\quad \mathbf{w}_1\cdot\mathbf{w}_2=ab+cd=0$ [using Eq. (ii)]

Example 48 $\mathbf{a}$, $\mathbf{b}$ *and* $\mathbf{c}$ *are three vectors such that* $\mathbf{a}\cdot\mathbf{a}=\mathbf{b}\cdot\mathbf{b}=\mathbf{c}\cdot\mathbf{c}=3$ *and* $|\mathbf{a}-\mathbf{b}|^2+|\mathbf{b}-\mathbf{c}|^2+|\mathbf{c}-\mathbf{a}|^2=27$, *then*

(a) $\mathbf{a}$, $\mathbf{b}$ and $\mathbf{c}$ are necessarily coplanar.

(b) $\mathbf{a}$, $\mathbf{b}$ and $\mathbf{c}$ represent sides of a triangle in magnitude and direction.

(c) $\mathbf{a}\cdot\mathbf{b}+\mathbf{b}\cdot\mathbf{c}+\mathbf{c}\cdot\mathbf{a}$ has the least value $-\dfrac{9}{2}$.

(d) $\mathbf{a}$, $\mathbf{b}$ and $\mathbf{c}$ represent orthogonal triad of vectors.

Sol. (a, b, c) Here, $|\mathbf{a}-\mathbf{b}|^2+|\mathbf{b}-\mathbf{c}|^2+|\mathbf{c}-\mathbf{a}|^2$

$=2(|\mathbf{a}|^2+|\mathbf{b}|^2+|\mathbf{c}|^2-\mathbf{a}\cdot\mathbf{b}-\mathbf{b}\cdot\mathbf{c}-\mathbf{c}\cdot\mathbf{a})$

$\Rightarrow \quad \mathbf{a}\cdot\mathbf{b}+\mathbf{b}\cdot\mathbf{c}+\mathbf{c}\cdot\mathbf{a}=-\dfrac{9}{2}$

Now, $|\mathbf{a}+\mathbf{b}+\mathbf{c}|^2=|\mathbf{a}|^2+|\mathbf{b}|^2+|\mathbf{c}|^2+2(\mathbf{a}\cdot\mathbf{b}+\mathbf{b}\cdot\mathbf{c}+\mathbf{c}\cdot\mathbf{a})$

$=3+3+3-2\left(\dfrac{9}{2}\right)=0$

$\therefore \quad \mathbf{a}+\mathbf{b}+\mathbf{c}=0$ ...(i)

Also, $\quad |\mathbf{a}+\mathbf{b}+\mathbf{c}|^2\geq 0$

$\Rightarrow \quad \mathbf{a}\cdot\mathbf{b}+\mathbf{b}\cdot\mathbf{c}+\mathbf{c}\cdot\mathbf{a}\geq-\dfrac{9}{2}$ ...(ii)

Thus, least value of $(\mathbf{a}\cdot\mathbf{b}+\mathbf{b}\cdot\mathbf{c}+\mathbf{c}\cdot\mathbf{a})$ is $-\dfrac{9}{2}$.

Example 49 *If unit vectors* $\hat{\mathbf{i}}$ *and* $\hat{\mathbf{j}}$ *are at right angles to each other and* $\mathbf{p}=3\hat{\mathbf{i}}+4\hat{\mathbf{j}}$, $\mathbf{q}=5\hat{\mathbf{i}}$, $4\mathbf{r}=\mathbf{p}+\mathbf{q}$ *and* $2\mathbf{s}=\mathbf{p}-\mathbf{q}$, *then*

(a) $|\mathbf{r}+k\mathbf{s}|=|\mathbf{r}-k\mathbf{s}|$ for all real k.

(b) $\mathbf{r}$ is perpendicular to $\mathbf{s}$.

(c) $\mathbf{r}+\mathbf{s}$ is perpendicular to $\mathbf{r}-\mathbf{s}$.

(d) $|\mathbf{r}|=|\mathbf{s}|=|\mathbf{p}|=|\mathbf{q}|$

Sol. (a, b, c) We have, $\mathbf{p}=3\hat{\mathbf{i}}+4\hat{\mathbf{j}}$ and $\mathbf{q}=5\hat{\mathbf{i}}$

Also, $4\mathbf{r}=\mathbf{p}+\mathbf{q}=3\hat{\mathbf{i}}+4\hat{\mathbf{j}}+5\hat{\mathbf{i}}=8\hat{\mathbf{i}}+4\hat{\mathbf{j}} \Rightarrow \mathbf{r}=2\hat{\mathbf{i}}+\hat{\mathbf{j}}$

and $\quad 2\mathbf{s}=\mathbf{p}-\mathbf{q}=3\hat{\mathbf{i}}+4\hat{\mathbf{j}}-5\hat{\mathbf{i}}=-2\hat{\mathbf{i}}+4\hat{\mathbf{j}} \Rightarrow \mathbf{s}=-\hat{\mathbf{i}}+2\hat{\mathbf{j}}$

Now, $\quad |\mathbf{r}+k\mathbf{s}|=|\mathbf{r}-k\mathbf{s}|$

$\Rightarrow |2\hat{\mathbf{i}}+\hat{\mathbf{j}}-k\hat{\mathbf{i}}+2k\hat{\mathbf{j}}|^2=|2\hat{\mathbf{i}}+\hat{\mathbf{j}}+k\hat{\mathbf{i}}-2k\hat{\mathbf{j}}|^2$

[on squaring both sides]

$\Rightarrow (2-k)^2+(1+2k)^2=(2+k)^2+(1-2k)^2$

Which is true for all values of k.

Now, $\quad \mathbf{r}\cdot\mathbf{s}=(2\hat{\mathbf{i}}+\hat{\mathbf{j}})\cdot(-\hat{\mathbf{i}}+2\hat{\mathbf{j}})=-2+2=0$

$\therefore \quad \mathbf{r}\perp\mathbf{s}$

Also, $(\mathbf{r}+\mathbf{s})\cdot(\mathbf{r}-\mathbf{s})=(\hat{\mathbf{i}}+3\hat{\mathbf{j}})(3\hat{\mathbf{i}}-\hat{\mathbf{j}})=3-3=0$

$\therefore \quad (\mathbf{r}+\mathbf{s})\perp(\mathbf{r}-\mathbf{s})$

Also, $\quad |\mathbf{r}|=\sqrt{(2)^2+1}=\sqrt{5}$

$|\mathbf{s}|=\sqrt{(-1)^2+(2)^2}=\sqrt{5}$

$|\mathbf{p}|=\sqrt{3^2+4^2}=5$

$|\mathbf{q}|=\sqrt{5^2}=5$

$\therefore \quad |\mathbf{r}|=|\mathbf{s}|$ and $|\mathbf{p}|=|\mathbf{q}|$

Example 50 *If vectors* $\mathbf{b}=(\tan\alpha, -1, 2\sqrt{\sin\alpha/2})$ *and* $\mathbf{c}=\left(\tan\alpha, \tan\alpha, -\dfrac{3}{\sqrt{\sin\alpha/2}}\right)$ *are orthogonal and vectors* $\mathbf{a}=(1, 3, \sin 2\alpha)$ *makes an obtuse angle with the Z-axis, then the value of* α *is*

(a) $\alpha=(4n+1)\pi+\tan^{-1}2$

(b) $\alpha=(4n+1)\pi-\tan^{-1}2$

(c) $\alpha=(4n+2)\pi+\tan^{-1}2$

(d) $\alpha=(4n+2)\pi-\tan^{-1}2$

Sol. (b, d), Since, $\mathbf{a} = (1, 3, \sin 2\alpha)$ makes an obtuse angle with the Z-axis, its z-component is negative.

Thus, $\quad -1 \le \sin 2\alpha < 0 \quad$ ...(i)

But $\quad \mathbf{b} \cdot \mathbf{c} = 0 \quad$ [$\because$ orthogonal]

$\tan^2\alpha - \tan\alpha - 6 = 0$

$\therefore \quad (\tan\alpha - 3)(\tan\alpha + 2) = 0 \Rightarrow \tan\alpha = 3, -2$

Now, $\quad \tan\alpha = 3.$

Therefore, $\quad \sin 2\alpha = \dfrac{2\tan\alpha}{1 + \tan^2\alpha} = \dfrac{6}{1+9} = \dfrac{3}{5}$

[not possible as $\sin 2\alpha < 0$]

Now, if $\tan\alpha = -2$,

$\Rightarrow \sin 2\alpha = \dfrac{2\tan\alpha}{1+\tan^2\alpha} = \dfrac{-4}{1+4} = \dfrac{-4}{5} \Rightarrow \tan 2\alpha > 0$

Hence, 2α is in the third quadrant.

Also, $\sqrt{\sin\alpha / 2}$ is meaningful.

If $0 < \sin\alpha / 2 < 1$, then

$\alpha = (4n+1)\pi - \tan^{-1}2$ and $\alpha = (4n+2)\pi - \tan^{-1}2$

Example 51 *If* $\alpha(\mathbf{a} \times \mathbf{b}) + \beta(\mathbf{b} \times \mathbf{c}) + \gamma(\mathbf{c} \times \mathbf{a}) = 0$, *then*

(a) $\mathbf{a}, \mathbf{b}, \mathbf{c}$ are coplanar, if all of $\alpha, \beta, \gamma \ne 0$

(b) $\mathbf{a}, \mathbf{b}, \mathbf{c}$ are coplanar, if any one of $\alpha, \beta, \gamma \ne 0$

(c) $\mathbf{a}, \mathbf{b}, \mathbf{c}$ are non-coplanar for any $\alpha, \beta, \gamma \ne 0$

(d) None of the above

Sol. (a, b) We have, $\alpha(\mathbf{a} \times \mathbf{b}) + \beta(\mathbf{b} \times \mathbf{c}) + \gamma(\mathbf{c} \times \mathbf{a}) = 0$

On taking dot product with $\mathbf{c}$, we have

$\alpha[\mathbf{a}\ \mathbf{b}\ \mathbf{c}] = 0$

Similarly, on taking dot product with b and c, we have

$\beta[\mathbf{a}\ \mathbf{b}\ \mathbf{c}] = 0$ and $\gamma[\mathbf{a}\ \mathbf{b}\ \mathbf{c}] = 0$

Now, even if one of $\alpha, \beta, \gamma \ne 0$, then we have $[\mathbf{a}\ \mathbf{b}\ \mathbf{c}] = 0$

$\Rightarrow$ $\mathbf{a}$, $\mathbf{b}$ and $\mathbf{c}$ are coplanar.

Example 52 *If* $\mathbf{a} = \hat{\mathbf{i}} + \hat{\mathbf{j}} + \hat{\mathbf{k}}$ *and* $\mathbf{b} = \hat{\mathbf{i}} - \hat{\mathbf{j}}$, *then the vectors* $(\mathbf{a} \cdot \hat{\mathbf{i}})\hat{\mathbf{i}} + (\mathbf{a} \cdot \hat{\mathbf{j}})\hat{\mathbf{j}} + (\mathbf{a} \cdot \hat{\mathbf{k}})\hat{\mathbf{k}}$, $(\mathbf{b} \cdot \hat{\mathbf{i}})\hat{\mathbf{i}} + (\mathbf{b} \cdot \hat{\mathbf{j}})\hat{\mathbf{j}} + (\mathbf{b} \cdot \hat{\mathbf{k}})\hat{\mathbf{k}}$ *and* $\hat{\mathbf{i}} + \hat{\mathbf{j}} - 2\hat{\mathbf{k}}$

(a) are mutually perpendicular

(b) are coplanar

(c) form a parallelopiped of volume 6 cu units

(d) form a parallelopiped of volume 3 cu units

Sol. (a, c) Given $\mathbf{a} = \hat{\mathbf{i}} + \hat{\mathbf{j}} + \hat{\mathbf{k}}$ and $\mathbf{b} = \hat{\mathbf{i}} - \hat{\mathbf{j}}$

$(\mathbf{a} \cdot \hat{\mathbf{i}})\hat{\mathbf{i}} + (\mathbf{a} \cdot \hat{\mathbf{j}})\hat{\mathbf{j}} + (\mathbf{a} \cdot \hat{\mathbf{k}})\hat{\mathbf{k}} = \hat{\mathbf{i}} + \hat{\mathbf{j}} + \hat{\mathbf{k}} = \mathbf{x}$ (say)

and $(b \cdot \hat{\mathbf{i}})\hat{\mathbf{i}} + (b \cdot \hat{\mathbf{j}})\hat{\mathbf{j}} + (b \cdot \hat{\mathbf{k}})\hat{\mathbf{k}} = \hat{\mathbf{i}} - \hat{\mathbf{j}} = \mathbf{y}$ (say)

and $\quad \hat{\mathbf{i}} + \hat{\mathbf{j}} - 2\hat{\mathbf{k}} = \mathbf{z}$ (say)

Clearly, $\quad \mathbf{x} \cdot \mathbf{y} = \mathbf{y} \cdot \mathbf{z} = \mathbf{z} \cdot \mathbf{x} = 0$

$\therefore$ $\mathbf{x}$, $\mathbf{y}$ and $\mathbf{z}$ are mutually perpendicular.

$\therefore$ Volume of parallelopiped $= \begin{vmatrix} 1 & 1 & 1 \\ 1 & -1 & 0 \\ 1 & 1 & -2 \end{vmatrix}$

$= 1(2-0) - 1(-2-0) + 1(1+1)$

$= 2 + 2 + 2 = 6$

$\because$ $\mathbf{x}$, $\mathbf{y}$ and $\mathbf{z}$ are not coplanar i.e. $[\mathbf{x}\ \mathbf{y}\ \mathbf{z}] \ne 0$

$\therefore$ Volume of parallelopiped formed by $\mathbf{x}$, $\mathbf{y}$ and $\mathbf{z}$ is 6 cu units.

JEE SCANNER

Example 53 Similar to PYQ Asked in JEE Adv. 2019

Let $\mathbf{a} = 3\hat{\mathbf{i}} - 3\hat{\mathbf{j}} + \hat{\mathbf{k}}$ *and* $\mathbf{b} = \hat{\mathbf{i}} + 3\hat{\mathbf{j}} - \hat{\mathbf{k}}$ *be two vectors. Consider a vector* $\mathbf{c} = \alpha\mathbf{a} + \beta\mathbf{b}$. $\alpha, \beta \in R$ *if the projection of* $\mathbf{c}$ *on the vector* $(\mathbf{a} + \mathbf{b})$ *in 4, then the minimum value of* $(\mathbf{c} - (\mathbf{a} \times \mathbf{b}))\mathbf{c}$ *equals* ....

Sol. Given, $\mathbf{a} = 3\hat{\mathbf{i}} - 3\hat{\mathbf{j}} + \hat{\mathbf{k}}$, $\mathbf{b} = \hat{\mathbf{i}} + 3\hat{\mathbf{j}} - \hat{\mathbf{k}}$

Projection of $\mathbf{c}$ on vector $(\mathbf{a} + \mathbf{b}) = \dfrac{\mathbf{c} \cdot (\mathbf{a} + \mathbf{b})}{|\mathbf{a} + \mathbf{b}|}$ ...(i)

Now, consider $|\mathbf{a} + \mathbf{b}| = \sqrt{9 + 0 + 0} = 3$

Also, $|\mathbf{a}| = \sqrt{9 + 9 + 1} = \sqrt{19}$, $|\mathbf{b}| = \sqrt{1 + 0 + 1} = \sqrt{11}$

$\mathbf{a} \cdot \mathbf{b} = 3 - 9 - 1 = -7$

From (i), we have $\quad \dfrac{\mathbf{c}(\mathbf{a} + \mathbf{b})}{|\mathbf{a} + \mathbf{b}|} = 4 \quad$ [given]

$\Rightarrow \quad (\alpha\mathbf{a} + \beta\mathbf{b}) \cdot (\mathbf{a} + \mathbf{b}) = 4|\mathbf{a} + \mathbf{b}|$

$\Rightarrow \alpha|\mathbf{a}|^2 + \alpha\mathbf{a} \cdot \mathbf{b} + \beta\mathbf{b} \cdot \mathbf{a} + \beta|\mathbf{b}|^2 = 4 \cdot 3$

$\Rightarrow \quad \alpha(\sqrt{19})^2 + \alpha(-7) + \beta(-7) + \beta(\sqrt{11})^2 = 12$

$\Rightarrow \quad 19\alpha - 7\alpha - 7\beta + 11\beta = 12 \Rightarrow 12\alpha + 4\beta = 12$

$\therefore \quad 3\alpha + \beta = 3$

Now, consider

$(\mathbf{c} - (\mathbf{a} \times \mathbf{b})) \cdot \mathbf{c} = (\alpha\mathbf{a} + \beta\mathbf{b} - \mathbf{a} \times \mathbf{b}) \cdot (\alpha\mathbf{a} + \beta\mathbf{b})$

$= \alpha|\mathbf{a}|^2 + \alpha\beta\,\mathbf{a} \cdot \mathbf{b} + \alpha\beta\mathbf{b} \cdot \mathbf{a} + \beta|\mathbf{b}|^2 - 0$

$= 19\alpha - 7\alpha\beta - 7\alpha\beta + 11\beta$

$= 19\alpha + 11\beta - 14\alpha\beta$

$= 19\alpha + 11(3 - 3\alpha) - 14\alpha(3 - 3\alpha)$

$= 19\alpha + 33 - 33\alpha - 42\alpha + 42\alpha^2$

$= 42\alpha^2 - 56\alpha + 33$

Let $\mathbf{x} = 42\alpha^2 - 56\alpha + 33$

Now, for the minimum of $\mathbf{x}$, find $\dfrac{d\mathbf{x}}{d\alpha}$

$\dfrac{d\mathbf{x}}{d\alpha} = 84\alpha - 56$

$\dfrac{d\mathbf{x}}{d\alpha} = 0 \Rightarrow 84\alpha - 56 \Rightarrow \alpha = \dfrac{2}{3}$

and $\quad \dfrac{d^2\mathbf{x}}{d\alpha^2} = 84 > 0$

So, $\alpha = \dfrac{2}{3}$ is point of minimum.

Hence, $(\mathbf{c} - (\mathbf{a} \times \mathbf{b}))\,\mathbf{c}$ is 23.67.

Skill Builder

Let $\mathbf{a} = 2\hat{\mathbf{i}} + \hat{\mathbf{j}} - \hat{\mathbf{k}}$ and $\mathbf{b} = \hat{\mathbf{i}} + 2\hat{\mathbf{j}} + \hat{\mathbf{k}}$ be two vectors. Consider a vector $\mathbf{c} = \alpha\mathbf{a} + \beta\mathbf{b}$. $\alpha, \beta \in R$ if the projection of $\mathbf{c}$ on the vector $(\mathbf{a} + \mathbf{b})$ in $3\sqrt{2}$, then the minimum value of $(\mathbf{c} - (\mathbf{a} \times \mathbf{b}))\mathbf{c}$ equals ....

For Sol.

Example 54 *If* $\mathbf{a}$ *is perpendicular to* $\mathbf{b}$ *and p is non-zero scalar such that* $p\mathbf{r}+(\mathbf{r}\cdot\mathbf{b})\mathbf{a}=\mathbf{c}$, *then* $\mathbf{r}$ *satisfy*

(a) $[\mathbf{r}\ \mathbf{a}\ \mathbf{c}]=0$ (b) $p^2\mathbf{r}=p\mathbf{a}-(\mathbf{c}\cdot\mathbf{a})\mathbf{b}$

(c) $p^2\mathbf{r}=p\mathbf{b}-(\mathbf{a}\cdot\mathbf{b})\mathbf{c}$ (d) $p^2\mathbf{r}=p\mathbf{c}-(\mathbf{b}\cdot\mathbf{c})\mathbf{a}$

Sol. (a, d) Given, $\mathbf{a}\cdot\mathbf{b}=0$ and $p\mathbf{r}+(\mathbf{r}\cdot\mathbf{b})\mathbf{a}=\mathbf{c}$ ... (i)

On taking dot product by $\mathbf{b}$, we get

$$p(\mathbf{r}\cdot\mathbf{b})+(\mathbf{r}\cdot\mathbf{b})\mathbf{a}\cdot\mathbf{b}=\mathbf{b}\cdot\mathbf{c}\Rightarrow p(\mathbf{r}\cdot\mathbf{b})=\mathbf{b}\cdot\mathbf{c}$$

$$\Rightarrow\quad p\left(\frac{\mathbf{c}-p\mathbf{r}}{\mathbf{a}}\right)=\mathbf{b}\cdot\mathbf{c}\Rightarrow p\mathbf{c}-p^2\mathbf{r}=(\mathbf{b}\cdot\mathbf{c})\mathbf{a}$$

$$\therefore\quad p^2r=p\mathbf{c}-(\mathbf{b}\cdot\mathbf{c})\mathbf{a}\Rightarrow\mathbf{r}=\frac{\mathbf{c}}{p}-\frac{(\mathbf{b}\cdot\mathbf{c})}{p^2}\mathbf{a}\Rightarrow[\mathbf{r}\ \mathbf{a}\ \mathbf{c}]=0$$

Example 55 *The volume of the parallelopiped whose coterminous edges are represented by the vectors* $2\mathbf{b}\times\mathbf{c}$, $3\mathbf{c}\times\mathbf{a}$ *and* $4\mathbf{a}\times\mathbf{b}$ *where,* $\mathbf{a}=(1+\sin\theta)\hat{\mathbf{i}}+\cos\theta\hat{\mathbf{j}}+\sin2\theta\hat{\mathbf{k}}$

$$\mathbf{b}=\sin\left(\theta+\frac{2\pi}{3}\right)\hat{\mathbf{i}}+\cos\left(\theta+\frac{2\pi}{3}\right)\hat{\mathbf{j}}+\sin\left(2\theta+\frac{4\pi}{3}\right)\hat{\mathbf{k}},$$

$$\mathbf{c}=\sin\left(\theta-\frac{2\pi}{3}\right)\hat{\mathbf{i}}+\cos\left(\theta-\frac{2\pi}{3}\right)\hat{\mathbf{j}}+\sin\left(2\theta-\frac{4\pi}{3}\right)\hat{\mathbf{k}}$$

is 18 *cu units, then the value of* θ *in the interval* $\left(0,\frac{\pi}{2}\right)$, *is/are*

(a) $\frac{\pi}{9}$ (b) $\frac{2\pi}{9}$ (c) $\frac{\pi}{3}$ (d) $\frac{4\pi}{9}$

Sol. (a, b, d) Volume $=|[2\mathbf{b}\times\mathbf{c}\ \ 3\mathbf{c}\times\mathbf{a}\ \ 4\mathbf{a}\times\mathbf{b}]|=18$

$$\Rightarrow\quad 24[\mathbf{a}\ \mathbf{b}\ \mathbf{c}]^2=18\Rightarrow|[\mathbf{a}\ \mathbf{b}\ \mathbf{c}]|=\frac{\sqrt{3}}{2}$$

$$\text{Now, }[\mathbf{a}\ \mathbf{b}\ \mathbf{c}]=\begin{vmatrix}(1+\sin\theta) & \cos\theta & \sin2\theta\\ \sin\left(\theta+\frac{2\pi}{3}\right) & \cos\left(\theta+\frac{2\pi}{3}\right) & \sin\left(\theta+\frac{4\pi}{3}\right)\\ \sin\left(\theta-\frac{2\pi}{3}\right) & \cos\left(\theta-\frac{2\pi}{3}\right) & \sin\left(2\theta-\frac{4\pi}{3}\right)\end{vmatrix}$$

On applying $R_1\to R_1+R_2+R_3$ and expanding, we get

$$|[\mathbf{a}\ \mathbf{b}\ \mathbf{c}]|=\sqrt{3}\,|\cos3\theta|=\frac{\sqrt{3}}{2}$$

$$\Rightarrow\quad\cos3\theta=\pm\frac{1}{2}\Rightarrow3\theta=\frac{\pi}{3},\frac{2\pi}{3},\frac{4\pi}{3}\Rightarrow\theta=\frac{\pi}{9},\frac{2\pi}{9},\frac{4\pi}{9}$$

Example 56 *If* $\mathbf{a}$, $\mathbf{b}$ *and* $\mathbf{c}$ *are three non-zero vectors, then which of the following statement(s) is/are true?*

(a) $\mathbf{a}\times(\mathbf{b}\times\mathbf{c})$, $\mathbf{b}\times(\mathbf{c}\times\mathbf{a})$, $\mathbf{c}\times(\mathbf{a}\times\mathbf{b})$ from a right handed system.

(b) $\mathbf{c}$, $(\mathbf{a}\times\mathbf{b})\times\mathbf{c}$, $\mathbf{a}\times\mathbf{b}$ from a right handed system

(c) $\mathbf{a}\cdot\mathbf{b}+\mathbf{b}\cdot\mathbf{c}+\mathbf{c}\cdot\mathbf{a}<0$, if $\mathbf{a}+\mathbf{b}+\mathbf{c}=0$

(d) $\dfrac{(\mathbf{a}\times\mathbf{b})\cdot(\mathbf{b}\times\mathbf{c})}{(\mathbf{b}\times\mathbf{c})\cdot(\mathbf{a}\times\mathbf{c})}=-1$, if $\mathbf{a}+\mathbf{b}+\mathbf{c}=0$

Sol. (b, c, d)

(a) $\mathbf{a}\times(\mathbf{b}\times\mathbf{c})+\mathbf{b}\times(\mathbf{c}\times\mathbf{a})+\mathbf{c}\times(\mathbf{a}\times\mathbf{b})=0$

$\therefore$ vector are coplanar, so do not form right hand system.

(b) $(\mathbf{a}\times\mathbf{b})\times\mathbf{c}$, $\mathbf{a}\times\mathbf{b}$, $\mathbf{c}$ in that order form right hand system.

$\therefore$ $\mathbf{c}$, $(\mathbf{a}\times\mathbf{b})\times\mathbf{c}$, $\mathbf{a}\times\mathbf{b}$ also form right hand system as they are in same cyclic order.

(c) $\mathbf{a}+\mathbf{b}+\mathbf{c}=0\Rightarrow|\mathbf{a}+\mathbf{b}+\mathbf{c}|^2=0$

$$\Rightarrow a^2+b^2+c^2=-2(\mathbf{a}\cdot\mathbf{b}+\mathbf{b}\cdot\mathbf{c}+\mathbf{c}\cdot\mathbf{a})$$

$$\Rightarrow\mathbf{a}\cdot\mathbf{b}+\mathbf{b}\cdot\mathbf{c}+\mathbf{c}\cdot\mathbf{a}<0\qquad[\because a^2+b^2+c^2>0]$$

(d) $\mathbf{a}+\mathbf{b}+\mathbf{c}=0\Rightarrow\mathbf{a}\times\mathbf{b}=\mathbf{b}\times\mathbf{c}=\mathbf{c}\times\mathbf{a}$

Example 57 *If* $\mathbf{a}\times(\mathbf{b}\times\mathbf{c})$ *is perpendicular to* $(\mathbf{a}\times\mathbf{b})\times\mathbf{c}$, *we may have*

(a) $(\mathbf{a}\cdot\mathbf{c})|\mathbf{b}|^2=(\mathbf{a}\cdot\mathbf{b})(\mathbf{b}\cdot\mathbf{c})$

(b) $\mathbf{a}\cdot\mathbf{b}=0$

(c) $\mathbf{a}\cdot\mathbf{c}=0$

(d) $\mathbf{b}\cdot\mathbf{c}=0$

Sol. (a, c) $\mathbf{a}\times(\mathbf{b}\times\mathbf{c})=(\mathbf{a}\cdot\mathbf{c})\mathbf{b}-(\mathbf{a}\cdot\mathbf{b})\mathbf{c}$

and $(\mathbf{a}\times\mathbf{b})\times\mathbf{c}=-(\mathbf{c}\cdot\mathbf{b})\mathbf{a}+(\mathbf{a}\cdot\mathbf{c})\mathbf{b}$

We have been given

$$(\mathbf{a}\times(\mathbf{b}\times\mathbf{c}))\cdot((\mathbf{a}\times\mathbf{b})\times\mathbf{c})=0$$

$$\therefore\quad((\mathbf{a}\cdot\mathbf{c})\mathbf{b}-(\mathbf{a}\cdot\mathbf{b})\mathbf{c})\cdot((\mathbf{a}\cdot\mathbf{c})\mathbf{b}-(\mathbf{c}\cdot\mathbf{b})\mathbf{a})=0$$

$$\text{or}\quad(\mathbf{a}\cdot\mathbf{c})^2|\mathbf{b}|^2-(\mathbf{a}\cdot\mathbf{c})(\mathbf{b}\cdot\mathbf{c})(\mathbf{a}\cdot\mathbf{b})$$

$$-(\mathbf{a}\cdot\mathbf{b})(\mathbf{a}\cdot\mathbf{c})(\mathbf{b}\cdot\mathbf{c})+(\mathbf{a}\cdot\mathbf{b})(\mathbf{b}\cdot\mathbf{c})(\mathbf{c}\cdot\mathbf{a})=0$$

$$\text{or}\quad(\mathbf{a}\cdot\mathbf{c})^2|\mathbf{b}|^2=(\mathbf{a}\cdot\mathbf{c})(\mathbf{a}\cdot\mathbf{b})(\mathbf{b}\cdot\mathbf{c})$$

$$\text{or}\quad(\mathbf{a}\cdot\mathbf{c})((\mathbf{a}\cdot\mathbf{c})(\mathbf{b}\cdot\mathbf{b})-(\mathbf{a}\cdot\mathbf{b})(\mathbf{b}\cdot\mathbf{c}))=0$$

$$\mathbf{a}\cdot\mathbf{c}=0$$

$$\text{or}\quad(\mathbf{a}\cdot\mathbf{c})|\mathbf{b}|^2=(\mathbf{a}\cdot\mathbf{b})(\mathbf{b}\cdot\mathbf{c})$$

Example 58 *The angles of a triangle having two of whose sides are represented by vectors* $\sqrt{3}(\hat{\mathbf{a}}\times\mathbf{b})$ *and* $\mathbf{b}-(\hat{\mathbf{a}}\cdot\mathbf{b})\hat{\mathbf{a}}$, *where* $\hat{\mathbf{b}}$ *is a non-zero vector and* $\hat{\mathbf{a}}$ *is a unit vector in the direction of* $\hat{\mathbf{a}}$, *are*

(a) $\tan^{-1}(\sqrt{3})$ (b) $\tan^{-1}(1/\sqrt{3})$

(c) $\cot^{-1}(0)$ (d) $\tan^{-1}(1)$

Sol. (a, b, c)

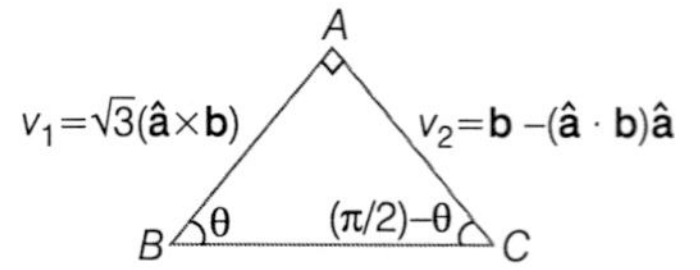

Consider $\mathbf{V}_1\cdot\mathbf{V}_2=0\Rightarrow A=90^\circ$

Using the sine law, $\dfrac{|\mathbf{b}-(\hat{\mathbf{a}}\cdot\mathbf{b})\hat{\mathbf{a}}|}{\sin\theta}=\dfrac{\sqrt{3}\,|\hat{\mathbf{a}}\times\hat{\mathbf{b}}|}{\cos\theta}$

$$\text{or}\quad\tan\theta=\frac{1}{\sqrt{3}}\frac{|\mathbf{b}-(\hat{\mathbf{a}}\cdot\mathbf{b})\hat{\mathbf{a}}|}{|\hat{\mathbf{a}}\times\hat{\mathbf{b}}|}=\frac{1}{\sqrt{3}}\frac{|(\hat{\mathbf{a}}\times\mathbf{b})\times\hat{\mathbf{a}}|}{|\hat{\mathbf{a}}\times\mathbf{b}|}$$

$$=\frac{1}{\sqrt{3}}\frac{|\hat{\mathbf{a}}\times\mathbf{b}|\,|\hat{\mathbf{a}}|\sin90^\circ}{|\hat{\mathbf{a}}\times\mathbf{b}|}=\frac{1}{\sqrt{3}}$$

Hence, $\theta=\dfrac{\pi}{6}$

Passage Based Questions

Passage I

(Ex. Nos. 59 and 60)

Let $\mathbf{a}=2\hat{\mathbf{i}}+3\hat{\mathbf{j}}-6\hat{\mathbf{k}}$, $\mathbf{b}=2\hat{\mathbf{i}}-3\hat{\mathbf{j}}+6\hat{\mathbf{k}}$ and $\mathbf{c}=-2\hat{\mathbf{i}}+3\hat{\mathbf{j}}+6\hat{\mathbf{k}}$. Let $\mathbf{a}_1$ be the projection of $\mathbf{a}$ on $\mathbf{b}$ and $\mathbf{a}_2$ be the projection of $\mathbf{a}_1$ on $\mathbf{c}$. Then,

Example 59 $\mathbf{a}_2$ *is equal to*

(a) $\frac{943}{49}(2\hat{\mathbf{i}}-3\hat{\mathbf{j}}-6\hat{\mathbf{k}})$ (b) $\frac{943}{49^2}(2\hat{\mathbf{i}}-3\hat{\mathbf{j}}-6\hat{\mathbf{k}})$

(c) $\frac{943}{49}(-2\hat{\mathbf{i}}+3\hat{\mathbf{j}}+6\hat{\mathbf{k}})$ (d) $\frac{943}{49^2}(-2\hat{\mathbf{i}}+3\hat{\mathbf{j}}+6\hat{\mathbf{k}})$

Sol. (b) $\mathbf{a}_1=\left[(2\hat{\mathbf{i}}+3\hat{\mathbf{j}}-6\hat{\mathbf{k}}).\frac{(2\hat{\mathbf{i}}-3\hat{\mathbf{j}}+6\hat{\mathbf{k}})}{7}\right]\frac{2\hat{\mathbf{i}}-3\hat{\mathbf{j}}+6\hat{\mathbf{k}}}{7}$

$$=\frac{-41}{49}(2\hat{\mathbf{i}}-3\hat{\mathbf{j}}+6\hat{\mathbf{k}})$$

$$\mathbf{a}_2=\frac{-41}{49}\left((2\hat{\mathbf{i}}-3\hat{\mathbf{j}}+6\hat{\mathbf{k}}).\frac{(-2\hat{\mathbf{i}}+3\hat{\mathbf{j}}+6\hat{\mathbf{k}})}{7}\right)\times\frac{(-2\hat{\mathbf{i}}+3\hat{\mathbf{j}}+6\hat{\mathbf{k}})}{7}$$

$$=\frac{-41}{(49)^2}(-4-9+36)(-2\hat{\mathbf{i}}+3\hat{\mathbf{j}}+6\hat{\mathbf{k}})$$

$$=\frac{943}{49^2}(2\hat{\mathbf{i}}-3\hat{\mathbf{j}}-6\hat{\mathbf{k}})$$

Example 60 $\mathbf{a}_1\,.\,\mathbf{b}$ *is equal to*

(a) -41 (b) $-\frac{41}{7}$

(c) 41 (d) 287

Sol. (a) $\mathbf{a}_1\cdot\mathbf{b}=-\frac{41}{49}(2\hat{\mathbf{i}}-3\hat{\mathbf{j}}+6\hat{\mathbf{k}})\cdot(2\hat{\mathbf{i}}-3\hat{\mathbf{j}}+6\hat{\mathbf{k}})$

$$=-41$$

Passage II

(Ex. Nos. 61 and 62)

Let $\mathbf{a}$ and $\mathbf{b}$ be two vectors perpendicular to each other and $|\mathbf{a}|=2$, $|\mathbf{b}|=3$ and $\mathbf{c}\times\mathbf{a}=\mathbf{b}$.

Example 61 *The least value of* $|\mathbf{c}-\mathbf{a}|$ *is*

(a) 1 (b) $\frac{1}{2}$ (c) $\frac{1}{4}$ (d) $\frac{3}{2}$

Example 62 *When* $|\mathbf{c}-\mathbf{a}|$ *is least the value of* α *(when* α *is angle between* $\mathbf{a}$ *and* $\mathbf{c}$*) equals*

(a) $\tan^{-1}\left(\frac{1}{2}\right)$ (b) $\tan^{-1}\left(\frac{3}{4}\right)$

(c) $\cos^{-1}\left(\frac{2}{3}\right)$ (d) None of these

Sol. For (Ex. Nos. 61 and 62)

Here, $|\mathbf{a}|=2$ and $|\mathbf{b}|=3$

$$\mathbf{c}\times\mathbf{a}=\mathbf{b}\Rightarrow|\mathbf{c}||\mathbf{a}|\sin\alpha=|\mathbf{b}|$$

$$\Rightarrow\quad|\mathbf{c}|=\frac{3}{2}\operatorname{cosec}\alpha$$

Consider, $|\mathbf{c}-\mathbf{a}|^2=|\mathbf{c}|^2-2(\mathbf{a}\,.\,\mathbf{c})+|\mathbf{a}|^2$

$$=\frac{9}{4}\operatorname{cosec}^2\alpha+4-2(2)\,.\left(\frac{3}{2}\right).\operatorname{cosec}\alpha\,.\cos\alpha$$

$$=\frac{25}{4}+\frac{9}{4}.\cot^2\alpha-6\cot\alpha$$

$$=\frac{25}{4}+\left(\frac{3}{2}\cot\alpha-2\right)^2-4$$

$$=\frac{9}{4}+\left(\frac{3}{2}\cot\alpha-2\right)^2\geq\frac{9}{4}$$

$$\therefore\quad|\mathbf{c}-\mathbf{a}|\geq\frac{3}{2}$$

and least possible when $\frac{3}{2}\cot\alpha=2\Rightarrow\tan\alpha=\frac{3}{4}$

$$\Rightarrow\quad\alpha=\tan^{-1}\frac{3}{4}$$

61. (d) **62.** (b)

Passage III

(Ex. Nos. 63 and 64)

Consider a triangular pyramid $ABCD$, the position vectors of whose angular points are $A(3,0,1)$, $B(-1,4,1)$, $C(5,2,3)$ and $D(0,-5,4)$. Let G be the point of intersection of the medians of ΔBCD.

Example 63 *The length of vector* $\mathbf{AG}$ *is*

(a) $\sqrt{17}$ (b) $\frac{\sqrt{51}}{3}$ (c) $\frac{3}{\sqrt{6}}$ (d) $\frac{\sqrt{59}}{4}$

Example 64 *Area of* ΔABC *in square units is*

(a) 24 (b) $8\sqrt{6}$

(c) $4\sqrt{6}$ (d) None of these

Sol. For (Ex. Nos. 63 and 64)

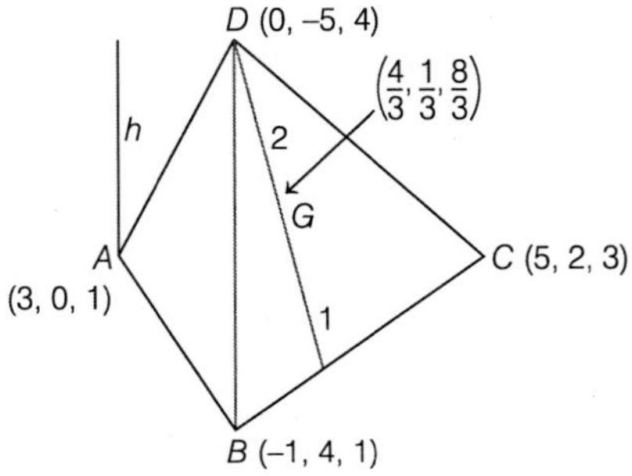

Point G is $\left(\frac{4}{3},\frac{1}{3},\frac{8}{3}\right)$.

Therefore, $|\mathbf{AG}|^2=\left(-\frac{5}{3}\right)^2+\frac{1}{9}+\left(\frac{5}{3}\right)^2=\frac{51}{9}$

Hence, $|\mathbf{AG}|=\frac{\sqrt{51}}{3}$

$\because \quad \mathbf{AB} = -4\hat{\mathbf{i}} + 4\hat{\mathbf{j}} + 0\hat{\mathbf{k}}$

$\therefore \quad \mathbf{AC} = 2\hat{\mathbf{i}} + 2\hat{\mathbf{j}} + 2\hat{\mathbf{k}}$

$$\therefore \quad \mathbf{AB} \times \mathbf{AC} = -8\begin{vmatrix} \hat{\mathbf{i}} & \hat{\mathbf{j}} & \hat{\mathbf{k}} \\ 1 & -1 & 0 \\ 1 & 1 & 1 \end{vmatrix}$$

$$= 8(\hat{\mathbf{i}} + \hat{\mathbf{j}} - 2\hat{\mathbf{k}})$$

Area of $\Delta ABC = \frac{1}{2}|\mathbf{AB} \times \mathbf{AC}| = 4\sqrt{6}$

63. (b) **64.** (c)

Passage IV

(Ex. Nos. 65 and 66)

Let A, B and C represent the vertices of a triangle, where A is the origin and B and C have position vectors $\mathbf{b}$ and $\mathbf{c}$ respectively. Points **M**, **N** and **P** are taken on sides **AB**, **BC** and **CA** respectively, such that $\frac{\mathbf{AM}}{\mathbf{AB}} = \frac{\mathbf{BN}}{\mathbf{BC}} = \frac{\mathbf{CP}}{\mathbf{CA}} = \alpha$

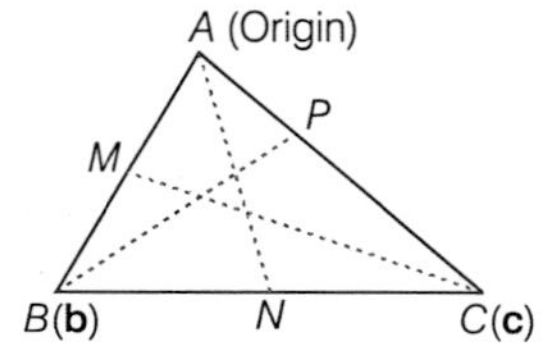

Example 65 $\mathbf{AN} + \mathbf{BP} + \mathbf{CM}$ *is*

(a) $3\alpha(\mathbf{b} + \mathbf{c})$ (b) $\alpha(\mathbf{b} + \mathbf{c})$

(c) $(1-\alpha)(\mathbf{b} + \mathbf{c})$ (d) 0

Sol. (d) Since $\frac{\mathbf{AM}}{\mathbf{AB}} = \alpha$,

$\therefore$ Position vector of $\mathbf{M} = \alpha\, \mathbf{b}$

Since, $\frac{\mathbf{BN}}{\mathbf{BC}} = \alpha$

$\therefore \quad \frac{\mathbf{BN}}{\mathbf{NC}} = \frac{\alpha}{1-\alpha}$

$\therefore$ Position vector of $\mathbf{N} = (1-\alpha)\mathbf{b} + \alpha\mathbf{c}$

Since, $\frac{\mathbf{CP}}{\mathbf{CA}} = \alpha$

$\therefore \quad \frac{\mathbf{AP}}{\mathbf{PC}} = \frac{1-\alpha}{\alpha}$

$\therefore$ Position vector of $\mathbf{p} = (1-\alpha)\mathbf{c}$

Now, $\quad \mathbf{AN} = (1-\alpha)\mathbf{b} + \alpha\mathbf{c}$

$\mathbf{BP} = (1-\alpha)\mathbf{c} - \mathbf{b}$

$\mathbf{CM} = \alpha\mathbf{b} - \mathbf{c}$

$\therefore$ $\mathbf{AN} + \mathbf{BP} + \mathbf{CM} = \mathbf{0}$

Example 66 *If* Δ *represents the area enclosed by the three vectors* **AN**, **BP** *and* **CM**, *then the value of* α *for which* Δ *is least*

(a) does not exist (b) $\frac{1}{2}$

(c) $\frac{1}{4}$ (d) None of these

Sol. (b) $\Delta = \frac{1}{2}|\mathbf{AN} \times \mathbf{BP}| = \frac{1}{2}|\{(1-\alpha)\mathbf{b} + \alpha\mathbf{c}\} \times \{(1-\alpha)\mathbf{c} - \mathbf{b}\}|$

$$= \frac{1}{2}|(1-\alpha)^2(\mathbf{b} \times \mathbf{c}) + \alpha(\mathbf{b} \times \mathbf{c})|$$

$$= \frac{1}{2}|\mathbf{b} \times \mathbf{c}|(\alpha^2 - \alpha + 1)$$

$$= \frac{1}{2}|\mathbf{b} \times \mathbf{c}|\left\{\left(\alpha - \frac{1}{2}\right)^2 + \frac{3}{4}\right\}$$

$\therefore$ Δ is least, if $\alpha = \frac{1}{2}$

Passage V

(Ex. Nos. 67 and 68)

Let **a**, **b** and **c** are non-zero unit vectors inclined pairwise with the same angle θ. p, q and r are non-zero scalars satisfying $\mathbf{a} \times \mathbf{b} + \mathbf{b} \times \mathbf{c} = p\mathbf{a} + q\mathbf{b} + r\mathbf{c}$

Example 67 *Volume of parallelopiped with edges* **a**, **b** *and* **c** *is*

(a) $p + (q + r)\cos\theta$ (b) $(p + q + r)\cos\theta$

(c) $2p - (q + r)\cos\theta$ (d) None of these

Example 68 *The value of* $\left(\frac{q}{p} + 2\cos\theta\right)$ *is*

(a) 1 (b) 0

(c) $2[\mathbf{a}\ \mathbf{b}\ \mathbf{c}]$ (d) None of these

Sol. For (Ex. Nos. 67 and 68)

Volume of parallelopiped $= [\mathbf{a}\ \mathbf{b}\ \mathbf{c}] = \mathbf{a} \cdot (\mathbf{b} \times \mathbf{c})$

Now, we have

$$\mathbf{a} \times \mathbf{b} + \mathbf{b} \times \mathbf{c} = p\mathbf{a} + q\mathbf{b} + r\mathbf{c}$$

$\Rightarrow \mathbf{a} \cdot (\mathbf{a} \times \mathbf{b}) + \mathbf{a} \cdot (\mathbf{b} \times \mathbf{c}) = p(\mathbf{a} \cdot \mathbf{a}) + q(\mathbf{a} \cdot \mathbf{b}) + r(\mathbf{a} \cdot \mathbf{c})$

$\Rightarrow [\mathbf{a}\ \mathbf{a}\ \mathbf{b}] + [\mathbf{a}\ \mathbf{b}\ \mathbf{c}] = p|\mathbf{a}|^2 + q|\mathbf{a}||\mathbf{b}|\cos\theta + r|\mathbf{a}||\mathbf{c}|\cos\theta$

$\Rightarrow \quad [\mathbf{a}\ \mathbf{b}\ \mathbf{c}] = p + q\cos\theta + r\cos\theta = p + (q + r)\cos\theta$

$\therefore$ Volume of parallelopiped $= p + (q + r)\cos\theta$

On taking dot products with **a**, **b** and **c** respectively, with given equation

$$[\mathbf{a}\ \mathbf{b}\ \mathbf{c}] = p + (q + r)\cos\theta \quad \text{...(i)}$$

$$\Rightarrow \quad 0 = (p + r)\cos\theta + q \quad \text{...(ii)}$$

$$\therefore \quad [\mathbf{a}\ \mathbf{b}\ \mathbf{c}] = (p + q)\cos\theta + r \quad \text{...(iii)}$$

From Eqs. (i) and (iii), $p = r$ substituting in Eq. (ii), we get

$$2p\cos\theta + q = 0$$

$$\Rightarrow \quad \frac{q}{p} + 2\cos\theta = 0$$

67. (a) **68.** (c)

Stem Based Questions

Stem I

(Ex. Nos. 69 and 70)

If *AP, BQ* and *CR* are the altitudes of acute ΔABC and $9\mathbf{AP} + 4\mathbf{BQ} + 7\mathbf{CR} = 0$.

Example 69 $\angle ACB$ *is equal to ....*

Example 70 $\angle ABC$ *is equal to ....*

Sol. For (Ex. Nos. 69 and 70)

Since, sum of three vectors $9\mathbf{AP}$, $4\mathbf{BQ}$ and $7\mathbf{CR}$ is zero, there is a triangle whose sides have lengths $9|\mathbf{AP}|$, $4|\mathbf{BQ}|$, $7|\mathbf{CR}|$ and are parallel to the corresponding vectors.

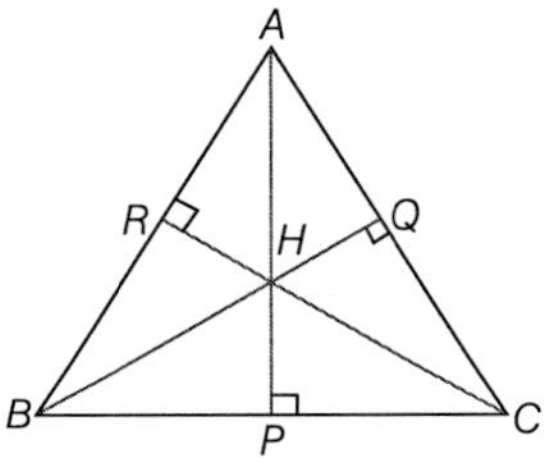

H is orthocentre.

$\Rightarrow \angle BHP = 90° - \angle QBC = \angle ACB$

$\Rightarrow$ Angle between **AP** and **BQ** equal to $\angle ACB$, similarly angle between **BQ** and **CR** be $\angle BAC$.

$$\Rightarrow \frac{AB^2}{7|\mathbf{CR}|} = \frac{BC^2}{9|\mathbf{AP}|} = \frac{AC^2}{4|\mathbf{BQ}|}$$

$$2\,\text{ar}(\Delta ABC) = |\mathbf{AB} \times \mathbf{CR}| = |\mathbf{BC} \times \mathbf{AP}|$$

$$= |\mathbf{CA} \times \mathbf{BQ}|$$

$$\Rightarrow \frac{c^2}{7} = \frac{a^2}{9} = \frac{b^2}{4}$$

$$\therefore \quad a : b : c = 3 : 2 : \sqrt{7}$$

69. $\cos C = \dfrac{a^2 + b^2 - c^2}{2ab} = \dfrac{1}{2} \Rightarrow \angle C = 60° = \dfrac{\pi}{3}$

70. $\cos B = \dfrac{a^2 + c^2 - b^2}{2ac} = \dfrac{2}{\sqrt{7}}$

Stem II

(Ex. Nos. 71 and 72)

If *ABC* is a triangle, right angled at *A*. The resultant of the forces acting along **AB** and **AC** with magnitude $\dfrac{1}{\mathbf{AB}}$ and $\dfrac{1}{\mathbf{AC}}$, respectively, is the force along **AD**, where *D* is the foot of the perpendicular from *A* onto *BC* and magnitude of *AD* is 0.25 units. If *E* is any point on *AC*, where $\mathbf{AB} = \lambda\mathbf{ED}$, $\mathbf{CD} = \beta\mathbf{ED}$ and $|\,\mathbf{AE} + \mathbf{CB}\,| = 12$ units.

Example 71 *Magnitude of resultant is equal to ....*

Sol. Given *ABC* is a triangle right angled at *A*.

$$|\mathbf{AB}| = \frac{1}{\mathbf{AB}}, |\mathbf{AC}| = \frac{1}{\mathbf{AC}}$$

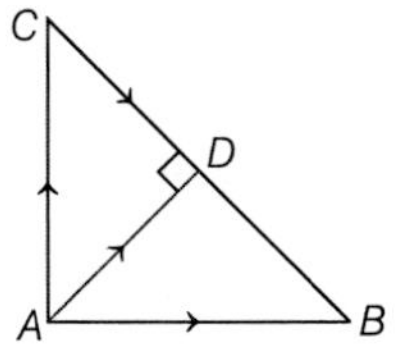

The magnitude of the resultant

$$= \sqrt{(\mathbf{AB})^2 + (\mathbf{AC})^2} = \sqrt{\left(\frac{1}{\mathbf{AB}}\right)^2 + \left(\frac{1}{\mathbf{AC}}\right)^2}$$

$$= \frac{\sqrt{\mathbf{AB}^2 + \mathbf{AC}^2}}{\mathbf{AB} \times \mathbf{AC}}$$

$$= \frac{\sqrt{\mathbf{BC}^2}}{\mathbf{AB} \times \mathbf{AC}} \qquad [\because AB^2 + AC^2 = BC^2]$$

$$= \frac{\mathbf{BC}}{\mathbf{AB} \times \mathbf{AC}} = \frac{\mathbf{BC}}{\mathbf{AD} \times \mathbf{BC}} = \frac{1}{\mathbf{AD}} = \frac{1}{0.25} = 4$$

Example 72 *If* $\lambda = 3$ *and* $\beta = 2$, *then* **ED** *is ....*

Sol. Given, *E* is the mid-point of *AC* and $\mathbf{AB} = \lambda\mathbf{ED}$, $\mathbf{CD} = \beta\mathbf{ED}$

In ΔABC, $\mathbf{AC} + \mathbf{CB} = \mathbf{AB}$ ...(i)

In ΔADC, $\mathbf{AC} + \mathbf{CD} = \mathbf{AD}$ ...(ii)

In ΔAED, $\mathbf{AE} + \mathbf{ED} = \mathbf{AD}$ ...(iii)

From Eqs. (ii) and (iii), we get

$$\mathbf{AE} + \mathbf{ED} = \mathbf{AC} + \mathbf{CD}$$

$$\Rightarrow \mathbf{AE} + \mathbf{ED} - \mathbf{CD} = \mathbf{AC}$$

$$\Rightarrow \mathbf{AE} + \mathbf{ED} - \mathbf{CD} + \mathbf{CB} = \mathbf{AB} \qquad \text{[using Eq. (i)]}$$

$$\Rightarrow \mathbf{AE} + \mathbf{ED} - \beta\mathbf{ED} + \mathbf{CB} = \lambda\mathbf{ED}$$

$$\Rightarrow \mathbf{AE} + \mathbf{CB} = \lambda\mathbf{ED} + \beta\mathbf{ED} - \mathbf{ED}$$

$$\Rightarrow \mathbf{ED}(\lambda + \beta - 1) = \mathbf{AE} + \mathbf{CB}$$

$$\Rightarrow \mathbf{ED} = \frac{\mathbf{AE} + \mathbf{CB}}{(\lambda + \beta - 1)} = \frac{1}{(\lambda + \beta - 1)}[\mathbf{AE} + \mathbf{CB}]$$

$$\therefore \quad \mathbf{ED} = \frac{12}{(3 + 2 - 1)} = \frac{12}{4} = 3 \text{ units}$$

Stem III

(Ex. Nos. 73 and 74)

Let vectors $\mathbf{x}_1 = (\cos\theta)\hat{\mathbf{i}} - (3\sin\theta)\hat{\mathbf{j}} - 2\hat{\mathbf{k}}$,

$\mathbf{x}_2 = (2\cos\theta)\hat{\mathbf{i}} - (\sin\theta)\hat{\mathbf{j}} + \hat{\mathbf{k}}$

and $\mathbf{x}_3 = (\cos\theta)\hat{\mathbf{i}} + (2\sin\theta)\hat{\mathbf{j}} + 3\hat{\mathbf{k}}$

be represent sides of a triangle, where $\theta \in \left[0, \dfrac{\pi}{2}\right)$. If area of the triangle is minimum and length of the median which bisects the side representing by $\mathbf{x}_3$ is *p*.

Example 73 *If h be the longest side of the triangle, then value of $5h^2$ is ....*

Example 74 *The value of $4p^2$ is equal to ....*

Sol. For (Ex. Nos. 73 and 74)

We have, $\mathbf{x}_1 = (\cos\theta)\hat{\mathbf{i}} - (3\sin\theta)\hat{\mathbf{j}} - 2\hat{\mathbf{k}}$

and $\mathbf{x}_2 = (2\cos\theta)\hat{\mathbf{i}} - (\sin\theta)\hat{\mathbf{j}} + \hat{\mathbf{k}}$

$$\therefore \quad \mathbf{x}_1 \times \mathbf{x}_2 = \begin{bmatrix} \hat{\mathbf{i}} & \hat{\mathbf{j}} & \hat{\mathbf{k}} \\ \cos\theta & -3\sin\theta & -2 \\ 2\cos\theta & -\sin\theta & 1 \end{bmatrix}$$

$$= \hat{\mathbf{i}}(-3\sin\theta - 2\sin\theta) - \hat{\mathbf{j}}(\cos\theta + 4\cos\theta) + \hat{\mathbf{k}}(-\sin\theta\cos\theta + 6\sin\theta\cos\theta)$$

$$= -5\sin\theta\hat{\mathbf{i}} - 5\cos\theta\hat{\mathbf{j}} + 5\sin\theta\cos\theta\hat{\mathbf{k}}$$

$$\therefore \text{Area of triangle} = \frac{1}{2}|\mathbf{x}_1 \times \mathbf{x}_2|$$

$$= \frac{1}{2}\sqrt{5^2(\sin^2\theta + \cos^2\theta + \sin^2\theta\cos^2\theta)}$$

$$= \frac{1}{2} \times 5\sqrt{1 + \sin^2\theta\cos^2\theta} = \frac{5}{2}\sqrt{1 + \frac{1}{4}\sin^2 2\theta}$$

Area of triangle will be minimum if

$$\sin 2\theta = 0 \Rightarrow \theta = 0$$

$$\therefore \quad \mathbf{x}_1 = \hat{\mathbf{i}} - 2\hat{\mathbf{k}},\ \mathbf{x}_2 = 2\hat{\mathbf{i}} + \hat{\mathbf{k}} \text{ and } \mathbf{x}_3 = \hat{\mathbf{i}} + 3\hat{\mathbf{k}}$$

$$\Rightarrow \quad |\mathbf{x}_1| = \sqrt{5},\ |\mathbf{x}_2| = \sqrt{5} \text{ and } |\mathbf{x}_3| = \sqrt{10}$$

$$\therefore \quad h = \sqrt{10} \Rightarrow 5h^2 = 5 \times 10 = 50 \text{ units}$$

$$\text{Also,} \quad p = \frac{\sqrt{10}}{2} \Rightarrow 4p^2 = 4 \times \frac{10}{4} = 10 \text{ units}$$

73. (50) **74.** (10)

Single Integer Answer Type Questions

Example 75 *Given that $\mathbf{u} = \hat{\mathbf{i}} - 2\hat{\mathbf{j}} + 3\hat{\mathbf{k}}$; $\mathbf{v} = 2\hat{\mathbf{i}} + \hat{\mathbf{j}} + 4\hat{\mathbf{k}}$; $\mathbf{w} = \hat{\mathbf{i}} + 3\hat{\mathbf{j}} + 3\hat{\mathbf{k}}$ and $(\mathbf{u}\cdot\mathbf{R} - 15)\hat{\mathbf{i}} + (\mathbf{v}\cdot\mathbf{R} - 30)\hat{\mathbf{j}} + (\mathbf{w}\cdot\mathbf{R} - 25)\hat{\mathbf{k}} = \mathbf{0}$. Then, the greatest integer less than or equal to $|\mathbf{R}|$ is*

Sol. (6) Let $\mathbf{R} = x\hat{\mathbf{i}} + y\hat{\mathbf{j}} + z\hat{\mathbf{k}}$

$$\mathbf{u} = \hat{\mathbf{i}} - 2\hat{\mathbf{j}} + 3\hat{\mathbf{k}};\ \mathbf{v} = 2\hat{\mathbf{i}} + \hat{\mathbf{j}} + 4\hat{\mathbf{k}};\ \mathbf{w} = \hat{\mathbf{i}} + 3\hat{\mathbf{j}} + 3\hat{\mathbf{k}}$$

$$(\mathbf{u}\cdot\mathbf{R} - 15)\hat{\mathbf{i}} + (\mathbf{v}\cdot\mathbf{R} - 30)\hat{\mathbf{j}} + (\mathbf{w}\cdot\mathbf{R} - 25)\hat{\mathbf{k}} = \mathbf{0} \quad \text{[given]}$$

So, $\mathbf{u}\cdot\mathbf{R} = 15 \Rightarrow x - 2y + 3z = 15$ ...(i)

$\mathbf{v}\cdot\mathbf{R} = 30 \Rightarrow 2x + y + 4z = 30$ ...(ii)

$\mathbf{w}\cdot\mathbf{R} = 25 \Rightarrow x + 3y + 3z = 25$ ...(iii)

On solving Eqs. (i), (ii) and (iii), we get

$$x = 4,\ y = 2,\ z = 5$$

Now, $|\mathbf{R}| = \sqrt{4^2 + 2^2 + 5^2} = \sqrt{45}$

$$[|\mathbf{R}|] = [\sqrt{45}] = 6$$

Example 76 *Let $\mathbf{u}$ be a vector on rectangular coordinate system with sloping angle 60°. Suppose that $|\mathbf{u} - \hat{\mathbf{i}}|$ is geometric mean of $|\mathbf{u}|$ and $|\mathbf{u} - 2\hat{\mathbf{i}}|$, where $\hat{\mathbf{i}}$ is the unit vector along the X-axis. Then, the value of $(\sqrt{2} + 1)|\mathbf{u}|$ is*

Sol. (1) Since, angle between $\mathbf{u}$ and $\hat{\mathbf{i}}$ is 60°, we have

$$\mathbf{u}\cdot\hat{\mathbf{i}} = |\mathbf{u}||\hat{\mathbf{i}}|\cos 60° = \frac{|\mathbf{u}|}{2}$$

Given that, $|\mathbf{u}|, |\mathbf{u} - \hat{\mathbf{i}}|, |\mathbf{u} - 2\hat{\mathbf{i}}|$ are in GP.

So, $|\mathbf{u} - \hat{\mathbf{i}}|^2 = |\mathbf{u}|\,|\mathbf{u} - 2\hat{\mathbf{i}}|$

Squaring both sides,

$$[|\mathbf{u}|^2 + |\hat{\mathbf{i}}|^2 - 2\mathbf{u}\cdot\hat{\mathbf{i}}]^2 = |\mathbf{u}|^2[|\mathbf{u}|^2 + 4|\hat{\mathbf{i}}|^2 - 4\mathbf{u}\cdot\hat{\mathbf{i}}]$$

$$\left(|\mathbf{u}|^2 + 1 - \frac{2|\mathbf{u}|}{2}\right)^2 = |\mathbf{u}|^2\left(|\mathbf{u}|^2 + 4 - \frac{4|\mathbf{u}|}{2}\right)$$

or $$|\mathbf{u}| + 2|\mathbf{u}| - 1 = 0$$

$$\Rightarrow \quad |\mathbf{u}|^2 = -\frac{2 \pm 2\sqrt{2}}{2}$$

or $$|\mathbf{u}| = \sqrt{2} - 1$$

$$\Rightarrow \quad (\sqrt{2} + 1)|\mathbf{u}| = (\sqrt{2} + 1)(\sqrt{2} - 1) = 2 - 1 = 1$$

Example 77 *Let $A(2\hat{\mathbf{i}} + 3\hat{\mathbf{j}} + 5\hat{\mathbf{k}})$, $B(-\hat{\mathbf{i}} + 3\hat{\mathbf{j}} + 2\hat{\mathbf{k}})$ and $C(\lambda\hat{\mathbf{i}} + 5\hat{\mathbf{j}} + \mu\hat{\mathbf{k}})$ are vertices of a triangle and its median through A is equally inclined to the positive directions of the axes, the value of $2\lambda - \mu$ is*

Sol. (4) Median through A is

$$\mathbf{AD} = \frac{\mathbf{AB} + \mathbf{AC}}{2}$$

$$\mathbf{AB} = -3\hat{\mathbf{i}} - 3\hat{\mathbf{k}}$$

$$\mathbf{AC} = (\lambda - 2)\hat{\mathbf{i}} + 2\hat{\mathbf{j}} + (\mu - 5)\hat{\mathbf{k}}$$

$$\mathbf{AD} = \frac{1}{2}[(\lambda - 5)\hat{\mathbf{i}} + 2\hat{\mathbf{j}} + (\mu - 8)\hat{\mathbf{k}}]$$

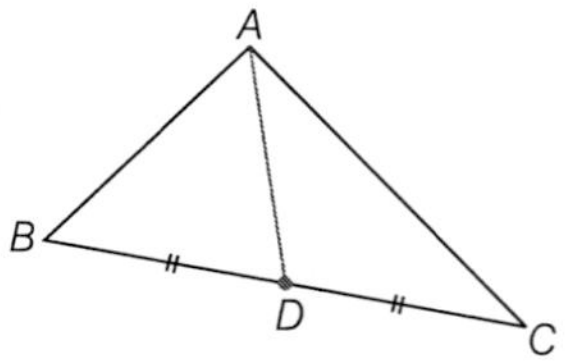

We have, **AD** is equally inclined to the positive direction of axes

$$\cos\theta = \frac{\frac{1}{2}[(\lambda - 5)\hat{\mathbf{i}} + 2\hat{\mathbf{j}} + (\mu - 8)\hat{\mathbf{k}}]\cdot\hat{\mathbf{i}}}{|\mathbf{AD}||\hat{\mathbf{i}}|}$$

$$= \frac{\frac{1}{2}[(\lambda - 5)\hat{\mathbf{i}} + 2\hat{\mathbf{j}} + (\mu - 8)\hat{\mathbf{k}}]\cdot\hat{\mathbf{j}}}{|\mathbf{AD}||\hat{\mathbf{j}}|}$$

$$= \frac{\frac{1}{2}[(\lambda - 5)\hat{\mathbf{i}} + 2\hat{\mathbf{j}} + (\mu - 8)\hat{\mathbf{k}}]\cdot\hat{\mathbf{k}}}{|\mathbf{AD}||\hat{\mathbf{k}}|}$$

$$\Rightarrow \quad \frac{\lambda-5}{2}=1=\frac{\mu-8}{2}$$

$$\Rightarrow \quad \lambda=7 \text{ and } \mu=10$$

$$\therefore \quad 2\lambda-\mu=14-10=4$$

Example 78 ■ *Three vectors* $\mathbf{a}(|\mathbf{a}|\neq 0)$, $\mathbf{b}$ *and* $\mathbf{c}$ *are such that* $\mathbf{a}\times\mathbf{b}=3\mathbf{a}\times\mathbf{c}$, *also* $|\mathbf{a}|=|\mathbf{b}|=1$ *and* $|\mathbf{c}|=\frac{1}{3}$. *If the angle between* $\mathbf{b}$ *and* $\mathbf{c}$ *is* $60°$ *and* $|\mathbf{b}-3\mathbf{c}|=\lambda|\mathbf{a}|$, *then the value of* $|\lambda|$ *is*

Sol. (1) We have, $\mathbf{a}\times\mathbf{b}=3\mathbf{a}\times\mathbf{c}$

$\Rightarrow \quad \mathbf{a}\times(\mathbf{b}-3\mathbf{c})=0$

$\Rightarrow$ $\mathbf{a}$ is parallel to $\mathbf{b}-3\mathbf{c}$.

Now, $\mathbf{b}-3\mathbf{c}=\lambda\mathbf{a}$

$\Rightarrow \quad |\mathbf{b}-3\mathbf{c}|^2=\lambda^2|\mathbf{a}|^2$

$\Rightarrow \quad |\mathbf{b}|^2+9|\mathbf{c}|^2-6(\mathbf{b}\cdot\mathbf{c})=\lambda^2|\mathbf{a}|^2$

$\Rightarrow \quad 1+9\times\frac{1}{9}-6\times1\times\frac{1}{3}\times\frac{1}{2}=\lambda^2(1)^2$

$\Rightarrow \quad 1+1-1=\lambda^2 \Rightarrow \lambda^2=1$

$\therefore \quad \lambda=\pm 1$

Hence, $\lambda=1$

Example 79 ■ *If* $\mathbf{a}$, $\mathbf{b}$ *and* $\mathbf{c}$ *are unit vectors such that* $\mathbf{a}\cdot\mathbf{b}=0=\mathbf{a}\cdot\mathbf{c}$ *and the angle between* $\mathbf{b}$ *and* $\mathbf{c}$ *is* $\frac{\pi}{3}$, *then the value of* $|\mathbf{a}\times\mathbf{b}-\mathbf{a}\times\mathbf{c}|$.

Sol. (1) $\mathbf{a}\cdot\mathbf{b}=0\Rightarrow\mathbf{a}\perp\mathbf{b}$

$\Rightarrow \quad \mathbf{a}\cdot\mathbf{c}=0\Rightarrow\mathbf{a}\perp\mathbf{c}$

$\Rightarrow \quad \mathbf{a}\perp(\mathbf{b}-\mathbf{c})$

$\therefore \quad |\mathbf{a}\times\mathbf{b}-\mathbf{a}\times\mathbf{c}|=|\mathbf{a}\times(\mathbf{b}-\mathbf{c})|$

$=|\mathbf{a}||\mathbf{b}-\mathbf{c}|=|\mathbf{b}-\mathbf{c}|$

Now, $|\mathbf{b}-\mathbf{c}|^2=|\mathbf{b}|^2+|\mathbf{c}|^2-2|\mathbf{b}||\mathbf{c}|\cos\frac{\pi}{3}$

$=2-2\times\frac{1}{2}=1$

$|\mathbf{b}-\mathbf{c}|=1$

Example 80 ■ *If the area of the triangle whose vertices are* $A(-1,1,2)$; $B(1,2,3)$ *and* $C(t,1,1)$ *is minimum, then the absolute value of parameter* t *is*

Sol. (2) $\mathbf{AB}=2\hat{\mathbf{i}}+\hat{\mathbf{j}}+\hat{\mathbf{k}}$, $\mathbf{AC}=(t+1)\hat{\mathbf{i}}+0\hat{\mathbf{j}}-\hat{\mathbf{k}}$

$$\mathbf{AB}\times\mathbf{AC}=\begin{vmatrix}\hat{\mathbf{i}} & \hat{\mathbf{j}} & \hat{\mathbf{k}}\\ 2 & 1 & 1\\ t+1 & 0 & -1\end{vmatrix}$$

$$=-\hat{\mathbf{i}}+(t+3)\hat{\mathbf{j}}-(t+1)\hat{\mathbf{k}}$$

$$|\mathbf{AB}\times\mathbf{AC}|=\sqrt{1+(t+3)^2+(t+1)^2}$$

$$=\sqrt{2t^2+8t+11}$$

Area of $\Delta ABC=\frac{1}{2}|\mathbf{AB}\times\mathbf{AC}|=\frac{1}{2}\sqrt{2t^2+8t+1}$

Let $f(t)=\Delta^2=\frac{1}{4}(2t^2+8t+1)$

$f'(t)=0\Rightarrow t=-2$

At $t=-2$, $f''(t)>0$

So, Δ is minimum at $t=-2$

$\therefore \quad |t|=2$

Example 81 ■ *Let* $\mathbf{OA}=\mathbf{a}$, $\mathbf{OB}=10\mathbf{a}+2\mathbf{b}$ *and* $\mathbf{OC}=\mathbf{b}$, *where* O, A *and* C *are non-collinear points. Let* p *denote the area of quadrilateral* $OACB$, *and let* q *denote the area of parallelogram with* OA *and* OC *as adjacent sides. If* $p=kq$, *then* k *is equal to*

Sol. (6) Here, $\mathbf{OA}=\mathbf{a}$, $\mathbf{OB}=10\mathbf{a}+2\mathbf{b}$, $\mathbf{OC}=\mathbf{b}$

q = Area of parallelogram with OA and OC as adjacent side.

$\therefore \quad q=|\mathbf{a}\times\mathbf{b}| \quad$ ...(i)

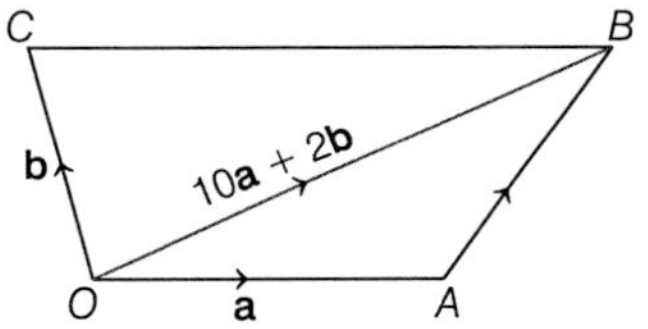

p = Area of quadrilateral $OABC$

= Area of ΔOAB + Area of ΔOBC

$=\frac{1}{2}|\mathbf{a}\times(10\mathbf{a}+2\mathbf{b})|+\frac{1}{2}|(10\mathbf{a}+2\mathbf{b})\times\mathbf{b}|$

$=|\mathbf{a}\times\mathbf{b}|+5|\mathbf{a}\times\mathbf{b}|$

$\therefore \quad p=6|\mathbf{a}\times\mathbf{b}|$ or $p=6q$ [from Eq. (i)]

$\therefore \quad k=6$

Example 82 ■ *If* $\mathbf{x}$ *and* $\mathbf{y}$ *are two non-zero and non-collinear vectors satisfying* $[(a-2)\alpha^2+(b-3)\alpha+c]\mathbf{x}+[(a-2)\beta^2+(b-3)\beta+c]\mathbf{y}+[(a-2)\gamma^2+(b-3)\gamma+c](\mathbf{x}\times\mathbf{y})=0$, *where* α, β *and* γ *are three distinct real numbers, then find the value of* $(a^2+b^2+c^2-4)$.

Sol. (9) Since, $\mathbf{x}$ and $\mathbf{y}$ are non-collinear vectors, therefore $\mathbf{x}$, $\mathbf{y}$ and $\mathbf{x}\times\mathbf{y}$ are non-coplanar vectors.

So, $[(a-2)\alpha^2+(b-3)\alpha+c]\mathbf{x}+[(a-2)\beta^2+(b-3)\beta+c]\mathbf{y}+[(a-2)\gamma^2+(b-3)\gamma+c](\mathbf{x}\times\mathbf{y})=0$

$\Rightarrow$ Coefficient of each vector $\mathbf{x}$, $\mathbf{y}$ and $\mathbf{x}\times\mathbf{y}$ is zero.

$(a-2)\alpha^2+(b-3)\alpha+c=0$

$(a-2)\beta^2+(b-3)\beta+c=0$

$(a-2)\gamma^2+(b-3)\gamma+c=0$

The above three equations will satisfy, if the coefficients of α, β and γ are zero because α, β and γ are three distinct real numbers

$a-2=0$ or $a=2$,

$b-3=0$ or $b=3$ and $c=0$

$\therefore \quad a^2+b^2+c^2=2^2+3^2+0^2=4+9=13$

Example 83 *Let* $\mathbf{v} = 2\hat{\mathbf{i}} + \hat{\mathbf{j}} - \hat{\mathbf{k}}$ *and* $\mathbf{w} = \hat{\mathbf{i}} + 3\hat{\mathbf{k}}$. *If* $\mathbf{u}$ *is unit vector and the maximum value of* $[\mathbf{u}\ \mathbf{v}\ \mathbf{w}] = \sqrt{\lambda}$, *then the value of* $(\lambda - 51)$ *is*

Sol. (8) We have, $[\mathbf{u}\ \mathbf{v}\ \mathbf{w}] = \mathbf{u} \cdot (\mathbf{v} \times \mathbf{w})$

$\Rightarrow \quad [\mathbf{u}\ \mathbf{v}\ \mathbf{w}] \le |\mathbf{u}|\,|\mathbf{v} \times \mathbf{w}| \qquad [\because \mathbf{a} \cdot \mathbf{b} \le |\mathbf{a}||\mathbf{b}|]$

$\Rightarrow \quad [\mathbf{u}\ \mathbf{v}\ \mathbf{w}] \le |\mathbf{v} \times \mathbf{w}| \qquad [\because |\mathbf{u}| = 1]$

Now, $$\mathbf{v} \times \mathbf{w} = \begin{vmatrix} \hat{\mathbf{i}} & \hat{\mathbf{j}} & \hat{\mathbf{k}} \\ 2 & 1 & -1 \\ 1 & 0 & 3 \end{vmatrix} = 3\hat{\mathbf{i}} - 7\hat{\mathbf{j}} - \hat{\mathbf{k}}$$

$\therefore \quad |\mathbf{v} \times \mathbf{w}| = \sqrt{9 + 49 + 1} = \sqrt{59}$

Hence, the maximum value of $[\mathbf{u}\ \mathbf{v}\ \mathbf{w}] = \sqrt{59}$

On comparing, we get $\lambda = 59$

$\therefore \quad \lambda - 51 = 8$

Example 84 *Let* $\mathbf{a} = \alpha\hat{\mathbf{i}} + 2\hat{\mathbf{j}} - 3\hat{\mathbf{k}}$, $\mathbf{b} = \hat{\mathbf{i}} + 2\alpha\hat{\mathbf{j}} - 2\hat{\mathbf{k}}$ *and* $\mathbf{c} = 2\hat{\mathbf{i}} - \alpha\hat{\mathbf{j}} + \hat{\mathbf{k}}$. *Then, the value of* 6α, *such that* $\{(\mathbf{a} \times \mathbf{b}) \times (\mathbf{b} \times \mathbf{c})\} \times (\mathbf{c} \times \mathbf{a}) = 0$, *is*

Sol. (4) $\mathbf{a} = \alpha\hat{\mathbf{i}} + 2\hat{\mathbf{j}} - 3\hat{\mathbf{k}}$, $\mathbf{b} = \hat{\mathbf{i}} + 2\alpha\hat{\mathbf{j}} - 2\hat{\mathbf{k}}$, $\mathbf{c} = 2\hat{\mathbf{i}} - \alpha\hat{\mathbf{j}} + \hat{\mathbf{k}}$

$\{(\mathbf{a} \times \mathbf{b}) \times (\mathbf{b} \times \mathbf{c})\} \times (\mathbf{c} \times \mathbf{a}) = \mathbf{0}$

or $\quad \{[\mathbf{a}\ \mathbf{b}\ \mathbf{c}]\mathbf{b} - [\mathbf{a}\ \mathbf{b}\ \mathbf{b}]\mathbf{c}\} \times (\mathbf{c} \times \mathbf{a}) = \mathbf{0}$

or $\quad [\mathbf{a}\ \mathbf{b}\ \mathbf{c}]\mathbf{b} \times (\mathbf{c} \times \mathbf{a}) = \mathbf{0}$

or $\quad [\mathbf{a}\ \mathbf{b}\ \mathbf{c}]((\mathbf{a} \cdot \mathbf{b})\mathbf{c} - (\mathbf{b} \cdot \mathbf{c})\mathbf{a}) = \mathbf{0}$

or $\quad [\mathbf{a}\ \mathbf{b}\ \mathbf{c}] = 0 \qquad [\because \mathbf{a}$ and $\mathbf{c}$ are not collinear$]$

$$\Rightarrow \quad \begin{vmatrix} \alpha & 2 & -3 \\ 1 & 2\alpha & -2 \\ 2 & -\alpha & 1 \end{vmatrix} = 0$$

or $\quad \alpha(2\alpha - 2\alpha) - 2(1 + 4) - 3(-\alpha - 4\alpha) = 0$

or $\quad 10 - 15\alpha = 0$

$\therefore \quad \alpha = \frac{2}{3} \Rightarrow 6\alpha = \frac{6 \times 2}{3} = 4$

Example 85 *Let* $\mathbf{A}$ *is a unit vector* $\mathbf{B} = 2\hat{\mathbf{i}} + \hat{\mathbf{j}} - \hat{\mathbf{k}}$ *and* $\mathbf{C} = \hat{\mathbf{i}} + 3\hat{\mathbf{k}}$, *and the maximum value of the* $[\mathbf{A}\ \mathbf{B}\ \mathbf{C}]$ *is* $\sqrt{p}$, *then the value of* $p - 50$ *is equal to ....*

Sol. (9) $\quad [\mathbf{A}\ \mathbf{B}\ \mathbf{C}] = \mathbf{A} \cdot (\mathbf{B} \times \mathbf{C})$

Now, $$\mathbf{B} \times \mathbf{C} = \begin{vmatrix} \hat{\mathbf{i}} & \hat{\mathbf{j}} & \hat{\mathbf{k}} \\ 2 & 1 & -1 \\ 1 & 0 & 3 \end{vmatrix}$$

$$= \hat{\mathbf{i}}(3 - 0) - \hat{\mathbf{j}}(6 + 1) + \hat{\mathbf{k}}(0 - 1)$$

$$= 3\hat{\mathbf{i}} - 7\hat{\mathbf{j}} - \hat{\mathbf{k}}$$

$\therefore \mathbf{A} \cdot (3\hat{\mathbf{i}} - 7\hat{\mathbf{j}} - \hat{\mathbf{k}}) = |\mathbf{A}|\sqrt{59}\cos\theta = 1 \times \sqrt{59}\cos\theta$

Maximum value of $[\mathbf{A}\ \mathbf{B}\ \mathbf{C}]$ occurs when $\theta = 0$

$\therefore$ Maximum value of the $[\mathbf{A}\ \mathbf{B}\ \mathbf{C}] = \sqrt{59}$

$\therefore \quad p - 50 = 9$

Example 86 *The work done by the force* $\mathbf{F} = 4\hat{\mathbf{i}} + 2\hat{\mathbf{j}} - 3\hat{\mathbf{k}}$ *acting on a particle such that the particle is displaced from point* $P(-5, 3, -2)$ *to point* $Q(-2, -1, -3)$ *is equal to ....*

Sol. (7) Given, $\mathbf{F} = 4\hat{\mathbf{i}} + 2\hat{\mathbf{j}} - 3\hat{\mathbf{k}}$

$$\mathbf{PQ} = (-2\hat{\mathbf{i}} - \hat{\mathbf{j}} - 3\hat{\mathbf{k}}) - (-5\hat{\mathbf{i}} + 3\hat{\mathbf{j}} - 2\hat{\mathbf{k}}) = 3\hat{\mathbf{i}} - 4\hat{\mathbf{j}} - \hat{\mathbf{k}}$$

$\therefore$ Work done $= \mathbf{F} \cdot \mathbf{PQ}$

$$= (4\hat{\mathbf{i}} + 2\hat{\mathbf{j}} - 3\hat{\mathbf{k}}) \cdot (3\hat{\mathbf{i}} - 4\hat{\mathbf{j}} - \hat{\mathbf{k}}) = 12 - 8 + 3 = 7 \text{ units}$$

Numerical Value Type Questions

Example 87 *The corner P of the square OPQR is folded up so that the plane OPQ is perpendicular to the plane OQR, if the angle between OP and QR is* $k\pi$, *then value of* $30k$ *is equal to ....*

Sol. (20) After folding OPQ, $PS \perp SQ$.

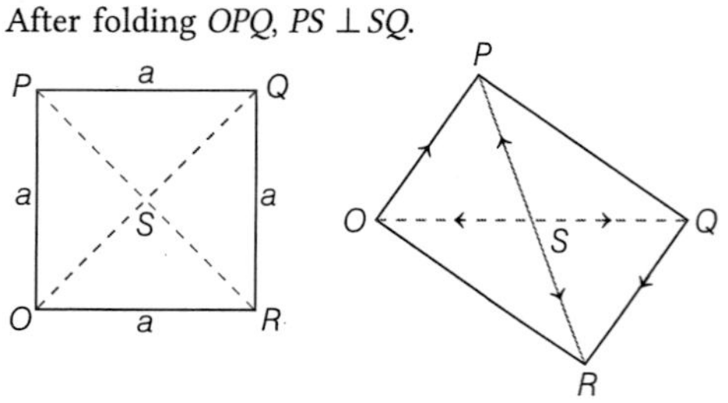

Here, $SQ \perp SR$, $SQ \perp PS$

Let $\mathbf{SR} = \frac{a}{\sqrt{2}}\hat{\mathbf{k}}$, $\mathbf{SQ} = \frac{a}{\sqrt{2}}\hat{\mathbf{i}}$ and $\mathbf{SP} = \frac{a}{\sqrt{2}}\hat{\mathbf{j}}$

$$\mathbf{OP} = -\mathbf{SO} + \mathbf{SP} = \frac{a}{\sqrt{2}}\hat{\mathbf{i}} + \frac{a}{\sqrt{2}}\hat{\mathbf{j}} = \frac{a}{\sqrt{2}}(\hat{\mathbf{i}} + \hat{\mathbf{j}})$$

$$\mathbf{QR} = \mathbf{SR} - \mathbf{SQ} = \frac{a}{\sqrt{2}}(\hat{\mathbf{k}} - \hat{\mathbf{i}})$$

$$|\mathbf{OP}| = \frac{a}{\sqrt{2}}\sqrt{2} = a \Rightarrow |\mathbf{QR}| = a$$

Cosine of angle between $\mathbf{OP}$ and $\mathbf{QR}$

$$= \frac{\mathbf{OP} \cdot \mathbf{QR}}{|\mathbf{OP}||\mathbf{QR}|} = \frac{a^2}{2}\frac{(\hat{\mathbf{i}} + \hat{\mathbf{j}}) \cdot (\hat{\mathbf{k}} - \hat{\mathbf{i}})}{a^2}$$

$$\Rightarrow \quad \cos\theta = \frac{1}{2}(-1) = -\frac{1}{2} \Rightarrow \theta = \frac{2\pi}{3}$$

$\therefore k = \frac{2}{3}$

$\therefore 30k = 20$

Example 88 *A circle is inscribed in an n-sided regular polygon* $A_1, A_2 \ldots, A_n$ *having each side a unit for any arbitrary point P on the circle.*

If $\sum_{i=1}^{n} (PA_i)^2 = n\frac{a^2}{\lambda}\left(\frac{1 + \cos^2 \pi/n}{\sin^2 \pi/n}\right)$, *then the value of* $\frac{\lambda}{10}$ *is*

....

Sol. (0.4) Let the centre of the incircle be the reference point.

Then, $\mathbf{PA}_i = \mathbf{OA}_i - \mathbf{OP}$

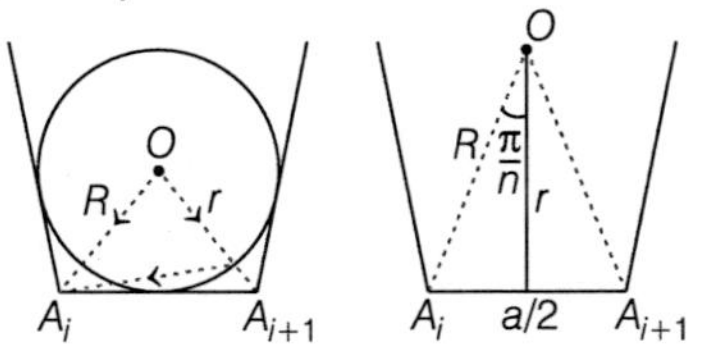

$$\mathbf{PA}_i \cdot \mathbf{PA}_i = (\mathbf{OA}_i - \mathbf{OP}) \cdot (\mathbf{OA}_i - \mathbf{OP})$$

$$(\mathbf{PA}_i)^2 = (|\mathbf{OA}_i|)^2 + (|\mathbf{OP}|)^2 - 2\mathbf{OA}_i \cdot \mathbf{OP}$$

$$\sum_{i=1}^{n} (\mathbf{PA}_i)^2 = \sum_{i=1}^{n} (|\mathbf{OA}_i|)^2 + (|\mathbf{OP}|^2) - 2\mathbf{OA}_i \cdot \mathbf{OP}$$

$$= nR^2 + nr^2 - 2\mathbf{OP} \cdot \sum_{i=1}^{n} \mathbf{OA}_i \quad \text{...(i)}$$

$$= n(R^2 + r^2) - 2\, OP \cdot (0)$$

Now, $$R = \frac{a}{2}\operatorname{cosec}\frac{\pi}{n}, r = \frac{a}{2}\cot\frac{\pi}{n} \quad \text{...(ii)}$$

$\therefore$ $$R^2 + r^2 = \frac{a^2}{4}\left(\operatorname{cosec}^2\frac{\pi}{n} + \cot^2\frac{\pi}{n}\right)$$

$$= \frac{a^2}{4}\left(\frac{1 + \cos^2 \pi/n}{\sin^2 \pi/n}\right) \quad \text{...(iii)}$$

$\therefore$ From Eqs. (i) and (iii), we get

$$\sum_{i=1}^{n} (PA_i)^2 = n\frac{a^2}{4}\left(\frac{1 + \cos^2 \pi/n}{\sin^2 \pi/n}\right)$$

$\therefore$ $$\frac{\lambda}{10} = 0.4$$

Example 89 *Let the area of a given $\Delta\, ABC$ be Δ. Points A_1, B_1 and C_1 are the mid-points of the sides BC, CA and AB, respectively. Point A_2 is the mid-point of CA, lines C_1A_1 and $A\,A_2$ meet the median BB_1 at E and D, respectively. If Δ_1 is the area of the quadrilateral A_1A_2DE, using vectors the value of $\frac{\Delta_1}{\Delta}$ is equal to ....*

Sol. (0.20) Let the position verctor of A, B and C be **a**, **b** and **c**, respectively.

We have, $\mathbf{AC}_1 = \frac{b}{2}$, $\mathbf{AB}_1 = \frac{c}{2}$, $\mathbf{AA}_2 = \frac{\mathbf{b}+\mathbf{c}}{2}$, $\mathbf{AA}_2 = \frac{3\mathbf{c}+\mathbf{b}}{4}$

Equation of the lines BB_1, AA_2 and C_1A_1 are

$$\mathbf{r} = \mathbf{b} + \lambda_1\left(\frac{\mathbf{c}}{2} - \mathbf{b}\right)$$

$$\mathbf{r} = \lambda_2 \frac{3\mathbf{c}+\mathbf{b}}{4} \quad \text{and} \quad \mathbf{r} = \frac{\mathbf{b}}{2} + \lambda_3\left(\frac{\mathbf{c}}{2}\right)$$

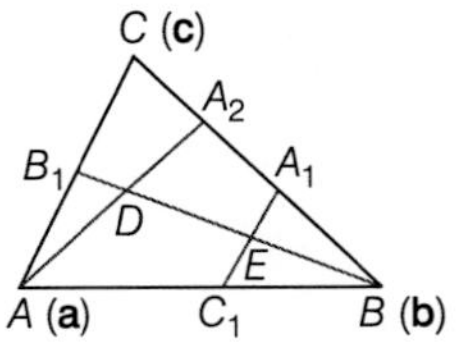

For the point D, we have

$$\mathbf{b} + \lambda_1\left(\frac{\mathbf{c}}{2} - \mathbf{b}\right) = \lambda_2\left(\frac{3\mathbf{c}+\mathbf{b}}{4}\right)$$

$$\mathbf{b}\left(1 - \lambda_1 - \frac{\lambda_2}{4}\right) + \frac{\mathbf{c}}{4}(2\lambda_1 - 3\lambda_2) = 0$$

$\Rightarrow$ $$\lambda_1 = \frac{6}{7}, \lambda_2 = \frac{4}{7}$$

$\therefore$ $$\mathbf{AD} = \frac{3\mathbf{c}+\mathbf{b}}{7}$$

For the point E, we have $\mathbf{b} + \lambda_1\left(\frac{\mathbf{c}}{2} - \mathbf{b}\right) = \frac{\mathbf{b}}{2} + \frac{\lambda_3}{2}\mathbf{c}$

$\Rightarrow$ $$\mathbf{b}\left(\frac{1}{2} - \lambda_1\right) + \frac{\mathbf{c}}{2}(\lambda_1 - \lambda_3) = 0$$

$\Rightarrow$ $$\lambda_1 = \lambda_3 = \frac{1}{2}$$

$\therefore$ $$\mathbf{AE} = \frac{2\mathbf{b}+\mathbf{c}}{4}$$

Now, $$\mathbf{EA}_2 = \frac{3\mathbf{c}+\mathbf{b}-2\mathbf{b}-\mathbf{c}}{4} = \frac{2\mathbf{c}-\mathbf{b}}{7}$$

$$\mathbf{DA}_1 = \frac{\mathbf{b}+\mathbf{c}}{2} - \frac{3\mathbf{c}+\mathbf{b}}{7} = \frac{5\mathbf{b}+\mathbf{c}}{14}$$

Area of quadrilateral $EA_1A_2\,D = \frac{1}{2}|\mathbf{EA}_2 \times \mathbf{DA}_1|$

$$= \frac{1}{112}|(2\mathbf{c}-\mathbf{b}) \times (5\mathbf{b}+\mathbf{c})| = \frac{1}{112}|10\mathbf{c} \times \mathbf{b} - \mathbf{b} \times \mathbf{c}|$$

$$= \frac{11}{112}|\mathbf{c} \times \mathbf{b}| = \frac{11}{56}\cdot\frac{1}{2}|\mathbf{c} \times \mathbf{b}| = \frac{11}{56}$$

and area of $\Delta ABC = \frac{1}{2}|\mathbf{b} \times \mathbf{c}|$

Thus, $\frac{\Delta_1}{\Delta} = 0.20$

Example 90 *If **a**, **b** and **c** represents the sides of tetrahedron and θ be an angle between **a** and **b**, ϕ be an angle between **a** and **c**, ψ be an angle between **b** and **c** and the volume of the tetrahedron is given by*

$$v^2 = \frac{a^2b^2c^2}{k}\begin{vmatrix} 1 & \cos\theta & \cos\theta \\ \cos\theta & 1 & \cos\psi \\ \cos\phi & \cos\psi & 1 \end{vmatrix}$$, *then the value of k is*

....

Sol. (36) OABC represent a tetrahedron, where

$\mathbf{OA} = \mathbf{a}, \mathbf{OB} = \mathbf{b}$ and $\mathbf{OC} = \mathbf{c}$ relative to O

Volume of tetrahedron $(v) = \frac{1}{6}[\mathbf{a} \cdot (\mathbf{b} \times \mathbf{c})]$

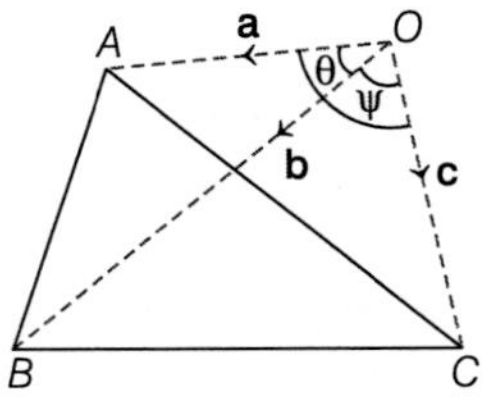

Also, $v^2 = \frac{1}{36}[\mathbf{a}\cdot(\mathbf{b}\times\mathbf{c})]^2 = \frac{1}{36}\begin{vmatrix} \mathbf{a}\cdot\mathbf{a} & \mathbf{a}\cdot\mathbf{b} & \mathbf{a}\cdot\mathbf{c} \\ \mathbf{b}\cdot\mathbf{a} & \mathbf{b}\cdot\mathbf{b} & \mathbf{b}\cdot\mathbf{c} \\ \mathbf{c}\cdot\mathbf{a} & \mathbf{c}\cdot\mathbf{b} & \mathbf{c}\cdot\mathbf{c}\end{vmatrix}$

$$= \frac{1}{36}\begin{vmatrix} a^2 & ab\cos\theta & ac\cos\phi \\ ab\cos\theta & b^2 & bc\cos\psi \\ ac\cos\phi & bc\cos\psi & c^2 \end{vmatrix}$$

$$= \frac{1}{36}a^2b^2c^2\begin{vmatrix} 1 & \cos\theta & \cos\phi \\ \cos\theta & 1 & \cos\psi \\ \cos\phi & \cos\psi & 1 \end{vmatrix}$$

$\Rightarrow \quad k = 36$

Example 91 *Let $h(\theta) = \int_{-(\hat{\mathbf{a}}\cdot\hat{\mathbf{b}})^2}^{|\hat{\mathbf{a}}\times\hat{\mathbf{b}}|^2}(2x+1)\,dx$, where θ is the angle between $\hat{\mathbf{a}}$ and $\hat{\mathbf{b}}$. If volume of the parallelopiped whose coterminous edges are represented by vectors $\hat{\mathbf{a}}$, $\hat{\mathbf{a}}\times\hat{\mathbf{b}}$ and $\hat{\mathbf{a}}\times(\hat{\mathbf{a}}\times\hat{\mathbf{b}})$ (where angle between $\hat{\mathbf{a}}$ and $\hat{\mathbf{b}}$ is taken from the equation $2h(\theta)-1=0$ is $\frac{m}{n}$, then the value of $\frac{m+n}{10}$ is ....*

Sol. (0.5) We have, $\hat{\mathbf{a}}\cdot\hat{\mathbf{b}} = |\hat{\mathbf{a}}||\hat{\mathbf{b}}|\cos\theta = \cos\theta$

and $\hat{\mathbf{a}}\times\hat{\mathbf{b}} = |\hat{\mathbf{a}}||\hat{\mathbf{b}}|\sin\theta = \sin\theta$

$\therefore \quad h(\theta) = \int_{-\cos^2\theta}^{\sin^2\theta}(2x+1)dx = [x^2+x]_{-\cos^2\theta}^{\sin^2\theta}$

$= (\sin^4\theta + \sin^2\theta) - (\cos^4\theta - \cos^2\theta)$

$= \sin^4\theta - \cos^4\theta + 1$

$= (\sin^2\theta)^2 - (\cos^2\theta)^2 + 1$

$= (\sin^2\theta + \cos^2\theta)(\sin^2\theta - \cos^2\theta) + 1$

$= \sin^2\theta - \cos^2\theta + 1$

$= 1 + \sin^2\theta - \cos^2\theta = \sin^2\theta + 1 - \cos^2\theta$

$= \sin^2\theta + \sin^2\theta = 2\sin^2\theta$

Volume of parallelopiped $= |[\hat{\mathbf{a}} \;\; \hat{\mathbf{a}}\times\hat{\mathbf{b}} \;\; \hat{\mathbf{a}}\times(\hat{\mathbf{a}}\times\hat{\mathbf{b}})]|$

$= |\hat{\mathbf{a}}\times(\hat{\mathbf{a}}\times\hat{\mathbf{b}})\cdot\hat{\mathbf{a}}\times(\hat{\mathbf{a}}\times\hat{\mathbf{b}})|$

$= |\hat{\mathbf{a}}\times(\hat{\mathbf{a}}\times\hat{\mathbf{b}})|^2$

$= |\hat{\mathbf{a}}|^2|\hat{\mathbf{a}}\times\hat{\mathbf{b}}|^2\sin^2 90°$

$= ||\hat{\mathbf{a}}||\hat{\mathbf{b}}|\sin\theta|^2 = \sin^2\theta$

Now, $\quad 2h(\theta) - 1 = 0$

$\Rightarrow \quad h(\theta) = \frac{1}{2} \Rightarrow 2\sin^2\theta = \frac{1}{2}$

$\Rightarrow \quad \sin^2\theta = \frac{1}{4} \Rightarrow \frac{m}{n} = \frac{1}{4}$

$\therefore \quad \frac{m+n}{10} = \frac{1+4}{10} = 0.5$

Example 92 *Let a three-dimensional vector $\mathbf{V}$ satisfy the condition, $2\mathbf{V} + \mathbf{V}\times(\hat{\mathbf{i}}+2\hat{\mathbf{j}}) = 2\hat{\mathbf{i}}+\hat{\mathbf{k}}$. If $9|\mathbf{V}|^2 = p^2$, then the value of $7\sqrt{6}p$ is equal to ....*

Sol. (42) We have, $2\mathbf{V} + \mathbf{V}\times(\hat{\mathbf{i}}+2\hat{\mathbf{j}}) = 2\hat{\mathbf{i}}+\hat{\mathbf{k}}$ ...(i)

On taking dot product with $(\hat{\mathbf{i}}+2\hat{\mathbf{j}})$, we get

$$2\mathbf{V}\cdot(\hat{\mathbf{i}}+2\hat{\mathbf{j}}) + (\mathbf{V}\times(\hat{\mathbf{i}}+2\hat{\mathbf{j}}))\cdot(\hat{\mathbf{i}}+2\hat{\mathbf{j}}) = (2\hat{\mathbf{i}}+\hat{\mathbf{k}})\cdot(\hat{\mathbf{i}}+2\hat{\mathbf{j}})$$

$\Rightarrow \quad 2\mathbf{V}\cdot(\hat{\mathbf{i}}+2\hat{\mathbf{j}}) = 2$

$\Rightarrow \quad \mathbf{V}(\hat{\mathbf{i}}+2\hat{\mathbf{j}}) = 1 \Rightarrow |\mathbf{V}\cdot(\hat{\mathbf{i}}+2\hat{\mathbf{j}})|^2 = 1$

$\Rightarrow \quad |\mathbf{V}|^2\cdot|(\hat{\mathbf{i}}+2\hat{\mathbf{j}})|^2\cos^2\theta = 1$

$\Rightarrow \quad |\mathbf{V}|^2 5(1-\sin^2\theta) = 1 \Rightarrow 5|\mathbf{V}|^2 - 5|\mathbf{V}|^2\sin^2\theta = 1$

$\Rightarrow \quad 5|\mathbf{V}|^2\sin^2\theta = 5|\mathbf{V}|^2 - 1$ ... (ii)

From Eq. (i), we have

$$|2\mathbf{V} + \mathbf{V}\times(\hat{\mathbf{i}}+2\hat{\mathbf{j}})|^2 = |2\hat{\mathbf{i}}+\hat{\mathbf{k}}|^2$$

$\Rightarrow \quad 4|\mathbf{V}|^2 + |\mathbf{V}\times(\hat{\mathbf{i}}+2\hat{\mathbf{j}})|^2 = 5$

$\Rightarrow \quad 4|\mathbf{V}|^2 + |\mathbf{V}|^2\cdot|\hat{\mathbf{i}}+2\hat{\mathbf{j}}|^2\sin^2\theta = 5$

$\Rightarrow \quad 4|\mathbf{V}|^2 + |\mathbf{V}|^2(5)\sin^2\theta = 5$

$\Rightarrow \quad 4|\mathbf{V}|^2 + 5|\mathbf{V}|^2 - 1 = 5$ [using Eq. (ii)]

$\Rightarrow \quad 9|\mathbf{V}|^2 = 6$

$\therefore \quad p^2 = 6 \Rightarrow p = \sqrt{6}$

$\therefore \quad 7\sqrt{6}p = 7\sqrt{6}(\sqrt{6}) = 42$

Matching Type Questions

Example 93 *Match the items of Column I with items of Column II.*

Column I	Column II
A. If $\|\mathbf{a}+\mathbf{b}\| = \|\mathbf{a}+2\mathbf{b}\|$, then angle between $\mathbf{a}$ and $\mathbf{b}$ is	p. 90°
B. If $\|\mathbf{a}+\mathbf{b}\| = \|\mathbf{a}-2\mathbf{b}\|$, then angle between $\mathbf{a}$ and $\mathbf{b}$ is	q. obtuse
C. If $\|\mathbf{a}+\mathbf{b}\| = \|\mathbf{a}-\mathbf{b}\|$ then angle between $\mathbf{a}$ and $\mathbf{b}$ is	r. 0°
D. Angle between $\mathbf{a}\times\mathbf{b}$ and a vector perpendicular to the vector $\mathbf{c}\times(\mathbf{a}\times\mathbf{b})$ is	s. acute

Sol. A → q; B → s; C → p; D → r

(A) $|\mathbf{a}+\mathbf{b}| = |\mathbf{a}+2\mathbf{b}|$

$a^2 + b^2 + 2\mathbf{a}\cdot\mathbf{b} = a^2 + 4b^2 + 4\mathbf{a}\cdot\mathbf{b}$ or $2\mathbf{a}\cdot\mathbf{b} = -3b^2 < 0$

Hence, the angle between **a** and **b** is obtuse.

(B) $|\mathbf{a}+\mathbf{b}| = |\mathbf{a}-2\mathbf{b}|$

or $a^2 + b^2 + 2\mathbf{a}\cdot\mathbf{b} = a^2 + 4b^2 - 4\mathbf{a}\cdot\mathbf{b}$ or $6\mathbf{a}\cdot\mathbf{b} = 3b^2 > 0$

Hence, the angle between **a** and **b** is acute.

(C) $|\mathbf{a}+\mathbf{b}| = |\mathbf{a}-\mathbf{b}| \Rightarrow \mathbf{a}\cdot\mathbf{b} = 0$

Hence, **a** is perpendicular to **b**.

(D) $\mathbf{c}\times(\mathbf{a}\times\mathbf{b})$ lies in the plane of vectors **a** and **b**.

A vector perpendicular to this plane is parallel to $\mathbf{a}\times\mathbf{b}$

Hence, the angle is 0°.

Example 94 ■ *Match the items of Column I with items of Column II.*

Column I	Column II
A. Let $\|\mathbf{a}\| = \|\mathbf{b}\| = 2$, $\mathbf{x} = \mathbf{a} + \mathbf{b}$, $\mathbf{y} = \mathbf{a} - \mathbf{b}$. If $\|\mathbf{x} \times \mathbf{y}\| = 2\{\lambda - (\mathbf{a} \cdot \mathbf{b})^2\}^{1/2}$, then the value of λ is	p. 4
B. The non-zero value of λ for which angle between $\lambda\hat{\mathbf{i}} + \hat{\mathbf{j}} + \hat{\mathbf{k}}$ and $\hat{\mathbf{i}} + \lambda\hat{\mathbf{j}} + \hat{\mathbf{k}}$ is $\frac{\pi}{3}$, is	q. 42
C. If $\|\mathbf{a}\| = \|\mathbf{b}\| = 1$ and $\|\mathbf{c}\| = 2$, then the maximum value of $\|\mathbf{a} - 2\mathbf{b}\|^2 + \|\mathbf{b} - 2\mathbf{c}\|^2 + \|\mathbf{c} - 2\mathbf{a}\|^2$ is	r. 16
D. If $a + 2b + 3c = 4$, and the least value of $a^2 + b^2 + c^2$ is $\frac{\lambda}{\mu}$, then $\lambda + \mu$ is equal to	s. 15

Sol. A → (r), B → (p), C → (q), D → (s)

(A) $\mathbf{x} \times \mathbf{y} = (\mathbf{a} + \mathbf{b}) \times (\mathbf{a} - \mathbf{b})$

$= \mathbf{a} \times \mathbf{a} - \mathbf{a} \times \mathbf{b} + \mathbf{b} \times \mathbf{a} - \mathbf{b} \times \mathbf{b}$

$= -2(\mathbf{a} \times \mathbf{b})$

LHS $= |\mathbf{x} \times \mathbf{y}| = |-2(\mathbf{a} \times \mathbf{b})| = 2|\mathbf{a}||\mathbf{b}|\sin\theta$

RHS $= 2(\lambda - (\mathbf{a} \cdot \mathbf{b})^2)^{\frac{1}{2}} = 2(\lambda - |\mathbf{a}|^2|\mathbf{b}|^2\cos^2\theta)^{1/2}$

$\because \quad 8\sin\theta = 2(\lambda - 16\cos^2\theta)^{1/2}$

$\Rightarrow \quad 16\sin^2\theta = \lambda - 16\cos^2\theta \Rightarrow 16(\sin^2\theta + \cos^2\theta) = \lambda$

$\therefore \quad \lambda = 16$

(B) We have, $\cos\frac{\pi}{3} = \frac{1}{2}$

$\Rightarrow \quad \frac{1}{2} = \frac{(\lambda\hat{\mathbf{i}} + \hat{\mathbf{j}} + \hat{\mathbf{k}}) \cdot (\hat{\mathbf{i}} + \lambda\hat{\mathbf{j}} + \hat{\mathbf{k}})}{\sqrt{\lambda^2 + 2}\sqrt{\lambda^2 + 2}}$

$\because \quad \frac{1}{2} = \frac{\lambda + \lambda + 1}{\lambda^2 + 2}$

$\Rightarrow \quad \lambda^2 + 2 = 2(2\lambda + 1) \Rightarrow \lambda^2 - 4\lambda = 0$

$\Rightarrow \quad \lambda(\lambda - 4) = 0$

$\Rightarrow \quad \lambda = 0$ and 4

$\therefore \quad \lambda = 4$

(C) We have,

$|\mathbf{a} - 2\mathbf{b}|^2 + |\mathbf{b} - 2\mathbf{c}|^2 + |\mathbf{c} - 2\mathbf{a}|^2$

$= |\mathbf{a}|^2 + 4|\mathbf{b}|^2 - 4\mathbf{a} \cdot \mathbf{b} + |\mathbf{b}|^2 + 4|\mathbf{c}|^2 - 4\mathbf{b} \cdot \mathbf{c} + |\mathbf{c}|^2 + 4|\mathbf{a}|^2 - 4\mathbf{c} \cdot \mathbf{a}$

$= 1 + 4 + 1 + 16 + 4 + 4 - 4(\mathbf{a} \cdot \mathbf{b} + \mathbf{b} \cdot \mathbf{c} + \mathbf{c} \cdot \mathbf{a})$

$= 30 - 4(\mathbf{a} \cdot \mathbf{b} + \mathbf{b} \cdot \mathbf{c} + \mathbf{c} \cdot \mathbf{a})$

We know that

$(\mathbf{a} + \mathbf{b} + \mathbf{c})^2 = \mathbf{a}^2 + \mathbf{b}^2 + \mathbf{c}^2 + 2(\mathbf{a} \cdot \mathbf{b} + \mathbf{b} \cdot \mathbf{c} + \mathbf{c} \cdot \mathbf{a}) \geq 0$

i.e. $1 + 1 + 4 + 2(\mathbf{a} \cdot \mathbf{b} + \mathbf{b} \cdot \mathbf{c} + \mathbf{c} \cdot \mathbf{a}) \geq 0$

$\Rightarrow \quad \mathbf{a} \cdot \mathbf{b} + \mathbf{b} \cdot \mathbf{c} + \mathbf{c} \cdot \mathbf{a} \geq -3$

$\Rightarrow \quad \geq 30 - 4(-3) \geq 30 + 12 \geq 42$

(D) Let the vector $\mathbf{p} = a\hat{\mathbf{i}} + b\hat{\mathbf{j}} + c\hat{\mathbf{k}}$ and $\mathbf{q} = \hat{\mathbf{i}} + 2\hat{\mathbf{j}} + 3\hat{\mathbf{k}}$

Now, $\cos\theta = \frac{a + 2b + 3c}{\sqrt{a^2 + b^2 + c^2}\sqrt{1^2 + 2^2 + 3^2}}$

$\Rightarrow \quad \cos^2\theta = \frac{(a + 2b + 3c)^2}{14(a^2 + b^2 + c^2)} \leq 1$ [on squaring both sides]

$\Rightarrow \quad a^2 + b^2 + c^2 \geq \frac{8}{7}$

So, $\lambda = 8$ and $\mu = 7$

Hence, $\lambda + \mu = 8 + 7 = 15$

Example 95 ■ *Match the items of Column I with items of Column II.*

Column I	Column II
A. Given two vectors $\mathbf{a} = 2\hat{\mathbf{i}} - 3\hat{\mathbf{j}} + 6\hat{\mathbf{k}}$, $\mathbf{b} = -2\hat{\mathbf{i}} + 2\hat{\mathbf{j}} - \hat{\mathbf{k}}$ and $\lambda = \frac{\text{Projection of } \mathbf{a} \text{ on } \mathbf{b}}{\text{Projection of } \mathbf{b} \text{ on } \mathbf{a}}$, then the value of 3λ is	p. 0
B. If $\mathbf{a} = \hat{\mathbf{i}} + 2\hat{\mathbf{j}} + 3\hat{\mathbf{k}}$, $\mathbf{b} = -\hat{\mathbf{i}} + 2\hat{\mathbf{j}} + \hat{\mathbf{k}}$, $\mathbf{c} = 3\hat{\mathbf{i}} + \hat{\mathbf{j}}$ and $\mathbf{a} + p\mathbf{b}$ is normal to $\mathbf{c}$, then p is	q. 7
C. Let $\mathbf{a}$, $\mathbf{b}$ and $\mathbf{c}$ be three non-zero vectors such that $\mathbf{a} + \mathbf{b} + \mathbf{c} = 0$, then $\lambda(\mathbf{a} \times \mathbf{b}) + \mathbf{c} \times \mathbf{b} + \mathbf{a} \times \mathbf{c} = 0$, where λ is equal to	r. 5
D. The points whose position vectors are $p\hat{\mathbf{i}} + q\hat{\mathbf{j}} + r\hat{\mathbf{k}}$, $q\hat{\mathbf{i}} + r\hat{\mathbf{j}} + p\hat{\mathbf{k}}$ and $r\hat{\mathbf{i}} + p\hat{\mathbf{j}} + q\hat{\mathbf{k}}$ are collinear, then the value of $(p^2 + q^2 + r^2 - pq - qr - rp)$ is	s. 2

Sol. A → (q), B → (r), C → (s), D → (p)

(A) Given, $\mathbf{a} = 2\hat{\mathbf{i}} - 3\hat{\mathbf{j}} + 6\hat{\mathbf{k}}$ and $\mathbf{b} = -2\hat{\mathbf{i}} + 2\hat{\mathbf{j}} - \hat{\mathbf{k}}$

Now, $\lambda = \frac{\text{Projection of } \mathbf{a} \text{ on } \mathbf{b}}{\text{Projection of } \mathbf{b} \text{ on } \mathbf{a}} = \frac{\left(\frac{\mathbf{a} \cdot \mathbf{b}}{|\mathbf{b}|}\right)}{\left(\frac{\mathbf{b} \cdot \mathbf{a}}{|\mathbf{a}|}\right)} = \frac{|\mathbf{a}|}{|\mathbf{b}|}$

$= \frac{\sqrt{2^2 + (-3)^2 + 6^2}}{\sqrt{(-2)^2 + 2^2 + (-1)^2}} = \frac{\sqrt{4 + 9 + 36}}{\sqrt{4 + 4 + 1}} = \frac{7}{3}$

$\therefore \quad 3\lambda = 7$

(B) Given, $\mathbf{a} = \hat{\mathbf{i}} + 2\hat{\mathbf{j}} + 3\hat{\mathbf{k}}$, $\mathbf{b} = -\hat{\mathbf{i}} + 2\hat{\mathbf{j}} + \hat{\mathbf{k}}$ and $\mathbf{c} = 3\hat{\mathbf{i}} + \hat{\mathbf{j}}$

Since, $\mathbf{a} + p\mathbf{b}$ is normal to $\mathbf{c}$

$\Rightarrow \quad (\mathbf{a} + p\mathbf{b}) \cdot \mathbf{c} = 0$

$\Rightarrow \quad [(1-p)\hat{\mathbf{i}} + (2+2p)\hat{\mathbf{j}} + (3+p)\hat{\mathbf{k}}] \cdot (3\hat{\mathbf{i}} + \hat{\mathbf{j}}) = 0$

$\Rightarrow \quad 3(1-p) + 2 + 2p = 0$

$\Rightarrow \quad 3 - 3p + 2 + 2p = 0$

$\therefore \quad p = 5$

(C) Given, $\mathbf{a} + \mathbf{b} + \mathbf{c} = 0$

$\Rightarrow \quad \mathbf{a} \times \mathbf{a} + \mathbf{a} \times \mathbf{b} + \mathbf{a} \times \mathbf{c} = \mathbf{a} \times 0$

$\Rightarrow \quad \mathbf{a} \times \mathbf{b} + \mathbf{a} \times \mathbf{c} = 0 \quad \text{...(i)}$

Also, $\mathbf{b} \times \mathbf{a} + \mathbf{b} \times \mathbf{b} + \mathbf{b} \times \mathbf{c} = \mathbf{b} \times 0$

$\Rightarrow \quad \mathbf{b} \times \mathbf{a} + \mathbf{b} \times \mathbf{c} = 0$

$\Rightarrow \quad -\mathbf{a} \times \mathbf{b} - \mathbf{c} \times \mathbf{b} = 0$

$\Rightarrow \quad \mathbf{a} \times \mathbf{b} + \mathbf{c} \times \mathbf{b} = 0 \quad \text{...(ii)}$

On adding Eqs. (i) and (ii), we get

$$2(\mathbf{a} \times \mathbf{b}) + \mathbf{c} \times \mathbf{b} + \mathbf{a} \times \mathbf{c} = 0$$

On comparing, we get $\lambda = 2$

(D) $\begin{vmatrix} p & q & r \\ q & r & p \\ r & p & q \end{vmatrix} = 0$

$\Rightarrow \quad (p+q+r)(p^2 + q^2 + r^2 - pq - qr - rp) = 0$

$\therefore \quad p^2 + q^2 + r^2 - pq - qr - rp = 0$

Example 96 *Match the items of Column I with items of Column II.*

Column I	Column II
A. If $\mathbf{a}$ and $\mathbf{b}$ are two unit vectors inclined at $\frac{\pi}{3}$, then $16[\mathbf{a}\ \mathbf{b} + \mathbf{a} \times \mathbf{b}\ \mathbf{b}]$ is	p. -12
B. If $\mathbf{b}$ and $\mathbf{c}$ are orthogonal unit vectors and $\mathbf{b} \times \mathbf{c} = \mathbf{a}$, then $[\mathbf{a} + \mathbf{b} + \mathbf{c}\ \ \mathbf{a} + \mathbf{b}\ \ \mathbf{b} + \mathbf{c}]$ is	q. 1
C. If $\|\mathbf{a}\| = \|\mathbf{b}\| = \|\mathbf{c}\| = 2$ and $\mathbf{a} \cdot \mathbf{b} = \mathbf{b} \cdot \mathbf{c} = \mathbf{c} \cdot \mathbf{a} = 2$, then $[\mathbf{a}\ \mathbf{b}\ \mathbf{c}] \cos 45^\circ$ is equal to	r. 3
D. $\mathbf{a} = 2\hat{\mathbf{i}} + 3\hat{\mathbf{j}} - \hat{\mathbf{k}}$, $\mathbf{b} = -\hat{\mathbf{i}} + 2\hat{\mathbf{j}} - 4\hat{\mathbf{k}}$, $\mathbf{c} = \hat{\mathbf{i}} + \hat{\mathbf{j}} + \hat{\mathbf{k}}$ and $\mathbf{d} = 3\hat{\mathbf{i}} + 2\hat{\mathbf{j}} + \hat{\mathbf{k}}$, then $\frac{1}{7}(\mathbf{a} \times \mathbf{b}) \cdot (\mathbf{c} \times \mathbf{d})$ is equal to	s. 4

Sol. A → (p); B → (q); C → (s); D → (r)

(A) Given $\mathbf{a}$ and $\mathbf{b}$ are two unit vectors, i.e. $|\mathbf{a}| = |\mathbf{b}| = 1$ and angle between them is $\frac{\pi}{3}$.

$$\sin\theta = \frac{|\mathbf{a} \times \mathbf{b}|}{|\mathbf{a}|\,|\mathbf{b}|} \Rightarrow \sin\frac{\pi}{3} = |\mathbf{a} \times \mathbf{b}|$$

$$\frac{\sqrt{3}}{2} = |\mathbf{a} \times \mathbf{b}|$$

Now, $[\mathbf{a}\ \ \mathbf{b} + \mathbf{a} \times \mathbf{b}\ \ \mathbf{b}] = [\mathbf{a}\ \mathbf{b}\ \mathbf{b}] + [\mathbf{a}\ \ \mathbf{a} \times \mathbf{b}\ \ \mathbf{b}]$

$= 0 + [\mathbf{a}\ \ \mathbf{a} \times \mathbf{b}\ \ \mathbf{b}] = (\mathbf{a} \times \mathbf{b}) \cdot (\mathbf{b} \times \mathbf{a})$

$= -(\mathbf{a} \times \mathbf{b}) \cdot (\mathbf{a} \times \mathbf{b}) = -|\mathbf{a} \times \mathbf{b}|^2 = -\frac{3}{4}$

(B) If $\mathbf{b}$ and $\mathbf{c}$ are orthogonal $\mathbf{b} \cdot \mathbf{c} = 0$

Also, it is given that $\mathbf{b} \times \mathbf{c} = \mathbf{a}$.

Now, $[\mathbf{a} + \mathbf{b} + \mathbf{c}\ \ \mathbf{a} + \mathbf{b}\ \ \mathbf{b} + \mathbf{c}]$

$= [\mathbf{a}\ \ \mathbf{a} + \mathbf{b}\ \ \mathbf{b} + \mathbf{c}] + [\mathbf{b} + \mathbf{c}\ \ \mathbf{a} + \mathbf{b}\ \ \mathbf{b} + \mathbf{c}]$

$= [\mathbf{a}\ \mathbf{b}\ \mathbf{c}] = \mathbf{a} \cdot (\mathbf{b} \times \mathbf{c})$

$= \mathbf{a} \cdot \mathbf{a} = |\mathbf{a}|^2 = 1$ (because $\mathbf{a}$ is a unit vector)

(C) We know that $[\mathbf{a} \times \mathbf{b}\ \ \mathbf{b} \times \mathbf{c}\ \ \mathbf{c} \times \mathbf{a}] = [\mathbf{a}\ \mathbf{b}\ \mathbf{c}]^2$

$$[\mathbf{a}\ \mathbf{b}\ \mathbf{c}]^2 = \begin{vmatrix} \mathbf{a} \cdot \mathbf{a} & \mathbf{a} \cdot \mathbf{b} & \mathbf{a} \cdot \mathbf{c} \\ \mathbf{b} \cdot \mathbf{a} & \mathbf{b} \cdot \mathbf{b} & \mathbf{b} \cdot \mathbf{c} \\ \mathbf{c} \cdot \mathbf{a} & \mathbf{c} \cdot \mathbf{b} & \mathbf{c} \cdot \mathbf{c} \end{vmatrix} = \begin{vmatrix} 4 & 2 & 2 \\ 2 & 4 & 2 \\ 2 & 2 & 4 \end{vmatrix} = 32$$

$\Rightarrow \quad [\mathbf{a}\ \mathbf{b}\ \mathbf{c}] = 4\sqrt{2}$

$\therefore [\mathbf{a}\ \mathbf{b}\ \mathbf{c}] \cos 45^\circ = 4$

(D) $(\mathbf{a} \cdot \mathbf{c})(\mathbf{b} \cdot \mathbf{d}) - (\mathbf{b} \cdot \mathbf{c})(\mathbf{a} \cdot \mathbf{d}) = 21$

$\therefore \quad \frac{1}{7}(\mathbf{a} \times \mathbf{c}) \cdot (\mathbf{c} \times \mathbf{d}) = 3$

Example 97 *Match the items of Column I with items of Column II.*

	Column I		Column II
A.	It $\mathbf{a} = 3\hat{\mathbf{i}} + 2\hat{\mathbf{k}}$ and $\mathbf{b} = 2\hat{\mathbf{j}} + \hat{\mathbf{k}}$ and $\mathbf{c}$ is a unit vector, then the maximum value of scalar triple product $[\mathbf{a}\ \mathbf{b}\ \mathbf{c}]$ is	p.	12
B.	Vectors $\mathbf{a}$ and $\mathbf{b}$ are inclined at an angle $\theta = 120^\circ$. If $\|\mathbf{a}\| = 1$, $\|\mathbf{b}\| = 2$, then $\{(\mathbf{a} + 3\mathbf{b}) \times (3\mathbf{a} - \mathbf{b})\}^2$ is equal to	q.	3
C.	If $\mathbf{a}, \mathbf{b}, \mathbf{c}$ and $\mathbf{d}$ are unit vectors, then $\|\mathbf{a} - \mathbf{b}\|^2 + \|\mathbf{b} - \mathbf{c}\|^2 + \|\mathbf{c} - \mathbf{d}\|^2 + \|\mathbf{d} - \mathbf{a}\|^2 + \|\mathbf{c} - \mathbf{a}\|^2 + \|\mathbf{b} - \mathbf{d}\|^2$ does not exceed	r.	300
D.	Let P, Q and R be points with position vectors $\mathbf{r}_1 = 3\hat{\mathbf{i}} - 2\hat{\mathbf{j}} - \hat{\mathbf{k}}$, $\mathbf{r}_2 = \hat{\mathbf{i}} + 3\hat{\mathbf{j}} + 4\hat{\mathbf{k}}$ and $\mathbf{r}_3 = 2\hat{\mathbf{i}} + \hat{\mathbf{j}} - 2\hat{\mathbf{k}}$ relative to an origin O. The distance of P from the plane OQR is	s.	$\sqrt{61}$

Sol. A → (s); B → (r); C → (p); D → (q)

(A) $\mathbf{a} = 3\hat{\mathbf{i}} + 2\hat{\mathbf{k}},\ \mathbf{b} = 2\hat{\mathbf{j}} + \hat{\mathbf{k}},\ |\mathbf{c}| = 1$

$$\mathbf{a} \times \mathbf{b} = \begin{vmatrix} \hat{\mathbf{i}} & \hat{\mathbf{j}} & \hat{\mathbf{k}} \\ 3 & 0 & 2 \\ 0 & 2 & 1 \end{vmatrix}$$

$$= \hat{\mathbf{i}}(-4) - \hat{\mathbf{j}}(3) + \hat{\mathbf{k}}(6)$$

$$= -4\hat{\mathbf{i}} - 3\hat{\mathbf{j}} + 6\hat{\mathbf{k}}$$

$$[\mathbf{a}\ \mathbf{b}\ \mathbf{c}] = (\mathbf{a} \times \mathbf{b}) \cdot \mathbf{c}$$

$$= (-4\hat{\mathbf{i}} - 3\hat{\mathbf{j}} + 6\hat{\mathbf{k}}) \cdot \mathbf{c}$$

⇒ The maximum value of $[\mathbf{a}\ \mathbf{b}\ \mathbf{c}] = |-4\hat{\mathbf{i}} - 3\hat{\mathbf{j}} + 6\hat{\mathbf{k}}|\,|\mathbf{c}|$

$$= \sqrt{61}$$

(B) Since, $\mathbf{a} \cdot \mathbf{b} = |\mathbf{a}|\,|\mathbf{b}| \cos 120°$

$$= 1 \cdot 2 \cdot \left(\frac{-1}{2}\right)$$

$$= -1$$

$$\{(\mathbf{a} + 3\mathbf{b}) \times (3\mathbf{a} - \mathbf{b})\}^2 = \{3\mathbf{a} \times \mathbf{a} - \mathbf{a} \times \mathbf{b} + 9\mathbf{b} \times \mathbf{a} - 3\mathbf{b} \times \mathbf{b}\}^2$$

$$= [0 - \mathbf{a} \times \mathbf{b} - 9\mathbf{a} \times \mathbf{b} - 0]^2$$

$$= [-10(\mathbf{a} \times \mathbf{b})]^2$$

$$= 100\,(\mathbf{a} \times \mathbf{b})^2$$

$$= 100\,(\mathbf{a}^2\mathbf{b}^2 - (\mathbf{a} \cdot \mathbf{b})^2)$$

$$= 100\,(4 - 1)$$

$$= 300$$

(C) We have,

$$0 < |a + b + c + d|^2 = |a|^2 + |b|^2 + |c|^2 + |d|^2$$
$$+ 2(a \cdot b + b \cdot c + c \cdot a + a \cdot d + c \cdot d + b \cdot d)$$
$$= 4 + 2\,(a \cdot b + b \cdot c + c \cdot a + a \cdot d + c \cdot d + b \cdot d)$$

So, $a \cdot b + b \cdot c + c \cdot a + a \cdot d + c \cdot d + b \cdot d \geq -2$

Now,

$$|a - b|^2 + |b - c|^2 + |c - d|^2 + |d - a|^2 + |c - a|^2 + |b - d|^2$$
$$= 2(|a|^2 + |b|^2 + |c|^2 + |d|^2 - (a \cdot b + c \cdot d + d \cdot a + a \cdot c + b \cdot d + b \cdot c))$$
$$\leq 2(4 + 2)$$
$$= 12$$

(D) Equation of the plane OQR is $r = \lambda r_2 + \mu r_3$

i.e. $\mathbf{r} \cdot (\mathbf{r}_2 \times \mathbf{r}_3) = 0$

So, the distance of P from the plane OQR is $\left|\dfrac{\mathbf{r}_1 \cdot (\mathbf{r}_2 \times \mathbf{r}_3)}{|\mathbf{r}_2 \times \mathbf{r}_3|}\right|$

$$\because \quad \mathbf{r}_2 \times \mathbf{r}_3 = \begin{vmatrix} \hat{\mathbf{i}} & \hat{\mathbf{j}} & \hat{\mathbf{k}} \\ 1 & 3 & 4 \\ 2 & 1 & -2 \end{vmatrix}$$

$$= \hat{\mathbf{i}}(-10) - \hat{\mathbf{j}}(-10) + \hat{\mathbf{k}}(1 - 6)$$

$$= -10\hat{\mathbf{i}} + 10\hat{\mathbf{j}} - 5\hat{\mathbf{k}}$$

$$\therefore \quad |\mathbf{r}_2 \times \mathbf{r}_3| = \sqrt{(10)^2 + (10)^2 + (5)^2} = 15$$

$$\therefore \text{ Required distance} = \frac{1}{15}\begin{vmatrix} 3 & -2 & -1 \\ 1 & 3 & 4 \\ 2 & 1 & -2 \end{vmatrix} = 3$$

EXERCISE 1
JEE Main Pattern

Single Option Correct Type Questions

1. If **a** has magnitude 5 and points North-East and vector **b** has magnitude 5 and points North-West, then $|\mathbf{a}-\mathbf{b}|$ is equal to

(a) 25 (b) 5 (c) $7\sqrt{3}$ (d) $5\sqrt{2}$

2. Let **a** and **b** be two unit vectors inclined at an angle θ, then $\sin(\theta/2)$ is equal to

(a) $\frac{1}{2}|\mathbf{a}-\mathbf{b}|$ (b) $\frac{1}{2}|\mathbf{a}+\mathbf{b}|$

(c) $|\mathbf{a}-\mathbf{b}|$ (d) $|\mathbf{a}+\mathbf{b}|$

3. If vector $\mathbf{a}=2\hat{\mathbf{i}}-3\hat{\mathbf{j}}+6\hat{\mathbf{k}}$ and vector $\mathbf{b}=-2\hat{\mathbf{i}}+2\hat{\mathbf{j}}-\hat{\mathbf{k}}$, then $\dfrac{\text{Projection of } \mathbf{a} \text{ on } \mathbf{b}}{\text{Projection of } \mathbf{b} \text{ on } \mathbf{a}}$ is equal to

(a) $\frac{3}{7}$ (b) $\frac{7}{3}$ (c) 3 (d) 7

4. If **a** and **b** are two vectors, then $(\mathbf{a}\times\mathbf{b})^2$ is equal to

(a) $\begin{vmatrix}\mathbf{a}\cdot\mathbf{b} & \mathbf{a}\cdot\mathbf{a}\\ \mathbf{b}\cdot\mathbf{b} & \mathbf{b}\cdot\mathbf{a}\end{vmatrix}$ (b) $\begin{vmatrix}\mathbf{a}\cdot\mathbf{a} & \mathbf{a}\cdot\mathbf{b}\\ \mathbf{b}\cdot\mathbf{a} & \mathbf{b}\cdot\mathbf{b}\end{vmatrix}$

(c) $\begin{vmatrix}\mathbf{a}\cdot\mathbf{b}\\ \mathbf{b}\cdot\mathbf{a}\end{vmatrix}$ (d) None of these

5. A force $\mathbf{F}=2\hat{\mathbf{i}}+\hat{\mathbf{j}}-\hat{\mathbf{k}}$ acts at a point *A* whose position vector is $2\hat{\mathbf{i}}-\hat{\mathbf{j}}$. The moment of **F** about the origin is

(a) $\hat{\mathbf{i}}+2\hat{\mathbf{j}}-4\hat{\mathbf{k}}$ (b) $\hat{\mathbf{i}}-2\hat{\mathbf{j}}-4\hat{\mathbf{k}}$

(c) $\hat{\mathbf{i}}+2\hat{\mathbf{j}}+4\hat{\mathbf{k}}$ (d) $\hat{\mathbf{i}}-2\hat{\mathbf{j}}+4\hat{\mathbf{k}}$

6. A vector whose modulus is $\sqrt{51}$ and makes the same angle with $\mathbf{a}=\dfrac{\hat{\mathbf{i}}-2\hat{\mathbf{j}}+2\hat{\mathbf{k}}}{3}$, $\mathbf{b}=\dfrac{-4\hat{\mathbf{i}}-3\hat{\mathbf{k}}}{5}$ and $\mathbf{c}=\hat{\mathbf{j}}$, will be

(a) $5\hat{\mathbf{i}}+5\hat{\mathbf{j}}+\hat{\mathbf{k}}$ (b) $5\hat{\mathbf{i}}+\hat{\mathbf{j}}-5\hat{\mathbf{k}}$

(c) $5\hat{\mathbf{i}}+\hat{\mathbf{j}}+5\hat{\mathbf{k}}$ (d) $\pm(5\hat{\mathbf{i}}-\hat{\mathbf{j}}-5\hat{\mathbf{k}})$

7. If $\mathbf{x}+\mathbf{y}+\mathbf{z}=\mathbf{0}$, $|\mathbf{x}|=|\mathbf{y}|=|\mathbf{z}|=2$ and θ is angle between **y** and **z**, then the value of $\operatorname{cosec}^2\theta+\cot^2\theta$ is equal to

(a) $4/3$ (b) $5/3$ (c) $1/3$ (d) 1

8. The value of *x* for which the angle between the vectors $\mathbf{a}=-3\hat{\mathbf{i}}+x\hat{\mathbf{j}}+\hat{\mathbf{k}}$ and $\mathbf{b}=x\hat{\mathbf{i}}+2x\hat{\mathbf{j}}+\hat{\mathbf{k}}$ is acute and the angle between **b** and *X*-axis lies between $\pi/2$ and π satisfy

(a) $x>0$ (b) $x<0$

(c) $x>1$ only (d) $x<-1$ only

9. If the vectors $3\mathbf{p}+\mathbf{q}$, $5\mathbf{p}-3\mathbf{q}$ and $2\mathbf{p}+\mathbf{q}$, $4\mathbf{p}-2\mathbf{q}$ are pairs of mutually perpendicular vectors, then $\sin(\mathbf{pq})$ is

(a) $\sqrt{55}/4$ (b) $\sqrt{55}/8$

(c) 3/16 (d) $\sqrt{247}/16$

10. Let $\mathbf{u}=\hat{\mathbf{i}}+\hat{\mathbf{j}}$, $\mathbf{v}=\hat{\mathbf{i}}-\hat{\mathbf{j}}$ and $\mathbf{w}=\hat{\mathbf{i}}+2\hat{\mathbf{j}}+3\hat{\mathbf{k}}$. If $\hat{\mathbf{n}}$ is a unit vector such that $\mathbf{u}\cdot\hat{\mathbf{n}}=0$ and $\mathbf{v}\cdot\hat{\mathbf{n}}=0$, then $|\mathbf{w}\cdot\hat{\mathbf{n}}|$ is equal to

(a) 1 (b) 2

(c) 3 (d) 0

11. Given a parallelogram *ABCD*. If $|\mathbf{AB}|=a$, $|\mathbf{AD}|=b$ and $|\mathbf{AC}|=c$, then $\mathbf{DB}\cdot\mathbf{AB}$ has the value

(a) $\dfrac{3a^2+b^2-c^2}{2}$ (b) $\dfrac{a^2+3b^2-c^2}{2}$

(c) $\dfrac{a^2-b^2+3c^2}{2}$ (d) None of these

12. For some non-zero vector **V**, if the sum of **V** and the vector obtained from **V** by rotating it by $\angle 2\alpha$ equals to the vector obtained from **V** by rotating it by $\angle\alpha$, then the value of α, is

(a) $2n\pi\pm\dfrac{\pi}{3}$ (b) $n\pi\pm\dfrac{\pi}{3}$

(c) $2n\pi\pm\dfrac{2\pi}{3}$ (d) $n\pi\pm\dfrac{2\pi}{3}$

13. In the isosceles ΔABC, $|\mathbf{AB}|=|\mathbf{BC}|=8$, a point *E* divides *AB* internally in the ratio 1 : 3, then the cosine of the angle between **CE** and **CA** is (where, $|\mathbf{CA}|=12$)

(a) $-\dfrac{3\sqrt{7}}{8}$ (b) $\dfrac{3\sqrt{8}}{17}$ (c) $\dfrac{3\sqrt{7}}{8}$ (d) $\dfrac{-3\sqrt{8}}{17}$

14. Given an equilateral ΔABC with side length equal to *a*. Let *M* and *N* be two points respectively, on the side *AB* and *AC* such that $\mathbf{AN}=k\mathbf{AC}$ and $\mathbf{AM}=\dfrac{\mathbf{AB}}{3}$. If **BN** and **CM** are orthogonal, then the value of *k* is

(a) $\frac{1}{5}$ (b) $\frac{1}{4}$ (c) $\frac{1}{3}$ (d) $\frac{1}{2}$

15. In a quadrilateral *ABCD*, **AC** is the bisector of the (**AB, AD**) which is $\dfrac{2\pi}{3}$, $15|\mathbf{AC}|=3|\mathbf{AB}|=5|\mathbf{AD}|$, then $\cos(\mathbf{BA},\mathbf{CD})$ is equal to

(a) $-\dfrac{\sqrt{14}}{7\sqrt{2}}$ (b) $-\dfrac{\sqrt{21}}{7\sqrt{3}}$ (c) $\dfrac{2}{\sqrt{7}}$ (d) $\dfrac{2\sqrt{7}}{14}$

16. If the distance from the point $P(1, 1, 1)$ to the line passing through the points $Q(0, 6, 8)$ and $R(-1, 4, 7)$ is expressed in the form $\sqrt{p/q}$, where p and q are coprime, then the value of $\dfrac{(p+q)(p+q-1)}{2}$ is equal to

(a) 4950 (b) 5050
(c) 5150 (d) None of these

17. The vector $\mathbf{c}$ is perpendicular to the vectors $\mathbf{a} = (2, -3, 1)$, $\mathbf{b} = (1, -2, 3)$ and satisfies the condition $\mathbf{c}\cdot(\hat{\mathbf{i}}+2\hat{\mathbf{j}}-7\hat{\mathbf{k}}) = 10$. Then, the vector $\mathbf{c}$ is equal to

(a) $(7, 5, 1)$ (b) $(-7, -5, -1)$
(c) $(1, 1, -1)$ (d) None of these

18. If vector $\hat{\mathbf{i}} + 2\hat{\mathbf{j}} + 2\hat{\mathbf{k}}$ is rotated through an angle of 90°, so as to cross the positive direction of Y-axis, then the vector in the new position is

(a) $-\dfrac{2}{\sqrt{5}}\hat{\mathbf{i}} + \sqrt{5}\hat{\mathbf{j}} - \dfrac{4}{\sqrt{5}}\hat{\mathbf{k}}$ (b) $\dfrac{2}{\sqrt{5}}\hat{\mathbf{i}} - \sqrt{5}\hat{\mathbf{j}} + \dfrac{4}{\sqrt{5}}\hat{\mathbf{k}}$
(c) $4\hat{\mathbf{i}} - \hat{\mathbf{j}} - \hat{\mathbf{k}}$ (d) None of these

19. Two adjacent sides of a parallelogram $ABCD$ are given by $\mathbf{AB} = 2\hat{\mathbf{i}} + 10\hat{\mathbf{j}} + 11\hat{\mathbf{k}}$ and $\mathbf{AD} = -\hat{\mathbf{i}} + 2\hat{\mathbf{j}} + 2\hat{\mathbf{k}}$. The side AD is rotated by an acute angle α in the plane of parallelogram, so that AD becomes AD'. If AD' makes a right angle with the side AB, then the cosine of angle α is given by

(a) $\dfrac{8}{9}$ (b) $\dfrac{\sqrt{17}}{9}$ (c) $\dfrac{1}{9}$ (d) $\dfrac{4\sqrt{5}}{9}$

20. If in a ΔABC, $\mathbf{BC} = \dfrac{\mathbf{e}}{|\mathbf{e}|} - \dfrac{\mathbf{f}}{|\mathbf{f}|}$ and $\mathbf{AC} = \dfrac{2\mathbf{e}}{|\mathbf{e}|}$; $|\mathbf{e}| \neq |\mathbf{f}|$, then the value of $\cos 2A + \cos 2B + \cos 2C$ must be

(a) -1 (b) 0 (c) 2 (d) $\dfrac{-3}{2}$

21. The ΔABC is such that the mid-points of the sides BC, CA, AB are $(l, 0, 0)$, $(0, m, 0)$, $(0, 0, n)$ respectively. Then, $\dfrac{AB^2 + BC^2 + CA^2}{l^2 + m^2 + n^2}$ is equal to

(a) 2 (b) 4 (c) 8 (d) 16

22. If $\mathbf{p}$ and $\mathbf{q}$ are two non-collinear vectors such that $(b-c)\,\mathbf{p}\times\mathbf{q} + (c-a)\mathbf{p} + (a-b)\mathbf{q} = \mathbf{0}$ where a, b and c are lengths of sides of a triangle, then the triangle is

(a) right angled
(b) obtuse angled
(c) equilateral
(d) right angled isosceles triangle

23. Let $\mathbf{a} = \hat{\mathbf{i}} + \hat{\mathbf{j}} + \hat{\mathbf{k}}$, $\mathbf{b} = -\hat{\mathbf{i}} + \hat{\mathbf{j}} + \hat{\mathbf{k}}$, $\mathbf{c} = \hat{\mathbf{i}} - \hat{\mathbf{j}} + \hat{\mathbf{k}}$ and $\mathbf{d} = \hat{\mathbf{i}} + \hat{\mathbf{j}} - \hat{\mathbf{k}}$. Then, the line of intersection of planes one determined by $\mathbf{a}$, $\mathbf{b}$ and other determined by $\mathbf{c}$, $\mathbf{d}$ is perpendicular to

(a) X-axis (b) Y-axis
(c) both X-axis and Y-axis (d) both Y-axis and Z-axis

24. The length of the edge of the regular tetrahedron $ABCD$ is a. Points E and F are taken on the edges AD and BD respectively, such that 'E' divides **DA** and 'F' divides **BD** in the ratio 2 : 1 each. Then, area of ΔCEF is

(a) $\dfrac{5a}{12\sqrt{3}}$ sq units (b) $\dfrac{a}{12\sqrt{3}}$ sq units
(c) $\dfrac{a^2}{12\sqrt{3}}$ sq units (d) $\dfrac{5a^2}{12\sqrt{3}}$ sq units

25. If two adjacent sides of two rectangles are represented by the vectors $\mathbf{p} = 5\mathbf{a} - 3\mathbf{b}$, $\mathbf{q} = -\mathbf{a} - 2\mathbf{b}$ and $\mathbf{r} = -4\mathbf{a} - \mathbf{b}$, $\mathbf{s} = -\mathbf{a} + \mathbf{b}$ respectively, then the angle between the vectors $\mathbf{x} = \dfrac{1}{3}(\mathbf{p} + \mathbf{r} + \mathbf{s})$ and $\mathbf{y} = \dfrac{1}{5}(\mathbf{r} + \mathbf{s})$

(a) $\pi - \cos^{-1}\left(\dfrac{19}{5\sqrt{43}}\right)$ (b) $\cos^{-1}\left(\dfrac{19}{5\sqrt{43}}\right)$
(c) $-\cos^{-1}\left(\dfrac{19}{5\sqrt{43}}\right)$ (d) $\pi - \cos^{-1}\left(\dfrac{19}{\sqrt{43}}\right)$

26. If the angle between the vectors $\mathbf{a} = \hat{\mathbf{i}} + (\cos x)\hat{\mathbf{j}} + \hat{\mathbf{k}}$ and $\mathbf{b} = (\sin^2 x - \sin x)\hat{\mathbf{i}} - (\cos x)\hat{\mathbf{j}} + (3 - 4\sin x)\hat{\mathbf{k}}$ is obtuse and $x \in \left(0, \dfrac{\pi}{2}\right)$, then the exhaustive set of values of x is equal to

(a) $x \in \left(0, \dfrac{\pi}{6}\right)$ (b) $x \in \left(\dfrac{\pi}{6}, \dfrac{\pi}{2}\right)$
(c) $x \in \left(\dfrac{\pi}{6}, \dfrac{\pi}{3}\right)$ (d) $x \in \left(\dfrac{\pi}{3}, \dfrac{\pi}{2}\right)$

27. If position vectors of the points A, B and C are $\mathbf{a}$, $\mathbf{b}$, $\mathbf{c}$ respectively and the points D and E divides line segments AC and AB in the ratio $2:1$ and $1:3$, respectively. Then, point of intersection of BD and EC divides EC in the ratio

(a) 2 : 1 (b) 1 : 3 (c) 1 : 2 (d) 3 : 2

Numerical Value Type Questions

28. Let $\mathbf{c}$ be a vector coplanar with the vectors $\mathbf{a} = 2\hat{\mathbf{i}} + 3\hat{\mathbf{j}} - \hat{\mathbf{k}}$ and $\mathbf{b} = \hat{\mathbf{j}} + \hat{\mathbf{k}}$, if $\mathbf{c}$ is perpendicular to $\mathbf{a}$ and $\mathbf{b}\cdot\mathbf{c} = 24$, then the value of $|\mathbf{c}|^2$ is ....

29. Given that $\mathbf{a} = \hat{\mathbf{i}} + \hat{\mathbf{j}} + \hat{\mathbf{k}}$, $\mathbf{c} = \hat{\mathbf{j}} - \hat{\mathbf{k}}$, $\mathbf{a}\cdot\mathbf{b} = 3$ and $\mathbf{a}\times\mathbf{b} = \mathbf{c}$, then $3|\mathbf{b}|^2$ is equal to ....

30. Let $\mathbf{a}$ and $\mathbf{b}$ be two unit vectors such that $\mathbf{a}\cdot\mathbf{b} = 0$ for some $x, y \in R$ let $\mathbf{c} = x\mathbf{a} + y\mathbf{b} + (\mathbf{a}\times\mathbf{b})$. If $|\mathbf{c}| = 2$ and the vector $\mathbf{c}$ is inclined at the same α to both $\mathbf{a}$ and $\mathbf{b}$, then the value of $\sin^2\alpha$ is ....

31. Given vector $\mathbf{A} = a\hat{\mathbf{i}} + b\hat{\mathbf{j}} + c\hat{\mathbf{k}}$, $\mathbf{B} = d\hat{\mathbf{i}} + 3\hat{\mathbf{j}} + 4\hat{\mathbf{k}}$ and $\mathbf{C} = 3\hat{\mathbf{i}} + \hat{\mathbf{j}} - 2\hat{\mathbf{k}}$ form a triangle such that $\mathbf{A} = \mathbf{B} + \mathbf{C}$, $a > b > c > d \geq 0$ and the area of triangle is $5\sqrt{6}$ sq units, then the value of $a^2 + b^2 + c^2 + d^2$ is ....

32. Let $\mathbf{a} = 2\hat{\mathbf{i}} + \hat{\mathbf{j}} - 2\hat{\mathbf{k}}$ and $\mathbf{b} = \hat{\mathbf{i}} + \hat{\mathbf{j}}$ let $\mathbf{c}$ be a vector such that $|\mathbf{c} - \mathbf{a}| = 3, |(\mathbf{a} \times \mathbf{b}) \times \mathbf{c}| = 3$ and the angle between $\mathbf{c}$ and $\mathbf{a} \times \mathbf{b}$ be 30°, then $\mathbf{a} \cdot \mathbf{c}$ is equal to ....

33. Given $\mathbf{a}$ and $\mathbf{b}$ are unit vector and $|\mathbf{a} + \mathbf{b}| = \sqrt{3}$, if $\mathbf{c}$ is vector such that $\mathbf{c} - \mathbf{a} - 2\mathbf{b} = 3(\mathbf{a} \times \mathbf{b})$, then the value of $\mathbf{b} \cdot \mathbf{c}$ is ....

34. If $a^2 + b^2 + c^2 = \frac{1}{2}$, then the maximum value of $3a + 4b + 5c$ is ....

35. If a is a real constant A, B and C are variable angles and $\sqrt{a^2 - 4} \tan A + a \tan B + \sqrt{a^2 + 4} \tan C = 6a$, then the least value of $\tan^2 A + \tan^2 B + \tan^2 C$ is ....

36. Let $\mathbf{OA} = \mathbf{a}, \mathbf{OB} = 2\mathbf{a} + 10\mathbf{b}, \mathbf{OC} = \mathbf{b}$ where O, A, C are non-collinear points. Let l denote the area of quadrilateral $OABC$. Let m denotes the area of parallelogram with $\mathbf{OA}$ and $\mathbf{OC}$ as adjacent sides. If $l = 2\lambda m$, then the value of λ is equal to ....

37. Let $\mathbf{a} = 2\hat{\mathbf{i}} + 3\hat{\mathbf{j}} - 6\hat{\mathbf{k}}, \mathbf{b} = 2\hat{\mathbf{i}} - 3\hat{\mathbf{j}} + 6\hat{\mathbf{k}}$. Let $\mathbf{a}_1$ be projection of $\mathbf{a}$ on $\mathbf{b}$, then $\mathbf{a}_1 \cdot \mathbf{b} = -\lambda$, then the value of λ is ....

38. Let $\alpha = 3\hat{\mathbf{i}} + \hat{\mathbf{j}}$ and $\beta = 2\hat{\mathbf{i}} - \hat{\mathbf{j}} + 3\hat{\mathbf{k}}$, if $\beta = \beta_1 - \beta_2$, where β_1 is parallel to α and β_2 is perpendicular to α, then $|\beta_1 \times \beta_2|^2$ is ....

39. $\mathbf{a}, \mathbf{b}$ and $\mathbf{c}$ are unit vectors such that $|\mathbf{a} + \mathbf{b} + 3\mathbf{c}| = 4$ angle between $\mathbf{a}$ and $\mathbf{b}$ is α, between $\mathbf{b}$ and $\mathbf{c}$ is β and between $\mathbf{a}$ and $\mathbf{c}$ varies $\left[\frac{\pi}{6}, \frac{2\pi}{3}\right]$, then the maximum value of $\cos \alpha + 3 \cos \beta$ is ....

40. If $\mathbf{a}$ and $\mathbf{b}$ are vectors perpendicular to each other and $|\mathbf{a}| = 2, |\mathbf{b}| = 3, \mathbf{c} \times \mathbf{a} = \mathbf{b}$, then least value of $|\mathbf{c} - \mathbf{a}|$ is ....

41. A parallelogram is constructed $3\mathbf{a} + \mathbf{b}$ and $\mathbf{a} - 4\mathbf{b}$, where $|\mathbf{a}| = 6$ and $|\mathbf{b}| = 8$ and $\mathbf{a}, \mathbf{b}$ are anti-parallel, then the length of longer diagonal is ....

42. Let ΔPQR be a triangle. Let $\mathbf{a} = \mathbf{QR}, \mathbf{b} = \mathbf{RP}$ and $\mathbf{c} = \mathbf{PQ}$, if $|\mathbf{a}| = 12, |\mathbf{b}| = 4\sqrt{3}$ and $\mathbf{b} \cdot \mathbf{c} = 24$, and the value of $|\mathbf{a} \times \mathbf{b} + \mathbf{c} \times \mathbf{a}| = \lambda\sqrt{3}$, then λ is equal to ....

Previous Years Questions

43. Let $\mathbf{a} = \hat{\mathbf{i}} + 2\hat{\mathbf{j}} + \hat{\mathbf{k}}, \mathbf{b} = 3(\hat{\mathbf{i}} - \hat{\mathbf{j}} + \hat{\mathbf{k}})$. Let $\mathbf{c}$ be the vector such that $\mathbf{a} \times \mathbf{c} = \mathbf{b}$ and $\mathbf{a} \cdot \mathbf{c} = 3$. Then, $\mathbf{a} \cdot ((\mathbf{c} \times \mathbf{b}) - \mathbf{b} - \mathbf{c})$ is equal to **[Single Correct Type, 2024 Main]**

(a) 32 (b) 24 (c) 20 (d) 36

44. Let a unit vector $\mathbf{u} = x\hat{\mathbf{i}} + y\hat{\mathbf{j}} + z\hat{\mathbf{k}}$ make angles $\frac{\pi}{2}, \frac{\pi}{3}$ and $\frac{2\pi}{3}$ with the vectors $\frac{1}{\sqrt{2}}\hat{\mathbf{i}} + \frac{1}{\sqrt{2}}\hat{\mathbf{k}}, \frac{1}{\sqrt{2}}\hat{\mathbf{j}} + \frac{1}{\sqrt{2}}\hat{\mathbf{k}}$ and $\frac{1}{\sqrt{2}}\hat{\mathbf{i}} + \frac{1}{\sqrt{2}}\hat{\mathbf{j}}$, respectively. If $\mathbf{v} = \frac{1}{\sqrt{2}}\hat{\mathbf{i}} + \frac{1}{\sqrt{2}}\hat{\mathbf{j}} + \frac{1}{\sqrt{2}}\hat{\mathbf{k}}$, then $|\mathbf{u} - \mathbf{v}|^2$ is equal to **[Single Correct Type, 2024 Main]**

(a) 9 (b) $\frac{5}{2}$ (c) 7 (d) $\frac{11}{2}$

45. Let $P(3, 2, 3)$, $Q(4, 6, 2)$ and $R(7, 3, 2)$ be the vertices of ΔPQR. Then, the $\angle QPR$ is **[Single Correct Type, 2024 Main]**

(a) $\frac{\pi}{6}$ (b) $\cos^{-1}\left(\frac{1}{18}\right)$

(c) $\cos^{-1}\left(\frac{7}{18}\right)$ (d) $\frac{\pi}{3}$

46. Let $\mathbf{OA} = \mathbf{a}$, $\mathbf{OB} = 12\mathbf{a} + 4\mathbf{b}$ and $\mathbf{OC} = \mathbf{b}$, where O is the origin. If S is the parallelogram with adjacent sides $\mathbf{OA}$ and $\mathbf{OC}$, then $\frac{\text{area of the quadrilateral } OABC}{\text{area of } S}$ is equal to **[Single Correct Type, 2024 Main]**

(a) 8 (b) 10 (c) 7 (d) 6

47. Let $A(2, 3, 5)$ and $C(-3, 4, -2)$ be opposite vertices of a parallelogram $ABCD$. If the diagonal $\mathbf{BD} = \hat{\mathbf{i}} + 2\hat{\mathbf{j}} + 3\hat{\mathbf{k}}$, then the area of the parallelogram is equal to **[Single Correct Type, 2024 Main]**

(a) $\frac{1}{2}\sqrt{410}$ (b) $\frac{1}{2}\sqrt{586}$ (c) $\frac{1}{2}\sqrt{306}$ (d) $\frac{1}{2}\sqrt{474}$

48. Let $\mathbf{a} = a_1\hat{\mathbf{i}} + a_2\hat{\mathbf{j}} + a_3\hat{\mathbf{k}}$ and $\mathbf{b} = b_1\hat{\mathbf{i}} + b_2\hat{\mathbf{j}} + b_3\hat{\mathbf{k}}$ be two vectors such that $|\mathbf{a}| = 1, \mathbf{a} \cdot \mathbf{b} = 2$ and $|\mathbf{b}| = 4$. If $\mathbf{c} = 2(\mathbf{a} \times \mathbf{b}) - 3\mathbf{b}$, then the angle between $\mathbf{b}$ and $\mathbf{c}$ is equal to **[Single Correct Type, 2024 Main]**

(a) $\cos^{-1}\left(\frac{2}{\sqrt{3}}\right)$ (b) $\cos^{-1}\left(-\frac{1}{\sqrt{3}}\right)$

(c) $\cos^{-1}\left(\frac{2}{3}\right)$ (d) $\cos^{-1}\left(-\frac{\sqrt{3}}{2}\right)$

49. Let $\mathbf{a} = \hat{\mathbf{i}} + \alpha\hat{\mathbf{j}} + \beta\hat{\mathbf{k}}, \alpha, \beta \in R$. Let a vector $\mathbf{b}$ be such that the angle between $\mathbf{a}$ and $\mathbf{b}$ is $\frac{\pi}{4}$ and $|\mathbf{b}|^2 = 6$. If $\mathbf{a} \cdot \mathbf{b} = 3\sqrt{2}$, then the value of $(\alpha^2 + \beta^2)|\mathbf{a} \times \mathbf{b}|^2$ is equal to **[Single Correct Type, 2024 Main]**

(a) 90 (b) 85 (c) 95 (d) 75

50. Let $\mathbf{a}$ and $\mathbf{b}$ be two vectors such that $|\mathbf{b}| = 1$ and $|\mathbf{b} \times \mathbf{a}| = 2$. Then, $|(\mathbf{b} \times \mathbf{a}) - \mathbf{b}|^2$ is equal to **[Single Correct Type, 2024 Main]**

(a) 1 (b) 3 (c) 4 (d) 5

51. Let $\mathbf{a} = 3\hat{\mathbf{i}} + \hat{\mathbf{j}} - 2\hat{\mathbf{k}}, \mathbf{b} = 4\hat{\mathbf{i}} + \hat{\mathbf{j}} + 7\hat{\mathbf{k}}$ and $\mathbf{c} = \hat{\mathbf{i}} - 3\hat{\mathbf{j}} + 4\hat{\mathbf{k}}$ be three vectors. If a vectors $\mathbf{p}$ satisfies $\mathbf{p} \times \mathbf{b} = \mathbf{c} \times \mathbf{b}$ and $\mathbf{p} \cdot \mathbf{a} = 0$, then $\mathbf{p} \cdot (\hat{\mathbf{i}} - \hat{\mathbf{j}} - \hat{\mathbf{k}})$ is equal to **[Single Correct Type, 2024 Main]**

(a) 36 (b) 32

(c) 24 (d) 28

52. Let $\mathbf{a} = -5\hat{\mathbf{i}} + \hat{\mathbf{j}} - 3\hat{\mathbf{k}}$, $\mathbf{b} = \hat{\mathbf{i}} + 2\hat{\mathbf{j}} - 4\hat{\mathbf{k}}$ and $\mathbf{c} = (((\mathbf{a} \times \mathbf{b}) \times \hat{\mathbf{i}}) \times \hat{\mathbf{i}}) \times \hat{\mathbf{i}}$. Then, $\mathbf{c} \cdot (-\hat{\mathbf{i}} + \hat{\mathbf{j}} + \hat{\mathbf{k}})$ is equal to **[Single Correct Type, 2024 Main]**

(a) -13 (b) -12 (c) -10 (d) -15

53. Consider a ΔABC where $A(1, 3, 2)$, $B(-2, 8, 0)$ and $C(3, 6, 7)$. If the angle bisector of $\angle BAC$ meets the line BC at D, then the length of the projection of the vector $\mathbf{AD}$ on the vector $\mathbf{AC}$ is **[Single Correct Type, 2024 Main]**

(a) $\frac{39}{2\sqrt{38}}$ (b) $\frac{\sqrt{38}}{2}$ (c) $\sqrt{19}$ (d) $\frac{37}{2\sqrt{38}}$

54. The least positive integral value of α, for which the angle between the vectors $\alpha\hat{\mathbf{i}} - 2\hat{\mathbf{j}} + 2\hat{\mathbf{k}}$ and $\alpha\hat{\mathbf{i}} + 2\alpha\hat{\mathbf{j}} - 2\hat{\mathbf{k}}$ is acute, is .... . **[Numerical Value Type, 2024 Main]**

55. Let $\mathbf{a} = 3\hat{\mathbf{i}} + 2\hat{\mathbf{j}} + \hat{\mathbf{k}}$, $\mathbf{b} = 2\hat{\mathbf{i}} - \hat{\mathbf{j}} + 3\hat{\mathbf{k}}$ and $\mathbf{c}$ be a vector such that $(\mathbf{a} + \mathbf{b}) \times \mathbf{c} = 2(\mathbf{a} \times \mathbf{b}) + 24\hat{\mathbf{j}} - 6\hat{\mathbf{k}}$ and $(\mathbf{a} - \mathbf{b} + \hat{\mathbf{i}}) \cdot \mathbf{c} = -3$. Then, $|\mathbf{c}|^2$ is equal to .... **[Numerical Value Type, 2024 Main]**

56. Let $\mathbf{a}$ and $\mathbf{b}$ be two vectors such that $|\mathbf{a}| = 1$, $|\mathbf{b}| = 4$ and $\mathbf{a} \cdot \mathbf{b} = 2$. If $\mathbf{c} = (2\mathbf{a} \times \mathbf{b}) - 3\mathbf{b}$ and the angle between $\mathbf{b}$ and $\mathbf{c}$ is α, then $192 \sin^2 \alpha$ is equal to .... **[Numerical Value Type, 2024 Main]**

57. Let $\mathbf{a} = \hat{\mathbf{i}} + \hat{\mathbf{j}} + \hat{\mathbf{k}}$, $\mathbf{b} = -\hat{\mathbf{i}} - 8\hat{\mathbf{j}} + 2\hat{\mathbf{k}}$ and $\mathbf{c} = 4\hat{\mathbf{i}} + c_2\hat{\mathbf{j}} + c_3\hat{\mathbf{k}}$ be three vectors such that $\mathbf{b} \times \mathbf{a} = \mathbf{c} \times \mathbf{a}$. If the angle between the vector $\mathbf{c}$ and the vector $3\hat{\mathbf{i}} + 4\hat{\mathbf{j}} + \hat{\mathbf{k}}$ is θ, then the greatest integer less than or equal to $\tan^2 \theta$ is .... **[Numerical Value Type, 2024 Main]**

58. Let $\mathbf{a} = 2\hat{\mathbf{i}} + \hat{\mathbf{j}} + \hat{\mathbf{k}}$ and $\mathbf{b}$ and $\mathbf{c}$ be two non-zero vectors such that $|\mathbf{a} + \mathbf{b} + \mathbf{c}| = |\mathbf{a} + \mathbf{b} - \mathbf{c}|$ and $\mathbf{b} \cdot \mathbf{c} = 0$. Consider the following two statements. **[Single Correct Type, 2023 Main]**

(A) $|\mathbf{a} + \lambda\mathbf{c}| \geq |\mathbf{a}|, \forall \lambda \in R$

(B) $\mathbf{a}$ and $\mathbf{c}$ are always parallel.

Then,

(a) Neither (A) nor (B) is correct.
(b) Both (A) and (B) are correct.
(c) Only (B) is correct.
(d) Only (A) is correct.

59. Let $\alpha = 4\hat{\mathbf{i}} + 3\hat{\mathbf{j}} + 5\hat{\mathbf{k}}$ and $\beta = \hat{\mathbf{i}} + 2\hat{\mathbf{j}} - 4\hat{\mathbf{k}}$. Let β_1 be parallel to α and β_2 be perpendicular to α. If $\beta = \beta_1 + \beta_2$, then the value of $5\beta_2 \cdot (\hat{\mathbf{i}} + \hat{\mathbf{j}} + \hat{\mathbf{k}})$ is **[Single Correct Type, 2023 Main]**

(a) 6 (b) 9 (c) 7 (d) 11

60. Let for a ΔABC, $\mathbf{AB} = -2\hat{\mathbf{i}} + \hat{\mathbf{j}} + 3\hat{\mathbf{k}}$, $\mathbf{CB} = \alpha\hat{\mathbf{i}} + \beta\hat{\mathbf{j}} + \gamma\hat{\mathbf{k}}$ and $\mathbf{CA} = 4\hat{\mathbf{i}} + 3\hat{\mathbf{j}} + \delta\hat{\mathbf{k}}$. If $\delta > 0$ and the area of the ΔABC is $5\sqrt{6}$, then $\mathbf{CB} \cdot \mathbf{CA}$ is equal to **[Single Correct Type, 2023 Main]**

(a) 60 (b) 54 (c) 108 (d) 120

61. Let $|\mathbf{a}| = 2$, $|\mathbf{b}| = 3$ and the angle between the vectors $\mathbf{a}$ and $\mathbf{b}$ be $\frac{\pi}{4}$. Then, $|(\mathbf{a} + 2\mathbf{b}) \times (2\mathbf{a} - 3\mathbf{b})|^2$ is equal to **[Single Correct Type, 2023 Main]**

(a) 841 (b) 882 (c) 482 (d) 441

62. Let $\mathbf{a} = \hat{\mathbf{i}} + 4\hat{\mathbf{j}} + 2\hat{\mathbf{k}}$, $\mathbf{b} = 3\hat{\mathbf{i}} - 2\hat{\mathbf{j}} + 7\hat{\mathbf{k}}$ and $\mathbf{c} = 2\hat{\mathbf{i}} - \hat{\mathbf{j}} + 4\hat{\mathbf{k}}$. If a vector $\mathbf{d}$ satisfies $\mathbf{d} \times \mathbf{b} = \mathbf{c} \times \mathbf{b}$ and $\mathbf{d} \cdot \mathbf{a} = 24$, then $|\mathbf{d}|^2$ is equal to **[Single Correct Type, 2023 Main]**

(a) 323 (b) 313 (c) 423 (d) 413

63. Let $\mathbf{a}$ be a non-zero vector parallel to the line of intersection of the two planes described by $\hat{\mathbf{i}} + \hat{\mathbf{j}}$, $\hat{\mathbf{i}} + \hat{\mathbf{k}}$ and $\hat{\mathbf{i}} - \hat{\mathbf{j}}$, $\hat{\mathbf{j}} - \hat{\mathbf{k}}$. If θ is the angle between the vector $\mathbf{a}$ and the vector $\mathbf{b} = 2\hat{\mathbf{i}} - 2\hat{\mathbf{j}} + \hat{\mathbf{k}}$ and $\mathbf{a} \cdot \mathbf{b} = 6$, then the ordered pair $(\theta, |\mathbf{a} \times \mathbf{b}|)$ is equal to **[Single Correct Type, 2023 Main]**

(a) $\left(\frac{\pi}{3}, 6\right)$ (b) $\left(\frac{\pi}{4}, 3\sqrt{6}\right)$ (c) $\left(\frac{\pi}{3}, 3\sqrt{6}\right)$ (d) $\left(\frac{\pi}{4}, 6\right)$

64. Let O be the origin and the position vector of the point P be $-\hat{\mathbf{i}} - 2\hat{\mathbf{j}} + 3\hat{\mathbf{k}}$. If the position vectors of the points A, B and C are $-2\hat{\mathbf{i}} + \hat{\mathbf{j}} - 3\hat{\mathbf{k}}$, $2\hat{\mathbf{i}} + 4\hat{\mathbf{j}} - 2\hat{\mathbf{k}}$ and $-4\hat{\mathbf{i}} + 2\hat{\mathbf{j}} - \hat{\mathbf{k}}$ respectively, then the projection of the vector $\mathbf{OP}$ on a vector perpendicular to the vectors $\mathbf{AB}$ and $\mathbf{AC}$ is **[Single Correct Type, 2023 Main]**

(a) $\frac{7}{3}$ (b) 3 (c) $\frac{8}{3}$ (d) $\frac{10}{3}$

65. The area of the quadrilateral $ABCD$ with vertices $A(2, 1, 1)$, $B(1, 2, 5)$, $C(-2, -3, 5)$ and $D(1, -6, -7)$ is equal to **[Single Correct Type, 2023 Main]**

(a) 54 (b) $8\sqrt{38}$ (c) 48 (d) $9\sqrt{38}$

66. Let $\mathbf{a} = 2\hat{\mathbf{i}} + 3\hat{\mathbf{j}} + 4\hat{\mathbf{k}}$, $\mathbf{b} = \hat{\mathbf{i}} - 2\hat{\mathbf{j}} - 2\hat{\mathbf{k}}$ and $\mathbf{c} = -\hat{\mathbf{i}} + 4\hat{\mathbf{j}} + 3\hat{\mathbf{k}}$. If $\mathbf{d}$ is a vector perpendicular to both $\mathbf{b}$ and $\mathbf{c}$, and $\mathbf{a} \cdot \mathbf{d} = 18$, then $|\mathbf{a} \times \mathbf{d}|^2$ is equal to **[Single Correct Type, 2023 Main]**

(a) 720 (b) 680 (c) 640 (d) 760

67. Let $\mathbf{a} = 2\hat{\mathbf{i}} - 7\hat{\mathbf{j}} + 5\hat{\mathbf{k}}$, $\mathbf{b} = \hat{\mathbf{i}} + \hat{\mathbf{k}}$ and $\mathbf{c} = \hat{\mathbf{i}} + 2\hat{\mathbf{j}} - 3\hat{\mathbf{k}}$ be three given vectors. If $\mathbf{r}$ is a vector such that $\mathbf{r} \times \mathbf{a} = \mathbf{c} \times \mathbf{a}$ and $\mathbf{r} \cdot \mathbf{b} = 0$, then $|\mathbf{r}|$ is equal to **[Single Correct Type, 2023 Main]**

(a) $\frac{11}{7}$ (b) $\frac{11}{5}\sqrt{2}$ (c) $\frac{\sqrt{914}}{7}$ (d) $\frac{11}{7}\sqrt{2}$

68. Let $\mathbf{a} = \hat{\mathbf{i}} + 2\hat{\mathbf{j}} + 3\hat{\mathbf{k}}$, $\mathbf{b} = \hat{\mathbf{i}} - \hat{\mathbf{j}} + 2\hat{\mathbf{k}}$ and $\mathbf{c} = 5\hat{\mathbf{i}} - 3\hat{\mathbf{j}} + 3\hat{\mathbf{k}}$ be three vectors. If $\mathbf{r}$ is a vector such that $\mathbf{r} \times \mathbf{b} = \mathbf{c} \times \mathbf{b}$ and $\mathbf{r} \cdot \mathbf{a} = 0$, then $25|\mathbf{r}|^2$ is equal to **[Single Correct Type, 2023 Main]**

(a) 560 (b) 449 (c) 339 (d) 336

69. Let $\mathbf{a}$ and $\mathbf{b}$ be two vectors. Let $|\mathbf{a}| = 1$, $|\mathbf{b}| = 4$ and $\mathbf{a} \cdot \mathbf{b} = 2$. If $\mathbf{c} = (2\mathbf{a} \times \mathbf{b}) - 3\mathbf{b}$, then the value of $\mathbf{b} \cdot \mathbf{c}$ is **[Single Correct Type, 2023 Main]**

(a) -84 (b) -60 (c) -24 (d) -48

70. If $\mathbf{a}=\hat{\mathbf{i}}+2\hat{\mathbf{k}}$, $\mathbf{b}=\hat{\mathbf{i}}+\hat{\mathbf{j}}+\hat{\mathbf{k}}$, $\mathbf{c}=7\hat{\mathbf{i}}-3\hat{\mathbf{j}}+4\hat{\mathbf{k}}$, $\mathbf{r}\times\mathbf{b}+\mathbf{b}\times\mathbf{c}=\mathbf{0}$ and $\mathbf{r}\cdot\mathbf{a}=0$. Then, $\mathbf{r}\cdot\mathbf{c}$ is equal to **[Single Correct Type, 2023 Main]**

(a) 34 (b) 36 (c) 30 (d) 32

71. Let $\mathbf{a}=4\hat{\mathbf{i}}+3\hat{\mathbf{j}}$ and $\mathbf{b}=3\hat{\mathbf{i}}-4\hat{\mathbf{j}}+5\hat{\mathbf{k}}$. If $\mathbf{c}$ is a vector such that $\mathbf{c}\cdot(\mathbf{a}\times\mathbf{b})+25=0$, $\mathbf{c}\cdot(\hat{\mathbf{i}}+\hat{\mathbf{j}}+\hat{\mathbf{k}})=4$ and projection of $\mathbf{c}$ on $\mathbf{a}$ is 1, then the projection of $\mathbf{c}$ on $\mathbf{b}$ equals **[Single Correct Type, 2023 Main]**

(a) $\frac{1}{5}$ (b) $\frac{3}{\sqrt{2}}$ (c) $\frac{5}{\sqrt{2}}$ (d) $\frac{1}{\sqrt{2}}$

72. The vector $\mathbf{a}=-\hat{\mathbf{i}}+2\hat{\mathbf{j}}+\hat{\mathbf{k}}$ is rotated through a right angle, passing through the Y-axis in its way and the resulting vector is $\mathbf{b}$. Then, the projection of $3\mathbf{a}+\sqrt{2}\mathbf{b}$ on $\mathbf{c}=5\hat{\mathbf{i}}+4\hat{\mathbf{j}}+3\hat{\mathbf{k}}$ is **[Single Correct Type, 2023 Main]**

(a) 1 (b) $\sqrt{6}$ (c) $3\sqrt{2}$ (d) $2\sqrt{3}$

73. Let $\mathbf{a}=3\hat{\mathbf{i}}+\hat{\mathbf{j}}-\hat{\mathbf{k}}$ and $\mathbf{c}=2\hat{\mathbf{i}}-3\hat{\mathbf{j}}+3\hat{\mathbf{k}}$. If $\mathbf{b}$ is a vector such that $\mathbf{a}=\mathbf{b}\times\mathbf{c}$ and $|\mathbf{b}|^2=50$, then $|72-|\mathbf{b}+\mathbf{c}|^2|$ is equal to .... **[Numerical Value Type, 2023 Main]**

74. Let $\mathbf{a}=\hat{\mathbf{i}}+2\hat{\mathbf{j}}+3\hat{\mathbf{k}}$ and $\mathbf{b}=\hat{\mathbf{i}}+\hat{\mathbf{j}}-\hat{\mathbf{k}}$. If $\mathbf{c}$ is a vector such that $\mathbf{a}\cdot\mathbf{c}=11$, $\mathbf{b}\cdot(\mathbf{a}\times\mathbf{c})=27$ and $\mathbf{b}\cdot\mathbf{c}=-\sqrt{3}|\mathbf{b}|$, then $|\mathbf{a}\times\mathbf{c}|^2$ is equal to .... . **[Numerical Value Type, 2023 Main]**

75. Let $\mathbf{a}=6\hat{\mathbf{i}}+9\hat{\mathbf{j}}+12\hat{\mathbf{k}}$, $\mathbf{b}=\alpha\hat{\mathbf{i}}+11\hat{\mathbf{j}}-2\hat{\mathbf{k}}$ and $\mathbf{c}$ vectors such that $\mathbf{a}\times\mathbf{c}=\mathbf{a}\times\mathbf{b}$. If $\mathbf{a}\cdot\mathbf{c}=-12$, $\mathbf{c}\cdot(\hat{\mathbf{i}}-2\hat{\mathbf{j}}+\hat{\mathbf{k}})=5$, then $\mathbf{c}\cdot(\hat{\mathbf{i}}+\hat{\mathbf{j}}+\hat{\mathbf{k}})$ is equal to .... **[Numerical Value Type, 2023 Main]**

76. Let $\mathbf{a}$, $\mathbf{b}$ and $\mathbf{c}$ be three vectors such that $|\mathbf{a}|=\sqrt{31}$, $4|\mathbf{b}|=|\mathbf{c}|=2$ and $2(\mathbf{a}\times\mathbf{b})=3(\mathbf{c}\times\mathbf{a})$. If the angle between $\mathbf{b}$ and $\mathbf{c}$ is $\frac{2\pi}{3}$, then $\left(\frac{\mathbf{a}\times\mathbf{c}}{\mathbf{a}\cdot\mathbf{b}}\right)$ is equal to .... **[Numerical Value Type, 2023 Main]**

77. Let $\mathbf{a}$ and $\mathbf{b}$ be two vectors such that $|\mathbf{a}|=\sqrt{14}$, $|\mathbf{b}|=\sqrt{6}$ and $|\mathbf{a}\times\mathbf{b}|=\sqrt{48}$. Then, $(\mathbf{a}\cdot\mathbf{b})^2$ is equal to .... **[Numerical Value Type, 2023 Main]**

78. Let $\mathbf{a}=\hat{\mathbf{i}}+2\hat{\mathbf{j}}+\lambda\hat{\mathbf{k}}$, $\mathbf{b}=3\hat{\mathbf{i}}-5\hat{\mathbf{j}}-\lambda\hat{\mathbf{k}}$, $\mathbf{a}\cdot\mathbf{c}=7$, $2\mathbf{b}\cdot\mathbf{c}+43=0$, $\mathbf{a}\times\mathbf{c}=\mathbf{b}\times\mathbf{c}$. Then, $|\mathbf{a}\cdot\mathbf{b}|$ is equal to .... **[Numerical Value Type, 2023 Main]**

79. Let $\lambda\in Z$, $\mathbf{a}=\lambda\hat{\mathbf{i}}+\hat{\mathbf{j}}-\hat{\mathbf{k}}$ and $\mathbf{b}=3\hat{\mathbf{i}}-\hat{\mathbf{j}}+2\hat{\mathbf{k}}$. Let $\mathbf{c}$ be a vector such that $(\mathbf{a}+\mathbf{b}+\mathbf{c})\times\mathbf{c}=\mathbf{0}$, $\mathbf{a}\cdot\mathbf{c}=-17$ and $\mathbf{b}\cdot\mathbf{c}=-20$. Then, $|\mathbf{c}\times(\lambda\hat{\mathbf{i}}+\hat{\mathbf{j}}+\hat{\mathbf{k}})|^2$ is equal to **[Single Correct Type, 2023 Main]**

(a) 53 (b) 46 (c) 62 (d) 49

80. Let a, b and c be three distinct real numbers, none equal to one. If the vectors $a\hat{\mathbf{i}}+\hat{\mathbf{j}}+\hat{\mathbf{k}}$, $\hat{\mathbf{i}}+b\hat{\mathbf{j}}+\hat{\mathbf{k}}$ and $\hat{\mathbf{i}}+\hat{\mathbf{j}}+c\hat{\mathbf{k}}$ are coplanar, then $\frac{1}{1-a}+\frac{1}{1-b}+\frac{1}{1-c}$ is equal to **[Single Correct Type, 2023 Main]**

(a) -2 (b) 1 (c) 2 (d) -1

81. Let $\mathbf{a}=2\hat{\mathbf{i}}+7\hat{\mathbf{j}}-\hat{\mathbf{k}}$, $\mathbf{b}=3\hat{\mathbf{i}}+5\hat{\mathbf{k}}$ and $\mathbf{c}=\hat{\mathbf{i}}-\hat{\mathbf{j}}+2\hat{\mathbf{k}}$. Let $\mathbf{d}$ be a vector which is perpendicular to both $\mathbf{a}$ and $\mathbf{b}$ and $\mathbf{c}\cdot\mathbf{d}=12$. Then, $(-\hat{\mathbf{i}}+\hat{\mathbf{j}}-\hat{\mathbf{k}})\cdot(\mathbf{c}\times\mathbf{d})$ is equal to **[Single Correct Type, 2023 Main]**

(a) 24 (b) 44 (c) 48 (d) 42

82. Let the vectors $\mathbf{u}_1=\hat{\mathbf{i}}+\hat{\mathbf{j}}+a\hat{\mathbf{k}}$, $\mathbf{u}_2=\hat{\mathbf{i}}+b\hat{\mathbf{j}}+\hat{\mathbf{k}}$ and $\mathbf{u}_3=c\hat{\mathbf{i}}+\hat{\mathbf{j}}+\hat{\mathbf{k}}$ be coplanar. If the vectors $\mathbf{v}_1=(a+b)\hat{\mathbf{i}}+c\hat{\mathbf{j}}+c\hat{\mathbf{k}}$, $\mathbf{v}_2=a\hat{\mathbf{i}}+(b+c)\hat{\mathbf{j}}+a\hat{\mathbf{k}}$ and $\mathbf{v}_3=b\hat{\mathbf{i}}+b\hat{\mathbf{j}}+(c+a)\hat{\mathbf{k}}$ are also coplanar, then $6(a+b+c)$ is equal to **[Single Correct Type, 2023 Main]**

(a) 12 (b) 0 (c) 4 (d) 6

83. Let the vectors $\mathbf{a}$, $\mathbf{b}$ and $\mathbf{c}$ represent three coterminous edges of a parallelopiped of volume V. Then, the volume of the parallelopiped, whose coterminous edges are represented by $\mathbf{a}$, $\mathbf{b}+\mathbf{c}$ and $\mathbf{a}+2\mathbf{b}+3\mathbf{c}$ is equal to **[Single Correct Type, 2023 Main]**

(a) V (b) $2V$ (c) $3V$ (d) $6V$

84. The sum of all values of α, for which the points whose position vectors are $\hat{\mathbf{i}}-2\hat{\mathbf{j}}+3\hat{\mathbf{k}}$, $2\hat{\mathbf{i}}-3\hat{\mathbf{j}}+4\hat{\mathbf{k}}$, $(\alpha+1)\hat{\mathbf{i}}+2\hat{\mathbf{k}}$ and $9\hat{\mathbf{i}}+(\alpha-8)\hat{\mathbf{j}}+6\hat{\mathbf{k}}$ are coplanar, is equal to **[Single Correct Type, 2023 Main]**

(a) 2 (b) -2 (c) 4 (d) 6

85. Let the position vectors of the points A, B, C and D be $5\hat{\mathbf{i}}+5\hat{\mathbf{j}}+2\lambda\hat{\mathbf{k}}$, $\hat{\mathbf{i}}+2\hat{\mathbf{j}}+3\hat{\mathbf{k}}$, $-2\hat{\mathbf{i}}+\lambda\hat{\mathbf{j}}+4\hat{\mathbf{k}}$ and $-\hat{\mathbf{i}}+5\hat{\mathbf{j}}+6\hat{\mathbf{k}}$. Let the set $S=\{\lambda\in R$: the points A, B, C and D are coplanar). Then, $\sum_{\lambda\in\Sigma}(\lambda+2)^2$ is equal to **[Single Correct Type, 2023 Main]**

(a) 25 (b) 41 (c) $\frac{37}{2}$ (d) 13

86. If $\mathbf{a}$, $\mathbf{b}$ and $\mathbf{c}$ are three non-zero vectors and $\hat{\mathbf{n}}$ is a unit vector perpendicular to $\mathbf{c}$ such that $\mathbf{a}=\alpha\mathbf{b}-\hat{\mathbf{n}}$, $(\alpha\neq0)$ and $\mathbf{b}\cdot\mathbf{c}=12$, then $|\mathbf{c}\times(\mathbf{a}\times\mathbf{b})|$ is equal to **[Single Correct Type, 2023 Main]**

(a) 6 (b) 15 (c) 12 (d) 9

87. Let $\lambda\in R$, $\mathbf{a}=\lambda\hat{\mathbf{i}}+2\hat{\mathbf{j}}-3\hat{\mathbf{k}}$, $\mathbf{b}=\hat{\mathbf{i}}-\lambda\hat{\mathbf{j}}+2\hat{\mathbf{k}}$. If $((\mathbf{a}+\mathbf{b})\times(\mathbf{a}\times\mathbf{b}))\times(\mathbf{a}-\mathbf{b})=8\hat{\mathbf{i}}-40\hat{\mathbf{j}}-24\hat{\mathbf{k}}$, then $|\lambda(\mathbf{a}+\mathbf{b})\times(\mathbf{a}-\mathbf{b})|^2$ is equal to **[Single Correct Type, 2023 Main]**

(a) 144 (b) 136 (c) 132 (d) 140

88. Let $\mathbf{a}$, $\mathbf{b}$ and $\mathbf{c}$ be three non-zero vectors such that $\mathbf{b}\cdot\mathbf{c}=0$ and $\mathbf{a}\times(\mathbf{b}\times\mathbf{c})=\frac{\mathbf{b}-\mathbf{c}}{2}$. If $\mathbf{d}$ be a vector such that $\mathbf{b}\cdot\mathbf{d}=\mathbf{a}\cdot\mathbf{b}$, then $(\mathbf{a}\times\mathbf{b})\cdot(\mathbf{c}\times\mathbf{d})$ is equal to **[Single Correct Type, 2023 Main]**

(a) $\frac{3}{4}$ (b) $-\frac{1}{4}$ (c) $\frac{1}{4}$ (d) $\frac{1}{2}$

89. Let $\mathbf{a}=-\hat{\mathbf{i}}-\hat{\mathbf{j}}+\hat{\mathbf{k}}$, $\mathbf{a}\cdot\mathbf{b}=1$ and $\mathbf{a}\times\mathbf{b}=\hat{\mathbf{i}}-\hat{\mathbf{j}}$. Then, $\mathbf{a}-6\mathbf{b}$ is equal to **[Single Correct Type, 2023 Main]**

(a) $3(\hat{\mathbf{i}}-\hat{\mathbf{j}}+\hat{\mathbf{k}})$ (b) $3(\hat{\mathbf{i}}+\hat{\mathbf{j}}+\hat{\mathbf{k}})$

(c) $3(\hat{\mathbf{i}}+\hat{\mathbf{j}}-\hat{\mathbf{k}})$ (d) $3(\hat{\mathbf{i}}-\hat{\mathbf{j}}-\hat{\mathbf{k}})$

90. Let $\mathbf{u} = \hat{\mathbf{i}} - \hat{\mathbf{j}} - 2\hat{\mathbf{k}}$, $\mathbf{v} = 2\hat{\mathbf{i}} + \hat{\mathbf{j}} - \hat{\mathbf{k}}$, $\mathbf{v} \cdot \mathbf{w} = 2$ and $\mathbf{v} \times \mathbf{w} = \mathbf{u} + \lambda \mathbf{v}$. Then, $\mathbf{u} \cdot \mathbf{w}$ is equal to **[Single Correct Type, 2023 Main]**

(a) 1 (b) $-2/3$ (c) $3/2$ (d) 2

91. Let $\mathbf{v} = \alpha\hat{\mathbf{i}} + 2\hat{\mathbf{j}} - 3\hat{\mathbf{k}}$, $\mathbf{w} = 2\alpha\hat{\mathbf{i}} + \hat{\mathbf{j}} - \hat{\mathbf{k}}$ and $\mathbf{u}$ be a vector such that $|\mathbf{u}| = \alpha > 0$. If the minimum value of the scalar triple product $|\mathbf{u}\ \mathbf{v}\ \mathbf{w}|$ is $-\alpha\sqrt{3401}$ and $|\mathbf{u} \cdot \hat{\mathbf{i}}|^2 = \frac{m}{n}$, where m and n are co-prime natural numbers, then $m + n$ is equal to .... **[Numerical Value Type, 2023 Main]**

92. Let $\mathbf{a}$, $\mathbf{b}$ and $\mathbf{c}$ be three non-zero non-coplanar vectors. Let the position vectors of four points A, B, C and D be $\mathbf{a} - \mathbf{b} + \mathbf{c}$, $\lambda\mathbf{a} - 3\mathbf{b} + 4\mathbf{c}$, $-\mathbf{a} + 2\mathbf{b} - 3\mathbf{c}$ and $2\mathbf{a} - 4\mathbf{b} + 6\mathbf{c}$, respectively. If $\mathbf{AB}$, $\mathbf{AC}$ and $\mathbf{AD}$ are coplanar, then λ is equal to .... **[Numerical Value Type, 2023 Main]**

93. Let a vector $\mathbf{a}$ has a magnitude 9. Let a vector $\mathbf{b}$ be such that for every $(x, y) \in \mathbf{R} \times \mathbf{R} - \{(0, 0)\}$, the vector $(x\mathbf{a} + y\mathbf{b})$ is perpendicular to the vector $(6y\mathbf{a} - 18x\mathbf{b})$. Then, the value of $|\mathbf{a} \times \mathbf{b}|$ is equal to **[Single Correct Type, 2022 Main]**

(a) $9\sqrt{3}$ (b) $27\sqrt{3}$ (c) 9 (d) 81

94. Let $\mathbf{a} = \alpha\hat{\mathbf{i}} + \hat{\mathbf{j}} - \hat{\mathbf{k}}$ and $\mathbf{b} = 2\hat{\mathbf{i}} + \hat{\mathbf{j}} - \alpha\hat{\mathbf{k}}$, $\alpha > 0$. If the projection of $\mathbf{a} \times \mathbf{b}$ on the vector $-\hat{\mathbf{i}} + 2\hat{\mathbf{j}} - 2\hat{\mathbf{k}}$ is 30, then α is equal to **[Single Correct Type, 2022 Main]**

(a) 15/2 (b) 8 (c) 13/2 (d) 7

95. Let $\mathbf{a}$ and $\mathbf{b}$ be two vectors such that $|\mathbf{a} + \mathbf{b}|^2 = |\mathbf{a}|^2 + 2|\mathbf{b}|^2$, $\mathbf{ab} = 3$ and $|\mathbf{a} \times \mathbf{b}|^2 = 75$. Then, $|\mathbf{a}|^2$ is equal to .... **[Numerical Value Type, 2022 Main]**

96. Let $\mathbf{a} = 3\hat{\mathbf{i}} + \hat{\mathbf{j}}$ and $\mathbf{b} = \hat{\mathbf{i}} + 2\hat{\mathbf{j}} + \hat{\mathbf{k}}$. Let $\mathbf{c}$ be a vector satisfying $\mathbf{a} \times (\mathbf{b} \times \mathbf{c}) = \mathbf{b} + \lambda\mathbf{c}$. If $\mathbf{b}$ and $\mathbf{c}$ are non-parallel, then the value of λ is **[Single Correct Type, 2022 Main]**

(a) -5 (b) 5 (c) 1 (d) -1

97. If $\mathbf{a} \cdot \mathbf{b} = 1$, $\mathbf{b} \cdot \mathbf{c} = 2$ and $\mathbf{c} \cdot \mathbf{a} = 3$, then the value of $[\mathbf{a} \times (\mathbf{b} \times \mathbf{c}), \mathbf{b} \times (\mathbf{c} \times \mathbf{a}), \mathbf{c} \times (\mathbf{b} \times \mathbf{a})]$ is **[Single Correct Type, 2022 Main]**

(a) 0 (b) $-6\,\mathbf{a} \cdot (\mathbf{b} \times \mathbf{c})$
(c) $12\,\mathbf{c} \cdot (\mathbf{a} \times \mathbf{b})$ (d) $-12\,\mathbf{b} \cdot (\mathbf{c} \times \mathbf{a})$

98. Let $\mathbf{a} = \hat{\mathbf{i}} - 2\hat{\mathbf{j}} + 3\hat{\mathbf{k}}$, $\mathbf{b} = \hat{\mathbf{i}} + \hat{\mathbf{j}} + \hat{\mathbf{k}}$ and $\mathbf{c}$ be a vector such that $\mathbf{a} + (\mathbf{b} \times \mathbf{c}) = \mathbf{0}$ and $\mathbf{b} \cdot \mathbf{c} = 5$. Then, the value of $3(\mathbf{c} \cdot \mathbf{a})$ is equal to .... **[Numerical Value Type, 2022 Main]**

99. Let $\mathbf{a}$ and $\mathbf{b}$ be two vectors such that $|2\mathbf{a} + 3\mathbf{b}| = |3\mathbf{a} + \mathbf{b}|$ and the angle between $\mathbf{a}$ and $\mathbf{b}$ is 60°. If $\frac{1}{8}\mathbf{a}$ is a unit vector, then $|\mathbf{b}|$ is equal to **[Single Correct Type, 2021 Main]**

(a) 4 (b) 6 (c) 5 (d) 8

100. If the projection of the vector $\hat{\mathbf{i}} + 2\hat{\mathbf{j}} + \hat{\mathbf{k}}$ on the sum of the two vectors $2\hat{\mathbf{i}} + 4\hat{\mathbf{j}} - 5\hat{\mathbf{k}}$ and $-\lambda\hat{\mathbf{i}} + 2\hat{\mathbf{j}} + 3\hat{\mathbf{k}}$ is 1, then λ is equal to .... **[Numerical Value Type, 2021 Main]**

101. Let $\mathbf{p} = 2\hat{\mathbf{i}} + 3\hat{\mathbf{j}} + \hat{\mathbf{k}}$ and $\mathbf{q} = \hat{\mathbf{i}} + 2\hat{\mathbf{j}} + \hat{\mathbf{k}}$ be two vectors. If a vector $\mathbf{r} = (\alpha\hat{\mathbf{i}} + \beta\hat{\mathbf{j}} + \gamma\hat{\mathbf{k}})$ is perpendicular to each of the vectors $(\mathbf{p} + \mathbf{q})$ and $(\mathbf{p} - \mathbf{q})$ and $|\mathbf{r}| = \sqrt{3}$, then $|\alpha| + |\beta| + |\gamma|$ is equal to .... **[Numerical Value Type, 2021 Main]**

102. Let a vector $\mathbf{a}$ be coplanar with vectors $\mathbf{b} = 2\hat{\mathbf{i}} + \hat{\mathbf{j}} + \hat{\mathbf{k}}$ and $\mathbf{c} = \hat{\mathbf{i}} - \hat{\mathbf{j}} + \hat{\mathbf{k}}$. If $\mathbf{a}$ is perpendicular to $\mathbf{d} = 3\hat{\mathbf{i}} + 2\hat{\mathbf{j}} + 6\hat{\mathbf{k}}$ and $|\mathbf{a}| = \sqrt{10}$. Then, a possible value of $[\mathbf{a}\ \mathbf{b}\ \mathbf{c}] + [\mathbf{a}\ \mathbf{b}\ \mathbf{d}] + [\mathbf{a}\ \mathbf{c}\ \mathbf{d}]$ is equal to **[Single Correct Type, 2021 Main]**

(a) -42 (b) -40
(c) -29 (d) -38

103. If (1, 5, 35), (7, 5, 5), (1, λ, 7) and (2λ, 1, 2) are coplanar, then the sum of all possible values of λ is **[Single Correct Type, 2021 Main]**

(a) $\frac{39}{5}$ (b) $-\frac{39}{5}$ (c) $\frac{44}{5}$ (d) $-\frac{44}{5}$

104. If $\mathbf{a}$ and $\mathbf{b}$ are unit vectors, then the greatest value of $\sqrt{3}|\mathbf{a} + \mathbf{b}| + |\mathbf{a} - \mathbf{b}|$ is .... **[Numerical Value Type, 2020 Main]**

105. Let $\mathbf{a} = \hat{\mathbf{i}} - 2\hat{\mathbf{j}} + \hat{\mathbf{k}}$ and $\mathbf{b} = \hat{\mathbf{i}} - \hat{\mathbf{j}} + \hat{\mathbf{k}}$ be two vectors. If $\mathbf{c}$ is a vector such that $\mathbf{b} \times \mathbf{c} = \mathbf{b} \times \mathbf{a}$ and $\mathbf{c} \cdot \mathbf{a} = 0$, then $\mathbf{c} \cdot \mathbf{b}$ is equal to **[Single Correct Type, 2020 Main]**

(a) 1/2 (b) $-3/2$
(c) $-1/2$ (d) -1

106. Let $A(3, 0, -1)$, $B(2, 10, 6)$ and $C(1, 2, 1)$ be the vertices of a triangle and M be the mid-point of AC. If G divides BM in the ratio 2 : 1, then $\cos(\angle GOA)$ (O being the origin) is equal to **[Single Correct Type, 2019 Main]**

(a) $\frac{1}{\sqrt{15}}$ (b) $\frac{1}{2\sqrt{15}}$ (c) $\frac{1}{\sqrt{30}}$ (d) $\frac{1}{6\sqrt{10}}$

107. Let $\mathbf{a} = 3\hat{\mathbf{i}} + 2\hat{\mathbf{j}} + 2\hat{\mathbf{k}}$ and $\mathbf{b} = \hat{\mathbf{i}} + 2\hat{\mathbf{j}} - 2\hat{\mathbf{k}}$ be two vectors. If a vector perpendicular to both the vectors $\mathbf{a} + \mathbf{b}$ and $\mathbf{a} - \mathbf{b}$ has the magnitude 12, then one such vector is **[Single Correct Type, 2019 Main]**

(a) $\pm 4(2\hat{\mathbf{i}} + 2\hat{\mathbf{j}} + \hat{\mathbf{k}})$ (b) $\pm 4(2\hat{\mathbf{i}} - 2\hat{\mathbf{j}} - \hat{\mathbf{k}})$
(c) $\pm 4(2\hat{\mathbf{i}} + 2\hat{\mathbf{j}} - \hat{\mathbf{k}})$ (d) $\pm 4(-2\hat{\mathbf{i}} - 2\hat{\mathbf{j}} + \hat{\mathbf{k}})$

108. The sum of the distinct real values of μ, for which the vectors, $\mu\hat{\mathbf{i}} + \hat{\mathbf{j}} + \hat{\mathbf{k}}$, $\hat{\mathbf{i}} + \mu\hat{\mathbf{j}} + \hat{\mathbf{k}}$, $\hat{\mathbf{i}} + \hat{\mathbf{j}} + m\hat{\mathbf{k}}$ are coplanar, is **[Single Correct Type, 2019 Main]**

(a) 2 (b) 0
(c) 1 (d) -1

EXERCISE 2
JEE Advanced Pattern

Single Option Correct Type Questions

1. If $\mathbf{a}\times(\mathbf{b}\times\mathbf{c})+(\mathbf{a}\cdot\mathbf{b})\,\mathbf{b}=(4-2\beta-\sin\alpha)\,\mathbf{b}+(\beta^2-1)\,\mathbf{c}$ and $(\mathbf{c}\cdot\mathbf{c})\,\mathbf{a}=\mathbf{c}$, where $\mathbf{b}$ and $\mathbf{c}$ are non-collinear and α, β are scalars, then

(a) $\alpha=(4n+1)\dfrac{\pi}{2}, n\in Z, \beta=1$ (b) $\alpha=(n+1)\,\pi, \beta=2$

(c) $\alpha=(n^2+1)\dfrac{\pi}{3}, \beta=2$ (d) $\alpha=(n^2-1)\dfrac{\pi}{4}, \beta=1$

2. Let O be an interior point of ΔABC such that $\mathbf{OA}+2\mathbf{OB}+3\mathbf{OC}=\mathbf{0}$ and areas of ΔABC, ΔAOB, ΔBOC and ΔAOC are denoted by A_1, A_2, A_3 and A_4 respectively, then value of $\dfrac{A_1}{\min(A_2, A_3, A_4)}$ is

(a) 4 (b) 6 (c) 7 (d) 5

3. If $\mathbf{b}$ and $\mathbf{c}$ are any two non-collinear unit vectors and $\mathbf{a}$ is any vector, then $(\mathbf{a}\cdot\mathbf{b})\,\mathbf{b}+(\mathbf{a}\cdot\mathbf{c})\,\mathbf{c}+\dfrac{\mathbf{a}\cdot(\mathbf{b}\times\mathbf{c})}{|\mathbf{b}\times\mathbf{c}|^2}(\mathbf{b}\times\mathbf{c})$ is equal to

(a) $\mathbf{a}$ (b) $\mathbf{b}$ (c) $\mathbf{c}$ (d) $\mathbf{a}+\mathbf{b}+\mathbf{c}$

4. If A, B, C, D are any four points in space, then the value of $|\mathbf{AB}\times\mathbf{CD}+\mathbf{BC}\times\mathbf{AD}+\mathbf{CA}\times\mathbf{BD}|$ is equal to

(a) area of ΔABC (b) $\dfrac{1}{2}$ area of ΔABC

(c) 2 area of ΔABC (d) None of these

5. A rigid body rotates about an axis through the origin with an angular velocity $10\sqrt{3}$ rad/s. If ω points in the direction of $\hat{\mathbf{i}}+\hat{\mathbf{j}}+\hat{\mathbf{k}}$, then the equation to the locus of the points having tangential speed 20 m/s is

(a) $x^2+y^2+z^2-xy-yz-zx-1=0$

(b) $x^2+y^2+z^2-2xy-2yz-2zx-1=0$

(c) $x^2+y^2+z^2-xy-yz-zx-2=0$

(d) $x^2+y^2+z^2-2xy-2yz-2zx-2=0$

6. A rigid body rotates with constant angular velocity ω about the line whose vector equation is, $\mathbf{r}=\lambda(\hat{\mathbf{i}}+2\hat{\mathbf{j}}+2\hat{\mathbf{k}})$. The speed of the particle at the instant it passes through the point with position vector $(2\hat{\mathbf{i}}+3\hat{\mathbf{j}}+5\hat{\mathbf{k}})$ is equal to

(a) $\omega\sqrt{2}$ (b) 2ω

(c) $\omega/\sqrt{2}$ (d) None of these

7. Consider ΔABC with $A=(\mathbf{a})$, $B=(\mathbf{b})$ and $C=(\mathbf{c})$. If $\mathbf{b}\cdot(\mathbf{a}+\mathbf{c})=\mathbf{b}\cdot\mathbf{b}+\mathbf{a}\cdot\mathbf{c}$, $|\mathbf{b}-\mathbf{a}|=3$ and $|\mathbf{c}-\mathbf{b}|=4$, then the angle between the medians **AM** and **BD** is

(a) $\pi-\cos^{-1}\left(\dfrac{1}{5\sqrt{13}}\right)$ (b) $\pi-\cos^{-1}\left(\dfrac{1}{13\sqrt{5}}\right)$

(c) $\cos^{-1}\left(\dfrac{1}{5\sqrt{13}}\right)$ (d) $\cos^{-1}\left(\dfrac{1}{13\sqrt{5}}\right)$

8. If $\mathbf{a}$ and $\mathbf{b}$ are unit vectors, then the vector defined as $\mathbf{V}=(\mathbf{a}\times\mathbf{b})\times(\mathbf{a}+\mathbf{b})$ is collinear to the vector

(a) $\mathbf{a}+\mathbf{b}$ (b) $\mathbf{b}-\mathbf{a}$

(c) $2\mathbf{a}-\mathbf{b}$ (d) $\mathbf{a}+2\mathbf{b}$

9. If $\mathbf{a}$ and $\mathbf{b}$ are orthogonal unit vectors, then for any non-zero vector $\mathbf{r}$, the vector $(\mathbf{r}\times\mathbf{a})$ is equal to

(a) $[\mathbf{r}\ \mathbf{a}\ \mathbf{b}]\,(\mathbf{a}+\mathbf{b})$ (b) $[\mathbf{r}\ \mathbf{a}\ \mathbf{b}]\,\mathbf{a}+(\mathbf{r}\cdot\mathbf{a})(\mathbf{a}\times\mathbf{b})$

(c) $[\mathbf{r}\ \mathbf{a}\ \mathbf{b}]\,\mathbf{b}+(\mathbf{r}\cdot\mathbf{b})(\mathbf{b}\times\mathbf{a})$ (d) $[\mathbf{r}\ \mathbf{a}\ \mathbf{b}]\,\mathbf{b}+(\mathbf{r}\cdot\mathbf{a})(\mathbf{a}\times\mathbf{b})$

10. If $\mathbf{a}$ is a unit vector and projection of $\mathbf{x}$ along $\mathbf{a}$ is 2 units and $(\mathbf{a}\times\mathbf{x})+\mathbf{b}=\mathbf{x}$, then $\mathbf{x}$ is equal to

(a) $\dfrac{1}{2}[2\mathbf{a}-\mathbf{b}+(\mathbf{a}\times\mathbf{b})]$ (b) $\dfrac{1}{2}[2\mathbf{a}+\mathbf{b}+(\mathbf{a}\times\mathbf{b})]$

(c) $[\mathbf{a}+(\mathbf{a}\times\mathbf{b})]$ (d) None of these

11. If $\mathbf{a}\cdot\mathbf{b}$ and $\mathbf{c}$ are any three non-zero vectors, then the component of $\mathbf{a}\times(\mathbf{b}\times\mathbf{c})$ perpendicular to $\mathbf{b}$ is

(a) $\mathbf{a}\times(\mathbf{b}\times\mathbf{c})+\dfrac{(\mathbf{a}\times\mathbf{b})\cdot(\mathbf{c}\times\mathbf{a})}{|\mathbf{b}|^2}\mathbf{b}$

(b) $\mathbf{a}\times(\mathbf{b}\times\mathbf{c})+\dfrac{(\mathbf{a}\times\mathbf{c})\cdot(\mathbf{a}\times\mathbf{b})}{|\mathbf{b}|^2}\mathbf{b}$

(c) $\mathbf{a}\times(\mathbf{b}\times\mathbf{c})+\dfrac{(\mathbf{b}\times\mathbf{c})\cdot(\mathbf{b}\times\mathbf{a})}{|\mathbf{b}|^2}\mathbf{b}$

(d) $\mathbf{a}\times(\mathbf{b}\times\mathbf{c})+\dfrac{(\mathbf{a}\times\mathbf{b})\cdot(\mathbf{b}\times\mathbf{c})}{|\mathbf{b}|^2}\mathbf{b}$

12. $\mathbf{a}$, $\mathbf{b}$ and $\mathbf{c}$ are three unit vectors, $\mathbf{a}$ and $\mathbf{b}$ are perpendicular to each other and vector $\mathbf{c}$ is equally inclined to both $\mathbf{a}$ and $\mathbf{b}$ at an angle θ. If $\mathbf{c}=\alpha\,\mathbf{a}+\beta\,\mathbf{b}+\gamma(\mathbf{a}\times\mathbf{b})$, where α, β and γ are constants, then

(a) $\alpha=\beta=-\cos\theta, \gamma^2=\cos2\theta$ (b) $\alpha=\beta=\cos\theta, \gamma^2=\cos2\theta$

(c) $\alpha=\beta=\cos\theta, \gamma^2=-\cos2\theta$ (d) $\alpha=\beta=-\cos\theta, \gamma^2=-\cos2\theta$

13. The perpendicular distance of a corner of a unit cube from a diagonal not passing through it is

(a) $\sqrt{\dfrac{3}{2}}$ (b) $\sqrt{\dfrac{2}{3}}$ (c) $\sqrt{\dfrac{3}{4}}$ (d) $\sqrt{\dfrac{4}{3}}$

14. Let **a**, **b** and **c** be three non-coplanar vectors and **d** be a non-zero vector, which is perpendicular to $\mathbf{a}+\mathbf{b}+\mathbf{c}$. Now, if $\mathbf{d}=(\sin x)(\mathbf{a}\times\mathbf{b})+(\cos y)(\mathbf{b}\times\mathbf{c})+2(\mathbf{c}\times\mathbf{a})$, then minimum value of x^2+y^2 is equal to

(a) π^2 (b) $\frac{\pi^2}{2}$ (c) $\frac{\pi^2}{4}$ (d) $\frac{5\pi^2}{4}$

15. If $\alpha(\mathbf{a}\times\mathbf{b})+\beta(\mathbf{b}\times\mathbf{c})+\gamma(\mathbf{c}\times\mathbf{a})=0$, then

(a) a, b and c are coplanar, if all of $\alpha, \beta, \gamma \neq 0$

(b) a, b and c are coplanar, if any one $\alpha, \beta, \gamma = 0$

(c) a, b and c are non-coplanar for any α, β, γ

(d) None of the above

16. Let area of faces,

$\Delta OAB=\lambda_1, \Delta OAC=\lambda_2, \Delta OBC=\lambda_3, \Delta ABC=\lambda_4$ and h_1, h_2, h_3, h_4 be perpendicular height from 0 to face ΔABC, A to the face ΔOBC, B to the face ΔOAC, C to the face ΔOAB, then the face

$$\frac{1}{3}\lambda_1 h_4 \cdot \frac{1}{3}\lambda_2 h_3 + \frac{1}{3}\lambda_3 h_2 + \frac{1}{3}\lambda_4 h_1$$

(a) $\frac{2}{3}|[\mathbf{AB}\ \mathbf{AC}\ \mathbf{OA}]|$ (b) $\frac{1}{3}|[\mathbf{AB}\ \mathbf{AC}\ \mathbf{OA}]|$

(c) $\frac{1}{3}|[\mathbf{OA}\ \mathbf{OB}\ \mathbf{OC}]|$ (d) None of these

17. The shortest distance between a diagonal of a unit cube and a diagonal of a face skew to it is

(a) $\frac{1}{2}$ (b) $\frac{1}{\sqrt{2}}$ (c) $\frac{1}{\sqrt{3}}$ (d) $\frac{1}{\sqrt{6}}$

18. Let $\mathbf{V}=2\hat{\mathbf{i}}+\hat{\mathbf{j}}+\hat{\mathbf{k}}$ and $\mathbf{W}=\hat{\mathbf{i}}+3\hat{\mathbf{k}}$. If **U** is a unit vector, then the maximum value of the scalar triple product $[\mathbf{U}\ \mathbf{V}\ \mathbf{W}]$ is

(a) -1 (b) $\sqrt{35}$ (c) $\sqrt{59}$ (d) $\sqrt{60}$

19. Let **a**, **b** and **c** are three vectors along the adjacent edges of a tetrahedron, if $|\mathbf{a}|=|\mathbf{b}|=|\mathbf{c}|=2$ and $\mathbf{a}\cdot\mathbf{b}=\mathbf{b}\cdot\mathbf{c}=\mathbf{c}\cdot\mathbf{a}=2$, then volume of tetrahedron is

(a) $\frac{1}{\sqrt{2}}$ (b) $\frac{2}{\sqrt{3}}$ (c) $\frac{\sqrt{3}}{2}$ (d) $\frac{2\sqrt{2}}{3}$

20. The angle θ between two non-zero vectors **a** and **b** satisfies the relation

$\cos\theta=(\mathbf{a}\times\hat{\mathbf{i}})\cdot(\mathbf{b}\times\hat{\mathbf{i}})+(\mathbf{a}\times\hat{\mathbf{j}})\cdot(\mathbf{b}\times\hat{\mathbf{j}})+(\mathbf{a}\times\hat{\mathbf{k}})\cdot(\mathbf{b}\times\hat{\mathbf{k}})$,

then the least value of $|\mathbf{a}|+|\mathbf{b}|$ is equal to (where $\theta\neq 90°$)

(a) $\frac{1}{2}$ (b) 2 (c) $\sqrt{2}$ (d) 4

21. Let O be the origin and let PQR be an arbitrary triangle. The point S is such that

$$\mathbf{OP}\cdot\mathbf{OQ}+\mathbf{OR}\cdot\mathbf{OS}=\mathbf{OR}\cdot\mathbf{OP}+\mathbf{OQ}\cdot\mathbf{OS}$$
$$=\mathbf{OQ}\cdot\mathbf{OR}+\mathbf{OP}\cdot\mathbf{OS}$$

Then, the ΔPQR has S as its

[Single Correct Type, 2017 Adv.]

(a) centroid (b) orthocentre

(c) incentre (d) circumcentre

More than One Correct Option Type Questions

22. If $\mathbf{a}\times(\mathbf{b}\times\mathbf{c})=(\mathbf{a}\times\mathbf{b})\times\mathbf{c}$, then

(a) $(\mathbf{c}\times\mathbf{a})\times\mathbf{b}=\mathbf{0}$ (b) $\mathbf{c}\times(\mathbf{a}\times\mathbf{b})=\mathbf{0}$

(c) $\mathbf{b}\times(\mathbf{c}\times\mathbf{a})=\mathbf{0}$ (d) $(\mathbf{c}\times\mathbf{a})\times\mathbf{b}=\mathbf{b}\times(\mathbf{c}\times\mathbf{a})=\mathbf{0}$

23. Let **a** and **b** be two non-collinear unit vectors. If $\mathbf{u}=\mathbf{a}-(\mathbf{a}\cdot\mathbf{b})\,\mathbf{b}$ and $\mathbf{v}=\mathbf{a}\times\mathbf{b}$, then $|\mathbf{v}|$ is

(a) $|\mathbf{u}|$ (b) $|\mathbf{u}|+|\mathbf{u}\cdot\mathbf{a}|$

(c) $|\mathbf{u}|+|\mathbf{u}\cdot\mathbf{b}|$ (d) $|\mathbf{u}|+\mathbf{u}\cdot(\mathbf{a}+\mathbf{b})$

24. Let **r** be a unit vector satisfying $\mathbf{r}\times\mathbf{a}=\mathbf{b}$, where $|\mathbf{a}|=\sqrt{3}$ and $|\mathbf{b}|=\sqrt{2}$. Then,

(a) $\mathbf{r}=\frac{2}{3}(\mathbf{a}+\mathbf{a}\times\mathbf{b})$ (b) $\mathbf{r}=\frac{1}{3}(\mathbf{a}+\mathbf{a}\times\mathbf{b})$

(c) $\mathbf{r}=\frac{2}{3}(\mathbf{a}-\mathbf{a}\times\mathbf{b})$ (d) $\mathbf{r}=\frac{1}{3}(-\mathbf{a}+\mathbf{a}\times\mathbf{b})$

25. If **a** and **b** are two vectors and angle between them is θ, then

(a) $|\mathbf{a}\times\mathbf{b}|^2+(\mathbf{a}\cdot\mathbf{b})^2=|\mathbf{a}|^2|\mathbf{b}|^2$

(b) $|\mathbf{a}\times\mathbf{b}|=(\mathbf{a}\cdot\mathbf{b})$, if $\theta=\pi/4$

(c) $\mathbf{a}\times\mathbf{b}=(\mathbf{a}\cdot\mathbf{b})\hat{\mathbf{n}}$ (where $\hat{\mathbf{n}}$ is a normal unit vector), if $\theta=\pi/4$

(d) $(\mathbf{a}\times\mathbf{b})\cdot(\mathbf{a}+\mathbf{b})=0$

26. If unit vectors **a** and **b** are inclined at an angle 2θ such that $|\mathbf{a}-\mathbf{b}|<1$ and $0\leq\theta\leq\pi$, then θ lies in the interval

(a) $[0,\pi/6)$ (b) $(5\pi/6,\pi]$

(c) $[\pi/6,\pi/2)$ (d) $(\pi/2,5\pi/6]$

27. **b** and **c** are non-collinear, if $\mathbf{a}\times(\mathbf{b}\times\mathbf{c})+(\mathbf{a}\cdot\mathbf{b})\mathbf{b}=(4-2x-\sin y)\mathbf{b}+(x^2-1)\mathbf{c}$ and $(\mathbf{c}\cdot\mathbf{c})\mathbf{a}=\mathbf{c}$. Then,

(a) $x=1$ (b) $x=-1$

(c) $y=(4n+1)\frac{\pi}{2}, n\in I$ (d) $y=(2n+1)\frac{\pi}{2}, n\in I$

28. If **a**, **b** and **c** be three non-zero vectors satisfying the condition $\mathbf{a}\times\mathbf{b}=\mathbf{c}$ and $\mathbf{b}\times\mathbf{c}=\mathbf{a}$, then which of the following always hold(s) good?

(a) **a**, **b** and **c** are orthogonal in pairs.

(b) $[\mathbf{a}\ \mathbf{b}\ \mathbf{c}]=|\mathbf{b}|$

(c) $[\mathbf{a}\ \mathbf{b}\ \mathbf{c}]=|\mathbf{c}|^2$

(d) $|\mathbf{b}|=|\mathbf{c}|$

29. Given the following information about the non-zero vectors **A**, **B** and **C**

(i) $(\mathbf{A}\times\mathbf{B})\times\mathbf{A}=\mathbf{0}$

(ii) $\mathbf{B}\cdot\mathbf{B}=4$

(iii) $\mathbf{A}\cdot\mathbf{B}=-6$

(iv) $\mathbf{B}\cdot\mathbf{C}=6$

Which one of the following holds good?

(a) $\mathbf{A}\times\mathbf{B}=\mathbf{0}$ (b) $\mathbf{A}\cdot(\mathbf{B}\times\mathbf{C})=0$

(c) $\mathbf{A}\cdot\mathbf{A}=8$ (d) $\mathbf{A}\cdot\mathbf{C}=-9$

30. Given three vectors
$\mathbf{U} = 2\hat{\mathbf{i}} + 3\hat{\mathbf{j}} - 6\hat{\mathbf{k}}$, $\mathbf{V} = 6\hat{\mathbf{i}} + 2\hat{\mathbf{j}} + 3\hat{\mathbf{k}}$ and $\mathbf{W} = 3\hat{\mathbf{i}} - 6\hat{\mathbf{j}} - 2\hat{\mathbf{k}}$
which of the following hold good for the vectors $\mathbf{U}, \mathbf{V}$ and $\mathbf{W}$?
(a) $\mathbf{U}$, $\mathbf{V}$ and $\mathbf{W}$ are linearly dependent
(b) $(\mathbf{U} \times \mathbf{V}) \times \mathbf{W} = \mathbf{0}$
(c) $\mathbf{U}$, $\mathbf{V}$ and $\mathbf{W}$ form a triplet of mutually perpendicular vectors
(d) $\mathbf{U} \times (\mathbf{V} \times \mathbf{W}) = \mathbf{0}$

31. Let $\mathbf{a} = 2\hat{\mathbf{i}} - \hat{\mathbf{j}} + \hat{\mathbf{k}}$, $\mathbf{b} = \hat{\mathbf{i}} + 2\hat{\mathbf{j}} - \hat{\mathbf{k}}$ and $\mathbf{c} = \hat{\mathbf{i}} + \hat{\mathbf{j}} - 2\hat{\mathbf{k}}$ be three vectors. A vector in the plane of $\mathbf{b}$ and $\mathbf{c}$ whose projection on $\mathbf{a}$ is of magnitude $\sqrt{\frac{2}{3}}$ is
(a) $2\hat{\mathbf{i}} + 3\hat{\mathbf{j}} - 3\hat{\mathbf{k}}$ (b) $2\hat{\mathbf{i}} + 3\hat{\mathbf{j}} + 3\hat{\mathbf{k}}$
(c) $-2\hat{\mathbf{i}} - \hat{\mathbf{j}} + 5\hat{\mathbf{k}}$ (d) $2\hat{\mathbf{i}} + \hat{\mathbf{j}} + 5\hat{\mathbf{k}}$

32. Three vectors $\mathbf{a}$ $(|\mathbf{a}| \neq 0)$, $\mathbf{b}$ and $\mathbf{c}$ are such that $\mathbf{a} \times \mathbf{b} = 3\mathbf{a} \times \mathbf{c}$. Also, $|\mathbf{a}| = |\mathbf{b}| = 1$ and $|\mathbf{c}| = \frac{1}{3}$. If the angle between $\mathbf{b}$ and $\mathbf{c}$ is 60°, then
(a) $\mathbf{b} = 3\mathbf{c} + \mathbf{a}$ (b) $\mathbf{b} = 3\mathbf{c} - \mathbf{a}$
(c) $\mathbf{a} = 6\mathbf{c} + 2\mathbf{b}$ (d) $\mathbf{a} = 6\mathbf{c} - 2\mathbf{b}$

33. If $\mathbf{a}$ and $\mathbf{b}$ are two unit vectors perpendicular to each other and $\mathbf{c} = \lambda_1\mathbf{a} + \lambda_2\mathbf{b} + \lambda_3(\mathbf{a} \times \mathbf{b})$, then the following is (are) true
(a) $\lambda_1 = \mathbf{a} \cdot \mathbf{c}$
(b) $\lambda_2 = |\mathbf{b} \times \mathbf{a}|$
(c) $\lambda_3 = |(\mathbf{a} \times \mathbf{b}) \times \mathbf{c}|$
(d) $\lambda_1 + \lambda_2 + \lambda_3 = (\mathbf{a} + \mathbf{b} + \mathbf{a} \times \mathbf{b}) \cdot \mathbf{c}$

34. Given three non-coplanar vectors
$\mathbf{OA} = \mathbf{a}, \mathbf{OB} = \mathbf{b}, \mathbf{OC} = \mathbf{c}$.
Let S be the centre of the sphere passing through the points, O, A, B, C if $\mathbf{OS} = \mathbf{x}$, then
(a) $\mathbf{x}$ must be linear combination of $\mathbf{a}, \mathbf{b}, \mathbf{c}$
(b) $\mathbf{x}$ must be linear combination of $\mathbf{b} \times \mathbf{c}$, $\mathbf{c} \times \mathbf{a}$ and $\mathbf{a} \times \mathbf{b}$
(c) $\mathbf{x} = \dfrac{a^2(\mathbf{b} \times \mathbf{c}) + b^2(\mathbf{c} \times \mathbf{a}) + c^2(\mathbf{a} \times \mathbf{b})}{2[\mathbf{a}\,\mathbf{b}\,\mathbf{c}]}$, $a = |\mathbf{a}|, b = |\mathbf{b}|, c = |\mathbf{c}|$
(d) $\mathbf{x} = \mathbf{a} + \mathbf{b} + \mathbf{c}$

35. If $\mathbf{a} = \hat{\mathbf{i}} + \hat{\mathbf{j}} + \hat{\mathbf{k}}$ and $\mathbf{b} = \hat{\mathbf{i}} - \hat{\mathbf{j}}$, then the vectors $(\mathbf{a} \cdot \hat{\mathbf{i}})\hat{\mathbf{i}} + (\mathbf{a} \cdot \hat{\mathbf{j}})\hat{\mathbf{j}} + (\mathbf{a} \cdot \hat{\mathbf{k}})\hat{\mathbf{k}}, (\mathbf{b} \cdot \hat{\mathbf{i}})\hat{\mathbf{i}} + (\mathbf{b} \cdot \hat{\mathbf{j}})\hat{\mathbf{j}} + (\mathbf{b} \cdot \hat{\mathbf{k}})\hat{\mathbf{k}}$ and $\hat{\mathbf{i}} + \hat{\mathbf{j}} - 2\hat{\mathbf{k}}$
(a) are mutually perpendicular.
(b) are coplanar.
(c) form a parallelopiped of volume 6 units.
(d) form a parallelopiped of volume 3 units.

36. If $\mathbf{a} = x\hat{\mathbf{i}} + y\hat{\mathbf{j}} + z\hat{\mathbf{k}}$, $\mathbf{b} = y\hat{\mathbf{i}} + z\hat{\mathbf{j}} + x\hat{\mathbf{k}}$, $\mathbf{c} = z\hat{\mathbf{i}} + x\hat{\mathbf{j}} + y\hat{\mathbf{k}}$, then $\mathbf{a} \times (\mathbf{b} \times \mathbf{c})$ is
(a) parallel to $(y - z)\hat{\mathbf{i}} + (z - x)\hat{\mathbf{j}} + (x - y)\hat{\mathbf{k}}$
(b) orthogonal to $\hat{\mathbf{i}} + \hat{\mathbf{j}} + \hat{\mathbf{k}}$
(c) orthogonal to $(y + z)\hat{\mathbf{i}} + (z + x)\hat{\mathbf{j}} + (x + y)\hat{\mathbf{k}}$
(d) parallel to $\hat{\mathbf{i}} + \hat{\mathbf{j}} + \hat{\mathbf{k}}$

37. If $\mathbf{a}$, $\mathbf{b}$ and $\mathbf{c}$ are three non-zero vectors, then which of the following statement (s) is/are true?
(a) $\mathbf{a} \times (\mathbf{b} \times \mathbf{c})$, $\mathbf{b} \times (\mathbf{c} \times \mathbf{a})$, $\mathbf{c} \times (\mathbf{a} \times \mathbf{b})$ form a right handed system
(b) $\mathbf{c}, (\mathbf{a} \times \mathbf{b}) \times \mathbf{c}, \mathbf{a} \times \mathbf{b}$ form a right handed system
(c) $\mathbf{a} \cdot \mathbf{b} + \mathbf{b} \cdot \mathbf{c} + \mathbf{c} \cdot \mathbf{a} < 0$, if $\mathbf{a} + \mathbf{b} + \mathbf{c} = \mathbf{0}$
(d) $\dfrac{(\mathbf{a} \times \mathbf{b}) \cdot (\mathbf{b} \times \mathbf{c})}{(\mathbf{b} \times \mathbf{c}) \cdot (\mathbf{a} \times \mathbf{c})} = -1$, if $\mathbf{a} + \mathbf{b} + \mathbf{c} = \mathbf{0}$

38. If $\mathbf{a}$ and $\mathbf{b}$ are any two unit vectors, then possible integers(s) in the range of $\dfrac{3|\mathbf{a} + \mathbf{b}|}{2} + 2|\mathbf{a} - \mathbf{b}|$ is
(a) 2 (b) 3 (c) 4 (d) 5

39. If $\mathbf{a}$ is perpendicular to $\mathbf{b}$ and p is non-zero scalar such that $p\,\mathbf{r} + (\mathbf{r} \cdot \mathbf{b})\,\mathbf{a} = \mathbf{c}$, then $\mathbf{r}$
(a) $[\mathbf{r}\;\mathbf{a}\;\mathbf{c}] = 0$ (b) $p^2\mathbf{r} = p\mathbf{a} - (\mathbf{c} \cdot \mathbf{a})\mathbf{b}$
(c) $p^2\mathbf{r} = p\mathbf{b} - (\mathbf{a} \cdot \mathbf{b})\mathbf{c}$ (d) $p^2\mathbf{r} = p\mathbf{c} - (\mathbf{b} \cdot \mathbf{c})\mathbf{a}$

40. In a four-dimensional space, where unit vectors along axes are $\hat{\mathbf{i}}, \hat{\mathbf{j}}, \hat{\mathbf{k}}$ and $\hat{\mathbf{l}}$ and $\mathbf{a}_1, \mathbf{a}_2, \mathbf{a}_3, \mathbf{a}_4$ are four non-zero vectors such that no vector can be expressed as linear combination of others and
$(\lambda - 1)(\mathbf{a}_1 - \mathbf{a}_2) + \mu(\mathbf{a}_2 + \mathbf{a}_3) + \gamma(\mathbf{a}_3 + \mathbf{a}_4 - 2\mathbf{a}_2)$
$+ \mathbf{a}_3 + \delta\mathbf{a}_4 = \mathbf{0}$, then
(a) $\lambda = 1$ (b) $\mu = -\frac{2}{3}$ (c) $\lambda = \frac{2}{3}$ (d) $\delta = \frac{1}{3}$

41. If $\mathbf{a}, \mathbf{b}, \mathbf{c}$ are non-zero, non-collinear vectors such that a vector $\mathbf{p} = ab\cos(2\pi - (\mathbf{a}, \mathbf{c}))\,\mathbf{c}$ and $\mathbf{q} = \mathbf{a}\mathbf{c}\cos(2\pi - (\mathbf{a}, \mathbf{b}))\,\mathbf{b}$, then $\mathbf{p} + \mathbf{q}$ is
(a) parallel to $\mathbf{a}$ (b) perpendicular to $\mathbf{a}$
(c) coplanar with $\mathbf{b}$ and $\mathbf{c}$ (d) coplanar with $\mathbf{a}$ and $\mathbf{c}$

42. Let $\mathbf{a}, \mathbf{b}, \mathbf{c}$ be three vectors such that each of them are non-collinear, $\mathbf{a} + \mathbf{b}$ and $\mathbf{b} + \mathbf{c}$ are collinear with $\mathbf{c}$ and $\mathbf{a}$ respectively and $\mathbf{a} + \mathbf{b} + \mathbf{c} = \mathbf{k}$. Then, $(|\mathbf{k}|, |\mathbf{k}|)$ lies on
(a) $y^2 = 4ax$ (b) $x^2 + y^2 - ax - by = 0$
(c) $x^2 - y^2 = 1$ (d) $|x| + |y| = 1$

43. Let $\mathbf{u} = \mathbf{u}_1\hat{\mathbf{i}} + \mathbf{u}_2\hat{\mathbf{j}} + \mathbf{u}_3\hat{\mathbf{k}}$ be a unit vector in R^3 and $\mathbf{w} = \frac{1}{\sqrt{6}}(\hat{\mathbf{i}} + \hat{\mathbf{j}} + 2\hat{\mathbf{k}})$. Given that there exists a vector $\mathbf{v}$ in R^3, such that $|\mathbf{u} + \mathbf{v}| = 1$ and $\mathbf{w} \cdot (\mathbf{u} + \mathbf{v}) = 1$. **[2016 Adv.]**
Which of the following statement(s) is/are correct?
(a) There is exactly one choice for such $\mathbf{v}$.
(b) There are infinitely many choices for such $\mathbf{v}$.
(c) If $\hat{\mathbf{u}}$ lies in the XY-plane, then $|\mathbf{u}_1| = |\mathbf{u}_2|$.
(d) If $\hat{\mathbf{u}}$ lies in the XY-plane, then $2|\mathbf{u}_1| = |\mathbf{u}_3|$.

44. Let ΔPQR be a triangle. Let $\mathbf{a} = \mathbf{QR}$, $\mathbf{b} = \mathbf{RP}$ and $\mathbf{c} = \mathbf{PQ}$. If $|\mathbf{a}| = 12$, $|\mathbf{b}| = 4\sqrt{3}$ and $\mathbf{b} \cdot \mathbf{c} = 24$, then which of the following is/are true? **[2015 Adv.]**
(a) $\dfrac{|\mathbf{c}|^2}{2} - |\mathbf{a}| = 12$ (b) $\dfrac{|\mathbf{c}|^2}{2} + |\mathbf{a}| = 30$
(c) $|\mathbf{a} \times \mathbf{b} + \mathbf{c} \times \mathbf{a}| = 48\sqrt{3}$ (d) $\mathbf{a} \cdot \mathbf{b} = -72$

Passage Based Questions

Passage I

(Q. Nos. 45 and 46)

- Consider three vectors $\mathbf{p}=\hat{\mathbf{i}}+\hat{\mathbf{j}}+\hat{\mathbf{k}}$, $\mathbf{q}=2\hat{\mathbf{i}}+4\hat{\mathbf{j}}-\hat{\mathbf{k}}$ and $\mathbf{r}=\hat{\mathbf{i}}+\hat{\mathbf{j}}+3\hat{\mathbf{k}}$ and let $\mathbf{s}$ be a unit vector, then

45. If $(\mathbf{p}\times\mathbf{q})\times\mathbf{r}=u\,\mathbf{p}+v\,\mathbf{q}+w\,\mathbf{r}$, then $(u+v+w)$ is equal to

(a) 8 (b) 2 (c) -2 (d) 4

46. The magnitude of the vector $(\mathbf{p}\cdot\mathbf{s})(\mathbf{q}\times\mathbf{r})+(\mathbf{q}\cdot\mathbf{s})(\mathbf{r}\times\mathbf{p})+(\mathbf{r}\cdot\mathbf{s})(\mathbf{p}\times\mathbf{q})$ is

(a) 4 (b) 8 (c) 18 (d) 2

Passage II

(Q. Nos. 47 and 48)

- Consider the three vectors $\mathbf{p}, \mathbf{q}$ and $\mathbf{r}$ such that $\mathbf{p}=\hat{\mathbf{i}}+\hat{\mathbf{j}}+\hat{\mathbf{k}}$ and $\mathbf{q}=\hat{\mathbf{i}}-\hat{\mathbf{j}}+\hat{\mathbf{k}}$; $\mathbf{p}\times\mathbf{r}=\mathbf{q}+c\mathbf{p}$ and $\mathbf{p}\cdot\mathbf{r}=2$

47. The value of $[\mathbf{p}\ \mathbf{q}\ \mathbf{r}]$ is

(a) $-\dfrac{5\sqrt{2}c}{|\mathbf{r}|}$ (b) $-\dfrac{8}{3}$

(c) 0 (d) greater than 0

48. If $\mathbf{x}$ is a vector such that $[\mathbf{p}\ \mathbf{q}\ \mathbf{r}]\mathbf{x}=(\mathbf{p}\times\mathbf{q})\times\mathbf{r}$, then $\mathbf{x}$ is

(a) $c\,(\hat{\mathbf{i}}-2\hat{\mathbf{j}}+\hat{\mathbf{k}})$

(b) a unit vector.

(c) indeterminate, as $[\mathbf{p}\ \mathbf{q}\ \mathbf{r}]$

(d) $-(\hat{\mathbf{i}}-2\hat{\mathbf{j}}+\hat{\mathbf{k}})/2$

Passage III

(Q. Nos. 49 and 50)

- Let P and Q are two points on the curve.
$y=\log_{1/2}(x-0.5)+\log_2\sqrt{4x^2-4x+1}$
and P is also on the circle $x^2+y^2=10$, Q lies inside the given circle such that its abscissa is an integer.

49. The coordinates of P are given by

(a) (1, 2) (b) (2, 4) (c) (3, 1) (d) (3, 5)

50. $\mathbf{OP}\cdot\mathbf{OQ}$, O being the origin is

(a) 4 or 7 (b) 4 or 2 (c) 2 or 3 (d) 7 or 8

Passage IV

(Q. Nos. 51 and 52)

- If $\mathbf{a}$, $\mathbf{b}$ and $\mathbf{c}$ are three given non-coplanar vectors and any arbitrary vector $\mathbf{r}$ is in space, where

$$\Delta_1=\begin{vmatrix}\mathbf{r}\cdot\mathbf{a} & \mathbf{b}\cdot\mathbf{a} & \mathbf{c}\cdot\mathbf{a}\\ \mathbf{r}\cdot\mathbf{b} & \mathbf{b}\cdot\mathbf{b} & \mathbf{c}\cdot\mathbf{b}\\ \mathbf{r}\cdot\mathbf{c} & \mathbf{b}\cdot\mathbf{c} & \mathbf{c}\cdot\mathbf{c}\end{vmatrix};\ \Delta_2=\begin{vmatrix}\mathbf{a}\cdot\mathbf{a} & \mathbf{r}\cdot\mathbf{a} & \mathbf{c}\cdot\mathbf{a}\\ \mathbf{a}\cdot\mathbf{b} & \mathbf{r}\cdot\mathbf{b} & \mathbf{c}\cdot\mathbf{b}\\ \mathbf{a}\cdot\mathbf{c} & \mathbf{r}\cdot\mathbf{c} & \mathbf{c}\cdot\mathbf{c}\end{vmatrix}$$

$$\Delta_3=\begin{vmatrix}\mathbf{a}\cdot\mathbf{a} & \mathbf{b}\cdot\mathbf{a} & \mathbf{r}\cdot\mathbf{a}\\ \mathbf{a}\cdot\mathbf{b} & \mathbf{b}\cdot\mathbf{b} & \mathbf{r}\cdot\mathbf{b}\\ \mathbf{a}\cdot\mathbf{c} & \mathbf{b}\cdot\mathbf{c} & \mathbf{r}\cdot\mathbf{c}\end{vmatrix};\ \Delta=\begin{vmatrix}\mathbf{a}\cdot\mathbf{a} & \mathbf{b}\cdot\mathbf{a} & \mathbf{c}\cdot\mathbf{a}\\ \mathbf{a}\cdot\mathbf{b} & \mathbf{b}\cdot\mathbf{b} & \mathbf{c}\cdot\mathbf{b}\\ \mathbf{a}\cdot\mathbf{c} & \mathbf{c}\cdot\mathbf{c} & \mathbf{c}\cdot\mathbf{c}\end{vmatrix}$$

51. The vector $\mathbf{r}$ is expressible in the form

(a) $\mathbf{r}=\dfrac{\Delta_1}{2\Delta}\mathbf{a}+\dfrac{\Delta_2}{2\Delta}\mathbf{b}+\dfrac{\Delta_3}{2\Delta}\mathbf{c}$

(b) $\mathbf{r}=\dfrac{2\Delta_1}{\Delta}\mathbf{a}+\dfrac{2\Delta_2}{\Delta}\mathbf{b}+\dfrac{2\Delta_3}{\Delta}\mathbf{c}$

(c) $\mathbf{r}=\dfrac{\Delta}{\Delta_1}\mathbf{a}+\dfrac{\Delta}{\Delta_2}\mathbf{b}+\dfrac{\Delta}{\Delta_3}\mathbf{c}$

(d) $\mathbf{r}=\dfrac{\Delta_1}{\Delta}\mathbf{a}+\dfrac{\Delta_2}{\Delta}\mathbf{b}+\dfrac{\Delta_3}{\Delta}\mathbf{c}$

52. The vector $\mathbf{r}$ is expressible as

(a) $\mathbf{r}=\dfrac{[\mathbf{r}\,\mathbf{b}\,\mathbf{c}]}{2[\mathbf{a}\,\mathbf{b}\,\mathbf{c}]}\mathbf{a}+\dfrac{[\mathbf{r}\mathbf{c}\mathbf{a}]}{2[\mathbf{a}\,\mathbf{b}\,\mathbf{c}]}\mathbf{b}+\dfrac{[\mathbf{r}\,\mathbf{a}\,\mathbf{b}]}{2[\mathbf{a}\,\mathbf{b}\,\mathbf{c}]}\mathbf{c}$

(b) $\mathbf{r}=\dfrac{2[\mathbf{r}\,\mathbf{b}\,\mathbf{c}]}{[\mathbf{a}\,\mathbf{b}\,\mathbf{c}]}\mathbf{a}+\dfrac{2[\mathbf{r}\,\mathbf{c}\,\mathbf{b}]}{[\mathbf{a}\,\mathbf{b}\,\mathbf{c}]}\mathbf{b}+\dfrac{2[\mathbf{r}\,\mathbf{a}\,\mathbf{b}]}{[\mathbf{a}\,\mathbf{b}\,\mathbf{c}]}\mathbf{c}$

(c) $\mathbf{r}=\dfrac{1}{[\mathbf{a}\,\mathbf{b}\,\mathbf{c}]}([\mathbf{r}\,\mathbf{b}\,\mathbf{c}]\mathbf{a}+[\mathbf{r}\,\mathbf{c}\,\mathbf{a}]\mathbf{b}+[\mathbf{r}\,\mathbf{a}\,\mathbf{b}]\,\mathbf{c})$

(d) None of the above

Passage V

(Q. Nos. 53 and 54)

- Let $g(x)=\int_0^x(3t^2+2t+9)\,dt$ and $f(x)$ be a decreasing function, $\forall\, x\ge 0$ such that $\mathbf{AB}=f(x)\hat{\mathbf{i}}+g(x)\hat{\mathbf{j}}$ and $\mathbf{AC}=g(x)\hat{\mathbf{i}}+f(x)\hat{\mathbf{j}}$ are the two smallest sides of a ΔABC whose circumcentre lies outside the triangle, $\forall\, x>0$.

53. Which of the following is true (for $x>0$)?

(a) $f(x)>0,\ g(x)<0$ (b) $f(x)<0,\ g(x)<0$

(c) $f(x)>0,\ g(x)>0$ (d) $f(x)<0, g(x)>0$

54. $\lim\limits_{t\to 0}\lim\limits_{x\to\infty}\left(\cot\left(\dfrac{\pi}{4}(1-t^2)\right)\right)^{f(x)\cdot g(x)}$ is equal to

(a) 0 (b) 1

(c) e (d) does not exist

Passage VI

(Q. Nos 55 and 56)

- Let $\mathbf{x}$, $\mathbf{y}$ and $\mathbf{z}$ be the vector, such that $|\mathbf{x}|=|\mathbf{y}|=|\mathbf{z}|=\sqrt{2}$ and $\mathbf{x}, \mathbf{y}, \mathbf{z}$ make angles of 60° with each other also,

$$\mathbf{x}\times(\mathbf{y}\times\mathbf{z})=\mathbf{a}$$
$$\mathbf{y}\times(\mathbf{z}\times\mathbf{x})=\mathbf{b}$$
and $$\mathbf{x}\times\mathbf{y}=\mathbf{c}\text{, then}$$

55. The value of $\mathbf{x}$ is

(a) $(\mathbf{a}+\mathbf{b})\times\mathbf{c}-(\mathbf{a}+\mathbf{b})$ (b) $(\mathbf{a}+\mathbf{b})-(\mathbf{a}+\mathbf{b})\times\mathbf{c}$

(c) $\dfrac{1}{2}\{(\mathbf{a}+\mathbf{b})\times\mathbf{c}-(\mathbf{a}+\mathbf{b})\}$ (d) None of these

56. The value of $\mathbf{y}$ is

(a) $\dfrac{1}{2}[(\mathbf{a}+\mathbf{b})+(\mathbf{a}+\mathbf{b})\times\mathbf{c}]$ (b) $2[(\mathbf{a}+\mathbf{b})+(\mathbf{a}+\mathbf{b})\times\mathbf{c}]$

(c) $4[(\mathbf{a}+\mathbf{b})+(\mathbf{a}+\mathbf{b})\times\mathbf{c}]$ (d) None of these

Passage VII
(Q. Nos. 57 and 58)

- **a, b** and **c** are non-zero unit vectors inclined pairwise with the same angle θ. p, q and r are non-zero scalars satisfying $\mathbf{a}\times\mathbf{b}+\mathbf{b}\times\mathbf{c}=p\mathbf{a}+q\mathbf{b}+r\mathbf{c}$. Now, answer the following questions.

57. $\frac{q}{p}+2\cos\theta$ is equal to

(a) 1 (b) $2[\mathbf{a}\ \mathbf{b}\ \mathbf{c}]$
(c) 0 (d) None of these

58. $|(p+q)\cos\theta+r|$ is equal to

(a) $(1+\cos\theta)\sqrt{1-2\cos\theta}$
(b) $2\sin^2\frac{\theta}{2}|\sqrt{1+2\cos\theta}|$
(c) $(1-\sin\theta)|\sqrt{1+2\cos\theta}|$
(d) None of the above

Stem Based Questions

Stem I
(Q. Nos. 59 and 60)

- Let **a**, **b** and **c** be three vectors having magnitudes 1, 2 and 3 units respectively, such that $|[\mathbf{a}\ \mathbf{b}\ \mathbf{c}]|=6$. If **r** is a unit vector coplanar with **b** and **c** and $\mathbf{r}\cdot\mathbf{b}=1$

59. Value of $4|(\mathbf{a}\times\mathbf{c})\times\mathbf{r}|^2$ is equal to ....

60. Value of $\sqrt{3}|[\mathbf{a}\ \mathbf{b}\ \mathbf{r}]|$ is equal to ....

Stem II
(Q. Nos. 61 and 62)

- Let **a** and **b** be two non-zero and non-collinear vectors ($|\mathbf{a}|=1$) such that vectors $3(\mathbf{a}\times\mathbf{b})$ and $2(\mathbf{b}-(\mathbf{a}\cdot\mathbf{b})\mathbf{a})$ represents two sides of a triangle. If area of the triangle is $\frac{3}{4}(|\mathbf{b}|^4+4)$.

61. Value of $[|\mathbf{b}|]$ is equal to ....

62. Value of $|\mathbf{b}|^2+2$ is equal to ....

Stem III
(Q. Nos. 63 and 64)

- Let O be the origin and **OX, OY, OZ** be three unit vectors in the directions of the sides **QR**, **RP** and **PQ** respectively, of a ΔPQR. [2017 Adv.]

63. If the ΔPQR varies, the minimum value of $\cos(P+Q)+\cos(Q+R)+\cos(R+P)$ is λ, then $2|\lambda|$ is equal to ....

64. $|\mathbf{OX}\times\mathbf{OY}|=\lambda\sin(P+Q)$, then λ is equal to ....

Single Integer Type Questions

65. Let $\hat{\mathbf{u}}$, $\hat{\mathbf{v}}$ and $\hat{\mathbf{w}}$ are three unit vectors, the angle between $\hat{\mathbf{u}}$ and $\hat{\mathbf{v}}$ is twice that of the angle between $\hat{\mathbf{u}}$ and $\hat{\mathbf{w}}$ and $\hat{\mathbf{v}}$ and $\hat{\mathbf{w}}$, then $[\hat{\mathbf{u}}\ \hat{\mathbf{v}}\ \hat{\mathbf{w}}]$ is equal to

66. If **a**, **b** and **c** are three vectors such that $[\mathbf{a}\ \mathbf{b}\ \mathbf{c}]=1$, then find the value of $[\mathbf{a}+\mathbf{b}\ \ \mathbf{b}+\mathbf{c}\ \ \mathbf{c}+\mathbf{a}]+[\mathbf{a}\times\mathbf{b}\ \ \mathbf{b}\times\mathbf{c}\ \ \mathbf{c}\times\mathbf{a}]+[\mathbf{a}\times(\mathbf{b}\times\mathbf{c})\ \ \mathbf{b}\times(\mathbf{c}\times\mathbf{a})\ \ \mathbf{c}\times(\mathbf{a}\times\mathbf{b})]$.

67. If $\hat{\mathbf{a}}$, $\hat{\mathbf{b}}$ and $\hat{\mathbf{c}}$ are three unit vectors and α, β and γ are scalars such that $\hat{\mathbf{c}}=\alpha\hat{\mathbf{a}}+\beta\hat{\mathbf{b}}+\gamma(\hat{\mathbf{a}}\times\hat{\mathbf{b}})$. If it is given that $\hat{\mathbf{a}}\cdot\hat{\mathbf{b}}=0$ and $\hat{\mathbf{c}}$ makes equal angle with both $\hat{\mathbf{a}}$ and $\hat{\mathbf{b}}$, then evaluate $\alpha^2+\beta^2+\gamma^2$.

68. The three vectors $\hat{\mathbf{i}}+\hat{\mathbf{j}}$, $\hat{\mathbf{j}}+\hat{\mathbf{k}}$ and $\hat{\mathbf{k}}+\hat{\mathbf{i}}$ taken two at a time form three planes. If V be the volume of the tetrahedron having adjacent sides as the three unit vectors drawn perpendicular to those three planes, then find the value of $9\sqrt{3}V$.

69. Let $\hat{\mathbf{c}}$ be a unit vector coplanar with $\mathbf{a}=\hat{\mathbf{i}}-\hat{\mathbf{j}}+2\hat{\mathbf{k}}$ and $\mathbf{b}=2\hat{\mathbf{i}}-\hat{\mathbf{j}}+\hat{\mathbf{k}}$ such that $\hat{\mathbf{c}}$ is perpendicular to **a**. If P be the projection of $\hat{\mathbf{c}}$ along **b**, where $P=\frac{\sqrt{11}}{k}$, then find k.

70. Let **a**, **b** and **c** are three vectors having magnitudes 1, 2 and 3, respectively satisfy the relation $[\mathbf{a}\ \mathbf{b}\ \mathbf{c}]=6$. If $\hat{\mathbf{d}}$ is a unit vector coplanar with **b** and **c** such that $\mathbf{b}\cdot\hat{\mathbf{d}}=1$, then evaluate $|(\mathbf{a}\times\mathbf{c})\cdot\hat{\mathbf{d}}|^2+|(\mathbf{a}\times\mathbf{c})\times\hat{\mathbf{d}}|^2$.

71. Let $A(2\hat{\mathbf{i}}+3\hat{\mathbf{j}}+5\hat{\mathbf{k}})$, $B(-\hat{\mathbf{i}}+3\hat{\mathbf{j}}+2\hat{\mathbf{k}})$ and $C(\lambda\hat{\mathbf{i}}+5\hat{\mathbf{j}}+\mu\hat{\mathbf{k}})$ are vertices of a triangle and its median through A is equally inclined to the positive directions of the axes. The value of $2\lambda-\mu$ is equal to

72. If V is the volume of the parallelopiped having three coterminous edges as **a**, **b** and **c** are the volume of the parallelopiped having three coterminous edges as
$\alpha=(\mathbf{a}\cdot\mathbf{a})\mathbf{a}+(\mathbf{a}\cdot\mathbf{b})\mathbf{b}+(\mathbf{a}\cdot\mathbf{c})\mathbf{c}$,
$\beta=(\mathbf{b}\cdot\mathbf{a})\mathbf{a}+(\mathbf{b}\cdot\mathbf{b})\mathbf{b}+(\mathbf{b}\cdot\mathbf{c})\mathbf{c}$ and
$\gamma=(\mathbf{c}\cdot\mathbf{a})\mathbf{a}+(\mathbf{c}\cdot\mathbf{b})\mathbf{b}+(\mathbf{c}\cdot\mathbf{c})\mathbf{c}$ is V^{λ}, then $\lambda=$

73. If M and N are the mid-point of the diagonals AC and BD, respectively of a quadrilateral $ABCD$, then $\mathbf{AB}+\mathbf{AD}+\mathbf{CB}+\mathbf{CD}=k\mathbf{MN}$, where $k=$.......

74. If $\mathbf{a}\times\mathbf{b}=\mathbf{c}$, $\mathbf{b}\times\mathbf{c}=\mathbf{a}$, $\mathbf{c}\times\mathbf{a}=\mathbf{b}$. If vectors **a**, **b** and **c** are forming a right handed system, then the volume of tetrahedron formed by vectors $3\mathbf{a}-2\mathbf{b}+2\mathbf{c}$, $-\mathbf{a}-2\mathbf{c}$ and $2\mathbf{a}-3\mathbf{b}+4\mathbf{c}$ is ....

75. Let **a** and **c** be unit vectors inclined at $\frac{\pi}{3}$ with each other. If $(\mathbf{a}\times(\mathbf{b}\times\mathbf{c}))\cdot(\mathbf{a}\times\mathbf{c})=5$, then $-[\mathbf{a}\ \mathbf{b}\ \mathbf{c}]-1=$ ....

76. Volume of parallelopiped formed by vectors $\mathbf{a} \times \mathbf{b}, \mathbf{b} \times \mathbf{c}$ and $\mathbf{c} \times \mathbf{a}$ is 36 sq units, then the volume of the parallelopiped formed by the vectors is $(pq)^2$, then $p+q$ is equal to ....

77. The volume of the tetrahedron whose vertices are the points with position vectors $\hat{\mathbf{i}}+\hat{\mathbf{j}}+\hat{\mathbf{k}}$, $-\hat{\mathbf{i}}-3\hat{\mathbf{j}}+7\hat{\mathbf{k}}, \hat{\mathbf{i}}+2\hat{\mathbf{j}}-7\hat{\mathbf{k}}$ and $3\hat{\mathbf{i}}-4\hat{\mathbf{j}}+\lambda\hat{\mathbf{k}}$ is 22, then the digit at unit place of λ is.

78. Volume of a tetrahedron whose coterminous edges are $\mathbf{a}, \mathbf{b}$ and $\mathbf{c}$ is 3 and volume of a parallelopiped whose coterminous edges are $\mathbf{a}+\mathbf{b}-\mathbf{c}$, $\mathbf{a}-\mathbf{b}, \mathbf{b}-\mathbf{c}$ is V. Then, units digit of V is.

79. Let $\mathbf{a}$ and $\mathbf{b}$ be two unit vectors such that $\mathbf{a}\cdot\mathbf{b}=0$. For some $x, y \in \mathbf{R}$, let $\mathbf{c}=x\mathbf{a}+y\mathbf{b}+(\mathbf{a}\times\mathbf{b})$. If $|\mathbf{c}|=2$ and the vector $\mathbf{c}$ is inclined at the same angle α to both $\mathbf{a}$ and $\mathbf{b}$, then the value of $8\cos^2\alpha$ is .... **[2018 Adv.]**

Numerical Value Type Questions

80. Two points P and Q are given in the rectangular cartesian coordinates in the curve $y=2^{x+2}$, such that $\mathbf{OP}\cdot\hat{\mathbf{i}}=-1$ and $\mathbf{OQ}\cdot\hat{\mathbf{i}}=2$, where $\hat{\mathbf{i}}$ is a unit vector along the X-axis. The magnitude of $\mathbf{OQ}-4\mathbf{OP}$ is ....

81. The perpendicular distance of $A(1, 4, -2)$ from the segment BC, where $B(2, 1, -2)$ and $C(0, -5, 1)$ is $\frac{3}{7}\sqrt{p}$, then the value of p is ....

82. A non-zero vector $\mathbf{a}$ is parallel to the line of intersection of the plane determined by the vectors, $\hat{\mathbf{i}}, \hat{\mathbf{i}}+\hat{\mathbf{j}}$ and the plane determined by the vectors $\hat{\mathbf{i}}-\hat{\mathbf{j}}$ and $\hat{\mathbf{i}}+\hat{\mathbf{k}}$. If the angle between $\mathbf{a}$ and $\hat{\mathbf{i}}-2\hat{\mathbf{j}}+2\hat{\mathbf{k}}$ is $\frac{\pi}{\lambda}$, then the value of $\frac{1}{\lambda}$ is equal to ....

83. The vector $\hat{\mathbf{i}}+2\hat{\mathbf{j}}+2\hat{\mathbf{k}}$ turns through a right angle while passing through the positive X-axis on the way. The vector in its new position is $x\hat{\mathbf{i}}+y\hat{\mathbf{j}}+z\hat{\mathbf{k}}$. Then, the value of $\sqrt{2}xyz$ is equal to ....

84. Let $\hat{\mathbf{u}}$ and $\hat{\mathbf{v}}$ be unit vectors and $\mathbf{w}$ is a vector such that $\hat{\mathbf{u}}\times\hat{\mathbf{v}}+\hat{\mathbf{u}}=\mathbf{w}$ and $\mathbf{w}\times\hat{\mathbf{u}}=\hat{\mathbf{v}}$, the value of $[\hat{\mathbf{u}}\ \hat{\mathbf{v}}\ \mathbf{w}]$ is equal to ....

85. $\mathbf{A}, \mathbf{B}$ and $\mathbf{C}$ are three vectors given by $2\hat{\mathbf{i}}+\hat{\mathbf{k}}, \hat{\mathbf{i}}+\hat{\mathbf{j}}+\hat{\mathbf{k}}$ and $4\hat{\mathbf{i}}-3\hat{\mathbf{j}}+7\hat{\mathbf{k}}$, then value of $\frac{1}{2}|\mathbf{R}|$ is ...., which satisfies the relation $\mathbf{R}\times\mathbf{B}=\mathbf{C}\times\mathbf{B}$ and $\mathbf{R}\cdot\mathbf{A}=0$.

86. Let $\mathbf{a}, \mathbf{b}$ and $\mathbf{c}$ be three mutually perpendicular vectors of equal magnitude. If the vector $\mathbf{x}$ satisfies the equation. $\mathbf{a}\times[(\mathbf{x}-\mathbf{b})\times\mathbf{a}]+\mathbf{b}\times[(\mathbf{x}-\mathbf{c})\times\mathbf{b}]+\mathbf{c}\times[(\mathbf{x}-\mathbf{a})\times\mathbf{c}]=0$ and $x=\frac{\mathbf{a}+\mathbf{b}+\mathbf{c}}{p}$, then value of $\frac{p^2}{5}$ is equal to ....

87. Arc AC of a circle subtends a right angle at the centre O. Point B divides the arc in the ratio 1 : 2. If $\mathbf{OA}=\mathbf{a}$ and $\mathbf{OB}=\mathbf{b}$ such that $\mathbf{OC}=k_1\mathbf{a}+k_2\mathbf{b}$, then the value of $\frac{5(k_1^2+k_2^2)}{2}$ is equal to ....

Matching Type Questions

88. Given two vectors $\mathbf{a}=-\hat{\mathbf{i}}+2\hat{\mathbf{j}}+2\hat{\mathbf{k}}$ and $\mathbf{b}=-2\hat{\mathbf{i}}+\hat{\mathbf{j}}+2\hat{\mathbf{k}}$. Match the Column I with Column II and mark the correct option from the codes given below.

	Column I		Column II
A.	A vector coplanar with $\mathbf{a}$ and $\mathbf{b}$	p.	$-3\hat{\mathbf{i}}+3\hat{\mathbf{j}}+4\hat{\mathbf{k}}$
B.	A vector which is perpendicular to both $\mathbf{a}$ and $\mathbf{b}$	q.	$2\hat{\mathbf{i}}-2\hat{\mathbf{j}}+3\hat{\mathbf{k}}$
C.	A vector which is equally inclined to $\mathbf{a}$ and $\mathbf{b}$	r.	$\hat{\mathbf{i}}+\hat{\mathbf{j}}$
D.	A vector which forms a triangle with $\mathbf{a}$ and $\mathbf{b}$	s.	$\hat{\mathbf{i}}-\hat{\mathbf{j}}+5\hat{\mathbf{k}}$

89. Volume of parallelepiped formed by vectors $\mathbf{a}\times\mathbf{b}, \mathbf{b}\times\mathbf{c}$ and $\mathbf{c}\times\mathbf{a}$ is 36 sq units.

	Column I		Column II
A.	Volume of parallelopiped formed by vectors $\mathbf{a}, \mathbf{b}$ and $\mathbf{c}$ is	p.	0 sq units
B.	Volume of tetrahedron formed by vectors $\mathbf{a}, \mathbf{b}$ and $\mathbf{c}$ is	q.	12 sq units
C.	Volume of parallelopiped formed by vectors $\mathbf{a}+\mathbf{b}, \mathbf{b}+\mathbf{c}$ and $\mathbf{c}+\mathbf{a}$ is	r.	6 sq units
D.	Volume of parallelopiped formed by vectors $\mathbf{a}-\mathbf{b}, \mathbf{b}-\mathbf{c}$ and $\mathbf{c}-\mathbf{a}$ is	s.	1 sq units

90. Match the statement of Column I with values of Column II.

	Column I		Column II
A.	Let $\mathbf{a}, \mathbf{b}$ and $\mathbf{c}$ be the three vectors such that $\mathbf{a}\cdot(\mathbf{b}+\mathbf{c})=\mathbf{b}\cdot(\mathbf{c}+\mathbf{a})=\mathbf{c}\cdot(\mathbf{a}+\mathbf{b})=0$ and $|\mathbf{a}|=1, |\mathbf{b}|=4, |\mathbf{c}|=8$, then $|\mathbf{a}+\mathbf{b}+\mathbf{c}|$ is equal to	p.	$\frac{5}{2}$
B.	If $\mathbf{a}_1, \mathbf{a}_2$ and $\mathbf{a}_3$ are vectors reciprocal to the non-coplanar vectors $\mathbf{b}_1, \mathbf{b}_2, \mathbf{b}_3$ then $[\mathbf{a}_1\ \mathbf{a}_2\ \mathbf{a}_3][\mathbf{b}_1\ \mathbf{b}_2\ \mathbf{b}_3]$ is equal to	q.	9
C.	$ABCD$ is a quadrilateral with $\mathbf{AB}=\mathbf{a}$, $\mathbf{AD}=\mathbf{b}$ and $\mathbf{AC}=2\mathbf{a}+3\mathbf{b}$. If its area is α times the area of the parallelogram with AB and AD as its adjacent sides, then α is equal to	r.	8
D.	If $\mathbf{d}=x(\mathbf{a}\times\mathbf{b})+y(\mathbf{b}\times\mathbf{c})+z(\mathbf{c}\times\mathbf{a})$ and $[\mathbf{a}\ \mathbf{b}\ \mathbf{c}]=\frac{1}{8}$, then $x+y+z=R(\mathbf{a}+\mathbf{b}+\mathbf{c})\cdot\mathbf{d}$, where $R=$ adjacent sides, then R is equal to	s.	1

Previous Years Questions

91. Let the position vectors of the points P, Q, R and S be

$\mathbf{a} = \hat{\mathbf{i}} + 2\hat{\mathbf{j}} - 5\hat{\mathbf{k}}$, $\mathbf{b} = 3\hat{\mathbf{i}} + 6\hat{\mathbf{j}} + 3\hat{\mathbf{k}}$, $\mathbf{c} = \frac{17}{5}\hat{\mathbf{i}} + \frac{16}{5}\hat{\mathbf{j}} + 7\hat{\mathbf{k}}$ and

$\mathbf{d} = 2\hat{\mathbf{i}} + \hat{\mathbf{j}} + \hat{\mathbf{k}}$, respectively. Then, which of the following statements is true? **[Single Correct Type, 2023 Adv.]**

(a) The points P, Q, R and S are not coplanar

(b) $\frac{\mathbf{b} + 2\mathbf{d}}{3}$ is the position vector of a point which divides PR internally in the ratio 5 : 4

(c) $\frac{\mathbf{b} + 2\mathbf{d}}{3}$ is the position vector of a point which divides PR externally in the ratio 5 : 4.

(d) The square of the magnitude of the vector $\mathbf{b} \times \mathbf{d}$ is 95

92. Let $\hat{\mathbf{i}}, \hat{\mathbf{j}}$ and $\hat{\mathbf{k}}$ be the unit vectors along the three positive coordinate axes.

Let $\mathbf{a} = 3\hat{\mathbf{i}} + \hat{\mathbf{j}} - \hat{\mathbf{k}}$, $\mathbf{b} = \hat{\mathbf{i}} + b_2\hat{\mathbf{j}} + b_3\hat{\mathbf{k}}$, $b_2, b_3 \in R$ and $\mathbf{c} = c_1\hat{\mathbf{i}} + c_2\hat{\mathbf{j}} + c_3\hat{\mathbf{k}}$, $c_1, c_2, c_3 \in R$ be three vectors such that $b_2 b_3 > 0$, $\mathbf{a} \cdot \mathbf{b} = 0$

and $\begin{bmatrix} 0 & -c_3 & c_2 \\ c_3 & 0 & -c_1 \\ -c_2 & c_1 & 0 \end{bmatrix} \begin{bmatrix} 1 \\ b_2 \\ b_3 \end{bmatrix} = \begin{bmatrix} 3 - c_1 \\ 1 - c_2 \\ -1 - c_3 \end{bmatrix}$.

Then, which of the following is/are true ? **[More than One Option Correct, 2022 Adv.]**

(a) $\mathbf{a} \cdot \mathbf{c} = 0$

(b) $\mathbf{b} \cdot \mathbf{c} = 0$

(c) $|\mathbf{b}| > \sqrt{10}$

(d) $|\mathbf{c}| \le \sqrt{11}$

93. Let O be the origin and $\mathbf{OA} = 2\hat{\mathbf{i}} + 2\hat{\mathbf{j}} + \hat{\mathbf{k}}$, $\mathbf{OB} = \hat{\mathbf{i}} - 2\hat{\mathbf{j}} + 2\hat{\mathbf{k}}$ and $\mathbf{OC} = \frac{1}{2}(\mathbf{OB} - \lambda\mathbf{OA})$, for some $\lambda > 0$. If $|\mathbf{OB} \times \mathbf{OC}| = \frac{9}{2}$, then which of the following statements is (are) TRUE? **[More than One Option Correct, 2021 Adv.]**

(a) Projection of $\mathbf{OC}$ on $\mathbf{OA}$ is $-\frac{3}{2}$.

(b) Area of the ΔOAB is $\frac{9}{2}$.

(c) Area of the ΔABC is $9/2$.

(d) The acute angle between the diagonals of the parallelogram with adjacent sides $\mathbf{OA}$ and $\mathbf{OC}$ is $\frac{\pi}{3}$.

94. Let $\mathbf{u}$, $\mathbf{v}$ and $\mathbf{w}$ be vectors in three-dimensional space, where $\mathbf{u}$ and $\mathbf{v}$ are unit vectors which are not perpendicular to each other and $\mathbf{u} \cdot \mathbf{w} = 1$, $\mathbf{v} \cdot \mathbf{w} = 1$, $\mathbf{w} \cdot \mathbf{w} = 4$.

If the volume of the parallelopiped, whose adjacent sides are represented by the vectors $\mathbf{u}$, $\mathbf{v}$ and $\mathbf{w}$, is $\sqrt{2}$, then the value of $|3\mathbf{u} + 5\mathbf{v}|$ is **[Numerical Value Type, 2021 Adv.]**

95. Let a and b be positive real numbers. Suppose $\mathbf{PQ} = a\hat{\mathbf{i}} + b\hat{\mathbf{j}}$ and $\mathbf{PS} = a\hat{\mathbf{i}} - b\hat{\mathbf{j}}$ are adjacent sides of a parallelogram $PQRS$. Let $\mathbf{u}$ and $\mathbf{v}$ be the projection vectors of $\mathbf{w} = \hat{\mathbf{i}} + \hat{\mathbf{j}}$ along $\mathbf{PQ}$ and $\mathbf{PS}$, respectively. If $|\mathbf{u}| + |\mathbf{v}| = |\mathbf{w}|$ and if the area of the parallelogram $PQRS$ is 8, then which of the following statements is/are TRUE?

[More than One Option Correct, 2020 Adv.]

(a) $a + b = 4$

(b) $a - b = 2$

(c) The length of the diagonal PR of the parallelogram $PQRS$ is 4

(d) $\mathbf{w}$ is an angle bisector of the vectors $\mathbf{PQ}$ and $\mathbf{PS}$

96. In a ΔPQR, let $\mathbf{a} = \mathbf{QR}$, $\mathbf{b} = \mathbf{RP}$ and $\mathbf{c} = \mathbf{PQ}$. If $|\mathbf{a}| = 3$, $|\mathbf{b}| = 4$ and $\frac{\mathbf{a} \cdot (\mathbf{c} - \mathbf{b})}{\mathbf{c} \cdot (\mathbf{a} - \mathbf{b})} = \frac{|\mathbf{a}|}{|\mathbf{a}| + |\mathbf{b}|}$, then the value of $|\mathbf{a} \times \mathbf{b}|^2$ is .... **[Numerical Value Type, 2020 Adv.]**

97. Let $\mathbf{a} = 2\hat{\mathbf{i}} + \hat{\mathbf{j}} - \hat{\mathbf{k}}$ and $\mathbf{b} = \hat{\mathbf{i}} + 2\hat{\mathbf{j}} + \hat{\mathbf{k}}$ be two vectors. Consider a vector $\mathbf{c} = \alpha\mathbf{a} + \beta\mathbf{b}$, $\alpha, \beta \in R$. If the projection of $\mathbf{c}$ on the vector $(\mathbf{a} + \mathbf{b})$ is $3\sqrt{2}$, then the minimum value of $(\mathbf{c} - (\mathbf{a} \times \mathbf{b})) \cdot \mathbf{c}$ equals ....

[Numerical Value Type, 2019 Adv.]

EXERCISE 3

Challenging Problems

1. Determine the values of c, so that for all real x, the vectors $cx\,\hat{\mathbf{i}} - 6\hat{\mathbf{j}} + 3\hat{\mathbf{k}}$ and $x\hat{\mathbf{i}} + 2\hat{\mathbf{j}} + 2cx\,\hat{\mathbf{k}}$ make an obtuse angle with each other.

2. Let I be the incentre of ΔABC. Using vectors prove that for any point P, $a(\mathbf{PA})^2 + b(\mathbf{PB})^2 + c(\mathbf{PC})^2$
$= a(\mathbf{IA})^2 + b(\mathbf{IB})^2 + c(\mathbf{IC})^2 + (a+b+c)(\mathbf{IP})^2$
where a, b and c have usual meanings.

3. If two circles intersect, prove by using vector method, that the line joining their centres is perpendicular to their common chord.

4. In ΔABC, points D, E and F are taken on the sides BC, CA and AB respectively, such that $\dfrac{BD}{DC} = \dfrac{CE}{EA} = \dfrac{AF}{AB} = n$. Using vectors, prove that
$$\Delta DEF = \frac{n^2 - n + 1}{(n+1)^2}\Delta\, ABC.$$

5. Let the area of a given $\Delta\, ABC$ be Δ. Points A_1, B_1 and C_1 are the mid-points of the sides BC, CA and AB, respectively. Point A_2 is the mid-point of CA, lines C_1A_1 and $A\,A_2$ meet the median BB_1 at E and D. If Δ is the area of the quadrilateral A_1A_2DE, using vectors prove that $\dfrac{\Delta_1}{\Delta} = \dfrac{11}{56}$.

6. Let ABC be an acute angled triangle with centriod G and the internal bisectors of angles A, B and C meets BC, CA and AB in M, N and K respectively, using vectors prove that if G lies on one of the sides of $\Delta\, MNK$, then one of the altitudes of $\Delta\, ABC$ equals the sum of other two.

7. Three poles of height x, $x+y$ and $x+z$ are posted at the vertices A, B and C of a triangular park of sides a, b and c, respectively. A plane sheet is mounted at the tops of the poles. If the plane of the sheet is inclined at an angle θ to the horizontal plane, prove using vector
$$\theta = \tan^{-1}\left\{\frac{\sqrt{\dfrac{y^2}{c^2} + \dfrac{z^2}{b^2} - \dfrac{2yz}{bc}\cos A}}{\sin A}\right\}.$$

8. Let $\hat{\mathbf{u}}$ and $\hat{\mathbf{v}}$ be unit vectors. If $\mathbf{w}$ is a vector such that $\mathbf{w} + (\mathbf{w}\times\mathbf{u}) = \mathbf{v}$, then prove that $|(\mathbf{u}\times\mathbf{v})\cdot\mathbf{w}| \le \dfrac{1}{2}$ and that the equality holds if and only if $\mathbf{u}$ is perpendicular to $\mathbf{v}$.

9. Prove that
$$\mathbf{R} + \frac{[\mathbf{R}.(\beta\times(\beta\times\alpha))]\alpha}{|\alpha\times\beta|^2} + \frac{\mathbf{R}.(\alpha\times(\alpha\times\beta))]\beta}{|\alpha\times\beta|^2} = \frac{[\mathbf{R}\,\alpha\,\beta\,](\alpha\times\beta)}{|\alpha\times\beta\,|^2},$$
where α, β are vectors.

10. A pyramid with vertex at the point P whose position vector is $4\hat{\mathbf{i}} + 2\hat{\mathbf{j}} + 2\sqrt{3}\,\hat{\mathbf{k}}$ has a regular hexagonal base $ABCDEF$. Position vectors of points A and B are $\hat{\mathbf{i}}$ and $\hat{\mathbf{i}} + 2\hat{\mathbf{j}}$. Centre of the base has the position vector $\hat{\mathbf{i}} + \hat{\mathbf{j}} + \sqrt{3}\,\hat{\mathbf{k}}$. Altitude drawn from P on the base meets the diagonal AD at point G. Find all possible position vectors of G. It is given that volume of the pyramid is $6\sqrt{3}$ cu units.

11. Let $\hat{\mathbf{a}}$, $\hat{\mathbf{b}}$ and $\hat{\mathbf{c}}$ be the non-coplanar unit vectors. The angle between $\hat{\mathbf{b}}$ and $\hat{\mathbf{c}}$ be α and angle between $\hat{\mathbf{c}}$ and $\hat{\mathbf{a}}$ be β and between $\hat{\mathbf{a}}$ and $\hat{\mathbf{b}}$ be γ. If $A(\hat{\mathbf{a}}\cos\alpha, 0)$, $B(\hat{\mathbf{b}}\cos\beta, 0)$ and $C(\hat{\mathbf{c}}\cos\gamma, 0)$, then show that in ΔABC.
$$\frac{|\hat{\mathbf{a}}\times(\hat{\mathbf{b}}\times\hat{\mathbf{c}})|}{\sin A} = \frac{|\hat{\mathbf{b}}\times(\hat{\mathbf{c}}\times\hat{\mathbf{a}})|}{\sin B} = \frac{|\hat{\mathbf{c}}\times(\hat{\mathbf{a}}\times\hat{\mathbf{b}})|}{\sin C}$$
$$= \frac{\pi|\,\hat{\mathbf{a}}(\hat{\mathbf{b}}\times\hat{\mathbf{c}})|}{|\Sigma\sin\alpha\cos\beta\cos\gamma\,\hat{\eta}|}$$
where, $\hat{\eta}_1 = \dfrac{\hat{\mathbf{b}}\times\hat{\mathbf{c}}}{|\hat{\mathbf{b}}\times\hat{\mathbf{c}}|}$, $\hat{\eta}_2 = \dfrac{\hat{\mathbf{c}}\times\hat{\mathbf{a}}}{|\hat{\mathbf{c}}\times\hat{\mathbf{a}}|}$ and $\hat{\eta}_3 = \dfrac{\hat{\mathbf{a}}\times\hat{\mathbf{b}}}{|\hat{\mathbf{a}}\times\hat{\mathbf{b}}|}$.

12. Given angles, A, B and C of $\Delta\, ABC$. Let M be the mid-point of segment AB and let D be the foot of the bisector of $\angle C$. Find the ratio of $\dfrac{\text{Area of } \Delta\, CDM}{\text{Area of } \Delta\, ABC}$ and also $\cos\phi = \cos\angle DCM$.

13. In the ΔABC a point P is taken on the side AB such that $AP : BP = 1:2$ and a point Q is taken on the side BC such that $CQ : BQ = 2:1$. If R be the point of intersection of lines AQ and CP, using vector find the area of $\Delta\, ABC$, if it is known that area of ΔABC is one unit.

14. The vector $\hat{\mathbf{i}} + 2\hat{\mathbf{j}} + 2\hat{\mathbf{k}}$ turns through a right angle while passing through the positive X-axis on the way. Find the vector in its new position.

15. Let $\hat{\mathbf{x}}$, $\hat{\mathbf{y}}$ and $\hat{\mathbf{z}}$ be unit vectors such that $\hat{\mathbf{x}} + \hat{\mathbf{y}} + \hat{\mathbf{z}} = \mathbf{a}$, $\hat{\mathbf{x}}\times(\hat{\mathbf{y}}\times\hat{\mathbf{z}}) = \mathbf{b}$, $(\hat{\mathbf{x}}\times\hat{\mathbf{y}})\times\hat{\mathbf{z}} = \mathbf{c}$, $\mathbf{a}\cdot\hat{\mathbf{x}} = \dfrac{3}{2}$, $\mathbf{a}\cdot\hat{\mathbf{y}} = \dfrac{7}{4}$ and $|\mathbf{a}| = 2$. Find $\mathbf{x}$, $\mathbf{y}$ and $\mathbf{z}$ in terms of $\mathbf{a}$, $\mathbf{b}$ and $\mathbf{c}$.

16. Given vectors $\mathbf{CB} = \mathbf{a}$, $\mathbf{CA} = \mathbf{b}$ and $\mathbf{CO} = \mathbf{x}$, where O is the centre of circle circumscribed about $\Delta\, ABC$, then find vector $\mathbf{x}$.

Answer Key

Exercise 1

1. (d)	2. (a)	3. (b)	4. (b)	5. (c)	6. (d)	7. (b)	8. (b)	9. (b)	10. (c)
11. (a)	12. (a)	13. (c)	14. (a)	15. (c)	16. (a)	17. (a)	18. (a)	19. (b)	20. (a)
21. (c)	22. (c)	23. (d)	24. (d)	25. (b)	26. (b)	27. (d)	28. (336)	29. (11)	30. (0.625)
31. (109)	32. (2)	33. (2.5)	34. (5)	35. (12)	36. (3)	37. (41)	38. (28.75)	39. (4)	40. (1.5)
41. (48)	42. (48)	43. (b)	44. (b)	45. (d)	46. (a)	47. (d)	48. (d)	49. (a)	50. (d)
51. (b)	52. (b)	53. (d)	54. (5)	55. (38)	56. (48)	57. (38)	58. (d)	59. (c)	60. (a)
61. (b)	62. (d)	63. (d)	64. (b)	65. (b)	66. (a)	67. (d)	68. (c)	69. (d)	70. (a)
71. (c)	72. (c)	73. (66)	74. (285)	75. (11)	76. (3)	77. (36)	78. (8)	79. (b)	80. (b)
81. (b)	82. (a)	83. (a)	84. (a)	85. (b)	86. (c)	87. (d)	88. (c)	89. (b)	90. (a)
91. (3501)	92. (2)	93. (b)	94. (d)	95. (14)	96. (a)	97. (a)	98. (0)	99. (c)	100. (5)
101. (3)	102. (a)	103. (c)	104. (4)	105. (c)	106. (a)	107. (b)	108. (d)		

Exercise 2

1. (a)	2. (b)	3. (a)	4. (d)	5. (c)	6. (a)	7. (a)	8. (b)	9. (c)	10. (b)
11. (d)	12. (c)	13. (b)	14. (d)	15. (a)	16. (a)	17. (d)	18. (b)	19. (d)	20. (c)
21. (b)	22. (a,c)	23. (a,c)	24. (b,d)	25. (a,b,c)	26. (a,b)	27. (a,c)	28. (a,c)	29. (a,b,d)	30. (b,c,d)
31. (a,c)	32. (a,b)	33. (a,d)	34. (a,b,c)	35. (a,c)	36. (a,b,c)	37. (b,c)	38. (b,c)	39. (a,d)	40. (a,b,d)
41. (b,c)	42. (a,b)	43. (b,c)	44. (a,c,d)	45. (b)	46. (a)	47. (b)	48. (d)	49. (c)	50. (a)
51. (d)	52. (c)	53. (d)	54. (a)	55. (c)	56. (a)	57. (c)	58. (b)	59. (27)	60. (3)
61. (1)	62. (4)	63. (3)	64. (1)	65. (0)	66. (3)	67. (1)	68. (2)	69. (6)	70. (9)
71. (4)	72. (3)	73. (4)	74. (2)	75. (9)	76. (5)	77. (1)	78. (18)	79. (3)	80. (10)
81. (26)	82. (0.25)	83. (2)	84. (1)	85. (34.5)	86. (0.8)	87. (17.5)			

88. (A) → (p,r), (B) → (q), (C) → (s), (D) → (p),
89. (A) → (r), (B) → (s), (C) → (q), (D) → (p),
90. (A) → (q), (B) → (s), (C) → (p), (D) → (r),

91. (b)	92. (b,c,d)	93. (b,c,d)	94. (7)	95. (a,c,d)	96. (108)	97. (18)

Solutions

Exercise 1 - JEE Main Pattern

1. Since, $\mathbf{a} \perp \mathbf{b} \Rightarrow \mathbf{a} \cdot \mathbf{b} = 0$

$$|\mathbf{a} - \mathbf{b}|^2 = (\mathbf{a} - \mathbf{b})^2 = \mathbf{a}^2 + \mathbf{b}^2 - 2\,\mathbf{a} \cdot \mathbf{b} = 25 + 25$$

$$\Rightarrow \quad |\mathbf{a} - \mathbf{b}| = 5\sqrt{2}$$

2. $|\mathbf{a} - \mathbf{b}| = \sqrt{1^2 + 1^2 - 2 \cdot 1^2 \cos\theta} = \sqrt{2(1 - \cos\theta)}$

$$= \sqrt{2} \times \sqrt{2} \sin\frac{\theta}{2} = 2\sin\frac{\theta}{2} \Rightarrow \sin\frac{\theta}{2} = \frac{|\mathbf{a} - \mathbf{b}|}{2}$$

3. Required value $= \dfrac{\mathbf{b} \cdot \mathbf{a}}{|\mathbf{b}|} \Big/ \dfrac{\mathbf{a} \cdot \mathbf{b}}{|\mathbf{a}|} = \dfrac{|\mathbf{a}|}{|\mathbf{b}|} = \dfrac{7}{3}$

4. $(\mathbf{a} \times \mathbf{b})^2 = a^2b^2 - (\mathbf{a} \cdot \mathbf{b})^2 = \begin{vmatrix} \mathbf{a} \cdot \mathbf{a} & \mathbf{a} \cdot \mathbf{b} \\ \mathbf{b} \cdot \mathbf{a} & \mathbf{b} \cdot \mathbf{b} \end{vmatrix}$

5. Force $(\mathbf{F}) = 2\hat{\mathbf{i}} + \hat{\mathbf{j}} - \hat{\mathbf{k}}$ and its position vector $= 2\hat{\mathbf{i}} - \hat{\mathbf{j}}$.
We know that the position vector of a force about origin $(\mathbf{r}) = (2\hat{\mathbf{i}} - \hat{\mathbf{j}}) - (0\hat{\mathbf{i}} + 0\hat{\mathbf{j}} + 0\hat{\mathbf{k}})$ or $\mathbf{r} = 2\hat{\mathbf{i}} - \hat{\mathbf{j}}$.

Therefore, moment of the force about origin

$$= \mathbf{r} \times \mathbf{F} = \begin{vmatrix} \hat{\mathbf{i}} & \hat{\mathbf{j}} & \hat{\mathbf{k}} \\ 2 & -1 & 0 \\ 2 & 1 & -1 \end{vmatrix} = \hat{\mathbf{i}} + 2\hat{\mathbf{j}} + 4\hat{\mathbf{k}}.$$

6. Let the required vector be $\mathbf{d} = d_1\hat{\mathbf{i}} + d_2\hat{\mathbf{j}} + d_3\hat{\mathbf{k}}$
where, $d_1^2 + d_2^2 + d_3^2 = 51$ [given] ...(i)

Now, each of the given vectors **a**, **b** and **c** is a unit vectors.

$$\cos\theta = \frac{\mathbf{d} \cdot \mathbf{a}}{|\mathbf{d}||\mathbf{a}|} = \frac{\mathbf{d} \cdot \mathbf{b}}{|\mathbf{d}||\mathbf{b}|} = \frac{\mathbf{d} \cdot \mathbf{c}}{|\mathbf{d}||\mathbf{c}|}$$

or $\quad \mathbf{d} \cdot \mathbf{a} = \mathbf{d} \cdot \mathbf{b} = \mathbf{d} \cdot \mathbf{c}$

[$\because |\mathbf{d}| = \sqrt{51}$ cancels out and $|\mathbf{a}| = |\mathbf{b}| = |\mathbf{c}| = 1$]

Hence, $\dfrac{1}{3}(d_1 - 2d_2 + 2d_3) = \dfrac{1}{5}(-4d_1 + 0d_2 - 3d_3) = d_2$

$\Rightarrow \quad d_1 - 5d_2 + 2d_3 = 0$

and $\quad 4d_1 + 5d_2 + 3d_3 = 0$

On solving, we get $\dfrac{d_1}{5} = \dfrac{d_2}{-1} = \dfrac{d_3}{-5} = \lambda$ (say)

On putting d_1, d_2 and d_3 in Eq. (i), we get $\lambda = \pm 1$
Hence, the required vectors are $\pm(5\hat{\mathbf{i}} - \hat{\mathbf{j}} - 5\hat{\mathbf{k}})$.

7. $\mathbf{x} + \mathbf{y} + \mathbf{z} = \mathbf{0} \Rightarrow \mathbf{x} = -(\mathbf{y} + \mathbf{z})$

$$|\mathbf{x}|^2 = (\mathbf{y} + \mathbf{z}) \cdot (\mathbf{y} + \mathbf{z})$$

$$\Rightarrow \quad |\mathbf{x}|^2 = |\mathbf{y}|^2 + |\mathbf{z}|^2 + 2\mathbf{y} \cdot \mathbf{z}$$

$$\Rightarrow \quad |\mathbf{x}|^2 = |\mathbf{y}|^2 + |\mathbf{z}|^2 + 2|\mathbf{y}||\mathbf{z}|\cos\theta$$

$$\Rightarrow \quad 4 = 4 + 4 + 2 \times 2 \times 2\cos\theta$$

$$\Rightarrow \quad \cos\theta = \frac{-1}{2}$$

$$\Rightarrow \quad \theta = 120^\circ$$

$\therefore \operatorname{cosec}^2 120^\circ + \cot^2 120^\circ$

$$= \left(\frac{2}{\sqrt{3}}\right)^2 + \left(-\frac{1}{\sqrt{3}}\right)^2 = \frac{4}{3} + \frac{1}{3} = \frac{5}{3}$$

8. For acute angle $\mathbf{a} \cdot \mathbf{b} > 0$

i.e. $\quad -3x + 2x^2 + 1 > 0$

$$\Rightarrow \quad (x - 1)(2x - 1) > 0 \Rightarrow x \in \left(-\infty, \frac{1}{2}\right) \cup (1, \infty) \qquad \text{...(i)}$$

For obtuse angle between **b** and X-axis, $\mathbf{b} \cdot \hat{\mathbf{i}} < 0$

$$\Rightarrow \qquad x < 0 \qquad \text{...(ii)}$$

Now, (i) $\cap$ (ii), we get $x < 0$.

9. $(3\mathbf{p} + \mathbf{q}) \cdot (5\mathbf{p} - 3\mathbf{q}) = 0$

or $\quad 15\mathbf{p}^2 - 3\mathbf{q}^2 = 4\mathbf{p} \cdot \mathbf{q}$ ...(i)

$(2\mathbf{p} + \mathbf{q}) \cdot (4\mathbf{p} - 2\mathbf{q}) = 0$ or $8\mathbf{p}^2 = 2\mathbf{q}^2 \Rightarrow \mathbf{q}^2 = 4\mathbf{p}^2$ ...(ii)

Now, $\quad \cos\theta = \dfrac{\mathbf{p} \cdot \mathbf{q}}{|\mathbf{p}||\mathbf{q}|}$

On substituting $\mathbf{q}^2 = 4\mathbf{p}^2$ in Eq. (i), we get

$$\Rightarrow \quad 3\mathbf{p}^2 = 4\mathbf{p} \cdot \mathbf{q}$$

$$\cos\theta = \frac{3}{4} \cdot \frac{\mathbf{p}^2}{|\mathbf{p}|2|\mathbf{p}|} = \frac{3}{8} \qquad [\because |\mathbf{q}| = 2|\mathbf{p}|]$$

$$\Rightarrow \quad \sin\theta = \frac{\sqrt{55}}{8}$$

10. $\hat{\mathbf{n}} = a_1\hat{\mathbf{i}} + a_2\hat{\mathbf{j}} + a_3\hat{\mathbf{k}}$, where, $a_1^2 + a_2^2 + a_3^2 = 1$

$\mathbf{u} \cdot \hat{\mathbf{n}} = 0 \Rightarrow a_1 + a_2 = 0$

Also, $\quad \mathbf{v} \cdot \hat{\mathbf{n}} = 0 \Rightarrow a_1 - a_2 = 0$

Hence, $\quad a_1 = a_2 = 0$

$\therefore \quad a_3 = 1$ or -1

$\therefore \quad \hat{\mathbf{n}} = \hat{\mathbf{k}}$ or $-\hat{\mathbf{k}}$

$$|\mathbf{w} \cdot \hat{\mathbf{n}}| = 3$$

11. To find $(\mathbf{a} - \mathbf{b}) \cdot \mathbf{a}$ i.e. $|\mathbf{a}|^2 - \mathbf{a} \cdot \mathbf{b}$ ...(i)

Now, $\quad \mathbf{a} + \mathbf{b} = \mathbf{c}$

$\Rightarrow |\mathbf{a}|^2 + |\mathbf{b}|^2 + 2\mathbf{a} \cdot \mathbf{b} = |\mathbf{c}|^2$ ...(ii)

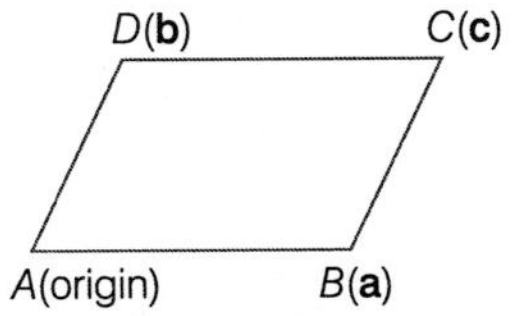

On substituting the value of $\mathbf{a} \cdot \mathbf{b}$ from Eq. (ii) in Eq. (i), we get

$$a^2 - \frac{1}{2}(c^2 - a^2 - b^2)$$

$$\Rightarrow \quad \frac{3a^2 + b^2 - c^2}{2}$$

12. Given, $\mathbf{V} + \mathbf{V}_1 = \mathbf{V}_2$

Also, $\mathbf{V} \cdot \mathbf{V}_1 = 2\alpha(\mathbf{V}_1)^2 = (\mathbf{V}_2 - \mathbf{V})^2$ and $\mathbf{V} \cdot \mathbf{V}_2 = \alpha$

Also, $|\mathbf{V}| = |\mathbf{V}_1| = |\mathbf{V}_2| = \lambda$ (say)

Hence, $\lambda^2 = 2\lambda^2 - 2\lambda^2 \cos\alpha \Rightarrow \cos\alpha = \frac{1}{2} = \cos\frac{\pi}{3}$

$\Rightarrow \alpha = 2n\pi \pm \frac{\pi}{3}, n \in I$

13. **Decoding the Question**

If a line segment of length x is divided by a point in $m : n$, then the length of each divided part is $\frac{xm}{m+n}$ and $\frac{xn}{m+n}$.

We can use this to find the length of vectors.

Given, $|\mathbf{b}| = |\mathbf{b} - \mathbf{c}| = 8$ and $|\mathbf{c}| = 12$ ...(i)

$\mathbf{AE} = \frac{\mathbf{b}}{4}$ and $\mathbf{EC} = \mathbf{c} - \frac{\mathbf{b}}{4}$

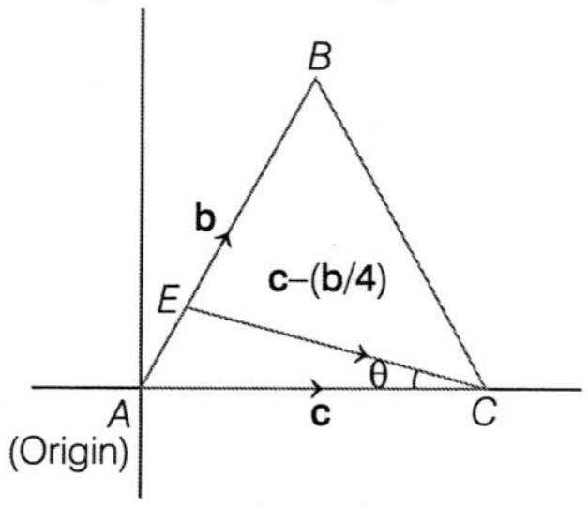

$$\cos\theta = \frac{\mathbf{c} \cdot \left(\mathbf{c} - \frac{\mathbf{b}}{4}\right)}{|\mathbf{c}|\left|\mathbf{c} - \frac{\mathbf{b}}{4}\right|} = \frac{\mathbf{c}^2 - \frac{\mathbf{c}\cdot\mathbf{b}}{4}}{12\left|\mathbf{c} - \frac{\mathbf{b}}{4}\right|} \quad \text{...(ii)}$$

From Eq. (i), $|\mathbf{b}| = 8, |\mathbf{c}| = 12$

$\therefore \quad |\mathbf{b} - \mathbf{c}|^2 = |\mathbf{b}|^2$

$\Rightarrow |\mathbf{b}|^2 + |\mathbf{c}|^2 - 2\mathbf{b}\cdot\mathbf{c} = |\mathbf{b}|^2 \Rightarrow \mathbf{b}\cdot\mathbf{c} = 72$ ...(iii)

and $\left|\mathbf{c} - \frac{\mathbf{b}}{4}\right|^2 = |\mathbf{c}|^2 + \frac{|\mathbf{b}|^2}{|16|} - \frac{\mathbf{b}\cdot\mathbf{c}}{2}$

$= 144 + 4 - 36 = 112$

$\therefore \quad \left|\mathbf{c} - \frac{\mathbf{b}}{4}\right| = 4\sqrt{7}$ ...(iv)

From Eqs. (ii), (iii) and (iv), we get

$$\cos\theta = \frac{144 - 18}{12 \times 4\sqrt{7}} = \frac{3\sqrt{7}}{8}$$

14. $\mathbf{BN} \cdot \mathbf{CM} = 0$

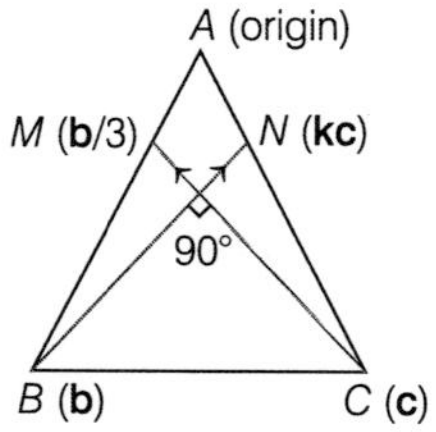

$$(k\mathbf{c} - \mathbf{b}) \cdot \left(\frac{\mathbf{b}}{3} - \mathbf{c}\right) = 0$$

$$\Rightarrow \frac{k}{3} \cdot \frac{a^2}{2} - ka^2 - \frac{a^2}{3} + \frac{a^2}{2} = 0 \Rightarrow \frac{k}{6} - k + \frac{1}{6} = 0$$

[$\because$ side length $= a$; $\therefore |\mathbf{b}| = |\mathbf{c}| = a$]

$$\frac{5k}{6} = \frac{1}{6} \Rightarrow k = \frac{1}{5}$$

15. Given, $15|\mathbf{AC}| = 3|\mathbf{AB}| = 5|\mathbf{AD}|$

Let $|\mathbf{AC}| = \lambda > 0$

$\therefore \quad |\mathbf{AB}| = 5\lambda$

$|\mathbf{AD}| = 3\lambda$

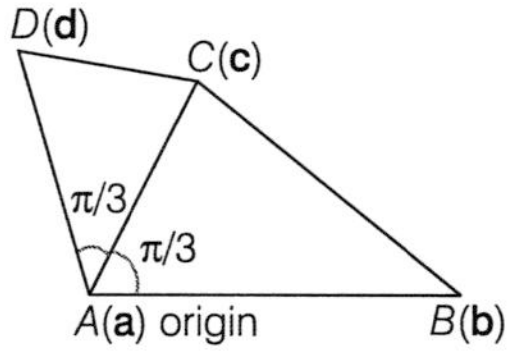

Now, $\cos(\mathbf{BA} \cdot \mathbf{CD}) = \frac{\mathbf{BA} \cdot \mathbf{CD}}{|\mathbf{BA}||\mathbf{CD}|} = \frac{-\mathbf{b}\cdot(\mathbf{d} - \mathbf{c})}{|\mathbf{b}||\mathbf{d} - \mathbf{c}|}$ ...(i)

Now, numerator of Eq. (i), we get

$$\mathbf{b}\cdot\mathbf{c} - \mathbf{b}\cdot\mathbf{d} = |\mathbf{b}||\mathbf{c}|\cos\frac{\pi}{3} - |\mathbf{b}||\mathbf{d}|\cos\frac{2\pi}{3}$$

$$= (5\lambda)(\lambda)\frac{1}{2} + 5\lambda(3\lambda)\frac{1}{2}$$

$$= \frac{5\lambda^2 + 15\lambda^2}{2} = 10\lambda^2$$

Denominator of Eq. (i),

$= |\mathbf{b}||\mathbf{d} - \mathbf{c}|$

Now, $|\mathbf{d} - \mathbf{c}|^2 = \mathbf{d}^2 + \mathbf{c}^2 - 2\mathbf{c}\cdot\mathbf{d}$

$$= 9\lambda^2 + \lambda^2 - 2(\lambda)(3\lambda)\frac{1}{2} = 10\lambda^2 - 3\lambda^2 = 7\lambda^2$$

$\therefore \quad |\mathbf{d} - \mathbf{c}| = \sqrt{7}\lambda$

Denominator of Eq. (i),

$= (5\lambda)\sqrt{7}\lambda = 5\sqrt{7}\lambda^2$

$$\therefore \cos(\mathbf{BA} \cdot \mathbf{CD}) = \frac{10\lambda^2}{5\sqrt{7}\lambda^2} = \frac{2}{\sqrt{7}}$$

16. $\mathbf{a} = -\hat{\mathbf{i}} - 2\hat{\mathbf{j}} - \hat{\mathbf{k}}$

$\mathbf{b} = \hat{\mathbf{i}} - 5\hat{\mathbf{j}} - 7\hat{\mathbf{k}}$

$|\mathbf{d}| = \frac{|\mathbf{a} \times \mathbf{b}|}{|\mathbf{a}|}$; $|\mathbf{a}| = \sqrt{6}$, $|\mathbf{b}| = \sqrt{75}$

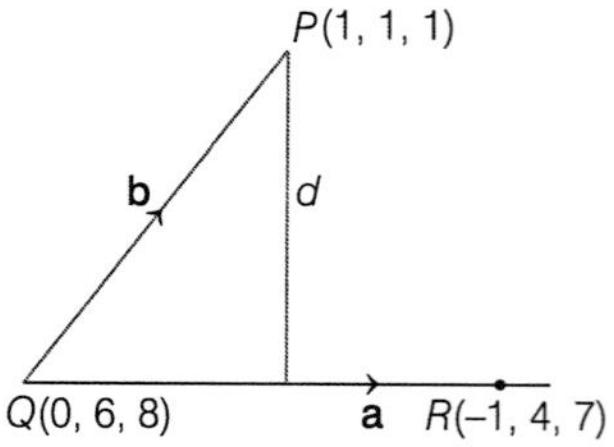

$|\mathbf{a} \times \mathbf{b}|^2 = |\mathbf{a}|^2|\mathbf{b}|^2 - (\mathbf{a}\cdot\mathbf{b})^2$

$= (6)(75) - (-1 + 10 + 7)^2 = 450 - 256 = 194$

$|\mathbf{a} \times \mathbf{b}| = \sqrt{194}$

$\therefore \quad d = \sqrt{\frac{194}{6}} = \sqrt{\frac{97}{3}}$

$\therefore \quad p + q = 100$

$$\Rightarrow \frac{(p+q)(p+q-1)}{2} = \frac{100 \times 99}{2} = 4950$$

17. Let $\mathbf{c} = \lambda(\mathbf{a} \times \mathbf{b})$

Hence, $\lambda(\mathbf{a} \times \mathbf{b}) \cdot (\hat{\mathbf{i}} + 2\hat{\mathbf{j}} - 7\hat{\mathbf{k}}) = 10$

$$\lambda \begin{vmatrix} 2 & -3 & 1 \\ 1 & -2 & 3 \\ 1 & 2 & -7 \end{vmatrix} = 10 \Rightarrow \lambda = -1$$

$\Rightarrow \quad \mathbf{c} = -(\mathbf{a} \times \mathbf{b})$

$\mathbf{a} = 2\hat{\mathbf{i}} - 3\hat{\mathbf{j}} + \hat{\mathbf{k}}$ and $\mathbf{b} = \hat{\mathbf{i}} - 2\hat{\mathbf{j}} + 3\hat{\mathbf{k}}$

$$\begin{vmatrix} \hat{\mathbf{i}} & \hat{\mathbf{j}} & \hat{\mathbf{k}} \\ 2 & -3 & 1 \\ 1 & -2 & 3 \end{vmatrix} = (-9+2)\hat{\mathbf{i}} - (5)\hat{\mathbf{j}} + (-4+3)\hat{\mathbf{k}} = (-7, -5, -1)$$

$\therefore \quad \mathbf{c} = (7, 5, 1)$

18. Since, $\hat{\mathbf{i}} + 2\hat{\mathbf{j}} + 2\hat{\mathbf{k}}$ is rotated, so as to cross Y-axis, the vector in new position.

Let the required vector be $x\hat{\mathbf{i}} + y\hat{\mathbf{j}} + z\hat{\mathbf{k}}$

where, $\quad x^2 + y^2 + z^2 = 9 \quad$ ...(i)

$x + 2y + 2z = 0 \quad$ ...(ii)

and $\quad \begin{vmatrix} x & y & z \\ 1 & 2 & 2 \\ 0 & 1 & 0 \end{vmatrix} \Rightarrow 2x - z = 0 \quad$ ...(iii)

On solving Eqs. (i), (ii) and (iii), we get

$$x = -\frac{2}{\sqrt{5}}, y = \sqrt{5}, z = \frac{-4}{\sqrt{5}}$$

$\therefore$ Required vector is $\frac{-2}{\sqrt{5}}\hat{\mathbf{i}} + \sqrt{5}\hat{\mathbf{j}} - \frac{4}{\sqrt{5}}\hat{\mathbf{k}}$.

19.

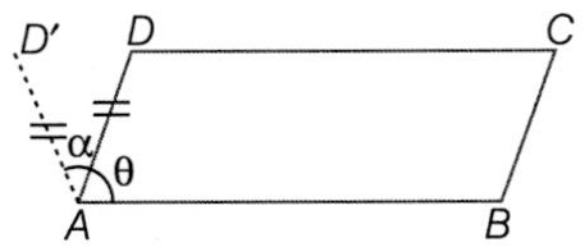

$$\cos\theta = \frac{\mathbf{AB} \cdot \mathbf{AD}}{|\mathbf{AB}||\mathbf{AD}|} = \frac{8}{9}$$

$\therefore \quad \cos^{-1}\left(\frac{8}{9}\right) + \alpha = \frac{\alpha}{2}$ by hypothesis

$\therefore \quad \sin\alpha = \frac{8}{9}$

$\therefore \quad \cos\alpha = \sqrt{1 - \frac{64}{81}} = \frac{\sqrt{17}}{9}$

20. $\quad \mathbf{BA} + \mathbf{AC} = \mathbf{BC}$

$\Rightarrow \quad \mathbf{BA} = \mathbf{BC} - \mathbf{AC}$

$\Rightarrow \quad \frac{\mathbf{e}}{|\mathbf{e}|} - \frac{\mathbf{f}}{|\mathbf{f}|} - \frac{2\mathbf{e}}{|\mathbf{e}|} = -\left(\frac{\mathbf{e}}{|\mathbf{e}|} + \frac{\mathbf{f}}{|\mathbf{f}|}\right)$

Now, $\quad \mathbf{BA} \cdot \mathbf{BC} = \left(\frac{\mathbf{e}}{|\mathbf{e}|} + \frac{\mathbf{f}}{|\mathbf{f}|}\right)\left(\frac{\mathbf{e}}{|\mathbf{e}|} - \frac{\mathbf{f}}{|\mathbf{f}|}\right) = 0$

$\Rightarrow \quad \angle B = 90°$

$\Rightarrow \quad \cos 2B = -1$

and $\cos 2A + \cos 2C = 2\cos(A + C)\cos(A - C) = 0$

$[\because A + C = 90°]$

$\Rightarrow \cos 2A + \cos 2B + \cos 2C = -1$

21. The mid-points of sides are $D(l, 0, 0)$, $E(0, m, 0)$ and $F(0, 0, n)$.

$$EF^2 = \frac{BC^2}{4} \Rightarrow BC^2 = 4(m^2 + n^2)$$

$$\frac{AB^2 + BC^2 + CA^2}{l^2 + m^2 + n^2} = 8$$

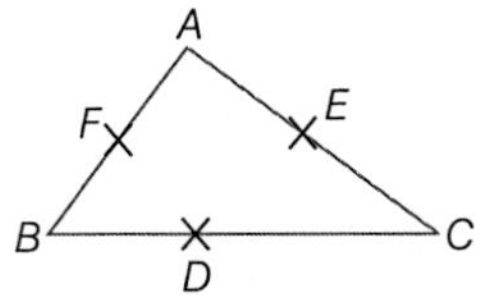

22. $\mathbf{p} \times \mathbf{q}$, $\mathbf{p}$, $\mathbf{q}$ are non-coplanar vectors

$\Rightarrow b - c = 0, c - a = 0, a - b = 0$

$\Rightarrow a = b = c$

$\Rightarrow \Delta$ is equilateral.

23. $(\mathbf{a} \times \mathbf{b}) \times (\mathbf{c} \times \mathbf{d}) = [\mathbf{a}\ \mathbf{b}\ \mathbf{d}]\mathbf{c} - [\mathbf{a}\ \mathbf{b}\ \mathbf{c}]\mathbf{d} = -4\mathbf{c} - 4\mathbf{d}$

$= -8\hat{\mathbf{i}}$, perpendicular to Y-axis, Z-axis

24. $|\mathbf{a}| = |\mathbf{b}| = |\mathbf{c}|$

$|\mathbf{b} - \mathbf{a}| = |\mathbf{b} - \mathbf{c}| = |\mathbf{c} - \mathbf{a}| = a$

$\mathbf{a} \cdot \mathbf{b} = \mathbf{b} \cdot \mathbf{c} = \mathbf{c} \cdot \mathbf{a} = \mathbf{AB} \cdot \mathbf{AC} = \mathbf{CA} \cdot \mathbf{CB} = \mathbf{BA} \cdot \mathbf{BC}$

$= a^2 \cos\frac{\pi}{3}$

$\Rightarrow \quad (\mathbf{EF})^2 = \frac{a^2}{\sqrt{3}} \Rightarrow \mathbf{EF} = \frac{a}{\sqrt{3}}$

$|\mathbf{CF}| = |\mathbf{CE}| = \frac{\sqrt{7}\mathbf{a}}{3}$ and $|\mathbf{CM}| = \frac{5a}{6}$

where, 'm' is middle point of **EF**.

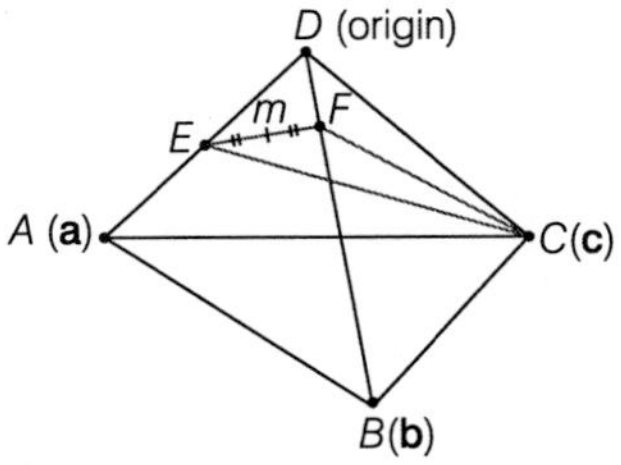

Area of $\Delta CEF = \frac{1}{2}|\mathbf{EF}||\mathbf{CM}|$

$= \frac{1}{2} \times \frac{a}{\sqrt{3}} \times \frac{5a}{6} = \frac{5a^2}{12\sqrt{3}}$ sq units

25. $\mathbf{p} \cdot \mathbf{q} = 0$ and $\mathbf{r} \cdot \mathbf{s} = 0$

$\Rightarrow \quad (5\mathbf{a} - 3\mathbf{b}) \cdot (-\mathbf{a} - 2\mathbf{b}) = 0$

$6\mathbf{b}^2 - 7\mathbf{a} \cdot \mathbf{b} - 5\mathbf{a}^2 = 0 \quad$ ...(i)

$\Rightarrow \quad (-4\mathbf{a} - \mathbf{b}) \cdot (-\mathbf{a} + \mathbf{b}) = 0$

$4\mathbf{a}^2 - \mathbf{b}^2 - 3\mathbf{a} \cdot \mathbf{b} = 0 \quad$ ...(ii)

Now, $\quad \mathbf{x} = \frac{1}{3}(\mathbf{p} + \mathbf{r} + \mathbf{s})$

$\mathbf{x} = \frac{1}{3}(5\mathbf{a} - 3\mathbf{b} - 4\mathbf{a} - \mathbf{b} - \mathbf{a} + \mathbf{b})$

$\therefore \quad \mathbf{x} = -\mathbf{b}$

$\mathbf{y} = \frac{1}{5}(\mathbf{r} + \mathbf{s}) = \frac{1}{5}(-5\mathbf{a}) = -\mathbf{a}$

Angle between $\mathbf{x}$ and $\mathbf{y}$ i.e. $\cos\theta = \frac{\mathbf{x} \cdot \mathbf{y}}{|\mathbf{x}||\mathbf{y}|} = \frac{\mathbf{a} \cdot \mathbf{b}}{|\mathbf{a}||\mathbf{b}|}$

From Eqs. (i) and (ii), we get

$$|\mathbf{a}|=\sqrt{\frac{25}{19}}\cdot\sqrt{\mathbf{a}\cdot\mathbf{b}} \quad\text{and}\quad |\mathbf{b}|=\sqrt{\frac{43}{19}}\sqrt{\mathbf{a}\cdot\mathbf{b}}$$

$$|\mathbf{a}|\,|\mathbf{b}|=\frac{\sqrt{25\times 43}}{19}(\mathbf{a}\cdot\mathbf{b})=\frac{19}{5\sqrt{43}}=\frac{\mathbf{a}\cdot\mathbf{b}}{|\mathbf{a}|\,|\mathbf{b}|}$$

$$\Rightarrow \quad \cos\theta=\frac{19}{5\sqrt{43}}$$

$$\therefore \quad \theta=\cos^{-1}\left(\frac{19}{5\sqrt{43}}\right)$$

26. $\because \mathbf{a}\cdot\mathbf{b}<0$

$$\Rightarrow \quad (\sin^2 x-\sin x)-\cos^2 x+3-4\sin x<0$$

$$\Rightarrow \quad 2\sin^2 x-5\sin x+2<0$$

$$\Rightarrow \quad \underbrace{(\sin x-2)}_{(-)\text{ve}}(2\sin x-1)<0$$

$$\Rightarrow \quad \sin x>\frac{1}{2} \Rightarrow x\in\left(\frac{\pi}{6},\frac{\pi}{2}\right)$$

27.

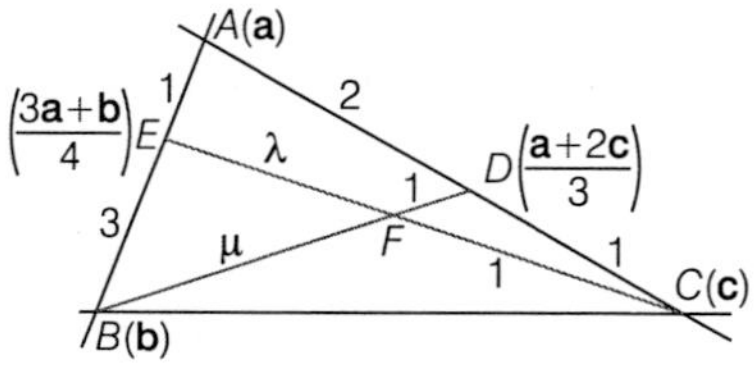

Positive vector of point $E=\dfrac{3\mathbf{a}+\mathbf{b}}{4}$

Position vector of point $D=\dfrac{\mathbf{a}+2\mathbf{c}}{3}$

Let point F divides EC in $\lambda:1$ and BD in $\mu:1$,

$$\text{then} \quad \frac{\mathbf{b}+\frac{\mu}{3}(\mathbf{a}+2\mathbf{c})}{\mu+1}=\frac{\lambda\mathbf{c}+\frac{3\mathbf{a}+\mathbf{b}}{4}}{\lambda+1}$$

$$\left[\mathbf{b}+\frac{\mu}{3}(\mathbf{a}+2\mathbf{c})\right](\lambda+1)=\left(\lambda\mathbf{c}+\frac{3\mathbf{a}+\mathbf{b}}{4}\right)(\mu+1)$$

On comparing the coefficient of **a**, **b** and **c**.

$$\Rightarrow \quad \frac{\mu(\lambda+1)}{3}=\frac{3(\mu+1)}{4} \quad \text{...(i)}$$

$$\Rightarrow \quad \lambda+1=\frac{\mu+1}{4} \quad \text{...(ii)}$$

$$\frac{2\mu}{3}(\lambda+1)=\lambda(\mu+1) \quad \text{...(iii)}$$

On solving, we get

$$\lambda=\frac{3}{2}$$

28. **c** is coplanar with **a** and **b**

$$\therefore \quad \mathbf{c}=\lambda\mathbf{a}+\mu\mathbf{b}$$

$$\mathbf{c}\cdot\mathbf{c}=\lambda\mathbf{a}\cdot\mathbf{c}+\mu\mathbf{b}\cdot\mathbf{c}$$

$$|\mathbf{c}|^2=0+24\mu \quad \text{...(i)} \ [\because \mathbf{a}\cdot\mathbf{c}=0,\ \mathbf{b}\cdot\mathbf{c}=24]$$

$$\mathbf{a}\cdot\mathbf{c}=\lambda|\mathbf{a}|^2+\mu\mathbf{a}\cdot\mathbf{b}$$

$$0=\lambda(14)+\mu(2) \quad [\because |\mathbf{a}|=\sqrt{14},\ \mathbf{a}\cdot\mathbf{b}=2]$$

$$\lambda=-\frac{1}{7}\mu \quad \text{...(ii)}$$

$$\mathbf{b}\cdot\mathbf{c}=\lambda(\mathbf{a}\cdot\mathbf{b})+\mu|\mathbf{b}|^2$$

$$24=2\lambda+2\mu$$

$$24=2\left(\frac{-\mu}{7}\right)+2\mu$$

$$\mu=\frac{12\times 7}{6}=14$$

$$\therefore \quad |\mathbf{c}|^2=24\mu=24\times 14=336$$

29. Given, $\mathbf{a}=\hat{\mathbf{i}}+\hat{\mathbf{j}}+\hat{\mathbf{k}}$, $\mathbf{c}=\hat{\mathbf{j}}-\hat{\mathbf{k}}$, $\mathbf{a}\cdot\mathbf{b}=3$ and $\mathbf{a}\times\mathbf{b}=\mathbf{c}$

$$\mathbf{a}\times\mathbf{c}=\begin{vmatrix}\hat{\mathbf{i}} & \hat{\mathbf{j}} & \hat{\mathbf{k}}\\ 1 & 1 & 1\\ 0 & 1 & -1\end{vmatrix}=-2\hat{\mathbf{i}}+\hat{\mathbf{j}}+\hat{\mathbf{k}}$$

$$\therefore \quad \mathbf{a}\times\mathbf{b}=\mathbf{c}$$

Cross product with **a**, we get

$$\mathbf{a}\times(\mathbf{a}\times\mathbf{b})=\mathbf{a}\times\mathbf{c}$$

$$(\mathbf{a}\cdot\mathbf{b})\,\mathbf{a}-(\mathbf{a}\cdot\mathbf{a})\,\mathbf{b}=\mathbf{a}\times\mathbf{c}$$

$$3\mathbf{a}-3\mathbf{b}=-2\hat{\mathbf{i}}+\hat{\mathbf{j}}+\hat{\mathbf{k}}$$

$$3\mathbf{b}=3(\hat{\mathbf{i}}+\hat{\mathbf{j}}+\hat{\mathbf{k}})-(-2\hat{\mathbf{i}}+\hat{\mathbf{j}}+\hat{\mathbf{k}})$$

$$3\mathbf{b}=5\hat{\mathbf{i}}+2\hat{\mathbf{j}}+2\hat{\mathbf{k}}$$

$$|9\mathbf{b}|^2=25+4+4=33$$

$$3|\mathbf{b}|^2=\frac{33}{3}=11$$

30. Given, $\mathbf{c}=x\mathbf{a}+y\mathbf{b}+\mathbf{a}\times\mathbf{b}$ ...(i)

and $\mathbf{a}\cdot\mathbf{b}=0, |\mathbf{c}|=2, |\mathbf{a}|=|\mathbf{b}|=1$

Let vector **c** make an angle α with vector **a** and **b**

$$\mathbf{a}\cdot\mathbf{c}=\mathbf{b}\cdot\mathbf{c}=2\cos\alpha$$

On taking dot product of Eq.(i) with **a** and **b**, we get

$$\mathbf{a}\cdot\mathbf{c}=x|\mathbf{a}|^2+y(\mathbf{a}\cdot\mathbf{b})+\mathbf{a}\cdot(\mathbf{a}\times\mathbf{b})$$

$$2\cos\alpha=x$$

Similarly, $2\cos\alpha=y$

Now, $|\mathbf{c}|^2=x^2+y^2+|\mathbf{a}\times\mathbf{b}|^2=2(4\cos^2\alpha)+1$

$$\Rightarrow \quad 4=8\cos^2\alpha+1$$

$$\Rightarrow \quad 4=8(1-\sin^2\alpha)+1$$

$$\Rightarrow \quad 8\sin^2\alpha=9-4=5$$

$$\Rightarrow \quad \sin^2\alpha=\frac{5}{8}=0.625$$

31. Given, $\mathbf{A}=\mathbf{B}+\mathbf{C}$

$$a\hat{\mathbf{i}}+b\hat{\mathbf{j}}+c\hat{\mathbf{k}}=(d+3)\hat{\mathbf{i}}+4\hat{\mathbf{j}}+2\hat{\mathbf{k}}$$

$$a=d+3,\ b=4 \text{ and } c=2$$

Now, area of $\Delta ABC=\dfrac{1}{2}|\mathbf{B}\times\mathbf{C}|$

$$=\frac{1}{2}\begin{vmatrix}\hat{\mathbf{i}} & \hat{\mathbf{j}} & \hat{\mathbf{k}}\\ d & 3 & 4\\ 3 & 1 & -2\end{vmatrix}$$

$$\Rightarrow \quad 5\sqrt{6}=\frac{1}{2}|-10\hat{\mathbf{i}}+(2d+12)\hat{\mathbf{j}}+(d-9)\hat{\mathbf{k}}|$$

$\Rightarrow \quad 600 = 100 + 4(d+6)^2 + (d-9)^2$

$\Rightarrow \quad d^2 + 6d - 55 = 0$

$\Rightarrow \quad (d+11)(d-5) = 0$

$\Rightarrow \quad d = -11, 5 \quad d \neq -11 \quad d > 0$

When $d = 5$, $a = d + 3 = 5 + 3 = 8$

$\therefore a^2 + b^2 + c^2 + d^2 = 8^2 + 4^2 + 2^2 + 5^2$

$= 64 + 16 + 4 + 25 = 109$

32. Given, $\mathbf{a} = 2\hat{\mathbf{i}} + \hat{\mathbf{j}} - 2\hat{\mathbf{k}}$, $\mathbf{b} = \hat{\mathbf{i}} + \hat{\mathbf{j}}$

$$\mathbf{a} \times \mathbf{b} = \begin{vmatrix} \hat{\mathbf{i}} & \hat{\mathbf{j}} & \hat{\mathbf{k}} \\ 2 & 1 & -2 \\ 1 & 1 & 0 \end{vmatrix} = 2\hat{\mathbf{i}} - 2\hat{\mathbf{j}} + \hat{\mathbf{k}}$$

$\Rightarrow \quad |\mathbf{a} \times \mathbf{b}| = \sqrt{4+4+1} = 3$

$\Rightarrow |(\mathbf{a} \times \mathbf{b}) \times \mathbf{c}| = |\mathbf{a} \times \mathbf{b}||\mathbf{c}| \sin 30° = 3$

$\Rightarrow \quad 3|\mathbf{c}| \times \frac{1}{2} = \frac{3}{2}|\mathbf{c}| = 3$

$\Rightarrow \quad |\mathbf{c}| = 2$

$\Rightarrow \quad |\mathbf{c} - \mathbf{a}|^2 = |\mathbf{c}|^2 + |\mathbf{a}|^2 - 2\mathbf{a} \cdot \mathbf{c}$

$\Rightarrow \quad 9 = 4 + 9 - 2\mathbf{a} \cdot \mathbf{c}$

$\Rightarrow \quad \mathbf{a} \cdot \mathbf{c} = 2$

33. Given, $|\mathbf{a}| = |\mathbf{b}| = 1, |\mathbf{a} + \mathbf{b}| = \sqrt{3}$

and $\quad \mathbf{c} - \mathbf{a} - 2\mathbf{b} = 3(\mathbf{a} \times \mathbf{b})$

$|\mathbf{a} + \mathbf{b}| = \sqrt{3}$

$\Rightarrow \quad |\mathbf{a} + \mathbf{b}|^2 = |\mathbf{a}|^2 + |\mathbf{b}|^2 + 2(\mathbf{a} \cdot \mathbf{b}) = 3$

$\Rightarrow \quad 1 + 1 + 2(\mathbf{a} \cdot \mathbf{b}) = 3$

$\Rightarrow \quad \mathbf{a} \cdot \mathbf{b} = \frac{1}{2}$

Now, $\quad \mathbf{c} - \mathbf{a} - 2\mathbf{b} = 3(\mathbf{a} \times \mathbf{b})$

$(\mathbf{c} - \mathbf{a} - 2\mathbf{b}) \cdot \mathbf{b} = 3(\mathbf{a} \times \mathbf{b}) \cdot \mathbf{b}$

$\mathbf{c} \cdot \mathbf{b} - \mathbf{a} \cdot \mathbf{b} - 2\mathbf{b} \cdot \mathbf{b} = 0$

$\mathbf{c} \cdot \mathbf{b} = \mathbf{a} \cdot \mathbf{b} + 2|\mathbf{b}|^2 = \frac{1}{2} + 2 = \frac{5}{2}$

$\mathbf{c} \cdot \mathbf{b} = \mathbf{b} \cdot \mathbf{c} = 2.5$

34. Let $\mathbf{u} = 3\hat{\mathbf{i}} + 4\hat{\mathbf{j}} + 5\hat{\mathbf{k}}$, $\mathbf{v} = a\hat{\mathbf{i}} + b\hat{\mathbf{j}} + c\hat{\mathbf{k}}$

$\mathbf{u} \cdot \mathbf{v} = 3a + 4b + 5c$

$\cos\theta = \frac{\mathbf{u} \cdot \mathbf{v}}{|\mathbf{u}||\mathbf{v}|}$

$\cos\theta = \frac{3a + 4b + 5c}{\sqrt{3^2 + 4^2 + 5^2}\sqrt{a^2 + b^2 + c^2}}$

$\cos\theta = \frac{3a + 4b + 5c}{\sqrt{50} \times \sqrt{\frac{1}{2}}} \qquad \left[\because a^2 + b^2 + c^2 = \frac{1}{2}\right]$

$\cos\theta = \frac{3a + 4b + 5c}{5}$

$\cos\theta \leq 1$

$\therefore \quad \frac{3a + 4b + 5c}{5} \leq 1$

$\Rightarrow \quad 3a + 4b + 5c = 5$

$\because$ Maximum value of $3a + 4b + 5c$ is 5.

35. Let $\mathbf{u} = \sqrt{a^2 - 4}\hat{\mathbf{i}} + a\hat{\mathbf{j}} + \sqrt{a^2 + 4}\hat{\mathbf{k}}$

$\mathbf{v} = \tan A\hat{\mathbf{i}} + \tan B\hat{\mathbf{j}} + \tan C\hat{\mathbf{k}}$

$\mathbf{u} \cdot \mathbf{v} = \sqrt{a^2 - 4} \tan A + a \tan B + \sqrt{a^2 + 4} \tan C = 6a$

$\cos\theta = \frac{\mathbf{u} \cdot \mathbf{v}}{|\mathbf{u}||\mathbf{v}|}$

$= \frac{6a}{(\sqrt{a^2 - 4 + a^2 + a^2 + 4})(\sqrt{\tan^2 A + \tan^2 B + \tan^2 C})}$

$\cos\theta = \frac{6a}{\sqrt{3a^2}\sqrt{\tan^2 A + \tan^2 B + \tan^2 C}}$

$\cos^2\theta = \frac{36a^2}{3a^2(\tan^2 A + \tan^2 B + \tan^2 C)}$

$\cos^2\theta \leq 1$

$\therefore 12 \leq \tan^2 A + \tan^2 B + \tan^2 C$

$\therefore$ Maximum value of $\tan^2 A + \tan^B + \tan^2 C = 12$

36. Area of quadrilateral $OABC = \Delta OAC + \Delta ABC$

$= \frac{1}{2}|\mathbf{OA} \times \mathbf{AC}| + \frac{1}{2}|\mathbf{AB} \times \mathbf{BC}|$

$= \frac{1}{2}|\mathbf{a} \times (\mathbf{b} - \mathbf{a})| + \frac{1}{2}|(10\mathbf{b} + \mathbf{a}) \times (-2\mathbf{a} - 9\mathbf{b})|$

$= \frac{1}{2}|\mathbf{a} \times \mathbf{b}| + \frac{1}{2}|11(\mathbf{a} \times \mathbf{b})|$

$= 6|\mathbf{a} \times \mathbf{b}|$

$l = 2\lambda m \qquad [\because m = \mathbf{a} \times \mathbf{b}]$

$\therefore \quad \lambda = 3$

37. Given, $\mathbf{a}_1$ is projection of $\mathbf{a}$ on $\mathbf{b}$

$\therefore \quad \mathbf{a}_1 = \frac{\mathbf{a} \cdot \mathbf{b}}{|\mathbf{b}|}$

$\Rightarrow \quad \mathbf{a}_1 = \frac{(\mathbf{a} \cdot \mathbf{b})\mathbf{b}}{|\mathbf{b}|^2}$

$\Rightarrow \quad \mathbf{a}_1 \cdot \mathbf{b} = \frac{(\mathbf{a} \cdot \mathbf{b})(\mathbf{b} \cdot \mathbf{b})}{|\mathbf{b}|^2} = \frac{(\mathbf{a} \cdot \mathbf{b})|\mathbf{b}|^2}{|\mathbf{b}|^2} = \mathbf{a} \cdot \mathbf{b}$

$\Rightarrow \quad \mathbf{a}_1 \cdot \mathbf{b} = \mathbf{a} \cdot \mathbf{b}$

$\Rightarrow \quad -\lambda = (2\hat{\mathbf{i}} + 3\hat{\mathbf{j}} - 6\hat{\mathbf{k}}) \cdot (2\hat{\mathbf{i}} - 3\hat{\mathbf{j}} + 6\hat{\mathbf{k}}) = 4 - 9 - 36 = -41$

$\therefore \quad \lambda = 41$

38. Given, $\alpha = 3\hat{\mathbf{i}} + \hat{\mathbf{j}}, \beta = 2\hat{\mathbf{i}} - \hat{\mathbf{j}} + 3\hat{\mathbf{k}}$

$\beta = \beta_1 - \beta_2$

Now, β_1 is parallel to α.

$\therefore \quad \beta_1 = \lambda\alpha = \lambda(3\hat{\mathbf{i}} + \hat{\mathbf{j}})$

and β_2 is perpendicular to α.

$\therefore \quad \beta_2 \cdot \alpha = 0$

$(\beta_1 - \beta) \cdot \alpha = 0 \qquad [\because \beta = \beta_1 - \beta_2]$

$\beta_1\alpha - \beta \cdot \alpha = 0$

$\lambda\alpha^2 - (2\hat{\mathbf{i}} - \hat{\mathbf{j}} + 3\hat{\mathbf{k}}) \cdot (3\hat{\mathbf{i}} + \hat{\mathbf{j}}) = 0$

$10\lambda = (6 - 1) = 5$

$\lambda = \frac{1}{2}$

$\therefore \quad \beta_2 = \beta_1 - \beta = \frac{1}{2}(3\hat{\mathbf{i}} + \hat{\mathbf{j}}) - (2\hat{\mathbf{i}} - \hat{\mathbf{j}} + 3\hat{\mathbf{k}})$

$= -\frac{1}{2}\hat{\mathbf{i}} + \frac{3}{2}\hat{\mathbf{j}} - 3\hat{\mathbf{k}}$

$$\text{Now, } \beta_1 \times \beta_2 = \begin{vmatrix} \hat{\mathbf{i}} & \hat{\mathbf{j}} & \hat{\mathbf{k}} \\ \frac{3}{2} & \frac{1}{2} & 0 \\ \frac{-1}{2} & \frac{3}{2} & -3 \end{vmatrix}$$

$= -\frac{3}{2}\hat{\mathbf{i}} + \frac{9}{2}\hat{\mathbf{j}} + \frac{5}{2}\hat{\mathbf{k}}$

$|\beta_1 \times \beta_2|^2 = \frac{9}{4} + \frac{81}{4} + \frac{25}{4} = \frac{115}{4} = 28.75$

39. Given, $\quad |\mathbf{a}| = |\mathbf{b}| = |\mathbf{c}| = 1$

$|\mathbf{a} + \mathbf{b} + 3\mathbf{c}| = 4$

$|\mathbf{a}|^2 + |\mathbf{b}|^2 + 9|\mathbf{c}|^2 + 2|\mathbf{a}||\mathbf{b}|\cos\alpha$

$\qquad + 6|\mathbf{b}||\mathbf{c}|\cos\beta + 6|\mathbf{a}||\mathbf{c}|\cos\gamma = 16$

$\Rightarrow \quad 1 + 1 + 9 + 2\cos\alpha + 6\cos\beta + 6\cos\gamma = 16$

$\Rightarrow \quad 2\cos\alpha + 6\cos\beta = 16 - 11 - 6\cos\gamma$

$\Rightarrow \quad 2\cos\alpha + 6\cos\beta = 5 - 6\cos\gamma \left[\gamma \in \left[\frac{\pi}{6}, \frac{2\pi}{3}\right]\right]$

$\Rightarrow \quad 2(\cos\alpha + 3\cos\beta) = 5 - 6\cos\gamma$

$\Rightarrow \quad \cos\alpha + 3\cos\beta = \frac{1}{2}(5 - 6\cos\gamma)$

$\cos\alpha + 3\cos\beta$ is maximum when $\gamma = \frac{2\pi}{3}$

$= \frac{1}{2}\left[5 - 6\cos\frac{2\pi}{3}\right]$

$= \frac{1}{2}\left[5 - 6 \times \left(-\frac{1}{2}\right)\right] = \frac{1}{2}(5 + 3) = 4$

40. Given, $\mathbf{c} \times \mathbf{a} = \mathbf{b}$

$|\mathbf{c} \times \mathbf{a}| = |\mathbf{b}|$

$|\mathbf{c}||\mathbf{a}|\sin\theta = |\mathbf{b}|$

$|\mathbf{c}| = \frac{3}{2\sin\theta} \qquad [\because |\mathbf{a}| = 2, |\mathbf{b}| = 3]$

$|\mathbf{c} - \mathbf{a}|^2 = |\mathbf{c}|^2 + |\mathbf{a}|^2 - 2|\mathbf{c}||\mathbf{a}|\cos\theta$

$= \frac{9}{4\sin^2\theta} + 4 - 2 \times \frac{3}{2\sin\theta} \times 2\cos\theta$

$= \frac{9}{4} + \left[\frac{3}{2}\cot\theta - 2\right]^2$

$\Rightarrow \quad |\mathbf{c} - \mathbf{a}|^2 \geq \frac{9}{4}$

$\Rightarrow \quad |\mathbf{c} - \mathbf{a}| \geq \frac{3}{2} = 1.5$

41. $(3\mathbf{a} + \mathbf{b}) \cdot (\mathbf{a} - 4\mathbf{b}) = 3|\mathbf{a}|^2 - 11\,\mathbf{a} \cdot \mathbf{b} - 4|\mathbf{b}|^2$

$= 3 \times 36 - 11 \times 6 \times 8\cos\pi - 4 \times 64$

$= 108 + 528 - 256 = 380 > 0$

$\therefore$ The angle between **a** and **b** is acute.

The longer diagonal is given by

$\mathbf{d} = (3\mathbf{a} + \mathbf{b}) + (\mathbf{a} - 4\mathbf{b}) = 4\mathbf{a} - 3\mathbf{b}$

Now, $|\mathbf{d}|^2 = |4\mathbf{a} - 3\mathbf{b}|^2 = 16|\mathbf{a}|^2 + 9|\mathbf{b}|^2 - 24|\mathbf{a}||\mathbf{b}|\cos\pi$

$= 16 \times 36 + 9 \times 64 - 24 \times 6 \times 8(-1)$

$= 16(36 + 36 + 72)$

$\Rightarrow \quad |\mathbf{d}| = \sqrt{16 \times 144} = 4 \times 12 = 48$

$\therefore$ Length of longer diagonal is 48.

42. Given, $\mathbf{a} + \mathbf{b} + \mathbf{c} = 0$

Cross product with **a**, we get

$\mathbf{a} \times \mathbf{a} + \mathbf{a} \times \mathbf{b} + \mathbf{a} \times \mathbf{c} = 0$

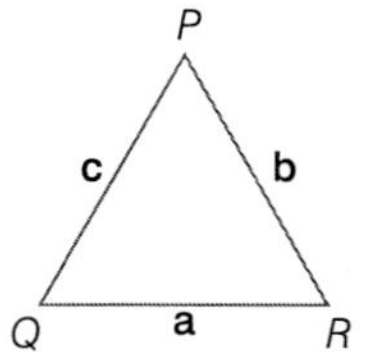

$\mathbf{a} \times \mathbf{b} = -\mathbf{a} \times \mathbf{c}$

$\mathbf{a} \times \mathbf{b} = \mathbf{c} \times \mathbf{a}$

$\therefore \quad |\mathbf{a} \times \mathbf{b} + \mathbf{c} \times \mathbf{a}| = |\mathbf{a} \times \mathbf{b} + \mathbf{a} \times \mathbf{b}| = 2|\mathbf{a} \times \mathbf{b}|$

$|\mathbf{a}|^2 = |\mathbf{b}|^2 + |\mathbf{c}|^2 + 2\mathbf{b} \cdot \mathbf{c}$

$144 = 48 + |\mathbf{c}|^2 + 2 \times 24$

$\Rightarrow \quad |\mathbf{c}|^2 = 48$

Again, $|\mathbf{c}|^2 = |\mathbf{a}|^2 + |\mathbf{b}|^2 + 2\mathbf{a} \cdot \mathbf{b}$

$\Rightarrow \quad \mathbf{a} \cdot \mathbf{b} = \frac{|\mathbf{c}|^2 - |\mathbf{a}|^2 - |\mathbf{b}|^2}{2}$

$\Rightarrow \quad \mathbf{a} \cdot \mathbf{b} = \frac{48 - 144 - 48}{2} = -72$

$\Rightarrow 2|\mathbf{a} \times \mathbf{b}| = 2\sqrt{|\mathbf{a}|^2|\mathbf{b}|^2 - (\mathbf{a} \cdot \mathbf{b})^2}$

$= 2\sqrt{(12)^2(4\sqrt{3})^2 - (-72)^2}$

$= 24\sqrt{48 - 36} = 48\sqrt{3}$

$\therefore \quad \lambda = 48$

43. Given, $\mathbf{a} = \hat{\mathbf{i}} + 2\hat{\mathbf{j}} + \hat{\mathbf{k}}$, $\mathbf{b} = 3(\hat{\mathbf{i}} - \hat{\mathbf{j}} + \hat{\mathbf{k}})$ and $\mathbf{a} \times \mathbf{c} = \mathbf{b}$

$\Rightarrow (\mathbf{a} \times \mathbf{c}) \cdot \mathbf{b} = \mathbf{b} \cdot \mathbf{b} = |\mathbf{b}|^2 = 27$

Now, $\mathbf{a} \cdot (\mathbf{c} \times \mathbf{b}) = [\mathbf{a}\ \ \mathbf{c}\ \ \mathbf{b}] = (\mathbf{a} \times \mathbf{c}) \cdot \mathbf{b} = 27 \qquad$ ...(i)

Now, $\quad \mathbf{a} \cdot \mathbf{b} = 3 - 6 + 3 = 0 \qquad$ ...(ii)

and $\quad \mathbf{a} \cdot \mathbf{c} = 3 \qquad$ [given] ...(iii)

Now, $\mathbf{a} \cdot ((\mathbf{c} \times \mathbf{b}) - \mathbf{b} - \mathbf{c}) = \mathbf{a} \cdot (\mathbf{c} \times \mathbf{b}) - \mathbf{a} \cdot \mathbf{b} - \mathbf{a} \cdot \mathbf{c}$

$= 27 - 0 - 3 = 24$

44. $\because$ Unit vector $\mathbf{u} = x\hat{\mathbf{i}} + y\hat{\mathbf{j}} + z\hat{\mathbf{k}}$ makes $\frac{\pi}{2}, \frac{\pi}{3}$ and $\frac{2\pi}{3}$ with the vectors $\frac{1}{\sqrt{2}}\hat{\mathbf{i}} + \frac{1}{\sqrt{2}}\hat{\mathbf{k}}$, $\frac{1}{\sqrt{2}}\hat{\mathbf{j}} + \frac{1}{\sqrt{2}}\hat{\mathbf{k}}$ and $\frac{1}{\sqrt{2}}\hat{\mathbf{i}} + \frac{1}{\sqrt{2}}\hat{\mathbf{j}}$, respectively.

Taking dot product of unit vector **u** with given vectors respectively, we have

$\frac{x}{\sqrt{2}} + \frac{z}{\sqrt{2}} = |\mathbf{u}|\sqrt{\frac{1}{2} + \frac{1}{2}} \cdot \cos\frac{\pi}{2} = 0$

$\Rightarrow \qquad x + z = 0 \qquad$ ...(i)

and $\frac{y}{\sqrt{2}} + \frac{z}{\sqrt{2}} = |\mathbf{u}| \sqrt{\frac{1}{2} + \frac{1}{2}} \cos \frac{\pi}{3}$

$\Rightarrow \quad \frac{y+z}{\sqrt{2}} = \frac{1}{2}$

$\Rightarrow \quad y + z = \frac{1}{\sqrt{2}}$ ...(ii)

and $\frac{x}{\sqrt{2}} + \frac{y}{\sqrt{2}} = |\mathbf{u}| \sqrt{\frac{1}{2} + \frac{1}{2}} \cos \frac{2\pi}{3}$

$\Rightarrow \quad \frac{x+y}{\sqrt{2}} = 1 \times 1 \times \frac{-1}{2}$

$\Rightarrow \quad x + y = \frac{-1}{\sqrt{2}}$ ...(iii)

On solving Eqs. (i), (ii) and (iii), we get

$$y = 0$$

$$\Rightarrow \quad x = \frac{-1}{\sqrt{2}}$$

$$z = \frac{1}{\sqrt{2}}$$

$$\Rightarrow \quad \mathbf{u} = \frac{-1}{\sqrt{2}}\hat{\mathbf{i}} + \frac{1}{\sqrt{2}}\hat{\mathbf{k}}$$

and $\quad \mathbf{v} = \frac{1}{\sqrt{2}}\hat{\mathbf{i}} + \frac{1}{\sqrt{2}}\hat{\mathbf{j}} + \frac{1}{\sqrt{2}}\hat{\mathbf{k}}$

$\therefore \quad \mathbf{u} - \mathbf{v} = -\sqrt{2}\,\hat{\mathbf{i}} - \frac{1}{\sqrt{2}}\hat{\mathbf{j}}$

$\Rightarrow |\mathbf{u} - \mathbf{v}|^2 = (\sqrt{2})^2 + \left(\frac{1}{\sqrt{2}}\right)^2 = 2 + \frac{1}{2} = \frac{5}{2}$

45. $P(3, 2, 3)$, $Q(4, 6, 2)$ and $R(7, 3, 2)$ be the vertices of ΔPQR.

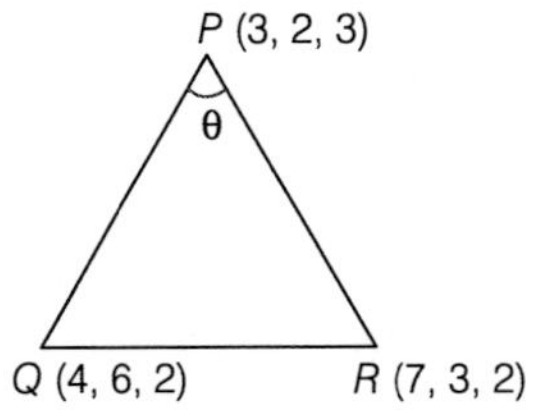

Let $\angle QPR = \theta$

$$\mathbf{QP} = -\hat{\mathbf{i}} - 4\hat{\mathbf{j}} + \hat{\mathbf{k}}$$

$$\mathbf{RP} = -4\hat{\mathbf{i}} - \hat{\mathbf{j}} + \hat{\mathbf{k}}$$

$\therefore \quad \cos\theta = \left| \frac{\mathbf{QP} \cdot \mathbf{RP}}{|\mathbf{QP}||\mathbf{RP}|} \right| = \left| \frac{4 + 4 + 1}{\sqrt{18}\sqrt{18}} \right|$

$$= \frac{9}{18} = \frac{1}{2}$$

So, $\quad \theta = \frac{\pi}{3}$

46. Given, $\mathbf{OA} = \mathbf{a}$, $\mathbf{OB} = 12\mathbf{a} + 4\mathbf{b}$ and $\mathbf{OC} = \mathbf{b}$

$\because$ S is parallelogram with adjacent sides OA and OC.

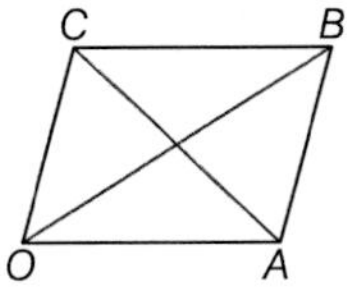

Area of quadrilateral

$$OABC = \frac{1}{2} |\bar{d}_1 \times \bar{d}_2| = \frac{1}{2} |\mathbf{OB} \times \mathbf{AC}|$$

$$= \frac{1}{2} |(12\mathbf{a} + 4\mathbf{b}) \times (\mathbf{b} - \mathbf{a})|$$

$$= \frac{1}{2} |12(\mathbf{a} \times \mathbf{b}) - 4(\mathbf{b} \times \mathbf{a})|$$

$$= \frac{1}{2} |16(\mathbf{a} \times \mathbf{b})|$$

$$= 8|\mathbf{a} \times \mathbf{b}|$$

Area of $S = |\mathbf{a} \times \mathbf{b}|$

$\therefore \quad \frac{\text{Area of quadrilateral } OABC}{\text{Area of } S} = 8$

47. Now, find diagonal

$\mathbf{AC} = (-3-2)\hat{\mathbf{i}} + (4-3)\hat{\mathbf{j}} + (-2-5)\hat{\mathbf{k}} = -5\hat{\mathbf{i}} + \hat{\mathbf{j}} - 7\hat{\mathbf{k}}$

and $\mathbf{BD} = \hat{\mathbf{i}} + 2\hat{\mathbf{j}} + 3\hat{\mathbf{k}}$

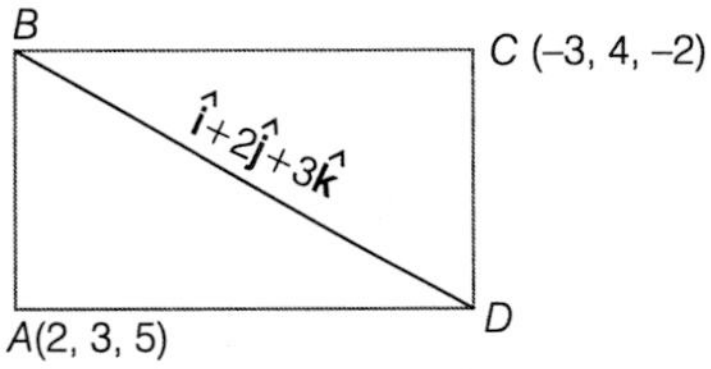

Hence, area of parallelogram $ABCD = \frac{1}{2} |\mathbf{AC} \times \mathbf{BD}|$

Now, $\mathbf{AC} \times \mathbf{BD} = \begin{vmatrix} \hat{\mathbf{i}} & \hat{\mathbf{j}} & \hat{\mathbf{k}} \\ -5 & 1 & -7 \\ 1 & 2 & 3 \end{vmatrix}$

$$= (3 + 14)\hat{\mathbf{i}} - (-15 + 7)\hat{\mathbf{j}} + (-10 - 1)\hat{\mathbf{k}}$$

$$= 17\hat{\mathbf{i}} + 8\hat{\mathbf{j}} - 11\hat{\mathbf{k}}$$

So, $|\mathbf{AC} \times \mathbf{BD}| = \sqrt{17^2 + 8^2 + 11^2} = \sqrt{474}$

Hence, area of parallelogram is $\frac{1}{2}\sqrt{474}$.

48. Given, $|\mathbf{a}| = 1$, $|\mathbf{b}| = 4$ and $\mathbf{a} \cdot \mathbf{b} = 2$ and $\mathbf{c} = 2(\mathbf{a} \times \mathbf{b}) - 3\mathbf{b}$

Dot product with $\mathbf{a}$ on both sides

$$\mathbf{c} \cdot \mathbf{a} = -6 \qquad \text{...(i)}$$

Dot product with $\mathbf{b}$ on both sides

$$\mathbf{b} \cdot \mathbf{c} = -48 \qquad \text{...(ii)}$$

$$\mathbf{c} \cdot \mathbf{c} = 4|\mathbf{a} \times \mathbf{b}|^2 + 9|\mathbf{b}|^2$$

$$|\mathbf{c}|^2 = 4[|\mathbf{a}|^2 |\mathbf{b}|^2 - (\mathbf{a} \cdot \mathbf{b})^2] + 9|\mathbf{b}|^2$$

$$= 4[(1)(4)^2 - (4)] + 9(16)$$

$$= 4[12] + 144 = 48 + 144$$

$$|\mathbf{c}|^2 = 192$$

$\therefore \quad \cos\theta = \frac{\mathbf{b} \cdot \mathbf{c}}{|\mathbf{b}||\mathbf{c}|}$

$$\cos\theta = \frac{-48}{\sqrt{192 \cdot 4}}$$

$\therefore \quad \theta = \cos^{-1}\left(\frac{-\sqrt{3}}{2}\right)$

49. Given, $\mathbf{a} = \hat{\mathbf{i}} + \alpha\hat{\mathbf{j}} + \beta\hat{\mathbf{k}}, \alpha, \beta \in R$.

Angle between $\mathbf{a}$ and $\mathbf{b} = \theta = \frac{\pi}{4}$

and $|\mathbf{b}|^2 = 6$

$\because \quad \mathbf{a}\cdot\mathbf{b} = 3\sqrt{2}$

$\therefore \quad |\mathbf{a}||\mathbf{b}|\cos\theta = 3\sqrt{2}$

$\Rightarrow \quad |\mathbf{a}|^2|\mathbf{b}|^2\cos^2\frac{\pi}{4} = 18$

$\Rightarrow \quad |\mathbf{a}|^2 \times 6 \times \frac{1}{2} = 18$

$\Rightarrow \quad |\mathbf{a}|^2 = 6$

$\therefore \quad 1 + \alpha^2 + \beta^2 = 6$

$\Rightarrow \quad \alpha^2 + \beta^2 = 5$

Now, $(\alpha^2 + \beta^2)|\mathbf{a}\times\mathbf{b}|^2 = 5|\mathbf{a}|^2|\mathbf{b}|^2\sin^2\theta$

$= 5 \times 6 \times 6 \times \frac{1}{2} = 90$

50. Given, $|\mathbf{b}| = 1$ and $|\mathbf{b}\times\mathbf{a}| = 2$

Let $\mathbf{d} = \mathbf{b}\times\mathbf{a}$

Now, for $|(\mathbf{b}\times\mathbf{a}) - \mathbf{b}|^2 = |\mathbf{d} - \mathbf{b}|^2$

$= |\mathbf{d}|^2 + |\mathbf{b}|^2 - 2\mathbf{d}\cdot\mathbf{b}$

$= |\mathbf{b}\times\mathbf{a}|^2 + |\mathbf{b}|^2 - 2(\mathbf{b}\times\mathbf{a})\cdot\mathbf{b}$

$= 4 + 1 - 0 = 5$

51. Given, $\mathbf{a} = 3\hat{\mathbf{i}} + \hat{\mathbf{j}} - 2\hat{\mathbf{k}}$, $\mathbf{b} = 4\hat{\mathbf{i}} + \hat{\mathbf{j}} + 7\hat{\mathbf{k}}$ and $\mathbf{c} = \hat{\mathbf{i}} - 3\hat{\mathbf{j}} + 4\hat{\mathbf{k}}$

$\therefore \quad \mathbf{p}\times\mathbf{b} = \mathbf{c}\times\mathbf{b}$

$\Rightarrow \quad \mathbf{p}\times\mathbf{b} - \mathbf{c}\times\mathbf{b} = 0$

$\Rightarrow \quad (\mathbf{p} - \mathbf{c})\times\mathbf{b} = 0$

$\therefore \quad \mathbf{p} - \mathbf{c} \parallel \mathbf{b}$

$\Rightarrow \quad \mathbf{p} - \mathbf{c} = \lambda\mathbf{b}$

$\Rightarrow \quad \mathbf{p} = \mathbf{c} + \lambda\mathbf{b}$

$\mathbf{p}\cdot\mathbf{a} = 0$ [given]

$0 = \mathbf{c}\cdot\mathbf{a} + \lambda\mathbf{a}\cdot\mathbf{b}$

$\lambda = -\frac{\mathbf{a}\cdot\mathbf{c}}{\mathbf{a}\cdot\mathbf{b}} = -\frac{(3-3-8)}{12+1-14}$

$= \frac{8}{-1} = -8$

$\therefore \mathbf{p} = \mathbf{c} - 8\mathbf{b} = -31\hat{\mathbf{i}} - 11\hat{\mathbf{j}} - 52\hat{\mathbf{k}}$

$\mathbf{p}\cdot(\hat{\mathbf{i}} - \hat{\mathbf{j}} - \hat{\mathbf{k}}) = -31 + 11 + 52 = 32$

52. Given, $\mathbf{a} = -5\hat{\mathbf{i}} + \hat{\mathbf{j}} - 3\hat{\mathbf{k}}$, $\mathbf{b} = \hat{\mathbf{i}} + 2\hat{\mathbf{j}} - 4\hat{\mathbf{k}}$

and $\mathbf{c} = (((\mathbf{a}\times\mathbf{b})\times\hat{\mathbf{i}})\times\hat{\mathbf{i}})\times\hat{\mathbf{i}}$

$$\mathbf{a}\times\mathbf{b} = \begin{vmatrix} \hat{\mathbf{i}} & \hat{\mathbf{j}} & \hat{\mathbf{k}} \\ -5 & 1 & -3 \\ 1 & 2 & -4 \end{vmatrix} = (-4+6)\,\hat{\mathbf{i}} - (20+3)\,\hat{\mathbf{j}} + (-10-1)\,\hat{\mathbf{k}}$$

$\mathbf{a}\times\mathbf{b} = 2\hat{\mathbf{i}} - 23\hat{\mathbf{j}} - 11\hat{\mathbf{k}}$

$$(\mathbf{a}\times\mathbf{b})\times\hat{\mathbf{i}} = \begin{vmatrix} \hat{\mathbf{i}} & \hat{\mathbf{j}} & \hat{\mathbf{k}} \\ 2 & -23 & -11 \\ 1 & 0 & 0 \end{vmatrix}$$

$= -11\hat{\mathbf{j}} + 23\hat{\mathbf{k}}$

$$((\mathbf{a}\times\mathbf{b})\times\hat{\mathbf{i}})\times\hat{\mathbf{i}} = \begin{vmatrix} \hat{\mathbf{i}} & \hat{\mathbf{j}} & \hat{\mathbf{k}} \\ 0 & -11 & 23 \\ 1 & 0 & 0 \end{vmatrix} = 23\hat{\mathbf{j}} + 11\hat{\mathbf{k}}$$

$$(((\mathbf{a}\times\mathbf{b})\times\hat{\mathbf{i}})\times\hat{\mathbf{i}})\times\hat{\mathbf{i}} = \begin{vmatrix} \hat{\mathbf{i}} & \hat{\mathbf{j}} & \hat{\mathbf{k}} \\ 0 & 23 & 11 \\ 1 & 0 & 0 \end{vmatrix} = 11\hat{\mathbf{j}} - 23\hat{\mathbf{k}}$$

$\therefore \quad \mathbf{c} = 11\hat{\mathbf{j}} - 23\hat{\mathbf{k}}$

$\mathbf{c}\cdot(-\hat{\mathbf{i}} + \hat{\mathbf{j}} + \hat{\mathbf{k}}) = (11\hat{\mathbf{j}} - 23\hat{\mathbf{k}})\cdot(-\hat{\mathbf{i}} + \hat{\mathbf{j}} + \hat{\mathbf{k}})$

$= 11 - 23 = -12$

53. We have, D divides BC in the ratio of $|\mathbf{AB}| : |\mathbf{AC}|$

$\therefore \quad \mathbf{AB} = -3\hat{\mathbf{i}} + 5\hat{\mathbf{j}} - 2\hat{\mathbf{k}}$ and $\mathbf{AC} = 2\hat{\mathbf{i}} + 3\hat{\mathbf{j}} + 5\hat{\mathbf{k}}$

$\therefore \quad |\mathbf{AB}| = \sqrt{9 + 25 + 4} = \sqrt{38}$

and $|\mathbf{AC}| = \sqrt{4 + 9 + 25} = \sqrt{38}$

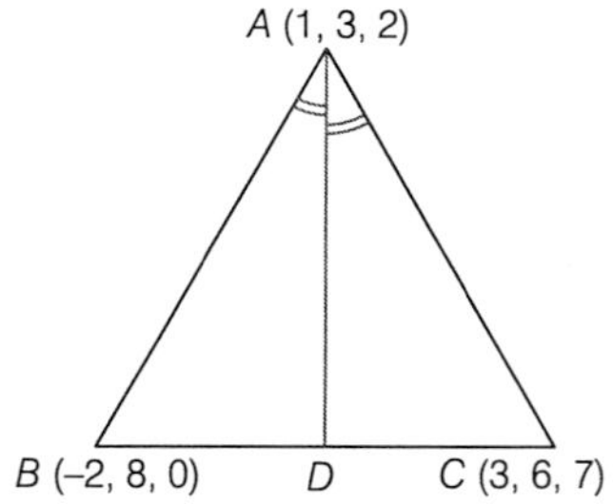

$\therefore \quad \frac{BD}{DC} = \frac{\sqrt{38}}{\sqrt{38}} = \frac{1}{1}$

So, D is mid-point of B and C.

So, $D\left(\frac{1}{2}, 7, \frac{7}{2}\right)$

Now, $\mathbf{AD} = -\frac{1}{2}\hat{\mathbf{i}} + 4\hat{\mathbf{j}} + \frac{3}{2}\hat{\mathbf{k}}$

$\therefore$ Projection of $\mathbf{AD}$ on $\mathbf{AC} = \frac{\mathbf{AD}\cdot\mathbf{DC}}{|\mathbf{AC}|} = \frac{-1 + 12 + \frac{15}{2}}{\sqrt{38}} = \frac{37}{2\sqrt{38}}$

54. Let θ be the acute angle between the vectors $\alpha\hat{\mathbf{i}} - 2\hat{\mathbf{j}} + 2\hat{\mathbf{k}}$ and $\alpha\hat{\mathbf{i}} + 2\alpha\hat{\mathbf{j}} - 2\hat{\mathbf{k}}$.

Now, $\cos\theta = \frac{(\alpha\hat{\mathbf{i}} - 2\hat{\mathbf{j}} + 2\hat{\mathbf{k}})\cdot(\alpha\hat{\mathbf{i}} + 2\alpha\hat{\mathbf{j}} - 2\hat{\mathbf{k}})}{\sqrt{\alpha^2 + 4 + 4}\sqrt{\alpha^2 + 4\alpha^2 + 4}}$

$\Rightarrow \quad \cos\theta = \frac{\alpha^2 - 4\alpha - 4}{\sqrt{\alpha^2 + 4 + 4}\sqrt{\alpha^2 + 4\alpha^2 + 4}}$

$\Rightarrow \quad \cos\theta = \frac{\alpha^2 - 4\alpha - 4}{\sqrt{\alpha^2 + 8}\sqrt{5\alpha^2 + 4}}$

$\Rightarrow \quad \alpha^2 - 4\alpha - 4 > 0$ [$\because \cos\theta > 0$ for acute angle]

$\Rightarrow \quad (\alpha - 2)^2 > 8$

$\Rightarrow \quad \alpha - 2 > 2\sqrt{2}$ or $\alpha - 2 < -2\sqrt{2}$

$\Rightarrow \quad \alpha > 2 + 2\sqrt{2}$ or $\alpha < 2 - 2\sqrt{2}$

$\Rightarrow x \in (-\infty, -0.82) \cup (4.82, \infty)$

Hence, least positive integral value of $\alpha = 5$.

55. Given, $\mathbf{a} = 3\hat{\mathbf{i}} + 2\hat{\mathbf{j}} + \hat{\mathbf{k}},\ \mathbf{b} = 2\hat{\mathbf{i}} - \hat{\mathbf{j}} + 3\hat{\mathbf{k}}$

$$\mathbf{a} \times \mathbf{b} = \begin{vmatrix} \hat{\mathbf{i}} & \hat{\mathbf{j}} & \hat{\mathbf{k}} \\ 3 & 2 & 1 \\ 2 & -1 & 3 \end{vmatrix} = 7\hat{\mathbf{i}} - 7\hat{\mathbf{j}} - 7\hat{\mathbf{k}}$$

Let $\mathbf{c} = x\hat{\mathbf{i}} + y\hat{\mathbf{j}} + z\hat{\mathbf{k}}$

$$(\mathbf{a} + \mathbf{b}) \times \mathbf{c} = 2(\mathbf{a} \times \mathbf{b}) + 24\hat{\mathbf{j}} - 6\hat{\mathbf{k}}$$

$$(5\hat{\mathbf{i}} + \hat{\mathbf{j}} + 4\hat{\mathbf{k}}) \times \mathbf{c} = 2(7\hat{\mathbf{i}} - 7\hat{\mathbf{j}} - 7\hat{\mathbf{k}}) + 24\hat{\mathbf{j}} - 6\hat{\mathbf{k}}$$

$$(5\hat{\mathbf{i}} + \hat{\mathbf{j}} + 4\hat{\mathbf{k}}) \times (x\hat{\mathbf{i}} + y\hat{\mathbf{j}} + z\hat{\mathbf{k}}) = 14\hat{\mathbf{i}} + 10\hat{\mathbf{j}} - 20\hat{\mathbf{k}}$$

$$\begin{vmatrix} \hat{\mathbf{i}} & \hat{\mathbf{j}} & \hat{\mathbf{k}} \\ 5 & 1 & 4 \\ x & y & z \end{vmatrix} = 14\hat{\mathbf{i}} + 10\hat{\mathbf{j}} - 20\hat{\mathbf{k}}$$

$$(z - 4y)\hat{\mathbf{i}} + (4x - 5z)\hat{\mathbf{j}} + (5y - x)\hat{\mathbf{k}} = 14\hat{\mathbf{i}} + 10\hat{\mathbf{j}} - 20\hat{\mathbf{k}}$$

$$z - 4y = 14$$
$$4x - 5z = 10$$
$$5y - x = -20$$
$$x = 5,\ y = -3 \text{ and } z = 2$$
$$|\mathbf{c}|^2 = x^2 + y^2 + z^2 = 25 + 9 + 4 = 38$$

56. Given, $|\mathbf{a}| = 1, |\mathbf{b}| = 4, \mathbf{a} \cdot \mathbf{b} = 2$

$\mathbf{c} = (2\mathbf{a} \times \mathbf{b}) - 3\mathbf{b}$, angle between $\mathbf{b}$ and $\mathbf{c} = \alpha$

Now, $\mathbf{a} \cdot \mathbf{b} = 2$

$$|a||b|\cos\theta = 2$$
$$1 \times 4\cos\theta = 2$$
$$\cos\theta = \frac{1}{2}$$

$\therefore$ Angle between $\mathbf{a}$ and $\mathbf{b}$

$$\theta = \frac{\pi}{3}$$
$$\mathbf{c} = (2\mathbf{a} \times \mathbf{b}) - 3\mathbf{b}$$
$$\mathbf{b} \cdot \mathbf{c} = \mathbf{b} \cdot (2\mathbf{a} \times \mathbf{b}) - 3 \cdot \mathbf{b} \cdot \mathbf{b}$$
$$|b||c|\cos\alpha = 0 - 3|b|^2$$
$$|c|\cos\alpha = -3|b| = -12 \quad \text{...(i)}$$

Again, $\mathbf{c} = 2\mathbf{a} \times \mathbf{b} - 3b$

$$|\mathbf{c}|^2 = (2\mathbf{a} \times \mathbf{b} - 3\mathbf{b})^2$$
$$= |2\mathbf{a} \times \mathbf{b}|^2 + 9|b|^2 - 6(2\mathbf{a} \times \mathbf{b}) \cdot \mathbf{b}$$
$$= 4|a|^2|b|^2\sin^2\frac{\pi}{3} + 9|\mathbf{b}|^2 - 0$$
$$= 4 \times 1 \times 16 \times \frac{3}{4} + 9 \times 16$$
$$= 48 + 144 = 192$$

By Eq. (i), $|c|^2\cos^2\alpha = 144$

$$\cos^2\alpha = \frac{144}{192}$$
$$\sin^2\alpha = 1 - \frac{144}{192} = \frac{192 - 144}{192}$$
$$\therefore \quad 192\sin^2\alpha = 48$$

57. We have, $\mathbf{a} = \hat{\mathbf{i}} + \hat{\mathbf{j}} + \hat{\mathbf{k}}, \mathbf{b} = -\hat{\mathbf{i}} - 8\hat{\mathbf{j}} + 2\hat{\mathbf{k}}$

and $\mathbf{c} = 4\hat{\mathbf{i}} + c_2\hat{\mathbf{j}} + c_3\hat{\mathbf{k}}$

Given, $\mathbf{b} \times \mathbf{a} = \mathbf{c} \times \mathbf{a}$

$$-10\hat{\mathbf{i}} + 3\hat{\mathbf{j}} + 7\hat{\mathbf{k}} = (c_2 - c_3)\hat{\mathbf{i}} + (c_3 - 4)\hat{\mathbf{j}} + (4 - c_2)\hat{\mathbf{k}}$$
$$c_2 - c_3 = -10,\ c_3 - 4 = 3,\ 4 - c_2 = 7$$
$$c_3 = 7,\ c_2 = -3$$

So, $\mathbf{c} = 4\hat{\mathbf{i}} - 3\hat{\mathbf{j}} + 7\hat{\mathbf{k}}$

Angle between c and $s(3\hat{\mathbf{i}} + 4\hat{\mathbf{j}} + \hat{\mathbf{k}})$ *is* θ.

$$\therefore \quad \cos\theta = \frac{12 - 12 + 7}{\sqrt{74} \cdot \sqrt{26}} \Rightarrow \frac{7}{\sqrt{74} \cdot \sqrt{26}}$$

Now, $\tan^2\theta = \sec^2\theta - 1 \Rightarrow \frac{74 \times 26}{49} - 1$

$$= \frac{1924 - 49}{49} = \frac{1875}{49} = 38.26$$

$\therefore \tan^2\theta = 38$

58. We have, $|\mathbf{a} + \mathbf{b} + \mathbf{c}| = |\mathbf{a} + \mathbf{b} - \mathbf{c}|$

$$\Rightarrow |\mathbf{a} + \mathbf{b} + \mathbf{c}|^2 = |\mathbf{a} + \mathbf{b} - \mathbf{c}|^2$$
$$\Rightarrow (\mathbf{a} + \mathbf{b} + \mathbf{c}) \cdot (\mathbf{a} + \mathbf{b} + \mathbf{c}) = (\mathbf{a} + \mathbf{b} - \mathbf{c}) \cdot (\mathbf{a} + \mathbf{b} - \mathbf{c})$$
$$\Rightarrow |\mathbf{a}|^2 + |\mathbf{b}|^2 + |\mathbf{c}|^2 + 2\mathbf{a} \cdot \mathbf{b} + 2\mathbf{b} \cdot \mathbf{c} + 2\mathbf{c} \cdot \mathbf{a}$$
$$= |\mathbf{a}|^2 + |\mathbf{b}|^2 + |\mathbf{c}|^2 + 2\mathbf{a} \cdot \mathbf{b} - 2\mathbf{b} \cdot \mathbf{c} - 2\mathbf{c} \cdot \mathbf{a}$$
$$\Rightarrow 4\,\mathbf{b} \cdot \mathbf{c} + 4\,\mathbf{c} \cdot \mathbf{a} = 0$$
$$\Rightarrow 4 \times 0 + 4\mathbf{c} \cdot \mathbf{a} = 0 \quad [\because \mathbf{b} \cdot \mathbf{c} = 0]$$
$$\Rightarrow 4\mathbf{c} \cdot \mathbf{a} = 0$$
$$\Rightarrow \mathbf{c} \cdot \mathbf{a} = 0$$

So, **a** and **c** are perpendicular to each other. So, Statement (B) is incorrect.

Again, we have

$$|\mathbf{a} + \lambda\mathbf{c}| \geq |\mathbf{a}|$$
$$\Rightarrow |\mathbf{a} + \lambda\mathbf{c}|^2 \geq |\mathbf{a}|^2$$
$$\Rightarrow (\mathbf{a} + \lambda\mathbf{c}) \cdot (\mathbf{a} + \lambda\mathbf{c}) \geq |\mathbf{a}|^2$$
$$\Rightarrow |\mathbf{a}|^2 + \lambda^2|\mathbf{c}|^2 + 2\lambda\mathbf{a} \cdot \mathbf{c} \geq |\mathbf{a}|^2$$
$$\Rightarrow \lambda^2|\mathbf{c}|^2 + 0 \geq 0 \quad [\because \mathbf{a} \cdot \mathbf{c} = 0]$$
$$\Rightarrow |\mathbf{c}| \geq 0$$

which is true as **c** is a non-zero vector.

So, Statement (A) is correct.

59. Given, $\alpha = 4\hat{\mathbf{i}} + 3\hat{\mathbf{j}} + 5\hat{\mathbf{k}},\ \beta = \mathbf{i} + 2\hat{\mathbf{j}} - 4\hat{\mathbf{k}}$

$\because \beta_1$ parallel to α.

$\therefore \beta_1 = \mu(4\hat{\mathbf{i}} + 3\hat{\mathbf{j}} + 5\hat{\mathbf{k}})$

$\because \quad \beta = \beta_1 + \beta_2 \Rightarrow \beta_2 = \beta - \beta_1$

$\therefore \beta_2 = (\hat{\mathbf{i}} + 2\hat{\mathbf{j}} - 4\hat{\mathbf{k}}) - \mu(4\hat{\mathbf{i}} + 3\hat{\mathbf{j}} + 5\hat{\mathbf{k}})$

$$\beta_2 = (1 - 4\mu)\hat{\mathbf{i}} + (2 - 3\mu)\hat{\mathbf{j}} - (4 + 5\mu)\hat{\mathbf{k}}$$

$\because \beta_2$ perpendicular to α, so its dot product = 0

$\therefore (1 - 4\mu)\,4 + (2 - 3\mu)\,3 - (4 + 5\mu)5 = 0$

$\Rightarrow \quad 4 - 16\mu + 6 - 9\mu - 20 - 25\mu = 0 \Rightarrow -10 - 50\mu = 0$

$$\therefore \quad \mu = \frac{-1}{5}$$

$\therefore$ The value of $5\beta_2 \cdot (\hat{\mathbf{i}} + \hat{\mathbf{j}} + \hat{\mathbf{k}})$

$$= 5\left\{\left(1 + \frac{4}{5}\right)\hat{\mathbf{i}} + \left(2 + \frac{3}{5}\right)\hat{\mathbf{j}} - \left(4 - \frac{5}{5}\right)\hat{\mathbf{k}}\right\} \cdot (\hat{\mathbf{i}} + \hat{\mathbf{j}} + \hat{\mathbf{k}})$$
$$= (9\hat{\mathbf{i}} + 13\hat{\mathbf{j}} - 15\hat{\mathbf{k}}) \cdot (\hat{\mathbf{i}} + \hat{\mathbf{j}} + \hat{\mathbf{k}}) = 9 + 13 - 15 = 7$$

60. **Decoding the Question**

In ΔABC, use $\mathbf{AB}+\mathbf{BC}+\mathbf{CA}=\mathbf{0}$ and then apply area of triangle formula.

Given that for a triangle

$\mathbf{AB}=-2\hat{\mathbf{i}}+\hat{\mathbf{j}}+3\hat{\mathbf{k}}$, $\mathbf{CB}=\alpha\hat{\mathbf{i}}+\beta\hat{\mathbf{j}}+\gamma\hat{\mathbf{k}}$ and $\mathbf{CA}=4\hat{\mathbf{i}}+3\hat{\mathbf{j}}+\delta\hat{\mathbf{k}}$

We know, $\mathbf{AB}+\mathbf{BC}+\mathbf{CA}=\mathbf{0}$

$$\Rightarrow (-2\hat{\mathbf{i}}+\hat{\mathbf{j}}+3\hat{\mathbf{k}})+(-\alpha\hat{\mathbf{i}}-\beta\hat{\mathbf{j}}-\gamma\hat{\mathbf{k}})+(4\hat{\mathbf{i}}+3\hat{\mathbf{j}}+\delta\hat{\mathbf{k}})=\mathbf{0}$$

$$\Rightarrow (-2-\alpha+4)\hat{\mathbf{i}}+(1-\beta+3)\hat{\mathbf{j}}+(3-\gamma+\delta)\hat{\mathbf{k}}=\mathbf{0}$$

$$\Rightarrow (-\alpha+2)\hat{\mathbf{i}}+(-\beta+4)\hat{\mathbf{j}}+(-\gamma+\delta+3)\hat{\mathbf{k}}=\mathbf{0}$$

On comparing both sides, we get

$$-\alpha+2=0-\beta+4=0$$

$$\alpha=2,\ \beta=4$$

and $-\gamma+\delta+3=0,\ -\gamma+\delta=-3$

Also, given the area of ΔABC is $5\sqrt{6}$.

Thus, $\frac{1}{2}|\mathbf{AB}\times\mathbf{AC}|=5\sqrt{6}\Rightarrow|\mathbf{AB}\times\mathbf{AC}|=10\sqrt{6}$ ...(i)

Now, $$\mathbf{AB}\times\mathbf{AC}=\begin{vmatrix}\hat{\mathbf{i}} & \hat{\mathbf{j}} & \hat{\mathbf{k}}\\ -2 & 1 & 3\\ 4 & 3 & \delta\end{vmatrix}$$

$$=\hat{\mathbf{i}}(\delta-9)+\hat{\mathbf{j}}(12+2\delta)+\hat{\mathbf{k}}(-6-4)$$

$$=\hat{\mathbf{i}}(\delta-9)+\hat{\mathbf{j}}(2\delta+12)-10\hat{\mathbf{k}}$$

From Eq. (i), we get

$$|\mathbf{AB}\times\mathbf{AC}|=10\sqrt{6}$$

$$\Rightarrow\sqrt{(\delta-9)^2+(2\delta+12)^2+100}=10\sqrt{6}$$

On squaring both sides, we get

$$(\delta-9)^2+(2\delta+12)^2+100=600$$

$$\Rightarrow\delta^2-18\delta+81+4\delta^2+48\delta+144-500=0$$

$$\Rightarrow 5\delta^2+30\delta-275=0$$

$$\therefore \delta=5\ (\delta>0)$$

So, $\delta-\gamma=-3$

$$-\gamma=-8\Rightarrow\gamma=8$$

Now, $\mathbf{CB}=2\hat{\mathbf{i}}+4\hat{\mathbf{j}}+8\hat{\mathbf{k}}$

$\mathbf{CA}=4\hat{\mathbf{i}}+3\hat{\mathbf{j}}+5\hat{\mathbf{k}}$

$\mathbf{CB}\cdot\mathbf{CA}=8+12+40=60$

61. Given that $|\mathbf{a}|=2$ and $|\mathbf{b}|=3$ and angle between the vector $\mathbf{a}$ and $\mathbf{b}$ be $\frac{\pi}{4}$.

$$\therefore |(\mathbf{a}+2\mathbf{b})\times(2\mathbf{a}-3\mathbf{b})|^2=|-3(\mathbf{a}\times\mathbf{b})+4(\mathbf{b}\times\mathbf{a})|^2$$

$$=|-3(\mathbf{a}\times\mathbf{b})-4(\mathbf{a}\times\mathbf{b})|^2$$

$$=\left|-7|\mathbf{a}|\times|\mathbf{b}|\times\sin\left(\frac{\pi}{4}\right)\right|^2$$

$$=\left|-7\times2\times3\times\frac{1}{\sqrt{2}}\right|^2$$

$$=49\times4\times9\times\frac{1}{2}$$

$$=882$$

62. Given, $\mathbf{a}=\hat{\mathbf{i}}+4\hat{\mathbf{j}}+2\hat{\mathbf{k}}$, $\mathbf{b}=3\hat{\mathbf{i}}-2\hat{\mathbf{j}}+7\hat{\mathbf{k}}$ and $\mathbf{c}=2\hat{\mathbf{i}}-\hat{\mathbf{j}}+4\hat{\mathbf{k}}$

Also, given $\mathbf{d}\cdot\mathbf{a}=24$ and $\mathbf{d}\times\mathbf{b}=\mathbf{c}\times\mathbf{b}$, then $(\mathbf{d}-\mathbf{c})\times\mathbf{b}=\mathbf{0}$

$$\Rightarrow \mathbf{d}-\mathbf{c}=\lambda\mathbf{b}\Rightarrow\mathbf{d}=\mathbf{c}+\lambda\mathbf{b}$$

Now, $$\mathbf{a}\cdot\mathbf{d}=\mathbf{a}\cdot(\mathbf{c}+\lambda\mathbf{b})=\mathbf{a}\cdot\mathbf{c}+\lambda(\mathbf{a}\cdot\mathbf{b})=6+\lambda(9)$$

$$\therefore 24=6+9\lambda\Rightarrow\lambda=2$$

$$\therefore \mathbf{d}=\mathbf{c}+2\mathbf{b}=(2\hat{\mathbf{i}}-\hat{\mathbf{j}}+4\hat{\mathbf{k}})+2(3\hat{\mathbf{i}}-2\hat{\mathbf{j}}+7\hat{\mathbf{k}})$$

$$=(8\hat{\mathbf{i}}-5\hat{\mathbf{j}}+18\hat{\mathbf{k}})$$

$$\therefore |\mathbf{d}|^2=64+25+324=413$$

63. We have, $\mathbf{a}$ is non-zero vector parallel to the line of intersection of the two planes described by

$$\hat{\mathbf{i}}+\hat{\mathbf{j}},\ \hat{\mathbf{i}}+\hat{\mathbf{k}}\text{ and }\hat{\mathbf{i}}-\hat{\mathbf{j}},\hat{\mathbf{j}}-\hat{\mathbf{k}}.$$

Let $\mathbf{x}_1$ and $\mathbf{x}_2$ are the normal vector to the plane $\hat{\mathbf{i}}+\hat{\mathbf{j}},\hat{\mathbf{i}}+\hat{\mathbf{k}}$ and $\hat{\mathbf{i}}-\hat{\mathbf{j}},\hat{\mathbf{j}}-\hat{\mathbf{k}}$, respectively.

$$\mathbf{x}_1=\begin{vmatrix}\hat{\mathbf{i}} & \hat{\mathbf{j}} & \hat{\mathbf{k}}\\ 1 & 1 & 0\\ 1 & 0 & 1\end{vmatrix}=\hat{\mathbf{i}}-\hat{\mathbf{j}}-\hat{\mathbf{k}}\text{ and }\mathbf{x}_2=\begin{vmatrix}\hat{\mathbf{i}} & \hat{\mathbf{j}} & \hat{\mathbf{k}}\\ 1 & -1 & 0\\ 0 & 1 & -1\end{vmatrix}=\hat{\mathbf{i}}+\hat{\mathbf{j}}+\hat{\mathbf{k}}$$

$$\mathbf{a}_1=\lambda|\mathbf{x}_1\times\mathbf{x}_2|$$

[$\because$ **a** is parallel to intersection of both planes]

$$a_1=\lambda\begin{vmatrix}\hat{\mathbf{i}} & \hat{\mathbf{j}} & \hat{\mathbf{k}}\\ 1 & -1 & -1\\ 1 & 1 & 1\end{vmatrix}$$

$$a_1=\lambda(-2\hat{\mathbf{j}}+2\hat{\mathbf{k}})$$

$\mathbf{a}\cdot\mathbf{b}=6$ [given]

$$\Rightarrow \lambda(0+4+2)=6\Rightarrow\lambda=1$$

$$\therefore \mathbf{a}=-2\hat{\mathbf{j}}+2\hat{\mathbf{k}}$$

$$\cos\theta=\frac{\mathbf{a}\cdot\mathbf{b}}{|\mathbf{a}||\mathbf{b}|}=\frac{6}{\sqrt{4+4}\sqrt{4+4+1}}=\frac{1}{\sqrt{2}}$$

$$\because \theta=\frac{\pi}{4}\Rightarrow\mathbf{a}\times\mathbf{b}=\begin{vmatrix}\hat{\mathbf{i}} & \hat{\mathbf{j}} & \hat{\mathbf{k}}\\ 0 & -2 & 2\\ 2 & -2 & 1\end{vmatrix}=2\hat{\mathbf{i}}+4\hat{\mathbf{j}}+4\hat{\mathbf{k}}$$

$$|\mathbf{a}\times\mathbf{b}|=\sqrt{4+16+16}=6$$

Hence, $(\theta,|\mathbf{a}\times\mathbf{b}|)=\left(\frac{\pi}{4},6\right)$

64. Given, $\mathbf{OP}=-\hat{\mathbf{i}}-2\hat{\mathbf{j}}+3\hat{\mathbf{k}}$, $\mathbf{OA}=-2\hat{\mathbf{i}}+\hat{\mathbf{j}}-3\hat{\mathbf{k}}$

$\mathbf{OB}=2\hat{\mathbf{i}}+4\hat{\mathbf{j}}-2\hat{\mathbf{k}}$ and $\mathbf{OC}=-4\hat{\mathbf{i}}+2\hat{\mathbf{j}}-\hat{\mathbf{k}}$

Now, $\mathbf{AB}=\mathbf{OB}-\mathbf{OA}$

$$=(2\hat{\mathbf{i}}+4\hat{\mathbf{j}}-2\hat{\mathbf{k}})-(-2\hat{\mathbf{i}}+\hat{\mathbf{j}}-3\hat{\mathbf{k}})=4\hat{\mathbf{i}}+3\hat{\mathbf{j}}+\hat{\mathbf{k}}$$

$\mathbf{AC}=\mathbf{OC}-\mathbf{OA}$

$$=(-4\hat{\mathbf{i}}+2\hat{\mathbf{j}}-\hat{\mathbf{k}})-(-2\hat{\mathbf{i}}+\hat{\mathbf{j}}-3\hat{\mathbf{k}})$$

$$=-2\hat{\mathbf{i}}+\hat{\mathbf{j}}+2\hat{\mathbf{k}}$$

The projection of vector **OP** on a vector perpendicular to the vector **AB** and **AC** is

$$\frac{\mathbf{OP}\cdot(\mathbf{AB}\times\mathbf{AC})}{|\mathbf{AB}\times\mathbf{AC}|}=\frac{(-\hat{\mathbf{i}}-2\hat{\mathbf{j}}+3\hat{\mathbf{k}})\cdot(5\hat{\mathbf{i}}-10\hat{\mathbf{j}}+10\hat{\mathbf{k}})}{|5\hat{\mathbf{i}}-10\hat{\mathbf{j}}+10\hat{\mathbf{k}}|}$$

$$=\frac{-5+20+30}{\sqrt{25+100+100}}=\frac{45}{15}=3$$

65.

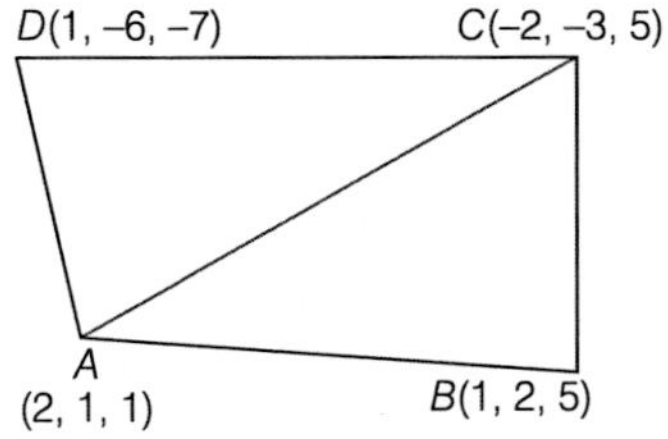

Required area of quadrilateral, $ABCD$

$$= \left|\frac{1}{2}(\mathbf{AB}\times\mathbf{AC}) + \frac{1}{2}(\mathbf{AC}\times\mathbf{AD})\right|$$

$$= \frac{1}{2}|(\mathbf{AB}\times\mathbf{AC}) - (\mathbf{AD}\times\mathbf{AC})| = \frac{1}{2}|(\mathbf{AB}-\mathbf{AD})\times\mathbf{AC}|$$

$$= \frac{1}{2}|\{(-\hat{\mathbf{i}}+\hat{\mathbf{j}}+4\hat{\mathbf{k}}) - (-\hat{\mathbf{i}}-7\hat{\mathbf{j}}-8\hat{\mathbf{k}})\}\times(-4\hat{\mathbf{i}}-4\hat{\mathbf{j}}+4\hat{\mathbf{k}})|$$

$$= \frac{1}{2}|(8\hat{\mathbf{j}}+12\hat{\mathbf{k}})\times(-4\hat{\mathbf{i}}-4\hat{\mathbf{j}}+4\hat{\mathbf{k}})|$$

$$= \frac{1}{2}\begin{vmatrix}\hat{\mathbf{i}} & \hat{\mathbf{j}} & \hat{\mathbf{k}}\\ 0 & 8 & 12\\ -4 & -4 & 4\end{vmatrix}$$

$$= \frac{1}{2}|(32+48)\hat{\mathbf{i}} - (0+48)\hat{\mathbf{j}} + (0+32)\hat{\mathbf{k}}|$$

$$= \frac{1}{2}|80\hat{\mathbf{i}} - 48\hat{\mathbf{j}} + 32\hat{\mathbf{k}}| = \frac{1}{2}\times 16\,|5\hat{\mathbf{i}}-3\hat{\mathbf{j}}+2\hat{\mathbf{k}}|$$

$$= 8\times\sqrt{25+9+4} = 8\sqrt{38}$$

66. Given, $\mathbf{a} = 2\hat{\mathbf{i}}+3\hat{\mathbf{j}}+4\hat{\mathbf{k}}$, $\mathbf{b} = \hat{\mathbf{i}}-2\hat{\mathbf{j}}-2\hat{\mathbf{k}}$ and $\mathbf{c} = -\hat{\mathbf{i}}+4\hat{\mathbf{j}}+3\hat{\mathbf{k}}$

$$\mathbf{b}\times\mathbf{c} = \begin{vmatrix}\hat{\mathbf{i}} & \hat{\mathbf{j}} & \hat{\mathbf{k}}\\ 1 & -2 & -2\\ -1 & 4 & 3\end{vmatrix}$$

$$= \hat{\mathbf{i}}(-6+8) - \hat{\mathbf{j}}(3-2) + \hat{\mathbf{k}}(4-2) = 2\hat{\mathbf{i}}-\hat{\mathbf{j}}+2\hat{\mathbf{k}}$$

$\therefore \quad \mathbf{d} = \lambda(\mathbf{b}\times\mathbf{c}) \Rightarrow \mathbf{d} = \lambda(2\hat{\mathbf{i}}-\hat{\mathbf{j}}+2\hat{\mathbf{k}})$

Since, $\quad \mathbf{a}\cdot\mathbf{d} = 18$

$\Rightarrow \lambda(4-3+8) = 18 \Rightarrow \lambda = 2$

$\therefore \quad \mathbf{d} = 2(2\hat{\mathbf{i}}-\hat{\mathbf{j}}+2\hat{\mathbf{k}})$

Now, $\quad |\mathbf{a}\times\mathbf{d}|^2 = |\mathbf{a}|^2|\mathbf{d}|^2 - (\mathbf{a}\cdot\mathbf{d})^2$

$$= (29)(36) - (18)^2 = 1044 - 324 = 720$$

67. We have, $\mathbf{a} = 2\hat{\mathbf{i}}-7\hat{\mathbf{j}}+5\hat{\mathbf{k}}$, $\mathbf{b} = \hat{\mathbf{i}}+\hat{\mathbf{k}}$, $\mathbf{c} = \hat{\mathbf{i}}+2\hat{\mathbf{j}}-3\hat{\mathbf{k}}$

Now, $\quad \mathbf{r}\times\mathbf{a} = \mathbf{c}\times\mathbf{a}$

$\mathbf{r}\times\mathbf{a} - \mathbf{c}\times\mathbf{a} = 0$

$\Rightarrow \quad (\mathbf{r}-\mathbf{c})\times\mathbf{a} = 0$

$\therefore \quad \mathbf{r}-\mathbf{c}\,||\,\mathbf{a}$

$\Rightarrow \quad \mathbf{r}-\mathbf{c} = \lambda\mathbf{a}$

$\Rightarrow \quad \mathbf{r} = \mathbf{c}+\lambda\mathbf{a}$

Now, $\quad \mathbf{r} = \mathbf{c}+\lambda\mathbf{a}$

$\Rightarrow \quad \mathbf{r}\cdot\mathbf{b} = \mathbf{c}\cdot\mathbf{b} + \lambda\,\mathbf{a}\cdot\mathbf{b}$

$\Rightarrow \quad 0 = (1+0-3) + \lambda(2+0+5)$

$\Rightarrow \quad 0 = -2+7\lambda \Rightarrow \lambda = \frac{2}{7}$

$\therefore \quad \mathbf{r} = \mathbf{c}+\frac{2}{7}\mathbf{a}$

$$= \hat{\mathbf{i}}+2\hat{\mathbf{j}}-3\hat{\mathbf{k}} + \frac{2}{7}(2\hat{\mathbf{i}}-7\hat{\mathbf{j}}+5\hat{\mathbf{k}}) = \frac{11}{7}\hat{\mathbf{i}} - \frac{11}{7}\hat{\mathbf{k}}$$

Now, $|\mathbf{r}| = \sqrt{\left(\frac{11}{7}\right)^2 + \left(-\frac{11}{7}\right)^2}$

$$= \sqrt{\frac{121}{49}+\frac{121}{49}} = \sqrt{\frac{2\times121}{49}} = \frac{11}{7}\sqrt{2}$$

68. We have,

$$\mathbf{a} = \hat{\mathbf{i}}+2\hat{\mathbf{j}}+3\hat{\mathbf{k}},\ \mathbf{b} = \hat{\mathbf{i}}-\hat{\mathbf{j}}+2\hat{\mathbf{k}} \text{ and } \mathbf{c} = 5\hat{\mathbf{i}}-3\hat{\mathbf{j}}+3\hat{\mathbf{k}}$$

Again, $\quad \mathbf{r}\times\mathbf{b} = \mathbf{c}\times\mathbf{b}$

$\Rightarrow \quad \mathbf{r}\times\mathbf{b} - \mathbf{c}\times\mathbf{b} = 0$

$\Rightarrow \quad (\mathbf{r}-\mathbf{c})\times\mathbf{b} = 0$

$\therefore \quad (\mathbf{r}-\mathbf{c})\,||\,\mathbf{b}$

$\therefore \quad \mathbf{r}-\mathbf{c} = \lambda\mathbf{b}$

$\Rightarrow \quad \mathbf{r} = \lambda\mathbf{b}+\mathbf{c}$

$$= \lambda(\hat{\mathbf{i}}-\hat{\mathbf{j}}+2\hat{\mathbf{k}}) + 5\hat{\mathbf{i}}-3\hat{\mathbf{j}}+3\hat{\mathbf{k}}$$

$$= (\lambda+5)\hat{\mathbf{i}} + (-\lambda-3)\hat{\mathbf{j}} + (2\lambda+3)\hat{\mathbf{k}}$$

Also, $\quad \mathbf{r}\cdot\mathbf{a} = 0$

$\Rightarrow ((\lambda+5)\hat{\mathbf{i}} + (-\lambda-3)\hat{\mathbf{j}} + (2\lambda+3)\hat{\mathbf{k}})\cdot(\hat{\mathbf{i}}+2\hat{\mathbf{j}}+3\hat{\mathbf{k}}) = 0$

$\Rightarrow \quad \lambda+5-2\lambda-6+6\lambda+9 = 0$

$\Rightarrow \quad 5\lambda+8 = 0$

$\Rightarrow \quad \lambda = -\frac{8}{5}$

$\therefore \quad \mathbf{r} = -\frac{8}{5}\mathbf{b}+\mathbf{c}$

$\Rightarrow \quad 5\mathbf{r} = -8\mathbf{b}+5\mathbf{c}$

$$= -8(\hat{\mathbf{i}}-\hat{\mathbf{j}}+2\hat{\mathbf{k}}) + 5(5\hat{\mathbf{i}}-3\hat{\mathbf{j}}+3\hat{\mathbf{k}}) = 17\hat{\mathbf{i}}-7\hat{\mathbf{j}}-\hat{\mathbf{k}}$$

$\therefore \quad 25|\mathbf{r}|^2 = (17)^2 + (-7)^2 + (-1)^2$

$$= 289+49+1 = 339$$

69. Given that $|\mathbf{a}| = 1$, $|\mathbf{b}| = 4$ and $\mathbf{a}\cdot\mathbf{b} = 2$ and $\mathbf{c} = (2\mathbf{a}\times\mathbf{b}) - 3\mathbf{b}$

Now, $\quad \mathbf{b}\cdot\mathbf{c} = \mathbf{b}\cdot[(2\mathbf{a}\times\mathbf{b}) - 3\mathbf{b}]$

$\Rightarrow \mathbf{b}\cdot(2\mathbf{a}\times\mathbf{b}) - 3\mathbf{b}\cdot\mathbf{b} = 0 - 3|\mathbf{b}|^2 \quad [\because \mathbf{b}\cdot(2\mathbf{a}\times\mathbf{b}) = 0]$

$\Rightarrow \quad -3(4)^2 = -48$

70. Given that $\mathbf{a} = \hat{\mathbf{i}}+2\hat{\mathbf{k}}$

$\mathbf{b} = \hat{\mathbf{i}}+\hat{\mathbf{j}}+\hat{\mathbf{k}}$

$\mathbf{c} = 7\hat{\mathbf{i}}-3\hat{\mathbf{j}}+4\hat{\mathbf{k}}$

$\mathbf{r}\times\mathbf{b} + \mathbf{b}\times\mathbf{c} = 0$ and $\mathbf{r}\cdot\mathbf{a} = 0$

$\Rightarrow \quad \mathbf{r}\times\mathbf{b} - \mathbf{c}\times\mathbf{b} = 0$

$\Rightarrow \quad (\mathbf{r}-\mathbf{c})\times\mathbf{b} = 0 \Rightarrow \mathbf{r} = \mathbf{c}+\lambda\mathbf{b}$

$\because \quad \mathbf{r}\cdot\mathbf{a} = 0$

So, $\quad (\mathbf{c}+\lambda\mathbf{b})\cdot\mathbf{a} = 0 \Rightarrow \mathbf{c}\cdot\mathbf{a} + \lambda\,\mathbf{b}\cdot\mathbf{a} = 0$

$\Rightarrow \quad (8+7) + \lambda\cdot 3 = 0$

$\Rightarrow \quad \lambda = -5 \Rightarrow \mathbf{r} = \mathbf{c}-5\mathbf{b}$

Now, $\mathbf{r}\cdot\mathbf{c} = (\mathbf{c}-5\mathbf{b})\cdot\mathbf{c} = \mathbf{c}\cdot\mathbf{c} - 5\mathbf{b}\cdot\mathbf{c}$

$$= 34$$

71. Let $\mathbf{a} = 4\hat{\mathbf{i}} + 3\hat{\mathbf{j}}$

and $\mathbf{b} = 3\hat{\mathbf{i}} - 4\hat{\mathbf{j}} + 5\hat{\mathbf{k}}$

Given, $\mathbf{c}\cdot(\mathbf{a}\times\mathbf{b}) + 25 = 0$, $\mathbf{c}\cdot(\hat{\mathbf{i}}+\hat{\mathbf{j}}+\hat{\mathbf{k}}) = 4$

and projection of **c** on **a** is 1.

Let $\mathbf{c} = c_1\hat{\mathbf{i}} + c_2\hat{\mathbf{j}} + c_3\hat{\mathbf{k}}$

$$\mathbf{a}\times\mathbf{b} = \begin{vmatrix} \hat{\mathbf{i}} & \hat{\mathbf{j}} & \hat{\mathbf{k}} \\ 4 & 3 & 0 \\ 3 & -4 & 5 \end{vmatrix} = 15\hat{\mathbf{i}} - 20\hat{\mathbf{j}} - 25\hat{\mathbf{k}}$$

$\therefore\ \mathbf{c}\cdot(\mathbf{a}\times\mathbf{b}) = 15c_1 - 20c_2 - 25c_3$

Given, $\mathbf{c}\cdot(\mathbf{a}\times\mathbf{b}) + 25 = 0$

$\Rightarrow\ 15c_1 - 20c_2 - 25c_3 + 25 = 0$ ... (i)

Also, $\mathbf{c}\cdot(\hat{\mathbf{i}}+\hat{\mathbf{j}}+\hat{\mathbf{k}}) = 4$

$\Rightarrow\ c_1 + c_2 + c_3 - 4 = 0$ ...(ii)

and projection of **c** on **a** is 1.

$\Rightarrow\ \dfrac{\mathbf{c}\cdot\mathbf{a}}{|\mathbf{a}|} = 1$

$\Rightarrow\ 4c_1 + 3c_2 - 5 = 0$ ...(iii)

On solving Eqs. (i), (ii) and (iii), we get

$c_1 = 2, c_2 = -1, c_3 = 3$

So, $\mathbf{c} = 2\hat{\mathbf{i}} - \hat{\mathbf{j}} + 3\hat{\mathbf{k}}$

Now, projection of **c** on **b** equals,

$$\frac{\mathbf{c}\cdot\mathbf{b}}{|\mathbf{b}|} = \frac{6+4+15}{5\sqrt{2}} = \frac{25}{5\sqrt{2}} = \frac{5}{\sqrt{2}}$$

72. $\mathbf{a} = -\hat{\mathbf{i}} + 2\hat{\mathbf{j}} + \hat{\mathbf{k}}$ is rotated through a right angle, passing through Y-axis, and resulted vector is **b**.

$\mathbf{b} = \lambda\,\mathbf{a}\times(\mathbf{a}\times\hat{\mathbf{j}})$

$$\mathbf{a}\times\hat{\mathbf{j}} = \begin{vmatrix} \hat{\mathbf{i}} & \hat{\mathbf{j}} & \hat{\mathbf{k}} \\ -1 & 2 & 1 \\ 0 & 1 & 0 \end{vmatrix} = -\hat{\mathbf{i}} + 0\hat{\mathbf{j}} - \hat{\mathbf{k}}$$

$$\Rightarrow \mathbf{a}\times(\mathbf{a}\times\hat{\mathbf{j}}) = \begin{vmatrix} \hat{\mathbf{i}} & \hat{\mathbf{j}} & \hat{\mathbf{k}} \\ -1 & 2 & 1 \\ -1 & 0 & -1 \end{vmatrix} = -2\hat{\mathbf{i}} - 2\hat{\mathbf{j}} + 2\hat{\mathbf{k}}$$

$\mathbf{b} = \lambda(-2\hat{\mathbf{i}} - 2\hat{\mathbf{j}} + 2\hat{\mathbf{k}})$

Also, $|\mathbf{a}| = |\mathbf{b}| \Rightarrow \sqrt{1+4+1} = \sqrt{(-2\lambda)^2 + (-2\lambda)^2 + (2\lambda)^2}$

$6 = 12\lambda^2 \Rightarrow \lambda^2 = \dfrac{1}{2} \Rightarrow \lambda = \pm\dfrac{1}{\sqrt{2}}$

[($\lambda = 1/\sqrt{2}$ rejected, $\because$ **b** makes acute angle with Y-axis)]

$\mathbf{b} = \dfrac{-1}{\sqrt{2}}(-2\hat{\mathbf{i}} - 2\hat{\mathbf{j}} + 2\hat{\mathbf{k}}) = -\sqrt{2}\,(-\hat{\mathbf{i}} - \hat{\mathbf{j}} + \hat{\mathbf{k}})$

Projection of $(3\mathbf{a} + \sqrt{2}\mathbf{b})$ on

$\mathbf{c} = (3\mathbf{a} + \sqrt{2}\mathbf{b})\cdot\dfrac{\mathbf{c}}{|\mathbf{c}|}$

$= (-3\hat{\mathbf{i}} + 6\hat{\mathbf{j}} + 3\hat{\mathbf{k}} + 2\hat{\mathbf{i}} + 2\hat{\mathbf{j}} - 2\hat{\mathbf{k}})\cdot\dfrac{(5\hat{\mathbf{i}} + 4\hat{\mathbf{j}} + 3\hat{\mathbf{k}})}{\sqrt{25+16+9}}$

$= \dfrac{(-\hat{\mathbf{i}} + 8\hat{\mathbf{j}} + \hat{\mathbf{k}})\cdot(5\hat{\mathbf{i}} + 4\hat{\mathbf{j}} + 3\hat{\mathbf{k}})}{5\sqrt{2}}$

$= \dfrac{-5+32+3}{5\sqrt{2}} = \dfrac{30}{5\sqrt{2}} = 3\sqrt{2}$

73. Given, $\mathbf{a} = 3\hat{\mathbf{i}} + \hat{\mathbf{j}} - \hat{\mathbf{k}}$

and $\mathbf{c} = 2\hat{\mathbf{i}} - 3\hat{\mathbf{j}} + 3\hat{\mathbf{k}}$

and given $\mathbf{a} = \mathbf{b}\times\mathbf{c}$

and $|\mathbf{a}| = \sqrt{11}$, $|\mathbf{c}| = \sqrt{22}$

$|\mathbf{a}| = |\mathbf{b}\times\mathbf{c}| = |\mathbf{b}|\,|\mathbf{c}|\sin\theta$

$\sqrt{11} = \sqrt{50}\,\sqrt{22}\sin\theta \Rightarrow \sin\theta = \dfrac{1}{10}$

$|\mathbf{b}+\mathbf{c}|^2 = |\mathbf{b}|^2 + |\mathbf{c}|^2 + 2\mathbf{b}\cdot\mathbf{c}$

$|\mathbf{b}|^2 + |\mathbf{c}|^2 + 2|\mathbf{b}|\,|\mathbf{c}|\cos\theta = 50 + 22 + 2\times\sqrt{50}\times\sqrt{22}\times\dfrac{\sqrt{99}}{10}$

$= 72 + 66$

Now, $|72 - |\mathbf{b}+\mathbf{c}|^2| = 66$

74. **Decoding the Question**

Use lagrange's identity formula $|\mathbf{a}\times\mathbf{b}| + (\mathbf{a}\cdot\mathbf{b})^2 = |\mathbf{a}|^2|\mathbf{b}|^2$

Given, $\mathbf{a} = \hat{\mathbf{i}} + 2\hat{\mathbf{j}} + 3\hat{\mathbf{k}}$, $\mathbf{b} = \hat{\mathbf{i}} + \hat{\mathbf{j}} - \hat{\mathbf{k}}$

$\mathbf{a}\cdot\mathbf{c} = 11$, $\mathbf{b}\cdot(\mathbf{a}\times\mathbf{c}) = 27$, $\mathbf{b}\cdot\mathbf{c} = -\sqrt{3}\,|\mathbf{b}|$

$\Rightarrow\ \mathbf{b}\cdot\mathbf{c} = -\sqrt{3}\times\sqrt{3}$ $[\because |\mathbf{b}| = \sqrt{1^2 + 1^2 + (-1)^2} = \sqrt{3}]$

$\Rightarrow\ \mathbf{b}\cdot\mathbf{c} = -3$

Let $\mathbf{c} = x\hat{\mathbf{i}} + y\hat{\mathbf{j}} + z\hat{\mathbf{k}}$

Then, using $\mathbf{a}\cdot\mathbf{c} = 11$

$\Rightarrow\ x + 2y + 3z = 11$ ...(i)

and using $\mathbf{b}\cdot\mathbf{c} = -3$

$\Rightarrow\ x + y - z = -3$ ...(ii)

and using $\mathbf{b}\cdot(\mathbf{a}\times\mathbf{c}) = 27$

$\Rightarrow\ (\mathbf{a}\times\mathbf{b})\cdot\mathbf{c} = -27$

$$\therefore\quad \mathbf{a}\times\mathbf{b} = \begin{vmatrix} \hat{\mathbf{i}} & \hat{\mathbf{j}} & \hat{\mathbf{k}} \\ 1 & 2 & 3 \\ 1 & 1 & -1 \end{vmatrix} = -5\hat{\mathbf{i}} + 4\hat{\mathbf{j}} - \hat{\mathbf{k}}$$

$\Rightarrow -5x + 4y - z = -27 \Rightarrow 5x - 4y + z = 27$ ...(iii)

On adding Eqs. (ii) and (iii), we get

$6x - 3y = 24$

$\Rightarrow\ 2x - y = 8$

$\Rightarrow\ y = 2x - 8$ ...(iv)

On multiplying Eq. (ii) with 3, then adding Eqs. (i) and (ii), we get

$4x + 5y = 2$

Using Eq. (iv), we get

$4x + 5(2x - 8) = 2$

$\Rightarrow\ x = 3$

From Eq. (iv), we get

$y = 2\times 3 - 8 = -2$

Now, from Eq. (i),

$3 + 2(-2) + 3z = 11$

$\Rightarrow\ z = 4$

So, $\mathbf{c} = 3\hat{\mathbf{i}} - 2\hat{\mathbf{j}} + 4\hat{\mathbf{k}}$

Now, $|\mathbf{a}\times\mathbf{c}|^2 = -(\mathbf{a}\cdot\mathbf{c})^2 + |\mathbf{a}|^2|\mathbf{c}|^2$

$= -(3 - 4 + 12)^2 + 14\times 29 = -121 + 406 = 285$

75. **Decoding the Question**

If $\mathbf{p} \times \mathbf{q} = 0$, then $\mathbf{p}$ is parallel to $\mathbf{q}$. Also, use dot product.

Given, $\mathbf{a} = 6\hat{\mathbf{i}} + 9\hat{\mathbf{j}} + 12\hat{\mathbf{k}}$

$$\mathbf{b} = \alpha\hat{\mathbf{i}} + 11\hat{\mathbf{j}} - 2\hat{\mathbf{k}}$$

$$\mathbf{a}\cdot\mathbf{b} = 6\alpha + 99 - 24 = 6\alpha + 75$$

$$|\mathbf{a}| = \sqrt{36 + 81 + 144} = \sqrt{261}$$

Since, $\mathbf{a}\times\mathbf{c} = \mathbf{a}\times\mathbf{b}, \mathbf{a}\cdot\mathbf{c} = -12$

and $\mathbf{c}\cdot(\hat{\mathbf{i}} - 2\hat{\mathbf{j}} + \hat{\mathbf{k}}) = 5$

$$\mathbf{a}\times\mathbf{c} = \mathbf{a}\times\mathbf{b}$$

$\Rightarrow$ $\mathbf{a}\times(\mathbf{c}-\mathbf{b}) = \mathbf{0}$

$\Rightarrow$ $\mathbf{c}-\mathbf{b} \parallel \mathbf{a}$

$\Rightarrow$ $\mathbf{c} = \mathbf{b} + \lambda\mathbf{a}$

Now, $\mathbf{c}\cdot\mathbf{a} = \mathbf{b}\cdot\mathbf{a} + \lambda|\mathbf{a}|^2$

$\Rightarrow 6\alpha + 75 + 261\lambda = -12$

$\Rightarrow$ $6\alpha + 261\lambda = -87$ ...(i)

Also, $(\mathbf{b} + \lambda\mathbf{a})\cdot(\hat{\mathbf{i}} - 2\hat{\mathbf{j}} + \hat{\mathbf{k}}) = 5$

$\Rightarrow (\alpha - 22 - 2) + \lambda(6 - 18 + 12) = 5$

$\Rightarrow$ $\alpha = 29$

From Eq. (i), $\lambda = -1$

Hence, $\mathbf{c}(\hat{\mathbf{i}} + \hat{\mathbf{j}} + \hat{\mathbf{k}}) = (\mathbf{b}-\mathbf{a})\cdot(\hat{\mathbf{i}} + \hat{\mathbf{j}} + \hat{\mathbf{k}}) = 11$

76. Given, $|\mathbf{a}| = \sqrt{31}$, $4|\mathbf{b}| = |\mathbf{c}| = 2$, $2(\mathbf{a}\times\mathbf{b}) = 3(\mathbf{c}\times\mathbf{a})$ and angle between $\mathbf{b}$ and $\mathbf{c}$ is $\frac{2\pi}{3}$.

Now, $2(\mathbf{a}\times\mathbf{b}) = 3(\mathbf{c}\times\mathbf{a})$

$\Rightarrow$ $3(\mathbf{c}\times\mathbf{a}) + 2(\mathbf{b}\times\mathbf{a}) = 0$

$\Rightarrow$ $(3\mathbf{c} + 2\mathbf{b})\times\mathbf{a} = 0$

$\therefore$ $(3\mathbf{c} + 2\mathbf{b}) \| \mathbf{a}$

$\Rightarrow$ $3\mathbf{c} + 2\mathbf{b} = \lambda\mathbf{a}$

$\Rightarrow$ $|3\mathbf{c} + 2\mathbf{b}| = |\lambda\mathbf{a}|$

$\Rightarrow$ $|3\mathbf{c} + 2\mathbf{b}|^2 = \lambda^2|\mathbf{a}|^2$

$\Rightarrow$ $(3\mathbf{c} + 2\mathbf{b})\cdot(3\mathbf{c} + 2\mathbf{b}) = \lambda^2|\mathbf{a}|^2$

$\Rightarrow$ $9|\mathbf{c}|^2 + 4|\mathbf{b}|^2 + 12\mathbf{c}\cdot\mathbf{b} = \lambda^2|\mathbf{a}|^2$

$\Rightarrow$ $9|\mathbf{c}|^2 + 4|\mathbf{b}|^2 + 12|\mathbf{c}||\mathbf{b}|\cos\frac{2\pi}{3} = \lambda^2|\mathbf{a}|^2$

$\Rightarrow 9(2)^2 + 4\left(\frac{1}{2}\right)^2 + 12\times 2\times\frac{1}{2}\times\left(-\frac{1}{2}\right) = \lambda^2(\sqrt{31})^2$

$\Rightarrow$ $36 + 1 - 6 = 31\lambda^2$

$\Rightarrow$ $31 = 31\lambda^2$

$\Rightarrow$ $\lambda^2 = 1 \Rightarrow \lambda = \pm 1$

$\therefore$ $3\mathbf{c} + 2\mathbf{b} = \pm\mathbf{a}$

Now, $3\mathbf{c} + 2\mathbf{b} = \pm\mathbf{a}$

$\Rightarrow$ $(3\mathbf{c} + 2\mathbf{b})\cdot\mathbf{b} = \pm\mathbf{a}\cdot\mathbf{b}$

$\Rightarrow$ $3\mathbf{c}\cdot\mathbf{b} + 2|\mathbf{b}|^2 = \pm\mathbf{a}\cdot\mathbf{b}$

$\Rightarrow$ $3|\mathbf{c}||\mathbf{b}|\cos\frac{2\pi}{3} + 2|\mathbf{b}|^2 = \mathbf{a}\cdot\mathbf{b}$

$\Rightarrow 3\times 2\times\frac{1}{2}\times\left(-\frac{1}{2}\right) + 2\left(\frac{1}{2}\right)^2 = \pm\mathbf{a}\cdot\mathbf{b}$

$\Rightarrow$ $-\frac{3}{2} + \frac{1}{2} = \pm\mathbf{a}\cdot\mathbf{b}$

$\Rightarrow$ $\mathbf{a}\cdot\mathbf{b} = \pm 1 \Rightarrow (\mathbf{a}\cdot\mathbf{b})^2 = 1$

Again, $|\mathbf{a}\times\mathbf{b}|^2 = |\mathbf{a}|^2|\mathbf{b}|^2 - |\mathbf{a}\cdot\mathbf{b}|^2$

$$= (\sqrt{31})^2\left(\frac{1}{2}\right)^2 - (1)^2 = \frac{31}{4} - 1 = \frac{27}{4}$$

Now, $3(\mathbf{c}\times\mathbf{a}) = 2(\mathbf{a}\times\mathbf{b})$

$\Rightarrow$ $\mathbf{c}\times\mathbf{a} = \frac{2}{3}\times(\mathbf{a}\times\mathbf{b})$

$\Rightarrow$ $|\mathbf{c}\times\mathbf{a}| = \frac{2}{3}|\mathbf{a}\times\mathbf{b}|$

$\Rightarrow$ $|\mathbf{c}\times\mathbf{a}|^2 = \frac{4}{9}|\mathbf{a}\times\mathbf{b}|^2 = \frac{4}{9}\times\frac{27}{4} = 3$

$\therefore$ $\left(\frac{\mathbf{a}\times\mathbf{c}}{\mathbf{a}\cdot\mathbf{b}}\right)^2 = \frac{3}{1} = 3$

77. We know that

$$|\mathbf{a}\cdot\mathbf{b}|^2 + |\mathbf{a}\times\mathbf{b}|^2 = |\mathbf{a}|^2|\mathbf{b}|^2$$

$\Rightarrow$ $|\mathbf{a}\cdot\mathbf{b}|^2 + (\sqrt{48})^2 = (\sqrt{14})^2(\sqrt{6})^2$

$\Rightarrow$ $|\mathbf{a}\cdot\mathbf{b}|^2 + 48 = 14\times 6$

$\Rightarrow$ $|\mathbf{a}\cdot\mathbf{b}|^2 + 48 = 84$

$\Rightarrow$ $|\mathbf{a}\cdot\mathbf{b}|^2 = 36$

78. Given, $\mathbf{a} = \hat{\mathbf{i}} + 2\hat{\mathbf{j}} + \lambda\hat{\mathbf{k}}$, $\mathbf{b} = 3\hat{\mathbf{i}} - 5\hat{\mathbf{j}} - \lambda\hat{\mathbf{k}}$

Let $\mathbf{c} = x\hat{\mathbf{i}} + y\hat{\mathbf{j}} + z\hat{\mathbf{k}}$

$\because$ Given, $\mathbf{a}\cdot\mathbf{c} = 7$

$\therefore$ $(\hat{\mathbf{i}} + 2\hat{\mathbf{j}} + \lambda\hat{\mathbf{k}})\cdot(x\hat{\mathbf{i}} + y\hat{\mathbf{j}} + z\hat{\mathbf{k}}) = 7$

$x + 2y + \lambda z = 7$ ...(i)

Also, $2\mathbf{b}\cdot\mathbf{c} + 43 = 0$

$2(3\hat{\mathbf{i}} - 5\hat{\mathbf{j}} - \lambda\hat{\mathbf{k}})\cdot(x\hat{\mathbf{i}} + y\hat{\mathbf{j}} + z\hat{\mathbf{k}}) + 43 = 0$

$6x - 10y - 2\lambda z + 43 = 0$ ...(ii)

Again, $\mathbf{a}\times\mathbf{c} = \mathbf{b}\times\mathbf{c}$

$$\therefore \begin{vmatrix} \hat{\mathbf{i}} & \hat{\mathbf{j}} & \hat{\mathbf{k}} \\ 1 & 2 & \lambda \\ x & y & z \end{vmatrix} = \begin{vmatrix} \hat{\mathbf{i}} & \hat{\mathbf{j}} & \hat{\mathbf{k}} \\ 3 & -5 & -\lambda \\ x & y & z \end{vmatrix}$$

$\Rightarrow \hat{\mathbf{i}}(2z - \lambda y) - \hat{\mathbf{j}}(z - \lambda x) + \hat{\mathbf{k}}(y - 2x)$

$$= \hat{\mathbf{i}}(-5z + \lambda y) - \hat{\mathbf{j}}(3z + \lambda x) + \hat{\mathbf{k}}(3y + 5x)$$

$\therefore$ On comparing, we get

$$2z - \lambda y = -5z + \lambda y$$

$\Rightarrow$ $7z = 2\lambda y$ ...(iii)

$\Rightarrow$ $z - \lambda x = 3z + \lambda x$

$\Rightarrow$ $-2z = 2\lambda x$ ...(iv)

and $y - 2x = 3y + 5x \Rightarrow -\mathbf{2}y = \mathbf{7}x$

On putting, $x = \frac{-2y}{7}$ in Eqs. (i) and (ii), we get

$$\frac{-2y}{7} + 2y + \lambda z = 7$$

$\Rightarrow$ $12y + 7\lambda z = 49$ ...(v)

Also, $6\left(\frac{-2y}{7}\right) - 10y - 2\lambda z + 43 = 0$

$$\frac{-12y - 70y - 14\lambda z}{7} = -43$$

$$\Rightarrow \quad 82y + 14\lambda z = 301 \quad \text{...(vi)}$$

$$\because \quad 7z = 2\lambda y$$

$$\Rightarrow \quad z = \frac{2\lambda y}{7}$$

From Eqs. (v) and (vi), we get

$$\therefore \quad 12y + 7\lambda\left(\frac{2\lambda y}{7}\right) = 49$$

$$12y + 2\lambda^2 y = 49 \quad \text{...(vii)}$$

Also, $82y + 14\lambda\left(\frac{2\lambda y}{7}\right) = 301$

$$82y + 4\lambda^2 y = 301 \quad \text{...(viii)}$$

Multiply by 2 in Eq. (vii), then subtract Eq. (viii) from it

$$24y + 4\lambda^2 y = 98$$

$$\Rightarrow \quad \underline{-82y - 4\lambda^2 y = -301}$$

$$\Rightarrow \quad 58y = 203$$

$$\Rightarrow \quad y = \frac{203}{58} = \frac{7}{2}$$

$$\therefore \quad x = \frac{-2y}{7} = \frac{-2}{7} \times \frac{7}{2} = -1$$

and $z = \frac{2\lambda}{7} \times \frac{7}{2} = \lambda \Rightarrow z = \lambda$

From Eq. (i), we get

$$-1 + 7 + \lambda^2 = 7$$

$$\Rightarrow \quad \lambda^2 = 1 \Rightarrow \lambda = \pm 1$$

$$\therefore \quad |\mathbf{a} \cdot \mathbf{b}| = |(\hat{\mathbf{i}} + 2\hat{\mathbf{j}} + \lambda\hat{\mathbf{k}}) \cdot (3\hat{\mathbf{i}} - 5\hat{\mathbf{j}} - \lambda\hat{\mathbf{k}})|$$

$$= |3 - 10 - \lambda^2| = |3 - 10 - 1| = |-8| = 8$$

79. We have, $(\mathbf{a} + \mathbf{b} + \mathbf{c}) \times \mathbf{c} = \mathbf{0}$

$$\Rightarrow \quad (\mathbf{a} + \mathbf{b}) \times \mathbf{c} + \mathbf{c} \times \mathbf{c} = \mathbf{0}$$

$$\Rightarrow \quad (\mathbf{a} + \mathbf{b}) \times \mathbf{c} = \mathbf{0} \quad [\because \mathbf{c} \times \mathbf{c} = 0]$$

$$\Rightarrow \quad \mathbf{c} = k(\mathbf{a} + \mathbf{b})$$

$$= k((\lambda\hat{\mathbf{i}} + \hat{\mathbf{j}} - \hat{\mathbf{k}}) + (3\hat{\mathbf{i}} - \hat{\mathbf{j}} + 2\hat{\mathbf{k}}))$$

$$= k((\lambda + 3)\hat{\mathbf{i}} + \hat{\mathbf{k}} \quad \text{...(i)}$$

Now, $\mathbf{a} \cdot \mathbf{c} = -17 \Rightarrow \lambda k(\lambda + 3) - k = -17$ ...(ii)

$\mathbf{b} \cdot \mathbf{c} = -20 \Rightarrow 3k(\lambda + 3) + 2k = -20$

$$\Rightarrow \quad \lambda = \frac{-20 - 11k}{3k} \quad \text{...(iii)}$$

On putting in Eq. (ii), we get

$$13k^2 + 413k + 400 = 0$$

$$\Rightarrow \quad k = -1, -\frac{400}{13}$$

$$\Rightarrow \quad \lambda = 3, \frac{-207}{60}$$

$$\because \quad \lambda \in Z$$

$$\Rightarrow \quad \lambda = 3 \text{ and } k = -1$$

$$\therefore \quad \mathbf{c} = -6\hat{\mathbf{i}} - \hat{\mathbf{k}}$$

Now, $\mathbf{c} \times (\lambda\hat{\mathbf{i}} + \hat{\mathbf{j}} + \hat{\mathbf{k}}) = (-6\hat{\mathbf{i}} - \hat{\mathbf{k}}) \times (3\hat{\mathbf{i}} + \hat{\mathbf{j}} + \hat{\mathbf{k}})$

$$= \begin{vmatrix} \hat{\mathbf{i}} & \hat{\mathbf{j}} & \hat{\mathbf{k}} \\ -6 & 0 & -1 \\ 3 & 1 & 1 \end{vmatrix} = \hat{\mathbf{i}} + 3\hat{\mathbf{j}} - 6\hat{\mathbf{k}}$$

$$\therefore \left| \mathbf{c} \times (\lambda\hat{\mathbf{i}} + \hat{\mathbf{j}} + \hat{\mathbf{k}}) \right|^2 = \left| \hat{\mathbf{i}} + 3\hat{\mathbf{j}} - 6\hat{\mathbf{k}} \right|^2$$

$$= 1^2 + 3^2 + (-6)^2 = 46$$

80. Since, the vectors $a\hat{\mathbf{i}} + \hat{\mathbf{j}} + \hat{\mathbf{k}}.\ \hat{\mathbf{i}} + b\hat{\mathbf{j}} + \hat{\mathbf{k}}$ and $\hat{\mathbf{i}} + \hat{\mathbf{j}} + c\hat{\mathbf{k}}$ are coplanar.

$$\therefore \quad \begin{vmatrix} a & 1 & 1 \\ 1 & b & 1 \\ 1 & 1 & c \end{vmatrix} = 0$$

On applying $R_3 \to R_3 - R_2$, we get

$$\begin{vmatrix} a & 1 & 1 \\ 1 & b & 1 \\ 0 & 1-b & c-1 \end{vmatrix} = 0$$

$$\Rightarrow a[b(c-1) - (1-b)] - 1[(c-1) + 1(1-b)] = 0$$

$$\Rightarrow \quad ab(c-1) - a(1-b) + (1-b) + (1-c) = 0$$

$$\Rightarrow \quad (1-c)(1-ab) + (1-b)(1-a) = 0$$

$$\Rightarrow \quad \frac{1}{1-c} = \frac{ab-1}{(1-a)(1-b)} \quad \text{...(i)}$$

$$\therefore \quad \frac{1}{1-a} + \frac{1}{1-b} + \frac{1}{1-c} = \frac{1}{1-a} + \frac{1}{1-b} + \frac{ab-1}{(1-a)(1-b)}$$

[using Eq. (i)]

$$= \frac{1-b+1-a+ab-1}{(1-a)(1-b)} = \frac{1-a-b+ab}{1-a-b+ab} = 1$$

81. **Decoding the Question**

If **p** is perpendicular to two vectors **q** and **r**, then $\mathbf{p} = k(\mathbf{q} \times \mathbf{r})$, k being any scalar.

We have, $\mathbf{a} = 2\hat{\mathbf{i}} + 7\hat{\mathbf{j}} - \hat{\mathbf{k}}$, $\mathbf{b} = 3\hat{\mathbf{i}} + 5\hat{\mathbf{k}}$ and $\mathbf{c} = \hat{\mathbf{i}} - \hat{\mathbf{j}} + 2\hat{\mathbf{k}}$

As **d** is perpendicular to both **a** and **b**,

$$\mathbf{d} = \lambda(\mathbf{a} \times \mathbf{b})$$

$$= \lambda \begin{vmatrix} \hat{\mathbf{i}} & \hat{\mathbf{j}} & \hat{\mathbf{k}} \\ 2 & 7 & -1 \\ 3 & 0 & 5 \end{vmatrix} = \lambda(35\hat{\mathbf{i}} - 13\hat{\mathbf{j}} - 21\hat{\mathbf{k}})$$

As $\mathbf{c} \cdot \mathbf{d} = 12$, $35\lambda + 13\lambda - 42\lambda = 12 \Rightarrow \lambda = 2$

$$\therefore \quad \mathbf{d} = 70\hat{\mathbf{i}} - 26\hat{\mathbf{j}} - 42\hat{\mathbf{k}}$$

Now, $(-\hat{\mathbf{i}} + \hat{\mathbf{j}} - \hat{\mathbf{k}}) \cdot (\mathbf{c} \times \mathbf{d}) = \begin{vmatrix} -1 & 1 & -1 \\ 1 & -1 & 2 \\ 70 & -26 & -42 \end{vmatrix} = 44$

82. $\mathbf{u}_1$, $\mathbf{u}_2$ and $\mathbf{u}_3$ are coplanar vectors.

$$\Rightarrow \quad \begin{vmatrix} 1 & 1 & a \\ 1 & b & 1 \\ c & 1 & 1 \end{vmatrix} = 0$$

$$\Rightarrow \quad (b-1) - (1-c) + a(1-bc) = 0$$

$$\Rightarrow \quad a + b + c - abc = 2 \quad \text{...(i)}$$

Again $\mathbf{v}_1$, $\mathbf{v}_2$ and $\mathbf{v}_3$ are coplanar.

$$\therefore \quad \begin{vmatrix} a+b & c & c \\ a & b+c & a \\ b & b & c+a \end{vmatrix} = 0$$

$$\Rightarrow \quad \begin{vmatrix} a+b & c & c \\ a & b+c & a \\ -2a & -2c & 0 \end{vmatrix} = 0 \quad [\because R_3 \to R_3 - (R_1 + R_2)]$$

On expanding along R_3, we get

$$-2a(ac - bc - c^2) + 2c(a^2 + ab - ac) = 0$$

$$\Rightarrow -2a^2c + 2abc + 2ac^2 + 2a^2c + 2abc - 2ac^2 = 0$$

$$\Rightarrow \quad 4abc = 0$$

$$\Rightarrow \quad abc = 0 \quad \text{...(ii)}$$

From Eqs. (i) and (ii), we get

$$a + b + c = 2$$

$$\Rightarrow \quad 6(a + b + c) = 12$$

83. When coterminous edges of a parallelopiped are **a**, **b** and **c** the volume of parallelopiped

$$V = [\mathbf{a}\ \mathbf{b}\ \mathbf{c}] \quad \text{...(i)}$$

When coterminous edges of a paralleopiped are **a**, **b** + **c** and **a** + 2**b** + 3**c**, then volume of parallelopiped

$$V = [\mathbf{a}\ \mathbf{b}+\mathbf{c}\ \ \mathbf{a}+2\mathbf{b}+3\mathbf{c}]$$

$$= \begin{vmatrix} 1 & 0 & 0 \\ 0 & 1 & 1 \\ 1 & 2 & 3 \end{vmatrix} [\mathbf{a}\ \mathbf{b}\ \mathbf{c}]$$

$$= 1\,(3 - 2)[\mathbf{a}\ \mathbf{b}\ \mathbf{c}]$$

$$= [\mathbf{a}\ \mathbf{b}\ \mathbf{c}] = V \quad \text{[using Eq. (i)]}$$

84. Let $\mathbf{OA} = \hat{\mathbf{i}} - 2\hat{\mathbf{j}} + 3\hat{\mathbf{k}}$

$$\mathbf{OB} = 2\hat{\mathbf{i}} - 3\hat{\mathbf{j}} + 4\hat{\mathbf{k}}$$

$$\mathbf{OC} = (\alpha + 1)\,\hat{\mathbf{i}} + 2\hat{\mathbf{k}}$$

and $\mathbf{OD} = 9\hat{\mathbf{i}} + (\alpha - 8)\,\hat{\mathbf{j}} + 6\hat{\mathbf{k}}$

$$\therefore \quad \mathbf{AB} = \hat{\mathbf{i}} - \hat{\mathbf{j}} + \hat{\mathbf{k}}$$

$$\mathbf{AC} = \alpha\hat{\mathbf{i}} + 2\hat{\mathbf{j}} - \hat{\mathbf{k}}$$

and $\mathbf{AD} = 8\hat{\mathbf{i}} + (\alpha - 6)\hat{\mathbf{j}} + 3\hat{\mathbf{k}}$

Since, given point are coplanar.

$$\therefore \quad [\mathbf{AB}\ \mathbf{AC}\ \mathbf{AD}] = 0$$

$$\Rightarrow \quad \begin{vmatrix} 1 & -1 & 1 \\ \alpha & 2 & -1 \\ 8 & \alpha - 6 & 3 \end{vmatrix} = 0$$

$$\Rightarrow 1\,(6 + \alpha - 6) + 1\,(3\alpha + 8) + 1\,(\alpha^2 - 6\alpha - 16) = 0$$

$$\Rightarrow \quad \alpha^2 - 2\alpha - 8 = 0$$

$$\Rightarrow \quad (\alpha - 4)(\alpha + 2) = 0$$

$$\Rightarrow \quad \alpha = 4, -2$$

$\therefore$ Sum of all values of $\alpha = 4 - 2 = 2$

85. Given, position vectors of the points A, B, C and D be $5\hat{\mathbf{i}} + 5\hat{\mathbf{j}} + 2\lambda\hat{\mathbf{k}}, \hat{\mathbf{i}} + 2\hat{\mathbf{j}} + 3\hat{\mathbf{k}}, -2\hat{\mathbf{i}} + \lambda\hat{\mathbf{j}} + 4\hat{\mathbf{k}}$ and $-\hat{\mathbf{i}} + 5\hat{\mathbf{j}} + 6\hat{\mathbf{k}}$, respectively.

$$\mathbf{AB} = (\hat{\mathbf{i}} + 2\hat{\mathbf{j}} + 3\hat{\mathbf{k}}) - (5\hat{\mathbf{i}} + 5\hat{\mathbf{j}} + 2\lambda\hat{\mathbf{k}})$$

$$= -4\hat{\mathbf{i}} - 3\hat{\mathbf{j}} + (3 - 2\lambda)\hat{\mathbf{k}}$$

$$\mathbf{AC} = (-2\hat{\mathbf{i}} + \lambda\hat{\mathbf{j}} + 4\hat{\mathbf{k}}) - (5\hat{\mathbf{i}} + 5\hat{\mathbf{j}} + 2\lambda\hat{\mathbf{k}})$$

$$= -7\hat{\mathbf{i}} + (\lambda - 5)\hat{\mathbf{j}} + (4 - 2\lambda)\hat{\mathbf{k}}$$

and $\mathbf{AD} = (-\hat{\mathbf{i}} + 5\hat{\mathbf{j}} + 6\hat{\mathbf{k}}) - (5\hat{\mathbf{i}} + 5\hat{\mathbf{j}} + 2\lambda\hat{\mathbf{k}}) = -6\hat{\mathbf{i}} + (6 - 2\lambda)\,\hat{\mathbf{k}}$

Since, points A, B, C and D are coplanar.

$$\therefore \quad [\mathbf{AB}\ \mathbf{AC}\ \mathbf{AD}] = 0$$

$$\Rightarrow \quad \begin{vmatrix} -4 & -3 & (3 - 2\lambda) \\ -7 & (\lambda - 5) & (4 - 2\lambda) \\ -6 & 0 & 6 - 2\lambda \end{vmatrix} = 0$$

$$\Rightarrow -6\,\{(-12 + 6\lambda) - (13\lambda - 15 - 2\lambda^2)\} + (6 - 2\lambda)\{-4\lambda + 20 - 21\} = 0$$

$$\Rightarrow -6(2\lambda^2 - 7\lambda + 3) + (6 - 2\lambda)(-4\lambda - 1) = 0$$

$$\Rightarrow \quad -12\lambda^2 + 42\lambda - 18 + 8\lambda^2 - 22\lambda - 6 = 0$$

$$\Rightarrow \quad -4\lambda^2 + 20\lambda - 24 = 0$$

$$\Rightarrow \quad \lambda^2 - 5\lambda + 6 = 0$$

$$\Rightarrow \quad (\lambda - 2)(\lambda - 3) = 0$$

$$\Rightarrow \quad \lambda = 2, 3$$

$$\therefore \quad \sum_{\lambda \in \Sigma} (\lambda + 2)^2 = (2 + 2)^2 + (3 + 2)^2$$

$$= 16 + 25 = 41$$

86. Given **a**, **b** and **c** are three non-zero vectors.

i.e. $|\mathbf{a}| = |\mathbf{b}| = |\mathbf{c}| \neq 0$

and $\hat{\mathbf{n}}$ is a unit vector and perpendicular to **c**

i.e. $|\hat{\mathbf{n}}| = 1$ with $\hat{\mathbf{n}} \perp \mathbf{c}$ i.e. $\hat{\mathbf{n}} \cdot \mathbf{c} = 0$

and $\mathbf{a} = \alpha\mathbf{b} - \hat{\mathbf{n}}$, where $\alpha \neq 0$ ...(i)

Also, $\mathbf{b} \cdot \mathbf{c} = 12$

From Eq. (i), we get

$$\mathbf{a} \cdot \mathbf{c} = \alpha\,(\mathbf{b} \cdot \mathbf{c}) - \hat{\mathbf{n}} \cdot \mathbf{c} \quad \text{[taking dot product with } \mathbf{c}]$$

$$\Rightarrow \mathbf{a} \cdot \mathbf{c} = \alpha(\mathbf{b} \cdot \mathbf{c}) \quad [\because \hat{\mathbf{n}} \cdot \mathbf{c} = 0] \text{... (ii)}$$

$$\therefore |\mathbf{c} \times (\mathbf{a} \times \mathbf{b})| = |(\mathbf{c} \cdot \mathbf{b})\mathbf{a} - (\mathbf{c} \cdot \mathbf{a})\mathbf{b}| \quad \text{[using vector triple product]}$$

$$= |(\mathbf{c} \cdot \mathbf{b})\mathbf{a} - \alpha(\mathbf{b} \cdot \mathbf{c})\mathbf{b}| \quad \text{[from Eq. (ii)]}$$

$$= |(\mathbf{c} \cdot \mathbf{b})|\,|\alpha\mathbf{b} - \mathbf{a}|$$

$$= 12 \times (|\hat{\mathbf{n}}|) \quad \text{[from Eq. (i)]}$$

$$= 12 \times 1 = 12$$

87. Given that $\mathbf{a} = \lambda\hat{\mathbf{i}} + 2\hat{\mathbf{j}} - 3\hat{\mathbf{k}}$

$$\mathbf{b} = \hat{\mathbf{i}} - \lambda\hat{\mathbf{j}} + 2\hat{\mathbf{k}},\ \lambda \in R$$

and $(\mathbf{a} + \mathbf{b}) \times (\mathbf{a} \times \mathbf{b}) \times (\mathbf{a} - \mathbf{b}) = 8\hat{\mathbf{i}} - 40\hat{\mathbf{j}} - 24\hat{\mathbf{k}}$

This is a vector triple product.

Now, solve LHS

$$= (\mathbf{a} + \mathbf{b}) \times (\mathbf{a} \times \mathbf{b}) \times (\mathbf{a} - \mathbf{b})$$

$$= (\mathbf{b} - \mathbf{a}) \times (\mathbf{a} + \mathbf{b}) \times (\mathbf{a} \times \mathbf{b})$$

$$= [(\mathbf{b} - \mathbf{a}) \cdot (\mathbf{a} \times \mathbf{b})]\,(\mathbf{a} + \mathbf{b}) - [(\mathbf{b} - \mathbf{a}) \cdot (\mathbf{a} + \mathbf{b})](\mathbf{a} \times \mathbf{b})$$

$$[\because \mathbf{a} \times \mathbf{b} \times \mathbf{c} = (\mathbf{a} \cdot \mathbf{c})\,\mathbf{b} - (\mathbf{a} \cdot \mathbf{b})\,\mathbf{c}]$$

$$= \mathbf{0} + ((\mathbf{a}-\mathbf{b})\cdot(\mathbf{a}+\mathbf{b}))(\mathbf{a}\times\mathbf{b})$$
$$= (|\mathbf{a}|^2 - |\mathbf{b}|^2)(\mathbf{a}\times\mathbf{b})$$
$$= [\lambda^2 + 4 + 9 - (1^2 + \lambda^2 + 4)](\mathbf{a}\times\mathbf{b})$$
$$= \lambda^2 + 13 - \lambda^2 - 5(\mathbf{a}\times\mathbf{b})$$
$$= 8(\mathbf{a}\times\mathbf{b})$$

Now, on putting LHS = RHS

$$8(\mathbf{a}\times\mathbf{b}) = 8(\hat{\mathbf{i}} - 5\hat{\mathbf{j}} - 3\hat{\mathbf{k}})$$
$$\mathbf{a}\times\mathbf{b} = \hat{\mathbf{i}} - 5\hat{\mathbf{j}} - 3\hat{\mathbf{k}}$$

Now, calculate $\mathbf{a}\times\mathbf{b}$

$$\mathbf{a}\times\mathbf{b} = \begin{vmatrix} \hat{\mathbf{i}} & \hat{\mathbf{j}} & \hat{\mathbf{k}} \\ \lambda & 2 & -3 \\ 1 & -\lambda & 2 \end{vmatrix}$$
$$= (4-3\lambda)\hat{\mathbf{i}} - (2\lambda+3)\hat{\mathbf{j}} - (\lambda^2+2)\hat{\mathbf{k}}$$
$$\Rightarrow (4-3\lambda)\hat{\mathbf{i}} - (2\lambda+3)\hat{\mathbf{j}} - (\lambda^2+2)\hat{\mathbf{k}} = \hat{\mathbf{i}} - 5\hat{\mathbf{j}} - 3\hat{\mathbf{k}}$$

On comparing both sides, we get

$$4 - 3\lambda = 1 \Rightarrow \lambda = 1$$

Therefore, $|\lambda(\mathbf{a}+\mathbf{b})\times(\mathbf{a}-\mathbf{b})|^2 = |(\mathbf{a}+\mathbf{b})\times(\mathbf{a}-\mathbf{b})|^2 \quad [\because \lambda = 1]$

$$= |\mathbf{a}\times\mathbf{a} - \mathbf{a}\times\mathbf{b} + \mathbf{b}\times\mathbf{a} - \mathbf{b}\times\mathbf{b}|^2$$
$$= |\mathbf{0} - \mathbf{a}\times\mathbf{b} - \mathbf{a}\times\mathbf{b} - \mathbf{0}|^2$$
$$= |-2(\mathbf{a}\times\mathbf{b})|^2 = 4|\mathbf{a}\times\mathbf{b}|^2$$
$$= 4\times(1^2 + 5^2 + 3^2)$$
$$[\because \mathbf{a}\times\mathbf{b} = \hat{\mathbf{i}} - 5\hat{\mathbf{j}} - 3\hat{\mathbf{k}}]$$
$$= 4\times(35)$$
$$= 140$$

88. Given, **a**, **b** and **c** are three non-zero vectors

$$\mathbf{b}\cdot\mathbf{c} = 0 \text{ and } \mathbf{a}\times(\mathbf{b}\times\mathbf{c}) = \frac{\mathbf{b}-\mathbf{c}}{2}$$
$$\Rightarrow \quad (\mathbf{a}\cdot\mathbf{c})\,\mathbf{b} - (\mathbf{a}\cdot\mathbf{b})\,\mathbf{c} = \frac{\mathbf{b}-\mathbf{c}}{2}$$
$$\Rightarrow \quad \mathbf{a}\cdot\mathbf{c} = \mathbf{a}\cdot\mathbf{b} = \frac{1}{2}$$

Also, $\mathbf{a}\cdot\mathbf{b} = \mathbf{b}\cdot\mathbf{d} = \frac{1}{2}$

$$(\mathbf{a}\times\mathbf{b})\cdot(\mathbf{c}\times\mathbf{d}) = \mathbf{a}\cdot[(\mathbf{b}\times(\mathbf{c}\times\mathbf{d})]$$
$$= \mathbf{a}\cdot[(\mathbf{b}\cdot\mathbf{d})\mathbf{c} - (\mathbf{b}\cdot\mathbf{c})\mathbf{d}]$$
$$= (\mathbf{b}\cdot\mathbf{d})(\mathbf{a}\cdot\mathbf{c}) - (\mathbf{b}\cdot\mathbf{c})(\mathbf{a}\cdot\mathbf{d})$$
$$= \frac{1}{2}\times\frac{1}{2} - (\mathbf{b}\cdot\mathbf{c})(\mathbf{a}\cdot\mathbf{d}) = \frac{1}{4} - 0$$
$$[\because \mathbf{b}\cdot\mathbf{c} = 0, \text{ given}]$$
$$= \frac{1}{4}$$

89. Given, $\mathbf{a} = -\hat{\mathbf{i}} - \hat{\mathbf{j}} + \hat{\mathbf{k}}$, $\mathbf{a}\cdot\mathbf{b} = 1$ and $\mathbf{a}\times\mathbf{b} = \hat{\mathbf{i}} - \hat{\mathbf{j}}$ ...(i)

On multiplying Eq. (i) by **a**, we get

$$\mathbf{a}\times(\mathbf{a}\times\mathbf{b}) = \mathbf{a}\times(\hat{\mathbf{i}} - \hat{\mathbf{j}})$$
$$\because \quad [\mathbf{a}\times(\mathbf{b}\times\mathbf{c}) = (\mathbf{a}\cdot\mathbf{c})\,\mathbf{b} - (\mathbf{a}\cdot\mathbf{b})\,\mathbf{c}]$$
$$\Rightarrow \text{So, } (\mathbf{a}\cdot\mathbf{b})\mathbf{a} - (\mathbf{a}\cdot\mathbf{a})\mathbf{b} = (-\hat{\mathbf{i}} - \hat{\mathbf{j}} + \hat{\mathbf{k}})\times(\hat{\mathbf{i}} - \hat{\mathbf{j}})$$

Now, we know that $\mathbf{a}\cdot\mathbf{a} = |\mathbf{a}|^2$

and $\quad |\mathbf{a}| = \sqrt{a_1^2 + a_2^2 + a_3^2}$

$$\Rightarrow \quad |\mathbf{a}| = \sqrt{(-1)^2 + (-1)^2 + (1)^2}$$
$$\Rightarrow \quad |\mathbf{a}| = \sqrt{3} \text{ or } |\mathbf{a}|^2 = 3$$

and $(-\hat{\mathbf{i}} - \hat{\mathbf{j}} + \hat{\mathbf{k}})\times(\hat{\mathbf{i}} - \hat{\mathbf{j}}) = \begin{vmatrix} \hat{\mathbf{i}} & \hat{\mathbf{j}} & \hat{\mathbf{k}} \\ -1 & -1 & 1 \\ 1 & -1 & 0 \end{vmatrix}$

$$= \hat{\mathbf{i}}(0-(-1)) - \hat{\mathbf{j}}(0-1) + \hat{\mathbf{k}}(1-(-1))$$
$$= \hat{\mathbf{i}} + \hat{\mathbf{j}} + 2\hat{\mathbf{k}}$$

So, $\quad \mathbf{a} - 3\mathbf{b} = \hat{\mathbf{i}} + \hat{\mathbf{j}} + 2\hat{\mathbf{k}}$

$$3\mathbf{b} = \mathbf{a} - (\hat{\mathbf{i}} + \hat{\mathbf{j}} + 2\hat{\mathbf{k}})$$
$$3\mathbf{b} = (-\hat{\mathbf{i}} - \hat{\mathbf{j}} + \hat{\mathbf{k}}) - (\hat{\mathbf{i}} + \hat{\mathbf{j}} + 2\hat{\mathbf{k}})$$
$$3\mathbf{b} = -2\hat{\mathbf{i}} - 2\hat{\mathbf{j}} - \hat{\mathbf{k}}$$

Now, $\quad \mathbf{a} - 6\mathbf{b} = \mathbf{a} - 2(3\mathbf{b})$

$$\Rightarrow \quad \mathbf{a} - 6\mathbf{b} = (-\hat{\mathbf{i}} - \hat{\mathbf{j}} + \hat{\mathbf{k}}) - 2(-2\hat{\mathbf{i}} - 2\hat{\mathbf{j}} - \hat{\mathbf{k}})$$
$$\Rightarrow \quad \mathbf{a} - 6\mathbf{b} = 3\hat{\mathbf{i}} + 3\hat{\mathbf{j}} + 3\hat{\mathbf{k}}$$

or $\quad \mathbf{a} - 6\mathbf{b} = 3(\hat{\mathbf{i}} + \hat{\mathbf{j}} + \hat{\mathbf{k}})$

90. Given, $\mathbf{u} = \hat{\mathbf{i}} - \hat{\mathbf{j}} - 2\hat{\mathbf{k}}$, $\mathbf{v} = 2\hat{\mathbf{i}} + \hat{\mathbf{j}} - \hat{\mathbf{k}}$

$$\mathbf{v}\cdot\mathbf{w} = 2 \quad \text{...(i)}$$

and $\quad \mathbf{v}\times\mathbf{w} = \mathbf{u} + \lambda\mathbf{v}$ ...(ii)

On taking dot product with **w** on Eq. (ii), we get

$$\mathbf{w}\cdot(\mathbf{v}\times\mathbf{w}) = \mathbf{u}\cdot\mathbf{w} + \lambda\mathbf{v}\cdot\mathbf{w}$$
$$\Rightarrow \quad 0 = \mathbf{u}\cdot\mathbf{w} + 2\lambda$$
$$\Rightarrow \quad \mathbf{u}\cdot\mathbf{w} = -2\lambda \quad \text{...(iii)}$$

So, our target is to find the value of λ and putting in Eq. (iii) to get our required result.

For this we take dot product again with **v** in Eq. (ii), we get

$$\mathbf{v}\cdot(\mathbf{v}\times\mathbf{w}) = \mathbf{u}\cdot\mathbf{v} + \lambda\mathbf{v}\cdot\mathbf{v}$$
$$\Rightarrow \quad 0 = (2 - 1 + 2) + \lambda(4 + 1 + 1)$$
$$\Rightarrow \quad \lambda = -\frac{1}{2}$$

Hence, $\quad \mathbf{u}\cdot\mathbf{w} = -2\left(-\frac{1}{2}\right)$ [from Eq. (iii)]

$$\Rightarrow \quad \mathbf{u}\cdot\mathbf{w} = 1$$

91. **Decoding the Question**

For minimum value of scalar triple product, we use $\theta = \pi$.

We have, $\mathbf{v} = \alpha\hat{\mathbf{i}} + 2\hat{\mathbf{j}} - 3\hat{\mathbf{k}}$, $\mathbf{w} = 2\alpha\hat{\mathbf{i}} + \hat{\mathbf{j}} - \hat{\mathbf{k}}$, $|\mathbf{u}| = \alpha$

Now, $[\mathbf{u}\ \mathbf{v}\ \mathbf{w}] = \mathbf{u}\cdot(\mathbf{v}\times\mathbf{w})$

$$= |\mathbf{u}|\,|\mathbf{v}\times\mathbf{w}|\cos\theta = \alpha\,|\mathbf{v}\times\mathbf{w}|\cos\theta$$
$$\therefore \quad [\mathbf{u}\ \mathbf{v}\ \mathbf{w}]_{min} = -\alpha\,|\mathbf{v}\times\mathbf{w}|$$
$$\therefore \quad -\alpha\,|\mathbf{v}\times\mathbf{w}| = -\alpha\sqrt{3401} \Rightarrow |\mathbf{v}\times\mathbf{w}| = \sqrt{3401}$$

Now, $\quad \mathbf{v}\times\mathbf{w} = \begin{vmatrix} \hat{\mathbf{i}} & \hat{\mathbf{j}} & \hat{\mathbf{k}} \\ \alpha & 2 & -3 \\ 2\alpha & 1 & -1 \end{vmatrix} = \hat{\mathbf{i}} - 5\alpha\hat{\mathbf{j}} - 3\alpha\hat{\mathbf{k}}$

Now, $|\mathbf{v}\times\mathbf{w}| = \sqrt{3401}$

$\Rightarrow \sqrt{(1)^2 + (-5\alpha)^2 + (-3\alpha)^2} = \sqrt{3401}$

$\Rightarrow \alpha = 10$ $[\because \alpha > 0]$

$\therefore \mathbf{v}\times\mathbf{w} = \hat{\mathbf{i}} - 50\hat{\mathbf{j}} - 30\hat{\mathbf{k}}$

Again, $\mathbf{u} = 10\left(-\dfrac{\mathbf{v}\times\mathbf{w}}{|\mathbf{v}\times\mathbf{w}|}\right)$

$= -10\left(\dfrac{\hat{\mathbf{i}} - 50\hat{\mathbf{j}} - 30\hat{\mathbf{k}}}{\sqrt{1+2500+900}}\right)$

$= \dfrac{-10}{\sqrt{3401}}(\hat{\mathbf{i}} - 50\hat{\mathbf{j}} - 30\hat{\mathbf{k}})$

Now, $|\mathbf{u}\cdot\hat{\mathbf{i}}|^2 = \left(\dfrac{-10}{\sqrt{3401}}\right)^2 = \dfrac{100}{3401}$

$\therefore m = 100, n = 3401$

So, $m + n = 3501$

92. We have, $A : \mathbf{a} - \mathbf{b} + \mathbf{c}$, $B : \lambda\mathbf{a} - 3\mathbf{b} + 4\mathbf{c}$,

$C : -\mathbf{a} + 2\mathbf{b} - 3\mathbf{c}$, $D : 2\mathbf{a} - 4\mathbf{b} + 6\mathbf{c}$

$\therefore \mathbf{AB} = (\lambda - 1)\mathbf{a} - 2\mathbf{b} + 3\mathbf{c}$,

$\mathbf{AC} = -2\mathbf{a} + 3\mathbf{b} - 4\mathbf{c}$

$\therefore \mathbf{AD} = \mathbf{a} - 3\mathbf{b} + 5\mathbf{c}$

If **AB**, **AC** and **AD** are coplanar, then $[\mathbf{AB}\ \mathbf{AC}\ \mathbf{AD}] = 0$

$$\Rightarrow \begin{vmatrix} \lambda-1 & -2 & 3 \\ -2 & 3 & -4 \\ 1 & -3 & 5 \end{vmatrix} [\mathbf{a}\ \ \mathbf{b}\ \ \mathbf{c}] = 0 \quad \text{...(i)}$$

Since, **a**, **b** and **c** are non-zero non-coplanar vectors, $[\mathbf{a}\ \mathbf{b}\ \mathbf{c}] \neq 0$

$\therefore$ Eq. (i) becomes,

$$\begin{vmatrix} \lambda-1 & -2 & 3 \\ -2 & 3 & -4 \\ 1 & -3 & 5 \end{vmatrix} = 0$$

$\Rightarrow (\lambda - 1)(15 - 12) + 2(-10 + 4) + 3(6 - 3) = 0$

$\Rightarrow 3(\lambda - 1) - 12 + 9 = 0$

$\Rightarrow 3(\lambda - 1) = 12 - 9 = 3$

$\Rightarrow \lambda - 1 = \dfrac{3}{3} = 1$

$\Rightarrow \lambda = 2$

93. We have, $|\mathbf{a}| = 9$ and $(x\mathbf{a} + y\mathbf{b})\cdot(6y\mathbf{a} - 18x\mathbf{b}) = 0$

$\Rightarrow 6xy|\mathbf{a}|^2 - 18x^2(\mathbf{a}\cdot\mathbf{b}) + 6y^2(\mathbf{a}\cdot\mathbf{b}) - 18xy|\mathbf{b}|^2 = 0$

$\Rightarrow 6xy(|\mathbf{a}|^2 - 3|\mathbf{b}|^2) + 6(\mathbf{a}\cdot\mathbf{b})(y^2 - 3x^2) = 0$

$\Rightarrow xy(|\mathbf{a}|^2 - 3|\mathbf{b}|^2) + (\mathbf{a}\cdot\mathbf{b})(y^2 - 3x^2) = 0$

This should hold, $\forall x, y \in \mathbf{R}\times\mathbf{R}$

$\therefore |\mathbf{a}|^2 = 3|\mathbf{b}|^2$ and $(\mathbf{a}\cdot\mathbf{b}) = 0$

Now, $|\mathbf{a}\times\mathbf{b}|^2 = |\mathbf{a}|^2|\mathbf{b}|^2 - (\mathbf{a}\cdot\mathbf{b})^2$

$= |\mathbf{a}|^2\cdot\dfrac{|\mathbf{a}|^2}{3}$

$\therefore |\mathbf{a}\times\mathbf{b}| = \dfrac{|\mathbf{a}|^2}{\sqrt{3}} = \dfrac{81}{\sqrt{3}} = 27\sqrt{3}$

94. Given, $\mathbf{a} = \alpha\hat{\mathbf{i}} + \hat{\mathbf{j}} - \hat{\mathbf{k}}$ and $\mathbf{b} = 2\hat{\mathbf{i}} + \hat{\mathbf{j}} - \alpha\hat{\mathbf{k}}$.

$\mathbf{a}\times\mathbf{b} = (1-\alpha)\hat{\mathbf{i}} + (\alpha^2 - 2)\hat{\mathbf{j}} + (\alpha - 2)\hat{\mathbf{k}}$

Now, projection of $\mathbf{a}\times\mathbf{b}$ on $-\hat{\mathbf{i}} + 2\hat{\mathbf{j}} - 2\hat{\mathbf{k}}$

$\Rightarrow \dfrac{(\mathbf{a}\times\mathbf{b})\cdot(-\hat{\mathbf{i}} + 2\hat{\mathbf{j}} - 2\hat{\mathbf{k}})}{3} = 30$

$\Rightarrow 2\alpha^2 - \alpha - 91 = 0$

$\Rightarrow \alpha = 7, \dfrac{-13}{2}$

$\therefore \alpha = 7$ $\left[\because \alpha \neq \dfrac{-13}{2}\right]$

95. Given vector equation is,

$|\mathbf{a} + \mathbf{b}|^2 = |\mathbf{a}|^2 + 2|\mathbf{b}|^2; \mathbf{a}\cdot\mathbf{b} = 3$

As, $|\mathbf{a}|^2 + |\mathbf{b}|^2 + 2\mathbf{a}\cdot\mathbf{b} = |\mathbf{a}|^2 + 2|\mathbf{b}|^2$

$\Rightarrow |\mathbf{b}|^2 = 2\mathbf{a}\cdot\mathbf{b} = 6$

$\Rightarrow |\mathbf{a}\times\mathbf{b}|^2 = 75$

$\Rightarrow |\mathbf{a}|^2|\mathbf{b}|^2 - (\mathbf{a}\cdot\mathbf{b})^2 = 75$

$\Rightarrow |\mathbf{a}|^2 6 - 9 = 75$

Therefore, $|\mathbf{a}|^2 = 14$

96. $\mathbf{a} = 3\hat{\mathbf{i}} + \hat{\mathbf{j}}$, $\mathbf{b} = \hat{\mathbf{i}} + 2\hat{\mathbf{j}} + \hat{\mathbf{k}}$

$\mathbf{a}\times(\mathbf{b}\times\mathbf{c}) = \mathbf{b} + \lambda\mathbf{c}$

$(\mathbf{a}\cdot\mathbf{c})\mathbf{b} - (\mathbf{a}\cdot\mathbf{b})\mathbf{c} = \mathbf{b} + \lambda\mathbf{c}$

$\Rightarrow \mathbf{a}\cdot\mathbf{c} = 1, \mathbf{a}\cdot\mathbf{b} = -\lambda$

$\Rightarrow (3\hat{\mathbf{i}} + \hat{\mathbf{j}})(\hat{\mathbf{i}} + 2\hat{\mathbf{j}} + \hat{\mathbf{k}}) = -\lambda$

$\Rightarrow 3 + 2 + 0 = -\lambda$

$\Rightarrow \lambda = -5$

97. Given, $\mathbf{a}\cdot\mathbf{b} = 1, \mathbf{b}\cdot\mathbf{c} = 2, \mathbf{c}\cdot\mathbf{a} = 3$

$\because \mathbf{a}\times(\mathbf{b}\times\mathbf{c}) = (\mathbf{a}\cdot\mathbf{c})\mathbf{b} - (\mathbf{a}\cdot\mathbf{b})\mathbf{c} = 3\mathbf{b} - \mathbf{c}$

$\because \mathbf{b}\times(\mathbf{c}\times\mathbf{a}) = (\mathbf{b}\cdot\mathbf{a})\mathbf{c} - (\mathbf{b}\cdot\mathbf{c})\mathbf{a} = \mathbf{c} - 2\mathbf{a}$

$\because \mathbf{c}\times(\mathbf{b}\times\mathbf{a}) = (\mathbf{c}\cdot\mathbf{a})\mathbf{b} - (\mathbf{c}\cdot\mathbf{b})\mathbf{a} = 3\mathbf{b} - 2\mathbf{a}$

Then, $[\mathbf{a}\times(\mathbf{b}\times\mathbf{c}), \mathbf{b}\times(\mathbf{c}\times\mathbf{a}), \mathbf{c}\times(\mathbf{b}\times\mathbf{a})]$

$= [3\mathbf{b} - \mathbf{c}\quad \mathbf{c} - 2\mathbf{a}\quad 3\mathbf{b} - 2\mathbf{a}]$

$= (3\mathbf{b} - \mathbf{c})\cdot[(\mathbf{c} - 2\mathbf{a})\times(3\mathbf{b} - 2\mathbf{a})]$

$= (3\mathbf{b} - \mathbf{c})\cdot[(3(\mathbf{c}\times\mathbf{b}) - 2(\mathbf{c}\times\mathbf{a}) - 6(\mathbf{a}\times\mathbf{b})]$

$= 0 - 6\mathbf{b}\cdot(\mathbf{c}\times\mathbf{a}) - 0 - 0 + 0 + 6\,\mathbf{c}\cdot(\mathbf{a}\times\mathbf{b}) = 0$

98. Given, $\mathbf{a} + (\mathbf{b}\times\mathbf{c}) = \mathbf{0}$

Now, $\mathbf{c}\cdot\mathbf{a} + \mathbf{c}\cdot\mathbf{b}\times\mathbf{c} = \mathbf{0}$

$\Rightarrow \mathbf{c}\cdot\mathbf{a} + [\mathbf{c}\ \mathbf{b}\ \mathbf{c}] = 0$

$\Rightarrow \mathbf{c}\cdot\mathbf{a} + 0 = \mathbf{0}$ or $3(\mathbf{c}\cdot\mathbf{a}) = 0$

99. Given, $|2\mathbf{a} + 3\mathbf{b}| = |3\mathbf{a} + \mathbf{b}|$,

then $|3\mathbf{a} + \mathbf{b}|^2 = |2\mathbf{a} + 3\mathbf{b}|^2$

$\Rightarrow (3\mathbf{a} + \mathbf{b})\cdot(3\mathbf{a} + \mathbf{b}) = (2\mathbf{a} + 3\mathbf{b})\cdot(2\mathbf{a} + 3\mathbf{b})$

$\Rightarrow 9|\mathbf{a}|^2 + |\mathbf{b}|^2 + 6|\mathbf{a}||\mathbf{b}|\cos 60°$

$= 4|\mathbf{a}|^2 + 9|\mathbf{b}|^2 + 12|\mathbf{a}||\mathbf{b}|\cos 60°$

$\Rightarrow 5|\mathbf{a}|^2 - 6|\mathbf{a}||\mathbf{b}|\cos 60° = 8|\mathbf{b}|^2$

$\Rightarrow \quad 5(8)^2 - 6\cdot 8\,|\mathbf{b}|\cos 60° = 8|\mathbf{b}|^2 \quad \left[\because \frac{1}{8}|\mathbf{a}| = 1 \Rightarrow |\mathbf{a}| = 8\right]$

$\Rightarrow \quad 40 - 3|\mathbf{b}| = |\mathbf{b}|^2$

$\Rightarrow \quad |\mathbf{b}|^2 + 3|\mathbf{b}| - 40 = 0$

$\Rightarrow \quad |\mathbf{b}| = -8$, (rejected) $|\mathbf{b}| = 5$

100. Sum of two vectors $= 2\hat{\mathbf{i}} + 4\hat{\mathbf{j}} - 5\hat{\mathbf{k}} + (-\lambda\hat{\mathbf{i}} + 2\hat{\mathbf{j}} + 3\hat{\mathbf{k}})$

$= (2-\lambda)\hat{\mathbf{i}} + 6\hat{\mathbf{j}} - 2\hat{\mathbf{k}}$

Projection $= 1 = \dfrac{1(2-\lambda) + 2(6) + 1\times(-2)}{\sqrt{(2-\lambda)^2 + 6^2 + 2^2}}$

$\Rightarrow \quad \dfrac{12-\lambda}{\sqrt{\lambda^2 - 4\lambda + 44}} = 1$

$\Rightarrow \quad (12-\lambda)^2 = \lambda^2 - 4\lambda + 44$

$\Rightarrow \quad 144 + \lambda^2 - 24\lambda = \lambda^2 - 4\lambda + 44$

$\Rightarrow \quad 100 = 20\lambda$

$\Rightarrow \quad \lambda = 5$

101. We have, $\mathbf{p} + \mathbf{q} = 3\hat{\mathbf{i}} + 5\hat{\mathbf{j}} + 2\hat{\mathbf{k}}$ and $\mathbf{p} - \mathbf{q} = \hat{\mathbf{i}} + \hat{\mathbf{j}}$

Now, $(\mathbf{p}+\mathbf{q})\times(\mathbf{p}-\mathbf{q}) = \begin{vmatrix} \hat{\mathbf{i}} & \hat{\mathbf{j}} & \hat{\mathbf{k}} \\ 3 & 5 & 2 \\ 1 & 1 & 0 \end{vmatrix}$

$= -2\hat{\mathbf{i}} + 2\hat{\mathbf{j}} - 2\hat{\mathbf{k}}$

$\therefore \quad \mathbf{r} = \lambda(-2\hat{\mathbf{i}} + 2\hat{\mathbf{j}} - 2\hat{\mathbf{k}})$

$|\mathbf{r}| = \pm 2\sqrt{3}\lambda = \sqrt{3} \Rightarrow \lambda = \pm\dfrac{1}{2}$

$\therefore |\alpha| + |\beta| + |\gamma| = 1 + 1 + 1 = 3$

102. Given, $\left\{\begin{array}{ll} \mathbf{b} = (2, 1, 1) & \mathbf{a} = \lambda\mathbf{b} + \mu\mathbf{c} \\ \mathbf{c} = (1, -1, 1) \text{ and} & \mathbf{a} \perp \mathbf{d} \\ \mathbf{d} = (3, 2, 6) & |\mathbf{a}| = \sqrt{10} \end{array}\right\}$

$\Rightarrow \quad \mathbf{a}\cdot\mathbf{d} = 0$

$\Rightarrow \quad (\lambda\mathbf{b} + \mu\mathbf{c})\cdot\mathbf{d} = 0$

$\Rightarrow \quad \lambda\mathbf{b}\cdot\mathbf{d} + \mu\mathbf{c}\cdot\mathbf{d} = 0$

$\Rightarrow \quad \lambda(6+2+6) + \mu(3-2+6) = 0$

$\Rightarrow \quad 14\lambda + 7\mu = 0$

$\Rightarrow \quad \mu = -2\lambda$

$\mathbf{a} = (2\lambda, \lambda, \lambda) + (\mu, -\mu, \mu)$

$= (2\lambda + \mu)\hat{\mathbf{i}} + (\lambda - \mu)\hat{\mathbf{j}} + (\lambda + \mu)\hat{\mathbf{k}}$

$= 0\hat{\mathbf{i}} + 3\lambda\hat{\mathbf{j}} - \lambda\hat{\mathbf{k}} = \lambda(3\hat{\mathbf{j}} - \hat{\mathbf{k}})$

Now, $\quad |\mathbf{a}| = \sqrt{10}$

$\Rightarrow \quad \lambda^2(3^2 + 1^2) = 10$

$\Rightarrow \quad \lambda^2 = 1 \Rightarrow \lambda = \pm 1$

$[\mathbf{a}\ \mathbf{b}\ \mathbf{c}] + [\mathbf{a}\ \mathbf{b}\ \mathbf{d}] + [\mathbf{a}\ \mathbf{c}\ \mathbf{d}] = [\mathbf{a}\ \mathbf{b}\ \mathbf{c}] + [\mathbf{a}\ \mathbf{b}+\mathbf{c}\ \mathbf{d}]$

$\left.\begin{array}{l} \mathbf{a} = \pm 1(3\hat{\mathbf{j}} - \hat{\mathbf{k}}) \\ \mathbf{b} = 2\hat{\mathbf{i}} + \hat{\mathbf{j}} + \hat{\mathbf{k}} \\ \mathbf{c} = \hat{\mathbf{i}} - \hat{\mathbf{j}} + \hat{\mathbf{k}} \end{array}\right\}, \mathbf{b} + \mathbf{c} = 3\hat{\mathbf{i}} + 2\hat{\mathbf{k}}$

$\mathbf{d} = 3\hat{\mathbf{i}} + 2\hat{\mathbf{j}} + 6\hat{\mathbf{k}}$

As, $\mathbf{a}$ is coplanar with $\mathbf{b}$ and $\mathbf{c}$.

So, $[\mathbf{a}\ \mathbf{b}\ \mathbf{c}] = 0$

$\pm\begin{vmatrix} 0 & 3 & -1 \\ 3 & 0 & 2 \\ 3 & 2 & 6 \end{vmatrix} = \pm(-36 - 6) = \pm 42$

103. Let $P(1, 5, 35)$, $Q(7, 5, 5)$, $R(1, \lambda, 7)$, $S(2\lambda, 1, 2)$

Given P, Q, R, S are coplanar.

Then, **PQ, PR, PS** lie on the same plane.

$\mathbf{PQ} = (7-1)\hat{\mathbf{i}} + (5-5)\hat{\mathbf{j}} + (5-35)\hat{\mathbf{k}} = 6\hat{\mathbf{i}} - 30\hat{\mathbf{k}}$

$\mathbf{PR} = (1-1)\hat{\mathbf{i}} + (\lambda-5)\hat{\mathbf{j}} + (7-35)\hat{\mathbf{k}} = (\lambda-5)\hat{\mathbf{j}} - 28\hat{\mathbf{k}}$

$\mathbf{PS} = (2\lambda-1)\hat{\mathbf{i}} + (1-5)\hat{\mathbf{j}} + (2-35)\hat{\mathbf{k}}$

$= (2\lambda-1)\hat{\mathbf{i}} - 4\hat{\mathbf{j}} - 33\hat{\mathbf{k}}$

$\because$ **PQ, PR** and **PS** lie on same plane, then

$\begin{vmatrix} 6 & 0 & -30 \\ 0 & \lambda-5 & -28 \\ 2\lambda-1 & -4 & -33 \end{vmatrix} = 0$

On expanding along first row, we get

$6[-33(\lambda-5) - 112] + 30[(2\lambda-1)(\lambda-5)] = 0$

$\Rightarrow \quad 6(-33\lambda + 53) + 30(2\lambda^2 - 11\lambda + 5) = 0$

$\Rightarrow \quad 60\lambda^2 - 528\lambda + 468 = 0$

$\Rightarrow \quad 5\lambda^2 - 44\lambda + 39 = 0 \quad$ ... (i)

Possible value of λ are roots of Eq. (i).

Then, the sum of all possible values of λ = Sum of roots of Eq. (i)

$= \dfrac{-(-44)}{5} = \dfrac{44}{5}$

$[\because ax^2 + bx + c = 0$, sum of roots $= -b/a]$

104. Let angle between $\mathbf{a}$ and $\mathbf{b}$ be θ.

$|\mathbf{a}+\mathbf{b}| = \sqrt{1 + 1 + 2\cos\theta} = 2\left|\cos\dfrac{\theta}{2}\right| \quad [\because |a| = |b| = 1]$

Similarly, $|\mathbf{a} - \mathbf{b}| = 2\left|\sin\dfrac{\theta}{2}\right|$

So, $\sqrt{3}|\mathbf{a}+\mathbf{b}| + |\mathbf{a}-\mathbf{b}| = 2\left[\sqrt{3}\left|\cos\dfrac{\theta}{2}\right| + \left|\sin\dfrac{\theta}{2}\right|\right]$

$\because$ Maximum value of $(a\cos\theta + b\sin\theta) = \sqrt{a^2 + b^2}$

$\therefore$ Maximum value $= 2\sqrt{(\sqrt{3})^2 + (1)^2} = 4$

105. Given vectors, $\mathbf{a} = \hat{\mathbf{i}} - 2\hat{\mathbf{j}} + \hat{\mathbf{k}}$ and $\mathbf{b} = \hat{\mathbf{i}} - \hat{\mathbf{j}} + \hat{\mathbf{k}}$ and $\mathbf{c}$, such that $\mathbf{b}\times\mathbf{c} = \mathbf{b}\times\mathbf{a}$

$\Rightarrow \mathbf{b}\times(\mathbf{c}-\mathbf{a}) = \mathbf{0} \Rightarrow \mathbf{b} \parallel \mathbf{c} - \mathbf{a}$

$\Rightarrow \mathbf{c} - \mathbf{a} = \lambda\mathbf{b} \Rightarrow \mathbf{c} = \mathbf{a} + \lambda\mathbf{b}$

$\Rightarrow \mathbf{c} = (1+\lambda)\hat{\mathbf{i}} - (2+\lambda)\hat{\mathbf{j}} + (1+\lambda)\hat{\mathbf{k}}$

$\because \mathbf{c}\cdot\mathbf{a} = 0 \quad$ [given]

$\Rightarrow (1+\lambda) + 2(2+\lambda) + (1+\lambda) = 0$

$\Rightarrow 4\lambda + 6 = 0 \quad \Rightarrow \lambda = -\dfrac{3}{2}$

$\therefore \quad \mathbf{c} = -\dfrac{1}{2}\hat{\mathbf{i}} - \dfrac{1}{2}\hat{\mathbf{j}} - \dfrac{1}{2}\hat{\mathbf{k}}$

So, $\mathbf{c}\cdot\mathbf{b} = -\dfrac{1}{2} + \dfrac{1}{2} - \dfrac{1}{2} = -\dfrac{1}{2}$

106. Given vertices of a ΔABC are $A(3, 0, -1)$, $B(2, 10, 6)$ and $C(1, 2, 1)$ and a point M is mid-point of AC.

An another point G divides BM in ratio $2 : 1$, so G is the centroid of ΔABC.

$$\therefore\ G\left(\frac{3+2+1}{3}, \frac{0+10+2}{3}, \frac{-1+6+1}{3}\right) = (2, 4, 2)$$

Now, $\cos(\angle GOA) = \dfrac{\mathbf{OG}\cdot\mathbf{OA}}{|\mathbf{OG}||\mathbf{OA}|}$,

where O is the origin.

$\because\quad \mathbf{OG} = 2\hat{\mathbf{i}} + 4\hat{\mathbf{j}} + 2\hat{\mathbf{k}} \Rightarrow |\mathbf{OG}| = \sqrt{4+16+4} = \sqrt{24}$

and $\quad |\mathbf{OA}| = 3\hat{\mathbf{i}} - \hat{\mathbf{k}} \Rightarrow |\mathbf{OA}| = \sqrt{9+1} = \sqrt{10}$

and $\quad \mathbf{OG}\cdot\mathbf{OA} = 6 - 2 = 4$

$$\therefore\ \cos(\angle GOA) = \frac{4}{\sqrt{24}\sqrt{10}} = \frac{1}{\sqrt{15}}$$

107. Given vectors are $\mathbf{a} = 3\hat{\mathbf{i}} + 2\hat{\mathbf{j}} + 2\hat{\mathbf{k}}$ and $\mathbf{b} = \hat{\mathbf{i}} + 2\hat{\mathbf{j}} - 2\hat{\mathbf{k}}$

Now, vectors $\mathbf{a} + \mathbf{b} = 4\hat{\mathbf{i}} + 4\hat{\mathbf{j}}$ and $\mathbf{a} - \mathbf{b} = 2\hat{\mathbf{i}} + 4\hat{\mathbf{k}}$

$\therefore$ A vector which is perpendicular to both the vectors $\mathbf{a} + \mathbf{b}$ and $\mathbf{a} - \mathbf{b}$ is

$$(\mathbf{a}+\mathbf{b})\times(\mathbf{a}-\mathbf{b}) = \begin{vmatrix} \hat{\mathbf{i}} & \hat{\mathbf{j}} & \hat{\mathbf{k}} \\ 4 & 4 & 0 \\ 2 & 0 & 4 \end{vmatrix}$$

$$= \hat{\mathbf{i}}(16) - \hat{\mathbf{j}}(16) + \hat{\mathbf{k}}(-8) = 8(2\hat{\mathbf{i}} - 2\hat{\mathbf{j}} - \hat{\mathbf{k}})$$

Then, the required vector along $(\mathbf{a}+\mathbf{b})\times(\mathbf{a}-\mathbf{b})$ having magnitude 12 is

$$\pm 12 \times \frac{8(2\hat{\mathbf{i}} - 2\hat{\mathbf{j}} - \hat{\mathbf{k}})}{8\times\sqrt{4+4+1}} = \pm 4(2\hat{\mathbf{i}} - 2\hat{\mathbf{j}} - \hat{\mathbf{k}})$$

108. Given vectors, $\mu\hat{\mathbf{i}} + \hat{\mathbf{j}} + \hat{\mathbf{k}}$, $\hat{\mathbf{i}} + \mu\hat{\mathbf{j}} + \hat{\mathbf{k}}$, $\hat{\mathbf{i}} + \hat{\mathbf{j}} + \mu\hat{\mathbf{k}}$ will be coplanar,

if $\quad \begin{vmatrix} \mu & 1 & 1 \\ 1 & \mu & 1 \\ 1 & 1 & \mu \end{vmatrix} = 0$

$\Rightarrow \mu(\mu^2 - 1) - 1(\mu - 1) + 1(1 - \mu) = 0$

$\Rightarrow\quad (\mu - 1)[\mu(\mu + 1) - 1 - 1] = 0 \Rightarrow (\mu - 1)[\mu^2 + \mu - 2] = 0$

$\Rightarrow\quad (\mu - 1)[(\mu + 2)(\mu - 1)] = 0 \Rightarrow \mu = 1 \text{ or } -2$

So, sum of the distinct real values of $\mu = 1 - 2 = -1$.

Exercise 2 - JEE Advanced Pattern

1. Given, $\mathbf{a}\times(\mathbf{b}\times\mathbf{c}) + (\mathbf{a}\cdot\mathbf{b})\,\mathbf{b} = (4 - 2\beta - \sin\alpha)\,\mathbf{b} + (\beta^2 - 1)\,\mathbf{c}$

$\Rightarrow (\mathbf{a}\cdot\mathbf{c})\,\mathbf{b} - (\mathbf{a}\cdot\mathbf{b})\,\mathbf{c} + (\mathbf{a}\cdot\mathbf{b})\,\mathbf{b}$

$$= (4 - 2\beta - \sin\alpha)\,\mathbf{b} + (\beta^2 - 1)\,\mathbf{c} \quad \text{...(i)}$$

Also, given $(\mathbf{c}\cdot\mathbf{c})\,\mathbf{a} = \mathbf{c} \Rightarrow |\mathbf{c}|^2\,\mathbf{a} = \mathbf{c} \Rightarrow |\mathbf{c}|^2(\mathbf{a}\cdot\mathbf{c}) = |\mathbf{c}|^2$

$\Rightarrow\quad \mathbf{a}\cdot\mathbf{c} = 1 \quad$ ...(ii)

From Eqs. (i) and (ii), we get

$$\mathbf{b} + (\mathbf{a}\cdot\mathbf{b})\,\mathbf{b} - (\mathbf{a}\cdot\mathbf{b})\,\mathbf{c} = (4 - 2\beta - \sin\alpha)\,\mathbf{b} + (\beta^2 - 1)\,\mathbf{c}$$

$\Rightarrow (1 + (\mathbf{a}\cdot\mathbf{b}))\,\mathbf{b} - (\mathbf{a}\cdot\mathbf{b})\,\mathbf{c} = (4 - 2\beta - \sin\alpha)\,\mathbf{b} + (\beta^2 - 1)\,\mathbf{c}$

On equating coefficient of **b** and **c**, we get

$$1 + (\mathbf{a}\cdot\mathbf{b}) = 4 - 2\beta - \sin\alpha \quad \text{...(iii)}$$

and $\quad \mathbf{a}\cdot\mathbf{b} = 1 - \beta^2 \quad$ ...(iv)

On subtracting Eq. (iv) from Eq. (iii), we get

$$1 = 3 - 2\beta - \sin\alpha + \beta^2$$

$\Rightarrow\quad \beta^2 - 2\beta + 2 = \sin\alpha \Rightarrow (\beta - 1)^2 + 1 = \sin\alpha$

Hence, $\sin\alpha \le 1$ and $(\beta - 1)^2 + 1 \ge 1$

$\therefore (\beta - 1)^2 = 0$ and $\sin\alpha = 1 = \sin\dfrac{\pi}{2}$

$\Rightarrow\quad \beta = 1$ and $\alpha = (4n + 1)\dfrac{\pi}{2}, n \in Z$

2. Let **a**, **b** and **c** are position vector of **A**, **B** and **C**, respectively.

Given, $\mathbf{OA} + 2\mathbf{OB} + 3\mathbf{OC} = 0 \Rightarrow \mathbf{a} + 2\mathbf{b} + 3\mathbf{c} = 0 \quad$ ...(i)

Taking cross product with **a** on Eq. (i), we get

$$\mathbf{a}\times\mathbf{a} + \mathbf{a}\times 2\mathbf{b} + \mathbf{a}\times 3\mathbf{c} = 0$$

$\Rightarrow\quad 2\mathbf{a}\times\mathbf{b} = -\mathbf{a}\times 3\mathbf{c}$

$\Rightarrow\quad 2\mathbf{a}\times\mathbf{b} = 3\mathbf{c}\times\mathbf{a} \Rightarrow \mathbf{a}\times\mathbf{b} = \dfrac{3}{2}\mathbf{c}\times\mathbf{a} \quad$ ...(ii)

Taking cross product with **b** on Eq. (i), we get

$$\mathbf{b}\times\mathbf{a} + 2\mathbf{b}\times\mathbf{b} + 3\mathbf{b}\times\mathbf{c} = 0$$

$\Rightarrow\quad -\mathbf{a}\times\mathbf{b} = -3\mathbf{b}\times\mathbf{c} \Rightarrow \mathbf{a}\times\mathbf{b} = 3\mathbf{b}\times\mathbf{c} \quad$ ...(iii)

From Eqs. (ii) and (iii), it is clear that area of ΔBOC is least.

$$\therefore\quad \frac{A_1}{A_3} = \frac{\frac{1}{2}|\mathbf{a}\times\mathbf{b} + \mathbf{b}\times\mathbf{c} + \mathbf{c}\times\mathbf{a}|}{\frac{1}{2}|\mathbf{b}\times\mathbf{c}|}$$

$$= \frac{\frac{1}{2}\left|\mathbf{a}\times\mathbf{b} + \frac{1}{3}\mathbf{a}\times\mathbf{b} + \frac{2}{3}\mathbf{a}\times\mathbf{b}\right|}{\frac{1}{2}\times\frac{1}{3}|\mathbf{a}\times\mathbf{b}|} = \frac{2|\mathbf{a}\times\mathbf{b}|}{\frac{1}{3}|\mathbf{a}\times\mathbf{b}|} = 6$$

3. Let $\hat{\mathbf{i}}$ be a unit vector in the direction of **b**, $\hat{\mathbf{j}}$ in the direction of **c**.

Note that $\mathbf{c} = \hat{\mathbf{j}}$ and $(\mathbf{b}\times\mathbf{c}) = |\mathbf{b}||\mathbf{c}|\sin\alpha\,\hat{\mathbf{k}} = \sin\alpha\,\hat{\mathbf{k}}$

where, $\hat{\mathbf{k}}$ is a unit vector perpendicular to **b** and **c**.

$\Rightarrow |\mathbf{b}\times\mathbf{c}| = \sin\alpha \Rightarrow \hat{\mathbf{k}} = \dfrac{\mathbf{b}\times\mathbf{c}}{|\mathbf{b}\times\mathbf{c}|}$

Let $\mathbf{a} = a_1\hat{\mathbf{i}} + a_2\hat{\mathbf{j}} + a_3\hat{\mathbf{k}}$

Now, $\mathbf{a}\cdot\mathbf{b} = \mathbf{a}\cdot\hat{\mathbf{i}} = \hat{\mathbf{i}}\cdot(a_1\hat{\mathbf{i}} + a_2\hat{\mathbf{j}} + a_3\hat{\mathbf{k}}) = a_1$

and $\mathbf{a}\cdot\mathbf{c} = \mathbf{a}\cdot\hat{\mathbf{j}} = \hat{\mathbf{j}}\cdot(a_1\hat{\mathbf{i}} + a_2\hat{\mathbf{j}} + a_3\hat{\mathbf{k}}) = a_2$

and $\mathbf{a}\cdot\dfrac{\mathbf{b}\times\mathbf{c}}{|\mathbf{b}\times\mathbf{c}|} = \mathbf{a}\cdot\hat{\mathbf{k}} = a_3$

$$\therefore\ (\mathbf{a}\cdot\mathbf{b})\mathbf{b} + (\mathbf{a}\cdot\mathbf{c})\mathbf{c} + \frac{\mathbf{a}\cdot(\mathbf{b}\times\mathbf{c})}{|\mathbf{b}\times\mathbf{c}|^2}(\mathbf{b}\times\mathbf{c}) = a_1\mathbf{b} + a_2\mathbf{c} + a_3\frac{(\mathbf{b}\times\mathbf{c})}{|\mathbf{b}\times\mathbf{c}|}$$

$$= a_1\hat{\mathbf{i}} + a_2\hat{\mathbf{j}} + a_3\hat{\mathbf{k}} = \mathbf{a}$$

4. Let the position vectors of points A, B, C, D be **a**, **b**, **c** and **d**, respectively.

Then, $\mathbf{AB} = \mathbf{b} - \mathbf{a}$, $\mathbf{BC} = \mathbf{c} - \mathbf{b}$, $\mathbf{AD} = \mathbf{d} - \mathbf{a}$,

$\mathbf{BD} = \mathbf{d} - \mathbf{b}$, $\mathbf{CA} = \mathbf{a} - \mathbf{c}$, $\mathbf{CD} = \mathbf{d} - \mathbf{c}$

Now, $|\mathbf{AB}\times\mathbf{CD} + \mathbf{BC}\times\mathbf{AD} + \mathbf{CA}\times\mathbf{BD}|$

$= |(\mathbf{b}-\mathbf{a})\times(\mathbf{d}-\mathbf{c}) + (\mathbf{c}-\mathbf{b})\times(\mathbf{d}-\mathbf{a}) + (\mathbf{a}-\mathbf{c})\times(\mathbf{d}-\mathbf{b})|$

$= |\mathbf{b}\times\mathbf{d} - \mathbf{a}\times\mathbf{d} - \mathbf{b}\times\mathbf{c} + \mathbf{a}\times\mathbf{c} + \mathbf{c}\times\mathbf{d} - \mathbf{c}\times\mathbf{a} - \mathbf{b}\times\mathbf{d}$
$+ \mathbf{b}\times\mathbf{a} + \mathbf{a}\times\mathbf{d} - \mathbf{a}\times\mathbf{b} - \mathbf{c}\times\mathbf{d} + \mathbf{c}\times\mathbf{b}|$

$= 2|\mathbf{a}\times\mathbf{b} + \mathbf{b}\times\mathbf{c} + \mathbf{c}\times\mathbf{a}| \quad$ ...(i)

Also, area of ΔABC

$$= \frac{1}{2}|\mathbf{AB} \times \mathbf{AC}| = \frac{1}{2}|(\mathbf{b}-\mathbf{a}) \times (\mathbf{c}-\mathbf{a})|$$

$$= \frac{1}{2}|\mathbf{b}\times\mathbf{c} - \mathbf{b}\times\mathbf{a} - \mathbf{a}\times\mathbf{c} + \mathbf{a}\times\mathbf{a}| = \frac{1}{2}|\mathbf{a}\times\mathbf{b} + \mathbf{b}\times\mathbf{c} + \mathbf{c}\times\mathbf{a}| \quad \text{...(ii)}$$

From Eqs. (i) and (ii), we get

$|\mathbf{AB}\times\mathbf{CD} + \mathbf{BC}\times\mathbf{AD} + \mathbf{CA}\times\mathbf{BD}|$

$2\,(2 \text{ area of } \Delta ABC) = 4 \text{ (area of } \Delta ABC)$

5. $\hat{\mathbf{n}} = \dfrac{\hat{\mathbf{i}}+\hat{\mathbf{j}}+\hat{\mathbf{k}}}{\sqrt{3}}$;

$$\omega = |\omega|\,\hat{\mathbf{n}} = 10(\hat{\mathbf{i}}+\hat{\mathbf{j}}+\hat{\mathbf{k}})$$

Now, $\mathbf{v} = \omega \times \mathbf{r} = 10\,(\hat{\mathbf{i}}+\hat{\mathbf{j}}+\hat{\mathbf{k}}) \times (x\hat{\mathbf{i}} + y\hat{\mathbf{j}} + z\hat{\mathbf{k}})$,

where **r** is the position vector of the point whose locus is to be determined.

Hence, $\mathbf{v} = 10\,[(z-y)\hat{\mathbf{i}} - (z-x)\hat{\mathbf{j}} + (y-x)\hat{\mathbf{k}}]$

$\therefore \quad |\mathbf{v}| = 10\sqrt{(x-y)^2 + (y-z)^2 + (z-x)^2}$

Hence, $2(x^2+y^2+z^2-xy-yz-zx) = 4$

$\Rightarrow \quad x^2+y^2+z^2-xy-yz-zx-2=0$

which is the equation of a cylinder.

6. $\hat{\mathbf{n}} = \dfrac{\hat{\mathbf{i}}+2\hat{\mathbf{j}}+2\hat{\mathbf{k}}}{3}$; $\omega = \dfrac{\omega}{3}(\hat{\mathbf{i}}+2\hat{\mathbf{j}}+2\hat{\mathbf{k}})$

$$\mathbf{v} = \omega \times \mathbf{r} = \frac{\omega}{3}\begin{vmatrix} \hat{\mathbf{i}} & \hat{\mathbf{j}} & \hat{\mathbf{k}} \\ 1 & 2 & 2 \\ 2 & 3 & 5 \end{vmatrix} = \frac{\omega}{3}(4\hat{\mathbf{i}} - \hat{\mathbf{j}} - \hat{\mathbf{k}})$$

$\therefore \quad |\mathbf{v}| = \dfrac{\omega}{3}\sqrt{18} = \omega\sqrt{2}$

7. $\mathbf{b}\cdot\mathbf{a} + \mathbf{b}\cdot\mathbf{c} = \mathbf{b}\cdot\mathbf{b} + \mathbf{a}\cdot\mathbf{c}$

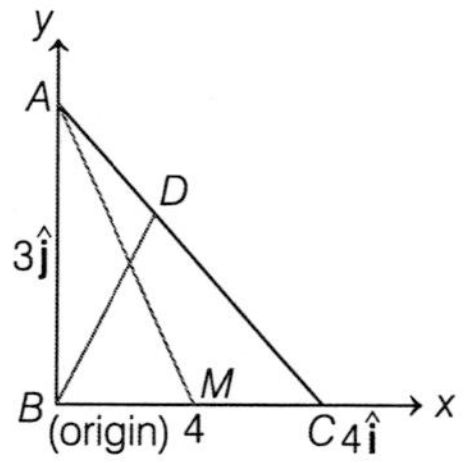

or $\quad \mathbf{b}\cdot(\mathbf{a}-\mathbf{b}) - \mathbf{c}\cdot(\mathbf{a}-\mathbf{b}) = 0$ or $(\mathbf{b}-\mathbf{c})\cdot(\mathbf{a}-\mathbf{b}) = 0$

$\Rightarrow$ **BC** and **AB** are perpendicular.

Now, find angle between **AM** and **BD**

where, $\quad \mathbf{AM} = 2\hat{\mathbf{i}} - 3\hat{\mathbf{j}}$, $\mathbf{BD} = \dfrac{4\hat{\mathbf{i}}+3\hat{\mathbf{j}}}{2}$

$$\therefore \cos\theta = \frac{\mathbf{AM}\cdot\mathbf{BD}}{|\mathbf{AM}||\mathbf{BD}|} = \frac{-1}{5\sqrt{13}} \Rightarrow \theta = \pi - \cos^{-1}\left(\frac{1}{5\sqrt{13}}\right)$$

8. $\mathbf{V} = (\mathbf{a}\times\mathbf{b})\times\mathbf{a} + (\mathbf{a}\times\mathbf{b})\times\mathbf{b}$

$= \mathbf{b} - (\mathbf{a}\cdot\mathbf{b})\mathbf{a} + (\mathbf{a}\cdot\mathbf{b})\mathbf{b} - \mathbf{a} = (\mathbf{b}-\mathbf{a}) + (\mathbf{b}-\mathbf{a})(\mathbf{a}\cdot\mathbf{b})$

$\mathbf{V} = (\mathbf{b}-\mathbf{a})(1+\mathbf{a}\cdot\mathbf{b}) = \lambda(\mathbf{b}-\mathbf{a})$

9. **Decoding the Question**

If **p** and **q** are orthogonal, then any vector $\mathbf{r}\times\mathbf{p}$ can be expressed as $\mathbf{r}\times\mathbf{p} = x\mathbf{p} + y\mathbf{q} + z(\mathbf{r}\times\mathbf{p})$.

Since, **a** and **b** are perpendicular, hence **a**, **b** and $\mathbf{a}\times\mathbf{b}$ are non-coplanar. Hence, any vector say $(\mathbf{r}\times\mathbf{a})$ can be expressed as

$\therefore \quad \mathbf{r}\times\mathbf{a} = x\mathbf{a} + y\mathbf{b} + z(\mathbf{a}\times\mathbf{b}) \quad \text{...(i)}$

Taking dot with **a**, $\quad 0 = x + 0 + 0 \Rightarrow x = 0$

Taking dot with **b**, $\quad [\mathbf{r}\ \mathbf{a}\ \mathbf{b}] = 0 + y + 0 \Rightarrow y = [\mathbf{r}\ \mathbf{a}\ \mathbf{b}]$

Taking dot with **r**, $\quad 0 = x\mathbf{a}\cdot\mathbf{r} + y\mathbf{r}\cdot\mathbf{b} + z[\mathbf{r}\ \mathbf{a}\ \mathbf{b}]$

$0 = [\mathbf{r}\ \mathbf{a}\ \mathbf{b}](\mathbf{r}\cdot\mathbf{b}) + z[\mathbf{r}\ \mathbf{a}\ \mathbf{b}] \Rightarrow z = -(\mathbf{r}\cdot\mathbf{b})$

Hence, $\quad \mathbf{r}\times\mathbf{a} = [\mathbf{r}\ \mathbf{a}\ \mathbf{b}]\,\mathbf{b} - (\mathbf{r}\cdot\mathbf{b})(\mathbf{a}\times\mathbf{b})$

$\mathbf{r}\times\mathbf{a} = [\mathbf{r}\ \mathbf{a}\ \mathbf{b}]\,\mathbf{b} + (\mathbf{r}\cdot\mathbf{b})(\mathbf{b}\times\mathbf{a})$

10. $(\mathbf{a}\times\mathbf{x}) + \mathbf{b} = \mathbf{x} \Rightarrow \mathbf{a}\times(\mathbf{a}\times\mathbf{x}) + (\mathbf{a}\times\mathbf{b}) = \mathbf{a}\times\mathbf{x}$

$(\mathbf{a}\cdot\mathbf{x})\,\mathbf{a} - (\mathbf{a}\cdot\mathbf{a})\,\mathbf{x} + (\mathbf{a}\times\mathbf{b}) = \mathbf{x} - \mathbf{b}$

Projection of **x** along **a** is 2 units.

$\Rightarrow \quad \dfrac{(\mathbf{a}\cdot\mathbf{x})}{|\hat{\mathbf{a}}|} = 2 \Rightarrow \mathbf{a}\cdot\mathbf{x} = 2$

So, $\quad \mathbf{x} = \dfrac{1}{2}[2\mathbf{a} + \mathbf{b} + (\mathbf{a}\times\mathbf{b})]$

11. We know, $\mathbf{a}\times(\mathbf{b}\times\mathbf{c}) = (\mathbf{a}\cdot\mathbf{c})\,\mathbf{b} - (\mathbf{a}\cdot\mathbf{b})\,\mathbf{c}$

Component of $\mathbf{a}\times(\mathbf{b}\times\mathbf{c})$ along **b** is

$$\left[\left\{\frac{(\mathbf{a}\cdot\mathbf{c})\mathbf{b} - (\mathbf{a}\cdot\mathbf{b})\mathbf{c}}{|\mathbf{b}|^2}\right\}\cdot\mathbf{b}\right]\mathbf{b} = \left(\frac{(\mathbf{a}\cdot\mathbf{c})(\mathbf{b}\cdot\mathbf{b}) - (\mathbf{a}\cdot\mathbf{b})(\mathbf{b}\cdot\mathbf{c})}{|\mathbf{b}|^2}\right)\mathbf{b}$$

So, component of $\mathbf{a}\times(\mathbf{b}\times\mathbf{c})$ perpendicular to **b** is

$$\mathbf{a}\times(\mathbf{b}\times\mathbf{c}) - \left(\frac{(\mathbf{a}\cdot\mathbf{c}(\mathbf{b}\cdot\mathbf{b}) - (\mathbf{a}\cdot\mathbf{b})(\mathbf{b}\cdot\mathbf{c})}{|\mathbf{b}|^2}\right)\mathbf{b}$$

$$= \mathbf{a}\times(\mathbf{b}\times\mathbf{c}) + \left(\frac{(\mathbf{a}\cdot\mathbf{b})(\mathbf{b}\cdot\mathbf{c}) - (\mathbf{a}\cdot\mathbf{c})(\mathbf{b}\cdot\mathbf{b})}{|\mathbf{b}|^2}\right)\mathbf{b}$$

$$= \mathbf{a}\times(\mathbf{b}\times\mathbf{c}) + \frac{(\mathbf{a}\times\mathbf{b})\cdot(\mathbf{b}\times\mathbf{c})}{|\mathbf{b}|^2}\,\mathbf{b}$$

12. We have, $\mathbf{c}\cdot\mathbf{a} = \mathbf{c}\cdot\mathbf{b} = \cos\theta$, $\mathbf{a}\cdot\mathbf{b} = 0$

Now, $\quad \mathbf{c} = \alpha\mathbf{a} + \beta\mathbf{b} + \gamma(\mathbf{a}\times\mathbf{b})$

On taking dot product of both sides with **a**, we get

$\mathbf{c}\cdot\mathbf{a} = \alpha = \cos\theta \quad [\because |\mathbf{a}|^2 = 1, \mathbf{a}\cdot\mathbf{b} = 0]$

Similarly, $\beta = \cos\theta$

Now, on taking dot product with $\mathbf{a}\times\mathbf{b}$, we get

$[\mathbf{c}\ \mathbf{a}\ \mathbf{b}] = \gamma|\mathbf{a}\times\mathbf{b}|^2 = \gamma$

Now, $[\mathbf{c}\ \mathbf{a}\ \mathbf{b}]^2 = [\mathbf{a}\ \mathbf{b}\ \mathbf{c}]^2$

$$= \begin{vmatrix} \mathbf{a}\cdot\mathbf{a} & \mathbf{a}\cdot\mathbf{b} & \mathbf{a}\cdot\mathbf{c} \\ \mathbf{b}\cdot\mathbf{a} & \mathbf{b}\cdot\mathbf{b} & \mathbf{b}\cdot\mathbf{c} \\ \mathbf{c}\cdot\mathbf{a} & \mathbf{a}\cdot\mathbf{b} & \mathbf{c}\cdot\mathbf{c} \end{vmatrix} = \begin{vmatrix} 1 & 0 & \cos\theta \\ 0 & 1 & \cos\theta \\ \cos\theta & \cos\theta & 1 \end{vmatrix}$$

$= 1 - \cos^2\theta + \cos\theta(-\cos\theta)$

Thus, $\quad \alpha = \beta = \cos\theta, \gamma^2 = -\cos 2\theta.$

13. From the figure the vector equation of **OP** is $\mathbf{r} = \lambda(\hat{\mathbf{i}} + \hat{\mathbf{j}} + \hat{\mathbf{k}})$

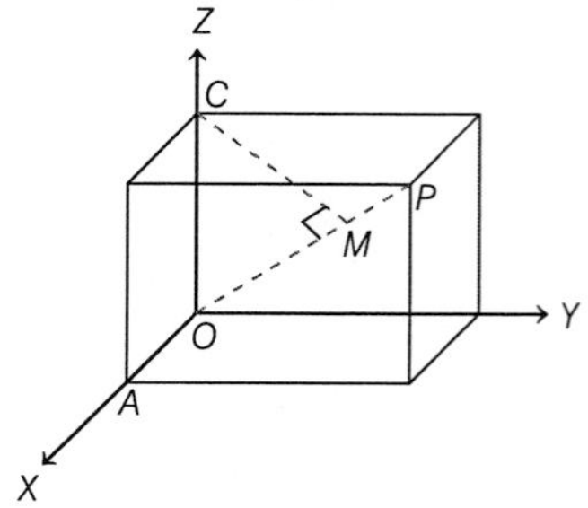

$\therefore \quad \mathbf{OM}$ = projection of **OC** on $\mathbf{OP} = \mathbf{OC}\cdot\mathbf{OP} = \dfrac{1}{\sqrt{3}}$

Now, $\quad CM^2 = OC^2 - OM^2 = 1 - \frac{1}{3} = \frac{2}{3}$

$\therefore \quad CM = \sqrt{\frac{2}{3}}$

14. $\mathbf{a}, \mathbf{b}$ and $\mathbf{c}$ are non-coplanar $\Rightarrow [\mathbf{a}\ \mathbf{b}\ \mathbf{c}] \neq 1$.
Also, $\mathbf{a} \times \mathbf{b}$, $\mathbf{b} \times \mathbf{c}$, $\mathbf{c} \times \mathbf{a}$ are non-coplanar.
Given, $\mathbf{d} = \sin x\, (\mathbf{a} \times \mathbf{b}) + \cos y\, (\mathbf{b} \times \mathbf{c}) + 2(\mathbf{c} \times \mathbf{a})$.
On taking dot product with $\mathbf{a} + \mathbf{b} + \mathbf{c}$, we get

$$\mathbf{0} = \sin x[\mathbf{a}\ \mathbf{b}\ \mathbf{c}] + \cos y[\mathbf{a}\ \mathbf{b}\ \mathbf{c}] + 2[\mathbf{a}\ \mathbf{b}\ \mathbf{c}]$$

$\Rightarrow \sin x + \cos y + 2 = 0 \Rightarrow \sin x + \cos y = -2$

$\Rightarrow \quad x = (4n - 1)\frac{\pi}{2}, y = (2n - 1)\pi, n \in z$

For least value of $x^2 + y^2$, $x = \frac{-\pi}{2}$ and $y = \pi$

and least value is $\frac{5\pi^2}{4}$.

15. We have, $\alpha(\mathbf{a} \times \mathbf{b}) + \beta\, (\mathbf{b} \times \mathbf{c}) + \gamma(\mathbf{c} \times \mathbf{a}) = 0$
Taking dot product with c, we have

$$\alpha[\mathbf{a}\ \mathbf{b}\ \mathbf{c}] + \beta[\mathbf{b}\ \mathbf{c}\ \mathbf{c}] + \gamma[\mathbf{c}\ \mathbf{a}\ \mathbf{c}] = 0$$

i.e. $\quad \alpha[\mathbf{a}\ \mathbf{b}\ \mathbf{c}] + 0 + 0 = 0 \Rightarrow \alpha[\mathbf{a}\ \mathbf{b}\ \mathbf{c}] = 0$

Similarly, on taking dot product with b and c, we have

$$\gamma\,[\mathbf{a}\ \mathbf{b}\ \mathbf{c}] = 0, \beta\,[\mathbf{a}\ \mathbf{b}\ \mathbf{c}] = 0$$

Now, even if all of $\alpha, \beta, \gamma \neq 0$, then we have $[\mathbf{a}\ \mathbf{b}\ \mathbf{c}] = 0$

$\Rightarrow$ **a, b** and **c** are coplanar.

16. $\frac{1}{3}\lambda_1 h_4 + \frac{1}{3}\lambda_2 h_3 + \frac{1}{3}\lambda_3 h_2 + \frac{1}{3}\lambda_4 h_1$

$= 4$ area the tetrahedron $OABC$

$= \frac{4}{6}|[\mathbf{AB}\ \ \mathbf{AC}\ \ \mathbf{OA}]| = \frac{2}{3}|[\mathbf{AB}\ \ \mathbf{AC}\ \ \mathbf{OA}]|$

17.

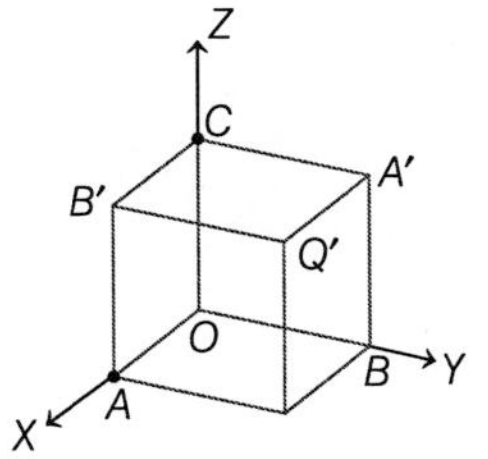

Equation of $OO' \Rightarrow \frac{x}{1} = \frac{y}{1} = \frac{z}{1} \Rightarrow \mathbf{r} = \mathbf{a} + t\mathbf{b}$

Equation of **AB** : $\frac{x-1}{-1} = \frac{y}{1} = \frac{z}{0} \Rightarrow (\alpha)\mathbf{r} = \mathbf{c} + s\mathbf{d}$,

where $\mathbf{a} = 0$, $\mathbf{b} = \hat{\mathbf{i}} + \hat{\mathbf{j}} + \hat{\mathbf{k}}$, $\mathbf{c} = \hat{\mathbf{i}}$, $\mathbf{d} = -\hat{\mathbf{i}} + \hat{\mathbf{j}}$

Shortest distance $= \frac{|(\mathbf{c} - \mathbf{a}) \cdot (\mathbf{b} \times \mathbf{d})|}{|\mathbf{b} \times \mathbf{d}|} = \frac{1}{\sqrt{6}}$

18. $\mathbf{V} \times \mathbf{W} = 3\hat{\mathbf{i}} - 5\hat{\mathbf{j}} - \hat{\mathbf{k}}$
Maximum value of $[\mathbf{U}\ \ \mathbf{V}\ \ \mathbf{W}] = |\mathbf{U}||\mathbf{V} \times \mathbf{W}| = 1 \cdot \sqrt{35} = \sqrt{35}$

19. Volume of tetrahedron $= \frac{1}{6}[\mathbf{a}\ \mathbf{b}\ \mathbf{c}]$

$$\text{Now, } [\mathbf{a}\ \mathbf{b}\ \mathbf{c}]^2 = \begin{vmatrix} \mathbf{a}\cdot\mathbf{a} & \mathbf{a}\cdot\mathbf{b} & \mathbf{a}\cdot\mathbf{c} \\ \mathbf{b}\cdot\mathbf{a} & \mathbf{b}\cdot\mathbf{b} & \mathbf{b}\cdot\mathbf{c} \\ \mathbf{c}\cdot\mathbf{a} & \mathbf{c}\cdot\mathbf{b} & \mathbf{c}\cdot\mathbf{c} \end{vmatrix} = \begin{vmatrix} 4 & 2 & 2 \\ 2 & 4 & 2 \\ 2 & 2 & 4 \end{vmatrix}$$

$= 4(12) + 2(-4) + 2\,(-4)$

Volume $= \frac{1}{6} \times 4\sqrt{2} = \frac{2\sqrt{2}}{3}$

20. Given, $\cos\theta = (\mathbf{a} \times \hat{\mathbf{i}}) \cdot (\mathbf{b} \times \hat{\mathbf{i}}) + (\mathbf{a} \times \hat{\mathbf{j}}) \cdot (\mathbf{b} \times \hat{\mathbf{j}})$
$\qquad + (\mathbf{a} \times \hat{\mathbf{k}}) \cdot (\mathbf{b} \times \hat{\mathbf{k}}) \quad$ ...(i)

Consider, $(\mathbf{a} \times \hat{\mathbf{i}}) \cdot (\mathbf{b} \times \hat{\mathbf{i}}) = [(\mathbf{a} \times \hat{\mathbf{i}})\mathbf{b}\ \hat{\mathbf{i}}] = ((\mathbf{a} \times \hat{\mathbf{i}}) \times \mathbf{b}) \cdot \hat{\mathbf{i}}$

$$((\mathbf{a} \cdot \mathbf{b})\hat{\mathbf{i}}) - (\hat{\mathbf{i}} \cdot \mathbf{b})\mathbf{a})\hat{\mathbf{i}} = (\mathbf{a} \cdot \mathbf{b})\,(\hat{\mathbf{i}} \cdot \hat{\mathbf{i}}) - (\hat{\mathbf{i}} \cdot \hat{\mathbf{b}})\,(\mathbf{a} \cdot \hat{\mathbf{i}})$$

$$= \mathbf{a} \cdot \mathbf{b} - \mathbf{a}_1\mathbf{b}_1$$

Similarly, $(\mathbf{a} \times \hat{\mathbf{j}}) \cdot (\mathbf{b} \times \hat{\mathbf{j}}) = \mathbf{a} \cdot \mathbf{b} - \mathbf{a}_2\mathbf{b}_2$

and $\quad (\mathbf{a} \times \hat{\mathbf{k}})\,(\mathbf{b} \times \hat{\mathbf{k}}) = \mathbf{a} \cdot \mathbf{b} - \mathbf{a}_3\mathbf{b}_3$

$\therefore$From Eq. (i), we get

$$\cos\theta = 3\mathbf{a} \cdot \mathbf{b} - (\mathbf{a}_1\mathbf{b}_1 + \mathbf{a}_2\mathbf{b}_2 + \mathbf{a}_3\mathbf{b}_3) = 3\mathbf{a} \cdot \mathbf{b} - \mathbf{a} \cdot \mathbf{b}$$

$\Rightarrow \quad \frac{\mathbf{a} \cdot \mathbf{b}}{|\mathbf{a}|\,|\mathbf{b}|} = 2\mathbf{a} \cdot \mathbf{b} \Rightarrow |\mathbf{a}|\,|\mathbf{b}| = \frac{1}{2}$

Now, use AM $\geq$ GM on $|\mathbf{a}|, |\mathbf{b}|$

$\therefore \frac{|\mathbf{a}| + |\mathbf{b}|}{2} \geq (|\mathbf{a}| \cdot |\mathbf{b}|)^{\frac{1}{2}} \Rightarrow |\mathbf{a}| + |\mathbf{b}| \geq \frac{2}{\sqrt{2}} \Rightarrow |\mathbf{a}| + |\mathbf{b}| \geq \sqrt{2}$

21. $\mathbf{OP} \cdot \mathbf{OQ} + \mathbf{OR} \cdot \mathbf{OS} = \mathbf{OR} \cdot \mathbf{OP} + \mathbf{OQ} \cdot \mathbf{OS}$

$\Rightarrow \mathbf{OP}(\mathbf{OQ} - \mathbf{OR}) + \mathbf{OS}(\mathbf{OR} - \mathbf{OQ}) = 0$

$\Rightarrow \quad (\mathbf{OP} - \mathbf{OS})(\mathbf{OQ} - \mathbf{OR}) = 0 \Rightarrow \mathbf{SP} \cdot \mathbf{RQ} = 0$

Similarly, $\mathbf{SR} \cdot \mathbf{PQ} = 0$ and $\mathbf{SQ} \cdot \mathbf{PR} = 0$

$\therefore S$ is orthocentre.

22. $\quad \mathbf{a} \times (\mathbf{b} \times \mathbf{c}) = (\mathbf{a} \times \mathbf{b}) \times \mathbf{c}$

or $\quad (\mathbf{a} \cdot \mathbf{c})\,\mathbf{b} - (\mathbf{a} \cdot \mathbf{b})\,\mathbf{c} = (\mathbf{a} \cdot \mathbf{c})\,\mathbf{b} - (\mathbf{c} \cdot \mathbf{b})\,\mathbf{a}$

or $\quad (\mathbf{a} \cdot \mathbf{b})\,\mathbf{c} - (\mathbf{c} \cdot \mathbf{b})\,\mathbf{a} = \mathbf{0}$

or $\quad \mathbf{b} \times (\mathbf{c} \times \mathbf{a}) = \mathbf{0}$ or $(\mathbf{c} \times \mathbf{a}) \times \mathbf{b} = \mathbf{0}$

or $\quad \mathbf{b} \times (\mathbf{c} \times \mathbf{a}) = (\mathbf{c} \times \mathbf{a}) \times \mathbf{b} = \mathbf{0}$

23. Let angle between **a** and **b** be θ

$$\mathbf{v} = \mathbf{a} \times \mathbf{b} = |\mathbf{a}|\,|\mathbf{b}|\sin\theta\,\hat{\mathbf{n}}$$

$\therefore \quad |\mathbf{v}| = \sin\theta, \quad \left[\because |\mathbf{a}| = 1, |\mathbf{b}| = 1, \mathbf{n} = \frac{(\mathbf{a} \times \mathbf{b})}{|\mathbf{a} \times \mathbf{b}|} = \frac{\mathbf{v}}{|\mathbf{v}|}\right]$

$$\mathbf{u} = \mathbf{a} - (\mathbf{a} \cdot \mathbf{b})\,\mathbf{b} = \mathbf{a} - \cos\theta\,\mathbf{b}$$

$$[\because \mathbf{a} \cdot \mathbf{b} = |\mathbf{a}|\,|\mathbf{b}|\cos\theta = \cos\theta]$$

$$\mathbf{u} \cdot \mathbf{u} = |\mathbf{u}|^2 = 1 + \cos^2\theta - 2\cos^2\theta = \sin^2\theta$$

$\therefore \quad |\mathbf{u}| = \sin\theta$

$$\mathbf{u} \cdot \mathbf{a} = \mathbf{a} \cdot \mathbf{a} - \cos\theta\,\mathbf{a} \cdot \mathbf{b} = 1 - \cos^2\theta = \sin^2\theta$$

$$\mathbf{u} \cdot \mathbf{b} = \mathbf{a} \cdot \mathbf{b} - \cos\theta\,\mathbf{b} \cdot \mathbf{b} = \cos\theta - \cos\theta = 0$$

$$\mathbf{u} \cdot (\mathbf{a} + \mathbf{b}) = (\mathbf{a} - \cos\theta\,\mathbf{b}) \cdot (\mathbf{a} + \mathbf{b})$$

$$= 1 + \cos\theta - \cos^2\theta - \cos\theta = 1 - \cos^2\theta = \sin^2\theta$$

24. $\mathbf{a} \times (\mathbf{r} \times \mathbf{a}) = \mathbf{a} \times \mathbf{b}$

$$3\,\mathbf{r} - (\mathbf{a} \cdot \mathbf{r})\,\mathbf{a} = \mathbf{a} \times \mathbf{b}$$

Also, $\quad |\mathbf{r} \times \mathbf{a}| = |\mathbf{b}|$

$\Rightarrow \quad \sin^2\theta = \frac{2}{3}$ or $(1 - \cos^2\theta) = \frac{2}{3}$ or $\frac{1}{3} = \cos^2\theta$

$\Rightarrow \quad \mathbf{a} \cdot \mathbf{r} = \pm 1 \Rightarrow 3\mathbf{r} \pm \mathbf{a} = \mathbf{a} \times \mathbf{b}$

or $\quad \mathbf{r} = \frac{1}{3}(\mathbf{a} \times \mathbf{b} \pm \mathbf{a})$

25. $\mathbf{a} \times \mathbf{b} = |\mathbf{a}|\,|\mathbf{b}|\sin\theta\,\hat{\mathbf{n}}$

or $\quad |\mathbf{a} \times \mathbf{b}| = |\mathbf{a}|\,|\mathbf{b}|\sin\theta$

or $\quad \sin\theta = \frac{|\mathbf{a} \times \mathbf{b}|}{|\mathbf{a}|\,|\mathbf{b}|} \quad$ ...(i)

$$\mathbf{a}\cdot\mathbf{b} = |\mathbf{a}||\mathbf{b}|\cos\theta \Rightarrow \cos\theta = \frac{|\mathbf{a}\cdot\mathbf{b}|}{|\mathbf{a}||\mathbf{b}|} \quad \text{...(ii)}$$

From Eqs. (i) and (ii), we get

$$\sin^2\theta + \cos^2\theta = 1$$

$$\Rightarrow \quad |\mathbf{a}\times\mathbf{b}|^2 + (\mathbf{a}\cdot\mathbf{b})^2 = |\mathbf{a}|^2|\mathbf{b}|^2$$

If $\theta = \pi/4$, then $\sin\theta = \cos\theta = 1/\sqrt{2}$.

Therefore, $|\mathbf{a}\times\mathbf{b}| = \frac{|\mathbf{a}||\mathbf{b}|}{\sqrt{2}}$ and $\mathbf{a}\cdot\mathbf{b} = \frac{|\mathbf{a}||\mathbf{b}|}{\sqrt{2}}$

$$\therefore \quad |\mathbf{a}\times\mathbf{b}| = \mathbf{a}\cdot\mathbf{b}$$

$$\mathbf{a}\times\mathbf{b} = |\mathbf{a}||\mathbf{b}|\sin\theta\,\hat{\mathbf{n}} = \frac{|\mathbf{a}||\mathbf{b}|}{\sqrt{2}}\hat{\mathbf{n}} = (\mathbf{a}\cdot\mathbf{b})\,\hat{\mathbf{n}}$$

26. We have, $|\mathbf{a}-\mathbf{b}|^2 = |\mathbf{a}|^2 + |\mathbf{b}|^2 - 2(\mathbf{a}\cdot\mathbf{b})$

or $\quad |\mathbf{a}-\mathbf{b}|^2 = |\mathbf{a}|^2 + |\mathbf{b}|^2 - 2|\mathbf{a}||\mathbf{b}|\cos 2\theta$

or $\quad |\mathbf{a}-\mathbf{b}|^2 = 2(1-\cos 2\theta) \quad [\because |\mathbf{a}| = |\mathbf{b}| = 1]$

$$= 4\sin^2\theta \text{ or } |\mathbf{a}-\mathbf{b}| = 2|\sin\theta|$$

Now, $\quad |\mathbf{a}-\mathbf{b}| < 1 \Rightarrow 2|\sin\theta| < 1$ or $|\sin\theta| < \frac{1}{2}$

$\Rightarrow \quad \theta \in [0, \pi/6)$ or $\theta \in (5\pi/6, \pi]$

27. $\mathbf{a}\times(\mathbf{b}\times\mathbf{c}) + (\mathbf{a}\cdot\mathbf{b})\,\mathbf{b} = (4-2x-\sin y)\,\mathbf{b} + (x^2-1)\,\mathbf{c}$

or $(\mathbf{a}\cdot\mathbf{c})\,\mathbf{b} - (\mathbf{a}\cdot\mathbf{b})\mathbf{c} + (\mathbf{a}\cdot\mathbf{b})\,\mathbf{b} = (4-2x-\sin y)\,\mathbf{b} + (x^2-1)\,\mathbf{c}$

Now, $\quad (\mathbf{c}\cdot\mathbf{c})\,\mathbf{a} = \mathbf{c}$.

Therefore, $(\mathbf{c}\cdot\mathbf{c})\,(\mathbf{a}\cdot\mathbf{c}) = (\mathbf{c}\cdot\mathbf{c})$ or $\mathbf{a}\,.\,\mathbf{c} = 1$

$\Rightarrow \quad 1 + \mathbf{a}\cdot\mathbf{b} = 4 - 2x - \sin y,\ x^2 - 1 = -(\mathbf{a}\cdot\mathbf{b})$

or $\quad 1 = 4 - 2x - \sin y + x^2 - 1$

or $\quad \sin y = x^2 - 2x + 2 = (x-1)^2 + 1$

But, $\sin y \le 1 \Rightarrow x = 1, \sin y = 1 \Rightarrow y = (4n+1)\frac{\pi}{2}, n \in I$

28. Clearly, $\mathbf{a}\cdot\mathbf{c} = 0$ and $\mathbf{b}\cdot\mathbf{c} = 0$. Also, $\mathbf{a}\cdot\mathbf{b} = 0$

$$\mathbf{a}\times\mathbf{b} = \mathbf{c}$$

Dot with $\mathbf{b} \Rightarrow \mathbf{b}\cdot\mathbf{c} = 0$

Similarly, $\quad \mathbf{b}\times\mathbf{c} = \mathbf{a}$

Dot with $\mathbf{b} \Rightarrow \mathbf{a}\cdot\mathbf{b} = 0$

Dot with $\mathbf{c} \Rightarrow \mathbf{a}\cdot\mathbf{c} = 0 \Rightarrow \mathbf{a}\cdot\mathbf{b} = \mathbf{b}\cdot\mathbf{c} = \mathbf{c}\cdot\mathbf{a} = 0$

Again, $\quad \frac{|\mathbf{a}||\mathbf{b}|}{|\mathbf{b}||\mathbf{c}|} = \frac{|\mathbf{c}|}{|\mathbf{a}|} \Rightarrow \frac{|\mathbf{a}|}{|\mathbf{c}|} = \frac{|\mathbf{c}|}{|\mathbf{a}|}$

$\Rightarrow \quad |\mathbf{a}| = |\mathbf{c}|$ and $|\mathbf{b}| = 1$

$\Rightarrow \quad (\mathbf{a}\times\mathbf{b})\cdot\mathbf{c} = |\mathbf{a}||\mathbf{b}||\mathbf{c}| = |\mathbf{a}|^2 = |\mathbf{c}|^2$

[children will assume $\mathbf{a} = \hat{\mathbf{i}}$; $\mathbf{b} = \hat{\mathbf{j}}$ and $\mathbf{c} = \hat{\mathbf{k}}$ but in this case all the four will be correct which will be wrong]

29. Given, $|\mathbf{A}||\mathbf{B}|\cos\theta = -6$; $|\mathbf{B}| = 2$ [given]

$$\mathbf{B}\cdot\mathbf{C} = |\mathbf{B}||\mathbf{C}|\cos\phi = 6$$

and $\quad (\mathbf{A}\times\mathbf{B})\times\mathbf{A} = \mathbf{0}$

$$(\mathbf{A}\cdot\mathbf{A})\mathbf{B} - (\mathbf{B}\cdot\mathbf{A})\mathbf{A} = \mathbf{0} \quad \text{...(i)}$$

$$(\mathbf{A}\cdot\mathbf{A}) = -6\mathbf{A}$$

$\therefore$ $\mathbf{A}$ and $\mathbf{B}$ are collinear and θ between $\mathbf{A}$ and $\mathbf{B}$ is π.

$\Rightarrow \quad \mathbf{A}\times\mathbf{B} = \mathbf{0} \Rightarrow$ (a) is correct.

$\Rightarrow \quad \mathbf{A}\cdot(\mathbf{B}\times\mathbf{C}) = (\mathbf{A}\times\mathbf{B})\cdot\mathbf{C} = \mathbf{0} \Rightarrow$ (b) is correct.

Also, $\quad \mathbf{A}\cdot\mathbf{B} = -6$ and $|\mathbf{B}| = 2$

$\therefore \quad |\mathbf{A}||\mathbf{B}|\cos\pi = -6 \Rightarrow |\mathbf{A}|\cdot(2) = 6$

$\Rightarrow \quad |\mathbf{A}| = 3 \Rightarrow \mathbf{A}\cdot\mathbf{A} = 9$

$\Rightarrow$ (c) is not correct.

Again, $\mathbf{A}\cdot\mathbf{C} = ?$

On taking dot with $\mathbf{C}$ in the Eq. (i), we get

$$9\,(\mathbf{B}\cdot\mathbf{C}) = -6\mathbf{A}\cdot\mathbf{C}$$

$$9\,(6) = -6\,(\mathbf{A}\cdot\mathbf{C}) \Rightarrow \mathbf{A}\cdot\mathbf{C} = -9$$

$\Rightarrow$ (d) is correct.

30. **Decoding the Question**

We know that a set of three non-coplanar vectors are linearly independent. Also, three vectors are said to be mutually perpendicular, if they are all perpendicular to each other.

It may be observed that

$$[\mathbf{U}\ \mathbf{V}\ \mathbf{W}] = \begin{vmatrix} 2 & 3 & -6 \\ 6 & 2 & 3 \\ 3 & -6 & -2 \end{vmatrix} = 343 \ne 0$$

$\Rightarrow$ **U**, **V** and **W** are non-coplanar, hence linearly independent

Further $\mathbf{U}\times\mathbf{V} = \mathbf{W}$ and $\mathbf{V}\times\mathbf{W} = \mathbf{U}$

They form a right handed triplet of mutually perpendicular vectors.

$\therefore \quad (\mathbf{U}\times\mathbf{V})\times\mathbf{W} = \mathbf{0}$ and $\mathbf{U}\times(\mathbf{V}\times\mathbf{W}) = \mathbf{0}$

31. Let the required vector be $\mathbf{d} = x\hat{\mathbf{i}} + y\hat{\mathbf{j}} + z\hat{\mathbf{k}}$. For this to be coplanar wih $\mathbf{b}$ and $\mathbf{c}$, we must have

$$\begin{vmatrix} x & y & z \\ 1 & 2 & -1 \\ 1 & 1 & -2 \end{vmatrix} = 0$$

$\Rightarrow \quad x(-4+1) + y(-1+2) + z(1-2) = 0$

$\Rightarrow \quad -3x + y - z = 0$

The projection of $\mathbf{d}$ on $\mathbf{a}$ is $\frac{|\mathbf{a}\cdot\mathbf{d}|}{|\mathbf{a}|}$.

So, $\sqrt{\frac{2}{3}} = \frac{1}{\sqrt{6}}|2x - y + z| \Rightarrow 2x - y + z = \pm 2$

The choices (a) and (c) satisfy the Eqs. (i) and (ii).

32. $\mathbf{a}\times(\mathbf{b}-3\mathbf{c}) = \mathbf{0} \Rightarrow \mathbf{b} - 3\mathbf{c} = \lambda\mathbf{a}$

$\Rightarrow |\mathbf{b}-3\mathbf{c}| = |\lambda\mathbf{a}| \Rightarrow 1 + 1 - 6.1\cdot\frac{1}{3}\cdot\frac{1}{2} = |\lambda| \Rightarrow \lambda = \pm 1$

$\therefore \quad \mathbf{b} - 3\mathbf{c} = \pm\mathbf{a}$

33. (a) is proved, if we take dot product of both sides with **a**.

(b) If we take dot product with **b**, then $\lambda_2 = \mathbf{b}\cdot\mathbf{c}$.

$\Rightarrow$ Option (b) is not true.

(c) If we take dot product of both sides with $\mathbf{a}\times\mathbf{b}$, we get

$$[\mathbf{c}\ \mathbf{b}\ \mathbf{a}] = \lambda_3[\mathbf{a}\times\mathbf{b}]^2 \Rightarrow \lambda_3 = [\mathbf{a}\ \mathbf{b}\ \mathbf{c}] \text{ or } \mathbf{c}\cdot(\mathbf{a}\times\mathbf{b})$$

$\Rightarrow$ Option (c) is wrong.

(d) is correct since $\lambda_1 + \lambda_2 + \lambda_3 = \mathbf{c}\cdot\mathbf{a} + \mathbf{b}\cdot\mathbf{c} + [\mathbf{a}\ \mathbf{b}\ \mathbf{c}]$.

34. (a) Since, **a**, **b** and **c**, are non-coplanar, option (a) is true.

Since, $\mathbf{b}\times\mathbf{c}$, $\mathbf{c}\times\mathbf{a}$, $\mathbf{a}\times\mathbf{b}$ are also non-coplanar.

(b) is also correct.

Since, $\mathbf{x} = \lambda(\mathbf{b}\times\mathbf{c}) + \mu(\mathbf{c}\times\mathbf{a}) + \nu(\mathbf{a}\times\mathbf{b})$

We have, $\lambda = \dfrac{\mathbf{a}\cdot\mathbf{x}}{[\mathbf{a}\ \mathbf{b}\ \mathbf{c}]}$, (on taking dot product with **a**)

μ and v have similar values.

Also, $|\mathbf{x}| = |\mathbf{a} - \mathbf{x}| \Rightarrow \mathbf{a}\cdot\mathbf{x} = \dfrac{a^2}{2}$, etc.

$\Rightarrow$ Option (c) is correct.

If (c) is correct (d) is ruled out.

35. $\alpha = (\mathbf{a}\cdot\hat{\mathbf{i}})\hat{\mathbf{i}} + (\mathbf{a}\cdot\hat{\mathbf{j}})\hat{\mathbf{j}} + (\mathbf{a}\cdot\hat{\mathbf{k}})\hat{\mathbf{k}} = \mathbf{a} = (1, 1, 1)$

$\beta = (\mathbf{b}\cdot\hat{\mathbf{i}})\hat{\mathbf{i}} + (\mathbf{b}\cdot\hat{\mathbf{j}})\hat{\mathbf{j}} + (\mathbf{b}\cdot\hat{\mathbf{k}})\hat{\mathbf{k}} = \mathbf{b} = (1, -1, 0)$

$\gamma = (1, 1, -2)$

$\therefore \quad \alpha\cdot\beta = \beta\cdot\gamma = \gamma\cdot\alpha = 0$

$\Rightarrow \alpha, \beta$ and γ are mutually perpendicular $\alpha, \beta, \gamma = 6$

Also, $[\alpha\ \ \beta\ \ \gamma] = 6$

So, α, β and γ form a parallelopiped of volume 6 units.

36. $\mathbf{a}\times(\mathbf{b}\times\mathbf{c}) = (\mathbf{a}\cdot\mathbf{c})\mathbf{b} - (\mathbf{a}\cdot\mathbf{b})\mathbf{c}$

$= (xz + yx + yz)(y\hat{\mathbf{i}} + z\hat{\mathbf{j}} + x\hat{\mathbf{k}})$
$\quad - (xy + yz + zx)(z\hat{\mathbf{i}} + x\hat{\mathbf{j}} + y\hat{\mathbf{k}})$

$= (xz + yx + yz)((y - z)\hat{\mathbf{i}} + (z - x)\hat{\mathbf{j}} + (x - y)\hat{\mathbf{k}})$

Clearly, perpendicular to $\hat{\mathbf{i}} + \hat{\mathbf{j}} + \hat{\mathbf{k}}$ and also to $(y + z)\hat{\mathbf{i}} + (z + x)\hat{\mathbf{j}} + (x + y)\hat{\mathbf{k}}$ as dot products are zeros.

Clearly, parallel to $(y - z)\hat{\mathbf{i}} + (z - x)\hat{\mathbf{j}} + (x - y)\hat{\mathbf{k}}$

37. $A \to \mathbf{a}\times(\mathbf{b}\times\mathbf{c}) + \mathbf{b}\times(\mathbf{c}\times\mathbf{a}) + \mathbf{c}\times(\mathbf{a}\times\mathbf{b}) = \mathbf{O}$

$\Rightarrow$ Vectors are coplanar, so do not form RHS

$B \to (\mathbf{a}\times\mathbf{b})\times\mathbf{c},\ \mathbf{a}\times\mathbf{b},\ \mathbf{c} = \mathbf{0}$ in that order form RHS

$\Rightarrow \mathbf{c}, (\mathbf{a}\times\mathbf{b})\times\mathbf{c}, \mathbf{a}\times\mathbf{b}$ also form RHS as they are in same cyclic order.

$C \to \mathbf{a} + \mathbf{b} + \mathbf{c} = \mathbf{0} \Rightarrow (\mathbf{a} + \mathbf{b} + \mathbf{c})^2 = 0$

$\Rightarrow \quad \mathbf{a}^2 + \mathbf{b}^2 + \mathbf{c}^2 = -2(\mathbf{a}\cdot\mathbf{b} + \mathbf{b}\cdot\mathbf{c} + \mathbf{c}\cdot\mathbf{a})$

Hence, $\quad \mathbf{a}\cdot\mathbf{b} + \mathbf{b}\cdot\mathbf{c} + \mathbf{c}\cdot\mathbf{a} < 0$

$D \to \mathbf{a} + \mathbf{b} + \mathbf{c} = \mathbf{0} \Rightarrow \mathbf{a}\times\mathbf{b} = \mathbf{b}\times\mathbf{c} = \mathbf{c}\times\mathbf{a}$

Using this we get result.

38. Let angle between **a** and **b** be θ.

We have, $|\mathbf{a}| = |\mathbf{b}| = 1$

Now, $|\mathbf{a} + \mathbf{b}| = 2\cos\dfrac{\theta}{2}$ and $|\mathbf{a} - \mathbf{b}| = 2\sin\dfrac{\theta}{2}$, where $\theta \in [0, \pi]$.

Consider, $F(\theta) = \dfrac{3}{2}\left(2\cos\dfrac{\theta}{2}\right) + 2\left(2\sin\dfrac{\theta}{2}\right)$

$\therefore \quad F(\theta) = 3\cos\dfrac{\theta}{2} + 4\sin\dfrac{\theta}{2}, \theta \in [0, \pi]$

$F'(\theta) = \dfrac{-3}{2}\sin\dfrac{\theta}{2} + 2\cos\dfrac{\theta}{2}$

Now, $\quad F'(\theta) = 0 \Rightarrow \tan\dfrac{\theta}{2} = \dfrac{4}{3}$

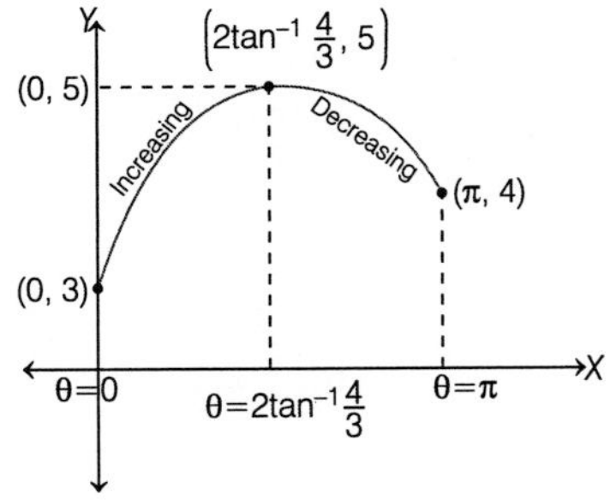

Clearly, $\quad F(0) = 3$

$$F\left(\theta = 2\tan^{-1}\frac{4}{3}\right) = 3\left(\frac{3}{5}\right) + 4\left(\frac{4}{5}\right) = \frac{9}{5} + \frac{16}{5} = \frac{25}{5} = 5$$

$$F(\theta = \pi) = 4$$

$\therefore \quad$ Range $= [3, 5]$

Hence, the possible integer(s) in the range of $F(\theta)$ in $[0, \pi]$ are 3 *viz*, 3, 4 and 5.

39. Let $\mathbf{r} = x\mathbf{a} + y\mathbf{b} + z(\mathbf{a}\times\mathbf{b})$ with **b**

$\mathbf{r}\cdot\mathbf{b} = 0 + y|\mathbf{b}|^2$

$\mathbf{a}(\mathbf{r}\cdot\mathbf{b}) = y(\mathbf{b})^2\mathbf{a} \Rightarrow \mathbf{c} - p\mathbf{r} = y|\mathbf{b}|^2\mathbf{a}$

$\mathbf{r} = \dfrac{1}{p}\mathbf{c} - \dfrac{y|\mathbf{b}|^2}{p}\mathbf{a}$

$\therefore \quad [\mathbf{r}\ \mathbf{a}\ \mathbf{c}] = 0$

Now, $\quad \mathbf{r}\cdot\mathbf{b} = \dfrac{1}{p}\mathbf{c}\cdot\mathbf{b}$

$\therefore \quad y|b|^2 = \dfrac{\mathbf{b}\cdot\mathbf{c}}{p}$

$\therefore \quad \mathbf{r} = \dfrac{1}{p}\mathbf{c} - \dfrac{1}{p^2}(\mathbf{b}\cdot\mathbf{c})\mathbf{a}$

40. **Decoding the Question**

A set of vectors is linearly independent, if all its coefficients are zero i.e. neither vector is a scalar multiple of the other.

$(\lambda - 1)(\mathbf{a}_1 - \mathbf{a}_2) + \mu(\mathbf{a}_2 + \mathbf{a}_3) + \gamma(\mathbf{a}_3 + \mathbf{a}_4 - 2\mathbf{a}_2) + \mathbf{a}_3 + \delta\mathbf{a}_4 = 0$

i.e. $(\lambda - 1)\mathbf{a}_1 + (1 - \lambda + \mu - 2\gamma)\mathbf{a}_2 + (\mu + \gamma + 1)\mathbf{a}_3 + (\gamma + \delta)\mathbf{a}_4 = 0$

Since $\mathbf{a}_1, \mathbf{a}_2, \mathbf{a}_3$ and $\mathbf{a}_4$ are linearly independent

$\therefore \quad \lambda - 1 = 0, 1 - \lambda + \mu - 2\gamma = 0, \mu + \gamma + 1 = 0$

$\gamma + \delta = 0$

i.e. $\quad \lambda = 1, \mu = 2\gamma, \mu + \gamma + 1 = 0, \gamma + \delta = 0$

i.e. $\quad \lambda = 1, \mu = -\dfrac{2}{3}, \gamma = -\dfrac{1}{3}, \delta = \dfrac{1}{3}$

41. $\mathbf{p} = ab\cos(2\pi - \theta)\mathbf{c}$, where θ is the angle between **a** and **c** and

$\mathbf{q} = ac\cos(\pi - \phi)\mathbf{b}$, where ϕ is the angle between **a** and **b** now

$\mathbf{p} + \mathbf{q} = (ab\cos\theta)\mathbf{c} - ac\cos\phi\mathbf{b} = (\mathbf{a}\cdot\mathbf{b})\mathbf{c} - (\mathbf{a}\cdot\mathbf{c})\mathbf{b} = \mathbf{a}\times(\mathbf{c}\times\mathbf{b})$

42. $\mathbf{a} + \mathbf{b} = \lambda\mathbf{c};\ \mathbf{b} + \mathbf{c} = \mu\mathbf{a}$

$\mathbf{a} - \mathbf{c} = \lambda\mathbf{c} - \mu\mathbf{a}$

$\mathbf{a}(1 + \mu) = \mathbf{c}(1 + \lambda)$

But **a** and **c** are non-collinear $\Rightarrow \mu = -1, \lambda = -1$

$\therefore \quad \mathbf{a} + \mathbf{b} + \mathbf{c} = 0 = \hat{\mathbf{k}} \quad \Rightarrow |\mathbf{k}| = 0$

$\Rightarrow (k, k) \equiv (0, 0)$ all the given curves pass through (0, 0).

43. Let θ be the angle between **u** and **v**.

$\therefore |\mathbf{u}\times\mathbf{v}| = 1 \Rightarrow |\mathbf{u}|\mathbf{v}|\sin\theta = 1$

$\therefore |\mathbf{v}|\sin\theta = 1 \qquad [\because |\mathbf{u}| = 1]$ ...(i)

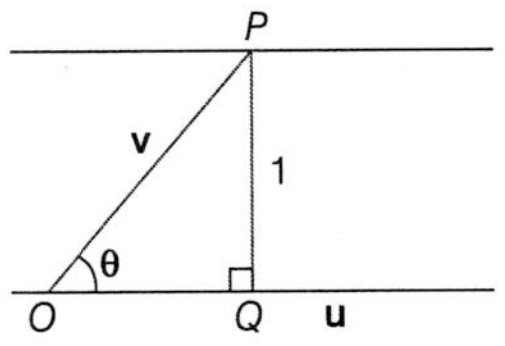

Clearly, there may be infinite vectors $\mathbf{OP} = \mathbf{v}$, such that P is always 1 unit distance from $\mathbf{u}$.

$\therefore$ Option (b) is correct.

Again, let ϕ be the angle between $\mathbf{w}$ and $\mathbf{u} \times \mathbf{v}$.

$$\therefore \quad \mathbf{w} \cdot (\mathbf{u} \times \mathbf{v}) = 1$$

$$\Rightarrow \quad |\mathbf{w}||\mathbf{u} \times \mathbf{v}| \cos\phi = 1 \Rightarrow \cos\phi = 1 \Rightarrow \phi = 0$$

Thus, $\mathbf{w} = \mathbf{u} \times \mathbf{v}$

Now, if $\hat{\mathbf{u}}$ lies in XY-plane, then

$$\mathbf{u} \times \mathbf{v} = \begin{vmatrix} \hat{\mathbf{i}} & \hat{\mathbf{j}} & \hat{\mathbf{k}} \\ u_1 & u_2 & 0 \\ v_1 & v_2 & v_3 \end{vmatrix} \text{ or } \mathbf{u} = u\hat{\mathbf{i}} + u_2\hat{\mathbf{j}}$$

$$\therefore \quad \mathbf{w} = (u_2v_3)\,\hat{\mathbf{i}} - (u_1v_3)\,\hat{\mathbf{j}} + (u_1v_2 - v_1u_2)\hat{\mathbf{k}} = \frac{1}{\sqrt{6}}(\hat{\mathbf{i}} + \hat{\mathbf{j}} + 2\hat{\mathbf{k}})$$

$$\therefore \quad u_2v_3 = \frac{1}{\sqrt{6}}, u_1v_3 = \frac{-1}{\sqrt{6}} \Rightarrow \frac{u_2v_3}{u_1v_3} = -1 \text{ or } |u_1| = |u_2|$$

$\therefore$ Option (c) is correct.

Now, if $\mathbf{u}$ lies in XZ-plane, then $\mathbf{u} = u_1\hat{\mathbf{i}} + u_3\hat{\mathbf{k}}$

$$\therefore \mathbf{u} \times \mathbf{v} = \begin{vmatrix} \hat{\mathbf{i}} & \hat{\mathbf{j}} & \hat{\mathbf{k}} \\ u_1 & 0 & u_3 \\ v_1 & v_2 & v_3 \end{vmatrix}$$

$$\Rightarrow \quad \mathbf{w} = (-v_2u_3)\,\hat{\mathbf{i}} - (u_1v_3 - u_3v_1)\,\hat{\mathbf{j}} + (u_1v_2)\,\hat{\mathbf{k}}$$

$$\Rightarrow \quad \hat{\mathbf{k}} = \frac{1}{\sqrt{6}}(\hat{\mathbf{i}} + \hat{\mathbf{j}} + 2\hat{\mathbf{k}}) \Rightarrow -v_2u_3 = \frac{1}{\sqrt{6}} \text{ and } u_1v_2 = \frac{2}{\sqrt{6}}$$

$$\therefore |u_1| = 2|u_3|$$

$\therefore$ Option (d) is incorrect.

44. Given, $|\mathbf{a}| = 12, |\mathbf{b}| = 4\sqrt{3}$

$$\mathbf{a} + \mathbf{b} + \mathbf{c} = \mathbf{0} \Rightarrow \mathbf{a} = -(\mathbf{b} + \mathbf{c})$$

We have, $|\mathbf{a}|^2 = |\mathbf{b} + \mathbf{c}|^2$

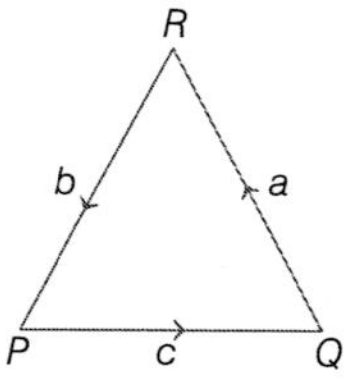

$$\Rightarrow \quad |\mathbf{a}|^2 = |\mathbf{b}|^2 + |\mathbf{c}|^2 + 2\mathbf{b} \cdot \mathbf{c}$$

$$\Rightarrow \quad 144 = 48 + |\mathbf{c}|^2 + 48 \qquad [\because \mathbf{b} \cdot \mathbf{c} = 24, \text{ given}]$$

$$\Rightarrow \quad |\mathbf{c}|^2 = 48 \Rightarrow |\mathbf{c}| = 4\sqrt{3}$$

Also, $|\mathbf{c}|^2 = |\mathbf{a}|^2 + |\mathbf{b}|^2 + 2\,\mathbf{a} \cdot \mathbf{b}$

$$\Rightarrow \quad 48 = 144 + 48 + 2\,\mathbf{a} \cdot \mathbf{b} \Rightarrow \mathbf{a} \cdot \mathbf{b} = -72$$

$\therefore$ Option (d) is correct.

Also, $\mathbf{a} \times \mathbf{b} = \mathbf{c} \times \mathbf{a}$

$$\Rightarrow \quad \mathbf{a} \times \mathbf{b} + \mathbf{c} \times \mathbf{a} = 2(\mathbf{a} \times \mathbf{b})$$

$$\Rightarrow \quad |\mathbf{a} \times \mathbf{b} + \mathbf{c} \times \mathbf{a}| = 2|\mathbf{a} \times \mathbf{b}| = 2\sqrt{|\mathbf{a}|^2|\mathbf{b}|^2 - (\mathbf{a} \cdot \mathbf{b})^2}$$

[by Lagrange's identity]

$$= 2\sqrt{(144)(48) - (-72)^2}$$

$$= 2(12)\sqrt{48 - 36} = 48\sqrt{3}$$

$\therefore$ Option (c) is correct.

Also, $\dfrac{|\mathbf{c}|^2}{2} - |\mathbf{a}| = 24 - 12 = 12$

$\therefore$ Option (a) is correct.

and $\dfrac{|\mathbf{c}|^2}{2} + |\mathbf{a}| = 24 + 12 = 36$

$\therefore$ Option (b) is not correct.

Solutions (Q.Nos. 45 and 46)

45. $(\mathbf{p} \times \mathbf{q}) \times \mathbf{r} = (\mathbf{p} \cdot \mathbf{r})\,\mathbf{q} - (\mathbf{q} \cdot \mathbf{r})\,\mathbf{p}$

$$\Rightarrow \quad u = -(\mathbf{q} \cdot \mathbf{r}) = -(2 + 4 - 3) = -3$$

$$v = \mathbf{p} \cdot \mathbf{r} = 1 + 1 + 3 = 5 \text{ and } w = 0$$

Hence, $u = -3, v = 5, w = 0 \Rightarrow u + v + w = 2$

46. $\because \mathbf{p}, \mathbf{q}$ and $\mathbf{r}$ are non-coplanar, therefore

$\mathbf{q} \times \mathbf{r}, \mathbf{r} \times \mathbf{p}$ and $\mathbf{p} \times \mathbf{q}$ are also non-coplanar

Hence, $\mathbf{s} = l(\mathbf{q} \times \mathbf{r}) + w(\mathbf{r} \times \mathbf{p}) + n(\mathbf{p} \times \mathbf{q})$

$$\therefore \quad l = \frac{\mathbf{s} \cdot \mathbf{p}}{[\mathbf{p}\ \mathbf{q}\ \mathbf{r}]}, w = \frac{\mathbf{s} \cdot \mathbf{q}}{[\mathbf{p}\ \mathbf{q}\ \mathbf{r}]}, n = \frac{\mathbf{s} \cdot \mathbf{r}}{[\mathbf{p}\ \mathbf{q}\ \mathbf{r}]}$$

Hence, $\mathbf{s}[\mathbf{p}\ \mathbf{q}\ \mathbf{r}] = (\mathbf{s} \cdot \mathbf{p})\,(\mathbf{q} \times \mathbf{r}) + (\mathbf{s} \cdot \mathbf{q})$

$$(\mathbf{r} \times \mathbf{p}) + (\mathbf{s} \cdot \mathbf{r})\,(\mathbf{p} \times \mathbf{q})$$

$$|(\mathbf{s} \cdot \mathbf{p})\,(\mathbf{q} \times \mathbf{r}) + (\mathbf{s} \cdot \mathbf{q})\,(\mathbf{r} \times \mathbf{p}) + (\mathbf{s} \cdot \mathbf{r})\,(\mathbf{p} \times \mathbf{q})|$$

$$= |\mathbf{s}\,[\mathbf{p}\ \mathbf{q}\ \mathbf{r}]|$$

$$= [\mathbf{p}\ \mathbf{q}\ \mathbf{r}]\,(\text{as } |\mathbf{s}| = 1)$$

$$\begin{vmatrix} 1 & 1 & 1 \\ 2 & 4 & -1 \\ 1 & 1 & 3 \end{vmatrix} = (12 + 1) - 1\,(6 + 1) + 1\,(2 - 4) = 13 - 7 - 2 = 4$$

Solutions (Q.Nos. 47 and 48)

47. Given, $\mathbf{p} = \hat{\mathbf{i}} + \hat{\mathbf{j}} + \hat{\mathbf{k}}; \mathbf{q} = \hat{\mathbf{i}} - \hat{\mathbf{j}} + \hat{\mathbf{k}}$

$$\mathbf{p} \times \mathbf{r} = \mathbf{q} + c\mathbf{p} \text{ and } \mathbf{p} \cdot \mathbf{r} = 2$$

$$\therefore \quad \mathbf{p} \times (\mathbf{p} \times \mathbf{r}) = \mathbf{p} \times (\mathbf{q} + c\mathbf{p}) \text{ and } \mathbf{p} \cdot (\mathbf{p} \times \mathbf{r}) = \mathbf{p} \cdot (\mathbf{q} + c\mathbf{p})$$

$$\therefore \quad (\mathbf{p} \cdot \mathbf{r})\mathbf{p} - (\mathbf{p} \cdot \mathbf{p})\mathbf{r} = \mathbf{p} \times \mathbf{q} + c\mathbf{0}$$

$$0 = \mathbf{p} \cdot \mathbf{q} + \mathbf{c}\,(\mathbf{p} \cdot \mathbf{p})$$

$$\therefore \quad (\mathbf{p} \cdot \mathbf{p})\mathbf{r} = (\mathbf{p} \cdot \mathbf{r})\mathbf{p} - \mathbf{p} \times \mathbf{q} \quad \text{...(i)}$$

$$c = -\frac{\mathbf{p} \cdot \mathbf{q}}{\mathbf{p} \cdot \mathbf{p}} \quad \text{...(ii)}$$

But $\mathbf{p} \cdot \mathbf{p} = |\mathbf{p}|^2 = \mathbf{p}^2 = 3$ ...(iii)

and $\mathbf{p} \cdot \mathbf{q} = 1 - 1 + 1 = 1$ ...(iv)

and $\mathbf{p} \times \mathbf{q} = \begin{vmatrix} \hat{\mathbf{i}} & \hat{\mathbf{j}} & \hat{\mathbf{k}} \\ 1 & 1 & 1 \\ 1 & -1 & 1 \end{vmatrix} = 2\hat{\mathbf{i}} - 2\hat{\mathbf{k}}$ ...(v)

Using Eqs. (iii), (iv) in Eq. (i) and Eq. (ii), we get

$$3\mathbf{r} = 2\mathbf{p} - 2\hat{\mathbf{i}} + 2\hat{\mathbf{k}} \text{ and } c = -\frac{1}{3} \quad \text{...(vi)}$$

$$\therefore \quad \mathbf{r} = \frac{1}{3}[2\hat{\mathbf{i}} + 2\hat{\mathbf{j}} + 2\hat{\mathbf{k}} - 2\hat{\mathbf{i}} + 2\hat{\mathbf{k}}]$$

$$\therefore \quad \mathbf{r} = \frac{2}{3}(\hat{\mathbf{j}} + 2\hat{\mathbf{k}}) \quad \text{...(vii)}$$

Now, $[\mathbf{p}\ \mathbf{q}\ \mathbf{r}] = \begin{vmatrix} 1 & 1 & 1 \\ 1 & -1 & 1 \\ 0 & \frac{2}{3} & \frac{4}{3} \end{vmatrix} = \left(\frac{-4}{3} - \frac{2}{3}\right) - 1\left(\frac{4}{3}\right) + 1\left(\frac{2}{3}\right)$

$$\therefore \quad [\mathbf{p}\ \mathbf{q}\ \mathbf{r}] = -2 - \frac{2}{3} = -\frac{8}{3} \quad \text{...(viii)}$$

48. $[\mathbf{p}\ \mathbf{q}\ \mathbf{r}]\,\mathbf{x} = (\mathbf{p}\times\mathbf{q})\times\mathbf{r} \Rightarrow -\frac{8}{3}\mathbf{x} = (\mathbf{p}\cdot\mathbf{r})\,\mathbf{q} - (\mathbf{q}\cdot\mathbf{r})\,\mathbf{p}$

$$\Rightarrow \left(-\frac{8}{3}\right)\mathbf{x} = 2\mathbf{q} - \frac{2\mathbf{p}}{3} \qquad \left[\mathbf{q}\cdot\mathbf{r} = \frac{2}{3}, \text{ verify yourself}\right]$$

$$\therefore \quad \mathbf{x} = -\frac{3}{8}\cdot\frac{2}{3}(3\mathbf{q}-\mathbf{p}) = -\frac{1}{4}(3\hat{\mathbf{i}} - 3\hat{\mathbf{j}} + 3\hat{\mathbf{k}} - \hat{\mathbf{i}} - \hat{\mathbf{j}} - \hat{\mathbf{k}})$$

$$= -\frac{1}{4}(2\hat{\mathbf{i}} - 4\hat{\mathbf{j}} + 2\hat{\mathbf{k}}) = -\frac{1}{2}(\hat{\mathbf{i}} - 2\hat{\mathbf{j}} + \hat{\mathbf{k}})$$

Solutions (Q.Nos. 49 and 50)

49. $y = \log_{1/2}\left(x - \frac{1}{2}\right) + \log_2\sqrt{(2x-1)^2}$

$$= \log_{1/2}\left(x - \frac{1}{2}\right) + \log_2(2x-1) \text{ but } x > \frac{1}{2}$$

$$y = 1$$

Since, P lies on the given circle $x^2 + y^2 = 10$ ...(i)

Now, putting $y = 1$ in Eq. (i), we get

$$x = \pm 3 \text{ but } x > \frac{1}{2}$$

$\therefore\ x = 3$ only.

Hence, coordinates of P is (3, 1).

$$P \equiv (3, 1)$$

50. $$\mathbf{OP} = 3\hat{\mathbf{i}} + \hat{\mathbf{j}}$$

$$\mathbf{Q} \equiv (1, 1) \text{ or } (2, 1)$$

$$\mathbf{OQ} = \hat{\mathbf{i}} + \hat{\mathbf{j}} \text{ or } 2\hat{\mathbf{i}} + \hat{\mathbf{j}}$$

$$\mathbf{OP}\cdot\mathbf{OQ} = 3 + 1 = 4 \text{ or } 6 + 1 = 7$$

Solutions (Q.Nos. 51 and 52)

51. Since, **a**, **b**, **c** are non-coplanar vectors, then

$$[\mathbf{a}\ \mathbf{b}\ \mathbf{c}] \neq 0 \Rightarrow [\mathbf{a}\ \mathbf{b}\ \mathbf{c}]^2 \neq 0$$

$$\Rightarrow \quad [\mathbf{a}\ \mathbf{b}\ \mathbf{c}]^2 = \begin{vmatrix} \mathbf{a}\cdot\mathbf{a} & \mathbf{b}\cdot\mathbf{a} & \mathbf{c}\cdot\mathbf{a} \\ \mathbf{a}\cdot\mathbf{b} & \mathbf{b}\cdot\mathbf{b} & \mathbf{c}\cdot\mathbf{b} \\ \mathbf{a}\cdot\mathbf{c} & \mathbf{b}\cdot\mathbf{c} & \mathbf{c}\cdot\mathbf{c} \end{vmatrix} \neq 0$$

Since, any vector **r** in space can be expressed as a linear combination of three non-coplanar vectors.

So, let $\mathbf{r} = l\mathbf{a} + m\mathbf{b} + n\mathbf{c}$ ...(i)

On taking dot product by **a**, **b** and **c** successively, we get

$$\mathbf{r}\cdot\mathbf{a} = l\mathbf{a}\cdot\mathbf{a} + m\mathbf{b}\cdot\mathbf{a} + n\mathbf{c}\cdot\mathbf{a} \quad \text{...(ii)}$$

$$\mathbf{r}\cdot\mathbf{b} = l\mathbf{a}\cdot\mathbf{b} + m\mathbf{b}\cdot\mathbf{b} + n\mathbf{c}\cdot\mathbf{b} \quad \text{...(iii)}$$

$$\mathbf{r}\cdot\mathbf{c} = l\mathbf{a}\cdot\mathbf{c} + m\mathbf{b}\cdot\mathbf{c} + n\mathbf{c}\cdot\mathbf{c} \quad \text{...(iv)}$$

Now, eliminating l, m and n from above 4 relations, we get

$$\begin{vmatrix} \mathbf{r} & \mathbf{a} & \mathbf{b} & \mathbf{c} \\ \mathbf{r}\cdot\mathbf{a} & \mathbf{a}\cdot\mathbf{a} & \mathbf{b}\cdot\mathbf{a} & \mathbf{c}\cdot\mathbf{a} \\ \mathbf{r}\cdot\mathbf{b} & \mathbf{a}\cdot\mathbf{b} & \mathbf{b}\cdot\mathbf{b} & \mathbf{c}\cdot\mathbf{b} \\ \mathbf{r}\cdot\mathbf{c} & \mathbf{a}\cdot\mathbf{c} & \mathbf{b}\cdot\mathbf{c} & \mathbf{c}\cdot\mathbf{c} \end{vmatrix} = 0$$

Now, on expanding along first row, we get

$$r = \left(\frac{\Delta_1}{\Delta}\right)\mathbf{a} + \left(\frac{\Delta_2}{\Delta}\right)\mathbf{b} + \left(\frac{\Delta_3}{\Delta}\right)\mathbf{c}$$

52. Since **a**, **b** and **c** are three non-coplanar vectors, then On three exists scalars x, y and z such that

$$\mathbf{r} = x\mathbf{a} + y\mathbf{b} + z\mathbf{c} \quad \text{...(i)}$$

On taking dot product by $\mathbf{b}\times\mathbf{c}$, $\mathbf{c}\times\mathbf{a}$ and $\mathbf{a}\times\mathbf{b}$ successively, we get

$$\mathbf{r}\cdot(\mathbf{b}\times\mathbf{c}) = (x\mathbf{a} + y\mathbf{b} + z\mathbf{c})\cdot(\mathbf{b}\times\mathbf{c}) = x[\mathbf{a}\ \mathbf{b}\ \mathbf{c}]$$

$$\mathbf{r}\cdot(\mathbf{c}\times\mathbf{a}) = y[\mathbf{b}\ \mathbf{c}\ \mathbf{a}]$$

$$\mathbf{r}\cdot(\mathbf{a}\times\mathbf{b}) = z[\mathbf{c}\ \mathbf{a}\ \mathbf{b}]$$

$$\because \quad x = \frac{[\mathbf{r}\ \mathbf{b}\ \mathbf{c}]}{[\mathbf{a}\ \mathbf{b}\ \mathbf{c}]},\ y = \frac{[\mathbf{r}\ \mathbf{c}\ \mathbf{a}]}{[\mathbf{a}\ \mathbf{b}\ \mathbf{c}]} \text{ and } z = \frac{[\mathbf{r}\ \mathbf{a}\ \mathbf{b}]}{[\mathbf{a}\ \mathbf{b}\ \mathbf{c}]}$$

On substituting the values of x, y, z in Eq. (i), we get

$$r = \left\{\frac{[\mathbf{r}\ \mathbf{b}\ \mathbf{c}]}{[\mathbf{a}\ \mathbf{b}\ \mathbf{c}]}\right\}\mathbf{a} + \left\{\frac{[\mathbf{r}\ \mathbf{c}\ \mathbf{a}]}{[\mathbf{a}\ \mathbf{b}\ \mathbf{c}]}\right\}\mathbf{b} + \left\{\frac{[\mathbf{r}\ \mathbf{a}\ \mathbf{b}]}{[\mathbf{a}\ \mathbf{b}\ \mathbf{c}]}\right\}\mathbf{c}$$

$$\text{or} \quad \mathbf{r} = \frac{1}{[\mathbf{a}\ \mathbf{b}\ \mathbf{c}]}\{[\mathbf{r}\ \mathbf{b}\ \mathbf{c}]\mathbf{a} + [\mathbf{r}\ \mathbf{c}\ \mathbf{a}]\,\mathbf{b} + [\mathbf{r}\ \mathbf{a}\ \mathbf{b}]\,\mathbf{c}\}$$

Solutions (Q.Nos. 53 and 54)

53. $\because\ g'(x) = 3x^2 + 2x + 0 > 0,\ \forall\ x \geq 0$

$\Rightarrow g(x)$ is an increasing function.

If circumcentre lies outside, then triangle is obtuse angle triangle and angle containing the given sides is obtuse angle.

Therefore, $(f(x)\hat{\mathbf{i}} + g(x)\hat{\mathbf{j}})\cdot(g(x)\hat{\mathbf{i}} + f(x)\hat{\mathbf{j}}) < 0$

$\Rightarrow \quad f(x)\cdot g(x) < 0$ ...(i)

$\Rightarrow \quad g(x) \uparrow \text{for} x \geq 0$

$\Rightarrow \quad g(x) > g(0) \forall x > 0$, also $g(0) = 0$

$\Rightarrow \quad g(x) > 0, \forall x > 0$, from (i) $\Rightarrow f(x) < 0$

$\therefore \quad f(x) < 0$ and $g(x) > 0\ \forall\ x > 0$

54. If $x \to \infty$, then $g(x) \to \infty$ and $f(x)$ is some negative number, then

$$\lim_{t\to 0}\lim_{x\to\infty}\Bigg(\underbrace{\cot\bigg(\underbrace{\frac{\pi}{4}\underbrace{(1-t^2)}_{1^-}}_{}\bigg)}_{1^+}\Bigg)^{\overbrace{f(x)\cdot g(x)}^{\to -\infty}} = 0$$

Solutions (Q.Nos. 55 and 56)

We have $|\mathbf{x}| = |\mathbf{y}| = |\mathbf{z}| = \sqrt{2}$ and **x**, **y**, **z** make angle of 60° with each other.

$$\therefore \quad \mathbf{x}\cdot\mathbf{y} = |\mathbf{x}|\,|\mathbf{y}|\cos 60^\circ = \sqrt{2}(\sqrt{2})\cdot\frac{1}{2} = 1 \quad \text{...(A)}$$

$$\mathbf{y}\cdot\mathbf{z} = |\mathbf{y}|\,|\mathbf{z}|\cos 60^\circ = \sqrt{2}(\sqrt{2})\left(\frac{1}{2}\right) = 1 \quad \text{...(B)}$$

$$\text{and} \quad \mathbf{x}\cdot\mathbf{z} = |\mathbf{x}|\,|\mathbf{z}|\cos 60^\circ = \sqrt{2}(\sqrt{2})\left(\frac{1}{2}\right) = 1 \quad \text{...(C)}$$

$$\mathbf{x}\cdot\mathbf{x} = |\mathbf{x}|^2 = 2 \quad \text{...(D)}$$

$$\mathbf{y}\cdot\mathbf{y} = |\mathbf{y}|^2 = 2 \text{ and } \mathbf{z}\cdot\mathbf{z} = |\mathbf{z}|^2 = 2 \quad \text{...(E)}$$

Now, $\mathbf{x}\times(\mathbf{y}\times\mathbf{z}) = \mathbf{a}$ and $\mathbf{y}\times(\mathbf{z}\times\mathbf{x}) = \mathbf{b}$ [given]

$\Rightarrow\ (\mathbf{x}\cdot\mathbf{z})\,\mathbf{y} - (\mathbf{x}\cdot\mathbf{y})\mathbf{z} = \mathbf{a}$ and $(\mathbf{y}\cdot\mathbf{x})\mathbf{z} - (\mathbf{y}\cdot\mathbf{z})\mathbf{x} = \mathbf{b}$

Thus, we have

$$\mathbf{y} - \mathbf{z} = \mathbf{a} \quad \text{[using (A) and (C)] ...(i)}$$

$$\mathbf{z} - \mathbf{x} = \mathbf{b} \quad \text{[using (A) and (B)] ...(ii)}$$

On adding Eqs. (i) and (ii),

$$\mathbf{y} - \mathbf{x} = \mathbf{a} + \mathbf{b} \quad \text{...(iii)}$$

Now, $\mathbf{x} \times \mathbf{y} = \mathbf{c}$ [given]

$\Rightarrow \mathbf{x} \times (\mathbf{x} \times \mathbf{y}) = \mathbf{x} \times \mathbf{c}$ [taking cross-product with **x**]

$\Rightarrow (\mathbf{x} \cdot \mathbf{y}) \times \mathbf{x} - (\mathbf{x} \cdot \mathbf{x})\mathbf{y} = \mathbf{x} \times \mathbf{c}$ [using (A) and (B)]

$\Rightarrow \mathbf{x} - 2\mathbf{y} = \mathbf{x} \times \mathbf{c}$ ...(iv)

Again, $\mathbf{x} \times \mathbf{y} = \mathbf{c}$

$\Rightarrow \mathbf{y} \times (\mathbf{x} \times \mathbf{y}) = \mathbf{y} \times \mathbf{c}$ (taking cross product with **y**)

$\Rightarrow (\mathbf{y} \cdot \mathbf{y})\mathbf{x} - (\mathbf{y} \cdot \mathbf{x})\mathbf{y} = \mathbf{y} \times \mathbf{c}$

$\Rightarrow 2\mathbf{x} - \mathbf{y} = \mathbf{y} \times \mathbf{c}$ [using (A) and (E)] ...(v)

On subtracting Eqs. (iv) and (v), we get

$\mathbf{x} + \mathbf{y} = (\mathbf{y} \times \mathbf{c}) - (\mathbf{x} \times \mathbf{c})$

$\Rightarrow \mathbf{x} + \mathbf{y} = (\mathbf{y} - \mathbf{x}) \times \mathbf{c}$

$\Rightarrow \mathbf{x} + \mathbf{y} = (\mathbf{a} + \mathbf{b}) \times \mathbf{c}$ [using Eq. (iii)] ...(vi)

On adding Eqs. (iii) and (vi), we get

$$2\mathbf{y} = (\mathbf{a} + \mathbf{b}) + (\mathbf{a} + \mathbf{b}) \times \mathbf{c} \Rightarrow \mathbf{y} = \frac{1}{2}[(\mathbf{a} + \mathbf{b}) + (\mathbf{a} + \mathbf{b}) \times \mathbf{c}]$$

On substituting the value of **y** in Eq. (iii), we get

$$\mathbf{x} = \frac{1}{2}[(\mathbf{a} + \mathbf{b}) + (\mathbf{a} + \mathbf{b}) \times \mathbf{c}] - (\mathbf{a} + \mathbf{b})$$

$$\Rightarrow \mathbf{x} = \frac{1}{2}[(\mathbf{a} + \mathbf{b}) \times \mathbf{c} - (\mathbf{a} + \mathbf{b})]$$

55. (c) 56. (a)

Solutions (Q.Nos. 57 and 58)

On taking dot products with **a**, **b** and **c** respectively, with given equation

$[\mathbf{a}\ \mathbf{b}\ \mathbf{c}] = p + (q + r)\cos\theta$ ...(i)

$0 = (p + r)\cos\theta + q$ ...(ii)

$[\mathbf{a}\ \mathbf{b}\ \mathbf{c}] = (p + q)\cos\theta + r$ ...(iii)

$$\text{Also, } [\mathbf{a}\ \mathbf{b}\ \mathbf{c}]^2 = \begin{vmatrix} 1 & \cos\theta & \cos\theta \\ \cos\theta & 1 & \cos\theta \\ \cos\theta & \cos\theta & 1 \end{vmatrix}$$

$$= 2\cos^2\theta - 3\cos^3\theta + 1 = (1 - \cos\theta)^2 (1 + 2\cos\theta)$$

$$\therefore v = |[\mathbf{a}\ \mathbf{b}\ \mathbf{c}]| = |1 - \cos\theta||\sqrt{1 + 2\cos\theta}|$$

$$= 2\sin^2\frac{\theta}{2}|\sqrt{1 + 2\cos\theta}|$$

From Eqs. (i) and (iii) $p = r$; on substituting in Eq. (ii), we get

$\therefore 2p\cos\theta + q = 0$

$\Rightarrow \dfrac{q}{p} + 2\cos\theta = 0$

57. (c) 58. (b)

Solutions (Q.Nos. 59 and 60)

We have, $|\mathbf{a}| = 1, |\mathbf{b}| = 2$ and $|\mathbf{c}| = 3$

Also, $|[\mathbf{a}\ \mathbf{b}\ \mathbf{c}]| = 6 = |\mathbf{a}||\mathbf{b}||\mathbf{c}|$

$\Rightarrow$ **a**, **b** and **c** are mutually perpendicular vectors.

Let $\mathbf{a} = \hat{\mathbf{i}}, \mathbf{b} = 2\hat{\mathbf{j}}$ and $\mathbf{c} = 3\hat{\mathbf{k}}$

Since, **r** is coplanar with **b** and **c**

$\therefore \mathbf{r} = x\mathbf{b} + y\mathbf{c} = x(2\hat{\mathbf{j}}) + y(3\hat{\mathbf{k}})$

On taking dot product with $2\hat{\mathbf{j}}$, we get

$$\mathbf{r} \cdot 2\hat{\mathbf{j}} = 4x \Rightarrow \mathbf{r} \cdot \mathbf{b} = 4x \Rightarrow 1 = 4x$$

$$\Rightarrow x = \frac{1}{4}$$

Now, $|\mathbf{r}|^2 = 4x^2 + 9y^2$

$$\Rightarrow 1 = 4\left(\frac{1}{4}\right)^2 + 9y^2$$

$$\Rightarrow 9y^2 = \frac{3}{4} \Rightarrow y^2 = \frac{1}{12} \Rightarrow y = \frac{1}{2\sqrt{3}}$$

$$\therefore \mathbf{r} = \frac{1}{2}\hat{\mathbf{j}} + \frac{\sqrt{3}}{2}\hat{\mathbf{k}}$$

$$\therefore |(\mathbf{a} \times \mathbf{c}) \times \mathbf{r}| = \left|(\hat{\mathbf{i}} \times 3\hat{\mathbf{k}}) \times \left(\frac{1}{2}\hat{\mathbf{j}} + \frac{\sqrt{3}}{2}\hat{\mathbf{k}}\right)\right|$$

$$= \left|3\hat{\mathbf{j}} \times \left(\frac{1}{2}\hat{\mathbf{j}} + \frac{\sqrt{3}}{2}\hat{\mathbf{k}}\right)\right| = \left|\frac{3\sqrt{3}}{2}\hat{\mathbf{i}}\right|$$

$$\Rightarrow 4|(\mathbf{a} \times \mathbf{c}) \times \mathbf{r}|^2 = 27$$

and also, $\sqrt{3}|[\mathbf{a}\ \mathbf{b}\ \mathbf{r}]| = \sqrt{3}|(\mathbf{a} \times \mathbf{b}) \cdot \mathbf{r}|$

$$= \sqrt{3}\left|(\hat{\mathbf{i}} \times 2\hat{\mathbf{j}}) \cdot \left(\frac{1}{2}\hat{\mathbf{j}} + \frac{\sqrt{3}}{2}\hat{\mathbf{k}}\right)\right|$$

$$= \sqrt{3}\left|2\hat{\mathbf{k}} \cdot \left(\frac{1}{2}\hat{\mathbf{j}} + \frac{\sqrt{3}}{2}\hat{\mathbf{k}}\right)\right| = 3$$

59. (27) 60. (3)

Solutions (Q.Nos. 61 and 62)

Let $\mathbf{x}_1 = 3(\mathbf{a} \times \mathbf{b})$

$\mathbf{x}_2 = 2(\mathbf{b} - (\mathbf{a} \cdot \mathbf{b})\,\mathbf{a})$

Here, $\mathbf{x}_1 \cdot \mathbf{x}_2 = 0$

$\Rightarrow \mathbf{x}_1$ and $\mathbf{x}_2$ are perpendicular.

Now, $|\mathbf{x}_1||3(\mathbf{a} \times \mathbf{b})| = 3|\mathbf{a}||\mathbf{b}|\sin\theta$

$= 3|\mathbf{b}|\sin\theta$ [$\because |\mathbf{a}| = 1$, given]

and $x_2 = 2(\mathbf{b} - (\mathbf{a} \cdot \mathbf{b})\mathbf{a})$

$= 2\sqrt{(\mathbf{b} - (\mathbf{a} \cdot \mathbf{b})\mathbf{a})^2}$

$= 2\sqrt{|\mathbf{b}|^2 - 2(\mathbf{a} \cdot \mathbf{b})^2 + (\mathbf{a} \cdot \mathbf{b})^2|\mathbf{a}|^2}$

$= 2\sqrt{|\mathbf{b}|^2 - (\mathbf{a} \cdot \mathbf{b})^2}$ [$\because |\mathbf{a}| = 1$]

$= 2\sqrt{|\mathbf{b}|^2 - |\mathbf{a}|^2|\mathbf{b}|^2\cos^2\theta}$

$= 2\sqrt{|\mathbf{b}|^2 - |\mathbf{b}|^2 \cdot \cos^2\theta}$ [$\because |\mathbf{a}| = 1$]

$= 2|\mathbf{b}|\sin\theta$

$\Rightarrow |\mathbf{x}_2| = 2|\mathbf{b}|\sin\theta$

$\therefore$ Area of triangle $= \dfrac{1}{2} \times 3|\mathbf{b}|\sin\theta \times 2|\mathbf{b}|\sin\theta$

$= 3|\mathbf{b}|^2\sin^2\theta = \dfrac{3}{4}(|\mathbf{b}|^4 + 4)$ [given]

$\Rightarrow |\mathbf{b}|^2\sin^2\theta = \dfrac{1}{4}(|\mathbf{b}|^4 + 4)$

$\Rightarrow (\le 4)4\sin^2\theta = |\mathbf{b}|^2 + \dfrac{4}{|\mathbf{b}|^2}(\ge 4) \Rightarrow |\mathbf{b}| = \sqrt{2}$

$\therefore [|\mathbf{b}|] = 1$ and $|\mathbf{b}|^2 + 2 = 2 + 2 = 4$

61. (1) 62. (4)

Solutions (Q.Nos. 63 and 64)

63. $\cos(P+Q)+\cos(Q+R)+\cos(R+P)$

$$=-(\cos R+\cos P+\cos Q)$$

In any triangle maximum value of $\cos P+\cos Q+\cos R=\frac{3}{2}$

Minimum value of $\cos(P+Q)+\cos(Q+R)+\cos(R+P)$ is $-\frac{3}{2}$.

$$\lambda=\frac{-3}{2} \text{ and } 2|\lambda|=3$$

64. $\sin R=\sin(P+Q)$

$\therefore\ \lambda=1$

65. Let the angle between **u** and **v** is 2θ and **w** and **u** is θ

$$[\hat{\mathbf{u}}\ \hat{\mathbf{v}}\ \hat{\mathbf{w}}]^2=\begin{vmatrix}\hat{\mathbf{u}}\cdot\hat{\mathbf{u}} & \hat{\mathbf{u}}\cdot\hat{\mathbf{v}} & \hat{\mathbf{u}}\cdot\hat{\mathbf{w}}\\ \hat{\mathbf{v}}\cdot\hat{\mathbf{u}} & \hat{\mathbf{v}}\cdot\hat{\mathbf{v}} & \hat{\mathbf{v}}\cdot\hat{\mathbf{w}}\\ \hat{\mathbf{w}}\cdot\hat{\mathbf{u}} & \hat{\mathbf{w}}\cdot\hat{\mathbf{v}} & \hat{\mathbf{w}}\cdot\hat{\mathbf{w}}\end{vmatrix}$$

$$=\begin{vmatrix}1 & \cos2\theta & \cos\theta\\ \cos2\theta & 1 & \cos\theta\\ \cos\theta & \cos\theta & 1\end{vmatrix}=0$$

$$\Rightarrow\quad [\hat{\mathbf{u}}\ \hat{\mathbf{v}}\ \hat{\mathbf{w}}]=0$$

66. Solving the equation by splitting in three parts.

$$\begin{aligned}\textbf{Part I}&=[\mathbf{a}+\mathbf{b}\ \ \mathbf{b}+\mathbf{c}\ \ \mathbf{c}+\mathbf{a}]\\&=(\mathbf{a}+\mathbf{b})\,[(\mathbf{b}+\mathbf{c})\times(\mathbf{c}+\mathbf{a})]\\&=(\mathbf{a}+\mathbf{b})[\mathbf{b}\times\mathbf{c}+\mathbf{b}\times\mathbf{a}+\mathbf{c}\times\mathbf{c}+\mathbf{c}\times\mathbf{a}]\\&=(\mathbf{a}+\mathbf{b})[\mathbf{b}\times\mathbf{c}+\mathbf{b}\times\mathbf{a}+\mathbf{0}+\mathbf{c}\times\mathbf{a}]\\&=[\mathbf{a}\ \mathbf{b}\ \mathbf{c}]+[\mathbf{a}\ \mathbf{b}\ \mathbf{a}]+[\mathbf{a}\ \mathbf{c}\ \mathbf{a}]+[\mathbf{b}\ \mathbf{b}\ \mathbf{c}]+[\mathbf{b}\ \mathbf{b}\ \mathbf{a}]+[\mathbf{b}\ \mathbf{c}\ \mathbf{a}]\\&=[\mathbf{a}\ \mathbf{b}\ \mathbf{c}]+0+0+0+0+[\mathbf{b}\ \mathbf{c}\ \mathbf{a}]\\&=2[\mathbf{a}\ \mathbf{b}\ \mathbf{c}]\end{aligned}$$

$$\begin{aligned}\textbf{Part II}&=[\mathbf{a}\times\mathbf{b}\ \ \mathbf{b}\times\mathbf{c}\ \ \mathbf{c}\times\mathbf{a}]\\&=(\mathbf{a}\times\mathbf{b})[(\mathbf{b}\times\mathbf{c})\times(\mathbf{c}\times\mathbf{a})]\\&=(\mathbf{a}\times\mathbf{b})([\mathbf{b}\ \mathbf{c}\ \mathbf{a}]\mathbf{c}-[\mathbf{b}\ \mathbf{c}\ \mathbf{c}]\mathbf{a})\\&=(\mathbf{a}\times\mathbf{b})([\mathbf{b}\ \mathbf{c}\ \mathbf{a}]\mathbf{c}-0)\\&=(\mathbf{a}\times\mathbf{b})(\mathbf{c}[\mathbf{a}\ \mathbf{b}\ \mathbf{c}])\\&=[\mathbf{a}\ \mathbf{b}\ \mathbf{c}]^2\end{aligned}$$

$$\begin{aligned}\textbf{Part III}&=[\mathbf{a}\times(\mathbf{b}\times\mathbf{c})\ \ \mathbf{b}\times(\mathbf{c}\times\mathbf{a})\ \ \mathbf{c}\times(\mathbf{a}\times\mathbf{b})]\\&=(\mathbf{a}\times(\mathbf{b}\times\mathbf{c}))\cdot((\mathbf{b}\times(\mathbf{c}\times\mathbf{a}))\times(\mathbf{c}\times(\mathbf{a}\times\mathbf{b})))\\&=0\end{aligned}$$

On adding parts I, II and II, we get

$$2[\mathbf{a}\ \mathbf{b}\ \mathbf{c}]+[\mathbf{a}\ \mathbf{b}\ \mathbf{c}]^2+0=2\times1+1^2=3$$

67. $\hat{\mathbf{a}}\cdot\hat{\mathbf{c}}=\hat{\mathbf{b}}\cdot\hat{\mathbf{c}}=\cos\theta$

$$\hat{\mathbf{c}}=\alpha\hat{\mathbf{a}}+\beta\hat{\mathbf{b}}+\gamma(\hat{\mathbf{a}}+\hat{\mathbf{b}})$$

On taking dot product with $\hat{\mathbf{a}}$ both sides $\cos\theta=\alpha$

On taking dot product with $\hat{\mathbf{b}}$ both sides $\cos\theta=\beta$

On taking dot product with $\hat{\mathbf{c}}$ both sides

$$1=\alpha\cos\theta+\beta\cos\theta+\gamma\,[\hat{\mathbf{a}}\ \hat{\mathbf{b}}\ \hat{\mathbf{c}}]$$

But $\quad [\hat{\mathbf{a}}\ \hat{\mathbf{b}}\ \hat{\mathbf{c}}]^2=\begin{bmatrix}1 & 0 & \cos\theta\\ 0 & 1 & \cos\theta\\ \cos\theta & \cos\theta & 1\end{bmatrix}=1-2\cos^2\theta$

So, $\quad 1=\cos^2\theta+\cos^2\theta+\gamma\sqrt{1-2\cos^2\theta}$

$\Rightarrow\quad \gamma=\sqrt{1-2\cos^2\theta}$

So, $\alpha^2+\beta^2+\gamma^2=1$

68. The three adjacent sides of tetrahedron is given by

$$\frac{(\hat{\mathbf{i}}+\hat{\mathbf{j}})\times(\hat{\mathbf{j}}+\hat{\mathbf{k}})}{|(\hat{\mathbf{i}}+\hat{\mathbf{j}})\times(\hat{\mathbf{j}}+\hat{\mathbf{k}})|},\ \frac{(\hat{\mathbf{j}}+\hat{\mathbf{k}})\times(\hat{\mathbf{k}}+\hat{\mathbf{i}})}{|(\hat{\mathbf{j}}+\hat{\mathbf{k}})\times(\hat{\mathbf{k}}+\hat{\mathbf{i}})|},\ \frac{(\hat{\mathbf{k}}+\hat{\mathbf{i}})\times(\hat{\mathbf{i}}+\hat{\mathbf{j}})}{|(\hat{\mathbf{k}}+\hat{\mathbf{i}})\times(\hat{\mathbf{i}}+\hat{\mathbf{j}})|}$$

i.e. $\quad \dfrac{\hat{\mathbf{i}}-\hat{\mathbf{j}}+\hat{\mathbf{k}}}{\sqrt{3}},\ \dfrac{\hat{\mathbf{i}}+\hat{\mathbf{j}}-\hat{\mathbf{k}}}{\sqrt{3}},\ \dfrac{-\hat{\mathbf{i}}+\hat{\mathbf{j}}+\hat{\mathbf{k}}}{\sqrt{3}}$

$$V=\frac{1}{6}\times\frac{1}{3\sqrt{3}}\left\|\begin{matrix}1 & -1 & 1\\ 1 & 1 & -1\\ -1 & 1 & 1\end{matrix}\right\|=\frac{2}{9\sqrt{3}}$$

So, $\quad 9\sqrt{3}V=2$

69. Let $\hat{\mathbf{c}}=x\mathbf{a}+y\,\mathbf{b}$, where x and y are scalars.

$\Rightarrow\quad \hat{\mathbf{c}}=x(\hat{\mathbf{i}}-\hat{\mathbf{j}}+2\hat{\mathbf{k}})+y(2\hat{\mathbf{i}}-\hat{\mathbf{j}}+\hat{\mathbf{k}})$

$\Rightarrow\quad \hat{\mathbf{c}}=\hat{\mathbf{i}}(x+2y)+\hat{\mathbf{j}}(-x-y)+\hat{\mathbf{k}}(2x+y)$

But $\quad \hat{\mathbf{c}}\cdot\mathbf{a}=0$

$$6x+5y=0\ \Rightarrow\ y=-\frac{6x}{5}$$

So, $\quad \hat{\mathbf{c}}=\dfrac{-7x}{5}\hat{\mathbf{i}}+\dfrac{x}{5}\hat{\mathbf{j}}+\dfrac{4x}{5}\hat{\mathbf{k}}$

We have, $\dfrac{49x^2+x^2+16x^2}{25}=1\ \Rightarrow\ x^2=\dfrac{25}{66}$

$\therefore\quad \hat{\mathbf{c}}=\pm\dfrac{5}{\sqrt{66}}\left(\dfrac{-7}{5}\hat{\mathbf{i}}+\dfrac{1}{5}\hat{\mathbf{j}}+\dfrac{4}{5}\hat{\mathbf{k}}\right)$

$$P=\frac{\hat{\mathbf{c}}\cdot\mathbf{b}}{|\mathbf{b}|}=\frac{\sqrt{11}}{6}$$

So, $\quad \dfrac{\sqrt{11}}{p}=6\ \Rightarrow\ k=6$

70. Let the angle between **a** and **b** is α and $\mathbf{a}\times\mathbf{b}$ and **c** is β.

$\therefore\quad |[\mathbf{a}\ \mathbf{b}\ \mathbf{c}]|=6$

$\Rightarrow\quad \sin\alpha\cos\beta=1\ \Rightarrow\ \sin\alpha=1,\ \cos\beta=1$

$\Rightarrow\quad \alpha=90^\circ,\ \beta=0^\circ$

$\Rightarrow$ **a**, **b** and **c** are mutually perpendicular.

Again, $[\mathbf{b}\ \mathbf{c}\ \hat{\mathbf{d}}]=0\Rightarrow\begin{vmatrix}4 & 0 & 1\\ 0 & 9 & \mathbf{c}\cdot\hat{\mathbf{d}}\\ 1 & \mathbf{c}\cdot\hat{\mathbf{d}} & 1\end{vmatrix}=0\Rightarrow\mathbf{c}\cdot\hat{\mathbf{d}}=\pm\dfrac{3\sqrt{3}}{2}$

We have, $\mathbf{a}\cdot\mathbf{b}=0$

$$|\mathbf{a}\times\mathbf{c}\cdot\hat{\mathbf{d}}|^2=\begin{vmatrix}1 & 0 & 0\\ 0 & 9 & \frac{3\sqrt{3}}{2}\\ 0 & \frac{3\sqrt{3}}{2} & 1\end{vmatrix}=9-\frac{27}{4}=\frac{9}{4}$$

$$|(\mathbf{a}\times\mathbf{c})\times\hat{\mathbf{d}}|^2=|(\mathbf{a}\cdot\hat{\mathbf{d}})\,\mathbf{c}-(\mathbf{c}\cdot\hat{\mathbf{d}})\mathbf{a}|^2=\left|\frac{3\sqrt{3}}{2}\mathbf{a}\right|^2=\frac{27}{4}$$

So, $\quad |\mathbf{a}\times\mathbf{c}\cdot\hat{\mathbf{d}}|^2+|(\mathbf{a}\times\mathbf{c})\times\hat{\mathbf{d}}|^2=\dfrac{36}{4}=9$

71. Position vector of $D = \frac{\lambda - 1}{2}\hat{\mathbf{i}} + 4\hat{\mathbf{j}} + \frac{\mu + 2}{2}\hat{\mathbf{k}}$

Direction ratio of AD $= \frac{\lambda - 5}{2}, 1, \frac{\mu - 8}{2}$

But direction ratios of AD should be $\frac{1}{\sqrt{3}}, \frac{1}{\sqrt{3}}, \frac{1}{\sqrt{3}}$.

$$\Rightarrow \quad \frac{\lambda - 5}{2} = 1 = \frac{\mu - 8}{2}$$

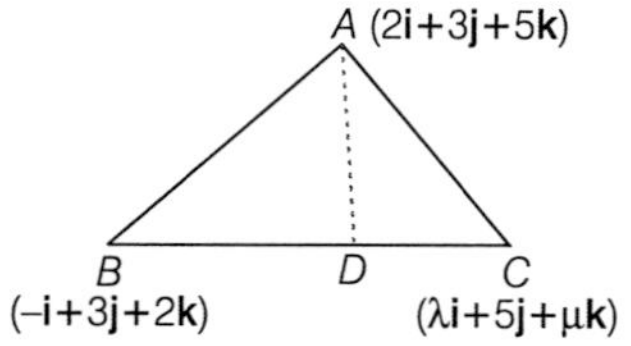

$$\lambda = 7, \mu = 10$$
$$2\lambda - \mu = 4$$

72. $V = [\mathbf{a}\ \mathbf{b}\ \mathbf{c}]$

$$[\alpha\ \beta\ \gamma] = \begin{vmatrix} \mathbf{a}\cdot\mathbf{a} & \mathbf{a}\cdot\mathbf{b} & \mathbf{a}\cdot\mathbf{c} \\ \mathbf{b}\cdot\mathbf{a} & \mathbf{b}\cdot\mathbf{b} & \mathbf{b}\cdot\mathbf{c} \\ \mathbf{c}\cdot\mathbf{a} & \mathbf{c}\cdot\mathbf{b} & \mathbf{c}\cdot\mathbf{c} \end{vmatrix} [\mathbf{a}\ \mathbf{b}\ \mathbf{c}]$$

$$= [\mathbf{a}\ \mathbf{b}\ \mathbf{c}]\,[\mathbf{a}\ \mathbf{b}\ \mathbf{c}]\,[\mathbf{a}\ \mathbf{b}\ \mathbf{c}] = V^3$$

$\therefore \quad \lambda = 3$

73. In ΔABD, N is the mid-point of BD.

$\therefore \quad \mathbf{AB} + \mathbf{AD} = 2\mathbf{AN}$ ...(i)

In ΔCBD, N is the mid-point of BD.

$\therefore \quad \mathbf{CB} + \mathbf{CD} = 2\mathbf{CN}$ ...(ii)

On adding Eqs. (i) and (ii), we have

$\mathbf{AB} + \mathbf{AD} + \mathbf{CB} + \mathbf{CD} = 2(\mathbf{AN} + \mathbf{CN})$ ...(iii)

In ΔANC, M is the mid-point of AC

$\therefore \quad \mathbf{AN} + \mathbf{CN} = 2\mathbf{MN}$

From Eq. (iii), we get

$\mathbf{AB} + \mathbf{AD} + \mathbf{CB} + \mathbf{CD} = 2(2\mathbf{MN}) = 4\mathbf{MN}$

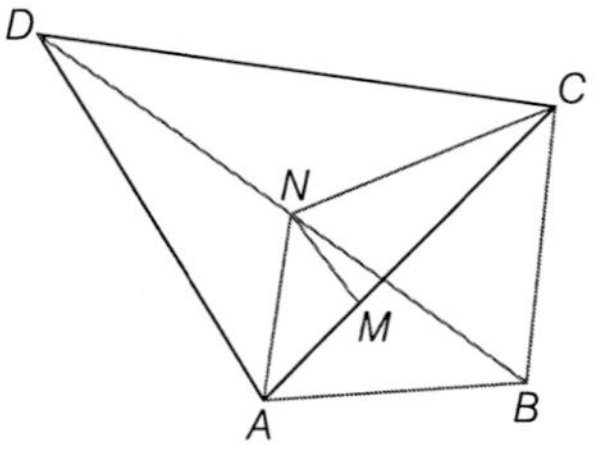

74. $|\mathbf{a}| = |\mathbf{b}| = |\mathbf{c}| = 1; [\mathbf{a}\ \mathbf{b}\ \mathbf{c}] = 1$

Volume of the tetrahedron $= \frac{1}{6} \left\| \begin{matrix} 3 & -2 & 2 \\ -1 & 0 & -2 \\ 2 & -3 & 4 \end{matrix} \right\| [\mathbf{a}\ \mathbf{b}\ \mathbf{c}] = 2$

75. $[\mathbf{a} \times (\mathbf{b} \times \mathbf{c})]\cdot(\mathbf{a} \times \mathbf{c}) = 5$

$\Rightarrow [(\mathbf{a}\cdot\mathbf{c})\mathbf{b} - (\mathbf{a}\cdot\mathbf{b})\mathbf{c}]\cdot(\mathbf{a} \times \mathbf{c}) = 5 \Rightarrow (\mathbf{a}\cdot\mathbf{c})\,[\mathbf{b}\ \mathbf{a}\ \mathbf{c}] = 5$

$\Rightarrow \quad [\mathbf{a}\ \mathbf{b}\ \mathbf{c}] = -10$

$\Rightarrow \quad -[\mathbf{a}\ \mathbf{b}\ \mathbf{c}] - 1 = +10 - 1 = 9$

76. $\begin{vmatrix} \mathbf{a}\cdot\mathbf{a} & \mathbf{a}\cdot\mathbf{b} & \mathbf{a}\cdot\mathbf{c} \\ \mathbf{b}\cdot\mathbf{a} & \mathbf{b}\cdot\mathbf{b} & \mathbf{b}\cdot\mathbf{c} \\ \mathbf{c}\cdot\mathbf{a} & \mathbf{c}\cdot\mathbf{b} & \mathbf{c}\cdot\mathbf{c} \end{vmatrix} = [\mathbf{a}\ \mathbf{b}\ \mathbf{c}]^2 = [\mathbf{a} \times \mathbf{b}\ \ \mathbf{b} \times \mathbf{c}\ \ \mathbf{c} \times \mathbf{a}]^2 = 36$

$$= 4 \times 9 = 2^2 \times 3^2$$

$\therefore \quad p + q = 5$

77. $\frac{1}{6}\begin{vmatrix} -2 & -4 & 6 \\ 0 & 1 & -8 \\ 2 & -5 & \lambda - 1 \end{vmatrix} = 22 \Rightarrow \lambda = 1$

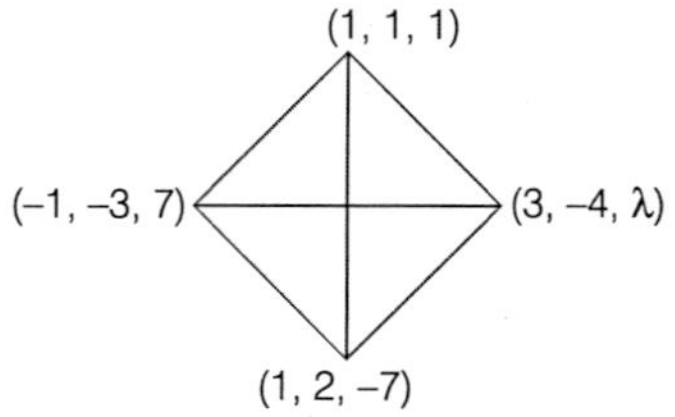

78. $\frac{1}{6}[\mathbf{a}\ \mathbf{b}\ \mathbf{c}] = 3 \Rightarrow [\mathbf{a}\ \mathbf{b}\ \mathbf{c}] = 18$

$V = [\mathbf{a} + \mathbf{b} - \mathbf{c}\ \ \mathbf{a} - \mathbf{b}\ \ \mathbf{b} - \mathbf{c}]$

$= (\mathbf{a} + \mathbf{b} - \mathbf{c})\cdot(\mathbf{a} - \mathbf{b}) \times (\mathbf{b} - \mathbf{c}) = \mathbf{a}\cdot(\mathbf{b} \times \mathbf{c}) = [\mathbf{a}\ \mathbf{b}\ \mathbf{c}] = 18$

79. Given that $|\mathbf{a}| = |\mathbf{b}| = 1, \mathbf{a}\cdot\mathbf{b} = 0, |\mathbf{c}| = 2$ and $\mathbf{c}$ makes angle α with both $\mathbf{a}$ and $\mathbf{b}$.

Also, $\mathbf{c} = x\mathbf{a} + y\mathbf{b} + \mathbf{a} \times \mathbf{b}$

$\mathbf{c}\cdot\mathbf{a} = |\mathbf{c}|\,|\mathbf{a}| \cos\alpha = 2\cos\alpha$

$\Rightarrow \quad x = 2\cos\alpha$

$\Rightarrow \mathbf{c}\cdot\mathbf{b} = 2\cos\alpha \Rightarrow y = 2\cos\alpha$

$\Rightarrow |\mathbf{c}|^2 = \mathbf{c}\cdot\mathbf{c} = |(2\cos\alpha)\mathbf{a} + (2\cos\alpha)\mathbf{b} + \mathbf{a} \times \mathbf{b}|^2$

$\Rightarrow (2)^2 = 4\cos^2\alpha + 4\cos^2\alpha + |\mathbf{a} \times \mathbf{b}|^2$

$\Rightarrow \quad 4 = 8\cos^2\alpha + 1 \quad [\because |\mathbf{a} \times \mathbf{b}| = 1 \times 1 \times \sin 90° = 1]$

$\Rightarrow \quad 8\cos^2\alpha = 3$

80. Let $P(x_1, y_1)$ and $Q(x_2, y_2)$ be the two points on $y = 2^{x+2}$

$\mathbf{OP}\cdot\hat{\mathbf{i}}$ = Projection of $\mathbf{OP}$ on the X-axis

$\Rightarrow \quad x_1 = -1 \quad [\because \mathbf{OP}\,.\,\hat{\mathbf{i}} = -1]$

Also, (x_1, y_1) lies on $y = 2^{x+2}$

$\therefore \quad y_1 = 2^{x_1 + 2} \Rightarrow y_1 = 2$

Also, $\mathbf{OQ}\cdot\hat{\mathbf{i}}$ = Projection of $\mathbf{OQ}$ on X-axis.

$\Rightarrow \quad x_2 = 2 \quad$ [given $\mathbf{OQ}\,.\,\hat{\mathbf{i}} = 2$]

As (x_2, y_2) lies on $y = 2^{x+2}$

$$y_2 = 2^{x_2 + 2};\ y_2 = 16$$

Thus, $\quad \mathbf{OP} = x_1\hat{\mathbf{i}} + y_1\hat{\mathbf{j}} = -\hat{\mathbf{i}} + 2\hat{\mathbf{j}}$

and $\quad \mathbf{OQ} = x_2\hat{\mathbf{i}} + y_2\hat{\mathbf{j}} = 2\hat{\mathbf{i}} + 16\hat{\mathbf{j}}$

$\Rightarrow \quad \mathbf{OQ} - 4\mathbf{OP} = 6\hat{\mathbf{i}} + 8\hat{\mathbf{j}}$

$\Rightarrow \quad |\mathbf{OQ} - 4\mathbf{OP}| = \sqrt{36 + 64} = 10$

81. Let $\mathbf{p} = \mathbf{BA}$ and $\mathbf{q} = \mathbf{BC}$

Now, required perpendicular distance $= AM = (BA)\sin\theta$

$= |\mathbf{p}| \sin\theta$ ...(i)

Consider, $|\mathbf{q} \times \mathbf{p}| = |\mathbf{q}||\mathbf{p}| \sin\theta$

On dividing by $|\mathbf{q}|$

$$\frac{|\mathbf{q} \times \mathbf{p}|}{|\mathbf{q}|} = |\mathbf{p}| \sin\theta \quad ...(ii)$$

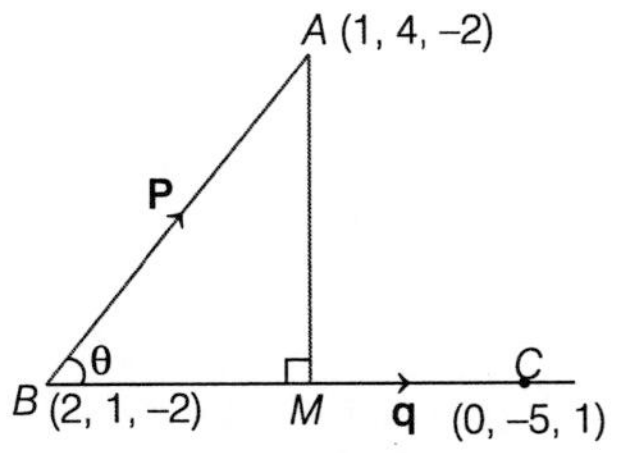

From Eqs. (i) and (ii), required perpendicular distance

$$= \frac{|\mathbf{q} \times \mathbf{p}|}{|\mathbf{q}|} \quad ...(iii)$$

where, $\mathbf{q} = \mathbf{BC} = -2\hat{\mathbf{i}} - 6\hat{\mathbf{j}} + 3\hat{\mathbf{k}}$

$\mathbf{p} = \mathbf{AB} = -\hat{\mathbf{i}} + 3\hat{\mathbf{j}}$

$\therefore \quad |\mathbf{q}| = \sqrt{4 + 36 + 9} = 7 \quad ...(iv)$

and $\mathbf{q} \times \mathbf{p} = \begin{vmatrix} \hat{\mathbf{i}} & \hat{\mathbf{j}} & \hat{\mathbf{k}} \\ -2 & -6 & 3 \\ -1 & 3 & 0 \end{vmatrix} = -9\hat{\mathbf{i}} - 3\hat{\mathbf{j}} - 12\hat{\mathbf{k}}$

$|\mathbf{q} \times \mathbf{p}| = \sqrt{81 + 9 + 144} = 3\sqrt{26} \quad ...(v)$

From Eqs. (iii), (iv) and (v), we get

Perpendicular distance $= \dfrac{3\sqrt{26}}{7}$

$\therefore \quad p = 26$

82. Let $\mathbf{a} = x\hat{\mathbf{i}} + y\hat{\mathbf{j}} + z\hat{\mathbf{k}}$

Now, $\mathbf{a}$, $\hat{\mathbf{i}}$ and $\hat{\mathbf{i}} + \hat{\mathbf{j}}$ are coplanar and $\mathbf{a}$, $\hat{\mathbf{i}} - \hat{\mathbf{j}}$ and $\hat{\mathbf{i}} + \hat{\mathbf{k}}$ are coplanar.

$\Rightarrow \quad [\mathbf{a}\ \hat{\mathbf{i}}\ \hat{\mathbf{i}} + \hat{\mathbf{j}}] = 0$ and $[\mathbf{a}\ \hat{\mathbf{i}} - \hat{\mathbf{j}}\ \hat{\mathbf{i}} + \hat{\mathbf{k}}] = 0$

$\Rightarrow \quad \begin{vmatrix} x & y & z \\ 1 & 0 & 0 \\ 1 & 1 & 0 \end{vmatrix} = 0$ and $\begin{vmatrix} x & y & z \\ 1 & -1 & 0 \\ 1 & 0 & 1 \end{vmatrix} = 0$

$\therefore \quad z = 0$ and $-x - y + z = 0$

$\Rightarrow \quad z = 0$ and $x + y = 0$

$\Rightarrow \quad y = -x$

$\therefore \quad \mathbf{a} = x\hat{\mathbf{i}} - x\hat{\mathbf{j}} \Rightarrow \mathbf{a} = \dfrac{\hat{\mathbf{i}} - \hat{\mathbf{j}}}{\sqrt{2}}$

Let the angle between $\mathbf{a}$ and $\hat{\mathbf{i}} - 2\hat{\mathbf{j}} + 2\hat{\mathbf{k}}$ be θ.

$$\cos\theta = \mathbf{a} \cdot \frac{\hat{\mathbf{i}} - 2\hat{\mathbf{j}} + 2\hat{\mathbf{k}}}{|\hat{\mathbf{i}} + 2\hat{\mathbf{j}} + 2\hat{\mathbf{k}}|} = \frac{(\hat{\mathbf{i}} - \hat{\mathbf{j}})}{\sqrt{2}} \cdot \frac{(\hat{\mathbf{i}} - 2\hat{\mathbf{j}} + 2\hat{\mathbf{k}})}{\sqrt{1 + 4 + 4}}$$

$$= \frac{(\hat{\mathbf{i}} - \hat{\mathbf{j}})\,(\hat{\mathbf{i}} - 2\hat{\mathbf{j}} + 2\hat{\mathbf{k}})}{\sqrt{2} \cdot 3} = \frac{1 + 2}{3\sqrt{2}} = \frac{1}{\sqrt{2}}$$

$\therefore \quad \theta = \dfrac{\pi}{4}$

$\therefore \quad \dfrac{1}{\lambda} = \dfrac{1}{4} = 0.25$

83. In the new position, let the vector be $x\hat{\mathbf{i}} + y\hat{\mathbf{j}} + z\hat{\mathbf{k}}$.

Since, it is perpendicular to the given vector.

$(x\hat{\mathbf{i}} + y\hat{\mathbf{j}} + z\hat{\mathbf{k}}) \cdot (\hat{\mathbf{i}} + 2\hat{\mathbf{j}} + 2\hat{\mathbf{k}}) = 0$

$\Rightarrow \quad x + 2y + 2z = 0 \quad ...(i)$

The magnitude is the new position which also remains the same.

$\Rightarrow \quad x^2 + y^2 + z^2 = 1 + 4 + 4 = 9 \quad ...(ii)$

The given vector, the vector in new position and the X-axis are coplanar.

$\Rightarrow \quad \begin{vmatrix} 1 & 0 & 0 \\ 1 & 2 & 2 \\ x & y & z \end{vmatrix} = 0$

$\Rightarrow \quad y = z$ and $x = -4y$ [using $x + 2y + 22 = 0$]

Hence, $\quad x^2 + y^2 + z^2 = 9$

$\Rightarrow \quad 16y^2 + y^2 + y^2 = 9$

$\Rightarrow \quad y^2 = \dfrac{1}{2}, y = \pm \dfrac{1}{\sqrt{2}}$

$\Rightarrow \quad x = \pm 2\sqrt{2}$

It is given that the vector passes through the positive X-axis.

$\Rightarrow \quad x = 2\sqrt{2}$ and $y = -\dfrac{1}{\sqrt{2}} = z$

Hence, the required vector is $\left(2\sqrt{2}\hat{\mathbf{i}} - \dfrac{1}{\sqrt{2}}\hat{\mathbf{j}} - \dfrac{1}{\sqrt{2}}\hat{\mathbf{k}}\right)$.

$\therefore \quad x = 2\sqrt{2}, y = -\dfrac{1}{\sqrt{2}}, z = -\dfrac{1}{\sqrt{2}}$

$\therefore \quad \sqrt{2}xyz = \sqrt{2} \times 2\sqrt{2} \times \left(-\dfrac{1}{\sqrt{2}}\right) \times \left(-\dfrac{1}{\sqrt{2}}\right) = 2$

84. $\hat{\mathbf{u}} \times \hat{\mathbf{v}} + \hat{\mathbf{u}} = \mathbf{w}$ and $\mathbf{w} \times \hat{\mathbf{u}} = \hat{\mathbf{v}}$

$\Rightarrow \quad (\hat{\mathbf{u}} \times \hat{\mathbf{v}} + \hat{\mathbf{u}}) \times \hat{\mathbf{u}} = \mathbf{w} \times \hat{\mathbf{u}}$

$\Rightarrow \quad (\hat{\mathbf{u}} \times \hat{\mathbf{v}}) \times \hat{\mathbf{u}} + \hat{\mathbf{u}} \times \hat{\mathbf{u}} = \hat{\mathbf{v}}$

$\Rightarrow \quad (\hat{\mathbf{u}} \cdot \hat{\mathbf{u}})\hat{\mathbf{v}} - (\hat{\mathbf{v}} \cdot \hat{\mathbf{u}})\hat{\mathbf{u}} + \hat{\mathbf{u}} \times \hat{\mathbf{u}} = \hat{\mathbf{v}}$

[using $\hat{\mathbf{u}} \cdot \hat{\mathbf{u}} = 1$ and $\hat{\mathbf{u}} \times \hat{\mathbf{u}} = 0$, since unit vectors]

$\Rightarrow \quad \hat{\mathbf{v}} - (\hat{\mathbf{v}} \cdot \hat{\mathbf{u}})\hat{\mathbf{u}} = \hat{\mathbf{v}}$

$\Rightarrow \quad (\hat{\mathbf{u}} \cdot \hat{\mathbf{v}})\hat{\mathbf{u}} = 0$

$\Rightarrow \quad \hat{\mathbf{u}} \cdot \hat{\mathbf{v}} = 0$

Now, $[\hat{\mathbf{u}}\ \hat{\mathbf{v}}\ \mathbf{w}]$

$\Rightarrow \quad \hat{\mathbf{u}} \cdot (\hat{\mathbf{v}} \times \mathbf{w}) = \hat{\mathbf{u}} \cdot [\hat{\mathbf{v}} \times (\hat{\mathbf{u}} \times \hat{\mathbf{v}} + \hat{\mathbf{u}})]$ [given, $\mathbf{w} = \hat{\mathbf{u}} \times \hat{\mathbf{v}} + \hat{\mathbf{u}}$]

$= \hat{\mathbf{u}} \cdot [\hat{\mathbf{v}} \times (\hat{\mathbf{u}} \times \hat{\mathbf{v}}) + \hat{\mathbf{v}} \times \hat{\mathbf{u}}]$

$= \hat{\mathbf{u}} \cdot [(\hat{\mathbf{v}} \cdot \hat{\mathbf{v}})\hat{\mathbf{u}} - (\hat{\mathbf{v}} \cdot \hat{\mathbf{u}})\,\hat{\mathbf{v}} + \hat{\mathbf{v}} \times \hat{\mathbf{u}}]$

[$\because \hat{\mathbf{u}} \cdot \hat{\mathbf{v}} = 0$ from Eq. (i)]

$= |\hat{\mathbf{v}}|^2 (\hat{\mathbf{u}} \cdot \hat{\mathbf{u}}) - \hat{\mathbf{u}} \cdot (\hat{\mathbf{v}} \times \hat{\mathbf{u}})$

$= |\hat{\mathbf{v}}|^2 |\hat{\mathbf{u}}|^2 - 0$ [$\because [\hat{\mathbf{u}}\ \hat{\mathbf{v}}\ \mathbf{w}] = 0$]

[$\because |\hat{\mathbf{u}}| = |\hat{\mathbf{v}}| = 1$]

$\Rightarrow \quad [\hat{\mathbf{u}}\ \hat{\mathbf{v}}\ \mathbf{w}] = 1$

85. We have, $\quad \mathbf{R} \times \mathbf{B} = \mathbf{C} \times \mathbf{B}$ and $\mathbf{R} \cdot \mathbf{A} = 0$

$\Rightarrow \quad \mathbf{A} \times (\mathbf{R} \times \mathbf{B}) = \mathbf{A} \times (\mathbf{C} \times \mathbf{B})$

$\Rightarrow \quad (\mathbf{A} \cdot \mathbf{B})\mathbf{R} - (\mathbf{A} \cdot \mathbf{R})\mathbf{B} = (\mathbf{A} \cdot \mathbf{B})\mathbf{C} - (\mathbf{A} \cdot \mathbf{C})\mathbf{B} \quad ...(i)$

where, $\quad \mathbf{A} = 2\hat{\mathbf{i}} + \hat{\mathbf{k}}, \mathbf{B} = \hat{\mathbf{i}} + \hat{\mathbf{j}} + \hat{\mathbf{k}}$

and $\quad \mathbf{C} = 4\hat{\mathbf{i}} - 3\hat{\mathbf{j}} + 7\hat{\mathbf{k}}$

$\therefore \quad \mathbf{A} \cdot \mathbf{B} = 2 + 1 = 3, \mathbf{A} \cdot \mathbf{C} = 8 + 7 = 15$

Hence, Eq. (i) reduces to

$3\mathbf{R} - 0 \cdot \mathbf{B} = 3\mathbf{C} - 15\mathbf{B}$

or $\quad \mathbf{R} = \mathbf{C} - 5\mathbf{B} = (4\hat{\mathbf{i}} - 3\hat{\mathbf{j}} + 7\hat{\mathbf{k}}) - 5(\hat{\mathbf{i}} + \hat{\mathbf{j}} + \hat{\mathbf{k}})$

$\therefore \quad \mathbf{R} = -\hat{\mathbf{i}} - 8\hat{\mathbf{j}} + 2\hat{\mathbf{k}}$

$\therefore \quad \dfrac{|\mathbf{R}|}{2} = \dfrac{69}{2} = 34.5$

86. Here,

$$\mathbf{a} \times [(\mathbf{x} - \mathbf{b}) \times \mathbf{a}] + \mathbf{b} \times [(\mathbf{x} - \mathbf{c}) \times \mathbf{b}] + \mathbf{c} \times [(\mathbf{x} - \mathbf{a}) \times \mathbf{c}] = 0$$

$$(\mathbf{a} \cdot \mathbf{a})(\mathbf{x} - \mathbf{b}) - [\mathbf{a} \cdot (\mathbf{x} - \mathbf{b})]\mathbf{a} + (\mathbf{b} \cdot \mathbf{b})(\mathbf{x} - \mathbf{c})$$
$$-[\mathbf{b} \cdot (\mathbf{x} - \mathbf{c})]\mathbf{b} + (\mathbf{c} \cdot \mathbf{c})(\mathbf{x} - \mathbf{a}) - [\mathbf{c} \cdot (\mathbf{x} - a)]\mathbf{c} = 0$$

$$\Rightarrow \lambda^2(\mathbf{x} - \mathbf{b}) - [\mathbf{a} \cdot \mathbf{x} - 0]\mathbf{a} + \lambda^2(\mathbf{x} - \mathbf{c}) - [\mathbf{b} \cdot \mathbf{x} - 0]\mathbf{b}$$
$$+ \lambda^2(\mathbf{x} - \mathbf{a}) - (\mathbf{c} \cdot \mathbf{x} - 0) = \mathbf{c} = 0$$

[using $\mathbf{a} \cdot \mathbf{b} = \mathbf{b} \cdot \mathbf{c} = \mathbf{c} \cdot \mathbf{a} = 0$ and $|\mathbf{a}| = |\mathbf{b}| = |\mathbf{c}| = \lambda$]

$$\Rightarrow \lambda^2[\mathbf{x} - \mathbf{b} + \mathbf{x} - \mathbf{c} + \mathbf{x} - \mathbf{a}]$$
$$= [(\mathbf{a} \cdot \mathbf{x})\mathbf{a} + (\mathbf{b} \cdot \mathbf{x})\mathbf{b} + (\mathbf{c} \cdot \mathbf{x})\mathbf{c}] \qquad \text{...(i)}$$

Let $\mathbf{x} = \alpha\mathbf{a} + \beta\mathbf{b} + \gamma\mathbf{c}$ ...(ii)

[$\mathbf{x}$ is linear combination of **a**, **b** and **c**]

From Eq. (i), $\lambda^2[3\mathbf{x} - (\mathbf{a} + \mathbf{b} + \mathbf{c})](\mathbf{a} \cdot \mathbf{x})$

$$\mathbf{a} + (\mathbf{b} \cdot \mathbf{x})\mathbf{b} + (\mathbf{c} \cdot \mathbf{x})\mathbf{c}$$

and from Eq. (ii),

$$\mathbf{a} \cdot \mathbf{x} = \lambda^2\alpha, \mathbf{b} \cdot \mathbf{x} = \lambda^2\beta, \mathbf{c} \cdot \mathbf{x} = \lambda^2\gamma$$

Above equation reduces to

$$\lambda^2\{3\mathbf{x} - (\mathbf{a} + \mathbf{b} + \mathbf{c})\} = \lambda^2(\mathbf{a}\alpha + \mathbf{b}\beta + \mathbf{c}\gamma)$$

$\Rightarrow \quad 3\mathbf{x} - (\mathbf{a} + \mathbf{b} + \mathbf{c}) = x$

$\Rightarrow \quad 2\mathbf{x} = \mathbf{a} + \mathbf{b} + \mathbf{c}$

$\Rightarrow \quad \mathbf{x} = \dfrac{\mathbf{a} + \mathbf{b} + \mathbf{c}}{2}$

$\therefore \quad \dfrac{p^2}{5} = \dfrac{4}{5} = 0.8$

87. Given, $AB : BC = 1 : 2$

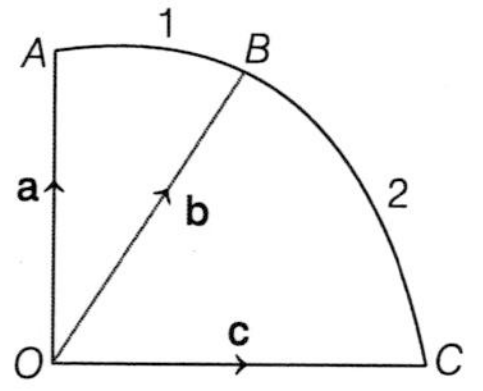

$\therefore \quad \angle AOB = 30°$ and $\angle BOC = 60°$

Since, **c** is coplanar with **a** and **b**.

$\therefore \quad \mathbf{c} = x_1\mathbf{a} + x_2\mathbf{b}$ ...(i)

Here, $|\mathbf{a}| = |\mathbf{b}| = |\mathbf{c}| = \lambda$ (let)

$\therefore \quad \mathbf{a} \cdot \mathbf{b} = |\mathbf{a}||\mathbf{b}|\cos 30°$

$$= \lambda^2\left(\frac{\sqrt{3}}{2}\right) = \frac{\sqrt{3}}{2}\lambda^2$$

$$\mathbf{b} \cdot \mathbf{c} = |\mathbf{b}||\mathbf{c}|\cos 60°$$

$$= \lambda^2\left(\frac{1}{2}\right) = \frac{\lambda^2}{2}$$

and $\quad \mathbf{a} \cdot \mathbf{c} = |\mathbf{a}||\mathbf{c}|\cos 90° = 0$

From Eq. (i), taking dot product with **c**, we get

$$\mathbf{c} \cdot \mathbf{c} = x_1\mathbf{a} \cdot \mathbf{c} + x_2\mathbf{b} \cdot \mathbf{c}$$

$$\Rightarrow \quad |\mathbf{c}|^2 = 0 + x_2\left(\frac{\lambda^2}{2}\right) \Rightarrow \lambda^2 = x_2\left(\frac{\lambda^2}{2}\right) \Rightarrow x_2 = 2$$

From Eq. (i), on taking dot product with **a**, we get

$$\mathbf{c} \cdot \mathbf{a} = x_1\mathbf{a} \cdot \mathbf{a} + x_2\mathbf{b} \cdot \mathbf{a}$$

$$\Rightarrow \quad 0 = x_1|\mathbf{a}|^2 + x_2\left(\frac{\sqrt{3}}{2}\lambda^2\right)$$

$$\Rightarrow \quad 0 = x_1\lambda^2 + 2\left(\frac{\sqrt{3}}{2}\lambda^2\right)$$

$$\Rightarrow \quad x_1 + \sqrt{3} = 0 \Rightarrow x_1 = -\sqrt{3}$$

On putting value of x_1 and x_2 in Eq. (i), we get

$$\mathbf{c} = -\sqrt{3}\mathbf{a} + 2\mathbf{b}$$

$\therefore \quad k_1 = -\sqrt{3}, k_2 = 2$

$\therefore \quad \dfrac{5(k_1^2 + k_2^2)}{2} = \dfrac{5(3 + 4)}{2} = \dfrac{35}{2} = 17.5$

88. (A) We know that 3 vectors are coplanar, if $x\mathbf{a} + y\mathbf{b} + z\mathbf{c} = 0$

Clearly, $-3\hat{\mathbf{i}} + 3\hat{\mathbf{j}} + 4\hat{\mathbf{k}}$ and $\hat{\mathbf{i}} + \hat{\mathbf{j}}$ are two vectors lie in the plane $(\mathbf{a} + \mathbf{b}$ and $\mathbf{a} - \mathbf{b})$.

(B) $\mathbf{a} \times \mathbf{b}$ is a vector which perpendicular to both **a** and **b**.

$$\therefore \quad \mathbf{a} \times \mathbf{b} = \begin{vmatrix} \hat{\mathbf{i}} & \hat{\mathbf{j}} & \hat{\mathbf{k}} \\ -1 & 2 & 2 \\ -2 & 1 & 2 \end{vmatrix} = \hat{\mathbf{i}}(4 - 2) - \hat{\mathbf{j}}(-2 + 4) + \hat{\mathbf{k}}(-1 + 4)$$
$$= 2\hat{\mathbf{i}} - 2\hat{\mathbf{j}} + 3\hat{\mathbf{k}}$$

(C) **c** is a vector which is equally inclined to **a** and **b**

$\therefore \quad \mathbf{c} \cdot \mathbf{a} = \mathbf{c} \cdot \mathbf{b}$

Clearly $\hat{\mathbf{i}} - \hat{\mathbf{j}} + 5\hat{\mathbf{k}}$ satisfies the condition.

(D) **a**, **b** and **c** are from the triangle

$\Rightarrow \quad \mathbf{AB} + \mathbf{BC} = \mathbf{AC}$

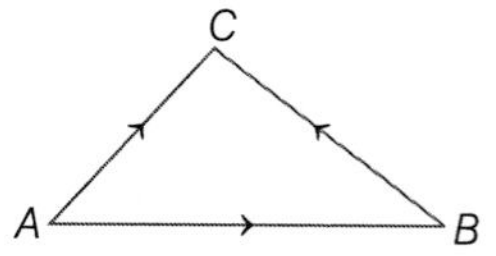

89. Given, $\quad [\mathbf{a} \times \mathbf{b} \;\; \mathbf{b} \times \mathbf{c} \;\; \mathbf{c} \times \mathbf{a}] = 36$

$[\mathbf{a}\;\mathbf{b}\;\mathbf{c}] = 6 \qquad [\because \text{volume} > 0]$

$\Rightarrow$ Volume of tetrahedron from by vectors

a, **b** and **c** is $\dfrac{1}{6}[\mathbf{a}\;\mathbf{b}\;\mathbf{c}] = 1$

$$[\mathbf{a} + \mathbf{b} \;\; \mathbf{b} + \mathbf{c} \;\; \mathbf{c} + \mathbf{a}] = 2[\mathbf{a}\;\mathbf{b}\;\mathbf{c}] = 12$$

$\mathbf{a} - \mathbf{b}$, $\mathbf{b} - \mathbf{c}$ and $\mathbf{c} - \mathbf{a}$ are coplanar

$\Rightarrow \quad [\mathbf{a} - \mathbf{b}\;\; \mathbf{b} - \mathbf{c}\;\; \mathbf{c} - \mathbf{a}] = 0$

90. **(A)** $\mathbf{a} \cdot \mathbf{b} + \mathbf{a} \cdot \mathbf{c} = \mathbf{b} \cdot \mathbf{c} + \mathbf{b} \cdot \mathbf{a} = 0$

$$\Rightarrow \quad \mathbf{b} \cdot \mathbf{c} = \mathbf{a} \cdot \mathbf{c} = -\mathbf{a} \cdot \mathbf{b} = -\frac{17}{2}$$

$$(\mathbf{a} + \mathbf{b} + \mathbf{c})^2 = |\mathbf{a}|^2 + |\mathbf{b}|^2 + |\mathbf{c}|^2 + 2\mathbf{a} \cdot \mathbf{b} + 2\mathbf{b} \cdot \mathbf{c} + 2\mathbf{c} \cdot \mathbf{a}$$
$$= (1)^2 + (4)^2 + (8)^2 + (\mathbf{a} \cdot \mathbf{b}) + (\mathbf{a} \cdot \mathbf{b})$$
$$+ (\mathbf{b} \cdot \mathbf{c}) + (\mathbf{b} \cdot \mathbf{c}) + (\mathbf{c} \cdot \mathbf{a}) + (\mathbf{c} \cdot \mathbf{a})$$
$$= 81 + (\mathbf{a} \cdot \mathbf{b} + \mathbf{c} \cdot \mathbf{a}) + (\mathbf{b} \cdot \mathbf{c} + \mathbf{a} \cdot \mathbf{b}) + (\mathbf{b} \cdot \mathbf{c} + \mathbf{c} \cdot \mathbf{a})$$
$$= 81 + \mathbf{a} \cdot (\mathbf{b} + \mathbf{c}) + \mathbf{b} \cdot (\mathbf{c} + \mathbf{a}) + \mathbf{c} \cdot (\mathbf{a} + \mathbf{b})$$
$$= 81 + 0 + 0 + 0 = 81$$

$$\Rightarrow \quad |\mathbf{a} + \mathbf{b} + \mathbf{c}| = 9$$

(B) $[\mathbf{a\ b\ c}]$, write in terms of $(\mathbf{a}_1\ \mathbf{a}_2\ \mathbf{a}_3\ \mathbf{b}_1\ \mathbf{b}_2\ \mathbf{b}_3)$

$$[\mathbf{d\ e\ f}] = \left[\frac{\mathbf{b}\times\mathbf{c}}{[\mathbf{a\ b\ c}]}\ \frac{\mathbf{c}\times\mathbf{a}}{[\mathbf{a\ b\ c}]}\ \frac{\mathbf{a}\times\mathbf{b}}{[\mathbf{a\ b\ c}]}\right] = \frac{1}{[\mathbf{a\ b\ c}]}$$

$$\Rightarrow [\mathbf{a\ b\ c}][\mathbf{d\ e\ f}] = 1$$

(C) $\alpha = \dfrac{\text{ar}(ABCD)}{\text{ar(parallelogram)}}$

$$= \left(\frac{\frac{1}{2}|\mathbf{a}\times(\mathbf{a}+3\mathbf{b})| + \frac{1}{2}|(2\mathbf{a}+3\mathbf{b})\times\mathbf{b}|}{|\mathbf{a}\times\mathbf{b}|}\right) = \frac{5}{2}$$

(D) $x = \dfrac{\mathbf{d}\cdot\mathbf{c}}{[\mathbf{a\ b\ c}]},\ y = \dfrac{\mathbf{d}\cdot\mathbf{a}}{[\mathbf{a\ b\ c}]},\ z = \dfrac{\mathbf{d}\cdot\mathbf{b}}{[\mathbf{a\ b\ c}]}$

$$x + y + z = \frac{\mathbf{d}\cdot(\mathbf{a}+\mathbf{b}+\mathbf{c})}{[\mathbf{a\ b\ c}]}$$

$$\Rightarrow \quad R = \frac{4}{[\mathbf{a\ b\ c}]} = 8$$

91. Given, $\mathbf{a} = \hat{\mathbf{i}} + 2\hat{\mathbf{j}} - 5\hat{\mathbf{k}},\ \mathbf{b} = 3\hat{\mathbf{i}} + 6\hat{\mathbf{j}} + 3\hat{\mathbf{k}},$

$$\mathbf{c} = \frac{17}{5}\hat{\mathbf{i}} + \frac{16}{5}\hat{\mathbf{i}} + 7\hat{\mathbf{k}} \text{ and } \mathbf{d} = 2\hat{\mathbf{i}} + \hat{\mathbf{j}} + \hat{\mathbf{k}}$$

Now, $\mathbf{PQ} = 2\hat{\mathbf{i}} + 4\hat{\mathbf{j}} + 8\hat{\mathbf{k}}$

$$\mathbf{PR} = \frac{12}{5}\hat{\mathbf{i}} + \frac{6}{5}\hat{\mathbf{j}} + 12\hat{\mathbf{k}}$$

$$\mathbf{PS} = \hat{\mathbf{i}} - \hat{\mathbf{j}} + 6\hat{\mathbf{k}}$$

So, $[\mathbf{PQ}\ \mathbf{PR}\ \mathbf{PS}] = \dfrac{1}{5}\begin{vmatrix} 2 & 4 & 8 \\ 12 & 6 & 60 \\ 1 & -1 & 6 \end{vmatrix} = 0$

So, option (a) is incorrect.

Since, $\dfrac{\mathbf{b}+2\mathbf{d}}{3} = \dfrac{(3\hat{\mathbf{i}}+6\hat{\mathbf{j}}+3\hat{\mathbf{k}}) + 2(2\hat{\mathbf{i}}+\hat{\mathbf{j}}+\hat{\mathbf{k}})}{3} = \dfrac{7\hat{\mathbf{i}}+8\hat{\mathbf{j}}+5\hat{\mathbf{k}}}{3}$

Using section formula for internal division,

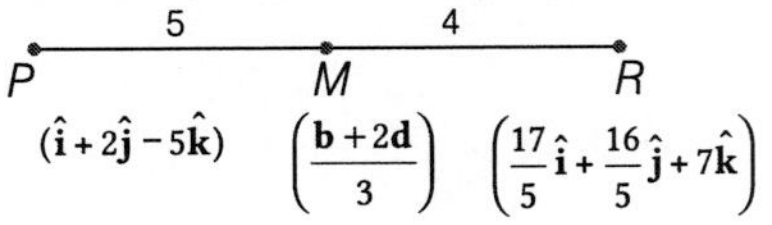

$$M = \frac{\left(5\times\frac{17}{5}\hat{\mathbf{i}} + 5\times\frac{16}{5}\hat{\mathbf{j}} + 5\times7\hat{\mathbf{k}}\right) + (4\hat{\mathbf{i}} + 8\hat{\mathbf{j}} - 20\hat{\mathbf{k}})}{5+4}$$

$$= \frac{21\hat{\mathbf{i}} + 24\hat{\mathbf{j}} + 15\hat{\mathbf{k}}}{9} = \frac{7\hat{\mathbf{i}} + 8\hat{\mathbf{j}} + 5\hat{\mathbf{k}}}{3} = \frac{\mathbf{b}+2\mathbf{d}}{3}$$

So, option (b) is correct.

Hence, there is no need to check another options because this is single choice based questions.

But for our practice, we check options (d).

$$|\mathbf{b}\times\mathbf{d}| = \begin{vmatrix} \hat{\mathbf{i}} & \hat{\mathbf{j}} & \hat{\mathbf{k}} \\ 3 & 6 & 3 \\ 2 & 1 & 1 \end{vmatrix} = |3\hat{\mathbf{i}} + 3\hat{\mathbf{j}} - 9\hat{\mathbf{k}}|$$

$$\Rightarrow \quad |\mathbf{b}\times\mathbf{d}| = \sqrt{9+9+81} = \sqrt{99}$$

$$\Rightarrow \quad |\mathbf{b}\times\mathbf{d}|^2 = 99 \neq 95$$

Hence, option (d) is incorrect.

92. Given, $\mathbf{a} = 3\hat{\mathbf{i}} + \hat{\mathbf{j}} - \hat{\mathbf{k}}$

$$\mathbf{b} = \hat{\mathbf{i}} + b_2\hat{\mathbf{j}} + b_3\hat{\mathbf{k}},\ b_2, b_3 \in R$$

$$\mathbf{c} = c_1\hat{\mathbf{i}} + c_2\hat{\mathbf{j}} + c_3\hat{\mathbf{k}},\ c_1, c_2, c_3 \in R$$

$$b_2\, b_3 > 0, \mathbf{a}\cdot\mathbf{b} = 0$$

$$3 + b_2 - b_3 = 0$$

$$b_3 - b_2 = 3$$

$$\begin{bmatrix} 0 & -c_3 & c_2 \\ c_3 & 0 & -c_1 \\ -c_2 & c_1 & 0 \end{bmatrix}\begin{bmatrix} 1 \\ b_2 \\ b_3 \end{bmatrix} = \begin{bmatrix} 3-c_1 \\ 1-c_2 \\ -1-c_3 \end{bmatrix}$$

$$\begin{bmatrix} -b_2c_3 + b_3c_2 \\ c_3 - c_1b_3 \\ -c_2 + c_1b_2 \end{bmatrix} = \begin{bmatrix} 3-c_1 \\ 1-c_2 \\ -1-c_3 \end{bmatrix}$$

On comparing, we get

$$b_3c_2 - b_2c_3 = 3 - c_1 \quad \text{...(i)}$$

$$c_3 - c_1b_3 = 1 - c_2 \quad \text{...(ii)}$$

$$c_1b_2 - c_2 = -1 - c_3 \quad \text{...(iii)}$$

Eq. (i) $\times\ \hat{\mathbf{i}}$ + Eq. (ii) $\times\ \hat{\mathbf{j}}$ + Eq. (iii) $\times\ \hat{\mathbf{k}}$

$$(b_3c_2 - b_2c_3)\,\hat{\mathbf{i}} + (c_3 - c_1b_3)\,\hat{\mathbf{j}} + (c_1b_2 - c_2)\,\hat{\mathbf{k}}$$

$$= (3\hat{\mathbf{i}} + \hat{\mathbf{j}} - \hat{\mathbf{k}}) - (c_1\hat{\mathbf{i}} + c_2\hat{\mathbf{j}} + c_3\hat{\mathbf{k}})$$

$$\mathbf{c}\times\mathbf{b} = \mathbf{a} - \mathbf{c}\,(\mathbf{c}\times\mathbf{b})\cdot\mathbf{b} = \mathbf{a}\cdot\mathbf{b} - \mathbf{c}\cdot\mathbf{b}$$

$$0 = 0 - \mathbf{c}\cdot\mathbf{b} \quad [\text{given, } \mathbf{a}\cdot\mathbf{b} = 0]$$

$$\mathbf{c}\cdot\mathbf{b} = 0$$

Option (b) is correct.

Similarly, $\mathbf{c}\times\mathbf{b} = \mathbf{a} - \mathbf{c}$

$$(\mathbf{c}\times\mathbf{b})\cdot\mathbf{c} = \mathbf{a}\cdot\mathbf{c} - \mathbf{c}\cdot\mathbf{c}$$

$$0 = \mathbf{a}\cdot\mathbf{c} - |\mathbf{c}|^2$$

$$\mathbf{a}\cdot\mathbf{c} = |\mathbf{c}|^2$$

$$|\mathbf{a}||\mathbf{c}|\cos\theta = |\mathbf{c}|^2$$

$$|\mathbf{a}| = \frac{|\mathbf{c}|}{\cos\theta} \neq 0$$

Option (a) is wrong.

$$|\mathbf{c}| = |\mathbf{a}|\cos\theta = \sqrt{9+1+1}\cos\theta$$

$$|\mathbf{c}| = \sqrt{11}\cos\theta \Rightarrow |\mathbf{c}| \leq \sqrt{11}$$

So, option (d) is correct.

Now, $\quad |\mathbf{b}| = \sqrt{1 + b_2^2 + b_3^2}$

Using, $\quad \mathbf{a}\cdot\mathbf{b} = 0$

$$b_3 - b_2 = 3$$

$$\Rightarrow b_3^2 + b_2^2 - 2b_2b_3 = 9 \quad [\text{squaring}]$$

$$\Rightarrow \quad 1 + b_3^2 + b_2^2 = 10 + 2b_2b_3$$

$$\Rightarrow \quad |\mathbf{b}| = \sqrt{10 + 2b_2b_3} \quad [\text{given, } b_2b_3 > 0]$$

$$|\mathbf{b}| > \sqrt{10}$$

So, option (c) is correct.

93. Given, $\mathbf{OA} = 2\hat{\mathbf{i}} + 2\hat{\mathbf{j}} + \hat{\mathbf{k}},\ \mathbf{OB} = \hat{\mathbf{i}} - 2\hat{\mathbf{j}} + 2\hat{\mathbf{k}}$

and $\quad \mathbf{OC} = \dfrac{1}{2}(\mathbf{OB} - \lambda\mathbf{OA})$

Also, $|\mathbf{OB}\times\mathbf{OC}| = \frac{9}{2}$ ...(i)

Now, $\mathbf{OB}\times\mathbf{OC} = \mathbf{OB}\times\frac{1}{2}(\mathbf{OB}-\lambda\mathbf{OA})$

$$= \frac{-\lambda}{2}\mathbf{OB}\times\mathbf{OA} = \frac{\lambda}{2}(\mathbf{OA}\times\mathbf{OB})$$

We need to find $\mathbf{OA}\times\mathbf{OB}$ for this,

$[\because \mathbf{a}\times\mathbf{b} = -\mathbf{b}\times\mathbf{a}$ and $\mathbf{a}\times\mathbf{a} = 0]$

$$\mathbf{OA}\times\mathbf{OB} = \begin{vmatrix} \hat{\mathbf{i}} & \hat{\mathbf{j}} & \hat{\mathbf{k}} \\ 2 & 2 & 1 \\ 1 & -2 & 2 \end{vmatrix} = 6\hat{\mathbf{i}} - 3\hat{\mathbf{j}} - 6\hat{\mathbf{k}} = 3(2\hat{\mathbf{i}} - \hat{\mathbf{j}} - 2\hat{\mathbf{k}})$$

So, $\mathbf{OB}\times\mathbf{OC} = \frac{3\lambda}{2}(2\hat{\mathbf{i}} - \hat{\mathbf{j}} - 2\hat{\mathbf{k}})$

From Eq. (i), $\left|\frac{3\lambda}{2}\sqrt{4+1+4}\right| = \frac{9}{2} \Rightarrow \left|\frac{9\lambda}{2}\right| = \frac{9}{2}$

$\Rightarrow \frac{9}{2}|\lambda| = \frac{9}{2} \Rightarrow |\lambda| = 1$

$\Rightarrow \lambda = \pm 1$

But $\lambda > 0$

$\therefore \lambda = 1$

So, $\mathbf{OC} = \frac{1}{2}(\mathbf{OB} - \mathbf{OA})$ $[\because \lambda = 1]$

$\Rightarrow \mathbf{OC} = \frac{1}{2}(-\hat{\mathbf{i}} - 4\hat{\mathbf{j}} + \hat{\mathbf{k}}) = -\frac{1}{2}\hat{\mathbf{i}} - 2\hat{\mathbf{j}} + \frac{1}{2}\hat{\mathbf{k}}$

Option (a)

Projection of $\mathbf{OC}$ and $\mathbf{OA} = \frac{\mathbf{OC}\cdot\mathbf{OA}}{|\mathbf{OA}|} = \frac{\frac{1}{2}(-2-8+1)}{3} = \frac{-3}{2}$

Option (b)

Area of $\Delta OAB = \frac{1}{2}|\mathbf{OA}\times\mathbf{OB}| = \frac{1}{2}|\mathbf{OA}||\mathbf{OB}|\sin 90°$

$$= \frac{1}{2}\times 3\times 3 = \frac{9}{2}$$

Option (c)

Area of the $\Delta ABC = \frac{1}{2}|\mathbf{AB}\times\mathbf{AC}| = \frac{1}{2}\left\|\begin{matrix} \hat{\mathbf{i}} & \hat{\mathbf{j}} & \hat{\mathbf{k}} \\ -1 & -4 & 1 \\ -5/2 & -4 & \frac{-1}{2} \end{matrix}\right\|$

$$= \frac{1}{2}|6\hat{\mathbf{i}} - 3\hat{\mathbf{j}} - 6\hat{\mathbf{k}}| = \frac{1}{2}\times 3\times 3 = \frac{9}{2}$$

Option (d)

The acute angle between the diagonals of the parallelogram with adjacent sides $\mathbf{OA}$ and $\mathbf{OC} = \theta$

$$\Rightarrow \frac{(\mathbf{OA}+\mathbf{OC})\cdot(\mathbf{OA}-\mathbf{OC})}{|\mathbf{OA}+\mathbf{OC}||\mathbf{OA}-\mathbf{OC}|} = \cos\theta$$

$$\Rightarrow \cos\theta = \frac{\left(\frac{3}{2}\hat{\mathbf{i}} + \frac{3}{2}\hat{\mathbf{k}}\right)\cdot\left(\frac{5}{2}\hat{\mathbf{i}} + 4\hat{\mathbf{j}} + \frac{1}{2}\hat{\mathbf{k}}\right)}{\frac{3}{2}\sqrt{2}\times\sqrt{\frac{90}{4}}}$$

$$= \frac{18}{3\sqrt{2}\times\sqrt{90}} = \frac{1}{\sqrt{5}} \neq \frac{1}{2} \quad [\therefore \theta \neq \pi/3]$$

94. Given, volume of the parallelopiped $= \sqrt{2}$

i.e. $[\mathbf{u}\ \mathbf{v}\ \mathbf{w}] = \sqrt{2}$, ... (i)

where $\mathbf{u}$, $\mathbf{v}$ and $\mathbf{w}$ are adjacent sides of parallelopiped.

Also, $[\mathbf{u}\ \mathbf{v}\ \mathbf{w}]^2 = \begin{vmatrix} \mathbf{u}\cdot\mathbf{u} & \mathbf{u}\cdot\mathbf{v} & \mathbf{u}\cdot\mathbf{w} \\ \mathbf{v}\cdot\mathbf{u} & \mathbf{v}\cdot\mathbf{v} & \mathbf{v}\cdot\mathbf{w} \\ \mathbf{w}\cdot\mathbf{u} & \mathbf{w}\cdot\mathbf{v} & \mathbf{w}\cdot\mathbf{w} \end{vmatrix} = 2$ [from Eq. (i)]

Let $\mathbf{u}\cdot\mathbf{v} = \lambda$ and substitute rest values, we get

$$\begin{vmatrix} 1 & \lambda & 1 \\ \lambda & 1 & 1 \\ 1 & 1 & 4 \end{vmatrix} = 2 \quad [\because \text{given } \mathbf{u}\cdot\mathbf{w} = 1, \mathbf{v}\cdot\mathbf{w} = 1, \mathbf{w}\cdot\mathbf{w} = 4]$$

$\Rightarrow 4\lambda^2 - 2\lambda = 0 \Rightarrow \mathbf{u}\cdot\mathbf{v} = 0$ (rejected)

or $\mathbf{u}\cdot\mathbf{v} = \frac{1}{2}$

$\therefore \mathbf{u}\cdot\mathbf{v} = \frac{1}{2}$

$\therefore |3\mathbf{u} + 5\mathbf{v}|^2 = 9|\mathbf{u}|^2 + 25|\mathbf{v}|^2 + 3\times 5\times 2\times \mathbf{u}\cdot\mathbf{v}$

$$= 9 + 25 + 30\times\frac{1}{2} = 49 \quad [\because |\mathbf{u}| = |\mathbf{v}| = 1, \text{ given}]$$

$\therefore |3\mathbf{u} + 5\mathbf{v}| = 7$

95. Given vectors $\mathbf{PQ} = a\hat{\mathbf{i}} + b\hat{\mathbf{j}}$ and $\mathbf{PS} = a\hat{\mathbf{i}} - b\hat{\mathbf{j}}$ are adjacent sides of a parallelogram $PQRS$,

so area of parallelogram $PQRS = |\mathbf{PQ}\times\mathbf{PS}| = 2ab = 8$ [given]

$\therefore ab = 4$ ... (i)

According to the question,

$|\mathbf{u}|$ = projection vector of $\mathbf{w} = \hat{\mathbf{i}} + \hat{\mathbf{j}}$ along $\mathbf{PQ}$

$$= \left|\frac{(\hat{\mathbf{i}}+\hat{\mathbf{j}})\cdot(a\hat{\mathbf{i}}+b\hat{\mathbf{j}})}{\sqrt{a^2+b^2}}\right| = \frac{|a+b|}{\sqrt{a^2+b^2}}$$

and similarly, $|\mathbf{v}| = |$ projection vector of $\mathbf{w} = \hat{\mathbf{i}} + \hat{\mathbf{j}}$ along $\mathbf{PS}$

$$= \frac{|(\hat{\mathbf{i}}+\hat{\mathbf{j}})\cdot(a\hat{\mathbf{i}}-b\hat{\mathbf{j}})|}{\sqrt{a^2+b^2}} = \frac{|a-b|}{\sqrt{a^2+b^2}}$$

$\because |\mathbf{u}| + |\mathbf{v}| = |\mathbf{w}|$

$\Rightarrow \frac{|a+b|}{\sqrt{a^2+b^2}} + \frac{|a-b|}{\sqrt{a^2+b^2}} = \sqrt{2}$

$\Rightarrow |a+b| + |a-b| = \sqrt{2}\sqrt{a^2+b^2}$

If $a \geq b > 0$, then $2a = \sqrt{2}\sqrt{a^2+b^2}$

$\Rightarrow 4a^2 = 2a^2 + 2b^2 \Rightarrow a^2 = b^2 \Rightarrow a = b$ ...(ii)

From Eqs. (i) and (ii), we get

$$a = 2 = b$$

$\therefore a + b = 4$

and the length of diagonal $PR = |a\hat{\mathbf{i}} + b\hat{\mathbf{j}} + a\hat{\mathbf{i}} - b\hat{\mathbf{j}}| = |2a\hat{\mathbf{i}}|$

$$= 2a = 4$$

and the angle bisector of vector $\mathbf{PQ}$ and $\mathbf{PS}$ is along the vector

$$\pm\frac{\lambda}{\sqrt{a^2+b^2}}[(a\hat{\mathbf{i}}+b\hat{\mathbf{j}}) \pm (a\hat{\mathbf{i}}-b\hat{\mathbf{j}})]$$

96. It is given that, in a ΔPQR

$$\mathbf{PQ} = \mathbf{c},\ \mathbf{QR} = \mathbf{a} \text{ and } \mathbf{RP} = \mathbf{b},$$

So, $\mathbf{a} + \mathbf{b} + \mathbf{c} = 0$

$\therefore \quad |\mathbf{a}|^2 + \mathbf{a}\cdot\mathbf{b} + \mathbf{a}\cdot\mathbf{c} = 0 \quad \ldots \text{(i)}$

and $\mathbf{a}\cdot\mathbf{b} + |\mathbf{b}|^2 + \mathbf{c}\cdot\mathbf{b} = 0 \quad \ldots \text{(ii)}$

and, also given that $|\mathbf{a}| = 3, |\mathbf{b}| = 4$

and $\dfrac{\mathbf{a}\cdot\mathbf{c} - \mathbf{a}\cdot\mathbf{b}}{\mathbf{c}\cdot\mathbf{a} - \mathbf{c}\cdot\mathbf{b}} = \dfrac{|\mathbf{a}|}{|\mathbf{a}| + |\mathbf{b}|} = \dfrac{3}{7}$

$\Rightarrow \; 7[(\mathbf{a}\cdot\mathbf{c}) - (\mathbf{a}\cdot\mathbf{b})] = 3[(\mathbf{c}\cdot\mathbf{a}) - (\mathbf{c}\cdot\mathbf{b})]$

From Eqs. (i) and (ii), on putting the values of $\mathbf{a}\cdot\mathbf{c}$ and $\mathbf{c}\cdot\mathbf{b}$, we get

$\Rightarrow \; 7[-9 - (\mathbf{a}\cdot\mathbf{b}) - (\mathbf{a}\cdot\mathbf{b})] = 3[-9 - (\mathbf{a}\cdot\mathbf{b}) + 16 + (\mathbf{a}\cdot\mathbf{b})]$

$\Rightarrow \; 7[-9 - 2(\mathbf{a}\cdot\mathbf{b})] = 3 \times 7$

$\Rightarrow \; \mathbf{a}\cdot\mathbf{b} = -6$

$\because \; |\mathbf{a}\times\mathbf{b}|^2 = (|\mathbf{a}||\mathbf{b}|)^2 - (\mathbf{a}\cdot\mathbf{b})^2$

$= 144 - 36 = 108$

97. Given vectors $\mathbf{a} = 2\hat{\mathbf{i}} + \hat{\mathbf{j}} - \hat{\mathbf{k}}$ and $\mathbf{b} = \hat{\mathbf{i}} + 2\hat{\mathbf{j}} + \hat{\mathbf{k}}$

So, $\mathbf{a} + \mathbf{b} = 3\hat{\mathbf{i}} + 3\hat{\mathbf{j}} \Rightarrow |\mathbf{a} + \mathbf{b}| = 3\sqrt{2}$

Since, it is given that projection of $\mathbf{c} = \alpha\mathbf{a} + \beta\mathbf{b}$ on the vector $(\mathbf{a} + \mathbf{b})$ is $3\sqrt{2}$, then

$$\frac{(\mathbf{a}+\mathbf{b})\cdot\mathbf{c}}{|\mathbf{a}+\mathbf{b}|} = 3\sqrt{2}$$

$\Rightarrow \; (\mathbf{a} + \mathbf{b}).(\alpha\mathbf{a} + \beta\mathbf{b}) = 18$

$\Rightarrow \; \alpha(\mathbf{a}\cdot\mathbf{a}) + \beta(\mathbf{a}\cdot\mathbf{b}) + \alpha(\mathbf{b}\cdot\mathbf{a}) + \beta(\mathbf{a}\cdot\mathbf{b}) = 18$

$\Rightarrow \; 6\alpha + 3\beta + 3\alpha + 6\beta = 18 \Rightarrow 9\alpha + 9\beta = 18$

$\Rightarrow \; (\alpha + \beta) = 2 \quad \ldots\text{(i)}$

Now, for minimum value of $[\mathbf{c} - (\mathbf{a}\times\mathbf{b})]\cdot\mathbf{c}$

$= (\alpha\mathbf{a} + \beta\mathbf{b} - (\mathbf{a}\times\mathbf{b}))\cdot(\alpha\mathbf{a} + \beta\mathbf{b})$

$= \alpha^2(\mathbf{a}\cdot\mathbf{a}) + \alpha\beta(\mathbf{a}\cdot\mathbf{b}) + \alpha\beta(\mathbf{a}\cdot\mathbf{b}) + \beta^2(\mathbf{b}\cdot\mathbf{b})$

$[\because (\mathbf{a}\times\mathbf{b})\cdot\mathbf{a} = 0 = (\mathbf{a}\times\mathbf{b})\cdot\mathbf{b}]$

$= 6\alpha^2 + 6\alpha\beta + 6\beta^2 = 6(\alpha^2 + \beta^2 + \alpha\beta)$

$= 6[(\alpha + \beta)^2 - \alpha\beta] = 6[4 - \alpha\beta]$

$= 6[4 - \alpha(2 - \alpha)] = 6[4 - 2\alpha + \alpha^2]$

The minimum value of $6(4 - 2\alpha + \alpha^2) = 6(3) = 18$

[As minimum value of $ax^2 + bx + c = -\dfrac{D}{4a}$, if $a > 0$]

Exercise 3 - Challenging Problems

1. Given, $\mathbf{a} = cx\hat{\mathbf{i}} - 6\hat{\mathbf{j}} + 3\hat{\mathbf{k}}$ and $\mathbf{b} = x\hat{\mathbf{i}} + 2\hat{\mathbf{j}} + 2cx\hat{\mathbf{k}}$

$\because$ **a** and **b** make an obtuse angle with each other.

$\therefore \quad \cos\theta = \dfrac{\mathbf{a}.\mathbf{b}}{|\mathbf{a}||\mathbf{b}|} < 0$

i.e. $\dfrac{cx^2 - 12 + 6cx}{\sqrt{c^2x^2 + 36 + 9}\sqrt{x^2 + 4 + 4c^2x^2}} < 0$

$\Rightarrow \; cx^2 + 6cx - 12 < 0 \quad \ldots\text{(i)}$

Now, two cases are possible.

Case I $\quad c \neq 0$

$\Rightarrow cx^2 + 6cx - 12$ is a quadratic equation which has real solution "iff $A < 0$ and $B^2 - 4AC < 0$"

i.e. if $c < 0$ and $36c^2 + 48c < 0$

i.e. if $c < 0$ and $12c(3c + 4) < 0 \Rightarrow 3c + 4 > 0 \quad [\because c > 0]$

$\Rightarrow \; -\dfrac{4}{3} < c < 0 \quad \ldots\text{(ii)}$

Case II $\quad c = 0$

$\Rightarrow -12 < 0$ which is an identity.

$\therefore \quad c = 0$ satisfy Eq. (i) $\quad \ldots$(iii)

$\therefore$ From Eqs. (ii) and (iii), we get $-\dfrac{4}{3} < c \leq 0$

2. We have, $\mathbf{IP} + \mathbf{IA} = \mathbf{PA}$

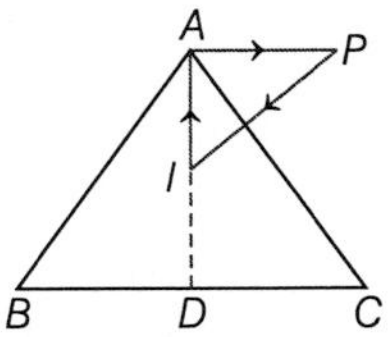

$\Rightarrow \; |\mathbf{PA}|^2 = |\mathbf{PI}|^2 + |\mathbf{IA}|^2 + 2\mathbf{PI}\cdot\mathbf{IA}$

$a|\mathbf{PA}|^2 = a|\mathbf{PI}|^2 + a|\mathbf{IA}|^2 + 2\mathbf{PI}\cdot(a\mathbf{IA}) \quad \ldots\text{(i)}$

Similarly, $b|\mathbf{PB}|^2 = b|\mathbf{PI}|^2 + b|\mathbf{IB}|^2 + 2\mathbf{PI}\cdot(b\,\mathbf{IB}) \quad \ldots\text{(ii)}$

$c|\mathbf{PC}|^2 = c|\mathbf{PI}|^2 + c|\mathbf{IC}|^2 + 2\mathbf{PI}\cdot(c\,\mathbf{IC}) \quad \ldots\text{(iii)}$

On adding Eqs. (i), (ii) and (iii), we get

$a|\mathbf{PA}|^2 + b|\mathbf{PB}|^2 + c|\mathbf{PC}|^2$

$= (a + b + c)|\mathbf{PI}|^2 + a|\mathbf{IA}|^2 + b|\mathbf{IB}|^2 + c|\mathbf{IC}|^2$

$+ 2\mathbf{PI}\cdot|a\mathbf{IA} + b\mathbf{IB} + c\mathbf{IC}|^2$

$\Rightarrow a|\mathbf{PA}|^2 + b|\mathbf{PB}|^2 + c|\mathbf{PC}|^2 = (a + b + c)$

$|\mathbf{PI}|^2 + a|\mathbf{IA}|^2 + b|\mathbf{IB}|^2 + c|\mathbf{IC}|^2$

$[\because a\mathbf{IA} + b\mathbf{IB} + c\mathbf{IC} = \mathbf{0}]$ shown as, since D be point of intersection of AI with side BC, we have $BD : DC = c : b$ and

$\mathbf{AI} : \mathbf{ID} = b + c : a \Rightarrow \mathbf{ID} = \dfrac{c\mathbf{IC} + b\mathbf{IB}}{b + c}$

and $\quad a\,\mathbf{AI} = (\mathbf{b} + \mathbf{c})\,\mathbf{ID}$

$a\,\mathbf{AI} = c\,\mathbf{IC} + b\,\mathbf{IB}$

$\Rightarrow a\,\mathbf{IA} + b\,\mathbf{IB} + c\,\mathbf{IC} = \mathbf{0}$

3. Let O be the centre of the first circle and C be the centre of second. Let a and b be the radii of the two circles. Position vector of C is **c** and AB be point of intersection of two circles.

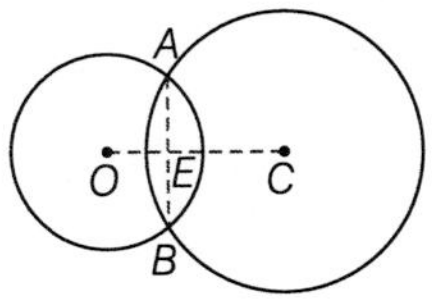

If **r** is the position vector of A.

$\Rightarrow \; \mathbf{CA} = \mathbf{OA} - \mathbf{OC} = \mathbf{r} - \mathbf{c} \quad \ldots\text{(i)}$

$[\because \mathbf{OA} = \mathbf{r}$ and $\mathbf{OC} = \mathbf{c}]$

Also, $\quad \mathbf{r}\cdot\mathbf{r} = a^2$ and $(\mathbf{r} - \mathbf{c})\cdot(\mathbf{r} - \mathbf{c}) = b^2 \quad \ldots\text{(ii)}$

Hence, at the point of intersection of two circle

$a^2 - 2\mathbf{r}\cdot\mathbf{c} + |\mathbf{c}|^2 = b^2 \Rightarrow \mathbf{r}\cdot\mathbf{c} = \dfrac{1}{2}[b^2 - a^2 - |\mathbf{c}|^2]$

If E is the point of intersection of OC and AB, then

$\mathbf{OA} = \mathbf{OE} + \mathbf{EA} = \lambda c + k_1\mathbf{AB}$

$\mathbf{OB} = \mathbf{OE} + \mathbf{EB} = \lambda c + k_2\mathbf{AB}$

$\Rightarrow \; 2\mathbf{OA}\cdot\mathbf{c} = 2\mathbf{r}\cdot\mathbf{c} = 2(\lambda\mathbf{c} + k_1\mathbf{AB})\cdot\mathbf{c} = \mathbf{a}^2 - \mathbf{b}^2 + |\mathbf{c}|^2$

and $\quad 2\,\mathbf{OB}\cdot\mathbf{c} = 2\mathbf{r}\cdot\mathbf{c} = 2(\lambda\mathbf{c} + k_2\mathbf{AB})\cdot\mathbf{c} = \mathbf{a}^2 - \mathbf{b}^2 + |\mathbf{c}|^2$

$\Rightarrow\ 2(\lambda\mathbf{c} - k_1\mathbf{AB})\cdot\mathbf{c} = 2\,(\lambda\mathbf{c} + k_2\mathbf{AB})\,\mathbf{c} \ \Rightarrow\ \mathbf{AB}\cdot\mathbf{c} = 0$

Hence, AB is perpendicular to OC.

4. Take A is the origin and let the position vectors of the points B and C be **b** and **c**, respectively.

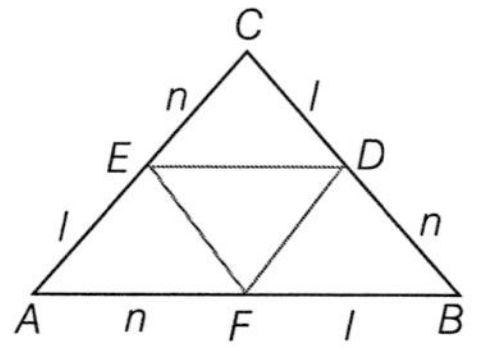

$\therefore$ The position vector of D, E and F are

$$\frac{n\mathbf{c} + \mathbf{b}}{\mathbf{n} + 1}, \frac{\mathbf{c}}{n+1}, \frac{n\mathbf{b}}{n+1}$$

$$\mathbf{FD} = \mathbf{AD} - \mathbf{AF} = \frac{n\mathbf{c} + \mathbf{b} - n\mathbf{b}}{n+1} = \frac{n\mathbf{c} + (1-n)\,\mathbf{b}}{n+1}$$

and $\quad \mathbf{EF} = \mathbf{AF} - \mathbf{AE} = \dfrac{n\mathbf{b} - \mathbf{c}}{n+1}$

Now, vector area of $\Delta ABC = \frac{1}{2}(\mathbf{b}\times\mathbf{c})$ and vector area of ΔDEF

$$= \frac{1}{2}\,(\mathbf{FD}\times\mathbf{FE})$$

$$= \frac{1}{2\,(n+1)^2}[(n\mathbf{b} - \mathbf{c})\times n\mathbf{c} + (1-n)\mathbf{b}]$$

$$= \frac{1}{2(n+1)^2}[n^2\mathbf{b}\times\mathbf{c} + (1-n)\,\mathbf{b}\times\mathbf{c}]$$

$$= \frac{1}{2(n+1)^2}[(n^2 - n + 1)\,(\mathbf{b}\times\mathbf{c})]$$

$$= \frac{n^2 - n + 1}{(n+1)^2}\,\Delta ABC$$

$\therefore$ Area of $\Delta\ DEF = \dfrac{n^2 - n + 1}{(n+1)^2}$ area of $\Delta\ ABC$

5. Let the position verctor of A, B and C be **a**, **b** and **c**, respectively.

We have, $\quad \mathbf{AC}_1 = \dfrac{b}{2}, \mathbf{AB}_1 = \dfrac{c}{2}$

$$\mathbf{AA}_2 = \frac{\mathbf{b} + \mathbf{c}}{2}, \mathbf{AA}_2 = \frac{3\mathbf{c} + \mathbf{b}}{4}$$

Equation of the lines BB_1, AA_2 and C_1A_1 are

$$\mathbf{r} = \mathbf{b} + \lambda_1\left(\frac{\mathbf{c}}{2} - \mathbf{b}\right), \mathbf{r} = \lambda_2\frac{3\mathbf{c} + \mathbf{b}}{4} \text{ and } \mathbf{r} = \frac{\mathbf{b}}{2} + \lambda_3\left(\frac{\mathbf{c}}{2}\right)$$

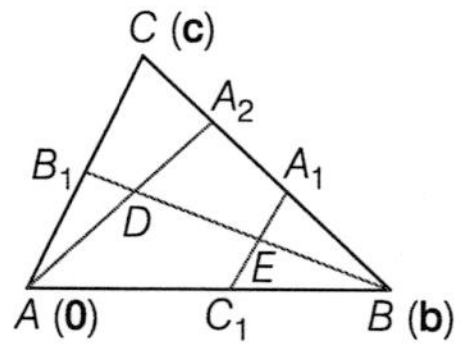

For the point D, we have

$$\mathbf{b} + \lambda_1\left(\frac{\mathbf{c}}{2} - \mathbf{b}\right) = \lambda_2\left(\frac{3\mathbf{c} + \mathbf{b}}{4}\right)$$

$$\mathbf{b}\left(1 - \lambda_1 - \frac{\lambda_2}{4}\right) + \frac{\mathbf{c}}{4}(2\lambda_1 - 3\lambda_2) = 0$$

$$\Rightarrow \qquad \lambda_1 = \frac{6}{7}, \lambda_2 = \frac{4}{7}$$

$$\therefore \qquad \mathbf{AD} = \frac{3\mathbf{c} + \mathbf{b}}{7}$$

For the point E, we have $\mathbf{b} + \lambda_1\left(\dfrac{\mathbf{c}}{2} - \mathbf{b}\right) = \dfrac{\mathbf{b}}{2} + \dfrac{\lambda_3}{2}\,\mathbf{c}$

$$\Rightarrow \qquad \mathbf{b}\left(\frac{1}{2} - \lambda_1\right) + \frac{\mathbf{c}}{2}(\lambda_1 - \lambda_3) = 0 \Rightarrow \lambda_1 = \lambda_3 = \frac{1}{2}$$

$$\therefore \qquad \mathbf{AE} = \frac{2\mathbf{b} + \mathbf{c}}{4}$$

Now, $\quad \mathbf{EA}_2 = \dfrac{3\mathbf{c} + \mathbf{b} - 2\mathbf{b} - \mathbf{c}}{4} = \dfrac{2\mathbf{c} - \mathbf{b}}{4}$

$$\mathbf{DA}_1 = \frac{\mathbf{b} + \mathbf{c}}{2} - \frac{3\mathbf{c} + \mathbf{b}}{7} = \frac{5\mathbf{b} + \mathbf{c}}{14}$$

Area of quadrilateral $EA_1A_2\ D = \frac{1}{2}\,|\mathbf{EA}_2\times\mathbf{DA}_1|$

$$= \frac{1}{112}\,|(2\mathbf{c} - \mathbf{b})\times(5\mathbf{b} + \mathbf{c})| = \frac{1}{112}\,|10\mathbf{c}\times\mathbf{b} - \mathbf{b}\times\mathbf{c}|$$

$$= \frac{11}{112}\,|\mathbf{c}\times\mathbf{b}| = \frac{11}{56}\cdot\frac{1}{2}\,|\mathbf{c}\times\mathbf{b}| = \frac{11}{56}$$

Hence, the required ratio is $\dfrac{11}{56}$.

6. Let G be on MK.

Let the position vectors of B and C with reference to origin A be **b** and **c**.

$\therefore \qquad BC = a,\ CA = b$ and $AB = c$

Now, $\quad \dfrac{BM}{MC} = \dfrac{c}{b}$

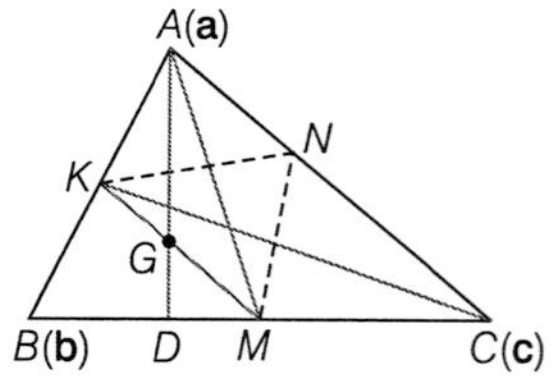

$\therefore$ Position vector of $M = \dfrac{b\mathbf{b} + c\mathbf{c}}{b + c}$

Similarly, position vector of $K = \dfrac{b\,\mathbf{b}}{a + b}$

$$\mathbf{MK} = \mathbf{PV} \text{ of } K - \mathbf{PV} \text{ of } M = \frac{b\mathbf{b}}{a+b} - \frac{b\mathbf{b} + c\mathbf{c}}{b+c}$$

PV of $G = \dfrac{\mathbf{b} + \mathbf{c}}{3}$

$$\mathbf{GK} = \mathbf{PV} \text{ of } \mathbf{K} - \mathbf{PV} \text{ of } \mathbf{G} = \frac{b\mathbf{b}}{a+b} - \frac{\mathbf{b} + \mathbf{c}}{3}$$

Since, G lies on MK, $\mathbf{MK}\times\mathbf{GK} = 0$

$$\Rightarrow \quad \left(\frac{b\mathbf{b}}{a+b} - \frac{b\mathbf{b} + c\mathbf{c}}{b+c}\right)\times\left(\frac{b\mathbf{b}}{a+b} - \frac{\mathbf{b} + \mathbf{c}}{3}\right) = 0$$

$$\Rightarrow \quad -\frac{b\mathbf{b}}{a+b}\times\frac{\mathbf{b} + \mathbf{c}}{3} - \frac{b\mathbf{b}\times c\mathbf{c}}{a+c}$$

$$\times\frac{b\mathbf{b}}{a+b} + \frac{b\mathbf{b} + c\mathbf{c}}{b+c}\times\frac{\mathbf{b} + \mathbf{c}}{3} = 0$$

$$\Rightarrow -\frac{b(\mathbf{b}\times\mathbf{c})}{3(a+b)} - \frac{\mathbf{bc}\,(\mathbf{c}\times\mathbf{b})}{(b+c)\,(a+b)} + \frac{\mathbf{b}\,(\mathbf{b}\times\mathbf{c})}{3\,(b+c)} + \frac{\mathbf{b}\,(\mathbf{c}\times\mathbf{b})}{3} = 0$$

$$\left[\frac{b}{3\,(a+b)} - \frac{bc}{(b+c)\,(a+b)} - \frac{b}{3(b+c)} + \frac{c}{3(b+c)}\right] (\mathbf{c}\times\mathbf{b}) = 0$$

$$\Rightarrow \frac{b}{3(a+b)} - \frac{bc}{(b+c)\,(a+b)} - \frac{b}{3(b+c)} + \frac{c}{3(b+c)} = 0$$

$$\Rightarrow b(b+c) - 3bc - b(a+b) + c(a+b) = 0$$

$$\Rightarrow b^2 + bc - 3bc - ab - b^2 + ac + bc = 0 \Rightarrow ac = ab + bc$$

$$\Rightarrow \frac{1}{b} = \frac{1}{c} + \frac{1}{a} \Rightarrow \frac{2\Delta}{b} = \frac{2\Delta}{c} + \frac{2\Delta}{a}$$

[where, Δ denotes area of $\Delta\ ABC$]

$\Rightarrow P_b = P_a + P_c$ denotes the altitudes drawn through A, B and C, respectively.

7. Let A', B' and C' be the tops of the poles at A, B and C, respectively. Through A' draw a $\Delta A'\ B_1C_1$ congruent to $\Delta\ ABC$ and parallel to the horizontal plane of the park.

Take $A'\ B_1$ as the X-axis and a line perpendicular to it as the Y-axis (in the plane of $\Delta\ A'\ B_1C_1$) and a line through A' and perpendicular to the plane $A'\ B_1C_1$ as the Z-axis.

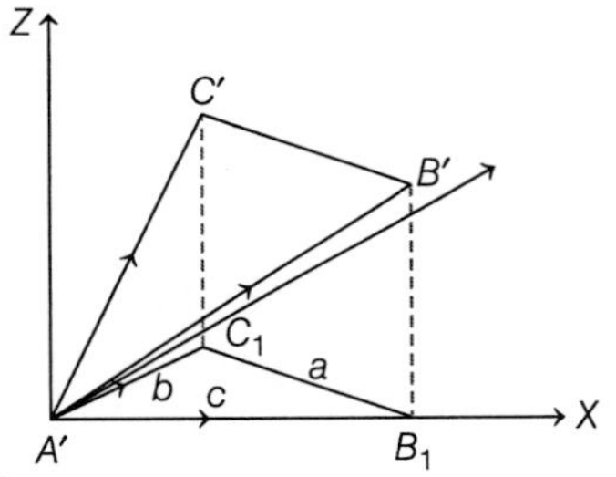

If $\hat{\mathbf{i}}$, $\hat{\mathbf{j}}$ and $\hat{\mathbf{k}}$ are the unit vectors along these axes, then

$$\mathbf{A'B_1} = c\hat{\mathbf{i}}$$
$$\mathbf{A'C_1} = (b\cos A)\hat{\mathbf{i}} + (b\sin A)\hat{\mathbf{j}}$$
$$\mathbf{A'B'} = c\hat{\mathbf{i}} + y\hat{\mathbf{k}}$$
$$\mathbf{A'C'} = (b\cos A)\hat{\mathbf{i}} + (b\sin A)\hat{\mathbf{j}} + z\hat{\mathbf{k}}$$

Since, the planes $A'\,B'\,C'$ is inclined at an angle θ to the plane $A'\,B_1C_1$, angle between the normals to the planes is $(\pi - \theta)$.

Obviously, the unit vector normal to the plane $A'\,B_1C_1$ is $\mathbf{k}$ and the normal vector to $A'\,B'\,C'$ is

$$[(b\cos A)\,\hat{\mathbf{i}} + (b\sin A)\,\hat{\mathbf{j}} + (z)\,\hat{\mathbf{k}}] \times (c\hat{\mathbf{i}} + y\hat{\mathbf{k}})$$
$$= (yb\sin A)\,\hat{\mathbf{i}} - (yb\cos A - zc)\hat{\mathbf{j}} - (bc\sin A)\hat{\mathbf{k}}$$

$$\cos(\pi - \theta) = \frac{[(yb\sin A)\hat{\mathbf{i}} - (yb\cos A - zc)\hat{\mathbf{j}} - (bc\sin A)\hat{\mathbf{k}}]\cdot\hat{\mathbf{k}}}{\sqrt{y^2b^2\sin^2 A + y^2b^2\cos^2 A + z^2c^2 - 2yzbc\cos A + b^2c^2\sin^2 A}}$$

$$\Rightarrow \cos\theta = \frac{\sin A}{\sqrt{\dfrac{y^2}{c^2} + \dfrac{z^2}{b^2} - \dfrac{2yz}{bc}\cos A + \sin^2 A}}$$

$$\Rightarrow \tan\theta = \frac{\sqrt{\dfrac{y^2}{c^2} + \dfrac{z^2}{b^2} - \dfrac{2yz}{bc}\cos A}}{\sin A}$$

8. $$\mathbf{w} + (\mathbf{w}\times\mathbf{u}) = \mathbf{v}$$

$$\Rightarrow \mathbf{w}\times\mathbf{u} = \mathbf{v} - \mathbf{w} \quad \text{...(i)}$$

$$\Rightarrow (\mathbf{w}\times\mathbf{u})^2 = \mathbf{v}^2 + \mathbf{w}^2 - 2\mathbf{v}\cdot\mathbf{w}$$

$$\Rightarrow 2\mathbf{v}\cdot\mathbf{w} = 1 + \mathbf{w}^2 - (\mathbf{u}\times\mathbf{w})^2 \quad \text{...(ii)}$$

Also, on taking dot product of Eq. (i) with $\mathbf{v}$, we get

$$\mathbf{w}\cdot\mathbf{v} + (\mathbf{w}\times\mathbf{u})\cdot\mathbf{v} = \mathbf{v}\cdot\mathbf{v}$$

$$\Rightarrow \mathbf{v}\cdot(\mathbf{w}\times\mathbf{u}) = 1 - \mathbf{w}\cdot\mathbf{v} \quad \text{...(iii)} \ [\because \mathbf{v}\cdot\mathbf{v} = |\mathbf{v}|^2 = 1]$$

Now, $\mathbf{v}\cdot(\mathbf{w}\times\mathbf{u}) = 1 - \frac{1}{2}[1 + \mathbf{w}^2 - (\mathbf{u}\times\mathbf{w})^2]$

[using Eqs. (ii) and (iii)]

$$= \frac{1}{2} - \frac{\mathbf{w}^2}{2} + \frac{(\mathbf{u}\times\mathbf{w})^2}{2} \quad [\because 0 \le \cos^2\theta \le 1]$$

$$= \frac{1}{2}(1 - \mathbf{w}^2 + \mathbf{w}^2\sin^2\theta) \quad \text{...(iv)}$$

As we know, $0 \le \mathbf{w}^2\cos^2\theta \le \mathbf{w}^2$

$$\therefore \frac{1}{2} \ge \frac{1 - \mathbf{w}^2\cos^2\theta}{2} \ge \frac{1 - \mathbf{w}^2}{2} \Rightarrow \frac{1 - \mathbf{w}^2\cos^2\theta}{2} \le \frac{1}{2} \quad \text{...(v)}$$

From Eqs. (iv) and (v), we get $|\mathbf{v}\cdot(\mathbf{w}\times\mathbf{u})| \le \frac{1}{2}$

Equality holds only when $\cos^2\theta = 0 \Rightarrow \theta = \frac{\pi}{2}$

i.e. $\mathbf{u} \perp \mathbf{w} = 0 \Rightarrow \mathbf{u}\cdot\mathbf{w} = 0$

$$\mathbf{w} + (\mathbf{w}\times\mathbf{u}) = \mathbf{v}$$
$$\mathbf{u}\cdot\mathbf{w} + \mathbf{u}\cdot(\mathbf{w}\times\mathbf{u}) = \mathbf{u}\cdot\mathbf{v}$$
$$0 + 0 = \mathbf{u}\cdot\mathbf{v}$$
$$\Rightarrow \mathbf{u}\cdot\mathbf{v} = 0 \Rightarrow \mathbf{u} \perp \mathbf{v}$$

9. α, β and $\alpha\times\beta$ are three non-coplanar vectors. Any vector $\mathbf{R}$ can be represented as a linear combination of these vectors.

$$\Rightarrow \mathbf{R} = k_1\alpha + k_2\beta + k_3(\alpha\times\beta) \quad \text{...(i)}$$

$$\Rightarrow \mathbf{R}\cdot(\alpha\times\beta) = k_3(\alpha\times\beta).(\alpha\times\beta) = k_3(\alpha\times\beta)^2$$

$$\Rightarrow k_3 = \frac{\mathbf{R}\cdot(\alpha\times\beta)}{|\alpha\times\beta|^2} = \frac{[\mathbf{R}\ \alpha\ \beta]}{|\alpha\times\beta|^2}$$

On taking dot product of Eq. (i) with $\alpha\times(\alpha\times\beta)$

$$\Rightarrow \mathbf{R}\cdot\alpha\times(\alpha\times\beta) = k_2[\alpha\times(\alpha\times\beta)]\cdot\beta$$

$$k_2[(\alpha.\beta)\alpha - (\alpha.\alpha)\beta].\beta = k_2[(\alpha.\beta)^2 - \alpha^2\beta^2] = -k_2|\alpha\times\beta|^2$$

$$\Rightarrow k_2 = \frac{-[\mathbf{R}\cdot\{\alpha\times(\alpha\times\beta)\}]}{|\alpha\times\beta|^2}$$

Similarly, $$k_1 = -\frac{[\mathbf{R}\cdot\{\beta\times(\beta\times\alpha)\}]}{|\alpha\times\beta|^2}$$

$$\Rightarrow \mathbf{R} = \frac{-[\mathbf{R}\cdot\{\beta\times(\beta\times\alpha)\}]\,\alpha}{|\alpha\times\beta|^2} - \frac{[\mathbf{R}\cdot\{\alpha\times(\alpha\times\beta)\}]\,\beta}{|\alpha\times\beta|^2} + \frac{[\mathbf{R}\cdot(\alpha\times\beta)](\alpha\times\beta)}{|\alpha\times\beta|^2}$$

$$\Rightarrow \mathbf{R} + \frac{[\mathbf{R}\cdot\{\beta\times(\beta\times\alpha)\}]\alpha}{|\alpha\times\beta|^2} + \frac{[\mathbf{R}\cdot\{\alpha\times(\alpha\times\beta)\}]\,\beta}{|\alpha\times\beta|^2} = \frac{[\mathbf{R}\cdot(\alpha\times\beta)]\,(\alpha\times\beta)}{|\alpha\times\beta|^2}$$

10. Let the centre of base be (0).

$$\mathbf{AB} = 2\hat{\mathbf{j}} \Rightarrow |\mathbf{AB}| = 2$$

$$\Delta OAB = \frac{1}{4}\cdot 4\sqrt{3} = \sqrt{3}$$

$\Rightarrow$ Base area $= 6\sqrt{3}$ sq units

Let height of the pyramid be h.

$$\Rightarrow \frac{1}{3}\cdot 6\sqrt{3}h = 6\sqrt{3} \Rightarrow h = 3 \text{ units}$$

$$\mathbf{AP} = 3\hat{\mathbf{i}} + 2\hat{\mathbf{j}} + 2\sqrt{3}\hat{\mathbf{k}}$$

$\Rightarrow \quad |\mathbf{AP}| = \sqrt{9+4+12} = 5$ units

$\Rightarrow \quad \mathbf{AG} = \sqrt{25-9} = 4$ units

$|\mathbf{AG}| = 4$ units

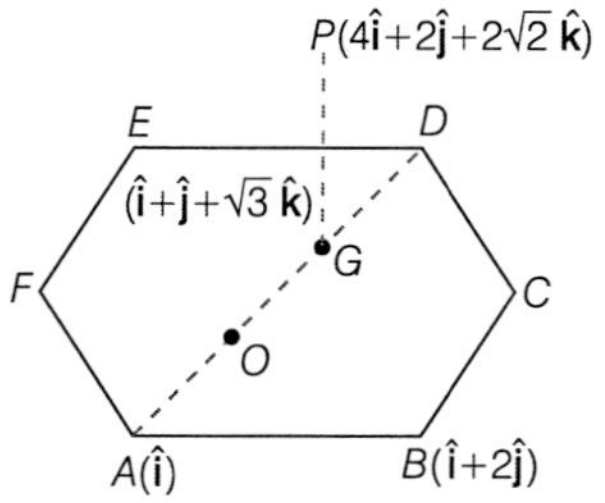

Now, **AG** and **AO** are collinear.

$\Rightarrow \quad \mathbf{AG} = \lambda\mathbf{AO} \Rightarrow |\mathbf{AG}| = |\lambda||\mathbf{AO}|$

$\Rightarrow \quad 2|\lambda| = 4 \Rightarrow |\lambda| = 2$

$\Rightarrow \quad \mathbf{AG} = \pm(\hat{\mathbf{i}} + \hat{\mathbf{j}} + \sqrt{3}\hat{\mathbf{k}})$

$\Rightarrow \quad \mathbf{G} = \pm 2(\hat{\mathbf{i}} + \hat{\mathbf{j}} + \sqrt{3}\hat{\mathbf{k}}) + \hat{\mathbf{i}}$

$$= -(\hat{\mathbf{i}} + 2\hat{\mathbf{j}} + 2\sqrt{3}\hat{\mathbf{k}}), 3\hat{\mathbf{i}} + 2\hat{\mathbf{j}} + 2\sqrt{3}\hat{\mathbf{k}}$$

11. We know from sine rule,

$$\frac{AB}{\sin C} = \frac{AC}{\sin B} = \frac{BC}{\sin A} = 2R = \frac{(AB)(BC)(CA)}{2(\Delta ABC)} \quad \text{...(i)}$$

$$BC = |\mathbf{BC}| = |\hat{\mathbf{c}}\cos\gamma - \hat{\mathbf{b}}\cos\beta|$$

$$= |(\hat{\mathbf{a}}\cdot\hat{\mathbf{b}})\hat{\mathbf{c}} - (\hat{\mathbf{c}}\cdot\hat{\mathbf{a}})\hat{\mathbf{b}}| = |\hat{\mathbf{a}} \times (\hat{\mathbf{b}} \times \hat{\mathbf{c}})|$$

Similarly, $\quad AC = |\mathbf{AC}| = |\hat{\mathbf{b}} \times (\hat{\mathbf{c}} \times \hat{\mathbf{a}})|$

and $\quad AB = |\mathbf{AB}| = |\hat{\mathbf{c}} \times (\hat{\mathbf{a}} \times \hat{\mathbf{b}})|$

Also, $\Delta ABC = \frac{1}{2}|\mathbf{BC} \times \mathbf{BA}|$

$$= \frac{1}{2}|(\hat{\mathbf{c}}\cos\gamma - \hat{\mathbf{b}}\cos\beta) \times (\hat{\mathbf{a}}\cos\alpha - \hat{\mathbf{b}}\cos\beta)|$$

$$= \frac{1}{2}|(\hat{\mathbf{c}} \times \hat{\mathbf{a}})\cos\alpha\cos\gamma + (\hat{\mathbf{b}} \times \hat{\mathbf{c}})\cos\gamma\cos\beta + (\hat{\mathbf{a}} \times \hat{\mathbf{b}})\cos\beta\cos\alpha|$$

$$= \frac{1}{2}|\hat{\eta}_1 \sin\alpha\cos\beta\cos\gamma + \hat{\eta}_2\sin\beta\cos\alpha\cos\gamma + \hat{\eta}_3\sin\gamma\cos\alpha\cos\beta|$$

$\Rightarrow \quad 2\Delta ABC = |\Sigma\hat{\eta}_1 \sin\alpha\cos\beta\cos\gamma|$

$\therefore$ Eq. (i) reduces to

$$\frac{|\hat{\mathbf{a}} \times (\hat{\mathbf{b}} \times \hat{\mathbf{c}})|}{\sin A} = \frac{|\hat{\mathbf{b}} \times (\hat{\mathbf{c}} \times \hat{\mathbf{a}})|}{\sin B} = \frac{|\hat{\mathbf{c}} \times (\hat{\mathbf{a}} \times \hat{\mathbf{b}})|}{\sin C}$$

$$= \frac{\pi|\hat{\mathbf{a}} \times (\hat{\mathbf{b}} \times \hat{\mathbf{c}})|}{|\Sigma \sin\alpha\cos\beta\cos\gamma\,\hat{\eta}|}$$

12. Here, $AM = MD$ and CD is angle bisector of $\angle C$.

$$\mathbf{CD} = \frac{a\mathbf{b} + b\mathbf{a}}{a+b} \text{ and } \mathbf{CM} = \frac{\mathbf{a}+\mathbf{b}}{2}$$

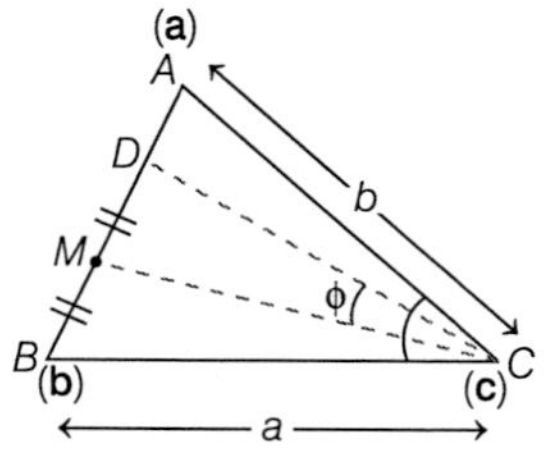

where, $\mathbf{a} = \mathbf{CB}$ and $\mathbf{b} = \mathbf{CA}$

Consequently,

$$\text{Area of } \Delta\, CDM = \frac{1}{2}(\mathbf{CD} \times \mathbf{CM}) = \frac{1}{2}\frac{(a\mathbf{b} + b\mathbf{a}) \times (\mathbf{a}+\mathbf{b})}{2(a+b)}$$

$$= \frac{a(\mathbf{b}\times\mathbf{a}) + a(\mathbf{b}\times\mathbf{b}) + b(\mathbf{a}\times\mathbf{a}) + b(\mathbf{a}\times\mathbf{b})}{4(a+b)}$$

$$= \frac{(b-a)(\mathbf{a}\times\mathbf{b})}{4(a+b)}$$

[using $\mathbf{a}\times\mathbf{a} = \mathbf{b}\times\mathbf{b} = \mathbf{0}$ and $\mathbf{b}\times\mathbf{a} = -\mathbf{a}\times\mathbf{b}$]

$$= \frac{b-a}{2(a+b)}\left(\frac{\mathbf{a}\times\mathbf{b}}{2}\right) = \frac{b-a}{2(a+b)} (\text{Area of } \Delta ABC)$$

$$\therefore \frac{\text{Area of } \Delta\, CDM}{\text{Area of } \Delta ABC} = \frac{(a-b)}{2(a+b)} = \frac{\sin A - \sin B}{2(\sin A + \sin B)}$$

Also, $\mathbf{CD} \,||\, (a\mathbf{b} + b\mathbf{a})$ and $\mathbf{CM} \,||\, (\mathbf{a}+\mathbf{b})$

$$\cos\phi = \frac{(a\mathbf{b} + b\mathbf{a})\cdot(\mathbf{a}+\mathbf{b})}{|a\mathbf{b} + b\mathbf{a}||\mathbf{a}+\mathbf{b}|}$$

$$= \frac{a|\mathbf{b}|^2 + b|\mathbf{a}|^2 + |\mathbf{a}||\mathbf{b}|(a+b)\cos C}{\sqrt{2a^2b^2 + 2a^2b^2\cos C}\sqrt{a^2+b^2+2ab\cos C}}$$

[where, $|\mathbf{a}| = a$ and $|\mathbf{b}| = b$]

$$= \frac{(a+b)\cos(C/2)}{\sqrt{a^2+b^2+2ab\cos C}}$$

$$= \frac{(\sin A + \sin B)\cos(C/2)}{\sqrt{\sin^2 A + \sin^2 B + 2\sin A \sin B \cos C}}$$

13. Let $A(\mathbf{O})$, $B(\mathbf{b})$, $C(\mathbf{c})$, $P(\mathbf{p})$, $Q(\mathbf{q})$, $R(\mathbf{r})$

We have, $p = \frac{b}{3}$ and $\mathbf{Q} = \frac{2\mathbf{b}+\mathbf{c}}{3}$

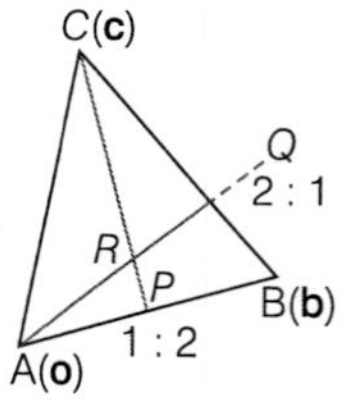

Equation of the line AQ, $\mathbf{r} = \lambda_1\left(\frac{2\mathbf{b}+\mathbf{c}}{3}\right)$

Equation of the line CP, $\mathbf{r} = \mathbf{c} + \lambda_2\left(\frac{\mathbf{b}}{3} - \mathbf{c}\right)$

R is the point of intersection of AQ and CP.

$\Rightarrow$ For point R, we have

$$\lambda_1\left(\frac{2\mathbf{b}+\mathbf{c}}{3}\right) = \mathbf{c} + \lambda_2\left(\frac{\mathbf{b}}{3} - \mathbf{c}\right)$$

$\Rightarrow \frac{2\lambda_1}{3} = \frac{\lambda_2}{3}$ (comparing coefficients of **b** and **c**)

and $\quad \frac{\lambda_1}{3} = 1 - \lambda_2$

On solving, we get $\lambda_1 = 3/7, \lambda_2 = 6/7$

$\Rightarrow \quad \mathbf{R} = \frac{1}{7}(2\mathbf{b}+\mathbf{c})$

Now, $\quad \mathbf{RB} = \mathbf{b} - \frac{1}{7}\cdot(2\mathbf{b}+\mathbf{c}) = \frac{5\mathbf{b}-\mathbf{c}}{7}$

$$\mathbf{RC} = \mathbf{c} - \frac{1}{7}(2\mathbf{b}+\mathbf{c}) = \frac{(6\mathbf{c}-2\mathbf{b})}{7}$$

$\therefore \quad |\mathbf{RB} \times \mathbf{RC}| = \frac{1}{49}(5\mathbf{b} - \mathbf{c}) \times (6\mathbf{c} - 2\mathbf{b})$

$= \frac{1}{49}(30\mathbf{b} \times \mathbf{c} + 2\mathbf{c} \times \mathbf{b}) = \frac{28}{49}(\mathbf{b} \times \mathbf{c})$

$\Rightarrow \quad |\mathbf{RB} \times \mathbf{RC}| = \frac{28}{49}|\mathbf{b} \times \mathbf{c}| = \frac{28}{49} \quad [(\text{area of } \Delta\, ABC) \cdot 2]$

$[\because \text{area of } \Delta\, BRC = 1]$

$\Rightarrow$ Area of $\Delta\, ABC = \frac{1}{2}|\mathbf{RB} \times \mathbf{RC}| \cdot \frac{49}{28} = (\text{Area of } \Delta\, BRC) \cdot \frac{49}{28}$

$\therefore$ Area of $\Delta ABC = \frac{49}{28}$ sq units

14. In the new position, let the vector be $x\hat{\mathbf{i}} + y\hat{\mathbf{j}} + z\hat{\mathbf{k}}$. Since, it is perpendicular to the given vector.

$(x\hat{\mathbf{i}} + y\hat{\mathbf{j}} + z\hat{\mathbf{k}}) \cdot (\hat{\mathbf{i}} + 2\hat{\mathbf{j}} + 2\hat{\mathbf{k}}) = 0$

$\Rightarrow \quad x + 2y + 2z = 0 \quad \text{...(i)}$

The magnitude is the new position which also remains the same.

$\Rightarrow \quad x^2 + y^2 + z^2 = 1 + 4 + 4 = 9 \quad \text{...(ii)}$

The given vector, the vector in new position and the X-axis are coplanar.

$$\Rightarrow \begin{vmatrix} 1 & 0 & 0 \\ 1 & 2 & 2 \\ x & y & z \end{vmatrix} = 0$$

$\Rightarrow \quad y = z \text{ and } x = -4y \quad [\text{using } x + 2y + 2z = 0]$

Hence, $\quad x^2 + y^2 + z^2 = 9 \Rightarrow 16y^2 + y^2 + y^2 = 9$

$\Rightarrow \quad y^2 = \frac{1}{2}, y = \pm\frac{1}{\sqrt{2}} \Rightarrow x = \pm 2\sqrt{2}$

It is given that the vector passes through the positive X-axis.

$\Rightarrow \quad x = 2\sqrt{2} \text{ and } y = 0 - \frac{1}{\sqrt{2}} = z$

Hence, the required vector is $\left(2\sqrt{2}\hat{\mathbf{i}} - \frac{1}{\sqrt{2}}\hat{\mathbf{j}} - \frac{1}{\sqrt{2}}\hat{\mathbf{k}}\right)$.

15. $\hat{\mathbf{x}} + \hat{\mathbf{y}} + \hat{\mathbf{z}} = \mathbf{a} \quad \text{...(i)}$

$\mathbf{a} \cdot \hat{\mathbf{x}} + \mathbf{a} \cdot \hat{\mathbf{y}} + \mathbf{a} \cdot \hat{\mathbf{z}} = \mathbf{a} \cdot \mathbf{a} = |\mathbf{a}|^2 = 4$

$\frac{3}{2} + \frac{7}{4} + \mathbf{a} \cdot \hat{\mathbf{z}} = 4 \Rightarrow \mathbf{a} \cdot \hat{\mathbf{z}} = \frac{3}{4} \quad \text{...(ii)}$

From Eq. (i), $\hat{\mathbf{x}} \cdot (\hat{\mathbf{x}} + \hat{\mathbf{y}} + \hat{\mathbf{z}}) = \hat{\mathbf{x}} \cdot \mathbf{a} = \mathbf{a} \cdot \hat{\mathbf{x}} = \frac{3}{2}$

$\Rightarrow \quad \hat{\mathbf{x}} \cdot \hat{\mathbf{x}} + \hat{\mathbf{x}} \cdot \hat{\mathbf{y}} + \hat{\mathbf{x}} \cdot \hat{\mathbf{z}} = \frac{3}{2}$

$\Rightarrow \quad 1 + \hat{\mathbf{x}} \cdot \hat{\mathbf{y}} + \hat{\mathbf{x}} \cdot \hat{\mathbf{z}} = \frac{3}{2}$

$\Rightarrow \quad \hat{\mathbf{x}} \cdot \hat{\mathbf{y}} + \hat{\mathbf{x}} \cdot \hat{\mathbf{z}} = \frac{1}{2} \quad \text{...(iii)}$

From Eq. (i), $\hat{\mathbf{y}} \cdot (\hat{\mathbf{x}} + \hat{\mathbf{y}} + \hat{\mathbf{z}}) = \hat{\mathbf{y}} \cdot \mathbf{a} = \frac{7}{4}$

$\hat{\mathbf{x}} \cdot \hat{\mathbf{y}} + 1 + \hat{\mathbf{y}} \cdot \hat{\mathbf{z}} = \frac{7}{4}$

$\hat{\mathbf{x}}.\hat{\mathbf{y}} + \hat{\mathbf{y}} \cdot \hat{\mathbf{z}} = \frac{3}{4} \quad \text{...(iv)}$

From Eq. (i), $\quad (\hat{\mathbf{x}} + \hat{\mathbf{y}} + \hat{\mathbf{z}})^2 = (\mathbf{a})^2$

$\Rightarrow \hat{\mathbf{x}} \cdot \hat{\mathbf{x}} + \hat{\mathbf{y}} \cdot \hat{\mathbf{y}} + \hat{\mathbf{z}} \cdot \hat{\mathbf{z}} + 2(\hat{\mathbf{x}} \cdot \hat{\mathbf{y}} + \hat{\mathbf{y}} \cdot \hat{\mathbf{z}} + \hat{\mathbf{z}} \cdot \hat{\mathbf{x}}) = |\mathbf{a}|^2$

$3 + 2(\hat{\mathbf{x}} \cdot \hat{\mathbf{y}} + \hat{\mathbf{y}} \cdot \hat{\mathbf{z}} + \hat{\mathbf{z}} \cdot \hat{\mathbf{x}}) = 4 \quad \text{...(v)}$

From Eqs. (iii), (iv) and (v), we get

$\hat{\mathbf{y}} \cdot \hat{\mathbf{z}} = 0, \hat{\mathbf{x}} \cdot \hat{\mathbf{z}} = -\frac{1}{4}, \hat{\mathbf{x}} \cdot \hat{\mathbf{y}} = \frac{3}{4}$

Now, $\quad \hat{\mathbf{x}} \times (\hat{\mathbf{y}} \times \hat{\mathbf{z}}) = \mathbf{b}$

$(\hat{\mathbf{x}} \cdot \hat{\mathbf{z}})\hat{\mathbf{y}} - (\hat{\mathbf{x}} \cdot \hat{\mathbf{y}})\hat{\mathbf{z}} = \mathbf{b}$

$-\frac{1}{4}\hat{\mathbf{y}} - \frac{3}{4}\hat{\mathbf{z}} = \mathbf{b} \quad \text{...(vi)}$

Again, $\quad (\hat{\mathbf{x}} \times \hat{\mathbf{y}}) \times \hat{\mathbf{z}} = \mathbf{c}$

$(\hat{\mathbf{x}} \cdot \hat{\mathbf{z}})\hat{\mathbf{y}} - (\hat{\mathbf{y}} \cdot \hat{\mathbf{z}})\hat{\mathbf{x}} = \mathbf{c}$

$\Rightarrow \quad -\frac{1}{4}\hat{\mathbf{y}} = \mathbf{c}$

$\hat{\mathbf{y}} = -4\mathbf{c} \quad [\text{from Eq. (vi)}]$

$\hat{\mathbf{z}} = \frac{4}{3}(\mathbf{c} - \mathbf{b})$

From Eq. (i), $\hat{\mathbf{x}} = \mathbf{a} - \hat{\mathbf{y}} - \hat{\mathbf{z}}$

$\hat{\mathbf{x}} = \frac{1}{3}(3\mathbf{a} + 4\mathbf{b} + 8\mathbf{c})$

$\hat{\mathbf{x}} = \frac{1}{3}(3\mathbf{a} + 4\mathbf{b} + 8\mathbf{c})$

$\hat{\mathbf{y}} = -4\mathbf{c}; \hat{\mathbf{z}} = \frac{4}{3}(\mathbf{c} - \mathbf{b})$

16. Here, $\mathbf{OC} = \mathbf{x}$, $\mathbf{CA} = \mathbf{b}$ and $\mathbf{CB} = \mathbf{a}$

$OA = \mathbf{b} - x$ and $OB = \mathbf{a} - x$

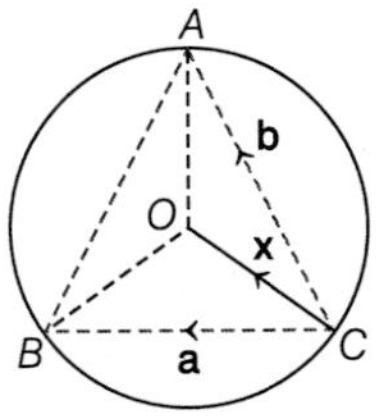

Now, $\quad \mathbf{OA}^2 = \mathbf{OB}^2 = \mathbf{OC}^2$

$\mathbf{x}^2 = (\mathbf{a} - \mathbf{x})^2 = (\mathbf{b} - \mathbf{x})^2$

$\Rightarrow \quad \mathbf{x} \cdot \mathbf{x} = (\mathbf{a} - \mathbf{x}) \cdot (\mathbf{a} - \mathbf{x}) = (\mathbf{b} - \mathbf{x})(\mathbf{b} - \mathbf{x})$

$\Rightarrow \quad \mathbf{x} \cdot \mathbf{x} = \mathbf{a} \cdot \mathbf{a} - 2\mathbf{a} \cdot \mathbf{x} + \mathbf{x} \cdot \mathbf{x} = \mathbf{b} \cdot \mathbf{b} - 2\mathbf{b} \cdot \mathbf{x} + \mathbf{x} \cdot \mathbf{x}$

$\mathbf{a} \cdot \mathbf{x} = \frac{\mathbf{a}^2}{2} \text{ and } \mathbf{b} \cdot \mathbf{x} = \frac{\mathbf{b}^2}{2} \quad \text{...(i)}$

Now, if we take $\mathbf{x} = \lambda\mathbf{a} + \mu\mathbf{b}$, then from Eq. (i)

$\lambda\mathbf{a}^2 + \mu \cdot \mathbf{a} \cdot \mathbf{b} = \frac{\mathbf{a}^2}{2} \quad \text{...(ii)}$

and $\quad \lambda\mathbf{a} \cdot \mathbf{b} + \mu\mathbf{b}^2 = \frac{b^2}{2} \quad \text{...(iii)}$

On solving Eqs. (ii) and (iii), we get

$\lambda = \frac{\mathbf{a}^2\mathbf{b}^2 - \mathbf{b}^2(\mathbf{a} \cdot \mathbf{b})}{2(\mathbf{a}^2\mathbf{b}^2) - (\mathbf{a} \cdot \mathbf{b})^2}$ and $\mu = \frac{\mathbf{a}^2\mathbf{b}^2 - \mathbf{a}^2(\mathbf{a} \cdot \mathbf{b})}{2(\mathbf{a}^2\mathbf{b}^2) - (\mathbf{a} \cdot \mathbf{b})^2}$

$\Rightarrow \quad \mathbf{x} = \frac{1}{2}\frac{\mathbf{a}^2\mathbf{b}^2 - \mathbf{b}^2(\mathbf{a} \cdot \mathbf{b})}{(\mathbf{a}^2\mathbf{b}^2) - (\mathbf{a} \cdot \mathbf{b})^2}\mathbf{a} + \frac{1}{2}\frac{\mathbf{a}^2\mathbf{b}^2 - \mathbf{a}^2(\mathbf{a} \cdot \mathbf{b})}{(\mathbf{a}^2\mathbf{b}^2) - (\mathbf{a} \cdot \mathbf{b})^2} \cdot \mathbf{b}$

"

Mathematics is, in its own ways, the poetry of logical ideas.

-Albert Einstein

3

Three Dimensional Coordinate System

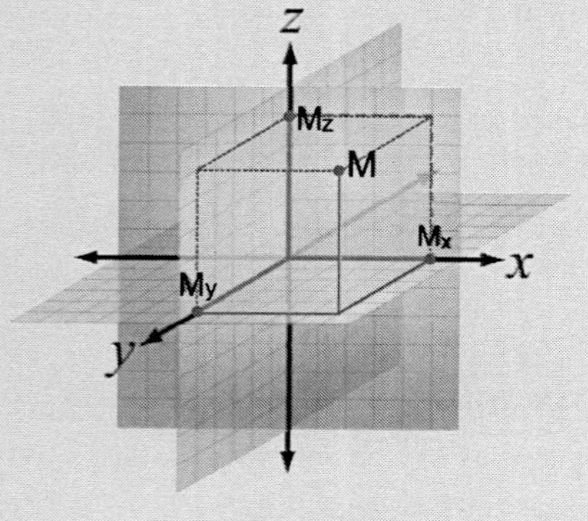

Learning Milestones

Milestone 1 Introduction to Three Dimensional Coordinate System

- Coordinates of a Point in Space
- Shifting of Origin
- Distance Formula
- Section Formula
- Direction Cosines and Direction Ratios of a Vector
- Projection of the Line Segment Joining Two Points on a Given Line

Milestone 2 Lines

- Equation of a Straight Line in Space
- Angle Between Two Lines
- Foot of Perpendicular and Distance of a Point From Line
- Reflection or Image of a Point in a Straight Line
- Shortest Distance Between Two Lines
- Point of Intersection of Lines

Milestone 3 Planes

- Equation of Plane in Various Form
- Angle Between Two Planes
- Family of Planes
- Two Sides of a Plane
- Distance of a Point from a Plane
- Equation of Planes Bisecting the Angle Between Two Planes
- Line and Plane
- Equation of a Plane Containing Two Intersecting Lines

Practice Milestones

Practice Milestone 1- JEE Main Pattern

Practice Milestone 2 - JEE Advanced Pattern

Practice Milestone 3 - Challenging Problems

Milestone 1 Introduction to Three Dimensional Coordinate System

• Coordinates of a Point in Space • Shifting of Origin • Distance Formula • Section Formula • Direction Cosines and Direction Ratios of a Vector • Projection of the Line Segment Joining Two Points on a Given Line

Let three mutually perpendicular lines $X'OX, Y'OY$ and $Z'OZ$ intersecting at O such that two of them $Y'OY$ and $Z'OZ$ lie in the plane of paper and third $X'OX$ is perpendicular to the plane of the paper and is projecting out from the plane of paper. The three mutually perpendicular lines be X, Y and Z-axes. They determine three mutually perpendicular planes called coordinate planes. These planes divides space in eight regions called octants.

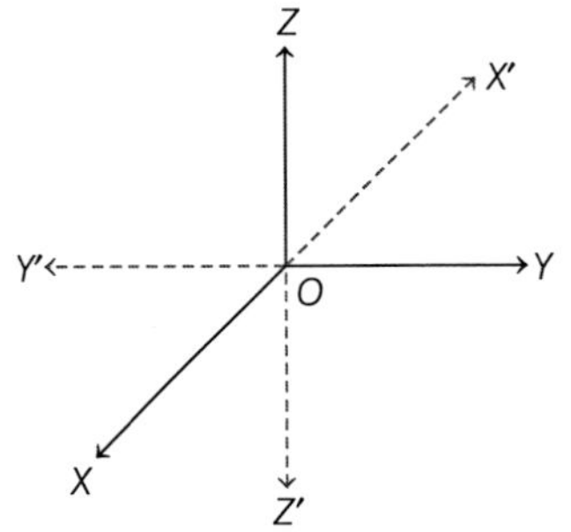

Here, OX, OY and OZ are positive axes and OX', OY' and OZ' are corresponding negative axes.

3.1 Coordinates of a Point in Space

Let P be a point in space. Through P, draw three planes parallel to the coordinate axes to meet the axes at A, B and C, respectively.

Let $OA = x$, $OB = y$ and $OC = z$. These three numbers taken in order are called **coordinates** of a point P and written as $P(x, y, z)$.

Thus, **x-coordinate of a point P** = Length of perpendicular from P to YZ-plane with proper sign.

y-coordinate of a point P = Length of perpendicular from P to ZX-plane with proper sign.

z-coordinate of a point P = Length of perpendicular from P to XY-plane with proper sign.

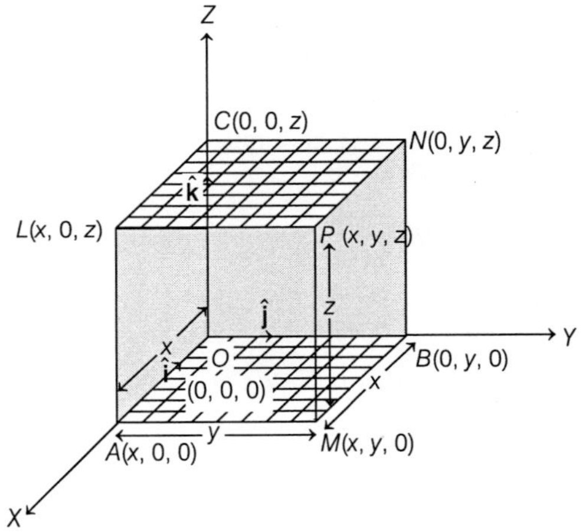

Sign of Coordinates

The sign of coordinates of the points in the octants in which the space is divided are given in the following table

Octants	I	II	III	IV	V	VI	VII	VIII
Coordinates	$XOYZ$	$X'OYZ$	$X'OY'Z$	$XOY'Z$	$XOYZ'$	$X'OYZ'$	$X'OY'Z'$	$XOY'Z'$
x	+	−	−	+	+	−	−	+
y	+	+	−	−	+	+	−	−
z	+	+	+	+	−	−	−	−

Example 1. Name the octants in which the following points lie.

$(1, 2, 3)$, $(4, -2, 3)$, $(4, -2, -5)$, $(4, 2, -5)$, $(-4, 2, -5)$, $(-4, 2, 5)$, $(-3, -1, 6)$, $(2, -4, -7)$

Sol. The name of octants in which given points lie, are given in the following table

Point	Octant	Name
(1, 2, 3)	I (all the coordinates are positive)	$XOYZ$
(4, – 2, 3)	IV (y-coordinate is negative)	$XOY'Z$
(4, – 2, – 5)	VIII (y and z-coordinates are negative)	$XOY'Z'$
(4, 2, – 5)	V (z-coordinate is negative)	$XOYZ'$
(–4, 2, – 5)	VI (x and z-coordinates are negative)	$X'OYZ'$
(–4, 2, 5)	II (x-coordinate is negative)	$X'OYZ$
(–3, –1, 6)	III (x and y-coordinates are negative)	$X'OY'Z$
(2, –4, –7)	VIII (y and z-coordinates are negative)	$XOY'Z'$

3.2 Shifting of Origin

Shifting the origin to another point without changing the directions of the axes is called the translation of axes.

Let the origin $O(0, 0, 0)$ be shifted to another point $O'(x', y', z')$ without changing the direction of axes. Let the new coordinates frame be $O'X'Y'Z'$.
Let $P(x, y, z)$ be a point with respect to the coordinate frame $OXYZ$. Then, coordinates of point P with respect to new coordinates frame $O'X'Y'Z'$ are (x_1, y_1, z_1), where $x_1 = x - x', y_1 = y - y', z_1 = z - z'$.

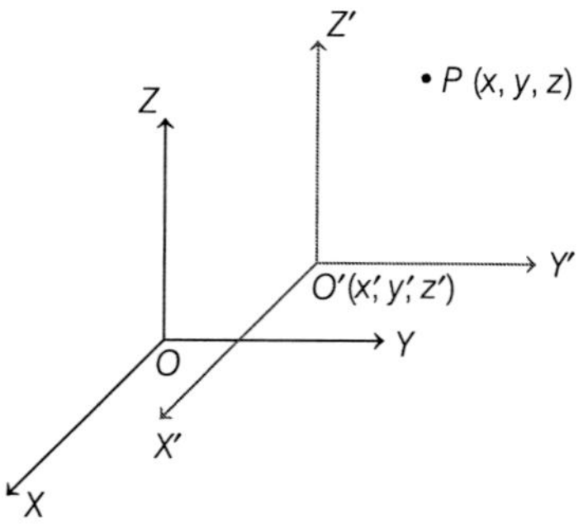

Example 2. If the origin is shifted to point $(1, 2, -3)$ without changing the directions of the axes, then find the new coordinates of the point $(0, 4, 5)$ with respect to new frame.

Sol. In the new frame $x_1 = x - x', y_1 = y - y', z_1 = z - z'$, where (x', y', z') is shifted origin.

$\Rightarrow \quad x_1 = 0 - 1 = -1, y_1 = 4 - 2 = 2, z_1 = 5 + 3 = 8$

Hence, the coordinates of the point with respect to the new coordinates frame are $(-1, 2, 8)$.

3.3 Distance Formula

The distance between the points $P(x_1, y_1, z_1)$ and $Q(x_2, y_2, z_2)$ is given by

$$PQ = \sqrt{(x_2 - x_1)^2 + (y_2 - y_1)^2 + (z_2 - z_1)^2}$$

Proof Let O be the origin and let $P(x_1, y_1, z_1)$ and $Q(x_2, y_2, z_2)$ be two given points.

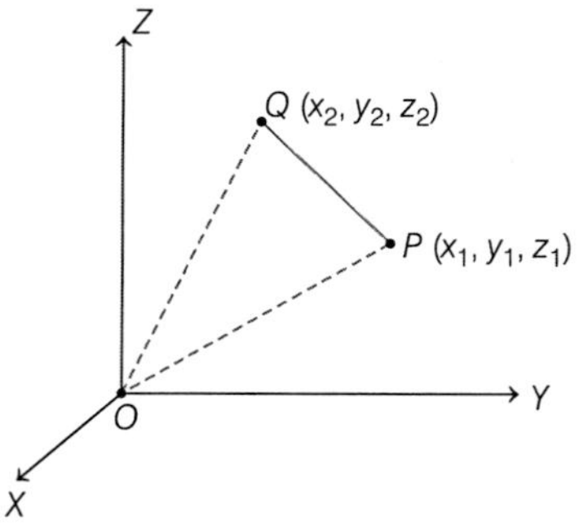

Then, $\mathbf{OP} = x_1\hat{\mathbf{i}} + y_1\hat{\mathbf{j}} + z_1\hat{\mathbf{k}}$, $\mathbf{OQ} = x_2\hat{\mathbf{i}} + y_2\hat{\mathbf{j}} + z_2\hat{\mathbf{k}}$

Now, $\mathbf{PQ}$ = Position vector of Q – Position vector of P

$$= \mathbf{OQ} - \mathbf{OP}$$
$$= (x_2\hat{\mathbf{i}} + y_2\hat{\mathbf{j}} + z_2\hat{\mathbf{k}}) - (x_1\hat{\mathbf{i}} + y_2\hat{\mathbf{j}} + z_1\hat{\mathbf{k}})$$
$$= (x_2 - x_1)\hat{\mathbf{i}} + (y_2 - y_1)\hat{\mathbf{j}} + (z_2 - z_1)\hat{\mathbf{k}}$$

$$\therefore \quad PQ = |\mathbf{PQ}|$$
$$= \sqrt{(x_2 - x_1)^2 + (y_2 - y_1)^2 + (z_2 - z_1)^2}$$

Hence, $PQ = \sqrt{(x_2 - x_1)^2 + (y_2 - y_1)^2 + (z_2 - z_1)^2}$

JEE Focus Points

- **Distance from origin** Let O be the origin and $P(x, y, z)$ be any point, then $OP = \sqrt{x^2 + y^2 + z^2}$
- **Distance of a point from coordinate axes** Let $P(x, y, z)$ be any point in the space. Let PA, PB and PC be the perpendiculars drawn from P to be axes OX, OY, OZ, respectively. Then,
  $$PA = \sqrt{y^2 + z^2}, \; PB = \sqrt{x^2 + z^2}, \; P = \sqrt{x^2 + y^2}$$
- **Distance of a point from XY, YZ and ZX-plane** Let $P(x, y, z)$ be any point in the space, then distance from
  XY-plane $= |z|$, YZ-plane $= |x|$, ZX-plane $= |y|$
- Three points $P(x_1, y_1, z_1)$, $Q(x_2, y_2, z_2)$ and $R(x_3, y_3, z_3)$ are collinear, then $PQ + QR = PR$

Example 3. Find the distance between the points $P(-2, 4, 1)$ and $Q(1, 2, -5)$.

Sol. We have, $PQ = \sqrt{(1 + 2)^2 + (2 - 4)^2 + (-5 - 1)^2}$

$$PQ = \sqrt{3^2 + (-2)^2 + (-6)^2}$$
$$= \sqrt{9 + 4 + 36}$$
$$= \sqrt{49} = 7 \text{ units}$$

Example 4. Find the distance of point $P(4, -6, 7)$ from X, Y and Z-axes and from XY, YZ and ZX-planes.

Sol. Distance of point $P(4, -6, 7)$ from X-axis

$$= \sqrt{y^2 + z^2} = \sqrt{(-6)^2 + 7^2} = \sqrt{36 + 49} = \sqrt{85}$$

Distance of point $P(4, -6, 7)$ from Y-axis

$$= \sqrt{x^2 + z^2} = \sqrt{4^2 + 7^2} = \sqrt{16 + 49} = \sqrt{65}$$

Distance of point $P(4, -6, 7)$ from Z-axis

$$= \sqrt{x^2 + y^2} = \sqrt{4^2 + (-6)^2} = \sqrt{16 + 36} = \sqrt{52}$$

Distance of point $P(4, -6, 7)$ from XY-plane $= |z| = 7$

Distance of point $P(4, -6, 7)$ from YZ-plane $= |x| = 4$

Distance of point $P(4, -6, 7)$ from ZX-plane $= |y| = |-6| = 6$

Example 5. Prove by using distance formula that the points $P(1, 2, 3)$, $Q(-1, -1, -1)$ and $R(3, 5, 7)$ are collinear.

Decoding the Question

With the help of distance formula, check whether the condition $AC = AB + BC$ is satisfied or not. If it is satisfied, then A, B and C are collinear otherwise not.

Sol. We have, $PQ = \sqrt{(-1-1)^2 + (-1-2)^2 + (-1-3)^2}$

$$= \sqrt{4 + 9 + 16} = \sqrt{29}$$

$$QR = \sqrt{(3+1)^2 + (5+1)^2 + (7+1)^2}$$

$$= \sqrt{16 + 36 + 64} = \sqrt{116} = 2\sqrt{29}$$

and $PR = \sqrt{(3-1)^2 + (5-2)^2 + (7-3)^2}$

$$= \sqrt{4 + 9 + 16} = \sqrt{29}$$

Since, $QR = QP + PR$

Therefore, the given points are collinear.

3.4 Section Formula

Vector Form

1. Section Formula for Internal Division

Let P and Q be two points whose position vectors are $\mathbf{r}_1$ and $\mathbf{r}_2$ respectively. Let R be a point on PQ dividing it in the ratio $m : n$. Then, the position vector of R is given by $\mathbf{r} = \dfrac{m\mathbf{r}_2 + n\mathbf{r}_1}{m + n}$.

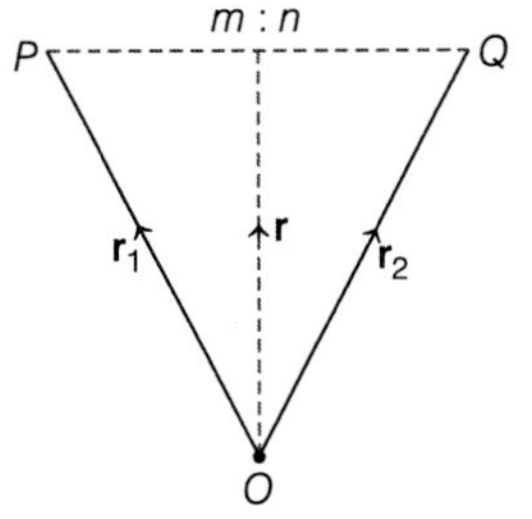

Proof Let O be the origin.

Then, $\mathbf{OP} = \mathbf{r}_1$, $\mathbf{OQ} = \mathbf{r}_2$ and $\mathbf{OR} = \mathbf{r}$

Now, $\dfrac{PR}{RQ} = \dfrac{m}{n}$

$$\Rightarrow \quad n\mathbf{PR} = m\mathbf{RQ}$$

$$\Rightarrow \quad n(\mathbf{OR} - \mathbf{OP}) = m(\mathbf{OQ} - \mathbf{OR})$$

$$\Rightarrow \quad n(\mathbf{r} - \mathbf{r}_1) = m(\mathbf{r}_2 - \mathbf{r})$$

$$\Rightarrow \quad (m + n)\mathbf{r} = m\mathbf{r}_2 + n\mathbf{r}_1$$

$$\Rightarrow \quad \mathbf{r} = \frac{m\mathbf{r}_2 + n\mathbf{r}_1}{m + n}$$

Mid-point formula Let P and Q be two points whose position vectors are given by $\mathbf{r}_1$ and $\mathbf{r}_2$ respectively. Then, the position vector of the mid-point R of PQ is given by, $\mathbf{r} = \dfrac{\mathbf{r}_1 + \mathbf{r}_2}{2}$.

2. Section Formula for External Division

Let P and Q be the points whose position vectors are $\mathbf{r}_1$ and $\mathbf{r}_2$ respectively. Let R be a point on PQ dividing it externally in the ratio $m : n$. Then, the position vector of R is given by,

$$\mathbf{r} = \frac{m\mathbf{r}_2 - n\mathbf{r}_1}{m - n}$$

Proof Let O be the origin.

Then, $\mathbf{OP} = \mathbf{r}_1$, $\mathbf{OQ} = \mathbf{r}_2$ and $\mathbf{OR} = \mathbf{r}$

Now, $\dfrac{PR}{QR} = \dfrac{m}{n}$

$$\Rightarrow \quad n\mathbf{PR} = m\mathbf{QR}$$

$$\Rightarrow \quad n(\mathbf{OR} - \mathbf{OP}) = m(\mathbf{OR} - \mathbf{OQ})$$

$$\Rightarrow \quad n(\mathbf{r} - \mathbf{r}_1) = m(\mathbf{r} - \mathbf{r}_2)$$

$$\Rightarrow \quad (m - n)\mathbf{r} = m\mathbf{r}_2 - n\mathbf{r}_1$$

$$\Rightarrow \quad \mathbf{r} = \left(\frac{m\mathbf{r}_2 - n\mathbf{r}_1}{m - n}\right)$$

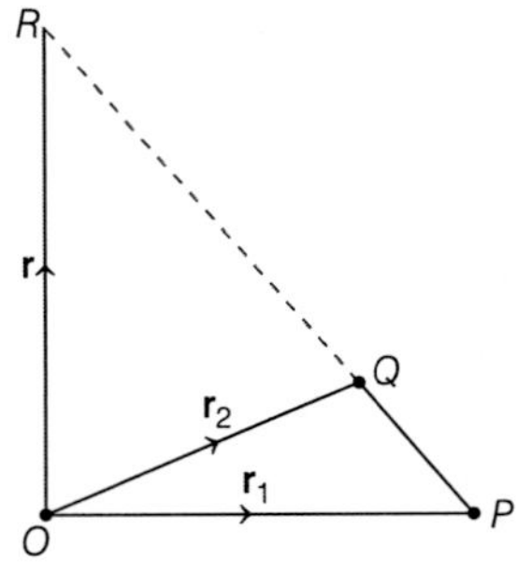

Cartesian Form

Consider two points $P(x_1, y_1, z_1)$ and $Q(x_2, y_2, z_2)$ of a line segment PQ and R be any point on PQ which divides PQ in ratio $m : n$.

1. If $R(x, y, z)$ is a point dividing the join of $P(x_1, y_1, z_1)$ and $Q(x_2, y_2, z_2)$ in the ratio $m : n$.

   Then, $x = \dfrac{mx_2 + nx_1}{m+n}, y = \dfrac{my_2 + ny_1}{m+n}, z = \dfrac{mz_2 + nz_1}{m+n}$

2. The coordinates of the mid-point of the joint of $P(x_1, y_1, z_1)$ and $Q(x_2, y_2, z_2)$ are

   $$\left(\frac{x_1 + x_2}{2}, \frac{y_1 + y_2}{2}, \frac{z_1 + z_2}{2}\right)$$

3. The coordinates of a point R which divides the join of $P(x_1, y_1, z_1)$ and $Q(x_2, y_2, z_2)$ externally in the ratio $m : n$ are

   $$\left(\frac{mx_2 - nx_1}{m-n}, \frac{my_2 - ny_1}{m-n}, \frac{mz_2 - nz_1}{m-n}\right)$$

4. The coordinates of centroid of triangle with vertices $(x_1, y_1, z_1), (x_2, y_2, z_2), (x_3, y_3, z_3)$ are

   $$\left(\frac{x_1 + x_2 + x_3}{3}, \frac{y_1 + y_2 + y_3}{3}, \frac{z_1 + z_2 + z_3}{3}\right)$$

5. Centroid of tetrahedron with vertices (x_1, y_1, z_1), (x_2, y_2, z_2), (x_3, y_3, z_3), (x_4, y_4, z_4) is

   $$\left(\frac{x_1 + x_2 + x_3 + x_4}{4}, \frac{y_1 + y_2 + y_3 + y_4}{4}, \frac{z_1 + z_2 + z_3 + z_4}{4}\right)$$

Example 6. Find the ratio in which plane $2x + 3y + 5z = 1$ divides the line joining the points $(1, 0, -3)$ and $(1, -5, 7)$.

Sol. Let $2x + 3y + 5z = 1$ divides $(1, 0, -3)$ and $(1, -5, 7)$ in the ratio of $k : 1$ at point P.

Then, $P = \left(\dfrac{k+1}{k+1}, \dfrac{-5k}{k+1}, \dfrac{7k-3}{k+1}\right)$ which must satisfy

$$2x + 3y + 5z = 1$$

$$\Rightarrow \quad 2\left(\frac{k+1}{k+1}\right) + 3\left(\frac{-5k}{k+1}\right) + 5\left(\frac{7k-3}{k+1}\right) = 1$$

$$\Rightarrow \quad 2k + 2 - 15k + 35k - 15 = k + 1$$

$$\Rightarrow \quad 21k = 14 \Rightarrow k = \frac{2}{3}$$

$\therefore$ $2x + 3y + 5z = 1$, divides $(1, 0, -3)$ and $(1, -5, 7)$ in the ratio of $2 : 3$.

Example 7. If $A(3, 2, -4)$, $B(5, 4, -6)$ and $C(9, 8, -10)$ are three collinear points, then find the ratio in which point C divides AB.

Sol. Let C divide AB in the ratio $\lambda : 1$.

Then, $C \equiv \left(\dfrac{5\lambda + 3}{\lambda + 1}, \dfrac{4\lambda + 2}{\lambda + 1}, \dfrac{-6\lambda - 4}{\lambda + 1}\right) = (9, 8, -10)$

On comparing, $5\lambda + 3 = 9\lambda + 9$ or $4\lambda = -6$

$$\therefore \quad \lambda = -\frac{3}{2}$$

Also, from $4\lambda + 2 = 8\lambda + 8$ and $-6\lambda - 4 = -10\lambda - 10$, we get the same value of λ.

$\therefore$ C divides AB in the ratio $3 : 2$ externally.

Example 8. Find the ratio in which the line joining the points $(1, 2, 3)$ and $(-3, 4, -5)$ is divided by XY-plane also, find the coordinates of the point of division.

> **Decoding the Question**
> First use section formula and then apply for XY-plane, z-coordinate is 0.

Sol. Let the line joining two points $A(1, 2, 3)$ and $B(-3, 4, -5)$ be divided by XY-plane at a point C in the ratio $k : 1$, then coordinates of C are

$$\left(\frac{-3k + 1}{k+1}, \frac{4k+2}{k+1}, \frac{-5k+3}{k+1}\right) \quad \text{...(i)}$$

In XY-plane, z-coordinate is 0.

$$\therefore \quad \frac{-5k + 3}{k+1} = 0 \Rightarrow k = \frac{3}{5}$$

So, the ratio is $3 : 5$.

On putting $k = \dfrac{3}{5}$ in Eq. (i), we get

Coordinates of C are $\left(\dfrac{-1}{2}, \dfrac{11}{4}, 0\right)$

3.5 Direction Cosines and Direction Ratios of a Vector

1. Direction Cosines (DC's)

If α, β and γ are the angles which a vector **OP** makes with the positive directions of the coordinate axes OX, OY and OZ respectively.

Then, $\cos\alpha$, $\cos\beta$ and $\cos\gamma$ are known as direction cosines of **OP** and are generally denoted by letters l, m and n, respectively.

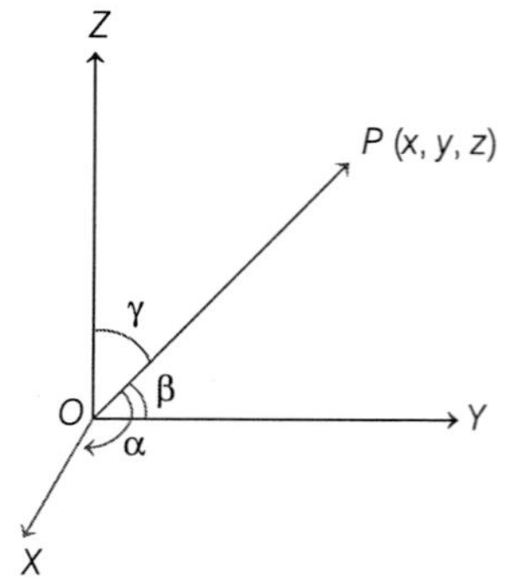

Thus, $l=\cos\alpha$; $m=\cos\beta$; $n=\cos\gamma$. The angles α, β and γ are known as direction angles and they satisfy the condition $0 \le \alpha, \beta, \gamma \le \pi$.

It can be seen from the figure

$$\cos\alpha = \frac{x}{OP}$$

Similarly, $$\cos\beta = \frac{y}{OP}$$

$$\cos\gamma = \frac{z}{OP}$$

where, OP is $|\mathbf{OP}|$.

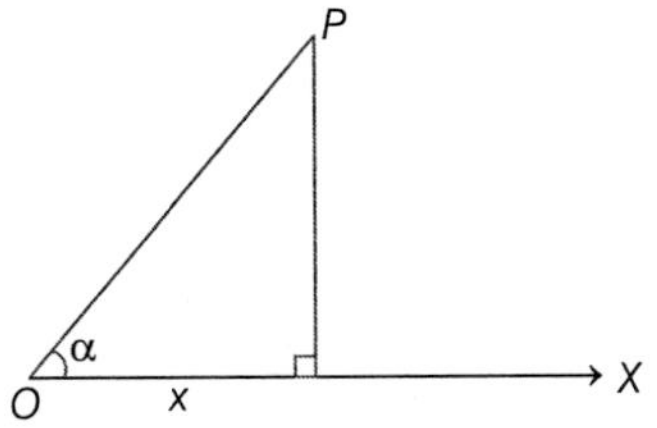

Clearly, $OP = \sqrt{x^2+y^2+z^2}$

So, $l^2+m^2+n^2 = \cos^2\alpha + \cos^2\beta + \cos^2\gamma$

$$= \frac{x^2+y^2+z^2}{OP^2}$$

$$= \frac{x^2+y^2+z^2}{x^2+y^2+z^2} = 1$$

$\therefore$ $l^2+m^2+n^2 = \cos^2\alpha+\cos^2\beta+\cos^2\gamma = 1$

$\therefore$ If $\mathbf{OP} = \mathbf{r} = x\hat{\mathbf{i}} + y\hat{\mathbf{j}} + z\hat{\mathbf{k}}$

Then, $\hat{\mathbf{r}} = l\hat{\mathbf{i}} + m\hat{\mathbf{j}} + n\hat{\mathbf{k}}$

By definition it follows that the direction cosines of the X-axis are $\cos 0°, \cos 90°, \cos 90°$ i.e. $(1, 0, 0)$.

Similarly, direction cosines of the Y and Z-axes are $(0, 1, 0)$ and $(0, 0, 1)$ respectively.

Example 9. What are the direction cosines of a line which is equally inclined to the coordinate axes?

Sol. If α, β and γ are the angles that a line makes with the coordinate axes, then if they are equally inclined.

$\Rightarrow \quad \alpha = \beta = \gamma$

Also, $l^2+m^2+n^2 = 1$

$\Rightarrow \quad \cos^2\alpha + \cos^2\beta + \cos^2\gamma = 1$

$\Rightarrow \quad \cos^2\alpha + \cos^2\alpha + \cos^2\alpha = 1$

$\Rightarrow \quad 3\cos^2\alpha = 1$

$\Rightarrow \quad \cos\alpha = \pm\frac{1}{\sqrt{3}} = \cos\beta = \cos\gamma$

$\therefore$ Direction cosines are

$$\left(\frac{1}{\sqrt{3}}, \frac{1}{\sqrt{3}}, \frac{1}{\sqrt{3}}\right) \text{ or } \left(-\frac{1}{\sqrt{3}}, -\frac{1}{\sqrt{3}}, -\frac{1}{\sqrt{3}}\right).$$

Example 10. A line OP through origin O is inclined at $30°$ and $45°$ to OX and OY, respectively. Find the angle at which it is inclined to OZ.

Sol. Let l, m and n be the direction cosines of the given vector.

$$l^2+m^2+n^2 = 1$$

where, $\alpha = 30°$ and $\beta = 45°$

$\therefore \quad \cos^2\alpha + \cos^2\beta + \cos^2\gamma = 1$

$\Rightarrow \quad \cos^2 30° + \cos^2 45° + \cos^2\gamma = 1$

$\Rightarrow \quad \left(\frac{\sqrt{3}}{2}\right)^2 + \left(\frac{1}{\sqrt{2}}\right)^2 + \cos^2\gamma = 1$

$\Rightarrow \quad \cos^2\gamma = 1 - \frac{3}{4} - \frac{1}{2}$

$\Rightarrow \quad \cos^2\gamma = \frac{4-3-2}{4}$

$\Rightarrow \quad \cos^2\gamma = -\frac{1}{4}$,

which is not possible.

$\therefore$ There exists no point which is inclined to 30° to X-axis and 45° to Y-axis.

Example 11. Find the direction cosines of a vector $\mathbf{r}$ which is equally inclined to OX, OY and OZ. If $|\mathbf{r}|$ is given, then find the total number of such vectors.

Sol. Let l, m and n be the direction cosines of $\mathbf{r}$.

Since, $\mathbf{r}$ is equally inclined with X, Y and Z-axes.

$\therefore \quad l^2+m^2+n^2 = 1$

$\Rightarrow \quad 3l^2 = 1 \quad [\because l = m = n]$

$\Rightarrow \quad l = \pm\frac{1}{\sqrt{3}}$

$\therefore$ Direction cosines of $\mathbf{r}$ are

$$\pm\frac{1}{\sqrt{3}}, \pm\frac{1}{\sqrt{3}}, \pm\frac{1}{\sqrt{3}}$$

Now, $\mathbf{r} = |\mathbf{r}|(l\hat{\mathbf{i}} + m\hat{\mathbf{j}} + n\hat{\mathbf{k}})$

$\Rightarrow \quad \mathbf{r} = |\mathbf{r}|\left(\pm\frac{1}{\sqrt{3}}\hat{\mathbf{i}} \pm \frac{1}{\sqrt{3}}\hat{\mathbf{j}} \pm \frac{1}{\sqrt{3}}\hat{\mathbf{k}}\right)$

Since, '+' and '–' signs can be arranged at three planes.

There are eight vectors (i.e. $2\times2\times2$) which are equally inclined to axes.

2. Direction Ratios (DR's)

Let l, m and n be the direction cosines of a vector $\mathbf{r}$ and a, b and c be three numbers such that a, b and c are proportional to l, m and n

i.e. $\frac{l}{a} = \frac{m}{b} = \frac{n}{c} = k$ or $(l, m, n) = (ka, kb, kc)$

$\Rightarrow (a, b, c)$ are direction ratios.

Relation between Direction Ratios and Direction Cosines

To obtain direction cosines from direction ratios, let a, b and c be direction ratios of a vector $\mathbf{r}$ having direction cosines l, m and n. Then,

$$l=\lambda a, m=\lambda b, n=\lambda c \qquad \text{[by definition]}$$

$$\therefore \quad l^2+m^2+n^2=1$$

$$\Rightarrow \quad a^2\lambda^2+b^2\lambda^2+c^2\lambda^2=1$$

$$\Rightarrow \quad \lambda=\pm\frac{1}{\sqrt{a^2+b^2+c^2}}$$

So,

$$l=\pm\frac{a}{\sqrt{a^2+b^2+c^2}},$$

$$m=\pm\frac{b}{\sqrt{a^2+b^2+c^2}},$$

and

$$n=\pm\frac{c}{\sqrt{a^2+b^2+c^2}}$$

JEE Focus Points

Concept Inside Video

- There can be infinitely many direction ratios for a given vector but the direction cosines are unique.
- The direction ratios of a line passing through two points $P(x_1, y_1, z_1)$ and $Q(x_2, y_2, z_2)$ are given by (x_2-x_1), (y_2-y_1) and (z_2-z_1).
- The direction ratios of two parallel lines are proportional, but the direction cosines of two parallel line are same set.

Example 12. Find the direction ratios and direction cosines of the line joining two points $(2,-4,5)$ and $(0,1,-1)$.

Sol. Given, two points $P(2,-4,5)$ and $Q(0,1,-1)$

Direction ratios of $PQ=(0-2),(1+4),(-1-5)$

$$=(-2,5,-6)$$

Now, direction cosines of

$$PQ=\left(\frac{-2}{\sqrt{4+25+36}},\frac{5}{\sqrt{4+25+36}},\frac{-6}{\sqrt{4+25+36}}\right)$$

$$=\left(\frac{-2}{\sqrt{65}},\frac{5}{\sqrt{65}},\frac{-6}{\sqrt{65}}\right)$$

JEE SCANNER

Example Similar to PYQ Asked in JEE Main 2016

PQR is a triangle with vertices $P(2,3,5)$, $Q(-1,3,2)$ and $R(x,5,z)$. If the median through P is equally inclined to the axes, then the values of x^2+z^2 is ......

Sol. Let PL is the median from point P to QR.

So, coordinates of point L are

$$\left(\frac{-1+x}{2},\frac{3+5}{2},\frac{2+z}{2}\right)=\left(\frac{x-1}{2},4,\frac{z+2}{2}\right)$$

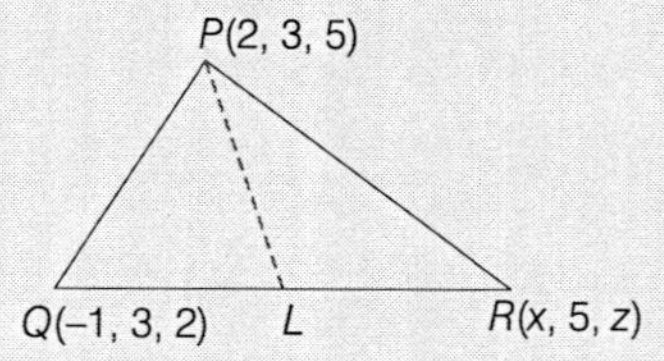

$\therefore$ Direction ratios of median through P are

$$\left(\frac{x-1}{2}-2,4-3,\frac{z+2}{2}-5\right)=\left(\frac{x-5}{2},1,\frac{z-8}{2}\right)$$

Since, median is equally inclined to the axes, therefore direction ratios must be equal

i.e. $$\frac{x-5}{2}=1=\frac{z-8}{2}$$

$$\Rightarrow \quad x-5=2$$

$$\Rightarrow \quad x=7$$

and $$z-8=2$$

$$\Rightarrow \quad z=10$$

$$\therefore \quad x^2+z^2=7^2+10^2$$

$$=49+100$$

$$=149$$

Skill Builder

For Sol.

ABC is a triangle with vertices $A(3,5,-3)$, $B(3,2,1)$ and $C(\lambda,-2,\mu)$. If the median through A is equally inclined to the axes, then find the value of $\lambda^3-\mu^3$.

- **For more practice** See Q.15 of Milestone Practice 1.

Example 13. If the points $(0,1,-2)$, $(3,\lambda,-1)$ and $(\mu,-3,-4)$ are collinear, then verify whether the point $(12,9,2)$ is also on the same line.

Sol. Let the points be A, B and C, whose coordinates are $(0,1,-2)$, $(3,\lambda,-1)$ and $(\mu,-3,-4)$ respectively.

Let $D=(12,9,2)$

$\Rightarrow$ DR's of $AB=(3-0,\lambda-1,-1+2)=(3,\lambda-1,1)$

DR's of $AC=(\mu-0,-3-1,-4-(-2))=(\mu,-4,-2)$

Since A, B and C are collinear.

$$\Rightarrow \quad \frac{3}{\mu}=\frac{\lambda-1}{-4}=\frac{1}{-2}\Rightarrow \mu=-6,\lambda=3$$

$\therefore$ Direction ratios of AB are $(3,2,1)$.

Now, direction ratios of AD are $(12-0,9-1,2-(-2))$ or $(12,8,4)$.

Here, $\quad \frac{3}{12}=\frac{2}{8}=\frac{1}{4}$

$\therefore \quad AB \parallel AD$

Since, AB and AD lie on same straight line.

Hence, the point $(12,9,2)$ is on the same line.

3. Angle between Two Vectors in Terms of Direction Cosines and Direction Ratios

Let $\mathbf{a}$ and $\mathbf{b}$ be two given vectors with direction cosines l_1,m_1,n_1 and l_2,m_2,n_2 respectively.

Then, $\mathbf{a}=l_1\hat{\mathbf{i}}+m_1\hat{\mathbf{j}}+n_1\hat{\mathbf{k}}$ and $\mathbf{b}=l_2\hat{\mathbf{i}}+m_2\hat{\mathbf{j}}+n_2\hat{\mathbf{k}}$

$\therefore \cos\theta=\dfrac{\mathbf{a}\cdot\mathbf{b}}{|\mathbf{a}|\cdot|\mathbf{b}|}$, where θ be the angle between $\mathbf{a}$ and $\mathbf{b}$.

$$\Rightarrow \cos\theta=\frac{(l_1\hat{\mathbf{i}}+m_1\hat{\mathbf{j}}+n_1\hat{\mathbf{k}})\cdot(l_2\hat{\mathbf{i}}+m_2\hat{\mathbf{j}}+n_2\hat{\mathbf{k}})}{|l_1\hat{\mathbf{i}}+m_1\hat{\mathbf{j}}+n_1\hat{\mathbf{k}}||l_2\hat{\mathbf{i}}+m_2\hat{\mathbf{j}}+n_2\hat{\mathbf{k}}|}$$

$$\Rightarrow \cos\theta=\frac{l_1l_2+m_1m_2+n_1n_2}{\sqrt{l_1^2+m_1^2+n_1^2}\sqrt{l_2^2+m_2^2+n_2^2}}$$

$$\Rightarrow \quad \cos\theta=l_1l_2+m_1m_2+n_1n_2 \qquad [\because l^2+m^2+n^2=1]$$

Also, $\sin^2\theta=1-\cos^2\theta$

$$=(l_1^2+m_1^2+n_1^2)(l_1^2+m_2^2+n_2^2)-(l_1l_2+m_1m_2+n_1n_2)^2$$

$$\Rightarrow \sin^2\theta=(m_1n_2-m_2n_1)^2+(n_1l_2-n_2l_1)^2+(l_1m_2-l_2m_1)^2$$

$$\Rightarrow \quad \sin\theta=\pm\sqrt{(m_1n_2-m_2n_1)^2+(n_1l_2-n_2l_1)^2+(l_1m_2-l_2m_1)^2}$$

JEE Focus Points

- Acute angle θ between the two lines having direction cosines l_1,m_1,n_1 and l_2,m_2,n_2 is given by
$$\cos\theta=|l_1l_2+m_1m_2+n_1n_2|.$$
$$\sin\theta=\sqrt{(l_1m_2-l_2m_1)^2+(m_1n_2-m_2n_1)^2+(n_1l_2-n_2l_1)^2}$$
- If a_1,b_1,c_1 and a_2,b_2,c_2 are the direction ratios of two lines, then the acute angle θ between them is given by
$$\cos\theta=\frac{|a_1a_2+b_1b_2+c_1c_2|}{\sqrt{a_1^2+b_1^2+c_1^2}\sqrt{a_2^2+b_2^2+c_2^2}}$$
$$\sin\theta=\frac{\sqrt{(a_1b_2-a_2b_1)^2+(b_1c_2-b_2c_1)^2+(c_1a_2-c_2a_1)^2}}{\sqrt{a_1^2+b_1^2+c_1^2}\sqrt{a_2^2+b_2^2+c_2^2}}$$
- The two lines with direction cosines l_1,m_1,n_1 and l_2,m_2,n_2 are perpendicular to each other, if
$$l_1l_2+m_1m_2+n_1n_2=0$$
- The two lines with direction cosines l_1,m_1,n_1 and l_2,m_2,n_2 are parallel to each other, if
$$\frac{l_1}{l_2}=\frac{m_1}{m_2}=\frac{n_1}{n_2}$$
- The two straight lines are perpendicular, if
$$a_1a_2+b_1b_2+c_1c_2=0$$
- The two straight lines are parallel, if
$$\frac{a_1}{a_2}=\frac{b_1}{b_2}=\frac{c_1}{c_2}$$

Example 14. Find the angle between the lines whose direction cosines are $\left(-\frac{\sqrt{3}}{4},\frac{1}{4},-\frac{\sqrt{3}}{2}\right)$ and $\left(-\frac{\sqrt{3}}{4},\frac{1}{4},\frac{\sqrt{3}}{2}\right)$.

Sol. Let θ be the required angle.

Then,
$$\cos\theta=l_1l_2+m_1m_2+n_1n_2$$
$$=\frac{3}{16}+\frac{1}{16}-\frac{3}{4}$$
$$=-\frac{1}{2}$$

$\therefore \quad \cos\theta=-\frac{1}{2}$

$\Rightarrow \quad \theta=120^\circ$

JEE SCANNER

Example Similar to PYQ Asked in JEE Main 2021

The angle between the lines whose direction cosines are given by $l+m+n=0$ and $2l^2+2m^2-n^2=0$, is

(a) $\frac{\pi}{3}$ (b) $\frac{\pi}{6}$ (c) $\cos^{-1}\left(\frac{-1}{3}\right)$ (d) $\cos^{-1}\left(\frac{-2}{3}\right)$

Sol. $l^2+m^2+n^2=1$

$$l+m+n=0 \quad ...(i)$$
$$\Rightarrow 2l^2+2m^2-n^2=0 \quad ...(ii)$$
$$\Rightarrow 2(l^2+m^2)-n^2=0$$
$$\Rightarrow 2(1-n^2)=n^2$$
$$\Rightarrow 3n^2=2$$
$$\Rightarrow n=\pm\sqrt{\frac{2}{3}} \quad ...(iii)$$
$$\Rightarrow 2(l^2+m^2)=n^2=[-(l+m)]^2 \quad ...(iv)$$
$$\Rightarrow 2l^2+2m^2=l^2+m^2+2lm$$
$$\Rightarrow l^2+m^2-2lm=0$$
$$\Rightarrow (l-m)^2=0 \Rightarrow l=m$$
$$\Rightarrow l+m=\mp\sqrt{\frac{2}{3}} \Rightarrow 2l=\mp\sqrt{\frac{2}{3}}$$
$$\therefore l=\pm\frac{1}{\sqrt{6}}, m=\pm\frac{1}{\sqrt{6}}$$

Direction cosines are $\left(\frac{1}{\sqrt{6}},\frac{1}{\sqrt{6}},\sqrt{\frac{2}{3}}\right)$ and $\left(\frac{1}{\sqrt{6}},\frac{1}{\sqrt{6}},-\sqrt{\frac{2}{3}}\right)$

or $\left(-\frac{1}{\sqrt{6}},-\frac{1}{\sqrt{6}},\sqrt{\frac{2}{3}}\right)$ and $\left(-\frac{1}{\sqrt{6}},-\frac{1}{\sqrt{6}},-\sqrt{\frac{2}{3}}\right)$.

Let θ be the angle between the lines, then

$$\cos\theta=\frac{1}{\sqrt{6}}\times\frac{1}{\sqrt{6}}+\frac{1}{\sqrt{6}}\times\frac{1}{\sqrt{6}}+\sqrt{\frac{2}{3}}\times\left(-\sqrt{\frac{2}{3}}\right)=\frac{1}{6}+\frac{1}{6}-\frac{2}{3}$$
$$\cos\theta=\frac{1}{3}-\frac{2}{3}=\frac{-1}{3}\Rightarrow\theta=\cos^{-1}\left(\frac{-1}{3}\right)$$

The angle between these lines in both the cases is $\cos^{-1}\left(-\frac{1}{3}\right)$.

Skill Builder

The angle between the lines whose direction cosines are given by $l+m+n=0$ and $l^2+m^2-n^2=0$, is

(a) $\frac{\pi}{4}$ (b) $\cos^{-1}\left(\frac{14}{7\sqrt{3}}\right)$

(c) $\cos^{-1}\left(\frac{12}{7\sqrt{3}}\right)$ (d) $\frac{\pi}{3}$

For Sol.

■ **For more practice** See Q.18 of Milestone Practice 1.

Example 15. Find the acute angle between two diagonal of a cube.

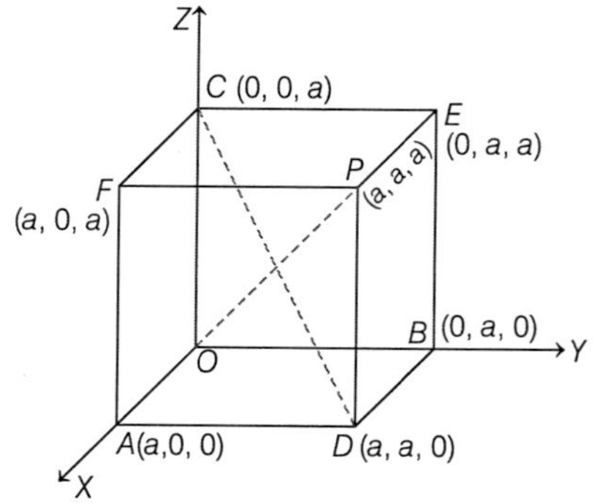

Sol. From the figure given below, the direction ratios of the diagonals OP and CD of a given cube are given by

$$a-0, a-0, a-0 \text{ and } a-0, a-0, 0-a$$

and hence their respective direction cosines are

$$\frac{a}{\sqrt{a^2+a^2+a^2}},\frac{a}{\sqrt{a^2+a^2+a^2}},\frac{a}{\sqrt{a^2+a^2+a^2}}$$

i.e. $\frac{1}{\sqrt{3}},\frac{1}{\sqrt{3}},\frac{1}{\sqrt{3}}$.

and $\frac{a}{\sqrt{a^2+a^2+a^2}},\frac{a}{\sqrt{a^2+a^2+a^2}},\frac{-a}{\sqrt{a^2+a^2+a^2}}$

i.e. $\frac{1}{\sqrt{3}},\frac{1}{\sqrt{3}},\frac{-1}{\sqrt{3}}$

Let θ be the angle between these diagonals, then

$$\cos\theta=\frac{1}{\sqrt{3}}\times\frac{1}{\sqrt{3}}+\frac{1}{\sqrt{3}}\times\frac{1}{\sqrt{3}}+\frac{1}{\sqrt{3}}\times\frac{-1}{\sqrt{3}}$$
$$=\frac{1}{3}+\frac{1}{3}-\frac{1}{3}=\frac{1}{3}$$
$$\Rightarrow \theta=\cos^{-1}\left(\frac{1}{3}\right)$$

Example 16. Find the direction cosines of the line which is perpendicular to the lines with direction cosines proportional to $(1,-2,-2)$ and $(0,2,1)$.

Sol. If l, m and n are the direction cosines of the line perpendicular to the given line, then

$$l\cdot(1)+m\cdot(-2)+n\cdot(-2)=0$$
$$\Rightarrow l-2m-2n=0 \quad ...(i)$$
and
$$l\cdot 0+m\cdot 2+n\cdot 1=0$$
$$0+2m+n=0 \quad ...(ii)$$

Then, from Eqs. (i) and (ii) by cross multiplication, we get

$$\frac{l}{2}=\frac{m}{-1}=\frac{n}{2}$$
$$\Rightarrow \frac{l}{2}=\frac{m}{-1}=\frac{n}{2}=\frac{\sqrt{l^2+m^2+n^2}}{\sqrt{4+1+4}}=\frac{1}{3}$$
$$[\because l^2+m^2+n^2=1]$$
$$\Rightarrow l=\frac{2}{3}, m=-\frac{1}{3} \text{ and } n=\frac{2}{3}$$

3.6 Projection of the Line Segment Joining Two Points on a Given Line

The projection of the line segment joining two given points (x_1, y_1, z_1) and (x_2, y_2, z_2) on the line having direction cosines l, m, n is given by

$l(x_2 - x_1) + m(y_2 - y_1) + n(z_2 - z_1)$ which is clear from the vector.

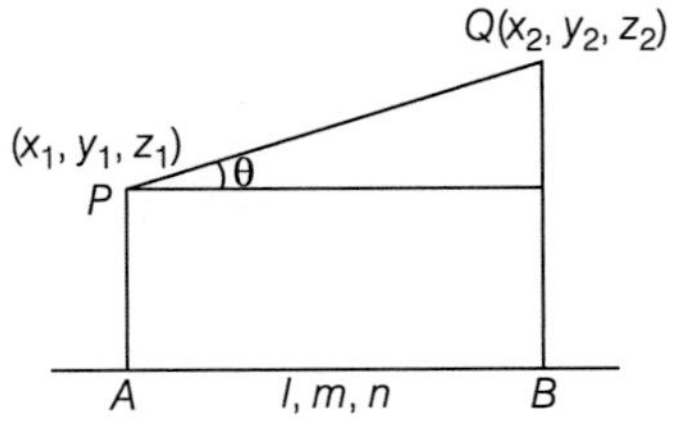

Clearly, $\mathbf{PQ} = (x_2 - x_1)\hat{\mathbf{i}} + (y_2 - y_1)\hat{\mathbf{j}} + (z_2 - z_1)\hat{\mathbf{k}}$

and the line $\mathbf{AB} = l\hat{\mathbf{i}} + m\hat{\mathbf{j}} + n\hat{\mathbf{k}}$

The projection of **PQ** on **AB**

$$= \frac{\mathbf{PQ} \cdot \mathbf{AB}}{|\mathbf{AB}|}$$

$$= \frac{l(x_2 - x_1) + m(y_2 - y_1) + n(z_2 - z_1)}{\sqrt{l^2 + m^2 + n^2}}$$

$$= l(x_2 - x_1) + m(y_2 - y_1) + n(z_2 - z_1)$$

$$[\because l^2 + m^2 + n^2 = 1]$$

JEE SPIKE

If P is a point (x_1, y_1, z_1), then projection of OP on a line whose direction cosines, l, m, n is $lx_1 + my_1 + nz_1$, where O is origin.

Example 17. Let $A(-1, 2, 1)$ and $B(4, 3, 5)$ be two given points. Find the projection of AB on a line which makes angle 120° and 135° with Y and Z-axes respectively and an acute angle with X-axis.

Sol. Let α be an acute angle that the given line make with X-axis.

Then, $\cos^2 \alpha + \cos^2 120° + \cos^2 135° = 1$

$$\Rightarrow \quad \cos^2 \alpha = 1 - \frac{1}{4} - \frac{1}{2} = \frac{4-2-1}{4} = \frac{1}{4}$$

$$\Rightarrow \quad \cos \alpha = \pm \frac{1}{2} \text{ but } \alpha \text{ is acute.}$$

$\therefore$ $\cos \alpha$ is positive.

$$\Rightarrow \quad \cos \alpha = \frac{1}{2} = \cos 60°$$

$$\Rightarrow \quad \alpha = 60°$$

Thus, the direction cosines of the given straight line are $\cos 60°$, $\cos 120°$, $\cos 135°$ i.e. $\frac{1}{2}, -\frac{1}{2}$ and $-\frac{1}{\sqrt{2}}$.

Hence, the projection of AB on the line

$$= \frac{1}{2}(4+1) - \frac{1}{2}(3-2) - \frac{1}{\sqrt{2}}(5-1) = \frac{5}{2} - \frac{1}{2} - 2\sqrt{2}$$

$$= (2 - 2\sqrt{2}) \text{ units}$$

Milestone Practice 3.1

1. Find the distance between the points $(k, k+1, k+2)$ and $(0, 1, 2)$.

2. Show that the points $(1, 2, 3)$, $(-1, -2, -1)$, $(2, 3, 2)$ and $(4, 7, 6)$ are the vertices of a parallelogram.

3. The maximum distance between the points $(3\sin\theta, 0, 0)$ and $(4\cos\theta, 0, 0)$ is equal to
   (a) 2 (b) 3 (c) 4 (d) 5

4. If the mid-points of the sides of a triangle are $(1, 5, -1)$, $(0, 4, -2)$ and $(2, 3, 4)$, then find its vertices.

5. If $A = (1, 2, 3)$, $B = (4, 5, 6)$, $C = (7, 8, 9)$ and D, E, F are the mid-points of the ΔABC, then find the centroid of the ΔDEF.

6. The ratio in which the plane $2x - 1 = 0$ divides the line joining $(-2, 4, 7)$ and $(3, -5, 8)$ is equal to
   (a) 1 : 1 (b) 1 : 2
   (c) 2 : 1 (d) None of these

7. A line makes angles α, β and γ with the coordinate axes. If $\alpha + \beta = 90°$, then the value of γ is equal to
   (a) 0° (b) 45° (c) 60° (d) 90°

8. If α, β and γ are angles made by a line with positive direction of X-axis, Y-axis and Z-axis respectively, then find the value of $\cos 2\alpha + \cos 2\beta + \cos 2\gamma$.

9. If $\cos\alpha$, $\cos\beta$, $\cos\gamma$ are the direction cosines of a line, then find the value of $\cos^2\alpha + (\cos\beta + \sin\gamma)(\cos\beta - \sin^2\gamma)$.

10. A line makes angles α, β, γ and δ with the four diagonals of a cube, then find the value of $\cos^2\alpha + \cos^2\beta + \cos^2\gamma + \cos^2\delta$.

11. The direction cosines of three mutually perpendicular lines are l_1, m_1, n_1; l_2, m_2, n_2 and l_3, m_3, n_3. Prove that the direction cosines of the line equally inclined to them are
$$\frac{l_1 + l_2 + l_3}{\sqrt{3}}, \frac{m_1 + m_2 + m_3}{\sqrt{3}}, \frac{n_1 + n_2 + n_3}{\sqrt{3}}.$$

12. A mirror and a source of light are situated at the origin O and at a point on OX, respectively. A ray of light from the source strikes the mirror and is reflected. If the direction ratios of the normal to the plane are $1, -1, 1$, then find the direction cosines of the reflected ray.

13. Find the direction cosines of line which is perpendicular to the lines with direction ratios $[1, -2, -2]$ and $[0, 2, 1]$.

14. Let $A(1, 2, 2)$, $B(2, 3, 6)$ and $C(3, 4, 12)$ be three points. Then, find the direction cosines of a line equally inclined with OA, OB and OC, where O is the origin.

15. PQR is a triangle in a plane with vertices $P(1, 3, 4)$, $Q(-2, 4, 2)$ and $R(\lambda, 3, \mu)$. If the median through P is equally inclined to the coordinates axes, then the value of $(\lambda^2 + \mu^2 + 2)$, is equal to
   (a) 50 (b) 76 (c) 150 (d) 200

16. Find the angle between the lines whose direction cosines are given by $l + m + n = 0$ and $3lm - 5mn + 2nl = 0$.

17. If the lines whose direction cosines satisfies the equations $al + bm + cn = 0$ and $fmn + gnl + hlm = 0$ are perpendicular, then find the value of $\frac{f}{a} + \frac{g}{b} + \frac{h}{c}$.

18. Find the angle between the lines, whose direction cosines satisfy the equations $l + m - n = 0$ and $l^2 + m^2 - n^2 = 0$

19. If $A(x_1, x_2, x_3)$ is a point on the line segment joining $B(2, 2, 4)$ and $C(3, 5, 6)$ such that the projections of OA on the axes are $\frac{13}{5}, \frac{19}{5}$ and $\frac{26}{5}$ respectively, then find the ratio in which A divides BC.

Answer Key

1. $\sqrt{3}k$	3. (d)	4. $A(1, 2, 3)$, $B(3, 4, 5)$ and $C(-1, 6, -7)$	5. (4, 5, 6)	6. (a)
7. (d)	8. -1	9. $\sin\gamma\,[(1 - \sin\gamma)(\sin\gamma + \cos\beta)]$	10. $\frac{4}{3}$	12. $-\frac{1}{3}, \frac{-2}{3}, \frac{2}{3}$
13. $\left(\frac{2}{3}, \frac{-1}{3}, \frac{2}{3}\right)$	14. $\left(-\frac{1}{\sqrt{3}}, \frac{1}{\sqrt{3}}, \frac{1}{\sqrt{3}}\right)$ or $\left(\frac{1}{\sqrt{3}}, -\frac{1}{\sqrt{3}}, -\frac{1}{\sqrt{3}}\right)$	15. (b)		
16. Right angle	17. 0	18. $\cos^{-1}\left(\frac{1}{2}\right)$	19. $\frac{3}{2} : 1$ or $3 : 2$	

For Detailed Solution

Milestone 2 Lines

• Equation of a Straight Line in Space • Angle Between Two Lines • Foot of Perpendicular and Distance of a Point From Line • Reflection or Image of a Point in a Straight Line • Shortest Distance Between Two Lines • Point of Intersection of Lines

3.7 Equation of a Straight Line in Space

A line (or straight line) is a curve such that all the points on the line segment joining any two points of it lies on it. A straight line in space is specified basically in two ways

(i) A line passing through a given point and parallel to a given vector.

(ii) A line passing through any two given points.

Equation of a Line Passing Through a Given Point and Parallel to a Given Vector

Vector Equation

The vector equation of a straight line which passes through a given point with position vector **a** and is parallel to a given vector **b** is

$$\mathbf{r} = \mathbf{a} + \lambda \mathbf{b},$$

where $\mathbf{r} = x\hat{\mathbf{i}} + y\hat{\mathbf{j}} + z\hat{\mathbf{k}}$ is the position vector of an arbitrary point P on the line and λ is a real number.

Let $\mathbf{a} = a_1\hat{\mathbf{i}} + a_2\hat{\mathbf{j}} + a_3\hat{\mathbf{k}}$ and $\mathbf{b} = b_1\hat{\mathbf{i}} + b_2\hat{\mathbf{j}} + b_3\hat{\mathbf{k}}$, where a_1, a_2, a_3 and b_1, b_2, b_3 are direction ratios of line **OA** and **EF**, respectively.

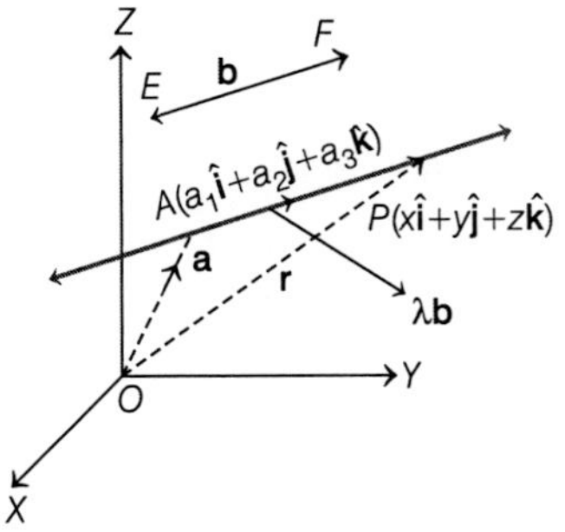

Proof Let A be the given point and let EF be the given line, then through A draw AP parallel to given line EF.

Let **b** be any vector parallel to the given line. Take any point O as the origin of reference. Let a the position vector of the given point A.

Let P be any point on the AP and let its position vector be **r**. Then, we have

$$\mathbf{r} = \mathbf{OP} = \mathbf{OA} + \mathbf{AP} = \mathbf{a} + \lambda\mathbf{b} \qquad [\text{where, } \mathbf{AP} = \lambda\mathbf{b}]$$

Hence, the vector equation of straight line

$$\mathbf{r} = \mathbf{a} + \lambda\mathbf{b} \qquad \text{...(i)}$$

JEE Focus Points

- The position vector of any point $P(x, y, z)$ on the line is $\mathbf{r} = x\hat{\mathbf{i}} + y\hat{\mathbf{j}} + z\hat{\mathbf{k}}$
- The vector equation of straight line passing through the origin and parallel to given vector **b** is $\mathbf{r} = \lambda\mathbf{b}$

Cartesian Equation

Let the coordinates of the given point A be (x_1, y_1, z_1) and the direction ratios of the line be a, b and c. Consider the coordinates of any point P be (x, y, z).

Then, $\mathbf{r} = x\hat{\mathbf{i}} + y\hat{\mathbf{j}} + z\hat{\mathbf{k}}; \mathbf{a} = x_1\hat{\mathbf{i}} + y_1\hat{\mathbf{j}} + z_1\hat{\mathbf{k}}$

and $\mathbf{b} = a\hat{\mathbf{i}} + b\hat{\mathbf{j}} + c\hat{\mathbf{k}}$

On substituting these values in (i) and equating the coefficients of $\hat{\mathbf{i}}$, $\hat{\mathbf{j}}$ and $\hat{\mathbf{k}}$, we get

$$x = x_1 + \lambda a,\ y = y_1 + \lambda b,\ z = z_1 + \lambda c$$

These are parametric equations of the line.

On eliminating the parameter λ, we get

$$\frac{x - x_1}{a} = \frac{y - y_1}{b} = \frac{z - z_1}{c}$$

Example 18. Find the equation of straight line parallel to $2\hat{\mathbf{i}} - \hat{\mathbf{j}} + 3\hat{\mathbf{k}}$ and passing through the point $(5, -2, 4)$.

Sol. **Vector form** Let $P = (5, -2, 4)$, then $\mathbf{OP} = 5\hat{\mathbf{i}} - 2\hat{\mathbf{j}} + 4\hat{\mathbf{k}} = \mathbf{a}$

Also, $\mathbf{b} = 2\hat{\mathbf{i}} - \hat{\mathbf{j}} + 3\hat{\mathbf{k}}$

So, equation of straight line passing through **a** and parallel to straight line whose direction ratios are **b** is given as

$$\mathbf{r} = \mathbf{a} + \lambda\mathbf{b}$$

$$\Rightarrow \quad \mathbf{r} = (5\hat{\mathbf{i}} - 2\hat{\mathbf{j}} + 4\hat{\mathbf{k}}) + \lambda(2\hat{\mathbf{i}} - \hat{\mathbf{j}} + 3\hat{\mathbf{k}})$$

Cartesian form Here, $(x_1, y_1, z_1) = (5, -2, 4)$ and parallel to straight line whose DR's are $(2, -1, 3)$, so equation of the straight line is $\frac{x-5}{2} = \frac{y+2}{-1} = \frac{z-4}{3}$.

JEE Focus Points

Concept Inside Video

- Parametric equation of straight line
$$\frac{x-x_1}{a} = \frac{y-y_1}{b} = \frac{z-z_1}{c} = \lambda$$
$\Rightarrow \quad x = x_1 + \lambda a,\ y = y_1 + \lambda b$ and $z = z_1 + \lambda c$
[where, λ being parameter]
- The cartesian equation of a line passing through origin and having direction ratios (a, b, c) is $\frac{x}{a} = \frac{y}{b} = \frac{z}{c}$.
- The cartesian equation of line
$$\frac{x-x_1}{a} = \frac{y-y_1}{b} = \frac{z-z_1}{c} = \lambda \text{ (let)}$$
is written in vector form as
$\mathbf{r} = (x_1\hat{\mathbf{i}} + y_1\hat{\mathbf{j}} + z_1\hat{\mathbf{k}}) + \lambda\,(a\hat{\mathbf{i}} + b\hat{\mathbf{j}} + c\hat{\mathbf{k}})$ and *vice-versa*.
- Since, X, Y and Z-axes pass through origin and have direction cosines $(1, 0, 0)$, $(0, 1, 0)$ and $(0, 0, 1)$.
$\therefore$ Their equations are
Equation of X-axis, $\frac{x-0}{1} = \frac{y-0}{0} = \frac{z-0}{0} \Rightarrow y = 0$ and $z = 0$
Equation of Y-axis, $\frac{x-0}{0} = \frac{y-0}{1} = \frac{z-0}{0} \Rightarrow x = 0$ and $z = 0$
Equation of Z-axis, $\frac{x-0}{0} = \frac{y-0}{0} = \frac{z-0}{1} \Rightarrow x = 0$ and $y = 0$

Example 19. Find the vector equation of a line passing through $(2, -1, 1)$ and parallel to the line whose equation is $\frac{x-3}{2} = \frac{y+1}{7} = \frac{z-2}{-3}$

Sol. Since, the required line is parallel to
$$\frac{x-3}{2} = \frac{y+1}{7} = \frac{z-2}{-3}$$
It follows that the required line passing through $A(2\hat{\mathbf{i}} - \hat{\mathbf{j}} + \hat{\mathbf{k}})$ has the direction of $2\hat{\mathbf{i}} + 7\hat{\mathbf{j}} - 3\hat{\mathbf{k}}$.

Hence, the vector equation of the required line is $\mathbf{r} = 2\hat{\mathbf{i}} - \hat{\mathbf{j}} + \hat{\mathbf{k}} + \lambda(2\hat{\mathbf{i}} + 7\hat{\mathbf{j}} - 3\hat{\mathbf{k}})$ where λ is a parameter.

Example 20. The cartesian equation of a line are $6x - 2 = 3y + 1 = 2z - 2$. Find its direction ratios and also find the vector equation of the line.

Sol. We know that $\frac{x-x_1}{a} = \frac{y-y_1}{b} = \frac{z-z_1}{c}$ is cartesian equation of straight line.

$\therefore \quad 6x - 2 = 3y + 1 = 2z - 2$

$\Rightarrow \quad 6\left(x - \frac{1}{3}\right) = 3\left(y + \frac{1}{3}\right) = 2(z - 1)$

$\Rightarrow \quad \frac{x - \frac{1}{3}}{\frac{1}{6}} = \frac{y + \frac{1}{3}}{\frac{1}{3}} = \frac{z-1}{\frac{1}{2}}$

$\Rightarrow \quad \frac{x - \frac{1}{3}}{1} = \frac{y + \frac{1}{3}}{2} = \frac{z-1}{3}$

which shows given line passes through $\left(\frac{1}{3}, -\frac{1}{3}, 1\right)$ and has direction ratios $(1, 2, 3)$.

$\therefore$ Its vector equation is
$$\mathbf{r} = \left(\frac{1}{3}\hat{\mathbf{i}} - \frac{1}{3}\hat{\mathbf{j}} + \hat{\mathbf{k}}\right) + \lambda(\hat{\mathbf{i}} + 2\hat{\mathbf{j}} + 3\hat{\mathbf{k}})$$

Equation of a Line Passing Through Two Given Points

Vector Equation

The vector equation of a line passing through two points whose position vectors $\mathbf{a}$ and $\mathbf{b}$ is
$$\mathbf{r} = \mathbf{a} + \lambda(\mathbf{b} - \mathbf{a}),$$
where $\mathbf{r}$ is the position vector of any point P on the line and λ is any scalar.

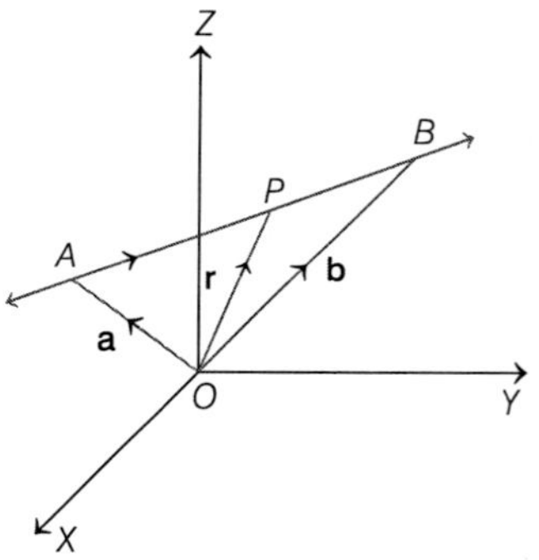

Proof Let O be the origin and A, B be the given points with position vectors $\mathbf{a}$ and $\mathbf{b}$, respectively.

Then, $\quad \mathbf{OP} = \mathbf{r}, \mathbf{OA} = \mathbf{a}$ and $\mathbf{OB} = \mathbf{b}$

Since, $\mathbf{AP}$ is collinear with $\mathbf{AB}$.

$\therefore \quad \mathbf{AP} = \lambda\ \mathbf{AB}$ for some scalar λ

$\Rightarrow \quad \mathbf{OP} - \mathbf{OA} = \lambda(\mathbf{OB} - \mathbf{OA})$

$\Rightarrow \quad \mathbf{r} - \mathbf{a} = \lambda(\mathbf{b} - \mathbf{a})$

$\Rightarrow \quad \mathbf{r} = \mathbf{a} + \lambda(\mathbf{b} - \mathbf{a})$

$\therefore$ Equation of straight line passing through $\mathbf{a}$ and $\mathbf{b}$.

$\Rightarrow \quad \mathbf{r} = \mathbf{a} + \lambda(\mathbf{b} - \mathbf{a})$

Cartesian Equation

The equation of a line passing through two points $A(x_1, y_1, z_1)$ and $B(x_2, y_2, z_2)$ is given by
$$\frac{x-x_1}{x_2-x_1} = \frac{y-y_1}{y_2-y_1} = \frac{z-z_1}{z_2-z_1},$$
where (x, y, z) are coordinates of any point on the line.

Proof Equation of straight line passing through $(x_1, y_1, z_1), (x_2, y_2, z_2)$.

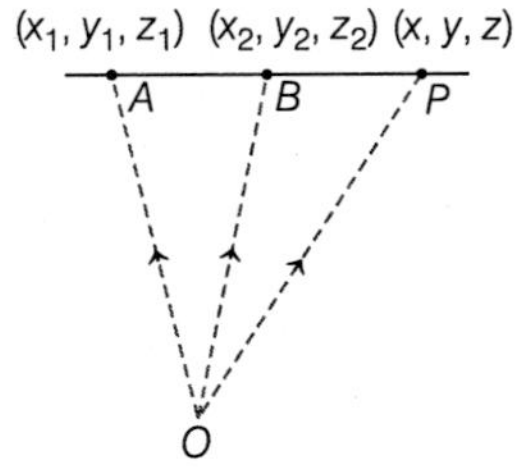

The direction ratios of $AB = (x_2 - x_1, y_2 - y_1, z_2 - z_1)$

The direction ratios of $AP = (x - x_1, y - y_1, z - z_1)$

Since, they are proportional

$$\frac{x - x_1}{x_2 - x_1} = \frac{y - y_1}{y_2 - y_1} = \frac{z - z_1}{z_2 - z_1}$$

Example 21. Find the vector equation of line passing through $A(3, 4, -7)$ and $B(1, -1, 6)$. Also, find its cartesian equations.

Sol. Since, the line passes through $A(3\hat{\mathbf{i}} + 4\hat{\mathbf{j}} - 7\hat{\mathbf{k}})$ and $B(\hat{\mathbf{i}} - \hat{\mathbf{j}} + 6\hat{\mathbf{k}})$, its vector equation is

$$\mathbf{r} = 3\hat{\mathbf{i}} + 4\hat{\mathbf{j}} - 7\hat{\mathbf{k}} + \lambda[(\hat{\mathbf{i}} - \hat{\mathbf{j}} + 6\hat{\mathbf{k}}) - (3\hat{\mathbf{i}} + 4\hat{\mathbf{j}} - 7\hat{\mathbf{k}})]$$

or $$\mathbf{r} = 3\hat{\mathbf{i}} + 4\hat{\mathbf{j}} - 7\hat{\mathbf{k}} - \lambda(2\hat{\mathbf{i}} + 5\hat{\mathbf{j}} - 13\hat{\mathbf{k}}) \quad \text{...(i)}$$

where λ is a parameter.

The cartesian equivalent of (i) is

$$\frac{x - 3}{2} = \frac{y - 4}{5} = \frac{z + 7}{-13}$$

Example 22. Find the equation of a line which passes through the point (2, 3, 4) and which has equal intercepts on the axes.

Sol. Since, lines has equal intercepts on axes, it is equally inclined to axes.

$\Rightarrow$ Line is along the $\mathbf{a} = (\hat{\mathbf{i}} + \hat{\mathbf{j}} + \hat{\mathbf{k}})$

$\Rightarrow$ Equation of line is $\frac{x - 2}{1} = \frac{y - 3}{1} = \frac{z - 4}{1}$

3.8 Angle between Two Lines

Vector Form

Let the vector equation of line L_1 and L_2 in space be $\mathbf{r} = \mathbf{a}_1 + \lambda\mathbf{b}_1$ and $\mathbf{r} = \mathbf{a}_2 + \mu\mathbf{b}_2$, respectively.

Let θ be the angle between two lines L_1 and L_2 is given by

$$\cos\theta = \frac{\mathbf{b}_1 \cdot \mathbf{b}_2}{|\mathbf{b}_1||\mathbf{b}_2|}$$

Cartesian Form

Let the cartesian equation of line L_1 and L_2 be

$$\frac{x - x_1}{a_1} = \frac{y - y_1}{b_1} = \frac{z - z_1}{c_1}$$

and $$\frac{x - x_2}{a_2} = \frac{y - y_2}{b_2} = \frac{z - z_2}{c_2}$$

Then, angle between the line L_1 and L_2 is given by

$$\cos\theta = \frac{a_1a_2 + b_1b_2 + c_1c_2}{\sqrt{a_1^2 + b_1^2 + c_1^2}\sqrt{a_2^2 + b_2^2 + c_2^2}}$$

JEE Focus Points

- **Condition for Perpendicularity**

  The lines are perpendicular, then

  $$\mathbf{b}_1 \cdot \mathbf{b}_2 = 0$$

  $$\Rightarrow \quad a_1a_2 + b_1b_2 + c_1c_2 = 0$$

- **Condition for Parallelism**

  The lines are parallel, then $\mathbf{b}_1 = \lambda\mathbf{b}_2$, where λ is any scalar.

  $$\Rightarrow \quad \frac{a_1}{a_2} = \frac{b_1}{b_2} = \frac{c_1}{c_2}$$

Example 23. Find the angle between the pair of lines

$$\mathbf{r} = 3\hat{\mathbf{i}} + 2\hat{\mathbf{j}} - 4\hat{\mathbf{k}} + \lambda(\hat{\mathbf{i}} + 2\hat{\mathbf{j}} + 2\hat{\mathbf{k}})$$

and $$\mathbf{r} = 5\hat{\mathbf{i}} - 2\hat{\mathbf{k}} + \mu(3\hat{\mathbf{i}} + 2\hat{\mathbf{j}} + 6\hat{\mathbf{k}})$$

Sol. Given line are

$$\mathbf{r} = (3\hat{\mathbf{i}} + 2\hat{\mathbf{j}} - 4\hat{\mathbf{k}}) + \lambda(\hat{\mathbf{i}} + 2\hat{\mathbf{j}} + 2\hat{\mathbf{k}})$$

and $$\mathbf{r} = (5\hat{\mathbf{i}} - 2\hat{\mathbf{k}}) + \mu(3\hat{\mathbf{i}} + 2\hat{\mathbf{j}} + 6\hat{\mathbf{k}})$$

We know that angle between $\mathbf{r} = \mathbf{a}_1 + \lambda\mathbf{b}_1$ and $\mathbf{r} = \mathbf{a}_2 + \mu\mathbf{b}_2$,

$$\cos\theta = \frac{\mathbf{b}_1 \cdot \mathbf{b}_2}{|\mathbf{b}_1||\mathbf{b}_2|}$$

$$\therefore \quad \cos\theta = \frac{(\hat{\mathbf{i}} + 2\hat{\mathbf{j}} + 2\hat{\mathbf{k}}) \cdot (3\hat{\mathbf{i}} + 2\hat{\mathbf{j}} + 6\hat{\mathbf{k}})}{\sqrt{1^2 + 2^2 + 2^2}\sqrt{3^2 + 2^2 + 6^2}}$$

$$= \frac{3 + 4 + 12}{\sqrt{9} \cdot \sqrt{49}}$$

$$= \frac{19}{21}$$

$$\therefore \quad \theta = \cos^{-1}\left(\frac{19}{21}\right)$$

Example 24. Find the angle between the pair of lines

$$-4x + 20 = -3y - 9, -4z + 28 = 0$$

and $$-2x = y - 1, 2y - 2 = -2z + 12$$

Sol. Given equation can be written in standard form

$$-4(x-5) = -3(y+3), -4(z-7) = 0$$

or $$\frac{x-5}{-3} = \frac{y+3}{-4} = \frac{z-7}{0}$$

and $$-2x = y-1, 2(y-1) = -2(z-6)$$

or $$\frac{x}{1} = \frac{y-1}{-2} = \frac{z-6}{2}$$

The direction ratios of the lines $(-3, -4, 0)$ and $(1, -2, 2)$.

Let θ be the acute angle between given line, then

$$\cos\theta = \frac{a_1a_2 + b_1b_2 + c_1c_2}{\sqrt{a_1^2+b_1^2+c_1^2}\sqrt{a_2^2+b_2^2+c_2^2}}$$

$$\Rightarrow \cos\theta = \frac{(-3)(1)+(-4)(-2)+(0)(2)}{\sqrt{9+16+0}\sqrt{1+4+4}}$$

$$\Rightarrow \cos\theta = \left(\frac{-3+8+0}{5\times 3}\right) = \frac{5}{5\times 3} = \frac{1}{3}$$

$$\Rightarrow \theta = \cos^{-1}\left(\frac{1}{3}\right)$$

Example 25. If the angle between the lines $\frac{x-3}{\alpha} = \frac{y+2}{-5} = \frac{z+5}{\beta}$ and $\frac{x}{1} = \frac{y}{0} = \frac{z}{1}$ is $\frac{\pi}{4}$, then find the minimum value of $\alpha+\beta$, where $\alpha, \beta > 0$.

Decoding the Question

For minimum value apply arithmetic mean is greater than or equal to geometric mean i.e. AM≥ GM

Sol. Direction ratios of given lines are $(\alpha, -5, \beta)$ and $(1, 0, 1)$.

Given, angle between the line is $\frac{\pi}{4}$.

$$\cos\frac{\pi}{4} = \frac{(\alpha)(1)+(-5)(0)+(\beta)(1)}{\sqrt{\alpha^2+25+\beta^2}\sqrt{1+0+1}}$$

$$\Rightarrow \frac{1}{\sqrt{2}} = \frac{\alpha+\beta}{(\sqrt{\alpha^2+\beta^2+25})(\sqrt{2})}$$

$$\Rightarrow \alpha+\beta = \sqrt{\alpha^2+\beta^2+25}$$

$$\Rightarrow (\alpha+\beta)^2 = \alpha^2+\beta^2+25$$

$$\Rightarrow \alpha^2+\beta^2+2\alpha\beta = \alpha^2+\beta^2+25$$

$$\Rightarrow \alpha\beta = \frac{25}{2}$$

$\because$ AM ≥ GM

$$\therefore \frac{\alpha+\beta}{2} \geq \sqrt{\alpha\beta}$$

$$\Rightarrow \alpha+\beta \geq 2\sqrt{\alpha\beta}$$

$$\Rightarrow \alpha+\beta \geq 2\sqrt{\frac{25}{2}}$$

$$\Rightarrow \alpha+\beta \geq 5\sqrt{2}$$

So, minimum value of $\alpha+\beta$ is $5\sqrt{2}$.

Example 26. Prove that the line $x = ay+b$, $z = cy+d$ and $x = a'y+b'$, $z = c'y+d'$ are perpendicular, if $aa'+cc'+1=0$.

Sol. We can write the equations of straight line as

$$\frac{x-b'}{a'} = y, y = \frac{z-d'}{c'}$$

$$\Rightarrow \frac{x-b'}{a'} = \frac{y-0}{1} = \frac{z-d'}{c'} \quad \text{...(i)}$$

and $$\frac{x-b}{a} = y, \; y = \frac{z-d}{c}$$

$$\Rightarrow \frac{x-b}{a} = \frac{y-0}{1} = \frac{z-d}{c} \quad \text{...(ii)}$$

We know that, $\frac{x-x_1}{a_1} = \frac{y-y_1}{b_1} = \frac{z-z_1}{c_1}$

and $\frac{x-x_2}{a_2} = \frac{y-y_2}{b_2} = \frac{z-z_2}{c_2}$

are perpendicular, if $a_1a_2+b_1b_2+c_1c_2 = 0$

$\therefore$ For the straight lines given by Eqs. (i) and (ii), to be perpendicular.

$$a'a + 1\cdot 1 + c'c = 0$$

$$\Rightarrow aa'+cc'+1 = 0$$

Example 27. Let the lines $\frac{x-1}{a} = \frac{y+1}{b} = \frac{z}{c}$ and $\frac{x+1}{b} = \frac{y-3}{c} = \frac{z-1}{a}$, where $a > b > c$ such that a, b and c are the roots of the equation $y^3+y^2-4y-4=0$. Then, find the angle between the lines.

Sol. Since, a, b and c are roots of the equation

$$y^3+y^2-4y-4=0$$

$$\therefore a+b+c = -1$$

and $$ab+bc+ca = -4$$

$$\therefore (a+b+c)^2 = a^2+b^2+c^2+2(ab+bc+ca)$$

$$\Rightarrow (-1)^2 = a^2+b^2+c^2+2(-4)$$

$$\Rightarrow a^2+b^2+c^2 = 9$$

Now, if θ be the angle between the lines.

$$\therefore \cos\theta = \left|\frac{ab+bc+ac}{\sqrt{a^2+b^2+c^2}\sqrt{b^2+c^2+a^2}}\right|$$

$$\Rightarrow \cos\theta = \left|\frac{ab+bc+ac}{(a^2+b^2+c^2)}\right| = \left|\frac{-4}{9}\right|$$

$$\Rightarrow \cos\theta = \frac{4}{9}$$

$$\Rightarrow \theta = \cos^{-1}\left(\frac{4}{9}\right)$$

JEE SCANNER

Example Similar to PYQ Asked in JEE Main 2021

The vector equation of line passing through (1, 1, 1) and perpendicular to two lines

$$\frac{x+2}{1}=\frac{y-3}{2}=\frac{z+1}{4}$$

and $$\frac{x-1}{2}=\frac{y-2}{3}=\frac{z-3}{4} \text{ is}$$

(a) $\mathbf{r}=\hat{\mathbf{i}}+\hat{\mathbf{j}}+\hat{\mathbf{k}}+\lambda(4\hat{\mathbf{i}}+4\hat{\mathbf{j}}-\hat{\mathbf{k}})$

(b) $\mathbf{r}=\hat{\mathbf{i}}+\hat{\mathbf{j}}+\hat{\mathbf{k}}+\lambda(-4\hat{\mathbf{i}}+4\hat{\mathbf{j}}-\hat{\mathbf{k}})$

(c) $\mathbf{r}=\hat{\mathbf{i}}+\hat{\mathbf{j}}+\hat{\mathbf{k}}+\lambda(4\hat{\mathbf{i}}-4\hat{\mathbf{j}}+\hat{\mathbf{k}})$

(d) $\mathbf{r}=\hat{\mathbf{i}}+\hat{\mathbf{j}}+\hat{\mathbf{k}}+\lambda(4\hat{\mathbf{i}}+4\hat{\mathbf{j}}+\hat{\mathbf{k}})$

Sol. (b) Any line passing through the point (1, 1, 1) is given by

$$\frac{x-1}{a}=\frac{y-1}{b}=\frac{z-1}{c} \quad \text{...(i)}$$

Now, the line (i) is perpendicular to the line

$$\frac{x+2}{1}=\frac{y-3}{2}=\frac{z+1}{4} \text{ and } \frac{x-1}{2}=\frac{y-2}{3}=\frac{z-3}{4}$$

where, direction ratios of these two lines are (1, 2, 4) and (2, 3, 4) respectively.

$$a+2b+4c=0 \quad \text{...(ii)}$$

$$2a+3b+4c=0 \quad \text{...(iii)}$$

On solving Eqs. (ii) and (iii) by cross-multiplication method, we get

$$\frac{a}{8-12}=\frac{b}{8-4}=\frac{c}{3-4}=\frac{a}{-4}=\frac{b}{4}=\frac{c}{-1}$$

Direction ratios of required line are $(-4, 4, -1)$.

$\therefore$ Equation of line is $\frac{x-1}{-4}=\frac{y-1}{4}=\frac{z-1}{-1}$

and vector equation is $\mathbf{r}=\hat{\mathbf{i}}+\hat{\mathbf{j}}+\hat{\mathbf{k}}+\lambda(-4\hat{\mathbf{i}}+4\hat{\mathbf{j}}-\hat{\mathbf{k}})$

Skill Builder

The vector equation of the line passing through (2, 1, 3) and perpendicular to the lines

$$\frac{x-2}{1}=\frac{y-4}{3}=\frac{z+1}{4}$$

and $$\frac{x-1}{3}=\frac{y+2}{2}=\frac{z+3}{5} \text{ is}$$

(a) $\mathbf{r}=2\hat{\mathbf{i}}-\hat{\mathbf{j}}+3\hat{\mathbf{k}}+7\lambda(\hat{\mathbf{i}}+\hat{\mathbf{j}}+\hat{\mathbf{k}})$

(b) $\mathbf{r}=2\hat{\mathbf{i}}+\hat{\mathbf{j}}+3\hat{\mathbf{k}}+7\lambda(\hat{\mathbf{i}}+\hat{\mathbf{j}}-\hat{\mathbf{k}})$

(c) $\mathbf{r}=\hat{\mathbf{i}}+\hat{\mathbf{j}}+3\hat{\mathbf{k}}+7\lambda(\hat{\mathbf{i}}-\hat{\mathbf{j}}-\hat{\mathbf{k}})$

(d) $\mathbf{r}=2\hat{\mathbf{i}}+\hat{\mathbf{j}}+\hat{\mathbf{k}}+7\lambda(\hat{\mathbf{i}}-\hat{\mathbf{j}}+\hat{\mathbf{k}})$

For Sol.

- **For more practice** See Q.7 of Milestone Practice 2.

3.9 Foot of Perpendicular and Distance of a Point from Line

Vector Form

Let L be the foot of the perpendicular drawn from $P(\alpha)$ on the line $\mathbf{r}=\mathbf{a}+\lambda\mathbf{b}$.

Since, $\mathbf{r}$ denotes the position vector of any point on the line $\mathbf{r}=\mathbf{a}+\lambda\mathbf{b}$, the position vector of L will be $(\mathbf{a}+\lambda\mathbf{b})$.

Directions ratios of $PL=\mathbf{a}-\alpha+\lambda\mathbf{b}$

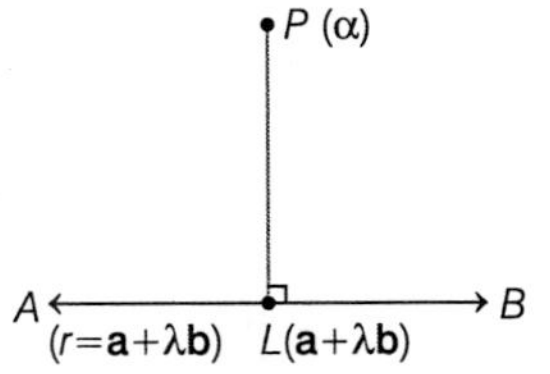

Since, **PL** is perpendicular to **b**,

$$(\mathbf{a}-\alpha+\lambda\mathbf{b})\cdot\mathbf{b}=0$$

$$\Rightarrow \quad (\mathbf{a}-\alpha)\cdot\mathbf{b}+\lambda\mathbf{b}\cdot\mathbf{b}=0 \Rightarrow \lambda=\frac{-(\mathbf{a}-\alpha)\cdot\mathbf{b}}{|\mathbf{b}|^2}$$

$\Rightarrow$ Position vector of L is $\mathbf{a}-\left(\frac{(\mathbf{a}-\alpha)\cdot\mathbf{b}}{|\mathbf{b}|^2}\right)\mathbf{b}$,

which is the foot of the perpendicular.

The length of perpendicular P on the given line is $|\mathbf{PL}|$.

Cartesian Form

Here, the equation of line AB is $\frac{x-x_1}{a}=\frac{y-y_1}{b}=\frac{z-z_1}{c}$

Let L be the foot of the perpendicular drawn from $P(\alpha, \beta, \gamma)$ on the line $\frac{x-x_1}{a}=\frac{y-y_1}{b}=\frac{z-z_1}{c}$.

Let the coordinates of L be $(x_1+a\lambda, y_1+b\lambda, z_1+c\lambda)$.

Then, the direction ratios of PL are $(x_1+a\lambda-\alpha, y_1+b\lambda-\beta, z_1+c\lambda-\gamma)$.

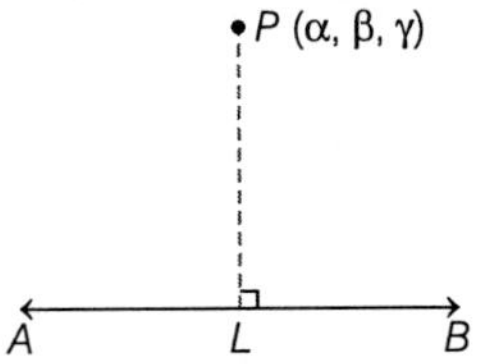

Direction ratios of AB are (a, b, c).

Since, PL is perpendicular to AB.

$$a(x_1+a\lambda-\alpha)+b(y_1+b\lambda-\beta)+c(z_1+c\lambda-\gamma)=0$$

$$\lambda=\frac{a(\alpha-x_1)+b(\beta-y_1)+c(\gamma+z_1)}{a^2+b^2+c^2}$$

On putting the value of λ in $(x_1+a\lambda, y_1+b\lambda, z_1+c\lambda)$, we get the foot of the perpendicular. Now, we can get distance PL using distance formula.

Example 28. Find the foot of perpendicular drawn from the point $2\hat{i} - \hat{j} + 5\hat{k}$ to the line $\mathbf{r} = (11\hat{i} - 2\hat{j} - 8\hat{k}) + \lambda(10\hat{i} - 4\hat{j} - 11\hat{k})$. Also, find the length of the perpendicular.

Sol. Let L be the foot of the perpendicular drawn from $P(2\hat{i} - \hat{j} + 5\hat{k})$ on the line

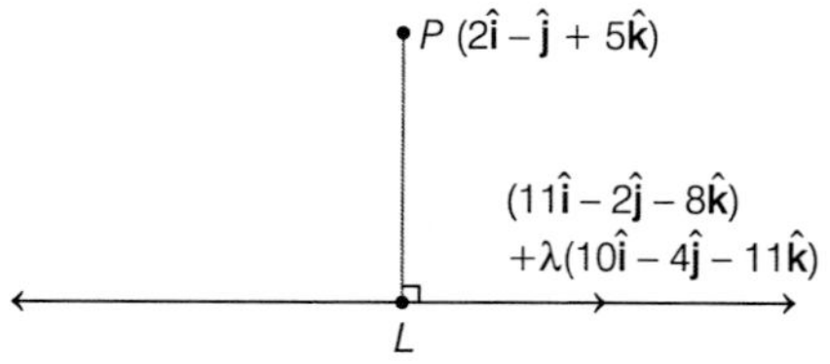

$$\mathbf{r} = (11\hat{i} - 2\hat{j} - 8\hat{k}) + \lambda(10\hat{i} - 4\hat{j} - 11\hat{k})$$

Let the position vector of L be

$$(11\hat{i} - 2\hat{j} - 8\hat{k}) + \lambda(10\hat{i} - 4\hat{j} - 11\hat{k})$$
$$= (11 + 10\lambda)\hat{i} + (-2 - 4\lambda)\hat{j} + (-8 - 11\lambda)\hat{k}$$

$\therefore$ $\mathbf{PL}$ = Position vector of L − Position vector of P

$$= (9 + 10\lambda)\hat{i} + (-1 - 4\lambda)\hat{j} + (-13 - 11\lambda)\hat{k}$$

Since, PL is perpendicular to the given line and parallel to

$$\mathbf{b} = 10\hat{i} - 4\hat{j} - 11\hat{k}$$

$$\Rightarrow \quad \mathbf{PL} \cdot \mathbf{b} = 0$$

$$\Rightarrow \{(9 + 10\lambda)\hat{i} + (-1 - 4\lambda)\hat{j} + (-13 - 11\lambda)\hat{k}\} \cdot (10\hat{i} - 4\hat{j} - 11\hat{k}) = 0$$

$$\Rightarrow \quad 10(9 + 10\lambda) - 4(-1 - 4\lambda) - 11(-13 - 11\lambda) = 0$$

$$\Rightarrow \quad \lambda = -1$$

On putting $\lambda = -1$, we get L as $(\hat{i} + 2\hat{j} + 3\hat{k})$

Now, $\quad \mathbf{PL} = (\hat{i} + 2\hat{j} + 3\hat{k}) - (2\hat{i} - \hat{j} + 5\hat{k})$

$$= (-\hat{i} + 3\hat{j} - 2\hat{k})$$

Hence, the length of perpendicular from P on the given line

$$= |\mathbf{PL}| = \sqrt{1 + 9 + 4} = \sqrt{14}$$

Example 29. Find the coordinates of the foot of the perpendicular drawn from point $A(1, 0, 3)$ to the join of points $B(4, 7, 1)$ and $C(3, 5, 3)$.

Sol. Let D be the foot of the perpendicular and let it divide BC in the ratio $\lambda : 1$.

Then, the coordinates of D are $\dfrac{3\lambda + 4}{\lambda + 1}, \dfrac{5\lambda + 7}{\lambda + 1}$ and $\dfrac{3\lambda + 1}{\lambda + 1}$.

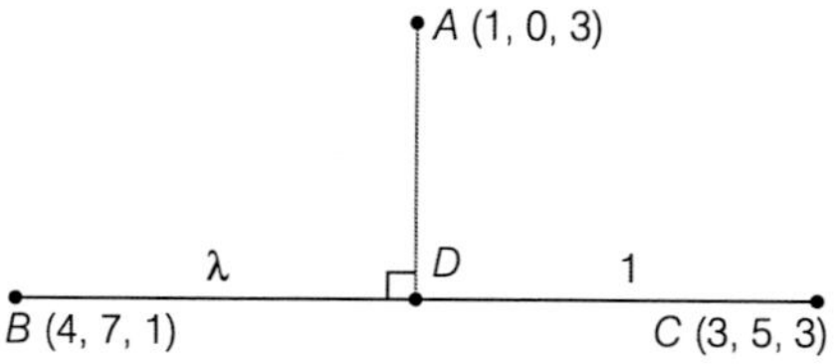

Direction ratios of $AD\left(\dfrac{3\lambda + 4}{\lambda + 1} - 1, \dfrac{5\lambda + 7}{\lambda + 1} - 0, \dfrac{3\lambda + 1}{\lambda + 1} - 3\right)$

$$= \left(\frac{2\lambda + 3}{\lambda + 1}, \frac{5\lambda + 7}{\lambda + 1}, \frac{-2}{\lambda + 1}\right)$$

Direction ratios of $BC = (-1, -2, 2)$

Now, $\quad \mathbf{AD} \perp \mathbf{BC}$

$$\Rightarrow \quad \mathbf{AD} \cdot \mathbf{BC} = 0$$

$$\Rightarrow \quad \frac{-1(2\lambda + 3)}{\lambda + 1} - 2\left(\frac{5\lambda + 7}{\lambda + 1}\right) - \frac{2 \times 2}{\lambda + 1} = 0$$

$$\Rightarrow \quad (2\lambda + 3) + 2(5\lambda + 7) + 4 = 0$$

$$\Rightarrow \quad \lambda = -\frac{7}{4}$$

$\Rightarrow$ Coordinates of D are $\dfrac{5}{3}, \dfrac{7}{3}$ and $\dfrac{17}{3}$.

Example 30. Find the length of perpendicular from $P(2, -3, 1)$ to the line $\dfrac{x+1}{2} = \dfrac{y-3}{3} = \dfrac{z+2}{-1}$

Sol. Given line is $\dfrac{x+1}{2} = \dfrac{y-3}{3} = \dfrac{z+2}{-1} = r$ ...(i)

and $P(2, -3, 1)$

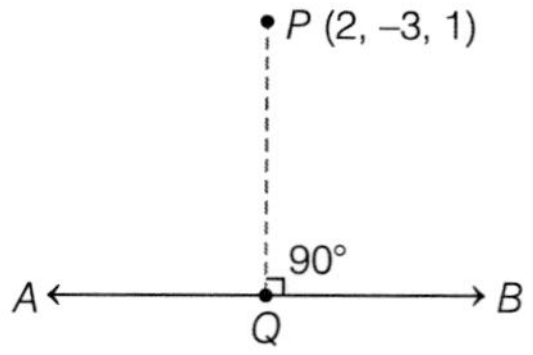

Coordinates of any point on line (i) may be taken as

$$(2r - 1, 3r + 3, -r - 2)$$

Let $\quad Q = (2r - 1, 3r + 3, -r - 2)$

Direction ratios of PQ are $(2r - 3, 3r + 6, -r - 3)$.

Direction ratios of AB are $(2, 3, -1)$.

Since, $PQ \perp AB$

$$2(2r - 3) + 3(3r + 6) - 1(-r - 3) = 0$$

$$\Rightarrow \quad r = -\frac{15}{14}$$

$$\therefore \quad Q = \left(-\frac{22}{7}, -\frac{3}{14}, -\frac{13}{14}\right)$$

$$PQ^2 = \left(2 + \frac{22}{7}\right)^2 + \left(-3 + \frac{3}{14}\right)^2 + \left(1 + \frac{13}{14}\right)^2 = \frac{531}{14}$$

$$PQ = \sqrt{\frac{531}{14}} \text{ units}$$

Example 31. Find the coordinates of those points on the line $\dfrac{x-1}{2} = \dfrac{y+2}{3} = \dfrac{z-3}{6}$ which are at a distance of 3 units from points $(1, -2, 3)$.

Sol. Here, $\dfrac{x-1}{2}=\dfrac{y+2}{3}=\dfrac{z-3}{6}$ ...(i)

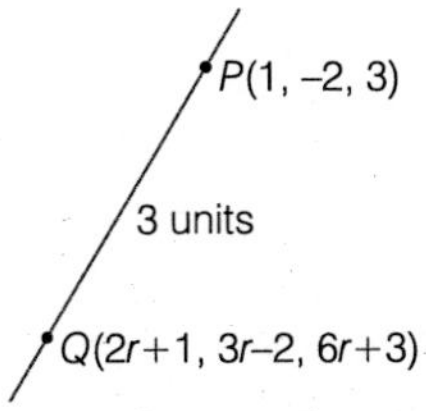

is the given straight line.

Let $P=(1,-2,3)$ on the straight line.

Here, direction ratios of line (i) are (2, 3, 6).

$\therefore$ Direction cosines of line (i) are $\dfrac{2}{7},\dfrac{3}{7},\dfrac{6}{7}$.

Equation of line (i) may be written as

$$\frac{x-1}{2/7}=\frac{y+2}{3/7}=\frac{z-3}{6/7} \quad \text{...(ii)}$$

Coordinates of any point on the line (ii) may be taken as

$\left(\dfrac{2}{7}r+1,\dfrac{3}{7}r-2,\dfrac{6}{7}r+3\right)$.

Let $Q\left(\dfrac{2}{7}r+1,\dfrac{3}{7}r-2,\dfrac{6}{7}r+3\right)$

$$PQ^2=\left(\frac{2r}{7}+1-1\right)^2+\left(\frac{3}{7}r-2+2\right)^2+\left(\frac{6r}{7}+3-3\right)^2$$

$$\Rightarrow \quad PQ^2=\frac{4r^2}{49}+\frac{9r^2}{49}+\frac{36r^2}{49}$$

$$\Rightarrow \quad PQ^2=\frac{49r^2}{49}$$

Given, $PQ=3$

$\therefore \quad r^2=9 \Rightarrow r=\pm 3$

Putting the value of r, we have

$$Q=\left(\frac{13}{7},\frac{-5}{7},\frac{39}{7}\right) \text{ or } \left(\frac{1}{7},\frac{-23}{7},\frac{3}{7}\right)$$

3.10 Reflection or Image of a Point in a Straight Line

Vector Form

To find the reflection or image of a point in a straight line in vector form. Let $P(\alpha)$ be the given point and $\mathbf{r}=\mathbf{a}+\lambda\mathbf{b}$ be the given line.

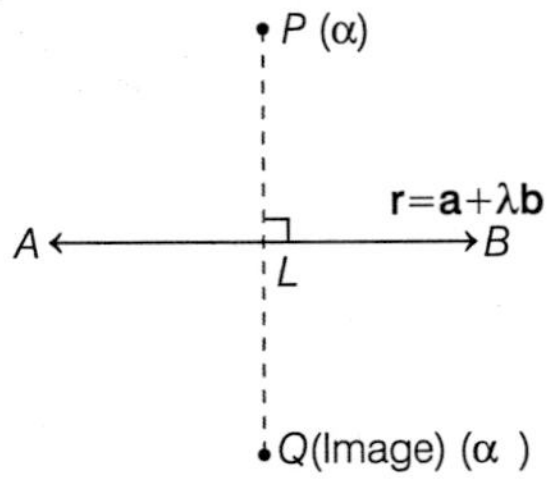

Let Q be the image of P in $\mathbf{r}=\mathbf{a}+\lambda\mathbf{b}$

$\therefore \quad \mathbf{PL}=\mathbf{a}+\lambda\mathbf{b}-\alpha$

Since, **PL** is perpendicular to the given line,

$\therefore \quad \mathbf{PL}\perp\mathbf{b}$

$\Rightarrow \quad \mathbf{PL}\cdot\mathbf{b}=0 \Rightarrow (\mathbf{a}+\lambda\mathbf{b}-\alpha)\cdot\mathbf{b}=0$

$$\Rightarrow \quad \lambda=-\frac{[(\mathbf{a}-\alpha)\cdot\mathbf{b}]}{|\mathbf{b}|^2}$$

$\therefore$ Position vector of L, $\mathbf{a}+\lambda\mathbf{b}=\mathbf{a}-\left(\dfrac{(\mathbf{a}-\alpha)\cdot\mathbf{b}}{|\mathbf{b}|^2}\right)\mathbf{b}$

Let Q be the image of point P and α' be the position vector.

Since, L is mid-point of PQ.

$$\Rightarrow \quad \frac{\alpha+\alpha'}{2}=\mathbf{a}-\left(\frac{(\mathbf{a}-\alpha)\cdot\mathbf{b}}{|\mathbf{b}|^2}\right)\mathbf{b}$$

$$\Rightarrow \quad \alpha'=2\mathbf{a}-\left(\frac{2(\mathbf{a}-\alpha)\cdot\mathbf{b}}{|\mathbf{b}|^2}\right)\mathbf{b}-\alpha$$

which is image of P on **r**.

Cartesian Form

To find the reflection or image of a point in a straight line in cartesian form.

Let $P(\alpha,\beta,\gamma)$ be the point and $\dfrac{x-x_1}{a}=\dfrac{y-y_1}{b}=\dfrac{z-z_1}{c}$ be the given line.

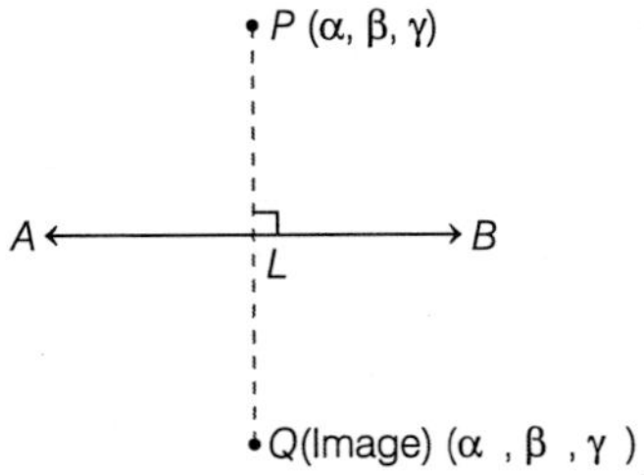

Let L be the foot of perpendicular from P to AB and let Q be the image of the point in the given line, where $PL=LQ$.

Let the coordinates of L be $(x_1+a\lambda, y_1+b\lambda, z_1+c\lambda)$.

Then, direction ratios of PL are

$$(x_1+a\lambda-\alpha, y_1+b\lambda-\beta, z_1+c\lambda-\gamma)$$

Since, PL is perpendicular to the given line, whose direction ratios are a, b and c.

$\therefore \quad (x_1+a\lambda-\alpha)\cdot a+(y_1+b\lambda-\beta)\cdot b+(z_1+c\lambda-\gamma)\cdot c=0$

$$\Rightarrow \quad \lambda=\frac{[a(\alpha-x_1)+b(\beta-y_1)+c(\gamma-z_1)]}{a^2+b^2+c^2}$$

On substituting λ, we get L, (foot of perpendicular)

Let coordinates of $Q(\alpha', \beta', \gamma')$ be image.

$\therefore$ Mid-point of PQ is L.

$$\therefore \quad \frac{\alpha+\alpha'}{2}=x_1+a\lambda, \frac{\beta+\beta'}{2}=y_1+b\lambda, \frac{\gamma+\gamma'}{2}=z_1+c\lambda$$

$$\therefore \quad \alpha'=2(x_1+a\lambda)-\alpha, \beta'=2(y_1+b\lambda)-\beta,$$
$$\gamma'=2(z_1+c\lambda)-\gamma$$

JEE SCANNER

Example Similar to PYQ Asked in JEE Main 2020

The image of the point (1, 6, 3) in the line $\frac{x}{1}=\frac{y-1}{2}=\frac{z-2}{3}$ *is* (α, β, γ), *then* $\alpha^2+\beta^2+\gamma^2$ *is equal to ....*

Sol. Let P be the given point and let L be the foot of perpendicular from P to the given line.

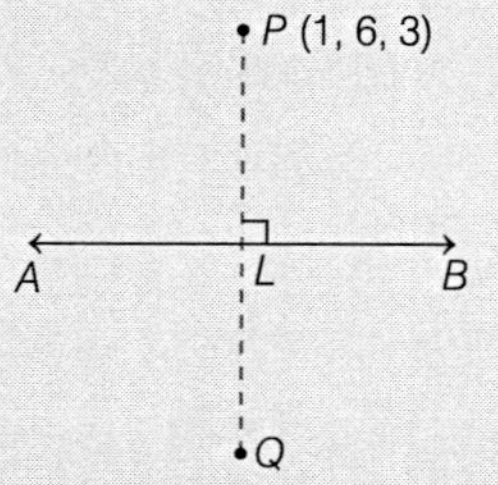

The coordinates of a general point on the given line are given by
$$\frac{x-0}{1}=\frac{y-1}{2}=\frac{z-2}{3}=\lambda$$

i.e. $\quad x=\lambda, y=2\lambda+1, z=3\lambda+2$

Let the coordinates of L be
$$(\lambda, 2\lambda+1, 3\lambda+2) \quad \text{...(i)}$$

So, direction ratios of PL are $(\lambda-1, 2\lambda-5, 3\lambda-1)$.

Direction ratios of the given line are (1, 2, 3) which is perpendicular to PL
$$(\lambda-1)\cdot 1+(2\lambda-5)\cdot 2+(3\lambda-1)\cdot 3=0 \Rightarrow \lambda=1$$

So, coordinates of L are (1, 3, 5).

Let $Q(x_1, y_1, z_1)$ be the image of $P(1, 6, 3)$ on given line.

Since, L is mid-point of PQ.

$$\therefore \quad 1=\frac{x_1+1}{2}, 3=\frac{y_1+6}{2}, 5=\frac{z_1+3}{2}$$

$$\Rightarrow \quad x_1=1, y_1=0, z_1=7$$

$\therefore$ Image of $P(1, 6, 3)$ in the given line is (1, 0, 7).

$\therefore \alpha^2+\beta^2+\gamma^2=1+0+49=50$

Skill Builder

The image of the point (1, 2, 3) in the line $\frac{x-1}{2}=\frac{y-2}{3}=\frac{z}{4}$ is (α, β, γ), then $\alpha+\beta+\gamma$ is equal to ....

For Sol.

■ **For more practice** See Q.11 of Milestone Practice 2.

3.11 Shortest Distance between Two Lines

If two lines in space intersect at a point, then the shortest distance between them is zero. Also, if two lines in space are parallel, then the shortest distance between them will be the perpendicular distance, i.e. the length of the perpendicular drawn from any point on one line onto the other line. Further, in a space, there are lines which are neither intersecting nor parallel. In fact, such pair of lines are non-coplanar and are called skew lines.

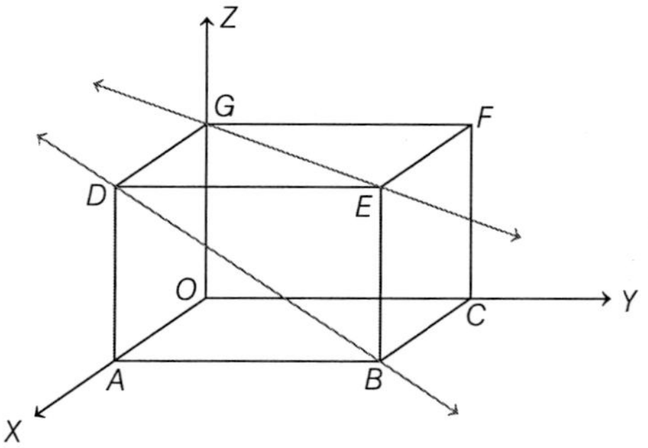

Line GE goes diagonally across the ceiling and line DB passes through one corner of the ceiling directly above A and goes diagonally down the wall. These lines are skew because they are not parallel and also never meet.

By the shortest distance between two lines, we mean the join of a point in one line with one point on the other line so that the length of the segment, so obtained is the smallest.

1. Shortest Distance between Two Skew Straight Lines

Line of Shortest Distance If l_1 and l_2 are two skew lines, then there is one and only one line perpendicular to each of lines l_1 and l_2 which is known as the line of shortest distance.

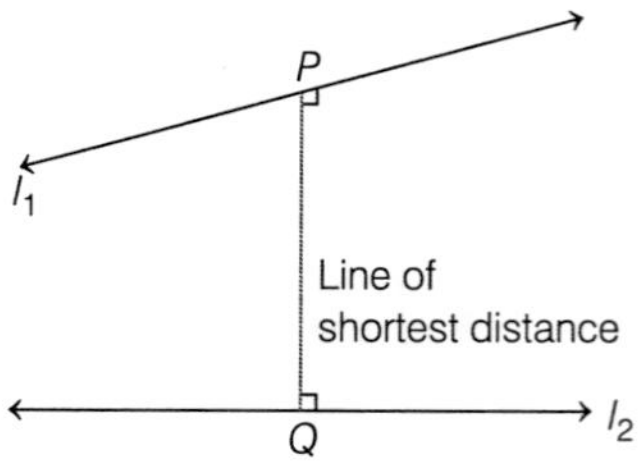

Here, distance PQ is called to be shortest distance.

JEE SPIKE

Shortest distance between two skew line is perpendicular to both the lines.

Vector Form

Let l_1 and l_2 be two lines whose equations are $\mathbf{r}=\mathbf{a}_1+\lambda\mathbf{b}_1$ and $\mathbf{r}=\mathbf{a}_2+\mu\mathbf{b}_2$, respectively.

Clearly, l_1 and l_2 pass through the points A and B with $\mathbf{a}_1$ and $\mathbf{a}_2$, respectively and are parallel to the vectors $\mathbf{b}_1$ and $\mathbf{b}_2$, respectively.

Since, **PQ** is perpendicular to both l_1 and l_2 which are parallel to $\mathbf{b}_1$ and $\mathbf{b}_2$.

$\therefore$ **PQ** is parallel to $\mathbf{b}_1\times\mathbf{b}_2$.

Let $\hat{\mathbf{n}}$ be a unit vector along **PQ**, then $\hat{\mathbf{n}}=\pm\dfrac{\mathbf{b}_1\times\mathbf{b}_2}{|\mathbf{b}_1\times\mathbf{b}_2|}$

$$\therefore \quad PQ=\text{Projection of } \mathbf{AB} \text{ on } \mathbf{PQ}$$

$$\Rightarrow \quad \mathbf{PQ}=\mathbf{AB}\cdot\hat{\mathbf{n}}$$

$$=\pm(\mathbf{a}_2-\mathbf{a}_1)\cdot\frac{(\mathbf{b}_1\times\mathbf{b}_2)}{|\mathbf{b}_1\times\mathbf{b}_2|}$$

$$=\pm\frac{(\mathbf{b}_1\times\mathbf{b}_2)(\mathbf{a}_2-\mathbf{a}_1)}{|\mathbf{b}_1\times\mathbf{b}_2|}$$

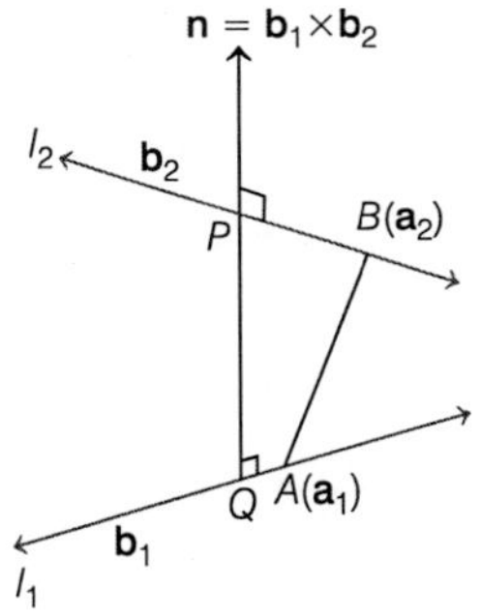

Hence, the distance $PQ=\left|\dfrac{(\mathbf{b}_1\times\mathbf{b}_2)\cdot(\mathbf{a}_2-\mathbf{a}_1)}{|\mathbf{b}_1\times\mathbf{b}_2|}\right|$

$$=\frac{[\mathbf{b}_1\ \ \mathbf{b}_2\ \ (\mathbf{a}_2-\mathbf{a}_1)]}{|\mathbf{b}_1\times\mathbf{b}_2|}$$

Condition for Lines to be Intersecting

The two lines are intersecting, if

$$\left|\frac{(\mathbf{b}_1\times\mathbf{b}_2)\cdot(\mathbf{a}_2-\mathbf{a}_1)}{|\mathbf{b}_1\times\mathbf{b}_2|}\right|=0$$

$$\Rightarrow \quad (\mathbf{b}_1\times\mathbf{b}_2)\cdot(\mathbf{a}_2-\mathbf{a}_1)=0$$

$$\Rightarrow \quad [\mathbf{b}_1\ \ \mathbf{b}_2\ \ (\mathbf{a}_2-\mathbf{a}_1)]=0$$

Cartesian Form

Let the two skew lines be

$$\frac{x-x_1}{a_1}=\frac{y-y_1}{b_1}=\frac{z-z_1}{c_1}$$

and $$\frac{x-x_2}{a_2}=\frac{y-y_2}{b_2}=\frac{z-z_2}{c_2}$$

Vector equations for these two lines are

$$\mathbf{r}=(x_1\hat{\mathbf{i}}+y_1\hat{\mathbf{j}}+z_1\hat{\mathbf{k}})+\lambda(a_1\hat{\mathbf{i}}+b_1\hat{\mathbf{j}}+c_1\hat{\mathbf{k}})$$

and $$\mathbf{r}=(x_2\hat{\mathbf{i}}+y_2\hat{\mathbf{j}}+z_2\hat{\mathbf{k}})+\mu(a_2\hat{\mathbf{i}}+b_2\hat{\mathbf{j}}+c_2\hat{\mathbf{k}})$$

$\because$ Shortest distance, $d=\left|\dfrac{(\mathbf{a}_2-\mathbf{a}_1)\cdot(\mathbf{b}_1\times\mathbf{b}_2)}{|\mathbf{b}_1\times\mathbf{b}_2|}\right|$

$$\Rightarrow d=\frac{\begin{vmatrix} x_2-x_1 & y_2-y_1 & z_2-z_1\\ a_1 & b_1 & c_1\\ a_2 & b_2 & c_2\end{vmatrix}}{\sqrt{(b_1c_2-b_2c_1)^2+(c_1a_2-a_1c_2)^2+(a_1b_2-a_2b_1)^2}}$$

Conditions for Lines to Intersect or coplanar

The lines are intersecting or coplanar, if shortest distance $=0$

$$\Rightarrow \quad \begin{vmatrix} x_2-x_1 & y_2-y_1 & z_2-z_1\\ a_1 & b_1 & c_1\\ a_2 & b_2 & c_2\end{vmatrix}=0$$

Example 32. Find the shortest distance between the lines $\mathbf{r}=(4\hat{\mathbf{i}}-\hat{\mathbf{j}})+\lambda(\hat{\mathbf{i}}+2\hat{\mathbf{j}}-3\hat{\mathbf{k}})$ and $\mathbf{r}=(\hat{\mathbf{i}}-\hat{\mathbf{j}}+2\hat{\mathbf{k}})+\mu(2\hat{\mathbf{i}}+4\hat{\mathbf{j}}-5\hat{\mathbf{k}})$.

Sol. We know that the shortest distance between the lines $\mathbf{r}=\mathbf{a}_1+\lambda\mathbf{b}_1$ and $\mathbf{r}=\mathbf{a}_2+\lambda\mathbf{b}_2$

$$\Rightarrow \quad d=\left|\frac{(\mathbf{a}_2-\mathbf{a}_1)\cdot(\mathbf{b}_1\times\mathbf{b}_2)}{|\mathbf{b}_1\times\mathbf{b}_2|}\right|$$

On comparing the given equation with the equations $\mathbf{r}=\mathbf{a}_1+\lambda\mathbf{b}_1$ and $\mathbf{r}=\mathbf{a}_2+\lambda\mathbf{b}_2$ respectively, we have $\mathbf{a}_1=4\hat{\mathbf{i}}-\hat{\mathbf{j}}$, $\mathbf{a}_2=\hat{\mathbf{i}}-\hat{\mathbf{j}}+2\hat{\mathbf{k}}$, $\mathbf{b}_1=\hat{\mathbf{i}}+2\hat{\mathbf{j}}-3\hat{\mathbf{k}}$ and $\mathbf{b}_2=2\hat{\mathbf{i}}+4\hat{\mathbf{j}}-5\hat{\mathbf{k}}$

Now, $\mathbf{a}_2-\mathbf{a}_1=-3\hat{\mathbf{i}}+0\hat{\mathbf{j}}+2\hat{\mathbf{k}}$

and $$\mathbf{b}_1\times\mathbf{b}_2=\begin{vmatrix}\hat{\mathbf{i}} & \hat{\mathbf{j}} & \hat{\mathbf{k}}\\ 1 & 2 & -3\\ 2 & 4 & -5\end{vmatrix}$$

$$=\hat{\mathbf{i}}(-10+12)-\hat{\mathbf{j}}(-5+6)+\hat{\mathbf{k}}(4-4)$$

$$=2\hat{\mathbf{i}}-\hat{\mathbf{j}}+0\hat{\mathbf{k}}$$

$$\therefore (\mathbf{a}_2-\mathbf{a}_1)\cdot(\mathbf{b}_1\times\mathbf{b}_2)=(-3\hat{\mathbf{i}}+0\hat{\mathbf{j}}+2\hat{\mathbf{k}})\cdot(2\hat{\mathbf{i}}-\hat{\mathbf{j}}+0\hat{\mathbf{k}})$$

$$=-6$$

and $$|\mathbf{b}_1\times\mathbf{b}_2|=\sqrt{4+1+0}=\sqrt{5}$$

$\therefore$ Shortest distance, $d=\left|\dfrac{(\mathbf{a}_2-\mathbf{a}_1)\cdot(\mathbf{b}_1\times\mathbf{b}_2)}{|\mathbf{b}_1\times\mathbf{b}_2|}\right|$

$$=\left|\frac{-6}{\sqrt{5}}\right|$$

$$=\frac{6}{\sqrt{5}}$$

JEE SCANNER

Example Similar to PYQ Asked in JEE Main 2023

The shortest distance between the lines $\frac{x-1}{2}=\frac{y-2}{3}=\frac{z-3}{4}$ *and* $\frac{x-2}{3}=\frac{y-4}{4}=\frac{z-5}{5}$ *is l, then the value of* $36l^2$ *is ....*

Sol. Given lines are

$$\frac{x-1}{2}=\frac{y-2}{3}=\frac{z-3}{4} \quad \text{...(i)}$$

and $$\frac{x-2}{3}=\frac{y-4}{4}=\frac{z-5}{5} \quad \text{...(ii)}$$

Here, $x_1 = 1, y_1 = 2, z_1 = 3;\ x_2 = 2, y_2 = 4, z_2 = 5$

$l_1 = 2, m_1 = 3, n_1 = 4;\ l_2 = 3, m_2 = 4, n_2 = 5$

Shortest distance between the lines (i) and (ii) are modulus of

$$= \frac{\begin{vmatrix} x_2 - x_1 & y_2 - y_1 & z_2 - z_1 \\ l_1 & m_1 & n_1 \\ l_2 & m_2 & n_2 \end{vmatrix}}{\sqrt{(l_1m_2 - l_2m_1)^2 + (m_1n_2 - m_2n_1)^2 + (l_1n_2 - l_2n_1)^2}} \quad \text{...(iii)}$$

$$\text{Now,} = \begin{vmatrix} x_2 - x_1 & y_2 - y_1 & z_2 - z_1 \\ l_1 & m_1 & n_1 \\ l_2 & m_2 & n_2 \end{vmatrix} = \begin{vmatrix} 1 & 2 & 2 \\ 2 & 3 & 4 \\ 3 & 4 & 5 \end{vmatrix}$$

$$= 1(15 - 16) - 2(10 - 12) + 2(8 - 9) = 1$$

Also, $(l_1m_2 - l_2m_1)^2 + (m_1n_2 - m_2n_1)^2 + (n_1l_2 - n_2l_1)^2$

$$= (8 - 9)^2 + (15 - 16)^2 + (10 - 12)^2 = 6$$

From Eq. (iii) shortest distance between lines (i) (ii), we get

$$= \left|\frac{1}{\sqrt{6}}\right| = \frac{1}{\sqrt{6}}$$

Here, $l = \frac{1}{\sqrt{6}}$

$\therefore\ 36l^2 = 36 \times \frac{1}{6} = 6$

Skill Builder

The shortest distance between the lines $\frac{x+2}{3}=\frac{y-3}{2}=\frac{z-2}{5}$ and $\frac{x-3}{1}=\frac{y+4}{4}=\frac{z-5}{3}$ is λ, then $39\lambda^2$ is equal to ....

For Sol.

- **For more practice** See Example 33 and Q.Nos. 13, 15 of Milestone Practice 2.

Example 33. Find the shortest distance, vector and cartesian equations of the lines, if the vector equation of the lines is given by

$$\mathbf{r} = (3\hat{\mathbf{i}} + 8\hat{\mathbf{j}} + 3\hat{\mathbf{k}}) + \lambda(3\hat{\mathbf{i}} - \hat{\mathbf{j}} + \hat{\mathbf{k}})$$

and $$\mathbf{r} = (-3\hat{\mathbf{i}} - 7\hat{\mathbf{j}} + 6\hat{\mathbf{k}}) + \mu(-3\hat{\mathbf{i}} + 2\hat{\mathbf{j}} + 4\hat{\mathbf{k}})$$

Sol. Given lines are

$$\mathbf{r} = (3\hat{\mathbf{i}} + 8\hat{\mathbf{j}} + 3\hat{\mathbf{k}}) + \lambda(3\hat{\mathbf{i}} - \hat{\mathbf{j}} + \hat{\mathbf{k}}) \quad \text{...(i)}$$

and $$\mathbf{r} = (-3\hat{\mathbf{i}} - 7\hat{\mathbf{j}} + 6\hat{\mathbf{k}}) + \mu(-3\hat{\mathbf{i}} + 2\hat{\mathbf{j}} + 4\hat{\mathbf{k}}) \quad \text{...(ii)}$$

Equation of lines (i) and (ii) in cartesian form,

$$AB: \frac{x-3}{3} = \frac{y-8}{-1} = \frac{z-3}{1} = \lambda \quad \text{...(iii)}$$

and $$CD: \frac{x+3}{-3} = \frac{y+7}{2} = \frac{z-6}{4} = \mu \quad \text{...(iv)}$$

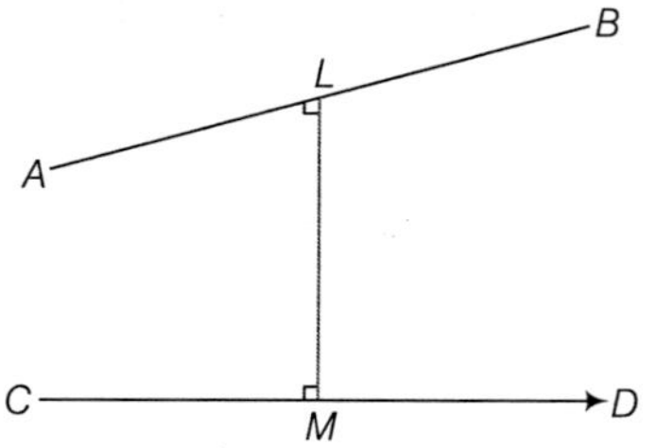

Let $L(3\lambda + 3, -\lambda + 8, \lambda + 3)$, $M(-3\mu - 3, 2\mu - 7, 4\mu + 6)$

Direction ratios of LM are

$$(3\lambda + 3\mu + 6, -\lambda - 2\mu + 15, \lambda - 4\mu - 3)$$

Since, $LM \perp AB$

$\therefore 3(3\lambda + 3\mu + 6) - 1(-\lambda - 2\mu + 15) + 1(\lambda - 4\mu - 3) = 0$

or $\quad 11\lambda + 7\mu = 0 \quad$ ...(v)

Again, $LM \perp CD$

$-3(3\lambda + 3\mu + 6) + 2(-\lambda - 2\mu + 15) + 4(\lambda - 4\mu - 3) = 0$

or $\quad -7\lambda - 29\mu = 0 \quad$ ...(vi)

On solving Eqs. (v) and (vi), we get

$$\lambda = 0 = \mu$$

$\therefore\quad L \equiv (3, 8, 3),\ M \equiv (-3, -7, 6)$

Hence, the shortest distance,

$$LM = \sqrt{(3+3)^2 + (8+7)^2 + (3-6)^2} = 3\sqrt{30} \text{ units}$$

$\therefore$ Vector equation of LM is

$$\mathbf{r} = 3\hat{\mathbf{i}} + 8\hat{\mathbf{j}} + 3\hat{\mathbf{k}} + t(6\hat{\mathbf{i}} + 15\hat{\mathbf{j}} - 3\hat{\mathbf{k}})$$

Also, the cartesian equation of LM is

$$\frac{x-3}{6} = \frac{y-8}{15} = \frac{z-3}{-3}$$

Shortest Distance between Parallel Lines

Let l_1 and l_2 be two parallel lines whose equations are $\mathbf{r} = \mathbf{a}_1 + \lambda\mathbf{b}$ or $\mathbf{r} = \mathbf{a}_2 + \mu\mathbf{b}$, respectively.

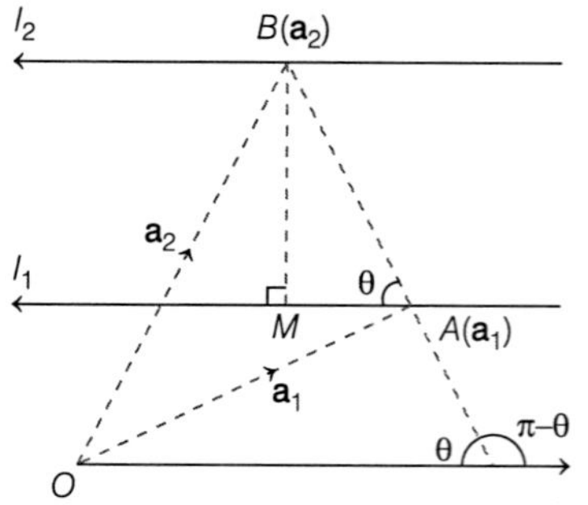

Clearly, l_1 and l_2 pass through the points A and B with position vectors $\mathbf{a}_1$ and $\mathbf{a}_2$, respectively and both are parallel to the vector $\mathbf{b}$, where BM is the shortest distance between l_1 and l_2.

Let θ be the angle between AB and l_1.

$$\therefore \quad \sin\theta = \frac{BM}{AB}$$

$$\Rightarrow \quad BM = AB\sin\theta = |\mathbf{AB}|\sin\theta$$

Now, $\quad |\mathbf{AB}\times\mathbf{b}| = |\mathbf{AB}||\mathbf{b}|\sin(\pi-\theta)$

$$|\mathbf{AB}||\mathbf{b}|\sin\theta = (|\mathbf{AB}|\sin\theta)|\mathbf{b}| = BM|\mathbf{b}|$$

$$\therefore \quad BM = \frac{|\mathbf{AB}\times\mathbf{b}|}{|\mathbf{b}|} = \frac{|(\mathbf{a}_2-\mathbf{a}_1)\times\mathbf{b}|}{|\mathbf{b}|}$$

$\therefore$ Shortest distance between parallel lines

$$\mathbf{r} = \mathbf{a}_1 + \lambda\mathbf{b}_1 \text{ and } \mathbf{r} = \mathbf{a}_2 + \mu\mathbf{b} \text{ is}$$

$$d = \frac{|(\mathbf{a}_2-\mathbf{a}_1)\times\mathbf{b}|}{|\mathbf{b}|}$$

Example 34. Find the shortest distance between lines $\mathbf{r} = (\hat{\mathbf{i}}+2\hat{\mathbf{j}}+\hat{\mathbf{k}})+\lambda(2\hat{\mathbf{i}}+\hat{\mathbf{j}}+2\hat{\mathbf{k}})$
and $\mathbf{r} = 2\hat{\mathbf{i}}-\hat{\mathbf{j}}-\hat{\mathbf{k}}+\mu(2\hat{\mathbf{i}}+\hat{\mathbf{j}}+2\hat{\mathbf{k}})$.

Sol. Here lines (i) and (ii) are passing through the points $\mathbf{a}_1 = \hat{\mathbf{i}}+2\hat{\mathbf{j}}+\hat{\mathbf{k}}$ and $\mathbf{a}_2 = 2\hat{\mathbf{i}}-\hat{\mathbf{j}}-\hat{\mathbf{k}}$, respectively, and are parallel to the vector $\mathbf{b} = 2\hat{\mathbf{i}}+\hat{\mathbf{j}}+2\hat{\mathbf{k}}$.

Hence, the shortest distance between the lines using the formula

$$\frac{|\mathbf{b}\times(\mathbf{a}_2-\mathbf{a}_1)|}{|\mathbf{b}|} = \frac{\begin{vmatrix}\hat{\mathbf{i}} & \hat{\mathbf{j}} & \hat{\mathbf{k}}\\ 2 & 1 & 2\\ 1 & -3 & -2\end{vmatrix}}{3}$$

$$= \frac{|4\hat{\mathbf{i}}-6\hat{\mathbf{j}}-7\hat{\mathbf{k}}|}{3}$$

$$= \frac{\sqrt{16+36+49}}{3} = \frac{\sqrt{101}}{3} \text{ units}$$

3.12 Point of Intersection of Lines

To check whether the two given lines intersect or not and to find the point of intersection (if intersect), which are defined below.

Vector Form

Suppose, two lines be

$$\mathbf{r} = (a_1\hat{\mathbf{i}}+a_2\hat{\mathbf{j}}+a_3\hat{\mathbf{k}})+\lambda(b_1\hat{\mathbf{i}}+b_2\hat{\mathbf{j}}+b_3\hat{\mathbf{k}}) \quad \text{...(i)}$$

and $\mathbf{r} = (a_1'\hat{\mathbf{i}}+a_2'\hat{\mathbf{j}}+a_3'\hat{\mathbf{k}})+\mu(b_1'\hat{\mathbf{i}}+b_2'\hat{\mathbf{j}}+b_3'\hat{\mathbf{k}})$ ...(ii)

If Eqs. (i) and (ii) intersect, then they have a common point.

So, we have $(a_1\hat{\mathbf{i}}+a_2\hat{\mathbf{j}}+a_3\hat{\mathbf{k}})+\lambda(b_1\hat{\mathbf{i}}+b_2\hat{\mathbf{j}}+b_3\hat{\mathbf{k}})$

$$= (a_1'\hat{\mathbf{i}}+a_2'\hat{\mathbf{j}}+a_3'\hat{\mathbf{k}})+\mu(b_1'\hat{\mathbf{i}}+b_2'\hat{\mathbf{j}}+b_3'\hat{\mathbf{k}})$$

$$\Rightarrow (a_1+\lambda b_1)\hat{\mathbf{i}}+(a_2+\lambda b_2)\hat{\mathbf{j}}+(a_3+\lambda b_3)\hat{\mathbf{k}}$$

$$= (a_1'+\mu b_1')\hat{\mathbf{i}}+(a_2'+\mu b_2')\hat{\mathbf{j}}+(a_3'+\mu b_3')\hat{\mathbf{k}}$$

$\therefore \quad a_1+\lambda b_1 = a_1'+\mu b_1', a_2+\lambda b_2 = a_2'+\mu b_2'$

and $a_3+\lambda b_3 = a_3'+\mu b_3'$

Now, find the value λ and μ by solving any two of above equations.

- If the value of λ and μ satisfy the third equation, then the two lines intersect, otherwise not.
- If intersect, then the point of intersection can be obtain by substituting the value of λ (or μ) in Eq. (i) [or Eq. (ii)].

Cartesian Form

Let two lines be

$$L_1 : \frac{x-x_1}{a_1} = \frac{y-y_1}{b_1} = \frac{z-z_1}{c_1} = \lambda \text{ (let)}$$

and $\quad L_2 : \dfrac{x-x_2}{a_2} = \dfrac{y-y_2}{b_2} = \dfrac{z-z_2}{c_2} = \mu$ (let)

Consider the coordinates of general points on L_1 and L_2,

i.e. $\quad (x_1+a_1\lambda, y_1+b_1\lambda, z_1+c_1\lambda) \quad$ ...(i)

and $\quad (x_2+a_2\mu, y_2+b_2\mu, z_2+c_2\mu) \quad$ ...(ii)

where, λ and μ are some real constants. If the lines L_1 and L_2 intersect, then they have a common point.

$$\therefore \quad (x_1+a_1\lambda, y_1+b_1\lambda, z_1+c_1\lambda) = (x_2+a_2\mu, y_2+b_2\mu, z_2+c_2\mu)$$

for some constants λ and μ.

$\Rightarrow x_1+a_1\lambda = x_2+a_2\mu, \; y_1+b_1\lambda = y_2+b_2\mu$

and $z_1+c_1\lambda = z_2+c_2\mu$

Now, find the value of λ and μ by solving any two of above equations.

- If the value of λ and μ satisfy the third equation, then the two lines intersect, otherwise not.
- If intersect, then the point of intersection can be obtain by substituting the value of λ (or μ) in Eq. (i) [or Eq. (ii)].

Example 35. The lines $\mathbf{r}=(\hat{\mathbf{i}}+\hat{\mathbf{j}}-\hat{\mathbf{k}})+\lambda(3\hat{\mathbf{i}}-\hat{\mathbf{j}})$ and $\mathbf{r}=(4\hat{\mathbf{i}}-\hat{\mathbf{k}})+\mu(2\hat{\mathbf{i}}+3\hat{\mathbf{k}})$ intersect each other. Then, find their point of intersection.

Sol. Given, lines are $\mathbf{r}=(\hat{\mathbf{i}}+\hat{\mathbf{j}}-\hat{\mathbf{k}})+\lambda(3\hat{\mathbf{i}}-\hat{\mathbf{j}})$ ...(i)

and $\mathbf{r}=(4\hat{\mathbf{i}}-\hat{\mathbf{k}})+\mu(2\hat{\mathbf{i}}+3\hat{\mathbf{k}})$ ...(ii)

Clearly, these lines will intersect, if

$$(\hat{\mathbf{i}}+\hat{\mathbf{j}}-\hat{\mathbf{k}})+\lambda(3\hat{\mathbf{i}}-\hat{\mathbf{j}})=(4\hat{\mathbf{i}}-\hat{\mathbf{k}})+\mu(2\hat{\mathbf{i}}+3\hat{\mathbf{k}}),$$

for some particualr values of λ and μ.

Collecting the like terms, we get

$$(1+3\lambda)\hat{\mathbf{i}}+(1-\lambda)\hat{\mathbf{j}}-\hat{\mathbf{k}}=(4+2\mu)\hat{\mathbf{i}}+(-1+3\mu)\hat{\mathbf{k}}$$

On equating the coefficient of $\hat{\mathbf{i}}$, we get

$$1+3\lambda=4+2\mu$$

$$\Rightarrow \quad 3\lambda-2\mu=3$$

On equating the coefficient $\hat{\mathbf{j}}$, we get

$$1-\lambda=0$$

$$\Rightarrow \quad \lambda=1$$

On equating the coefficient of $\hat{\mathbf{k}}$, we get

$$-1=-1+3\mu$$

$$\Rightarrow \quad \mu=0$$

$\therefore \mu=0$ and $\lambda=1$

Also, these value satisfy $3\lambda-2\mu=3$, therefore the given lines intersect.

On putting $\lambda=1$ in Eq. (i), we get

$$\mathbf{r}=(\hat{\mathbf{i}}+\hat{\mathbf{j}}-\hat{\mathbf{k}})+1(3\hat{\mathbf{i}}-\hat{\mathbf{j}})$$

$$=4\hat{\mathbf{i}}+0\hat{\mathbf{j}}-\hat{\mathbf{k}}$$

Hence, the point of intersection of given lines is $(4, 0, -1)$.

Alternate Solution

Given, equation is $\mathbf{r}=\hat{\mathbf{i}}+\hat{\mathbf{j}}-\hat{\mathbf{k}}+\lambda(3\hat{\mathbf{i}}-\hat{\mathbf{j}})$

and $\mathbf{r}=4\hat{\mathbf{i}}-\hat{\mathbf{k}}+\mu(2\hat{\mathbf{i}}+3\hat{\mathbf{k}})$

$$\Rightarrow \quad \frac{x-1}{3}=\frac{y-1}{-1}=\frac{z+1}{0}=\lambda \text{ (let)} \quad \text{...(i)}$$

and $$\frac{x-4}{2}=\frac{y}{0}=\frac{z+1}{3}=\lambda \text{ (let)} \quad \text{...(ii)}$$

From Eq. (i),

$$x=3\lambda+1, y=-\lambda+1, z=-1$$

On putting x, y and z in Eq. (ii), we get

$$\frac{3\lambda+1-4}{2}=\frac{-\lambda+1}{0}$$

$$\Rightarrow \quad -\lambda+1=0$$

$$\Rightarrow \quad \lambda=1$$

Intersecting part is $x-1=3$

$$\Rightarrow \quad x=4$$

$$y-1=-1, y=0$$

$$z+1=0, \quad z=-1$$

$\therefore$ Point of intersection $=(4, 0, -1)$

JEE SCANNER

Example Similar to PYQ Asked in JEE Main 2022

If a line with direction ratios 2:1:1 intersects the lines $\frac{x-1}{2}=\frac{y-2}{3}=\frac{z-3}{4}$ *and* $\frac{x-2}{1}=\frac{y+1}{2}=\frac{z+2}{3}$ *at P and Q, then the value of* $(PQ)^2$ *is ....*

Sol. Given lines are

$$\frac{x-1}{2}=\frac{y-2}{3}=\frac{z-3}{4} \quad \text{...(i)}$$

and $$\frac{x-2}{1}=\frac{y+1}{2}=\frac{z+2}{3} \quad \text{...(ii)}$$

Any point on the line (i) is

$$(2\lambda+1, 3\lambda+2, 4\lambda+3).$$

$\therefore$ Point P is $(2\lambda+1, 3\lambda+2, 4\lambda+3)$

and any point on the line (ii) is

$$(\mu+2, 2\mu-1, 3\mu-2).$$

$\therefore$ Point Q is $(\mu+2, 2\mu-1, 3\mu-2)$.

Now, direction ratios of PQ are

$$2\lambda+1-\mu-2, 3\lambda+2-2\mu+1, 4\lambda+3-3\mu+2$$

i.e. $2\lambda-\mu-1, 3\lambda-2\mu+3, 4\lambda-3\mu+5$

Since, lines (i) and (ii) are parallel.

$$\therefore \quad \frac{2\lambda-\mu-1}{2}=\frac{3\lambda-2\mu+3}{1}=\frac{4\lambda-3\mu+5}{1}$$

I II III

On taking I and II, we get

$$2\lambda-\mu-1=2(3\lambda-2\mu+3)$$

$$\Rightarrow \quad 2\lambda-\mu-1=6\lambda-4\mu+6$$

$$\Rightarrow \quad 4\lambda-3\mu+7=0 \quad \text{...(iii)}$$

On taking II and III, we get

$$3\lambda-2\mu+3=4\lambda-3\mu+5 \Rightarrow \lambda-\mu+2=0 \quad \text{...(iv)}$$

On solving Eqs. (iii) and (iv), we get

$$\lambda=-1 \text{ and } \mu=1$$

$\therefore$ Coordinates of P are $(-1, -1, -1)$ and coordinates of Q are $(3, 1, 1)$.

$$\therefore \quad PQ=\sqrt{(3+1)^2+(1+1)^2+(1+1)^2}$$

$$=\sqrt{16+4+4}=\sqrt{24}=2\sqrt{6}$$

$$\therefore \quad PQ^2=24$$

Skill Builder

If a line with direction ratios 3:2:4 intersects the lines $\frac{x-2}{3}=\frac{y-1}{2}=\frac{z-3}{5}$ and $\frac{x-4}{1}=\frac{y+2}{3}=\frac{z+3}{2}$ at A and B, then the value of $(AB)^2$ is ....

For Sol.

- **For more practice** See Q. 17 of Milestone Practice 2.

Example 36. Find the equation of a line which passes through the point (1, 1, 1) and intersects the lines $\frac{x-1}{2}=\frac{y-2}{3}=\frac{z-3}{4}$ and $\frac{x+2}{1}=\frac{y-3}{2}=\frac{z+1}{4}$.

Sol. Any line passing through the point (1, 1, 1) is

$$\frac{x-1}{a}=\frac{y-1}{b}=\frac{z-1}{c} \quad ...(i)$$

This line intersects the line

$$\frac{x-1}{2}=\frac{y-2}{3}=\frac{z-3}{4}$$

if $a:b:c \neq 2:3:4$ and $\begin{vmatrix} 1-1 & 2-1 & 3-1 \\ a & b & c \\ 2 & 3 & 4 \end{vmatrix}=0$

$$\Rightarrow \quad a-2b+c=0 \quad ...(ii)$$

Again, line (i) intersects line

$$\frac{x-(-2)}{1}=\frac{y-3}{2}=\frac{z-(-1)}{4}$$

if $a:b:c \neq 1:2:4$ and $\begin{vmatrix} -2-1 & 3-1 & -1-1 \\ a & b & c \\ 1 & 2 & 4 \end{vmatrix}=0$

$$\Rightarrow \quad 6a+5b-4c=0 \quad ...(iii)$$

From (ii) and (iii) by cross multiplication, we have

$$\frac{a}{8-5}=\frac{b}{6+4}=\frac{c}{5+12}$$

$$\Rightarrow \quad \frac{a}{3}=\frac{b}{10}=\frac{c}{17}$$

So, the required lines is

$$\frac{x-1}{3}=\frac{y-1}{10}=\frac{z-1}{17}$$

Example 37. If the straight line $x=-1+s, y=3-\lambda s, z=1+\lambda s$ and $x=\frac{t}{2}, y=1+t, z=2-t$, with parameters s and t respectively are coplanar, then find λ.

Sol. The given lines $\frac{x+1}{1}=\frac{y-3}{-\lambda}=\frac{z-1}{\lambda}=s$

$\frac{x-0}{\frac{1}{2}}=\frac{y-1}{1}=\frac{y-2}{-1}=t$ are coplanar, if

$$\begin{vmatrix} 0+1 & 1-3 & 2-1 \\ 1 & -\lambda & \lambda \\ 1/2 & 1 & -1 \end{vmatrix}=0$$

$$\Rightarrow \begin{vmatrix} 1 & -2 & 1 \\ 1 & -\lambda & \lambda \\ 1/2 & 1 & -1 \end{vmatrix}=0$$

$$\Rightarrow 1(\lambda-\lambda)+2\left(-1-\frac{\lambda}{2}\right)+1\left(1+\frac{\lambda}{2}\right)=0$$

Hence, $\lambda=-2$

Milestone Practice 3.2

1. A line passes through the point with position vector $2\hat{i}-3\hat{j}+4\hat{k}$ and is in the direction of $3\hat{i}+4\hat{j}-5\hat{k}$. Find the equation of the line in vector and cartesian forms.
2. The cartesian equation of a line is $\frac{x-3}{2}=\frac{y+1}{-2}=\frac{z-3}{5}$. Find the vector equation of the line.
3. If $\mathbf{r}=(\hat{i}+2\hat{j}+3\hat{k})+\lambda(\hat{i}-\hat{j}+\hat{k})$ and $\mathbf{r}=(\hat{i}+2\hat{j}+3\hat{k})+\mu(\hat{i}+\hat{j}-\hat{k})$ are two lines, then find the equation of acute angle bisectors of two lines.
4. Find the angle between the pairs of line $\mathbf{r}=3\hat{i}+2\hat{j}-4\hat{k}+\lambda(\hat{i}+2\hat{j}+2\hat{k})$, $\hat{r}=5\hat{i}-2\hat{j}+\mu(3\hat{i}+2\hat{j}+6\hat{k})$
5. The angle between the lines $2x=3y=-z$ and $6x=-y=-4z$, is equal to
   (a) 0° (b) 45° (c) 60° (d) 90°
6. Find the equation of the line drawn through the point (1, 0, 2) to meet at right angles the line $\frac{x+1}{3}=\frac{y-2}{-2}=\frac{z+1}{-1}$.
7. Find the equation of line through (1, 2, −1) and perpendicular to each of the lines $\frac{x}{1}=\frac{y}{0}=\frac{z}{-1}$ and $\frac{x}{3}=\frac{y}{4}=\frac{z}{5}$.
8. Find the points where line $\frac{x-2}{3}=\frac{y+4}{-5}=\frac{z}{2}$ intersects XY, YZ and ZX-planes.
9. The point $A(3,-2,4)$ is shifted parallel to the line $\frac{x}{\sqrt{3}}=\frac{y-1}{2}=\frac{z+1}{3}$ by distance 1 unit, then find the coordinates of P in the new position.

10. Find the coordinates of a point on the line $\frac{x-1}{2}=\frac{y+1}{-3}=z$ at a distance $4\sqrt{14}$ units from the point $(1,-1,0)$.

11. The image of the point (1, 2, 3) in the line $\frac{x-6}{3}=\frac{y-7}{2}=\frac{z-7}{-2}$, is

(a) (5, 8, 15)
(b) (8, 5, 15)
(c) (8, 15, 5)
(d) (15, 8, 5)

12. Two lines $L_1: x=5, \frac{y}{3-\alpha}=\frac{z}{-2}$ and $L_2: x=\alpha$, $\frac{y}{-1}=\frac{z}{2-\alpha}$ are intersecting. Then, the sum of values of α, is

(a) 0 (b) 5 (c) 10 (d) 15

13. Find the magnitude of the shortest distance between the lines $\frac{x}{2}=\frac{y}{-3}=\frac{z}{1}$ and $\frac{x-2}{3}=\frac{y-1}{-5}=\frac{z+2}{2}$.

14. Find the perpendicular distance of the point $(1,1,1)$ from the line $\frac{x-2}{2}=\frac{y+3}{2}=\frac{z}{-1}$.

15. The shortest distance between the lines $\frac{x}{2}=\frac{y}{2}=\frac{z}{1}$ and $\frac{x+2}{-2}=\frac{y-4}{8}=\frac{y-5}{4}$ lies in the interval (λ, μ). Then, the value of $\lambda+\mu$ is

(a) 0 (b) 5 (c) 10 (d) 15

16. Show that the two lines $\frac{x-1}{2}=\frac{y-2}{3}=\frac{z-3}{4}$ and $\frac{x-4}{5}=\frac{y-1}{2}=z$ intersect. Find also the point of intersection of these lines.

17. A line from the origin meets the lines $\frac{x-2}{1}=\frac{y-1}{-2}=\frac{z+1}{1}$ and $\frac{x-\frac{8}{3}}{2}=\frac{y+3}{-1}=\frac{z-1}{1}$ at P and Q, respectively. If distance $PQ=l$, then find value of $[l]$, where [ ] denotes the greatest integer function.

18. Find the coordinates of the point P on the line $\mathbf{r}=(\hat{\mathbf{i}}+\hat{\mathbf{j}}+\hat{\mathbf{k}})+\lambda(-\hat{\mathbf{i}}+\hat{\mathbf{j}}+\hat{\mathbf{k}})$ which is nearest to the origin.

19. Find the centroid of the triangle formed by the point (0, 0, 0) and the point of intersection of line $\frac{x-1}{1}=\frac{y-1}{2}=\frac{z-1}{1}$ with $x=0$ and $y=0$.

20. If the line $\frac{x-2}{3}=\frac{y-1}{2}=\frac{z-1}{-1}$ intersects the curve $x^2-y^2=p^2, z=0$, then p is equal to

(a) $\pm\sqrt{6}$
(b) $\pm 2\sqrt{6}$
(c) $\pm 3\sqrt{6}$
(d) None of the above

21. If the straight lines $\frac{x-1}{k}=\frac{y-2}{2}=\frac{z-3}{3}$ and $\frac{x-2}{3}=\frac{y-3}{k}=\frac{z-1}{2}$ intersect at a point, then find the value of k.

22. If l_1 and l_2 are two skew lines such that A, B are two distinct points on l_1 and C, D are two distinct points on l_2, then prove that AC cannot be parallel to BD.

23. A line with direction cosines proportional to 2, 1, 2 meets each of the line $x=y+a=z$ and $x+a=2y=2z$, find the coordinates of each of the points of intersection.

Answer Key

1. $\frac{x-2}{3}=\frac{y-(-3)}{4}=\frac{z-4}{-5}$ **2.** $\mathbf{r}=\mathbf{r}_1+\lambda\mathbf{a}=(3\hat{\mathbf{i}}-\hat{\mathbf{j}}+3\hat{\mathbf{k}})+\lambda(2\hat{\mathbf{i}}-2\hat{\mathbf{j}}+5\hat{\mathbf{k}})$

3. $\hat{\mathbf{i}}+2\hat{\mathbf{j}}+3\hat{\mathbf{k}}+\lambda(-2\hat{\mathbf{j}}+2\hat{\mathbf{k}})$ **4.** $\theta=\cos^{-1}\left(\frac{19}{21}\right)$ **5.** (d) **6.** $\frac{x-1}{1}=\frac{y}{-2}=\frac{z-2}{7}$

7. $L: \frac{x-1}{4}=\frac{y-2}{-8}=\frac{z+1}{4}$, $\mathbf{r}=(\hat{\mathbf{i}}+2\hat{\mathbf{j}}-\hat{\mathbf{k}})+\lambda(4\hat{\mathbf{i}}-8\hat{\mathbf{j}}+4\hat{\mathbf{k}})$ **8.** $\left(-\frac{2}{5}, 0, -\frac{8}{5}\right)$

9. $\left(\frac{12+\sqrt{3}}{4}, -\frac{3}{2}, \frac{19}{4}\right)$ and $\left(\frac{12-\sqrt{3}}{4}, -\frac{5}{2}, \frac{13}{4}\right)$ **10.** $(9,-13,4)$ or $(-7,11,-4)$ **11.** (a) **12.** (c)

13. $\frac{1}{\sqrt{3}}$ units **14.** $\frac{1}{3}\sqrt{137}$ **15.** (b) **16.** $(-1,-1,-1)$ **17.** 2 **18.** $\left(\frac{4}{3}, \frac{2}{3}, \frac{2}{3}\right)$

19. $\left(\frac{1}{6}, -\frac{1}{3}, \frac{1}{6}\right)$ **20.** (d) **21.** $-5, \frac{5}{2}$ **23.** $P(3a, 2a, 3a)$ and $Q(a, 0, a)$

For Detailed Solution

Milestone 3 Planes

• Equation of Plane in Various Form • Angle Between Two Planes • Family of Planes
• Two Sides of a Plane • Distance of a Point from a Plane • Equation of Planes Bisecting the Angle Between Two Planes • Line and Plane • Equation of a Plane Containing Two Intersecting Lines

A **plane** is a surface such that if any two points are taken on it, the line segment joining them lies completely on the surface.

General Form General equation of the first degree in x, y, z always represents a plane.

The general equation of plane is $ax + by + cz + d = 0$.

Proof Let first degree equation in x, y and z be

$$ax + by + cz + d = 0 \quad \text{...(i)}$$

In order to prove that Eq. (i) is the equation of plane, it is sufficient to show that every point on the line joining two points lies on the surface represented by Eq. (i).

Let $P(x_1, y_1, z_1)$ and $Q(x_2, y_2, z_2)$ be two points on the surface represented by Eq. (i).

Then, $$ax_1 + by_1 + cz_1 + d = 0 \quad \text{...(ii)}$$

and $$ax_2 + by_2 + cz_2 + d = 0 \quad \text{...(iii)}$$

Let R be any arbitrary point on the line segment joining P and Q. Suppose R divides PQ in the ratio $\lambda : 1$.

$\therefore$ R is $\left(\dfrac{x_1 + \lambda x_2}{1+\lambda}, \dfrac{y_1 + \lambda y_2}{1+\lambda}, \dfrac{z_1 + \lambda z_2}{1+\lambda}\right)$

We are to show that R lies on the surface represented by Eq. (i) for all values of λ. For this, it is sufficient to prove that R satisfy Eq. (i)

On putting this value of R in LHS of Eq. (i), we obtain

$$a\left(\frac{x_1 + \lambda x_2}{\lambda + 1}\right) + b\left(\frac{y_1 + \lambda y_2}{\lambda + 1}\right) + c\left(\frac{z_1 + \lambda z_2}{\lambda + 1}\right) + d$$

$$= \frac{1}{\lambda + 1}\{(ax_1 + by_1 + cz_1) + \lambda(ax_2 + by_2 + cz_2)\}$$

$$= \frac{1}{\lambda + 1}[0 + 0] \quad \text{[using Eqs. (ii) and (iii)]}$$

$$= 0$$

which shows that the point R lies on Eq. (i). Since, R is an arbitrary point on the line segment joining P and Q.

$\therefore$ Every point on PQ lies on the surface represented by Eq. (i).

Hence, $ax + by + cz + d = 0$ is equation of plane.

Equation of a Plane Passing Through a Given Point

The general equation of a plane passing through a given point (x_1, y_1, z_1) is $a(x - x_1) + b(y - y_1) + c(z - z_1) = 0$, where a, b and c are constants.

Proof The general equation of plane is

$$ax + by + cz + d = 0 \quad \text{...(i)}$$

If it passes through (x_1, y_1, z_1)

$$\Rightarrow \quad ax_1 + by_1 + cz_1 + d = 0 \quad \text{...(ii)}$$

On subtracting Eq. (i) from Eq. (ii), we get

$$a(x - x_1) + b(y - y_1) + c(z - z_1) = 0$$

which is the equation of a plane passing through a given point (x_1, y_1, z_1).

Example 38. Show that the four points $(0, -1, -1)$, $(-4, 4, 4)$, $(4, 5, 1)$ and $(3, 9, 4)$ are coplanar. Find the equation of the plane containing them.

Sol. We shall find the equation of a plane passing through any three out of the given four points and show that the fourth point satisfies the equation.

Now, any plane passing through $(0, -1, -1)$ is

$$a(x - 0) + b(y + 1) + c(z + 1) = 0 \quad \text{...(i)}$$

If it passes through $(-4, 4, 4)$, we have

$$a(-4) + b(5) + c(5) = 0 \quad \text{...(ii)}$$

Also, if plane passes through $(4, 5, 1)$,we have

$$a(4) + b(6) + c(2) = 0$$

$$\Rightarrow \quad 2a + 3b + c = 0 \quad \text{...(iii)}$$

On solving Eqs. (ii) and (iii) by cross multiplication method, we obtain

$$\frac{a}{-5} = \frac{b}{7} = \frac{c}{-11} = k$$

On putting in Eq. (i), we get

$$-5kx + 7k(y + 1) - 11k(z + 1) = 0$$

$$\Rightarrow \quad -5x + 7y - 11z - 4 = 0$$

[required equation of plane]

Clearly, the fourth point namely (3, 9, 4) satisfies this equation. Hence, the given points are coplanar and the equation of plane containing those points, is

$5x - 7y + 11z + 4 = 0$

3.13 Equation of Plane in Various Form

A plane is determined uniquely, if

(i) The normal to the plane and its distance from the origin is given i.e. the equation of a plane in normal form.

(ii) It passes through a point and is perpendicular to a given direction.

(iii) It passes through three given non-collinear points.

Equation of Plane in Normal Form

Vector Form

The vector equation of a plane normal to unit vector $\hat{\mathbf{n}}$ and at a distance d from the origin is $\mathbf{r}\cdot\hat{\mathbf{n}} = d$.

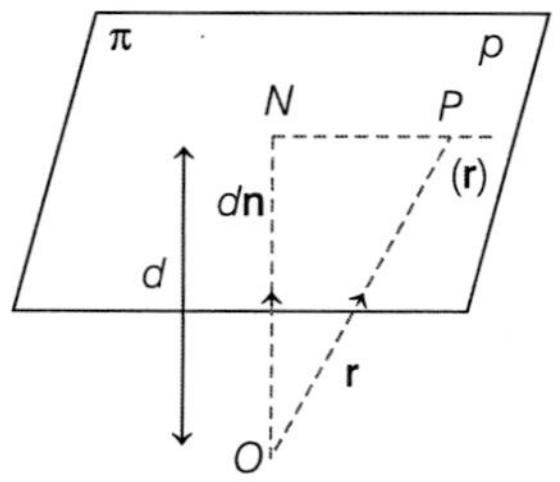

Proof. Let O be the origin and let ON be the perpendicular from O to the given plane π such that $\mathbf{ON} = d\hat{\mathbf{n}}$, where d is perpendicular distance of plane from origin.

Let P be a point on the plane, with position vector $\mathbf{r}$, so that $\mathbf{OP} = \mathbf{r}$

Now, $\mathbf{NP} \perp \mathbf{ON}$

$\Rightarrow \quad \mathbf{NP}\cdot\mathbf{ON} = 0 \quad$ ...(i)

$\Rightarrow \quad (\mathbf{OP} - \mathbf{ON})\cdot\mathbf{ON} = 0$

$\Rightarrow \quad (\mathbf{r} - d\hat{\mathbf{n}})\cdot d\hat{\mathbf{n}} = 0$

$\Rightarrow \quad \mathbf{r}\cdot d\hat{\mathbf{n}} - d^2\hat{\mathbf{n}}\cdot\hat{\mathbf{n}} = 0$

$\Rightarrow \quad d\mathbf{r}\cdot\hat{\mathbf{n}} - d^2|\mathbf{n}|^2 = 0 \quad [\because d \neq 0]$

$\Rightarrow \quad \mathbf{r}\cdot\hat{\mathbf{n}} - d = 0 \quad [\because |\hat{\mathbf{n}}| = 1]$

$\Rightarrow \quad \mathbf{r}\cdot\hat{\mathbf{n}} = d \quad$ ...(ii)

Hence, the required equation of the plane is $\mathbf{r}\cdot\hat{\mathbf{n}} = d$.

The equation $\mathbf{r}\cdot\mathbf{n} = d$ is in normal form, if $\mathbf{n}$ is a unit vector and d is the distance of the plane from the origin. If $\mathbf{n}$ is not a unit vector, then to reduce the equation $\mathbf{r}\cdot\mathbf{n} = d$ to normal form, we reduce the equation $\mathbf{r}\cdot\mathbf{n} = d$ to normal form by dividing both sides by $|\mathbf{n}|$, we get

$$\frac{\mathbf{r}\cdot\mathbf{n}}{|\mathbf{n}|} = \frac{d}{|\mathbf{n}|}$$

$$\Rightarrow \quad \mathbf{r}\cdot\mathbf{n} = \frac{d}{|\mathbf{n}|} = p \text{ (distance from the origin)}$$

Cartesian Form

Equation (ii) gives the vector equation of a plane, where $\hat{\mathbf{n}}$ is the unit vector normal to the plane. Let $P(x, y, z)$ be any point on the plane.

Then, $\quad \mathbf{OP} = \mathbf{r} = x\hat{\mathbf{i}} + y\hat{\mathbf{j}} + z\hat{\mathbf{k}}$

Let l, m and n be the direction cosines of $\hat{\mathbf{n}}$.

Then, $\quad \hat{\mathbf{n}} = (l\hat{\mathbf{i}} + m\hat{\mathbf{j}} + n\hat{\mathbf{k}})$

Therefore, (ii) gives

$$(x\hat{\mathbf{i}} + y\hat{\mathbf{j}} + z\hat{\mathbf{k}})\cdot(l\hat{\mathbf{i}} + m\hat{\mathbf{j}} + n\hat{\mathbf{k}}) = d \text{ or } lx + my + nz = d \quad \text{...(iii)}$$

This is the cartesian equation of the plane in the normal form.

JEE SPIKE

Vector equation of a plane is $\mathbf{r}\cdot(a\hat{i} + b\hat{j} + c\hat{k}) = d$ and cartesian equation of plane is $ax + by + cz = d$, when a, b, c are the direction ratios of the normal to the plane.

Example 39. Find the vector equation of plane which is at a distance of 8 units from the origin and which is normal to the vector $2\hat{i} + \hat{j} + 2\hat{k}$.

Sol. Here, $d = 8$ and $n = 2\hat{\mathbf{i}} + \hat{\mathbf{j}} + 2\hat{\mathbf{k}}$

$$\hat{\mathbf{n}} = \frac{\mathbf{n}}{|\mathbf{n}|} = \frac{2\hat{\mathbf{i}} + \hat{\mathbf{j}} + 2\hat{\mathbf{k}}}{\sqrt{2^2 + 1^2 + 2^2}} = \frac{2\hat{\mathbf{i}} + \hat{\mathbf{j}} + 2\hat{\mathbf{k}}}{3}$$

Hence, the required equation of plane is, $\mathbf{r}\cdot\hat{\mathbf{n}} = d$

$$\Rightarrow \quad \mathbf{r}\cdot\left(\frac{2\hat{\mathbf{i}} + \hat{\mathbf{j}} + 2\hat{\mathbf{k}}}{3}\right) = 8$$

$$\Rightarrow \quad \mathbf{r}\cdot(2\hat{\mathbf{i}} + \hat{\mathbf{j}} + 2\hat{\mathbf{k}}) = 24$$

Example 40. Reduce the equation $\mathbf{r}\cdot(3\hat{i} - 4\hat{j} + 12\hat{k}) = 5$ to normal form and hence find the length of perpendicular from the origin to the plane.

Sol. The given equation of plane is

$$\mathbf{r}\cdot(3\hat{\mathbf{i}} - 4\hat{\mathbf{j}} + 12\hat{\mathbf{k}}) = 5 \text{ or } \mathbf{r}\cdot\mathbf{n} = 5$$

where, $\quad \mathbf{n} = 3\hat{\mathbf{i}} - 4\hat{\mathbf{j}} + 12\hat{\mathbf{k}}$

Since, $|\mathbf{n}| = \sqrt{9 + 16 + 144} = 13 \neq 1$, therefore the given equation is not the normal form.

To reduce to normal form we divide both sides by $|\mathbf{n}|$

i.e. $$\frac{\mathbf{r}\cdot\mathbf{n}}{|\mathbf{n}|} = \frac{5}{|\mathbf{n}|}$$

or $$\mathbf{r}\cdot\left(\frac{3}{13}\hat{\mathbf{i}} - \frac{4}{13}\hat{\mathbf{j}} + \frac{12}{13}\hat{\mathbf{k}}\right) = \frac{5}{13}.$$

This is the normal form of the equation of given plane and length perpendicular $= \dfrac{5}{13}$.

Vector Equation of a Plane Passing Through a Given Point and Normal to a Given Vector

Vector Form

The vector equation of a plane passing through a point having position vector $\mathbf{a}$ and normal to vector $\mathbf{n}$ is $(\mathbf{r}-\mathbf{a})\cdot\mathbf{n}=0$.

Proof Suppose the plane π passes through a point having position vector $\mathbf{a}$ and is normal to the vector $\mathbf{n}$. Let O be the origin and $\mathbf{r}$ be the position vector of any point P on the plane π. Then, $\mathbf{OP}=\mathbf{r}$.

Since, $\mathbf{AP}$ lies in the plane and $\mathbf{n}$ is a normal to the plane π.

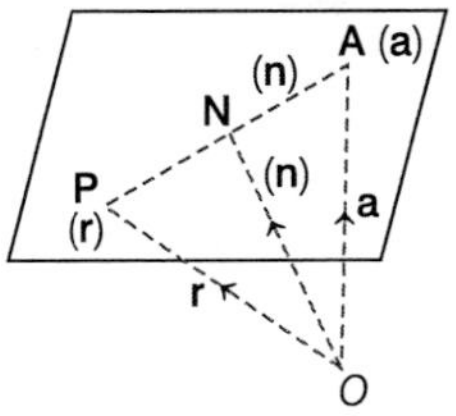

$\therefore \quad \mathbf{AP}\perp\mathbf{n} \Rightarrow \mathbf{AP}\cdot\mathbf{n}=0$

$\Rightarrow \quad (\mathbf{r}\cdot\mathbf{a})\cdot\mathbf{n}=0 \quad [\because \mathbf{AP}=\mathbf{r}-\mathbf{a}]$

Hence, the required equation of the plane is

$$(\mathbf{r}-\mathbf{a})\cdot\mathbf{n}=0$$

The above equation can be written as $\mathbf{r}\cdot\mathbf{n}=\mathbf{d}$,

where $\mathbf{d}=\mathbf{a}\cdot\mathbf{n}$ (known as scalar product of plane)

Cartesian Form

If $\mathbf{r}=x\hat{\mathbf{i}}+y\hat{\mathbf{j}}+z\hat{\mathbf{k}}$, $\mathbf{a}=x_1\hat{\mathbf{i}}+y_1\hat{\mathbf{j}}+z_1\hat{\mathbf{k}}$ and $\mathbf{n}=a\hat{\mathbf{i}}+b\hat{\mathbf{j}}+c\hat{\mathbf{k}}$,

then $(\mathbf{r}-\mathbf{a})=(x-x_1)\hat{\mathbf{i}}+(y-y_1)\hat{\mathbf{j}}+(z-z_1)\hat{\mathbf{k}}$

Then equation of the plane can be written as

$(x-x_1)\hat{\mathbf{i}}+(y-y_1)\hat{\mathbf{j}}+(z-z_1)\hat{\mathbf{k}}\cdot(a\hat{\mathbf{i}}+b\hat{\mathbf{j}}+c\hat{\mathbf{k}})=0$

$\Rightarrow \quad a(x-x_1)+b(y-y_1)+c(z-z_1)=0$

Thus, the coefficients of x, y and z in the cartesian equation of a plane are the direction ratios of the normal to the plane.

Example 41. Find the equation of the plane passing through the point (2, 3, 1) having (5, 3, 2) as the direction ratios of the normal to the plane.

Sol. The equation of the plane passing through (x_1, y_1, z_1) and perpendicular to the line with direction ratios a, b and c is given by $a(x-x_1)+b(y-y_1)+c(z-z_1)=0$.

Now, since the plane passes through (2, 3, 1) and is perpendicular to the line having direction ratios (5, 3, 2), the equation of the plane is given by

$$5(x-2)+3(y-3)+2(z-1)=0 \text{ or } 5x+3y+2z=21.$$

Example 42. The foot of the perpendicular drawn from the origin to a plane is (12, – 4, 3). Find the equation of the plane.

Sol. Since, $P(12,-4,3)$ is the foot of the perpendicular from the origin to the plane OP is normal to the plane π.

Thus, the direction ratios of normal to the plane are 12, –4 and 3.

Now, since the plane passes through (12,– 4 , 3), its equation is given by

$$12(x-12)-4(y+4)+3(z-3)=0$$

or $$12x-4y+3z-169=0$$

Example 43. A vector $\mathbf{n}$ of magnitude 8 units is inclined to X-axis at 45°, Y-axis at 60° and an acute angle with Z-axis. If a plane passes through a point $(\sqrt{2},-1,1)$ and is normal to $\mathbf{n}$, then find its equation in vector form.

Sol. Let γ be the angle made by $\mathbf{n}$ with Z-axis, then direction cosines of $\mathbf{n}$ are

$$l=\cos 45°=\frac{1}{\sqrt{2}},\ m=\cos 60°=\frac{1}{2} \text{ and } n=\cos\gamma$$

$$\therefore\ l^2+m^2+n^2=1 \Rightarrow \frac{1}{2}+\frac{1}{4}+n^2=1 \Rightarrow n^2=\frac{1}{4}$$

$$n=\frac{1}{2} \left[\text{neglecting } n=-\frac{1}{2} \text{ as } \gamma \text{ is acute} : n>0\right]$$

We have, $|\mathbf{n}|=8$

$$\mathbf{n}=|\mathbf{n}|(l\hat{\mathbf{i}}+m\hat{\mathbf{j}}+n\hat{\mathbf{k}})$$

$$\mathbf{n}=8\left(\frac{1}{\sqrt{2}}\hat{\mathbf{i}}+\frac{1}{2}\hat{\mathbf{j}}+\frac{1}{2}\hat{\mathbf{k}}\right)=4\sqrt{2}\hat{\mathbf{i}}+4\hat{\mathbf{j}}+4\hat{\mathbf{k}}$$

The required plane passes through the point $(\sqrt{2},-1,1)$ having position vector

$$\mathbf{a}=\sqrt{2}\hat{\mathbf{i}}-\hat{\mathbf{j}}+\hat{\mathbf{k}}$$

So, its vector equation is $(\mathbf{r}-\mathbf{a})\cdot\mathbf{n}=0$

$\Rightarrow \quad \hat{\mathbf{r}}\cdot\hat{\mathbf{n}}=\hat{\mathbf{a}}\cdot\hat{\mathbf{n}}$

$\Rightarrow \mathbf{r}\cdot(4\sqrt{2}\hat{\mathbf{i}}+4\hat{\mathbf{j}}+4\hat{\mathbf{k}})=(\sqrt{2}\hat{\mathbf{i}}-\hat{\mathbf{j}}+\hat{\mathbf{k}})\cdot(4\sqrt{2}\hat{\mathbf{i}}+4\hat{\mathbf{j}}+4\hat{\mathbf{k}})$

$\Rightarrow \mathbf{r}\cdot(4\sqrt{2}\hat{\mathbf{i}}+4\hat{\mathbf{j}}+4\hat{\mathbf{k}})=8 \Rightarrow \mathbf{r}\cdot(\sqrt{2}\hat{\mathbf{i}}+\hat{\mathbf{j}}+\hat{\mathbf{k}})=2$

Equation of a Plane Passing through Three Given Points

Vector Form

Vector form of the equation of the plane passing through three points A, B and C having position vectors $\mathbf{a}$, $\mathbf{b}$ and $\mathbf{c}$ respectively.

Let $\mathbf{r}$ be the position vector of any point P in the plane.

Here, the vector $\mathbf{AP}=\mathbf{r}-\mathbf{a}$, $\mathbf{AB}=\mathbf{b}-\mathbf{a}$ and $\mathbf{AC}=\mathbf{c}-\mathbf{a}$ are coplanar.

Hence, $\quad (\mathbf{r}-\mathbf{a})\cdot\{(\mathbf{b}-\mathbf{a})\times(\mathbf{c}-\mathbf{a})\}=0$

$\Rightarrow \quad (\mathbf{r}-\mathbf{a})\cdot(\mathbf{b}\times\mathbf{c}-\mathbf{b}\times\mathbf{a}-\mathbf{a}\times\mathbf{c}+\mathbf{a}\times\mathbf{a})=0$

$\Rightarrow \quad (\mathbf{r}-\mathbf{a})\cdot(\mathbf{b}\times\mathbf{c}+\mathbf{a}\times\mathbf{b}+\mathbf{c}\times\mathbf{a})=0$

$$\Rightarrow \mathbf{r}\cdot(\mathbf{b}\times\mathbf{c}+\mathbf{a}\times\mathbf{b}+\mathbf{c}\times\mathbf{a})$$
$$=\mathbf{a}\cdot(\mathbf{b}\times\mathbf{c})+\mathbf{a}\cdot(\mathbf{a}\times\mathbf{b})+\mathbf{a}\cdot(\mathbf{c}\times\mathbf{a})$$
$$\Rightarrow [\mathbf{r}\ \mathbf{b}\ \mathbf{c}]+[\mathbf{r}\ \mathbf{a}\ \mathbf{b}]+[\mathbf{r}\ \mathbf{c}\ \mathbf{a}]=[\mathbf{a}\ \mathbf{b}\ \mathbf{c}]$$

which is the required equation of the plane.

Cartesian Form

Let the plane be passing through points $A(x_1, y_1, z_1)$, $B(x_2, y_2, z_2)$ and $C(x_3, y_3, z_3)$.

Let $P(x, y, z)$ be any point on the plane.

Then, vectors **PA**, **BA** and **CA** are coplanar.

$$[\mathbf{PA}\ \ \mathbf{BA}\ \ \mathbf{CA}]=0$$

$$\Rightarrow \begin{vmatrix} x-x_1 & y-y_1 & z-z_1 \\ x_2-x_1 & y_2-y_1 & z_2-z_1 \\ x_3-x_1 & y_3-y_1 & z_3-z_1 \end{vmatrix}=0,$$

which is the required equation of the plane.

Concept Inside Video

JEE Focus Points

- If p is the length of perpendicular from the origin on this plane, then $p=[\mathbf{a}\ \mathbf{b}\ \mathbf{c}]/n$, where $n=|\mathbf{a}\times\mathbf{b}+\mathbf{b}\times\mathbf{c}+\mathbf{c}\times\mathbf{a}|$.
- Four points **a, b, c** and **d** are coplanar if **d** lies on the plane containing **a, b** and **c**.

  or $\quad \mathbf{d}\cdot[\mathbf{a}\times\mathbf{b}+\mathbf{b}\times\mathbf{c}+\mathbf{c}\times\mathbf{a}]=[\mathbf{a}\ \mathbf{b}\ \mathbf{c}]$

  or $\quad [\mathbf{d}\ \mathbf{a}\ \mathbf{b}]+[\mathbf{d}\ \mathbf{b}\ \mathbf{c}]+[\mathbf{d}\ \mathbf{c}\ \mathbf{a}]=[\mathbf{a}\ \mathbf{b}\ \mathbf{c}]$

Example 44. Find equation of plane passing through the points $P(1, 1, 1)$, $Q(3, -1, 2)$ and $R(-3, 5, -4)$.

Sol. Let the equation of plane passing through (1, 1, 1) be $a(x-1)+b(y-1)+c(z-1)=0$, as it passes through the points Q and R.

$\therefore \quad 2a-2b+c=0$ and $-4a+4b-5c=0$

Now, solving by cross multiplication method, we get

$$\frac{a}{10-4}=\frac{b}{-4+10}=\frac{c}{8-8}=k$$

$$\therefore \quad a=6k,\ b=6k,\ c=0$$

On substituting in Eq. (i), we get

$$6(x-1)+6(y-1)+0=0$$

i.e. $x+y=2$, which is the required equation.

Alternate Solution

Equation of plane passing through (x_1, y_1, z_1), (x_2, y_2, z_2) and (x_3, y_3, z_3) is

$$\begin{vmatrix} x-x_1 & y-y_1 & z-z_1 \\ x_2-x_1 & y_2-y_1 & z_2-z_1 \\ x_3-x_1 & y_3-y_1 & z_3-z_1 \end{vmatrix}=0$$

i.e. $$\begin{vmatrix} x-1 & y-1 & z-1 \\ 3-1 & -1-1 & 2-1 \\ -3-1 & 5-1 & -4-1 \end{vmatrix}=0$$

On solving, we get

$$x+y=2$$

Example 45. Find the equation of the plane passing through $A(2, 2, -1)$, $B(3, 4, 2)$ and $C(7, 0, 6)$. Also, find a unit vector perpendicular to this plane.

Sol. Here, $(x_1, y_1, z_1)\equiv(2, 2, -1)$, $(x_2, y_2, z_2)\equiv(3, 4, 2)$ and $(x_3, y_3, z_3)\equiv(7, 0, 6)$.

Then, the equation of the plane is

$$\begin{vmatrix} x-x_1 & y-y_1 & z-z_1 \\ x_2-x_1 & y_2-y_1 & z_2-z_1 \\ x_3-x_1 & y_3-y_1 & z_3-z_1 \end{vmatrix}=0$$

or $$\begin{vmatrix} x-2 & y-2 & z-(-1) \\ 3-2 & 4-2 & 2-(-1) \\ 7-2 & 0-2 & 6-(-1) \end{vmatrix}=0$$

or $$5x+2y-3z=17$$

A normal vector to this plane is $\mathbf{d}=5\hat{\mathbf{i}}+2\hat{\mathbf{j}}-3\hat{\mathbf{k}}$ ...(i)

Therefore, a unit vector normal to (i) is given by

$$\hat{\mathbf{n}}=\frac{\mathbf{d}}{|\mathbf{d}|}=\frac{5\hat{\mathbf{i}}+2\hat{\mathbf{j}}-3\hat{\mathbf{k}}}{\sqrt{25+4+9}}=\frac{1}{\sqrt{38}}(5\hat{\mathbf{i}}+2\hat{\mathbf{j}}-3\hat{\mathbf{k}})$$

Equation of a Plane Passing Through a Given Point and Parallel to Two Given Vectors

Vector Form

Let a plane pass through $A(\mathbf{a})$ and is parallel to the plane formed by two vectors **b** and **c**. Since, **AP** lies in the plane and **b** and **c** are two non-collinear vectors,

$$\mathbf{AP}=\lambda\mathbf{b}+\mu\mathbf{c} \Rightarrow \mathbf{r}-\mathbf{a}=\lambda\mathbf{b}+\mu\mathbf{c} \Rightarrow \mathbf{r}=\mathbf{a}+\lambda\mathbf{b}+\mu\mathbf{c}$$

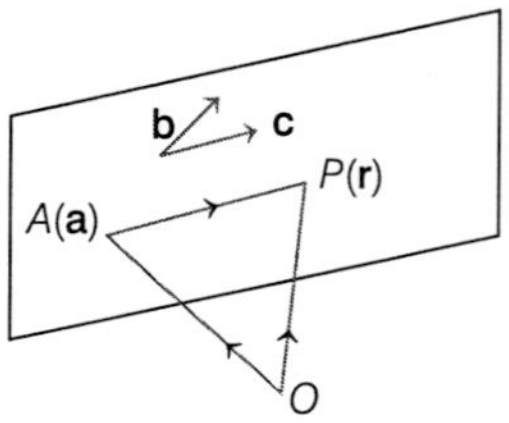

Here, λ and μ are arbitrary scalars.

This form is also called the parametric form of the plane. It can also be written in the non-parametric form as

$$(\mathbf{r}-\mathbf{a})\cdot(\mathbf{b}\times\mathbf{c})=0 \quad \text{or} \quad [\mathbf{r}\ \mathbf{b}\ \mathbf{c}]=[\mathbf{a}\ \mathbf{b}\ \mathbf{c}]$$

Cartesian Form

From $(\mathbf{r}-\mathbf{a})\cdot(\mathbf{b}\times\mathbf{c})=0$, we have $[\mathbf{r}-\mathbf{a}\ \mathbf{b}\ \mathbf{c}]$

$$\Rightarrow \begin{vmatrix} x-x_1 & y-y_1 & z-z_1 \\ x_2 & y_2 & z_2 \\ x_3 & y_3 & z_3 \end{vmatrix}=0$$ which is the required equation of the plane, where $\mathbf{b}=x_2\hat{\mathbf{i}}+y_2\hat{\mathbf{j}}+z_2\hat{\mathbf{k}}$ and $\mathbf{c}=x_3\hat{\mathbf{i}}+y_3\hat{\mathbf{j}}+z_3\hat{\mathbf{k}}$.

Example 46. Find the vector equation of the following planes in cartesian form
$\mathbf{r}=\hat{\mathbf{i}}-\hat{\mathbf{j}}+\lambda(\hat{\mathbf{i}}+\hat{\mathbf{j}}+\hat{\mathbf{k}})+\mu(\hat{\mathbf{i}}-2\hat{\mathbf{j}}+3\hat{\mathbf{k}})$.

Sol. The equation of the plane is

$$\mathbf{r}=\hat{\mathbf{i}}-\hat{\mathbf{j}}+\lambda(\hat{\mathbf{i}}+\hat{\mathbf{j}}+\hat{\mathbf{k}})+\mu(\hat{\mathbf{i}}-2\hat{\mathbf{j}}+3\hat{\mathbf{k}}).$$

Let $\mathbf{r}=x\hat{\mathbf{i}}+y\hat{\mathbf{j}}+z\hat{\mathbf{k}}$

Hence, the equation is

$$(x\hat{\mathbf{i}}+y\hat{\mathbf{j}}+z\hat{\mathbf{k}})-(\hat{\mathbf{i}}-\hat{\mathbf{j}})=\lambda(\hat{\mathbf{i}}+\hat{\mathbf{j}}+\hat{\mathbf{k}})+\mu(\hat{\mathbf{i}}-2\hat{\mathbf{j}}+3\hat{\mathbf{k}})$$

Thus, the vectors $(x\hat{\mathbf{i}}+y\hat{\mathbf{j}}+z\hat{\mathbf{k}})-(\hat{\mathbf{i}}-\hat{\mathbf{j}}),\ \hat{\mathbf{i}}+\hat{\mathbf{j}}+\hat{\mathbf{k}},\ \hat{\mathbf{i}}-2\hat{\mathbf{j}}+3\hat{\mathbf{k}}$ are coplanar.

Therefore, the equation of the plane is

$$\begin{vmatrix} x-1 & y-(-1) & z-0 \\ 1 & 1 & 1 \\ 1 & -2 & 3 \end{vmatrix}=0$$

or $$5x-2y-3z-7=0$$

Intercept Form of a Plane

The equation of a plane having intercepting lengths a, b and c with X-axis, Y-axis and Z-axis respectively, is

$$\frac{x}{a}+\frac{y}{b}+\frac{z}{c}=1$$

Proof Let O be the origin and let OX, OY and OZ be the coordinate axes.

Let the plane meets the coordinate axes at the points P, Q and R, respectively such that

$OP=a$, $OQ=b$ and $P=c$. Then, the coordinates of the points are $P(a,0,0)$, $Q(0,b,0)$ and $R(0,0,c)$.

Let the equation of plane be

$$Ax+By+Cz+D=0 \quad \text{...(i)}$$

Since, Eq. (i) passes through $(a,0,0)$, $(0,b,0)$ and $(0,0,c)$, we have

$$Aa+D=0 \Rightarrow A=\frac{-D}{a}$$

$$Bb+D=0 \Rightarrow B=\frac{-D}{b}$$

$$Cc+D=0 \Rightarrow C=\frac{-D}{b}$$

On putting these values in Eq. (i),we get required equation of plane as

$$\frac{-D}{a}x-\frac{D}{b}y-\frac{D}{c}z=-D$$

$$\Rightarrow \quad \frac{x}{a}+\frac{y}{b}+\frac{z}{c}=1$$

Example 47. A plane meets the coordinates axes in A, B and C such that the centroid of the ΔABC is the point (p,q,r), find the equation of the plane.

Sol. Let the required equation of plane be

$$\frac{x}{a}+\frac{y}{b}+\frac{z}{c}=1 \quad \text{...(i)}$$

Then, the coordinates of A, B and C are $A(a,0,0)$, $B(0,b,0)$ and $C(0,0,c)$ respectively. So, the centroid of the ΔABC,

$$\left(\frac{a}{3},\frac{b}{3},\frac{c}{3}\right)$$

But the coordinate of the centroid are (p,q,r).

$$\therefore \quad \frac{a}{3}=p,\ \frac{b}{3}=q,\ \frac{c}{3}=r$$

On putting the values of a, b and c in Eq. (i), we get The required plane as

$$\frac{x}{3p}+\frac{y}{3q}+\frac{z}{3r}=1$$

$$\Rightarrow \quad \frac{x}{p}+\frac{y}{q}+\frac{z}{r}=3$$

3.14 Angle between Two Planes

Vector Form

The angle between two planes is defined as the angle between their normals.

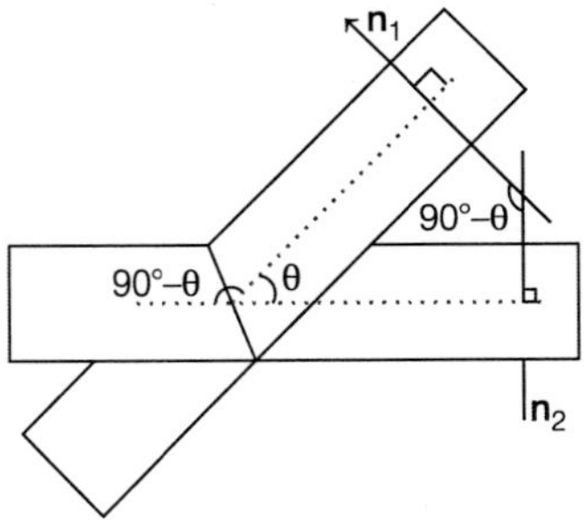

Let θ be the angle between planes $\mathbf{r}\cdot\mathbf{n}_1=d_1$ and $\mathbf{r}\cdot\mathbf{n}_2=d_2$ then

$$\cos\theta=\frac{\mathbf{n}_1\cdot\mathbf{n}_2}{|\mathbf{n}_1||\mathbf{n}_2|}$$

Concept Inside Video

JEE Focus Points

- **Condition for Perpendicularity**

  If the planes $\mathbf{r}\cdot\mathbf{n}_1=d_1$ and $\mathbf{r}\cdot\mathbf{n}_2=\mathbf{d}_2$ are perpendicular, then $\mathbf{n}_1$ and $\mathbf{n}_2$ are perpendicular. Therefore, $\mathbf{n}_1\cdot\mathbf{n}_2=0$

- **Condition for Parallelism**

  If the planes $\mathbf{r}\cdot\mathbf{n}_1=d_1$ and $\mathbf{r}\cdot\mathbf{n}_2=d_2$ are parallel, there exists the scalar λ such that

  $$\mathbf{n}_1=\lambda\mathbf{n}_2$$

Cartesian Form

If the planes are $a_1x + b_1y + c_1z + d = 0$

and $a_2x + b_2y + c_2z + d_2 = 0$

$$\Rightarrow \cos\theta = \frac{a_1a_2 + b_1b_2 + c_1c_2}{\sqrt{a_1^2 + b_1^2 + c_1^2}\sqrt{a_2^2 + b_2^2 + c_2^2}}$$

JEE Focus Points

- Condition for parallelism

$$\frac{a_1}{a_2} = \frac{b_1}{b_2} = \frac{c_1}{c_2} = \lambda$$

- Condition for perpendicularity

$$a_1a_2 + b_1b_2 + c_1c_2 = 0$$

Concept Inside Video

Example 48. Find the angle between the planes $2x + y - 2x + 3 = 0$ and $\mathbf{r}\cdot(6\hat{\mathbf{i}} + 3\hat{\mathbf{j}} + 2\hat{\mathbf{k}}) = 5$.

Sol. Normals along the given planes are $2\hat{\mathbf{i}} + \hat{\mathbf{j}} - 2\hat{\mathbf{k}}$ and $6\hat{\mathbf{i}} + 3\hat{\mathbf{j}} + 2\hat{\mathbf{k}}$.

Then angle between planes,

$$\theta = \cos^{-1}\frac{(2\hat{\mathbf{i}} + \hat{\mathbf{j}} - 2\hat{\mathbf{k}})\cdot(6\hat{\mathbf{i}} + 3\hat{\mathbf{j}} + 2\hat{\mathbf{k}})}{\sqrt{(2)^2 + (1)^2 + (-2)^2}\sqrt{(6)^2 + (3)^2 + (2)^2}} = \cos^{-1}\frac{11}{21}$$

Example 49. Show that $ax + by + r = 0$, $by + cz + p = 0$ and $cz + ax + q = 0$ are perpendicular to XY, YZ and ZX planes, respectively.

Sol. The planes $a_1x + b_1y + c_1z + d_1 = 0$ and $a_2x + b_2y + c_2z + d_2 = 0$ are perpendicular to each other if and only if $a_1a_2 + b_1b_2 + c_1c_2 = 0$.

The equation of XY, YZ and ZX planes are $z = 0$, $x = 0$ and $y = 0$, respectively.

Now, we have to show that $z = 0$ is perpendicular to

$$ax + by + r = 0.$$

It follows immediately, since $a(0) + b(0) + (0)(1) = 0$, other parts can be done similarly.

3.15 Family of Planes

Plane Parallel to a Given Plane

Since parallel planes have the same normal vector, so equation of a plane parallel to $\mathbf{r}\cdot\mathbf{n} = d_1$ is of the form $\mathbf{r}\cdot\mathbf{n} = d_2$, where d_2 is determined by the given conditions.

In **cartesian form**, if $ax + by + cz + d = 0$ be the given plane then the plane parallel to this plane is $ax + by + cz + k = 0$.

Example 50. Find the equation of the plane through the point $(1, 4, -2)$ and parallel to the plane $-2x + y - 3z = 7$.

Sol. Let the equation of a plane parallel to the plane $-2x + y - 3z = 7$ be

$$-2x + y - 3z + k = 0 \quad \text{...(i)}$$

This passes through $(1, 4, -2)$, therefore

$$(-2)(1) + 4 - 3(-2) + k = 0$$

$$\Rightarrow \quad -2 + 4 + 6 + k = 0$$

$$\Rightarrow \quad k = -8$$

On putting $k = -8$ in Eq. (i), we obtain

$$-2x + y - 3z - 8 = 0$$

or $$-2x + y - 3z = 8$$

This is the equation of the required plane.

Example 51. Find the equation of the plane passing through $(3, 4, -1)$, which is parallel to the plane $\mathbf{r}\cdot(2\hat{\mathbf{i}} - 3\hat{\mathbf{j}} + 5\hat{\mathbf{k}}) + 7 = 0$.

Sol. The equation of any plane which is parallel to $\mathbf{r}\cdot(2\hat{\mathbf{i}} - 3\hat{\mathbf{j}} + 5\hat{\mathbf{k}}) + 7 = 0$ is

$$\mathbf{r}\cdot(2\hat{\mathbf{i}} - 3\hat{\mathbf{j}} + 5\hat{\mathbf{k}}) + \lambda = 0$$

or $$2x - 3y + 5z + \lambda = 0$$

Further (i) will pass through $(3, 4, -1)$

if $(2)(3) + (-3)(4) + 5(-1) + \lambda = 0$

or $$-11 + \lambda = 0 \Rightarrow \lambda = 11$$

Thus, the equation of the required plane is

$$\mathbf{r}\cdot(2\hat{\mathbf{i}} - 3\hat{\mathbf{j}} + 5\hat{\mathbf{k}}) + 11 = 0$$

Equation of any Plane Passing Through the Line of Intersection of Two Plane

The equation of the plane passing through the line of intersection of the planes

$a_1x + b_1y + c_1z + d_1 = 0$ and $a_2x + b_2y + c_2z + d_2 = 0$ is $(a_1x + b_1y + c_1z + d_1) + k(a_2x + b_2y + c_2z + d_2) = 0$

Proof Let the given plane be

$$a_1x + b_1y + c_1z + d_1 = 0 \quad \text{...(i)}$$

and $$a_2x + b_2y + c_2z + d_2 = 0 \quad \text{...(ii)}$$

$\therefore$ Required plane is

$$(a_1x + b_1y + c_1z + d_1) + k(a_2x + b_2y + c_2z + d_2) = 0 \quad \text{...(iii)}$$

Clearly, plane (iii) represents the equation of plane.

Let (α, β, γ) be a point on the line of intersection of planes (i) and (ii), then P lies on planes (i) and (ii).

$\therefore$ $$a_1\alpha + b_1\beta + c_1\gamma + d_1 = 0 \quad \text{...(iv)}$$

and $$a_2\alpha + b_2\beta + c_2\gamma + d_2 = 0 \quad \text{...(v)}$$

Now, multiply by k in plane (v) and then adding planes (iv) and (v), we get

$$(a_1\alpha + b_1\beta + c_1\gamma + d_1) + k(a_2\alpha + b_2\beta + c_2\gamma + d_2) = 0$$

$\Rightarrow P(\alpha, \beta, \gamma)$ lies on plane (iii).

Hence, plane (iii) passes through each point on the line of intersection of planes (i) and (ii).

Thus, plane (iii) is the equation of plane passing through the line of intersection of planes (i) and (ii).

Vector Form

Equation of planes passing through the line of intersection of planes $\mathbf{r}\cdot\mathbf{n}_1 = d_1$ and $\mathbf{r}\cdot\mathbf{n}_2 = d_2$ is

$$(\mathbf{r}\cdot\mathbf{n}_1 - d_1) + k(\mathbf{r}\cdot\mathbf{n}_2 - d_2) = 0$$

or $$\mathbf{r}\cdot(\mathbf{n}_1 + k\mathbf{n}_2) = d_1 + kd_2,$$

k being any scalar.

JEE SCANNER

Example Similar to PYQ Asked in JEE Main 2023

If the equation of the plane containing the line of intersection of the plane $x+y+z-6=0$ and $2x+3y+4z+5=0$ and passing through the point $(1,1,1)$ is $\alpha x+\beta y+\gamma z=69$, then the value of $\alpha+\beta+\gamma$ is

Sol. The equation of a plane through the line of intersection of the given plane is

$$(x+y+z-6)+\lambda(2x+3y+4z+5)=0 \quad ...(i)$$

If line (i) passes through (1, 1, 1), we have

$$-3+14\lambda=0 \Rightarrow \lambda=\frac{3}{14}$$

On putting $\lambda=\frac{3}{14}$ in line (i), we obtain the equation of the required plane as

$$(x+y+z-6)+\frac{3}{14}(2x+3y+4z+5)=0$$

$$\Rightarrow \quad 20x+23y+26z-69=0$$

Here, $\alpha=20, \beta=23, \gamma=26$

$\therefore\ \alpha+\beta+\gamma=20+23+26=69$

Skill Builder

For Sol.

If the equation of the plane containing the line of intersection of the plane $x+y+z-12=0$ and $2x+4y+5z+15=0$ and passing through the point $(1,2,3)$ is $\alpha x+\beta y+\gamma z=195$, then the value of $\alpha+\beta+\gamma$ is ....

- **For more practice** See Q. 6 of Milestone Practice 3.

Example 52. Find the planes passing through the intersection of planes $\mathbf{r}\cdot(2\hat{\mathbf{i}}-3\hat{\mathbf{j}}+4\hat{\mathbf{k}})=1$ and $\mathbf{r}\cdot(\hat{\mathbf{i}}-\hat{\mathbf{j}})+4=0$ and perpendicular to planes $\mathbf{r}\cdot(2\hat{\mathbf{i}}-\hat{\mathbf{j}}+\hat{\mathbf{k}})=-8$.

Sol. The equation of any plane through the line of intersection of the given planes is

$$[\mathbf{r}\cdot(2\hat{\mathbf{i}}-3\hat{\mathbf{j}}+4\hat{\mathbf{k}})-1]+\lambda[\mathbf{r}\cdot(\hat{\mathbf{i}}-\hat{\mathbf{j}})+4]=0$$

$$\mathbf{r}\cdot[(2+\lambda)\hat{\mathbf{i}}-(3+\lambda)\hat{\mathbf{j}}+4\hat{\mathbf{k}}]=1-4\lambda \quad ...(i)$$

If it is perpendicular to $\mathbf{r}\cdot(2\hat{\mathbf{i}}-\hat{\mathbf{j}}+\hat{\mathbf{k}})+8=0$, then

$$[(2+\lambda)\hat{\mathbf{i}}-(3+\lambda)\hat{\mathbf{j}}+4\hat{\mathbf{k}}]\cdot(2\hat{\mathbf{i}}-\hat{\mathbf{j}}+\hat{\mathbf{k}})=0$$

$$2(2+\lambda)+(3+\lambda)+4=0$$

$$\lambda=\frac{-11}{3}$$

On putting $\lambda=-\frac{11}{3}$ in line (i), we obtain the equation of the required plane as

$$\mathbf{r}\cdot(-5\hat{\mathbf{i}}+2\hat{\mathbf{j}}+12\hat{\mathbf{k}})=47$$

3.16 Two Sides of a Plane

Let $ax+by+cz+d=0$ be the plane, then the points (x_1, y_1, z_1) and (x_2, y_2, z_2) lie on the same side or opposite side according as

$$\frac{ax_1+by_1+cz_1+d}{ax_2+by_2+cz_2+d} > 0 \text{ or } < 0$$

Proof Here equation of plane is,

$$ax+by+cz+d=0 \quad ...(i)$$

Given plane divide the line segment joining P and Q at R internally in the ratio $m:n$.

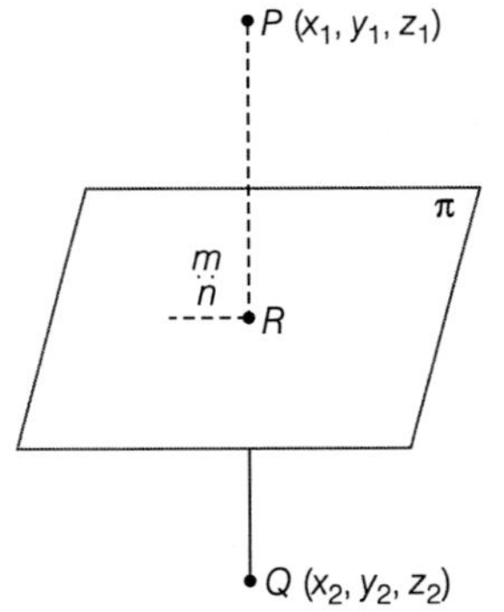

Then, $R\left(\frac{mx_2+nx_1}{m+n}, \frac{my+ny_1}{m+n}, \frac{mz_2+nz_1}{m+n}\right)$

Since, R lies on the plane (i).

$$\therefore\ a\left(\frac{mx_2+nx_1}{m+n}\right)+b\left(\frac{my_2+ny_1}{m+n}\right)+c\left(\frac{mz_2+nz_1}{m+n}\right)+d=0$$

$$\Rightarrow\ a(mx_2+nx_1)+b(my_2+ny_1)+c(mz_2+nz_1)+d(m+n)=0$$

$$\Rightarrow\ m(ax_2+by_2+cz_2+d)+n(ax_1+by_1+cz_1+d)=0$$

$$\Rightarrow\ \frac{m}{n}=-\frac{(ax_1+by_1+cz_1+d)}{(ax_2+by_2+cz_2+d)} \quad ...(ii)$$

Now, if $ax_1+by_1+cz_1+d$ and $ax_2+by_2+cz_2+d$

are of same sign $\frac{m}{n}<0$ [external division]

are of opposite sign $\frac{m}{n}>0$ [internal division]

$\therefore$ If $\dfrac{ax_1 + by_1 + cz_1 + d}{ax_2 + by_2 + cz_2 + d} > 0$ [same side]

$\dfrac{ax_1 + by_1 + cz_1 + d}{ax_2 + by_2 + cz_2 + d} < 0$ [opposite side]

Example 53. Find the interval of α for which $(\alpha, \alpha^2, \alpha)$ and $(3, 2, 1)$ lies on same side of $x + y - 4z + 2 = 0$.

Sol. $(\alpha, \alpha^2, \alpha)$ and $(3, 2, 1)$ lies on same side of $x + y - 4z + 2 = 0$

$\therefore (\alpha + \alpha^2 - 4\alpha + 2)(3 + 2 - 4 + 2) > 0$

$\Rightarrow \alpha^2 - 3\alpha + 2 > 0$

$(\alpha - 1)(\alpha - 2) > 0$

$\Rightarrow \alpha \in (-\infty, 1) \cup (2, \infty)$

3.17 Distance of a Point from a Plane

Vector Form

The length of the perpendicular from a point having position vector $\mathbf{a}$ to the plane $\mathbf{r} \cdot \mathbf{n} = d$ is given by

$$PM = \frac{|\mathbf{a} \cdot \mathbf{n} - d|}{|\mathbf{n}|}$$

Proof. Let π be the given plane and $P(\mathbf{a})$ be the given point. Let PM be the length of perpendicular from P to the plane π.

Since, line PM passes through $P(\mathbf{a})$ and is parallel to the vector $\mathbf{n}$ which is normal to the plane π. So, vector equation of line PM is

$$\mathbf{r} = \mathbf{a} + \lambda \mathbf{n} \qquad \text{...(i)}$$

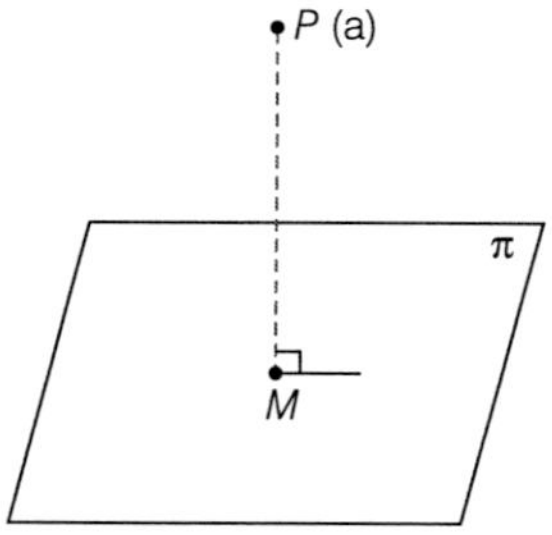

Point M is the intersection of Eq. (i) and the given plane π.

$\therefore (\mathbf{a} + \lambda\mathbf{n}) \cdot \mathbf{n} = d$

$\Rightarrow \mathbf{a} \cdot \mathbf{n} + \lambda \mathbf{n} \cdot \mathbf{n} = d$

$\Rightarrow \lambda = \dfrac{d - (\mathbf{a} \cdot \mathbf{n})}{|\mathbf{n}|^2}$

On putting the value of λ in Eq. (i), we obtain the position vector of M given by

$$\mathbf{r} = \mathbf{a} + \left(\frac{d - \mathbf{a} \cdot \mathbf{n}}{|\mathbf{n}|^2}\right)\mathbf{n}$$

$\mathbf{PM}$ = Position vector of M − Position vector of P

$= \mathbf{a} + \left(\dfrac{d - (\mathbf{a} \cdot \mathbf{n})}{|\mathbf{n}|^2}\right)\mathbf{n} - \mathbf{a}$

$\mathbf{PM} = \left(\dfrac{d - (\mathbf{a} \cdot \mathbf{n})}{|\mathbf{n}|^2}\right)\mathbf{n}$

$\Rightarrow PM = |\mathbf{PM}| = \left|\dfrac{(d - \mathbf{a} \cdot \mathbf{n})\,\mathbf{n}}{|\mathbf{n}|^2}\right|$

$= \dfrac{|d - (\mathbf{a} \cdot \mathbf{n})|\,|\mathbf{n}|}{|\mathbf{n}|^2} = \dfrac{|d - (\mathbf{a} \cdot \mathbf{n})|}{|\mathbf{n}|}$

Thus, the length of perpendicular from a point having position vector $\mathbf{a}$ on the plane $\mathbf{r} \cdot \mathbf{n} = d$ is $\dfrac{|\mathbf{a} \cdot \mathbf{n} - d|}{|\mathbf{n}|}$

Cartesian Form

The length of perpendicular from a point $P(x_1, y_1, z_1)$ to the plane $ax + by + cz + d = 0$. Then, the equation of PM is

$$\frac{x - x_1}{a} = \frac{y - y_1}{b} = \frac{z - z_1}{c}$$

and length, $PM = \dfrac{|(ax_1 + by_1 + cz_1 + d)|}{\sqrt{a^2 + b^2 + c^2}}$

Example 54. Find the distance of the point $(2, 1, 0)$ from the plane $2x + y + 2z + 5 = 0$.

Sol. We know that the distance of the point (x_1, y_1, z_1) from the plane $ax + by + cz + d = 0$ is

$$\frac{|ax_1 + by_1 + cz_1 + d|}{\sqrt{a^2 + b^2 + c^2}}$$

Hence, required distance $= \dfrac{|2 \times 2 + 1 + 2 \times 0 + 5|}{\sqrt{2^2 + 1^2 + 2^2}} = \dfrac{10}{3}$ units

Distance between the Parallel Planes

The distance between two parallel planes

$$ax + by + cz + d_1 = 0 \text{ and } ax + by + cz + d_2 = 0$$

is given by $d = \left|\dfrac{(d_2 - d_1)}{\sqrt{a^2 + b^2 + c^2}}\right|$

Proof Let d = Difference of the length of perpendicular from origin to the two planes.

$$= \left|\frac{|d_1|}{\sqrt{a^2 + b^2 + c^2}} - \frac{|d_2|}{\sqrt{a^2 + b^2 + c^2}}\right|.$$

if d_1 and d_2 are of same side $= \left|\dfrac{d_1 - d_2}{\sqrt{a^2 + b^2 + c^2}}\right|$

Vector Form

The distance between two parallel plane $\mathbf{r} \cdot \mathbf{n} = d_1$ and $\mathbf{r} \cdot \mathbf{n} = d_2$ is given by

$$d = \frac{|d_1 - d_2|}{|\mathbf{n}|}$$

JEE SCANNER

Example Similar to PYQ Asked in JEE Main 2019

If the plane $2x - y + 2z + 3 = 0$ has the distances $\frac{1}{3}$ and $\frac{2}{3}$ units from the plane $4x - 2y + 4z + \lambda = 0$ and $2x - y + 2z + \mu = 0$ respectively, then the maximum value of $\lambda + \mu$ is ....

Sol. The given plane is

$$2x - y + 2z + 3 = 0 \text{ or } 4x - 2y + 4z + 6 = 0 \qquad \text{...(i)}$$

$\Rightarrow$ Plane (i) is parallel to the plane $4x - 2y + 4z + \lambda = 0$

Distance between two plane is $\left|\frac{\lambda - 6}{\sqrt{16 + 4 + 16}}\right| = \frac{1}{3}$

$$\Rightarrow \quad \frac{|\lambda - 6|}{\sqrt{36}} = \frac{1}{3}$$

$$\Rightarrow \quad |\lambda - 6| = \frac{6}{3} = 2$$

$$\Rightarrow \quad \lambda = 8, 4$$

Again, distance between $2x - y + 2z + 3 = 0$ and $2x - y + 2z + \mu = 0$ is

$$\frac{|\mu - 3|}{\sqrt{4 + 1 + 4}} = \frac{2}{3} \Rightarrow |\mu - 3| = 2 \Rightarrow \mu = 5, 1$$

$\therefore$ Maximum value $= 8 + 5 = 13$

Skill Builder

For Sol.

If the plane $12x + 3y + 4z + 15 = 0$ has the distance $\frac{1}{13}$ and $\frac{5}{13}$ units from the plane $24x + 6y + 8z + \alpha = 0$ and $12x + 3y + 4z + \beta = 0$ respectively, then the minimum value of $\alpha + \beta$ is ....

- **For more practice** See Q. 14 of Milestone Practice 3.

Example 55. Find the distance between the parallel planes $x + 2y - 2z + 1 = 0$ and $2x + 4y - 4z + 5 = 0$.

Sol. We know that distance between parallel planes

$ax + by + cz + d_1 = 0$ and $ax + by + cz + d_2 = 0$ is,

$$\frac{|d_1 - d_2|}{\sqrt{a^2 + b^2 + c^2}}$$

$\therefore$ Distance between $x + 2y - 2z + 1 = 0$ and $x + 2y - 2z + \frac{5}{2} = 0$ is

$$\frac{\left|\frac{5}{2} - 1\right|}{\sqrt{1 + 4 + 4}} = \frac{1}{2} \text{ units}$$

3.18 Equation of Planes Bisecting the Angle between Two Planes

Equation of the planes bisecting the angle between the planes.

$a_1x + b_1y + c_1z + d_1 = 0$ and $a_2x + b_2y + c_2z + d_2 = 0$ is

$$\frac{a_1x + b_1y + c_1z + d_1}{\sqrt{a_1^2 + b_1^2 + c_1^2}} = \pm \frac{a_2x + b_2y + c_2z + d_2}{\sqrt{a_2^2 + b_2^2 + c_2^2}}$$

Proof Given planes are

$$a_1x + b_1y + c_1z + d_1 = 0 \qquad \text{...(i)}$$

and

$$a_2x + b_2y + c_2z + d_2 = 0 \qquad \text{...(ii)}$$

Let $P(x, y, z)$ be a point on the plane bisecting the angle between planes (i) and (ii).

Let PL and PM be the length of perpendiculars from P to planes (i) and (ii).

$\therefore \quad PL = PM$

$$\Rightarrow \left|\frac{a_1x + b_1y + c_1z + d_1}{\sqrt{a_1^2 + b_1^2 + c_1^2}}\right| = \left|\frac{a_2x + b_2y + c_2z + d_2}{\sqrt{a_2^2 + b_2^2 + c_2^2}}\right|$$

$$\frac{a_1x + b_1y + c_1z + d_1}{\sqrt{a_1^2 + b_1^2 + c_1^2}} = \pm \frac{a_2x + b_2y + c_2z + d_2}{\sqrt{a_2^2 + b_2^2 + c_2^2}}$$

This is equation of planes bisecting the angles between the planes (i) and (ii).

Vector Form

Equation of planes bisecting the angle between planes $\mathbf{r} \cdot \mathbf{n}_1 = d_1$ and $\mathbf{r} \cdot \mathbf{n}_2 = d_2$ are

$$\left|\frac{\mathbf{r} \cdot \mathbf{n}_1 - d_1}{\mathbf{n}_1}\right| = \left|\frac{\mathbf{r} \cdot \mathbf{n}_2 - d_2}{\mathbf{n}_2}\right|$$

$$\Rightarrow \quad \frac{\mathbf{r} \cdot \mathbf{n}_1 - d_1}{\mathbf{n}_1} = \pm \frac{\mathbf{r} \cdot \mathbf{n}_2 - d_2}{\mathbf{n}_2}$$

$$\Rightarrow \quad \mathbf{r} \cdot \frac{\mathbf{n}_1}{|\mathbf{n}_1|} \pm \mathbf{r} \cdot \frac{\mathbf{n}_2}{|\mathbf{n}_1|} = \frac{d_1}{|\mathbf{n}_1|} \pm \frac{d_2}{|\mathbf{n}_2|}$$

$$\Rightarrow \quad \mathbf{r} \cdot (\hat{\mathbf{n}}_1 \pm \hat{\mathbf{n}}_2) = \frac{d_1}{|\mathbf{n}_1|} \pm \frac{d_2}{|\mathbf{n}_2|}$$

Bisector of the Angle between the Two Planes Containing the Origin

Let the equation of the two planes be

$$a_1x + b_1y + c_1z + d_1 = 0 \quad \text{...(i)}$$

and $$a_2x + b_2y + c_2z + d_2 = 0 \quad \text{...(ii)}$$

where, d_1 and d_2 are positive, then equation of the bisector of the angle between the planes (i) and (ii) containing the origin is

$$\frac{a_1x + b_1y + c_1z + d_1}{\sqrt{a_1^2 + b_1^2 + c_1^2}} = \frac{a_2x + b_2y + c_2z + d_2}{\sqrt{a_2^2 + b_2^2 + c_2^2}}$$

Concept Inside Video

JEE Focus Points

- If $\frac{a_1x + b_1y + c_1z + d_1}{\sqrt{a_1^2 + b_1^2 + c_1^2}} = \frac{a_2x + b_2y + c_2z + d_2}{\sqrt{a_2^2 + b_2^2 + c_2^2}}$, then bisects that angle between the plane which contains the origin.
- If $\frac{a_1x + b_1y + c_1z + d_1}{\sqrt{a_1^2 + b_1^2 + c_1^2}} = -\frac{a_2x + b_2y + c_2z + d_2}{\sqrt{a_2^2 + b_2^2 + c_2^2}}$, then bisects that angle between the plane that does not contains the origin.
- If $a_1a_2 + b_1b_2 + c_1c_2 < 0$, then origin lies in the acute angle,
- If $a_1a_2 + b_1b_2 + c_1c_2 > 0$, then origin lies in the obtuse angle,

Example 56. Find the equation of the bisector planes of the angles between the planes $2x - y + 2z + 3 = 0$ and $3x - 2y + 6z + 8 = 0$ and specify the plane which bisects the acute angle and the plane which bisects the obtuse angle.

Sol. The two given planes are

$$2x - y + 2z + 3 = 0$$

and $$3x - 2y + 6z + 8 = 0$$

where, d_1 and $d_2 > 0$

and $a_1a_2 + b_1b_2 + c_1c_2 = 6 + 2 + 12 > 0$

$$\therefore \quad \frac{a_1x + b_1y + c_1z + d_1}{\sqrt{a_1^2 + b_1^2 + c_1^2}} = -\frac{a_2x + b_2y + c_2z + d_2}{\sqrt{a_2^2 + b_2^2 + c_2^2}}$$

[acute angle bisector]

and $$\frac{a_1x + b_1y + c_1z + d_1}{\sqrt{a_1^2 + b_1^2 + c_1^2}} = \frac{a_2x + b_2y + c_2z + d_2}{\sqrt{a_2^2 + b_2^2 + c_2^2}}$$

[obtuse angle bisector]

i.e. $$\frac{2x - y + 2z + 3}{\sqrt{4 + 1 + 4}} = \pm \frac{3x - 2y + 6z + 8}{\sqrt{9 + 4 + 36}}$$

$$\Rightarrow \quad (14x - 7y + 14z + 21) = \pm (9x - 6y + 18z + 24)$$

On taking positive sign on the right hand side, we get

$$5x - y - 4z - 3 = 0 \quad \text{[obtuse angle bisector]}$$

and taking negative sign on the right hand side, we get

$$23x - 13y + 32z + 45 = 0 \quad \text{[acute angle bisector]}$$

3.19 Line and Plane

Line of Intersection of Two Planes

Let two non-parallel planes are $\mathbf{r} \cdot \mathbf{n}_1 = d_1$ and $\mathbf{r} \cdot \mathbf{n}_2 = d_2$

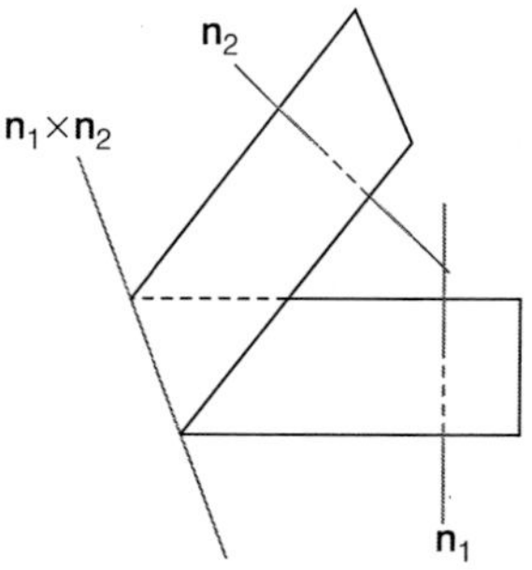

Now, line of intersection of planes is perpendicular to vector $\mathbf{n}_1$ and $\mathbf{n}_2$.

$\therefore$ Line of intersection is parallel to vector $\mathbf{n}_1 \times \mathbf{n}_2$.

If we wish to find the equation of line of intersection of planes

$$a_1x + b_1y + c_1z - d_1 = 0$$

and $$a_2x + b_2y + c_2z - d_2 = 0,$$

then we find any point on the line by putting $z = 0$ (say), then we can find corresponding values of x and y by solving equations

$$a_1x + b_1y - d_1 = 0$$

and $$a_2x + b_2y - d_2 = 0$$

Thus, by fixing the value of $z = \lambda$, we can find the corresponding value of x and y in terms of λ.

After getting x, y and z in terms of λ, we can find the equation of line in symmetric form.

Example 57 Reduce the equation of line $x - y + 2z = 5$ and $3x + y + z = 6$ in symmetrical form.

Or

Find the line of intersection of planes $x - y + 2z = 5$ and $3x + y + z = 6$.

Sol. Given $x - y + 2z = 5, 3x + y + z = 6$.

Let $z = \lambda$

Then, $x - y = 5 - 2\lambda$

and $3x + y = 6 - \lambda$

On solving these two equations,

$$4x = 11 - 3\lambda$$

and $$4y = 4x - 20 + 8\lambda = -9 + 5\lambda$$

The equation of the line is

$$\frac{4x - 11}{-3} = \frac{4y + 9}{5} = \frac{z - 0}{1}.$$

JEE SCANNER

Example Similar to PYQ Asked in JEE Main 2021

The distance of the point $(-3, -4, -1)$ from the line of intersection of the planes $x+y+z-1=0$ and $4x+y-2z+2=0$ is l, then $4l^2$ is ....

Sol. Given, $x+y+z-1=0$ and $4x+y-2z+2=0$

On putting $z=\lambda$ in both equations, we get

$$x+y=1-\lambda \quad \text{...(i)}$$

$$4x+y=2\lambda-2 \quad \text{...(ii)}$$

On solving Eqs. (i) and (ii) we get

$$3x=3\lambda-3 \Rightarrow x=\lambda-1$$

and $$y=\lambda-1+y=1-\lambda \Rightarrow y=-2(\lambda-1)$$

The equation of line is

$$\frac{x+1}{1}=\frac{y+1}{-2}=\frac{z}{1}=\lambda$$

Equation of line is $\mathbf{r}=-\hat{\mathbf{i}}-\hat{\mathbf{j}}+\lambda(\hat{\mathbf{i}}-2\hat{\mathbf{j}}+\hat{\mathbf{k}})$

Distance from point $(-3,-4,-1)$ to the line $\mathbf{r}=-\hat{\mathbf{i}}-\hat{\mathbf{j}}+\lambda(\hat{\mathbf{i}}-2\hat{\mathbf{j}}+\hat{\mathbf{k}})$ is

$$d=\frac{|((-1+3)\hat{\mathbf{i}}+(-1+4)\hat{\mathbf{j}}+(0+1)\hat{\mathbf{k}})\times(\hat{\mathbf{i}}-2\hat{\mathbf{j}}+\hat{\mathbf{k}})|}{|\hat{\mathbf{i}}-2\hat{\mathbf{j}}+\hat{\mathbf{k}}|}$$

$$d=\frac{|(2\hat{\mathbf{i}}+3\hat{\mathbf{j}}+\hat{\mathbf{k}})\times(\hat{\mathbf{i}}-2\hat{\mathbf{j}}+\hat{\mathbf{k}})|}{(\hat{\mathbf{i}}-2\hat{\mathbf{j}}+\hat{\mathbf{k}})}$$

$$d=\frac{|5\hat{\mathbf{i}}-\hat{\mathbf{j}}-7\hat{\mathbf{k}}|}{|\hat{\mathbf{i}}-2\hat{\mathbf{j}}+\hat{\mathbf{k}}|}=\frac{\sqrt{25+1+49}}{\sqrt{1+4+1}}=\frac{\sqrt{75}}{\sqrt{6}}=\frac{5\sqrt{3}}{\sqrt{6}}=\frac{5}{\sqrt{2}}=\frac{5\sqrt{2}}{2}$$

$$\therefore \quad 4l^2=4\times\frac{25}{2}=50$$

Skill Builder

The distance of the point $(-1,-2,-3)$ from the line of intersection of the planes $x+y+z-1=0$ and $4x-y-6z+6=0$ is l, then $6l^2$ is equal to ......

For Sol.

■ **For more practice** See Q. 17 of Milestone Practice 3.

Angle between a Line and a Plane

The angle between a line and a plane is the complement of the angle between the line and the normal to the plane.

If the equation of the line is $\mathbf{r}=\mathbf{a}+\lambda\mathbf{b}$ and that of the plane is $\mathbf{r}\cdot\mathbf{n}=d$, then angle θ between the line and the normal to the plane is $\cos\theta=\left|\frac{\mathbf{b}\cdot\mathbf{n}}{|\mathbf{b}||\mathbf{n}|}\right|$.

So, the angle ϕ between the line and the plane is given by $90°-\theta$.

$$\sin\phi=\left|\frac{\mathbf{b}\cdot\mathbf{n}}{|\mathbf{b}||\mathbf{n}|}\right| \text{ or } \phi=\sin^{-1}\left|\frac{\mathbf{b}\cdot\mathbf{n}}{|\mathbf{b}||\mathbf{n}|}\right|$$

Line $\mathbf{r}=\mathbf{a}+\lambda\mathbf{b}$ and plane $\mathbf{r}\cdot\mathbf{n}=d$ are perpendicular if $\mathbf{b}=\lambda\mathbf{n}$ or $\mathbf{b}\times\mathbf{n}=\mathbf{0}$ and parallel, if $\mathbf{b}\perp\mathbf{n}$ or $\mathbf{b}\cdot\mathbf{n}=0$.

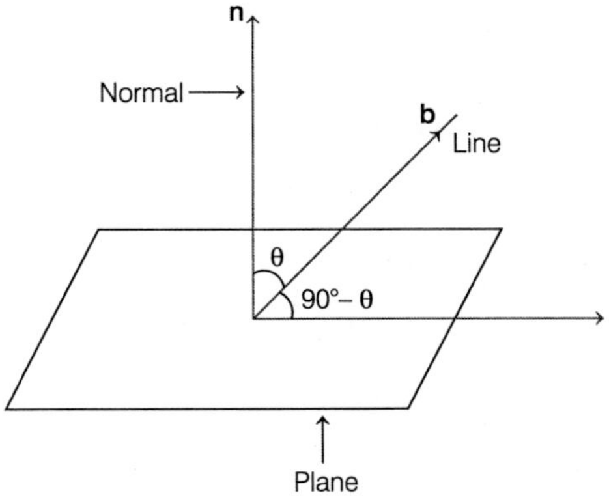

Example 58. Find the angle between the line $\mathbf{r}=\hat{\mathbf{i}}+2\hat{\mathbf{j}}-\hat{\mathbf{k}}+\lambda(\hat{\mathbf{i}}-\hat{\mathbf{j}}+\hat{\mathbf{k}})$ and the plane $\mathbf{r}\cdot(2\hat{\mathbf{i}}-\hat{\mathbf{j}}+\hat{\mathbf{k}})=4$.

Sol. We know that if θ is the angle between the lines $\mathbf{r}=\mathbf{a}+\lambda\mathbf{b}$ and $\mathbf{r}\cdot\mathbf{n}=p$, then

$$\sin\theta=\left|\frac{\mathbf{b}\cdot\mathbf{n}}{|\mathbf{b}||\mathbf{n}|}\right|$$

Therefore, if θ is the angle between $\mathbf{r}=\hat{\mathbf{i}}+2\hat{\mathbf{j}}-\hat{\mathbf{k}}+\lambda(\hat{\mathbf{i}}-\hat{\mathbf{j}}+\hat{\mathbf{k}})$ and $\mathbf{r}\cdot(2\hat{\mathbf{i}}-\hat{\mathbf{j}}+\hat{\mathbf{k}})=4$

Then, $$\sin\theta=\left|\frac{(\hat{\mathbf{i}}-\hat{\mathbf{j}}+\hat{\mathbf{k}})\cdot(2\hat{\mathbf{i}}-\hat{\mathbf{j}}+\hat{\mathbf{k}})}{|\hat{\mathbf{i}}-\hat{\mathbf{j}}+\hat{\mathbf{k}}||2\hat{\mathbf{i}}-\hat{\mathbf{j}}+\hat{\mathbf{k}}|}\right|$$

$$=\frac{2+1+1}{\sqrt{1+1+1}\sqrt{4+1+1}}$$

$$=\frac{4}{\sqrt{3}\sqrt{6}}=\frac{4}{3\sqrt{2}}$$

$$\Rightarrow \quad \theta=\sin^{-1}\left(\frac{4}{3\sqrt{2}}\right)$$

Intersection of a Line and a Plane

To find the point of intersection of the line $\frac{x-x_1}{l}=\frac{y-y_1}{m}=\frac{z-z_1}{n}$ and the plane $ax+by+cz+d=0$.

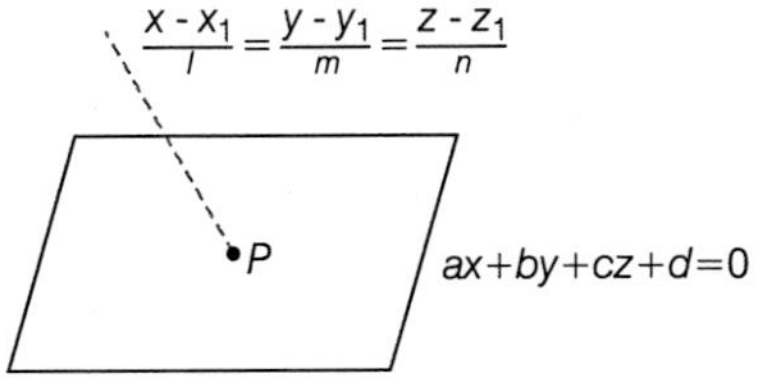

Let $\frac{x-x_1}{l}=\frac{y-y_1}{m}=\frac{z-z_1}{n}=r$

$\therefore \quad (x=rl+x_1, y=mr+y_1, z=nr+z_1)$ ...(i)

be a point in the plane say P.

It must satisfy the equation of plane.

$\therefore \quad a(x_1 + lr) + b(y_1 + mr) + c(z_1 + nr) + d = 0$

$\Rightarrow \quad (ax_1 + by_1 + cz_1 + d) + r(al + bm + cn) = 0$

$\Rightarrow \quad r = -\dfrac{(ax_1 + by_1 + cz_1 + d)}{al + bm + cn}$

On substituting the value of r Eq. (i), we get the coordinates of the required point of intersection.

JEE Focus Points

Concept Inside Video

- **Condition for a Line to be Parallel to a Plane**

  Let line $\dfrac{x - x_1}{l} = \dfrac{y - y_1}{m} = \dfrac{z - z_1}{n}$ be parallel to plane $ax + by + cz + d = 0$ iff;

  $$\theta = 0 \text{ or } \pi \text{ or } \sin\theta = 0$$

  $$\Rightarrow \quad al + bm + cm = 0$$

- **Condition for a Line to Lie in the Plane**

  Condition for $\dfrac{x - x_1}{l} = \dfrac{y - y_1}{m} = \dfrac{z - z_1}{n}$ to lie in the plane $ax + by + cz + d = 0$ are

  $$al + bm + cn = 0$$

  and $\quad ax_1 + by_1 + cz_1 + d = 0$

- A line will be in a plane iff
  - the normal to the plane is perpendicular to the line.
  - a point on the line in the plane.

Example 59. Find the equation of plane passing through the point (0, 7, −7) and containing the line $\dfrac{x+1}{-3} = \dfrac{y-3}{2} = \dfrac{z+2}{1}$.

Sol. Let the equation of the plane passing through the point $(0, 7, -7)$ be $a(x - 0) + b(y - 7) + c(z + 7) = 0$ ...(i)

The line $\dfrac{x+1}{-3} = \dfrac{y-3}{2} = \dfrac{z+2}{1}$ passes through the point $(-1, 3, -2)$ and has direction ratios $-3, 2, 1$. If (i) contains this line, it must pass through $(-1, 3, -2)$ and must be parallel to the line. Therefore,

$$a(-1) + b(3 - 7) + c(-2 + 7) = 0$$

i.e. $\quad a(-1) + b(-4) + c(5) = 0$ ...(ii)

and $\quad -3a + 2b + 1c = 0$ ...(iii)

On solving Eqs. (ii) and (iii) by cross multiplication, we get

$$\frac{a}{-14} = \frac{b}{-14} = \frac{c}{-14}$$

$\Rightarrow \quad \dfrac{a}{1} = \dfrac{b}{1} = \dfrac{c}{1} = \lambda \text{ (let)}$

$\Rightarrow \quad a = \lambda, b = \lambda, c = \lambda$

On putting the values of a, b, c in (i), we obtain

$$\lambda(x - 0) + \lambda(y - 7) + \lambda(z + 7) = 0$$

$\Rightarrow \quad x + y + z = 0$

This is the equation of the required plane.

Example 60. Find the distance between the point with position vector $-\hat{i} - 5\hat{j} - 10\hat{k}$ and the point of intersection of the line $\dfrac{x-2}{3} = \dfrac{y+1}{4} = \dfrac{z-2}{12}$ with the plane $x - y + z = 5$.

Sol. The coordinates of any point on the line $\dfrac{x-2}{3} = \dfrac{y+1}{4} = \dfrac{z-2}{12} = r$ (let) are $(3r + 2, 4r - 1, 12r + 2)$

If it lies on the plane $x - y + z = 5$, then

$$3r + 2 - 4r + 1 + 12r + 2 = 5$$

$\Rightarrow \quad 11r = 0$

$\Rightarrow \quad r = 0$

On putting $r = 0$ in (i), we obtain $(2, -1, 2)$ as the coordinates of the point of intersection of the given line and plane.

Required distance = Distance between points $(-1, -5, -10)$

and $\quad (2, -1, 2) = \sqrt{(2+1)^2 + (-1+5)^2 + (2+10)^2}$

$= \sqrt{9 + 16 + 144}$

$= \sqrt{169}$

$= 13$ units

Example 61. Find the distance of the point (1, −2, 3) from the plane $x - y + z = 5$ measured parallel to the line $\dfrac{x-1}{2} = \dfrac{y-3}{3} = \dfrac{z+2}{-6}$.

Sol. Equation of the given plane is

$$x - y + z = 5 \quad \text{...(i)}$$

and equation of the given line is

$$\frac{x-1}{2} = \frac{y-3}{3} = \frac{z+2}{-6} \quad \text{...(ii)}$$

$\therefore$ Equation of the line passing through the point $(1, -2, 3)$ and parallel to line (ii).

$$\frac{x-1}{2} = \frac{y+2}{3} = \frac{z-3}{-6} = \lambda \text{ (let)} \quad \text{...(iii)}$$

Any point on the line (iii) is

$$Q(2\lambda + 1, 3\lambda - 2, -6\lambda + 3)$$

Point Q lies in the plane (i).

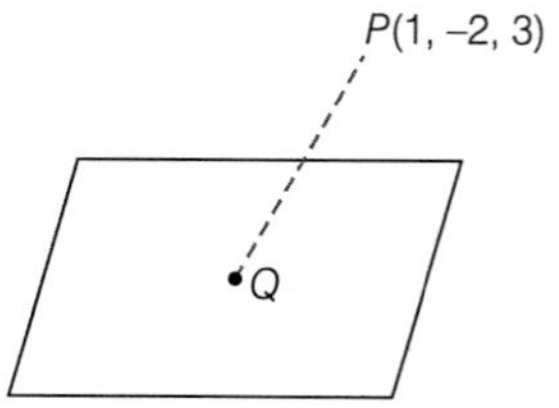

$\therefore \quad (2\lambda + 1) - (3\lambda - 2) + (-6\lambda + 3) = 5 \Rightarrow -7\lambda + 6 = 5$

$\Rightarrow \quad -7\lambda = -1 \Rightarrow \lambda = \dfrac{1}{7}$

$\therefore$ Coordinates of Q are $\left(\frac{2}{7}+1, \frac{3}{7}-2, -\frac{6}{7}+3\right)$.

i.e. $\left(\frac{9}{7}, \frac{-11}{7}, \frac{15}{7}\right)$

$$\therefore \quad PQ = \sqrt{\left(\frac{9}{7}-1\right)^2 + \left(\frac{-11}{7}+2\right)^2 + \left(\frac{15}{7}-3\right)^2}$$

$$= \sqrt{\left(\frac{2}{7}\right)^2 + \left(\frac{3}{7}\right)^2 + \left(\frac{-6}{7}\right)^2}$$

$$= \sqrt{\frac{4+9+36}{49}}$$

$$= \sqrt{\frac{49}{49}} = 1$$

Alternate Solution

Equation of plane is $x - y + z - 5 = 0$

Distance of the point $(1, -2, 3)$ from the plane $x - y + z - 5 = 0$ is

$$PR = \left|\frac{1+2+3-5}{\sqrt{1+1+1}}\right| = \frac{1}{\sqrt{3}}$$

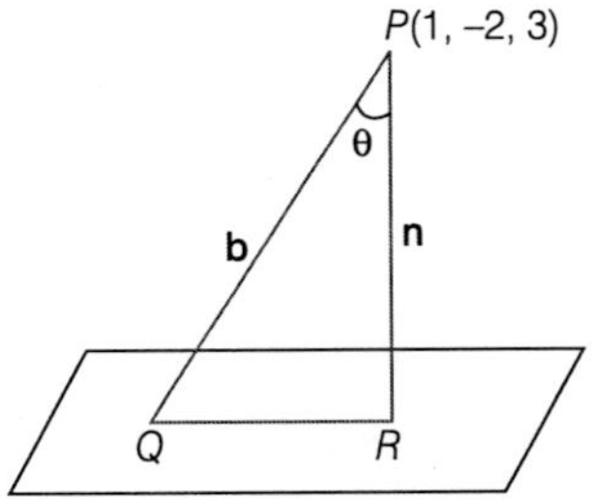

Direction ratios of $PQ = (2, 3, -6)$

Direction ratios of PQ are normal vector of plane aree $(1, -1, 1)$.

$\therefore$ Angle between PQ and PR

$$\cos\theta = \frac{(2)(1) + (3)(-1) + (-6)(1)}{\sqrt{2^2 + 3^2 + (-6)^2}\sqrt{(1)^2 + (-1)^2 + (1)^2}}$$

$$= \left|\frac{2-3-6}{\sqrt{49}\sqrt{3}}\right|$$

$$= \frac{1}{\sqrt{3}}$$

Also, $\cos\theta = \frac{PR}{PQ}$

$$PQ = \frac{PR}{\cos\theta}$$

$$= \frac{1}{\sqrt{3}} \times \frac{\sqrt{3}}{1} = 1$$

$\therefore$ Length $PQ = 1$ unit

3.20 Equation of a Plane Containing Two Intersecting Lines

The equation of the plane containing two given straight lines

$$\frac{x-x_1}{a_1} = \frac{y-y_1}{b_1} = \frac{z-z_1}{c_1} \text{ and } \frac{x-x_2}{a_2} = \frac{y-y_2}{b_2} = \frac{z-z_2}{c_2}$$

$$\begin{vmatrix} x-x_1 & y-y_1 & z-z_1 \\ a_1 & b_1 & c_1 \\ a_2 & b_2 & c_2 \end{vmatrix} = 0$$

or

$$\begin{vmatrix} x-x_2 & y-y_2 & z-z_2 \\ a_1 & b_1 & c_1 \\ a_2 & b_2 & c_2 \end{vmatrix} = 0$$

These lines will coplanar if

$$\begin{vmatrix} x_2-x_1 & y_2-y_1 & z_2-z_1 \\ a_1 & b_1 & c_1 \\ a_2 & b_2 & c_2 \end{vmatrix} = 0$$

Vector Form

The lines $\mathbf{r} = \mathbf{a}_1 + \lambda\mathbf{b}_1$ and $\mathbf{r} = \mathbf{a}_2 + \lambda\mathbf{b}_2$ are coplanar, then

$$[\mathbf{a}_1\ \mathbf{b}_1\ \mathbf{b}_2] = [\mathbf{a}_2\ \mathbf{b}_1\ \mathbf{b}_2]$$

and the equation of plane containing them is

$$[\mathbf{r}\ \mathbf{b}_1\ \mathbf{b}_2] = [\mathbf{a}_1\ \mathbf{b}_1\ \mathbf{b}_2] \text{ or } [\mathbf{r}\ \mathbf{b}_1\ \mathbf{b}_2] = [\mathbf{a}_2 \mathbf{b}_1\ \mathbf{b}_2]$$

Example 62. Find the vector equation of the plane that contains the lines $\mathbf{r} = (5\hat{\mathbf{i}} + 7\hat{\mathbf{j}} - 3\hat{\mathbf{k}}) + \lambda(4\hat{\mathbf{i}} + 4\hat{\mathbf{j}} - 5\hat{\mathbf{k}})$ and $\mathbf{r} = (8\hat{\mathbf{i}} + 4\hat{\mathbf{j}} + 5\hat{\mathbf{k}}) + \mu\ (7\hat{\mathbf{i}} + \hat{\mathbf{j}} + 3\hat{\mathbf{k}})$.

Sol. The two given lines pass through the point having position vector $\mathbf{a}_1 = 5\hat{\mathbf{i}} + 7\hat{\mathbf{j}} - 3\hat{\mathbf{k}}$ and $\mathbf{a}_2 = 8\hat{\mathbf{i}} + 4\hat{\mathbf{j}} + 5\hat{\mathbf{k}}$ and are parallel to the vectors $\mathbf{b}_1 = 4\hat{\mathbf{i}} + 4\hat{\mathbf{j}} - 5\hat{\mathbf{k}}$ and $\mathbf{b}_2 = 7\hat{\mathbf{i}} + \hat{\mathbf{j}} + 3\hat{\mathbf{k}}$.

$\therefore$ The plane containing the given lines also passes through the point with position vector $\mathbf{a}_1 = 5\hat{\mathbf{i}} + 7\hat{\mathbf{j}} - 3\hat{\mathbf{k}}$.

Since, the plane contains the line which are parallel to the vector $\mathbf{b}_1$ and $\mathbf{b}_2$ respectively.

$\therefore$ The normal vector of plane

$$\mathbf{n} = \mathbf{b}_1 \times \mathbf{b}_2 = \begin{vmatrix} \hat{\mathbf{i}} & \hat{\mathbf{j}} & \hat{\mathbf{k}} \\ 4 & 4 & -5 \\ 7 & 1 & 3 \end{vmatrix} = 17\hat{\mathbf{i}} - 47\hat{\mathbf{j}} - 24\hat{\mathbf{k}}$$

Thus, vector equation of the required plane is

$$(\mathbf{r} - \mathbf{a}) \cdot \mathbf{n} = 0 \Rightarrow \mathbf{r} \cdot \mathbf{n} - \mathbf{a} \cdot \mathbf{n} = 0$$

$$\Rightarrow \mathbf{r} \cdot (17\hat{\mathbf{i}} - 47\hat{\mathbf{j}} - 24\hat{\mathbf{k}}) - (5\hat{\mathbf{i}} + 7\hat{\mathbf{j}} - 3\hat{\mathbf{k}})(17\hat{\mathbf{i}} - 47\hat{\mathbf{j}} - 24\hat{\mathbf{k}}) = 0$$

$$\Rightarrow \quad \mathbf{r} \cdot (17\hat{\mathbf{i}} - 47\hat{\mathbf{j}} - 24\hat{\mathbf{k}}) + 172 = 0$$

JEE SCANNER

Example Similar to PYQ Asked in JEE Main 2022

If the lines $\frac{x+\alpha}{3}=\frac{y+3}{5}=\frac{z+5}{7}$ *and* $\frac{x-2}{1}=\frac{y-4}{4}=\frac{z-6}{7}$ *are coplanar, then the distance of the plane containing these two lines from the point* $(\alpha, -2, \alpha)$ *is*

(a) $2\sqrt{6}$ (b) $\sqrt{6}$ (c) $\frac{1}{\sqrt{6}}$ (d) $2\sqrt{3}$

Sol. We know that the line $\frac{x-x_1}{a_1}=\frac{y-y_1}{b_1}=\frac{z-z_1}{c_1}$

and $\frac{x-x_2}{a_2}=\frac{y-y_2}{b_2}=\frac{z-z_2}{c_2}$ are coplanar, if

$$\begin{vmatrix} x_2-x_1 & y_2-y_1 & z_2-z_1 \\ a_1 & b_1 & c_1 \\ a_2 & b_2 & c_2 \end{vmatrix}=0$$

and the equation of the plane containing these two lines is

$$\begin{vmatrix} x-x_1 & y-y_1 & z-z_1 \\ a_1 & b_1 & c_1 \\ a_2 & b_2 & c_2 \end{vmatrix}=0$$

Here, $x_1=-\alpha, y_1=-3, z_1=-5,$
$x_2=2, \quad y_2=4, \quad z_2=6,$
$a_1=3, \quad b_1=5, \quad c_1=7,$
$a_2=1, \quad b_2=4, \quad c_2=7$

$$\therefore \begin{vmatrix} x_2-x_1 & y_2-y_1 & z_2-z_1 \\ a_1 & b_1 & c_1 \\ a_2 & b_2 & c_2 \end{vmatrix}=\begin{vmatrix} 2+\alpha & 7 & 11 \\ 3 & 5 & 7 \\ 1 & 4 & 7 \end{vmatrix}=0$$

$\Rightarrow \quad (2+\alpha)(7)-98-77=0 \Rightarrow \alpha=1$

So, the given lines are coplanar.

The equation of the plane containing the lines is

$$\begin{vmatrix} x+1 & y+3 & z+5 \\ 3 & 5 & 7 \\ 1 & 4 & 7 \end{vmatrix}=0$$

or $(x+1)(35-28)-(y+3)(21-7)+(z+5)(12-5)=0$

or $x-2y+z=0$

Distance of point $(1,-2,1)$ from the plane $x-2y+z=0$ is

$$\frac{|1-2(-2)+1|}{\sqrt{1^2+(-2)^2+1^2}}=\left|\frac{1+4+1}{\sqrt{6}}\right|=\sqrt{6} \text{ units}$$

Skill Builder

The lines $\frac{x+1}{3}=\frac{y+3}{5}=\frac{z+5}{7}$ and $\frac{x-\alpha}{1}=\frac{y-4}{4}=\frac{z-6}{7}$ are coplanar, then the distance of the plane containing these two lines from the point $(\alpha, -\alpha, \alpha)$ is

(a) $\frac{8}{\sqrt{6}}$ (b) $2\sqrt{6}$ (c) $\frac{4\sqrt{6}}{3}$ (d) $\frac{2\sqrt{6}}{3}$

For Sol.

■ **For more practice** See Q. 28 of Milestone Practice 3.

Image of a Point in a Plane

To find the image of the point (α, β, γ) in the plane

$$ax+by+cz+d=0 \quad \text{...(i)}$$

Let $Q(x_1, y_1, z_1)$ be the image of point P in the plane (i).

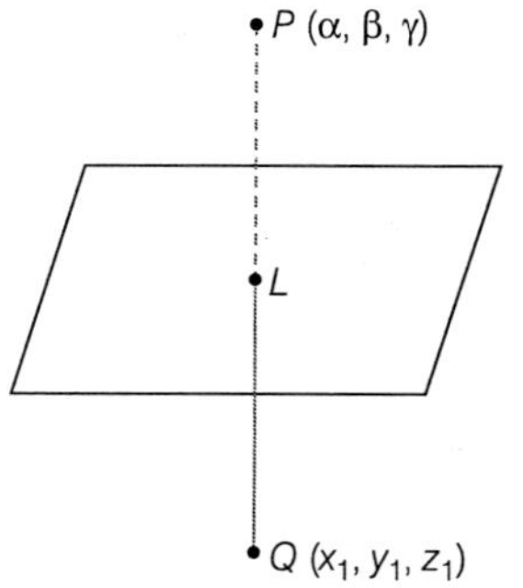

Let PQ meet plane (i) at L, direction ratios of normal to plane (i) are (a, b, c), since PQ perpendicular of plane (i).

So, direction ratios of PQ are a, b, c.

$\Rightarrow$ Equation of line PQ is,

$$\frac{x-\alpha}{a}=\frac{y-\beta}{b}=\frac{z-\gamma}{c}=r \text{ (let)}$$

Coordinates of any point on line PQ may be taken as

$$(ar+\alpha, br+\beta, cr+\gamma)$$

Let $Q(ar+\alpha, br+\beta, cr+\gamma)$

Since, L is the middle point of PQ.

$$\therefore \quad L=\left(\alpha+\frac{ar}{2}, \beta+\frac{br}{2}, \gamma+\frac{cr}{2}\right)$$

Since, L lies on plane (i), we get

$$a\left(\frac{ar}{2}+\alpha\right)+b\left(\frac{br}{2}+\beta\right)+c\left(\frac{cr}{2}+\gamma\right)+d=0$$

$$\Rightarrow \quad (a^2+b^2+c^2)\frac{r}{2}=-(a\alpha+b\beta+c\gamma+d)$$

$$\Rightarrow \quad r=\frac{-2(a\alpha+b\beta+c\gamma+d)}{a^2+b^2+c^2}$$

JEE SPIKE

If x_1, y_1, z_1 is image of point α, β, γ in the plane $ax+by+cz+d=0$

Then, $\frac{x_1-\alpha}{a}=\frac{y_1-\beta}{b}=\frac{z_1-\gamma}{c}$
$=\frac{-2(a\alpha+b\beta+c\gamma+d)}{a^2+b^2+c^2}$

JEE SCANNER

Example Similar to PYQ Asked in JEE Main 2022

If the image of the point $P(3,5,7)$ in the plane $2x+y+z=0$ is (a, b, c), then the value of $a^2+b^2+c^2$ is

Sol. Given plane is $2x+y+z=0$ ...(i)

and the point $P(3, 5, 7)$

DR's of normal to the plane (i) are 2, 1, 1.

Let Q be the image of a point P in plane (i).

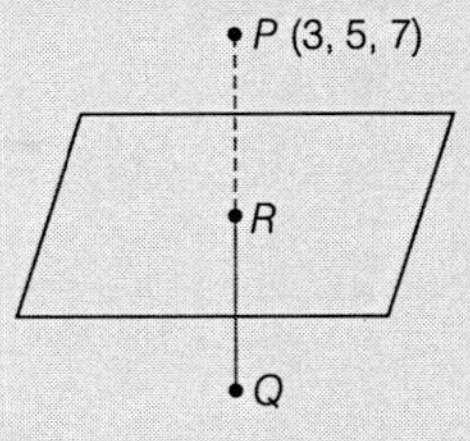

$\therefore$ Equation of line PR is $\dfrac{x-3}{2}=\dfrac{y-5}{1}=\dfrac{z-7}{1}=r$

Let $R(2r+3, r+5, r+7)$

Since, R lies on plane (i).

$\therefore \quad 2(2r+3)+(r+5)+(r+7)=0;\ 6r+18=0$

$\therefore \quad r=-3$

$\therefore \quad R\equiv(-3, 2, 4)$

Let $\quad Q\equiv(\alpha, \beta, \gamma)$

Since, R is mid-point of PQ.

$\therefore \ -3=\dfrac{\alpha+3}{2} \Rightarrow \alpha=-9;\quad 2=\dfrac{\beta+5}{2} \Rightarrow \beta=-1$

$4=\dfrac{\gamma+7}{2} \Rightarrow \gamma=1$

$\therefore \quad Q\equiv(-9, -1, 1)$

Here, $a=-9, b=-1$ and $c=1$

$\therefore\ a^2+b^2+c^2=81+1+1=83$

Time Saving Technique

a, b, c are image of $(3,5,7)$ in the plane $2x+y+z=0$

$\therefore \dfrac{a-3}{2}=\dfrac{b-5}{1}=\dfrac{c-z}{1}=\dfrac{-2(2\times3+5\times1+7\times1)}{2^2+1^2+1^2}$

$\dfrac{a-3}{2}=\dfrac{b-5}{1}=\dfrac{c-7}{1}=\dfrac{-2(6+5+7)}{6}=-6$

$a=-12+3, b=-6+5, c=7-6$

$a=-9, b=-1, c=1$

$\therefore\ a^2+b+c^2=81+1+1=83$

Skill Builder

For Sol.

If the image of the point $A(1, 2, 3)$ in the plane $3x-y+z=0$ is (α, β, γ), then the value of $\alpha+2\beta-\gamma$ is ....

- **For more practice** See Q. 30, 31 of Milestone Practice 3.

Example 63. Find the length and the foot of the perpendicular from the point $(7,14,5)$ to the plane $2x+4y-z=2$.

Sol. The required length $=\dfrac{2(7)+4(14)-(5)-2}{\sqrt{2^2+4^2+1^2}}$

$=\dfrac{14+56-5-2}{\sqrt{4+16+1}}$

$=\dfrac{63}{\sqrt{21}}$

$=3\sqrt{21}$ units

Let the coordinates of the foot of the perpendicular from the point $P(7, 14, 5)$ be $M(\alpha, \beta, \gamma)$.

Then, the direction ratios of PM are

$$\alpha-7, \beta-14 \text{ and } \gamma-5.$$

Therefore, the direction ratios of the normal to the plane are $\alpha-7, \beta-14$ and $\gamma-5$.

But the direction ratios of normal to the given plane $2x+4y-z=2$ are 2, 4 and -1.

Hence, $\dfrac{\alpha-7}{2}=\dfrac{\beta-14}{4}=\dfrac{\gamma-5}{-1}=k$

$\therefore \quad \alpha=2k+7, \beta=4k+14$ and $\gamma=-k+5$ ...(i)

Since, α, β and γ lie on the plane $2x+4y-z=2$,

$2\alpha+4\beta-\gamma=2$

$\Rightarrow \quad 2(7+2k)+4(14+4k)-(5-k)=2$

$\Rightarrow \quad 14+4k+56+16k-5+k=2$

$\Rightarrow \quad 21k=-63$

$\Rightarrow \quad k=-3$

Now, on putting $k=-3$ in (i), we get

$$\alpha=1, \beta=2 \text{ and } \gamma=8$$

Hence, the foot of the perpendicular is (1, 2, 8).

Time Saving Technique

Let α, β, γ be foot of perpendicular from the point $(7,14,5)$ to the plane $2x+4y-z=2$

$\therefore \quad \dfrac{\alpha-7}{2}=\dfrac{\beta-14}{4}=\dfrac{\gamma-5}{-1}$

$=\dfrac{-1[2(7)+4(14)-(1)(5)-2]}{2^2+4^2+(-1)^2}$

$\dfrac{\alpha-7}{2}=\dfrac{\beta-14}{4}=\dfrac{\gamma-5}{-1}=\dfrac{-(14+56-5-2)}{4+16+1}=-3$

$\alpha=-6+7, \beta=-12+14, \gamma=3+5$

$\alpha=1, \quad \beta=2, \quad \gamma=8$

$\therefore$ Foot of perpendicular $(1,2,8)$

Distance $=\sqrt{(1-7)^2+(2-14)^2+(8-5)^2}$

$=\sqrt{36+144+9}$

$=\sqrt{189}$

$=3\sqrt{21}$ units

Example 64. Find the image of the line $\frac{x-1}{9}=\frac{y-2}{-1}=\frac{z+3}{-3}$ in the plane $3x-3y+10z-26=0$.

Sol.

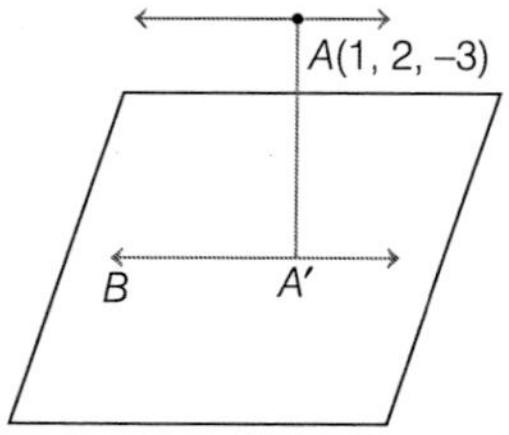

$$\frac{x-1}{9}=\frac{y-2}{-1}=\frac{z+3}{-3} \quad \text{...(i)}$$

$$3x-3y+10z-26=0 \quad \text{...(ii)}$$

The direction ratios of the line are 9, – 1 and – 3 and direction ratios of the normal to the given plane are 3, – 3 and 10.

Since, $9\cdot3+(-1)(-3)+(-3)10=0$ and the point $(1, 2, -3)$ of line (i) does not lie in plane (ii) for $3\cdot1-3\cdot2+10\cdot(-3)-26\neq0$, line (i) is parallel to plane (ii).

Let A' be the image of point $A(1, 2, -3)$ in plane (ii).

Then, the image of the line (i) in the plane (ii) is the line through A' and parallel to the line (i).

Let point A' be (p, q, r).

Then, $\frac{p-1}{3}=\frac{q-2}{-3}=\frac{r+3}{10}$

$$=-\frac{(3(1)-3(2)+10(-3)-26)}{9+9+100}=\frac{1}{2}$$

The point $A'\left(\frac{5}{2},\frac{1}{2},2\right)$

The equation of line BA' is $\frac{x-\left(\frac{5}{2}\right)}{9}=\frac{y-\left(\frac{1}{2}\right)}{-1}=\frac{z-2}{-3}$

Milestone Practice 3.3

1. Find the equation of plane passing through the point (1, 2, 3) and having the vector $\mathbf{r}=2\hat{i}-\hat{j}+3\hat{k}$ normal to it.
2. Show that the four points $(0,-1,0)$, $(2,1,-1)$, $(1,1,1)$ and $(3,3,0)$ are coplanar. Also, find equation of plane through them.
3. Find a unit vector normal to the plane through the points (1, 1, 1), (– 1, 2, 3) and (2, – 1, 3).
4. A plane meets coordinates axes at A, B and C respectively, such that position vector of centroid of ΔABC is $(2\hat{i}-5\hat{j}+8\hat{k})$, then the equation of plane is
   (a) $20x-8y+5z=120$ (b) $8x-20y+5z=120$
   (c) $20x-y+5z=120$ (d) None of these
5. If the plane $\frac{x}{2}+\frac{y}{3}+\frac{z}{4}=\frac{1}{2}$ intersects X, Y and Z-axes at P, Q and R respectively, then find volume of the tetrahedron $OPQR$, where O is the origin.
6. Find the equation of plane passing through the line of intersection of planes $3x+4y-4=0$ and $x+7y+3z+1=0$ and also through origin.
7. Find the equation of the planes parallel to the plane $x-2y+2z-3=0$. Which is at a unit distance from the point $(1,2,3)$.
8. Find the distance between the line $\mathbf{r}=(2\hat{i}-2\hat{j}+3\hat{k})+\lambda(\hat{i}-\hat{j}+4\hat{k})$ and the plane $\mathbf{r}\cdot(\hat{i}+5\hat{j}+\hat{k})=5$.
9. Find the equation of a plane which passes through the point (1, 2, 3) and which is at the maximum distance from the point (– 1, 0, 2).
10. Find the equation of plane which passes through the point (1, 2, 0) and which is perpendicular to the plane $x-y+z=3$ and $2x+y-z+4=0$.
11. Find the planes passing through the intersection of planes $\mathbf{r}\cdot(\hat{i}-3\hat{j}+5\hat{k})=2$ and $\mathbf{r}\cdot(\hat{i}-\hat{j})+8=0$ and perpendicular to planes $\mathbf{r}\cdot(\hat{i}-\hat{j}+\hat{k})=-4$.
12. A plane passes through $(1,-2,1)$ and is perpendicular to two planes $2x-2y+z=0$ and $x-y+2z=4$. Find the distance of the plane from the point (1, 2, 2).
13. Find the shortest distance between the planes $2x+y+z-1=0=3x+y+2z-2$ and $x=y=z$.
14. If the plane $2x-y+2z+6=0$ has the distance $\frac{1}{6}$ and $\frac{4}{3}$ units from the plane $4x-2y+4z+\alpha=0$ and $2x-y+2z+\beta=0$ respectively then, find the maximum value of $\alpha+\beta$.
15. Find equation of angle bisector of plane $x+2y+3z-1=0$ and $2x-3y+z+4=0$.

16. Find the equation of the bisector planes of the angles between the plane $x + 2y + 2z = 19$ and $4x - 3y + 12z + 3 = 0$ and specify the plane which bisects the acute angle and the plane which bisects the obtuse angle.

17. Find the distance of point $(1, 2, 3)$ from the line of intersection of planes $2x + y + z - 4 = 0$ and $4x + y - 2z + 6 = 0$.

18. Find the angle between the line $\frac{x+1}{2} = \frac{y}{3} = \frac{z-3}{6}$ and the plane $3x + y + z = 7$.

19. If the angle between the line $x = \frac{y-1}{2} = \frac{z-3}{k}$ and plane $x + 2y + 3z = 4$ is $\cos^{-1}\left(\sqrt{\frac{5}{14}}\right)$, then the value of k is

(a) $\frac{3}{2}$ (b) $\frac{5}{2}$ (c) $\frac{2}{3}$ (d) $\frac{2}{5}$

20. Find the equation of the plane passing through the line $\frac{x-1}{2} = \frac{y+1}{-1} = \frac{z}{3}$ and parallel to the direction whose direction numbers are 3, 4, 2.

21. Find the distance of the point $(1, -5, 9)$ from the plane $x - y + z = 5$ measured along the straight line $x = y = z$.

22. Find the equation of the plane which passes through the point $(3, 4, -5)$ and contains the line $\frac{x+1}{2} = \frac{y-1}{3} = \frac{z+2}{-1}$.

23. Find the distance of the point $(-1, -5, -10)$ from the point of intersection of the line $\frac{x-2}{2} = \frac{y+1}{4} = \frac{z-2}{12}$ and plane $x - y + z = 5$.

24. The distance of the point $(-2, 3, -4)$ from the line $\frac{x+2}{3} = \frac{2y+3}{4} = \frac{3z+4}{5}$, measured parallel to the plane $4x + 12y - 3z + 1 = 0$ is

(a) $\frac{17}{2}$ units (b) $\frac{7}{2}$ units (c) $\frac{13}{2}$ units (d) $\frac{19}{2}$ units

25. Find the value of k for which the planes $kx + 4y + z = 0$, $4x + ky + 2z = 0$ and $2x + 2y + z = 0$ intersect in a straight line.

26. Find the equation of plane of the projection of the line $\frac{x-1}{2} = \frac{y+1}{-1} = \frac{z-3}{4}$ on the plane $x + 2y + z = 9$.

27. Find the direction cosines of the projection of the line $\frac{x}{-2} = \frac{y-1}{1} = \frac{z+1}{-1}$ on the plane $2x + y - 3z = 5$.

28. If the lines $\frac{x-\alpha}{4} = \frac{y-7}{4} = \frac{z+3}{-5}$ and $\frac{x-8}{7} = \frac{y-4}{1} = \frac{z-5}{3}$ are coplanar, then the distance of the plane containing these two lines from the point $\left(-\alpha, \frac{\alpha}{5}, \frac{\alpha}{5}\right)$ is equal to ....

29. Are the lines $3x - 2y + z + 5 = 0 = 2x + 3y + 4z - 4$ and $\frac{x+4}{3} = \frac{y+6}{5} = \frac{z-1}{-2}$ intersect? If yes, then find their point of intersection and equation of the plane in which they lie.

30. Find image of point $(1, 3, 4)$ in the plane $2x - y + z + 3 = 0$.

31. Find the equation of the image of the plane $x - 2y + 2z - 3 = 0$ in the plane $x + y + z - 1 = 0$.

Answer Key

1. $\mathbf{r}\cdot(2\hat{\mathbf{i}} - \hat{\mathbf{j}} + 3\hat{\mathbf{k}}) = 9$

2. $4x - 3y + 2z = 3$

3. $\frac{2\hat{\mathbf{i}} + 2\hat{\mathbf{j}} + \hat{\mathbf{k}}}{3}$

4. (a)

5. $\frac{1}{2}$

6. $7x + 32y + 12z = 0$

7. $P_1 : x - 2y + 2z - 6 = 0$, $P_2 : x - 2y + 2z = 0$

8. $\frac{10}{3\sqrt{3}}$

9. $2x + 2y + z = 9.$

10. $y + z - 2 = 0$

11. $\mathbf{r}(-7\hat{\mathbf{i}} + 3\hat{\mathbf{j}} + 10\hat{\mathbf{k}}) = 76$

12. $2\sqrt{2}$

13. $\frac{1}{\sqrt{2}}$

14. 23

15. $3x - y + 4z + 3 = 0$

16. $\mathbf{r}(25\hat{\mathbf{i}} + 7\hat{\mathbf{j}} + 62\hat{\mathbf{k}}) - 238 = 0$

17. $\frac{\sqrt{34}}{\sqrt{13}}$

18. $\theta = \sin^{-1}\left(\frac{15}{7\sqrt{11}}\right)$

19. (c)

20. $14x - 5y - 11z = 19$

21. $10\sqrt{3}$

22. $3x - y + 3z + 10 = 0$

23. 13

24. (a)

25. 2, 4

26. $9x - 2y - 5z + 4 = 0$

27. $\left(-\frac{18}{7}, -\frac{13}{7}, 0\right)$

28. $\frac{16}{\sqrt{3074}}$

29. $(2, 4, -3)$

30. $x_1 = -3, y_1 = -5, z_1 = 2$

31. $7x + 13y + 15z + 15 = 0$

For Detailed Solution

JEE Pattern EXAMPLES

Single Option Correct Type Questions

Example 1 *The points* $(5, -4, 2)$ $(4, -3, 1)$, $(7, -6, 4)$ *and* $(8, -7, 5)$ *are the vertices of*

(a) a rectangle (b) a square
(c) a parallelogram (d) None of these

Sol. (c) Let $A(5, -4, 2)$, $B(4, -3, 1)$, $C(7, -6, 4)$ and $D(8, -7, 5)$

$$\mathbf{AB} = -\hat{\mathbf{i}} + \hat{\mathbf{j}} - \hat{\mathbf{k}},\ \mathbf{BC} = 3\hat{\mathbf{i}} - 3\hat{\mathbf{j}} + 3\hat{\mathbf{k}}$$

$$\mathbf{CD} = \hat{\mathbf{i}} - \hat{\mathbf{j}} + \hat{\mathbf{k}} \text{ and } \mathbf{DA} = -3\hat{\mathbf{i}} + 3\hat{\mathbf{j}} - 3\hat{\mathbf{k}}$$

Clearly $\mathbf{AB} \parallel \mathbf{CD}$ and $\mathbf{BC} \parallel \mathbf{DA}$

Also, $\mathbf{AB} \cdot \mathbf{BC} = -9 \neq 0$

$\therefore$ *ABCD* is a parallelogram.

Example 2 *In* ΔABC *the mid-point of the sides AB, BC and CA are respectively* $(l, 0, 0)$, $(0, m, 0)$ *and* $(0, 0, n)$. *Then,* $\dfrac{AB^2 + BC^2 + CA^2}{l^2 + m^2 + n^2}$ *is equal to*

(a) 2 (b) 4 (c) 8 (d) 16

Sol. (c) From the figure,

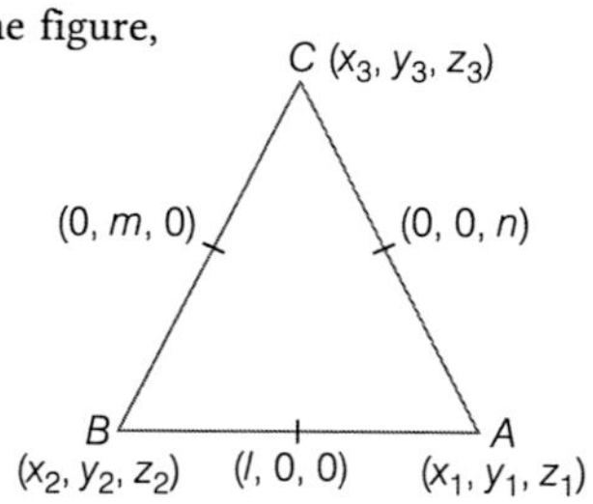

$$x_1 + x_2 = 2l,\ y_1 + y_2 = 0,\ z_1 + z_2 = 0$$

$$x_2 + x_3 = 0,\ y_2 + y_3 = 2m,\ z_2 + z_3 = 0$$

and $x_1 + x_3 = 0,\ y_1 + y_3 = 0,\ z_1 + z_3 = 2n$

On solving, we get

$$x_1 = l,\ x_2 = l,\ x_3 = -l$$

$$y_1 = -m,\ y_2 = m,\ y_3 = m$$

and $z_1 = n,\ z_2 = -n,\ z_3 = n$

$\therefore$ Coordinates are $A(l, -m, n)$, $B(l, m, -n)$ and $C(-l, m, n)$

$$\therefore \frac{AB^2 + BC^2 + CA^2}{l^2 + m^2 + n^2} = \frac{(4m^2 + 4n^2) + (4l^2 + 4n^2) + (4l^2 + 4m^2)}{l^2 + m^2 + n^2} = 8$$

JEE SCANNER

Example 3 Similar to PYQ Asked in JEE Main 2024

Let (α, β, γ) *be the mirror image of point* $(2, 3, 4)$ *in the line* $\dfrac{x-2}{1} = \dfrac{y-3}{2} = \dfrac{z-4}{3}$. *Then,* $\alpha + 2\beta + 3\gamma$ *is equal to*

(a) 12 (b) 20 (c) 18 (d) 19

Sol. (b) Let $\dfrac{x-2}{1} = \dfrac{y-3}{2} = \dfrac{z-4}{3} = \lambda$ and $P(2, 3, 4)$ and $Q(\alpha, \beta, \gamma)$.

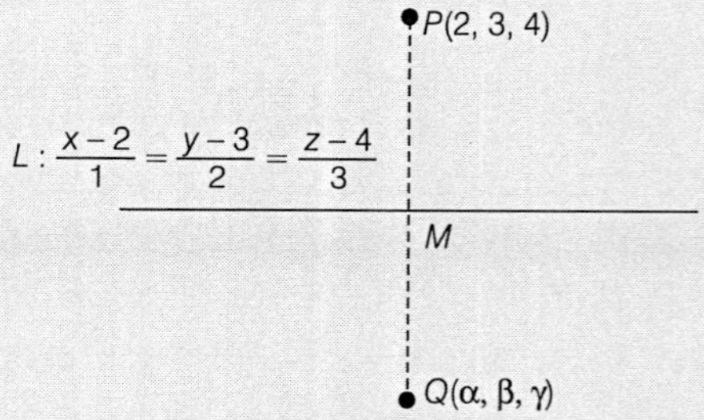

$\therefore$ DR's of $PQ : (\alpha - 2, \beta - 3, \gamma - 4)$

DR's of line $L : 1, 2, 3$

$\because$ L is perpendicular to PQ

$\therefore 1(\alpha - 2) + 2(\beta - 3) + 3(\gamma - 4) = 0$

$\Rightarrow \alpha + 2\beta + 3\gamma = 20$

Skill Builder

Let (α, β, γ) be the mirror image of the point $(-1, 3, 4)$ in the line $\dfrac{x-3}{2} = \dfrac{y-4}{5} = \dfrac{z-6}{3}$.
Then $2\alpha + 5\beta + 3\gamma$ is equal to

(a) 29 (b) 27
(c) 25 (d) 23

For Sol.

Example 4 *The angle between the lines* $2x = 3y = -z$ *and* $6x = -y = -4z$ *is*

(a) 30° (b) 45° (c) 60° (d) 90°

Sol. (d) Given, equation of lines can be rewritten as

$$\frac{x}{1/2} = \frac{y}{1/3} = \frac{z}{-1} \text{ and } \frac{x}{1/6} = \frac{y}{-1} = \frac{z}{-1/4}$$

$$\therefore \cos\theta = \frac{a_1a_2 + b_1b_2 + c_1c_2}{\sqrt{a_1^2 + b_1^2 + c_1^2}\sqrt{a_2^2 + b_2^2 + c_2^2}}$$

$$= \frac{\frac{1}{2}\times\frac{1}{6} + \frac{1}{3}\times(-1) - 1\times\left(-\frac{1}{4}\right)}{\sqrt{\frac{1}{4}+\frac{1}{9}+1}\sqrt{\frac{1}{36}+1+\frac{1}{16}}} = \frac{\frac{1}{12} - \frac{1}{3} + \frac{1}{4}}{\sqrt{\frac{1}{4}+\frac{1}{9}+1}\sqrt{\frac{1}{36}+1+\frac{1}{16}}}$$

$$\Rightarrow \cos\theta = 0 \Rightarrow \theta = 90^\circ$$

Example 5 *A line makes the same angle θ with X-axis and Z-axis. If the angle β, which it makes with Y-axis, is such that $\sin^2\beta = 3\sin^2\theta$, then the value of $\cos^2\theta$ is*

(a) $\frac{1}{5}$ (b) $\frac{2}{5}$ (c) $\frac{3}{5}$ (d) $\frac{2}{3}$

Sol. (c) Since, $\cos^2\theta + \cos^2\beta + \cos^2\theta = 1$ $[\because l^2 + m^2 + n^2 = 1]$

$\Rightarrow 2\cos^2\theta + 1 - \sin^2\beta = 1$

$\Rightarrow 2\cos^2\theta + 1 - 3\sin^2\theta = 1$ $[\because \sin^2\beta = 3\sin^2\theta]$

$\Rightarrow 2\cos^2\theta - 3(1 - \cos^2\theta) = 0$

$\Rightarrow 5\cos^2\theta = 3 \Rightarrow \cos^2\theta = \frac{3}{5}$

Example 6 *The projection of a line segment on the coordinate axes are 2, 3, 6. Then, the length of the line segment is*

(a) 7 (b) 5 (c) 1 (d) 11

Sol. (a) Let the length of the line segment be r and its direction cosines be l, m, n. Then, its projections on the coordinate axes are lr, mr, nr.

$\therefore \quad lr = 2, mr = 3$ and $nr = 6$

$\Rightarrow l^2r^2 + m^2r^2 + n^2r^2 = 4 + 9 + 36$

$\Rightarrow r^2(l^2 + m^2 + n^2) = 49 \Rightarrow r^2 = 49 \Rightarrow r = 7$

$[\because l^2 + m^2 + n^2 = 1$ and $r > 0]$

Example 7 *The equation of the straight line through the origin and parallel to the line $(b+c)x + (c+a)y + (a+b)z = k = (b-c)x + (c-a)y + (a-b)z$ are*

(a) $\frac{x}{b^2-c^2} = \frac{y}{c^2-a^2} = \frac{z}{a^2-b^2}$

(b) $\frac{x}{b} = \frac{y}{b} = \frac{z}{a}$

(c) $\frac{x}{a^2-bc} = \frac{y}{b^2-ca} = \frac{z}{c^2-ab}$

(d) None of the above

Sol. (c) Equations of straight line through the origin are

$$\frac{x-0}{l} = \frac{y-0}{m} = \frac{z-0}{n}$$

where, $l(b+c) + m(c+a) + n(a+b) = 0$

and $l(b-c) + m(c-a) + n(a-b) = 0$

On solving, $\frac{l}{2(a^2-bc)} = \frac{m}{2(b^2-ca)} = \frac{n}{2(c^2-ab)}$

Equations of the straight line are

$$\frac{x}{a^2-bc} = \frac{y}{b^2-ca} = \frac{z}{c^2-ab}.$$

JEE SCANNER

Example 8 Similar to PYQ Asked in JEE Main 2024

The distance of the point $Q(0, 1, -1)$ from the line passing through the point $P(2, -4, 3)$ and perpendicular to the lines $\mathbf{r} = (-\hat{i} + 2\hat{k}) + \lambda(\hat{i} + 2\hat{j} + 3\hat{k}), \lambda \in R$ and $\mathbf{r} = (2\hat{i} - \hat{j} + 3\hat{k}) + \mu(-2\hat{i} + 3\hat{j} + 4\hat{k}), \mu \in R$ is

(a) $\frac{1}{75}\sqrt{37249}$ units (b) $\frac{1}{75}\sqrt{40274}$ units

(c) $\frac{1}{75}\sqrt{36525}$ units (d) $\frac{1}{75}\sqrt{37250}$ units

Sol. (c) Given, $L_1 : \mathbf{r}_1 = (-\hat{i} + 2\hat{k}) + \lambda(\hat{i} + 2\hat{j} + 3\hat{k})$

and $L_2 : \mathbf{r} = (2\hat{i} - \hat{j} + 3\hat{k}) + \mu(-2\hat{i} + 3\hat{j} + 4\hat{k})$

Let L be a line which passes through $(2, -4, 3)$ and perpendicular to L_1, L_2 both

$$\mathbf{b} = \begin{vmatrix} \hat{i} & \hat{j} & \hat{k} \\ 1 & 2 & 3 \\ -2 & 3 & 4 \end{vmatrix} = -\hat{i} - 10\hat{j} + 7\hat{k}$$

$\therefore$ Equation of line L

$$\mathbf{r} = 2\hat{i} - 4\hat{j} + 3\hat{k} + \lambda(-\hat{i} - 10\hat{j} + 7\hat{k})$$
$$= (2-\lambda)\hat{i} - (4+10\lambda)\hat{j} + (3+7\lambda)\hat{k}$$

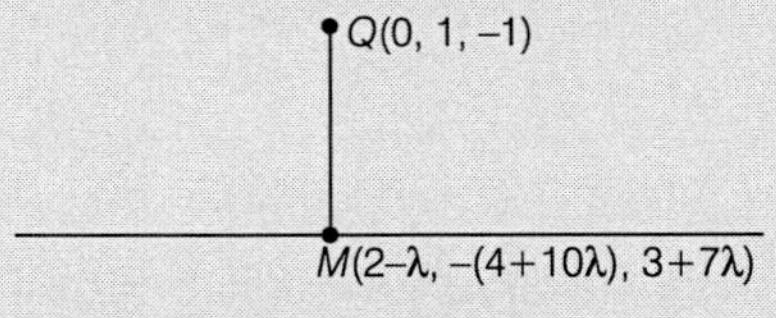

$$\mathbf{QM} = (2-\lambda)\hat{i} - (10\lambda + 5)\hat{j} + (7\lambda + 4)\hat{k}$$

Now, $\mathbf{QM} \cdot (-\hat{i} - 10\hat{j} + 7\hat{k}) = 0$ $[\because \mathbf{QM} \perp L]$

$\Rightarrow -(2-\lambda) + 10(10\lambda + 5) + 7(7\lambda + 4) = 0$

$\Rightarrow -2 + \lambda + 100\lambda + 50 + 49\lambda + 28 = 0$

$\Rightarrow 150\lambda = -76 \Rightarrow \lambda = \frac{-38}{75}$

$$\mathbf{QM} = \left(2 + \frac{38}{75}\right)\hat{i} - \left(10\left(\frac{-38}{75}\right) + 5\right)\hat{j} + \left(7\left(-\frac{38}{75}\right) + 4\right)\hat{k}$$

$$= \frac{188}{75}\hat{i} + \frac{5}{75}\hat{j} + \frac{34}{75}\hat{k} = \frac{1}{75}(188\hat{i} + 5\hat{j} + 34\hat{k})$$

$\therefore$ Required distance $= |\mathbf{QM}| = \frac{1}{75}\sqrt{(188)^2 + (5)^2 + (34)^2}$

$$= \frac{1}{75}\sqrt{35344 + 25 + 1156} = \frac{1}{75}\sqrt{36525} \text{ units}$$

Skill Builder

The distance of the point $Q(0, 1, 1)$ from the line passing through the point $P(1, 2, 3)$ and perpendicular to the lines $\mathbf{r} = (-\hat{i} + 2\hat{j}) + \lambda(-2\hat{i} + 3\hat{j} + 5\hat{k}), \lambda \in R$ and $\mathbf{r} = (\hat{i} - 3\hat{j} + 6\hat{k}) + \mu(-\hat{i} + \hat{j} + 2\hat{k}), \mu \in R$ is

(a) $\frac{4}{3}$ units (b) $\frac{5}{3}$ units

(c) $\frac{1}{3}\sqrt{41}$ units (d) $\frac{1}{3}\sqrt{42}$ units

For Sol.

Example 9 *A mirror and a source of light are situated at the origin O and at a point on OX, respectively. A ray of light from the source strikes the mirror and is reflected. If the direction ratios of the normal to the plane are proportional to 1, –1, 1, then direction cosines of the reflected ray are*

(a) $\frac{1}{3}, \frac{2}{3}, \frac{2}{3}$ (b) $-\frac{1}{3}, \frac{2}{3}, \frac{2}{3}$

(c) $-\frac{1}{3}, -\frac{2}{3}, -\frac{2}{3}$ (d) $-\frac{1}{3}, -\frac{2}{3}, \frac{2}{3}$

Sol. (d) Let the source of light be situated at $A(a, 0, 0)$, where, $a \neq 0$.

Let OA be the incident ray, OB be the reflected ray and ON be the normal to the mirror at O.

$$\therefore \quad \angle AON = \angle NOB = \frac{\theta}{2} \quad \text{(say)}$$

Direction ratios of **OA** are proportional to a, 0, 0 and so its direction cosines are 1, 0, 0.

Direction cosines of ON are $\frac{1}{\sqrt{3}}, \frac{-1}{\sqrt{3}}, \frac{1}{\sqrt{3}}$

$$\therefore \quad \cos\frac{\theta}{2} = \frac{1}{\sqrt{3}}$$

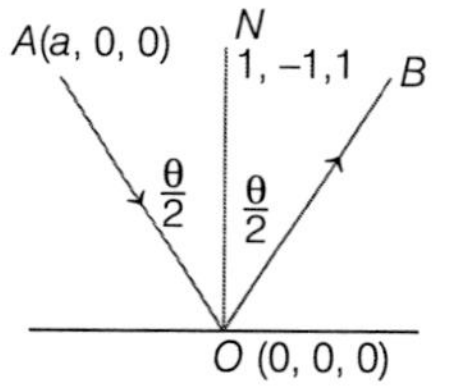

Let l, m, n be the direction cosines of the reflected ray OB.

Then, $\frac{l+1}{2\cos\frac{\theta}{2}} = \frac{1}{\sqrt{3}}, \frac{m+0}{2\cos\frac{\theta}{2}} = -\frac{1}{\sqrt{3}}$ and $\frac{n+0}{2\cos\frac{\theta}{2}} = \frac{1}{\sqrt{3}}$

$$\Rightarrow \quad l = \frac{2}{3} - 1, m = -\frac{2}{3}, n = \frac{2}{3}$$

$$\Rightarrow \quad l = -\frac{1}{3}, m = -\frac{2}{3}, n = \frac{2}{3}$$

Hence, direction cosines of the reflected ray are $-\frac{1}{3}, -\frac{2}{3}, \frac{2}{3}$.

Example 10 *If the direction cosines of two lines are such that $l + m + n = 0$, $l^2 + m^2 - n^2 = 0$, then the angle between them is*

(a) π (b) $\frac{\pi}{3}$ (c) $\frac{\pi}{4}$ (d) $\frac{\pi}{6}$

Sol. (b) If l, m, n are direction cosines of two lines are such that

$$l + m + n = 0 \quad \text{...(i)}$$

and $$l^2 + m^2 - n^2 = 0 \quad \text{...(ii)}$$

$$\Rightarrow \quad l^2 + m^2 - (-l - m)^2 = 0 \Rightarrow 2lm = 0 \Rightarrow l = 0 \text{ or } m = 0$$

If $l = 0$, then $n = -m \Rightarrow l : m : n = 0 : 1 : -1$

and if $m = 0$, then $n = -l \Rightarrow l : m : n = 1 : 0 : -1$

$$\therefore \quad \cos\theta = \frac{0 + 0 + 1}{\sqrt{0 + 1 + 1}\sqrt{0 + 1 + 1}} = \frac{1}{2} \Rightarrow \theta = \frac{\pi}{3}$$

JEE SCANNER

Example 11 Similar to PYQ Asked in JEE Main 2022

Let O be the origin and M and N be the points on the lines $\frac{x-4}{3} = \frac{y-3}{2} = \frac{z-5}{4}$ and $\frac{x-2}{6} = \frac{y+1}{3} = \frac{z-3}{2}$ respectively, such that MN is the shortest distance between the given lines. Then, $\frac{(500 \times 125)}{750}(\mathbf{OM} \cdot \hat{\mathbf{j}}) + (\mathbf{ON} \cdot \hat{\mathbf{j}})$ is equal to ....

Sol. Let $M(3\lambda + 4, 2\lambda + 3, 4\lambda + 5)$ and $N(6\mu + 2, 3\mu - 1, 2\mu + 3)$ be two points on given lines.

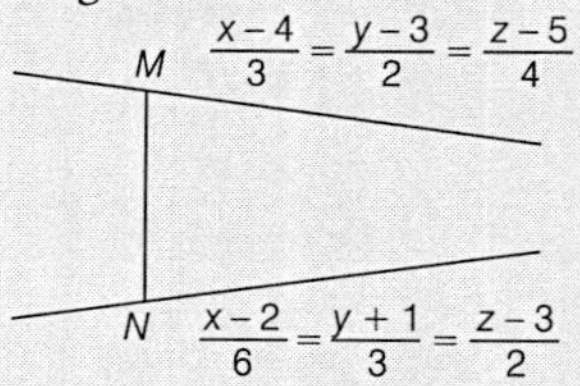

Here, $\mathbf{b}_1 = 3\hat{\mathbf{i}} + 2\hat{\mathbf{j}} + 4\hat{\mathbf{k}}$ and $\mathbf{b}_2 = 6\hat{\mathbf{i}} + 3\hat{\mathbf{j}} + 2\hat{\mathbf{k}}$

$\therefore$ $\mathbf{MN} \perp \mathbf{b}_1$ and $\mathbf{MN} \perp \mathbf{b}_2$

$$\therefore \quad \mathbf{MN} \cdot \mathbf{b}_1 = 0$$

$$\Rightarrow 3(6\mu - 3\lambda - 2) + 2(3\mu - 2\lambda - 4) + 4(2\mu - 4\lambda - 2) = 0$$

$$\Rightarrow \quad 18\mu - 9\lambda - 6 + 6\mu - 4\lambda - 8 + 8\mu - 16\lambda - 8 = 0$$

$$\Rightarrow \quad 32\mu - 29\lambda = 22 \quad \text{...(i)}$$

$$\therefore \quad \mathbf{MN} \cdot \mathbf{b}_2 = 0$$

$$\Rightarrow 6(6\mu - 3\lambda - 2) + 3(3\mu - 2\lambda - 4) + 2(2\mu - 4\lambda - 2) = 0$$

$$\Rightarrow \quad 36\mu - 18\lambda - 12 + 9\mu - 6\lambda - 12 + 4\mu - 8\lambda - 4 = 0$$

$$\Rightarrow \quad 49\mu - 32\lambda = 28 \quad \text{...(ii)}$$

On solving Eqs. (i) and (ii), we get

$$\mu = \frac{272}{1000} \text{ and } \lambda = \frac{-458}{1000}; \quad \mu = \frac{34}{125} \text{ and } \lambda = \frac{-229}{500}$$

$$\therefore M\left[3\left(\frac{-229}{500}\right) + 4, 2\left(\frac{-229}{500}\right) + 3, 4\left(\frac{-229}{500}\right) + 5\right]$$

$$= M\left(\frac{1313}{500}, \frac{1042}{500}, \frac{1584}{500}\right)$$

$$\therefore N\left(6 \times \frac{34}{125} + 2, 3 \times \frac{34}{125} - 1, 2 \times \frac{34}{125} + 3\right) = N\left(\frac{454}{125}, \frac{23}{125}, \frac{443}{125}\right)$$

So, $\mathbf{OM} = \frac{1}{500}(1313\hat{\mathbf{i}} + 1042\hat{\mathbf{j}} + 1584\hat{\mathbf{k}})$

$\mathbf{ON} = \frac{1}{125}(454\hat{\mathbf{i}} + 23\hat{\mathbf{j}} + 443\hat{\mathbf{k}})$

$\mathbf{OM} \cdot \hat{\mathbf{j}} = \frac{1042}{500}$ and $\mathbf{ON} \cdot \hat{\mathbf{j}} = \frac{23}{125}$

Hence, $\frac{500 \times 125}{750}[(\mathbf{OM} \cdot \hat{\mathbf{j}}) + (\mathbf{ON} \cdot \hat{\mathbf{j}})] = \frac{141750}{750} = 189$

Skill Builder

Let O be the origin and M and N be the points on the $\frac{x-1}{0} = \frac{y}{2} = \frac{z-2}{0}$ and $\frac{x+1}{0} = \frac{y+2}{0} = \frac{z}{1}$ respectively, such that MN is the shortest distance between the given lines. Then, $|\mathbf{OM} \cdot \mathbf{ON}|$ is equal to ....

For Sol.

Example 12 *A straight line 'L' cuts the lines AB, AC and AD of a parallelogram ABCD at points B_1, C_1 and D_1, respectively. If $\mathbf{AB}_1 = \lambda_1 \mathbf{AB}$, $\mathbf{AD}_1 = \lambda_2 \mathbf{AD}$ and $\mathbf{AC}_1 = \lambda_3 \mathbf{AC}$, where $\lambda_1, \lambda_2, \lambda_3$ are scalars real numbers, then $\frac{1}{\lambda_3}$ is equal to*

(a) $\frac{1}{\lambda_1} + \frac{1}{\lambda_2}$ (b) $\frac{1}{\lambda_1} - \frac{1}{\lambda_2}$

(c) $-\lambda_1 + \lambda_2$ (d) $\lambda_1 + \lambda_2$

Sol. (a) Let $\mathbf{AB} = \mathbf{a}$, $\mathbf{AD} = \mathbf{b}$, then $\mathbf{AC} = \mathbf{a} + \mathbf{b}$

Given, $\mathbf{AB}_1 = \lambda_1 \mathbf{a}$, $\mathbf{AD}_1 = \lambda_2 \mathbf{b}$, $\mathbf{AC}_1 = \lambda_3(\mathbf{a} + \mathbf{b})$

$$\mathbf{B}_1\mathbf{D}_1 = \mathbf{AD}_1 - \mathbf{AB}_1 = \lambda_2 \mathbf{b} - \lambda_1 \mathbf{a}$$

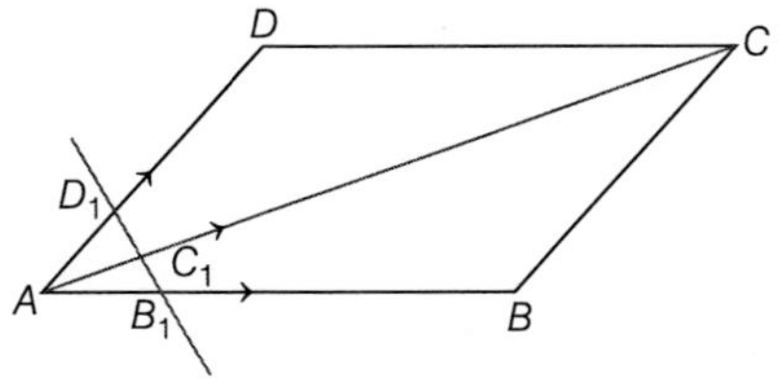

Since, vectors $\mathbf{D}_1\mathbf{C}_1$ and $\mathbf{B}_1\mathbf{D}_1$ are collinear, we have $\mathbf{D}_1\mathbf{C}_1 = k\,\mathbf{B}_1\mathbf{D}_1$ for some $k \in R$.

$$\Rightarrow \quad \mathbf{AC}_1 - \mathbf{AD}_1 = k \cdot \mathbf{B}_1\mathbf{D}_1$$

$$\Rightarrow \quad \lambda_3(\mathbf{a} + \mathbf{b}) - \lambda_2 \mathbf{b} = k \cdot (\lambda_2 \mathbf{b} - \lambda_1 \mathbf{a})$$

$$\Rightarrow \quad \lambda_3 \mathbf{a} + (\lambda_3 - \lambda_2)\mathbf{b} = k \cdot \lambda_2 \mathbf{b} - k \cdot \lambda_1 \mathbf{a}$$

Thus, $\lambda_3 = -k\lambda_1$ and $\lambda_3 - \lambda_2 = k\lambda_2$

$$\Rightarrow \quad k = \frac{-\lambda_3}{\lambda_1} = \frac{\lambda_3 - \lambda_2}{\lambda_2}$$

$$\Rightarrow \quad \lambda_1\lambda_2 = \lambda_1\lambda_3 + \lambda_2\lambda_3$$

$$\Rightarrow \quad \frac{1}{\lambda_3} = \frac{1}{\lambda_1} + \frac{1}{\lambda_2}$$

Example 13 *The line $\frac{x-2}{3} = \frac{y+1}{2} = \frac{z-1}{-1}$ intersects the curve $xy = c^2$, $z = 0$, if c is equal to*

(a) ± 1 (b) $\pm \frac{1}{3}$

(c) $\pm \sqrt{5}$ (d) None of these

Sol. (c) At the point on the line where it intersects the given curve, we have $z = 0$, so that

$$\frac{x-2}{3} = \frac{y+1}{2} = \frac{0-1}{-1}$$

$$\Rightarrow \quad \frac{x-2}{3} = 1 \text{ and } \frac{y+1}{2} = 1$$

$$\Rightarrow \quad x = 5 \text{ and } y = 1.$$

On putting these values of x and y in $xy = c^2$, we get

$$c^2 = 5 \Rightarrow c = \pm\sqrt{5}$$

JEE SCANNER

Example 14 Similar to PYQ Asked in JEE Main 2024

The lines $\frac{x-2}{0} = \frac{y}{2} = \frac{z+3}{-1}$ and $\frac{x-1}{1} = \frac{y+3}{-3} = \frac{z+1}{1}$ intersect at the point P. If the distance of P from the line $\frac{x-1}{2} = \frac{y-1}{-3} = \frac{z+1}{1}$ is l, then $7l^2$ is equal to ....

Sol. Let $L_1 : \frac{x-2}{0} = \frac{y}{2} = \frac{z+3}{-1} = \lambda$ (let) ...(i)

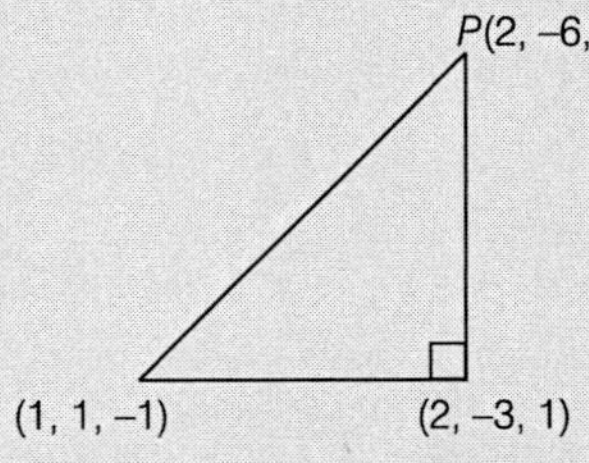

any point on the line (i) is $(2, 2\lambda, -\lambda - 3)$

and $\frac{x-1}{1} = \frac{y+3}{-3} = \frac{z+1}{1} = \mu$ (let) ...(ii)

any point on the line (ii) is $(\mu + 1, -3\mu - 3, \mu - 1)$

Since, lines (i) and (ii) intersecting.

$\therefore \quad \mu + 1 = 2, -3\mu - 3 = 2\lambda$ and $\mu - 1 = -\lambda - 3$

$\Rightarrow \quad \mu = 1, -3(1) - 3 = 2\lambda \Rightarrow \mu = 1, \lambda = -3$

So, $P(2, -6, 0)$

Projection of $\hat{\mathbf{i}} - 7\hat{\mathbf{j}} + \hat{\mathbf{k}}$ on $2\hat{\mathbf{i}} - 3\hat{\mathbf{j}} + \hat{\mathbf{k}}$

$$\frac{2 + 21 + 1}{\sqrt{4 + 9 + 1}} = \frac{24}{\sqrt{14}}$$

$$\therefore \quad l^2 = 51 - \frac{576}{14} = \frac{138}{14} = \frac{69}{7}$$

$$\therefore \quad 7l^2 = 69$$

Skill Builder

The lines $\frac{x-1}{2} = \frac{y-2}{3} = \frac{z-3}{4}$ and $\frac{x-4}{5} = \frac{y-1}{2} = z$ intersect at the point P. If the distance of P from the line $\frac{x-1}{1} = \frac{y+1}{2} = \frac{z-2}{-3}$ is l, then $2l^2$ is equal to ......

For Sol.

Example 15 *If the position vectors of the points A and B are $3\hat{\mathbf{i}} + \hat{\mathbf{j}} + 2\hat{\mathbf{k}}$ and $\hat{\mathbf{i}} - 2\hat{\mathbf{j}} - 4\hat{\mathbf{k}}$ respectively, then the equation of the plane through B and perpendicular to **AB** is*

(a) $2x + 3y + 6z + 28 = 0$ (b) $3x + 2y + 6z = 28$

(c) $2x - 3y + 6z + 28 = 0$ (d) $3x - 2y + 6z = 28$

Sol. (a) We have, $\mathbf{AB} = -2\hat{\mathbf{i}} - 3\hat{\mathbf{j}} - 6\hat{\mathbf{k}}$

So, vector equation of the plane is

$$|\mathbf{r} - (\hat{\mathbf{i}} - 2\hat{\mathbf{j}} - 4\hat{\mathbf{k}})| \cdot \mathbf{AB} = 0$$

$$\Rightarrow \quad \mathbf{r} \cdot (-2\hat{\mathbf{i}} - 3\hat{\mathbf{j}} - 6\hat{\mathbf{k}}) = (\hat{\mathbf{i}} - 2\hat{\mathbf{j}} - 4\hat{\mathbf{k}}) \cdot (-2\hat{\mathbf{i}} - 3\hat{\mathbf{j}} - 6\hat{\mathbf{k}})$$

$$\Rightarrow \quad -2x - 3y - 6z = -2 + 6 + 24$$

$$\Rightarrow \quad 2x + 3y + 6z + 28 = 0$$

Example 16 *The equation of the plane passing through the mid-point of the line points* (1, 2, 3) *and* (3, 4, 5) *and perpendicular to it is*

(a) $x + y + z = 9$ (b) $x + y + z = -9$

(c) $2x + 3y + 4z = 9$ (d) $2x + 3y + 4z = -9$

Sol. (a) The DR's of the joining of the points (1,2, 3) and (3, 4, 5) and (3 − 1, 4 − 2, 5 − 3), ie. (2, 2, 2).

Also, the mid-point of the join of the points (1, 2, 3) and (3, 4, 5) is (2, 3, 4).

∴ Equation of plane which passes through (2, 3, 4) and the DR's of its normal are (2, 2, 2) is

$$2(x - 2) + 2(y - 3) + 2(z - 4) = 0$$

$$\Rightarrow \quad x + y + z - 9 = 0$$

$$\Rightarrow \quad x + y + z = 9$$

Example 17 *Equation of the plane that contains the lines* $\mathbf{r} = (\hat{\mathbf{i}} + \hat{\mathbf{j}}) + \lambda(\hat{\mathbf{i}} + 2\hat{\mathbf{j}} - \hat{\mathbf{k}})$ *and,* $\mathbf{r} = (\hat{\mathbf{i}} + \hat{\mathbf{j}}) + \mu(-\hat{\mathbf{i}} + \hat{\mathbf{j}} - 2\hat{\mathbf{k}})$ *is*

(a) $\mathbf{r} \cdot (2\hat{\mathbf{i}} + \hat{\mathbf{j}} - 3\hat{\mathbf{k}}) = -4$ (b) $\mathbf{r} \times (-\hat{\mathbf{i}} + \hat{\mathbf{j}} + \hat{\mathbf{k}}) = 0$

(c) $\mathbf{r} \cdot (-\hat{\mathbf{i}} + \hat{\mathbf{j}} + \hat{\mathbf{k}}) = 0$ (d) None of these

Sol. (c) The lines are parallel to the vectors $\mathbf{b}_1 = \hat{\mathbf{i}} + 2\hat{\mathbf{j}} - \hat{\mathbf{k}}$ and $\mathbf{b}_2 = -\hat{\mathbf{i}} + \hat{\mathbf{j}} - 2\hat{\mathbf{k}}$.

Therefore, the plane is normal to the vector

$$\mathbf{n} = \mathbf{b}_1 \times \mathbf{b}_2 = \begin{vmatrix} \hat{\mathbf{i}} & \hat{\mathbf{j}} & \hat{\mathbf{k}} \\ 1 & 2 & -1 \\ -1 & 1 & -2 \end{vmatrix} = -3\hat{\mathbf{i}} + 3\hat{\mathbf{j}} + 3\hat{\mathbf{k}}$$

The required plane passes through $(\hat{\mathbf{i}} + \hat{\mathbf{j}})$ and is normal to the vector $\mathbf{n}$.

Therefore, its equation is

$$\mathbf{r} \cdot \mathbf{n} = \mathbf{a} \cdot \mathbf{n}$$

$$\Rightarrow \mathbf{r} \cdot (-3\hat{\mathbf{i}} + 3\hat{\mathbf{j}} + 3\hat{\mathbf{k}}) = (\hat{\mathbf{i}} + \hat{\mathbf{j}}) \cdot (-3\hat{\mathbf{i}} + 3\hat{\mathbf{j}} + 3\hat{\mathbf{k}})$$

$$\Rightarrow \mathbf{r} \cdot (-3\hat{\mathbf{i}} + 3\hat{\mathbf{j}} + 3\hat{\mathbf{k}}) = -3 + 3 \Rightarrow \mathbf{r} \cdot (-\hat{\mathbf{i}} + \hat{\mathbf{j}} + \hat{\mathbf{k}}) = 0$$

Example 18 *The distance between the line* $\mathbf{r} = 2\hat{\mathbf{i}} - 2\hat{\mathbf{j}} + 3\hat{\mathbf{k}} + \lambda(\hat{\mathbf{i}} - \hat{\mathbf{j}} + 4\hat{\mathbf{k}})$ *and the plane* $\mathbf{r} \cdot (\hat{\mathbf{i}} + 5\hat{\mathbf{j}} + \hat{\mathbf{k}}) = 5$, *is*

(a) $\dfrac{10}{9}$ (b) $\dfrac{10}{3\sqrt{3}}$

(c) $\dfrac{10}{3}$ (d) None of these

Sol. (b) Clearly, the given line passes through the point $\mathbf{a} = 2\hat{\mathbf{i}} - 2\hat{\mathbf{j}} + 3\hat{\mathbf{k}}$ and is parallel to the vector $\mathbf{b} = \hat{\mathbf{i}} - \hat{\mathbf{j}} + 4\hat{\mathbf{k}}$.

The plane is normal to the vector $\mathbf{n} = \hat{\mathbf{i}} + 5\hat{\mathbf{j}} + \hat{\mathbf{k}}$.

We have, $\mathbf{b} \cdot \mathbf{n} = 1 - 5 + 4 = 0$

So, the line is parallel to the plane.

∴ Required distance

= Length of the perpendiculars from a point on the line to the given plane.

= Length of the perpendicular from $(2\hat{\mathbf{i}} - 2\hat{\mathbf{j}} + 3\hat{\mathbf{k}})$ to the given plane.

$$= \left| \frac{(2\hat{\mathbf{i}} - 2\hat{\mathbf{j}} + 3\hat{\mathbf{k}}) \cdot (\hat{\mathbf{i}} + 5\hat{\mathbf{j}} + \hat{\mathbf{k}}) - 5}{\sqrt{1 + 25 + 1}} \right|$$

$$= \left| \frac{2 - 10 + 3 - 5}{3\sqrt{3}} \right|$$

$$= \frac{10}{3\sqrt{3}}$$

Example 19 *If the plane* $\dfrac{x}{2} + \dfrac{y}{3} + \dfrac{z}{4} = 1$, *cuts the coordinate axes in A, B, C, then the area of* ΔABC *is*

(a) $\sqrt{29}$ sq units (b) $\sqrt{41}$ sq units

(c) $\sqrt{61}$ sq units (d) None of these

Sol. (c) The given plane cuts the coordinate axes in $A(2, 0, 0)$, $B(0, 3, 0)$ and $C(0, 0, 4)$.

$$\therefore \text{Area of } \Delta ABC = \frac{1}{2} AB \times AC \times \sin \angle BAC$$

Now, $AB = \sqrt{4 + 9 + 0} = \sqrt{13}$, $AC = \sqrt{4 + 0 + 16} = \sqrt{20}$

$$\cos \angle BAC = \frac{\mathbf{AB} \cdot \mathbf{AC}}{|\mathbf{AB}||\mathbf{AC}|} = \frac{(-2\hat{\mathbf{i}} + 3\hat{\mathbf{j}}) \cdot (-2\hat{\mathbf{i}} + 4\hat{\mathbf{k}})}{\sqrt{4 + 9}\sqrt{4 + 16}}$$

$$\Rightarrow \cos \angle BAC = \frac{4 + 0 + 0}{\sqrt{13}\sqrt{20}} = \frac{4}{\sqrt{13}\sqrt{20}} = \frac{2}{\sqrt{65}}$$

$$\Rightarrow \sin \angle BAC = \sqrt{1 - \frac{4}{65}} = \sqrt{\frac{61}{65}}$$

Hence, area of $\Delta ABC = \dfrac{1}{2} \times \sqrt{13} \times \sqrt{20} \times \sqrt{\dfrac{61}{65}} = \sqrt{61}$ sq units

Example 20 *The distance of the point* (1, −2, 3) *from the plane* $x - y + z = 5$ *measured parallel to the line* $\dfrac{x}{2} = \dfrac{y}{3} = \dfrac{z - 1}{-6}$ *is*

(a) 1 (b) 2

(c) 4 (d) None of these

Sol. (a) The equation of the line passing through $P(1, -2, 3)$ and parallel to the given line is

$$\frac{x - 1}{2} = \frac{y + 2}{3} = \frac{z - 3}{-6}$$

Suppose it meets the plane $x - y + z = 5$ at the point Q given by

$$\frac{x-1}{2} = \frac{y+2}{3} = \frac{z-3}{-6} = \lambda$$

i.e. $(2\lambda + 1, 3\lambda - 2, -6\lambda + 3)$

This lies on $x - y + z = 5$.

Therefore, $2\lambda + 1 - 3\lambda + 2 - 6\lambda + 3 = 5$

$$\Rightarrow \quad -7\lambda = -1 \Rightarrow \lambda = \frac{1}{7}$$

So, the coordinates of Q are $\left(\frac{9}{7}, -\frac{11}{7}, \frac{15}{7}\right)$.

Hence, the required distance $PQ = \sqrt{\frac{4}{49} + \frac{9}{49} + \frac{36}{49}} = 1.$

Example 21 ■ *The length of the perpendicular from the origin to the plane passing through the point* **a** *and containing the line* $\mathbf{r} = \mathbf{b} + \lambda\mathbf{c}$ *is*

(a) $\dfrac{[\mathbf{a}\ \mathbf{b}\ \mathbf{c}]}{|\mathbf{a}\times\mathbf{b} + \mathbf{b}\times\mathbf{c} + \mathbf{c}\times\mathbf{a}|}$

(b) $\dfrac{[\mathbf{a}\ \mathbf{b}\ \mathbf{c}]}{|\mathbf{a}\times\mathbf{b} + \mathbf{b}\times\mathbf{c}|}$

(c) $\dfrac{[\mathbf{a}\ \mathbf{b}\ \mathbf{c}]}{|\mathbf{b}\times\mathbf{c} + \mathbf{c}\times\mathbf{a}|}$

(d) $\dfrac{[\mathbf{a}\ \mathbf{b}\ \mathbf{c}]}{|\mathbf{a}\times\mathbf{b} + \mathbf{c}\times\mathbf{a}|}$

Sol. (c) The plane passing through **a** and containing the line $\mathbf{r} = \mathbf{b} + \lambda\mathbf{c}$ also passes through the point **b** and is parallel to the vector **c**. So, it is normal to the vector $(\mathbf{a} - \mathbf{b}) \times \mathbf{c}$.

Thus, the equation of the plane is

$$(\mathbf{r} - \mathbf{a}) \cdot |(\mathbf{a} - \mathbf{b}) \times \mathbf{c}| = 0$$

$$\Rightarrow \quad (\mathbf{r} - \mathbf{a}) \cdot (\mathbf{a}\times\mathbf{c} - \mathbf{b}\times\mathbf{c}) = 0$$

$$\Rightarrow \quad \mathbf{r} \cdot (\mathbf{a}\times\mathbf{c} - \mathbf{b}\times\mathbf{c}) = \mathbf{a} \cdot (\mathbf{a}\times\mathbf{c} - \mathbf{b}\times\mathbf{c})$$

$$\Rightarrow \quad \mathbf{r} \cdot (\mathbf{a}\times\mathbf{c} - \mathbf{b}\times\mathbf{c}) = -\mathbf{a} \cdot (\mathbf{b}\times\mathbf{c})$$

$$\Rightarrow \quad \mathbf{r} \cdot (\mathbf{b}\times\mathbf{c} + \mathbf{c}\times\mathbf{a}) - [\mathbf{a}\ \mathbf{b}\ \mathbf{c}] = 0$$

$\therefore$ Length of the perpendicular from the origin to this plane

$$= \left|\frac{\mathbf{0} \cdot (\mathbf{b}\times\mathbf{c} + \mathbf{c}\times\mathbf{a}) - [\mathbf{a}\ \mathbf{b}\ \mathbf{c}]}{|\mathbf{b}\times\mathbf{c} + \mathbf{c}\times\mathbf{a}|}\right|$$

$$= \frac{[\mathbf{a}\ \mathbf{b}\ \mathbf{c}]}{|\mathbf{b}\times\mathbf{c} + \mathbf{c}\times\mathbf{a}|}$$

Example 22 ■ *If* $P(0, 1, 0)$ *and* $Q(0, 0, 1)$ *are two points, then the projection of* **PQ** *on the plane* $x + y + z = 3$ *is*

(a) 2 (b) 3 (c) $\sqrt{2}$ (d) $\sqrt{3}$

Sol. (c) The projection of PQ on the given plane is $PQ \cos\theta$, where θ is the angle between PQ and the plane.

Let **n** be a vector normal to the plane.

We have, $\mathbf{PQ} = -\hat{\mathbf{j}} + \hat{\mathbf{k}}$ and $\mathbf{n} = \hat{\mathbf{i}} + \hat{\mathbf{j}} + \hat{\mathbf{k}}$

$$\therefore \quad \sin\theta = \frac{\mathbf{PQ} \cdot \mathbf{n}}{|\mathbf{PQ}||\mathbf{n}|} = 0$$

$\Rightarrow$ **PQ** is parallel to the plane.

Hence, the projection of **PQ** on the given plane

$$= |\mathbf{PQ}| \cos\theta$$

$$= |\mathbf{PQ}| = \sqrt{1+1} = \sqrt{2}$$

Example 23 ■ *The equation of the plane through the intersection of the planes* $x + y + z = 1$ *and* $2x + 3y - z + 4 = 0$ *and parallel to X-axis, is*

(a) $y - 3z + 6 = 0$ (b) $3y - z + 6 = 0$

(c) $y + 3z + 6 = 0$ (d) $3y - 2z + 6 = 0$

Sol. (a) The equation of the plane through the intersection of the planes $x + y + z = 1$ and $2x + 3y - z + 4 = 0$ is

$$(x + y + z - 1) + \lambda(2x + 3y - z + 4) = 0$$

or, $(2\lambda + 1)x + (3\lambda + 1)y + (1 - \lambda)z + 4\lambda - 1 = 0$ ...(i)

It is parallel to X-axis i.e. $\frac{x}{1} = \frac{y}{0} = \frac{z}{0}$

$$\therefore \quad 1(2\lambda + 1) + 0 \times (3\lambda + 1) + 0(1 - \lambda) = 0$$

$$\Rightarrow \quad \lambda = -\frac{1}{2}$$

On substituting $\lambda = -\frac{1}{2}$ in Eq. (i), we get

$y - 3z + 6 = 0$ as the equation of the required plane.

Example 24 ■ *A plane passes through the point* $(1, 1, 1)$. *If b, c, a are the direction ratios of a normal to the plane where a, b, c* $(a < b < c)$ *are the prime factors of* 2001, *then the equation of the plane* II *is*

(a) $29x + 31y + 3z = 63$ (b) $23x + 29y - 29z = 23$

(c) $23x + 29y + 3z = 55$ (d) $31x + 37y + 3z = 71$

Sol. (c) The equation of the plane is

$$b(x - 1) + c(y - 1) + a(z - 1) = 0 \quad ...(i)$$

Now, $2001 = 3 \times 23 \times 29$

$$\therefore \quad a < b < c \Rightarrow a = 3, b = 23 \text{ and } c = 29.$$

On substituting the values of a, b, c in Eq. (i), we obtain $23x + 29y + 3z = 55$ as the equation of the required plane.

Example 25 ■ *A tetrahedron has vertices at* $O(0, 0, 0)$, $A(1, 2, 1)$, $B(2, 1, 3)$ *and* $C(-1, 1, 2)$. *Then, the angle between the faces OAB and ABC will be*

(a) 90° (b) $\cos^{-1}\left(\frac{19}{35}\right)$

(c) $\cos^{-1}\left(\frac{17}{31}\right)$ (d) 30°

Decoding the Question

First find **OA**, **OB**, **AB** and **AC**, then find vectors normal to *OAB* and *ABC*. After this, use formula $\cos\theta = \dfrac{\mathbf{a}_1 \cdot \mathbf{a}_2}{|\mathbf{a}_1||\mathbf{a}_2|}$

Sol. (b) Let $\mathbf{n}_1$ and $\mathbf{n}_2$ be the vectors normal to the faces OAB and ABC.

Then, $\mathbf{n}_1 = \mathbf{OA} \times \mathbf{OB} = \begin{vmatrix} \hat{\mathbf{i}} & \hat{\mathbf{j}} & \hat{\mathbf{k}} \\ 1 & 2 & 1 \\ 2 & 1 & 3 \end{vmatrix} = 5\hat{\mathbf{i}} - \hat{\mathbf{j}} - 3\hat{\mathbf{k}}$

and $\mathbf{n}_2 = \mathbf{AB} \times \mathbf{AC} = \begin{vmatrix} \hat{\mathbf{i}} & \hat{\mathbf{j}} & \hat{\mathbf{k}} \\ 1 & -1 & 2 \\ -2 & -1 & 1 \end{vmatrix} = \hat{\mathbf{i}} - 5\hat{\mathbf{j}} - 3\hat{\mathbf{k}}$

If θ is the angle between the faces OAB and ABC, then

$$\cos\theta = \frac{\mathbf{n}_1 \cdot \mathbf{n}_2}{|\mathbf{n}_1||\mathbf{n}_2|}$$

$$\Rightarrow \quad \cos\theta = \frac{5+5+9}{\sqrt{25+1+9}\sqrt{1+25+9}} = \frac{19}{35}$$

$$\Rightarrow \quad \theta = \cos^{-1}\left(\frac{19}{35}\right)$$

Example 26 *The vector equation of the plane through the point $(2, 1, -1)$ and passing through the line of intersection of the plane $\mathbf{r}\cdot(\hat{\mathbf{i}} + 3\hat{\mathbf{j}} - \hat{\mathbf{k}}) = 0$ and $\mathbf{r}\cdot(\hat{\mathbf{j}} + 2\hat{\mathbf{k}}) = 0$, is*

(a) $\mathbf{r}\cdot(\hat{\mathbf{i}} + 9\hat{\mathbf{j}} + 11\hat{\mathbf{k}}) = 0$ (b) $\hat{\mathbf{r}}\cdot(\hat{\mathbf{i}} + 9\hat{\mathbf{j}} + 11\hat{\mathbf{k}}) = 6$

(c) $\hat{\mathbf{r}}\cdot(\hat{\mathbf{i}} - 3\hat{\mathbf{j}} - 13\hat{\mathbf{k}}) = 0$ (d) None of these

Sol. (a) The vector equation of a plane through the line of intersection of the plane $\mathbf{r}\cdot(\hat{\mathbf{i}} + 3\hat{\mathbf{j}} - \hat{\mathbf{k}}) = 0$ and $\mathbf{r}\cdot(\hat{\mathbf{j}} + 2\hat{\mathbf{k}}) = 0$ can be written as

$$\mathbf{r}\cdot(\hat{\mathbf{i}} + 3\hat{\mathbf{j}} + - \hat{\mathbf{k}}) + \lambda\{\mathbf{r}\cdot(\hat{\mathbf{j}} + 2\hat{\mathbf{k}})\} = 0 \quad \text{...(i)}$$

This passes through $2\hat{\mathbf{i}} + \hat{\mathbf{j}} - \hat{\mathbf{k}}$.

$$\therefore \quad (2\hat{\mathbf{i}} + \hat{\mathbf{j}} - \hat{\mathbf{k}})\cdot(\hat{\mathbf{i}} + 3\hat{\mathbf{j}} - \hat{\mathbf{k}}) + \lambda(2\hat{\mathbf{i}} + \hat{\mathbf{j}} - \hat{\mathbf{k}})\cdot(\hat{\mathbf{j}} + 2\hat{\mathbf{k}}) = 0$$

$$\Rightarrow \quad (2+3+1) + \lambda(0+1-2) = 0$$

$$\Rightarrow \quad \lambda = 6$$

On putting the value of λ in Eq. (i), we get the equation of the required plane as

$$\mathbf{r}\cdot(\hat{\mathbf{i}} + 9\hat{\mathbf{j}} + 11\hat{\mathbf{k}}) = 0$$

Example 27 *The vector equation of the plane through the point $\hat{\mathbf{i}} + 2\hat{\mathbf{j}} - \hat{\mathbf{k}}$ and perpendicular to the line of intersection of the plane $\mathbf{r}\cdot(3\hat{\mathbf{i}} - \hat{\mathbf{j}} + \hat{\mathbf{k}}) = 1$ and $\mathbf{r}\cdot(\hat{\mathbf{i}} + 4\hat{\mathbf{j}} - 2\hat{\mathbf{k}}) = 2$, is*

(a) $\mathbf{r}\cdot(2\hat{\mathbf{i}} + 7\hat{\mathbf{j}} - 13\hat{\mathbf{k}}) = 1$ (b) $\mathbf{r}\cdot(2\hat{\mathbf{i}} - 7\hat{\mathbf{j}} - 13\hat{\mathbf{k}}) = 1$

(c) $\mathbf{r}\cdot(2\hat{\mathbf{i}} + 7\hat{\mathbf{j}} + 13\hat{\mathbf{k}}) = 0$ (d) None of these

Sol. (b) The line of intersection of the planes

$$\mathbf{r}\cdot(3\hat{\mathbf{i}} - \hat{\mathbf{j}} + \hat{\mathbf{k}}) = 1 \text{ and } \mathbf{r}\cdot(\hat{\mathbf{i}} + 4\hat{\mathbf{j}} - 2\hat{\mathbf{k}}) = 2$$

is common to both the planes. Therefore, it is perpendicular to normals to the two planes, i.e.

$$\mathbf{n}_1 = 3\hat{\mathbf{i}} - \hat{\mathbf{j}} + \hat{\mathbf{k}} \text{ and } \mathbf{n}_2 = \hat{\mathbf{i}} + 4\hat{\mathbf{j}} - 2\hat{\mathbf{k}}$$

Hence, it is parallel to the vector $\mathbf{n}_1 \times \mathbf{n}_2 = -2\hat{\mathbf{i}} + 7\hat{\mathbf{j}} + 13\hat{\mathbf{k}}$.

Thus, we have to find the equation of the plane passing through $\mathbf{a} = \hat{\mathbf{i}} + 2\hat{\mathbf{j}} - \hat{\mathbf{k}}$ and normal to the vector $\mathbf{n} = \mathbf{n}_1 \times \mathbf{n}_2$.

The equation of the required plane is

$$(\mathbf{r} - \mathbf{a})\cdot\mathbf{n} = 0 \Rightarrow \mathbf{r}\cdot\mathbf{n} = \mathbf{a}\cdot\mathbf{n}$$

$$\Rightarrow \quad \mathbf{r}\cdot(-2\hat{\mathbf{i}} + 7\hat{\mathbf{j}} + 13\hat{\mathbf{k}}) = (\hat{\mathbf{i}} + 2\hat{\mathbf{j}} - \hat{\mathbf{k}})\cdot(-2\hat{\mathbf{i}} + 7\hat{\mathbf{j}} + 13\hat{\mathbf{k}})$$

$$\Rightarrow \quad \mathbf{r}\cdot(2\hat{\mathbf{i}} - 7\hat{\mathbf{j}} - 13\hat{\mathbf{k}}) = 1$$

Example 28 *The cartesian equation of the plane $\mathbf{r} = (1 + \lambda - \mu)\hat{\mathbf{i}} + (2 - \lambda)\hat{\mathbf{j}} + (3 - 2\lambda + 2\mu)\hat{\mathbf{k}}$, is*

(a) $2x + y = 5$ (b) $2x - y = 5$

(c) $2x + z = 5$ (d) $2x - z = 5$

Sol. (c) We have,

$$\mathbf{r} = (1 + \lambda - \mu)\hat{\mathbf{i}} + (2 - \lambda)\hat{\mathbf{j}} + (3 - 2\lambda + 2\mu)\hat{\mathbf{k}}$$

$$\Rightarrow \quad \mathbf{r} = (\hat{\mathbf{i}} + 2\hat{\mathbf{j}} + 3\hat{\mathbf{k}}) + \lambda(\hat{\mathbf{i}} - \hat{\mathbf{j}} - 2\hat{\mathbf{k}}) + \mu(-\hat{\mathbf{i}} + 2\hat{\mathbf{k}})$$

which is a plane passing through $\mathbf{a} = \hat{\mathbf{i}} + 2\hat{\mathbf{j}} + 3\hat{\mathbf{k}}$ and parallel to the vectors $\mathbf{b} = \hat{\mathbf{i}} - \hat{\mathbf{j}} - 2\hat{\mathbf{k}}$ and $\mathbf{c} = -\hat{\mathbf{i}} + 2\hat{\mathbf{k}}$.

Therefore, it is normal to the vector

$$\mathbf{n} = \mathbf{b} \times \mathbf{c} = -2\hat{\mathbf{i}} - \hat{\mathbf{k}}$$

Hence, its vector equation is

$$(\mathbf{r} - \mathbf{a})\cdot\mathbf{n} = 0$$

$$\Rightarrow \quad \mathbf{r}\cdot\mathbf{n} = \mathbf{a}\cdot\mathbf{n}$$

$$\Rightarrow \quad \mathbf{r}\cdot(-2\hat{\mathbf{i}} - \hat{\mathbf{k}}) = -2 - 3 \Rightarrow \mathbf{r}\cdot(2\hat{\mathbf{i}} + \hat{\mathbf{k}}) = 5$$

So, the cartesian equation of the plane is

$$(x\hat{\mathbf{i}} + y\hat{\mathbf{j}} + z\hat{\mathbf{k}})\cdot(2\hat{\mathbf{i}} + \hat{\mathbf{k}}) = 5 \Rightarrow 2x + z = 5$$

Example 29 *A variable plane is at a distance, k from the origin and meets the coordinates axis in A, B and C. Then, the locus of the centroid of ΔABC is*

(a) $x^{-2} + y^{-2} + z^{-2} = k^{-2}$

(b) $x^{-2} + y^{-2} + z^{-2} = 4k^{-2}$

(c) $x^{-2} + y^{-2} + z^{-2} = 16k^{-2}$

(d) $x^{-2} + y^{-2} + z^{-2} = 9k^{-2}$

Sol. (d) Let the equation of the variable plane be $\frac{x}{a} + \frac{y}{b} + \frac{z}{c} = 1$.

This meets the coordinates axes at $A(a, 0, 0)$, $B(0, b, 0)$ and $C(0, 0, c)$.

Let (α, β, γ) be the coordinates of the centroid of ΔABC.

Then, $\alpha = \frac{a}{3}, \beta = \frac{b}{3}, \gamma = \frac{c}{3} \Rightarrow a = 3\alpha, b = 3\beta, c = 3\gamma$ ...(i)

The plane is at a distance, k from the origin.

$$\therefore \quad \left|\frac{\frac{0}{a} + \frac{0}{b} + \frac{0}{c} - 1}{\sqrt{\frac{1}{a^2} + \frac{1}{b^2} + \frac{1}{c^2}}}\right| = k \Rightarrow \frac{1}{a^2} + \frac{1}{b^2} + \frac{1}{c^2} = \frac{1}{k^2}$$

$$\Rightarrow \quad \alpha^{-2} + \beta^{-2} + \gamma^{-2} = 9k^{-2}$$

Hence, the locus of (α, β, γ) is $x^{-2} + y^{-2} + z^{-2} = 9k^{-2}$

More than One Correct Option Type Questions

Example 30 *The direction ratios of the line $x-y+z-5=0=x-3y-6$ are*

(a) 3, 1, – 2 (b) 2, – 4, 1

(c) $\frac{3}{\sqrt{14}}, \frac{1}{\sqrt{14}}, \frac{-2}{\sqrt{14}}$ (d) $\frac{2}{\sqrt{21}}, \frac{-4}{\sqrt{21}}, \frac{1}{\sqrt{21}}$

Sol. (a, c) Let the DR's of line are a, b and c.

As the line is perpendicular to both the planes

$$\Rightarrow \quad a-b+c=0 \Rightarrow a-3b+0\cdot c=0$$

$$\Rightarrow \quad \frac{a}{3}=\frac{b}{1}=\frac{c}{-2}$$

$\therefore$ Direction ratios of lines are $(3, 1, -2)$ or $\left(\frac{3}{\sqrt{14}}, \frac{1}{\sqrt{14}}, \frac{-2}{\sqrt{14}}\right)$.

Example 31 *The equation of the line $x+y+z-1=0$, $4x+y-2z+2=0$ written in the symmetrical form is*

(a) $\frac{x+1}{1}=\frac{y-2}{-2}=\frac{z-0}{1}$ (b) $\frac{x}{1}=\frac{y}{-2}=\frac{z-1}{1}$

(c) $\frac{x+\frac{1}{2}}{1}=\frac{y-1}{-2}=\frac{z-\frac{1}{2}}{1}$ (d) $\frac{x-1}{2}=\frac{y+2}{-1}=\frac{z-2}{2}$

Sol. (a, b, c, d) $x+y+z-1=0,\ 4x+y-2z+2=0$

Let DR's of line are a, b and c.

As the line is perpendicular to both the plane.

$$\therefore \quad a+b+c=0 \Rightarrow 4a+b-2c=0$$

On solving, we get $\frac{a}{-3}=\frac{b}{6}=\frac{c}{-3}$

$\therefore$ Direction ratios of the line are $(-3, 6, -3)$ i.e. $<1, -2, 1>$

Let $z=k$, then $x=k-1, y=2-2k$

i.e. $(k-1, 2-2k, k)$ is any point on the line.

$\therefore (-1, 2, 0), (0, 0, 1), \left(-\frac{1}{2}, 1, \frac{1}{2}\right)$ and $(1, -2, 2)$ are points on the line.

Example 32 *The direction cosines of the lines bisecting the angle between the line whose direction cosines are l_1, m_1, n_1 and l_2, m_2, n_2 and the angle between these lines is θ, are*

(a) $\frac{l_1+l_2}{\cos\frac{\theta}{2}}, \frac{m_1+m_2}{\cos\frac{\theta}{2}}, \frac{n_1+n_2}{\cos\frac{\theta}{2}}$

(b) $\frac{l_1+l_2}{2\cos\frac{\theta}{2}}, \frac{m_1+m_2}{2\cos\frac{\theta}{2}}, \frac{n_1+n_2}{2\cos\frac{\theta}{2}}$

(c) $\frac{l_1+l_2}{\sin\frac{\theta}{2}}, \frac{m_1+m_2}{\sin\frac{\theta}{2}}, \frac{n_1+n_2}{\sin\frac{\theta}{2}}$

(d) $\frac{l_1-l_2}{2\sin\frac{\theta}{2}}, \frac{m_1-m_2}{2\sin\frac{\theta}{2}}, \frac{n_1-n_2}{2\sin\frac{\theta}{2}}$

Sol. (b, d) Distance ratio of the bisector are

$$<l_1+l_2, m_1+m_2, n_1+n_2>$$
$$=\sqrt{(l_1+l_2)^2+(m_1+m_2)^2+(n_1+n_2)^2}$$
$$=\sqrt{2+2(l_1l_2+m_1m_2+n_1n_2)}$$
$$=\sqrt{2+2\cos\theta}=2\cos\frac{\theta}{2}$$

$\therefore$ Direction cosines are $\left\langle \frac{l_1+l_2}{2\cos\frac{\theta}{2}}, \frac{m_1+m_2}{2\cos\frac{\theta}{2}}, \frac{n_1+n_2}{2\cos\frac{\theta}{2}} \right\rangle$.

Distance ratios of the other bisector are

$$<l_1-l_2, m_1-m_2, n_1-n_2> \sqrt{(l_1-l_2)^2+(m_1-m_2)^2+(n_1-n_2)^2}$$
$$=2\sin\frac{\theta}{2}$$

$\therefore$ Direction cosines of the bisector are

$$\left\langle \frac{l_1-l_2}{2\sin\frac{\theta}{2}}, \frac{m_1-m_2}{2\sin\frac{\theta}{2}}, \frac{n_1-n_2}{2\sin\frac{\theta}{2}} \right\rangle$$

Example 33 *Consider the planes $3x-6y+2z+5=0$ and $4x-12y+3z=3$. The planes $67x+162y+47z+44=0$ bisects the angle between the planes which*

(a) contains origin. (b) is acute.

(c) is obtuse. (d) None of these

Sol. (a,b)
$$3x-6y+2z+5=0 \quad \text{...(i)}$$
$$-4x+12y-3z+3=0 \quad \text{...(ii)}$$
$$\frac{3x-6y+2z+5}{\sqrt{9+36+4}}=\frac{-4x+12y-3z+3}{\sqrt{16+144+9}}$$

Bisects the angle between the planes that contains the origin.

$$13(3x-6y+2z+5)=7(-4x+12y-3z+3)$$
$$39x-78y+26z+65=-28x+84y-21z+21$$
$$67x-162y+47z+44=0 \quad \text{...(iii)}$$

Let θ be the angle between Eqs. (i) and (iii), then find $\cos\theta$ and then we obtain $|\tan\theta|<1$.

Example 34 *Consider the equation of line AB is $\frac{x}{2}=\frac{y}{-3}=\frac{z}{6}$. Through a point $P(1, 2, 5)$ line PN is drawn perpendicular to AB and line PQ is drawn parallel to the plane $3x+4y+5z=0$ to meet AB is Q. Then,*

(a) the coordinates of N are $\left(\frac{52}{49}, -\frac{78}{49}, \frac{156}{49}\right)$.

(b) the coordinates of Q are $\left(3, -\frac{9}{2}, 9\right)$.

(c) the equation of PN is $\frac{x-1}{3}=\frac{y-2}{-176}=\frac{z-5}{-89}$

(d) coordinates of N are $\left(\frac{156}{49}, \frac{52}{49} -\frac{78}{49}\right)$.

Sol. (a,b,c) Equation of line AB is $\frac{x}{2}=\frac{y}{-3}=\frac{z}{6}$

Its DR's are $<2,-3,6>$

Let the coordinates be $<2r,-3r,6r>$

DR's of PN are $<2r-1,-3r-2,6r-5>$

It is perpendicular to AB.

$$\therefore \quad 2(2r-1)-3(-3r-2)+6(6r-5)=0$$
$$4r-2+9r+6+36r-30=0$$
$$49r=26 \text{ i.e. } r=\frac{26}{49}$$

(a) $\therefore$ Coordinates of N are $\left(\frac{52}{49},-\frac{78}{49},\frac{156}{49}\right)$.

(b) Let the coordinates of Q be $(2r,-3r,6r)$, then DR's of PQ are $<2r-1,-3r-2,6r-5>$. Since, PQ is parallel to the plane.

$$\therefore \quad 3(2r-1)+4(-3r-2)+5(6r-5)=0$$
$$6r-3-12r-8+30r-25=0$$
$$24r=36,\ r=\frac{3}{2}$$

$\therefore$ Coordinates of Q are $\left(3,-\frac{9}{2},9\right)$.

Equation of PN is $\frac{x-1}{3}=\frac{y-2}{-176}=\frac{z-5}{-89}$.

Example 35 *The equation of a plane is $2x-y-3z=5$ and $A(1,1,1)$, $B(2,1,-3)$, $C(1,-2,-2)$ and $D(-3,1,2)$ are four points. Which of the following line segment are intersected by the plane?*

(a) AD (b) AB (c) AC (d) BC

Sol. (b, c) For $A(1,1,1)$, $2x-y-3z-5=2-1-3-5<0$

For $B(2,1,-3)$, $2x-y-3z-5=4-1+9-5>0$

For $C(1,-2,-2)$, $2x-y-3z-5=2+2+6-5>0$.

For $D(-3,1,2)$, $2x-y-3z-5=-6-1-6-5=-18<0$

A, D are on one side of the plane and B, C are on the other side, the line segments AB, AC, BD, CD intersect the plane.

Example 36 *The coordinates of a point on the line $\frac{x-1}{2}=\frac{y+1}{-3}=z$ at a distance $4\sqrt{14}$ from the point $(1,-1,0)$ are*

(a) $(9,-13,4)$

(b) $(8\sqrt{14}+1,-12\sqrt{14}-1,4\sqrt{14})$

(c) $(-7,11,-4)$

(d) $(-8\sqrt{14}+1,12\sqrt{14}-1,-4\sqrt{14})$

Sol. (a, c) The coordinates of any point on the given line are $(2r+1,-3r-1,r)$

The distance of this point from the point $(1,-1,0)$ is given to be $4\sqrt{14}$.

$$\Rightarrow \quad (2r)^2+(-3r)^2+(r)^2=(4\sqrt{14})^2$$
$$\Rightarrow \quad 14r^2=16\times 14 \Rightarrow r=\pm 4$$

So, the coordinates of the required point are

$$(9,-13,4) \text{ or } (-7,11,-4).$$

Example 37 *Equation of a plane passing through the lines $2x-y+z-3=0$, $3x+y+z-5=0$ and which is at a distance of $\frac{1}{\sqrt{6}}$ from the point $(2,1,-1)$ is*

(a) $2x-y+z-3=0$

(b) $3x+y+z-5=0$

(c) $62x+29y+19z-105=0$

(d) $x+2y-2=0$

Sol. (a,c) Equation of a plane through the given line is $2x-y+z-3+\lambda(3x+y+z-5)=0$

$$\Rightarrow \quad (2+3\lambda)x+(\lambda-1)y+(\lambda+1)z-(3+5\lambda)=0$$

So,
$$\frac{1}{\sqrt{6}}=\frac{2(2+3\lambda)+(\lambda-1)-(\lambda+1)-3-5\lambda}{\sqrt{(2+3\lambda)^2+(\lambda-1)^2+(\lambda+1)^2}}$$
$$\Rightarrow \quad 11\lambda^2+12\lambda+6=6(\lambda-1)^2=6(\lambda^2-2\lambda+1)$$
$$\Rightarrow \quad 5\lambda^2+24\lambda=0 \Rightarrow \lambda=0 \text{ or } \lambda=-\frac{24}{5}.$$

Thus, the equation of the required planes are

$$2x-y+z-3=0 \text{ or } 62x+29y+19z-105=0.$$

Example 38 *The plane passing through the point $(-2,-2,2)$ and containing the line joining the points $(1,1,1)$ and $(1,-1,2)$ makes intercepts of lengths a, b, c respectively on the axes of x, y and z respectively, then*

(a) $a=3b$ (b) $b=2c$

(c) $a+b+c=12$ (d) $a+2b+2c=0$

Sol. (a,b,d) Equation of any plane passing through $(-2,-2,2)$ is

$$A(x+2)+B(y+2)+C(z-2)=0$$

Since, it contains the line joining $(1,1,1)$ and $(1,-1,2)$ these points also lie on this plane.

$$\Rightarrow \quad 3A+3B-C=0 \text{ and } 3A+B+0=0$$
$$\Rightarrow \quad \frac{A}{1}=\frac{B}{-3}=\frac{C}{-6}.$$

So, the equation of the plane is

$$(x+2)-3(y+2)-6(z-2)=0$$

or
$$x-3y-6z+8=0 \text{ or } \frac{x}{-8}+\frac{y}{\frac{8}{3}}+\frac{z}{\frac{8}{6}}=1$$
$$\Rightarrow \quad a=-8,\ b=\frac{8}{3},\ c=\frac{8}{6}$$
$$\Rightarrow \quad a=-3b,\ b=2c \text{ and } a+2b+2c=0$$

Passage Based Questions

Passage I

(Ex. Nos. 39 and 40)

Two line whose equation are $\frac{x-3}{2}=\frac{y-2}{3}=\frac{z-1}{4}$ and $\frac{x-2}{3}=\frac{y-3}{2}=\frac{z-2}{3}$ lie in the same plane, then

Example 39 *Point of intersection of the lines lies on*

(a) $3x + y + z = 20$ (b) $2x + y + z = 25$

(c) $3x + 2y + z = 24$ (d) $x = y = z$

Example 40 *Angle between the plane containing both the lines and the plane $4x + y + 2z = 0$ is equal to*

(a) $\frac{\pi}{3}$ (b) $\frac{\pi}{2}$ (c) $\frac{\pi}{6}$ (d) $\cos^{-1}\frac{2}{\sqrt{186}}$

Sol. (Ex. 39 and 40)

39. (d) Let $\frac{x-3}{2} = \frac{y-2}{3} = \frac{z-1}{4} = r_1$

$\Rightarrow \quad x = 3 + 2r_1,\ y = 2 + 3r_1,\ z = 1 + 4r_1$

It will lie on $\frac{x-2}{3} = \frac{y-3}{2} = \frac{z-2}{3} \Rightarrow r_1 = 1$

So, point of intersection is (5, 5, 5).

40. (b) Equation of plane contains both lines

$$\begin{vmatrix} x-3 & y-2 & z-1 \\ 2 & 3 & 4 \\ 3 & 2 & 3 \end{vmatrix} = 0$$

$$(x-3)(1) + (y-2)(12-6) + (z-1)(4-9) = 0$$

$$x + 6y - 5z = 10$$

Angle between plane $x + 6y - 5z = 10$ and $4x + y + 2z = 0$ is

$$\cos\theta = \frac{(1)(4) + 6(1) + (-5)(2)}{\sqrt{1+36+25}\,\sqrt{16+1+4}} \Rightarrow \cos\theta = 0 \Rightarrow \theta = \frac{\pi}{2}$$

Thus, the angle is $\frac{\pi}{2}$.

Passage II

(Ex. Nos. 41 and 42)

Let $a_1x + b_1y + c_1z + d_1 = 0$ and $a_2x + b_2y + c_2z + d_2 = 0$ be two planes, where $d_1, d_2 > 0$. Then, origin lies in acute angle, if $a_1a_2 + b_1b_2 + c_1c_2 < 0$ and origin lies in obtuse angle, if $a_1a_2 + b_1b_2 + c_1c_2 > 0$.

Further point (x_1, y_1, z_1) and origin both lie either in acute angle or in obtuse angle. If $(a_1x_1 + b_1y_1 + c_1z_1 + d_1)(a_2x_1 + b_2y_1 + c_2z_1 + d_2) > 0$.

One of (x_1, y_1, z_1) and origin lie in acute and the other in obtuse angle; if $(a_1x_1 + b_1y_1 + c_1z_1 + d_1)(a_2x_1 + b_2y_1 + c_2z_1 + d_2) < 0$.

Example 41 *Given that planes $2x + 3y - 4z + 7 = 0$ and $x - 2y + 3z - 5 = 0$. If a point P is $(1, -2, 3)$, then*

(a) O and P both lie in acute angle between the planes.

(b) O and P both lie in obtuse angle.

(c) O lies in acute angle, P lies in obtuse angle.

(d) O lies in obtuse angle, P lies an acute angle.

Example 42 *Given the planes $x + 2y - 3z + 2 = 0$ and $x - 2y + 3z + 7 = 0$, if the point P is $(1, 2, 2)$, then*

(a) O and P both lie in acute angle between the planes.

(b) O and P both lie in obtuse angle.

(c) O lies in acute angle, P lie in obtuse angle.

(d) O lies in obtuse angle, P lies in acute angle.

Sol. (Ex. 41 and 42)

41. (b) Equation of the second plane is $-x + 2y - 3z + 5 = 0$

$2(-1) + 3\cdot 2 + (-4)(-3) > 0$

$\therefore$ Origin lies in obtuse angle.

$$(2\times 1 + 3(-2) - 4\times 3 + 7)(-1 + 2(-2) - 3\times 3 + 5)$$
$$= (2 - 6 - 12 + 7)(-1 - 4 - 9 + 5) > 0$$

$\therefore P$ lies in obtuse angle.

42. (a) $1 - 4 - 9 < 0$

$\therefore$ Origin lies in acute angle.

Further $(1 + 4 - 6 + 2)(1 - 4 + 6 + 7) > 0$

$\therefore$ The point P lies in acute angle.

Passage III

(Ex. Nos. 43 and 44)

In a parallelogram $OABC$ with position vectors of A is $3\hat{\mathbf{i}} + 4\hat{\mathbf{j}}$ and C is $4\hat{\mathbf{i}} + 3\hat{\mathbf{j}}$ with reference to O as origin. A point E is taken on the side BC which divides it in the ratio of $2:1$. Also, the line segment AE intersects the line bisecting the $\angle AOC$ internally at P. CP when extended meets AB at point F.

Example 43 *The equation of line parallel to* **CP** *and passing through* (2, 3, 4) *is*

(a) $\frac{x-2}{1} = \frac{y-3}{5}, z = 4$ (b) $\frac{x-2}{1} = \frac{y-3}{6}, z = 4$

(c) $\frac{x-2}{2} = \frac{y-3}{5}, z = 3$ (d) $\frac{x-2}{3} = \frac{y-3}{5}, z = 3$

Example 44 *The equation of plane containing line AC and at a maximum distance from B is*

(a) $\mathbf{r}\cdot(\hat{\mathbf{i}} + \hat{\mathbf{j}}) = 7$ (b) $\mathbf{r}\cdot(\hat{\mathbf{i}} - \hat{\mathbf{j}}) = 7$

(c) $\mathbf{r}\cdot(2\hat{\mathbf{i}} - \hat{\mathbf{j}}) = 7$ (d) $\mathbf{r}\cdot(3\hat{\mathbf{i}} + 4\hat{\mathbf{j}}) = 7$

Sol. (Ex 43 and 44)

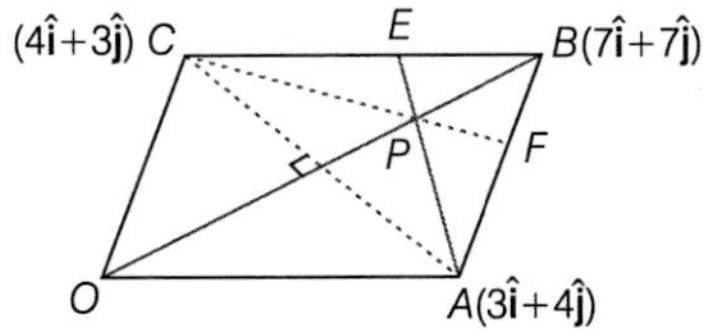

43. (b) Here, $\mathbf{OB} = 7\hat{\mathbf{i}} + 7\hat{\mathbf{j}}$, $\mathbf{OE} = 5\hat{\mathbf{i}} + \frac{13}{3}\hat{\mathbf{j}}$, $\mathbf{OP} = \frac{21}{5}(\hat{\mathbf{i}} + \hat{\mathbf{j}})$

$$\text{DR's of CP} = \left[\left(\frac{21}{5} - 4\right), \left(\frac{21}{5} - 3\right), 0\right]$$

Direction ratios of **CP** are (1, 6, 0), then equation of line passing through (2, 3, 4) and parallel to **CP** is

$$\frac{x-2}{1} = \frac{y-3}{6} = \frac{z-4}{0}$$

44. (a) The plane containing line AC and at a maximum distance from B must be perpendicular to the plane $OABC$.

Since, $OABC$ is rhombus, so **OB** must normal to the plane. So, equation of required plane is

$$[\mathbf{r}-4\hat{\mathbf{i}}-3\hat{\mathbf{j}}]\cdot(\hat{\mathbf{i}}+\hat{\mathbf{j}})=0 \Rightarrow \mathbf{r}\cdot(\hat{\mathbf{i}}+\hat{\mathbf{j}})=7$$

Passage IV

(Ex. Nos. 45 and 46)

A ray of light comes along the line $L=0$ and strikes the plane mirror kept along the plane $P=0$ at B. $A(2,1,6)$ is a point on the line $L=0$ whose image about $P=0$ is A'. It is given that $L=0$ is $\frac{x-2}{3}=\frac{y-1}{4}=\frac{z-6}{5}$ and $P=0$ is $x+y-2z=3$.

Example 45 *The coordinates of A' are*

(a) (6, 5, 2) (b) (6, 5, – 2)
(c) (6, – 5, 2) (d) None of these

Example 46 *If $L_1=0$ is the reflected ray, then its equation is*

(a) $\frac{x+10}{4}=\frac{y-5}{4}=\frac{z+2}{3}$ (b) $\frac{x+10}{3}=\frac{y+15}{5}=\frac{z+14}{5}$

(c) $\frac{x+10}{4}=\frac{y+15}{5}=\frac{z+14}{3}$ (d) None of these

Sol. (Ex 45 and 46)

45. (b) Let $A'(x_2, y_2, z_2)$ be the image of $A(2,1,6)$ about mirror $x+y-2z=3$. Then,

$$\frac{x_2-2}{1}=\frac{y_2-1}{1}=\frac{z_2-6}{-2}=\frac{-2(2+1-12-3)}{1^2+1^2+2^2}=4$$

$$\Rightarrow \quad (x_2, y_2, z_2)\equiv(6,5,-2)$$

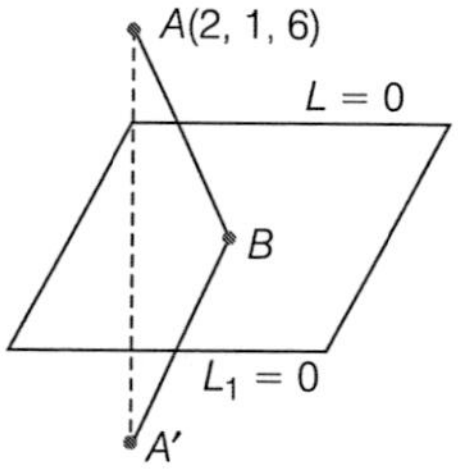

46. (c) Let $\frac{x-2}{3}=\frac{y-1}{4}=\frac{z-6}{5}=\lambda$

$x=2+3\lambda, y=1+4\lambda, z=6+5\lambda$ lies on plane $x+y-2z=3$

$$\Rightarrow \quad 2+3\lambda+1+4\lambda-2(6+5\lambda)=3$$

$$\Rightarrow \quad 3+7\lambda-12-10\lambda=3$$

$$\Rightarrow \quad -3\lambda=12 \Rightarrow \lambda=-4$$

Point $B\equiv(-10,-15,-14)$

The equation of the reflected ray $L_1=0$ is the line joining $A'(x_2, y_2, z_2)$ and $B(-10,-15,-14)$.

$$\frac{x+10}{16}=\frac{y+15}{20}=\frac{z+14}{12}$$

or $$\frac{x+10}{4}=\frac{y+15}{5}=\frac{z+14}{3}$$

Passage V

(Ex. Nos. 47 and 48)

The line of greatest slope on an inclined plane P_1 is the line in the plane P_1 which is perpendicular to the line of intersection of the plane P_1 and a horizontal plane P_2.

Example 47 *Assuming the plane $4x-3y+7z=0$ to be horizontal, the direction cosines of the line of greatest slope in the plane $2x+y-5z=0$ are*

(a) $\frac{3}{\sqrt{11}}, \frac{-1}{\sqrt{11}}, \frac{1}{\sqrt{11}}$ (b) $\frac{3}{\sqrt{11}}, \frac{1}{\sqrt{11}}, \frac{-1}{\sqrt{11}}$

(c) $\frac{-3}{\sqrt{11}}, \frac{1}{\sqrt{11}}, \frac{1}{\sqrt{11}}$ (d) None of these

Example 48 *The coordinates of a point on the plane $2x+y-5z=0$, $2\sqrt{11}$ unit away from the line of intersection of $2x+y-5z=0$ and $4x-3y+7z=0$ are*

(a) (6, 2, – 2) (b) (3, 1, – 1)
(c) (6, – 2, 2) (d) (1, 3, – 1)

Sol. (Ex. 47 and 48)

47. (a) Plane P_1 is of the form $\mathbf{r}\cdot\mathbf{n}_1=0$, where $\mathbf{n}_1=(4,-3,7)$

Plane P_2 is of the form $\mathbf{r}\cdot\mathbf{n}_2=0$, where $\mathbf{n}_2=(2,1,-5)$

The vector **b** along the line of intersection of planes is

$$\mathbf{n}_1\times\mathbf{n}_2=(4,17,5)=\mathbf{n}_3$$

Since, the line of greatest slope is perpendicular to $\mathbf{n}_3$ and $\mathbf{n}_2$ the vector along the line of greatest slope

$$=\mathbf{n}_2\times\mathbf{n}_3=(3,-1,1)=\mathbf{n}_4$$

and the unit vector

$$\mathbf{n}_4=\hat{\mathbf{n}}=\left(\frac{3}{\sqrt{11}}, \frac{-1}{\sqrt{11}}, \frac{1}{\sqrt{11}}\right)$$

48. (c) Since, (0, 0, 0) is a point on both planes, it lies on the line of intersection.

Hence, the equation a line of greatest slope can be

$$\frac{x}{3}=\frac{y}{-1}=\frac{z}{1}$$

The point on the line $\frac{x}{3}=\frac{y}{-1}=\frac{z}{1}$ at a distance $2\sqrt{11}$ units from the origin is given by $\frac{x}{\frac{3}{\sqrt{11}}}=\frac{y}{\frac{-1}{\sqrt{11}}}=\frac{z}{1}=2\sqrt{11}$

The point is $(6,-2,2)$.

Stem Based Questions

Stem I

(Ex. Nos. 49 and 50)

A ray of light emanating from a point $P(1,2,3)$ and strikes a line mirror $L: \frac{x+2}{1}=\frac{y-3}{2}=\frac{z-1}{3}$ at point M, after reflection it passes through the point $Q(3,6,9)$.

Example 49 *If the equation of the plane passing through the points P, M and Q is $ax + by - cz + d = 0$, then the value of $a + b + c + d$ is ....*

Example 50 *Find the value of $(MP + MQ)^2$.*

Sol. (Ex. 49 and 50)

$$\frac{x+2}{1} = \frac{y-3}{2} = \frac{z-1}{3} = \lambda \text{ [let]}$$

Let any point on the mirror be $M(\lambda - 2, 2\lambda + 3, 3\lambda + 1)$.

Since, ΔPMQ is an isosceles triangle.

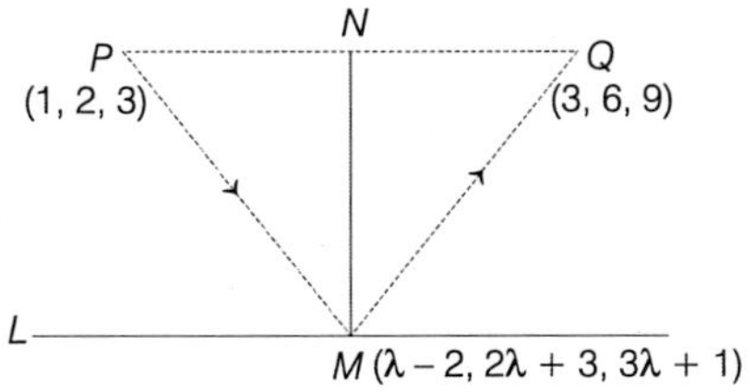

$\therefore$ Let N be the mid-point of PQ.

Position vector of $\mathbf{ON} = 2\hat{\mathbf{i}} + 4\hat{\mathbf{j}} + 6\hat{\mathbf{k}}$

Direction ratios of MN are $\lambda - 4, 2\lambda - 1, 3\lambda - 5$.

Since, NM perpendicular to given line.

$$\therefore 1(\lambda - 4) + 2(2\lambda - 1) + 3(3\lambda - 5) = 0$$

$$\Rightarrow \quad \lambda - 4 + 4\lambda - 2 + 9\lambda - 15 = 0$$

$$\Rightarrow \quad 14\lambda - 21 = 0 \Rightarrow \lambda = \frac{21}{14} = \frac{3}{2}$$

$\therefore M(\lambda - 2, 2\lambda + 3, 3\lambda + 1)$

i.e. $M\left(\frac{3}{2} - 2, 2\left(\frac{3}{2}\right) + 3, 3\left(\frac{3}{2}\right) + 1\right) = M\left(-\frac{1}{2}, 6, \frac{11}{2}\right)$

Equation of plane passing through the point $P(1, 2, 3)$ is

$$A(x - 1) + B(y - 2) + C(z - 3) = 0 \quad \text{...(i)}$$

Eq. (i) passes through the point (3, 6, 9).

$$\therefore \quad A(3 - 1) + B(6 - 2) + C(9 - 3) = 0 \Rightarrow 2A + 4B + 6C = 0$$

$$\Rightarrow \quad A + 2B + 3C = 0 \quad \text{....(ii)}$$

Eq. (i) passes through $\left(-\frac{1}{2}, 6, \frac{11}{2}\right)$

$$\therefore A\left(-\frac{1}{2} - 1\right) + B(6 - 2) + C\left(\frac{11}{2} - 3\right) = 0$$

$$\Rightarrow \quad -\frac{3}{2}A + 4B + \frac{5}{2}C = 0$$

$$\Rightarrow \quad -3A + 8B + 5C = 0 \quad \text{...(iii)}$$

From Eqs. (ii) and (iii), we get

$$\frac{A}{10 - 24} = \frac{B}{-9 - 5} = \frac{C}{8 + 6}$$

$$\Rightarrow \quad \frac{A}{-14} = \frac{B}{-14} = \frac{C}{14} \Rightarrow \frac{A}{1} = \frac{B}{1} = \frac{C}{-1}$$

$\therefore$ Required equation of plane is

$$(x - 1) + (y - 2) - 1(z - 3) = 0$$

$$\Rightarrow \quad x - 1 + y - 2 - z + 3 = 0 \Rightarrow x + y - z = 0$$

$$\therefore a = 1, b = 1, c = 1, d = 0$$

$$\therefore a + b + c + d = 1 + 1 + 1 + 0 = 3$$

Now, $MP + MQ = 2MP$

$$= 2\sqrt{\left(-1 - \frac{1}{2}\right)^2 + (6 - 2)^2 + \left(\frac{11}{2} - 3\right)^2}$$

$$= 2\sqrt{\frac{9}{4} + 16 + \frac{25}{4}}$$

$$= 2\sqrt{\frac{9 + 64 + 25}{4}} = 2\sqrt{\frac{98}{4}} = 7\sqrt{2}$$

$$\therefore \quad (MP + MQ)^2 = (7\sqrt{2})^2 = 49 \times 2 = 98$$

49. (3) **50.** (98)

Stem II

(Ex. Nos. 51 and 52)

If a line passing through $(-2, 1, p_1)$ and $(4, 1, 2)$ is perpendicular to the vector $2\hat{\mathbf{i}} - 7\hat{\mathbf{j}} - 6\hat{\mathbf{k}}$ and parallel to the plane containing the vectors $\hat{\mathbf{i}} + p_2\hat{\mathbf{k}}$ and $p_2\hat{\mathbf{j}} + p_1\hat{\mathbf{k}}$, then

Example 51 *Value of $p_1 + 4$ is equal to ....*

Example 52 *If the value of p_2 is $\frac{t}{3}$, then $(t + 3)$ is equal to ....*

Sol. (Ex. 51 and 52)

51. (4) Let **a** along the line that passes through the points $(-2, 1, p_1)$ and $(4, 1, 2)$.

$$\therefore \quad \mathbf{a} = 6\hat{\mathbf{i}} + 0\hat{\mathbf{j}} + (2 - p_1)\hat{\mathbf{k}}$$

It is given that **a** is perpendicular to $(2\hat{\mathbf{i}} - 7\hat{\mathbf{j}} - 6\hat{\mathbf{k}})$.

$$\therefore \quad 6 \times 2 + 0 \times (-7) + (2 - p_1) \times (-6) = 0$$

$$\Rightarrow \quad 12 - 12 + 6p_1 = 0 \Rightarrow p_1 = 0$$

$$\Rightarrow \quad p_1 + 4 = 0 + 4 = 4$$

$$\therefore \quad \mathbf{a} = 6\hat{\mathbf{i}} + 2\hat{\mathbf{k}}$$

52. (4) Normal vector to the plane $\hat{\mathbf{i}} + p_2\hat{\mathbf{k}}$ and $p_2\hat{\mathbf{j}} + p_1\hat{\mathbf{k}}$ is

$$\hat{\mathbf{n}} = \begin{vmatrix} \hat{\mathbf{i}} & \hat{\mathbf{j}} & \hat{\mathbf{k}} \\ 1 & 0 & p_2 \\ 0 & p_2 & p_1 \end{vmatrix} = \begin{vmatrix} \hat{\mathbf{i}} & \hat{\mathbf{j}} & \hat{\mathbf{k}} \\ 1 & 0 & p_2 \\ 0 & p_2 & 0 \end{vmatrix}$$

$$= \hat{\mathbf{i}}(0 - p_2^2) - \hat{\mathbf{j}}(0 - 0) + \hat{\mathbf{k}}(p_2 - 0) = -p_2^2\hat{\mathbf{i}} + p_2\hat{\mathbf{k}}$$

Since, **a** is perpendicular to $\hat{\mathbf{n}}$.

$$\therefore \quad (6\hat{\mathbf{i}} + 2\hat{\mathbf{k}}) \cdot (-p_2^2\hat{\mathbf{i}} + p_2\hat{\mathbf{k}}) = 0$$

$$\Rightarrow \quad -6p_2^2 + 2p_2 = 0 \Rightarrow 2p_2(-3p_2 + 1) = 0$$

$$\Rightarrow \quad p_2 = 0 \text{ or } -3p_2 + 1 = 0$$

$$\Rightarrow \quad p_2 = 0, \frac{1}{3}$$

$$\therefore \quad t = 1$$

$$\therefore \quad t + 3 = 1 + 3 = 4$$

Single Integer Answer Type Questions

Example 53 *If the perpendicular distance of the point (6, 5, 8) from the Y-axis is 5λ units, then λ is equal to ......*

Sol. (2) Foot of perpendicular from (6, 5, 8) on Y-axis is (0, 5, 0).

Required distance $= \sqrt{(6-0)^2 + (5-5)^2 + (8-0)^2} = 10$ units

$$\Rightarrow \quad 5\lambda = 10 \Rightarrow \lambda = \frac{10}{5} = 2$$

Example 54 *A parallelopiped is formed by planes drawn through the points (2, 3, 5) and (5, 9, 7) parallel to the coordinate planes. The length of the diagonal of the parallelopiped is ......*

Sol. (7) The length of the edges are given by $a = 5 - 2 = 3$, $b = 9 - 3 = 6$, $c = 7 - 5 = 2$, so length of the diagonal

$$= \sqrt{a^2 + b^2 + c^2} = \sqrt{9 + 36 + 4} = 7 \text{ units}$$

Example 55 *If the shortest distance between the lines $\frac{x-3}{3} = \frac{y-8}{-1} = \frac{z-3}{1}$ and $\frac{x+3}{-3} = \frac{y+7}{2} = \frac{z-6}{4}$ is $\lambda\sqrt{30}$ units, then the value of λ is ......*

Decoding the Question

Use formula, short distance between lines $\mathbf{r} = \mathbf{a}_1 + \lambda \mathbf{b}_1$ and $\mathbf{r} = \mathbf{a}_2 + \lambda \mathbf{b}_2$ is $d = \left| \frac{(\mathbf{b}_1 \times \mathbf{b}_2) \cdot (\mathbf{a}_2 - \mathbf{a}_1)}{|\mathbf{b}_1 \times \mathbf{b}_2|} \right|$.

Sol. (3) Given, lines are

$$\mathbf{r} = 3\hat{\mathbf{i}} + 8\hat{\mathbf{j}} + 3\hat{\mathbf{k}} + \lambda(3\hat{\mathbf{i}} - \hat{\mathbf{j}} + \hat{\mathbf{k}})$$

$$\mathbf{r} = (-3\hat{\mathbf{i}} - 7\hat{\mathbf{j}} + 6\hat{\mathbf{k}}) + \mu(-3\hat{\mathbf{i}} + 2\hat{\mathbf{j}} + 4\hat{\mathbf{k}})$$

where λ and μ are parameters.

Shortest distance

$$= \frac{(3\hat{\mathbf{i}} - \hat{\mathbf{j}} + \hat{\mathbf{k}}) \times (-3\hat{\mathbf{i}} + 2\hat{\mathbf{j}} + 4\hat{\mathbf{k}}) \cdot [(-3-3)\hat{\mathbf{i}} + (-7-8)\hat{\mathbf{j}} + (6-3)\hat{\mathbf{k}}]}{|(3\hat{\mathbf{i}} - \hat{\mathbf{j}} + \hat{\mathbf{k}}) \times (-3\hat{\mathbf{i}} + 2\hat{\mathbf{j}} + 4\hat{\mathbf{k}})|}$$

$$= \frac{(-6\hat{\mathbf{i}} - 15\hat{\mathbf{j}} + 3\hat{\mathbf{k}}) \times (-6\hat{\mathbf{j}} - 15\hat{\mathbf{k}} + 3\hat{\mathbf{k}})}{\sqrt{36 + 225 + 9}}$$

$$= \sqrt{270} = 3\sqrt{30} \text{ units}$$

Example 56 *If the planes $x - cy - bz = 0$, $cx - y + az = 0$ and $bx + ay - z = 0$ pass through a line, then the value of $a^2 + b^2 + c^2 + 2abc$ is ......*

Sol. (1) Given, planes are

$$x - cy - bz = 0 \quad \text{...(i)}$$

$$cx - y + az = 0 \quad \text{...(ii)}$$

$$bx + ay - z = 0 \quad \text{(iii)}$$

Equation of planes passing through the line of intersection of planes (i) and (ii) may be taken as

$$(x - cy - bz) + \lambda(cx - y + az) = 0 \quad \text{...(iv)}$$

Now, planes (iii) and (iv) are same.

$$\therefore \quad \frac{1 + c\lambda}{b} = \frac{-(c + \lambda)}{a} = \frac{-b + a\lambda}{-1}$$

By eliminating λ, we get $a^2 + b^2 + c^2 + 2abc = 1$

Example 57 *If the line $\frac{x-4}{1} = \frac{y-2}{1} = \frac{z-k}{2}$ lies exactly on the plane $2x - 4y + z = 7$, the value of k is ......*

Sol. (7) The point $(4, 2, k)$ must satisfy the plane.

So, $\quad 8 - 8 + k = 7 \Rightarrow k = 7$

Example 58 *If the centroid of the tetrahedron OABC, where A, B, C are the points $(a, 2, 3)$, $(1, b, 2)$ and $(2, 1, c)$ be $(1, 2, 3)$, then the point (a, b, c) is at distance $5\sqrt{\lambda}$ units from origin, then λ must be equal to ....*

Sol. (3) $1 = \frac{a + 1 + 2 + 0}{4}$, $2 = \frac{2 + b + 1 + 0}{4}$, $3 = \frac{3 + 2 + c + 0}{4}$

$\Rightarrow \quad a = 1, b = 5$ and $c = 7$

$\Rightarrow$ Distance of centroid from origin is

$$\sqrt{1 + 25 + 49} = \sqrt{75} = 5\sqrt{3} \text{ units} \Rightarrow \lambda = 3$$

Example 59 *If the circumcentre of the triangle whose vertices are $(3, 2, -5)$, $(-3, 8, -5)$ and $(-3, 2, 1)$ is $(-1, \lambda, -3)$ the integer λ must be equal to ....*

Sol. (4) Equating the distances of circumcentre $(-1, \lambda, -3)$ from $(3, 2, -5)$ and $(-3, 8, -5)$ we get

$$(-1-3)^2 + (\lambda+2)^2 + (-3+5)^2 = (-1+3)^2 + (\lambda-8)^2 + (-3+5)^2$$

$$\Rightarrow \quad \lambda = 4$$

Example 60 *If $\mathbf{P}_1\mathbf{P}_2$ is perpendicular to $\mathbf{P}_2\mathbf{P}_3$, then the value of k is, where $P_1(k, 1, -1)$, $P_2(2k, 0, 2)$ and $P_3(2 + 2k, k, 1)$ is ....*

Sol. (3) DR's of $\mathbf{P}_1\mathbf{P}_2 = (k, -1, 3)$

DR's of $\mathbf{P}_2\mathbf{P}_3 = (2, k, -1)$

$\because \quad \mathbf{P}_1\mathbf{P}_2 \perp \mathbf{P}_2\mathbf{P}_3$

$\therefore \quad k(2) - k - 3 = 0 : k = 3$

Example 61 *Let the equation of the plane containing line $x - y - z - 4 = 0 = x + y + 2z - 4$ and parallel to the line of intersection of the planes $2x + 3y + z = 1$ and $x + 3y + 2z = 2$ be $x + Ay + Bz + C = 0$. Then, the values of $|A + B + C - 4|$ is ....*

Sol. (15) A plane containing line of intersection of the given planes is

$$x - y - z - 4 + \lambda(x + y + 2z - 4) = 0$$

i.e. $(\lambda + 1)x + (\lambda - 1)y + (2\lambda - 1)z - 4(\lambda + 1) = 0 \quad \text{...(i)}$

vector normal to it

$$\mathbf{V} = (\lambda + 1)\hat{\mathbf{i}} + (\lambda - 1)\hat{\mathbf{j}} + (2\lambda - 1)\hat{\mathbf{k}}$$

Now, the vector along the line of intersection of the planes $2x + 3y + z - 1 = 0$ and $x + 3y + 2z - 2 = 0$ is given by

$$\mathbf{n} = \begin{vmatrix} \hat{\mathbf{i}} & \hat{\mathbf{j}} & \hat{\mathbf{k}} \\ 2 & 3 & 1 \\ 1 & 3 & 2 \end{vmatrix} = 3(\hat{\mathbf{i}} - \hat{\mathbf{j}} + \hat{\mathbf{k}})$$

As $\mathbf{n}$ is parallel to the plane (i), therefore $\mathbf{n} \cdot \mathbf{V} = 0$

$$(\lambda + 1) - (\lambda - 1) + (2\lambda - 1) = 0 \Rightarrow 2 + 2\lambda - 1 = 0 \Rightarrow \lambda = \frac{-1}{2}$$

Hence, the required plane is $\frac{x}{2} - \frac{3y}{2} - 2z - 2 = 0$

$$x - 3y - 4z - 4 = 0$$

Hence, $|A + B + C - 4| = 15$

Example 62 *Let $P(a, b, c)$ be any point on the plane $3x + 2y + z = 7$. Then, find the least value of $2(a^2 + b^2 + c^2)$.*

> **Decoding the Question**
>
> If $\mathbf{a} = a_1\hat{\mathbf{i}} + a_2\hat{\mathbf{j}} + a_3\hat{\mathbf{k}}$ and $\mathbf{b} = b_1\hat{\mathbf{i}} + b_2\hat{\mathbf{j}} + b_3\hat{\mathbf{k}}$, then for least value use $|\mathbf{a}|^2|\mathbf{b}|^2 > (\mathbf{a} \cdot \mathbf{b})^2$.

Sol. (7) Here, $P(a, b, c)$ lie on plane.

$\therefore 3a + 2b + c = 7$

Let $\mathbf{u} = a\hat{\mathbf{i}} + b\hat{\mathbf{j}} + c\hat{\mathbf{k}}$ and $\mathbf{v} = 3\hat{\mathbf{i}} + 2\hat{\mathbf{j}} + \hat{\mathbf{k}}$

$$|\mathbf{u}|^2 |\mathbf{v}|^2 > (\mathbf{u} \cdot \mathbf{v})^2$$

$$(a^2 + b^2 + c^2)(9 + 4 + 1) > (3a + 2b + c)^2$$

$$a^2 + b^2 + c^2 > \frac{49}{14} > \frac{7}{2}$$

$$\therefore \quad 2(a^2 + b^2 + c^2) \geq 7$$

Numerical Value Type Questions

Example 63 *The equation of motion of rockets are*

$$x = 2t,\ y = -4t,\ z = 4t,$$

where the time 't' is given in second and the coordinates of a moving point in kilometres. At what distance will the rocket be from the starting point $O(0, 0, 0)$ in 10s.

Sol. (60) Eliminating 't' from the given equations, we get the equation of the path,

$$\frac{x}{2} = \frac{y}{-4} = \frac{z}{4} \text{ or } \frac{x}{1} = \frac{y}{-2} = \frac{z}{2}$$

Thus, the path of the rocket represents a straight line passing through the origin.

For $t = 10$ s

We have, $x = 20$, $y = -40$, $z = 40$

and $|\mathbf{r}| = |\mathbf{OM}| = \sqrt{x^2 + y^2 + z^2}$

$$= \sqrt{400 + 1600 + 1600} = 60 \text{ km}$$

Example 64 *If a variable plane forms a tetrahedron of constant volume $64k^3$ with the coordinate planes, such that the locus of the centroid of the tetrahedron is $xyz = \lambda k^3$, then the value of $\frac{\lambda}{10}$ is ....*

Sol. (0.6) Let the variable plane intersects the coordinate axes at $A(a, 0, 0)$, $B(0, b, 0)$ and $C(0, 0, c)$. Then, the equation of the plane will be

$$\frac{x}{a} + \frac{y}{b} + \frac{z}{c} = 1 \quad \text{...(i)}$$

Let $P(\alpha, \beta, \gamma)$ be the centroid of tetrahedron $OABC$, then

$$\alpha = \frac{a}{4}, \beta = \frac{b}{4} \text{ and } \gamma = \frac{c}{4} \text{ or } a = 4\alpha, b = 4\beta \text{ and } c = 4\gamma$$

$\Rightarrow$ Volume of tetrahedron $= \frac{1}{3}$ (Area of ΔAOB) $\cdot OC$

$$\Rightarrow \quad 64k^3 = \frac{1}{3}\left(\frac{1}{2}ab\right)c = \frac{abc}{6}$$

$$\Rightarrow \quad 64k^3 = \frac{(4\alpha)(4\beta)(4\gamma)}{6} \Rightarrow k^3 = \frac{\alpha\beta\gamma}{6}$$

$\therefore$ Required locus of $P(\alpha, \beta, \gamma)$ is $xyz = 6k^3$.

Therefore, $\frac{\lambda}{10} = \frac{6}{10} = 0.6$

Example 65 *The shortest distance between any two opposite edges of a tetrahedron formed by the planes $y + z = 0$, $x + z = 0$, $x + y = 0$, $x + y + z = \sqrt{3}a$ is $\sqrt{pa}$. Then, the value of $3p^2$ is equal to ....*

> **Decoding the Question**
>
> Let $OABC$ is tetrahedron. First find coordinates of points O and C, then find direction cosines. After this, apply formula of short distance between OA and BC.

Sol. (12) Here, planes

$y + z = 0$, $z + x = 0$, $x + y = 0$ meet at $O(0, 0, 0)$.

Let the tetrahedron be $OABC$.

Let the equation of one of the pair of opposite edges OA and BC be

$$y + z = 0,\ x + z = 0 \quad \text{...(i)}$$

and $$x + y = 0,\ x + y + z = \sqrt{3}a \quad \text{...(ii)}$$

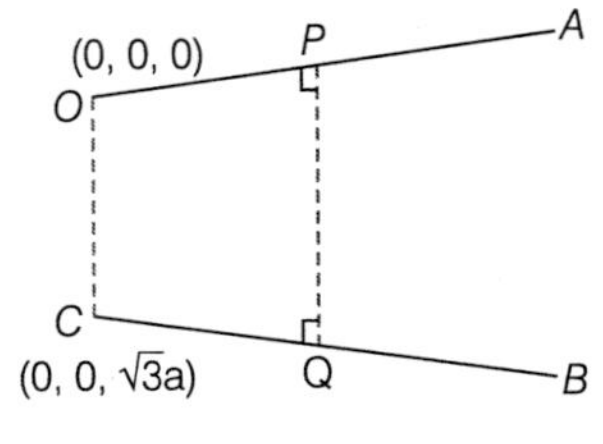

Eqs. (i) and (ii) can be expressed in symmetrical form as

$$\frac{x - 0}{1} = \frac{y - 0}{1} = \frac{z - 0}{-1} \quad \text{...(iii)}$$

and $$\frac{x - 0}{1} = \frac{y - 0}{-1} = \frac{z - \sqrt{3}a}{0} \quad \text{...(iv)}$$

DR's of OA and BC are $(1, 1, -1)$ and $(1, -1, 0)$.

Let PQ be the shortest distance between OA and BC having direction cosines (l, m, n).

$\therefore PQ$ is perpendicular to both OA and BC.

$$l + m - n = 0 \quad \text{...(v)}$$

$$l - m = 0 \quad \text{...(vi)}$$

On solving Eqs. (v) and (vi), we get

$$\frac{l}{1}=\frac{m}{1}=\frac{n}{2}=k$$

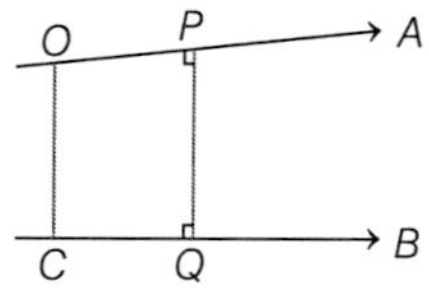

Also, $l^2+m^2+n^2=1$

$\therefore$ $k^2+k^2+4k^2=1$

$\Rightarrow$ $k=\frac{1}{\sqrt{6}}$

$\therefore$ $l=\frac{1}{\sqrt{6}}=m$ and $n=\frac{2}{\sqrt{6}}$

Shortest distance between OA and BC,

i.e. $PQ=$ Length of projection of OC and PQ

$$=|(x_2-x_1)l+(y_2-y_1)m+(z_2-z_1)n|$$

$$=\left|0\cdot\frac{1}{\sqrt{6}}+0\cdot\frac{1}{\sqrt{6}}+\sqrt{3}a\cdot\frac{2}{\sqrt{6}}\right|=\sqrt{2}a \text{ units}$$

$\therefore p=2$

Therefore, $3p^2=3\times4=12$

Example 66 *The plane denoted by $P_1:4x+7y+4z+81=0$ is rotated through a right angle about its line of intersection with the plane $P_2:5x+3y+10z=25$. If the plane in its new position be denoted by P, and the distance of this plane from the origin is d, then the value of [d] (where [.] represents greatest integer less than or equal to k) is ......*

Sol. (14) $4x+7y+4z+81=0$ ...(i)

$5x+3y+10z=25$ ...(ii)

Equation of plane passing through their line of intersection is

$$(4x+7y+4z+81)+\lambda(5x+3y+10z-25)=0$$

or $(4+5\lambda)x+(7+3\lambda)y+(4+10\lambda)z+81-25\lambda=0$ ...(iii)

plane (iii) is perpendicular to (i), so

$$4(4+5\lambda)+7(7+3\lambda)+4(4+10\lambda)=0$$

$\therefore$ $\lambda=-1$

From (iii), equation of plane is

$-x+4y-6z+106=0$ ...(iv)

Distance of (iv) from (0, 0, 0) $=\frac{106}{\sqrt{1+16+36}}=\frac{106}{\sqrt{53}}$ units

$\therefore$ $[d]=14$

Example 67 *The distance of the point $P(-2, 3, -4)$ from the line $\frac{x+2}{3}=\frac{2y+3}{4}=\frac{3z+4}{5}$ measured parallel to the plane $4x+12y-3z+1=0$ is d, then find the value of 2d is ....*

Sol. (17) Line through point $P(-2, 3, -4)$ and parallel to the given line $\frac{x+2}{3}=\frac{2y+3}{4}=\frac{3z+4}{5}$ is

$$\frac{x+2}{3}=\frac{y+\frac{3}{2}}{2}=\frac{z+\frac{4}{3}}{\frac{5}{3}}=\lambda$$

Any point on this line is $Q\left[3\lambda-2, 2\lambda-\frac{3}{2}, \frac{5}{3}\lambda-\frac{4}{3}\right]$.

Direction ratios of PQ are $\left[3\lambda, \frac{4\lambda-9}{2}, \frac{5\lambda+8}{3}\right]$

Now, PQ is parallel to the given plane $4x+12y-3z+1=0$

$\Rightarrow$ line is perpendicular to the normal to the plane

$\Rightarrow$ $4(3\lambda)+12\left(\frac{4\lambda-9}{2}\right)-3\left(\frac{5\lambda+8}{3}\right)=0$

$\Rightarrow$ $\lambda=2 \Rightarrow Q\left(4, \frac{5}{2}, 2\right)$

$\Rightarrow$ $PQ=\sqrt{(6)^2+\left(\frac{5}{2}-3\right)^2+(6)^2}=\frac{17}{2}$

$\therefore$ $2d=17$

Example 68 *The position vectors of the four angular points of a tetrahedron OABC are (0, 0, 0), (0, 0, 2), (0, 4, 0) and (6, 0, 0), respectively. A point P inside the tetrahedron is at the same distance 'r' from the four plane faces of the tetrahedron. Then, the value of 9r is ....*

Sol. (6) The given points are $O(0, 0, 0)$, $A(0, 0, 2)$, $B(0, 4, 0)$ and $C(6, 0, 0)$

Here, three faces of tetrahedron are XY, YZ, ZX-planes.

Since point P is equidistance from ZX, XY and YZ-planes, its coordinates are $P(r, r, r)$.

Equation of plane ABC is

$2x+3y+6z=12$ [from intercept form]

P is also at distance r from plane ABC

$\Rightarrow$ $\frac{|2r+3r+6r-12|}{\sqrt{4+9+36}}=r \Rightarrow |11r-12|=7r$

$\Rightarrow$ $11r-12=\pm7r \Rightarrow r=\frac{12}{18}, 3$

$\therefore$ $r=2/3$ [as $r<2$]

$\therefore$ $9r=9\times\frac{2}{3}=6$

Example 69 *Value of λ do the planes $x-y+z+1=0$, $\lambda x+3y+2z-3=0$, $3x+\lambda y+z-2=0$ form a triangular prism must be ......*

Sol. (4) The equation of the given planes can be written as

$$x-y+z+1=0$$

$$\lambda x+3y+2z-3=0$$

$$3x+\lambda y+z-2=0$$

The rectangular array is

$$\left\|\begin{matrix}1 & -1 & 1 & 1\\ \lambda & 3 & 2 & -3\\ 3 & \lambda & 1 & -2\end{matrix}\right\|=0$$

$\therefore$ $\Delta_4=\begin{vmatrix}1 & -1 & 1\\ \lambda & 3 & 2\\ 3 & \lambda & 1\end{vmatrix}$

On applying $C_2 \to C_2 + C_1$ and $C_3 \to C_3 - C_1$, then

$$\Delta_4 = \begin{vmatrix} 1 & 0 & 0 \\ \lambda & 3+\lambda & 2-\lambda \\ 3 & 3+\lambda & -2 \end{vmatrix} = (\lambda - 4)(\lambda + 3) \quad \text{... (i)}$$

Also, $$\Delta_1 = \begin{vmatrix} -1 & 1 & 1 \\ 3 & 2 & -3 \\ \lambda & 1 & -2 \end{vmatrix}$$

On applying $C_2 \to C_2 + C_1$ and $C_3 \to C_3 + C_1$, then

$$\Delta_1 = \begin{vmatrix} -1 & 0 & 0 \\ 3 & 5 & 0 \\ \lambda & \lambda+1 & \lambda-2 \end{vmatrix} = -5(\lambda - 2) \quad \text{... (ii)}$$

$$\Delta_2 = \begin{vmatrix} 1 & 1 & 1 \\ \lambda & 2 & -3 \\ 3 & 1 & -2 \end{vmatrix}$$

On applying $C_2 \to C_2 - C_1$ and $C_3 \to C_3 - C_1$, then

$$\Delta_2 = \begin{vmatrix} 1 & 0 & 0 \\ \lambda & 2-\lambda & -3-\lambda \\ 3 & -2 & -5 \end{vmatrix} = 3\lambda - 16 \quad \text{... (iii)}$$

$$\Delta_3 = \begin{vmatrix} 1 & -1 & 1 \\ \lambda & 3 & -3 \\ 3 & \lambda & -2 \end{vmatrix}$$

On applying $C_2 \to C_2 + C_1$ and $C_3 \to C_3 - C_1$, then

$$\Delta_3 = \begin{vmatrix} 1 & 0 & 0 \\ \lambda & 3+\lambda & -3-\lambda \\ 3 & 3+\lambda & -5 \end{vmatrix} = (\lambda + 3)(\lambda - 2) \quad \text{... (iv)}$$

If the given planes form a triangular prism, then we know that $\Delta_4 = 0$ and none of $\Delta_1, \Delta_2, \Delta_3$ is zero. Here, from Eqs. (i), (ii), (iii) and (iv) we find that if $\lambda = 4$, then $\Delta_4 = 0$ and none of Δ_1, Δ_2, Δ_3 is zero. Consequently for $\lambda = 4$, then given planes form a triangular prism.

Example 70 *If the lattice point $P(x, y, z)$; $x, y, z > 0$ and $x, y, z \in I$ with least value of z such that the 'P' lies on the planes $7x + 6y + 2z = 272$ and $x - y + z = 16$, then the value of $(x + y + z)$ is equal to ....*

Sol. (46) $7x + 6y + 2z = 272$ and $x - y + z = 16$

$$\Rightarrow \quad 5x + 8y = 240 \Rightarrow x = 48 - \frac{8}{5}y$$

Let $y = 5\lambda$, $\lambda \in I \Rightarrow x = 48 - 8\lambda$

and $z = 16 + y - x = 13\lambda - 32$

But $x > 0$, $y > 0$ and $z > 0 \quad \Rightarrow 48 - 8\lambda > 0 \Rightarrow \lambda > \frac{48}{8}$

$\Rightarrow \lambda \le 5$ and $13\lambda - 32 > 0 \Rightarrow \lambda > \frac{32}{13} \Rightarrow \lambda \ge 3$

$\therefore \quad \lambda \in [3, 5]$

$\therefore \quad z_{\min} = 39 - 32 = 7 \Rightarrow x = 24, y = 15$

$\therefore \quad x + y + z - 42 = 4$

$\Rightarrow \quad x + y + z = 46$

Example 71 *If the line $x = y = z$ intersect the line $x\sin A + y\sin B + z\sin C - 2d^2 = 0$ $= x\sin 2A + y\sin 2B + z\sin C - d^2$, where A, B, C are the internal angles of a triangle and $\sin\frac{A}{2}\sin\frac{B}{2}\sin\frac{C}{2} = k$, then the value of 40k is equal to ....*

Sol. (2.5) The given two lines are intersect each other, then

$$\frac{a_1\alpha + b_1\beta + c_1\gamma + d_1}{a_1 l + b_1 m + c_1 n} = \frac{a_2\alpha + b_2\beta + c_2\gamma + d_2}{a_2 l + b_2 m + c_2 n}$$

$$\Rightarrow \quad \frac{-2d^2}{\sin A + \sin B + \sin C} = \frac{-d^2}{\sin 2A + \sin 2B + \sin 2C}$$

$$\Rightarrow \quad \sin\frac{A}{2}\sin\frac{B}{2}\sin\frac{C}{2} = \frac{1}{16}$$

$\therefore \quad k = \frac{1}{16}$

Thus, $40k = 2.5$

Example 72 *The number of real values of k for which the lines $\frac{x}{1} = \frac{y-1}{k} = \frac{z}{-1}$ and $\frac{x-k}{2k} = \frac{y-k}{3k-1} = \frac{z-2}{k}$ are coplanar, is ....*

Sol. (1) $[\mathbf{c} - \mathbf{a}\ \mathbf{b}\ \mathbf{c}] = 0 \quad \Rightarrow \quad \begin{vmatrix} k & k-1 & 2 \\ 1 & k & -1 \\ 2k & 3k-1 & k \end{vmatrix} = 0$

$$\Rightarrow \quad k^3 - 4k^2 + 8k - 2 = 0$$

Here, $f'(k) = 3k^2 - 8k + 8 > 0, \forall k \in R$

[$\because$ its discriminate is negative]

$\therefore$ The equation has only one real root.

Matching Type Questions

Example 73 *Match the entries between following two columns.*

	Column I		Column II
A.	If the line $\frac{x-1}{1} = \frac{y+1}{-2} = \frac{z+1}{\lambda}$ lies in the plane $3x - 2y + 5z = 0$, then λ is equal to	p.	$\sin^{-1}\sqrt{\frac{6}{25}}$
B.	If $(3, \lambda, \mu)$ is a point on the line $2x + y + z - 3 = 0 = x - 2y + z - 1$, then $\lambda + \mu$ is equal to	q.	$-\frac{7}{5}$
C.	The angle between the line $x = y = z$ and the plane $4x - 3y + 5z = 2$ is	r.	-3
D.	The angle between the planes $x + y + z = 0$ and $3x - 4y + 5z = 0$ is	s.	$\cos^{-1}\sqrt{\frac{8}{75}}$

Sol. (A) $\to$ (q), (B) $\to$ (r), (C) $\to$ (p), (D) $\to$ (s)

(A) $3 \cdot 1 - 2(-2) + 5(\lambda) = 0 \Rightarrow \lambda = -\frac{7}{5}$

(B) Point $(3, \lambda, \mu)$ lies on $2x + y + z - 3 = x - 2y + z - 1$

$\Rightarrow 3 \cdot 2 + \lambda + \mu - 3 = 0$ and $3 - 2\lambda + \mu - 1 = 0$

$\Rightarrow \quad \lambda + \mu + 3 = 0$ and $2\lambda - \mu - 2 = 0$

So, $\quad \lambda + \mu = -3$

(C) $\sin\theta = \dfrac{1 \cdot 4 + 1(-3) + 1 \cdot 5}{\sqrt{1^2 + 1^2 + 1^2}\sqrt{16 + 9 + 25}} = \dfrac{6}{\sqrt{3}\sqrt{50}}$

$$\theta = \sin^{-1}\sqrt{\frac{6}{25}}$$

(D) $\cos\theta = \dfrac{1 \cdot 3 + 1(-4) + 1 \cdot 5}{\sqrt{3}\sqrt{16 + 9 + 25}} = \dfrac{4}{\sqrt{3}\sqrt{50}}$

$$\theta = \cos^{-1}\sqrt{\frac{8}{75}}$$

Example 74 *Match the following.*

	Column I	Column II
A.	$\frac{x-1}{2} = \frac{y-2}{3} = \frac{z-3}{4}$ and $\frac{x-1}{3} = \frac{y-3}{4} = \frac{z-5}{5}$ are	p. coincident
B.	$\frac{x-1}{2} = \frac{y-2}{3} = \frac{z-3}{4}$ and $\frac{x-3}{2} = \frac{y-5}{3} = \frac{z-7}{4}$ are	q. parallel and different
C.	$\frac{x-2}{5} = \frac{y+3}{4} = \frac{5-z}{2}$ and $\frac{x-7}{5} = \frac{y-1}{4} = \frac{z-2}{-2}$ are	r. skew
D.	$\frac{x-3}{2} = \frac{y+2}{3} = \frac{z-4}{5}$ and $\frac{x-3}{3} = \frac{y-2}{2} = \frac{z-7}{5}$ are	s. intersecting in a point

Sol. (A) $\rightarrow$ (s), (B) $\rightarrow$ (p), (C) $\rightarrow$ (q), (D) $\rightarrow$ (r)

(A) Both the lines pass through the point $(7, 11, 15)$.

(B) $< 2, 3, 4 >$ are direction ratios of both the lines. Also, the point $(1, 2, 3)$ is common to both.

$\therefore$ The lines are coincident.

(C) $< 5, 4, -2 >$ are direction ratios of both the lines.

$\therefore$ The lines are parallel.

Also, $x = 2 + 5\lambda, y = -3 + 4\lambda, z = 5 - 2\lambda$

$$\therefore \quad \frac{2 + 5\lambda - 7}{5} = \frac{-3 + 4\lambda - 1}{4} = \frac{5 - 2\lambda - 2}{-2}$$

i.e. $\quad \lambda - 1 = \lambda - 1 = \dfrac{3 - 2\lambda}{-2}$

$\therefore$ No value of λ.

Thus, the lines are parallel and different.

(D) $< 2, 3, 5 >$ and $<3, 2, 5 >$ are direction ratios of first and second line, respectively.

Example 75 *Match the followings.*

Column I	Column II
A. The coordinates of a point on the line $x = 4y + 5, z = 3y - 6$ at a distance 3 from the point $(5, 3, -6)$ are	p. $(-1, -2, 0)$
B. The plane containing the lines $\frac{x-2}{3} = \frac{y+3}{5} = \frac{z+5}{7}$ and parallel to $\hat{\mathbf{i}} + 4\hat{\mathbf{j}} + 7\hat{\mathbf{k}}$ has the point	q. $(5, 0, -6)$
C. A line passes through two points $A(2, -3, -1)$ and $B(8, -1, 2)$. The coordinates of a point on this line nearer to the origin and at a distance of 14 units from A is/are	r. $(2, 5, 7)$
D. The coordinates of the foot of the perpendicular from the point $(3, -1, 11)$ on the line $\frac{x}{2} = \frac{y-2}{3} = \frac{z-3}{4}$ are	s. $(14, 1, 5)$

Sol. (A) $\rightarrow$ (q), (B) $\rightarrow$ (p), (C) $\rightarrow$ (s), (D) $\rightarrow$ (r)

(A) The given line is $x = 4y + 5, z = 3y - 6$,

or $\quad \dfrac{x-5}{4} = y, \quad \dfrac{z+6}{3} = y$

or $\quad \dfrac{x-5}{4} = \dfrac{y}{1} = \dfrac{z+6}{3} = \lambda$ (let)

Any point on the line is of the form $(4\lambda + 5, \lambda, 3\lambda - 6)$.

The distance between $(4\lambda + 5, \lambda, 3\lambda - 6)$ and $(5, 3, -6)$ is 3 units (given).

Therefore, $(4\lambda + 5 - 5)^2 + (\lambda - 3)^2 + (3\lambda - 6 + 6)^2 = 9$

$\Rightarrow \quad 16\lambda^2 + \lambda^2 + 9 - 6\lambda + 9\lambda^2 = 9$

$\Rightarrow \quad 26\lambda^2 - 6\lambda = 0$

$\Rightarrow \quad \lambda = 0, \dfrac{3}{13}$

The point is $(5, 0, -6)$.

(B) The equation of the plane containing the lines $\dfrac{x-2}{3} = \dfrac{y+3}{5} = \dfrac{z+5}{7}$ and parallel to $\hat{\mathbf{i}} + 4\hat{\mathbf{j}} + 7\hat{\mathbf{k}}$.

$$\begin{vmatrix} x-2 & y+3 & z+5 \\ 1 & 4 & 7 \\ 3 & 5 & 7 \end{vmatrix} = 0 \Rightarrow x - 2y + z - 3 = 0$$

Point $(-1, -2, 0)$ lies on this plane.

(C) The line passing through points $A(2, -3, -1)$ and $B(8, -1, 2)$ is $\dfrac{x-2}{8-2} = \dfrac{y+3}{-1+3} = \dfrac{z+1}{2+1}$

or $\quad \dfrac{x-2}{6} = \dfrac{y+3}{2} = \dfrac{z+1}{3} = \lambda$ (let)

Any point on this line is of the form $P(6\lambda + 2, 2\lambda - 3, 3\lambda - 1)$, whose distance from point $A(2, -3, -1)$ is 14 units.

Therefore, $\quad PA = 14 \Rightarrow PA^2 = (14)^2$

$\Rightarrow \quad (6\lambda)^2 + (2\lambda)^2 + (3\lambda)^2 = 196$

$\Rightarrow \quad 49\lambda^2 = 196 \Rightarrow \lambda^2 = 4 \Rightarrow \lambda = \pm 2$

Therefore, the required points are (14, 1, 5) and (– 10, – 7, – 7). The point nearer to the origin is (14, 1, 5).

(D) Any point on line AB, $\frac{x}{2} = \frac{y-2}{3} = \frac{z-3}{4} = \lambda$ is $M(2\lambda, 3\lambda + 2, 4\lambda + 3)$.

Therefore, the direction ratios of PM are $2\lambda - 3, 3\lambda + 3$ and $4\lambda - 8$.

But $\quad PM \perp AB$

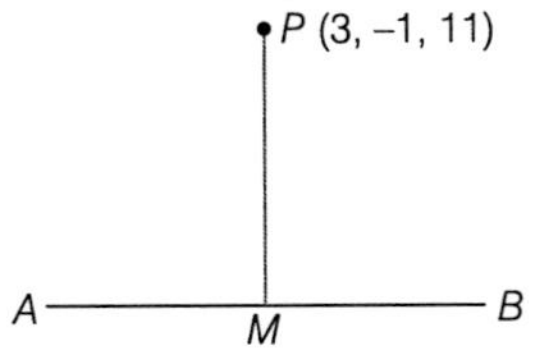

$$\therefore \quad 2(2\lambda - 3) + 3(3\lambda + 3) + 4(4\lambda - 8) = 0$$

$$4\lambda - 6 + 9\lambda + 9 + 16\lambda - 32 = 0$$

$$29\lambda - 29 = 0; \ \lambda = 1$$

Therefore, foot of the perpendicular is $M(2, 5, 7)$.

Example 76 ■ *Match the followings.*

Column I	Column II
A. Image of the point (3, 5, 7) in the plane $2x + y + z = -18$ is	p. (– 1, – 1, – 1)
B. The point of intersection of the line $\frac{x-2}{-3} = \frac{y-1}{2} = \frac{z-3}{2}$ and the plane $2x + y - z = 3$ is	q. (– 21, – 7, – 5)
C. The foot of the perpendicular from the point (1, 1, 2) to the plane $2x - 2y + 4z + 5 = 0$ is	r. $\left(\frac{5}{2}, \frac{2}{3}, \frac{8}{3}\right)$
D. The intersection point of the lines $\frac{x-1}{2} = \frac{y-2}{3} = \frac{z-3}{4}$ and $\frac{x-4}{5} = \frac{y-1}{2} = z$ is	s. $\left(-\frac{1}{12}, \frac{25}{12}, \frac{2}{12}\right)$

Sol. (A) → (q), (B) → (r), (C) → (s), (D) → (p)

(A) If the required image is (x, y, z), then

$$\frac{x-3}{2} = \frac{y-5}{1} = \frac{z-7}{1}$$

$$= -\frac{2(6 + 5 + 7 + 18)}{2^2 + 1^2 + 1^2} = -12 \text{ or } (-21, -7, -5).$$

(B) Any point on the line $\frac{x-2}{-3} = \frac{y-1}{2} = \frac{z-3}{2} = \lambda$ is

$(-3\lambda + 2, 2\lambda + 1, 2\lambda + 3)$, which lies on plane $2x + y - z = 3$.

Therefore, $\quad -6\lambda + 4 + 2\lambda + 1 - 2\lambda - 3 = 3$

$$\Rightarrow \quad -6\lambda = 1 \Rightarrow \lambda = -\frac{1}{6}$$

Therefore, the point is $\left(\frac{5}{2}, \frac{2}{3}, \frac{8}{3}\right)$.

(C) If (x, y, z) is required foot of the perpendicular, then

$$\frac{x-1}{2} = \frac{y-1}{-2} = \frac{z-2}{4} = \frac{(2 - 2 + 8 + 5)}{2^2 + (-2)^2 + 4^2}$$

or $$(x, y, z) \equiv \left(\frac{-1}{12}, \frac{25}{12}, \frac{-2}{12}\right)$$

(D) Any point on the line $\frac{x-1}{2} = \frac{y-2}{3} = \frac{z-3}{4} = \lambda$ is $P(2\lambda + 1, 3\lambda + 2, 4\lambda + 3)$, which satisfies the line

$$\frac{x-4}{5} = \frac{y-1}{2} = \frac{z}{1}$$

or $$\frac{2\lambda + 1 - 4}{5} = \frac{3\lambda + 2 - 1}{2} = \frac{4\lambda + 3}{1} \Rightarrow \lambda = -1$$

The required point is (– 1, – 1, – 1).

Example 77 ■ $\frac{x-2}{3} = \frac{y-3}{4} = \frac{z-4}{5}$

Column I	Column II
A. Point on the line at a distance $10\sqrt{2}$ units from (2, 3, 4)	p. (– 1, – 1, – 1)
B. Point on the line common to the plane $x + y + z + 3 = 0$	q. (2, 3, 4)
C. Point on the line at a distance $\sqrt{29}$ units from the origin.	r. (8, 11, 14)
D. Point on the line common to the plane $x + y - z + 3 = 0$	s. (– 4, – 5, – 6)

Sol. (A) → (r, s), (B) → (p), (C) → (q), (D) → (s)

Any point on the line is

$$(3r + 2, 4r + 3, 5r + 4)$$

(A) $(3r + 2 - 2)^2 + (4r + 3 - 3)^2 + (5r + 4 - 4)^2 = 200$

$$\Rightarrow \quad (9 + 16 + 25)r^2 = 200$$

$$\Rightarrow \quad r = \pm 2$$

For $r = 2$, the point is (8, 11, 14),

For $r = -2$ it is (– 4, – 5, – 6)

(B) $3r + 2 + 4r + 3 + 5r + 4 + 3 = 0$

$$\Rightarrow \quad 12r + 12 = 0$$

$$\Rightarrow \quad r = -1$$

and the point on the line common to the plane is (– 1, – 1, – 1).

(C) $(3r + 2)^2 + (4r + 3)^2 + (5r + 4)^2 = 29$

$$50r^2 + 76r = 0$$

$$\Rightarrow \quad r = 0, r = -\frac{76}{50}$$

For $r = 0$, the point is (2, 3, 4).

(D) $3r + 2 + 4r + 3 - 5r - 4 + 3 = 0$

$$\Rightarrow \quad 2r + 4 = 0$$

$$\Rightarrow \quad r = -2$$

∴ The point on the line common to the plane is (–4, –5, –6).

EXERCISE 1

JEE Main Pattern

Single Option Correct Type Questions

1. Ratio in which the ZX-plane divides the join of (1, 2, 3) and (4, 2, 1).
(a) 1 : 1 internally
(b) 1 : 1 externally
(c) 2 : 1 internally
(d) 2 : 1 externally

2. If $P(3, 2, -4)$, $Q(5, 4, -6)$ and $R(9, 8, -10)$ are collinear, then R divides PQ in the ratio
(a) 3 : 2 internally
(b) 3 : 2 externally
(c) 2 : 1 internally
(d) 2 : 1 externally

3. $A(3, 2, 0)$, $B(5, 3, 2)$ and $C(-9, 6, -3)$ are the vertices of a ΔABC. If the bisector of $\angle BAC$ meets BC at D, then coordinates of D are
(a) $\left(\frac{19}{8}, \frac{57}{16}, \frac{17}{16}\right)$ (b) $\left(-\frac{19}{8}, \frac{57}{16}, \frac{17}{16}\right)$
(c) $\left(\frac{19}{8}, -\frac{57}{16}, \frac{17}{16}\right)$ (d) None of these

4. A line passes through the points $(6, -7, -1)$ and $(2, -3, 1)$. The direction cosines of the line, so directed that the angle made by it with the positive direction of X-axis is acute, are
(a) $\frac{2}{3}, -\frac{2}{3}, -\frac{1}{3}$ (b) $-\frac{2}{3}, \frac{2}{3}, \frac{1}{3}$
(c) $\frac{2}{3}, -\frac{2}{3}, \frac{1}{3}$ (d) $\frac{2}{3}, \frac{2}{3}, \frac{1}{3}$

5. If P is a point in space such that **OP** is inclined to OX at 45° and OY to 60°, then **OP** is inclined to OZ at
(a) 75° (b) 60° or 120°
(c) 75° or 105° (d) 255°

6. The number of planes that are equidistant from four non-coplanar points is
(a) 3 (b) 4
(c) 7 (d) 9

7. If lines $x = y = z$ and $x = \frac{y}{2} = \frac{z}{3}$ and third line passing through (1, 1, 1) form a triangle of area $\sqrt{6}$ units, then point of intersection of third line with second line will be
(a) (1, 2, 3) (b) (2, 4, 6)
(c) $\left(\frac{4}{3}, \frac{8}{3}, \frac{12}{3}\right)$ (d) None of these

8. The line $\frac{x+6}{5} = \frac{y+10}{3} = \frac{z+14}{8}$ is the hypotenuse of an isosceles right angled triangle whose opposite vertex is (7, 2, 4). Then, which of the following is not the side of the triangle ?
(a) $\frac{x-7}{2} = \frac{y-2}{-3} = \frac{z-4}{6}$ (b) $\frac{x-7}{3} = \frac{y-2}{6} = \frac{z-4}{2}$
(c) $\frac{x-7}{3} = \frac{y-2}{5} = \frac{z-4}{-1}$ (d) None of these

9. Consider the following 3 lines in space
$L_1 : \mathbf{r} = 3\hat{\mathbf{i}} - \hat{\mathbf{j}} + 2\hat{\mathbf{k}} + \lambda(2\hat{\mathbf{i}} + 4\hat{\mathbf{j}} - \hat{\mathbf{k}})$
$L_2 : \mathbf{r} = \hat{\mathbf{i}} + \hat{\mathbf{j}} - 3\hat{\mathbf{k}} + \mu(4\hat{\mathbf{i}} + 2\hat{\mathbf{j}} + 4\hat{\mathbf{k}})$
$L_3 : \mathbf{r} = 3\hat{\mathbf{i}} + 2\hat{\mathbf{j}} - 2\hat{\mathbf{k}} + t(2\hat{\mathbf{i}} + \hat{\mathbf{j}} + 2\hat{\mathbf{k}})$
Then, which one of the following pair(s) is/are in the same plane ?
(a) Only L_1L_2 (b) Only L_2L_3
(c) Only L_3L_1 (d) L_1L_2 and L_2L_3

10. Let $\mathbf{r} = \mathbf{a} + \lambda\mathbf{l}$ and $\mathbf{r} = \mathbf{b} + \mu\mathbf{m}$ be two lines in space, where $\mathbf{a} = 5\hat{\mathbf{i}} + \hat{\mathbf{j}} + 2\hat{\mathbf{k}}$, $\mathbf{b} = -\hat{\mathbf{i}} + 7\hat{\mathbf{j}} + 8\hat{\mathbf{k}}$, $\mathbf{l} = -4\hat{\mathbf{i}} + \hat{\mathbf{j}} - \hat{\mathbf{k}}$, and $\mathbf{m} = 2\hat{\mathbf{i}} - 5\hat{\mathbf{j}} - 7\hat{\mathbf{k}}$, then the position vector of a point which lies on both of these lines, is
(a) $\hat{\mathbf{i}} + 2\hat{\mathbf{j}} + \hat{\mathbf{k}}$
(b) $2\hat{\mathbf{i}} + \hat{\mathbf{j}} + \hat{\mathbf{k}}$
(c) $\hat{\mathbf{i}} + \hat{\mathbf{j}} + 2\hat{\mathbf{k}}$
(d) non-existent as the lines are skew

11. L_1 and L_2 are two lines whose vector equations are
$L_1 : \mathbf{r} = \lambda[(\cos\theta + \sqrt{3})\hat{\mathbf{i}} + (\sqrt{2}\sin\theta)\hat{\mathbf{j}} + (\cos\theta - \sqrt{3})\hat{\mathbf{k}}]$
and $L_2 : \mathbf{r} = \mu(a\hat{\mathbf{i}} + b\hat{\mathbf{j}} + c\hat{\mathbf{k}})$, where, λ and μ are scalars and α is the acute angle between L_1 and L_2. If the angle α is independent of θ, then the value of α is
(a) $\frac{\pi}{6}$ (b) $\frac{\pi}{4}$ (c) $\frac{\pi}{3}$ (d) $\frac{\pi}{2}$

12. The vector equations of two lines L_1 and L_2 are respectively,
$$\mathbf{r} = 17\hat{\mathbf{i}} - 9\hat{\mathbf{j}} + 9\hat{\mathbf{k}} + \lambda(3\hat{\mathbf{i}} + \hat{\mathbf{j}} + 5\hat{\mathbf{k}})$$
and $$\mathbf{r} = 15\hat{\mathbf{i}} - 8\hat{\mathbf{j}} - \hat{\mathbf{k}} + \mu(4\hat{\mathbf{i}} + 3\hat{\mathbf{j}})$$
I. L_1 and L_2 are skew lines.
II. (11, −11, −1) is the point of intersection of L_1 and L_2.
III. (−11, 11, 1) is the point of intersection of L_1 and L_2.

IV. $\cos^{-1}\left(\frac{3}{\sqrt{35}}\right)$ is the acute angle between, L_1 and L_2.

Then, which of the following is true ?

(a) II and IV (b) I and IV
(c) Only IV (d) III and IV

13. The plane XOZ divides the join of $(1, -1, 5)$ and $(2, 3, 4)$ in the ratio $\lambda : 1$, then λ is

(a) -3 (b) $-\frac{1}{3}$ (c) 3 (d) $\frac{1}{3}$

14. The vector equations of the two lines L_1 and L_2 are given by $L_1 : \mathbf{r} = (2\hat{\mathbf{i}} + 9\hat{\mathbf{j}} + 13\hat{\mathbf{k}}) + \lambda(\hat{\mathbf{i}} + 2\hat{\mathbf{j}} + 3\hat{\mathbf{k}})$

and $L_2 : \mathbf{r} = (-3\hat{\mathbf{i}} + 7\hat{\mathbf{j}} + p\hat{\mathbf{k}}) + \mu(-\hat{\mathbf{i}} + 2\hat{\mathbf{j}} - 3\hat{\mathbf{k}})$.

Then, the lines L_1 and L_2 are

(a) skew lines for all $p \in R$
(b) intersecting for all $p \in R$ and the point of intersection is $(-1, 3, 4)$
(c) intersecting lines for $p = -2$
(d) intersecting for all real $p \in R$

15. The value of a for which the lines $\frac{x-2}{1} = \frac{y-9}{2} = \frac{z-13}{3}$ and $\frac{x-a}{-1} = \frac{y-7}{2} = \frac{z+2}{-3}$ intersect, is

(a) -5 (b) -2 (c) 5 (d) -3

16. The lines $\frac{x-2}{1} = \frac{y-3}{1} = \frac{z-4}{-k}$ and $\frac{x-1}{k} = \frac{y-4}{2} = \frac{z-5}{1}$ are coplanar, if

(a) $k = 0$ or -1 (b) $k = 1$ or -1
(c) $k = 0$ or -3 (d) $k = 3$ or -3

17. The line $\frac{x-2}{3} = \frac{y+1}{2} = \frac{z-1}{-1}$ intersects the curve $xy = c^2$, in XY-plane, if c is equal to

(a) ± 1 (b) $\pm\frac{1}{3}$
(c) $\pm\sqrt{5}$ (d) None of these

18. The angle between the lines AB and CD, where $A = (0, 0, 0)$, $B = (1, 1, 1)$, $C = (-1, -1, -1)$ and $D = (0, 1, 0)$ is given by

(a) $\cos\theta = \frac{1}{\sqrt{3}}$ (b) $\cos\theta = \frac{4}{3\sqrt{2}}$
(c) $\cos\theta = \frac{1}{\sqrt{5}}$ (d) $\cos\theta = \frac{1}{2\sqrt{2}}$

19. The direction ratios of line L_1 passing through $P(1, 3, 4)$ and perpendicular to line L_2 $\frac{x-1}{2} = \frac{y-2}{3} = \frac{z-3}{4}$ (where, L_1 and L_2 are coplanar) are

(a) 14, 8, 1 (b) -14, 8, -1
(c) 14, -8, -1 (d) -14, -8, 1

20. The angle between the lines whose direction cosines are given by the equations $l^2 + m^2 - n^2 = 0, l + m + n = 0$ is

(a) $\cos^{-1}(2\sqrt{3})$ (b) $\cos^{-1}\sqrt{3}$
(c) $\frac{\pi}{3}$ (d) $\frac{\pi}{2}$

21. Let $\mathbf{a} = \hat{\mathbf{i}} + \hat{\mathbf{j}}$ and $\mathbf{b} = 2\hat{\mathbf{i}} - \hat{\mathbf{k}}$, then the point of intersection of the lines $\mathbf{r} \times \mathbf{a} = \mathbf{b} \times \mathbf{a}$ and $\mathbf{r} \times \mathbf{b} = \mathbf{a} \times \mathbf{b}$ is

(a) $(3, -1, 1)$ (b) $(3, 1, -1)$
(c) $(-3, 1, 1)$ (d) $(-3, -1, -1)$

22. The coordinates of the point P on the line $\mathbf{r} = (\hat{\mathbf{i}} + \hat{\mathbf{j}} + \hat{\mathbf{k}}) + \lambda(-\hat{\mathbf{i}} + \hat{\mathbf{j}} - \hat{\mathbf{k}})$ which is nearest to the origin is

(a) $\left(\frac{2}{3}, \frac{4}{3}, \frac{2}{3}\right)$ (b) $\left(-\frac{2}{3}, -\frac{4}{3}, \frac{2}{3}\right)$
(c) $\left(\frac{2}{3}, \frac{4}{3}, -\frac{2}{3}\right)$ (d) None of these

23. The 3-dimensional vectors $\mathbf{v}_1$, $\mathbf{v}_2$ and $\mathbf{v}_3$ satisfying $\mathbf{v}_1 \cdot \mathbf{v}_1 = 4, \mathbf{v}_1 \cdot \mathbf{v}_2 = -2, \mathbf{v}_1 \cdot \mathbf{v}_3 = 6, \mathbf{v}_2 \cdot \mathbf{v}_2 = 2$, $\mathbf{v}_2 \cdot \mathbf{v}_3 = -5, \mathbf{v}_3 \cdot \mathbf{v}_3 = 29$, then $\mathbf{v}_3$ may be

(a) $-3\hat{\mathbf{i}} + 2\hat{\mathbf{j}} \pm 4\hat{\mathbf{k}}$ (b) $3\hat{\mathbf{i}} - 2\hat{\mathbf{j}} \pm 4\hat{\mathbf{k}}$
(c) $-2\hat{\mathbf{i}} + 3\hat{\mathbf{j}} \pm 4\hat{\mathbf{k}}$ (d) $2\hat{\mathbf{i}} + 3\hat{\mathbf{j}} \pm 4\hat{\mathbf{k}}$

24. A ray of light is sent through the point $P(1, 2, 3)$ and is reflected on the XY-plane. If the reflected ray passes through the point $Q(3, 2, 5)$, then the equation of the reflected ray is

(a) $\frac{x-3}{1} = \frac{y-2}{0} = \frac{z-5}{1}$ (b) $\frac{x-3}{1} = \frac{y-2}{0} = \frac{z-5}{-4}$
(c) $\frac{x-3}{1} = \frac{y-2}{0} = \frac{z-5}{4}$ (d) $\frac{x-1}{1} = \frac{y-2}{0} = \frac{z-3}{4}$

25. Let S be the set of all values of λ, for which the shortest distance between the lines $\frac{1-x}{-2} = \frac{2-y}{-3} = \frac{z-3}{4}$ and $\frac{x-2}{3} = \frac{y-4}{4} = \frac{z-\lambda}{5}$ is $\frac{1}{\sqrt{6}}$. Then, $\sum_{\lambda \in S} \lambda^2$ is equal to

(a) 34 (b) 80
(c) 130 (d) 74

Numerical Value Type Questions

26. Let α be the angle between the lines whose direction cosines satisfy the equation $l + m + n = 0$ and $l^2 = m^2 + n^2$, then the value of $\sin^4\alpha + \cos^4\alpha$ is ....

27. If the angle between the line, $\frac{x}{2} = \frac{y}{2} = \frac{z}{1}$ and $\frac{5-x}{-2} = \frac{7y-14}{p} = \frac{z-3}{4}$ is $\sin^{-1}\frac{\sqrt{5}}{3}$, then the value of p is ....

28. The shortest distance between the line $\frac{x-1}{1}=\frac{y-1}{1}=\frac{z-1}{1}$ and $\frac{x-2}{1}=\frac{y-3}{1}=\frac{z-4}{1}$ is λ, then λ^2 is ....

29. Two line $\frac{x-3}{1}=\frac{y+1}{3}=\frac{z-6}{-1}$ and $\frac{x+5}{7}=\frac{y-2}{-6}=\frac{z-3}{4}$ intersect at point Q. The image of point Q in XY-plane is (α, β, γ), then $\alpha^2+\beta^2+\gamma^2$ is ....

30. Let $\lambda, \mu \in R$. If the mirror image of point $P(\lambda, 6, 9)$ with respect to the line $\frac{x-3}{7}=\frac{y-2}{5}=\frac{z-1}{-9}$ is $(20, \mu, -\lambda-9)$, then the value of $|\lambda|+|\mu|$ is ....

31. Let P and Q be the points on the line $\frac{x+3}{8}=\frac{y-4}{2}=\frac{z+1}{2}$ which are at a distance of 6 units from the point $R(1, 2, 3)$, then the area of ΔPQR is .... (in sq units).

32. Let a line having direction ratios $(1, -4, 2)$ intersect the line $\frac{x-7}{3}=\frac{y-1}{-1}=\frac{z+2}{1}$ at $P(\alpha, \beta, \gamma)$ and $\frac{x}{2}=\frac{y-7}{3}=\frac{z}{1}$ at $Q(p, q, r)$, then the value of $|(\alpha+\beta+\gamma)(p+q+r)|$ is ....

33. The foot of perpendicular of the point $P(1, 8, 4)$ to the line joining the points $Q(0, -1, 3)$ and $R(2, -3, -1)$ is (α, β, γ), then the value of $3(\alpha+\beta+\gamma)$ is ....

34. If two lines $L_1 \equiv \frac{x-2}{3}=\frac{y+1}{-2}$, $z=2$ and line $L_2=\frac{x-1}{1}=\frac{2y+3}{\alpha}=\frac{z+5}{2}$ are perpendicular, then angle between the line L_2 and $L_3=\frac{1-x}{3}=\frac{2y-1}{-4}=\frac{z}{4}$ is $\cos^{-1}\left(\frac{p}{q}\right)$, then $p+q$ is equal to .... (where p and q are relatively prime)

35. The length of perpendicular drawn from the point $(0, 2, \lambda)$ on the line $\mathbf{r}=-3\hat{\mathbf{i}}+\hat{\mathbf{j}}-4\hat{\mathbf{k}}+\mu(5\hat{\mathbf{i}}+2\hat{\mathbf{j}}+3\hat{\mathbf{k}})$ is $\sqrt{21}$ units. Let S be the set of all values of λ, then $29\sum_{\lambda \in S}|\lambda|$ is equal to ....

36. If a point $P(\alpha, \beta, \gamma)$ lie on the line $\frac{x+2}{3}=\frac{y+1}{2}=\frac{z-3}{2}$ at a distance of $3\sqrt{2}$ from the point $(1, 2, 3)$, then the value of $17(\alpha+\beta+\gamma)$ is ...., where α, β, γ lie in first octant.

37. The distance, of the point $(7, -2, 11)$ from the line $\frac{x-6}{1}=\frac{y-4}{0}=\frac{z-8}{3}$ along the line $\frac{x-7}{2}=\frac{y+2}{-3}=\frac{z-11}{6}$, is ....

38. If the length of the perpendicular drawn from the point $P(1, 2, k)$, $k<4$ on the line $\frac{x-6}{3}=\frac{y-7}{2}=\frac{z-7}{-2}$ is 7 units and $Q(\alpha_1, \alpha_2, \alpha_3)$ is the image of the point P in this line, then $k+\sum_{i=1}^{3}\alpha_i$ is equal to ....

Previous Year Questions

39. If the mirror image of the point $P(3, 4, 9)$ in the line $\frac{x-1}{3}=\frac{y+1}{2}=\frac{z-2}{1}$ is (α, β, γ), then $14(\alpha+\beta+\gamma)$ is **[Single Correct Type, 2024 Main]**

(a) 132 (b) 138 (c) 108 (d) 102

40. Let P and Q be the points on the line $\frac{x+3}{8}=\frac{y-4}{2}=\frac{z+1}{2}$ which are at a distance of 6 units from the point $R(1, 2, 3)$. If the centroid of the ΔPQR is (α, β, γ), then $\alpha^2+\beta^2+\gamma^2$ is **[Single Correct Type, 2024 Main]**

(a) 18 (b) 26 (c) 36 (d) 24

41. If the shortest distance between the lines $\frac{x-\lambda}{-2}=\frac{y-2}{1}=\frac{z-1}{1}$ and $\frac{x-\sqrt{3}}{1}=\frac{y-1}{-2}=\frac{z-2}{1}$ is 1, then the sum of all possible values of λ is **[Single Correct Type, 2024 Main]**

(a) 0 (b) $3\sqrt{3}$ (c) $2\sqrt{3}$ (d) $-2\sqrt{3}$

42. The shortest distance between lines L_1 and L_2, where $L_1: \frac{x-1}{2}=\frac{y+1}{-3}=\frac{z+4}{2}$ and L_2 is the line passing through the points $A(-4, 4, 3)$, $B(-1, 6, 3)$ and perpendicular to the line $\frac{x-3}{-2}=\frac{y}{3}=\frac{z-1}{1}$ is **[Single Correct Type, 2024 Main]**

(a) $\frac{121}{\sqrt{221}}$ (b) $\frac{24}{\sqrt{117}}$ (c) $\frac{42}{\sqrt{117}}$ (d) $\frac{141}{\sqrt{221}}$

43. Let (α, β, γ) be the mirror image of the point $(2, 3, 5)$ in the line $\frac{x-1}{2}=\frac{y-2}{3}=\frac{z-3}{4}$. Then, $2\alpha+3\beta+4\gamma$ is equal to **[Single Correct Type, 2024 Main]**

(a) 34 (b) 31 (c) 33 (d) 32

44. The distance of the point $Q(0, 2, -2)$ from the line passing through the point $P(5, -4, 3)$ and perpendicular to the lines $\mathbf{r}=(-3\hat{\mathbf{i}}+2\hat{\mathbf{k}})+\lambda(2\hat{\mathbf{i}}+3\hat{\mathbf{j}}+5\hat{\mathbf{k}})$, $\lambda \in R$ and $\mathbf{r}=(\hat{\mathbf{i}}-2\hat{\mathbf{j}}+\hat{\mathbf{k}})+\mu(-\hat{\mathbf{i}}+3\hat{\mathbf{j}}+2\hat{\mathbf{k}})$, $\mu \in R$ is **[Single Correct Type, 2024 Main]**

(a) $\sqrt{20}$ (b) $\sqrt{86}$ (c) $\sqrt{54}$ (d) $\sqrt{74}$

45. Let $L_1 : \mathbf{r} = (\hat{\mathbf{i}} - \hat{\mathbf{j}} + 2\hat{\mathbf{k}}) + \lambda(\hat{\mathbf{i}} - \hat{\mathbf{j}} + 2\hat{\mathbf{k}}), \lambda \in R$, $L_2 : \mathbf{r} = (\hat{\mathbf{j}} - \hat{\mathbf{k}}) + \mu(3\hat{\mathbf{i}} + \hat{\mathbf{j}} + p\hat{\mathbf{k}}), \mu \in R$ and $L_3 : \mathbf{r} = \delta(l\hat{\mathbf{i}} + m\hat{\mathbf{j}} + n\hat{\mathbf{k}}), \delta \in R$ be three lines such that L_1 is perpendicular to L_2 and L_3 is perpendicular to both L_1 and L_2. Then, the point which lies on L_3 is

[Single Correct Type, 2024 Main]

(a) (−1, 7, 4) (b) (1, 7, −4)
(c) (1, −7, 4) (d) (−1, −7, 4)

46. Let (α, β, γ) be the foot of perpendicular from the point (1, 2, 3) on the line $\frac{x+3}{5} = \frac{y-1}{2} = \frac{z+4}{3}$. Then, $19(\alpha + \beta + \gamma)$ is equal to **[Single Correct Type, 2024 Main]**

(a) 101 (b) 99 (c) 100 (d) 102

47. Let PQR be a triangle with $R(-1, 4, 2)$. Suppose $M(2, 1, 2)$ is the mid-point of PQ. The distance of the centroid of ΔPQR from the point of intersection of the lines $\frac{x-2}{0} = \frac{y}{2} = \frac{z+3}{-1}$ and $\frac{x-1}{1} = \frac{y+3}{-3} = \frac{z+1}{1}$ is

[Single Correct Type, 2024 Main]

(a) 9 (b) 69 (c) $\sqrt{69}$ (d) $\sqrt{99}$

48. Let the image of the point (1, 0, 7) in the line $\frac{x}{1} = \frac{y-1}{2} = \frac{z-2}{3}$ be the point (α, β, γ). Then, which one of the following points lies on the line passing through (α, β, γ) and making angles $\frac{2\pi}{3}$ and $\frac{3\pi}{4}$ with Y-axis and Z-axis respectively and an acute angle with X-axis?

[Single Correct Type, 2024 Main]

(a) $(1, -2, 1 + \sqrt{2})$ (b) $(1, 2, 1 - \sqrt{2})$
(c) $(3, -4, 3 + 2\sqrt{2})$ (d) $(3, 4, 3 - 2\sqrt{2})$

49. The distance of the point $(7, -2, 11)$ from the line $\frac{x-6}{1} = \frac{y-4}{0} = \frac{z-8}{3}$ along the line $\frac{x-5}{2} = \frac{y-1}{-3} = \frac{z-5}{6}$, is **[Single Correct Type, 2024 Main]**

(a) 14 (b) 12 (c) 18 (d) 21

50. Let the line of the shortest distance between the lines $L_1 : \mathbf{r} = (\hat{\mathbf{i}} + 2\hat{\mathbf{j}} + 3\hat{\mathbf{k}}) + \lambda(\hat{\mathbf{i}} - \hat{\mathbf{j}} + \hat{\mathbf{k}})$ and $L_2 : \mathbf{r} = (4\hat{\mathbf{i}} + 5\hat{\mathbf{j}} + 6\hat{\mathbf{k}}) + \mu(\hat{\mathbf{i}} + \hat{\mathbf{j}} - \hat{\mathbf{k}})$ intersect L_1 and L_2 at P and Q, respectively. If (α, β, γ) is the mid-point of the line segment PQ, then $2(\alpha + \beta + \gamma)$ is equal to ....

[Numerical Value Type, 2024 Main]

51. A line passes through $A(4, -6, -2)$ and $B(16, -2, 4)$. The point $P(a, b, c)$, where a, b, c are non-negative integers on the line AB lies at a distance of 21 units from the point A. The distance between the points $P(a, b, c)$ and $Q(4, -12, 3)$ is equal to ....

[Numerical Value Type, 2024 Main]

52. Let Q and R be the feet of perpendiculars from the point $P(a, a, a)$ on the lines $x = y, z = 1, x = -y$ and $z = -1$, respectively. If $\angle QPR$ is a right angle, then $12a^2$ is equal to .... **[Numerical Value Type, 2024 Main]**

53. Let a line passing through the point (−1, 2, 3) intersect the lines $L_1 : \frac{x-1}{3} = \frac{y-2}{2} = \frac{z+1}{-2}$ at $M(\alpha, \beta, \gamma)$ and $L_2 : \frac{x+2}{-3} = \frac{y-2}{-2} = \frac{z-1}{4}$ at $N(a, b, c)$. Then, the value of $\frac{(\alpha + \beta + \gamma)^2}{(a + b + c)^2}$ equals ....

[Numerical Value Type, 2024 Main]

54. If d_1 is the shortest distance between the lines $x + 1 = 2y = -12z$, $x = y + 2 = 6z - 6$ and d_2 is the shortest distance between the lines $\frac{x-1}{2} = \frac{y+8}{-7} = \frac{z-4}{5}$, $\frac{x-1}{2} = \frac{y-2}{1} = \frac{z-6}{-3}$, then the value of $\frac{32\sqrt{3}d_1}{d_2}$ is ....

[Numerical Value Type, 2024 Main]

55. Let O be the origin, and M and N be the points on the lines $\frac{x-5}{4} = \frac{y-4}{1} = \frac{z-5}{3}$ and $\frac{x+8}{12} = \frac{y+2}{5} = \frac{z+11}{9}$ respectively, such that MN is the shortest distance between the given lines. Then, $\mathbf{OM} \cdot \mathbf{ON}$ is equal to ....

[Numerical Value Type, 2024 Main]

56. A line with direction ratios 2, 1, 2 meets the lines $x = y + 2 = z$ and $x + 2 = 2y = 2z$ respectively, at the points P and Q. If the length of the perpendicular from the point (1, 2, 12) to the line PQ is l, then l^2 is ....

[Numerical Value Type, 2024 Main]

57. The lines $\frac{x-2}{2} = \frac{y}{-2} = \frac{z-7}{16}$ and $\frac{x+3}{4} = \frac{y+2}{3} = \frac{z+2}{1}$ intersect at the point P. If the distance of P from the line $\frac{x+1}{2} = \frac{y-1}{3} = \frac{z-1}{1}$ is l, then $14l^2$ is equal to ....

[Numerical Value Type, 2024 Main]

58. Let the line L pass through the point (0, 1, 2), intersect the line $\frac{x-1}{2} = \frac{y-2}{3} = \frac{z-3}{4}$ and be parallel to the plane $2x + y - 3z = 4$. Then, the distance of the point $P(1, -9, 2)$ from the line L is

[Single Correct Type, 2023 Main]

(a) $\sqrt{74}$ (b) $\sqrt{54}$ (c) $\sqrt{69}$ (d) 9

59. Let S be the set of all values of λ, for which the shortest distance between the lines $\frac{x-\lambda}{0} = \frac{y-3}{4} = \frac{z+6}{1}$ and $\frac{x+\lambda}{3} = \frac{y}{-4} = \frac{z-6}{0}$ is 13. Then, $8\left|\sum_{\lambda \in S} \lambda\right|$ is equal to

[Single Correct Type, 2023 Main]

(a) 304 (b) 302 (c) 306 (d) 308

60. The line, that is coplanar to the line $\frac{x+3}{-3}=\frac{y-1}{1}=\frac{z-5}{5}$, is **[Single Correct Type, 2023 Main]**

(a) $\frac{x+1}{-1}=\frac{y-2}{2}=\frac{z-5}{4}$ (b) $\frac{x+1}{-1}=\frac{y-2}{2}=\frac{z-5}{5}$

(c) $\frac{x-1}{-1}=\frac{y-2}{2}=\frac{z-5}{5}$ (d) $\frac{x+1}{1}=\frac{y-2}{2}=\frac{z-5}{5}$

61. Let the lines $l_1:\frac{x+5}{3}=\frac{y+4}{1}=\frac{z-\alpha}{-2}$ and $l_2: 3x+2y+z-2=0=x-3y+2z-13$ be coplanar. If the point $P(a,b,c)$ on l_1 is nearest to the point $Q(-4,-3,2)$, then $|a|+|b|+|c|$ is equal to **[Single Correct Type, 2023 Main]**

(a) 14 (b) 12 (c) 10 (d) 8

62. Let the line $\frac{x}{1}=\frac{6-y}{2}=\frac{z+8}{5}$ intersect the lines $\frac{x-5}{4}=\frac{y-7}{3}=\frac{z+2}{1}$ and $\frac{x+3}{6}=\frac{3-y}{3}=\frac{z-6}{1}$ at the points A and B respectively. Then, the distance of the mid-point of the line segment AB from the plane $2x-2y+z=14$ is **[Single Correct Type, 2023 Main]**

(a) 4 (b) 3 (c) $\frac{11}{3}$ (d) $\frac{10}{3}$

63. For $a, b \in Z$ and $|a-b| \le 10$, let the angle between the plane $P: ax+y-z=b$ and the line $l: x-1=a-y=z+1$ be $\cos^{-1}\left(\frac{1}{3}\right)$. If the distance of the point $(6,-6,4)$ from the plane P is $3\sqrt{6}$, then a^4+b^2 is equal to **[Single Correct Type, 2023 Main]**

(a) 48 (b) 85 (c) 32 (d) 25

64. Let the shortest distance between the lines $L:\frac{x-5}{-2}=\frac{y-\lambda}{0}=\frac{z+\lambda}{1}$, $\lambda \ge 0$ and $L_1: x+1=y-1=4-z$ be $2\sqrt{6}$. If (α, β, γ) lies on L, then which of the following is not possible? **[Single Correct Type, 2023 Main]**

(a) $\alpha-2\gamma=19$ (b) $\alpha+2\gamma=24$

(c) $2\alpha-\gamma=9$ (d) $2\alpha+\gamma=7$

65. The distance of the point $P(4,6,-2)$ from the line passing through the point $(-3,2,3)$ and parallel to a line with direction ratios $3, 3, -1$ is equal to **[Single Correct Type, 2023 Main]**

(a) $\sqrt{14}$ (b) 3 (c) $2\sqrt{3}$ (d) $\sqrt{6}$

66. The foot of perpendicular of the point $(2, 0, 5)$ on the line $\frac{x+1}{2}=\frac{y-1}{5}=\frac{z+1}{-1}$ is (α, β, γ). Then, which of the following is not correct? **[Single Correct Type, 2023 Main]**

(a) $\frac{\beta}{\gamma}=-\frac{1}{5}$ (b) $\frac{\gamma}{\alpha}=\frac{5}{8}$

(c) $\frac{\alpha}{\beta}=-8$ (d) $\frac{\alpha\beta}{\gamma}=\frac{4}{15}$

67. Consider the lines L_1 and L_2 given by

$L_1:\frac{x-1}{2}=\frac{y-3}{1}=\frac{z-2}{2}$; $L_2:\frac{x-2}{1}=\frac{y-2}{2}=\frac{z-3}{3}$

A line L_3 having direction ratios $1,-1,-2$, intersects L_1 and L_2 at the points P and Q, respectively. Then, the length of line segment PQ is **[Single Correct Type, 2023 Main]**

(a) $4\sqrt{3}$ (b) 4 (c) $2\sqrt{6}$ (d) $3\sqrt{2}$

68. Let a line l pass through the origin and be perpendicular to the lines $\mathbf{r}=(\hat{\mathbf{i}}-11\hat{\mathbf{j}}-7\hat{\mathbf{k}})+\lambda(\hat{\mathbf{i}}+2\hat{\mathbf{j}}+3\hat{\mathbf{k}}), \lambda \in R$ and $l_2: \mathbf{r}=(-\hat{\mathbf{i}}+\hat{\mathbf{k}})+\mu(2\hat{\mathbf{i}}+2\hat{\mathbf{j}}+\hat{\mathbf{k}}), \mu \in R$.

If P is the point of intersection of l and l_1, and $Q(\alpha, \beta, \gamma)$ is the foot of perpendicular from P on l_2. Then, $9(\alpha+\beta+\gamma)$ is equal to .... **[Numerical Value Type, 2023 Main]**

69. If the lines $\frac{x-1}{2}=\frac{2-y}{-3}=\frac{z-3}{\alpha}$ and $\frac{x-4}{5}=\frac{y-1}{2}=\frac{z}{\beta}$ intersect, then the magnitude of the minimum value of $8\alpha\beta$ is .... **[Numerical Value Type, 2023 Main]**

70. One vertex of a rectangular parallelopiped is at the origin O and the lengths of its edges along X, Y and Z axes are 3, 4 and 5 units respectively. Let P be the vertex $(3, 4, 5)$. Then, the shortest distance between the diagonal OP and an edge parallel to Z-axis, not passing through O or P is .... **[Numerical Value Type, 2023 Main]**

71. Let a line L pass through the point $P(2, 3, 1)$ and be parallel to the line $x+3y-2z-2=0=x-y+2z$. If the distance of L from the point $(5,3,8)$ is α, then $3\alpha^2$ is equal to .... **[Numerical Value Type, 2023 Main]**

72. Let the coordinates of one vertex of ΔABC be $A(0, 2, \alpha)$ and the other two vertices lie on the line $\frac{x+\alpha}{5}=\frac{y-1}{2}=\frac{z+4}{3}$. For $\alpha \in Z$, if the area of ΔABC is 21 sq units and the line segment BC has length $2\sqrt{21}$ units, then α^2 is equal to .... **[Numerical Value Type, 2023 Main]**

73. If the shortest distance between the line joining the points $(1, 2, 3)$ and $(2, 3, 4)$ and the line $\frac{x-1}{2}=\frac{y+1}{-1}=\frac{z-2}{0}$ is α, then $28\alpha^2$ is equal to .... **[Numerical Value Type, 2023 Main]**

74. Let the foot of perpendicular of the point $P(3, -2, -9)$ on the plane passing through the points $(-1, -2, -3)$, $(9, 3, 4)$, $(9, -2, 1)$ be $Q(\alpha, \beta, \gamma)$. Then, distance of Q from the origin is **[Single Correct Type, 2023 Main]**

(a) $\sqrt{29}$ (b) $\sqrt{42}$ (c) $\sqrt{35}$ (d) $\sqrt{38}$

75. Let N be the foot of perpendicular from the point $P(1, -2, 3)$ on the line passing through the points $(4, 5, 8)$ and $(1, -7, 5)$. Then, the distance of N from the plane $2x - 2y + z + 5 = 0$ is **[Single Correct Type, 2023 Main]**

(a) 9 (b) 7 (c) 6 (d) 8

76. Let the equation of plane passing through the line of intersection of the planes $x + 2y + az = 2$ and $x - y + z = 3$ be $5x - 11y + bz = 6a - 1$. For $c \in Z$, if the distance of this plane from the point $(a, -c, c)$ is $\frac{2}{\sqrt{a}}$, then $\frac{a+b}{c}$ is equal to **[Single Correct Type, 2023 Main]**

(a) 2 (b) -4 (c) -2 (d) 4

77. Let P be the plane passing through the points $(5, 3, 0)$, $(13, 3, -2)$ and $(1, 6, 2)$. For, $\alpha \in N$, if the distances of the points $A(3, 4, \alpha)$ and $B(2, \alpha, a)$ from the plane P are 2 and 3 respectively, then the positive value of a is **[Single Correct Type, 2023 Main]**

(a) 3 (b) 6 (c) 5 (d) 4

78. Let the line passing through the points $P(2, -1, 2)$ and $Q(5, 3, 4)$ meet the plane $x - y + z = 4$ at the point R. Then, the distance of the point R from the plane $x + 2y + 3z + 2 = 0$ measured parallel to the line $\frac{x-7}{2} = \frac{y+3}{2} = \frac{z-2}{1}$ is equal to **[Single Correct Type, 2023 Main]**

(a) $\sqrt{189}$ (b) $\sqrt{31}$ (c) 3 (d) $\sqrt{61}$

79. If equation of the plane that contains the point $(-2, 3, 5)$ and is perpendicular to each of the planes $2x + 4y + 5z = 8$ and $3x - 2y + 3z = 5$ is $\alpha x + \beta y + \gamma z + 97 = 0$, then $\alpha + \beta + \gamma =$ **[Single Correct Type, 2023 Main]**

(a) 17 (b) 18 (c) 16 (d) 15

80. Let (α, β, γ) be the image of the point $P(2, 3, 5)$ in the plane $2x + y - 3z = 6$. Then, $\alpha + \beta + \gamma$ is equal to **[Single Correct Type, 2023 Main]**

(a) 10 (b) 12
(c) 5 (d) 9

81. Let the image of the point $P(1, 2, 6)$ in the plane passing through the points $A(1, 2, 0)$, $B(1, 4, 1)$ and $C(0, 5, 1)$ be $Q(\alpha, \beta, \gamma)$. Then, $(\alpha^2 + \beta^2 + \gamma^2)$ is equal to **[Single Correct Type, 2023 Main]**

(a) 70 (b) 76
(c) 62 (d) 65

82. If the equation of the plane containing the line $x + 2y + 3z - 4 = 0 = 2x + y - z + 5$ and perpendicular to the plane $\mathbf{r} = (\hat{\mathbf{i}} - \hat{\mathbf{j}}) + \lambda(\hat{\mathbf{i}} + \hat{\mathbf{j}} + \hat{\mathbf{k}}) + \mu(\hat{\mathbf{i}} - 2\hat{\mathbf{j}} + 3\hat{\mathbf{k}})$ is $ax + by + cz = 4$, then $(a - b + c)$ is equal to **[Single Correct Type, 2023, Main]**

(a) 20 (b) 24 (c) 18 (d) 22

83. A plane P contains the line of intersection of the plane $\mathbf{r} \cdot (\hat{\mathbf{i}} + \hat{\mathbf{j}} + \hat{\mathbf{k}}) = 6$ and $\mathbf{r} \cdot (2\hat{\mathbf{i}} + 3\hat{\mathbf{j}} + 4\hat{\mathbf{k}}) = -5$. If P passes through the point $(0, 2, -2)$, then the square of distance of the point $(12, 12, 18)$ from the plane P is **[Single Correct Type, 2023 Main]**

(a) 620 (b) 155
(c) 1240 (d) 310

84. Let the image of the point $P(2, -1, 3)$ in the plane $x + 2y - z = 0$ be Q. Then, the distance of the plane $3x + 2y + z + 29 = 0$ from the point Q is **[Single Correct Type, 2023 Main]**

(a) $\frac{24\sqrt{2}}{7}$ (b) $2\sqrt{14}$
(c) $\frac{22\sqrt{2}}{7}$ (d) $3\sqrt{14}$

85. The plane, passing through the points $(0, -1, 2)$ and $(-1, 2, 1)$ and parallel to the line passing through $(5, 1, -7)$ and $(1, -1, -1)$, also passes through the point **[Single Correct Type, 2023 Main]**

(a) $(2, 0, 1)$ (b) $(-2, 5, 0)$
(c) $(1, -2, 1)$ (d) $(0, 5, -2)$

86. The distance of the point $(-1, 2, 3)$ from the plane $\mathbf{r} \cdot (\hat{\mathbf{i}} - 2\hat{\mathbf{j}} + 3\hat{\mathbf{k}}) = 10$ parallel to the line of the shortest distance between the lines $\mathbf{r} = (\hat{\mathbf{i}} - \hat{\mathbf{j}}) + \lambda(2\hat{\mathbf{i}} + \hat{\mathbf{k}})$ and $\mathbf{r} = (2\hat{\mathbf{i}} - \hat{\mathbf{j}}) + \mu(\hat{\mathbf{i}} - \hat{\mathbf{j}} + \hat{\mathbf{k}})$ is **[Single Correct Type, 2023 Main]**

(a) $3\sqrt{6}$ (b) $2\sqrt{6}$
(c) $2\sqrt{5}$ (d) $3\sqrt{5}$

87. Let the plane $P: 4x - y + z = 10$ be rotated by an angle $\frac{\pi}{2}$ about its line of intersection with the plane $x + y - z = 4$. If α is the distance of the point $(2, 3, -4)$ from the new position of the plane P, then 35α is equal to **[Single Correct Type, 2023 Main]**

(a) 126 (b) 90
(c) 85 (d) 105

88. Let P be the point of intersection of the line $\frac{x+3}{3} = \frac{y+2}{1} = \frac{1-z}{2}$ and the plane $x + y + z = 2$. If the distance of the point P from the plane $3x - 4y + 12z = 32$ is q, then q and $2q$ are the roots of the equation **[Single Correct Type, 2023 Main]**

(a) $x^2 - 18x + 72 = 0$ (b) $x^2 + 18x + 72 = 0$
(c) $x^2 - 18x - 72 = 0$ (d) $x^2 + 18x - 72 = 0$

89. Let two vertices of a ΔABC be (2, 4, 6) and (0, – 2, – 5), and its centroid be (2, 1, – 1). If the image of the third vertex in the plane $x + 2y + 4z = 11$ is (α, β, γ), then $\alpha\beta + \beta\gamma + \gamma\alpha$ is equal to **[Single Correct Type, 2023 Main]**

(a) 70 (b) 74 (c) 72 (d) 76

90. Let P be the plane passing through the line $\frac{x-1}{1} = \frac{y-2}{-3} = \frac{z+5}{7}$ and the point (2, 4, – 3). If the image of the point (– 1, 3, 4) in the plane P is (α, β, γ), then $\alpha + \beta + \gamma$ is equal to **[Single Correct Type, 2023 Main]**

(a) 9 (b) 11
(c) 12 (d) 10

91. If the equation of the plane passing through the line of intersection of the planes $2x - y + z = 3$, $4x - 3y + 5z + 9 = 0$ and parallel to the line $\frac{x+1}{-2} = \frac{y+3}{4} = \frac{z-2}{5}$ is $ax + by + cz + 6 = 0$, then $a + b + c$ is equal to **[Single Correct Type, 2023 Main]**

(a) 14 (b) 15
(c) 12 (d) 13

92. Let the plane P passess through the intersection of the planes $2x + 3y - z = 2$ and $x + 2y + 3z = 6$ and be perpendicular to the plane $2x + y - z + 1 = 0$. If d is the distance of P from the point (– 7, 1, 1), then d^2 is equal to **[Single Correct Type, 2023 Main]**

(a) $\frac{25}{83}$ (b) $\frac{250}{82}$
(c) $\frac{250}{83}$ (d) $\frac{15}{53}$

93. Let the plane $P: 8x + \alpha_1 y + \alpha_2 z + 12 = 0$ be parallel to the line $L: \frac{x+2}{2} = \frac{y-3}{3} = \frac{z+4}{5}$. If the intercept of P on the Y-axis is 1, then the distance between P and L is **[Single Correct Type, 2023 Main]**

(a) $\sqrt{7/2}$ (b) $\frac{6}{\sqrt{14}}$
(c) $\sqrt{14}$ (d) $\sqrt{2/7}$

94. Let P be the plane. passing through the point (1, – 1, – 5) and perpendicular to the line joining the points (4, 1, – 3) and (2, 4, 3). Then, the distance of P from the point (3, – 2, 2) is **[Single Correct Type, 2023 Main]**

(a) 7 (b) 6
(c) 4 (d) 5

95. The foot of perpendicular from the origin O to a plane P which meets the coordinate axes at the points A, B, C is $(2, a, 4)$, $a \in N$. If the volume of the tetrahedron $OABC$ is 144 cu units, then which of the following points is not on P? **[Single Correct Type, 2023 Main]**

(a) (0, 6, 3) (b) (3, 0, 4)
(c) (0, 4, 4) (d) (2, 2, 4)

96. If a plane passes through the points $(-1, k, 0)$, $(2, k, -1)$, (1, 1, 2) and is parallel to the line $\frac{x-1}{1} = \frac{2y+1}{2} = \frac{z+1}{-1}$, then the value of $\frac{k^2+1}{(k-1)(k-2)}$ is **[Single Correct Type, 2023 Main]**

(a) $\frac{17}{5}$ (b) $\frac{5}{17}$ (c) $\frac{6}{13}$ (d) $\frac{13}{6}$

97. The line l_1 passes through the point (2,6,2) and is perpendicular to the plane $2x + y - 2z = 10$. Then, the shortest distance between the line l_1 and the line $\frac{x+1}{2} = \frac{y+4}{-3} = \frac{z}{2}$ is **[Single Correct Type, 2023 Main]**

(a) 13/3 (b) 9 (c) 7 (d) 19/3

98. A vector **v** in the first octant is inclined to the X-axis at 60°, to the Y-axis at 45° and to the Z-axis at an acute angle. If a plane passing through the points $(\sqrt{2}, -1, 1)$ and (a, b, c) is normal to **v**, then **[Single Correct Type, 2023 Main]**

(a) $a + b + \sqrt{2}c = 1$ (b) $a + \sqrt{2}b + c = 1$
(c) $\sqrt{2}a + b + c = 1$ (d) $\sqrt{2}a - b + c = 1$

99. The plane $2x - y + z = 4$ intersects the line segment joining the points $A(a, -2, 4)$ and $B(2, b, -3)$ at the point C in the ratio 2 : 1 and the distance of the point C from the origin is $\sqrt{5}$. If $ab < 0$ and P is the point $(a - b, b, 2b - a)$, then CP^2 is equal to **[Single Correct Type, 2023 Main]**

(a) $\frac{97}{3}$ (b) $\frac{17}{3}$ (c) $\frac{16}{3}$ (d) $\frac{73}{3}$

100. If the lines $\frac{x-1}{1} = \frac{y-2}{2} = \frac{z+3}{1}$ and $\frac{x-a}{2} = \frac{y+2}{3} = \frac{z-3}{1}$ intersect at the point P, then the distance of the point P from the plane $z = a$ is **[Single Correct Type, 2023 Main]**

(a) 22 (b) 10 (c) 28 (d) 16

101. The distance of the point (– 1, 9, – 16) from the plane $2x + 3y - z = 5$ measured parallel to the line $\frac{x+4}{3} = \frac{2-y}{4} = \frac{z-3}{12}$ is **[Single Correct Type, 2023 Main]**

(a) $20\sqrt{2}$ (b) 26 (c) 31 (d) $13\sqrt{2}$

102. If the foot of the perpendicular drawn from (1, 9, 7) to the line passing through the point (3, 2, 1) and parallel to the planes $x + 2y + z = 0$ and $3y - z = 3$ is (α, β, γ), then $\alpha + \beta + \gamma$ is equal to **[Single Correct Type, 2023 Main]**

(a) – 1 (b) 5
(c) 3 (d) 1

103. Let the plane containing the line of intersection of the planes $P_1 : x + (\lambda + 4)y + z = 1$ and $P_2 : 2x + y + z = 2$ pass through the points $(0, 1, 0)$ and $(1, 0, 1)$. Then, the distance of the point $(2\lambda, \lambda, -\lambda)$ from the plane P_2 is

[Single Correct Type, 2023 Main]

(a) $2\sqrt{6}$ (b) $4\sqrt{6}$
(c) $5\sqrt{6}$ (d) $3\sqrt{6}$

104. Let the plane P contain the line $2x + y - z - 3 = 0 = 5x - 3y + 4z + 9$ and be parallel to the line $\frac{x+2}{2} = \frac{3-y}{-4} = \frac{z-7}{5}$. Then, the distance of the point $A(8, -1, -19)$ from the plane P measured parallel to the line $\frac{x}{-3} = \frac{y-5}{4} = \frac{2-z}{-12}$ is equal to ....

[Numerical Value Type, 2023 Main]

105. Let the line $l : x = \frac{1-y}{-2} = \frac{z-3}{\lambda}$, $\lambda \in R$ meet the plane $P : x + 2y + 3z = 4$ at the point (α, β, γ). If the angle between the line l and the plane P is $\cos^{-1}\left(\sqrt{\frac{5}{14}}\right)$, then $\alpha + 2\beta + 6\gamma$ is equal to ....

[Numerical Value Type, 2023 Main]

106. Let the foot of perpendicular from the point $A(4, 3, 1)$ on the plane $P : x - y + 2z + 3 = 0$ be N. If $B(5, \alpha, \beta)$, $\alpha, \beta \in Z$ is a point on plane P such that the area of the ΔABN is $3\sqrt{2}$, then $\alpha^2 + \beta^2 + \alpha\beta$ is equal to ....

[Numerical Value Type, 2023 Main]

107. Let λ_1 and λ_2 be the values of λ for which the points $\left(\frac{5}{2}, 1, \lambda\right)$ and $(-2, 0, 1)$ are at equal distance from the plane $2x + 3y - 6z + 7 = 0$. If $\lambda_1 > \lambda_2$, then the distance of the point $(\lambda_1 - \lambda_2, \lambda_2, \lambda_1)$ from the line $\frac{x-5}{1} = \frac{y-1}{2} = \frac{z+7}{2}$ is ....

[Numerical Value Type, 2023 Main]

108. Let $\alpha x + \beta y + \gamma z = 1$ be the equation of a plane passing through the point $(3, -2, 5)$ and perpendicular to the line joining the points $(1, 2, 3)$ and $(-2, 3, 5)$. Then, the value of $\alpha\beta\gamma$ is equal to ....

[Numerical Value Type, 2023 Main]

109. The point of intersection C of the plane $8x + y + 2z = 0$ and the line joining the points $A(-3, -6, 1)$ and $B(2, 4, -3)$ divides the line segment AB internally in the ratio $k : 1$. If a, b, c ($|a|, |b|, |c|$ are coprime) are the direction ratios of the perpendicular from the point C on the line $\frac{1-x}{1} = \frac{y+4}{2} = \frac{z+2}{3}$, then $|a + b + c|$ is equal to ....

[Numerical Value Type, 2023 Main]

110. Let the line $L : \frac{x-1}{2} = \frac{y+1}{-1} = \frac{z-3}{1}$ intersect the plane $2x + y + 3z = 16$ at the point P. Let the point Q be the foot of perpendicular from the point $R(1, -1, -3)$ on the line L. If α is the area of ΔPQR, then α^2 is equal to ....

[Numerical Value Type, 2023 Main]

111. Let the equation of the plane P containing the line $x + 10 = \frac{8-y}{2} = z$ be $ax + by + 3z = 2(a + b)$ and the distance of the plane P from the point $(1, 27, 7)$ be c. Then, $a^2 + b^2 + c^2$ is equal to ....

[Numerical Value Type, 2023 Main]

112. Let the equation of the plane passing through the line $x - 2y - z - 5 = 0 = x + y + 3z - 5$ and parallel to the line $x + y + 2z - 7 = 0 = 2x + 3y + z - 2$ be $ax + by + cz = 65$. Then, the distance of the point (a, b, c) from the plane $2x + 2y - z + 16 = 0$ is ....

[Numerical Value Type, 2023 Main]

113. If two straight lines whose direction cosines are given by the relations $l + m - n = 0$ and $3l^2 + m^2 + cnl = 0$ are parallel, then the positive value of c is

[Single Correct Type, 2022 Main]

(a) 6 (b) 4
(c) 3 (d) 2

114. Let $P(-2, -1, 1)$ and $Q\left(\frac{56}{17}, \frac{43}{17}, \frac{111}{17}\right)$ be the vertices of the rhombus $PQRS$. If the direction ratios of the diagonal RS are $\alpha, -1, \beta$, where both α and β are integers of minimum absolute values, then $\alpha^2 + \beta^2$ is equal to ....

[Numerical Value Type, 2022 Main]

115. If the length of the perpendicular drawn from the point $P(a, 4, 2)$, $a > 0$ on the line $\frac{x+1}{2} = \frac{y-3}{3} = \frac{z-1}{-1}$ is $2\sqrt{6}$ units and $Q(\alpha_1, \alpha_2, \alpha_3)$ is the image of the point P in this line, then $a + \sum_{i=1}^{3} \alpha_i$ is equal to

[Single Correct Type, 2022 Main]

(a) 7 (b) 8
(c) 12 (d) 14

116. The shortest distance between the lines $\frac{x+7}{-6} = \frac{y-6}{7} = z$ and $\frac{7-x}{2} = y - 2 = z - 6$ is

[Single Correct Type, 2022 Main]

(a) $2\sqrt{29}$ units (b) 1 unit
(c) $\sqrt{\frac{37}{29}}$ units (d) $\frac{\sqrt{29}}{2}$ units

117. If the two lines $l_1 : \frac{x-2}{3} = \frac{y+1}{-2}, z = 2$ and $l_2 : \frac{x-1}{1} = \frac{2y+3}{\alpha} = \frac{z+5}{2}$ are perpendicular, then an angle between the lines l_2 and $l_3 : \frac{1-x}{3} = \frac{2y-1}{-4} = \frac{z}{4}$ is

[Single Correct Type, 2022 Main]

(a) $\cos^{-1}\left(\frac{29}{4}\right)$ (b) $\sec^{-1}\left(\frac{29}{4}\right)$

(c) $\cos^{-1}\left(\frac{2}{29}\right)$ (d) $\cos^{-1}\left(\frac{2}{\sqrt{29}}\right)$

118. Consider a ΔABC whose vertices are $A(0, \alpha, \alpha)$, $B(\alpha, 0, \alpha)$ and $C(\alpha, \alpha, 0)$, $\alpha > 0$. Let D be a point moving on the line $x + z - 3 = 0 = y$ and G be the centroid of ΔABC. If the minimum length of GD is $\sqrt{\frac{57}{2}}$, then α is equal to ....

[Numerical Value Type, 2022 Main]

119. If the shortest distance between the lines $\mathbf{r} = (-\hat{\mathbf{i}} + 3\hat{\mathbf{k}}) + \lambda(\hat{\mathbf{i}} - a\hat{\mathbf{j}})$ and $\mathbf{r} = (-\hat{\mathbf{j}} + 2\hat{\mathbf{k}}) + \mu(\hat{\mathbf{i}} - \hat{\mathbf{j}} + \hat{\mathbf{k}})$ is $\sqrt{\frac{2}{3}}$, then the integral value of a is equal to .... .

[Numerical Value Type, 2022 Main]

120. A vector $\mathbf{a}$ is parallel to the line of intersection of the plane determined by the vectors $\hat{\mathbf{i}}, \hat{\mathbf{i}} + \hat{\mathbf{j}}$ and the plane determined by the vectors $\hat{\mathbf{i}} - \hat{\mathbf{j}}, \hat{\mathbf{i}} + \hat{\mathbf{k}}$. The obtuse angle between $\mathbf{a}$ and the vector $\mathbf{b} = \hat{\mathbf{i}} - 2\hat{\mathbf{j}} + 2\hat{\mathbf{k}}$.

[Single Correct Type, 2022 Main]

(a) $\frac{3\pi}{4}$ (b) $\frac{2\pi}{3}$ (c) $\frac{4\pi}{5}$ (d) $\frac{5\pi}{6}$

121. A plane E is perpendicular to the two planes $2x - 2y + z = 0$ and $x - y + 2z = 4$ and passes through the point $P(1, -1, 1)$. If the distance of the plane E from the point $Q(a, a, 2)$ is $3\sqrt{2}$, then$(PQ)^2$ is equal to

[Single Correct Type, 2022 Main]

(a) 9 units (b) 12 units

(c) 21 units (d) 33 units

122. In the mirror image of the point (2, 4, 7) in the plane $3x - y + 4z = 2$ is (a, b, c), then $2a + b + 2c$ is equal to

[Single Correct Type, 2022 Main]

(a) 54 (b) 50 (c) -6 (d) -42

123. The acute angle between the planes P_1 and P_2, when P_1 and P_2 are the planes passing through the intersection of the planes $5x + 8y + 13z - 29 = 0$ and $8x - 7y + z - 20 = 0$ and the points (2, 1, 3) and (0, 1, 2) respectively, is

[Single Correct Type, 2022 Main]

(a) $\frac{\pi}{3}$ (b) $\frac{\pi}{4}$ (c) $\frac{\pi}{6}$ (d) $\frac{\pi}{12}$

124. Let the points on the plane P be equidistant from the points $(-4, 2, 1)$ and $(2, -2, 3)$. Then, the acute angle between the plane P and the plane $2x + y + 3z = 1$ is

[Single Correct Type, 2022 Main]

(a) $\frac{\pi}{6}$ (b) $\frac{\pi}{4}$ (c) $\frac{\pi}{3}$ (d) $\frac{5\pi}{12}$

125. Let $P_1 : \mathbf{r} \cdot (2\hat{\mathbf{i}} + \hat{\mathbf{j}} - 3\hat{\mathbf{k}}) = 4$ be a plane. Let P_2 be another plane which passes through the points $(2, -3, 2)$, $(2, -2, -3)$ and $(1, -4, 2)$. If the direction ratios of the line of intersection of P_1 and P_2 be $16, \alpha, \beta$, then the value of $\alpha + \beta$ is equal to .... **[Numerical Value Type, 2022 Main]**

126. If the foot of the perpendicular from the point $A(-1, 4, 3)$ on the plane $P : 2x + my + nz = 4$, is $\left(-2, \frac{7}{2}, \frac{3}{2}\right)$, then the distance of the point A from the plane P, measured parallel to a line with direction ratios $3, -1, -4$, is equal to **[Single Correct Type, 2022 Main]**

(a) 1 (b) $\sqrt{26}$ (c) $2\sqrt{2}$ (d) $\sqrt{14}$

127. The distance of the point $(3, 2, -1)$ from the plane $3x - y + 4z + 1 = 0$ along the line $\frac{2-x}{2} = \frac{y-3}{2} = \frac{z+1}{1}$ is equal to **[Single Correct Type, 2022 Main]**

(a) 9 units (b) 6 units

(c) 3 units (d) 2 units

128. Let the foot of the perpendicular from the point (1, 2, 4) on the line $\frac{x+2}{4} = \frac{y-1}{2} = \frac{z+1}{3}$ be P. Then, the distance of P from the plane $3x + 4y + 12z + 23 = 0$

[Single Correct Type, 2022 Main]

(a) 5 units (b) $\frac{50}{13}$ units (c) 4 units (d) $\frac{63}{13}$ units

129. Let Q be the mirror image of the point $P(1, 0, 1)$ with respect to the plane $S : x + y + z = 5$. If a line L passing through $(1, -1, -1)$, parallel to the line PQ meets the plane S at R, then QR^2 is equal to

[Single Correct Type, 2022 Main]

(a) 2 (b) 5 (c) 7 (d) 11

130. Let d be the distance between the foot of perpendiculars of the points $P(1, 2 - 1)$ and $Q(2, -1, 3)$ on the plane $-x + y + z = 1$. Then, d^2 is equal to...... .

[Numerical Value Type, 2022 Main]

131. Let the line $\frac{x-3}{7} = \frac{y-2}{-1} = \frac{z-3}{-4}$ intersect the plane containing the lines $\frac{x-4}{1} = \frac{y+1}{-2} = \frac{z}{1}$ and $4ax - y + 5z - 7a = 0 = 2x - 5y - z - 3$, $a \in R$ at the point $P(\alpha, \beta, \gamma)$. Then, the value of $\alpha + \beta + \gamma$ equals ....

[Numerical Value Type, 2022 Main]

132. Let the lines $L_1 : \mathbf{r} = \lambda(\hat{\mathbf{i}}+2\hat{\mathbf{j}}+3\hat{\mathbf{k}}), \lambda \in R$

$L_2 : \mathbf{r}=(\hat{\mathbf{i}}+3\hat{\mathbf{j}}+\hat{\mathbf{k}})+\mu(\hat{\mathbf{i}}+\hat{\mathbf{j}}+5\hat{\mathbf{k}}); \mu \in R$

intersect at the point S. If a plane $ax + by - z + d = 0$ passes through S and is parallel to both the lines L_1 and L_2, then the value of $a + b + d$ is equal to ....

[Numerical Value Type, 2022 Main]

133. Let α be the angle between the lines whose direction cosines satisfy the equations $l + m - n$ and $l^2 + m^2 - n^2 = 0$. Then, the value of $\sin^4 \alpha + \cos^4 \alpha$ is

[Single Correct Type, 2021, 18, 14, 13 Main]

(a) 3/4 (b) 5/8 (c) 1/2 (d) 3/8

134. If the foot of the perpendicular from point (4, 3, 8) on the line $L_1 : \frac{x-a}{l} = \frac{y-2}{3} = \frac{z-b}{4}, l \neq 0$ is (3, 5, 7), then the shortest distance between the line L_1 and line $L_2 : \frac{x-2}{3} = \frac{y-4}{4} = \frac{z-5}{5}$ is equal to

[Single Correct Type, 2021 Main]

(a) 1/2 (b) $1/\sqrt{6}$

(c) $\sqrt{2/3}$ (d) $1/\sqrt{3}$

135. If the mirror image of the point (1, 3, 5) with respect to the plane $4x - 5y + 2z = 8$ is (α, β, γ), then $5(\alpha + \beta + \gamma)$ equals **[Single Correct Type, 2021 Main]**

(a) 47 (b) 43

(c) 39 (d) 41

136. Consider the three planes

$P_1 : 3x + 15y + 21z = 9,$

$P_2 : x - 3y - z = 5$

and $P_3 : 2x + 10y + 14z = 5$

Then, which one of the following is true ?

[Single Correct Type, 2021 Main]

(a) P_1 and P_2 are parallel.

(b) P_1 and P_3 are parallel.

(c) P_2 and P_3 are parallel.

(d) P_1, P_2 and P_3 all are parallel.

137. Let P be a plane $lx + my + nz = 0$ containing the line, $\frac{1-x}{1} = \frac{y+4}{2} = \frac{z+2}{3}$. If plane P divides the line segment AB joining points $A(-3, -6, 1)$ and $B(2, 4, -3)$ in ratio $k : 1$, then the value of k is equal to

[Single Correct Type, 2021 Main]

(a) 1.5 (b) 3

(c) 2 (d) 4

138. If the lines $\frac{x-k}{1} = \frac{y-2}{2} = \frac{z-3}{3}$ and $\frac{x+1}{3} = \frac{y+2}{2} = \frac{z+3}{1}$ are coplanar, then the value of k is ....

[Numerical Value Type, 2021 Main]

139. The mirror image of the point (1, 2, 3) in a plane is $\left(-\frac{7}{3}, -\frac{4}{3}, -\frac{1}{3}\right)$. Which of the following points lies on this plane? **[Single Correct Type, 2020 Main]**

(a) (1, – 1, 1) (b) (– 1, – 1, 1)

(c) (1, 1, 1) (d) (– 1, – 1, – 1)

140. The distance of the point having position vector $-\hat{\mathbf{i}}+2\hat{\mathbf{j}}+6\hat{\mathbf{k}}$ from the straight line passing through the point (2, 3, – 4) and parallel to the vector, $6\hat{\mathbf{i}}+3\hat{\mathbf{j}}-4\hat{\mathbf{k}}$ is

[Single Correct Type, 2019 Main]

(a) $2\sqrt{13}$ units (b) $4\sqrt{3}$ units

(c) 6 units (d) 7 units

141. A plane which bisects the angle between the two given planes $2x - y + 2z - 4 = 0$ and $x + 2y + 2z - 2 = 0$, passes through the point **[Single Correct Type, 2019 Main]**

(a) (1, – 4, 1) (b) (1, 4, – 1)

(c) (2, 4, 1) (d) (2, – 4, 1)

142. If the line $\frac{x-2}{3} = \frac{y+1}{2} = \frac{z-1}{-1}$ intersects the plane $2x + 3y - z + 13 = 0$ at a point P and the plane $3x + y + 4z = 16$ at a point Q, then PQ is equal to

[Single Correct Type, 2019 Main]

(a) 14 (b) $\sqrt{14}$

(c) $2\sqrt{7}$ (d) $2\sqrt{14}$

EXERCISE 2

JEE Advanced Pattern

Single Option Correct Type Questions

1. The position vectors of points **a** and **b** are $\hat{\mathbf{i}}-\hat{\mathbf{j}}+3\hat{\mathbf{k}}$ and $3\hat{\mathbf{i}}+3\hat{\mathbf{j}}+3\hat{\mathbf{k}}$ respectively. The equation of a plane is $\mathbf{r}\cdot(5\hat{\mathbf{i}}+2\hat{\mathbf{j}}-7\hat{\mathbf{k}})+9=0$. The points **a** and **b**

(a) lie on the plane.
(b) lie on the same side of the plane.
(c) lie on the opposite side of the plane.
(d) None of the above

2. Let L_1 be the line $\mathbf{r}_1=2\hat{\mathbf{i}}+\hat{\mathbf{j}}-\hat{\mathbf{k}}+\lambda(\hat{\mathbf{i}}+2\hat{\mathbf{k}})$ and let L_2 be the another line $\mathbf{r}_2=3\hat{\mathbf{i}}+\hat{\mathbf{j}}+\alpha(\hat{\mathbf{i}}+\hat{\mathbf{j}}-\hat{\mathbf{k}})$. Let π be the plane which contains the line L_1 and is parallel to L_2. The distance of the plane π from the origin is

(a) $\sqrt{\frac{2}{7}}$ (b) $\frac{1}{7}$
(c) $\sqrt{6}$ (d) None of these

3. The length of projection of the line segment joining the points $(1, 0, -1)$ and $(-1, 2, 2)$ on the plane $x+3y-5z=6$, is equal to

(a) 2 (b) $\sqrt{\frac{271}{53}}$
(c) $\sqrt{\frac{472}{31}}$ (d) $\sqrt{\frac{474}{35}}$

4. A plane passing through (1, 1, 1) cuts positive direction of coordinate axes at A, B and C, then the volume of tetrahedron $OABC$ satisfies

(a) $V\le\frac{9}{2}$ (b) $V\ge\frac{9}{2}$
(c) $V=\frac{9}{2}$ (d) None of these

5. Two systems of rectangular axes have the same origin. If a plane cuts them at distance a, b, c and a', b', c' from the origin, then

(a) $\frac{1}{a^2}+\frac{1}{b^2}+\frac{1}{c^2}+\frac{1}{a'^2}+\frac{1}{b'^2}+\frac{1}{c'^2}=0$
(b) $\frac{1}{a^2}-\frac{1}{b^2}-\frac{1}{c^2}+\frac{1}{a'^2}-\frac{1}{b'^2}-\frac{1}{c'^2}=0$
(c) $\frac{1}{a^2}+\frac{1}{b^2}+\frac{1}{c^2}-\frac{1}{a'^2}-\frac{1}{b'^2}-\frac{1}{c'^2}=0$
(d) $\frac{1}{a^2}-\frac{1}{b^2}+\frac{1}{c^2}-\frac{1}{a'^2}+\frac{1}{b'^2}-\frac{1}{c'^2}=0$

6. A variable plane forms a tetrahedron of constant volume $64K^3$ with the coordinate planes and the origin, then locus of the centroid of the tetrahedron is

(a) $x^3+y^3+z^3=6k^3$ (b) $xyz=6k^3$
(c) $x^2+y^2+z^2=4k^2$ (d) $x^{-2}+y^{-2}+z^{-2}=4k^{-2}$

7. Consider the plane $(x, y, z)=(0, 1, 1)+\lambda(1, -1, 1)+\mu(2, -1. 0)$. The distance of this plane from the origin is

(a) $\frac{1}{3}$ (b) $\frac{\sqrt{3}}{2}$ (c) $\sqrt{\frac{3}{2}}$ (d) $\frac{2}{\sqrt{3}}$

8. A straight line is given by $\mathbf{r}=(1+t)\hat{\mathbf{i}}+3t\hat{\mathbf{j}}+(1-t)\hat{\mathbf{k}}$, where $t\in R$. If this line lies in the plane $x+y+cz=d$, then the value of $(c+d)$ is

(a) -1 (b) 1
(c) 7 (d) 9

9. The distance of the point $(-1, -5, -10)$ from the point of intersection of the line $\frac{x-2}{2}=\frac{y+1}{4}=\frac{z-2}{12}$ and the plane $x-y+z=5$ is

(a) $2\sqrt{11}$ units (b) $\sqrt{126}$ units
(c) 13 units (d) 14 units

10. The three vectors $\hat{\mathbf{i}}+\hat{\mathbf{j}}, \hat{\mathbf{j}}+\hat{\mathbf{k}}, \hat{\mathbf{k}}+\hat{\mathbf{i}}$ taken two at a time form three planes. The three unit vectors drawn perpendicular to these three planes form a parallelopiped of volume

(a) $\frac{1}{3}$ (b) 4 (c) $3\frac{\sqrt{3}}{4}$ (d) $\frac{4}{3\sqrt{3}}$

11. The orthogonal projection A' of the point A with position vector (1, 2, 3) on the plane $3x-y+4z=0$ is

(a) $(-1, 3, -1)$ (b) $\left(-\frac{1}{2}, \frac{5}{2}, 1\right)$
(c) $\left(\frac{1}{2}, -\frac{5}{2}, -1\right)$ (d) $(6., -7, -5)$

12. The equation of the line passing through (1, 1, 1) and perpendicular to the line of intersection of the planes $x+2y-4z=0$ and $2x-y+2z=0$ is

(a) $\frac{x-1}{5}=\frac{1-y}{1}=\frac{z-1}{2}$ (b) $\frac{x-1}{-5}=\frac{1-y}{1}=\frac{z-1}{2}$
(c) $\frac{x-1}{0}=\frac{1-y}{-10}=\frac{z-1}{-5}$ (d) $\frac{x-1}{-10}=\frac{y-1}{0}=\frac{z-1}{-5}$

13. A variable plane at a distance of 1 unit from the origin cuts the axes at A, B and C. If the centroid $D(x, y, z)$ of ΔABC satisfies the relation $\frac{1}{x^2} + \frac{1}{y^2} + \frac{1}{z^2} = K$, then the value of K is

(a) 3 (b) 1 (c) $\frac{1}{3}$ (d) 9

14. A tetrahedron has vertices $O(0, 0, 0)$, $A(1, 2, 1)$, $B(2, 1, 3)$ and $C(-1, 1, 2)$. Then, the angle between the faces OAB and ABC will be

(a) $\cos^{-1}\left(\frac{19}{35}\right)$ (b) $\cos^{-1}\left(\frac{17}{31}\right)$

(c) $30°$ (d) $90°$

15. The plane $x - y - z = 4$ is rotated through an angle $90°$ about its line of intersection with the plane $x + y + 2z = 4$. Then, the equation of the plane in its new position is

(a) $x + y + 4z = 20$ (b) $x + 5y + 4z = 20$

(c) $x + y - 4z = 20$ (d) $5x + y + 4z = 20$

16. A, B, C and D are four points in space. Then, $AC^2 + BD^2 + AD^2 + BC^2 \geq$

(a) $AB^2 + CD^2$ (b) $\frac{1}{AB^2} - \frac{1}{CD^2}$

(c) $\frac{1}{CD^2} - \frac{1}{AB^2}$ (d) None of these

17. If $|x_1| > |y_1| + |z_1|, |y_2| > |x_2| + |z_2|, |z_3| > |x_3| + |y_3|$, then $x_1\hat{\mathbf{i}} + y_1\hat{\mathbf{j}} + z_1\hat{\mathbf{k}}$, $x_2\hat{\mathbf{i}} + y_2\hat{\mathbf{j}} + z_2\hat{\mathbf{k}}$ and $x_3\hat{\mathbf{i}} + y_3\hat{\mathbf{j}} + z_3\hat{\mathbf{k}}$ are

(a) perpendicular (b) collinear

(c) coplanar (d) non-coplanar

18. The position vector of the point of intersection of three planes $\mathbf{r} \cdot \mathbf{n}_1 = q_1$, $\mathbf{r} \cdot \mathbf{n}_2 = q_2$, $\mathbf{r} \cdot \mathbf{n}_3 = q_3$, where $\mathbf{n}_1, \mathbf{n}_2$ and $\mathbf{n}_3$ are non-coplanar vectors, is

(a) $\frac{1}{[\mathbf{n}_1\ \mathbf{n}_2\ \mathbf{n}_3]}[q_3(\mathbf{n}_1 \times \mathbf{n}_2) + q_1(\mathbf{n}_2 \times \mathbf{n}_3) + q_2(\mathbf{n}_3 \times \mathbf{n}_1)]$

(b) $\frac{1}{[\mathbf{n}_1\ \mathbf{n}_2\ \mathbf{n}_3]}[q_1(\mathbf{n}_1 \times \mathbf{n}_2) + q_2(\mathbf{n}_2 \times \mathbf{n}_3) + q_3(\mathbf{n}_3 \times \mathbf{n}_1)]$

(c) $-\frac{1}{[\mathbf{n}_3\ \mathbf{n}_1\ \mathbf{n}_2]}[q_1(\mathbf{n}_1 \times \mathbf{n}_2) + q_2(\mathbf{n}_2 \times \mathbf{n}_3) + q_3(\mathbf{n}_3 \times \mathbf{n}_1)]$

(d) None of the above

19. A pentagon is formed by cutting a triangular corner from a rectangular piece of paper. The five sides of the pentagon have length 13, 19, 20, 25 and 31 not necessarily in that order. The area of the pentagon is

(a) 459 sq units

(b) 600 sq units

(c) 680 sq units

(d) 745 sq units

20. The locus of a point which moves in such a way that its distance from the line $\frac{x}{1} = \frac{y}{1} = \frac{z}{-1}$ is twice the distance from the plane $x + y + z = 0$ is

(a) $x^2 + y^2 + z^2 - 5x - 3y - 3z = 0$

(b) $x^2 + y^2 + z^2 + 5x + 3y + 3z = 0$

(c) $x^2 + y^2 + z^2 - 5xy - 3yz - 3zx = 0$

(d) $x^2 + y^2 + z^2 + 5xy + 3yz + 3zx = 0$

21. The shortest distance between any two opposite edges of the tetrahedron formed by planes $x + y = 0$, $y + z = 0$, $z + x = 0$, $x + y + z = a$ is constant, equal to

(a) $2a$ units (b) $\frac{2a}{\sqrt{6}}$ units

(c) $\frac{a}{\sqrt{6}}$ units (d) $\frac{2a}{\sqrt{3}}$ units

22. The shortest distance from (1, 1, 1) to the line of intersection of the pair of planes $xy + yz + zx + y^2 = 0$ is

(a) $\sqrt{\frac{8}{3}}$ units (b) $\frac{2}{\sqrt{3}}$ units (c) $\frac{1}{\sqrt{3}}$ unit (d) $\frac{2}{3}$ unit

23. $A = \begin{bmatrix} l_1 & m_1 & n_1 \\ l_2 & m_2 & n_2 \\ l_3 & m_3 & n_3 \end{bmatrix}$ and $B = \begin{bmatrix} p_1 & q_1 & r_1 \\ p_2 & q_2 & r_2 \\ p_3 & q_3 & r_3 \end{bmatrix}$, where p_i, q_i, r_i are the cofactors of the elements l_i, m_i, n_i for $i = 1, 2, 3$. If (l_1, m_1, n_1), (l_2, m_2, n_2) and (l_3, m_3, n_3) are the direction cosines of three mutually perpendicular lines, then (p_1, q_1, r_1), (p_2, q_2, r_2) and (p_3, q_3, r_3) are

(a) the direction cosines of three mutually perpendicular lines

(b) the direction ratios of three mutually perpendicular lines which are not direction cosines

(c) the direction cosines of three lines which need not be perpendicular

(d) the direction ratios but not the direction cosines of three lines which need not be perpendicular

24. In a regular tetrahedron, if the distance between the mid-points of opposite edges is unity, its volume is

(a) $\frac{1}{3}$ cu unit (b) $\frac{1}{2}$ cu unit

(c) $\frac{1}{\sqrt{2}}$ cu unit (d) $\frac{1}{6\sqrt{2}}$ cu unit

25. A variable plane makes intercepts on X, Y and Z-axes and it makes a tetrahedron of volume 64 cu units. The locus of foot of perpendicular from origin on this plane is

(a) $(x^2 + y^2 + z^2)^3 = 384\, xyz$

(b) $xyz = 681$

(c) $(x + y + z)\left(\frac{1}{x} + \frac{1}{y} + \frac{1}{z}\right)^2 = 16$

(d) $xyz\,(x + y + z) = 81$

More than One Correct Option Type Questions

26. Consider the family of planes $x + y + z = c$, where c is a parameter intersecting the coordinate axes at P, Q and R and α, β and γ are the angles made by each member of this family with positive X, Y and Z-axes. Which of the following interpretations hold good for this family?

(a) Each member of this family is equally inclined with coordinate axes.

(b) $\sin^2 \alpha + \sin^2 \beta + \sin^2 \gamma = 1$

(c) $\cos^2 \alpha + \cos^2 \beta + \cos^2 \gamma = 2$

(d) For $c = 3$ area of the ΔPQR is $3\sqrt{3}$ sq units.

27. Equation of the line through the point (1, 1, 1) and intersecting the lines $2x - y - z - 2 = 0 = x + y + z - 1$ and $x - y - z - 3 = 0 = 2x + 4y - z - 4$

(a) $x - 1 = 0, 7x + 17y - 3z - 134 = 0$

(b) $x - 1 = 0, 9x + 15y - 5z - 19 = 0$

(c) $x - 1 = 0, \frac{y-1}{1} = \frac{z-1}{3}$

(d) $x - 2y + 2z - 1 = 0, 9x + 15y - 5z - 19 = 0$

28. Through a point $P(h, k, l)$ a plane is drawn at right angles to OP to meet the coordinate axes in A, B and C. If $OP = p$, A_{xy} is area of projection of ΔABC on XY-plane, A_{yz} is area of projection of ΔABC on YZ-plane, then

(a) $\Delta = \left|\frac{p^5}{hkl}\right|$

(b) $\Delta = \left|\frac{p^5}{2hkl}\right|$

(c) $\frac{A_{xy}}{A_{yz}} = \left|\frac{l}{h}\right|$

(d) $\frac{A_{xy}}{A_{yz}} = \left|\frac{h}{l}\right|$

29. Which of the following statements is/are correct?

(a) If $\mathbf{n} \cdot \mathbf{a} = 0$, $\mathbf{n} \cdot \mathbf{b} = 0$ and $\mathbf{n} \cdot \mathbf{c} = 0$ for some non-zero vector $\mathbf{n}$, then $[\mathbf{a}\ \mathbf{b}\ \mathbf{c}] = 0$

(b) There exist a vector making angles 30° and 45° with X-axis and Y-axis.

(c) Locus of point for which $x = 3$ and $y = 4$ is a line parallel to the Z-axis whose distance from the Z-axis is 5.

(d) The vertices of regular tetrahedron are O, A, B, C where 'O' is the origin. The vector $\mathbf{OA} + \mathbf{OB} + \mathbf{OC}$ is perpendicular to the plane ABC.

30. Which of the following is/are correct about a tetrahedron ?

(a) Centroid of a tetrahedron lies on lines joining any vertex to the centroid opposite face.

(b) Centroid of a tetrahedron lies on the lines joining the mid point of the opposite faces.

(c) Distance of centroid from all the vertices are equal.

(d) None of the above

31. A variable plane cutting coordinate axes in A, B, C is at a constant distance from the origin. Then, the locus of centroid of the ΔABC is

(a) $x^{-2} + y^{-2} + z^{-2} = 16$

(b) $x^{-2} + y^{-2} + z^{-2} = 9$

(c) $\frac{1}{9}\left\{\frac{1}{x^2} + \frac{1}{y^2} + \frac{1}{z^2}\right\}^{-1} = 0$

(d) $x + y = 0$

32. The line $\frac{x-2}{3} = \frac{y+1}{2} = \frac{z-1}{-1}$ intersects the curve $x^2 + y^2 = r^2, z = 0$, then

(a) Equation of the plane through (0, 0, 0) perpendicular to the given line is $3x + 2y - z = 0$

(b) $r = \pm\sqrt{26}$

(c) $r = 6$

(d) $r = 7$

33. A vector equally inclined to the vectors $\hat{\mathbf{i}} - \hat{\mathbf{j}} + \hat{\mathbf{k}}$ and $\hat{\mathbf{i}} + \hat{\mathbf{j}} - \hat{\mathbf{k}}$, then the plane containing them is

(a) $\frac{\hat{\mathbf{i}} + \hat{\mathbf{j}} - \hat{\mathbf{k}}}{\sqrt{3}}$ (b) $\hat{\mathbf{j}} - \hat{\mathbf{k}}$

(c) $2\hat{\mathbf{i}}$ (d) $\hat{\mathbf{i}}$

34. A plane passes through a fixed point (a, b, c) and cuts the axes in A, B, C. The locus of a point equidistant from origin, A, B and C must be

(a) $ayz + bzx + cxy = 2xyz$ (b) $\frac{a}{x} + \frac{b}{y} + \frac{c}{z} = 1$

(c) $\frac{a}{x} + \frac{b}{y} + \frac{c}{z} = 2$ (d) $\frac{a}{x} + \frac{b}{y} + \frac{c}{z} = 3$

35. Let $\mathbf{A}$ be vector parallel to line of intersection of planes P_1 and P_2. Plane P_1 is parallel to the vectors $2\hat{\mathbf{j}} + 3\hat{\mathbf{k}}$ and $4\hat{\mathbf{j}} - 3\hat{\mathbf{k}}$ and that P_2 is parallel to $\hat{\mathbf{j}} - \hat{\mathbf{k}}$ and $3\hat{\mathbf{i}} + 3\hat{\mathbf{j}}$, then the angle between vector $\mathbf{A}$ and a given vector $2\hat{\mathbf{i}} + \hat{\mathbf{j}} - 2\hat{\mathbf{k}}$ is

(a) $\frac{\pi}{2}$ (b) $\frac{\pi}{4}$

(c) $\frac{\pi}{6}$ (d) $\frac{3\pi}{4}$

36. Consider the lines $x = y = z$ and the line $2x + y + z - 1 = 0 = 3x + y + 2z - 2$, then

(a) the shortest distance between the two lines is $\frac{1}{\sqrt{2}}$ unit.

(b) the shortest distance between the two lines is $\sqrt{2}$ units.

(c) plane containing 2nd line parallel to 1st line is $y - z + 1 = 0$.

(d) the shortest distance between the two lines is $\frac{\sqrt{3}}{2}$ units.

37. A line segment has length 63 and direction ratios are 3, −2,6. The components of the line vector are
(a) −27, 18, 54 (b) 27, −18, −54
(c) 27, −18, 54 (d) −27, 18, −54

38. The points $A(4, 5, 10)$, $B(2, 3, 4)$ and $C(1, 2, -1)$ are three vertices of a parallelogram $ABCD$, then
(a) vector equation of AB is $2\hat{\mathbf{i}} + 3\hat{\mathbf{j}} + 4\hat{\mathbf{k}} + \lambda(\hat{\mathbf{i}} + \hat{\mathbf{j}} + 3\hat{\mathbf{k}})$.
(b) cartesian equation of BC is $\frac{x-2}{1} = \frac{y-3}{1} = \frac{z-4}{5}$
(c) coordinates of D are (3, 4, 5).
(d) $ABCD$ is a rectangle.

39. Consider a pyramid $OPQRS$ located in the first octant $(x \geq 0, y \geq 0, z \geq 0)$ with O as origin, and OP and OR along the X-axis and the Y-axis, respectively. The base $OPQR$ of the pyramid is a square with $OP = 3$. The point S is directly above the mid-point T of diagonal OQ such that $TS = 3$. Then,
(a) the acute angle between OQ and OS is $\pi/3$
(b) the equation of the plane containing the ΔOQS is $x - y = 0$
(c) the length of the perpendicular from P to the plane containing the ΔOQS is $3/\sqrt{2}$
(d) the perpendicular distance from O to the straight line containing RS is $\sqrt{15/2}$

40. A rod of length 2 units whose one end is $(1, 0, -1)$ and other end touches the plane $x - 2y + 2z + 4 = 0$, then
(a) The rod sweeps the figure whose volume is π cu units.
(b) The area of the region which the rod traces on the plane is 2π.
(c) The length of projection of the rod on the plane is $\sqrt{3}$ units.
(d) The centre of the region which the rod traces on the plane is $\left(\frac{2}{3}, \frac{2}{3}, \frac{-5}{3}\right)$.

41. The volume of a right triangular prism $ABCA_1B_1C_1$ is equal to 3. Find the coordinates of the vertex A_1, if the coordinates of the base vertices of the prism are $A(1, 0, 1)$, $B(2, 0, 0)$ and $C(0, 1, 0)$.
(a) (− 2, 0, 2) (b) (0, − 2, 0)
(c) (0, 2, 0) (d) (2, 2, 2)

42. Let a plane passes through origin and is parallel to the line $\frac{x-1}{2} = \frac{y+3}{-1} = \frac{z+1}{-2}$ such that distance between plane and the line is $\frac{5}{3}$. Then, equation of the plane is
(a) $x - 2y + 2z = 0$ (b) $x - 2y - 2z = 0$
(c) $2x + 2y + z = 0$ (d) $x + y + z = 0$

43. $OABC$ is a regular tetrahedron of side unity, then
(a) the length of perpendicular from one vertex to opposite face is $\sqrt{2/3}$ units.
(b) the perpendicular distance from mid-point of $\overline{OA}$ to the plane ABC is $1/\sqrt{6}$ unit.
(c) the angle between two skew edges is $\pi/2$
(d) the distance of centroid of the tetrahedron from any vertex is $\sqrt{3/8}$ unit.

44. In R^3, let L be a straight line passing through the origin. Suppose that all the points on L are at a constant distance from the two planes $P_1 : x + 2y - z + 1 = 0$ and $P_2 : 2x - y + z - 1 = 0$. Let M be the locus of the foot of the perpendiculars drawn from the points on L to the plane P_1. Which of the following point(s) lie(s) on M ?
(a) $\left(0, -\frac{5}{6}, -\frac{2}{3}\right)$ (b) $\left(-\frac{1}{6}, -\frac{1}{3}, \frac{1}{6}\right)$
(c) $\left(-\frac{5}{6}, 0, \frac{1}{6}\right)$ (d) $\left(-\frac{1}{3}, 0, \frac{2}{3}\right)$

45. A variable plane which remains at a constant distance P from the origin (0) cuts the coordinate axes in A, B, C
(a) Locus of centroid of tetrahedron $OABC$ is $x^2y^2 + y^2z^2 + z^2x^2 = \frac{16}{p^2}x^2y^2z^2$
(b) Locus of centroid of tetrahedron $OABC$ is $x^2y^2 + y^2z^2 + z^2x^2 = \frac{4}{p^2}x^2y^2z^2$
(c) Parametric equation of the centroid of the tetrahedron is of the form $\left(\frac{P}{4}\sec\alpha\sec\beta, \frac{P}{4}\sec\alpha \operatorname{cosec}\beta, \frac{P}{4}\operatorname{cosec}\alpha\right)$, $\alpha, \beta \in (0, 2\pi) - \{\pi/2, \pi, 3\pi/2\}$
(d) None of the above

Passage Based Questions

Passage I
(Q. Nos. 46 and 47)

■ Let $A(1, 2, 3)$, $B(0, 0, 1)$ and $C(-1, 1, 1)$ are the vertices of ΔABC.

46. The equation of internal angle bisector through A to side BC is
(a) $\mathbf{r} = \hat{\mathbf{i}} + 2\hat{\mathbf{j}} + 3\hat{\mathbf{k}} + \mu(3\hat{\mathbf{i}} + 2\hat{\mathbf{j}} + 3\hat{\mathbf{k}})$
(b) $\mathbf{r} = \hat{\mathbf{i}} + 2\hat{\mathbf{j}} + 3\hat{\mathbf{k}} + \mu(3\hat{\mathbf{i}} + 4\hat{\mathbf{j}} + 3\hat{\mathbf{k}})$
(c) $\mathbf{r} = \hat{\mathbf{i}} + 2\hat{\mathbf{j}} + 3\hat{\mathbf{k}} + \mu(3\hat{\mathbf{i}} + 3\hat{\mathbf{j}} + 2\hat{\mathbf{k}})$
(d) $\mathbf{r} = \hat{\mathbf{i}} + 2\hat{\mathbf{j}} + 3\hat{\mathbf{k}} + \mu(3\hat{\mathbf{i}} + 3\hat{\mathbf{j}} + 4\hat{\mathbf{k}})$

47. The equation of altitude through B to side AC is
(a) $\mathbf{r} = \mathbf{k} + t(7\hat{\mathbf{i}} - 10\hat{\mathbf{j}} + 2\hat{\mathbf{k}})$ (b) $\mathbf{r} = \mathbf{k} + t(-7\hat{\mathbf{i}} + 10\hat{\mathbf{j}} + 2\hat{\mathbf{k}})$
(c) $\mathbf{r} = \mathbf{k} + t(7\hat{\mathbf{i}} - 10\hat{\mathbf{j}} - 2\hat{\mathbf{k}})$ (d) $\mathbf{r} = \mathbf{k} + t(7\hat{\mathbf{i}} + 10\hat{\mathbf{j}} + 2\hat{\mathbf{k}})$

Passage II
(Q. Nos. 48 and 49)

■ Consider a plane $x + y - z = 1$ and the point $A(1, 2, -3)$. A line L has the equation $x = 1 + 3r$, $y = 2 - r$, $z = 3 + 4r$

48. The coordinates of a point B of line L, such that AB is parallel to the plane, are
(a) (10, − 1, 15) (b) (−5, 4, −5)
(c) (4, 1, 7) (d) (−8, 5, −9)

49. Equation of the plane containing the line L and the point A has the equation

(a) $x - 3y + 5 = 0$ (b) $x + 3y - 7 = 0$
(c) $3x - y - 1 = 0$ (d) $3x + y - 5 = 0$

Passage III
(Q. Nos. 50 and 51)

- Consider a triangular pyramid $ABCD$ the position vector of whose angular points are $A(3, 0, 1)$, $B(-1, 4, 1)$, $C(5, 2, 3)$ and $D(0, -5, 4)$. Let G be the point of intersection of the medians of the ΔBCD.

50. The length of the perpendicular from the vertex D on the opposite face is

(a) $\frac{14}{\sqrt{6}}$ (b) $\frac{2}{\sqrt{6}}$
(c) $\frac{3}{\sqrt{6}}$ (d) None of these

51. Equation of the plane ABC is

(a) $x + y + 2z = 5$ (b) $x - y - 2z = 1$
(c) $2x + y - 2z = 4$ (d) $x + y - 2z = 1$

Passage IV
(Q. Nos. 52 and 53)

- A line L_1 passing through a point with position vector $\mathbf{p} = \hat{\mathbf{i}} + 2\hat{\mathbf{j}} + 3\hat{\mathbf{k}}$ and parallel to $\mathbf{a} = \hat{\mathbf{i}} + 2\hat{\mathbf{j}} + 3\hat{\mathbf{k}}$, Another line L_2 passing through a point with position vector $2\hat{\mathbf{i}} + 3\hat{\mathbf{j}} + 3\hat{\mathbf{k}}$ and parallel to $\mathbf{b} = 3\hat{\mathbf{i}} + \hat{\mathbf{j}} + 2\hat{\mathbf{k}}$.

52. Equation of plane equidistant from line L_1 and L_2 is

(a) $\hat{\mathbf{r}} \cdot (\hat{\mathbf{i}} - 7\hat{\mathbf{j}} - 5\hat{\mathbf{k}}) = 3$ (b) $\hat{\mathbf{r}} \cdot (\hat{\mathbf{i}} + 7\hat{\mathbf{j}} + 5\hat{\mathbf{k}}) = 3$
(c) $\hat{\mathbf{r}} \cdot (\hat{\mathbf{i}} - 7\hat{\mathbf{j}} - 5\hat{\mathbf{k}}) = 9$ (d) $\hat{\mathbf{r}} \cdot (\hat{\mathbf{i}} + 7\hat{\mathbf{j}} - 5\hat{\mathbf{k}}) = 9$

53. Equation of a line passing through the point $(2, -3, 2)$ and equally inclined to the line L_1 and L_2 may be equal to

(a) $\frac{x-2}{2} = \frac{y-3}{-1} = \frac{z-2}{1}$
(b) $\frac{x-2}{2} = y + 3 = z - 2$
(c) $\frac{x-2}{-4} = \frac{y+3}{3} = \frac{z-5}{2}$
(d) $\frac{x+2}{4} = \frac{y+3}{3} = \frac{z-2}{-5}$

Passage V
(Q. Nos. 54 and 55)

- For positive l, m and n, if the planes $x = ny + mz, y = lz + nx, z = mx + ly$ intersect in a straight line, then

54. $\cos^{-1} l + \cos^{-1} m + \cos^{-1} n$ is equal to

(a) 90° (b) 50°
(c) 180° (d) None of these

55. The equation of the straight line is $\frac{x}{a} = \frac{y}{b} = \frac{z}{c}$, where the ordered traid (a, b, c) is

(a) $\sqrt{1 - l^2}, \sqrt{1 - m^2}, \sqrt{1 - n^2}$
(b) l, m and n
(c) $\frac{1}{\sqrt{1 - l^2}}, \frac{m}{\sqrt{1 - m^2}}$ and $\frac{n}{\sqrt{1 - n^2}}$
(d) None of the above

Passage VI
(Q. Nos. 56 and 57)

- If $\mathbf{a} = 6\hat{\mathbf{i}} + 7\hat{\mathbf{j}} + 7\hat{\mathbf{k}}$, $\mathbf{b} = 3\hat{\mathbf{i}} + 2\hat{\mathbf{j}} - 2\hat{\mathbf{k}}$, $P(1, 2, 3)$

56. The position vector of L, the foot of the perpendicular from P on the line $\mathbf{r} = \mathbf{a} + \lambda\mathbf{b}$ is

(a) $6\hat{\mathbf{i}} + 7\hat{\mathbf{j}} + 7\hat{\mathbf{k}}$ (b) $3\hat{\mathbf{i}} + 2\hat{\mathbf{j}} - 2\hat{\mathbf{k}}$
(c) $3\hat{\mathbf{i}} + 5\hat{\mathbf{j}} + 9\hat{\mathbf{k}}$ (d) $9\hat{\mathbf{i}} + 9\hat{\mathbf{j}} + 5\hat{\mathbf{k}}$

57. The image of the point P in the line $\mathbf{r} = \mathbf{a} + \lambda\mathbf{b}$ is

(a) $(11, 12, 11)$ (b) $(5, 2, -7)$
(c) $(5, 8, 15)$ (d) $(17, 16, 7)$

Passage VII
(Q. Nos. 58 and 59)

- $A(-2, 2, 3)$ and $B(13, -3, 13)$ and L is a line through A.

58. Coordinates of the point P which divides the join of A and B in the ratio $2 : 3$ internally are

(a) $\left(\frac{33}{5}, -\frac{2}{5}, 9\right)$ (b) $(4, 0, 7)$
(c) $\left(\frac{32}{5}, -\frac{12}{5}, \frac{17}{5}\right)$ (d) $(20, 0, 35)$

59. Equation of a line L, perpendicular to the line AB is

(a) $\frac{x+2}{15} = \frac{y-2}{-5} = \frac{z-3}{10}$ (b) $\frac{x-2}{3} = \frac{y+2}{13} = \frac{z+3}{2}$
(c) $\frac{x+2}{3} = \frac{y-2}{13} = \frac{z-3}{2}$ (d) $\frac{x-2}{15} = \frac{y+2}{-5} = \frac{z+3}{10}$

Passage VIII
(Q. Nos. 60 and 61)

- The vector equation of a plane is a relation satisfied by position vectors of all the points on the plane. If P is a plane and $\hat{\mathbf{n}}$ is a unit vector through origin which is perpendicular to the plane P, then vector equation of the plane must be $\mathbf{r} . \hat{\mathbf{n}} = d$, where d represents perpendicular distance of plane p from origin.

60. If A is a point vector $\mathbf{a}$, then perpendicular distance of A from the plane $\mathbf{r} . \hat{\mathbf{n}} = d$ must be

(a) $|d + \mathbf{a}\hat{\mathbf{n}}|$ (b) $|d - \mathbf{a}\hat{\mathbf{n}}|$
(c) $|\mathbf{a}| - d|$ (d) $|d - \hat{\mathbf{a}}|$

61. If **b** be the foot of perpendicular from A to the plane $\mathbf{r}.\hat{\mathbf{n}} = d$, then **b** must be
(a) $\mathbf{a} + (d - \mathbf{a}.\hat{\mathbf{n}})\,\hat{\mathbf{n}}$
(b) $\mathbf{a} - (d - \mathbf{a}.\hat{\mathbf{n}})\,\hat{\mathbf{n}}$
(c) $\mathbf{a} + \mathbf{a}.\hat{\mathbf{n}}$
(d) $\mathbf{a} - \mathbf{a}.\hat{\mathbf{n}}$

Stem Based Questions

Stem I
(Q. Nos. 62 and 63)

- Let the line L passes through the point $P(1, 0, 3)$ intersect the line $\frac{x}{2} = \frac{y-1}{3} = \frac{z-2}{1}$ at Q and parallel to the plane $x + y + z = 2$.

62. If the distance between P and Q is $\sqrt{\frac{k_1}{k_2}}$, then the value of $k_1 + k_2$ is equal to ………

63. If the angle between the line L and $\frac{x}{2} = \frac{y-1}{3} = \frac{z-2}{1}$ is $\cos^{-1}\left(\frac{a_1}{\sqrt{a_2}}\right)$, then the value of $|a_1 - a_2|$ is equal to ...

Stem II
(Q. Nos. 64 and 65)

- Consider the lines

$$L_1 : \frac{x+1}{3} = \frac{y+2}{1} = \frac{z+1}{2} \text{ and } L_2 : \frac{x-2}{1} = \frac{y+2}{2} = \frac{z-3}{3}$$

64. If the shortest distance between L_1 and L_2 is $\frac{p}{5\sqrt{q}}$, then value of pq is equal to ……….

65. If the distance of the point (1, 1, 1) from the plane passing through the point $(-1, -2, -1)$ and whose normal is perpendicular to both the lines L_1 and L_2 is $\frac{13}{\sqrt{\lambda}}$, then the value of λ is ………

Stem III
(Q. Nos. 66 and 67)

- Let $A(2, 3, 5), B(-1, 3, 2), C(\lambda, 5, \mu)$ are the vertices of a triangle and its median through A i.e. AD is equally inclined to the coordinates axes.
On the basis of the above information answer the following

66. The value of $2\lambda - \mu$ is equal to ………

67. Projection of AB on BC is $\frac{-\lambda\sqrt{3}}{\sqrt{11}}$, then λ is equal to ………

Stem IV
(Q. Nos. 68 and 69)

- Given four points $A(2, 1, 0), B(1, 0, 1), C(3, 0, 1)$ and $D(0, 0, 2)$. Point D lies on a line L orthogonal to the plane determined by the points A, B and C.

68. The equation of the plane ABC is $\alpha x + \beta y + \gamma z = \delta$, then $\alpha + \beta + \gamma + \delta$ is equal to ………

69. The perpendicular distance of D from the plane ABC is λ, then $\sqrt{2}\,\lambda$ is equal to ………

Single Integer Type Questions

70. In a tetrahedron $OABC$, if $\mathbf{OA} = \hat{\mathbf{i}}$, $\mathbf{OB} = \hat{\mathbf{i}} + \hat{\mathbf{j}}$ and $\mathbf{OC} = \hat{\mathbf{i}} + 2\hat{\mathbf{j}} + \hat{\mathbf{k}}$, if shortest distance between edges OA and BC is m, then $\sqrt{2}m$ is equal to ……
(where, O is the origin)

71. A parallelopiped is formed by planes drawn through the points (2, 4, 5) and (5, 9, 7) parallel to the coordinate planes. The length of the diagonal of the parallelopiped is ………

72. If the shortest distance between the lines $\frac{x-3}{3} = \frac{y-8}{-1} = \frac{z-3}{1}$ and $\frac{x+3}{-3} = \frac{y+7}{2} = \frac{z-6}{4}$ is $\lambda\sqrt{30}$ units, then the value of λ is ………

73. If the planes $x - cy - bz = 0$, $cx - y + az = 0$ and $bx + ay - z = 0$ pass through a line, then the values of $a^2 + b^2 + c^2 + 2abc$ is ………..

74. If XZ-plane divide the join of point (2, 3, 4) and $(1, -1, 5)$ in the ratio $\lambda : 1$, then the integer λ should be equal to ……

75. If the ΔABC whose vertices are $A(-1, 1, 1)$, $B(1, -1, 1)$ and $C(1, 1, -1)$ is projected on XY-plane, then the area of the projected triangles is ……….

76. The equation of a plane which bisects the line joining (1, 5, 7) and $(-3, 1, -1)$ is $x + y + 2z = \lambda$, then λ must be ………..

77. The shortest distance between origin and a point on the space curve $x = 2\sin t$, $y = 2\cos t$, $z = 3t$ is ………..

78. Let P be a point in the first octant, whose image Q in the plane $x + y = 3$ (that is, the line segment PQ is perpendicular to the plane $x + y = 3$ and the mid-point of PQ lies in the plane $x + y = 3$) lies on the Z-axis. Let the distance of P from the X-axis be 5. If R is the image of P in the XY-plane, then the length of PR is ……… .

Numerical Value Type Questions

79. If the angle between the lines whose direction cosines has the relation $l+m+n=0$ and $2l^2+2m^2-n^2=0$ is $\cos^{-1}\left(\frac{-1}{k}\right)$, then the value of $\frac{k}{5}$ is equal to ....

80. If the point on the line $\frac{x+2}{3}=\frac{y+1}{2}=\frac{z-3}{2}$ at a distance of $3\sqrt{2}$ from the point (1, 2, 3) is $\left(\frac{a_1}{17}, \frac{a_2}{17}, \frac{a_3}{17}\right)$, then $(a_1+a_2+a_3)$ is equal to ....

81. A line passes through $(2,-1,3)$ and is perpendicular to the lines $\mathbf{r}\cdot(\hat{\mathbf{i}}+\hat{\mathbf{j}}-\hat{\mathbf{k}})+\lambda(2\hat{\mathbf{i}}-2\hat{\mathbf{j}}+\hat{\mathbf{k}})$ and $\mathbf{r}=(2\hat{\mathbf{i}}-\hat{\mathbf{j}}-3\hat{\mathbf{k}})+\mu(\hat{\mathbf{i}}+2\hat{\mathbf{j}}+2\hat{\mathbf{k}})$ is $(2\hat{\mathbf{i}}-\hat{\mathbf{j}}+3\hat{\mathbf{k}})+\mu(b_1\hat{\mathbf{i}}+b_2\hat{\mathbf{j}}+b_3\hat{\mathbf{k}})$, then the value of $\left|\frac{b_1b_2b_3}{5}\right|$ is equal to ....

82. If the equations of the two lines through the origin which intersect the line $\frac{x-3}{2}=\frac{y-3}{1}=\frac{z}{1}$ at angle of $\frac{\pi}{3}$ each is $\frac{x}{1}=\frac{y}{a}=\frac{z}{-1}$ and $\frac{x}{-1}=\frac{y}{b}=\frac{z}{-2}$, then value of $(a+b)^3$ is ....

83. Vertices B and C of ΔABC lie along the line $\frac{x+2}{2}=\frac{y-1}{1}=\frac{z-0}{4}$. The area of the triangle given that A has coordinates $(1,-1,2)$ and line segment BC has length 5 is $\sqrt{\frac{k_1}{k_2}}$, then the value of k_1+k_2 is equal to ......

84. If the distance of the point of intersection of the line $\frac{x-2}{3}=\frac{y+1}{4}=\frac{z-2}{12}$ and the plane $x-y+z=5$ from the point $(-1,-5,-10)$ is $2d$, then the value of d is ....

85. If the equation of the image of the plane $x-2y+2z-3=0$ in the plane $x+y+z-1=0$ is $ax+by+cz+d=0$, then the value of $|a+b+c+d|$ is equal to ....

86. Let G_1, G_2 and G_3 be the centroids of the triangular faces OBC, OCA and OAB of a tetrahedron $OABC$. If V_1 denotes the volume of tetrahedron $OABC$ and V_2 that of the parallelepiped with OG_1, OG_2 and OG_3 as three concurrent edges, then the value of V_1/V_2 is .... (where O is the origin)

87. A variable plane which remains at a constant distance p from the origin cuts the coordinate axes in A, B, C. The locus of the centroid of the tetrahedron $OABC$ is $x^2y^2+y^2z^2+z^2x^2=\frac{k}{p^2}x^2y^2z^2$, then $\frac{k}{5}$ is ....

88. If (l_1, m_1, n_1); (l_2, m_2, n_2) are DC's of two lines, then $(l_1m_2-l_2m_1)^2+(m_1n_2-m_2n_1)^2+(n_1l_2-n_2l_1)^2+(l_1l_2+m_1m_2+n_1n_2)^2=\lambda$, then the value of $\frac{\lambda}{2}$ is ....

89. If the coordinates (x, y, z) of the point S which is equidistant from the points $O(0,0,0)$, $A(n^5,0,0)$ $B(0,n^4,0)$, $C(0,0,n)$ obey the relation $2(x+y+z)+1=0$. If $n\in Z$, then $\frac{|n|}{5}=$ .... ($|\cdot|$ is the modulus function).

Matching Type Questions

90. Consider the following four pairs of line in Column I and match them with one or more entries in Column II.

Column I	Column II
(A) $L_1: x=1+t, y=t, z=2-5t$ $L_2: r=(2,1,-3)+\lambda(2,2,-10)$	(p) non-coplanar lines
(B) $L_1: \frac{x-1}{2}=\frac{y-3}{2}=\frac{z-2}{-1}$ $L_2: \frac{x-2}{1}=\frac{y-6}{-1}=\frac{z+2}{-1}$	(q) lines lie in a unique plane
(C) $L_1: x=-6t, y=1+9t, z=-3t$ $L_2: x=1+2s, y=4-3s, z=s$	(r) infinite planes containing both the lines
(D) $L_1: \frac{x}{1}=\frac{y-1}{2}=\frac{z-2}{3}$ $L_2: \frac{x-3}{-4}=\frac{y-2}{-3}=\frac{z-1}{2}$	(s) lines are not intersecting at a unique point

91. $P(0,3,-2)$, $Q(3,7,-1)$ and $R(1,-3,-1)$ are 3 given points. Let L_1 be the line passing through P and Q and L_2 be the line through R and parallel to the vector $\mathbf{V}=\hat{\mathbf{i}}+\hat{\mathbf{k}}$.

Column I	Column II
(A) Perpendicular distance of P from L_1	(p) $7\sqrt{3}$
(B) Shortest distance between L_1 and L_2	(q) 2
(C) Area of the ΔPQR	(r) 6
(D) Distance from (0, 0, 0) to the plane PQR	(s) $\frac{19}{\sqrt{147}}$

92. Consider the lines

$$L_1 : \frac{x-1}{2} = \frac{y}{-1} = \frac{z+3}{1},\ L_2 : \frac{x-4}{1} = \frac{y+3}{1} = \frac{z+3}{2}$$

and the planes $P_1 : 7x + y + 2z = 3, P_2 : 3x + 5y - 6z = 4$. Let $ax + by + cz = d$ the equation of the plane passing through the point of intersection of lines L_1 and L_2 and perpendicular to planes P_1 and P_2.

Match List I with List II and select the correct answer using the code given below the lists.

Column I		Column II	
(A)	$a =$	(p)	13
(B)	$b =$	(q)	– 3
(C)	$c =$	(r)	1
(D)	$d =$	(s)	– 2

93. A variable plane cuts the *X*, *Y* and *Z*-axes at the points, *A*, *B* and *C* respectively, such that the volume of the tetrahedron *OABC* remain constant equal to 32 cu units and *O* is the origin of the coordinate system.

Column I	Column II
(A) The locus of the centroid of the tetrahedron is	(p) $xyz = 24$
(B) The locus of the point equidistant from *O*, *A*, *B* and *C* is	(q) $(x^2 + y^2 + z^2) = 192\ xyz$
(C) The locus of the foot of perpendicular from origin to the plane is	(r) $xyz = 3$
(D) If *PA*, *PB* and *PC* are mutually perpendicular, then the locus of *P* is	(s) $(x^2 + y^2 + z^2)^3 = 1536\ xyz$

94. Match the Columns.

Column I	Column II
(A) The intersection point of the lines $\frac{x-1}{2} = \frac{y-2}{3} = \frac{z-3}{4}$ and $\frac{x-4}{5} = \frac{y-1}{2} = z$ is	(p) (2,5,7)
(B) Line $\frac{x-2}{3} = \frac{y-3}{4} = \frac{z-4}{5}$, the point on the line at a distance $10\sqrt{2}$ units from (2,3,4)	(q) (2, 3, 4)
(C) Point on the line $\frac{x-2}{3} = \frac{y-3}{4} = \frac{z-4}{5}$ at a distance $\sqrt{29}$ units from the origin	(r) $(-1,-1,-1)$
(D) Coordinates of the foot of the perpendicular from the point $P(3,-1,11)$ on the line $\frac{x}{2} = \frac{y-2}{3} = \frac{z-3}{4}$	(s) (8,11,14)

Previous Years Questions

95. Let *Q* be the cube with the set of vertices $\{(x_1, x_2, x_3) \in R^3 : x_1, x_2, x_3 \in \{0, 1\}\}$. Let *F* be the set of all twelve lines containing the diagonals of the six faces of the cube *Q*. Let *S* be the set of all four lines containing the main diagonals of the cube *Q*; for instance, the line passing through the vertices (0, 0, 0) and (1, 1, 1) is in *S*. For lines l_1 and l_2, let $d(l_1, l_2)$ denote the shortest distance between them. Then, the maximum value of $d(l_1, l_2)$, as l_1 varies over *F* and l_2 varies over *S*, is

[Single Correct Type, 2023 Adv.]

(a) $\frac{1}{\sqrt{6}}$ (b) $\frac{1}{\sqrt{8}}$ (c) $\frac{1}{\sqrt{3}}$ (d) $\frac{1}{\sqrt{12}}$

96. Let *P* be the plane $\sqrt{3}x + 2y + 3z = 16$ and let $S = \{\alpha\hat{\mathbf{i}} + \beta\hat{\mathbf{j}} + \gamma\hat{\mathbf{k}} : \alpha^2 + \beta^2 + \gamma^2 = 1$ and the distance of (α, β, γ) from the plane *P* is $7/2\}$.

Let **u**, **v** and **w** be three distinct vectors in *S* such that $[\mathbf{u} - \mathbf{v}] = [\mathbf{v} - \mathbf{w}] = [\mathbf{w} - \mathbf{u}]$. Let *V* be the volume of the parallelopiped determined by vectors **u**, **v** and **w**. Then, the value of $\frac{80}{\sqrt{3}} V$ is ....

[Numerical Value Type, 2023 Adv.]

97. Let l_1 and l_2 be the lines $\mathbf{r}_1 = \lambda(\hat{\mathbf{i}} + \hat{\mathbf{j}} + \hat{\mathbf{k}})$ and $\mathbf{r}_2 = (\hat{\mathbf{j}} - \hat{\mathbf{k}}) + \mu(\hat{\mathbf{i}} + \hat{\mathbf{k}})$, respectively. Let *X* be the set of all the planes *H* that contain the line l_1. For a plane *H*, let $d(H)$ denote the smallest possible distance between the points of l_2 and *H*. Let H_0 be a plane in *X* for which $d(H_0)$ is the maximum value of $d(H)$ as *H* varies over all planes in *X*.

Match each entry in **List-I** to the correct entries in **List-II**.

[Matching Type, 2023 Adv.]

List-I		List-II	
(P)	The value of $d(H_0)$ is	(1)	$\sqrt{3}$
(Q)	The distance of the point (0, 1, 2) from H_0 is	(2)	$\frac{1}{\sqrt{3}}$
(R)	The distance of origin from H_0 is	(3)	0
(S)	The distance of origin from the point of intersection of planes $y = z, x = 1$ and H_0 is	(4)	$\sqrt{2}$
		(5)	$\frac{1}{\sqrt{2}}$

The correct option is

	P	Q	R	S		P	Q	R	S
(a)	2	4	5	1	(b)	5	4	3	1
(c)	2	1	3	2	(d)	5	1	4	2

Match the conditions/expressions in Column I with values statements in Column II.

98. Let S be the reflection of a point Q with respect to the plane given by $\mathbf{r} = -(t+p)\hat{\mathbf{i}} + t\hat{\mathbf{j}} + (1+p)\hat{\mathbf{k}}$, where t, p are real parameters and $\hat{\mathbf{i}}, \hat{\mathbf{j}}, \hat{\mathbf{k}}$ are the unit vectors along the three positive coordinate axes. If the position vectors of Q and S are $10\hat{\mathbf{i}} + 15\hat{\mathbf{j}} + 20\hat{\mathbf{k}}$ and $\alpha\hat{\mathbf{i}} + \beta\hat{\mathbf{j}} + \gamma\hat{\mathbf{k}}$ respectively, then which of the following is/are TRUE ?

[More than One Option Correct, 2022 Adv.]

(a) $3(\alpha + \beta) = -101$
(b) $3(\beta + \gamma) = -71$
(c) $3(\gamma + \alpha) = -86$
(d) $3(\alpha + \beta + \gamma) = -121$

99. Let P_1 and P_2 be two planes given by

$P_1 : 10x + 15y + 12z - 60 = 0$
$P_2 : -2x + 5y + 4z - 20 = 0$

Which of the following straight lines can be an edge of some tetrahedron whose two faces lie on P_1 and P_2?

[More than One Option Correct, 2022 Adv.]

(a) $\dfrac{x-1}{0} = \dfrac{y-1}{0} = \dfrac{z-1}{5}$

(b) $\dfrac{x-6}{-5} = \dfrac{y}{2} = \dfrac{z}{3}$

(c) $\dfrac{x}{-2} = \dfrac{y-4}{5} = \dfrac{z}{4}$

(d) $\dfrac{x}{1} = \dfrac{y-4}{-2} = \dfrac{z}{3}$

100. Let L_1 and L_2 be the following straight lines.

$L_1 : \dfrac{x-1}{1} = \dfrac{y}{-1} = \dfrac{z-1}{3}$ and $L_2 : \dfrac{x-1}{-3} = \dfrac{y}{-1} = \dfrac{z-1}{1}$.

Suppose the straight line $L : \dfrac{x-\alpha}{l} = \dfrac{y-1}{m} = \dfrac{z-\gamma}{-2}$ lies in the plane containing L_1 and L_2 and passes through the point of intersection of L_1 and L_2. If the line L bisects the acute angle between the lines L_1 and L_2, then which of the following statements is/are TRUE?

[More than One Option Correct, 2020 Adv.]

(a) $\alpha - \gamma = 3$
(b) $l + m = 2$
(c) $\alpha - \gamma = 1$
(d) $l + m = 0$

101. Let $\alpha, \beta, \gamma, \delta$ be real numbers such that $\alpha^2 + \beta^2 + \gamma^2 \neq 0$ and $\alpha + \gamma = 1$. Suppose the point $(3, 2, -1)$ is the mirror image of the point $(1, 0, -1)$ with respect to the plane $\alpha x + \beta y + \gamma z = \delta$. Then, which of the following statements is/are TRUE?

[More than One Option Correct, 2020 Adv.]

(a) $\alpha + \beta = 2$
(b) $\delta - \gamma = 3$
(c) $\delta + \beta = 4$
(d) $\alpha + \beta + \gamma = \delta$

102. Three lines $L_1 : \mathbf{r} = \lambda\hat{\mathbf{i}}, \lambda \in R$, $L_2 : \mathbf{r} = \hat{\mathbf{k}} + \mu\hat{\mathbf{j}}, \mu \in R$ and $L_3 : \mathbf{r} = \hat{\mathbf{i}} + \hat{\mathbf{j}} + v\hat{\mathbf{k}}, v \in R$ are given. For which point(s) Q on L_2 can we find a point P on L_1 and a point R on L_3, so that P, Q and R are collinear?

[More than One Option Correct, 2019 Adv.]

(a) $\hat{\mathbf{k}}$
(b) $\hat{\mathbf{k}} + \hat{\mathbf{j}}$
(c) $\hat{\mathbf{k}} + \dfrac{1}{2}\hat{\mathbf{j}}$
(d) $\hat{\mathbf{k}} - \dfrac{1}{2}\hat{\mathbf{j}}$

103. Let L_1 and L_2 denote the lines $\mathbf{r} = \hat{\mathbf{i}} + \lambda(-\hat{\mathbf{i}} + 2\hat{\mathbf{j}} + 2\hat{\mathbf{k}})$, $\lambda \in R$ and $\mathbf{r} = \mu(2\hat{\mathbf{i}} - \hat{\mathbf{j}} + 2\hat{\mathbf{k}}), \mu \in R$ respectively. If L_3 is a line which is perpendicular to both L_1 and L_2 and cuts both of them, then which of the following options describe(s) L_3? **[More than One Option Correct, 2019 Adv.]**

(a) $\mathbf{r} = \dfrac{2}{9}(2\hat{\mathbf{i}} - \hat{\mathbf{j}} + 2\hat{\mathbf{k}}) + t(2\hat{\mathbf{i}} + 2\hat{\mathbf{j}} - \hat{\mathbf{k}}), t \in R$

(b) $\mathbf{r} = \dfrac{1}{3}(2\hat{\mathbf{i}} + \hat{\mathbf{k}}) + t(2\hat{\mathbf{i}} + 2\hat{\mathbf{j}} - \hat{\mathbf{k}}), t \in R$

(c) $\mathbf{r} = \dfrac{2}{9}(4\hat{\mathbf{i}} + \hat{\mathbf{j}} + \hat{\mathbf{k}}) + t(2\hat{\mathbf{i}} + 2\hat{\mathbf{j}} - \hat{\mathbf{k}}), t \in R$

(d) $\mathbf{r} = t(2\hat{\mathbf{i}} + 2\hat{\mathbf{j}} - \hat{\mathbf{k}}), t \in R$

104. Three lines are given by $\mathbf{r} = \lambda\hat{\mathbf{i}}, \lambda \in R$, $\mathbf{r} = \mu(\hat{\mathbf{i}} + \hat{\mathbf{j}}), \mu \in R$ and $\mathbf{r} = v(\hat{\mathbf{i}} + \hat{\mathbf{j}} + \hat{\mathbf{k}}), v \in R$. Let the lines cut the plane $x + y + z = 1$ at the points A, B and C respectively. If the area of the ΔABC is Δ then the value of $(6\Delta)^2$ equals ……….

[Numerical Value Type, 2019 Adv.]

EXERCISE 3
Challenging Problems

1. The plane $ax + by = 0$ is rotated through an angle α about its line of intersection with the plane $z = 0$. Show that the equation to the plane in new position is
$ax + by \pm z\sqrt{a^2 + b^2} \tan\alpha = 0.$

2. Assuming the plane $4x - 3y + 7z = 0$ to be horizontal, find the equation of the line of greatest slope through the point (2, 1, 1) in the plane $2x + y - 5z = 0$.

3. Let *PM* be the perpendicular from the point *P*(1, 2, 3) to *XY*-plane. If *OP* makes an angle θ with the positive direction of the *Z*-axis and *OM* makes an angle ϕ with the positive direction of *X*-axis, where *O* is the origin, then find θ and ϕ.

4. Find the perpendicular distance of a corner of a unit cube from a diagonal not passing through it.

5. Show that the line segments joining the points (4, 7, 8), (– 1, – 2, 1) and (2, 3, 4) (1, 2, 5) intersect. Verify whether the four points concyclic.

6. If *P* be any point on the plane $lx + my + nz = p$ and *Q* be a point on the line *OP* such that $OP \cdot OQ = p^2$, show that the locus of the point *Q* is
$$p(lx + my + nz) = x^2 + y^2 + z^2.$$

7. Find the reflection of the plane $ax + by + cz + d = 0$ in the plane $a'x + b'y + c'z + d' = 0$.

8. Prove that the two lines whose direction cosines are connected by the two relations $al + bm + cn = 0$ and $ul^2 + vm^2 + wn^2 = 0$ are perpendicular, if
$$a^2(v + w) + b^2(w + u) + c^2(u + v) = 0$$
and parallel, if $\dfrac{a^2}{u} + \dfrac{b^2}{v} + \dfrac{c^2}{w} = 0$.

9. A point *P* moves on the plane $\dfrac{x}{a} + \dfrac{y}{b} + \dfrac{z}{c} = 1$ which is fixed. The plane through *P* perpendicular to *OP* meets the axes in *A*, *B* and *C*. The planes through *A*, *B* and *C* parallel to *YZ*, *ZX*, *XY*-planes intersect in *Q*. Prove that if the axis *bc* rectangular, then the locus of *Q* is
$$\frac{1}{x^2} + \frac{1}{y^2} + \frac{1}{z^2} = \frac{1}{ax} + \frac{1}{by} + \frac{1}{cz}.$$

10. Find the equation of the plane through the intersection of the planes $x + 3y + 6 = 0$ and $3x - y - 4z = 0$, whose perpendicular distance from the origin is unity.

11. Find the equation of the image of the plane $x - 2y + 2z - 3 = 0$ in the plane $x + y + z - 1 = 0$.

Answer Key

■ Exercise 1

1. (b)	2. (b)	3. (a)	4. (a)	5. (b)	6. (c)	7. (b)	8. (c)	9. (d)	10. (a)
11. (a)	12. (b)	13. (d)	14. (c)	15. (d)	16. (c)	17. (c)	18. (b)	19. (c)	20. (c)
21. (b)	22. (a)	23. (b)	24. (c)	25. (d)	26. (0.625)	27. (3.5)	28. (2)	29. (69)	30. (88)
31. (18)	32. (99)	33. (16)	34. (33)	35. (304)	36. (210)	37. (14)	38. (31)	39. (c)	40. (a)
41. (c)	42. (d)	43. (c)	44. (d)	45. (a)	46. (a)	47. (c)	48. (d)	49. (a)	50. (21)
51. (22)	52. (12)	53. (196)	54. (16)	55. (9)	56. (65)	57. (108)	58. (a)	59. (c)	60. (b)
61. (c)	62. (a)	63. (c)	64. (b)	65. (a)	66. (a)	67. (c)	68. (5)	69. (18)	70. (2.4)
71. (158)	72. (9)	73. (18)	74. (b)	75. (b)	76. (b)	77. (d)	78. (c)	79. (d)	80. (a)
81. (d)	82. (d)	83. (a)	84. (d)	85. (b)	86. (b)	87. (a)	88. (a)	89. (b)	90. (d)
91. (a)	92. (c)	93. (c)	94. (d)	95. (b)	96. (d)	97. (b)	98. (b)	99. (b)	100. (c)
101. (b)	102. (b)	103. (d)	104. (26)	105. (11)	106. (7)	107. (9)	108. (6)	109. (10)	110. (180)
111. (355)	112. (9)	113. (a)	114. (450)	115. (b)	116. (a)	117. (b)	118. (6)	119. (2)	120. (a)
121. (c)	122. (c)	123. (a)	124. (c)	125. (28)	126. (b)	127. (c)	128. (a)	129. (b)	130. (26)
131. (12)	132. (5)	133. (b)	134. (b)	135. (a)	136. (b)	137. (c)	138. (1)	139. (a)	140. (d)
141. (d)	142. (d)								

■ Exercise 2

1. (c)	2. (a)	3. (d)	4. (b)	5. (c)	6. (b)	7. (c)	8. (d)	9. (c)	10. (d)
11. (b)	12. (a)	13. (d)	14. (a)	15. (d)	16. (a)	17. (d)	18. (a)	19. (d)	20. (d)
21. (b)	22. (a)	23. (a)	24. (a)	25. (a)	26. (a,b,c)	27. (b,c)	28. (b,c)	29. (a,c,d)	30. (a,b)
31. (b,c)	32. (a,b)	33. (c,d)	34. (a,c)	35. (b,d)	36. (a,c)	37. (c,d)	38. (a,b,c)	39. (b,c,d)	40. (a,c,d)
41. (b,d)	42. (a,c)	43. (a,b,c,d)	44. (a,b)	45. (a,b)	46. (d)	47. (b)	48. (d)	49. (b)	50. (a)
51. (d)	52. (d)	53. (b)	54. (c)	55. (a)	56. (c)	57. (c)	58. (b)	59. (c)	60. (b)
61. (a)	62. (79)	63. (420)	64. (51)	65. (75)	66. (4)	67. (8)	68. (3)	69. (1)	70. (1)
71. (7)	72. (3)	73. (1)	74. (3)	75. (2)	76. (8)	77. (2)	78. (8)	79. (0.6)	80. (210)
81. (0.8)	82. (27)	83. (1803)	84. (6.5)	85. (10)	86. (2.25)	87. (3.2)	88. (0.5)	89. (0.2)	

90. (A) → r, (B) → q, (C) → q.s (D) → p.s

91. (A) → r, (B) → q, (C) → p (D) → s

92. (A) → r, (B) → q, (C) → s (D) → p

93. (A) → r, (B) → p, (C) → q (D) → s

94. (A) → r, (B) → s, (C) → p (D) → q

95. (a) 96. (45) 97. (b) 98. (a,b,c) 99. (a,b) 100. (a,b)

101. (a,b,c) 102. (c,d) 103. (a,b,c) 104. (0.75)

Solutions

Exercise 1 - JEE Main Pattern

1. Suppose ZX-plane divides the join of (1, 2, 3) and (4, 2, 1) in the ratio $\lambda : 1$. Then, the coordinates of the point of division are

$$\left(\frac{4\lambda+1}{\lambda+1}, \frac{2\lambda+2}{\lambda+1}, \frac{\lambda+3}{\lambda+1}\right)$$

This point lies on ZX-plane

$\therefore$ y-coordinate $= 0 \Rightarrow \dfrac{2\lambda+2}{\lambda+1} = 0 \Rightarrow \lambda = -1$

Hence, ZX-plane divides the join of (1, 2, 3) and (4, 2, 1) externally in the ratio 1 : 1.

Alternate Solution

We know that the ZX-plane divides the segment joining $P(x_1, y_1, z_1)$ and $Q(x_2, y_2, z_2)$ in the ratio $-y_1 : y_2$.

$\therefore$ ZX-plane divides the join of (1, 2, 3) and (4, 2, 1) in the ratio $-1:1$ i.e. 1 : 1 externally.

2. Suppose R divides PQ in the ratio $\lambda : 1$.

Then, the coordinates of R are $\left(\dfrac{5\lambda+3}{\lambda+1}, \dfrac{4\lambda+2}{\lambda+1}, \dfrac{-6\lambda-4}{\lambda+1}\right)$.

But, the coordinates of R are given as (9, 8, −10).

$\therefore$ $\dfrac{5\lambda+3}{\lambda+1} = 9, \quad \dfrac{4\lambda+2}{\lambda+1} = 8$

and $\dfrac{-6\lambda-4}{\lambda+1} = -10 \Rightarrow \lambda = -\dfrac{3}{2}$

Hence, R divides PQ externally in the ratio 3 : 2.

3. $\because$ $AB = 3$ units and $AC = 13$ units

D divides BC in the ratio $AB : AC$ i.e. 3 : 13.

Therefore, coordinates of D are

$$\left(\frac{3\times -9+13\times 5}{3+13}, \frac{3\times 6+13\times 3}{3+13}, \frac{3\times -3+13\times 2}{3+13}\right) \text{ or } \left(\frac{19}{8}, \frac{57}{16}, \frac{17}{16}\right).$$

4. Let l, m, n be the direction cosines of the given line. Then, as it makes an acute angle with X-axis. Therefore, $l > 0$. The line passes through (6, −7, −1) and (2, −3, 1). Therefore, its direction ratios are $6-2, -7+3, -1-1$ or $4, -4, -2$ or $2, -2, -1$.

Hence, the direction cosines of the given line are $\dfrac{2}{3}, -\dfrac{2}{3}, -\dfrac{1}{3}$.

5. We have, $\alpha = 45°$ and $\beta = 60°$

Suppose **OP** makes angle γ with OZ.

Then, $\cos^2\alpha + \cos^2\beta + \cos^2\gamma = 1$

$\Rightarrow \left(\dfrac{1}{\sqrt{2}}\right)^2 + \left(\dfrac{1}{2}\right)^2 + \cos^2\gamma = 1 \Rightarrow \cos^2\gamma = \dfrac{1}{4}$

$\Rightarrow \cos\gamma = \pm\dfrac{1}{2} \Rightarrow \gamma = 60°$ or $120°$

6. Let the point be A, B, C and D.

The number of planes which have three points on one side and the fourth point on other side is 4. The number of planes which have two points on each side of the plane is 3.

$\Rightarrow$ Number of planes is 7.

7.

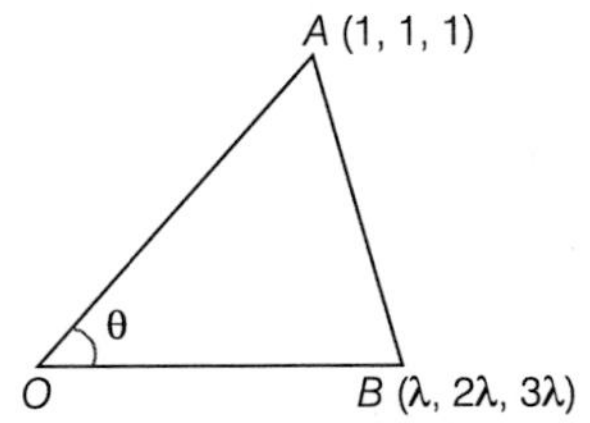

Let any point of second line be $(\lambda, 2\lambda, 3\lambda)$.

$$\cos\theta = \frac{6}{\sqrt{42}}, \cos\theta = \frac{\mathbf{OA}\cdot\mathbf{OB}}{|\mathbf{OA}||\mathbf{OB}|}, \sin\theta = \frac{\sqrt{6}}{\sqrt{42}}$$

$\therefore$ $\Delta_{OAB} = \dfrac{1}{2}(OA)OB\sin\theta$

$= \dfrac{1}{2}\sqrt{3}\lambda\sqrt{14}\times\dfrac{\sqrt{6}}{\sqrt{42}}$

$= \sqrt{6}$

$\Rightarrow$ $\lambda = 2$

So, B is (2, 4, 6).

8. Given one vertex $A(7, 2, 4)$ and line

$$\frac{x+6}{5} = \frac{y+10}{3} = \frac{z+14}{8}$$

General point on above line, $B \equiv (5\lambda-6, 3\lambda-10, 8\lambda-14)$

Direction ratios of line AB are $< 5\lambda-13, 3\lambda-12, 8\lambda-18 >$

Direction ratios of line BC are $< 5, 3, 8 >$

Since, angle between AB and BC is $\dfrac{\pi}{4}$.

$$\cos\frac{\pi}{4} = \frac{(5\lambda-13)5 + 3(3\lambda-12) + 8(8\lambda-18)}{\sqrt{5^2+3^2+8^2}\cdot\sqrt{(5\lambda-13)^2+(3\lambda-12)^2+(8\lambda-18)^2}}$$

On squaring and solving, we get $\lambda = 3, 2$

Hence, the equation of lines are

$$\frac{x-7}{2} = \frac{y-2}{-3} = \frac{z-4}{6} \text{ and } \frac{x-7}{3} = \frac{y-2}{6} = \frac{z-4}{2}$$

9. L_1L_2 intersecting; L_2L_3 parallel; L_3L_1 skew.

10. $\lambda = \mu = 1$ (point of intersection of two lines)

$\Rightarrow$ $\mathbf{r} = \mathbf{a} + \mathbf{l}$ or $\mathbf{b} + \mathbf{m}$, i.e. $\mathbf{r} = \hat{\mathbf{i}} + 2\hat{\mathbf{j}} + \hat{\mathbf{k}}$

11. Both the lines pass through origin.

Line L_1 is parallel to the vector.

$\mathbf{V}_1 = (\cos\theta + \sqrt{3})\hat{\mathbf{i}} + (\sqrt{2}\sin\theta)\hat{\mathbf{j}} + (\cos\theta - \sqrt{3})\hat{\mathbf{k}}$ and L_2 is parallel to the vector $\mathbf{V}_2 = a\hat{\mathbf{i}} + b\hat{\mathbf{j}} + c\hat{\mathbf{k}}$

$\therefore \quad \cos\alpha = \dfrac{\mathbf{V}_1 \cdot \mathbf{V}_2}{|\mathbf{V}_1||\mathbf{V}_2|}$

$= \dfrac{a(\cos\theta + \sqrt{3}) + (b\sqrt{2})\sin\theta + c(\cos\theta - \sqrt{3})}{\sqrt{a^2+b^2+c^2}\sqrt{(\cos\theta+\sqrt{3})^2 + 2\sin^2\theta + (\cos\theta - \sqrt{3})^2}}$

$= \dfrac{(a+c)\cos\theta + b\sqrt{2}\sin\theta + (a-c)\sqrt{3}}{\sqrt{a^2+b^2+c^2}\sqrt{2+6}}$

In order that $\cos\alpha$ is independent of θ.

$a + c = 0$ and $b = 0$

$\therefore \quad \cos\alpha = \dfrac{2a\sqrt{3}}{a\sqrt{2}\cdot 2\sqrt{2}} = \dfrac{\sqrt{3}}{2} \Rightarrow \alpha = \dfrac{\pi}{6}$

12. Given lines are skew lines and angle between them

$= \cos^{-1}\left[\dfrac{12+3+0}{\sqrt{35}\sqrt{25}}\right]$

$= \cos^{-1}\dfrac{3}{\sqrt{35}}$

13. y-coordinate of P is zero.

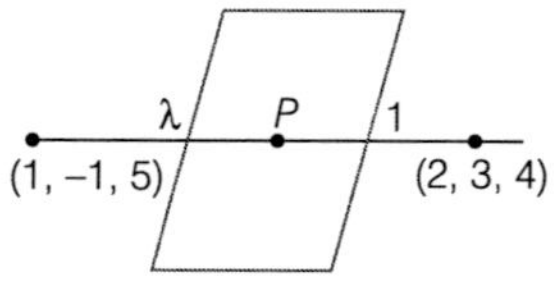

$\Rightarrow \quad 0 = \dfrac{3\lambda + (-1)}{\lambda + 1}$

$\Rightarrow \quad \lambda = \dfrac{1}{3}$

14. Intersecting, if

$\begin{vmatrix} 5 & 2 & 13-p \\ 1 & 2 & 3 \\ -1 & 2 & -3 \end{vmatrix} = \begin{vmatrix} 5 & 2 & 13-p \\ 0 & 4 & 0 \\ -1 & 2 & -3 \end{vmatrix} \quad [\because R_2 \to R_2 + R_3]$

$\Rightarrow \quad -4(-15 + 13 - p) = 0$

$\therefore \quad p = -2$

Alternate Solution

$(\lambda + 2) = -(\mu + 3) \quad \ldots(i)$

$2\lambda + 9 = 2\mu + 7 \quad \ldots(ii)$

$3\lambda + 13 = p - 3\mu \quad \ldots(iii)$

From Eq. (i), $\mu = -(\lambda + 5)$

On putting in Eq. (ii), $2\lambda + 9 = -2(\lambda + 5) + 7$

$\Rightarrow \quad \lambda = -3$

Now, from Eq. (iii), $-9 + 13 = p + 6 \quad [\because \mu = -2]$

$\Rightarrow \quad p = -2$

15. $\begin{vmatrix} 2-a & 9-7 & 13-(-2) \\ 1 & 2 & 3 \\ -1 & 2 & -3 \end{vmatrix} = 0$

$\Rightarrow (2-a)(-6-6) + 15(2+2) = 0$

$\Rightarrow \quad a = -3$

16. The given lines are coplanar, if

$\begin{vmatrix} 2-1 & 3-4 & 4-5 \\ 1 & 1 & -k \\ k & 2 & 1 \end{vmatrix} = 0 \Rightarrow \begin{vmatrix} 1 & -1 & -1 \\ 1 & 1 & -k \\ k & 2 & 1 \end{vmatrix} = 0$

$\Rightarrow \quad \begin{vmatrix} 1 & 0 & 0 \\ 1 & 2 & 1-k \\ k & k+2 & 1+k \end{vmatrix} = 0$

$[\because C_2 \to C_2 + C_1 \text{ and } C_3 \to C_3 + C_1]$

$\Rightarrow \quad 2(1+k) - (k+2)(1-k) = 0$

if $\quad k^2 + 3k = 0 \Rightarrow k = 0$ or -3

17. On putting $z = 0$ in the line given $x = 5$ and $y = 1$

$\Rightarrow \quad 5 \cdot 1 = c^2$

Hence, $c = \pm\sqrt{5}$

18. Direction ratios of AB are $1 : 1 : 1$.

Direction ratios of CD are $1 : 2 : 1$.

Angle between AB and CD,

$\cos\theta = \dfrac{1\times1 + 1\times2 + 1\times1}{\sqrt{3}\sqrt{6}} = \dfrac{4}{3\sqrt{2}}$

19. Let coordinates of any point taken on L_2 is $Q \equiv (1+2\lambda, 2+3\lambda, 3+4\lambda)$.

Direction ratios of $PQ = 2\lambda, 3\lambda - 1, 4\lambda - 1$

Now, $(2\lambda)2 + (3\lambda - 1)3 + (4\lambda - 1)4 = 0 \Rightarrow 29\lambda = 7$

$\Rightarrow \quad \lambda = \dfrac{7}{29}$

Direction ratios of line PQ are $(14, -8, -1)$.

20. $l + m + n = 0, l^2 + m^2 - n^2 = 0$

$\Rightarrow \quad l^2 + m^2 - (-l - m)^2 = 0 \Rightarrow 2lm = 0$ i.e. $l = 0$ or $m = 0$

If $l = 0, m = -n$ and if $m = 0, l = -n$

Since, DR's of the two lines are $0, 1, -1$ and $1, 0, -1$

$\cos\theta = \dfrac{0\times1 + 1\times0 + (-1)\times(-1)}{\sqrt{2}\sqrt{2}} = \dfrac{1}{2} \Rightarrow \theta = \dfrac{\pi}{3}$

21. Let $\quad \mathbf{r} \times \mathbf{a} = \mathbf{b} \times \mathbf{a}$

$\Rightarrow \quad (\mathbf{r} - \mathbf{b}) \times \mathbf{a} = \mathbf{0} \Rightarrow \mathbf{r} = \mathbf{b} + t\mathbf{a}$

Similarly, other line $\mathbf{r} = \mathbf{a} + k\mathbf{b}$, where t and k are scalars.

Now, $\mathbf{a} + k\mathbf{b} = \mathbf{b} + t\mathbf{a}$

$\Rightarrow \quad t = 1, k = 1 \quad$ [equating the coefficients of $\mathbf{a}$ and $\mathbf{b}$]

$\therefore \quad \mathbf{r} = \mathbf{a} + \mathbf{b} = \hat{\mathbf{i}} + \hat{\mathbf{j}} + 2\hat{\mathbf{i}} - \hat{\mathbf{k}} = 3\hat{\mathbf{i}} + \hat{\mathbf{j}} - \hat{\mathbf{k}}$ i.e. $(3, 1, -1)$

22. Let the point P be (x, y, z), then the vector $x\hat{\mathbf{i}} + y\hat{\mathbf{j}} + z\hat{\mathbf{k}}$ will lie on the line.

$\Rightarrow (x-1)\hat{\mathbf{i}} + (y-1)\hat{\mathbf{j}} + (z-1)\hat{\mathbf{k}} = -\lambda\hat{\mathbf{i}} + \lambda\hat{\mathbf{j}} - \lambda\hat{\mathbf{k}}$

$\Rightarrow \quad x = 1 - \lambda, y = 1 + \lambda$ and $z = 1 - \lambda$

Now, point P in nearest to the origin.

$\Rightarrow \quad D = (1-\lambda)^2 + (1+\lambda)^2 + (1-\lambda)^2$

$\Rightarrow \quad \dfrac{dD}{d\lambda} = -4(1-\lambda) + 2(1+\lambda) = 0 \Rightarrow \lambda = \dfrac{1}{3}$

So, the point P is $\left(\dfrac{2}{3}, \dfrac{4}{3}, \dfrac{2}{3}\right)$.

23. We have, $|\mathbf{v}_1| = 2, |\mathbf{v}_2| = \sqrt{2}$ and $|\mathbf{v}_3| = \sqrt{29}$

If θ is the angle between $\mathbf{v}_1$ and $\mathbf{v}_2$, then

$$2\sqrt{2}\cos\theta = -2$$

$$\Rightarrow \quad \cos\theta = -\frac{1}{\sqrt{2}} \Rightarrow \theta = 135^\circ$$

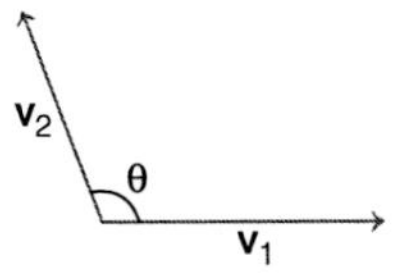

Let $\mathbf{v}_1 = 2\mathbf{i}, \mathbf{v}_2 = -\hat{\mathbf{i}} + \hat{\mathbf{j}}$ and $\mathbf{v}_3 = \alpha\hat{\mathbf{i}} + \beta\hat{\mathbf{j}} + \gamma\hat{\mathbf{k}}$

Since, $\quad \mathbf{v}_3 \cdot \mathbf{v}_1 = 6 = 2\alpha$

$\Rightarrow \quad \alpha = 3$

Also, $\quad \mathbf{v}_3 \cdot \mathbf{v}_2 = -5 = -\alpha + \beta \Rightarrow \beta = -2$

and $\quad \mathbf{v}_3 \cdot \mathbf{v}_3 = 29 = \alpha^2 + \beta^2 + \gamma^2 \Rightarrow \gamma = \pm 4$

$\therefore \quad \mathbf{v}_3 = 3\hat{\mathbf{i}} - 2\hat{\mathbf{j}} \pm 4\hat{\mathbf{k}}$

24. Here P and Q lie on the same side of XY-plane

Image $P(1, 2, 3)$ on the XY-plane is $P'(1, 2, -3)$

Reflected ray is $P'Q \Rightarrow \dfrac{x-3}{2} = \dfrac{y-2}{0} = \dfrac{z-5}{8}$

$$\Rightarrow \quad \frac{x-3}{1} = \frac{y-2}{0} = \frac{z-5}{4}$$

25. Given, line are $\dfrac{1-x}{-2} = \dfrac{2-y}{-3} = \dfrac{z-3}{4}$

and $\quad \dfrac{x-2}{3} = \dfrac{y-4}{4} = \dfrac{z-\lambda}{5}$

Also, we write $\dfrac{x-1}{2} = \dfrac{y-2}{3} = \dfrac{z-3}{4}$

and $\quad \dfrac{x-2}{3} = \dfrac{y-4}{4} = \dfrac{z-\lambda}{5}$

Here, $\quad \mathbf{a}_1 = \hat{\mathbf{i}} + 2\hat{\mathbf{j}} + 3\hat{\mathbf{k}}$ and $\mathbf{b}_1 = 2\hat{\mathbf{i}} + 3\hat{\mathbf{j}} + 4\hat{\mathbf{k}}$

and $\quad \mathbf{a}_2 = 2\hat{\mathbf{i}} + 4\hat{\mathbf{j}} + \lambda\hat{\mathbf{k}}$ and $\mathbf{b}_2 = 3\hat{\mathbf{i}} + 4\hat{\mathbf{j}} + 5\hat{\mathbf{k}}$

$\therefore (\mathbf{a}_2 - \mathbf{a}_1) = \hat{\mathbf{i}} + 2\hat{\mathbf{j}} + (\lambda - 3)\hat{\mathbf{k}}$

$$\text{So, } \mathbf{b}_1 \times \mathbf{b}_2 = \begin{vmatrix} \hat{\mathbf{i}} & \hat{\mathbf{j}} & \hat{\mathbf{k}} \\ 2 & 3 & 4 \\ 3 & 4 & 5 \end{vmatrix} = -\hat{\mathbf{i}} + 2\hat{\mathbf{j}} - \hat{\mathbf{k}}$$

$\therefore |\mathbf{b}_1 \times \mathbf{b}_2| = \sqrt{1 + 4 + 1} = \sqrt{6}$

$$\text{Shortest distance} = \frac{(\mathbf{a}_2 - \mathbf{a}_1) \cdot (\mathbf{b}_1 \times \mathbf{b}_2)}{|\mathbf{b}_1 \times \mathbf{b}_2|}$$

$$= \frac{(\hat{\mathbf{i}} + 2\hat{\mathbf{j}} + (\lambda - 3)\hat{\mathbf{k}}) \cdot (-\hat{\mathbf{i}} + 2\hat{\mathbf{j}} - \hat{\mathbf{k}})}{\sqrt{6}}$$

$$= \left| \frac{-1 + 4 - \lambda + 3}{\sqrt{6}} \right|$$

$$\because \quad \frac{1}{\sqrt{6}} = \left| \frac{6 - \lambda}{\sqrt{6}} \right|$$

$\Rightarrow \quad |6 - \lambda| = 1$

$\Rightarrow \quad 6 - \lambda = \pm 1$

$\Rightarrow \quad \lambda = 6 \pm 1 \Rightarrow \lambda = 7, 5$

$\therefore \ \Sigma\lambda^2 = 7^2 + 5^2 = 49 + 25 = 74$

26. Given, $l + m + n = 0 \quad$ ...(i)

and $\quad l^2 = m^2 + n^2 \quad$ ...(ii)

As we know, $\quad l^2 + m^2 + n^2 = 1$

From Eq. (ii), $\quad 2l^2 = 1 \Rightarrow l = \pm \dfrac{1}{\sqrt{2}} \quad$ ...(iii)

Now, from Eq. (i), $\quad m + n = -l$

$\Rightarrow \quad (m + n)^2 = l^2$

$\Rightarrow \quad m^2 + n^2 + 2mn = l^2$

$\Rightarrow \quad 2mn = 0 \quad$ [using Eq. (ii)]

$\Rightarrow \quad m = 0$ or $n = 0$

When $m = 0$, then from Eq. (i), $l = -n$

$$\frac{1}{\sqrt{2}}, 0, \frac{-1}{\sqrt{2}} \quad \text{[using Eq. (iii)]}$$

When $n = 0$, then from Eq. (i), $l = -m$

$$\frac{1}{\sqrt{2}}, \frac{-1}{\sqrt{2}}, 0 \quad \text{[using Eq. (iii)]}$$

$$\therefore \quad \cos\alpha = \frac{\frac{1}{2} + 0 + 0}{\sqrt{\frac{1}{2} + \frac{1}{2}}\sqrt{\frac{1}{2} + \frac{1}{2}}} = \frac{1}{2}$$

$$\cos\alpha = \frac{1}{2} \text{ and } \sin\alpha = \frac{\sqrt{3}}{2}$$

$$\therefore \ \sin^4\alpha + \cos^4\alpha = \left(\frac{\sqrt{3}}{2}\right)^4 + \left(\frac{1}{2}\right)^4$$

$$= \frac{9}{16} + \frac{1}{16} = \frac{10}{16} = \frac{5}{8} = 0.625$$

27. Given, line $\dfrac{x}{2} = \dfrac{y}{2} = \dfrac{z}{1}$ and $\dfrac{5-x}{-2} = \dfrac{7y-14}{p} = \dfrac{z-3}{4}$

Angle between lines is $\sin^{-1}\left(\dfrac{\sqrt{5}}{3}\right)$

$$\because \ \sin^{-1}\left(\frac{\sqrt{5}}{3}\right) = \cos^{-1}\left(\frac{\sqrt{9-5}}{3}\right) = \cos^{-1}\frac{2}{3}$$

Here, $a_1 = 2, b_1 = 2, c_1 = 1$ and $a_2 = 2, b_2 = p/7, c_2 = 4$

$$\cos\theta = \frac{a_1 a_2 + b_1 b_2 + c_1 c_2}{\sqrt{a_1^2 + b_1^2 + c_1^2}\sqrt{a_2^2 + b_2^2 + c_2^2}}$$

$$\cos\left(\cos^{-1}\left(\frac{2}{3}\right)\right) = \frac{2 \times 2 + 2 \times p/7 + 1 \times 4}{\sqrt{4 + 4 + 1}\sqrt{4 + \frac{p^2}{49} + 16}}$$

$$\Rightarrow \quad \frac{2}{3} = \frac{4 + \frac{2p}{7} + 4}{3\sqrt{20 + \frac{p^2}{49}}}$$

$$\Rightarrow \quad 2\sqrt{20 + \frac{p^2}{49}} = 8 + \frac{2p}{7} \Rightarrow \sqrt{20 + \frac{p^2}{49}} = 4 + \frac{p}{7}$$

$$\Rightarrow \quad 20 + \frac{p^2}{49} = 16 + \frac{8p}{7} + \frac{p^2}{49}$$

$$\Rightarrow \quad \frac{8p}{7} = 4 \Rightarrow p = \frac{7}{2} = 3.5$$

28.

> **Decoding the Question**
> First check whether the lines are parallel or not. If lines are parallel, then apply formula,
> Distance between two parallel lines $= \left|\dfrac{(\mathbf{a}_2 - \mathbf{a}_1)\times\mathbf{b}}{|\mathbf{b}|}\right|$

Given, line $\dfrac{x-1}{1} = \dfrac{y-1}{1} = \dfrac{z-1}{1}$ and $\dfrac{x-2}{1} = \dfrac{y-3}{1} = \dfrac{z-4}{1}$

Since, these lines are parallel.

$\because$ Distance between the lines $= \dfrac{|(\mathbf{a}_2 - \mathbf{a}_1)\times\mathbf{b}|}{|\mathbf{b}|}$

Here, $\mathbf{a}_1 = \hat{\mathbf{i}} + \hat{\mathbf{j}} + \hat{\mathbf{k}}$

$\mathbf{a}_2 = 2\hat{\mathbf{i}} + 3\hat{\mathbf{j}} + 4\hat{\mathbf{k}}$ and $\mathbf{b} = \hat{\mathbf{i}} + \hat{\mathbf{j}} + \hat{\mathbf{k}}$

$$\because\ (\mathbf{a}_2 - \mathbf{a}_1)\times\mathbf{b} = \begin{vmatrix} \hat{\mathbf{i}} & \hat{\mathbf{j}} & \hat{\mathbf{k}} \\ 1 & 2 & 3 \\ 1 & 1 & 1 \end{vmatrix} = -\hat{\mathbf{i}} + 2\hat{\mathbf{j}} - \hat{\mathbf{k}}$$

$$\Rightarrow \quad \text{Distance} = \frac{|-\hat{\mathbf{i}} + 2\hat{\mathbf{j}} - \hat{\mathbf{k}}|}{|\hat{\mathbf{i}} + \hat{\mathbf{j}} + \hat{\mathbf{k}}|} \Rightarrow \frac{\sqrt{1+4+1}}{\sqrt{1+1+1}} = \frac{\sqrt{6}}{\sqrt{3}} = \sqrt{2} \text{ units}$$

$\because \quad \lambda = \sqrt{2} \Rightarrow \lambda^2 = 2$

29. Let $L_1 \equiv \dfrac{x-3}{1} = \dfrac{y+1}{3} = \dfrac{z-6}{-1} = \lambda$

and $L_2 \equiv \dfrac{x+5}{7} = \dfrac{y-2}{-6} = \dfrac{z-3}{4} = \mu$

Point on L_1 is $(\lambda + 3, 3\lambda - 1, -\lambda + 6)$

and point on L_2 is $(7\mu - 5, -6\mu + 2, 4\mu + 3)$.

As, the line L_1 and L_2 intersect at Q.

$\therefore \quad \lambda + 3 = 7\mu - 5$ and $3\lambda - 1 = -6\mu + 2$

$\Rightarrow \quad \lambda - 7\mu = -8$ ...(i)

and $\quad 3\lambda + 6\mu = 3 \Rightarrow \lambda + 2\mu = 1$ ...(ii)

On solving Eqs. (i) and (ii), we get

$\lambda = -1, \mu = 1$

$\therefore$ Coordinates of Q are $(2, -4, 7)$.

$\therefore$ Image of point Q in XY-plane is $(2, -4, -7)$.

Now, $\alpha = 2, \beta = -4, \gamma = -7$

$\therefore\ \alpha^2 + \beta^2 + \gamma^2 = 4 + 16 + 49 = 69$

30. Given, $P = (\lambda, 6, 9)$ and image of point P is $Q(20, \mu, -\lambda - 9)$.

$\because$ Mid-point of PQ is $\left(\dfrac{\lambda + 20}{2}, \dfrac{6+\mu}{2}, \dfrac{-\lambda}{2}\right)$.

Now, mid-point of PQ is lie on the line $\dfrac{x-3}{7} = \dfrac{y-2}{5} = \dfrac{z-1}{-9}$.

$$\because \frac{\frac{\lambda+20}{2} - 3}{7} = \frac{\frac{6+\mu}{2} - 2}{5} = \frac{\frac{-\lambda}{2} - 1}{-9} \Rightarrow \frac{\lambda+14}{7} = \frac{\mu+2}{5} = \frac{\lambda+2}{9}$$

$\because \quad \lambda = -56$ and $\mu = -32$

$\therefore \quad |\lambda| + |\mu| = 56 + 32 = 88$

31. Given, line $\dfrac{x+3}{8} = \dfrac{y-4}{2} = \dfrac{z+1}{2} = \lambda$

Point P on line is $(8\lambda - 3, 2\lambda + 4, 2\lambda - 1)$.

Also, given $PR = 6$, where $R(1, 2, 3)$.

$\Rightarrow \quad PR^2 = 36$

$\Rightarrow (8\lambda - 4)^2 + (2\lambda + 2)^2 + (2\lambda - 4)^2 = 36 \Rightarrow \lambda = 0, 1$

$\therefore\ P = (-3, 4 - 1)$ and $Q(5, 6, 1)$.

Area of $\Delta PQR = \dfrac{1}{2}|\mathbf{PQ} \times \mathbf{PR}|$

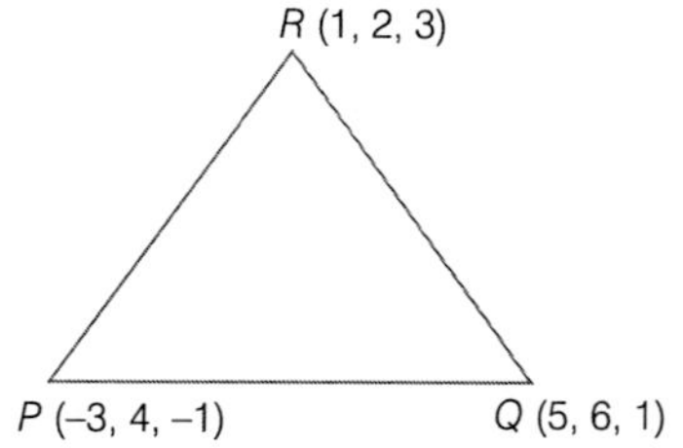

$$\mathbf{PQ} = 8\hat{\mathbf{i}} + 2\hat{\mathbf{j}} + 2\hat{\mathbf{k}}$$

$$\mathbf{PR} = 4\hat{\mathbf{i}} - 2\hat{\mathbf{j}} + 4\hat{\mathbf{k}}$$

$$\mathbf{PQ} \times \mathbf{PR} = \begin{vmatrix} \hat{\mathbf{i}} & \hat{\mathbf{j}} & \hat{\mathbf{k}} \\ 8 & 2 & 2 \\ 4 & -2 & 4 \end{vmatrix} = 12\hat{\mathbf{i}} - 24\hat{\mathbf{j}} - 24\hat{\mathbf{k}}$$

$$|\mathbf{PQ} \times \mathbf{QR}| = \sqrt{144 + 576 + 576} = \sqrt{1296} = 36$$

Hence, area of $\Delta PQR = \dfrac{1}{2} \times 36 = 18$ sq units

32. Point P lie on line $\dfrac{x-7}{3} = \dfrac{y-1}{-1} = \dfrac{z+2}{1} = \lambda$

$\therefore\ P(3\lambda + 7, -\lambda + 1, \lambda - 2)$

and point Q lie on line $\dfrac{x}{2} = \dfrac{y-7}{3} = \dfrac{z}{1} = \mu$

$\therefore\ Q(2\mu, 3\mu + 7, \mu)$

Now, direction ratios of PQ are $(1, -4, 2)$.

and direction ratios of $PQ(3\lambda - 2\mu + 7, -\lambda - 3\mu - 6, \lambda - \mu - 2)$

$$\therefore \quad \underset{\text{I}}{\frac{3\lambda - 2\mu + 7}{1}} = \underset{\text{II}}{\frac{-\lambda - 3\mu - 6}{-4}} = \underset{\text{III}}{\frac{\lambda - \mu - 2}{2}}$$

On taking (I) and (II),

$-12\lambda + 8\mu - 28 = -\lambda - 3\mu - 6 \Rightarrow \lambda - \mu + 2 = 0$ ...(i)

On taking (II) and (III), we get

$-2\lambda - 6\mu - 12 = -4\lambda + 4\mu + 8 \Rightarrow \lambda - 5\mu - 10 = 0$ ...(ii)

On solving Eqs. (i) and (ii), we get

$\lambda = -5$ and $\mu = -3$

$\because \quad P(-8, 6, -7)$ and $Q(-6, -2, -3)$

$\therefore \quad |(\alpha + \beta + \gamma)(p + q + r)| = |(-8 + 6 - 7)(-6 - 2 - 3)|$

$|(-9) \times (-11)| = |99| = 99$

33. Equation of line joining point $Q(0, -1, 3)$ and $R(2, -3, -1)$ is

$$\frac{x}{2} = \frac{y+1}{-2} = \frac{z-3}{-4}$$

$$\Rightarrow \quad \frac{x}{1} = \frac{y+1}{-1} = \frac{z-3}{-2} = \lambda$$

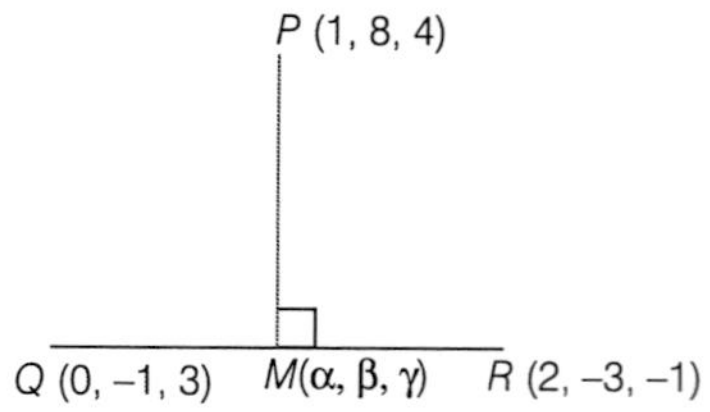

Let foot of perpendicular of P on QR be M.

Now, point M are $(\lambda, -\lambda-1, -2\lambda+3)$.

Direction ratios of line PM are $(\lambda-1, -\lambda-9, -2\lambda-1)$.

PM is perpendicular on QR.

$\because 1(\lambda-1)-1(-\lambda-9)-2(-2\lambda-1)=0 \Rightarrow \lambda=-\dfrac{5}{3}$

$\therefore$ Coordinates of M are $\left(\dfrac{-5}{3}, \dfrac{2}{3}, \dfrac{19}{3}\right)$.

$\because \alpha=\dfrac{-5}{3}, \beta=\dfrac{2}{3}$ and $\gamma=\dfrac{19}{3}$

$$3(\alpha+\beta+\gamma)=3\left(\frac{-5+2+19}{3}\right)=16$$

34. Given line $L_1 \equiv \dfrac{x-2}{3}=\dfrac{y+1}{-2}=\dfrac{z-2}{0}$

and $L_2 \equiv \dfrac{x-1}{1}=\dfrac{2y+3}{\alpha}=\dfrac{z+5}{2}$ are perpendicular.

$\therefore (3)(1)-(2)\left(\dfrac{\alpha}{2}\right)+(0)(2)=0$

$\Rightarrow \alpha=3$

Now, angle between line

$$L_2=\frac{x-1}{1}=\frac{2y+3}{3}=\frac{z+5}{2}$$

and $L_3=\dfrac{1-x}{3}=\dfrac{2y-1}{-4}=\dfrac{z}{4}$

$$\therefore \cos\theta=\frac{(1)(-3)+\left(\frac{3}{2}\right)\left(\frac{-4}{2}\right)+(2)(4)}{\sqrt{1+\frac{9}{4}+4}\sqrt{9+4+16}}$$

$$\Rightarrow \cos\theta=\frac{-3-3+8}{\sqrt{\frac{29}{4}}\sqrt{29}}=\frac{2\times2}{29}=\frac{4}{29}$$

$$\Rightarrow \theta=\cos^{-1}\left(\frac{4}{29}\right)$$

Hence, $p+q=4+29=33$

35. Given, point $(0, 2, \lambda)$ and equation of line

$$\mathbf{r}=-3\hat{\mathbf{i}}+\hat{\mathbf{j}}-4\hat{\mathbf{k}}+\mu(5\hat{\mathbf{i}}+2\hat{\mathbf{j}}+3\hat{\mathbf{k}})$$

Length of perpendicular from point $(0, 2, \lambda)$ to the line

$$\mathbf{r}=-3\hat{\mathbf{i}}+\hat{\mathbf{j}}-4\hat{\mathbf{k}}+\mu(5\hat{\mathbf{i}}+2\hat{\mathbf{j}}+3\hat{\mathbf{k}})$$

$$=\left|\frac{[3\hat{\mathbf{i}}+\hat{\mathbf{j}}+(\lambda+4)\hat{\mathbf{k}}]\times(5\hat{\mathbf{i}}+2\hat{\mathbf{j}}+3\hat{\mathbf{k}})}{(5\hat{\mathbf{i}}+2\hat{\mathbf{j}}+3\hat{\mathbf{k}})}\right|$$

So, $[3\hat{\mathbf{i}}+\hat{\mathbf{j}}+(\lambda+4)\hat{\mathbf{k}}]\times(5\hat{\mathbf{i}}+2\hat{\mathbf{j}}+3\hat{\mathbf{k}})=\begin{vmatrix}\hat{\mathbf{i}} & \hat{\mathbf{j}} & \hat{\mathbf{k}}\\ 3 & 1 & \lambda+4\\ 5 & 2 & 3\end{vmatrix}$

$$=(-5-2\lambda)\hat{\mathbf{i}}+(5\lambda+11)\hat{\mathbf{j}}+\hat{\mathbf{k}}$$

$$\therefore \sqrt{21}=\frac{\sqrt{(-5-2\lambda)^2+(5\lambda+11)^2+(1)^2}}{\sqrt{25+4+9}}$$

$\Rightarrow 21\times38=25+4\lambda^2+20\lambda+25\lambda^2+110\lambda+121+1$

[on squaring both sides]

$\Rightarrow 29\lambda^2+130\lambda-651=0$

$\Rightarrow (29\lambda-87)(29\lambda+217)=0$

$\Rightarrow \lambda=3, \dfrac{-217}{29}$

$\because 29\left(3+\dfrac{217}{29}\right)=\dfrac{29(87+217)}{29}=304$

36. The coordinates of any point lie on the line

$$\frac{x+2}{3}=\frac{y+1}{2}=\frac{z-3}{2}=\lambda$$

or $x=3\lambda-2, y=2\lambda-1, z=2\lambda+3$

Distance between points $(3\lambda-2, 2\lambda-1, 2\lambda+3)$ and $(1, 2, 3)$ is $3\sqrt{2}$.

$\because (3\lambda-2-1)^2+(2\lambda-1-2)^2+(2\lambda+3-3)^2=(3\sqrt{2})^2$

$\Rightarrow 9(\lambda-1)^2+(2\lambda-3)^2+4\lambda^2=18$

$\Rightarrow 17\lambda^2-30\lambda=0$

$\Rightarrow \lambda=0, \dfrac{30}{17}$

$\because$ Points are $(-2, -1, 3)$ and $\left(\dfrac{56}{17}, \dfrac{43}{17}, \dfrac{111}{17}\right)$.

Since α, β and γ are lie in first octant.

Hence, $17(\alpha+\beta+\gamma)=17\left(\dfrac{56+43+111}{17}\right)=210$

37. Point $(7, -2, 11)$ lie on the line $\dfrac{x-7}{2}=\dfrac{y+2}{-3}=\dfrac{z-11}{6}$.

$\because$ Also, equation of line is $\dfrac{x-7}{2}=\dfrac{y+2}{-3}=\dfrac{z-11}{6}=\lambda$

$$x=2\lambda+7, y=-3\lambda-2, z=6\lambda+11$$

Also, this point lie on the line

$$\frac{x-6}{1}=\frac{y-4}{0}=\frac{z-8}{3}$$

$$\therefore \frac{2\lambda+7-6}{1}=\frac{-3\lambda-2-4}{0}=\frac{6\lambda+11-8}{3}$$

$\Rightarrow -3\lambda-6=0 \Rightarrow \lambda=-2$

So, points are $3, 4, -1$

Distance between the points $(7, -2, 11)$ and $(3, 4, -1)$ is

$\sqrt{(7-3)^2+(-2-4)^2+(11+1)^2}=\sqrt{16+36+144}$

$=\sqrt{196}=14$ units

38. Given, line $\dfrac{x-6}{3}=\dfrac{y-7}{2}=\dfrac{z-7}{-2}=\lambda$

$$x=3\lambda+6, y=2\lambda+7, z=-2\lambda+7$$

Line l and PM are perpendicular to each other.

Direction ratios of PM are $(3\lambda+5)$, $(2\lambda+5)$ and $(-2\lambda+7-k)$ and direction ratios of line l are $3, 2, -2$.

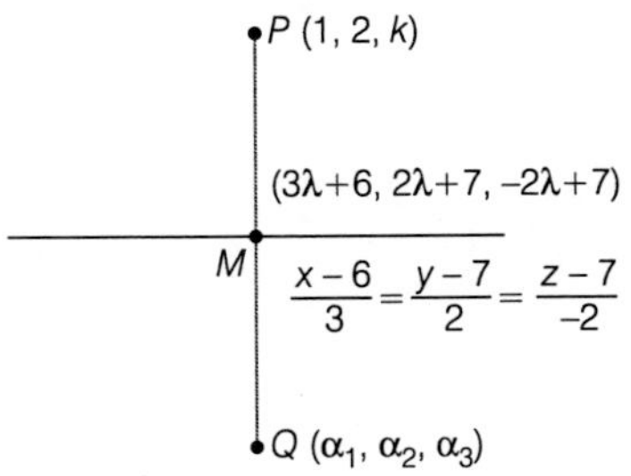

$\therefore \quad 3(3\lambda + 5) + 2(2\lambda + 5) - 2(-2\lambda + 7 - k) = 0$

$\Rightarrow \quad 9\lambda + 15 + 4\lambda + 10 + 4\lambda - 14 + 2k = 0$

$\Rightarrow \quad 17\lambda + 11 + 2k = 0$

$\Rightarrow \quad k = \dfrac{-17\lambda - 11}{2}$

Also, $PM^2 = (7)^2 = 49$

$\therefore \quad (3\lambda + 5)^2 + (2\lambda + 5)^2 + (-2\lambda + 7 - k)^2 = 49$

$\Rightarrow \quad (3\lambda + 5)^2 + (2\lambda + 5)^2 + \left(-2\lambda + 7 + \dfrac{17\lambda + 11}{2}\right)^2 = 49$

$\Rightarrow 9\lambda^2 + 30\lambda + 25 + 4\lambda^2 + 20\lambda + 25 + \dfrac{(13\lambda + 25)^2}{4} = 49$

$\Rightarrow 4(9\lambda^2 + 30\lambda + 25 + 4\lambda^2 + 20\lambda + 25) + 169\lambda^2 + 625 + 650\lambda$

$= 49 \times 4$

$\Rightarrow \quad 221\lambda^2 + 850\lambda + 629 = 0$

$\Rightarrow \quad (\lambda + 1)(221\lambda + 629) = 0$

$\Rightarrow \quad \lambda = -1, \dfrac{-629}{221}$

Given, $k < 4$

$k = \dfrac{17 - 11}{2} = 3$

So, point M is (3, 5, 9).

$\because$ M is the mid-point of PQ.

$\therefore \quad 3 = \dfrac{1 + \alpha_1}{2}, 5 = \dfrac{2 + \alpha_2}{2}, 9 = \dfrac{\alpha_3 + 3}{2}$

$\alpha_1 = 5, \alpha_2 = 8, \alpha_3 = 15$

$\because k + \sum_{i=1}^{3} \alpha_i = k + \alpha_1 + \alpha_2 + \alpha_3 = 3 + 5 + 8 + 15 = 31$

39. Given, equation of line $\dfrac{x - 1}{3} = \dfrac{y + 1}{2} = \dfrac{z - 2}{1} = \lambda$

Then, any point on given line $Q(3\lambda + 1, 2\lambda - 1, \lambda + 2)$ and $P(3, 4, 9)$.

Direction ratios of PQ are $(3\lambda - 2, 2\lambda - 5, \lambda - 7)$.

and given line is perpendicular to PQ.

So, $< 3\lambda - 2, 2\lambda - 5, \lambda - 7 > \cdot < 3, 2, 1 > = 0$

$\Rightarrow \quad 9\lambda - 6 + 4\lambda - 10 + \lambda - 7 = 0$

$\Rightarrow \quad 14\lambda - 23 = 0 \Rightarrow \lambda = \dfrac{23}{14}$

So, $Q\left(\dfrac{83}{14}, \dfrac{32}{14}, \dfrac{51}{14}\right)$

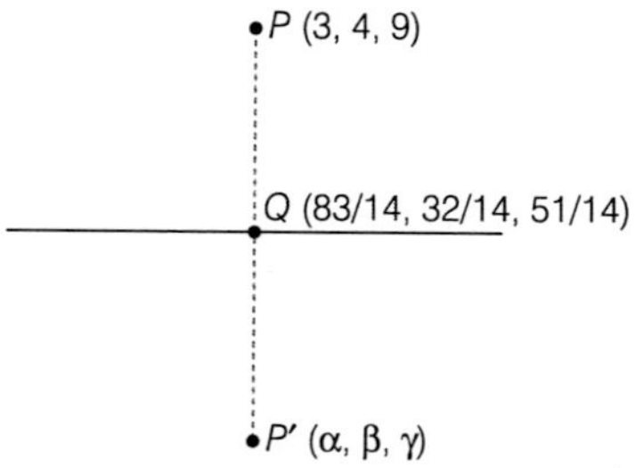

Q is mid-point of P and P'.

$\therefore \quad \dfrac{\alpha + 3}{2} = \dfrac{83}{14} \Rightarrow \alpha = \dfrac{62}{7}$

$\dfrac{\beta + 4}{2} = \dfrac{32}{14} \Rightarrow \beta = \dfrac{4}{7}$

$\dfrac{\gamma + 9}{2} = \dfrac{51}{14} \Rightarrow \gamma = -\dfrac{12}{7}$

Now, $14(\alpha + \beta + \gamma) = 14\left(\dfrac{62 + 4 - 12}{7}\right) = 108$

40. **Decoding the Question**

First find the coordinates of the median and then find the coordinates of centroid of the triangle by section formula.

Given, line is $\dfrac{x + 3}{8} = \dfrac{y - 4}{2} = \dfrac{z + 1}{2} = \lambda$.

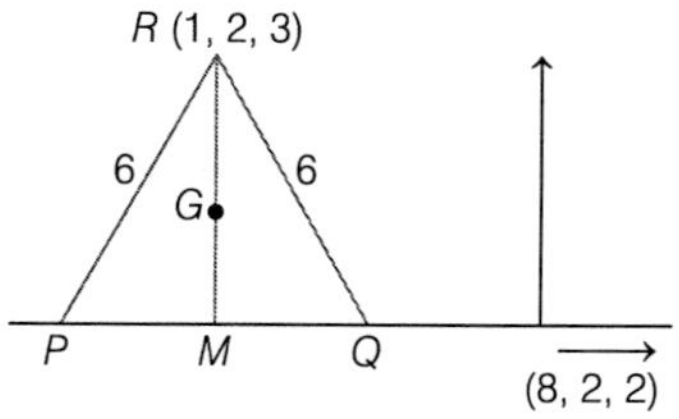

Let M be mid-point of PQ and perpendicular to given line.

G is centroid of ΔPQR

such that $RG : GM = 2 : 1$

So, coordinates of $M(8\lambda - 3, 2\lambda + 4, 2\lambda - 1)$

Now, $\quad \mathbf{RM} \cdot (8\hat{\mathbf{i}} + 2\hat{\mathbf{j}} + 2\hat{\mathbf{k}}) = 0$

$\Rightarrow \quad 8\cdot(8\lambda - 4) + 2(2\lambda + 2) + 2(2\lambda - 4) = 0 \Rightarrow 72\lambda - 36 = 0$

$\therefore \quad \lambda = \dfrac{1}{2}$

So, $M(1, 5, 0)$.

$\therefore$ Centroid $G\left(\dfrac{2 \times 1 + 1 \times 1}{3}, \dfrac{2 \times 5 + 1 \times 2}{3}, \dfrac{2 \times 0 + 1 \times 3}{3}\right)$

$\Rightarrow \quad G(1, 4, 1)$

$\therefore \quad \alpha^2 + \beta^2 + \gamma^2 = 18$

41. Given equation

$\dfrac{x - \lambda}{-2} = \dfrac{y - 2}{1} = \dfrac{z - 1}{1}$

and $\quad \dfrac{x - \sqrt{3}}{1} = \dfrac{y - 1}{-2} = \dfrac{z - 2}{1}$

$$\text{SD} = \left| \frac{\begin{vmatrix} \lambda - \sqrt{3} & 1 & -1 \\ -2 & 1 & 1 \\ 1 & -2 & 1 \end{vmatrix}}{\sqrt{(1 + 2)^2 + (-2 - 1)^2 + (4 - 1)^2}} \right|$$

$\Rightarrow \quad \pm 1 = \dfrac{(\lambda - \sqrt{3})(3) - 1(-3) - 1(3)}{\sqrt{9 + 9 + 9}}$

$\Rightarrow \quad \pm 3\sqrt{3} = 3\lambda - 3\sqrt{3} + 3 - 3$

$\Rightarrow \quad 3\lambda = 3\sqrt{3} \pm 3\sqrt{3} \Rightarrow \lambda = \sqrt{3} \pm \sqrt{3} \Rightarrow \lambda = 2\sqrt{3}, 0$

$\therefore$ Sum of all $\lambda = 2\sqrt{3} + 0 = 2\sqrt{3}$

42. $L_1 : \dfrac{x - 1}{2} = \dfrac{y + 1}{-3} = \dfrac{z + 4}{2}$

$L_1 : \mathbf{r} = (\hat{\mathbf{i}} - \hat{\mathbf{j}} - 4\hat{\mathbf{k}}) + \lambda(2\hat{\mathbf{i}} - 3\hat{\mathbf{j}} + 2\hat{\mathbf{k}})$

L_2 passes through $A(-4, 4, 3)$ and $B(-1, 6, 3)$.

DR's of $L_2: -1-(-4), 6-4, 3-3 \equiv 3, 2, 0$

$$L_2: \frac{x+4}{3} = \frac{y-4}{2} = \frac{z-3}{0}$$

$$L_2: \mathbf{r} = (-4\hat{\mathbf{i}} + 4\hat{\mathbf{j}} + 3\hat{\mathbf{k}}) + \mu\,(3\hat{\mathbf{i}} + 2\hat{\mathbf{j}} + 0\hat{\mathbf{k}})$$

$$\mathbf{a}_2 - \mathbf{a}_1 = -5\hat{\mathbf{i}} + 5\hat{\mathbf{j}} + 7\hat{\mathbf{k}}$$

$$\mathbf{b}_1 = 2\hat{\mathbf{i}} - 3\hat{\mathbf{j}} + 2\hat{\mathbf{k}},$$

$$\mathbf{b}_2 = 3\hat{\mathbf{i}} + 2\hat{\mathbf{j}} + 0\hat{\mathbf{k}}$$

$$\text{SD} = \left| \frac{(\mathbf{a}_2 - \mathbf{a}_1)\cdot(\mathbf{b}_1 \times \mathbf{b}_2)}{|\mathbf{b}_1 \times \mathbf{b}_2|} \right|$$

$$\mathbf{b}_1 \times \mathbf{b}_2 = \begin{vmatrix} \hat{\mathbf{i}} & \hat{\mathbf{j}} & \hat{\mathbf{k}} \\ 2 & -3 & 2 \\ 3 & 2 & 0 \end{vmatrix} = -4\hat{\mathbf{i}} + 6\hat{\mathbf{j}} + 13\hat{\mathbf{k}}$$

$$|\mathbf{b}_1 \times \mathbf{b}_2| = \sqrt{16 + 36 + 169} = \sqrt{221}$$

$$\text{SD} = \left| \frac{(-5\hat{\mathbf{i}} + 5\hat{\mathbf{j}} + 7\hat{\mathbf{k}})\cdot(-4\hat{\mathbf{i}} + 6\hat{\mathbf{j}} + 13\hat{\mathbf{k}})}{\sqrt{221}} \right|$$

$$= \frac{20 + 30 + 91}{\sqrt{221}} = \frac{141}{\sqrt{221}}$$

43. Let $\frac{x-1}{2} = \frac{y-2}{3} = \frac{z-3}{4} = \lambda$

and $P(2, 3, 5)$ and $Q(\alpha, \beta, \gamma)$.

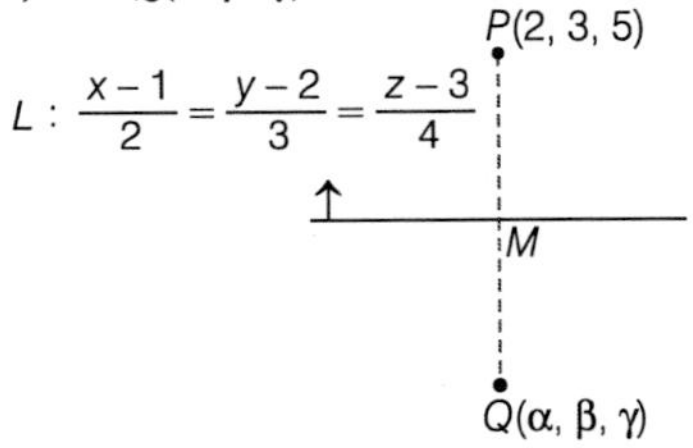

$\therefore$ DR's of $PQ: (\alpha - 2, \beta - 3, \gamma - 5)$

DR's of line $L: 2, 3, 4$

$\because$ L is perpendicular to PQ.

$\therefore\ 2(\alpha - 2) + 3(\beta - 3) + 4(\gamma - 5) = 0 \Rightarrow 2\alpha + 3\beta + 4\gamma = 33$

44. $L_1: \mathbf{r} = (-3\hat{\mathbf{i}} + 2\hat{\mathbf{k}}) + \lambda(2\hat{\mathbf{i}} + 3\hat{\mathbf{j}} + 5\hat{\mathbf{k}})$

$L_2: \mathbf{r} = (\hat{\mathbf{i}} - 2\hat{\mathbf{j}} + \hat{\mathbf{k}}) + \mu(-\hat{\mathbf{i}} + 3\hat{\mathbf{j}} + 2\hat{\mathbf{k}})$

Let L be a line which passes through $(5, -4, 3)$ and perpendicular to L_1, L_2 both

$$\mathbf{b} = \begin{vmatrix} \hat{\mathbf{i}} & \hat{\mathbf{j}} & \hat{\mathbf{k}} \\ 2 & 3 & 5 \\ -1 & 3 & 2 \end{vmatrix} = \hat{\mathbf{i}}(-9) - \hat{\mathbf{j}}(9) + \hat{\mathbf{k}}(9) = -9\hat{\mathbf{i}} - 9\hat{\mathbf{j}} + 9\hat{\mathbf{k}}$$

$\therefore$ Equation of line L

$$\mathbf{r} = 5\hat{\mathbf{i}} - 4\hat{\mathbf{j}} + 3\hat{\mathbf{k}} + \lambda(-9\hat{\mathbf{i}} - 9\hat{\mathbf{j}} + 9\hat{\mathbf{k}}) = 5\hat{\mathbf{i}} - 4\hat{\mathbf{j}} + 3\hat{\mathbf{k}} - 9\lambda(\hat{\mathbf{i}} + \hat{\mathbf{j}} - \hat{\mathbf{k}})$$

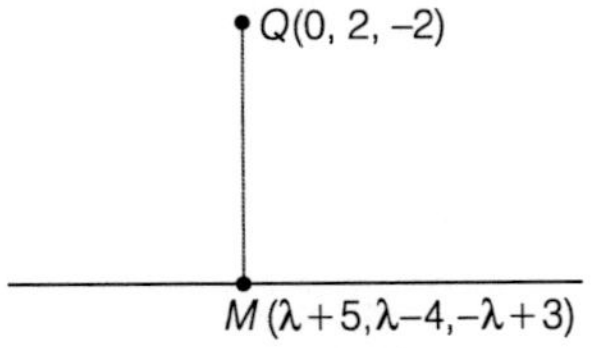

$$\frac{x-5}{1} = \frac{y+4}{1} = \frac{z-3}{-1}$$

$$\mathbf{QM} = (\lambda + 5)\hat{\mathbf{i}} + (\lambda - 6)\hat{\mathbf{j}} + (-\lambda + 5)\hat{\mathbf{k}}$$

$$\mathbf{QM}\cdot(\hat{\mathbf{i}} + \hat{\mathbf{j}} - \hat{\mathbf{k}}) = 0$$

$\Rightarrow\quad \lambda + 5 + \lambda - 6 + \lambda - 5 = 0$

$\Rightarrow\quad 3\lambda = 6 \Rightarrow \lambda = 2$

$\mathbf{QM} = 7\hat{\mathbf{i}} - 4\hat{\mathbf{j}} + 3\hat{\mathbf{k}}$

$\therefore$ Required distance $= |\mathbf{QM}|$

$$= \sqrt{49 + 16 + 9} = \sqrt{74} \text{ units}$$

45. Given, $L_1: \mathbf{r} = (\hat{\mathbf{i}} - \hat{\mathbf{j}} + 2\hat{\mathbf{k}}) + \lambda(\hat{\mathbf{i}} - \hat{\mathbf{j}} + 2\hat{\mathbf{k}})$,

$L_2: \mathbf{r} = (\hat{\mathbf{j}} - \hat{\mathbf{k}}) + \mu(3\hat{\mathbf{i}} + \hat{\mathbf{j}} + p\hat{\mathbf{k}})$

and $L_3: \mathbf{r} = \delta(l\hat{\mathbf{i}} + m\hat{\mathbf{j}} + n\hat{\mathbf{k}})$

$\therefore\quad L_1 \perp L_2 \Rightarrow \mathbf{b}_1 \cdot \mathbf{b}_2 = 0$

$\Rightarrow\quad 3 - 1 + 2p = 0 \Rightarrow p = -1$

$\because$ L_3 is perpendicular to L_1 and L_2.

$\therefore$ Parallel vector of $L_3 = k\,(\mathbf{b}_1 \times \mathbf{b}_2)$

$$= \begin{vmatrix} \hat{\mathbf{i}} & \hat{\mathbf{j}} & \hat{\mathbf{k}} \\ 1 & -1 & 2 \\ 3 & 1 & -1 \end{vmatrix}$$

$$= \hat{\mathbf{i}}(-1) - \hat{\mathbf{j}}(-7) + \hat{\mathbf{k}}(1 + 3)$$

$$= -\hat{\mathbf{i}} + 7\hat{\mathbf{j}} + 4\hat{\mathbf{k}}$$

Equation of line L_3 can be assumed

$\Rightarrow\quad \mathbf{r} = \delta(-\hat{\mathbf{i}} + 7\hat{\mathbf{j}} + 4\hat{\mathbf{k}})$

$\therefore$ L_3 will be passes through $(-1, 7, 4)$.

46. We have, $\frac{x+3}{5} = \frac{y-1}{2} = \frac{z+4}{3} = \lambda$ (let)

Now, the coordinates of any point Q on the line are

$$x = 5\lambda - 3,\ y = 2\lambda + 1,\ z = 3\lambda - 4$$

and given point is $P(1, 2, 3)$.

The direction ratios of PQ are $5\lambda - 4, 2\lambda - 1, 3\lambda - 7$ and the direction ratios of the given line are 5, 2, 3.

If PQ perpendicular line, then

$5(5\lambda - 4) + 2(2\lambda - 1) + 3(3\lambda - 7) = 0$

$\Rightarrow\ 25\lambda - 20 + 4\lambda - 2 + 9\lambda - 21 = 0$

$\Rightarrow\quad 38\lambda = 43 \Rightarrow \lambda = \frac{43}{38}$

Now, the foot of the perpendicular is $\frac{101}{38}, \frac{124}{38}, \frac{-23}{38}$.

So, $\alpha = \frac{101}{38}, \beta = \frac{62}{19}, \gamma = \frac{-23}{38}$

So, $19(\alpha + \beta + \gamma) = 101$

47. Given, lines are $\frac{x-2}{0} = \frac{y}{2} = \frac{z+3}{-1} = \lambda$ (let) ...(i)

Any point on the line (i) is $(2, 2\lambda, -\lambda - 3)$

and $\frac{x-1}{1} = \frac{y+3}{-3} = \frac{z+1}{1} = \mu$ (let) ...(ii)

Any point on the line (ii) is $(\mu + 1, -3\mu - 3, \mu - 1)$

Since, lines (i) and (ii) are intersecting

$\therefore\ \mu + 1 = 2, -3\mu - 3 = 2\lambda$ and $\mu - 1 = -\lambda - 3$

$\Rightarrow\quad \mu = 1, -3(1) - 3 = 2\lambda \Rightarrow \mu = 1, \lambda = -3$

$\therefore$ Point of intersection of both lines is $(2, -6, 0)$

Since, G(centroid) divides RM in $2:1$

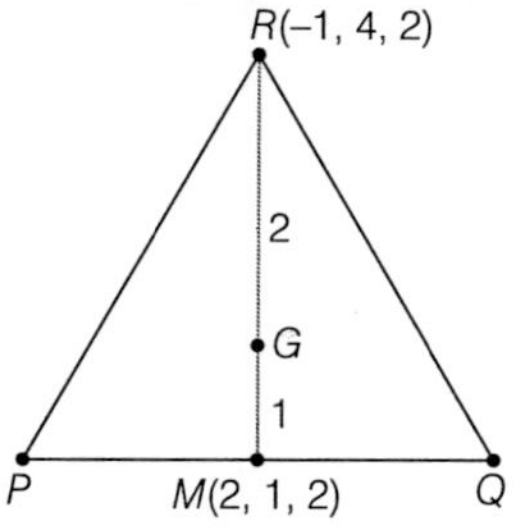

$$\therefore G \equiv \left(\frac{2\times 2-1}{2+1}, \frac{2\times 1+1\times 4}{2+1}, \frac{2\times 2+1\times 2}{2+1}\right)$$

$$\equiv (1, 2, 2)$$

$\therefore$ Distance of the centroid from the point of intersection of both lines $= \sqrt{(2-1)^2+(-6-2)^2+(0-2)^2}$

$$= \sqrt{1+64+4} = \sqrt{69} \text{ units}$$

48. Let $L_1 : \dfrac{x-0}{1} = \dfrac{y-1}{2} = \dfrac{z-2}{3} = k$

$\therefore$ Coordinates of M can be taken as

$$x = k, y = 2k+1, z = 3k+2$$

i.e. $M \equiv (k, 2k+1, 3k+2)$

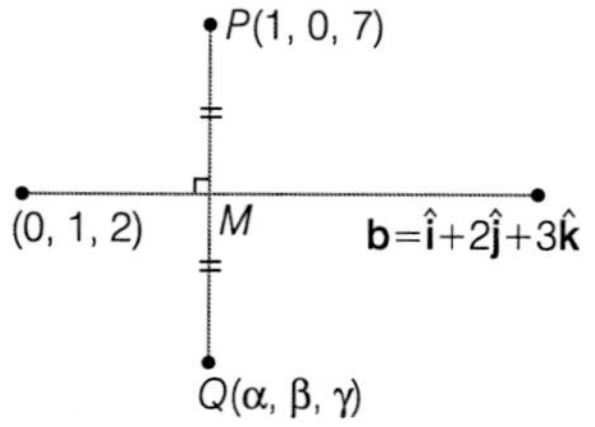

Now, $\mathbf{PM} = (k-1)\hat{\mathbf{i}} + (2k+1)\hat{\mathbf{j}} + (3k-5)\hat{\mathbf{k}}$

$\because$ $\mathbf{PM} \perp L_1$

$\therefore$ $\mathbf{PM}\cdot\mathbf{b} = 0$

$\Rightarrow$ $k-1+4k+2+9k-15=0$ $\quad$ [as $\mathbf{b} = \hat{\mathbf{i}}+2\hat{\mathbf{j}}+3\hat{\mathbf{k}}$]

$\Rightarrow$ $k = 1;$

$\therefore$ $M \equiv (1, 3, 5)$

Now, here M is mid-point of $\mathbf{P}$ and $\mathbf{Q}$.

$\therefore$ $\mathbf{Q} = 2\mathbf{M} - \mathbf{P}$

$\Rightarrow$ $\mathbf{Q} = (2\hat{\mathbf{i}}+6\hat{\mathbf{j}}+10\hat{\mathbf{k}}) - (\hat{\mathbf{i}}+7\hat{\mathbf{k}}) \Rightarrow \mathbf{Q} = \hat{\mathbf{i}}+6\hat{\mathbf{j}}+3\hat{\mathbf{k}}$

$\therefore$ $(\alpha, \beta, \gamma) = (1, 6, 3)$

Let required line having direction cosines $< l, m, n >$.

Given, $m = -\dfrac{1}{2}$ and $n = -\dfrac{1}{\sqrt{2}}$

According to the question,

$\because$ $l^2+m^2+n^2 = 1 \Rightarrow l^2 = \dfrac{1}{4} \Rightarrow l = \dfrac{1}{2}$

[$\because$ line makes an acute angle with X-axis]

Therefore, equation of line passes through $(1, 6, 3)$ will be

$$\mathbf{r} = (\hat{\mathbf{i}}+6\hat{\mathbf{j}}+3\hat{\mathbf{k}}) + \mu\left(\frac{1}{2}\hat{\mathbf{i}} - \frac{1}{2}\hat{\mathbf{j}} - \frac{1}{\sqrt{2}}\hat{\mathbf{k}}\right)$$

Option (d) satisfying for $\mu = 4$.

49. Given equation of lines are

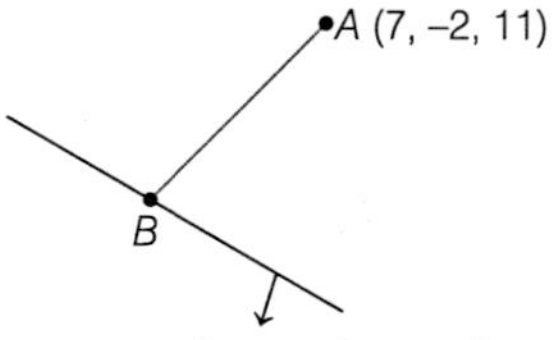

$$\frac{x-6}{1} = \frac{y-4}{0} = \frac{z-8}{3}$$

$$\frac{x-6}{1} = \frac{y-4}{0} = \frac{z-8}{3} \quad ...(i)$$

and $$\frac{x-5}{2} = \frac{y-1}{-3} = \frac{z-5}{6} = \lambda \text{ (let)} \quad ...(ii)$$

Let $A \equiv (7, -2, 11)$

Any point B taken on Eq. (ii) as $(2\lambda+5, -3\lambda+1, 6\lambda+5)$.

$\because$ Point B lies on Eq. (i).

$$\therefore \underset{\text{(iii)}}{\frac{2\lambda+5-6}{1}} = \underset{\text{(iv)}}{\frac{-3\lambda+1-4}{0}} = \underset{\text{(v)}}{\frac{6\lambda+5-8}{3}}$$

From Eqs. (iii) and (iv), we get

$$-3\lambda - 3 = 0 \Rightarrow \lambda = -1$$

So, $B \equiv (3, 4, -1)$

Hence, $AB = \sqrt{(7-3)^2+(-2-4)^2+(11+1)^2}$

$$= \sqrt{16+36+144} = \sqrt{196} = 14$$

50. **PQ** is perpendicular to L_1 and L_2

$$(3+\mu-\lambda, 3+\mu+\lambda, 3-\mu-\lambda)$$

$$(3+\mu-\lambda)(1) + (3+\mu+\lambda)(-1) + (3-\mu-\lambda)(1) = 0$$

$\Rightarrow$ $-3\lambda - \mu + 3 = 0 \quad ...(i)$

$\Rightarrow$ $(3+\mu-\lambda)(1) + (3+\mu+\lambda)(1) + (3-\mu-\lambda)(-1) = 0$

$\Rightarrow$ $\lambda + 3\mu + 3 = 0 \quad ...(ii)$

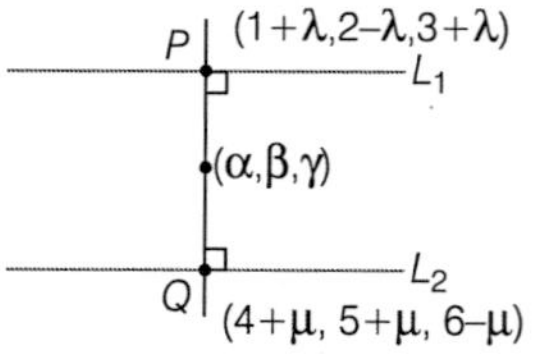

On solving Eqs. (i) and (ii), we get

$$8\mu = -12, \mu = \frac{-3}{2}, \lambda = \frac{3}{2}$$

$$P\left(\frac{5}{2}, \frac{1}{2}, \frac{9}{2}\right) \text{ and } Q\left(\frac{5}{2}, \frac{7}{2}, \frac{15}{2}\right)$$

$$\alpha = \frac{5}{2}, \beta = 2, \gamma = 6$$

Hence, $2(\alpha+\beta+\gamma) = 21$

51. Line passing through $A(4, -6, -2)$ and $B(16, -2, 4)$

$$L : \frac{x-4}{12} = \frac{y+6}{4} = \frac{z+2}{6}$$

$$L : \frac{x-4}{6} = \frac{y+6}{2} = \frac{z+2}{3} = \lambda \text{ (let)}$$

$$x = 6\lambda + 4, y = 2\lambda - 6, z = 3\lambda - 2$$

Let $P(6\lambda + 4, 2\lambda - 6, 3\lambda - 2)$

$$PA = 21$$

$$\sqrt{(6\lambda)^2 + (2\lambda)^2 + (3\lambda)^2} = 21$$

$$\lambda = 3$$

$P(22, 0, 7) \equiv P(a, b, c)$

$Q(4, -12, 3)$

$PQ = \sqrt{18^2 + 12^2 + 4^2} = 22$

52. $x = y, z = 1 \rightarrow$ Line $[L_1]$

$$\frac{x}{1} = \frac{y}{1} = \frac{z-1}{0}$$

Let point Q on line $(\lambda, \lambda, 1)$

$x = -y, z = -1 \rightarrow$ Line $[L_2]$

$$\frac{x}{1} = \frac{y}{-1} = \frac{z+1}{0}$$

Let point R on line $L_2\ (\mu, -\mu, -1)$

Given, point $P(a, a, a)$

$$\mathbf{PQ} \cdot \mathbf{b}_1 = 0, \quad \mathbf{PR} \cdot \mathbf{b}_2 = 0$$

$$(a - \lambda) + (a - \lambda) + 0 = 0$$

$$(a - \mu) + (a + \mu)(-1) + 0 = 0$$

$$a = \lambda, \quad \mu = 0$$

$\because \quad \angle QPR = 90°$

$$\mathbf{PQ} \cdot \mathbf{PR} = 0$$

$\Rightarrow \quad (\lambda - a)(\mu - a) + (\lambda - a)(-\mu + a) + (a - 1)(a + 1) = 0$

$\Rightarrow \quad 0 + 0 + a^2 - 1 = 0$

$\Rightarrow \quad a^2 = 1$

$\therefore \quad 12a^2 = 12$

53. $L_1 : \dfrac{x-1}{3} = \dfrac{y-2}{2} = \dfrac{z+1}{-2}, \quad L_2 : \dfrac{x+2}{-3} = \dfrac{y-2}{-2} = \dfrac{z-1}{4}$

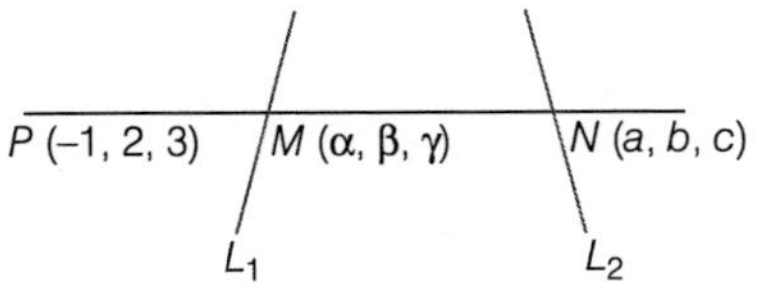

Let a point on L_1

$\Rightarrow (3\lambda + 1, 2\lambda + 2, -2\lambda - 1) = M(\alpha, \beta, \gamma)$

$$\alpha + \beta + \gamma = 3\lambda + 2 \quad \text{...(i)}$$

Similarly, on L_2

$\Rightarrow (-3\mu - 2, -2\mu + 2, 4\mu + 1) = N(a, b, c)$

$$a + b + c = -\mu + 1 \quad \text{...(ii)}$$

$\therefore$ **PM** || **PN**

$$\frac{3\lambda + 1 + 1}{-3\mu - 2 + 1} = \frac{2\lambda + 2 - 2}{-2\mu + 2 - 2} = \frac{-2\lambda - 1 - 3}{4\mu + 1 - 3}$$

$$\Rightarrow \quad \frac{3\lambda + 2}{-3\mu - 1} = \frac{2\lambda}{-2\mu} = \frac{-2\lambda - 4}{4\mu - 2}$$

$\Rightarrow -3\lambda\mu - 2\mu = -3\lambda\mu - \lambda;$

$\Rightarrow \quad \lambda = 2\mu$

and $4\lambda\mu - 2\lambda = 4\lambda\mu - 8$

$2\lambda = 8, \lambda = 4$

$\therefore \quad \lambda = 4$ and $\mu = 2$

Required value $\dfrac{(\alpha + \beta + \gamma)^2}{(a + b + c)^2} = \dfrac{(3\lambda + 2)^2}{(-\mu + 1)^2}$ [from Eqs. (i) and (ii)]

$$= \frac{14^2}{1^2} = 196$$

54. Given lines are

$$\frac{x+1}{1} = \frac{y-0}{1/2} = \frac{z-0}{-1/12} : L_1$$

and $\quad \dfrac{x-0}{1} = \dfrac{y+2}{1} = \dfrac{z-1}{1/6} : L_2$

Here, $x_1 = -1, y_1 = 0, z_1 = 0$

$$a_1 = 1, b_1 = \frac{1}{2}, c_1 = -1/12$$

and $\quad x_2 = 0, y_2 = -2, z_2 = 1$

$$a_2 = 1, b_2 = 1, c_2 = \frac{1}{6}$$

Now, $d = \left| \dfrac{\begin{vmatrix} x_2 - x_1 & y_2 - y_1 & z_2 - z_1 \\ a_1 & b_1 & c_1 \\ a_2 & b_2 & c_2 \end{vmatrix}}{\sqrt{(a_1 b_2 - a_2 b_1)^2 + (b_1 c_2 - b_2 c_1)^2 + (c_1 a_2 - c_2 a_1)^2}} \right|$

So, $d_1 = \left| \dfrac{\begin{vmatrix} 0+1 & -2 & 1 \\ 1 & 1/2 & -1/12 \\ 1 & 1 & 1/6 \end{vmatrix}}{\sqrt{\left(1 - \frac{1}{2}\right)^2 + \left(\frac{1}{12} + \frac{1}{12}\right)^2 + \left(-\frac{1}{12} - \frac{1}{6}\right)^2}} \right|$

$$= \left| \frac{\begin{vmatrix} 1 & -2 & 1 \\ 1 & 1/2 & -1/12 \\ 1 & 1 & 1/6 \end{vmatrix}}{\sqrt{\frac{1}{4} + \frac{1}{36} + \frac{1}{16}}} \right| \left| \frac{\left(\frac{1}{12} + \frac{1}{12}\right) + 2\left(1/6 + \frac{1}{12}\right) + (1 - 1/2)}{\sqrt{\frac{36 + 4 + 9}{144}}} \right|$$

$$= \frac{12}{7} \times \left[\frac{1}{6} + \frac{1}{2} + \frac{1}{2}\right] = 2$$

Similarly, $d_2 = \left| \dfrac{\begin{vmatrix} 0 & 10 & 2 \\ 2 & -7 & 5 \\ 2 & 1 & -3 \end{vmatrix}}{\sqrt{256 + 256 + 256}} \right|$

$$= \frac{1}{16\sqrt{3}}[0 - 10(-6 - 10) + 2(2 + 14)]$$

$$= \frac{1}{16\sqrt{3}}(160 + 32) = \frac{12}{\sqrt{3}}$$

Now, $\frac{32\sqrt{3}d_1}{d_2} = \frac{32\sqrt{3}\times 2}{12/\sqrt{3}} = 16$

Time Saving Technique

We have, $L_1: \frac{x+1}{1} = \frac{y-0}{1/2} = \frac{z-0}{-1/12}$

$L_2: \frac{x-0}{1} = \frac{y+2}{1} = \frac{z-1}{1/6}$

$d_1 = \left|\frac{(\mathbf{a}_2 - \mathbf{a}_1)\cdot(\mathbf{b}_1 \times \mathbf{b}_2)}{|(\mathbf{b}_1 \times \mathbf{b}_2)|}\right| = 2$

Similarly, we can find

$d_2 = \frac{12}{\sqrt{3}}$

So, $\frac{d_1 32\sqrt{3}}{d_2} = \frac{2\times 32\times\sqrt{3}\times\sqrt{3}}{12} = 16$

55. Let $M(4\lambda+5, \lambda+4, 3\lambda+5)$ and $N(12\mu-8, 5\mu-2, 9\mu-11)$ be two points on given lines.

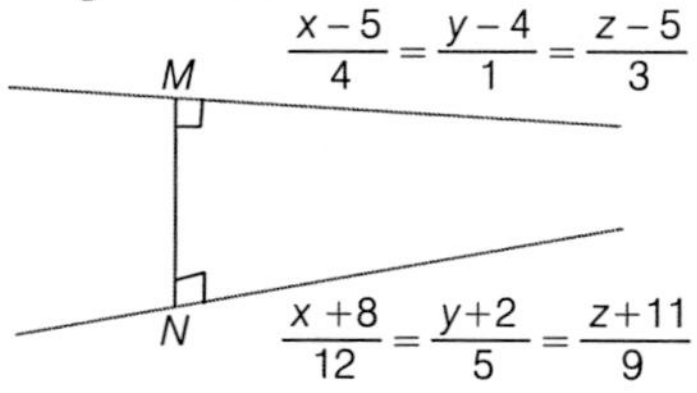

$\therefore$ $\mathbf{MN} \perp \mathbf{b}_1$ and $\mathbf{MN} \perp \mathbf{b}_2$

$\mathbf{MN}\cdot\mathbf{b}_1 = 0$

$4(12\mu - 4\lambda - 13) + 1(5\mu - \lambda - 6) + 3(9\mu - 3\lambda - 16) = 0$

$\Rightarrow \quad 48\mu - 16\lambda - 52 + 5\mu - \lambda - 6 + 27\mu - 9\lambda - 48 = 0$

$\Rightarrow \quad 80\mu - 26\lambda = 106$

$\Rightarrow \quad 40\mu - 13\lambda = 53$ ...(i)

$\mathbf{MN}\cdot\mathbf{b}_2 = 0$

$12(12\mu - 4\lambda - 13) + 5(5\mu - \lambda - 6) + 9(9\mu - 3\lambda - 16) = 0$

$\Rightarrow 144\mu - 48\lambda - 156 + 25\mu - 5\lambda - 30 + 81\mu - 27\lambda - 144 = 0$

$\Rightarrow \quad 250\mu - 80\lambda = 330$

$\Rightarrow \quad 25\mu - 8\lambda = 33$ ...(ii)

On solving Eqs. (i) and (ii), we get

$\mu = 1, \ \lambda = -1$

$\therefore M = (1, 3, 2)$ and $N = (4, 3, -2)$

$\mathbf{OM} = \hat{\mathbf{i}} + 3\hat{\mathbf{j}} + 2\hat{\mathbf{k}}$

$\mathbf{ON} = 4\hat{\mathbf{i}} + 3\hat{\mathbf{j}} - 2\hat{\mathbf{k}}$

$\mathbf{OM}\cdot\mathbf{ON} = 4 + 9 - 4 = 9$

56. Given, lines are $x = y + 2 = z$

$\Rightarrow \quad \frac{x}{1} = \frac{y-(-2)}{1} = \frac{z}{1} = t$ (let) ...(i)

Let any point on the line (i) be $P(t, t-2, t)$

and any point on the $x + 2 = 2y = 2z$ is $Q(2s-2, s, s)$.

$\therefore$ Direction ratios of PQ are $2s - 2 - t, s - t + 2, s - t$

$\therefore \quad \frac{2s-2-t}{2} = \frac{s-t+2}{1} = \frac{s-t}{2}$

$\Rightarrow \quad t = 6$ and $s = 2$

$\therefore \quad P \equiv (6, 4, 6)$ and $Q \equiv (2, 2, 2)$

Equation of line PQ is

$\frac{x-2}{2} = \frac{y-2}{1} = \frac{z-2}{2} = \lambda$ (let) ...(ii)

Let any point on the line (ii) be $F(2\lambda+2, \lambda+2, 2\lambda+2)$ and let $A(1, 2, 12)$

$\therefore$Direction ratio of AF is $2\lambda+1, \lambda, 2\lambda-10$.

Here, $\mathbf{AF}\cdot\mathbf{PQ} = 0$

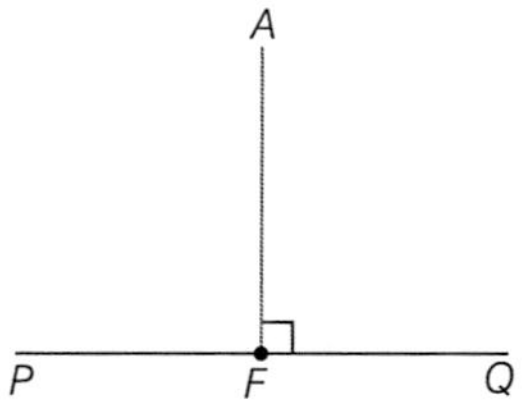

$\Rightarrow \quad (2\lambda+1)(2) + (\lambda)(1) + (2\lambda-10)(2) = 0$

$\Rightarrow \quad 4\lambda + 2 + \lambda + 4\lambda - 20 = 0$

$\Rightarrow \quad 9\lambda = 18$

$\Rightarrow \quad \lambda = 2$

$\therefore \quad F \equiv (6, 4, 6)$

$\therefore \quad AF = \sqrt{(6-1)^2 + (4-2)^2 + (6-12)^2}$

$= \sqrt{25 + 4 + 36} = \sqrt{65}$

$\therefore \quad l^2 = 65$

57. Let $L_1: \frac{x-2}{2} = \frac{y}{-2} = \frac{z-7}{16} = \lambda$ (let)

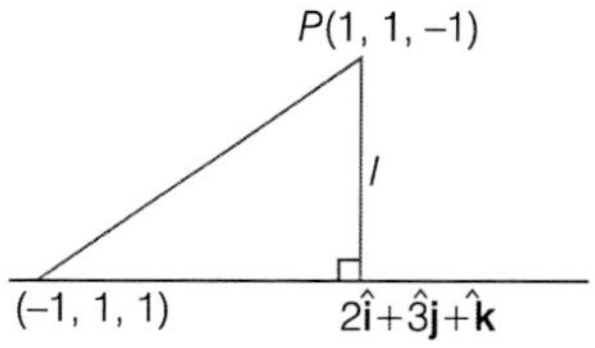

and $L_2: \frac{x+3}{4} = \frac{y+2}{3} = \frac{z+2}{1} = \mu$ (let)

any point taken on L_1 as $(2\lambda+2, -2\lambda, 16\lambda+7)$

and any point taken on L_2 as $(4\mu-3, 3\mu-2, \mu-2)$

According to the question,

$2\lambda + 2 = 4\mu - 3$ ...(i)

$-2\lambda = 3\mu - 2$ ...(ii)

$16\lambda + 7 = \mu - 2$ ...(iii)

On solving Eqs. (i) and (ii), we get

$\mu = 1$ and $\lambda = -\frac{1}{2}$ and these values satisfies Eq. (iii).

So, $P \equiv (1, 1, -1)$

Now, line $\frac{x+1}{2} = \frac{y-1}{3} = \frac{z-1}{1}$ passes through $(-1, 1, 1)$ and having DR's $< 2, 3, 1 >$ [as shown in figure]

Now, projection of $2\hat{\mathbf{i}} + 0\hat{\mathbf{j}} + (-2)\hat{\mathbf{k}}$ on $2\hat{\mathbf{i}} + 3\hat{\mathbf{j}} + \hat{\mathbf{k}}$ is

$= \frac{4-2}{\sqrt{4+9+1}} = \frac{2}{\sqrt{14}}$

$\therefore \quad l^2 = 8 - \frac{4}{14} = \frac{108}{14}$

$\Rightarrow \quad 14l^2 = 108$

58. Given line, $\frac{x-1}{2} = \frac{y-2}{3} = \frac{z-3}{4} = \lambda$ ...(i)

$\therefore$ Any point on the line $A(2\lambda + 1, 3\lambda + 2, 4\lambda + 3)$.

Since, line L pass through the point $B(0, 1, 2)$ and intersects line (i).

$\therefore$ Direction ratios of AB are

$$0 - 2\lambda - 1, 1 - 3\lambda - 2, 2 - 4\lambda - 3$$

i.e. $$-2\lambda - 1, -3\lambda - 1, -4\lambda - 1$$

Line L parallel to the plane $2x + y - 3z = 4$

$\therefore 2(-2\lambda - 1) + 1(-3\lambda - 1) - 3(-4\lambda - 1) = 0$

$\Rightarrow \quad -4\lambda - 2 - 3\lambda - 1 + 12\lambda + 3 = 0$

$\Rightarrow \quad 5\lambda = 0 \Rightarrow \lambda = 0$

$\therefore$ Direction ratios of $AB = -1, -1, -1$ i.e. 1, 1, 1

$\therefore$ Equation of line L is

$$\frac{x-0}{1} = \frac{y-1}{1} = \frac{z-2}{1} = \mu$$

$\Rightarrow \quad x = \mu, y = \mu + 1, z = \mu + 2$

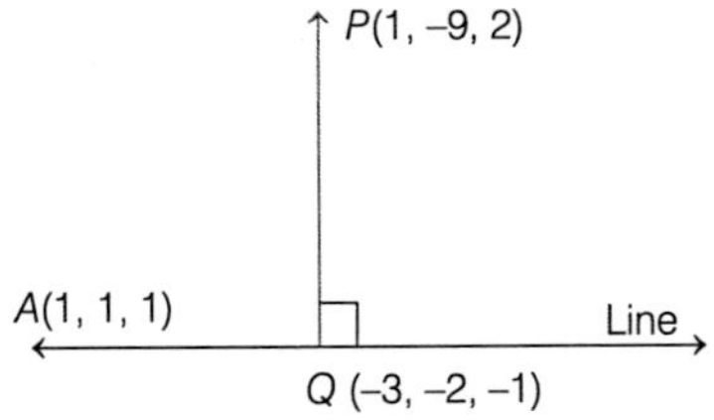

$\therefore$ Distance radius of $PQ = \mu - 1, \mu + 10, \mu$

Since, $PQ \perp L$

$\therefore \quad 1(\mu - 1) + 1(\mu + 10) + \mu(1) = 0$

$\Rightarrow \quad \mu - 1 + \mu + 10 + \mu = 0$

$\Rightarrow \quad 3\mu + 9 = 0 \Rightarrow \mu = -3$

$\therefore Q$ is $(-3, -2, -1)$

$\therefore$ Distance of the point $P(1, -9, 2)$ from the line L is

$$\sqrt{(-3-1)^2 + (-2+9)^2 + (-1-2)^2} = \sqrt{16 + 49 + 9} = \sqrt{74}$$

59. The given lines are

$$\frac{x-\lambda}{0} = \frac{y-3}{4} = \frac{z+6}{1}$$

$$\frac{x+\lambda}{3} = \frac{y}{-4} = \frac{z-6}{0}$$

and shortest distance is 13 units.

We know, formula for shortest distance,

$$\text{SD} = \frac{\begin{vmatrix} x_2 - x_1 & y_2 - y_1 & z_2 - z_1 \\ a_1 & b_1 & c_1 \\ a_2 & b_2 & c_2 \end{vmatrix}}{\left|\begin{vmatrix} \hat{\mathbf{i}} & \hat{\mathbf{j}} & \hat{\mathbf{k}} \\ a_1 & b_1 & c_1 \\ a_2 & b_2 & c_2 \end{vmatrix}\right|} = \left|\frac{\begin{vmatrix} 2\lambda & 3 & -12 \\ 0 & 4 & 1 \\ 3 & -4 & 0 \end{vmatrix}}{\left|\begin{vmatrix} \hat{\mathbf{i}} & \hat{\mathbf{j}} & \hat{\mathbf{k}} \\ 0 & 4 & 1 \\ 3 & -4 & 0 \end{vmatrix}\right|}\right|$$

$$= \left|\frac{2\lambda \times (4) + 3(3) - 12(-12)}{|4\hat{\mathbf{i}} + 3\hat{\mathbf{j}} - 12\hat{\mathbf{k}}|}\right|$$

$$= \frac{|8\lambda + 153|}{\sqrt{16 + 9 + 144}} = \frac{|8\lambda + 153|}{13}$$

According to the question,

$$\frac{|8\lambda + 153|}{13} = 13 \Rightarrow |8\lambda + 153| = 169$$

$\Rightarrow \quad 8\lambda + 153 = 169 \Rightarrow \lambda = \frac{16}{8} = 2$

or $\quad (8\lambda + 153) = -169 \Rightarrow 8\lambda = -322$

$\Rightarrow \quad \lambda = \frac{-322}{8} = \frac{-161}{4}$

Let S be the set of all values of λ.

So, $8\left|\sum_{\lambda \in S} \lambda\right| = 8\left|2 - \frac{161}{4}\right| = 8\left|\frac{-153}{4}\right| = 306$

60. **Decoding the Question**

Condition of coplanarity is

$$\begin{vmatrix} x_2 - x_1 & a_1 & a_2 \\ y_2 - y_1 & b_1 & b_2 \\ z_2 - z_1 & c_1 & c_2 \end{vmatrix} = 0$$

where a_1, b_1, c_1 are direction cosines of Ist line and a_2, b_2, c_2 are direction cosines of 2nd line.

Points $(-3, 1, 5)$ and $(-1, 2, 4)$, we get

$$\begin{vmatrix} -2 & -3 & -1 \\ -1 & 1 & 2 \\ 0 & 5 & 4 \end{vmatrix} = -2(4 - 10) - 3(4) - 1(-5)$$

$$= 12 - 12 + 5 = 5 \neq 0$$

Points $(-3, 1, 5)$ and $(-1, 2, 5)$, we get

$$\begin{vmatrix} -2 & -3 & -1 \\ -1 & 1 & 2 \\ 0 & 5 & 5 \end{vmatrix} = -2(5 - 10) - 3(5) - 1(-5)$$

$$= 10 - 15 + 5 = 0$$

Points $(-3, 1, 5)$ and $(-1, 2, 5)$, we get

$$\begin{vmatrix} -4 & -3 & -1 \\ -1 & 1 & 2 \\ 0 & 5 & 5 \end{vmatrix} = -4(5 - 10) - 3(5) - 1(-5)$$

$$= 20 - 15 + 5 = 10 \neq 0$$

Points $(-3, 1, 5)$ and $(1, 2, 5)$, we get

$$\begin{vmatrix} -2 & -3 & 1 \\ -1 & 1 & 2 \\ 0 & 5 & 5 \end{vmatrix} = -2(-5) - 3(5) + 1(-5)$$

$$= 10 - 15 - 5 = -10 \neq 0$$

Hence, the line $\frac{x+3}{-3} = \frac{y-1}{1} = \frac{z-5}{5}$ coplanar with the line $\frac{x+1}{-1} = \frac{y-2}{2} = \frac{z-5}{5}$.

61. We have, $l_2 : 3x + 2y + z - 2 = 0 = x - 3y + 2z - 13$ is intersection of planes

$$3x + 2y + z - 2 = 0 \text{ and } x - 3y + 2z - 13 = 0$$

Let $x = 1, 3 + 2y + z - 2 = 0$

$\Rightarrow \quad 2y + z + 1 = 0$ ...(i)

and $\quad 1 - 3y + 2z - 13 = 0$

$\Rightarrow \quad -3y + 2z - 12 = 0$ ...(ii)

$\therefore$ Point (1, – 2, 3) lies on l_2.

Let direction ratios of l_2 be $< l, m, n >$.

Since, it's the intersection of both planes, so it is perpendicular to normals of both planes.

$$\therefore \quad 3l + 2m + n = 0 \quad \text{...(iii)}$$

$$l - 3m + 2n = 0 \quad \text{...(iv)}$$

From Eqs. (iii) and (iv), we get $\frac{l}{-7} = \frac{m}{5} = \frac{n}{11}$

So, direction ratios of $l_2 : < -7, 5, 11 >$.

Now, $l_1 : \frac{x+5}{3} = \frac{y+4}{1} = \frac{z-\alpha}{-2}$

$\therefore$ Direction ratios of $l_1 : < 3, 1, -2 >$ and $(-5, -4, \alpha)$ is a point on l_1.

Since, l_1 and l_2 are coplanar.

$$\therefore \begin{vmatrix} 1-(-5) & -2-(-4) & 3-\alpha \\ 3 & 1 & -2 \\ -7 & 5 & 11 \end{vmatrix} = 0$$

$$\Rightarrow \begin{vmatrix} 6 & 2 & 3-\alpha \\ 3 & 1 & -2 \\ -7 & 5 & 11 \end{vmatrix} = 0$$

On applying $R_1 \to R_1 - 2R_2$, we get

$$\begin{vmatrix} 0 & 0 & 7-\alpha \\ 3 & 1 & -2 \\ -7 & 5 & 11 \end{vmatrix} = 0$$

$$\Rightarrow \quad 7 - \alpha = 0 \Rightarrow \alpha = 7$$

Let $(3k-5, k-4, -2k+7)$ be a point on l_1.

For $P(a, b, c)$,

$$a = 3k - 5,\ b = k - 4,\ c = -2k + 7$$

Direction ratios of PQ

$$= < 3k - 5 - (-4), k - 4 - (-3), -2k + 7 - 2 >$$
$$= < 3k - 1, k - 1, 5 - 2k >$$

For nearest point, $PQ \perp l_1$

$\Rightarrow 3(3k-1) + 1(k-1) - 2(5-2k) = 0 \Rightarrow k = 1$

$\therefore \quad a = -2, b = -3, c = 5$

$\therefore |a| + |b| + |c| = |-2| + |-3| + |5| = 10$

62. We have, $\frac{x}{1} = \frac{6-y}{2} = \frac{z+8}{5}$ intersect the line

$$\frac{x-5}{4} = \frac{y-7}{3} = \frac{z+2}{1} \text{ and } \frac{x+3}{6} = \frac{3-y}{3} = \frac{z-6}{1}$$

Now, $$\frac{x}{1} = \frac{6-y}{2} = \frac{z+8}{5} = \lambda \quad \text{...(i)}$$

$$\Rightarrow \quad x = \lambda, y = 6 - 2\lambda, z = 5\lambda - 8$$

Also, $$\frac{x-5}{4} = \frac{y-7}{3} = \frac{z+2}{1} = k \quad \text{...(ii)}$$

$$\Rightarrow \quad x = 4k + 5, y = 3k + 7, z = k - 2$$

and $$\frac{x+3}{6} = \frac{3-y}{3} = \frac{z-6}{1} = \mu \quad \text{...(iii)}$$

$$\Rightarrow \quad x = 6\mu - 3, y = 3 - 3\mu, z = \mu + 6$$

On solving Eqs (i) and (ii), we get

$$\lambda = 1, k = -1$$

$\therefore$ Coordinates of A are $(1, 4, -3)$.

On solving Eqs. (i) and (ii), we get

$$\lambda = 3, \mu = 1$$

$\therefore$ Coordinates of B are $(3, 0, 7)$.

Coordinates of mid-point of AB are $\left(\frac{1+3}{2}, \frac{4+0}{2}, \frac{-3+7}{2}\right)$

or (2, 2, 2).

Perpendicular distance of mid-point of AB from the plane $2x - 2y + z = 14$ is

$$\frac{|2(2) - 2(2) + 2 - 14|}{\sqrt{2^2 + (-2)^2 + 1^2}} = 4$$

63. Let θ be the angle between the plane and the line

Now, $$\sin\theta = \frac{a \times 1 + 1 \times (-1) + (-1) \times 1}{\sqrt{a^2 + 1^2 + (-1)^2} \cdot \sqrt{1^2 + 1^2 + 1^2}}$$

$$\Rightarrow \quad \sqrt{1 - \cos^2\theta} = \frac{(a-2)}{\sqrt{a^2+2}\sqrt{3}}$$

$$\Rightarrow \quad \sqrt{1 - \frac{1}{9}} = \frac{(a-2)}{\sqrt{3(a^2+2)}} \quad \left[\because \cos\theta = \frac{1}{3}\right]$$

$$\Rightarrow \quad \frac{8}{9} = \frac{(a-2)^2}{3(a^2+2)}$$

$$\Rightarrow \quad 3(a-2)^2 = 8a^2 + 16 \Rightarrow 5a^2 + 12a + 4 = 0$$

$$\Rightarrow \quad a = -2, -\frac{2}{5}$$

$$\because \quad a \in Z \Rightarrow a = -2$$

Distance of $(6, -6, 4)$ from the plane $-2x + y - z - b = 0$ is $3\sqrt{6}$

$$\Rightarrow \quad \frac{|-2(6) + 1(-6) - 1(4) - b|}{\sqrt{(-2)^2 + 1^2 + (-1)^2}} = 3\sqrt{6}$$

$$\Rightarrow \quad |b + 22| = 3\sqrt{6} \times \sqrt{6} = 18$$

$$\Rightarrow \quad b + 22 = \pm 18$$

$$\Rightarrow \quad b = -4, -40$$

$$\because \quad |a - b| \le 10 \Rightarrow b = -4$$

$$\Rightarrow \quad a^4 + b^2 = (-2)^4 + (-4)^2 = 32$$

64. Given equations of lines are

$$L : \frac{x-5}{-2} = \frac{y-\lambda}{0} = \frac{z+\lambda}{1}$$

and $$L_1 : \frac{x+1}{1} = \frac{y-1}{1} = \frac{4-z}{1} \text{ or } \frac{x+1}{1} = \frac{y-1}{1} = \frac{z-4}{-1}$$

We have, $\mathbf{a}_1 = 5\hat{\mathbf{i}} + \lambda\hat{\mathbf{j}} - \lambda\hat{\mathbf{k}}$, $\mathbf{b}_1 = -2\hat{\mathbf{i}} + 0\hat{\mathbf{j}} + \hat{\mathbf{k}}$

$$\mathbf{a}_2 = -\hat{\mathbf{i}} + \hat{\mathbf{j}} + 4\hat{\mathbf{k}},\ \mathbf{b}_2 = \hat{\mathbf{i}} + \hat{\mathbf{j}} - \hat{\mathbf{k}}$$

Now, $\mathbf{a}_2 - \mathbf{a}_1 = -6\hat{\mathbf{i}} + (1-\lambda)\hat{\mathbf{j}} + (4+\lambda)\hat{\mathbf{k}}$

$$\mathbf{b}_1 \times \mathbf{b}_2 = \begin{vmatrix} \hat{\mathbf{i}} & \hat{\mathbf{j}} & \hat{\mathbf{k}} \\ -2 & 0 & 1 \\ 1 & 1 & -1 \end{vmatrix} = -\hat{\mathbf{i}} - \hat{\mathbf{j}} - 2\hat{\mathbf{k}}$$

$$\therefore \quad (\mathbf{a}_2 - \mathbf{a}_1) \cdot (\mathbf{b}_1 \times \mathbf{b}_2)$$
$$= [-6\hat{\mathbf{i}} + (1-\lambda)\hat{\mathbf{j}} + (4+\lambda)\hat{\mathbf{k}}] \cdot [-\hat{\mathbf{i}} - \hat{\mathbf{j}} - 2\hat{\mathbf{k}}]$$
$$= 6 - 1 + \lambda - 8 - 2\lambda = -3 - \lambda$$

and $$|\mathbf{b}_1 \times \mathbf{b}_2| = \sqrt{(-1)^2 + (-1)^2 + (-2)^2} = \sqrt{6}$$

Again, according to the question,

$$\left|\frac{(\mathbf{a}_2-\mathbf{a}_1)\cdot(\mathbf{b}_1\times\mathbf{b}_2)}{|\mathbf{b}_1\times\mathbf{b}_2|}\right|=2\sqrt{6}$$

$$\Rightarrow \quad \left|\frac{-3-\lambda}{\sqrt{6}}\right|=2\sqrt{6}$$

$$\Rightarrow \quad |-3-\lambda|=12$$

$$\Rightarrow \quad -(3+\lambda)=\pm 12 \Rightarrow \lambda=9,-15$$

But, $\lambda \geq 0$; $\lambda=9$

So, equation of line L is

$$\frac{x-5}{-2}=\frac{y-9}{0}=\frac{z+9}{1}$$

Since, (α, β, γ) lies on L, so

$(\alpha, \beta, \gamma)=(-2k+5, 9, k-9)$, where $k \in R$

$\therefore \quad \alpha=-2k+5$ and $\gamma=k-9$

Again, $\alpha+2\gamma=-2k+5+2k-18$

$=-13$

So, $\alpha+2\gamma=24$ is not possible.

65. Equation of line passing through $(-3, 2, 3)$ and parallel to a line with direction ratios $(3, 3, -1)$

$$L: \frac{x+3}{3}=\frac{y-2}{3}=\frac{z-3}{-1}=\lambda$$

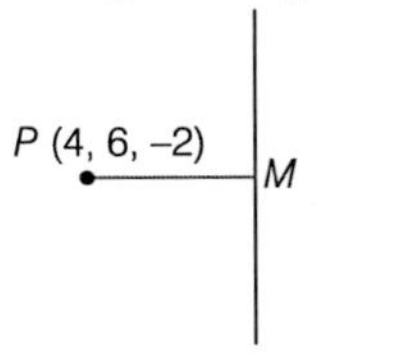

$$L: x=3\lambda-3, y=3\lambda+2, z=-\lambda+3$$

Let $M(3\lambda-3, 3\lambda+2, -\lambda+3)$

Direction ratios of line

$PM: (3\lambda-3-4, 3\lambda+2-6, -\lambda+3+2)$

$\equiv(3\lambda-7, 3\lambda-4, -\lambda+5)$

Direction ratios of line $L: 3, 3, -1$

We know that if two lines are perpendicular, then

$$a_1a_2+b_1b_2+c_1c_2=0$$

Here, $PM \perp L$

$\Rightarrow \quad 3(3\lambda-7)+3(3\lambda-4)-1(-\lambda+5)=0$

$\Rightarrow \quad 19\lambda-38=0 \Rightarrow \lambda=2$

So, point $M(3, 8, 1)$

Distance $PM=\sqrt{(3-4)^2+(8-6)^2+(1+2)^2}$

$=\sqrt{1+4+9}=\sqrt{14}$ units

66. Given, equation of line $\frac{x+1}{2}=\frac{y-1}{5}=\frac{z+1}{-1}$

Foot of perpendicular from P (2, 0, 5) to given lines is (α, β, γ).

Direction ratios of given line are $(2, 5, -1)$.

Direction vector $\mathbf{a}=2\hat{\mathbf{i}}+5\hat{\mathbf{j}}-\hat{\mathbf{k}}$

and line passes thorugh $=(-1, 1, -1)$

Now, let's suppose

$$\frac{x+1}{2}=\frac{y-1}{5}=\frac{z+1}{-1}=\lambda$$

or $\quad x=2\lambda-1, y=5\lambda+1, z=-\lambda-1$

Let the foot of perpendicular from point $P(2, 0, 5)$ on the line is $(\alpha, \beta, \gamma) \equiv A(2\lambda-1, 5\lambda+1, -\lambda-1)$

Now, $\mathbf{PA}=$ Position vector of $A-$ Position vector of P

$=[(2\lambda-1)\hat{\mathbf{i}}+(5\lambda+1)\hat{\mathbf{j}}+(-\lambda-1)\hat{\mathbf{k}}]-(2\hat{\mathbf{i}}+5\hat{\mathbf{k}})$

$\mathbf{PA}=(2\lambda-3)\hat{\mathbf{i}}+(5\lambda+1)\hat{\mathbf{j}}+(-\lambda-6)\hat{\mathbf{k}}$

Now, $\mathbf{PA} \perp$ (direction of line)

Now, $\mathbf{PA} \perp \mathbf{a}$. So, $\mathbf{PA}\cdot\mathbf{a}=0$

$[(2\lambda-3)\hat{\mathbf{i}}+(5\lambda+1)\hat{\mathbf{j}}+(-\lambda-6)\hat{\mathbf{k}}]\cdot[2\hat{\mathbf{i}}+5\hat{\mathbf{j}}-\hat{\mathbf{k}}]=0$

So, $\quad 2(2\lambda-3)+5(5\lambda+1)+(\lambda+6)=0$

$\Rightarrow \quad 30\lambda=-5$

$\Rightarrow \quad \lambda=-\frac{1}{6}$

So, $A \equiv(2\lambda-1, 5\lambda+1, -\lambda-1)$

$$A \equiv\left[2\left(\frac{-1}{6}\right)-1, 5\left(-\frac{1}{6}\right)+1, -\left(\frac{-1}{6}\right)-1\right]$$

$$A \equiv\left(-\frac{4}{3}, \frac{1}{6}, -\frac{5}{6}\right) \equiv(\alpha, \beta, \gamma)$$

or $\alpha=-\frac{4}{3}, \beta=\frac{1}{6}, \gamma=\frac{-5}{6}$

$$\therefore \quad \frac{\beta}{\gamma}=\frac{\left(\frac{1}{6}\right)}{\left(-\frac{5}{6}\right)}=\frac{-1}{5}$$

67.

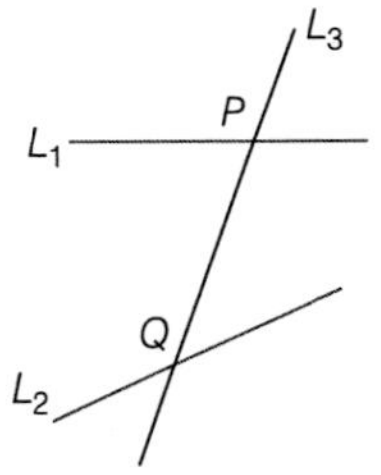

We have, $L_1: \frac{x-1}{2}=\frac{y-3}{1}=\frac{z-2}{2}=\lambda$

$x=2\lambda+1, y=\lambda+3, z=2\lambda+2$

Let $P(2\lambda+1, \lambda+3, 2\lambda+2)$

$$L_2: \frac{x-2}{1}=\frac{y-2}{2}=\frac{z-3}{3}=\mu$$

$x=\mu+2, y=2\mu+2, z=3\mu+3$

Let $Q(\mu+2, 2\mu+2, 3\mu+3)$.

Direction ratios of line PQ

$=(2\lambda+1-\mu-2, \lambda+3-2\mu-2, 2\lambda+2-3\mu-3)$

$=(2\lambda-\mu-1, \lambda-2\mu+1, 2\lambda-3\mu-1)$

Given, direction ratios of $L_3: 1, -1, -2$ and L_3 and PQ are same line

So, $\frac{2\lambda-\mu-1}{1}=\frac{\lambda-2\mu+1}{-1}=\frac{2\lambda-3\mu-1}{-2}$

On taking, $\frac{2\lambda-\mu-1}{1}=\frac{\lambda-2\mu+1}{-1}$

$\Rightarrow \quad 2\lambda-\mu-1=-\lambda+2\mu-1$

$\Rightarrow \quad 3\lambda=3\mu \Rightarrow \lambda=\mu \quad$ ...(i)

On taking, $\frac{\lambda - 2\mu + 1}{-1} = \frac{2\lambda - 3\mu - 1}{-2}$

$\Rightarrow \quad 2\lambda - 4\mu + 2 = 2\lambda - 3\mu - 1 \Rightarrow \mu = 3$

From Eq. (i), $\quad \lambda = \mu = 3$

Now, $P(7, 6, 8)$ and $Q(5, 8, 12)$.

Length of segment, $PQ = \sqrt{(7-5)^2 + (6-8)^2 + (8-12)^2}$

$= \sqrt{4 + 4 + 16} = \sqrt{24} = 2\sqrt{6}$ units

68. We have, $l_1: \mathbf{r} = (\hat{\mathbf{i}} - 11\hat{\mathbf{j}} - 7\hat{\mathbf{k}}) + \lambda(\hat{\mathbf{i}} + 2\hat{\mathbf{j}} + 3\hat{\mathbf{k}}), \lambda \in R$

and $\quad l_2: \mathbf{r} = (-\hat{\mathbf{i}} + \hat{\mathbf{k}}) + \mu(2\hat{\mathbf{i}} + 2\hat{\mathbf{j}} + \hat{\mathbf{k}}), \mu \in R$

Let direction ratios of line l be a, b and c.

Equation of line l, $\mathbf{r} = (0\hat{\mathbf{i}} + 0\hat{\mathbf{j}} + 0\hat{\mathbf{k}}) + \delta(a\hat{\mathbf{i}} + b\hat{\mathbf{j}} + c\hat{\mathbf{k}})$

$= \delta(a\hat{\mathbf{i}} + b\hat{\mathbf{j}} + c\hat{\mathbf{k}})$

As line l is perpendicular to l_1 and l_2,

$$a\hat{\mathbf{i}} + b\hat{\mathbf{j}} + c\hat{\mathbf{k}} = \begin{vmatrix} \hat{\mathbf{i}} & \hat{\mathbf{j}} & \hat{\mathbf{k}} \\ 1 & 2 & 3 \\ 2 & 2 & 1 \end{vmatrix}$$

$$= -4\hat{\mathbf{i}} + 5\hat{\mathbf{j}} - 2\hat{\mathbf{k}}$$

Equation line $l: \mathbf{r} = \delta(-4\hat{\mathbf{i}} + 5\hat{\mathbf{j}} - 2\hat{\mathbf{k}})$

As P is the intersecting point of l and l_1

$-4\delta = 1 + \lambda, 5\delta = -11 + 2\lambda, -2\delta = -7 + 3\lambda$

After solving the above three equation, we get

$\delta = -1$ and $\lambda = 3$

Coordinates of point P are $(4, -5, 2)$.

Q is a point on line l_2.

Let coordinates of Q be $(-1 + 2\mu, 2\mu, 1 + \mu)$

$\mathbf{PQ} = (-5 + 2\mu)\hat{\mathbf{i}} + (2\mu + 5)\hat{\mathbf{j}} + (\mu - 1)\hat{\mathbf{k}}$

$\mathbf{PQ} \cdot (2\hat{\mathbf{i}} + 2\hat{\mathbf{j}} + \hat{\mathbf{k}}) = 0 \qquad [\because PQ \perp l_2]$

$\Rightarrow \quad 2(-5 + 2\mu) + 2(2\mu + 5) + \mu - 1 = 0$

$\Rightarrow \quad 9\mu - 1 = 0$

$\Rightarrow \quad \mu = \frac{1}{9}$

$\therefore \quad \alpha = -1 + \frac{2}{9} = \frac{-7}{9}, \beta = 2 \times \frac{1}{9} = \frac{2}{9}, \; r = 1 + \frac{1}{9} = \frac{10}{9}$

Hence, $\quad 9(\alpha + \beta + \gamma) = 9\left(-\frac{7}{9} + \frac{2}{9} + \frac{10}{9}\right) = 5$

69. Given lines $\quad \frac{x-1}{2} = \frac{2-y}{-3} = \frac{z-3}{\alpha}$

$$\frac{x-1}{2} = \frac{y-2}{3} = \frac{z-3}{\alpha} = \lambda \qquad \text{...(i)}$$

Any point on the line (i),

$x = 2\lambda + 1, y = 3\lambda + 2, z = \alpha\lambda + 3$

and line $\frac{x-4}{5} = \frac{y-1}{2} = \frac{z}{\beta} = \mu \qquad \text{...(ii)}$

any point on line (ii),

$\Rightarrow \quad x = 5\mu + 4, y = 2\mu + 1, z = \beta\mu$

Since, given lines intersects

$\therefore \quad 2\lambda + 1 = 5\mu + 4 \qquad \text{...(iii)}$

$3\lambda + 2 = 2\mu + 1 \qquad \text{...(iv)}$

and $\quad \alpha\lambda + 3 = \beta\mu \qquad \text{...(v)}$

On solving Eqs. (iii) and (iv), we get

$\lambda = -1, \mu = -1$

On putting value of λ and μ in Eq. (v), we get

$\alpha(-1) + 3 = -\beta \Rightarrow \alpha = \beta + 3$

Now, $8\alpha\beta = 8(\beta + 3)(\beta)$

$= 8(\beta^2 + 3\beta) = 8\left(\beta^2 + 3\beta + \frac{9}{4} - \frac{9}{4}\right)$

$= 8\left[\left(\beta + \frac{3}{2}\right)^2 - \frac{9}{4}\right] = 8\left(\beta + \frac{3}{2}\right)^2 - 18$

Here, minimum value $= -18$

$\therefore$ Magnitude of the minimum value of $8\alpha\beta$ is 18.

70.

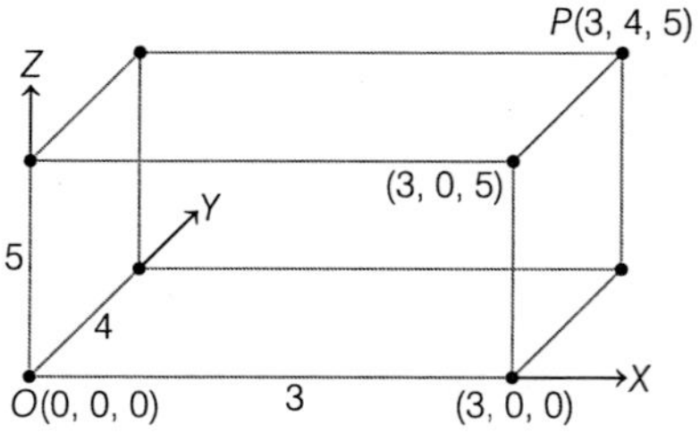

Equation of OP is

$$\frac{x-0}{3-0} = \frac{y-0}{4-0} = \frac{z-0}{5-0}$$

$\Rightarrow \quad \frac{x}{3} = \frac{y}{4} = \frac{z}{5} \qquad \text{...(i)}$

Equation of edge parallel to Z-axis is

$$\frac{x-3}{0} = \frac{y-0}{0} = \frac{z-5}{1} \qquad \text{...(ii)}$$

$$\therefore \text{ Shortest distance} = \frac{\begin{vmatrix} x_2 - x_1 & y_2 - y_1 & z_2 - z_1 \\ a_1 & b_1 & c_1 \\ a_2 & b_2 & c_2 \end{vmatrix}}{\sqrt{a}}$$

Here, $x_1 = 0, y_1 = 0, z_1 = 0$

$x_2 = 3, y_2 = 0, z_2 = 5$

$a_1 = 3, b_1 = 4, c_1 = 5$

$a_2 = 0, b_2 = 0, c_2 = 1$

$$\therefore \begin{vmatrix} x_2 - x_1 & y_2 - y_1 & z_2 - z_1 \\ a_1 & b_1 & c_1 \\ a_2 & b_2 & c_2 \end{vmatrix} = \begin{vmatrix} 3 & 0 & 5 \\ 3 & 4 & 5 \\ 0 & 0 & 1 \end{vmatrix} = 4(3) = 12$$

and $\sqrt{(a_1b_2 - a_2b_1)^2 + (b_1c_2 - b_2c_1)^2 + (c_1a_2 - c_2a_1)^2}$

$= \sqrt{0 + (4-0)^2 + (0-3)^2} = \sqrt{16 + 9} = 5$

Hence, the required shortest distance $= \frac{12}{5}$ units

71. We have to find direction ratios of line

$$\begin{vmatrix} \hat{\mathbf{i}} & \hat{\mathbf{j}} & \hat{\mathbf{k}} \\ 1 & 3 & -2 \\ 1 & -1 & 2 \end{vmatrix} = \hat{\mathbf{i}}(6-2) - \hat{\mathbf{j}}(2+2) + \hat{\mathbf{k}}(-1-3)$$

$$= \hat{\mathbf{i}}(6-2) - \hat{\mathbf{j}}(4) + \hat{\mathbf{k}}(-1-3) = 4\hat{\mathbf{i}} - 4\hat{\mathbf{j}} - 4\hat{\mathbf{k}}$$

Then, equation of line

$$\frac{x-2}{1}=\frac{y-3}{-1}=\frac{z-1}{-1}=\lambda$$

Let $M(\lambda+2, -\lambda+3, -\lambda+1)$

Direction ratios of MQ

$$=<\lambda+2-5, -\lambda+3-3, -\lambda+1-8>$$
$$=<\lambda-3, -\lambda, -\lambda-7>$$

$\because L \perp MQ$

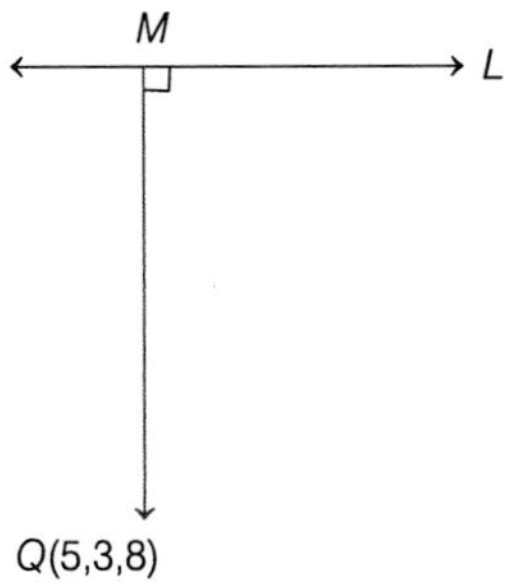

Then, $(\lambda-3)(1)+(-\lambda)(-1)+(-\lambda-7)(-1)=0$

$\Rightarrow \quad \lambda-3+\lambda+\lambda+7=0$

$\Rightarrow \quad 3\lambda=-4$

$\Rightarrow \quad \lambda=-\frac{4}{3}$

$$\therefore \quad M=\left(-\frac{4}{3}+2, \frac{4}{3}+3, \frac{4}{3}+1\right)=\left(\frac{2}{3}, \frac{13}{3}, \frac{7}{3}\right)$$

and $MQ=\alpha$, then

$$3\alpha^2=3\left[\left(5-\frac{2}{3}\right)^2+\left(3-\frac{13}{3}\right)^2+\left(8-\frac{7}{3}\right)^2\right]$$
$$=3\left[\frac{169}{9}+\frac{16}{9}+\frac{289}{9}\right]$$
$$=3\left(\frac{474}{9}\right)=\frac{474}{3}=158$$

72. We have, B and C lying on $\frac{x+\alpha}{5}=\frac{y-1}{2}=\frac{z+4}{3}$

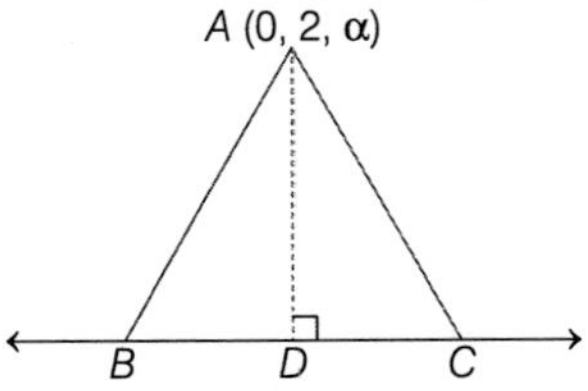

Also, $A(0, 2, \alpha)$, ar$(ABC)=21$ sq units, $BC=2\sqrt{21}$ units

$\Rightarrow \quad \frac{1}{2}\times BC \times AD=21$

$\Rightarrow \quad \frac{1}{2}\times 2\sqrt{21}\times AD=21$

$\Rightarrow \quad AD=\sqrt{21}$ units

Let $D(5h-\alpha, 2h+1, 3h-4)$

$\Rightarrow <AD>=<5h-\alpha-0, 2h+1-2, 3h-4-\alpha>$

$$=<5h-\alpha, 2h-1, 3h-\alpha-4>$$

Direction ratios of line BC are $<5, 2, 3>$

Since, $AD \perp BC$,

$\therefore$ Dot product of direction ratios $=0$

$\Rightarrow 5(5h-\alpha)+2(2h-1)+3(3h-\alpha-4)=0$

$\Rightarrow \quad (5^2+2^2+3^2)h=5\alpha+2+3\alpha+12$

$\Rightarrow \quad 38h=8\alpha+14$

$\Rightarrow \quad h=\frac{4\alpha+7}{19}$ ...(i)

$$\therefore \text{Coordinates of } D=\left(\frac{20\alpha+35}{19}-\alpha, \frac{8\alpha+14}{19}+1, \frac{12\alpha+21}{19}-4\right)$$

i.e. $D\left(\frac{\alpha+35}{19}, \frac{8\alpha+33}{19}, \frac{12\alpha-55}{19}\right)$.

Using distance formula for points i.e., if $P(x_1, y_1, z_1)$ and $Q(x_2, y_2, z_2)$, then

$PQ=\sqrt{(x_2-x_1)^2+(y_2-y_1)^2+(z_2-z_1)^2}$

We get,

$$AD^2=\left(\frac{\alpha+35}{19}-0\right)^2+\left(\frac{8\alpha+33}{19}-2\right)^2+\left(\frac{12\alpha-55}{19}-\alpha\right)^2$$

$$\Rightarrow (\sqrt{21})^2=\frac{(\alpha+35)^2}{19^2}+\frac{(8\alpha+33-38)^2}{19^2}+\frac{(12\alpha-55-19\alpha)^2}{19^2}$$

$\Rightarrow \quad 114\alpha^2+760\alpha-3306=0$

$\Rightarrow \quad 3\alpha^2+20\alpha-87=0$

$$\Rightarrow \quad \alpha=\frac{-20\pm\sqrt{(20)^2-4\cdot 3\cdot(-87)}}{2\cdot 3}$$
$$=\frac{-20\pm\sqrt{400+1044}}{2\cdot 3}$$
$$=\frac{-20\pm 38}{6}=\frac{-20+38}{6}, \frac{-20-38}{6}$$
$$=3, \frac{-58}{6}$$

Rejecting $\alpha=\frac{-58}{6} \Rightarrow \alpha^2=9$

73. The line C_1 joining the points (1, 2, 3) and (2, 3, 4) is

$$L_1: \frac{x-1}{1}=\frac{y-2}{1}=\frac{z-3}{1}$$

Position vector of point $(1, 2, 3)=\hat{\mathbf{i}}+2\hat{\mathbf{j}}+3\hat{\mathbf{k}}=\mathbf{a}_1$

Direction ratios of line $=(1, 1, 1)$

So, direction vectors of $L_1=\hat{\mathbf{i}}+\hat{\mathbf{j}}+\hat{\mathbf{k}}=\mathbf{b}_1$

Now, $L_2: \frac{x-1}{2}=\frac{y+1}{-1}=\frac{z-2}{0}$

Point on $L_2 \equiv (1, -1, 2)$

Position vector of point $=\mathbf{a}_2=\hat{\mathbf{i}}-\hat{\mathbf{j}}+2\hat{\mathbf{k}}$

Direction ratios of line $L_2=(2, -1, 0)$

So, direction vector of $L_2=2\hat{\mathbf{i}}-\hat{\mathbf{j}}+0\hat{\mathbf{k}}$ or $\mathbf{b}_2=2\hat{\mathbf{i}}-\hat{\mathbf{j}}$

Now, shortest distance between 2 skew lines $=d$

$$d=\left|\frac{(\mathbf{a}_1-\mathbf{a}_2)\cdot(\mathbf{b}_1\times\mathbf{b}_2)}{|\mathbf{b}_1\times\mathbf{b}_2|}\right|$$

Now, $\mathbf{a}_1-\mathbf{a}_2=(\hat{\mathbf{i}}+2\hat{\mathbf{j}}+3\hat{\mathbf{k}})-(\hat{\mathbf{i}}-\hat{\mathbf{j}}+2\hat{\mathbf{k}})$

So, $\quad \mathbf{a}_1-\mathbf{a}_2=3\hat{\mathbf{j}}+\hat{\mathbf{k}}$

Now, $\mathbf{b}_1\times\mathbf{b}_2=(\hat{\mathbf{i}}+\hat{\mathbf{j}}+\hat{\mathbf{k}})\times(2\hat{\mathbf{i}}-\hat{\mathbf{j}})$

So, $\mathbf{b}_1 \times \mathbf{b}_2 = \begin{vmatrix} \hat{\mathbf{i}} & \hat{\mathbf{j}} & \hat{\mathbf{k}} \\ 1 & 1 & 1 \\ 2 & -1 & 0 \end{vmatrix} = \hat{\mathbf{i}}(0-(-1)) - \hat{\mathbf{j}}(0-2) + \hat{\mathbf{k}}(-1-2)$

So, $\mathbf{b}_1 \times \mathbf{b}_2 = \hat{\mathbf{i}} + 2\hat{\mathbf{j}} - 3\hat{\mathbf{k}}$

So, $|\mathbf{b}_1 \times \mathbf{b}_2| = \sqrt{1+4+9} = \sqrt{14}$

Now, $(\mathbf{a}_1 - \mathbf{a}_2) \cdot (\mathbf{b}_1 \times \mathbf{b}_2) = (3\hat{\mathbf{j}} + \hat{\mathbf{k}}) \cdot (\hat{\mathbf{i}} + 2\hat{\mathbf{j}} - 3\hat{\mathbf{k}})$

So, $(\mathbf{a}_1 - \mathbf{a}_2) \cdot (\mathbf{b}_1 \times \mathbf{b}_2) = 0 + 6 - 3 = 3$

Now, $d = \left|\dfrac{3}{\sqrt{14}}\right|$

So, $\alpha = \dfrac{3}{\sqrt{14}}$

So, $28\alpha^2 = 28\left(\dfrac{3}{\sqrt{14}}\right)^2$

$\Rightarrow 28\alpha^2 = 18$

74. $(-1, -2, -3)(9, 3, 4), (9, -2, 1)$

Equation of plane, $\begin{vmatrix} x+1 & y+2 & z+3 \\ -10 & -5 & -7 \\ -10 & 0 & -4 \end{vmatrix} = 0$

$$(x+1)[20] + 10[-4y-8] - 10[-7y-14+5z+15] = 0$$

$$20x + 20 - 40y - 80 + 70y + 140 - 50z - 150 = 0$$

$$20x + 30y - 50z - 70 = 0$$

$$2x + 3y - 5z = 7$$

Now, $P(3, -2, -9)$ and $Q(\alpha, \beta, \gamma)$

$$\mathbf{PQ} = (\alpha - 3)\,\hat{\mathbf{i}} + (\beta + 2)\,\hat{\mathbf{j}} + (\gamma + 9)\,\hat{\mathbf{k}}$$

$$\mathbf{N} = 2\hat{\mathbf{i}} + 3\hat{\mathbf{j}} - 5\hat{\mathbf{k}}$$

$$\mathbf{PQ} \,||\, \mathbf{N} \Rightarrow \frac{\alpha - 3}{2} = \frac{\beta + 2}{3} = \frac{\gamma + 9}{-5} = \lambda$$

$$\frac{\alpha - 3}{2} = \lambda \Rightarrow \alpha = 2\lambda + 3, \frac{\beta + 2}{3} = \lambda$$

$$\Rightarrow 3\lambda - 2 = \beta; \frac{\gamma + 9}{-5} = \lambda \Rightarrow -5\lambda - 9 = \gamma$$

$\because$ $2x + 3y - 5z = 7$

(α, β, γ) lies on plane $2\alpha + 3\beta - 5\gamma = 7$

$$2(2\lambda + 3) + 3(3\lambda - 2) - 5(-5\lambda - 9) = 7$$

$$4\lambda + 6 + 9\lambda - 6 + 25\lambda + 45 - 7 = 0$$

$$25\lambda + 13\lambda + 38 = 0$$

$$38\lambda = -38$$

$$\lambda = -1$$

$\lambda = -1 \Rightarrow \alpha = 2(-1) + 3 = 1, \beta = 3(-1) - 2 = -5,$

$\gamma = -5\lambda - 9 = -4$

$Q(1, -5, -4)$ and $O(0, 0, 0)$

$$QO = \sqrt{(1)^2 + (-5)^2 + (-4)^2}$$

$$= \sqrt{1 + 25 + 16}$$

$$= \sqrt{42}$$

75. Equation of the line, $\dfrac{x-4}{4-1} = \dfrac{y-5}{5-(-7)} = \dfrac{z-8}{8-5}$

$$\Rightarrow \frac{x-4}{3} = \frac{y-5}{12} = \frac{z-8}{3} = K \text{ (let)}$$

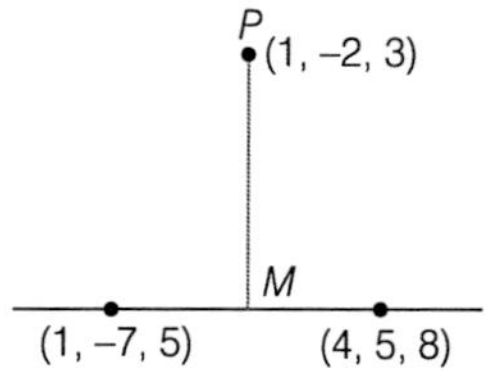

Thus, $x = 3K + 4, y = 12K + 5, z = 3K + 8$

Hence, $M \equiv (3K + 4, 12K + 5, 3K + 8)$

$P \equiv (1, -2, 3)$

$\therefore$ $\mathbf{PM} = (3K + 4 - 1)\,\hat{\mathbf{i}} + (12K + 5 + 2)\hat{\mathbf{j}} + (3K + 8 - 3)\hat{\mathbf{k}}$

$= (3K + 3)\hat{\mathbf{i}} + (12K + 7)\hat{\mathbf{j}} + (3K + 5)\hat{\mathbf{k}}$

Now, vector equation of line passigng through (4, 5, 8) and $(1, -7, 5)$ is $3\hat{\mathbf{i}} + 12\hat{\mathbf{j}} + 3\hat{\mathbf{k}}$ (say n)

Thus, $\mathbf{PM} \cdot \mathbf{n} = 0$

$\Rightarrow$ $3(3K + 3) + 12(12K + 7) + 3(3K + 5) = 0$

$\Rightarrow$ $9K + 9 + 144K + 84 + 9K + 15 = 0$

$\Rightarrow$ $162K + 108 = 0$

$\Rightarrow$ $K = \dfrac{-108}{162} = \dfrac{-6}{9} = \dfrac{-2}{3}$

Thus, $M \equiv \left[3 \cdot \left(\dfrac{-2}{3}\right) + 4, 12\left(-\dfrac{2}{3}\right) + 5, 3 \cdot \left(\dfrac{-2}{3}\right) + 8\right]$

$= (-2 + 4, -8 + 5, -2 + 8) = (2, -3, 6)$

Now, distance of $M \equiv (2, -3, 6)$ from the plane $2x - 2y + z + 5 = 0$ is

$$\left|\frac{2(2) - 2(-3) + 6 + 5}{\sqrt{(2)^2 + (-2)^2 + (1)^2}}\right| = \left|\frac{4 + 6 + 6 + 5}{\sqrt{9}}\right|$$

$$= \left|\frac{21}{3}\right|$$

$$= |7|$$

$= 7$ units

76. Let the equation of plane passing through the line of intersection of the planes, $x + 2y + az = 2$ and $x - y + z = 3$ is

$$(x + 2y + az - 2) + \lambda(x - y + z - 3) = 0$$

$\Rightarrow (1 + \lambda)x + (2 - \lambda)y + (a + \lambda)z + (-2 - 3\lambda) = 0$ ...(i)

Given that $5x - 11y + bz = 6a - 1$ ...(ii)

Thus, Eqs. (i) and Eqs. (ii) are parallel.

So, $\dfrac{1+\lambda}{5} = \dfrac{2-\lambda}{-11} = \dfrac{a+\lambda}{b} = \dfrac{2+3\lambda}{6a-1}$

I II III IV

On taking I and II, we get

$$\lambda = -\frac{7}{2}$$

Now, taking I and IV, we get

$$\frac{1 - \frac{7}{2}}{5} = \frac{2 + 3\left(\frac{-7}{2}\right)}{6a - 1}$$

$$\Rightarrow \quad -\frac{1}{2} = \frac{-17}{2(6a-1)}$$

$$\Rightarrow \quad 6a = 17 + 1 = 18$$

$$\Rightarrow \quad a = 3$$

Similarly, $b = 1$

Thus, the equation of plane is

$$5x - 11y + z = 17 \qquad \text{[from Eq. (ii)]}$$

Now, the distance of this from the point $(3, -c, c)$ is

$$\left| \frac{15 + 11c + c - 17}{\sqrt{25 + 121 + 1}} \right| = \frac{2}{\sqrt{a}} \qquad \text{[given]}$$

$$\Rightarrow \quad \pm\left[\frac{12c - 2}{\sqrt{147}}\right] = \frac{2}{\sqrt{3}} \Rightarrow c = -1 \text{ or } \frac{4}{3}$$

But $c \in Z$ [given]

$\therefore \quad c = -1$

$$\therefore \quad \frac{a+b}{c} = \frac{3+1}{-1} = -4$$

77. Given, plane P is passing through $(5, 3, 0)$, $(13, 3, -2)$ and $(1, 6, 2)$.

Distances of points $A(3, 4, \alpha)$, $B(2, \alpha, a)$ from plane P are 2 and 3, respectively.

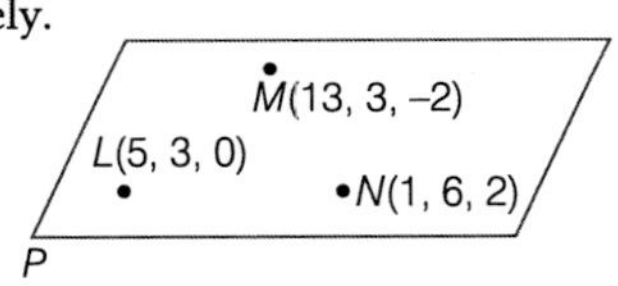

$$P: \begin{vmatrix} x-5 & y-3 & z-0 \\ 12 & -3 & -4 \\ 4 & -3 & -2 \end{vmatrix} = 0$$

$$\Rightarrow \quad -6(x-5) + 8(y-3) - 24(z-0) = 0$$

$$\Rightarrow \quad -6x + 8y - 24z + 30 - 24 = 0$$

$$\Rightarrow \quad P: 3x - 4y + 12z = 3$$

$\therefore$ Distance of $A(3, 4, \alpha)$ from plane $P = 2$

$$\Rightarrow \quad \left| \frac{3 \times 3 - 4 \times 4 + 12\alpha - 3}{\sqrt{3^2 + (-4)^2 + 12^2}} \right| = 2 \Rightarrow \frac{|12\alpha - 10|}{13} = 2$$

$$\Rightarrow \quad 12\alpha - 10 = \pm 26 \Rightarrow 12\alpha = 36, -16$$

$$\Rightarrow \quad \alpha = 3, -4/3$$

$\therefore \alpha \in N \Rightarrow \alpha = 3$

Also, distance of $B(2, \alpha, a)$ from plane $P = 3$

$$\Rightarrow \quad \left| \frac{3 \times 2 - 4\alpha + 12a - 3}{\sqrt{3^2 + (-4)^2 + 12^2}} \right| = 3$$

$$\Rightarrow \quad |12a - 4\alpha + 3| = 39$$

For $\alpha = 3$ | For $\alpha = \dfrac{-4}{3}$

$|12a - 9| = 39$ | $\left| 12a + \dfrac{25}{3} \right| = 39$

$12a = 48, -30$ | $12a = \dfrac{92}{3}, -\dfrac{142}{3}$

$$\Rightarrow \quad a = 4, \frac{-5}{2}$$

$\therefore \quad a = 4 \qquad [\because a > 0]$

Hence, the positive value of a is 4.

78. The line passing through the points $P(2, -1, 2)$ and $Q(5, 3, 4)$ is

$$\frac{x-5}{5-2} = \frac{y-3}{3-(-1)} = \frac{z-4}{4-2}$$

$$\Rightarrow \quad \frac{x-5}{3} = \frac{y-3}{4} = \frac{z-4}{2} = \lambda \text{ (let)}$$

$\therefore x = 3\lambda + 5, y = 4\lambda + 3, z = 2\lambda + 4$

This line meet the plane $x - y + z = 4$ at the point R.

So, $R \equiv (3\lambda + 5, 4\lambda + 3, 2\lambda + 4)$

Now, $(3\lambda + 5) - (4\lambda + 3) + (2\lambda + 4) = 4$

$$\Rightarrow \quad \lambda = -2$$

$$\Rightarrow \quad R \equiv (-1, -5, 0)$$

The equation of line passing through $P(-1, -5, 0)$ and parallel to the line $\dfrac{x-7}{2} = \dfrac{y+3}{2} = \dfrac{z-2}{1}$ is

$$\frac{x+1}{2} = \frac{y+5}{2} = \frac{z-0}{1} = \mu \text{ (let)}$$

$$\therefore \quad x = 2\mu - 1, y = 2\mu - 5, z = \mu$$

Thus, the point $(2\mu - 1, 2\mu - 5, \mu)$ lines on the plane

$$x + 2y + 3z + 2 = 0$$

$$\Rightarrow (2\mu - 1) + 2(2\mu - 5) + 3(\mu) + 2 = 0$$

$$\Rightarrow \quad 2\mu + 4\mu + 3\mu - 1 - 10 + 2 = 0$$

$$\Rightarrow \quad 9\mu = 9 \Rightarrow \mu = 1$$

Thus, the point is $(1, -3, 1)$

Say, $\quad Q \equiv (1, -3, 1)$

Now, distance of the point $R(-1, -5, 0)$ from $(1, -3, 1)$ is

$$\sqrt{(1+1)^2 + (-3+5)^2 + (1)^2} = \sqrt{4 + 4 + 1}$$

$$= \sqrt{9} = 3 \text{ units}$$

79. The equation of plane that passes through the point $(-2, 3, 5)$ is

$$a(x+2) + b(y-3) + c(z-5) = 0 \qquad \text{...(i)}$$

The plane is perpendicular to

$$2x + 4y + 5z = 8 \text{ and } 3x - 2y + 3z = 5$$

$$\Rightarrow \quad 2a + 4b + 5c = 0 \qquad \text{...(ii)}$$

$$\text{and} \quad 3a - 2b + 3c = 0 \qquad \text{...(iii)}$$

On solving Eqs. (ii) and (iii), we get

$$\frac{a}{22} = \frac{b}{9} = \frac{c}{-16}$$

Equation of plane $22(x+2) + 9(y-3) - 16(z-5) = 0$

$$\Rightarrow \quad 22x + 9y - 16z + 97 = 0$$

Here, $\alpha = 22, \beta = 9, \gamma = -16$

$$\therefore \quad \alpha + \beta + \gamma = 22 + 9 - 16 = 15$$

80. We have, (α, β, γ) be the image of the point $P(2, 3, 5)$ in the plane $2x + y - 3z = 6$

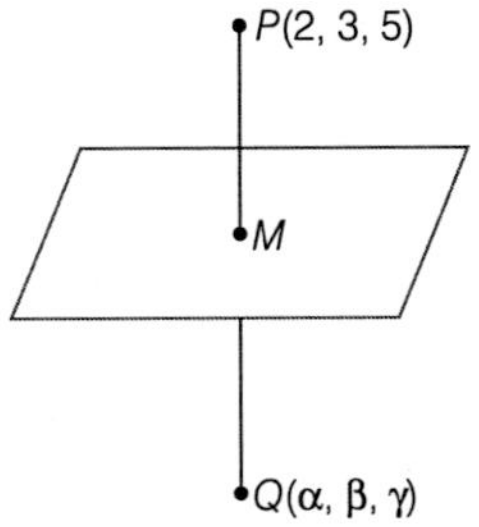

Direction ratios of $PQ = 2, 1, -3$

Equation of PQ is $\frac{x-2}{2} = \frac{y-3}{1} = \frac{z-5}{-3}$

Let M be the point on the plane such that it also lies on PQ.

$$\frac{x-2}{2} = \frac{y-3}{1} = \frac{z-5}{-3} = K$$

$\Rightarrow \quad x = 2 + 2K, y = K + 3, Z = 5 - 3K$

Coordinates of M are $(2 + 2K, \ K + 3, \ 5 - 3K)$

M lies on the plane.

$$2(2 + 2K) + K + 3 - 3(5 - 3K) = 6 \Rightarrow K = 1$$

$\therefore$ Coordinates of M are $(4, 4, 2)$.

M is also mid-point of PQ

$$\frac{\alpha + 2}{2} = 4, \frac{\beta + 3}{2} = 4, \frac{\gamma + 5}{2} = 2$$

$$\alpha = 6, \beta = 5, \gamma = -1$$

$\therefore \quad \alpha + \beta + \gamma = 6 + 5 - 1 = 10$

81. We have, $A(1, 2, 0)$, $B(1, 4, 1)$ and $C(0, 5, 1)$ are the points through which a plane passes.

Equation of plane is

$$\begin{vmatrix} x-1 & y-2 & z-0 \\ 1-1 & 4-2 & 1-0 \\ 0-1 & 5-2 & 1-0 \end{vmatrix} = 0$$

$\Rightarrow \quad x + y - 2z - 3 = 0$

$\because$ Image of point $P(1, 2, 6)$ is $Q(\alpha, \beta, \gamma)$

$$\therefore \quad \frac{\alpha - 1}{1} = \frac{\beta - 2}{1} = \frac{\gamma - 6}{-2}$$

$$= \frac{-2[1 + 2 - 2(6) - 3]}{1^2 + 1^2 + (-2)^2}$$

$$\Rightarrow \quad \frac{\alpha - 1}{1} = \frac{\beta - 2}{1} = \frac{\gamma - 6}{-2} = 4$$

$\Rightarrow \quad \alpha = 5, \beta = 6, \gamma = -2$

Hence, $\alpha^2 + \beta^2 + \gamma^2 = 5^2 + 6^2 + (-2)^2 = 65$

82. Given planes $x + 2y + 3z - 4 = 0$ ...(i)

and $\quad 2x + y - z + 5 = 0$ ...(ii)

Equation of plane containing line of intersection of planes (i) and (ii) is given by

$$(x + 2y + 3z - 4) + \lambda(2x + y - z + 5) = 0$$

$\Rightarrow (1 + 2\lambda)x + (2 + \lambda)y + (3 - \lambda)z + (5\lambda - 4) = 0$ ...(iii)

which is perpendicular to

$$\mathbf{r} = (\hat{\mathbf{i}} - \hat{\mathbf{j}}) + \lambda(\hat{\mathbf{i}} + \hat{\mathbf{j}} + \hat{\mathbf{k}}) + \mu(\hat{\mathbf{i}} - 2\hat{\mathbf{j}} + 3\hat{\mathbf{k}}) \quad \text{...(iv)}$$

Normal to the plane (iv) is given by

$$\begin{vmatrix} \hat{\mathbf{i}} & \hat{\mathbf{j}} & \hat{\mathbf{k}} \\ 1 & 1 & 1 \\ 1 & -2 & 3 \end{vmatrix} = 5\hat{\mathbf{i}} - 2\hat{\mathbf{j}} - 3\hat{\mathbf{k}} \quad \text{...(v)}$$

Planes (iii), (iv) and normal (v) are perpendicular

$\therefore \quad 5(1 + 2\lambda) - 2(2 + \lambda) - 3(3 - \lambda) = 0$

$$\Rightarrow \quad \lambda = \frac{8}{11}$$

Equation of plane, $\frac{27}{11}x + \frac{30}{11}y + \frac{25}{11}z - \frac{4}{11} = 0$

$\Rightarrow \quad 27x + 30y + 25z = 4$

On comparing with $ax + by + cz = 4$, we have

$$a = 27, b = 30, c = 25$$

Hence, $a - b + c = 27 - 30 + 25 = 22$

83. Given equation of planes

$$\mathbf{r} \cdot (\hat{\mathbf{i}} + \hat{\mathbf{j}} + \hat{\mathbf{k}}) = 6$$

$\Rightarrow \quad x + y + z = 6$ ...(i)

and $\quad \mathbf{r} \cdot (2\hat{\mathbf{i}} + 3\hat{\mathbf{j}} + 4\hat{\mathbf{k}}) = -5$

$\Rightarrow \quad 2x + 3y + 4z = -5$ ...(ii)

Equation of plane passing through the intersection of planes (i) and (ii)

$$(x + y + z - 6) + \lambda(2x + 3y + 4z + 5) = 0$$

$\Rightarrow (1 + 2\lambda)x + (1 + 3\lambda)y + (1 + 4\lambda)z + (-6 + 5\lambda) = 0$ ...(iii)

Plane (i) passes through the point $(0, 2, -2)$

$\therefore \quad (1 + 3\lambda)(2) + (1 + 4\lambda)(-2) + (-6 + 5\lambda) = 0$

$\Rightarrow \quad 2 + 6\lambda - 2 - 8\lambda - 6 + 5\lambda = 0$

$\Rightarrow \quad 3\lambda - 6 = 0$

$\Rightarrow \quad \lambda = 2$

$\therefore$ Equation of plane is $5x + 7y + 9z + 4 = 0$.

$\therefore$ Distance of the point $(12, 12, 18)$ from the plane

$$d = \frac{5 \times 12 + 7 \times 12 + 9 \times 18 + 4}{\sqrt{5^2 + 7^2 + 9^2}}$$

$$= \frac{60 + 84 + 162 + 4}{\sqrt{155}}$$

$$= \frac{310}{\sqrt{155}}$$

$$\therefore \quad d^2 = \frac{310 \times 310}{155}$$

$= 620$ units

84. Let the image of $P(2, -1, 3)$ in the plane $x + 2y - z = 0$ be Q.

Then, $\frac{x-2}{1} = \frac{y+1}{2} = \frac{z-3}{-1} = \frac{-2(2 - 2 - 3)}{(1)^2 + (2)^2 + (-1)^2}$

$$\Rightarrow \quad \frac{x-2}{1} = \frac{y+1}{2} = \frac{z-3}{-1} = 1$$

$\Rightarrow \quad x = 3, y = 1, z = 2$

So, Q is $(3, 1, 2)$.

Now, distance of $Q(3, 1, 2)$ from the plane $3x + 2y + z + 29 = 0$ is d.

Then, $d = \left| \frac{3(3) + 2(1) + 1(2) + 29}{\sqrt{(3)^2 + (2)^2 + (1)^2}} \right|$

$$= \left| \frac{9 + 2 + 2 + 29}{\sqrt{9 + 4 + 1}} \right|$$

$$= \frac{42}{\sqrt{14}}$$

$= 3\sqrt{14}$ units

85. To find the plane, passing through the points (0, −1, 2) and (−1, 2, 1) and parallel to the line passing through (5, 1, −7) and (1, −1, −1).

So Ist find the normal vector

$$\hat{\mathbf{n}} = \begin{vmatrix} \hat{\mathbf{i}} & \hat{\mathbf{j}} & \hat{\mathbf{k}} \\ 4 & 2 & -6 \\ -1 & 3 & -1 \end{vmatrix}$$

$$= \hat{\mathbf{i}}(-2+18) + \hat{\mathbf{j}}(6+4) + \hat{\mathbf{k}}(12+2)$$

$$= 16\hat{\mathbf{i}} + 10\hat{\mathbf{j}} + 14\hat{\mathbf{k}}$$

So, the plane is $16x + 10y + 14z - d = 0$

Passing through (0, −1, 2) so, $d = 18$

∴ The equation of plane is

$$16x + 10y + 14z - 18 = 0$$

$$\Rightarrow \quad 8x + 5y + 7z = 9$$

Clearly, from the given options we conclude that (2, 0, 1), (1, −2, 1), (0, 5, −2) does not satisfied the above equation of plane.

So, only (−2, 5, 0) satisfied.

86. Let $L_1 : \mathbf{r} = (\hat{\mathbf{i}} - \hat{\mathbf{j}}) + \lambda(2\hat{\mathbf{i}} + \hat{\mathbf{k}})$

and $L_2 : \mathbf{r} = (2\hat{\mathbf{i}} - \hat{\mathbf{j}}) + \mu(\hat{\mathbf{i}} - \hat{\mathbf{j}} + \hat{\mathbf{k}})$

$$\therefore \quad \hat{\mathbf{n}} = \begin{vmatrix} \hat{\mathbf{i}} & \hat{\mathbf{j}} & \hat{\mathbf{k}} \\ 2 & 0 & 1 \\ 1 & -1 & 1 \end{vmatrix}$$

$$= \hat{\mathbf{i}}(1) - \hat{\mathbf{j}}(2-1) + \hat{\mathbf{k}}(-2-0)$$

$$= \hat{\mathbf{i}} - \hat{\mathbf{j}} - 2\hat{\mathbf{k}}$$

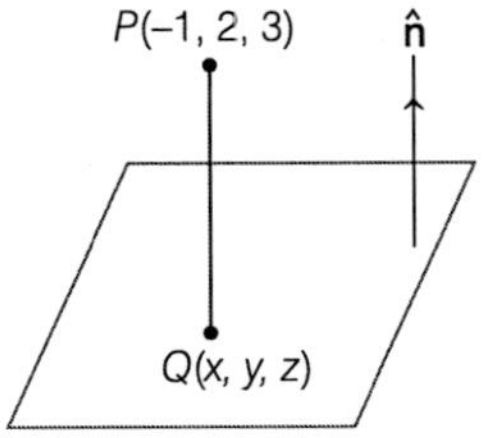

Thus, the equation of line along shortest distance of L_1 and L_2 is

$$\frac{x+1}{1} = \frac{y-2}{-1} = \frac{z-3}{-2} = k \text{ (let)}$$

$$\therefore \quad x = k - 1, y = -k + 2, z = -2k + 3$$

Now, $(x, y, z) = (k - 1, -k + 2, -2k + 3)$ the point lie on the plane $x - 2y + 3z = 10$ is

$$(k-1) - 2(2-k) + 3(-2k+3) = 10$$

$$\Rightarrow \quad k = -2$$

Hence, $Q = (-3, 4, 7)$

Thus, $PQ = \sqrt{(-1+3)^2 + (2-4)^2 + (3-7)^2}$

$$= \sqrt{(2)^2 + (-2)^2 + (-4)^2}$$

$$= \sqrt{4 + 4 + 16}$$

$$= \sqrt{24}$$

$$= 2\sqrt{6} \text{ units}$$

87. Plane $P : 4x - y + z = 10$

Plane $Q : x + y - z = 4$

Let direction ratios of their line of intersection be < l, m, n >.

$$\therefore \quad 4l - m + n = 0 \quad \text{...(i)}$$

$$l + m - n = 0 \quad \text{...(ii)}$$

From Eqs. (i) and (ii), we get

$$\frac{l}{0} = \frac{m}{1} = \frac{n}{1}$$

∴Direction ratios of line of intersection are < 0, 1, 1 >.

Let $y = 1$

$$\therefore \quad 4x - y + z = 10 \quad \text{...(iii)}$$

$$x + y - z = 4 \quad \text{...(iv)}$$

From Eqs. (iii) and (iv), we get

$$x = \frac{14}{5}, z = \frac{-1}{5}$$

∴ Line of intersection passes through $\left(\frac{14}{5}, 1, -\frac{1}{5}\right)$.

Let plane after rotation be R.

Since $R \perp P$,

∴ Normal of $R \perp$ normal of P.

Let direction ratios of normal of R be < a, b, c >

$$\Rightarrow \quad 4a - b + c = 0 \quad \text{...(v)}$$

Also, R passes through line of intersection.

So, normal of $R \perp$ line.

$$\Rightarrow \quad a(0) + b + c = 0 \quad \text{...(vi)}$$

From Eqs. (v) and (vi), we get

$$\frac{a}{1} = \frac{b}{2} = \frac{c}{-2}$$

So, equation of R is $1\left(x - \frac{14}{5}\right) + 2(y-1) - 2\left(z + \frac{1}{5}\right) = 0$

i.e. $5x + 10y - 10z - 26 = 0$

Distance of (2, 3, − 4) from

$$R = \frac{|5(2) + 10(3) - 10(-4) - 26|}{\sqrt{5^2 + 10^2 + (-10)^2}}$$

$$= \frac{18}{5} \text{ units} = \alpha \quad \text{[given]}$$

$\Rightarrow \quad 35\alpha = 126$

88. Given, equation of line is

$$\frac{x+3}{3} = \frac{y+2}{1} = \frac{1-z}{2} = k \text{ (let)}$$

$$\therefore \quad x = 3k - 3, y = k - 2, z = 1 - 2k$$

Since, given that

$$p \equiv (3k-3, k-2, 1-2k)$$

given be the point of intersection of the line and the plane $x + y + z = 2$

So, $(3k - 3) + (k - 2) + (1 - 2k) = 2$

$$\Rightarrow \quad 2k - 4 = 2$$

$$\Rightarrow \quad k = 3$$

Thus $P = (6, 1, -5)$.

Now, distance of point P from the plane $3x - 4y + 12z = 32$ is

$$q = \left| \frac{18 - 4 - 60 - 32}{\sqrt{9 + 16 + 144}} \right| = \left| \frac{-78}{\sqrt{169}} \right|$$

$$\Rightarrow \quad q = \left| \frac{-78}{13} \right| = \frac{78}{13} = 6$$

$$\therefore \quad q = 6$$

$$\Rightarrow \quad 2q = 12$$

Thus, q and $2q$ are roots of the equation $x^2 - 18x + 72 = 0$

89. Given that, two vertices of a ΔABC be $A(2, 4, 6)$ and $B(0, -2, -5)$ and $G = \text{centroid} = (2, 1, -1)$ [given]

Let the other vertex be $C(x, y, z)$.

Now, $(2, 1, -1) \equiv \left(\frac{2 + 0 + x}{3}, \frac{4 - 2 + y}{3}, \frac{6 - 5 + z}{3} \right)$

$\Rightarrow \quad (x, y, z) \equiv (4, 1, -4)$

Hence, the vertex is $C(4, 1, -4)$.

Now, it image of $C(4, 1, -4)$ in the plane $x + 2y + 4z = 11$ is $D(\alpha, \beta, \gamma)$

So, $\frac{\alpha - 4}{1} = \frac{\beta - 1}{2} = \frac{\gamma + 4}{4} = k$ (let)

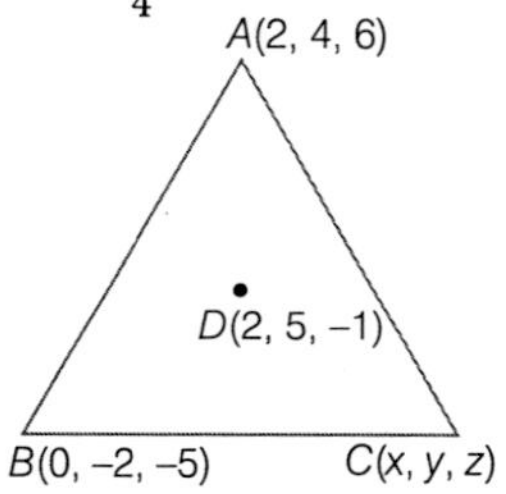

$\Rightarrow \quad \alpha = k + 4, \beta = 2k + 1, \gamma = 4k - 4$

Then, coordinates of D are $(k + 4, 2k + 1, 4k - 4)$.

Let E be the mid-point of CD which lies on the plane $x + 2y + 4z = 11$.

Then, coordinates of E are

$$\left(\frac{k + 8}{2}, \frac{2k + 2}{2}, \frac{4k - 8}{2} \right) = \left(\frac{k + 8}{2}, k + 1, 2k - 4 \right)$$

Since, E lines on the plane, $x + 2y + 4z - 11 = 0$

So, $\frac{k + 8}{2} + 2k + 2 + 8k - 16 - 11 = 0$

$$\Rightarrow \quad \frac{k + 8 + 4k + 4 + 16k - 54}{2} = 0$$

$$\Rightarrow \quad 21k = 42$$

$$\Rightarrow \quad k = 2$$

Hence, $D \equiv (6, 5, 4) \equiv (\alpha, \beta, \gamma)$

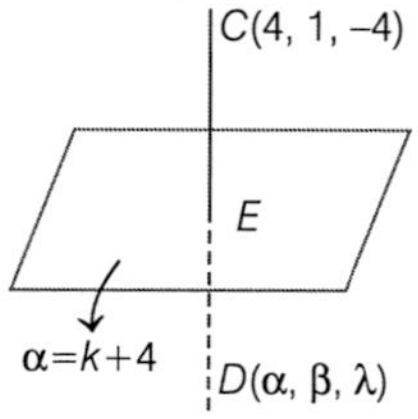

So, $\alpha = 6, \beta = 5, \gamma = 4$

Now, $\alpha\beta + \beta\gamma + \gamma\alpha = 6 \times 5 + 5 \times 4 + 4 \times 6$
$= 30 + 20 + 24 = 74$

90.

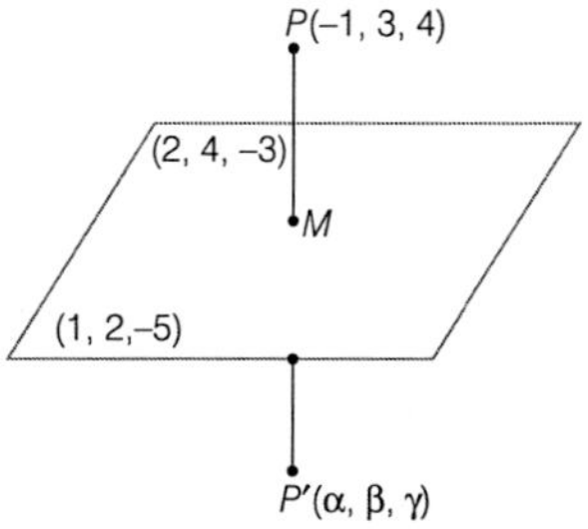

Equation of plane

$$\begin{vmatrix} x - 1 & y - 2 & z + 5 \\ 1 & 2 & 2 \\ 1 & -3 & 7 \end{vmatrix} = 0$$

$$\Rightarrow \quad 4x - y - z - 7 = 0$$

$$\therefore \quad \frac{\alpha - (-1)}{4} = \frac{\beta - 3}{-1} = \frac{\gamma - 4}{-1}$$

$$= \frac{-2(4(-1) - 3 - 4 - 7)}{4^2 + 1^2 + 1^2} = 2$$

$$\Rightarrow \quad \alpha = 8 - 1$$

$$\beta = -2 + 3, \gamma = -2 + 4$$

$$\Rightarrow \quad \alpha = 7, \beta = 1, \gamma = 2$$

$$\therefore \quad \alpha + \beta + \gamma = 10$$

91. Equation of any plane through the intersection of given planes is

$$(2x - y + z - 3) + \lambda(4x - 3y + 5z + 9) = 0 \quad \text{...(i)}$$

$$\Rightarrow (2 + 4\lambda)x + (-1 - 3\lambda)y + (1 + 5\lambda)z + (-3 + 9\lambda) = 0 \quad \text{...(ii)}$$

Plane (i) is parallel to given line.

$$\therefore \quad (-2)(2 + 4\lambda) + 4(-1 - 3\lambda) + 5(1 + 5\lambda) = 0$$

$$\Rightarrow \quad 5\lambda - 3 = 0$$

$$\Rightarrow \quad \lambda = \frac{3}{5}$$

On putting the value of λ in Eq. (i), we get

$$(2x - y + z - 3) + \frac{3}{5}(4x - 3y + 5z + 9) = 0$$

$$\Rightarrow \quad 11x - 7y + 10z + 6 = 0$$

$$\therefore \quad a = 11, b = -7, c = 10 \text{ and } d = 6$$

$$\therefore \quad a + b + c = 11 - 7 + 10 = 14$$

92. Equation of plane passing through the intersection of the planes $2x + 3y - z = 2$ and $x + 2y + 3z = 6$ is

$$2x + 3y - z - 2 + \lambda(x + 2y + 3z - 6) = 0$$

$$\Rightarrow \quad (2 + \lambda)x + (3 + 2\lambda)y + (-1 + 3\lambda)z - 2 - 6\lambda = 0$$

Since, above plane is perpendicular to the plane $2x + y - z + 1 = 0$, then

$$2(2 + \lambda) + 1(3 + 2\lambda) - 1(-1 + 3\lambda) = 0$$

$$\Rightarrow \quad 4 + 2\lambda + 3 + 2\lambda + 1 - 3\lambda = 0$$

$$\Rightarrow \quad \lambda = -8$$

So, equation of plane is

$$-6x - 13y - 25z + 46 = 0$$

$$\Rightarrow \quad 6x + 13y + 25z - 46 = 0$$

Now, distance of point $(-7, 1, 1)$ from the plane $6x + 13y + 25z - 46 = 0$ is d, then

$$d = \left| \frac{6(-7) + 13(1) + 25(1) - 46}{\sqrt{(6)^2 + (13)^2 + (25)^2}} \right|$$

$$= \left| \frac{-42 + 13 + 25 - 46}{\sqrt{36 + 169 + 625}} \right| = \frac{50}{\sqrt{830}}$$

$$\therefore \quad d^2 = \frac{2500}{830} = \frac{250}{83} \text{ units}$$

93.

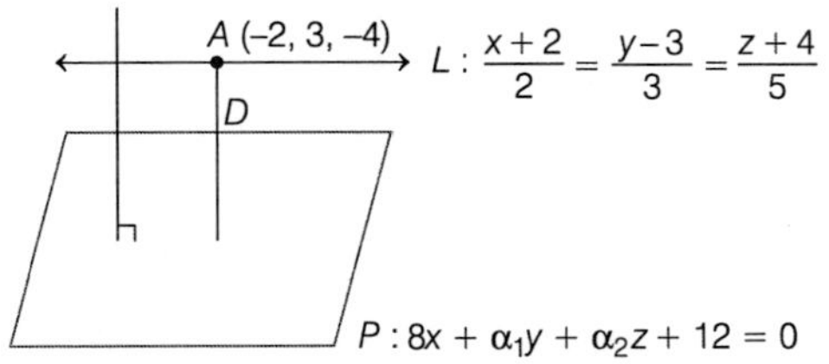

Since, line L is perpendicular to the normal to the plane P, so

$$2 \times 8 + 3\alpha_1 + 5\alpha_2 = 0$$

$$\Rightarrow \quad 16 + 3\alpha_1 + 5\alpha_2 = 0 \quad \ldots\text{(i)}$$

Again, equation of plane is

$$\Rightarrow \quad 8x + \alpha_1 y + \alpha_2 z = -12$$

$$\Rightarrow \quad \frac{8x}{-12} + \frac{\alpha_1 y}{-12} + \frac{\alpha_2 z}{-12} = 1$$

$$\Rightarrow \quad \frac{x}{\left(\frac{-3}{2}\right)} + \frac{y}{\left(\frac{-12}{\alpha_1}\right)} + \frac{z}{\left(\frac{-12}{\alpha_2}\right)} = 1$$

Now, y-intercept = 1

$$\Rightarrow \quad \frac{-12}{\alpha_1} = 1 \Rightarrow \alpha_1 = -12$$

On putting $\alpha_1 = -12$ in Eq. (i), we get

$$16 - 36 + 5\alpha_2 = 0$$

$$\Rightarrow \quad \alpha_2 = 4$$

Hence, the equation of plane P is

$$8x - 12y + 4z + 12 = 0$$

$$\Rightarrow \quad 2x - 3y + z + 3 = 0$$

Now, distance between plane P and line L

= Distance of point $(-2, 3, -4)$ from plane P

$$= \left| \frac{2(-2) - 3(3) + 1(-4) + 3}{\sqrt{(2)^2 + (-3)^2 + (1)^2}} \right|$$

$$= \left| \frac{-4 - 9 - 4 + 3}{\sqrt{4 + 9 + 1}} \right| = \frac{14}{\sqrt{14}} = \sqrt{14} \text{ units}$$

94.

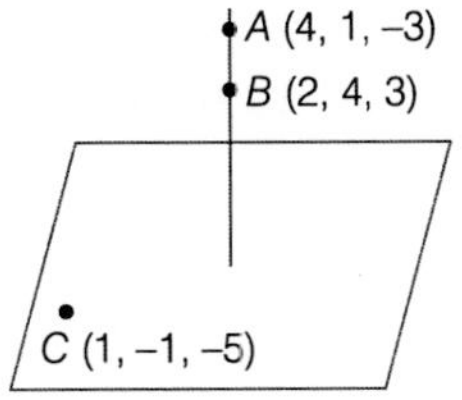

Direction ratios of the normal to the plane

= Direction ratios of line AB

$= 4 - 2 : 1 - 4 : -3 - 3$

$= 2 : -3 : -6$

Equation of plane is

$$2(x - 1) - 3(y + 1) - 6(z + 5) = 0$$

$$\Rightarrow \quad 2x - 3y - 6z - 35 = 0 \quad \ldots\text{(i)}$$

Hence, perpendicular distance of plane (i) from point $(3, -2, 2)$ is given as

$$\text{Distance} = \left| \frac{2 \times 3 - 3 \times (-2) - 6 \times 2 - 35}{\sqrt{(2)^2 + (-3)^2 + (-6)^2}} \right|$$

$$= \frac{35}{7} = 5 \text{ units}$$

95.

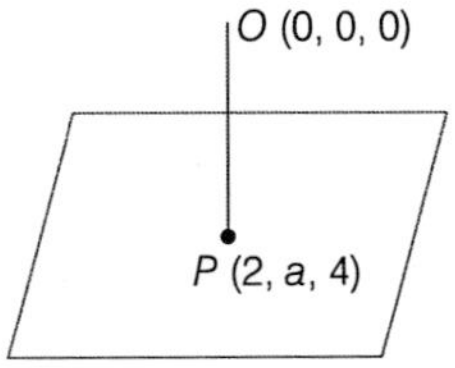

Equation of plane is

$$2(x - 2) + a(y - a) + 4(z - 4) = 0$$

$$\Rightarrow \quad 2x + ay + 4z = 20 + a^2$$

$$\Rightarrow \quad \frac{x}{\left(\frac{20 + a^2}{2}\right)} + \frac{y}{\left(\frac{20 + a^2}{a}\right)} + \frac{z}{\left(\frac{20 + a^2}{4}\right)} = 1$$

$\therefore$ Intercept on axes are $\frac{20 + a^2}{2}, \frac{20 + a^2}{a}, \frac{20 + a^2}{4}$, respectively.

So, $A\left(\frac{20 + a^2}{2}, 0, 0\right)$, $B\left(0, \frac{20 + a^2}{a}, 0\right)$ and $C\left(0, 0, \frac{20 + a^2}{4}\right)$

$\therefore$ Volume of tetrahedron $OABC$

$$= \frac{1}{6}\left(\frac{20 + a^2}{2}\right)\left(\frac{20 + a^2}{a}\right)\left(\frac{20 + a^2}{4}\right)$$

$$\Rightarrow \quad \frac{(20 + a^2)^3}{48a} = 144 \quad \text{[given]}$$

$$\Rightarrow \quad \left(\frac{20 + a^2}{12}\right)^3 = 4a$$

Let $\quad a = 2\lambda^3$

$$\Rightarrow \quad \left(\frac{20 + 4\lambda^6}{12}\right)^3 = 8\lambda^3$$

$$\Rightarrow \quad \frac{20 + 4\lambda^6}{12} = 2\lambda$$

$$\Rightarrow \quad 5 + \lambda^6 = 6\lambda$$

$$\Rightarrow \quad \lambda^6 - 6\lambda + 5 = 0$$

$$\Rightarrow \quad \lambda = 1 \Rightarrow \lambda^3 = 1$$

$$\Rightarrow \quad a = 2 \quad [\because a = 2\lambda^3]$$

So, equation of plane becomes

$$2x + 2y + 4z = 24$$

$$\Rightarrow \quad x + y + 2z = 12$$

Only, (3, 0, 4) does not satisfy above the equation of plane.

96. Given points are $(-1, k, 0)$, $(2, k, -1)$ and $(1, 1, 2)$, then equation of plane.

$$\begin{vmatrix} x-2 & y-k & z-(-1) \\ -1-2 & k-k & 0-(-1) \\ 1-2 & 1-k & 2-(-1) \end{vmatrix} = 0$$

$$\Rightarrow \quad \begin{vmatrix} x-2 & y-k & z+1 \\ -3 & 0 & 1 \\ -1 & 1-k & 3 \end{vmatrix} = 0$$

$$\Rightarrow (x-2)[0-(1-k)] - (y-k)[(3)(-3)-(-1)(1)] + (z+1)[-3(1-k)-0] = 0$$

$$\Rightarrow (x-2)(k-1) - (y-k)(-9+1) + (z+1)(3k-3) = 0$$

$$\Rightarrow (k-1)x + 8y + z(3k-3) + 3k - 3 - 8k - 2k + 2 = 0$$

$$\Rightarrow (k-1)x + 8y + z(3k-3) - 7k - 1 = 0$$

The plane is parallel to the line and $(k-1)$, 8, $(3k-3)$ are normal vectors.

So, dot product of normal vectors with the direction vectors of lines will be zero.

Then, $\quad (k-1)1 + 8(1) + (3k-3)(-1) = 0$

$$\Rightarrow k - 1 + 8 - 3k + 3 = 0$$

$$\Rightarrow 2k = 10$$

$$\Rightarrow k = 5$$

Therefore, $\dfrac{k^2+1}{(k-1)(k-2)} = \dfrac{(5)^2+1}{(5-1)(5-2)}$

$$= \frac{26}{4 \times 3} = \frac{13}{6}$$

97. Let $l_2 : \dfrac{x+1}{2} = \dfrac{y+4}{-3} = \dfrac{z}{2}$ ...(i)

Given, l_1 is a line passing through the point (2, 6, 2) and perpendicular to the plane $2x + y - 2z = 10$ ...(ii)

So, equation of l_1 is $\dfrac{x-2}{a} = \dfrac{y-6}{b} = \dfrac{z-2}{c}$, where a, b, c are direction ratios of l_1. Since, l_1 is perpendicular to the plane (ii). So, direction ratios of l_1 is same as direction ratios of normal to the plane (ii).

So, $\quad a = 2, b = 1, c = -2$

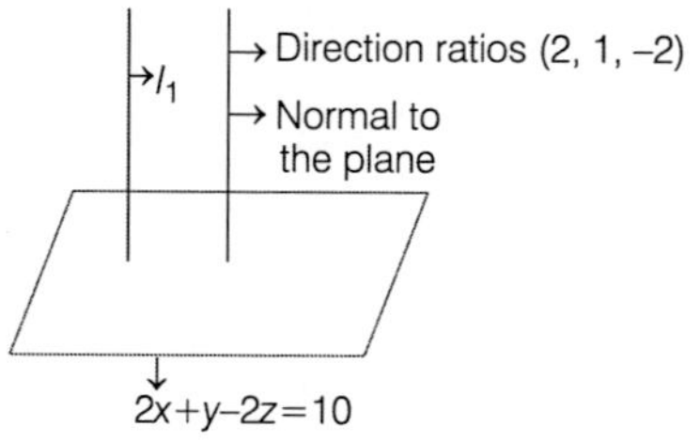

Hence, the equation of l_1 is

$$\frac{x-2}{2} = \frac{y-6}{1} = \frac{z-2}{-2} \quad \text{... (iii)}$$

Here, $\mathbf{AB} = (2-(-1)\hat{\mathbf{i}} + (6-(-4))\hat{\mathbf{j}} + (2-0)\hat{\mathbf{k}}$

$$= 3\hat{\mathbf{i}} + 10\hat{\mathbf{j}} + 2\hat{\mathbf{k}}$$

$$\mathbf{PQ} = \begin{vmatrix} \hat{\mathbf{i}} & \hat{\mathbf{j}} & \hat{\mathbf{k}} \\ 2 & 1 & -2 \\ 2 & -3 & 2 \end{vmatrix}$$

$$= \hat{\mathbf{i}}(2-6) - \hat{\mathbf{j}}(4+4) + \hat{\mathbf{k}}(-6-2) = -4\hat{\mathbf{i}} - 8\hat{\mathbf{j}} - 8\hat{\mathbf{k}}$$

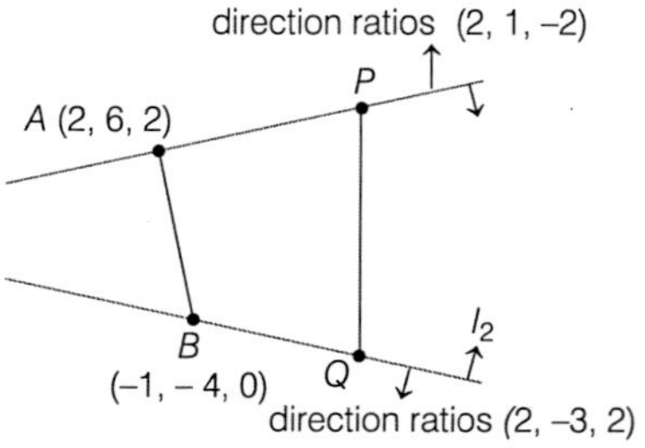

$$\therefore \ \mathbf{AB} \cdot \mathbf{PQ} = (3\hat{\mathbf{i}} + 10\hat{\mathbf{j}} + 2\hat{\mathbf{k}}) \cdot (-4\hat{\mathbf{i}} - 8\hat{\mathbf{j}} - 8\hat{\mathbf{k}})$$

$$= -12 - 80 - 16 = -108$$

and $\quad |\mathbf{PQ}| = PQ = \sqrt{(-4)^2 + (-8)^2 + (-8)^2}$

$$= \sqrt{16 + 64 + 64} = \sqrt{144} = 12$$

$$\therefore \text{ Shortest distance} = \left| \frac{\mathbf{AB} \cdot \mathbf{PQ}}{|\mathbf{PQ}|} \right| = \left| \frac{-108}{12} \right| = 9$$

98. Given that $\quad l = \cos 60° = \dfrac{1}{2}$

$$m = \cos 45 = \frac{1}{\sqrt{2}}$$

$$n = n$$

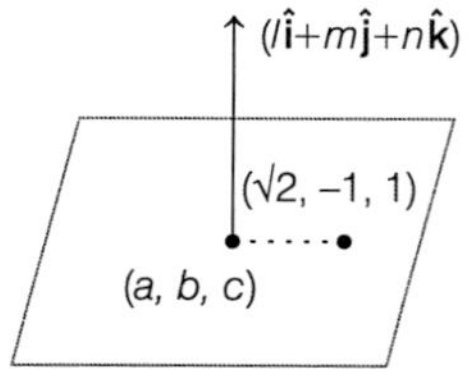

We know that $\quad l^2 + m^2 + n^2 = 1$

$$\frac{1}{4} + \frac{1}{2} + n^2 = 1$$

$$n^2 = 1 - \frac{3}{4} = \frac{1}{4} \Rightarrow n = \pm \frac{1}{2}$$

$$\Rightarrow \quad n = -\frac{1}{2} \quad \text{[reject acute angle]}$$

So, $\quad n = \dfrac{1}{2}$

Now, $l = \dfrac{1}{2}$, $m = \dfrac{1}{\sqrt{2}}$, $n = \dfrac{1}{2}$

Now, equation of a plane passing through (a, b, c) and $(\sqrt{2}, -1, 1)$ and normal to the vector $\mathbf{v} = \dfrac{1}{2}\hat{\mathbf{i}} + \dfrac{1}{\sqrt{2}}\hat{\mathbf{j}} + \dfrac{1}{2}\hat{\mathbf{k}}$ is given by,

$$(a - \sqrt{2})\frac{1}{2} + (b+1)\frac{1}{\sqrt{2}} + (c-1)\frac{1}{2} = 0$$

$$\Rightarrow \quad a + \sqrt{2}b + c = 1$$

99. The plane $2x - y + z = 4$ intersects the line segment joining the points $A(a, -2, 4)$ and $B(2, b, -3)$ at point C in the ratio $2:1$.

So, coordinates of C will be $\left(\frac{4+a}{3}, \frac{2b-2}{3}, \frac{-2}{3}\right)$.

C will satisfy the equation of the plane $2x - y + z = 4$

$$\therefore \quad 2\left(\frac{4+a}{3}\right) - \left(\frac{2b-2}{3}\right) + \left(\frac{-2}{3}\right) = 4$$

$$\Rightarrow \quad \frac{8 + 2a - 2b + 2 - 2}{3} = 4$$

$$\Rightarrow \quad 2a - 2b + 8 = 12$$

$$\Rightarrow \quad 2a - 2b = 4$$

$$\Rightarrow \quad a - b = 2$$

$$\Rightarrow \quad b = a - 2 \quad \text{...(i)}$$

Now, distance of the point C from origin O is,

$$\sqrt{\left(\frac{4+a}{3}\right)^2 + \left(\frac{2b-2}{3}\right)^2 + \left(\frac{-2}{3}\right)^2} = \sqrt{5}$$

$$\Rightarrow \quad (4+a)^2 + (2b-2)^2 + 4 = 45$$

$$\Rightarrow \quad 16 + a^2 + 8a + 4b^2 + 4 - 8b = 41$$

$$\Rightarrow \quad 5a^2 - 16a + 11 = 0$$

$$\Rightarrow \quad a = \frac{11}{5}, 1$$

For $a = \frac{11}{5}, b = \frac{11}{5} - 2 = \frac{1}{5}$

For $a = 1, b = 1 - 2 = -1$

As, $ab < 0 \Rightarrow a = 1, b = -1$

So, $P(a - b, b, 2b - a) = P(2, -1, -3)$

and $C\left(\frac{5}{3}, -\frac{4}{3}, \frac{-2}{3}\right)$

$$\therefore \quad (CP)^2 = \left(2 - \frac{5}{3}\right)^2 + \left(-1 + \frac{4}{3}\right)^2 + \left(-3 + \frac{2}{3}\right)^2$$

$$= \frac{1 + 1 + 49}{9} = \frac{51}{9} = \frac{17}{3}$$

100. Suppose, the lines are

$$L_1 \equiv \frac{x-1}{1} = \frac{y-2}{2} = \frac{z+3}{1} = \lambda \text{ (let)}$$

$$L_2 \equiv \frac{x-a}{2} = \frac{y+2}{3} = \frac{z-3}{1} = \mu \text{ (let)}$$

$$\therefore \quad x = \lambda + 1, y = 2\lambda + 2, z = \lambda - 3$$

$$\text{and} \quad x = 2\mu + a, y = 3\mu - 2, z = \mu + 3$$

$\because$ L_1 and L_2 intersect.

$$\therefore \quad 2\lambda + 2 = 3\mu - 2 \text{ and } \lambda - 3 = \mu + 3$$

$$\Rightarrow \quad -2\lambda + 3\mu = 4 \text{ and } \lambda - \mu = 6$$

On solving, we get

$$\mu = 16, \ \lambda = 22$$

$$\therefore \quad \lambda + 1 = 2\mu + a$$

$$\Rightarrow \quad 23 = 32 + a \Rightarrow a = -9$$

$\therefore$ Point of intersection $P = (23, 46, 19)$

Distance of P from the plane $z = -9$ is

$$= \left|\frac{19 + 9}{\sqrt{0 + 0 + 1}}\right| = 28$$

101. Given, equation of plane is

$$2x + 3y - z = 5 \quad \text{...(i)}$$

and equation of line is

$$\frac{x+4}{3} = \frac{2-y}{4} = \frac{z-3}{12}$$

$$\Rightarrow \quad \frac{x+4}{3} = \frac{y-2}{-4} = \frac{z-3}{12} \quad \text{...(ii)}$$

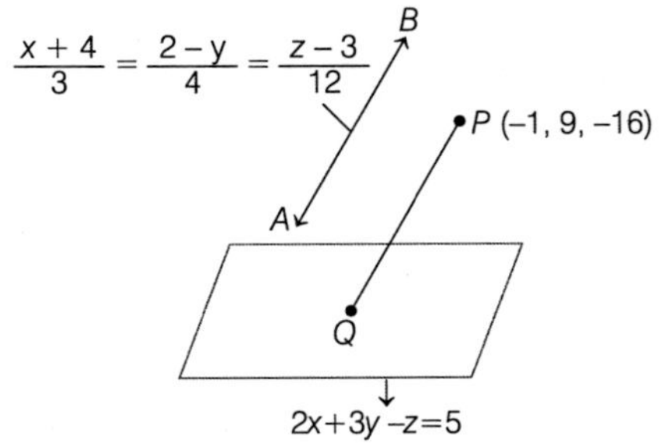

Direction ratios of Eq. (ii) are $3, -4, 12$.

Also, let $P \equiv (-1, 9, -16)$

Now, equation of any line parallel to the line (ii) and passing through the point P is given by

$$\frac{x-(-1)}{3} = \frac{y-9}{-4} = \frac{z-(-16)}{12}$$

$$\text{i.e.} \quad \frac{x+1}{3} = \frac{y-9}{-4} = \frac{z+16}{12} \quad \text{...(iii)}$$

Now, coordinates of a general point taken on line (iii) are $Q \cdot (3\lambda - 1, -4\lambda + 9, 12\lambda - 16)$, where λ is a parameter.

Since, Q lies on the given plane or you can say that the Q is the point of intersection of line and plane.

Then, $6\lambda - 2 - 12\lambda + 27 - 12\lambda + 16 = 5$

$$\Rightarrow \quad \lambda = 2$$

So, $Q \equiv (5, 1, 8)$

Hence, the distance, $PQ = \sqrt{(5+1)^2 + (1-9)^2 + (8+16)^2}$

$$= \sqrt{36 + 64 + 576} = 26 \text{ units}$$

102. Vector perpedicular to the perpendicular of the planes $x + 2y + z = 0$ and $3y - z = 3$ is

$$\mathbf{b} = \begin{vmatrix} \hat{\mathbf{i}} & \hat{\mathbf{j}} & \hat{\mathbf{k}} \\ 1 & 2 & 1 \\ 0 & 3 & -1 \end{vmatrix}$$

$$= \hat{\mathbf{i}}(-2-3) - \hat{\mathbf{j}}(-1) + \hat{\mathbf{k}}(3)$$

$$= -5\hat{\mathbf{i}} + \hat{\mathbf{j}} + 3\hat{\mathbf{k}}$$

$\therefore$ Equation of line parallel to **b** and passing through $(3, 2, 1)$ is

$$\frac{x-3}{-5} = \frac{y-2}{1} = \frac{z-1}{3} = r \text{ (let)}$$

$$\therefore \quad x = -5r + 3, \ y = r + 2, z = 3r + 1$$

$\Rightarrow$ $Q(-5r + 3, r + 2, 3r + 1)$

Given, point $P(1, 9, 7)$

Direction ratios of PQ are $-5r + 2, r - 7, 3r - 6$, which is perpendicular to **b**.

$\therefore \quad -5(-5r+2)+1(r-7)+3(3r-6)=0 \Rightarrow r=1$

$\therefore \quad Q(-2, 3, 4)$

Hence, $\alpha+\beta+\gamma=5$

103. Given eqations of the two planes are

$$P_1: x+(\lambda+4)y+z-1=0$$

and $P_2:\ 2x+y+z-2=0$

$\therefore$ Equation of plane through the line of intersection of the two planes is

$$(x+(\lambda+4)y+z-1)+\mu(2x+y+z-2)=0 \qquad \text{...(i)}$$

which passes through (0, 1, 0) and (1, 0, 1).

$\therefore \quad (0+(\lambda+4)\times 1+0-1)+\mu(0+1+0-2)=0$

$\therefore \quad \mu=\lambda+3 \qquad \text{...(ii)}$

Also, $(1+0+1-1)+\mu(2+0+1-2)=0$

$\Rightarrow \quad 1+\mu=0 \Rightarrow \mu=-1$

From Eq. (ii),

$$-1=\lambda+3 \Rightarrow \lambda=-4$$

$\therefore$ From Eq. (i),

$(x+0+z-1)+(-1)(2x+y+z-2)=0$

$\Rightarrow \quad -x-y+1=0$

$\Rightarrow \quad x+y=1$

$\because$ Point from which the distance is to be calculated is, $P(2\lambda, \lambda, -\lambda)$

i.e. $\quad P(-8, -4, 4)$

$\therefore$ The required distance of P from plane P_2 is,

$$=\left|\frac{2(-8)+(-4)+4-2}{\sqrt{4+1+1}}\right|$$

$$=\left|\frac{-16-2}{\sqrt{6}}\right|$$

$$=\frac{18}{\sqrt{6}}=3\sqrt{6} \text{ units}$$

104. (26) Let the plane P contain the line $2x+y-z-3=0$ and $5x-3y+4z+9=0$ is

$$(2x+y-z-3)+\lambda(5x-3y+4z+9)=0 \ [\lambda=\text{constant}]$$

$$=(2+5\lambda)x+(1-3\lambda)y+(-1+4\lambda)z+(-3+9\lambda)=0$$

which is parallel to the line

$$\frac{x+2}{2}=\frac{3-y}{-4}=\frac{z-7}{5}$$

So, $\quad 2(2+5\lambda)+4(1-3\lambda)+5(-1+4\lambda)=0$

$\Rightarrow \quad 4+10\lambda+4-12\lambda-5+20\lambda=0$

$\Rightarrow \quad 18\lambda=-3$

$\Rightarrow \quad \lambda=-\frac{1}{6}$

So, plane $P: 7x+9y-10z-27=0$

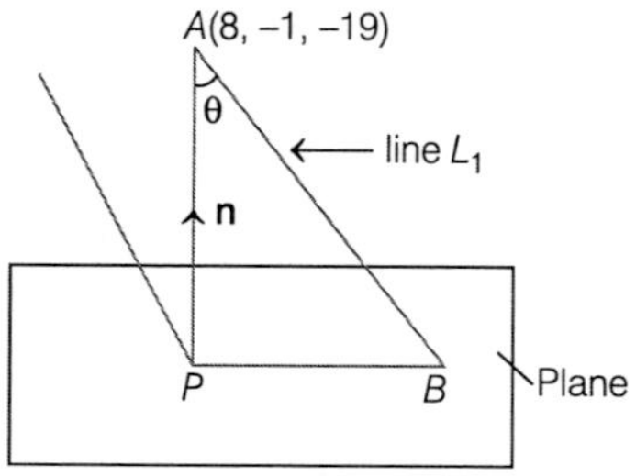

Thus, equation of line AB is

$$\frac{x-8}{-3}=\frac{y+1}{4}=\frac{z+19}{12}=K \text{ (let)}$$

$\therefore \quad x=-3K+8, y=4K-1,$

$\quad z=12K-19$

Thus, $B\equiv(-3K+8, 4K-1, 12K-19)$

Since, the point B line on plane 'P'

So, $7(-3k+8)+9(4K-1)-10(12K-19)=27$

$\Rightarrow \quad -21K+56+36K-9-120K+190=27$

$\Rightarrow \quad -105K=27+9-190-56$

$\Rightarrow \quad -105K=-210$

$\Rightarrow \quad K=2$

$\therefore \quad B=(2, 7, 5)$

So, distance from point $A(8, -1, -19)$ to point $B(2, 7, 5)$ is

$$\sqrt{(8-2)^2+(-1-7)^2+(-19-5)^2}=\sqrt{36+64+576}$$

$$=\sqrt{676}=26 \text{ units}$$

105. Given, line $l: x=\frac{y-1}{2}=\frac{z-3}{\lambda}; \lambda\in R$ and $P: x+2y+3z=4$

l and P meet at (α, β, γ).

Also, angle between line and plane is $\cos^{-1}\left(\sqrt{\frac{5}{14}}\right)$.

Now, if angle between line and plane is θ.

Then, $\sin\theta=\frac{\mathbf{n}_1\cdot\mathbf{n}_2}{|\mathbf{n}_1||\mathbf{n}_2|}$

where, $\mathbf{n}_1=$ Normal vector of plane $P=\hat{\mathbf{i}}+2\hat{\mathbf{j}}+3\hat{\mathbf{k}}$

and $\quad \mathbf{n}_2=$ Vector along line $l=\hat{\mathbf{i}}+2\hat{\mathbf{j}}+\lambda\hat{\mathbf{k}}$

$\Rightarrow \quad \sin\theta=\frac{3}{\sqrt{14}}=\frac{1+4+3\lambda}{\sqrt{14}\sqrt{\lambda^2+5}}$

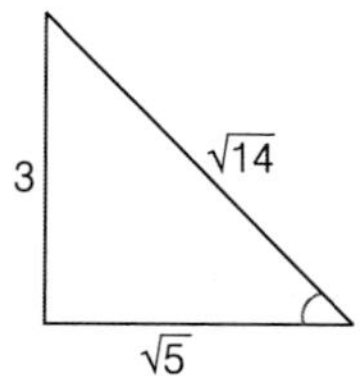

$\Rightarrow \quad \frac{9}{14}=\frac{(5+3\lambda)^2}{14(\lambda^2+5)}$

$\Rightarrow \quad 9\lambda^2+45=25+9\lambda^2+30\lambda$

$\Rightarrow \quad 30\lambda=20$

$\Rightarrow \quad \lambda=\frac{2}{3}$

Then, $l: x=\frac{y-1}{2}=\frac{z-3}{\left(\frac{2}{3}\right)}=k$

Now, any point on line l will be $\left(k, 2k+1, \frac{2k}{3}+3\right)$,

which will lie on plane P, for intersection

$\Rightarrow \quad k+2(2k+1)+3\left(\frac{2k}{3}+3\right)=4$

$\Rightarrow \quad 7k+11=4 \Rightarrow k=-1$

Thus, the points of intersection is $\left(-1, -1, \frac{7}{3}\right)$.

$\Rightarrow \alpha = -1, \beta = -1, \gamma = \frac{7}{3}$

So, $\alpha + 2\beta + 6\gamma = -1 - 2 + 14 = 11$

Hence, $\alpha + 2\beta + 6\gamma = 11$

106. We have, equation of plane P is

$$x - y + 2z + 3 = 0$$

$B(5, \alpha, \beta)$ lies on the plane P,

so $5 - \alpha + 2\beta + 3 = 0$

$\Rightarrow \qquad \alpha = 2\beta + 8$

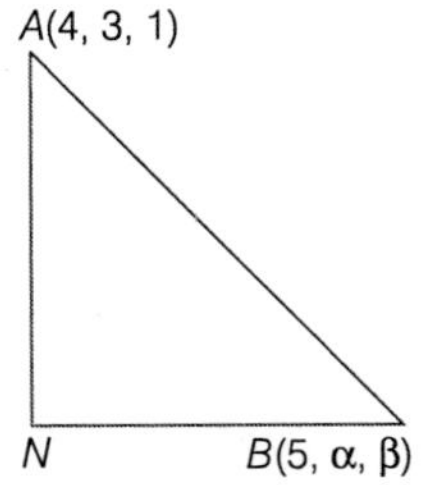

Direction ratios of AN are $< 1, -1, 2 >$

Equation of AN is

$$\frac{x-4}{1} = \frac{y-3}{-1} = \frac{z-1}{2}$$

Coordinates of N: $\frac{x-4}{1} = \frac{y-3}{-1} = \frac{z-1}{2}$

$$= \frac{-(4-3+2+3)}{1+1+4}$$

$$= -1$$

$\Rightarrow \qquad x = 3, y = 4, z = -1$

$\therefore$ Coordinates of N are $(3, 4, -1)$

Area of $\Delta ABN = \frac{1}{2} \times AN \times BN = 3\sqrt{2}$

$\Rightarrow \frac{1}{2} \times \sqrt{6} \times BN = 3\sqrt{2} \Rightarrow BN = 2\sqrt{3}$

$\Rightarrow \qquad \sqrt{(5-3)^2 + (\alpha - 4)^2 + (\beta + 1)^2} = 2\sqrt{3}$

$\Rightarrow \qquad 4 + (2\beta + 4)^2 + (\beta + 1)^2 = 12$

$\Rightarrow \qquad 4 + 4\beta^2 + 16 + 16\beta + \beta^2 + 2\beta + 1 = 12$

$\Rightarrow \qquad 5\beta^2 + 18\beta + 9 = 0$

$\Rightarrow \qquad (5\beta + 3)(\beta + 3) = 0$

$\Rightarrow \qquad \beta = -3$

$[\because \beta \in Z, \text{ so rejecting } \beta = \frac{-3}{5}]$

$\Rightarrow \alpha = 2\beta + 8 = 2(-3) + 8 = 2$

$\therefore \alpha^2 + \beta^2 + \alpha\beta = (2)^2 + (-3)^2 + 2 \times (-3) = 7$

107. Given plane

$$2x + 3y - 6z + 7 = 0 \qquad \text{...(i)}$$

Points let $A\left(\frac{5}{2}, 1, \lambda\right)$ and $B(-2, 0, 1)$ are at equal distance from plane.

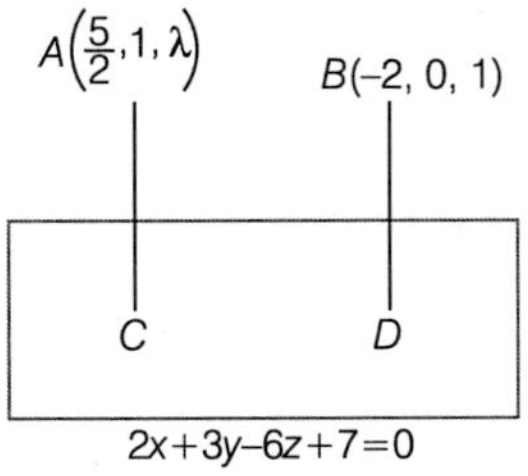

$\because \qquad AC = BD = \left|\frac{5 + 3 - 6\lambda + 7}{\sqrt{4 + 9 + 36}}\right|$

$$= \left|\frac{-4 - 6 + 7}{\sqrt{4 + 9 + 36}}\right|$$

$\Rightarrow \qquad 15 - 6\lambda = \pm 3$

$\Rightarrow \qquad 6\lambda = 12, 18$

$\Rightarrow \qquad \lambda = 2, 3$

$\Rightarrow \qquad \lambda_1 > \lambda_2$

$\therefore \qquad \lambda_1 = 3, \lambda_2 = 2$

Points $(\lambda_1 - \lambda_2, \lambda_2, \lambda_1) = (1, 2, 3)$

Distance of $P(1, 2, 3)$ from the line

$$\frac{x-5}{1} = \frac{y-1}{2} = \frac{z+7}{2} = \mu \text{ (let)}$$

Q is a point on line, i.e. $Q(\mu + 5, 2\mu + 1, 2\mu - 7)$

DR's of PQ: $\mu + 4, 2\mu - 1, 2\mu - 10$

DR's of line : 1, 2, 2

PQ is perpendicular to line.

$\Rightarrow (\mu + 4) \cdot 1 + (2\mu - 1) \cdot 2 + (2\mu - 10) 2 = 0$

$\Rightarrow \qquad \mu = 2$

$Q(7, 5, -3)$

$$PQ = \sqrt{36 + 9 + 36} = 9$$

108. We have, equation of plane is $\alpha x + \beta y + \gamma z = 1$

Since, plane passes through the point $(3, -2, 5)$,

so $\qquad 3\alpha - 2\beta + 5\gamma = 1 \qquad$ ...(i)

Again, direction ratios of line joining the points (1, 2, 3) and $(-2, 3, 5)$ are $1 + 2 : 2 - 3 : 3 - 5$ i.e., $3 : -1 : -2$

Since, plane is perpendicular to the line, so

$$\frac{\alpha}{3} = \frac{\beta}{-1} = \frac{\gamma}{-2} = \lambda$$

$\Rightarrow \qquad \alpha = 3\lambda, \beta = -\lambda, \gamma = -2\lambda$

On putting $\alpha = 3\lambda, \beta = -\lambda, \gamma = -2\lambda$ in Eq. (i), we get

$$9\lambda + 2\lambda - 10\lambda = 1$$

$\Rightarrow \qquad \lambda = 1$

$\therefore \qquad \alpha = 3, \beta = -1, \gamma = -2$

So, $\alpha\beta\gamma = (3)(-1)(-2) = 6$

109. It is given that C divides $A(-3, -6, 1)$ and $B(2, 4, -3)$ in the ratio $k : 1$.

Then, coordinates of C are $\left(\frac{2k-3}{k+1}, \frac{4k-6}{k+1}, \frac{-3k+1}{k+1}\right)$.

Since, C lies on the plane $8x + y + 2z = 0$.

So, $8\left(\frac{2k-3}{k+1}\right)+\frac{4k-6}{k+1}+2\left(\frac{-3k+1}{k+1}\right)=0$

$\Rightarrow \quad 16k-24+4k-6-6k+2=0$

$\Rightarrow \quad 14k-28=0$

$\Rightarrow \quad k=2$

$\therefore$ Coordinates of C are $\left(\frac{1}{3},\frac{2}{3},\frac{-5}{3}\right)$.

Now, any point of line $\frac{x-1}{-1}=\frac{y+4}{2}=\frac{z+2}{3}=\lambda$ is $D(-\lambda+1, 2\lambda-4, 3\lambda-2)$.

$\therefore$ Direction ratios of CD

$$=-\lambda+1-\frac{1}{3}:2\lambda-4-\frac{2}{3}:3\lambda-2+\frac{5}{3}$$

$$=\frac{2}{3}-\lambda:2\lambda-\frac{14}{3}:3\lambda-\frac{1}{3}$$

Since, CD perpendicular to line, then

$$-1\left(\frac{2}{3}-\lambda\right)+2\left(2\lambda-\frac{14}{3}\right)+3\left(3\lambda-\frac{1}{3}\right)=0$$

$\Rightarrow \quad -\frac{2}{3}+\lambda+4\lambda-\frac{28}{3}+9\lambda-1=0$

$\Rightarrow \quad 14\lambda-11=0$

$\Rightarrow \quad \lambda=\frac{11}{14}$

$\therefore$ Direction ratios of $CD=\frac{2}{3}-\frac{11}{14}:2\left(\frac{11}{14}\right)-\frac{14}{3}:3\left(\frac{11}{14}\right)-\frac{1}{3}$

$$=\frac{28-33}{42}:\frac{66-196}{42}:\frac{99-14}{42}$$

$$=-5:-130:85=1:26:-17$$

$\therefore \quad a=1, b=26, c=-17$

So, $|a+b+c|=|1+26-17|=10$

110. Given equation of line is

$$L:\frac{x-1}{2}=\frac{y+1}{-1}=\frac{z-3}{1}=\lambda \text{ (let)}$$

Any point of line L has coordinates $(2\lambda+1, -\lambda-1, \lambda+3)$.

$\therefore$ Coordinates of point P are $(2\lambda+1, -\lambda-1, \lambda+3)$.

Since, P lies on the plane $2x+y+3z=16$

$\therefore \quad 2(2\lambda+1)+(-\lambda-1)+3(\lambda+3)=16$

$\Rightarrow \quad 6\lambda=6$

$\Rightarrow \quad \lambda=1$

$\therefore$ Coordinates of P are $(3,-2,4)$.

Again, Q is foot of perpendicular from $R(1,-1,-3)$ on the line L, then coordinates of Q are $(2\lambda+1, -\lambda-1, \lambda+3)$.

Now, direction ratios of QR are

$<2\lambda+1-1, -\lambda-1+1, \lambda+3+3>$ i.e. $<2\lambda, -\lambda, \lambda+6>$

$\because QR\perp L$, then

$$2(2\lambda)+(-1)(-\lambda)+1(\lambda+6)=0$$

$\Rightarrow \quad \lambda=-1$

So, coordinates of Q are $(-1,0,2)$.

Now, vertices of ΔPQR are $P(3,-2,4)$, $Q(-1,0,2)$ and $R(1,-1,-3)$.

Again, $\mathbf{PR}=(3-1)\hat{\mathbf{i}}+(-2+1)\hat{\mathbf{j}}+(4+3)\hat{\mathbf{k}}$

$$=2\hat{\mathbf{i}}-\hat{\mathbf{j}}+7\hat{\mathbf{k}}$$

and $\quad \mathbf{PQ}=(-1-3)\hat{\mathbf{i}}+(0+2)\hat{\mathbf{j}}+(2-4)\hat{\mathbf{k}}$

$$=-4\hat{\mathbf{i}}+2\hat{\mathbf{j}}-2\hat{\mathbf{k}}$$

Also, $\mathbf{PR}\times\mathbf{PQ}=\begin{vmatrix}\hat{\mathbf{i}} & \hat{\mathbf{j}} & \hat{\mathbf{k}}\\ 2 & -1 & 7\\ -4 & 2 & -2\end{vmatrix}$

$$=-12\hat{\mathbf{i}}-24\hat{\mathbf{j}}+0\hat{\mathbf{k}}$$

$\therefore \quad |\mathbf{PR}\times\mathbf{PQ}|=\sqrt{(-12)^2+(-24)^2+(0)^2}$

$$=\sqrt{144+576}=\sqrt{720}$$

Now, $\text{ar}(\Delta PQR)=\frac{1}{2}|\mathbf{PR}\times\mathbf{PQ}|$

$$=\frac{1}{2}\times\sqrt{720}$$

But $\quad \text{ar}(\Delta PQR)=\alpha$

$\therefore \quad \alpha=\frac{1}{2}\sqrt{720}$

$\Rightarrow \quad \alpha^2=\frac{1}{4}\times 720=180$

111. We have, the line $\frac{x+10}{1}=\frac{y-8}{-2}=\frac{z-0}{1}$.

i.e. $(-10,8,0)$ lies on the line with direction ratios $<1,-2,1>$.

Equation of plane is $ax+by+3z=2(a+b)$.

So, its normal's direction ratios are $<a,b,3>$.

Since, plane contains the given line, so $(-10,8,0)$ lies on the plane

$\Rightarrow \quad a(-10)+b(8)+3(0)=2(a+b)$

$\Rightarrow \quad -10a+8b=2a+2b$

$\Rightarrow \quad 12a=6b$

$\Rightarrow \quad b=2a \qquad \text{...(i)}$

Also, line will be perpendicular to normal of plane, so dot product of their direction ratios will be zero.

i.e. $\quad (a)(1)+(b)(-2)+(3)(1)=0$

$\Rightarrow \quad a-2b+3=0$

$\Rightarrow \quad a-2(2a)+3=0 \qquad$ [from Eq. (i)]

$\Rightarrow \quad a-4a+3=0$

$\Rightarrow \quad 3=3a$

$\Rightarrow \quad a=1 \qquad \text{...(ii)}$

$\therefore \quad b=2 \qquad \text{...(iii)}$

$\Rightarrow$ Equation of plane is $x+2y+3z=6 \qquad \text{...(iv)}$

So, distance of $(1,27,7)$ from the plane

$$c=\frac{|(1)+2(27)+3(7)-6|}{\sqrt{1^2+2^2+3^2}}=\frac{70}{\sqrt{14}}$$

$\Rightarrow \quad c^2=\frac{70\times 70}{14}=350 \qquad \text{...(v)}$

From Eqs. (ii), (iii) and (v), we get

$$a^2+b^2+c^2=1^2+2^2+350=355$$

112. Equation of plane passing through the intersection of

$$x - 2y - z - 5 = 0 \text{ and } x + y + 3z - 5 = 0$$

$$P : (x - 2y - z - 5) + \lambda(x + y + 3z - 5) = 0$$

$$P : (1 + \lambda)x + (-2 + \lambda)y + (-1 + 3\lambda)\, z - 5(1 + \lambda) = 0 \quad \text{...(i)}$$

Above plane is parallel to line of intersection of

$$x + y + 2z - 7 = 0 \text{ and } 2x + 3y + z - 2 = 0$$

So, $\begin{vmatrix} 1+\lambda & -2+\lambda & -1+3\lambda \\ 1 & 1 & 2 \\ 2 & 3 & 1 \end{vmatrix} = 0$

$\Rightarrow -5(1 + \lambda) + 3(-2 + \lambda) + (-1 + 3\lambda) = 0$

$\Rightarrow \quad -5 - 5\lambda - 6 + 3\lambda - 1 + 3\lambda = 0 \Rightarrow \lambda = 12$

On putting $\lambda = 12$ in Eq. (i)

So, equation of plane is $13x + 10y + 35z = 65$

On comparing with $ax + by + cz = 65$

$$a = 13, b = 10, c = 35$$

Hence, the distance of point (13, 10, 35) from the plane $2x + 2y - z + 16 = 0$ is

$$= \left|\frac{26 + 20 - 35 + 16}{\sqrt{2^2 + 2^2 + (-1)^2}}\right| = \left|\frac{27}{3}\right| = 9 \text{ units}$$

113. Given, equations are

$$l + m - n = 0 \Rightarrow n = l + m$$

Now, put the value of n in another equation, then

$$3l^2 + m^2 + cl\,(l + m) = 0$$

$\Rightarrow \quad (3 + c)l^2 + clm + m^2 = 0$

$\Rightarrow \quad (3 + c)\left(\frac{l}{m}\right)^2 + c\left(\frac{l}{m}\right) + 1 = 0 \quad \text{...(i)}$

Given, that lines are parallel.

Then, roots of Eq. (i) must be equal.

$\Rightarrow \quad D = 0$

$\Rightarrow \quad c^2 - 4(3 + c) = 0$

$\Rightarrow \quad c^2 - 4c - 12 = 0$

$\Rightarrow \quad (c - 6)(c + 2) = 0$

$\Rightarrow \quad c = 6$ or $c = -2$.

Therefore, positive value of $c = 6$.

114. $RS \equiv (\alpha, -1, \beta)$

$\therefore$ Direction ratios of $PQ \equiv \left(\frac{56}{17} + 2, \frac{43}{17} + 1, \frac{111}{17} - 1\right)$

$$\equiv \left(\frac{90}{17}, \frac{60}{17}, \frac{94}{17}\right)$$

$\Rightarrow \quad \frac{90}{17}\alpha + \frac{60}{17}(-1) + \frac{94}{17}\beta = 0$

$\Rightarrow \quad 90\alpha + 94\beta = 60$

$\Rightarrow \quad \beta = \frac{60 - 90\alpha}{94}$

$\Rightarrow \quad \beta = \frac{30(2 - 3\alpha)}{94}$

$\Rightarrow \quad \beta = -30\,\frac{(3\alpha - 2)}{94}$

$\Rightarrow \quad \beta = \frac{-15}{47}(3\alpha - 2)$

$\Rightarrow \quad \frac{\beta}{-15} = \frac{3\alpha - 2}{47}$

$\Rightarrow \quad \beta = 15, \alpha = -15$

$\therefore \quad \alpha^2 + \beta^2 = 225 + 225 = 450$

115.

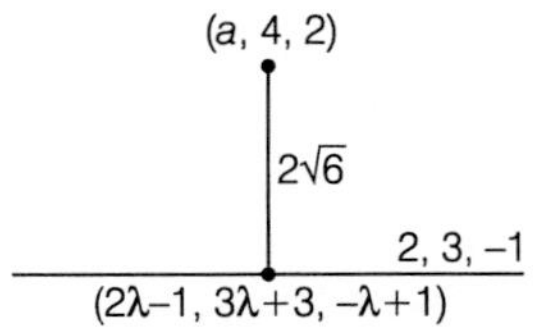

Given, line is $\frac{x + 1}{2} = \frac{y - 3}{3} = \frac{z - 1}{-1} = \lambda$

$$x = 2\lambda - 1, y = 3\lambda + 3, z = -\lambda + 1$$

$\Rightarrow \quad (2\lambda - 1 - a)2 + (3\lambda - 1)3 + (-\lambda - 1)(-1) = 0$

$\Rightarrow \quad 4\lambda - 2 - 2a + 9\lambda - 3 + \lambda + 1 = 0$

$\Rightarrow \quad 14\lambda - 4 - 2a = 0$

$\Rightarrow \quad 7\lambda - 2 - a = 0$

and $\quad (2\lambda - 1 - a)^2 + (3\lambda - 1)^2 + (\lambda + 1)^2 = 24$

$\Rightarrow \quad (5\lambda - 1)^2 + (3\lambda - 1)^2 + (\lambda + 1)^2 = 24$

$\Rightarrow \quad 35\lambda^2 - 14\lambda - 21 = 0$

$\Rightarrow \quad (\lambda - 1)(35\lambda + 21) = 0$

For $\lambda = 1 \Rightarrow a = 5$

Let $(\alpha_1, \alpha_2, \alpha_3)$ be reflection of point P

$$\alpha_1 + 5 = 2, \ \alpha_2 + 4 = 12, \ \alpha_3 + 2 = 0$$

$$\alpha_1 = -3, \ \alpha_2 = 8, \ \alpha_3 = -2$$

$\therefore \quad a + \alpha_1 + \alpha_2 + \alpha_3 = 8$

116. Given that first line, $L_1 : \frac{x + 7}{-6} = \frac{y - 6}{7} = \frac{z - 0}{1}$

Any point on the line $\mathbf{a}_1 \equiv (-7, 6, 0)$

and L_1 parallel to $\mathbf{b}_1 \equiv (-6, 7, 1)$

and second line, $L_2 ; \frac{x - 7}{-2} = \frac{y - 2}{1} = \frac{z - 6}{1}$

Then, any point on it $\mathbf{a}_2$ is (7, 2, 6) and the line L_2 is parallel to $\mathbf{b}_2$ is (– 2, 1, 1).

Thus, the shortest distance between line L_1 and L_2 is

$$\left|\frac{(\mathbf{a}_2 - \mathbf{a}_1) \cdot (\mathbf{b}_1 \times \mathbf{b}_2)}{|\mathbf{b}_1 \times \mathbf{b}_2|}\right| = \left|\frac{(14, -4, 6) \cdot (3, 2, 4)}{\sqrt{3^2 + 2^2 + 4^2}}\right|$$

$$= \left|\frac{42 - 8 + 24}{\sqrt{29}}\right| = \frac{58}{\sqrt{29}} = 2\sqrt{29} \text{ units}$$

117. $l_1 : \frac{x-2}{3} = \frac{y+1}{-2} = \frac{z-2}{0}$

$$a_1 = 3, b_1 = -2, c_1 = 0$$

$$l_2 : \frac{x-1}{1} = \frac{y + \left(\frac{3}{2}\right)}{\left(\frac{\alpha}{2}\right)} = \frac{z+5}{2}$$

$$a_2 = 1, b_2 = \frac{\alpha}{2}, c_2 = 2$$

Given, that l_1 perpendicular to l_2.

$\therefore \quad a_1 a_2 + b_1 b_2 + c_1 c_2 = 0$

$\Rightarrow \quad 3 - \alpha + 0 = 0$

$\Rightarrow \quad \alpha = 3$

$\Rightarrow \quad a_2 = 1, b_2 = \frac{3}{2}, c_2 = 2$

Now, $l_3 : \frac{x-1}{-3} = \frac{y - \left(\frac{1}{2}\right)}{-2} = \frac{z-0}{4}$

$a_3 = -3, b_3 = -2, c_3 = 4$

Angle between l_2 and l_3 is given by,

$$\cos\theta = \frac{|a_2 a_3 + b_2 b_3 + c_2 c_3|}{\sqrt{a_2^2 + b_2^2 + c_2^2}\sqrt{a_3^2 + b_3^2 + c_3^2}}$$

$$= \frac{|-3 - 3 + 8|}{\sqrt{1 + \frac{9}{4} + 4}\sqrt{9 + 4 + 16}}$$

$\Rightarrow \quad \cos\theta = \frac{4}{\sqrt{29}\sqrt{29}}$

$\Rightarrow \quad \theta = \cos^{-1}\left(\frac{4}{29}\right)$

$\Rightarrow \quad \theta = \sec^{-1}\left(\frac{29}{4}\right)$

118. Centroid of $\Delta ABC = G\left(\frac{2\alpha}{3}, \frac{2\alpha}{3}, \frac{2\alpha}{3}\right)$

Given, equation of line is $\frac{x}{1} = \frac{z-3}{-1} = \frac{y}{0} = \lambda$

$x = \lambda, y = 0, z = -\lambda + 3$

$\therefore D(\lambda, 0, -\lambda + 3)$ be any point on given line

$$\therefore \quad GD = \left(\sqrt{\left(\lambda - \frac{2\alpha}{3}\right)^2 + \left(\frac{2\alpha}{3}\right)^2 + \left(-\lambda + 3 - \frac{2\alpha}{3}\right)^2}\right)$$

$$GD_1 = \left(\lambda - \frac{2\alpha}{3}\right)^2 + \left(\frac{2\alpha}{3}\right)^2 + \left(-\lambda + 3 - \frac{2\alpha}{3}\right)^2$$

$$\frac{dGD_1}{d\lambda} = 2\left(\lambda - \frac{2\alpha}{3}\right) - 2\left(-\lambda + 3 - \frac{2\alpha}{3}\right)$$

$\Rightarrow 4\lambda - 6 = 0 \quad \Rightarrow \lambda = 3/2$

$$\therefore \text{ Minimum } GD = \sqrt{\left(\frac{3}{2} - \frac{2\alpha}{3}\right)^2 + \left(\frac{2\alpha}{3}\right)^2 + \left(-\frac{3}{2} + 3 - \frac{2\alpha}{3}\right)^2}$$

$$= \sqrt{\frac{57}{2}}$$

$$= \sqrt{\left(\frac{9 - 4\alpha}{6}\right)^2 + \frac{4\alpha^2}{9} + \left(\frac{9 - 4\alpha}{6}\right)^2}$$

$\Rightarrow \quad \frac{57}{2} = \frac{24\alpha^2 - 72\alpha + 81}{18}$

$\Rightarrow \alpha^2 - 3\alpha - 18 = 0$

$\Rightarrow \quad \alpha = -3, 6$

$\therefore \quad \alpha = 6 \quad [\because \alpha > 0]$

119. Given that $\mathbf{r} = (-\hat{\mathbf{i}} + 3\hat{\mathbf{k}}) + \lambda(\mathbf{i} - a\hat{\mathbf{j}})$

and $\quad \mathbf{r} = (-\hat{\mathbf{j}} + 2\hat{\mathbf{k}}) + \mu(\hat{\mathbf{i}} - \hat{\mathbf{j}} + \hat{\mathbf{k}})$

So, let $\mathbf{b}_1 = \hat{\mathbf{i}} - a\hat{\mathbf{j}}$ and $\mathbf{b}_2 = \hat{\mathbf{i}} - \hat{\mathbf{j}} + \hat{\mathbf{k}}$

$$\mathbf{b}_1 \times \mathbf{b}_2 = \begin{vmatrix} \hat{\mathbf{i}} & \hat{\mathbf{j}} & \hat{\mathbf{k}} \\ 1 & -a & 0 \\ 1 & -1 & 1 \end{vmatrix} = -a\hat{\mathbf{i}} - \hat{\mathbf{j}} + (a-1)\hat{\mathbf{k}}$$

Let $\quad \mathbf{a}_1 = -\hat{\mathbf{i}} + 3\hat{\mathbf{k}}$ and $\mathbf{a}_2 = -\hat{\mathbf{j}} + 2\hat{\mathbf{k}}$

$\therefore \quad \mathbf{a}_1 - \mathbf{a}_2 = (-\hat{\mathbf{i}} + 3\hat{\mathbf{k}}) - (-\hat{\mathbf{j}} + 2\hat{\mathbf{k}})$

$= -\hat{\mathbf{i}} + \hat{\mathbf{j}} + \hat{\mathbf{k}}$

Thus, shortest distance $= \left|\frac{(\mathbf{a}_1 - \mathbf{a}_2)\cdot(\mathbf{b}_1 \times \mathbf{b}_2)}{|\mathbf{b}_1 \times \mathbf{b}_2|}\right|$

$$\Rightarrow \quad \sqrt{\frac{2}{3}} = \left|\frac{(-\hat{\mathbf{i}} + \hat{\mathbf{j}} + \hat{\mathbf{k}})\cdot(-a\hat{\mathbf{i}} - \hat{\mathbf{j}} + (a-1)\hat{\mathbf{k}})}{\sqrt{a^2 + 1 + (a-1)^2}}\right|$$

$$\Rightarrow \quad \sqrt{\frac{2}{3}} = \left|\frac{2(a-1)}{\sqrt{a^2 + 1 + (a-1)^2}}\right|$$

$\Rightarrow \quad 6(a^2 - 2a + 1) = 2a^2 - 2a + 2$

$\Rightarrow \quad 4a^2 - 10a + 4 = 0$

$\Rightarrow \quad 2a^2 - 5a + 2 = 0$

$\Rightarrow \quad (a-2)(2a-1) = 0$

Thus, $a = 2$ or $\frac{1}{2}$

Hence, the integral value of a is 2.

120. Normal vectors can be determined by cross product.

So, $\mathbf{n}_1 = \hat{\mathbf{i}} \times (\hat{\mathbf{i}} \times \hat{\mathbf{j}}) = \hat{\mathbf{k}}$ and $\mathbf{n}_2 = (\hat{\mathbf{i}} + \hat{\mathbf{k}}) \times (\hat{\mathbf{i}} - \hat{\mathbf{j}}) = \hat{\mathbf{i}} + \hat{\mathbf{j}} - \hat{\mathbf{k}}$

Line of intersection along $\mathbf{n}_1 \times \mathbf{n}_2 = \hat{\mathbf{k}} \times (\hat{\mathbf{i}} + \hat{\mathbf{j}} - \hat{\mathbf{k}}) = -\hat{\mathbf{i}} + \hat{\mathbf{j}}$

DR's of $\mathbf{a} = -\hat{\mathbf{i}} + \hat{\mathbf{j}}$

DR's of $\mathbf{b} = \hat{\mathbf{i}} - 2\hat{\mathbf{j}} + 2\hat{\mathbf{k}}$

$\mathbf{a} \cdot \mathbf{b} = -3$ and $(\mathbf{a} \times \mathbf{b}) = 0$

$$\cos\theta = \frac{-3}{\sqrt{2} \times 3} \Rightarrow \theta = \frac{3\pi}{4}$$

121. Normal of plane E

$$\mathbf{n} = \begin{vmatrix} \hat{\mathbf{i}} & \hat{\mathbf{j}} & \hat{\mathbf{k}} \\ 2 & -2 & 1 \\ 1 & -1 & 2 \end{vmatrix} = -3\hat{\mathbf{i}} - 3\hat{\mathbf{j}}$$

$\therefore \quad \mathbf{n} = \hat{\mathbf{i}} + \hat{\mathbf{j}}$

Equation plane E,

$1(x-1) + 1(y+1) + 0(y-1) = 0$

$\Rightarrow \quad x + y = 0 \quad$ ...(i)

Distance from $Q(a, a, 2)$ from plane (i) is

$$d = \left|\frac{a + a}{\sqrt{1+1}}\right| \Rightarrow \left|\frac{2a}{\sqrt{2}}\right| = 3\sqrt{2} \text{ units}$$

$\Rightarrow \quad a = \pm 3$

$\therefore \quad PQ^2 = (2)^2 + 4^2 + 1 = 21$ units

122. The image or reflection (x, y, z) of a point (x_1, y_1, z_1) in a plane $ax + by + cz + d = 0$ is given by

$$\frac{x - x_1}{a} = \frac{y - y_1}{b} = \frac{z - z_1}{c} = \frac{-2(ax_1 + by_1 + cz_1 + d)}{a^2 + b^2 + c^2}$$

$$\Rightarrow \frac{a-2}{3} = \frac{b-4}{-1} = \frac{c-7}{4} = \frac{-2(6-4+28-2)}{9+1+16} = -\frac{28}{13}$$

$$\therefore a = 2 - \frac{84}{13} \Rightarrow a = -\frac{58}{13}$$

$$b = 4 + \frac{28}{13} \Rightarrow b = \frac{80}{13}$$

$$c = 7 - \frac{112}{13} \Rightarrow c = \frac{-21}{13}$$

$$\because 2a + b + 2c = \frac{-116 + 80 - 42}{13} = -\frac{78}{13} = -6$$

123. Equation of plane passing through the intersection of given planes is

$$(5 + 8\lambda)x + (8 - 7\lambda)y + (13 + \lambda)z - (29 + 20\lambda) = 0$$

Since, P_1 passes through (2, 1, 3)

$$\Rightarrow (10 + 16\lambda) + (8 - 7\lambda) + (39 + 3\lambda) - (29 + 20\lambda) = 0$$

$$\Rightarrow -8\lambda + 28 = 0$$

$$\Rightarrow \lambda = \frac{7}{2}$$

$\therefore$ DR's of normal to P_1

$$< 33, \frac{-33}{2}, \frac{33}{2} > \text{ or } < 1, \frac{-1}{2}, \frac{1}{2} >$$

Since, P_2 passes through (0, 1, 2)

$$\Rightarrow 8 - 7\lambda + 26 + 2\lambda - (29 + 20\lambda) = 0$$

$$\Rightarrow 5 - 25\lambda = 0$$

$$\Rightarrow \lambda = \frac{1}{5}$$

DR's of normal to P_2

$$< \frac{33}{5}, \frac{33}{5}, \frac{66}{5} > \text{ or } < 1, 1, 2 >$$

$$\text{Angle between normals} = \frac{\left(\hat{\mathbf{i}} - \frac{1}{2}\hat{\mathbf{j}} + \frac{1}{2}\hat{\mathbf{k}}\right) \cdot (\hat{\mathbf{i}} + \hat{\mathbf{j}} + 2\hat{\mathbf{k}})}{\frac{\sqrt{3}}{2} \cdot \sqrt{6}}$$

$$\cos\theta = \frac{1 - 1/2 + 1}{3} = \frac{1}{2} \Rightarrow \theta = \frac{\pi}{3}$$

124. Let the point on the plane 'P' be (x, y, z).

Given that the points on the plane P be equidistance from the points (–4, 2, 1) and (2, –2, 3).

Thus, $(x + 4)^2 + (y - 2)^2 + (z - 1)^2 = (x - 2)^2 + (y + 2)^2 + (z - 3)^2$

$$\Rightarrow x^2 + 16 + 8x + y^2 + 4 - 4y + z^2 - 2z + 1 = x^2 - 4x + 4 + y^2 + 4y + 4 + z^2 - 6z + 9$$

$$\Rightarrow 12x - 8y + 4z = -4$$

$$\Rightarrow 3x - 2y + z = -1 \quad \text{...(i)}$$

Given, that $2x + y + 3z = 1$ ...(ii)

Let θ be an acute angle between the plane 'P' and the plane $2x + y + 3z = 1$

$$\therefore \cos\theta = \left|\frac{3\times2 - 2\times1 + 3\times1}{\sqrt{(3)^2 + (-2)^2 + 1^2} \cdot \sqrt{(2)^2 + (1)^2 + (3^2)}}\right| = \left|\frac{6 - 2 + 3}{\sqrt{14}\cdot\sqrt{14}}\right| = \frac{7}{14} = \frac{1}{2}$$

Thus, $\cos\theta = \frac{1}{2} \Rightarrow \theta = \cos^{-1}\left(\frac{1}{2}\right) = \frac{\pi}{3}$

125. $P_1 : \mathbf{r} \cdot (2\hat{\mathbf{i}} + \hat{\mathbf{j}} - 3\hat{\mathbf{k}}) = 4$

$P_1 : 2x + y - 3z = 4$

$$P_2 = \begin{vmatrix} x-2 & y+3 & z-2 \\ 0 & 1 & -5 \\ -1 & -1 & 0 \end{vmatrix} = 0$$

$$\Rightarrow -5x + 5y + z + 23 = 0$$

Let a, b, c be the DR's of line of intersection.

Then, $a = \frac{16\lambda}{15}; b = \frac{13\lambda}{15}; c = \frac{15\lambda}{15}$

$\therefore \quad \alpha = 13$ and $\beta = 15$

$$\alpha + \beta = 28$$

126.

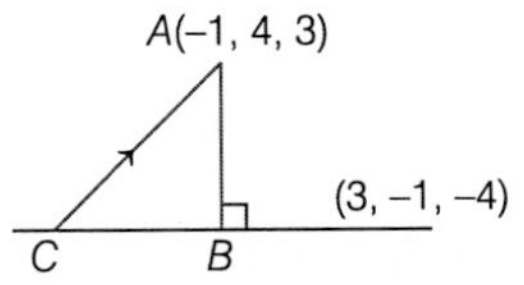

Let B be foot of perpendicular coordinates of $B = \left(-2, \frac{7}{2}, \frac{3}{2}\right)$.

$\therefore$ Direction ratios of line AB are < 2, 1, 3 >, so $m = 1$, $n = 3$

So, equation of AC is

$$\frac{x+1}{3} = \frac{y-4}{-1} = \frac{z-3}{-4} = \lambda$$

Point C is $(3\lambda - 1, -\lambda + 4, -4\lambda + 3)$.

$\because C$ lies on the plane.

$\therefore \quad 6\lambda - 2 - \lambda + 4 - 12\lambda + 9 = 4 \Rightarrow \lambda = 1$

$\Rightarrow \quad C(2, 3, -1) \Rightarrow AC = \sqrt{26}$

127. Equation of straight line passes through $P(3, 2, -1)$ and parallel to given line is

$$\frac{x-3}{-2} = \frac{y-2}{2} = \frac{z+1}{1} = \lambda \quad \text{...(i)}$$

$\therefore Q(-2\lambda + 3, 2\lambda + 2, \lambda - 1)$ be any point in line (i) and it is also lines on given plane.

$$\therefore 3(-2\lambda + 3) - 1(2\lambda + 2) + 4(\lambda - 1) + 1 = 0$$

$$\Rightarrow -4\lambda + 4 = 0$$

$$\Rightarrow \lambda = 1$$

$\therefore Q(1, 4, 0)$

Now, distance, $PQ = \sqrt{(1-3)^2 + (4-2)^2 + (0+1)^2} = 3$ units

128. Let the coordinates of foot of perpendicular be (x, y, z).

Take $\frac{x+2}{4}=\frac{y-1}{2}=\frac{z+1}{3}=\lambda$

$(x, y, z)=(4\lambda-2, 2\lambda+1, 3\lambda-1)$

Equation of line from point A to point P

$=(4\lambda-3)\hat{\mathbf{i}}+(2\lambda-1)\hat{\mathbf{j}}+(3\lambda-5)\hat{\mathbf{k}}$

Line passes through the vector $\mathbf{b}$.

Then, $\mathbf{b}=4\hat{\mathbf{i}}+2\hat{\mathbf{j}}+3\hat{\mathbf{k}}$

So, $\mathbf{AP}\cdot\mathbf{b}=0$

$\Rightarrow 4(4\lambda-3)+2(2\lambda-1)+3(3\lambda-5)=0$

$\Rightarrow 29\lambda=12+2+15=29$

$\Rightarrow \lambda=1$

Now, put the value of λ in the value of point P.

Then, $P=(2, 3, 2)$

Distance of point P from the plane $3x+4y+12z+23=0$.

Required distance, $d=\left|\frac{6+12+24+23}{\sqrt{9+16+144}}\right|$,

$\Rightarrow d=\left|\frac{65}{13}\right|=5$ units

129.

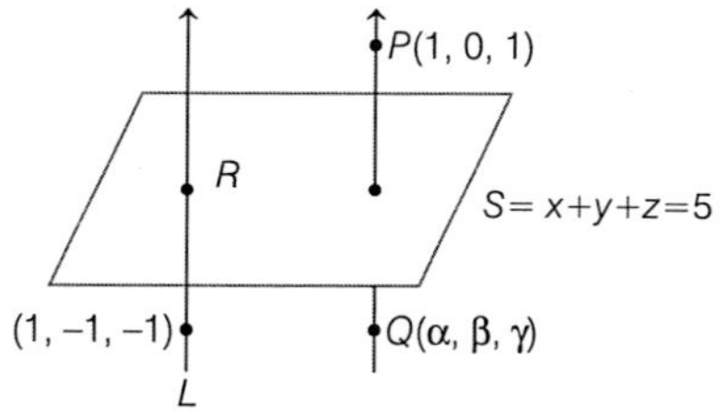

Given, a line L is parallel to PQ direction, then ratios of line L is $<1, 1, 1>$.

Apply formula for image of point on the plane $\frac{-2(ax_1+by_1+cz_1+d)}{a^2+b^2+c^2}$.

$$\frac{\alpha-1}{1}=\frac{\beta-0}{1}=\frac{\gamma-1}{1}=\frac{-2(2-5)}{3}$$

$\alpha=3, \beta=2, \gamma=3; Q\equiv(3, 2, 3)$

Here, line $L \parallel PQ$.

Equation of line L is shown below

$$\frac{x-1}{1}=\frac{y+1}{1}=\frac{z+1}{1}=\mu$$

Here point $R, \mu+1, \mu-1, \mu-1$ is intersection point of plane $x+y+z=5$.

$3\mu-1=5 \Rightarrow \mu=2$

So, point R is $(3, 1, 1)$; $QR^2=5$

130. Points $P\equiv(1, 2, -1)$ and $Q\equiv(2, -1, 3)$

Plane : $-x+y+z=1$ ... (i)

Let foot of the perpendicular of points P and Q be F_1 and F_2, respectively.

Line PF_1 : $\frac{x-1}{-1}=\frac{y-2}{1}=\frac{z+1}{1}=\lambda$

$F_1\equiv(1-\lambda, 2+\lambda, -1+\lambda)$

$-(1-\lambda)+(2+\lambda)+(-1+\lambda)=1$ [from Eq. (i)]

$\Rightarrow -1+\lambda+2+\lambda-1+\lambda=1 \Rightarrow \lambda=\frac{1}{3}$

$F_1\equiv\left(\frac{2}{3}, \frac{7}{3}, -\frac{2}{3}\right)$

Similarly, $F_2\equiv\left(\frac{5}{3}, -\frac{2}{3}, \frac{10}{3}\right)$

$\therefore F_1F_2=\sqrt{\left(\frac{5}{3}-\frac{2}{3}\right)^2+\left(-\frac{2}{3}-\frac{7}{3}\right)^2+\left(\frac{10}{3}+\frac{2}{3}\right)^2}$

$=\sqrt{(1)^2+(-3)^2+(4)^2}=\sqrt{1+9+16}=\sqrt{26}=d$

$\Rightarrow d^2=26$

131. Equation of plane passing through P_1 and P_2 is

$4ax-y+5z-7a+\lambda(2x-5y-z-3)=0$

$(4, -1, 0)$ will satisfy it

$16a+1-7a+\lambda(8+5-3)=0$

$\Rightarrow 9a+1+10\lambda=0$ ...(i)

Normal vector to the plane A is $(4a+2\lambda, -1-5\lambda, 5-\lambda)$ a vector along the line which contained the plane A is $\hat{\mathbf{i}}-2\hat{\mathbf{j}}+\hat{\mathbf{k}}$

$\therefore 4a+2\lambda+2+10\lambda+5-\lambda=0$

$\Rightarrow 11\lambda+4a+7=0$ ...(ii)

On solving Eqs. (i) and (ii), we get

$a=1, \lambda=-1$

Now, equation of plane

$x+2y+3z-2=0$

Let the point in the line $\frac{x-3}{7}=\frac{y-2}{-1}=\frac{z-3}{-4}=k$ is

$(7k+3, -k+2, -4k+3)$ satisfy the equation of plane A;

$7k+3-2k+4+9-12k-2=0$

$\Rightarrow k=2$

So, $\alpha+\beta+\gamma=2k+8=12$

132. Both the lines lie in the same plane with L_1 is $\mathbf{r}=\lambda(\hat{\mathbf{i}}+2\hat{\mathbf{j}}+3\hat{\mathbf{k}})$ and L_2 : $\mathbf{r}=(\hat{\mathbf{i}}+3\hat{\mathbf{j}}+\hat{\mathbf{k}})+\mu(\hat{\mathbf{i}}+\hat{\mathbf{j}}+5\hat{\mathbf{k}})$

$\therefore$ Equation of the plane is $\begin{vmatrix} x & y & z \\ 1 & 2 & 3 \\ 1 & 1 & 5 \end{vmatrix}=0$

$\Rightarrow 7x-2y-z=0$

Direction ratios of normal to the plane $<7, -2, -1>$.

Put the values of $a=7, b=-2, c=-1, d=0$

$a+b+d=5$

133. Given that

$l+m-n=0 \Rightarrow l=n-m$ ...(i)

and $l^2+m^2-n^2=0$ ...(ii)

On substituting l from Eq. (i) into Eq. (ii), we get

$(n-m)^2+m^2-n^2=0$

$\Rightarrow 2m(m-n)=0$

$\Rightarrow m=0$ or $m=n$

Case I If $m=0$,

$l=n$ [from Eq. (i)]

We know that

$$l^2 + m^2 + n^2 = 1 \Rightarrow l^2 = \frac{1}{2} \Rightarrow l_1, l_2 = \frac{1}{\sqrt{2}}, \frac{-1}{\sqrt{2}} \text{ respectively.}$$

$\because \quad l = n \Rightarrow n_1, n_2 = \frac{1}{\sqrt{2}}, \frac{-1}{\sqrt{2}}$ respectively.

$\therefore \left(\frac{1}{\sqrt{2}}, 0, \frac{1}{\sqrt{2}}\right)$ or $\left(\frac{-1}{\sqrt{2}}, 0, \frac{-1}{\sqrt{2}}\right)$ are direction cosines of line L_1.

Case II If $m = n$

$\Rightarrow \quad l = 0$ [from Eq. (i)]

$\Rightarrow \quad l^2 + m^2 + n^2 = 1 \Rightarrow m^2 = 1/2$

$\Rightarrow \quad m_1, m_2 = \frac{1}{\sqrt{2}}, \frac{-1}{\sqrt{2}}$ respectively.

$\because \quad m = n \Rightarrow n_1, n_2 = \frac{1}{\sqrt{2}}, \frac{-1}{\sqrt{2}}$ respectively.

$\therefore \left(0, \frac{1}{\sqrt{2}}, \frac{1}{\sqrt{2}}\right)$ or $\left(0, \frac{-1}{\sqrt{2}}, \frac{-1}{\sqrt{2}}\right)$ are direction cosines of line L_2.

Now, $\cos \alpha = l_1 l_2 + m_1 m_2 + n_1 n_2$

$$= 0 + 0 \pm \frac{1}{2} = \pm \frac{1}{2}$$

$\Rightarrow \quad \cos^2 \alpha = \frac{1}{4} \Rightarrow \sin^2 \alpha = \frac{3}{4}$

So, $\sin^4 \alpha + \cos^4 \alpha = \frac{5}{8}$

134. $L_1 \Rightarrow \frac{x-a}{l} = \frac{y-2}{3} = \frac{z-b}{4}$

Foot of perpendicular from $A(4, 3, 8)$ to L_1 is $B(3, 5, 7)$.

$$\mathbf{AB} = \mathbf{OB} - \mathbf{OA}$$

$$= (3\hat{\mathbf{i}} + 5\hat{\mathbf{j}} + 7\hat{\mathbf{k}}) - (4\hat{\mathbf{i}} + 3\hat{\mathbf{j}} + 8\hat{\mathbf{k}}) = -\hat{\mathbf{i}} + 2\hat{\mathbf{j}} - \hat{\mathbf{k}}$$

Now, **AB** is perpendicular to direction cosine of L_1,

So, $\quad (-\hat{\mathbf{i}} + 2\hat{\mathbf{j}} - \hat{\mathbf{k}}) \cdot (l\hat{\mathbf{i}} + 3\hat{\mathbf{j}} + 4\hat{\mathbf{k}}) = 0$

$\Rightarrow \quad -l + 6 - 4 = 0 \Rightarrow l = 2$

As, (3, 5, 7) lies on L_1,

$$\frac{3-a}{2} = \frac{5-2}{3} = \frac{7-b}{4}$$

$$3 - a = 2$$

So, $a = 1, 7 - b = 4 \Rightarrow b = 3$

$$L_1 = \frac{x-1}{2} = \frac{y-2}{3} = \frac{z-3}{4}$$

and $L_2 = \frac{x-2}{3} = \frac{y-4}{4} = \frac{z-5}{5}$

$\therefore$ Shortest distance will be along common normal.

So, common normal $= \begin{vmatrix} \hat{\mathbf{i}} & \hat{\mathbf{j}} & \hat{\mathbf{k}} \\ 2 & 3 & 4 \\ 3 & 4 & 5 \end{vmatrix}$

$\Rightarrow \quad \mathbf{n} = -\hat{\mathbf{i}} + 2\hat{\mathbf{j}} - \hat{\mathbf{k}}$

$\Rightarrow \quad \hat{\mathbf{n}} = 1/\sqrt{6}\,(-\hat{\mathbf{i}} + 2\hat{\mathbf{j}} - \hat{\mathbf{k}})$

Shortest distance will be the projection of $(2-1)\hat{\mathbf{i}} + (4-2)\hat{\mathbf{j}} + (5-3)\hat{\mathbf{k}}$ or $\hat{\mathbf{i}} + 2\hat{\mathbf{j}} + 2\hat{\mathbf{k}}$ along $\hat{\mathbf{n}}$.

$\Rightarrow \quad (\hat{\mathbf{i}} + 2\hat{\mathbf{j}} + 2\hat{\mathbf{k}}) \frac{(-\hat{\mathbf{i}} + 2\hat{\mathbf{j}} - \hat{\mathbf{k}})}{\sqrt{6}} = \frac{-1+4-2}{\sqrt{6}} = \frac{1}{\sqrt{6}}$

135. Given, point $P(1, 3, 5)$ has the mirror image $Q(\alpha, \beta, \gamma)$ with respect to plane $4x - 5y + 2z = 8$

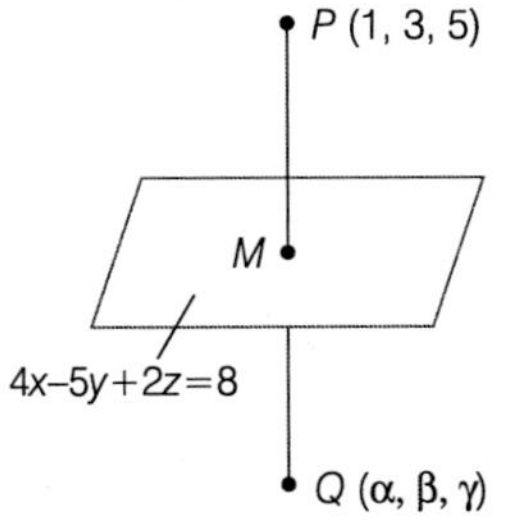

Then, M be the mid-point of line joining point P and Q and M lies on given plane.

Coordinates of $M(a, b, c)$ are as follows

$$a = \frac{\alpha+1}{2}, b = \frac{\beta+3}{2}, c = \frac{\gamma+5}{2}$$

$\because$ M lies on plane, then

$$4a - 5b + 2c = 8$$

$$4\left(\frac{\alpha+1}{2}\right) - 5\left(\frac{\beta+3}{2}\right) + 2\left(\frac{\gamma+5}{2}\right) = 8 \quad \text{...(i)}$$

Also, PQ is perpendicular to plane

$$\frac{\alpha-1}{4} = \frac{\beta-3}{-5} = \frac{\gamma-5}{2} = \lambda \quad \text{(say)}$$

$\Rightarrow \quad \alpha = 4\lambda + 1, \beta = 3 - 5\lambda, \gamma = 2\lambda + 5 \quad$ ...(ii)

Use Eq. (ii) in Eq. (i), we get

$$2(4\lambda + 2) - 5\left(\frac{6 - 5\lambda}{2}\right) + 2\lambda + 10 = 8$$

$\Rightarrow \quad 8\lambda + 4 - 15 + \frac{25\lambda}{2} + 2\lambda + 10 = 8$

$\Rightarrow \quad \lambda = \frac{2}{5}$

$\therefore \quad \alpha = 4\lambda + 1 = 4\left(\frac{2}{5}\right) + 1 = \frac{13}{5}$

$$\beta = 3 - 5\left(\frac{2}{5}\right) = \frac{5}{5} = 1$$

and $\gamma = 5 + 2\left(\frac{2}{5}\right) = \frac{29}{5}$

$\therefore \quad 5(\alpha + \beta + \gamma) = 5\left(\frac{13}{5} + 1 + \frac{29}{5}\right) = 47$

136. Given, $P_1 \Rightarrow 3x + 15y + 21z = 9$

$P_2 \Rightarrow x - 3y - z = 5$

$P_3 \Rightarrow 2x + 10y + 14z = 5$

Consider plane P_1, it can be written as

$$3x + 15y + 21z = 9 \text{ or } x + 5y + 7z = 3$$

Again, consider plane P_3, it can be written as,

$$2x + 10y + 14z = 5$$

or $\quad x + 5y + 7z = \frac{5}{2}$

Hence, P_1 and P_3 are parallel.

137. $P \Rightarrow lx + my + nz = 0$

P contains L_1

$$L_1 \Rightarrow \frac{x-1}{-1} = \frac{y+4}{2} = \frac{z+2}{3}$$

So, $(1, -4, -2)$ lies on plane.

$$l - 4m - 2n = 0 \quad \text{...(i)}$$

And $(-1, 2, 3)$ will be perpendicular to (l, m, n).

$$-l + 2m + 3n = 0 \quad \text{... (ii)}$$

Adding Eqs. (i) and (ii),

$$-2m + n = 0 \Rightarrow n = 2m$$

$$l - 4m - 4m = 0 \Rightarrow l = 8m$$

So, $l = 8m$ and $n = 2m$

Plane $\Rightarrow 8x + y + 2z = 0$

Now, $A(-3, -6, 1)$ and $B(2, 4, -3)$.

Plane P divides AB in the ratio of $k:1$.

Let plane P intersect the line AB at point O.

So, $O = \left(\dfrac{2k-3}{k+1}, \dfrac{4k-6}{k+1}, \dfrac{-3k+1}{k+1}\right)$

And O lies on plane P,

So, $8(2k-3) + (4k-6) + 2(-3k+1) = 0$

$\Rightarrow \quad 14k - 28 = 0$

$\therefore \quad k = 2$

138. Given lines, $\dfrac{x-k}{1} = \dfrac{y-2}{2} = \dfrac{z-3}{3}$ and $\dfrac{x+1}{3} = \dfrac{y+2}{2} = \dfrac{z+3}{1}$ are coplanar.

So, $\begin{vmatrix} k+1 & 4 & 6 \\ 1 & 2 & 3 \\ 3 & 2 & 1 \end{vmatrix} = 0$

$\Rightarrow \ (k+1)(2-6) - 4(1-9) + 6(2-6) = 0$

$\Rightarrow \quad -4k - 4 + 32 - 24 = 0$

$\Rightarrow \quad -4k + 4 = 0 \Rightarrow k = 1$

139. Since, the mirror image of the point $A(1, 2, 3)$ in a plane is $B\left(-\dfrac{7}{3}, -\dfrac{4}{3}, -\dfrac{1}{3}\right)$, then mid-point of AB lies in the plane and DR's of line AB are the DR's, of normal to the plane.

Now, mid-point of AB is

$$P\left(\frac{1-\frac{7}{3}}{2}, \frac{2-\frac{4}{3}}{2}, \frac{3-\frac{1}{3}}{2}\right) = P\left(-\frac{2}{3}, \frac{1}{3}, \frac{4}{3}\right)$$

and DR's of line AB is

$$\left(1+\frac{7}{3}, 2+\frac{4}{3}, 3+\frac{1}{3}\right) \approx \left(\frac{10}{3}, \frac{10}{3}, \frac{10}{3}\right) \approx (1, 1, 1)$$

$\therefore$ Equation of the plane is

$$1\left(x+\frac{2}{3}\right) + 1\left(y-\frac{1}{3}\right) + 1\left(z-\frac{4}{3}\right) = 0$$

$\Rightarrow \quad x + y + z = 1$

From the option the point $(1, -1, 1)$ satisfy the plane $x + y + z = 1$.

140. Let point P whose position vector is $(-\hat{\mathbf{i}} + 2\hat{\mathbf{j}} + 6\hat{\mathbf{k}})$ and a straight line passing through $Q(2, 3, -4)$ parallel to the vector $\mathbf{n} = 6\hat{\mathbf{i}} + 3\hat{\mathbf{j}} - 4\hat{\mathbf{k}}$.

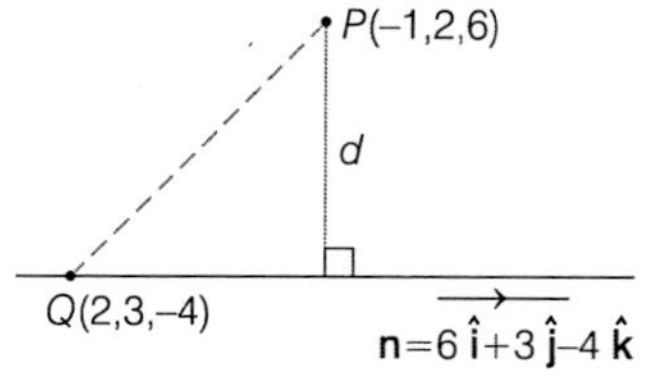

$\because$ Required distance d = Projection of line segment PQ perpendicular to vector $\mathbf{n}$

$$= \frac{|\mathbf{PQ} \times \mathbf{n}|}{|\mathbf{n}|}$$

Now, $\quad \mathbf{PQ} = 3\hat{\mathbf{i}} + \hat{\mathbf{j}} - 10\hat{\mathbf{k}}$, so

$$\mathbf{PQ} \times \mathbf{n} = \begin{vmatrix} \hat{\mathbf{i}} & \hat{\mathbf{j}} & \hat{\mathbf{k}} \\ 3 & 1 & -10 \\ 6 & 3 & -4 \end{vmatrix} = 26\hat{\mathbf{i}} - 48\hat{\mathbf{j}} + 3\hat{\mathbf{k}}$$

So, $\quad d = \dfrac{\sqrt{(26)^2 + (48)^2 + (3)^2}}{\sqrt{(6)^2 + (3)^2 + (4)^2}} = \sqrt{\dfrac{676 + 2304 + 9}{36 + 9 + 16}}$

$$= \sqrt{\frac{2989}{61}} = \sqrt{49} = 7 \text{ units}$$

141. Equation of given planes are

$$2x - y + 2z - 4 = 0 \quad \text{...(i)}$$

and $\quad x + 2y + 2z - 2 = 0 \quad$ ...(ii)

Now, equation of planes bisecting the angles between the planes (i) and (ii) are

$$\frac{2x - y + 2z - 4}{\sqrt{4+1+4}} = \pm \frac{x + 2y + 2z - 2}{\sqrt{1+4+4}}$$

$\Rightarrow \quad 2x - y + 2z - 4 = \pm(x + 2y + 2z - 2)$

On taking (+ve) sign, we get a plane

$$x - 3y = 2 \quad \text{...(iii)}$$

On taking (– ve) sign, we get a plane

$$3x + y + 4z = 6 \quad \text{...(iv)}$$

Now, from the given options, the point $(2, -4, 1)$ satisfy the plane of angle bisector $3x + y + 4z = 6$

142. Equation of given line is

$$\frac{x-2}{3} = \frac{y+1}{2} = \frac{z-1}{-1} = r \text{ (let)} \quad \text{...(i)}$$

Now, coordinates of a general point over given line are $R(3r + 2, 2r - 1, -r + 1)$.

Let the coordinates of point P are $(3r_1 + 2, 2r_1 - 1, -r_1 + 1)$ and Q are $(3r_2 + 2, 2r_2 - 1, -r_2 + 1)$.

Since, P is the point of intersection of line (i) and the plane $2x + 3y - z + 13 = 0$, so

$$2(3r_1 + 2) + 3(2r_1 - 1) - (-r_1 + 1) + 13 = 0$$

$\Rightarrow \quad 6r_1 + 4 + 6r_1 - 3 + r_1 - 1 + 13 = 0$

$\Rightarrow \quad 13r_1 + 13 = 0$

$\Rightarrow \quad r_1 = -1$

So, point $P(-1, -3, 2)$

and similarly for point 'Q', we get

$$3(3r_2 + 2) + (2r_2 - 1) + 4(-r_2 + 1) = 16$$

$$\Rightarrow \quad 7r_2 = 7$$

$$\Rightarrow \quad r_2 = 1$$

So, point is $Q(5, 1, 0)$.

Now, $PQ = \sqrt{(5+1)^2 + (1+3)^2 + 2^2}$

$= \sqrt{36 + 16 + 4} = \sqrt{56} = 2\sqrt{14}$

Exercise 2 - JEE Advanced Pattern

1. The position vectors of two given points are $\mathbf{a} = \hat{\mathbf{i}} - \hat{\mathbf{j}} + 3\hat{\mathbf{k}}$ and $\mathbf{b} = 3\hat{\mathbf{i}} + 3\hat{\mathbf{j}} + 3\hat{\mathbf{k}}$ and the equation of the given plane is

$$\mathbf{r} \cdot (5\hat{\mathbf{i}} + 2\hat{\mathbf{j}} - 7\hat{\mathbf{k}}) + 9 = 0$$

or $\quad \mathbf{r}.\mathbf{n} + d = 0$

We have, $\quad \mathbf{a}.\mathbf{n} + d = (\hat{\mathbf{i}} - \hat{\mathbf{j}} + 3\hat{\mathbf{k}}) \cdot (5\hat{\mathbf{i}} + 2\hat{\mathbf{j}} - 7\hat{\mathbf{k}}) + 9$

$= 5 - 2 - 21 + 9 < 0$

and $\quad \mathbf{b}.\mathbf{n} + d = (3\hat{\mathbf{i}} + 3\hat{\mathbf{j}} + 3\hat{\mathbf{k}}) \cdot (5\hat{\mathbf{i}} + 2\hat{\mathbf{j}} - 7\hat{\mathbf{k}}) + 9$

$= 15 + 6 - 21 + 9 > 0$

So, the points **a** and **b** are on the opposite sides of the plane.

2. Equation of the plane containing L_1,

$$A(x-2) + B(y-1) + C(z+1) = 0$$

where $A + 2C = 0$; $A + B - C = 0$

$\Rightarrow \quad A = -2C, B = 3C, C = C$

$\Rightarrow$ Plane is $-2(x-2) + 3(y-1) + z + 1 = 0$

or $\quad 2x - 3y - z - 2 = 0$

Hence, $p = \left|\dfrac{-2}{\sqrt{14}}\right| = \sqrt{\dfrac{2}{7}}$

3. Let $A(1, 0, -1), B(-1, 2, 2)$

Direction ratios of segment AB are $< 2, -2, -3 >$.

$$\cos\theta = \frac{|1 \times 2 + 3(-2) - 5(-3)|}{\sqrt{1+9+25}\sqrt{4+4+9}}$$

$$= \frac{11}{\sqrt{17}\sqrt{35}} = \frac{11}{\sqrt{595}}$$

Length of projection $= |AB \sin\theta|$

$$= \sqrt{(2)^2 + (2)^2 + (3)^2} \times \sqrt{1 - \frac{121}{595}}$$

$$= \sqrt{17}\frac{\sqrt{474}}{\sqrt{17}\sqrt{35}} = \sqrt{\frac{474}{35}} \text{ units}$$

4. Let the equation of the plane be $\dfrac{x}{a} + \dfrac{y}{b} + \dfrac{z}{c} = 1$

$$\Rightarrow \quad \frac{1}{a} + \frac{1}{b} + \frac{1}{c} = 1$$

$\Rightarrow$ Volume of tetrahedron $OABC = V = \dfrac{1}{6}[a\ b\ c]$

Now, $\quad (abc)^{1/3} \ge \dfrac{3}{\dfrac{1}{a} + \dfrac{1}{b} + \dfrac{1}{c}} \ge 3$ (GM $\ge$ HM)

$\Rightarrow \quad [a\ b\ c] \ge 27$

$\Rightarrow \quad V \ge \dfrac{9}{2}$

5. The planes are $\dfrac{x}{a} + \dfrac{y}{b} + \dfrac{z}{c} = 1$

and $\quad \dfrac{x}{a'} + \dfrac{y}{b'} + \dfrac{z}{c'} = 1$

Since, the perpendicular distance of the origin on the planes is same, therefore

$$\left|\frac{-1}{\sqrt{\frac{1}{a^2} + \frac{1}{b^2} + \frac{1}{c^2}}}\right| = \left|\frac{-1}{\sqrt{\frac{1}{a'^2} + \frac{1}{b'^2} + \frac{1}{c'^2}}}\right|$$

$$\Rightarrow \quad \frac{1}{a^2} + \frac{1}{b^2} + \frac{1}{c^2} - \frac{1}{a'^2} - \frac{1}{b'^2} - \frac{1}{c'^2} = 0$$

6. $\dfrac{x_1}{4} = u, \dfrac{y_1}{4} = v, \dfrac{z_1}{4} = w$

$$x_1 = 4u, y_1 = 4v, z_1 = 4w$$

$$V = \frac{1}{6}\begin{vmatrix} 4u & 0 & 0 \\ 0 & 4v & 0 \\ 0 & 0 & 4w \end{vmatrix} = \left(\frac{64}{6}\right)uvw$$

$$\therefore \quad 64\left(\frac{uvw}{6}\right) = 64k^3$$

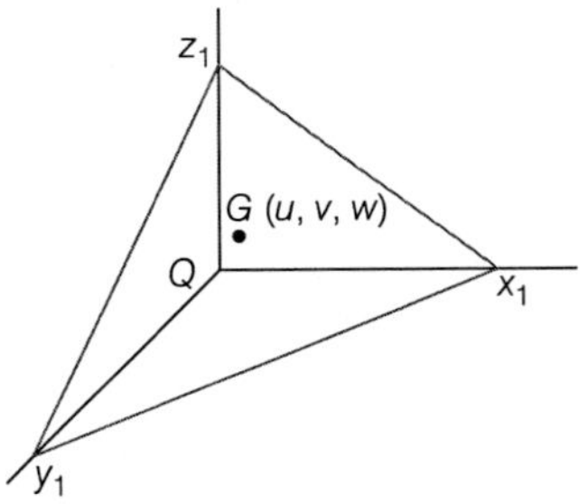

$$xyz = 6k^3$$

7. $\mathbf{r} = \mathbf{a} + \gamma\mathbf{b} + \mu\mathbf{c}$

On taking dot with $\mathbf{b} \times \mathbf{c}$

$[\mathbf{r}\ \mathbf{b}\ \mathbf{c}] = [\mathbf{a}\ \mathbf{b}\ \mathbf{c}]$ $\quad$ [where, $\mathbf{a} = (0, 1, 1)$]

$\mathbf{b} = (1, -1, 1)$ and $\mathbf{c} = (2, -1, 0)$

$$[\mathbf{a}\ \mathbf{b}\ \mathbf{c}] = \begin{vmatrix} 0 & 1 & 1 \\ 1 & -1 & 1 \\ 2 & -1 & 0 \end{vmatrix} = 0 - (0 - 2) + 1(-1 + 2) = 3$$

and $$[\mathbf{r}\ \mathbf{b}\ \mathbf{c}] = \begin{vmatrix} x & y & z \\ 1 & -1 & 1 \\ 2 & -1 & 0 \end{vmatrix} = x(0 + 1) - y(0 - 2) + z(-1 + 2)$$

$$= x + 2y + z$$

Hence, the equation of plane is $x + 2y + z = 3$

$$\therefore \quad p = \left|\frac{-3}{\sqrt{6}}\right| = \sqrt{\frac{3}{2}}$$

8. Equation of line is

$$\mathbf{r} = \hat{\mathbf{i}} + 0\hat{\mathbf{j}} + \hat{\mathbf{k}} + t(\hat{\mathbf{i}} + 3\hat{\mathbf{j}} - \hat{\mathbf{k}}) \quad \text{...(i)}$$

Eq. (i) lies in $x + y + cz = d$

$\therefore \quad 1 + 0 + c = d$

$1 + c = d$

Also, $1 \cdot 1 + 1 \cdot 3 + c(-1) = 0$

$c = 4$

$\therefore \quad 1 + 4 = d$

$\Rightarrow \quad d = 5$

$\Rightarrow \quad (c + d) = 4 + 5 = 9$

9. Any point on $\dfrac{x-2}{2} = \dfrac{y+1}{4} = \dfrac{z-2}{12}$ can be $(2r + 2, 4r - 1, 12r + 2)$

which lies on $x - y + z = 5$

$\therefore \quad (2r + 2) - (4r - 1) + 12r + 2 = 5$

$\Rightarrow \quad r = 0$

$\therefore$ Point on the plane $\equiv (2, -1, 2)$

Distance between $(2, -1, 2)$ and $(-1, -5, -10)$

$$= \sqrt{(2+1)^2 + (-1+5)^2 + (2+10)^2}$$

$= 13$ units

10. $(\hat{\mathbf{i}} + \hat{\mathbf{j}}) \times (\hat{\mathbf{j}} + \hat{\mathbf{k}}) = \hat{\mathbf{i}} - \hat{\mathbf{j}} + \hat{\mathbf{k}} \Rightarrow$ Unit vector perpendicular as to the plane of $\hat{\mathbf{i}} + \hat{\mathbf{j}}$ and $\hat{\mathbf{j}} + \hat{\mathbf{k}}$ is $\dfrac{1}{\sqrt{3}}(\hat{\mathbf{i}} - \hat{\mathbf{j}} + \hat{\mathbf{k}})$.

Similarly, other two unit vectors are

$\dfrac{1}{\sqrt{3}(\hat{\mathbf{i}} + \hat{\mathbf{j}} - \hat{\mathbf{k}})}$ and $\dfrac{1}{\sqrt{3}}(-\hat{\mathbf{i}} + \hat{\mathbf{j}} + \hat{\mathbf{k}})$.

$$V = [\hat{\mathbf{n}}_1, \hat{\mathbf{n}}_2, \hat{\mathbf{n}}_3] = \frac{1}{3\sqrt{3}}\begin{vmatrix} 1 & -1 & 1 \\ 1 & 1 & -1 \\ -1 & 1 & 1 \end{vmatrix} = \frac{4}{3\sqrt{3}}$$

Alternate Solution

Let $\mathbf{a} = \hat{\mathbf{i}} + \hat{\mathbf{j}}$, $\mathbf{b} = \hat{\mathbf{j}} + \hat{\mathbf{k}}$ and $\mathbf{c} = \hat{\mathbf{k}} + \hat{\mathbf{i}}$.

Now, $[\mathbf{a} \times \mathbf{b}, \mathbf{b} \times \mathbf{c}, \mathbf{c} \times \mathbf{a}] = [\mathbf{a}\ \mathbf{b}\ \mathbf{c}]^2$

$$= \begin{vmatrix} 1 & 1 & 0 \\ 0 & 1 & 1 \\ 1 & 0 & 1 \end{vmatrix}^2 = [1(1) - 1(0-1)]^2 = 4$$

Hence, the actual volume with unit vectors

$$= \frac{4}{|\mathbf{a} \times \mathbf{b}|\,|\mathbf{b} \times \mathbf{c}|\,|\mathbf{c} \times \mathbf{a}|}$$

Now, $|\mathbf{a} \times \mathbf{b}| = \sqrt{a^2b^2 - (\mathbf{a} \cdot \mathbf{b})^2} = \sqrt{4 - 1} = \sqrt{3}$ etc.

$$V_{\text{actual}} = \frac{4}{3\sqrt{3}}$$

11. $\mathbf{n} = 3\hat{\mathbf{i}} - \hat{\mathbf{j}} + 4\hat{\mathbf{k}}$

Line through A are parallel to $\mathbf{n}$ is

$$\mathbf{r} = \hat{\mathbf{i}} + 2\hat{\mathbf{j}} + 3\hat{\mathbf{k}} + \lambda(3\hat{\mathbf{i}} - \hat{\mathbf{j}} + 4\hat{\mathbf{k}})$$

$$= (3\lambda + 1)\hat{\mathbf{i}} + (2 - \lambda)\hat{\mathbf{j}} + (3 + 4\lambda)\hat{\mathbf{k}} \quad \text{...(i)}$$

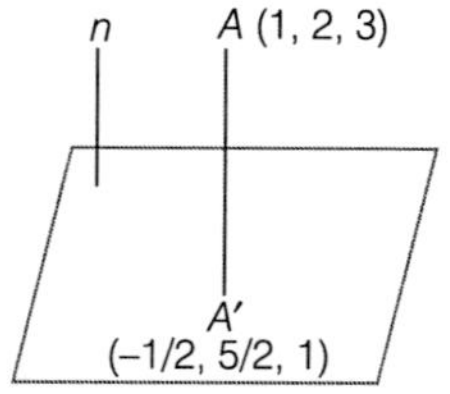

Hence, Eq. (i) must satisfy the plane

$$3x - y + 4z = 0$$

$\Rightarrow \quad 3(3\lambda + 1) - (2 - \lambda) + 4(3 + 4\lambda) = 0$

$\Rightarrow \quad 26\lambda + 13 = 0 \Rightarrow \lambda = -\dfrac{1}{2}$

Hence, A' is $\left(-\dfrac{1}{2}, \dfrac{5}{2}, 1\right)$ which is the foot of the perpendicular from A on the given plane.

12. On solving $x + 2y - 4z = 0$ and $2x - y + 2z = 0$, we get

$$\frac{x}{0} = \frac{y}{-10} = \frac{z}{-5}$$

One point P on line is $(0, -10t, -5t)$ and $Q \equiv (1, 1, 1)$

Direction ratio of $PQ \equiv (1, 1 + 10t, 1 + 5t)$

$$0 - 10 - 100t - 5 - 25t = 0$$

$\Rightarrow \quad t = -\dfrac{3}{25} \Rightarrow P \equiv \left(0, \dfrac{6}{5}, \dfrac{3}{5}\right)$

$\therefore$ Direction ratios of PQ are $(5, -1, 2)$.

Hence, the required equation $\dfrac{x-1}{5} = \dfrac{1-y}{1} = \dfrac{z-1}{2}$.

13. Let $\dfrac{x}{a} + \dfrac{y}{b} + \dfrac{z}{c} = 1$ be the variable.

So that, $\left|\dfrac{1}{\sqrt{\dfrac{1}{a^2} + \dfrac{1}{b^2} + \dfrac{1}{c^2}}}\right| = 1$

Then, the coordinates of ΔABC are $A(a, 0, 0)$, $B(0, b, 0)$ and $C(0, 0, c)$.

The centroid of ΔABC is $\left(\dfrac{a}{3}, \dfrac{b}{3}, \dfrac{c}{3}\right)$.

$$x = \frac{a}{3}, y = \frac{b}{3}, z = \frac{c}{3} \Rightarrow a = 3x, b = 3y \text{ and } c = 3z$$

$$\frac{1}{x^2} + \frac{1}{y^2} + \frac{1}{z^2} = 9$$

14. Angle between the faces = Angle between the normals

$\mathbf{n}_1$ = Vector normal to face OAB

$$= \mathbf{OA} \times \mathbf{OB} = \begin{vmatrix} \hat{\mathbf{i}} & \hat{\mathbf{j}} & \hat{\mathbf{k}} \\ 1 & 2 & 1 \\ 2 & 1 & 3 \end{vmatrix} = 5\hat{\mathbf{i}} - \hat{\mathbf{j}} - 3\hat{\mathbf{k}}$$

$\mathbf{n}_2$ = Vector normal to face ABC

$$= \mathbf{AB} \times \mathbf{AC} = \begin{vmatrix} \hat{\mathbf{i}} & \hat{\mathbf{j}} & \hat{\mathbf{k}} \\ 1 & -1 & 2 \\ -2 & -1 & 1 \end{vmatrix} = \hat{\mathbf{i}} - 5\hat{\mathbf{j}} - 3\hat{\mathbf{k}}$$

Angle between faces $= \cos^{-1}\dfrac{\mathbf{n}_1 \cdot \mathbf{n}_2}{[\mathbf{n}_1][\mathbf{n}_2]} = \cos^{-1}\left(\dfrac{19}{35}\right)$

15. Given equation of planes are

$$x - y - z - 4 = 0,\ x + y + 2z - 4 = 0$$

Required plane is of the form

$$(x - y - z - 4) + \lambda(x + y + 2z - 4) = 0$$

Since, this plane is perpendicular to the plane $x - y - z - 4 = 0$

$\therefore \quad 1 + \lambda + (\lambda - 1)(-1) + (2\lambda - 1)(-1) = 0, \lambda = \dfrac{3}{2}$

$\therefore$ Required plane $5x + y + 4z = 20$

16. Let the position vector of A, B, C, D be $\mathbf{a}$, $\mathbf{b}$, $\mathbf{c}$ and $\mathbf{d}$ respectively.

Then, $AC^2 + BD^2 + AD^2 + BC^2$

$$= (\mathbf{c}-\mathbf{a})\cdot(\mathbf{c}-\mathbf{a}) + (\mathbf{d}-\mathbf{b})\cdot(\mathbf{d}-\mathbf{b}) + (\mathbf{d}-\mathbf{a})\cdot(\mathbf{d}-\mathbf{a}) + (\mathbf{c}-\mathbf{b})\cdot(\mathbf{c}-\mathbf{b})$$

$$= |\mathbf{c}|^2 + |\mathbf{a}|^2 - 2\mathbf{a}\cdot\mathbf{c} + |\mathbf{d}|^2 + |\mathbf{b}|^2 - 2\mathbf{d}\cdot\mathbf{b} + |\mathbf{d}|^2 + |\mathbf{a}|^2 - 2\mathbf{a}\cdot\mathbf{d} + |\mathbf{c}|^2 + |\mathbf{b}|^2 - 2\mathbf{b}\cdot\mathbf{c}$$

$$= |\mathbf{a}|^2 + |\mathbf{b}|^2 - 2\mathbf{a}\cdot\mathbf{b} + |\mathbf{c}|^2 + |\mathbf{d}|^2 - 2\mathbf{c}\cdot\mathbf{d} + |\mathbf{a}|^2 + |\mathbf{b}|^2 + |\mathbf{c}|^2 + |\mathbf{d}|^2 + 2\mathbf{a}\cdot\mathbf{b} + 2\mathbf{c}\cdot\mathbf{d} - 2\mathbf{a}\cdot\mathbf{c} - 2\mathbf{b}\cdot\mathbf{d} - 2\mathbf{a}\cdot\mathbf{d} - 2\mathbf{b}\cdot\mathbf{c}$$

$$= (\mathbf{a}-\mathbf{b})\cdot(\mathbf{a}-\mathbf{b}) + (\mathbf{c}-\mathbf{d})\cdot(\mathbf{c}-\mathbf{d}) + (\mathbf{a}+\mathbf{b}-\mathbf{c}-\mathbf{d})\cdot(\mathbf{a}+\mathbf{b}-\mathbf{c}-\mathbf{d})$$

$$= AB^2 + CD^2 + (\mathbf{a}+\mathbf{b}-\mathbf{c}-\mathbf{d})\cdot(\mathbf{a}+\mathbf{b}-\mathbf{c}-\mathbf{d})$$

$$\geq AB^2 + CD^2$$

17. If the given vectors are coplanar, then $\begin{vmatrix} x_1 & y_1 & z_1 \\ x_2 & y_2 & z_2 \\ x_3 & y_3 & z_3 \end{vmatrix} = 0$

The set of equation

$$x_1x + y_1y + z_1z = 0,\quad x_2x + y_2y + z_2z = 0$$
$$x_3x + y_3y + z_3z = 0$$

has a non-trivial solution.

Let the given set has a non-trivial solution x, y, z without loss of generality, we can assume that $x \geq y \geq z$.

For the given equation $x_1x + y_1y + z_1z = 0$, we have

$$x_1x = -y_1y - z_1z$$

$\Rightarrow \quad |x_1x| = |y_1y + z_1z| \leq |y_1y| + |z_1z|$

$\Rightarrow \quad |x_1x| \leq |y_1x| + |z_1x|$

$\Rightarrow \quad |x_1| < |y_1| + |z_1|$

Which is a contradiction to the given inequality.

$$|x_1| > |y_1| + |z_1|$$

Similarly, the other inequalities rule out the possibility of a non-trivial solution.

Therefore, the given equations have only a trivial solution.

So, the given vectors are non-coplanar.

18. The vectors $\mathbf{n}_1 \times \mathbf{n}_2$, $\mathbf{n}_2 \times \mathbf{n}_3$ and $\mathbf{n}_3 \times \mathbf{n}_1$ are non-coplanar vectors, so every vector can be written as

$$\mathbf{r} = a(\mathbf{n}_1 \times \mathbf{n}_2) + b(\mathbf{n}_2 \times \mathbf{n}_3) + c(\mathbf{n}_3 \times \mathbf{n}_1)$$

On substituting this value in $\mathbf{r}\cdot\mathbf{n}_1 = q_1$, $\mathbf{a}, \mathbf{b}$, we get

$$a(\mathbf{n}_1 \times \mathbf{n}_2)\cdot\mathbf{n}_1 + b(\mathbf{n}_2 \times \mathbf{n}_3)\cdot\mathbf{n}_1 + c(\mathbf{n}_3 \times \mathbf{n}_1)\cdot\mathbf{n}_1 = q_1$$

$$b[\mathbf{n}_1\ \mathbf{n}_2\ \mathbf{n}_3] = q_1 \Rightarrow b = \frac{q_1}{[\mathbf{n}_1\ \mathbf{n}_2\ \mathbf{n}_3]}$$

Since, the required point of intersection will have the position vector,

$$\mathbf{r} = \frac{1}{[\mathbf{n}_1\ \mathbf{n}_2\ \mathbf{n}_3]}\,[q_3(\mathbf{n}_1 \times \mathbf{n}_2) + q_1(\mathbf{n}_2 \times \mathbf{n}_3) + q_2(\mathbf{n}_3 \times \mathbf{n}_1)]$$

19. Since, $r^2 + s^2 = e^2$

$\Rightarrow \quad e = 31$ or $e = 19$ is not possible.

Therefore, e equals 13, 20 or 25.

The possibility for triplet $\{r, s, e\}$ are $\{5, 12, 13\}$, $\{12, 16, 20\}$, $\{15, 20, 25\}$, $\{7, 24, 25\}$.

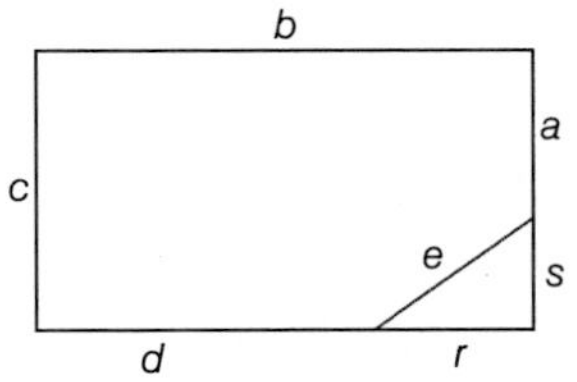

Since, 16, 15 and 24 do not appear among any of pair wise differences of 13, 19, 20, 25, 31

$\Rightarrow a = 19, b = 25, c = 31, d = 20, e = 13$

Hence, the required area = 745 sq units.

20. Given equation of line is $\frac{x}{1} = \frac{y}{1} = \frac{z}{-1} = r$ (say)

Let $Q \equiv (r, r, -r)$

PQ perpendicular to $\frac{x}{1} = \frac{y}{1} = \frac{z}{-1}$

$\therefore \quad (\alpha - r)\cdot 1 + (\beta - r)\cdot 1 + (\gamma + r)(-1) = 0$

$\Rightarrow \quad r = \frac{\alpha + \beta - \gamma}{3}$

$\therefore \quad PQ^2 = \frac{2}{3}\{\alpha^2 + \beta^2 + \gamma^2 - \alpha\beta + \beta\gamma + \gamma\}$

But $PQ = 2$

{perpendicular distance from $P(\alpha, \beta, \gamma)$ to plane $x + y + z = 0$}

$\therefore \quad \frac{2}{3}(\alpha^2 + \beta^2 + \gamma^2 - \alpha\beta + \beta\gamma + \gamma\alpha) = 4\left\{\frac{\alpha + \beta + \gamma}{\sqrt{3}}\right\}^2$

$\therefore \quad \alpha^2 + \beta^2 + \gamma^2 + 5\alpha\beta + 3\beta\gamma + 3\gamma\alpha = 0$

Hence, the locus of required point is

$$x^2 + y^2 + z^2 + 5xy + 3yz + 3zx = 0$$

21. $\mathbf{b}_1 \times \mathbf{b}_2 = \begin{vmatrix} \hat{\mathbf{i}} & \hat{\mathbf{j}} & \hat{\mathbf{k}} \\ -1 & 1 & 1 \\ 0 & 1 & -1 \end{vmatrix} = -2\hat{\mathbf{i}} - \hat{\mathbf{j}} - \hat{\mathbf{k}}$

and $\mathbf{a}_1 - \mathbf{a}_2 = a\hat{\mathbf{i}} - a\hat{\mathbf{j}} + a\hat{\mathbf{k}}$

$\therefore \quad \text{SD} = \frac{|(-2\hat{\mathbf{i}} - \hat{\mathbf{j}} - \hat{\mathbf{k}})\cdot(a\hat{\mathbf{i}} - a\hat{\mathbf{j}} + a\hat{\mathbf{k}})|}{\sqrt{(-2)^2 + (-1)^2 + (-1)^2}}$

$$= \frac{|-2a + a - a|}{\sqrt{6}} = \frac{2a}{\sqrt{6}} \text{ units}$$

22. $y(x + y) + z(x + y) = 0$

$\Rightarrow \quad (x + y)(y + z) = 0$

$\Rightarrow \quad x + y = 0 \Rightarrow$ DR's are $\mathbf{b}_1 = (1, 1, 0)$

and $\quad y + z = 0 \Rightarrow$ DR's are $\mathbf{b}_2 = (0, 1, 1)$

Now, $\quad \mathbf{b}_1 \times \mathbf{b}_2 = \begin{vmatrix} \hat{\mathbf{i}} & \hat{\mathbf{j}} & \hat{\mathbf{k}} \\ 1 & 1 & 0 \\ 0 & 1 & 1 \end{vmatrix} = (1, -1, 1)$

and $\quad \mathbf{a}_2 - \mathbf{a}_1 = (1, 1, 1) - (0, 0, 0) = (1, 1, 1)$

$\therefore \quad \text{SD} = \frac{|(1, 1, 1) \times (1, -1, 1)|}{|(1, -1, 1)|}$

$$= \frac{|(-2, 0, 2)|}{|(1, -1, 1)|}$$

$$= \frac{\sqrt{4 + 0 + 4}}{\sqrt{1 + 1 + 1}} = \sqrt{\frac{8}{3}} \text{ units}$$

23. Let $\mathbf{a} = l_1\hat{\mathbf{i}} + m_1\hat{\mathbf{j}} + n_1\hat{\mathbf{k}}$, $\mathbf{b} = l_2\hat{\mathbf{i}} + m_2\hat{\mathbf{j}} + n_2\hat{\mathbf{k}}$ and $\mathbf{c} = l_3\hat{\mathbf{i}} + m_3\hat{\mathbf{j}} + n_3\hat{\mathbf{k}}$

Given that **a, b, c** are three mutually perpendicular unit vectors.

Then, $p_1\hat{\mathbf{i}} + q_1\hat{\mathbf{j}} + r_1\hat{\mathbf{k}} = \mathbf{b}\times\mathbf{c} = \mathbf{a}$

[$\because$ $\mathbf{b}\times\mathbf{c}$ parallel to **a** and $\mathbf{b}\times\mathbf{c}$, **a** are unit vectors]

Similarly, $p_2\hat{\mathbf{i}} + q_2\hat{\mathbf{j}} + r_2\hat{\mathbf{k}} = \mathbf{c}\times\mathbf{a} = \mathbf{b}$

and $p_3\hat{\mathbf{i}} + q_3\hat{\mathbf{j}} + r_3\hat{\mathbf{k}} = \mathbf{a}\times\mathbf{b} = \mathbf{c}$

These vectors are also mutually perpendicular unit vectors.

24. **a, b, c** be PV of A, B, C, $|\mathbf{a}| = |\mathbf{b}| = |\mathbf{c}| = K$

$$\mathbf{OD} = \frac{\mathbf{a}}{2}\left|\,|\mathbf{OE}| = \frac{\mathbf{b}+\mathbf{c}}{2}\right|$$

Given, $|\mathbf{DE}| = 1 \Rightarrow \left|\dfrac{\mathbf{b}+\mathbf{c}-\mathbf{a}}{2}\right| = 1 \Rightarrow |\mathbf{b}+\mathbf{c}-\mathbf{a}| = 2$

$$\Rightarrow \quad 3k^2 + 2k^2\left(\frac{1}{2} - \frac{1}{2} - \frac{1}{2}\right) = 4$$

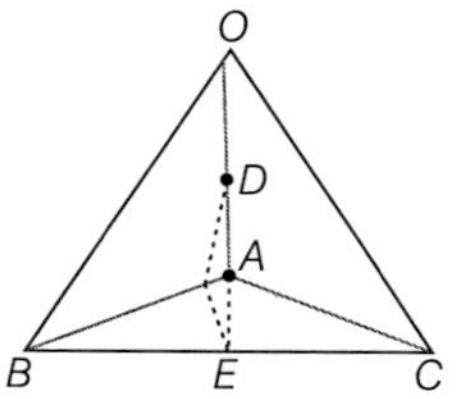

$$\Rightarrow \quad K = \sqrt{2}$$

$$\text{Volume} = \frac{1}{3}(\text{base area} \times \text{height})$$

$$= \frac{1}{3}\left(\frac{\sqrt{3}}{4}(k)^2 \times \sqrt{\frac{2}{3}}k\right) = \frac{1}{3}$$

25. The plane equation in the intercept forms is $\dfrac{x}{a} + \dfrac{y}{b} + \dfrac{z}{c} = 1$.

Volume of tetrahedron $OABC$ is

$$v = \frac{[abc]}{6} = 64 \Rightarrow [abc] = 384$$

Foot of perpendicular from (0, 0, 0) on this plane is

$$\frac{x}{1/a} = \frac{y}{1/b} = \frac{z}{1/c} = \frac{1}{\frac{1}{a^2}+\frac{1}{b^2}+\frac{1}{c^2}} = k$$

$$\Rightarrow \quad x = \frac{k}{a}, y = \frac{k}{b}, z = \frac{k}{c}$$

and $$\frac{1}{k} = \frac{1}{a^2} + \frac{1}{b^2} + \frac{1}{c^2}$$

$$\Rightarrow \quad \frac{1}{k} = \frac{x^2+y^2+z^2}{k^2} \Rightarrow x^2 + y^2 + z^2 = k$$

$\therefore$ $(x^2 + y^2 + z^2)^3 = k^3 = (abc)\,xyz = 384\,xyz$ is the required locus.

26. Vector normal to the plane

$$\mathbf{n} = \hat{\mathbf{i}} + \hat{\mathbf{j}} + \hat{\mathbf{k}}$$

$$\mathbf{V}_x = \hat{\mathbf{i}}, \mathbf{V}_y = \hat{\mathbf{j}}, \mathbf{V}_z = \hat{\mathbf{k}}$$

$$\cos(90^\circ - \alpha) = \frac{\mathbf{V}_x \cdot \mathbf{n}}{|\mathbf{n}|} \Rightarrow \sin\alpha = \frac{1}{\sqrt{3}}$$

Similarly, $\sin\beta = \dfrac{1}{\sqrt{3}}$ and $\sin\gamma = \dfrac{1}{\sqrt{3}}$

Hence, $\sum \sin^2\alpha = 1$ and $\sum \cos^2\alpha = 2$

Also, plane is equally inclined with the coordinate axes.

Also, $A = \dfrac{1}{2}\sqrt{9^2 + 9^2 + 9^2} = \dfrac{9\sqrt{3}}{2}$.

27. $2x - y - z - 2 + \lambda(x + y + z - 1) = 0$ satisfies (1, 1, 1)

$$2 - 1 - 1 - 2 + \lambda(3 - 1) = 0 \Rightarrow \lambda = 1$$

$$x = 1 \quad \text{...(i)}$$

$$x - y - z - 3 + \mu(2x + 4y - z - 4) = 0$$

$$-4 + \mu(1) = 0 \Rightarrow \mu = 4$$

$$x - y - z - 3 + 4(2x + 4y - z - 4) = 0$$

$$9x + 15y - 5z - 19 = 0 \quad \text{...(ii)}$$

From Eqs. (i) and (ii), we get

$$x - 1 = 0, 9x + 15y - 5z - 19 = 0$$

$a = 0$ and $c = 3b$

$$x - 1 = 0, \frac{y-1}{1} = \frac{z-1}{3}$$

28. $OP = \sqrt{h^2 + k^2 + l^2}$

Direction ratios of OP are $\left(\dfrac{h}{p}, \dfrac{k}{p}, \dfrac{l}{p}\right)$.

Equation of plane is $\dfrac{hx}{p} + \dfrac{ky}{p} + \dfrac{lz}{p} = p$

$$A\left(\frac{p^2}{h}, 0, 0\right), B\left(0, \frac{p^2}{k}, 0\right), C\left(0, 0, \frac{p^2}{l}\right)$$

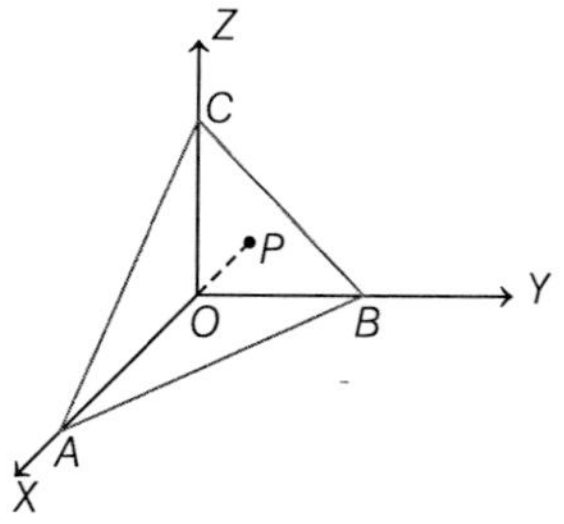

29. (a) Since, $\mathbf{n}\cdot\mathbf{a} = \mathbf{n}\cdot\mathbf{b} = \mathbf{n}\cdot\mathbf{c} = \mathbf{0}$

$\therefore$ **a, b** and **c** are coplanar.

$\therefore$ $[\mathbf{a}, \mathbf{b}, \mathbf{c}] = 0$

(b) $\cos^3 30^\circ + \cos^2 45^\circ + \cos^2\gamma = 1$

$\therefore$ $\sin^2\gamma = \dfrac{3}{4} + \dfrac{1}{2} = \dfrac{5}{4}$ which is not possible.

(c) Obvious

(d) $\mathbf{AB}\times\mathbf{BC}$ is perpendicular to the plane ABC.

$$\mathbf{AB}\times\mathbf{BC} = (\mathbf{OB} - \mathbf{OA})\times(\mathbf{OC} - \mathbf{OB})$$
$$= \mathbf{OB}\times\mathbf{OC} - \mathbf{OA}\times\mathbf{OC} + \mathbf{OA}\times\mathbf{OB}$$
$$= \mathbf{OA}\times\mathbf{OB} + \mathbf{OB}\times\mathbf{OC} + \mathbf{OA}\times\mathbf{OB}$$

i.e. $\mathbf{a}\times\mathbf{b} + \mathbf{b}\times\mathbf{c} + \mathbf{c}\times\mathbf{a}$ is perpendicular the plane ABC.

$$(\mathbf{a}+\mathbf{b}+\mathbf{c})\times(\mathbf{a}\times\mathbf{b}+\mathbf{b}\times\mathbf{c}+\mathbf{c}\times\mathbf{a})$$
$$=\{(\mathbf{a}+\mathbf{b}+\mathbf{c})\cdot\mathbf{c}\}\mathbf{b}-\{(\mathbf{a}+\mathbf{b}+\mathbf{c})\cdot\mathbf{a}\}\mathbf{b}$$
$$+\{(\mathbf{a}+\mathbf{b}+\mathbf{c})\cdot\mathbf{c}\}\,\mathbf{b}-\{(\mathbf{a}+\mathbf{b}+\mathbf{c})\cdot\mathbf{b}\}\times\mathbf{c}$$
$$+\{(\mathbf{a}+\mathbf{b}+\mathbf{c})\cdot\mathbf{a}\}\mathbf{c}-\{(\mathbf{a}+\mathbf{b}+\mathbf{c})\cdot\mathbf{a}\}\mathbf{a}$$
$$=(\mathbf{a}+\mathbf{b}+\mathbf{c})\cdot(\mathbf{b}-\mathbf{c})\mathbf{a}+(\mathbf{a}+\mathbf{b}+\mathbf{c})$$
$$\cdot(\mathbf{c}-\mathbf{a})\mathbf{b}+\{(\mathbf{a}+\mathbf{b}+\mathbf{c})\cdot(\mathbf{a}-\mathbf{b})\}\mathbf{c}$$
$$=(\mathbf{a}\cdot\mathbf{b}-\mathbf{a}\cdot\mathbf{c}+\mathbf{b}^2-\mathbf{c}^2)\mathbf{a}+(\mathbf{b}\cdot\mathbf{c}-\mathbf{b}\cdot\mathbf{a}$$
$$+(\mathbf{c}^2-\mathbf{a}^2)\mathbf{b}+(\mathbf{a}^2-\mathbf{b}^2+\mathbf{c}\cdot\mathbf{a}-\mathbf{c}-\mathbf{b})\mathbf{c}=\mathbf{0}$$

Thus, the statement is true.

30. Let $A(\mathbf{a})$, $B(\mathbf{d})$, $C(\mathbf{c})$ and $D(\mathbf{d})$ be the vertices of a tetrahedron, then centroid of the tetrahedron is

$$\frac{\mathbf{a}+\mathbf{b}+\mathbf{c}+\mathbf{d}}{4}$$

centroid G_1 of the face BCD is $\frac{\mathbf{b}+\mathbf{c}+\mathbf{d}}{3}$

Now, centroid of the tetrahedron G_1 divides AG_1 in the ratio $3:1$.

i.e. $$\frac{3(\mathbf{b}+\mathbf{c}+\mathbf{d})+\mathbf{a}}{3+1}=\frac{\mathbf{a}+\mathbf{b}+\mathbf{c}+\mathbf{a}}{4}$$

$\therefore$ C lies on AG_1.

(b) The edges AB and CD. Let E be the mid-point of AB and F be the mid-point of CD

$\therefore$Positive vector of E is $\frac{\mathbf{a}+\mathbf{b}}{2}$.

Positive vector of F is $\frac{\mathbf{c}+\mathbf{a}}{2}$.

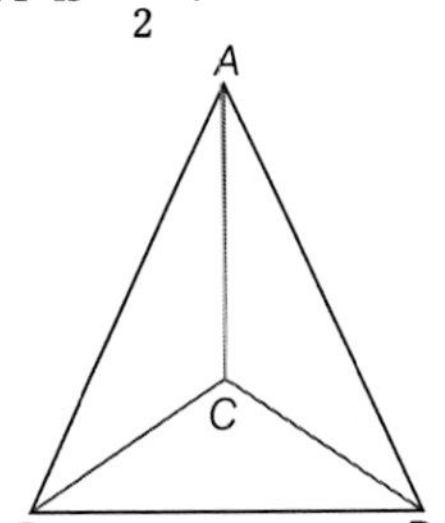

Mid-point of EF is $\frac{\mathbf{a}+\mathbf{b}+\mathbf{c}+\mathbf{d}}{4}$ which is the centroid of the tetrahedron $ABCD$.

31. Let the plane be $\frac{x}{a}+\frac{y}{b}+\frac{z}{c}=1$

$$\left|\frac{1}{\sqrt{\left(\frac{1}{a}\right)^2+\left(\frac{1}{b}\right)^2+\left(\frac{1}{c}\right)^2}}\right|=1 \text{ or } \frac{1}{a^2}+\frac{1}{b^2}+\frac{1}{c^2}=1$$

The plane cuts the coordinates axes at $A(a, 0, 0)$, $B(0, b, 0)$, $c(0, 0, c)$. The centroid of ΔABC is

$$\left(\frac{a}{3},\frac{b}{3},\frac{c}{3}\right)=(x, y, z)\text{ (let)}$$

$$x^{-2}+y^{-2}+z^{-2}=9$$

or $$\frac{1}{9}\left\{\frac{1}{x^2}+\frac{1}{y^2}+\frac{1}{z^2}\right\}^{-1}=0$$

32. For the given curve $z=0$, therefore, the line and the curve meet, where $\frac{x-2}{3}=\frac{y+1}{2}=\frac{0-1}{-1}$

i.e. where $\frac{x-2}{3}=1$, $\frac{y+1}{2}=1$ i.e. where $x=5$, $y=1$

So, the given line and the given curve meet in the point $(5, 1, 0)$.

Since, this point lies on the curve also, therefore,

$$5^2+1^2=r^2$$

$$\Rightarrow\quad r^2=(\sqrt{26})^2\Rightarrow r=\pm\sqrt{26}$$

33. A vector coplanar with given vectors is $(1+\lambda)\hat{\mathbf{i}}+(\lambda-1)\hat{\mathbf{j}}+(1-\lambda)\hat{\mathbf{k}}$. Since, it is equally inclined to the two given vectors

$$\frac{(1+\lambda)\hat{\mathbf{i}}+(\lambda-1)\hat{\mathbf{j}}+(1-\lambda)\hat{\mathbf{k}}}{|(1+\lambda)\hat{\mathbf{i}}+(\lambda-1)\hat{\mathbf{j}}+(1-\lambda)\hat{\mathbf{k}}|}\cdot\frac{(\hat{\mathbf{i}}-\hat{\mathbf{j}}+\hat{\mathbf{k}})}{\sqrt{3}}$$
$$=\frac{(1+\lambda)\hat{\mathbf{i}}+(\lambda-1)\hat{\mathbf{j}}+(1-\lambda)\hat{\mathbf{k}}}{|(1+\lambda)\hat{\mathbf{i}}+(\lambda-1)\hat{\mathbf{j}}+(1-\lambda)\hat{\mathbf{k}}|}\cdot\frac{(\hat{\mathbf{i}}+\hat{\mathbf{j}}-\hat{\mathbf{k}})}{\sqrt{3}}$$

$$\therefore\quad \lambda=1$$

Required vector is $2\hat{\mathbf{i}}$ or $\hat{\mathbf{i}}$.

34. Let A, B, C be $(\alpha, 0, 0)$, $(0, \beta, 0)$ and $(0, 0, \gamma)$ respectively, then the plane ABC is $\frac{x}{\alpha}+\frac{y}{\beta}+\frac{z}{\gamma}=1$

Since, it always passes through a, b, c

$$\frac{a}{\alpha}+\frac{b}{\beta}+\frac{c}{\gamma}=1 \qquad \text{...(i)}$$

If p is (u, v, w), then $OP^2=AP^2=BP^2=CP^2$

$$\Rightarrow\quad u^2+v^2+w^2=(u-\alpha)^2+v^2+w^2$$
$$=\ldots\Rightarrow\alpha=\frac{u}{2},\beta=\frac{v}{2},\gamma=\frac{w}{2}$$

On putting α, β, γ in Eq. (i), we get

$$\frac{a}{u}+\frac{b}{v}+\frac{c}{w}=2$$

$\Rightarrow$ Locus of (u, v, w) is $\frac{a}{x}+\frac{b}{y}+\frac{c}{z}=2$

35. Normal of plane P_1 is

$$\mathbf{n}_1=(2\hat{\mathbf{j}}+3\hat{\mathbf{k}})\times(4\hat{\mathbf{j}}-3\hat{\mathbf{k}})=-18\hat{\mathbf{i}}$$

Normal to plane P_2 is

$$\mathbf{n}_2=(\hat{\mathbf{j}}-\hat{\mathbf{k}})\times(3\hat{\mathbf{i}}+3\hat{\mathbf{j}})=3\hat{\mathbf{i}}-3\hat{\mathbf{j}}-3\hat{\mathbf{k}}$$

$\therefore$ **A** is parallel to $(\mathbf{n}_1<\mathbf{n}_2)=\pm(-54\hat{\mathbf{j}}-54\hat{\mathbf{k}})$

$\therefore$ Angle between **A** and $2\hat{\mathbf{i}}+\hat{\mathbf{j}}-2\hat{\mathbf{k}}$ is

$$\cos\theta=\pm\frac{(-54\hat{\mathbf{j}}+54\hat{\mathbf{k}})\cdot(2\hat{\mathbf{i}}+\hat{\mathbf{j}}-2\hat{\mathbf{k}})}{54\sqrt{2.3}}=\pm\frac{1}{\sqrt{2}}$$

$$\theta=\frac{\pi}{4}\text{ or }\frac{3\pi}{4}$$

36. Any plane through the second line is

$$2x+y+z-1+k(3x+y+2z-2)=0$$

If this is parallel to the first line, then

$$(2+3k)+(1+k)+(1+2k)=0\Rightarrow k=-\frac{2}{3}$$

$\Rightarrow$ Plane is $2x + y + z - 1 - \frac{2}{3}(3x + y + 2z - 2) = 0$

or $y - z + 1 = 0$. The required SD must be distance of this plane from any point on the line $x = y = z$ say $(1, 1, 1)$

$$\Rightarrow \quad SD = \frac{1 - 1 + 1}{\sqrt{0^2 + 1^2 + (-1)^2}} = \frac{1}{\sqrt{2}} \text{ units}$$

37. Let the components of the line segment vector be a, b, c, then

$$a^2 + b^2 + c^2 = (63)^2 \quad \text{...(i)}$$

also $\quad \frac{a}{3} = \frac{b}{-2} = \frac{c}{6} = \lambda$ (let), then

$$a = 3\lambda, b = -2\lambda \text{ and } c = 6\lambda$$

and from Eq. (i), we have

$$9\lambda^2 + 4\lambda^2 + 36\lambda^2 = (63)^2 \Rightarrow 49\lambda^2 = (63)^2$$

$$\Rightarrow \quad \lambda = \pm\frac{63}{7} = \pm 9$$

The required components are $27, -18, 54$ or $-27, 18, -54$.

38. Direction ratios of AB are $4 - 2, 5 - 3, 10 - 4$ or $1, 1, 3$. So AB in parallel to the vector $\hat{\mathbf{i}} + \hat{\mathbf{j}} + 3\hat{\mathbf{k}}$ and passes through $B(2, 3, 4)$, the vector $2\hat{\mathbf{i}} + 3\hat{\mathbf{j}} + 4\hat{\mathbf{k}}$, its equation is

$$2\hat{\mathbf{i}} + 3\hat{\mathbf{j}} + 4\hat{\mathbf{k}} + \lambda(\hat{\mathbf{i}} + \hat{\mathbf{j}} + 3\hat{\mathbf{k}}).$$

Similarly, BC passes through the points $B(2, 3, 4)$ and its direction ratios are $2 - 1, 3 - 2, 4 + 1$ or $1, 1, 5$.

So, its cartesian equation is

$$\frac{x-2}{1} = \frac{y-3}{1} = \frac{z-4}{5}$$

Next, if D is (a, b, c), then since $ABCD$ is a parallelogram mid-point of AC and BD is same. (diagonals of a parallelogram bisect each other)

$$\Rightarrow \quad \left(\frac{a+2}{2}, \frac{b+3}{2}, \frac{c+4}{2}\right) = \left(\frac{5}{2}, \frac{7}{2}, \frac{9}{2}\right)$$

$$\Rightarrow \quad (a, b, c) = (3, 4. 5)$$

AB is not perpendicular to BC because

$$1 \times 1 + 1 \times 1 + 3 \times 5 \neq 0.$$

$ABCD$ is not a rectangle.

39. Given, square base $OP = OR = 3$

$\therefore \quad P(3,0,0), R = (0,3,0)$

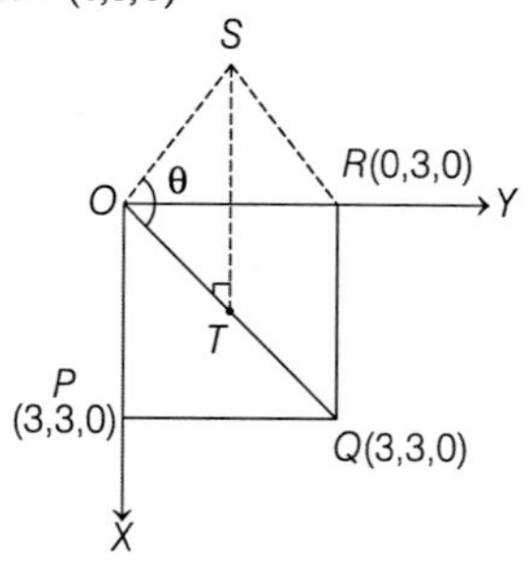

Also, mid-point of OQ is $T\left(\frac{3}{2}, \frac{3}{2}, 0\right)$.

Since, S is directly above the mid-point T of diagonal OQ and $ST = 3$ i.e. $S\left(\frac{3}{2}, \frac{3}{2}, 3\right)$.

Here, DR's of OQ $(3, 3, 0)$ and DR's of $OS\left(\frac{3}{2}, \frac{3}{2}, 3\right)$.

$$\therefore \cos\theta = \frac{\frac{9}{2} + \frac{9}{2}}{\sqrt{9 + 9 + 0}\sqrt{\frac{9}{4} + \frac{9}{4} + 9}} = \frac{9}{\sqrt{18} \cdot \sqrt{\frac{27}{2}}} = \frac{1}{\sqrt{3}}$$

$\therefore$ Option (a) is incorrect.

Now, equation of the plane containing the ΔOQS is

$$\begin{vmatrix} x & y & z \\ 3 & 3 & 0 \\ 3/2 & 3/2 & 3 \end{vmatrix} = 0 \Rightarrow \begin{vmatrix} x & y & z \\ 1 & 1 & 0 \\ 1 & 1 & 2 \end{vmatrix} = 0$$

$$\Rightarrow \quad x(2 - 0) - y(2 - 0) + z(1 - 1) = 0$$

$$\Rightarrow \quad 2x - 2y = 0 \text{ or } x - y = 0$$

$\therefore$ Option (b) is correct.

Now, length of the perpendicular from $P(3, 0, 0)$ to the plane containing ΔOQS is $\frac{|3 - 0|}{\sqrt{1 + 1}} = \frac{3}{\sqrt{2}}$

$\therefore$ Option (c) is correct.

Here, equation of RS is

$$\frac{x - 0}{3/2} = \frac{y - 3}{-3/2} = \frac{z - 0}{3} = \lambda \Rightarrow x = \frac{3}{2}\lambda, y = -\frac{3}{2}\lambda + 3, z = 3\lambda$$

To find the distance from $O(0, 0, 0)$ to RS.

Let M be the foot of perpendicular.

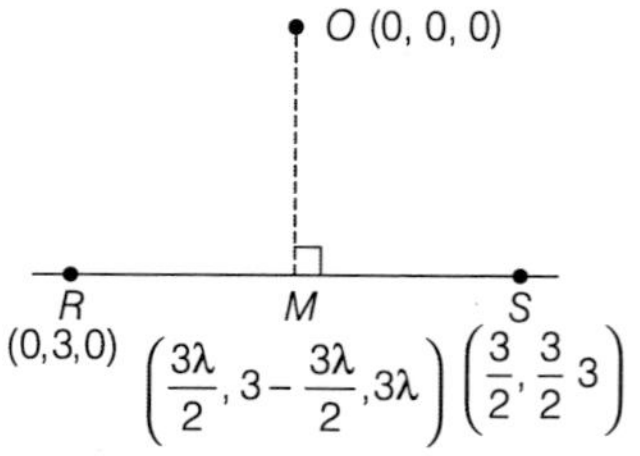

$$\because \quad \overline{OM} \perp \overline{RS} \Rightarrow \overline{OM} \cdot \overline{RS} = 0$$

$$\Rightarrow \quad \frac{9\lambda}{4} - \frac{3}{2}\left(3 - \frac{3\lambda}{2}\right) + 3(3\lambda) = 0 \Rightarrow \lambda = \frac{1}{3}$$

$$\therefore \quad M\left(\frac{1}{2}, \frac{5}{2}, 1\right) \Rightarrow OM = \sqrt{\frac{1}{4} + \frac{25}{4} + 1} = \sqrt{\frac{30}{4}} = \sqrt{\frac{15}{2}}$$

$\therefore$ Option (d) is correct.

40. The rod sweeps out the figure which is a cone.

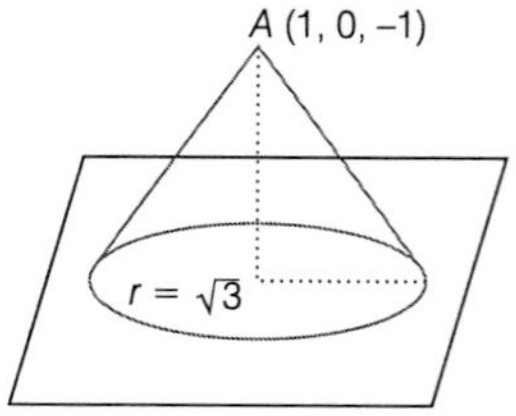

The distance of point $A(1, 0, -1)$ from the plane is $\frac{|1 - 2 + 4|}{\sqrt{9}} = 1$ unit.

The slant height l of the cone is 2 units.

Then, the radius of the base of the cone is

$$\sqrt{l^2 - 1} = \sqrt{4 - 1} = \sqrt{3}.$$

Hence, the volume of the cone is $\frac{\pi}{3}(\sqrt{3})^2 \cdot 1 = \pi$ cubic units.

Area of the circle on the plane which the rod traces is 3π.

Also, the centre of the circle is $Q(x, y, z)$.

Then, $$\frac{x-1}{1} = \frac{y-0}{-2} = \frac{z+1}{2} = \frac{-(1-0-2+4)}{l^2+(-2)^2+2^2}$$

or $$Q(x, y, z) \equiv \left(\frac{2}{3}, \frac{2}{3}, \frac{-5}{3}\right).$$

41. Volume = Area of base × height

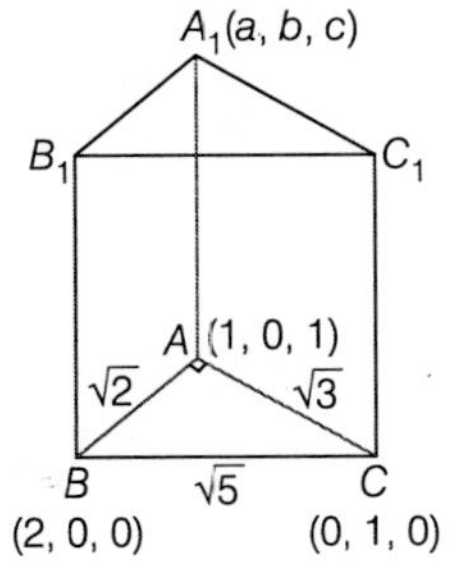

$$3 = \frac{1}{2} \times \sqrt{2} \times \sqrt{3} \times h$$
$$h = \sqrt{6}$$
$$(A_1A)^2 = h^2 = 6$$
$$\mathbf{A_1A} \cdot \mathbf{AB} = 0$$
$$\mathbf{A_1A} \cdot \mathbf{AC} = 0$$
$$\mathbf{AA_1} \cdot \mathbf{BC} = 0$$

On solving, we get position vector of A_1 are $(0, -2, 0)$ or $(2, 2, 2)$.

42. Let the equation of plane be $lx + my + nz = 0$, where l, m, n be d.c's $\Rightarrow l^2 + m^2 + n^2 = 1 \rightarrow$ (i)

Given line $\frac{x-1}{2} = \frac{y+3}{-1} = \frac{z+1}{-2} \Rightarrow 2l - m - 2n = 0 \rightarrow$ (ii)

Also, $$\frac{l-3m-n}{\sqrt{l^2+m^2+n^2}} = \frac{5}{3} \Rightarrow l - 3m - n = \frac{5}{3} \rightarrow \text{(iii)}$$

On solving Eqs. (i), (ii) and (iii), we get equation of plane as
$$x - 2y + 2z = 0 \quad \text{or} \quad 2x + 2y + z = 0.$$

43. (a) Height $= h = \sqrt{1 - \frac{1}{3}} = \sqrt{\frac{2}{3}}$

(b) Required distance $= \frac{1}{2}\left(\sqrt{\frac{2}{3}}\right) = \frac{1}{\sqrt{6}}$

(c) Angle $= \frac{\pi}{2}$

(d) Required distance $= \frac{3}{4}(h) = \frac{3}{4}\left(\sqrt{\frac{2}{3}}\right) = \sqrt{\frac{3}{8}}$

44. Since, L is at constant distance from two planes P_1 and P_2.

Therefore, L is parallel to the line through intersection of P_1 and P_2.

$$\text{DR's of } L = \begin{vmatrix} \hat{\mathbf{i}} & \hat{\mathbf{j}} & \hat{\mathbf{k}} \\ 1 & 2 & -1 \\ 2 & -1 & 1 \end{vmatrix}$$
$$= \hat{\mathbf{i}}(2-1) - \hat{\mathbf{j}}(1+2) + \hat{\mathbf{k}}(-1-4) = \hat{\mathbf{i}} - 3\hat{\mathbf{j}} - 5\hat{\mathbf{k}}$$

$\therefore$ DR's of L are $(1, -3, -5)$ passing through $(0, 0, 0)$.

Now, equation of L is $\frac{x-0}{1} = \frac{y-0}{-3} = \frac{z-0}{-5}$.

For any point on L, $\frac{x}{1} = \frac{y}{-3} = \frac{z}{-5} = \lambda$ [say]

i.e. $P(\lambda, -3\lambda, -5\lambda)$

If (α, β, γ) is foot of perpendicular from P on P_1, then
$$\frac{\alpha-\lambda}{1} = \frac{\beta+3\lambda}{2} = \frac{\gamma+5\lambda}{-1} = k \quad \text{[say]}$$
$$\Rightarrow \quad \alpha = \lambda + k, \beta = 2k - 3\lambda, \gamma = -k - 5\lambda$$

which satisfy $P_1 : x + 2y - z + 1 = 0$
$$\Rightarrow (\lambda + k) + 2(2k - 3\lambda) - (-k - 5\lambda) + 1 = 0 \Rightarrow k = -\frac{1}{6}$$
$$\therefore x = -\frac{1}{6} + \lambda, y = -\frac{1}{3} - 3\lambda, z = \frac{1}{6} - 5\lambda$$

which satisfy options (a) and (b).

45. Let (l, m, n) be the direction cosines of the line perpendicular to the plane.

$\Rightarrow$ Equation of the plane $lx + my + nz = p$
$$\frac{x}{\left(\frac{p}{l}\right)} + \frac{y}{\left(\frac{p}{m}\right)} + \frac{z}{\left(\frac{p}{n}\right)} = 1$$

$A(p/l, 0, 0), B(0, p/m, 0), C(0, 0, p/n)$

Centroid of tetrahedron $OABC$ is
$$(x, y, z) = \left(\frac{p}{4l}, \frac{p}{4m}, \frac{p}{4n}\right)$$

Using, $l^2 + m^2 + n^2 = 1$
$$x^2y^2 + y^2z^2 + z^2x^2 = \frac{16}{p^2}x^2y^2z^2 \Rightarrow \frac{1}{x^2} + \frac{1}{y^2} + \frac{1}{z^2} = \frac{16}{p^2}$$

On putting $x = \frac{p}{4}\sec\alpha\sec\beta$, $y = \frac{p}{4}\sec\alpha \operatorname{cosec}\beta$, $z = \frac{p}{4}\operatorname{cosec}\alpha$
$$\frac{1}{x} = \frac{4}{p}\cos\alpha\cos\beta, \frac{1}{y} = \frac{4}{p}\cos\alpha\sin\beta, \frac{1}{z} = \frac{4}{p}\sin\alpha$$
$$\left(\frac{1}{x}\right)^2 + \left(\frac{1}{y}\right)^2 + \left(\frac{1}{z}\right)^2 = \frac{16}{p^2}[\cos^2\alpha\cos^2\beta + \cos^2\alpha\sin^2\beta + \sin^2\alpha]$$
$$= \frac{16}{p^2}[\cos^2\alpha + \sin^2\alpha] = \frac{16}{p^2}$$

■ Solution (Q. Nos. 46 and 47)

46. Here, ΔABC is an isosceles with $AB = AC$

So, internal bisector of A is perpendicular to BC.

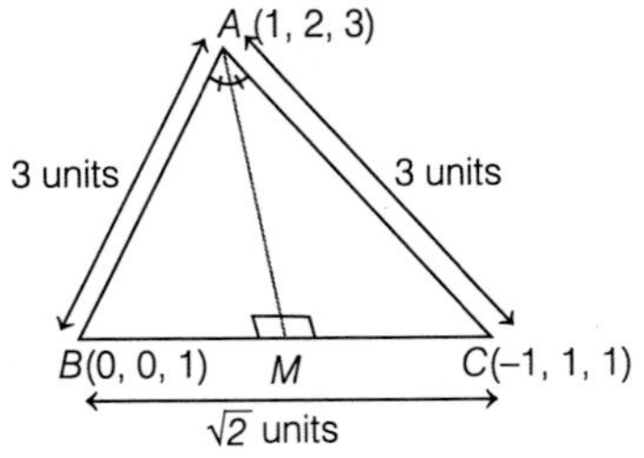

$\Delta AMB \cong \Delta AMC$ (RHS rule)

M is mid-point of BC.

So, $$M \equiv \left(\frac{-1}{2}, \frac{1}{2}, 1\right)$$

$\therefore$ Equation of internal bisector through A to side BC is

$$\mathbf{r} = (\hat{\mathbf{i}} + 2\hat{\mathbf{j}} + 3\hat{\mathbf{k}}) + \mu'\left(\frac{3}{2}\hat{\mathbf{i}} + \frac{3}{2}\hat{\mathbf{j}} + 2\hat{\mathbf{k}}\right)$$

$$\Rightarrow \quad \mathbf{r} = (\hat{\mathbf{i}} + 2\hat{\mathbf{j}} + 3\hat{\mathbf{k}}) + \mu(3\hat{\mathbf{i}} + 3\hat{\mathbf{j}} + 4\hat{\mathbf{k}}) \quad \left[\because \mu = \frac{\mu'}{2}\right]$$

47. Now, equation of AC is

$$\mathbf{r} = (\hat{\mathbf{i}} + 2\hat{\mathbf{j}} + 3\hat{\mathbf{k}}) + \lambda(2\hat{\mathbf{i}} + \hat{\mathbf{j}} + 2\hat{\mathbf{k}})$$

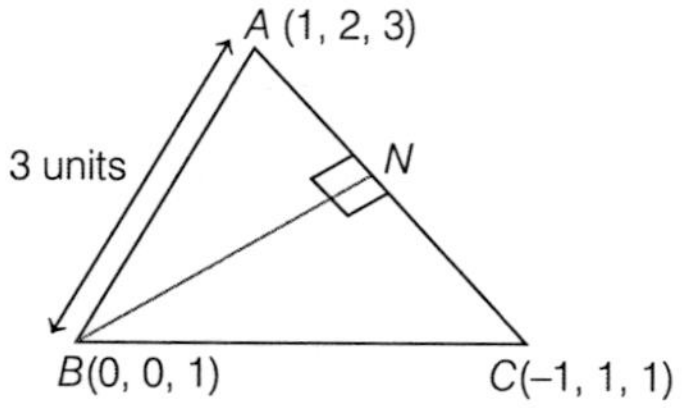

Also, $$\mathbf{BN} = (1 + 2\lambda)\hat{\mathbf{i}} + (2 + \lambda)\hat{\mathbf{j}} + 2(1 + \lambda)\hat{\mathbf{k}}$$

$$\Rightarrow \quad \mathbf{BN} \cdot (2\hat{\mathbf{i}} + \hat{\mathbf{j}} + 2\hat{\mathbf{k}}) = 0$$

$$\Rightarrow \quad 2(1 + 2\lambda) + (2 + \lambda) + 4(1 + \lambda) = 0 \Rightarrow \lambda = \frac{-8}{9}$$

Position vector of $\mathbf{N} = \dfrac{-7\hat{\mathbf{i}} + 10\hat{\mathbf{j}} + 11\hat{\mathbf{k}}}{9}$

Equation of altitude through B to side AC is

$$\mathbf{r} = \hat{\mathbf{k}} + t'\left(-\frac{7}{9}\hat{\mathbf{i}} + \frac{10}{9}\hat{\mathbf{j}} + \frac{11}{9}\hat{\mathbf{k}} - \hat{\mathbf{k}}\right)$$

$$\mathbf{r} = \hat{\mathbf{k}} + t(-7\hat{\mathbf{i}} + 10\hat{\mathbf{j}} + 2\hat{\mathbf{k}}) \quad \left[\because t = \frac{t'}{9}\right]$$

■ Solution (Q. Nos. 48 and 49)

48. Line $\dfrac{x-1}{3} = \dfrac{y-2}{-1} = \dfrac{z-3}{4} = r$

Any point $B \equiv 3r + 1, 2 - r, 3 + 4r$ (on the line L)

$$\mathbf{AB} = 3r, -r, 4r + 6$$

Hence, $\mathbf{AB}$ is parallel to $x + y - z = 1$.

Hence, $3r - r - 4r - 6 = 0$

$$2r = -6\,; \quad r = -3$$

Hence, B is $(-8, 5, -9)$.

49. Equation of plane containing the line L is

$$A(x-1) + B(y-2) + C(z-3) = 0$$

where, $3A - B + 4C = 0$ ...(ii)

$\therefore$ Eq. (i) also contains the point $A(1, 2, -1)$

Hence, $C = 0, 3A = B$

Equation of plane $x - 1 + 3(y - 2) = 9$

$$x + 3y - 7 = 0$$

■ Solution (Q. Nos. 50 and 51)

50. $h = |\text{Projection of } \mathbf{AD} \text{ on } \mathbf{n}|$

$$\mathbf{AD} = -3\hat{\mathbf{i}} - 5\hat{\mathbf{j}} + 3\hat{\mathbf{k}}$$

$$= \left|\frac{\mathbf{AD} \cdot \mathbf{n}}{|\mathbf{n}|}\right| = \left|\frac{(-3\hat{\mathbf{i}} - 5\hat{\mathbf{j}} + 3\hat{\mathbf{k}})(\hat{\mathbf{i}} + \hat{\mathbf{j}} - 2\hat{\mathbf{k}})}{\sqrt{6}}\right|$$

$$= \left|\frac{-3-5-6}{\sqrt{6}}\right| = \frac{14}{\sqrt{6}}$$

51. Equation of the plane ABC

$$A(x-3) + By + (z-1) = 0$$

where, $A = 1, B = 1, C = -2$

$$\therefore \quad x - 3 + y - 2z + 2 = 0 \Rightarrow x + y - 2z = 1$$

■ Solution (Q. Nos. 52 and 53)

52. Line L_1 is parallel to $\mathbf{a} = \hat{\mathbf{i}} + 2\hat{\mathbf{j}} + 3\hat{\mathbf{k}}$

Line L_2 is parallel to $\mathbf{b} = 3\hat{\mathbf{i}} + \hat{\mathbf{j}} + 2\hat{\mathbf{k}}$

Normal to the plane perpendicular to line L_1 and L_2 is

$$\mathbf{a} \times \mathbf{b} = (\hat{\mathbf{i}} + 7\hat{\mathbf{j}} - 5\hat{\mathbf{k}})$$

and plane passes through the point with positive vector

$$= \frac{3}{2}\hat{\mathbf{i}} + \frac{5}{2}\hat{\mathbf{j}} + 2\hat{\mathbf{k}}$$

Equation of plane is $\mathbf{r} \cdot (\hat{\mathbf{i}} + 7\hat{\mathbf{j}} - 5\hat{\mathbf{k}}) = 9$

53. Angle bisector of vector $\mathbf{a}$ and $\mathbf{b}$ is,

$$\mathbf{r}_1 = \frac{1}{\sqrt{14}}(2\hat{\mathbf{i}} - \hat{\mathbf{j}} - \hat{\mathbf{k}}) \text{ and } \mathbf{r}_2 = \frac{1}{\sqrt{14}}(4\hat{\mathbf{i}} + 3\hat{\mathbf{j}} + 5\hat{\mathbf{k}})$$

Hence, the plane with either $(2, -1, -1)$ or $(4, 3, 5)$ as the direction ratio of normal and passing through $(2, -3, 2)$ is the required plane.

$\therefore$ Equation of line is $\dfrac{x-2}{2} = \dfrac{y+3}{-1} = \dfrac{z-2}{-1}$

and $$\frac{x-2}{4} = \frac{y+3}{3} = \frac{z-2}{5}$$

$$\therefore \quad \frac{x-2}{2} = y + 3 = z - 2 \text{ or } \frac{x-2}{4} = \frac{y+3}{3} = \frac{z-2}{5}$$

■ Solutions (Q. Nos. 54 and 55)

The three plane intersect in a straight line. All three plane pass through origin (clearly).

$$\begin{vmatrix} 1 & -n & -m \\ n & -1 & l \\ m & l & -1 \end{vmatrix} = 1(1 - l^2) + n(-n - lm) - m(nl + m)$$

$$1 = l^2 + m^2 + n^2 + 2lmn$$

Let $l = \cos\theta_1, m = \cos\theta_2, n = \cos\theta_3$ [since, $l, m, n \in (0, 1)$]

$$\cos^2\theta_1 + \cos^2\theta_2 + \cos^2\theta_3 + 2\cos\theta_1\cos\theta_2\cos\theta_3 = 1$$

$$\cos^2\theta_1 + (2\cos\theta_2\cos\theta_3)\cos\theta_1 + \cos^2\theta_2 + \cos^2\theta_3 - 1 = 0$$

$\cos\theta_1$

$$= \frac{-2\cos\theta_2\cos\theta_3 \pm \sqrt{4\cos^2\theta_2\cos^2\theta_3 - 4\cos^2\theta_2 - 4\cos^2\theta_3 + 4}}{2}$$

$$= -\cos\theta_2\cos\theta_3 \pm \sqrt{1 - \cos\theta_2}\sqrt{1 - \cos^2\theta_3}$$

$$\Rightarrow \quad \cos\theta_1 = (\cos\theta_2\cos\theta_3 - \sin\theta_2\sin\theta_3)$$

$$\Rightarrow \quad \cos\theta_1 = -\cos(\theta_2 + \theta_3)$$

Hence, $$\theta_1 + \theta_2 + \theta_3 = \pi$$

$$\Rightarrow \quad ny + mz = \frac{y - lz}{n}$$

$$\Rightarrow \quad n^2y + mnz = y - lz$$

$$\Rightarrow \quad (1 + mn)z = (1 - n^2)y$$

$$\therefore \quad \frac{z}{y} = \frac{1 - n^2}{1 + mn} \Rightarrow \frac{x - ny}{m} = \frac{y - nx}{1}$$

$$\Rightarrow \quad lx - nly = my - mnx$$

$$\Rightarrow \quad (l + mn)x = (m + nl)y$$

$$\therefore \quad \frac{y}{x} = \frac{l + mn}{m + nl}$$

$$\Rightarrow \quad \frac{y - lz}{n} = \frac{z - ly}{m}$$

$$\Rightarrow \quad my - mlz = nz - nly \Rightarrow (m + nl)y = (n + ml)z$$

$$\therefore \quad \frac{z}{y} = \frac{m + nl}{n + ml} = \frac{\sin\theta_1 \sin\theta_3}{\sin\theta_2 \sin\theta_1} = \frac{\sin\theta_3}{\sin\theta_2}$$

$$\therefore \quad \frac{x}{y} = \frac{m + nl}{l + mn} = \frac{\sin\theta_1}{\sin\theta_2}$$

$$\Rightarrow \quad \frac{x}{\sin\theta_1} = \frac{y}{\sin\theta_2} = \frac{z}{\sin\theta_3}$$

Hence, $\dfrac{x}{\sqrt{1 - l^2}} = \dfrac{y}{\sqrt{l - m^2}} = \dfrac{z}{\sqrt{1 - n^2}}$

Hence, ordered traid $(a, b, c) \equiv (\sqrt{1-l^2}, \sqrt{1-m^2}, \sqrt{1-n^2})$

▪ Solution (Q. Nos. 56 and 57)

56. Let the position vector of L be $\mathbf{a} + \lambda \mathbf{b}$

$$= (6 + 3\lambda)\hat{\mathbf{i}} + (7 + 2\lambda)\hat{\mathbf{j}} + (7 - 2\lambda)\hat{\mathbf{k}}$$

So, $\mathbf{PL} = (6 + 3\lambda)\hat{\mathbf{i}} + (7 + 2\lambda)\hat{\mathbf{j}} + (7 - 2\lambda)\hat{\mathbf{k}} - (\hat{\mathbf{i}} + 2\hat{\mathbf{j}} + 3\hat{\mathbf{k}})$

$$= (5 + 3\lambda)\,\hat{\mathbf{i}} + (5 + 2\lambda)\,\hat{\mathbf{j}} + (4 - 2\lambda)\,\hat{\mathbf{k}}$$

Since, **PL** is perpendicular to the given line which is parallel to $\mathbf{b} = 3\hat{\mathbf{i}} + 2\hat{\mathbf{j}} - 2\hat{\mathbf{k}}$

$$\Rightarrow \quad 3(5 + 3\lambda) + 2(5 + 2\lambda) - 2(4 - 2\lambda) = 0$$

$\Rightarrow \lambda = -1$ and thus the position vector of L is $3\hat{\mathbf{i}} + 5\hat{\mathbf{j}} + 9\hat{\mathbf{k}}$

57. Let the position vector of Q, the image of P in the given line be $x_1\hat{\mathbf{i}} + y_1\hat{\mathbf{j}} + z_1\hat{\mathbf{k}}$, then L is the mid-point of PQ.

$$\Rightarrow \quad 3\hat{\mathbf{i}} + 5\hat{\mathbf{j}} + 9\hat{\mathbf{k}} = \frac{\hat{\mathbf{i}} + 2\hat{\mathbf{j}} + 3\hat{\mathbf{k}} + x_1\hat{\mathbf{i}} + y_1\hat{\mathbf{j}} + z_1\hat{\mathbf{k}}}{2}$$

$$\Rightarrow \quad \frac{x_1 + 1}{2} = 3, \ \frac{y_1 + 2}{2} = 5, \ \frac{z_1 + 3}{2} = 9$$

$$\Rightarrow \quad x_1 = 5, y_1 = 8, z_1 = 15$$

$\Rightarrow$ Image of P in the line is (5, 8, 15).

▪ Solution (Q. Nos. 58 and 59)

58. The required coordinates are

$$\left(\frac{2 \times 13 + 3(-2)}{2 + 3}, \frac{2 \times (-3) + 3(2)}{2 + 3}, \frac{2 \times 13 + 3 \times 3}{2 + 3}\right) = (4, 0, 7)$$

59. Direction ratios of AB are $13 + 2, -3 - 2, 13 - 3$.

i.e. $15, -5, 10$

Let the equation of the required line L be $\dfrac{x + 2}{l} = \dfrac{y - 2}{m} = \dfrac{z - 3}{n}$

Then, $15l - 5m + 10n = 0$, which satisfied by option (c).

▪ Solution (Q. Nos. 60 and 61)

60. Equation $\mathbf{r} = \mathbf{a} + t\hat{\mathbf{n}}$ is line passing through $\mathbf{a}$ and parallel to $\hat{\mathbf{n}}$. This will meet the plane $\mathbf{r} \cdot \hat{\mathbf{n}} = d$ at point for which

$$(\mathbf{a} + t\,\hat{\mathbf{n}}) \,.\, \hat{\mathbf{n}} = d \Rightarrow t = d - \mathbf{a} \,.\, \hat{\mathbf{n}}$$

Required distance $= |\mathbf{a} + (d - \mathbf{a}.\hat{\mathbf{n}})\hat{\mathbf{n}} - \mathbf{a}| = |d - \mathbf{a}.\hat{\mathbf{n}}|$

61. Foot of the perpendicular from the point A to plane $\mathbf{r}.\hat{\mathbf{n}} = d$

$$= \mathbf{a} + (d - \mathbf{a}.\hat{\mathbf{n}})\,\hat{\mathbf{n}}$$

▪ Solution (Q. Nos. 62 and 63)

Given line is $\dfrac{x}{2} = \dfrac{y - 1}{3} = \dfrac{z - 2}{1} = \lambda$ (let)

Any point on the line is $Q(2\lambda, 3\lambda + 1, \lambda + 2)$.

$\therefore$ Direction ratios of PQ are

$2\lambda - 1, 3\lambda + 1 - 0, \lambda + 2 - 3$ i.e. $2\lambda - 1, 3\lambda + 1, \lambda - 1$.

Since, PQ is parallel to the plane $x + y + z = 2$

$$\therefore \quad (2\lambda - 1)(1) + (3\lambda + 1)(1) + (\lambda - 1)(1) = 0$$

$$\Rightarrow \quad 2\lambda - 1 + 3\lambda + 1 + \lambda - 1 = 0$$

$$\Rightarrow \quad 6\lambda - 1 = 0$$

$$\Rightarrow \quad \lambda = \frac{1}{6}$$

$\therefore$ Coordinates of Q are $\left(\dfrac{2}{6}, \dfrac{3}{6} + 1, \dfrac{1}{6} + 2\right)$ i.e $\left(\dfrac{1}{3}, \dfrac{3}{2}, \dfrac{13}{6}\right)$.

$$\therefore PQ = \sqrt{\left(1 - \frac{1}{3}\right)^2 + \left(0 - \frac{3}{2}\right)^2 + \left(3 - \frac{13}{6}\right)^2}$$

$$= \sqrt{\frac{4}{9} + \frac{9}{4} + \frac{25}{36}} = \sqrt{\frac{16 + 81 + 25}{36}} = \sqrt{\frac{122}{36}} = \sqrt{\frac{61}{18}}$$

Direction ratios of PQ are

$$2\left(\frac{1}{6}\right) - 1, 3\left(\frac{1}{6}\right) + 1, \frac{1}{6} - 1 \text{ i.e. } -\frac{2}{3}, \frac{3}{2}, -\frac{5}{6}$$

$\therefore$ Equation of line L is $\dfrac{x - 1}{\frac{2}{3}} = \dfrac{y}{-\frac{3}{2}} = \dfrac{z - 3}{\frac{5}{6}}$.

Angle between line L and line $\dfrac{x}{2} = \dfrac{y - 1}{3} = \dfrac{z - 2}{1}$

$$\therefore \cos\theta = \left|\frac{2\left(\frac{2}{3}\right) + 3\left(-\frac{3}{2}\right) + 1\left(\frac{5}{6}\right)}{\sqrt{4 + 9 + 1}\sqrt{\frac{4}{9} + \frac{9}{4} + \frac{25}{36}}}\right|$$

$$= \left|\frac{\frac{4}{3} - \frac{9}{2} + \frac{5}{6}}{\sqrt{14}\sqrt{\frac{61}{18}}}\right| = \left|\frac{-\frac{14}{6}}{\sqrt{14 \times \frac{61}{18}}}\right| = \frac{7}{3} \times \frac{3}{\sqrt{427}}$$

$$\Rightarrow \quad \theta = \cos^{-1}\left(\frac{7}{\sqrt{427}}\right)$$

62. $k_1 + k_2 = 61 + 18 = 79$

63. $|a_1 - a_2| = |7 - 427| = 420$

■ **Solution** (Q. Nos. 64 and 65)

64. Vector equation of given lines L_1 and L_2 are

$$\mathbf{r} = -\hat{\mathbf{i}} - 2\hat{\mathbf{j}} - \hat{\mathbf{k}} + \lambda_1(3\hat{\mathbf{i}} + \hat{\mathbf{j}} + 2\hat{\mathbf{k}})$$

and $\mathbf{r} = 2\hat{\mathbf{i}} - 2\hat{\mathbf{j}} + 3\hat{\mathbf{k}} + \lambda_2(\hat{\mathbf{i}} + 2\hat{\mathbf{j}} + 3\hat{\mathbf{k}})$

Let $\mathbf{OA} = -\hat{\mathbf{i}} - 2\hat{\mathbf{j}} - \hat{\mathbf{k}}$ and $\mathbf{OB} = 2\hat{\mathbf{i}} - 2\hat{\mathbf{j}} + 3\hat{\mathbf{k}}$

$\therefore \quad \mathbf{AB} = 3\hat{\mathbf{i}} + 4\hat{\mathbf{k}}$

Let $\mathbf{n}_1 = 3\hat{\mathbf{i}} + \hat{\mathbf{j}} + 2\hat{\mathbf{k}}$, $\mathbf{n}_2 = \hat{\mathbf{i}} + 2\hat{\mathbf{j}} + 3\hat{\mathbf{k}}$

$$\therefore \mathbf{n}_1 \times \mathbf{n}_2 = \begin{vmatrix} \hat{\mathbf{i}} & \hat{\mathbf{j}} & \hat{\mathbf{k}} \\ 3 & 1 & 2 \\ 1 & 2 & 3 \end{vmatrix} = \hat{\mathbf{i}}(3-4) - \hat{\mathbf{j}}(9-2) + \hat{\mathbf{k}}(6-1)$$

$$= -\hat{\mathbf{i}} - 7\hat{\mathbf{j}} + 5\hat{\mathbf{k}}$$

$$\therefore \text{Shortest distance between } L_1 \text{ and } L_2 = \left| \frac{[\mathbf{AB} \ \ \mathbf{n}_1 \ \ \mathbf{n}_2]}{|\mathbf{n}_1 \times \mathbf{n}_2|} \right|$$

$$\text{Here, } [\mathbf{AB} \ \ \mathbf{n}_1 \ \ \mathbf{n}_2] = \begin{vmatrix} 3 & 0 & 4 \\ 3 & 1 & 2 \\ 1 & 2 & 3 \end{vmatrix}$$

$$= 3(3-4) - 0(9-2) + 4(6-1)$$

$$= 3(-1) + 4(5) = -3 + 20 = 17$$

$\therefore$ Shortest distance between lines L_1 and L_2

$$= \left| \frac{[\mathbf{AB} \ \ \mathbf{n}_1 \ \ \mathbf{n}_2]}{\mathbf{n}_1 \times \mathbf{n}_2} \right| = \left| \frac{17}{\sqrt{1+49+25}} \right| = \frac{17}{5\sqrt{3}} \text{ units}$$

$\therefore \quad p = 17, q = 3$

Hence, $pq = 17 \times 3 = 51$

65. Let $\mathbf{a} = -\hat{\mathbf{i}} - 2\hat{\mathbf{j}} - \hat{\mathbf{k}}$ and $\mathbf{n} = \mathbf{n}_1 \times \mathbf{n}_2$

$\therefore$ Equation of plane passing through point $\mathbf{a}$ and perpendicular to both lines is

$$\mathbf{r} \cdot \mathbf{n} = \mathbf{a} \cdot \mathbf{n}$$

$$\Rightarrow \mathbf{r} \cdot (-\hat{\mathbf{i}} - 7\hat{\mathbf{j}} + 5\hat{\mathbf{k}}) = (-\hat{\mathbf{i}} - 2\hat{\mathbf{j}} - \hat{\mathbf{k}}) \cdot (-\hat{\mathbf{i}} - 7\hat{\mathbf{j}} + 5\hat{\mathbf{k}})$$

$$= 1 + 14 - 5 = 10$$

$$\Rightarrow \quad \mathbf{r} \cdot (-\hat{\mathbf{i}} - 7\hat{\mathbf{j}} + 5\hat{\mathbf{k}}) = 10 \qquad \text{...(i)}$$

$\therefore$ Perpendicular distance from point (1, 1, 1) to the plane (i) is

$$\frac{|(\hat{\mathbf{i}} + \hat{\mathbf{j}} + \hat{\mathbf{k}})(-\hat{\mathbf{i}} - 7\hat{\mathbf{j}} + 5\hat{\mathbf{k}}) - 10|}{|\mathbf{n}|} = \frac{|-3-10|}{\sqrt{75}} = \frac{13}{\sqrt{75}}$$

$\therefore \quad \lambda = 75$

■ **Solution** (Q. Nos. 66 and 67)

66. Mid-point of $BC = \left(\frac{\lambda - 1}{2}, \frac{5+3}{2}, \frac{\mu + 2}{2} \right)$

DR's $\quad AD = \left(\frac{\lambda - 5}{2}, 1, \frac{\mu - 8}{2} \right)$

AD is equally inclined to axes $\Rightarrow \lambda = 7, \mu = 10, 2\lambda - \mu = 4$

67. $A(2, 3, 5)\ B(-1, 3, 2)\ C(7, 5, 10)$

Projection of $\mathbf{AB} = -3\hat{\mathbf{i}} - 3\hat{\mathbf{k}}$ on $\mathbf{BC} = 8\hat{\mathbf{i}} + 2\hat{\mathbf{j}} + 8\hat{\mathbf{k}}$

$$\frac{\mathbf{AB} \cdot \mathbf{BC}}{|\mathbf{BC}|} = \frac{-8\sqrt{3}}{\sqrt{11}}$$

Hence, $\lambda = 8$

■ **Solution** (Q. Nos. 68 and 69)

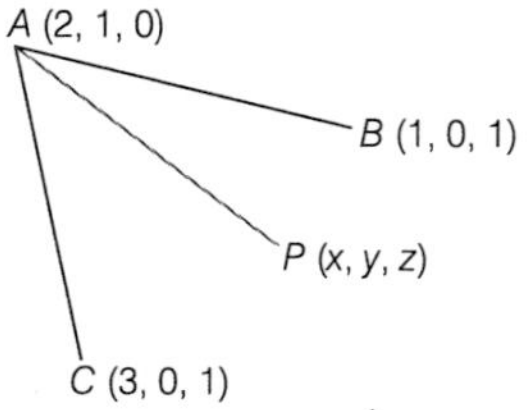

$$\begin{vmatrix} x-2 & y-1 & z \\ -1 & -1 & 1 \\ 1 & -1 & 1 \end{vmatrix} = 0$$

$$\Rightarrow (x-2)[(-1)-(-1)] - (y-1)[(-1)-1] + z[1+1] = 0$$

$$\Rightarrow \quad 2(y-1) + 2z = 0$$

$$\Rightarrow \quad y + z - 1 = 0$$

The vector normal to the plane is $\mathbf{r} = 0\hat{\mathbf{i}} + \hat{\mathbf{j}} + \hat{\mathbf{k}}$

$\therefore \alpha + \beta + \gamma + \delta = 0 + 1 + 1 + 1 = 3$

The equation of the line through (0, 0, 2) and parallel to $\mathbf{n}$ is

$$\mathbf{r} = 2\hat{\mathbf{k}} + \lambda(\hat{\mathbf{j}} + \hat{\mathbf{k}})$$

The perpendicular distance of $D(0, 0, 2)$ from plane.

Hence, $\lambda = 1$

[$\because$ perpendicular distance of D from the plane ABC is $\frac{1}{\sqrt{2}}$]

68. 3   69. 1

70. Shortest distance

$$= \frac{|\mathbf{OB} \cdot (\mathbf{OA} \times \mathbf{BC})|}{|\mathbf{OA} \times \mathbf{BC}|} = \frac{|(\hat{\mathbf{i}} + \hat{\mathbf{j}}) \cdot (\hat{\mathbf{i}} \times (\hat{\mathbf{j}} \times \hat{\mathbf{k}}))|}{\hat{\mathbf{i}} \times (\hat{\mathbf{j}} + \hat{\mathbf{k}})} = \frac{1}{\sqrt{2}} \text{ units}$$

$$\Rightarrow \quad \sqrt{2}m = 1$$

71. The length of the edges are given by $a = 5 - 2 = 3$, $b = 9 - 3 = 6$ and $c = 7 - 5 = 2$, so length of the diagonal

$$= \sqrt{a^2 + b^2 + c^2} = \sqrt{9 + 36 + 4} = 7 \text{ units}$$

72. Given lines are

$\mathbf{r} = (3\hat{\mathbf{i}} + 8\hat{\mathbf{j}} + 3\hat{\mathbf{k}}) + \lambda(3\hat{\mathbf{i}} - \hat{\mathbf{j}} + \hat{\mathbf{k}}) \Rightarrow \mathbf{r} = (3, 8, 3) + \lambda(3, -1, 1)$

and $\mathbf{r} = (-3\hat{\mathbf{i}} - 7\hat{\mathbf{j}} + 6\hat{\mathbf{k}}) + \mu(-3\hat{\mathbf{i}} + 2\hat{\mathbf{j}} + 4\hat{\mathbf{k}})$

$\Rightarrow \quad \mathbf{r} = (-3, -7, 6) + \mu(-3, 2, 4)$

where, λ and μ are parameters

Shortest distance

$$= \frac{(-3-3)\hat{\mathbf{i}} + (-7-8)\hat{\mathbf{j}} + (6-3)\hat{\mathbf{k}} \cdot [(3\hat{\mathbf{i}} - \hat{\mathbf{j}} + \hat{\mathbf{k}}) \times (-3\hat{\mathbf{i}} + 2\hat{\mathbf{j}} + 4\hat{\mathbf{k}})]}{|(3, -1, 1) \times (-3, 2, 4)|}$$

$$= \frac{(-6, -15, 3) \cdot (-6, -15, 3)}{\sqrt{36 + 225 + 9}} = \frac{270}{\sqrt{270}}$$

$$= \sqrt{270} = 3\sqrt{30} \text{ units} = \lambda\sqrt{30}$$

$\therefore \quad \lambda = 3$

73. Given planes are

$$x - cy - bz = 0 \qquad \text{...(i)}$$

$$cx - y + az = 0 \qquad \text{...(ii)}$$

$$bx + acy - z = 0 \qquad \text{...(iii)}$$

Equation of plane passing through the line of intersection of planes (i) and (ii) may be taken as

$$(x - cy - bz) + \lambda(cx - y + az) = 0 \qquad \text{...(iv)}$$

Now, on eliminating λ, we get

$$a^2 + b^2 + c^2 + 2abc = 1$$

74. We must have $\dfrac{\lambda(-1)+1\times 3}{\lambda+1}=0 \Rightarrow \lambda=3$

$\therefore \quad \lambda=3$

75. The coordinates of vertices of projected triangle will be $A'(-1, 1, 0)$, $B'(1, -1, 0)$, $C'(1, 1, 0)$.

Area of triangle $=\dfrac{1}{2}\begin{vmatrix}-1 & 1 & 1\\ 1 & -1 & 1\\ 1 & 1 & 1\end{vmatrix}$ (Two dimension area formula)

$= 2$ sq units

76. Plane must pass through $\left(\dfrac{1-3}{2}, \dfrac{5+1}{2}, \dfrac{7-1}{2}\right)$ or $(-1, 3, 3)$.

$\Rightarrow \quad -1+3+2\times 3=\lambda \Rightarrow \lambda=8$

77. $x^2+y^2+z^2=$ square of distance from origin

$4\sin^2 t+4\cos^2 t+9t^2=4+9t^2$

which is shortest at $t=0$

$\Rightarrow$ Shortest distance $=2$ units

78. Let $P(\alpha, \beta, \gamma)$ and R is image of P in the xy-plane.

$\therefore R(\alpha, \beta, -\gamma)$

Also, Q is the image of P in the plane $x+y=3$

$\therefore \quad \dfrac{x-\alpha}{1}=\dfrac{y-\beta}{1}=\dfrac{z-\gamma}{0}=\dfrac{-2(\alpha+\beta-3)}{2}$

$x=3-\beta, y=3-\alpha, z=\gamma$

Since, Q is lies on Z-axis.

$\therefore \quad \beta=3, \alpha=3, z=\gamma$

$\therefore \quad P(3, 3, \gamma)$

Given, distance of P from X-axis be 5.

$\therefore \quad 5=\sqrt{3^2+\gamma^2} \Rightarrow 25-9=\gamma^2 \Rightarrow \gamma=\pm 4$

Then, $PR=|2\gamma|=|2\times 4|=8$

79. We have, $\quad l+m+n=0 \quad$ ...(i)

and $\quad 2l^2+2m^2-n^2=0 \quad$ ...(ii)

Now, $\quad 2(l^2+m^2)-n^2=0$

$\Rightarrow \quad 2(1-n^2)-n^2=0 \quad [\because l^2+m^2+n^2=1]$

$\Rightarrow \quad 3n^2=2 \Rightarrow n=\pm\sqrt{\dfrac{2}{3}}$

Again, $\quad 2(l^2+m^2)=n^2$

$\Rightarrow \quad 2[(l+m)^2-2lm]=(-(l+m))^2 \Rightarrow l=m$

$\therefore \quad l+m=\pm\sqrt{\dfrac{2}{3}} \Rightarrow 2l=\pm\sqrt{\dfrac{2}{3}}$

$\Rightarrow \quad l=\pm\dfrac{1}{\sqrt{6}}=m$

$\therefore$ Direction cosines are

$\left(\dfrac{1}{\sqrt{6}}, \dfrac{1}{\sqrt{6}}, \sqrt{\dfrac{2}{3}}\right)\left(\dfrac{1}{\sqrt{6}}, \dfrac{1}{\sqrt{6}}, -\sqrt{\dfrac{2}{3}}\right)$

or $\quad \left(-\dfrac{1}{\sqrt{6}}, -\dfrac{1}{\sqrt{6}}, \sqrt{\dfrac{2}{3}}\right)$ and $\left(-\dfrac{1}{\sqrt{6}}, -\dfrac{1}{\sqrt{6}}, -\sqrt{\dfrac{2}{3}}\right)$

The angle between the lines in both the cases is $\cos^{-1}\left(\dfrac{-1}{3}\right)$.

$\therefore k=3$

Therefore, $\dfrac{k}{5}=0.6$

80. The coordinates of any point on the line $\dfrac{x+2}{3}=\dfrac{y+1}{2}=\dfrac{z-3}{2}=\lambda$ are given by $(3\lambda-2, 2\lambda-1, 2\lambda+3)$.

The distance between the above point and $(1, 2, 3)$ is $3\sqrt{2}$.

$\therefore \quad \sqrt{(3\lambda-2-1)^2+(2\lambda-1-2)^2+(2\lambda+3-3)^2}=3\sqrt{2}$

$\Rightarrow \quad \lambda=\dfrac{30}{17}, 0$

$\therefore$ Required points are $(-2, -1, 3)$ and $\left(\dfrac{56}{17}, \dfrac{43}{17}, \dfrac{111}{17}\right)$.

$\therefore a_1=56, a_2=43, a_3=111$

Therefore, $a_1+a_2+a_3=56+43+111=210$

81. The required line is perpendicular to the lines which are parallel to vectors $\mathbf{b}_1=2\hat{\mathbf{i}}-2\hat{\mathbf{j}}+\hat{\mathbf{k}}$ and $\mathbf{b}_2=\hat{\mathbf{i}}+2\hat{\mathbf{j}}+2\hat{\mathbf{k}}$ respectively. So, it is parallel to the vector $\mathbf{b}=\mathbf{b}_1\times\mathbf{b}_2$.

Now, $\mathbf{b}=\mathbf{b}_1\times\mathbf{b}_2=\begin{vmatrix}\hat{\mathbf{i}} & \hat{\mathbf{j}} & \hat{\mathbf{k}}\\ 2 & -2 & 1\\ 1 & 2 & 2\end{vmatrix}=-6\hat{\mathbf{i}}-3\hat{\mathbf{j}}+6\hat{\mathbf{k}}$

Thus, the required line passes through the point $(2, -1, 3)$ and is parallel to the vector $\mathbf{b}=-6\hat{\mathbf{i}}-3\hat{\mathbf{j}}+6\hat{\mathbf{k}}$.

So, its vector equation is

$\mathbf{r}=(2\hat{\mathbf{i}}-\hat{\mathbf{j}}+3\hat{\mathbf{k}})+\lambda(-6\hat{\mathbf{i}}-3\hat{\mathbf{j}}+6\hat{\mathbf{k}})$

or $\quad \mathbf{r}=(2\hat{\mathbf{i}}-\hat{\mathbf{j}}+3\hat{\mathbf{k}})+\mu(2\hat{\mathbf{i}}+\hat{\mathbf{j}}-2\hat{\mathbf{k}})$, where $\mu=-3\lambda$.

$\therefore b_1=2, b_2=1, b_3=-2$

Therefore, $\left|\dfrac{b_1b_2b_3}{5}\right|=0.8$

82. The coordinates of any point on the line $\dfrac{x-3}{2}=\dfrac{y-3}{1}=\dfrac{z}{1}$ are given by $\dfrac{x-3}{2}=\dfrac{y-3}{1}=\dfrac{z}{1}=\lambda$

So, let the coordinates of A be $(2\lambda+3, \lambda+3, \lambda)$.

Let the line through $O(0, 0, 0)$ and making an angle $\dfrac{\pi}{3}$ with the given line be along OA.

Then, its $d'r$ are proportional to

$2\lambda+3-0, \lambda+3-0, \lambda-0$ or $2\lambda+3, \lambda+3, \lambda$

The direction ratios of the given line are proportional to 2, 1, 1.

It is given that the angle between the given line and the line along OA is $\dfrac{\pi}{3}$.

$\therefore \quad \cos\dfrac{\pi}{3}=\dfrac{(2\lambda+3)\times 2+(\lambda+3)\times 1+\lambda\times 1}{\sqrt{(2\lambda+3)^2+(\lambda+3)^2+\lambda^2}\sqrt{2^2+1^2+1^2}}$

$=\dfrac{6\lambda+9}{\sqrt{6\lambda^2+18\lambda+18}\sqrt{6}}$

$\therefore \quad \lambda=-1, -2.$

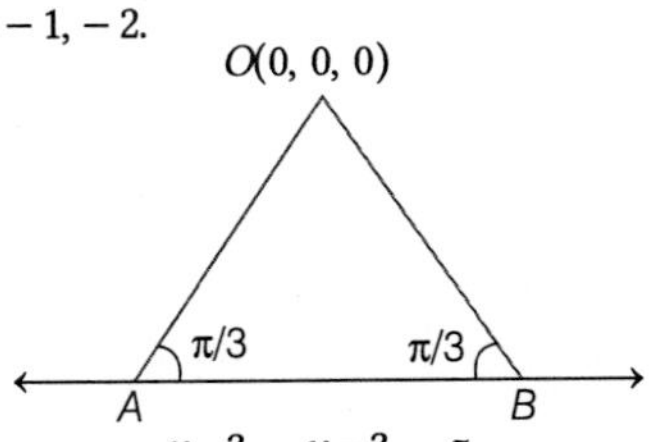

$\dfrac{x-3}{2}=\dfrac{y-3}{1}=\dfrac{z}{1}$

Putting these values of λ in the coordinates of A i.e. $(2\lambda + 3, \lambda + 3, \lambda)$, we find the coordinates of A and B i.e. $A(1, 2, -1)$ and $B(-1, 1, -2)$.

So, the equations of OA and OB are

$$\frac{x-0}{1-0} = \frac{y-0}{2-0} = \frac{z-0}{-1-0}$$

$$\frac{x-0}{-1-0} = \frac{y-0}{1-0} = \frac{z-0}{-2-0}$$

or $$\frac{x}{1} = \frac{y}{2} = \frac{z}{-1} \text{ and } \frac{x}{-1} = \frac{y}{1} = \frac{z}{-2}$$

$\therefore a = 2$ and $b = 1$

Therefore, $(a+b)^3 = 27$

83. Clearly, height h of ΔABC is the length of perpendicular from $A(1, -1, 2)$ to the line $\frac{x+2}{2} = \frac{y-1}{1} = \frac{z-0}{4}$ which passes through $P(-2, 1, 0)$ and is parallel to $\mathbf{b} = 2\hat{\mathbf{i}} + \hat{\mathbf{j}} + 4\hat{\mathbf{k}}$.

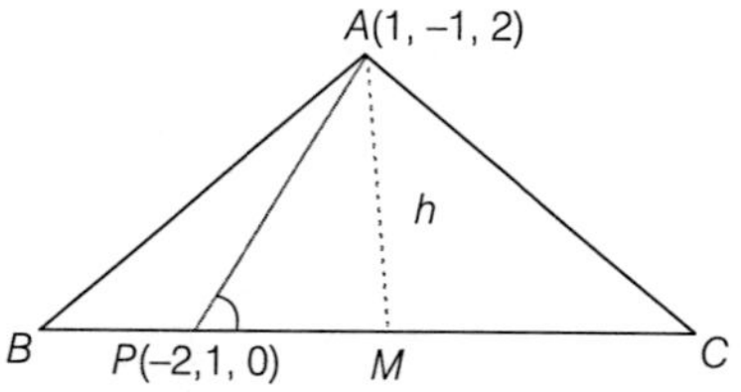

$\therefore$ $$h = \frac{|\mathbf{PA} \times \mathbf{b}|}{|\mathbf{b}|}$$

Now, $\mathbf{PA} = -3\hat{\mathbf{i}} + 2\hat{\mathbf{j}} - 2\hat{\mathbf{k}}$ and $\mathbf{b} = 2\hat{\mathbf{i}} + \hat{\mathbf{j}} + 4\hat{\mathbf{k}}$

$\therefore$ $$\mathbf{PA} \times \mathbf{b} = \begin{vmatrix} \hat{\mathbf{i}} & \hat{\mathbf{j}} & \hat{\mathbf{k}} \\ -3 & 2 & -2 \\ 2 & 1 & 4 \end{vmatrix} = 10\hat{\mathbf{i}} - 8\hat{\mathbf{j}} - 7\hat{\mathbf{k}}$$

$\therefore$ $$|\mathbf{PA} \times \mathbf{b}| = \sqrt{10^2 + 8^2 + (-7)^2} = \sqrt{213}$$

and $$|\mathbf{b}| = \sqrt{2^2 + 1^2 + 4^2} = \sqrt{21}$$

$\therefore$ $$h = \frac{|\mathbf{PA} \times \mathbf{b}|}{|\mathbf{b}|} = \frac{\sqrt{213}}{\sqrt{21}} = \sqrt{\frac{71}{7}}$$

It is given that the length of BC is 5 units.

$\therefore$ Area of $\Delta ABC = \frac{1}{2}(BC \times h) = \frac{1}{2} \times 5 \times \sqrt{\frac{71}{7}} = \sqrt{\frac{1775}{28}}$ sq units

$\therefore k_1 = 1775$ and $k_2 = 28$

Therefore, $k_1 + k_2 = 1803$

84. Given line is $\frac{x-2}{3} = \frac{y+1}{4} = \frac{z-2}{12} = r$ (say)

Any point on the line is $(3r+2, 4r-1, 12r+2)$.

If it lies on the plane $x - y + z = 5$, then

$$(3r+2) - (4r-1) + (12r+2) = 5 \Rightarrow r = 0$$

Hence, point of intersection is $(2, -1, 2)$.

Its distance from $(-1, -5, -10)$ is

$$\sqrt{(2+1)^2 + (-1+5)^2 + (2+10)^2} = \sqrt{9 + 16 + 144}$$
$$= \sqrt{169} = 13 \text{ units}$$

$\therefore 2d = 13 \Rightarrow d = 6.5$

85. The image of the plane

$$x - 2y + 2z - 3 = 0 \quad \text{...(i)}$$

in the plane $$x + y + z - 1 = 0 \quad \text{...(ii)}$$

passes through the line of intersection of the given planes.

Therefore, the equation of such a plane is

$$(x - 2y + 2z - 3) + t(x + y + z - 1) = 0$$

$$\Rightarrow (1+t)x + (-2+t)y + (2+t)z - 3 - t = 0 \quad \text{...(iii)}$$

Now, plane (ii) makes the same angle with plane (i) and image plane (iii). Thus,

$$\frac{1-2+2}{3\sqrt{3}} = \pm \frac{1+t-2+t+2+t}{\sqrt{3}\sqrt{(t+1)^2 + (t-2)^2 + (2+t)^2}}$$

$$\Rightarrow \quad t = 0, -\frac{2}{3}$$

For $t = 0$, we get plane (i); hence for image plane, $t = -\frac{2}{3}$

The equation of the image plane

$$3(x - 2y + 2z - 3) - 2(x + y + z - 1) = 0$$

$$\Rightarrow \quad x - 8y + 4z - 7 = 0$$

$\because a = 1, b = -8, c = 4, d = -7$

Therefore, $|a + b + c + d| = 10$

86. Taking O as the origin, let the position vectors of A, B and C be $\mathbf{a}$, $\mathbf{b}$, $\mathbf{c}$ respectively, then the position vectors of G_1, G_2 and G_3 are

$$\frac{\mathbf{b}+\mathbf{c}}{3}, \frac{\mathbf{c}+\mathbf{a}}{3} \text{ and } \frac{\mathbf{a}+\mathbf{b}}{3}$$

$$V_1 = \frac{1}{6}[\mathbf{a}\ \mathbf{b}\ \mathbf{c}] \text{ and } V_2 = [\mathbf{OG}_1\ \mathbf{OG}_2\ \mathbf{OG}_3]$$

$$\Rightarrow \quad V_2 = \frac{1}{27}[\mathbf{b}+\mathbf{c}\ \mathbf{c}+\mathbf{a}\ \mathbf{a}+\mathbf{b}] = \frac{2}{27}[\mathbf{a}\ \mathbf{b}\ \mathbf{c}]$$

$$\Rightarrow \quad V_2 = \frac{2}{27} \times 6V_1$$

$$\Rightarrow \quad 9V_2 = 4V_1$$

$$\therefore \quad \frac{V_1}{V_2} = 2.25$$

87. Let the equation of planes is $lx + my + nz = p$

$\therefore A = \left(\frac{p}{l}, 0, 0\right), B = \left(0, \frac{p}{m}, 0\right), C = \left(0, 0, \frac{p}{n}\right)$ respectively

$$\text{Centroid of } OABC = \left(\frac{p}{4l}, \frac{p}{4m}, \frac{p}{4n}\right) = (x_1, y_1, z_1) \text{ (say)}$$

$\because$ $$l^2 + m^2 + n^2 = 1$$

$\therefore$ $$\frac{p^2}{16x_1^2} + \frac{p^2}{16y_1^2} + \frac{p^2}{16z_1^2} = 1 \Rightarrow x_1^2y_1^2 + y_1^2z_1^2 + z_1^2x_1^2 = \frac{16}{p^2}x_1^2y_1^2z_1^2$$

$\therefore$ $$k = 16$$

$\therefore$ $$\frac{k}{5} = 3.2$$

88. $l_1^2 + m_1^2 + n_1^2 = 1, l_2^2 + m_2^2 + n_2^2 = 1$

$$(l_1^2 + m_1^2 + n_1^2)(l_2^2 + m_2^2 + n_2^2) - (l_1l_1 + m_1m_2 + n_1n_2)^2$$
$$= (m_1n_2 - m_2n_1)^2 + (n_1l_2 - n_2l_1)^2 + (l_1m_2 - l_2m_1)^2$$

$$(l_1m_2 - l_2m_1)^2 + (m_1n_2 - m_2n_1)^2 + (n_1l_2 - n_2l_1)^2$$
$$+ (l_1l_2 + m_1m_2 + n_1n_2)^2 = 1$$

Hence, $\frac{\lambda}{2} = 0.5$

89. Coordinates of the point, $S = \left(\frac{n^5}{2}, \frac{n^4}{2}, \frac{n}{2}\right)$

$\Rightarrow \quad 2 \times \left(\frac{n^5}{2} + \frac{n^4}{2} + \frac{n}{2}\right) = -1$

$\Rightarrow \quad n(n^4 + n^3 + 1) = -1$

$n = -1$ is the only solution.

Hence, $\frac{|n|}{5} = 0.2$

90. **(A)** $L_1 : \frac{x-1}{1} = \frac{y-0}{1} = \frac{z-2}{-5}$; $\mathbf{V}_1 = \hat{\mathbf{i}} + \hat{\mathbf{j}} - 5\hat{\mathbf{k}}$;

$L_2 : \frac{x-2}{2} = \frac{y-1}{2} = \frac{z+3}{-10}$; $\mathbf{V}_2 = 2(\hat{\mathbf{i}} + \hat{\mathbf{j}} - 5\hat{\mathbf{k}})$

Hence, lines are parallel and both contains the points (1, 0, 2) and (2, 1, – 3) Coincident lines both L_1 and L_2 may lie in an infinite number of planes.

(B) $\left.\begin{array}{l}\mathbf{V}_1 = 2\hat{\mathbf{i}} + 2\hat{\mathbf{j}} - \hat{\mathbf{k}} \\ \mathbf{V}_2 = \hat{\mathbf{i}} - 2\hat{\mathbf{j}} + 3\hat{\mathbf{k}}\end{array}\right]$

$\Rightarrow$ Lines not parallel

Also, both intersect at (3, 5, 1)

Hence, the lines are intersecting, hence they lie on a unique plane.

(C) $L_1 : \frac{x-0}{-6} = \frac{y-1}{9} = \frac{z-0}{-3} = t$

$L_2 : \frac{x-1}{2} = \frac{y-4}{-3} = \frac{z-0}{1} = s$

$\left[\begin{array}{l} L_1 \text{ is parallel to } -6\hat{\mathbf{i}} + 9\hat{\mathbf{j}} - 3\hat{\mathbf{k}} \\ L_2 \text{ is parallel to } 2\hat{\mathbf{i}} - 3\hat{\mathbf{j}} + \hat{\mathbf{k}}\end{array}\right]$

$\Rightarrow$ Lines parallel but not coincident.

Since, (0, 1, 0) does not lie on L_2, not intersecting.

Hence, L_1, L_2 lies in unique planes.

(D) Lines are skew can be verified.

91. $L_1 : \frac{x}{3} = \frac{y-3}{4} = \frac{z+2}{1}$ ...(i) (passing through P and Q)

$L_2 : \frac{x-1}{1} = \frac{y-3}{0} = \frac{z+1}{1}$ ...(ii)

(passing through R and parallel to $\mathbf{v} = \hat{\mathbf{i}} + \hat{\mathbf{k}}$)

(A) Distance of $P(0, 3, -2)$ from L_2

$\mathbf{PN} = (t+1)\,\hat{\mathbf{i}} - 6\hat{\mathbf{j}} + 2(t-1)\,\hat{\mathbf{k}}$

Now, $\quad \mathbf{PN} \cdot \mathbf{V} = 0$

$[(t+1)\hat{\mathbf{i}} - 6\hat{\mathbf{j}} + (t+1)\hat{\mathbf{k}}] \cdot (\hat{\mathbf{i}} + \hat{\mathbf{k}}) = 0$

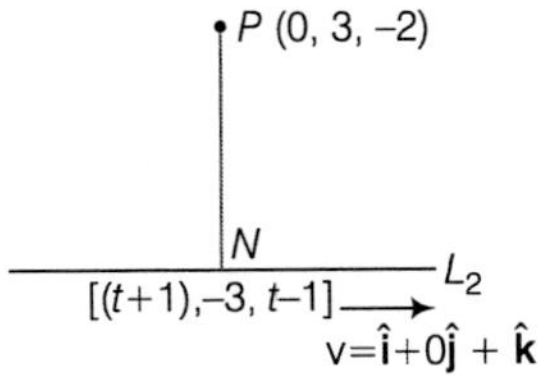

$(t+1) + (t+1) = 0\,;\; t = -1$

Hence, $\mathbf{PN} = 6\hat{\mathbf{j}}$

$|\mathbf{PN}| = |-6\hat{\mathbf{j}}| = 6$ units

(B) Distance between L_1 and L_2

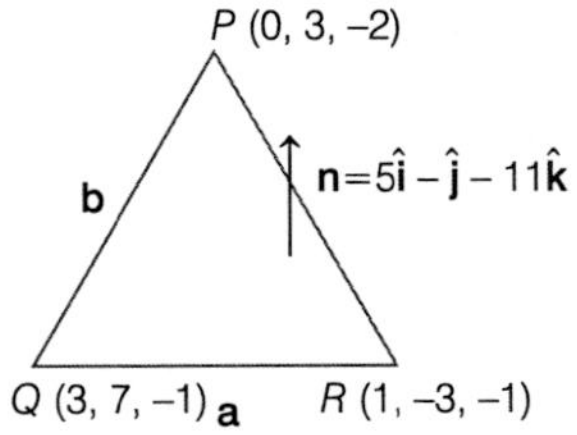

Equation of plane containing L_1 and parallel to L_2

$$Ax + B(y-3) + C(z+2) = 0$$

where, $\quad 3A + 4B + C = 0$

and $\quad A + B + C = 0$

$$A + C = 0$$

$$C = \lambda,\ A = -\lambda,\ B = +\lambda/2$$

$\therefore$ Equation of plane

$$-\lambda x + \frac{\lambda}{2}(y-3) + \lambda(z+2) = 0$$

$$2x - y + 3 - 2z - 4 = 0$$

$$2x - y - 2z = 1 \quad \text{...(i)}$$

Now, distance of the point (1, – 3, – 1) lying on the line L_1 from the plane (i)

$$d = \left|\frac{2+3+2-1}{3}\right| = 2 \text{ units}$$

(C) Area of ΔPQR

$\mathbf{QR} = a = 2\hat{\mathbf{i}} + 10\hat{\mathbf{j}} + 0\hat{\mathbf{k}}$

$\mathbf{QP} = b = 3\hat{\mathbf{i}} + 4\hat{\mathbf{j}} + \hat{\mathbf{k}}$

$$\mathbf{a} \times \mathbf{b} = 2\begin{vmatrix}\hat{\mathbf{i}} & \hat{\mathbf{j}} & \hat{\mathbf{k}} \\ 1 & 5 & 0 \\ 3 & 4 & 1\end{vmatrix}$$

$$= 2[\hat{\mathbf{i}}(5) - \hat{\mathbf{j}}(1) + \hat{\mathbf{k}}(4-15)] = 2[5\hat{\mathbf{i}} - \hat{\mathbf{j}} - 11\hat{\mathbf{k}}]$$

$$\frac{|\mathbf{a} \times \mathbf{b}|}{2} = \sqrt{25+1+121} = \sqrt{147} = \sqrt{3 \cdot 49} = 7\sqrt{3}$$

(D) Distance of (0, 0, 0) from PQR

Equation of plane PQR is $(r - p) \cdot n$

$$= [x\hat{\mathbf{i}} + (y-3)\hat{\mathbf{j}} + (z+2)\hat{\mathbf{k}}] \cdot [5\hat{\mathbf{i}} - \hat{\mathbf{j}} - 11\hat{\mathbf{k}}]$$

$$= 5x - (y-3) - 11(z+2) = 0$$

$$= 5x - y - 11z - 19 = 0$$

Distance from (0, 0, 0) of the plane

$$d = \left|\frac{19}{\sqrt{25+1+121}}\right| = \frac{19}{\sqrt{147}} \text{ units}$$

92. $L_1 : \frac{x-1}{2} = \frac{y-0}{-1} = \frac{z-(-3)}{1}$

Normal of plane $P : \mathbf{n} = \begin{vmatrix}\hat{\mathbf{i}} & \hat{\mathbf{j}} & \hat{\mathbf{k}} \\ 7 & 1 & 2 \\ 3 & 5 & -6\end{vmatrix}$

$$= \hat{\mathbf{i}}(-16) - \hat{\mathbf{j}}(-42-6) + \hat{\mathbf{k}}(32)$$

$$= -16\hat{\mathbf{i}} + 48\hat{\mathbf{j}} + 32\hat{\mathbf{k}}$$

DR's of normal $\mathbf{n} = \hat{\mathbf{i}} - 3\hat{\mathbf{j}} - 2\hat{\mathbf{k}}$

Point of intersection of L_1 and L_2.

$\Rightarrow \quad 2K_1 + 1 = K_2 + 4$

and $\quad -k_1 = k_2 - 3 \Rightarrow k_1 = 2$ and $k_2 = 1$

$\therefore$ Point of intersection $(5, -2, -1)$

Now equation of plane,

$$1\cdot(x-5) - 3(y+2) - 2(z+1) = 0$$

$$\Rightarrow \quad x - 3y - 2z - 13 = 0$$

$$\Rightarrow \quad x - 3y - 2z = 13$$

$\therefore a \to 1, b \to -3, c \to -2, d \to 13$

93. Given, $\frac{abc}{6} = 32$, where A, B and C are respectively, $(a, 0, 0)$, $(0, b, 0)$, $(0, 0, c)$.

(A) Centroid of tetrahedron $(x, y, z) = \left(\frac{a}{4}, \frac{b}{4}, \frac{c}{4}\right)$

$$a = 4x, b = 4y, c = 4z$$

$$64xyz = 32 \times 6$$

$$xyz = 3$$

(B) Equidistant point $(x, y, z) \equiv \left(\frac{a}{2}, \frac{b}{2}, \frac{c}{2}\right)$

$$a = 2x, b = 2y, c = 2z$$

$$8xyz = 32 \times 6$$

$$xyz = 24$$

(C) The equation of the plane is $\frac{x}{a} + \frac{y}{b} + \frac{z}{c} = 1$

$\therefore$ Foot of the perpendicular from the origin

$$\equiv (x, y, z) \equiv \left(\frac{1/a}{\sum 1/a^2}, \frac{1/b}{\sum 1/b^2}, \frac{1/c}{\sum 1/c^2}\right)$$

$$\frac{1}{ax} = \frac{1}{by} = \frac{1}{cz} = t$$

where, $\quad t = \frac{1}{a^2} + \frac{1}{b^2} + \frac{1}{c^2} = \sum \frac{1}{a^2}$

or $\quad t = (x^2 + y^2 + z^2)t^2$

$$t = \frac{1}{x^2 + y^2 + z^2}$$

and $\quad x = \frac{x^2 + y^2 + z^2}{x}, b = \frac{x^2 + y^2 + z^2}{y}, c = \frac{x^2 + y^2 + z^2}{z}$

Now, $\quad abc = 6 \times 32$

$$(x^2 + y^2 + z^2) = 192\, xyz$$

(D) Let P be (x, y, z), then $PA \perp PB$

$$\Rightarrow \quad a(x-a) + y(y-b) + zz = 0$$

$$\Rightarrow \quad ax + by = x^2 + y^2 + z^2$$

$$PB \perp PC$$

$$\Rightarrow \quad ax + b(y-b) + c(z-c) = 0$$

$$\Rightarrow \quad by + cz = x^2 + y^2 + z^2$$

$$\therefore \quad \frac{a}{1/x} = \frac{b}{1/y} = \frac{c}{1/z}$$

$$a = \frac{x^2 + y^2 + z^2}{2x}, b = \frac{x^2 + y^2 + z^2}{2y}$$

and $\quad c = \frac{x^2 + y^2 + z^2}{2z}$

$$\therefore \quad abc = 6 \times 32$$

$$\Rightarrow \quad (x^2 + y^2 + z^2)^3 = 192 \times 8xyz = 1536\, xyz$$

94. **(A)** Any point on line $\frac{x-1}{2} = \frac{y-2}{3} = \frac{z-3}{4} = \lambda$ is $P(2\lambda + 1, 3\lambda + 2, 4\lambda + 3)$, which satisfies the line

$$\frac{x-4}{5} = \frac{y-1}{2} = \frac{z}{1}$$

$$\Rightarrow \quad \frac{2\lambda + 1 - 4}{5} = \frac{3\lambda + 2 - 1}{2} = \frac{4\lambda + 3}{1} \Rightarrow \lambda = -1$$

Then, the required point is $(-1, -1, -1)$.

(B) Given line $\frac{x-2}{3} = \frac{y-3}{4} = \frac{z-4}{5} = r$ (let)

Any point on the line is $(3r + 2, 4r + 3, 5r + 4)$. distance from this point to $(2, 3, 4)$ is $10\sqrt{2}$ unit.

So, $(3r + 2 - 2)^2 + (4r + 3 - 3)^2 + (5r + 4 - 4)^2 = 200$

$$\Rightarrow \quad 50r^2 = 200$$

$$\Rightarrow \quad r^2 = 4 \Rightarrow r = \pm 2$$

Hence, the points are $(8, 11, 14)$ and $(-4, -5, -6)$.

(C) Given line $\frac{x-2}{3} = \frac{y-3}{4} = \frac{z-4}{5}$

Any point on this line is $(3r + 2, 4r + 3, 5r + 4)$.

Distance from the origin is $\sqrt{29}$ units.

So, $(3r + 2)^2 + (4r + 3)^2 + (5r + 4)^2 = 29$

$$\Rightarrow \quad 50r^2 + 76r = 0$$

$$\Rightarrow \quad r = 0, r = -\frac{76}{50}$$

For $r = 0$, the point is $(2, 3, 4)$.

(D) Any point on line AB

$$\frac{x}{2} = \frac{y-2}{3} = \frac{z-3}{4} = \lambda \text{ (let)}$$

is $M(2\lambda, 3\lambda + 2, 4\lambda + 3)$

The direction ratios of PM are

$$2\lambda - 3, 3\lambda + 3, 4\lambda - 8.$$

But $PM \perp AB$

$$\therefore \quad 2(2\lambda - 3) + 3(3\lambda + 3) + 4(4\lambda - 8) = 0$$

$$\Rightarrow \quad 4\lambda - 6 + 9\lambda + 9 + 16\lambda - 32 = 0$$

$$\Rightarrow \quad 29\lambda - 29 = 0$$

$$\Rightarrow \quad \lambda = 1$$

Therefore, the foot of perpendicular is $M(2, 5, 7)$.

95. Equation of line OQ is

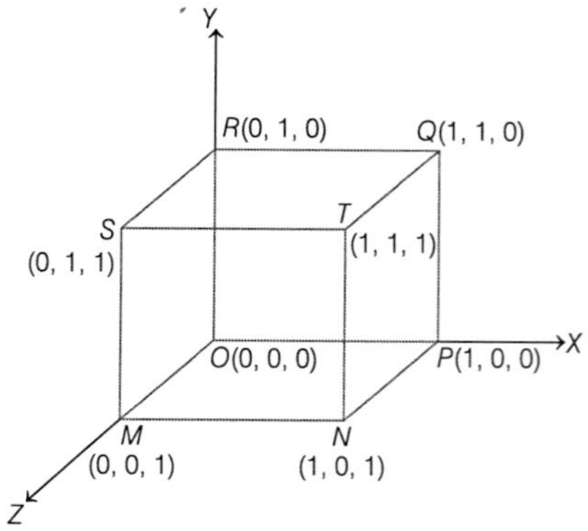

$$\mathbf{r}_1 = (0\hat{\mathbf{i}} + 0\hat{\mathbf{j}} + 0\hat{\mathbf{k}}) + \lambda[(1-0)\hat{\mathbf{i}} + (1-0)\hat{\mathbf{j}} + (0-0)\hat{\mathbf{k}}]$$

$\Rightarrow \mathbf{r}_1 = \mathbf{0} + \lambda(\hat{\mathbf{i}} + \hat{\mathbf{j}})$ ...(i)

Also, equation of the diagonal NR is given by

$$\mathbf{r}_2 = (0\hat{\mathbf{i}} + 1\hat{\mathbf{j}} + 0\hat{\mathbf{k}}) + \mu((1-0)\hat{\mathbf{i}} + (0-1)\hat{\mathbf{j}} + (1-0)\hat{\mathbf{k}}))$$

$\Rightarrow \mathbf{r}_2 = \hat{\mathbf{j}} + \mu(\hat{\mathbf{i}} - \hat{\mathbf{j}} + \hat{\mathbf{k}})$ ...(ii)

Hence, shortest distance (SD) is given by

$$\left|\frac{\hat{\mathbf{j}}\cdot(\hat{\mathbf{i}} - \hat{\mathbf{j}} - 2\hat{\mathbf{k}})}{\sqrt{6}}\right| = \left|\frac{-1}{\sqrt{6}}\right| = \frac{1}{\sqrt{6}} \text{ units}$$

96. Given, $|\mathbf{u} - \mathbf{v}| = |\mathbf{v} - \mathbf{w}| = |\mathbf{w} - \mathbf{u}|$ ...(i)

Eq. (i) implies that ΔABC is an equilateral triangle.

Also, given distances of A, B, C from

$$P = \frac{7}{2} \Rightarrow QD = \frac{7}{2}$$

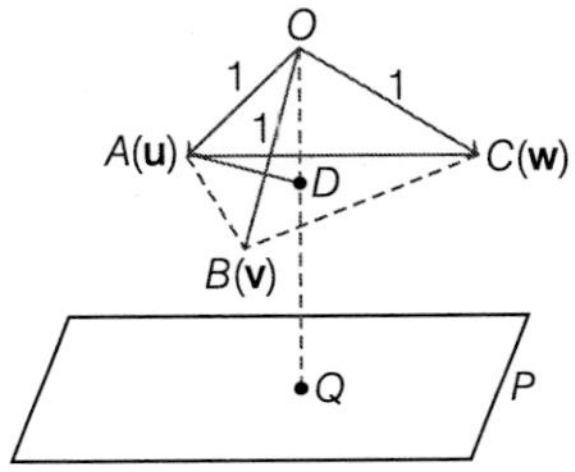

Also, distance of plane P from origin = 4

$\Rightarrow$ $OQ = 4$

$\therefore$ $OD = OQ - QD = 4 - \frac{7}{2} = \frac{1}{2}$

Hence, $AD = \sqrt{OA^2 - OD^2} = \frac{\sqrt{3}}{2} = R$

So, D is the circumcentre of ΔABC.

$\therefore$ $AS = R\cos 30°$

$\Rightarrow$ $AB = 2R\cos 30°$

$\Rightarrow$ $AB = 2 \times \frac{\sqrt{3}}{2} \times \frac{\sqrt{3}}{2}$

$\Rightarrow$ $AB = \frac{3}{2}$

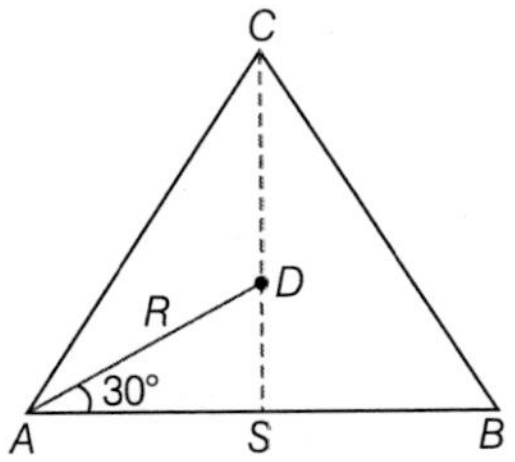

$\therefore$ Area of $\Delta ABC = \frac{\sqrt{3}}{4}\left(\frac{3}{2}\right)^2 = \frac{9\sqrt{3}}{16}$

Now, volume of tetrahedron with coterminous edges **u, v, w**

$$= \frac{1}{3}(\text{ar}(\Delta ABC)) \times OD = \frac{1}{3} \times \frac{9\sqrt{3}}{16} \times \frac{1}{2}$$

$$= \frac{3\sqrt{3}}{32}$$

Hence, volume of parallelopiped with coterminous edges

$$\mathbf{u}, \mathbf{v}, \mathbf{w} = 6 \times \frac{3\sqrt{3}}{32} = \frac{9\sqrt{3}}{16} = V$$

Therefore, $\frac{80V}{\sqrt{3}} = \frac{80}{\sqrt{3}} \times \frac{9\sqrt{3}}{16} = 45$

97. $l_1 = \mathbf{r}_1 = \lambda(\hat{\mathbf{i}} + \hat{\mathbf{j}} + \hat{\mathbf{k}})$

$l_2 = \mathbf{r}_2 = (\hat{\mathbf{j}} - \hat{\mathbf{k}}) + \mu(\hat{\mathbf{i}} + \hat{\mathbf{k}})$

According to the situation, μ_0 will be the plane containing the line l_1 and parallel to l_2.

$\therefore$ Normal vector of plane parallel to l_1

$$\text{and } l_2 = \begin{vmatrix} \hat{\mathbf{i}} & \hat{\mathbf{j}} & \hat{\mathbf{k}} \\ 1 & 1 & 1 \\ 1 & 0 & 1 \end{vmatrix} = \hat{\mathbf{i}}(1) - \hat{\mathbf{j}}(1-1) + \hat{\mathbf{k}}(-1) = \hat{\mathbf{i}} - \hat{\mathbf{k}}$$

$\therefore$ $\mu_0 : x - z = k$ at (0, 0, 0)

So, $0 - 0 = k \Rightarrow k = 0$

Hence, the plane $\mu_0 = x - z = 0$

(P) $d(\mu_0)$ = Perpendicular distance from point $(0, 1, -1)$ on l_2 to plane

$$= \left|\frac{0-(-1)}{\sqrt{1^2 + (-1)^2}}\right|$$

$$= \left|\frac{1}{\sqrt{2}}\right| = \frac{1}{\sqrt{2}}$$

(Q) $d = \left|\frac{0-2}{\sqrt{2}}\right| = \sqrt{2}$

(R) $d = \left|\frac{0-0}{\sqrt{2}}\right| = 0$

(S) Point of intersection will be (1, 1, 1).

$\therefore$ $d = \sqrt{1+1+1} = \sqrt{3}$

98. Let equation of plane be

$$\mathbf{r} = -(t+p)\hat{\mathbf{i}} + t\hat{\mathbf{j}} + (1+p)\hat{\mathbf{k}}$$

$$\mathbf{r} = \hat{\mathbf{k}} + t(-\hat{\mathbf{i}} + \hat{\mathbf{j}}) + p(-\hat{\mathbf{i}} + \hat{\mathbf{k}})$$

So, equation of plane in standard form is

$$[\mathbf{r} - \hat{\mathbf{k}}, -\hat{\mathbf{i}} + \hat{\mathbf{j}}, -\hat{\mathbf{i}} + \hat{\mathbf{k}}] = 0$$

$\therefore$ $x + y + z = 1$ ...(i)

Given that the position vectors of Q and S are $10\hat{\mathbf{i}} + 15\hat{\mathbf{j}} + 20\hat{\mathbf{k}}$ and $\alpha\hat{\mathbf{i}} + \beta\hat{\mathbf{j}} + \gamma\hat{\mathbf{k}}$, respectively.

Thus, coordinates of $Q \equiv (10, 15, 20)$

and coordinates of $S \equiv (\alpha, \beta, \gamma)$.

$$\therefore \quad \frac{\alpha - 10}{1} = \frac{\beta - 15}{1} = \frac{\gamma - 20}{1}$$

$$= \frac{-2(10 + 15 + 20 - 1)}{3}$$

$$\Rightarrow \quad \frac{\alpha - 10}{1} = \frac{\beta - 15}{1} = \frac{\gamma - 20}{1} = \frac{-88}{3}$$

$\Rightarrow \quad \alpha = 10 - \frac{88}{3} = -\frac{58}{3}, \beta = 15 - \frac{88}{3} = \frac{-43}{3}$

and $\quad \gamma = 20 - \frac{88}{3} = \frac{-28}{3}$

$\therefore \quad 3(\alpha + \beta) = 3\left(\frac{-58}{3} - \frac{43}{3}\right) = -101$

and $\quad 3(\beta + \gamma) = 3\left(-\frac{43}{3} - \frac{28}{3}\right) = -71$

$3(\gamma + \alpha) = 3\left(-\frac{28}{3} - \frac{58}{3}\right) = -86$

and $3(\alpha + \beta + \gamma) = 3\left(-\frac{58}{3} - \frac{43}{3} - \frac{28}{3}\right)$

$= 3\left(-\frac{129}{3}\right) = -129$

Thus, option (a), (b), (c) are correct.

99. Equation of pair of given planes is

$P_1 : (10x + 15y + 12z - 60) = 0$

$P_2 : (-2x + 5y + 4z - 20) = 0$

We will be find a general point of each line and we will solve it with P. If we get more than one value of variable λ, then the line can be edge of given tetrahedron.

For option (a),

The point is $(1, 1, 5\lambda + 1)$.

So, $(60\lambda - 23)(20\lambda - 17) = 0$

$\Rightarrow \quad \lambda = \frac{23}{60}, \lambda = \frac{17}{20}$

So, it can be edges of tetrahedron.

For option (b),

The point is $(-5\lambda + 6, 2\lambda, 3\lambda)$.

So, $(16\lambda)(32\lambda - 32) = 0$

$\Rightarrow \quad \lambda = 0, \lambda = 1$

So, it can be edges of tetrahedron.

For option (c),

The point is $(-2\lambda, 5\lambda + 4, 4\lambda)$

So, $(103\lambda)(45\lambda) = 0$

$\Rightarrow \quad \lambda = 0$ and $\lambda = 0$

So, it cannot be the edges of tetrahedron.

For option (d),

The point is $(\lambda, -2\lambda + 4, 3\lambda)$

$\Rightarrow \quad (16\lambda)(0) = 0$

So, it cannot be edge of tetrahedron.

100. Equation of given straight lines

$L_1 : \frac{x-1}{1} = \frac{y}{-1} = \frac{z-1}{3}$

and $\quad L_2 : \frac{x-1}{-3} = \frac{y}{-1} = \frac{z-1}{1}$

having vector form respectively, are

$\mathbf{r} = (\hat{\mathbf{i}} + \hat{\mathbf{k}}) + \lambda(\hat{\mathbf{i}} - \hat{\mathbf{j}} + 3\hat{\mathbf{k}})$

and $\mathbf{r} = (\hat{\mathbf{i}} + \hat{\mathbf{k}}) + \lambda(-3\hat{\mathbf{i}} - \hat{\mathbf{j}} + \hat{\mathbf{k}})$

$\because \quad (\hat{\mathbf{i}} - \hat{\mathbf{j}} + 3\hat{\mathbf{k}}) \cdot (-3\hat{\mathbf{i}} - \hat{\mathbf{j}} + \hat{\mathbf{k}}) = -3 + 1 + 3 = 1$ is positive.

$\therefore$ Angle between supporting line vectors of lines L_1 and L_2 is acute, and point of intersection of given lines L_1 and L_2 is $(1, 0, 1)$.

Now, vector along the acute angle bisector of vectors $(\hat{\mathbf{i}} - \hat{\mathbf{j}} + 3\hat{\mathbf{k}})$ and $(-3\hat{\mathbf{i}} - \hat{\mathbf{j}} + \hat{\mathbf{k}})$ is $(-\hat{\mathbf{i}} - \hat{\mathbf{j}} + 2\hat{\mathbf{k}})$ or $(\hat{\mathbf{i}} + \hat{\mathbf{j}} - 2\hat{\mathbf{k}})$.

It is given that line

$L : \frac{x-\alpha}{l} = \frac{y-1}{m} = \frac{z-\gamma}{-2}$ is the bisector of the acute angle between the lines L_1 and L_2,

so $l = 1$ and $m = 1$

and $\quad \frac{1-\alpha}{1} = \frac{0-1}{1} = \frac{1-\gamma}{-2}$

$\Rightarrow \quad \alpha = 2, \gamma = -1$

$\therefore \quad \alpha - \gamma = 3, l + m = 2$

101. Since, the point $A(3, 2, -1)$ is the mirror image of the point $B(1, 0, -1)$ with respect to the plane $\alpha x + \beta y + \gamma z = \delta$, then

$\frac{\alpha}{3-1} = \frac{\beta}{2-0} = \frac{\gamma}{(-1)-(-1)}$

$\Rightarrow \quad \frac{\alpha}{1} = \frac{\beta}{1} = \frac{\gamma}{0}$

$\Rightarrow \quad \gamma = 0$

it is given that $\alpha + \gamma = 1$

$\Rightarrow \quad \alpha = 1$, so $\beta = 1$.

and the mid-point of AB, $M(2, 1, -1)$ lies on the given plane, so

$2\alpha + \beta - \gamma = \delta$

$\Rightarrow \quad 2(1) + (1) - 0 = \delta$

$\Rightarrow \quad \delta = 3$

$\therefore \quad \alpha + \beta = 2, \delta - \gamma = 3, \delta + \beta = 4,$

$\alpha + \beta + \gamma = 2 \neq 3 = \delta$

102. Given lines,

$L_1 : \mathbf{r} = \lambda\hat{\mathbf{i}}, \lambda \in R$ ...(i)

$L_2 : \mathbf{r} = \mu\hat{\mathbf{j}} + \hat{\mathbf{k}}, \mu \in R$ ...(ii)

and $L_3 : \mathbf{r} = \hat{\mathbf{i}} + \hat{\mathbf{j}} + v\hat{\mathbf{k}}, v \in R$ ...(iii)

Now, let the point P on $L_1 = (\lambda, 0, 0)$

the point Q on $L_2 = (0, \mu, 1)$ and the point R on $L_3 = (1, 1, v)$

For collinearity of points P, Q and R, there should be a non-zero scalar 'm', such that $\mathbf{PQ} = m\,\mathbf{PR}$

$\Rightarrow \quad (-\lambda\hat{\mathbf{i}} + \mu\hat{\mathbf{j}} + \hat{\mathbf{k}}) = m[(1-\lambda)\hat{\mathbf{i}} + \hat{\mathbf{j}} + v\hat{\mathbf{k}}]$

$\Rightarrow \quad \frac{\lambda}{\lambda - 1} = \frac{\mu}{1} = \frac{1}{v}$

$\Rightarrow \quad v = \frac{1}{\mu}$ and $\lambda = \frac{\mu}{\mu - 1}$

where, $\mu \neq 0$ and $\mu \neq 1$

$\Rightarrow \quad Q \neq \hat{\mathbf{k}}$ and $Q \neq \hat{\mathbf{k}} + \hat{\mathbf{j}}$

Hence, Q can not have coordinates $(0, 0, 1)$ and $(0, 1, 1)$.

Hence, options (c) and (d) are correct.

103. Given lines

$L_1 : \mathbf{r} = \hat{\mathbf{i}} + \lambda(-\hat{\mathbf{i}} + 2\hat{\mathbf{j}} + 2\hat{\mathbf{k}}), \lambda \in R$

and $L_2 : \mathbf{r} = \mu(2\hat{\mathbf{i}} - \hat{\mathbf{j}} + 2\hat{\mathbf{k}}), \mu \in R$

and since line L_3 is perpendicular to both lines L_1 and L_2.
Then, a vector along L_3 will be,

$$\begin{vmatrix} \hat{\mathbf{i}} & \hat{\mathbf{j}} & \hat{\mathbf{k}} \\ -1 & 2 & 2 \\ 2 & -1 & 2 \end{vmatrix} = \hat{\mathbf{i}}(4+2) - \hat{\mathbf{j}}(-2-4) + \hat{\mathbf{k}}(1-4)$$

$$= 6\hat{\mathbf{i}} + 6\hat{\mathbf{j}} - 3\hat{\mathbf{k}} = 3(2\hat{\mathbf{i}} + 2\hat{\mathbf{j}} - \hat{\mathbf{k}}) \quad \text{...(i)}$$

Now, let a general point on line L_1.
$P(1-\lambda, 2\lambda, 2\lambda)$ and on line L_2.
As, $Q(2\mu, -\mu, 2\mu)$ and let P and Q are point of intersection of lines L_1, L_3 and L_2, L_3, so direction ratios of

$$L_3\ (2\mu + \lambda - 1, -\mu - 2\lambda, 2\mu - 2\lambda) \quad \text{...(ii)}$$

Now, $\dfrac{2\mu + \lambda - 1}{2} = \dfrac{-\mu - 2\lambda}{2} = \dfrac{2\mu - 2\lambda}{-1}$ [from Eqs.(i) and (ii)]

$$\Rightarrow \quad \lambda = \frac{1}{9} \text{ and } \mu = \frac{2}{3}$$

So, $P\left(\frac{8}{9}, \frac{2}{9}, \frac{2}{9}\right)$ and $Q\left(\frac{4}{9}, -\frac{2}{9}, \frac{4}{9}\right)$

Now, we can take equation of line L_3 as $\mathbf{r} = \mathbf{a} + t(2\hat{\mathbf{i}} + 2\hat{\mathbf{j}} - \hat{\mathbf{k}})$, where $\mathbf{a}$ is position vector of any point on line L_3 and possible vector of $\mathbf{a}$ are

$$\left(\frac{8}{9}\hat{\mathbf{i}} + \frac{2}{9}\hat{\mathbf{j}} + \frac{2}{9}\hat{\mathbf{k}}\right) \text{ or } \left(\frac{4}{9}\hat{\mathbf{i}} - \frac{2}{9}\hat{\mathbf{j}} + \frac{4}{9}\hat{\mathbf{k}}\right) \text{ or } \left(\frac{2}{3}\hat{\mathbf{i}} + \frac{1}{3}\hat{\mathbf{k}}\right)$$

Hence, options (a), (b) and (c) are correct.

104. Given three lines

$\mathbf{r} = \lambda\hat{\mathbf{i}}, \lambda \in R$, $\mathbf{r} = \mu(\hat{\mathbf{i}} + \hat{\mathbf{j}}), \mu \in R$ and $\mathbf{r} = v(\hat{\mathbf{i}} + \hat{\mathbf{j}} + \hat{\mathbf{k}}), v \in R$

cuts the plane $x + y + z = 1$ at the points A, B and C, respectively.

So, for point A, put $(\lambda, 0, 0)$ in the plane, we get

$$\lambda + 0 + 0 = 1$$
$$\Rightarrow \quad \lambda = 1$$
$$\Rightarrow \quad A \equiv (1, 0, 0).$$

Similarly, for point B, put $(\mu, \mu, 0)$ in the plane, we get

$$\mu + \mu + 0 = 1$$
$$\Rightarrow \quad \mu = \frac{1}{2}$$
$$\Rightarrow \quad B \equiv \left(\frac{1}{2}, \frac{1}{2}, 0\right)$$

and for point C, put (v, v, v) in the plane we get

$$v + v + v = 1$$
$$\Rightarrow \quad v = \frac{1}{3}$$
$$\Rightarrow \quad C \equiv \left(\frac{1}{3}, \frac{1}{3}, \frac{1}{3}\right)$$

Now, area of $\Delta ABC = \frac{1}{2}|\overrightarrow{AB} \times \overrightarrow{AC}| = \Delta$

$$\because \quad \mathbf{AB} = -\frac{1}{2}\hat{\mathbf{i}} + \frac{1}{2}\hat{\mathbf{j}}$$

and $\quad \mathbf{AC} = -\frac{2}{3}\hat{\mathbf{i}} + \frac{1}{3}\hat{\mathbf{j}} + \frac{1}{3}\hat{\mathbf{k}}$

$$\therefore \mathbf{AB} \times \mathbf{AC} = \begin{vmatrix} \hat{\mathbf{i}} & \hat{\mathbf{j}} & \hat{\mathbf{k}} \\ -1/2 & 1/2 & 0 \\ -2/3 & 1/3 & 1/3 \end{vmatrix}$$

$$= \hat{\mathbf{i}}\left(\frac{1}{6}\right) - \hat{\mathbf{j}}\left(-\frac{1}{6}\right) + \hat{\mathbf{k}}\left(-\frac{1}{6} + \frac{2}{6}\right)$$

$$= \frac{1}{6}(\hat{\mathbf{i}} + \hat{\mathbf{j}} + \hat{\mathbf{k}})$$

$$\Rightarrow \quad |\mathbf{AB} \times \mathbf{AC}| = \frac{1}{6}\sqrt{3}$$

$$= \frac{1}{2\sqrt{3}}$$

$$\Rightarrow \quad \Delta = \frac{1}{4\sqrt{3}}$$

$$\Rightarrow \quad (6\Delta)^2 = 36\frac{1}{16 \times 3}$$

$$= \frac{3}{4} = 0.75$$

Exercise 3 - Challenging Problems

1. Given planes are

$$ax + by = 0 \quad \text{...(i)}$$

and $\quad z = 0 \quad$ ...(ii)

$\therefore$ Equation of any plane passing through the line of intersection of planes (i) and (ii) may be taken as,

$$ax + by + kz = 0 \quad \text{...(iii)}$$

The direction cosines of a normal to the plane (iii) are

$$\frac{a}{\sqrt{a^2 + b^2 + k^2}}, \frac{b}{\sqrt{a^2 + b^2 + k^2}}, \frac{k}{\sqrt{a^2 + b^2 + k^2}}$$

The direction cosines of a normal to the plane (i) are

$$\frac{a}{\sqrt{a^2 + b^2}}, \frac{b}{\sqrt{a^2 + b^2}}, 0$$

Since, the angle between the planes (i) and (iii) is α.

$$\therefore \quad \cos\alpha = \frac{a \cdot a + b \cdot b + k \cdot 0}{\sqrt{a^2 + b^2 + k^2}\sqrt{a^2 + b^2}}$$

$$= \sqrt{\frac{a^2 + b^2}{a^2 + b^2 + k^2}}$$

$$k^2 \cos^2\alpha = \alpha^2(1 - \cos^2\alpha) + b^2(1 - \cos^2\alpha)$$

$$k^2 = \frac{(a^2 + b^2)\sin^2\alpha}{\cos^2\alpha}$$

On putting in Eq. (iii) $k = \pm\sqrt{a^2 + b^2}\tan\alpha$, we get equation of plane as,

$$ax + by \pm z\sqrt{a^2 + b^2}\tan\alpha = 0.$$

2. The required line passing through the point (2, 1, 1) in the plane $2x + y - 5z = 0$ and is having greatest slope, so it must be perpendicular to the line of intersection of the planes

$$2x + y - 5z = 0 \quad \text{...(i)}$$

and $\quad 4x - 3y + 7z = 0 \quad$ ...(ii)

Let the DR's of the line of intersection of Eqs. (i) and (ii) are a, b, c.

$$2a + b - 5c = 0$$

and $$4a - 3b + 7c = 0$$

(as DR's of straight line (a, b, c) is perpendicular to DR's of normal to both the planes)

$$\frac{a}{4} = \frac{b}{17} = \frac{c}{5}$$

Now, let the direction ratio of required line be proportional to l, m and n, then its equation be

$$\frac{x-2}{l} = \frac{y-1}{m} = \frac{z-1}{n}$$

where, $2l + m - 5n = 0$ and $4l + 17m + 5n = 0$

So, $$\frac{l}{3} = \frac{m}{-1} = \frac{n}{1}$$

Thus, the required line is $\dfrac{x-2}{3} = \dfrac{y-1}{-1} = \dfrac{z-1}{1}$

3. Here, P be (x, y, z) shown as,

then, $x = r \sin\theta \cdot \cos\phi$, $y = r \sin\theta \sin\phi$, $z = r\cos\theta$ ...(i)

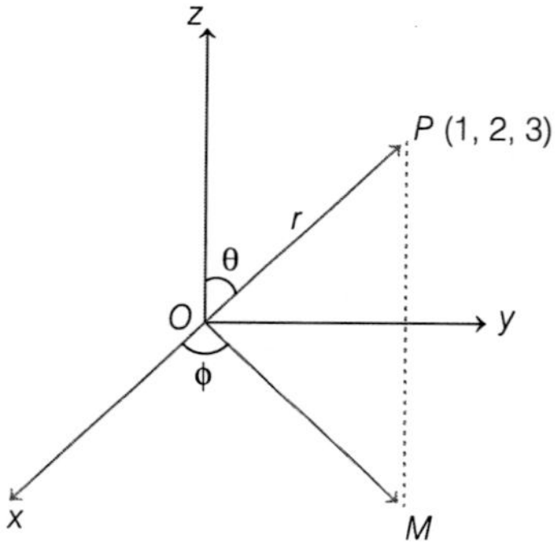

$\Rightarrow$ $1 = r\sin\theta \cdot \cos\phi$, $2 = r\sin\theta\sin\phi$, $3 = r\cos\theta$

$\Rightarrow$ $1^2 + 2^2 + 3^2 = r^2\sin^2\theta\cos^2\phi + r^2\sin^2\theta\sin^2\phi + r^2\cos^2\theta$

$$= r^2\sin^2\theta(\cos^2\phi + \sin^2\phi) + r^2\cos^2\theta$$

$$= r^2\sin^2\theta + r^2\cos^2\theta = r^2$$

$\Rightarrow$ $$r = \pm\sqrt{14}$$

$\therefore$ From Eq. (i), we have

$$\sin\theta\cos\phi = + \frac{1}{\sqrt{14}},$$

$$\sin\theta\sin\phi = \frac{2}{\sqrt{14}}, \cos\theta = \frac{3}{\sqrt{14}}$$

[neglecting – ve sign as acute angles]

$\therefore$ $$\frac{\sin\theta\sin\phi}{\sin\theta\cos\phi} = \frac{2}{1}$$

and $$\tan\theta = \frac{\sin\theta}{\cos\theta} = \frac{\sqrt{5}}{3}$$

$\Rightarrow$ $$\tan\phi = 2 \text{ and } \tan\theta = \frac{\sqrt{5}}{3}$$

$\Rightarrow$ $$\phi = \tan^{-1} 2 \text{ and } \theta = \tan^{-1}\left(\frac{\sqrt{5}}{3}\right)$$

4. Let the edges OA, OB, OC of the unit cube be along OX, OY and OZ, respectively. Since, $OA = OB = OC = 1$ unit

$\therefore$ $$\mathbf{OA} = \hat{\mathbf{i}}, \mathbf{OB} = \hat{\mathbf{j}}, \mathbf{OC} = \hat{\mathbf{k}}$$

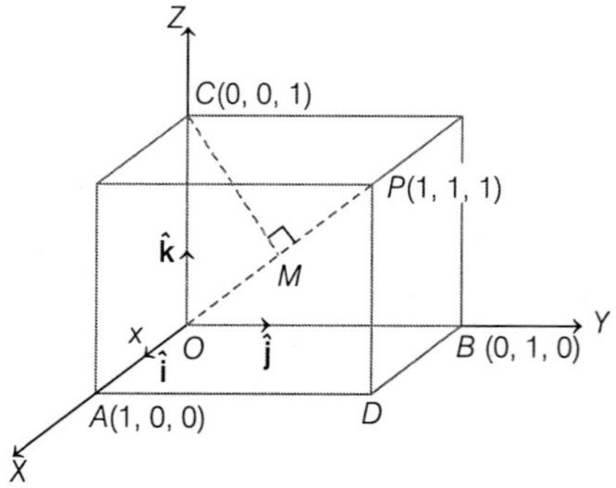

Let CM be perpendicular from the corner C on the diagonal OP. The vector equation of OP is

$$\mathbf{r} = \lambda(\hat{\mathbf{i}} + \hat{\mathbf{j}} + \hat{\mathbf{k}})$$

$\therefore$ OM = Projection of **OC** on **OP**

$$= \mathbf{OC} \cdot \mathbf{OP}$$

$$= \hat{\mathbf{k}}\,\frac{(\hat{\mathbf{i}} + \hat{\mathbf{j}} + \hat{\mathbf{k}})}{\sqrt{3}} = \frac{1}{\sqrt{3}}$$

Now, $$OC^2 = OM^2 + CM^2$$

$\Rightarrow$ $$CM^2 = |OC|^2 - OM^2 = 1 - \frac{1}{3} = \frac{2}{3}$$

$\Rightarrow$ $$CM = \sqrt{\frac{2}{3}}$$

5. Here, $A(4, 7, 8)$, $B(-1, -2, 1)$, $C(2, 3, 4)$ and $D(1, 2, 5)$. If the lines AB and CD intersect at P, then let

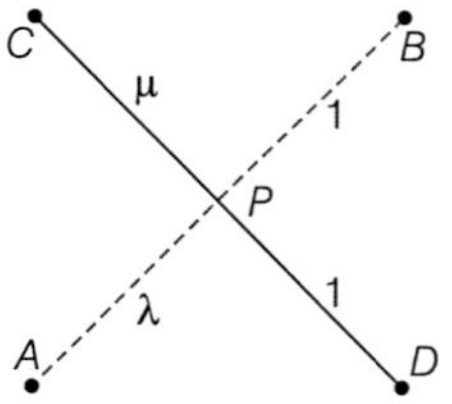

$$\frac{AP}{PB} = \frac{\lambda}{1} \text{ and } \frac{CP}{PD} = \frac{\mu}{1}$$

Then, $$P\left(\frac{-\lambda+4}{\lambda+1}, \frac{-2\lambda+7}{\lambda+1}, \frac{\lambda+8}{\lambda+1}\right) = \left(\frac{\mu+2}{\mu+1}, \frac{2\mu+3}{\mu+1}, \frac{5\mu+4}{\mu+1}\right)$$

$\Rightarrow$ $$\frac{-\lambda+4}{\lambda+1} = \frac{\mu+2}{\mu+1}, \frac{-2\lambda+7}{\lambda+1} = \frac{2\mu+3}{\mu+1}$$

$$\frac{\lambda+8}{\lambda+1} = \frac{5\mu+4}{\mu+1}$$

$\Rightarrow$ $$\frac{-(\lambda+1)+5}{\lambda+1} = \frac{(\mu+1)+1}{\mu+1}$$

$$\frac{-2(\lambda+1)+9}{\lambda+1} = \frac{2(\mu+1)+1}{\mu+1}$$

$$\frac{(\lambda+1)+7}{\lambda+1} = \frac{5(\mu+1)-1}{\mu+1}$$

$$\Rightarrow \quad -1+\frac{5}{\lambda+1}=1+\frac{1}{\mu+1}$$

$$-2+\frac{9}{\lambda+1}=2+\frac{1}{\mu+1};$$

$$1+\frac{7}{\lambda+1}=5-\frac{1}{(\mu+1)}$$

Let $\frac{1}{\lambda+1}=x$ and $\frac{1}{\mu+1}=y$

$$\Rightarrow \quad 5x-y=2; 9x-y=4; 7x+y=4$$

On solving, $x=\frac{1}{2}, y=\frac{1}{2}$

$$\Rightarrow \quad \lambda+1=2, \mu+1=2$$

$$\lambda=1, \mu=1$$

Clearly, if $\lambda=1$ and $\mu=1$,

AB and CD bisects each other.

$$\therefore \quad P=\left(\frac{3}{2},\frac{5}{2},\frac{9}{2}\right)$$

Now, $AP=\sqrt{\left(4-\frac{3}{2}\right)^2+\left(7-\frac{5}{2}\right)^2+\left(8-\frac{9}{2}\right)^2}$

$$=\frac{\sqrt{155}}{2}=PB$$

Also, $CP=\sqrt{\left(2-\frac{3}{2}\right)^2+\left(3-\frac{5}{2}\right)^2+\left(4-\frac{9}{2}\right)^2}$

$$=\frac{\sqrt{3}}{2}=PD$$

We know four points A, B, C and D are concylic, if

$$AP\cdot PB=PC\cdot PD$$

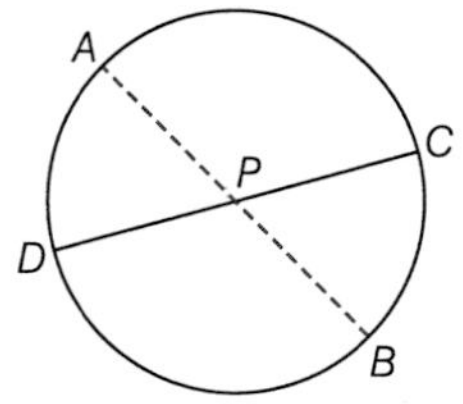

But here, $AP\cdot PB=\frac{155}{4}$ and $PC\cdot PD=\frac{3}{4}$

$\therefore$ Points are non-concyclic.

6. Let $P(\alpha,\beta,\gamma)$ and $Q(x_1, y_1, z_1)$

DR's of OP are (α,β,γ) and DR's of OQ are (x_1, y_1, z_1).

$\because$ O, Q and P are collinear.

$$\therefore \quad \frac{\alpha}{x_1}=\frac{\beta}{y_1}=\frac{\gamma}{z_1}=k \text{ (let)} \quad \text{...(i)}$$

Since, $P(\alpha,\beta,\gamma)$ lie on the plane

$$lx+my+nz=p, \; l\alpha+m\beta+n\gamma=p$$

Since, $P(\alpha, \beta, \gamma)$ lie on the plane $lx+my+nz=p$,
$l\alpha+m\beta+n\gamma \pm p$

$$\Rightarrow \quad klx_1+kmy_1+knz_1=p \quad \text{[using Eq. (i)] ...(ii)}$$

Since, $OP\cdot OQ=p^2$

$$\therefore \quad \sqrt{\alpha^2+\beta^2+\gamma^2}\cdot\sqrt{x_1^2+y_1^2+z_1^2}=p^2$$

$$\sqrt{k^2x_1^2+k^2y_1^2+k^2z_1^2}\cdot\sqrt{x_1^2+y_1^2+z_1^2}=p^2$$

$$\Rightarrow \quad k(x_1^2+y_1^2+z_1^2)=p^2 \quad \text{...(iii)}$$

From Eqs. (ii) and (iii), we get

$$\frac{lx_1+my_1+nz_1}{x_1^2+y_1^2+z_1^2}=\frac{1}{p}$$

$$\Rightarrow \quad p(lx_1+my_1+nz_1)=(x_1^2+y_1^2+z_1^2)$$

Hence, the locus of Q

$$\Rightarrow \quad p(lx+my+nz)=x^2+y^2+z^2$$

7. Given planes are

$$ax+by+cz+d=0 \quad \text{...(i)}$$

and $\quad a'x+b'y+c'z+d'=0 \quad$ ...(ii)

Let $P(\alpha,\beta,\gamma)$ be an arbitrary point in the plane (i) and $Q(p,q,r)$ be the reflection of the point P in plane (ii).

Locus of Q will be the required reflection of plane (i) in plane (ii), let L be the mid-point of PQ.

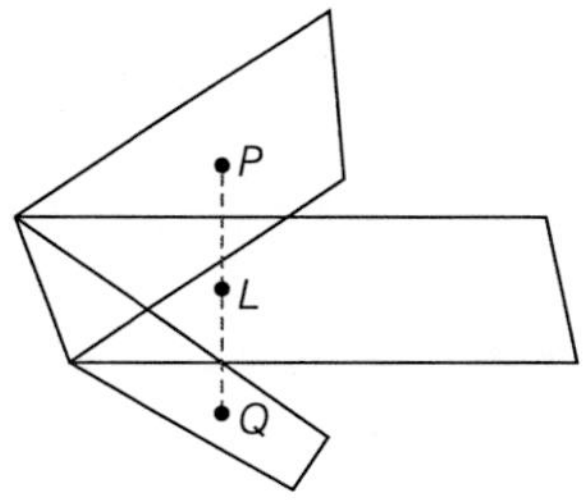

Then, $\quad L\left(\frac{p+\alpha}{2},\frac{q+\beta}{2},\frac{r+\gamma}{2}\right)$

L lies in plane (ii), we get

$$\therefore \quad a'\left(\frac{p+\alpha}{2}\right)+b'\left(\frac{q+\beta}{2}\right)+c'\left(\frac{r+\gamma}{2}\right)+d'=0$$

$$\Rightarrow \quad a'(p+\alpha)+b'(q+\beta)+c'(r+\gamma)+2d'=0 \quad \text{...(iii)}$$

DR's of PQ are $\alpha-p, \beta-q, \gamma-r$.

Since, PQ perpendicular on plane Eq. (iii), we get

$$\frac{\alpha-p}{a'}=\frac{\beta-q}{b'}=\frac{\gamma-r}{c'}=k \text{ (let)}$$

$$\therefore \quad \alpha=p+a'k, \beta=q+b'k, \gamma=r+c'k$$

On putting the values of α, β and γ in Eq. (iii), we get

$$a'(2p+ka')+b'(2q+kb')+c(2r+kc')+2d'=0$$

$$\Rightarrow 2(a'p+b'q+c'r+d')=-k(a'^2+b'^2+c'^2) \quad \text{...(iv)}$$

Since, $P(\alpha,\beta,\gamma)$ lies on plane (i), we get

$$a\alpha+b\beta+c\gamma+d=0$$

$$\Rightarrow a(p+ka')+n(q+kb')+c(r+kc')+d=0$$

$$\therefore \quad k=-\frac{(ap+bq+cr+d)}{(aa'+bb'+cc')}$$

On putting the value of k in Eq. (iv), we get

$$2(a'p + b'q + c'r + d') = \frac{(a'^2 + b'^2 + c'^2)(ap + bq + cr + d)}{aa' + bb' + cc'}$$

∴ Locus of $Q\,(p, q, r)$.
i.e. equation reflection of plane (i) in plane (ii) is,

$$2(aa' + bb' + cc')(a'x + b'y + c'z + d') = (a'^2 + b'^2 + c'^2)(ax + by + cz + d)$$

8. Elimination n between the given relations, we get

$$ul^2 + vm^2 + w\left(\frac{al + bm}{-c}\right)^2 = 0$$

$$\Rightarrow (c^2u + a^2w)\frac{l^2}{m^2} + 2abw.\frac{l}{m} + (b^2w + c^2v) = 0 \quad ...(i)$$

$$\therefore \frac{l_1}{m_1}\cdot\frac{l_2}{m_2} = \text{product of roots} = \frac{b^2w + c^2v}{c^2u + a^2w}$$

or $$\frac{l_1l_2}{b^2w + c^2v} = \frac{m_1m_2}{c^2u + a^2w} = \frac{n_1n_2}{a^2v + b^2u} \quad \text{[by symmetry]}$$

If lines are perpendicular, then

$$l_1l_2 + m_1m_2 + n_1n_2 = 0$$

$$\Rightarrow a^2(v + w) + b^2(w + u) + c^2(u + v) = 0$$

Again, if the lines be parallel, then their DC are equal, so that the roots of Eq. (i) should be equal, i.e. discriminate = 0

$$\therefore \quad 4a^2b^2w^2 - 4(c^2u + a^2w)(b^2w + c^2v) = 0$$

$$\Rightarrow a^2c^2vw + b^2c^2uw + c^4uv = 0$$

$$\Rightarrow \frac{a^2}{u} + \frac{b^2}{v} + \frac{c^2}{w} = 0$$

9. If the coordinates of the point P be (α, β, γ).

Then, $$\frac{\alpha}{a} + \frac{\beta}{\beta} + \frac{\gamma}{c} = 1 \quad ...(i)$$

Again DC of OP are proportional to α, β, γ and hence these are also the DR of the normal to the plane which is perpendicular to OP and since it passes through P, its equation is

$$\alpha(x - \alpha) + \beta(y - \beta) + \gamma(z - \gamma) = 0$$

or $$\alpha x + \beta y + \gamma z = \alpha^2 + \beta^2 + \gamma^2 \quad ...(ii)$$

It meets the axes in A, B, C and hence the coordinates of these points are $\left(\frac{\alpha^2 + \beta^2 + \gamma^2}{\alpha}, 0, 0\right)$ etc.

The equation of the plane through A and parallel to the YZ-plane is $x = \frac{\alpha^2 + \beta^2 + \gamma^2}{\alpha}$.

Similarly, the equations of other planes are

$$y = \frac{\alpha^2 + \beta^2 + \gamma^2}{\beta} \text{ and } z = \frac{\alpha^2 + \beta^2 + \gamma^2}{\gamma}.$$

The locus of their point of intersection is obtained by elimination α, β, γ between the three equations of the planes and relation (i)

$$\frac{1}{x^2} + \frac{1}{y^2} + \frac{1}{z^2} = \frac{\alpha^2 + \beta^2 + \gamma^2}{(\alpha^2 + \beta^2 + \gamma^2)^2} = \frac{1}{\alpha^2 + \beta^2 + \gamma^2}$$

Again, $$\frac{1}{ax} + \frac{1}{by} + \frac{1}{cz} = \frac{\left(\frac{\alpha}{a}\right) + \left(\frac{\beta}{b}\right) + \left(\frac{\gamma}{c}\right)}{\alpha^2 + \beta^2 + \gamma^2} = \frac{1}{\alpha^2 + \beta^2 + \gamma^2} \quad \text{[from Eq. (i)]}$$

$$\therefore \quad \frac{1}{x^2} + \frac{1}{y^2} + \frac{1}{z^2} = \frac{1}{ax} + \frac{1}{by} + \frac{1}{cz}$$

10. Any plane through the intersection of given planes is
$(x + 3y + 6 + \lambda\,(3x - y - 4z) = 0$
or $(1 + 3\lambda)x + (3 - \lambda)y - 4\lambda z + 6 = 0 \quad ...(i)$
Its perpendicular distance from $(0, 0, 0)$ is 1.

$$\therefore \quad \left|\frac{6}{\sqrt{(1 + 3\lambda)^2 + (3 - \lambda)^2 + (-4\lambda)^2}}\right| = 1$$

$\Rightarrow \lambda = \pm 1$

∴ Required planes are

$$2x + y - 2z + 3 = 0 \text{ and} x - 2y - 2z - 3 = 0.$$

11. The image of the plane

$$x - 2y + 2z - 3 = 0 \quad ...(i)$$

in the plane $$x + y + z - 1 = 0 \quad ...(ii)$$

passes through the line of intersection of the given planes. Therefore, the equation of such a plane is

$$(x - 2y + 2z - 3) + t(x + y + z - 1) = 0$$

$$\Rightarrow (1 + t)x + (-2 + t)y + (2 + t)z - 3 - t = 0 \quad ...(iii)$$

Now, plane (ii) makes the same angle with plane (i) and image plane (iii). Thus,

$$\frac{1 - 2 + 2}{3\sqrt{3}} = \pm\frac{1 + t - 2 + t + 2 + t}{\sqrt{3}\sqrt{(t + 1)^2 + (t - 2)^2 + (2 + t)^2}}$$

$$\Rightarrow \quad t = 0, -\frac{2}{3}$$

For $t = 0$, we get plane (i); hence for image plane, $t = -\frac{2}{3}$

The equation of the image plane

$$3(x - 2y + 2z - 3) - 2(x + y + z - 1) = 0$$

$$\Rightarrow \quad x - 8y + 4z - 7 = 0$$